American Journal of Psychiatry
Journal of Abnormal Psychology

Delacatto Theory

A PSYCHOLOGICAL APPROACH TO ABNORMAL BEHAVIOR

LEONARD P. ULLMANN
University of Hawaii

LEONARD KRASNER
State University of New York at Stony Brook

PRENTICE-HALL, INC., Englewood Cliffs, New Jersey

a psychological approach to abnormal behavior

SECOND EDITION

Library of Congress Cataloging in Publication Data

ULLMANN, LEONARD P
   A psychological approach to abnormal behavior.

   (Prentice-Hall psychology series)
   Bibliography: p.
   Includes indexes.
   1. Psychology, Pathological.   1. Krasner, Leonard, joint author.   II. Title.
RC454.U4 1975   616.8′9   74-28271
ISBN 0-13-732545-2

A PSYCHOLOGICAL APPROACH TO ABNORMAL BEHAVIOR
second edition
Leonard P. Ullmann / Leonard Krasner

© 1975, 1969 by Prentice-Hall, Inc., Englewood Cliffs, New Jersey

All rights reserved.
No part of this book may be reproduced
in any form or by any means
without permission in writing from the publisher.

Printed in the United States of America

10 9 8 7 6 5 4 3 2 1

PRENTICE-HALL INTERNATIONAL, INC., *London*
PRENTICE-HALL OF AUSTRALIA, PTY. LTD., *Sydney*
PRENTICE-HALL OF CANADA, LTD., *Toronto*
PRENTICE-HALL OF INDIA PRIVATE LIMITED, *New Delhi*
PRENTICE-HALL OF JAPAN, INC., *Tokyo*

Prentice-Hall Psychology Series, Richard S. Lazarus, editor

*To Kaloha and Miriam;
our children, Nancy and Mike,
Wendy, David, Charles, and Stefanie;
our mothers, Irma and Helen;
and the memory of our fathers,
Siegfried and Samuel.*

contents

preface xix

prologue 1

    TRADITIONAL ABNORMAL PSYCHOLOGY, 3
    PURPOSES OF STUDYING ABNORMAL PSYCHOLOGY, 4
    ABOUT THIS BOOK, 5
    SUMMARY, 6

1 defining abnormality 8

    The Psychiatric Emergency, 9
    The Importance of Definitions of Mental Illness, 11
    OPERATIONAL DEFINITIONS OF ABNORMALITY, 11
    ADDITIONAL THEORETICAL CONSIDERATIONS, 15
        Unitary or Separate Behaviors, 15
        Necessarily Socially Deviant, 16
        Values Other than Social Conformity, 16
    OTHER DEFINITIONS OF ABNORMALITY, 17
    PREFATORY CONSIDERATIONS, 22
    AN OUTLINE OF CATEGORIES, 24
        Comments on DSM-II, 27
        DSM-II as a Definition of Mental Illness and Health, 28
    SOME DATA, 28
    SUMMARY, 30

2 an alternative approach 31

    WHAT IS "RIGHT" BEHAVIOR AND WHO DEFINES IT? 33
        Behavior Likely to be Called Abnormal, 33
    WHO DOES THE LABELING? 35
    WHAT ARE THE CONSEQUENCES OF LABELING? 35
    THE DEVELOPMENT AND MAINTENANCE OF PRO-SOCIAL BEHAVIOR, 36
        The Physiological Environment: Genetic Endowment, 36
        The Physiological Environment: Bodily Function, 37
        The Physiological Environment: Ecological Considerations, 38
        Summary of Physiological Bases of Pro-Social Behavior, 38
    THE BEHAVIORAL SETTING: PHYSICAL AND SOCIAL, 38
        Social Organization, 39

POLITICAL AND ECONOMIC CONSIDERATIONS, 40
   Historical Perspective, 40
   Summary of Contexts, 40
THE ROLE OF LEARNING, 41
CONDITIONS LEADING TO BEHAVIOR BEING EVALUATED AS CHANGEWORTHY, 42
   Skills, 42
   Learning How and When to Label, 43
   Self-Labeling, 44
   The Consequences of Failure to Attend, 45
   Overt Behavior and Reinforcement, 46
   The Learning of Behaviors Aversive to Others, 48
THE DEMOGRAPHIC PERSPECTIVE, 50
CHANGING BEHAVIOR, 51
SUMMARY, 52

3 scientific method 54

DECISION MAKING, 55
OPERATIONAL DEFINITIONS, 57
SAMPLING, 60
STATISTICAL ANALYSIS, 62
RELIABILITY AND VALIDITY, 65
THE USE OF THE SINGLE CASE, 66
SUMMARY, 67

4 learning principles 68

   Behavior Terminating an Aversive Stimulus, 71
   The Effects of Satiation, 72
   The Function of Discriminative Stimuli, 73
FROM DISCRIMINATIVE STIMULI TO GENERALIZED REINFORCERS, 75
   Schedules of Reinforcement, 79
   The Shaping of Behavior, 79
   Prompting and Fading, 81
LANGUAGE AND OTHER COMPLEX OPERANT BEHAVIORS, 81
   The Effects of Verbalization as Stimulus, 83
   Language and Labeling, 83
IMITATION AND MODELING, 84
   Formation of Abstractions, 85
THE TRAINING OF ATTENTION, 85
THE INTERRELATION OF OPERANT AND RESPONDENT BEHAVIOR, 86
SUMMARY, 87

5 social roles and deviant behavior

THE ROLE ENACTMENTS OF HYPNOSIS, PLACEBO,
EXPERIMENTER BIAS, AND OTHER
SOCIALLY SANCTIONED "ABNORMAL" BEHAVIOR 88

ROLE ENACTMENTS, 89
EXPECTANCY AND PERFORMANCE, 95

contents   ix

THE "SICK" SOCIAL ROLE, 96
    Effects of "Sick-role" (Medical Model) 96
OUTPATIENT PSYCHOTHERAPY, 97
    Summary, 99
PLACEBO RESPONSES, 100
    The Placebo Reactor, 103
    The Placebo, 103
    Placebo Effectiveness, 103
    Placebo Reaction and Role Enactment, 104
    Role Enactment and the Demand Characteristics of a Situation, 105
    Summary, 106
HYPNOSIS, 107
    Summary, 111
THE PSYCHOLOGICAL EXPERIMENT, 112
SUMMARY, 114

6 approaches to abnormality
ANCIENT AND MEDIEVAL 115

SOME MODELS, 116
    Orientation, 119
"PRIMITIVE MAN," 119
INDIA, 120
CHINA, 121
THE GREEKS, 121
HELLENIC AND ROMAN PERIOD, 123
MIDDLE AGES, 124
THE NEAR EAST, 127
THE DISSENTERS, 127
THE DEVELOPMENT OF ASYLUMS, 129
SUMMARY, 129

7 approaches to abnormality
MODERN 130

FORERUNNERS OF PSYCHOTHERAPY, 131
    The Bernheim-Charcot Controversy, 132
    Philosophical and Other Predecessors of Psychological Approaches, 133
MORAL TREATMENT, 135
THE DECLINE OF MORAL TREATMENT, 137
THE ORGANIC POINT OF VIEW, 139
    The Organic Viewpoint and Mental Retardation, 141
    Physical Approaches to Behavior Change, 142
THE BEHAVIORAL APPROACH, 144
THE PROFESSIONS, 148
SUMMARY, 150

8 Freud and psychoanalysis 151

PSYCHOANALYSIS AS TREATMENT, 153
PSYCHOANALYSIS AS THEORY, 155
SUMMARY, 160

9 the conceptual impact of Freud
SYMPTOM, PERSONALITY, AND ANXIETY 161

SYMPTOM, 162
ANXIETY AND SYMPTOM, 165
PERSONALITY, 166
ANXIETY, 170
ON PSYCHOANALYSIS AS AN INTELLECTUAL SYSTEM, 172
SUMMARY, 173

10 social and societal contexts 174

LABELING AS BEHAVIOR, 175
   The Social Function of Labeling, 177
SOCIAL EVENTS LEADING TO THE LABEL "ABNORMAL," 180
   Cross-cultural Incidence of Mental Disorders, 182
   Epidemiological Studies, 183
   Ecological and Social Class Studies of Mental Disorders, 185
LEARNING TO BE NORMALLY ABNORMAL, 187
   Rule Learning, Rule Following, and Abnormality, 191
   Labeling: A Further Step In Being Normally Abnormal, 192
LEARNING TO BE A BUGHOUSER, 196
SUMMARY, 200

11 behavioral evaluation
DIAGNOSIS AND ASSESSMENT 202

RELIABILITY OF PSYCHIATRIC DIAGNOSIS, 203
   Consistency Over Time and Place, 207
   Evaluation, 208
EMPIRICAL APPROACHES, 209
PSYCHOLOGICAL TESTS, 213
   Projective Tests, 214
   Standardized Tests, 215
   Personality Inventories, 217
SOME THINGS TO CONSIDER, 217
   Other Considerations, 218
   How Were the Data Collected? 219
   Illusory Correlation, 219
DATA FOR BEHAVIORAL DECISIONS, 219
SUMMARY, 221

contents

12 behavior modification 223

CONCEPTS OF BEHAVIORAL CHANGE, 224
FROM FREUD TO ROGERS, 225
DISSATISFACTION WITH EVOCATIVE THERAPY, 227
    Group Treatment, 227
    Psychotherapy as a Process of Control of Behavior, 231
METHOD OF CHANGE: BEHAVIOR THERAPY, 233
    The Training of Assertive Responses, 233
    The Use of Sexual Responses, 234
    The Development of Relaxation Responses, 235
    The Use of Conditioned Avoidance Responses, 235
    Evocative Therapy as a Behavioral Technique, 236
    Response Modeling, 236
    The Use of Negative Practice, 237
    Extinction of Response, 237
    Positive Reinforcement of Selected Responses, 237
    Stimulus Deprivation and Satiation, 237
    Self-modification, 237
    Cognitions: Talking to Oneself, 238
    Other Techniques, 239
THE IMPLICIT DEMAND CHARACTERISTICS IN BEHAVIOR MODIFICATION, 239
    Behavior Change and Attitude Change, 242
EVALUATIONS OF PSYCHOTHERAPY EFFECTIVENESS, 243
    Experimental Evidence of the Effectiveness of Systematic Desensitization, 245
SUMMARY, 247

13 neuroses I
MAJOR ROLE-PLAYING COMPONENTS 248

DSM-II: DEFINITIONS AND GENERAL COMMENTS, 249
    General Approach, 250
HYSTERICAL NEUROSIS, 250
    Hysterical Behavior: Definitions, 250
    A Behavioral Reformulation, 253
    A Sociopsychological Formulation of Hysteria, 254
CLINICAL OBSERVATIONS AND TREATMENT OF HYSTERIA, 257
    A Reformulation of Dissociative Behavior, 260
    Illustrative Cases, 261
DEPRESSIVE NEUROSIS, 263
SUMMARY, 266

14 neuroses II

TENSIONAL COMPONENTS 267

PHOBIC BEHAVIOR, 268
General Discussion, 268
REFORMULATION OF PHOBIC BEHAVIOR, 269
ILLUSTRATIONS OF TREATMENT PROCEDURES, 272
Desensitization in Practice, 273
Use of Rapport, 273
"Anxiety-Relief" Responses, 273
Systematic Desensitization, 274
Group Therapy by Desensitization, 274
Modeling, 276
Contact Desensitization, 276
Operant Procedures, 276
Reactive Inhibition and Implosion, 276
A General Comment: Behavior Therapy and Seduction, 278
OBSESSIVE-COMPULSIVE BEHAVIOR, 278
General Discussion, 278
A Reformulation, 279
Behavioral Treatment of Obsessive-Compulsive Acts, 280
DIFFUSE ANXIOUS BEHAVIOR, 282
General Discussion, 282
HYPOCHONDRIACAL BEHAVIOR, 285
General Remarks, 285
DEPERSONALIZATION BEHAVIOR, 285
General Comments, 286
NEURASTHENIC BEHAVIOR, 286
General Comments, 286
OTHER NEUROSES, 287
Discussion, 287
SUMMARY, 288

15 special symptom behaviors and transient situational disturbances 289

SPECIAL SYMPTOMS, 290
General Discussion, 290
Speech Disturbance, 290
Learning Disturbance, 290
Sleep Problems, 290
Tic and Other Psychomotor Problems, 290
Other Target Behaviors, 295
Feeding Problems, 295
Enuresis and Encopresis, 298
Cephalagia, 298
Overeating, 298
GENERAL COMMENTS, 299
TRANSIENT SITUATIONAL DISTURBANCE, 299
General Discussion, 301
Panic as a Paradigm of the Transient Situational Disturbances, 302

CIVILIAN DISASTER, 303
WAR NEUROSIS, 304
PRISONERS OF WAR, 305
A NOTE ON SLEEP DEPRIVATION, 308
SUMMARY, 308

16 psychophysiological disorders 310

HISTORY OF THE CONCEPT, 311
CAUTIONS IN THE USE OF THE CONCEPT, 312
THE INTERNAL AND EXTERNAL ENVIRONMENT, 313
THEORIES OF ORIGIN OF PSYCHOPHYSIOLOGICAL DISORDERS, 314
    Hereditary, 314
    Somatic Weakness, 314
    Stress Theory, 314
    Inherited Autonomic Patterns, 314
    Psychological Theories, 314
    Conditioning, 316
HYPNOSIS AND PHYSIOLOGICAL CHANGE, 319
    A Summary Statement, 320
CLINICAL APPLICATIONS, 321
    Skin Problems, 321
    Bronchial Asthma, 322
    Gastrointestinal Reactions, 323
    Genito-urinary Reactions, 324
    Hypertension, 325
    Headaches, 325
SUMMARY, 325

17 schizophrenic behavior
A DESCRIPTION 327

GENERAL DISCUSSION, 328
A DESCRIPTION OF SCHIZOPHRENIA, 330
TYPES OF SCHIZOPHRENIA, 334
    Other Types of Schizophrenia, 336
FACTOR ANALYSIS OF "SYMPTOMATIC" BEHAVIOR, 338
ADDITIONAL DIMENSIONS IN THE STUDY OF SCHIZOPHRENIA, 339
THE PROCESS-REACTIVE DIMENSION, 339
    Other Dimensions, 340
ATTEMPTS TO GENERALIZE ABOUT SCHIZOPHRENIA, 342
    A Genetic View, 343
    Other Theories, 346
    Impression Management, 347
IDEOLOGICAL-SOCIOLOGICAL THEORIES, 348
    Linguistic Analysis, 349
IS THE CONCEPT SCHIZOPHRENIA VIABLE? 350
SUMMARY, 351

18 the sociopsychological formulation and treatment of schizophrenia 352

BACKGROUND, 353
A FORMULATION OF SCHIZOPHRENIA, 357
GETTING TO THE HOSPITAL, 361
SCHIZOPHRENIA AND THE HOSPITAL, 362
DEDUCTIONS FROM THE HOSPITAL SITUATION, 366
    The Hospital and Schizophrenic Behaviors, 366
    Effects of Hospital Practices, 369
BEYOND THE HOSPITAL, 371
EXPERIMENTS IN THE SOCIOPSYCHOLOGICAL MODEL, 372
    Disorganization of Thinking, 372
    Apathy, 372
    Social Withdrawal, 375
    Bizarre or Aversive Verbalization, 377
    A Word About Experiments, 378
APPLICATIONS OF CONCEPTS: TREATMENT, 378
    Family Treatment, 380
TOKEN ECONOMIES, 380
    The Token Economy and Staff Training, 384
THE TOKEN ECONOMY: EVALUATIONS, 386
SUMMARY, 387

19 extreme affective behavior 388

    Historical Background, 389
MANIC BEHAVIOR, 390
DEPRESSIVE BEHAVIOR, 391
INVOLUTIONAL MELANCHOLIA, 393
A SOCIOPSYCHOLOGICAL FORMULATION, 394
TREATMENT OF DEPRESSION, 397
SUMMARY, 399

20 personality disorders with particular reference to paranoid behavior 400

    Discussion, 402
PARANOID BEHAVIOR, 402
PARANOID STATES, 403
FORMULATIONS OF PARANOIA, 404
    Freud's Formulation, 404
    Cameron's Formulation, 405
    Lemert's Formulation, 406
A SOCIOPSYCHOLOGICAL FORMULATION, 410
TREATMENT OF PARANOID BEHAVIOR, 413
OTHER PERSONALITY DISORDERS, 414
    A Note On Labeling by Experts, 415
SUMMARY, 416

21 sexual behavior 417

DEFINITIONS OF SEXUAL NORMALITY, 419
A SOCIOPSYCHOLOGICAL APPROACH, 423
    General Comments, 426
    Problems and Solutions, 423
    Ejaculatory Incompetence, 431
    Unusual Stimuli, 431
ETHICAL CONSIDERATIONS, 440
SUMMARY, 441

22 addictive behavior 443

DEFINING ADDICTION, 444
ALCOHOLISM, 445
    Effects of Alcohol, 447
    History of Alcohol, 449
    Theories of Alcoholism, 451
    Learning Formulations of Alcoholism, 450
A SOCIOPSYCHOLOGICAL FORMULATION, 451
TREATMENT OF ALCOHOLISM, 452
    Behavioral Approaches, 453
    Drinking Behavior, 453
    Specific Social-Learning Procedures, 454
    Aversion Procedures, 455
    Desensitization of Drinking Behavior, 456
    Operant and Controlled Drinking Approaches, 456
    Social-Group Approaches, 457
    Summary, 458
DRUG ADDICTION, 458
    Drug Usage, 459
HISTORICAL BACKGROUND, 459
THE EFFECTS OF SPECIFIC DRUGS, 462
    Heroin and Morphine, 463
    Barbiturates, 463
    Amphetamines, 464
    Cocaine, 464
    Marijuana, 464
    Hallucinogenic Drugs, 465
TREATMENT, 466
SUMMARY, 468

23 children's behavior 469

    Changeworthy Behavior, 470
HISTORICAL DEVELOPMENT, 471
PROBLEMS OF DESCRIPTION, 472
FEARFUL BEHAVIOR, 475
    Training Parents, 477
    On Punishment and Parental Attitudes, 481

Parental Attitudes, 482
The Battered Child, 483
Summary, 484
Some Behavioral Techniques, 484
Modeling, 487
Summary, 488
CONDUCT PROBLEMS, 489
CLASSROOM BEHAVIOR, 495
HYPERACTIVITY, 495
Treatment, 497
TOILET TRAINING, 498
Summary, 500
AUTISM AND CHILDHOOD SCHIZOPHRENIA, 501
Behavioral Approaches to Autism, 503
SUMMARY, 510

24 retardation 512

CLINICAL SUBCATEGORIES, 513
The Diagnosis of Retardation, 514
Physiological Defects, 517
CULTURAL-FAMILIAL RETARDATION, 519
A Social View of Retardation, 521
Retardation: The Braginskys' Alternative Paradigm, 521
A BEHAVIORAL VIEW OF RETARDATION, 522
BEHAVIORAL TREATMENT OF THE RETARDED, 524
Self-help Behavior, 524
Speech, 525
Work, 525
Classroom Behavior, 525
TOKEN-ECONOMY WORK WITH RETARDATES, 526
SUMMARY, 528

25 brain syndromes and geriatrics 530

CLASSIFICATION OF BRAIN SYNDROMES, 531
SOME SPECIFIC ORGANIC DISEASES, 532
Huntington's Chorea, 532
Alzheimer's Disease, 532
Pick's Disease, 532
Parkinson's Disease, 532
Epidemic Encephalitis, 533
EFFECTS OF REMOVAL OF BRAIN TISSUE, 533
ASSESSMENT OF BRAIN DAMAGE, 535
TREATMENT OF AN ILLUSTRATIVE PROBLEM BEHAVIOR, 536
BEING OLD IN A YOUNG WORLD: SENILITY—MAYBE, 537
"Senile Dementia," 539
EPILEPSY, 540
SUMMARY, 542

26 conflict with the prevailing society

ANTISOCIAL AND DYSSOCIAL BEHAVIOR 543

THE HISTORY OF A LABEL, 545
DESCRIPTION AND THEORIES OF PSYCHOPATHY, 546
   Heredity and the Sociopath, 548
   Family Relations of the Sociopath, 549
   Role-Taking and Sociopathy, 550
   The Sociopath and Conditionability, 550
   Stimulation-Seeking and the Sociopath, 550
   A Sociopsychological Formulation of Antisocial (Psychopathic) Behavior, 551
DYSSOCIAL REACTIONS, 554
JUVENILE DELINQUENCY, 556
   Treatment of Delinquency, 559
   Prevention of Delinquency, 562
SUMMARY, 563

27 placing limits on personal behavior

OTHER CHANGEWORTHY BEHAVIORS 564

PORNOGRAPHY AND OBSCENITY, 565
   Cursing and Wall-Writing, 567
GAMBLING, 569
SMOKING CIGARETTES, 570
EXISTENTIAL PROBLEMS: A BEHAVIORAL APPROACH, 571
SUICIDE, 575
   Research Problems, 576
   Categories of Suicide, 576
   Theories of Suicide, 576
   Suicide Prevention, 579
   Self-mutilation, 580
SUMMARY, 581

28 increasing prosocial behavior

"POSITIVE DEVIANCE" 582

CHARACTERISTICS OF THE PROSOCIAL PERSON, 584
SELF AND SELF-CONTROL, 585
HELPING STRANGERS, 586
   Bystander Effect, 587
   "Passers-by" Studies, 588
   Field Experiments: Good Citizens, 589
   Summary, 590
   Aspects of Moral Behavior, 590
   Rules, 591
   Some Empirical Studies, 592

SPECIFIC POSITIVE BEHAVIORS, 593
   In the Classroom, 594
   Token Economy in the Classroom, 594
   Intellectual Targets, 595
   How to Approach Situations, 596
   The Classroom as a Planned Environment, 596
   Work, 597
   Caring for the Environment, 597
   Behavior Therapy Procedures as Part of Other Treatment Programs, 597
CHANGING ROLES, CHANGING SOCIETY: WOMEN'S LIB AS CREATIVE DEVIANCE, 598
SUMMARY, 601

29 humanism, human behavior, and the concept of abnormality   602

   Areas of Choice (Ethical Concern), 604
   Genetic Engineering, 604
   Biofeedback, 604
   Population Control, 605
   Death and Life, and Style of Life, 605
   Hardware: Information Storage and Retrieval, 606
   The Production of Research, 606
   Application of Research, 607
SPECIFYING LIMITS OF BEHAVIOR: RIGHTS OF PEOPLE, 607
   Children and Parents, 607
   Patients and Practitioners, 608
   Encounter-Sensitivity Training, 608
   Behavior Therapy, 610
LAW AND MEDICINE, 613
PROBLEMS OF CHANGE: PSYCHOTHERAPY, 614
COMMUNITY AS "PATIENT," 616
   Community Mental Health in Action, 618
   Conditions of Service Delivery: Crisis Intervention, 620
SUMMARY, 620

references   623

name index   725

subject index   757

preface

First of all, this is a book about people. It is about how people get along with other people, the things they learn to do, and the concepts other people have about such adjustments.

In dealing with people, we will make the assumption that the more accurately we perceive people and what they do, the better we will be able to deal with them, to serve others, and to attain our own humanity and decency. We think the scientific method offers the best way yet devised for checking the accuracy of our observations, and therefore we will use it.

We will deal with what people do and not with abstractions. We will talk about people who are called "schizophrenic" and about people who are considered appropriate for professional assistance. But neither in this book nor in our professional work do we treat an abstraction such as schizophrenia, hysteria, or sexual perversion. Rather, we are always dealing with people who at certain times act in various ways that lead to labels, categorizations, and the application of abstractions. It follows that, because of its crucial importance, we place considerable emphasis on investigating the labeling process itself.

That the labels and the things labeled (people and acts) must not be confused does not mean that such abstractions do not serve a number of purposes. What we hope to do is to give the reader a good grasp of the current labels, what they mean, and how they are used, but we plan to do so within the context that such labeling is professional behavior or, more precisely, the behavior of professional people. The field of abnormal psychology is a human endeavor: it involves people dealing with each other. What professionals do not only affects the people they treat but also reflects the society that has trained them and in which they serve. We will, therefore, pay a great deal of attention to the concepts and acts of the professional person who is as deeply involved in the definition and outcome of the interpersonal drama called abnormal behavior as the person who is thought of as a schizophrenic, a lunatic, or a patient.

We will try to look at ourselves and others as clearly and honestly as we can, Just as abnormal psychology is a human enterprise, so a book about abnormal psychology is a limited, imperfect attempt that may help, may be a step forward but, by the nature of the material and our approach to it, is never completely finished or completely the truth. As authors, we are faced with limitations of space in this book and of time in the reader's life. We are faced with a field that moves from physiology to anthropology, from tranquilizers and electric convulsive therapy to encounter groups, sit-ins, and marriage. We must select our topics, and our selection reflects the times in which we live and our own responses (biases if you will) to those times.

This second edition was written because a great deal of new information became available in the five years since we wrote the first edition. Although some of this material is included because it strengthens our viewpoint, other new information and ideas presented have made our previous writing so dated that even middle-aged college professors should be and are embarrassed by it.

Our view of the field of abnormal psychology is illustrated by the changes in public and professional interest that have led to behaviors not considered to be a problem a decade ago becoming the subject of concern. Conversely, other behaviors previously considered to be abnormal are now being reevaluated. Among such topics are: existential problems, abortion, use of marijuana, women's social role, homosexuality, racism, the youth and the elderly as minority groups, pornography, poverty, personal responsibility within a defined social role (e.g., in the military or in a bureaucracy), and human ecology (both in terms of population and pollution).

If the authors as individuals have a worry, it is not that the world changes, much less that concepts of appropriate behavior change, but that every year seems to bring new social interests that compete with last year's genuine concern. It is as if there were an implicit election (in the mass media) each year of the "problem of the year." The only rules of the game are that it must be a *new* problem. Problems are defined one year and promises are made for remediation. Newspapers, magazines, books, television, and movies sell the new; we are concerned that recognition of problems and promised solutions will take the place of the slower, much more laborious process of understanding and evaluating the effects of solutions (if and when the promises are kept). Rather than moving from last year's pet problem to this year's popular cause, we think a general orientation towards interpersonal behavior will be more rewarding. We are worried that recognition of a problem will be mistaken for solution, that personal sympathy will be confused with genuine activity, and that currency will be confused with relevancy. We think that the pressure to sell in the popular media and the pressure to make a showing, or seem to make a showing, in the applied and political arenas must be buttressed by the scholarly approach that our universities still permit. Therefore, we use current concerns as examples of principles that are more general and more enduring.

To return to our first sentence: this is a book about people, how they get along with other people, and how they may regard these interactions. The content of abnormal psychology is interesting and important in itself, but also it provides an example of more general concepts. We are both the students and the people being studied: this, then, is a book about people, ourselves included. The field of abnormal psychology is *not* a separate, puzzling, or unique field. It is about all of us as people.

The information explosion continues. Even as we read page proofs for this edition, we become aware of new articles and examples that we would have liked to include.

In terms of organization of the book, the revision of the American Psychiatric Association's *Diagnostic and Statistical Manual* in 1968, hereafter called DSM-II, has had a major impact. We think that there are both strengths and weaknesses in the DSM-II changes, and we will discuss them at the appropriate times.

Two chapters have been assimilated into others. We have moved the Chapter 6 of the first edition, "A Formulation of Abnormal Behavior," into the Chapter 2 rather than waiting until we had covered the background material on scientific method and learning. Even though the statement is now intellectually weaker if taken by itself, it is better pedagogically to state the viewpoint early and let the remainder of the volume speak for itself. Chapter 11 of the first edition, "The Roots of Behavior Modification," has been eliminated; most of the material covered there is found in the present chapter on history (Chapter 7).

With the space saved, we have introduced two major new chapters. The first (Chapter 27) deals with behaviors and problems not explicitly covered in DSM-II but which people find disturbing and worthy of change—for example, behaviors such as viewing pornography, and "existential" problems (which are not recognized in either DSM-I or DSM-II yet receive considerable attention in our clinics and publications).

A second new chapter (28) deals with behavior that is pleasing rather than disturbing and that is societally encouraged rather than discouraging. Self-control and altruism are two prime examples in this chapter.

Because of space limitations, every new item meant deletion of some former material. Every page and paragraph represents a matter of choice. A frequent instance was whether to keep a classic breakthrough study or replace it with a more recent and usually more complex one. We have not been consistent in our choices, although we favored the classic material if for no other reason than that the designs are usually easier for students to grasp. Certainly every professional reader will be able to think of many good studies that deserved inclusion and would have strengthened the presentation. We are all too cognizant of our deficiencies and can only state two of our chosen self-limitations. The first is that this is a book on a *psychological approach*. We present relatively little on surgical, chemical, or electrical forms of therapy, or biochemical and metabolic hypotheses, and refer the interested reader to volumes such as Mendels (1973), and Hammer, Salzinger and Sutton (1973). Second, we often provide a list of references, but we preferred to present some material in useful detail rather than encyclopedic bibliographies. An example of this latter may be found in our work for fellow professionals, such as Krasner (1971) on behavior therapy.

We hope that the word "approach" in the title will apply to the reader who is a student as well as to the authors' efforts. We can only present an *approach*, a coming-nearer, a start on work, an approximation, and *not* a consummation. We find the field ever-changing, exciting, and challenging. We hope the reader will join us.

ACKNOWLEDGMENTS

We are grateful to have this opportunity to thank publicly the many people who made this book possible, particularly the multitude of investigators whose work has helped create this book. To each and every one cited in the reference section we offer our thanks. Professors Richard Lazarus, Richard Blanton, and Henry E. Adams provided us with many valuable suggestions: the faults that remain are our responsibility. Peggy Harra contributed by long and valiant typing. Grant Number 11938 from the National Institute of Mental Health, U. S. Public Health Service, assisted us in support of research described in the book.

Many authors and publishers have consented to having their material quoted in this volume, and we are happy to acknowledge their kindness. The special credit lines that were requested are listed here; other quotations are acknowledged within the text by parenthetical reference to the bibliography.

The following articles are copyrighted by the American Psychological Association and are quoted by permission of the authors and the Association from the journals named:

B. M. Braginsky, M. Grosse, and K. Ring, "Controlling Outcomes through Impression-Management: An Experimental Study of the Manipulative Tactics of Mental Patients," *Journal of Consulting Psychology,* 1966, *30,* 295-300.

T. L. McInnis and L. P. Ullmann, "Positive and Negative Reinforcement with Short- and Long-Term Hospitalized Schizophrenics in a Probability Learning Situation," *Journal of Abnormal Psychology,* 1967, *72,* 157-162.

H. O. Schmidt and C. P. Fonda, "The Reliability of Psychiatric Diagnosis: A New Look," *Journal of Abnormal and Social Psychology,* 1956, *52,* 262-267.

E. Zigler and L. Phillips, "Psychiatric Diagnosis and Symptomatology," *Journal* of *Abnormal and Social Psychology*, 1961, *63*, 69-75.

Permssion to quote from other works came from the following:

American Psychiatric Association. Diagnostic and statistical manual of mental disorders. 2nd ed. (DSM-II.) © 1968.

A. T. Beck, C. H. Ward, M. Mendelson, J. E. Mock, and J. K. Erbaugh, "Reliability of Psychiatric Diagnosis. II: A Study of Consistency of Clinical Judgments and Ratings," *American Journal of Psychiatry*, 1962, *119*, 351-357. © 1962 by the American Psychiatric Association.

Dale Carnegie, *How to Win Friends and Influence People* (New York: Simon & Schuster, Inc., 1936). Reprinted by permission of Simon & Schuster, Inc.; Angus & Robertson Ltd., Sydney; and World's Work Ltd., London.

Otto Fenichel, *The Psychoanalytic Theory of Neurosis*. Excerpt reprinted by permission of W. W. Norton & Co., Inc. © 1945 by W. W. Norton & Co.

M. G. Sandifer, Jr., C. Pettus, and D. Quade, "A Study of Psychiatric Diagnosis," *Journal of Nervous and Mental Disease*, 1964, *139*, 350-356. © 1964 by The Williams & Wilkins Co., Baltimore.

H. N. Sloane, Jr. and B. D. MacAulay, eds., Operant Procedures in Remedial Speech and Language Training, pp. 63-64. © 1968 by Houghton Mifflin Co.

M. K. Termelin, Suggestion Effects in Psychiatric Diagnosis, *Journal of Nervous and Mental Disease*, 1968, *147*, 349-353. © 1968 by The Williams & Wilkins Co., Baltimore.

G. Zilboorg and G. W. Henry, *A History of Medical Psychology* (New York: W. W. Norton & Company, Inc., 1941). © 1941 by W. W. Norton & Co., Inc.

January 1975

Honolulu, Hawaii
Stony Brook, New York

A PSYCHOLOGICAL APPROACH TO ABNORMAL BEHAVIOR

prologue

The central idea of this book is that the behaviors traditionally called abnormal are no different, either quantitatively or qualitatively, in their development and maintenance from other behaviors. This book traces the conceptual research and therapeutic implications of not labeling any behavior, *ipso facto,* as abnormal or as an indication of "mental illness."

In general conversation the word "abnormal" is used to signify that something is unexpected, irregular, and different from the normal or predictable state of affairs.

> . . . normal behavior does not awaken the need for scientific explanation. We know our strivings, our hopes. We know what hurts our feelings, what pleases us, and how our aims and feelings determine our behavior. At least we think we know. Only when human behavior and feelings become abnormal—for instance when a person becomes depressed or elated without any obvious reasons, when he sees and hears things that do not exist, when he is afraid without being threatened—do we need some special explanation. [Alexander and Selesnick, 1968, p. 32.]

The mutual interdependence of people often makes the accurate prediction of other persons' behavior crucial for survival. For example, when driving a car, use of the proper side of the road and the proper responses to traffic lights are literally matters of life and death. In social life, there are formal and informal expectations that are valuable to both the individual and those around him. Breaking these rules may be termed *deviance.* When the rules are written laws, deviance may be called criminal. There is an area of behavior, however, where formal rules may not be broken but where unexpected behavior is seriously upsetting to other people, such as friends, parents, spouses, neighbors, teachers, and policemen, or to the person himself. For the purposes of this book, *abnormality is the sort of deviance that calls for and sanctions the professional attention of psychiatrists, clinical psychologists, and other "mental health" professionals.*

It is apparent from this definition that the area of abnormality will vary from place to place, time to time, and person to person. An example is style of dress. A man wearing clothes proper for a woman or an adult wearing what is typical for a child would also be considered unusual, unexpected, and different in a noteworthy manner. An example of how the context of a specific action determines the consequences of a social evaluation occurred when the *Chicago Daily News* (January 18, 1969, p. 12) printed a photograph of two males in dresses passing two coeds in slacks. The men were protesting the fact that the women were wearing trousers in class. However, the caption clearly indicated that the school officials had sanctioned the stunt. With a "good reason," behavior that might otherwise have led to a referral to a physician or policeman was permissible. The particular garb is not in and of itself unusual; questions of who, when, and where must be taken into consideration. When considering abnormal behavior, it is crucial to include the context of the act rather than the act by itself.

Calling an act abnormal has a number of

consequences. Of importance here is that the label sanctions a type of social control. In the past century, in our culture, the profession which has been most intimately associated with the forms of deviance subsumed under the heading "abnormal psychology" has been medicine. Following the pattern of physical medicine, the presence of a "disease" justifies the activities of a medical specialist. The next section will therefore deal with the association of this tradition with the present volume.

TRADITIONAL ABNORMAL PSYCHOLOGY

If abnormal behavior is the result of some pattern of disease, abnormal psychology would be the study of diseases such as neuroses and psychoses. A quick review of the titles of the chapters of this book from 13 onwards indicates little departure from these groupings of behaviors. The book, in fact, uses the word "abnormal" in its title and the system of diagnostic categories of the American Psychiatric Association. There are a number of reasons why this has been done despite our view that what is called abnormal does not differ in itself from what is called normal behavior.

First, although this book questions the usefulness of the *conceptual* framework of traditional abnormal psychology, there is no question of the *reality* of the behaviors involved. When, for example, a person washes his hands 25 times within a period of 6 hours, there is no argument about what he is doing or that such behavior may have important consequences for his life and for others around him. The question, rather, is whether it is valuable to call such behavior abnormal, sick, or obsessive-compulsive. This book uses traditional categories to outline *the behaviors* to be dealt with. The traditional categories are a starting point indicating the types of behavior currently viewed as abnormal in our society.

Second, the traditional categories are used because the teacher, lawyer, clinician, researcher, and general reader should be conversant with the materials which historically have come to be included in this area. Both the professional person and the educated layman should be familiar with the language—the labels as well as the concepts—used to communicate about people.

These methods of communication influence further behavior. How a situation or an individual is labeled affects how people perceive, evaluate, and react to it. For example, if the reader were told that both authors of this book are paranoid and that the book was published to illustrate how nearly plausible such disturbed characters can be, he probably would react differently to it than if he were told the authors are no more poorly adjusted than most professors of psychology. Because labels influence behavior, it is essential that current ways of talking about abnormal behavior be presented to determine how they developed and what they imply.

There is another reason for organizing material within the traditional framework. A historical perspective is helpful, if not absolutely necessary, for the appreciation of new concepts. Ideas do not develop in an intellectual vacuum, and all ideas, especially those about human behavior, have a continuing history. Formulations of human behavior are best understood within the contexts in which they developed.

Finally, given the present book's socio-psychological frame of reference, abnormal behavior must be studied in the context of a given time, place, and person. The study of abnormal behavior reveals much about a culture by telling what behaviors in it are selected as deviant, what behaviors are ignored as irrelevant, and what behaviors are considered appropriate. Cultures are revealed in many ways, and the identification and treatment of unusual behaviors tells much about a society's way of life, especially its framework of roles within which individual behavior takes place.

PURPOSES OF STUDYING ABNORMAL PSYCHOLOGY

By some estimates, abnormal psychology deals with up to 25 percent of the population. If one includes four million individuals classified as mentally retarded, eight million categorizable as "neurotic," three quarters of a million patients in mental hospitals, three quarters of a million alcoholics, a quarter of a million incarcerated criminals, and all the people who have "psychosomatic" disorders, behavior problems, or who are functioning inadequately, it becomes startlingly obvious that the field encompasses a large percentage of the population. Because of the number of people involved and the nature of their problems, abnormal psychology has professional relevance for physicians, social workers, judges, occupational therapists, nurses, journalists, teachers, ministers, novelists, actors, lawyers, and many others.

A knowledge of abnormal psychology is prerequisite for being an educated person. There are ramifications of abnormal psychology for the taxpayer in terms of decisions about taxes for treatment programs. There are legal ramifications in terms of criminal responsibility and civil contracts. The study of abnormal psychology helps give a critical appreciation of the subject matter of plays, movies, television, novels, newspapers, Greek tragedy, and the Bible.[1] Certain aspects of this field, particularly those originating with Freud, are part of contemporary language and thought. Further, as noted above, the manner in which the unfortunates of a society are treated, whether they be the mentally ill, the unemployed, a minority group, or the aged, reflects that society's values.

Abnormal psychology as the study of unexpected behaviors is intrinsically interesting.

[1] A number of anthologies provide examples of literary descriptions of behavior (Fadiman and Kewman, 1973; Kaplan, 1964; Rabkin, 1966; Stone and Stone, 1966).

One of my favourite aunts was an incurable soprano. If you happened to meet her on the corner of Fifth Avenue while waiting for a bus, she would open her mouth wide and sing scales, trying to make you do as much. She wore her hat hanging off the back of her head or tilted over one ear. A rose was always stuck in her hair. Long hatpins emerged dangerously, not from her hat, but from her hair. Her trailing dresses swept up the dust of the streets. She invariably wore a feather boa. She was an excellent cook and made beautiful tomato jelly. Whenever she wasn't at the piano, she could be found in the kitchen or reading the ticker-tape. She was an inveterate gambler. She had a strange complex about germs and was forever wiping her furniture with Lysol. But she had such extraordinary charm that I really loved her. I cannot say her husband felt as much. After he had fought with her for over thirty years, he tried to kill her and one of her sons by hitting them with a golf club. Not succeeding, he rushed to the reservoir where he drowned himself with heavy weights tied to his feet. [Guggenheim, 1960, pp. 18–19.]

"Abnormal" acts are dramatic, puzzling, exciting, alien, and yet very near to all people. There is a plethora of professional and popular terms for unusual behavior: mental illness, mental disorder, mental disease, behavior disorder, neuropsychiatric disability, psychological disorder, emotional disorder, nervous breakdown, personality disorder, bizarre, peculiar, sick, maladjusted, immoral, crazy, odd, eccentric, irrational, and many others. The behaviors referred to may range from poor study habits to rape, from stuttering to amnesia, from dropping out of school to divorce, from excessive hand-washing to low back pains. In fact, it seems that almost any human behavior might, under one circumstance or another, be included.

Finally, abnormal psychology is worth studying because no other branch of human knowledge is as filled with misinformation, dogma, quackery, and fear-arousing stimuli. Since this is a vital area of human behavior about which there has been relatively little clear-cut and objective scientific information, the field has led the sincere do-gooder, the power-mad, the would-be healer, the self-anointed prophet, and even the confused and misguided professional to make dogmatic, frightening, hopeful, misleading, frantic, and erroneous statements and promises.

Conley, Conwell, and Arrill (1967) estimated the annual cost of mental illness at 20 billion dollars, while Carey (1972) cites one expert's opinion that, "60 million Americans are borderline schizophrenics or exhibit other deviant mental behavior in the schizophrenic category." Many standard textbooks have statements such as, "If present trends continue, approximately one person in ten now living in this country will at some time require professional treatment. . . . Abnormal behavior has for good reason been designated the country's Number One health problem." (Coleman, 1972, p. 4.) If the reader feels frightened by such statements and starts wondering if he is one of the ten, he is reacting appropriately. If the reader is confused by the claims and counterclaims of the various approaches to psychotherapy, he is again reacting appropriately. If the reader feels perplexed and even irritated when three prominent psychiatrists testify that the defendant at a famous murder trial is insane and three other prominent psychiatrists testify that the defendant is sane, he is again reacting appropriately. These matters *are* frightening, irritating, and confusing. The material in this text is intended to facilitate the understanding and evaluation of such social phenomena.

ABOUT THIS BOOK

"Abnormal" and its synonyms imply that a behavior or an individual is different, unlawful, inappropriate, disruptive, and not understandable by usual criteria. This book takes the position that abnormal psychology is a title of convenience. Unfortunately, most of the terms which are often substituted for "abnormal," such as "deviant," "disorganized," "ineffective," or "maladjusted," imply a distinction between two types of people, the sick and the healthy, the normal and the abnormal, the adjusted and the maladjusted. The view presented in this volume is that human behavior is not dichotomous but rather can and should be dealt with through a single set of principles. Behavior that is reacted to as "abnormal" or "bad" is the reasonable outcome of past and present circumstances. Much of this book will be devoted to demonstrating that this formulation of what has been called abnormal leads to greater understanding and more effective response to behavior. Using a new language and approach may lead to new ways of dealing with people.

In striving toward this goal, this book will make use of three sources of concepts: the scientific method of investigation, the social learning concepts derived from psychological experiments, and the specific tasks and experiences with which psychologists have become associated. In terms of scientific method, there will be discussion of topics such as operational definitions, methods of demonstration, hypothesis formulation, and independent and dependent variables. The materials dealing with social learning formulations will be drawn from psychologists, psychiatrists, and sociologists whose research has emphasized the effects of environmental events on the learning of human behavior. In terms of psychological practice, there will be a focus on current behavior modification procedures.

The presentation of material in this book is intended as an introduction to abnormal psychology, not as an encyclopedic coverage of the field. It is hoped that the student will be lured to the library to follow up material he finds exciting.

A psychological approach to abnormal behavior will be manifest in many ways. Terms such as "experimental" and "control" will occur with the same frequency that terms such as "id" and "ego" may appear in other volumes. Learning concepts will be used frequently. Such use may answer the question rightly posed in elementary psychology courses, "How can we make use of all this?" In addition, examples of the way psychological principles are applied in life situations should make them clearer and more meaningful to the reader.

Instead of illustrations that stress the oddity of abnormal behavior, the reader will find in this book an attempt to describe the unity of behavior. Thus, throughout there will be illustrations of ideas, experiments, and samples of behavior. There will be presented, in other words, a scientific outlook on life rather than a mass of rapidly dated specific information. Ideally the student will obtain a background that he can use in evaluating new ideas, other people, and his own behavior.

This book is not aimed at making therapists, but is intended to help develop citizens and parents who will not be swayed by every new "discovery" reported in newspapers and magazines. In terms of this goal it is more important that the student be able to evaluate new material than it is for him to possess various bits of information. It is hoped that after reading this book the student faced with new material in this field will routinely ask questions such as "Where is the control group?" and "What are the reinforcing contingencies?"

If it is correct that no behavior is intrinsically abnormal and that social determinants play a crucial role in the designation of abnormality, profound questions of value arise. Abnormal psychology touches upon perennial philosophical questions such as "What is good behavior?" and "How do the individuals within a society determine the value of different kinds of behaviors?" The material to be discussed in this book should help clarify the moral and ethical issues involved in abnormal psychology.

Every effort will be made to integrate treatment with diagnosis. The descriptions of behaviors considered abnormal will be presented together with examples of their treatment. Instead of a nebulous "and the person was referred for therapy," there will be illustrations of what can be done to modify the behavior described. In this regard the book will touch on and introduce some two dozen different therapeutic procedures. These illustrations of the application of psychological techniques will be the vehicle for demonstrating the use of learning procedures. If a direct application of concepts derived from "normal" learning is effective, many traditional beliefs about abnormality will be found to be questionable.

On a practical level, this book starts out with a theory about abnormality and then tries to see how well the concept works in practice. If thinking in different terms about supposedly abnormal people leads to greater effectiveness in understanding and dealing with them, the present viewpoint will be bolstered. On a theoretical level, many words which are traditionally considered to designate real things will be found to be unnecessary and, to the extent that they misdirect attention, even pernicious.

The entire thrust of science is a movement toward freedom from misconception. The goal of education in science is an openness to experience that will enable the individual to know the world and to react effectively to it rather than to remain in bondage to the shadows of his ignorance. In dealing with abnormal behavior, the focus is the understanding of and appropriate response to fellow human beings. Responding to others with a freedom from bias seems a necessary condition for treating them with dignity and decency. This book is an attempted step in that direction.

SUMMARY

For social life to be possible, people must be able to predict with some degree of accuracy the responses of their fellows. The failure to live up to social expectations is called *deviance,* and the special subclass of deviance which currently sanctions the intervention of the mental health professions is called *abnormal behavior.* This definition stems from a view that abnormal behavior is a label of convenience and that in actuality behavior considered abnormal is no different in its development and maintenance from behavior considered normal. It also stresses that no act by itself can be called abnormal, but rather that the social context of the act and actor must be taken into account.

Given this view, the traditional formulations of abnormal psychology will be examined to provide a background for developing newer concepts, to give the reader a knowledge of the vocabulary currently used by many workers in the field, and to provide a systematic way to include the behaviors considered abnormal in this society at this point in time. The method of this volume will be to present concepts and data to help the reader develop skill in evaluating new materials. While there are many practical and intellectually challenging reasons for studying abnormal behavior, the ultimate goal of this book is that of all scientific and educational endeavors: the increase of intellectual freedom that will lead people to respond to their fellow human beings with decency and dignity.

defining abnormality

1

In the Prologue, abnormality was defined as behavior violating interpersonal expectations in a manner that sanctions intervention of mental health practitioners. This definition emphasizes that labeling a person as abnormal is a social act within a definite context of time, place, and person. The act of designating someone as abnormal is a human behavior and therefore as much a proper subject for empirical investigation by social scientists as the supposedly abnormal acts themselves. This first chapter will acquaint the student with the range of approaches to the concept of abnormality.

The Psychiatric Emergency

A good start is a look at conditions leading to the intervention of a mental health practitioner. The single most critical situation is probably what has been called a psychiatric emergency: someone—a person, his relatives, or the police—asks for immediate service. The emergent situation calls for prompt action. Glasscote and his colleagues surveyed the majority of facilities in the United States providing emergency psychiatric service within a relatively comprehensive mental health program. Of 174 facilities surveyed, 154 replied to a questionnaire, and of these only 20 said they had a *formal* definition of a psychiatric emergency, and "none of these as set forth would meet dictionary standards." (Glasscote et al., 1966, p. 9.) The facilities defined an emergent patient as one who is dangerous to himself or to others; one who calls himself—or whose relatives call—an emergency; or one who is so evaluated by a physician. In addition to those with more formal definitions, 69 facilities gave *working* definitions. Of these, 22 said they treated a patient as emergent if he or a relative asserted that he was a psychiatric emergency; another 17 used as their criterion that the individual was considered a danger to himself or to others, and 21 others accepted the opinion of a referring or examining physician that the patient was emergent.

As Glasscote et al. note, these definitions tell why facilities are willing to see persons, but they do not tell what is disturbing such people. The findings concerning the definition of a psychiatric emergency may be summarized by the following excerpt: "Dr. Stuart Knox, commenting at our emergency service conference, characterized the emergent patient as one 'who finds that his adaptive capabilities have been reduced to the point where he cannot cope with his current problem without outside assistance.' This criterion can be applied not only to the patient, Dr. Knox says, but to the family doctor or to the police when they have been called in." (Glasscote et al., 1966, p. 10.)

In short, *someone, whether the patient or another member of the community, finds the facilities of a psychiatric service a solution to a problem.* Glasscote et al. make the point in this way: "Thus, classification as a *psychiatric* emergency seems largely contingent on one's being conceived of as a *social* emergency. Of course many social emergencies are not psychiatric emergencies, but virtually all psychiatric emergencies are simultaneously social emergencies . . . other kinds of disturbed behavior, if they are to be considered psychiatric emergencies, must also be perceived as social emergencies that carry a threat, whether immediate or remote." (p. 11.)

In practice, however, there is a shift from a focus on social behavior to a set of abstractions. This shift is pointed out by Jackson (1964, p. 45):

It is unlikely that people are very often committed to state mental hospitals solely because they are unhappy or suffering; most often they are committed only when their behavior is such that they impose inconvenience, embarrassment, or suffering upon others. Thus, although the diagnostic categories employed may be psychiatric, the symptoms from which illness is inferred relate to social behavior.

Discharge from hospitalization is similarly based on social competence rather than strict psychiatric categorization. Rock, Jacobson, and Janopaul (1968) cite the following excerpts from interviews and field observations: "The mere fact that a patient's illness is in full remission is not sufficient for discharge. The discharge also hinges on what he is returning to in the community. . . . the main point discussed was the ability of the patient to support himself or be supported in the community." (p. 217.)

In short, there is social behavior that is a problem to someone and calls for a response. A bar association task force made the following observations: "For many . . . hospitalization is predicated not so much on their mental illness as on the fact that the state mental hospital offers the only public custodial care program available." (Rock, Jacobson, and Janopaul, 1968, p. 171.) "In effect the only mechanism for invoking state assistance in the care of the mentally ill is commitment, which shifts financial responsibility immediately and completely to the state." (Rock, Jacobson, and Janopaul, 1968, p. 176.)

An example (Plog and Edgerton, 1969) of a social agreement to solve a problem follows:

A few years ago, when Mutiso was about 35 years old, he killed a 6-year-old girl, not to mention two goats and a chicken. Mutiso attacked the girl and the animals in broad daylight and killed all of them with a large knife. He was in a great rage, and members of his clan finally had to tie him to a tree until he calmed down enough to explain his actions. Mutiso explained that the child was a witch who had been causing his cattle and goats to sicken and die. He claimed that he had warned the child, but when the animals continued to die, he decided to kill the "witch." Then, he killed the nearby animals "as compensation."

After hearing Mutiso's story, members of his clan met to determine their proper course. By Kamba law, the clan is responsible for paying compensation whenever one of their members harms the property or life of a member of another clan. In a murder case, they would ordinarily have considerable compensation to pay. In this instance, they were unusually reluctant to pay compensation because Mutiso was considered by his fellow clansmen to be a "worthless" person—poor, irresponsible and a troublemaker. Mutiso's claim that the girl he killed was a witch was plausible, for even very young girls can be witches, but in this case there was no solid evidence to support his claim. Hence, Mutiso's action could not be excused, and compensation would apparently be required. However, since Mutiso previously had been in disputes that required the payment of clan compensation, his clansmen were most reluctant to pay for his misdeeds again. While the clan was debating the proper course to follow, a European police official heard of the "murder" of the child and took Mutiso into custody, saying indiscreetly that Mutiso must be "insane" to have done such a thing.

Mutiso's clansmen leaped at this interpretation with eager acceptance, for if Mutiso were found to be insane, they would be required to pay little compensation, or perhaps none at all. The clansmen agreed among themselves to testify to Mutiso's madness, and they appear to have won Mutiso's agreement to such a plea. As one old man recalled it, "We told him that if the Europeans found him guilty of murder, he would hang. But if he were only insane, he would go away to the hospital in Nairobi. He agreed that he was insane." ...

I visited Mutiso in the mental hospital, three years after his commitment. He occasionally spoke bizarrely, saying such things as, "You only think I am an African; actually I am English," or "I am king of the Kenya cowboys," or "This is a place for killing cows." But he was also capable of quite competent conduct, as witness the fact that he was nominally in charge of three wards of African patients. Indeed, the psychiatrist in charge stated that he was by no means certain that Mutiso was psychotic and added his own speculation that his legal insanity was contrived to escape "the noose." *He quickly added, however, that he could not prove his belief, so Mutiso was still in the hospital.* . . .

Finally, I asked Mutiso directly if he were mad. His answer, though rhetorical, is worth repeating: "Am I crazy? Of course, I am. Everyone is. You are crazy, too. *If everyone were not crazy, would I be here?*" [Italics added; pp. 63–65.]

The Importance of Definitions of Mental Illness

The immediately succeeding material in this chapter will be based on the *provisional assumption* that there is indeed some distinction between normal and abnormal behavior. In this manner, it will be possible to determine the usefulness of such an assumption.

Many important *social* acts depend on the designation of certain behaviors as deviant from normal or as abnormal. There are *societal* decisions of criminal responsibility, legal competence, and commitment to hospitals which are based on notions of normality and abnormality. The definition of abnormality is also crucial for *research*: if one group of people can be clearly specified as normal and another as abnormal, the two groups may be compared. Biochemical, life history, or other differences can be identified and made the subject of further study, and improved methods of treatment and prevention may result. If clear-cut ways of distinguishing between normality and abnormality cannot be devised, then the presence of normal people in the abnormal group and abnormal people in the normal group will lead to errors that obscure the presumed differences between the groups.

A definition of abnormality should have certain characteristics. The first has already been implied: the definition of "abnormal" should include all the people who are indeed abnormal and none of the people who are not. To the extent that abnormal people are not so designated and normal people are, the definition leads to error. Further, a definition must be consistently applied by different people and by the same person at different times. This is achieved by specifying the characteristics to be attended to by the labeler or the operations needed to find a person who fits the definition. This procedure is what is meant by obtaining an *operational definition*.

OPERATIONAL DEFINITIONS OF ABNORMALITY

This section will deal with procedures that have been used in research to define normality and abnormality. Scott (1958a) discussed six operational definitions of mental illness found in the psychological and psychiatric literature.

1. *Mental illness may be defined as exposure to psychiatric treatment.* This frequently used definition equates mental illness with "being under psychiatric treatment" and usually is confined to hospital treatment rather than including out-patient therapy. Mental illness, then, means that someone, such as a psychiatrist, relative, or the patient himself, has made the judgment that the person needs to receive the treatment officially sanctioned by society.

There are a number of difficulties with this definition. Many people are unhappy, bizarre, or act in ways that disturb others but do not come to the attention of psychiatrists or receive treatment. There is a limitation on the number of people who can be designated mentally ill by this definition, because there are limited numbers of personnel and facilities for treatment. Resources such as hospitals and psychiatrists are concentrated in wealthier states. By this definition, the population of Washington, D.C., where the admission rate is 48.9 per 1,000, is "crazier" than that of Arizona, where the rate is 6.1 per 1,000 (UPI, 1973). This may be true, but the test should not be in terms of the availability of psychiatrists or hospital beds in the particular state. Labeling of patients may also reflect regional differences in tolerance of deviant behaviors, differences in the manner and accuracy with which records are kept, and cultural differences between psychiatrists and patients.

2. *Maladjustment may be equivalent to mental illness.* The immediate question arising from this definition is "adjustment to what?" In a pluralistic society such as ours, different groups have different expectancies of what is good, appropriate, or normal behavior. Even different professionals who deal with the same children may have different definitions of what constitutes good adjustment. For example, teachers and psychologists may differ about whether a quiet, shy child who never talks out of turn and always does exactly what the teacher wants is particularly well adjusted. The necessity for considering varying frames of reference and the demands of different social structures pose obstacles to the establishment of a consistent operational definition. There seems to be no specific behavior that in and of itself is considered sick or healthy by all people everywhere. Observations by the anthropologist Margaret Mead on the Mundugumor (1935), who live in a society where it is right and proper to cheat, aggress against, and get the best of one's neighbor, emphasize this point. The average Mundugumor is suspicious, hostile, and self-centered. He thinks everyone is out to get him; therefore, the best thing he can do is to get "them" first. In our society, such behavior would be called maladjusted, paranoid, and mentally ill. In short, behavior as such is not adjusted or maladjusted but is judged as one or the other in terms of specific times, places, and persons.

3. *Psychiatric diagnosis may be the criterion for mental illness.* A person exhibiting a particular set of symptoms, i.e., a syndrome which can be found in psychiatric texts, may be labeled mentally ill by a psychiatrist. In addition to the uneven geographical distribution of psychiatrists mentioned in the first operational definition, the use of psychiatric diagnosis as a definition of abnormality has other serious difficulties. One problem is that the person has to come to the psychiatrist's attention. Patients are usually brought to the psychiatrist by parents, school authorities, police, neighbors, or themselves. Thus, while the diagnosis may be given by a professional, *who* gets to be diagnosed is decided by nonprofessionals. This then brings the problem back to social norms and the second definition given immediately above: what is tolerated by a particular group of people and what these people do when someone's behavior becomes intolerable to *them.*

People whom a psychiatrist sees in his usual practice are neither randomly selected nor exhaustive of the population of those who are disturbed or have problems. Scheff (1966a, pp. 47–50) indicates that the untreated greatly outnumber the treated, the estimates ranging from 8:1 to 20:1. If most people who display the syndrome can manage to live without psychiatric assistance, it may be reasonably hypothesized that there is something more than the syndrome, in and of itself, which is crucial for the designation of abnormality.

A second problem is that professional people assigning diagnoses may disagree *defining abnormality*

with one another because of inadequacies in the system of categorization, differences in populations served, differences in societal implications of the decisions made, or differences in the training, socioeconomic background, or the diagnostic tools used by the professional person.

A final problem is that defining abnormality as a label given by a particular profession involves two assumptions. The first assumption is that abnormality is literally mental illness; i.e., a disease.

A crucial question then becomes what do psychiatrists mean when they talk of illness or disease? Woodruff, Goodwin, and Guze (1974) present a strong expression of the disease viewpoint:

> When the term "disease" is used, this is what is meant: a disease is a cluster of symptoms and/or signs with a more or less predictable course. Symptoms are what patients tell you; signs are what you see. The cluster may be associated with physical abnormality or may not. The essential point is that it results in consultation with a physician who specializes in recognizing, preventing and, sometimes, curing diseases.
>
> It is hard for many people to think of psychiatric problems as diseases. For one thing, psychiatric problems usually consist of symptoms—complaints about thoughts and feelings—or behavior disturbing to others. Rarely are there signs—a fever, a rash. Almost never are there laboratory tests to confirm the diagnosis. What people say changes from time to time, as does behavior. It is usually harder to agree about symptoms than about signs. But whatever the psychiatric problems are, they have this in common with "real" diseases—they result in consultation with a physician and are associated with pain, suffering, disability, and death.
>
> Whether homosexuality, for example, is a disease like measles is not the issue. Homosexuals see psychiatrists, occasionally for homosexuality. Homosexuality can be defined precisely and has a "natural history." It is included as a diagnostic category because it leads to psychiatric consultation, meets the criteria for a useful category, and—as long as this persists—is a subject physicians should know something about.
>
> Another objection to the disease or medical "model" arises from a misconception about disease. Disease often is equated with physical abnormality. In fact, a disease is a category used by physicians, as "apples" is a category used by grocers. It is a useful category if precise and if the encompassed phenomena are stable over time. Diseases are conventions and may not "fit" anything in nature at all. Through the centuries, diseases have come and gone, some more useful than others, and there is no guarantee that our present "diseases"—medical or psychiatric—will represent the same clusters of symptoms and signs a hundred years from now that they do today." [Woodruff, Goodwin, and Guze, 1974, pp x-xi.]

By this definition, disease is whatever the physician deals with. In this regard, it is particularly interesting that the American Psychiatric Association, first by a vote of its board of directors and then by its membership, decided in 1974 to no longer consider homosexuality as pathological. It is also interesting to ask the reader whether a college student, whose status has a "natural history" (including a cure known as graduation), would qualify as having a disease? Do fatigue, irritability, and dislike of psychology texts qualify as symptoms and/or signs? And is the use of the campus counseling center a necessary part of the syndrome? If mental illness is a disease, there is the further assumption that the categorization given by a single professional group is sufficient as an operational definition. Because of the important consequences of receiving a "diagnosis" there is a societal danger in delegating such a responsibility to a single segment of the population.

4. *Mental illness may be defined subjectively.* This definition depends upon the person himself saying that he is mentally ill, unhappy, or in need of help. It may be a useful working definition in some populations, such as upper-middle-class neurotics and college students; but there are indi-

viduals who deny that anything is wrong with them whose very degree of denial may be an indication of abnormality. Further, there are real situations which, viewed objectively, are so difficult that a person should rightfully feel upset. It is sometimes true that if you can keep your head when all around you are losing theirs, you don't understand the situation. A person is considered unusual and possibly abnormal if he does not show signs of distress in situations that sadden most people. Finally, people learn under what circumstances, in what manner, and to whom to report personal distress. These considerations lead back to social learning concepts that are not consistent with a discontinuity between normal and abnormal behavior.

5. *Mental illness may be defined by objective psychological tests.* This definition involves behavior on tests, such as personality inventories, aimed at assessing the extent of disordered psychological processes or deviation from a "normal" population. There is one immediate advantage of a standardized psychological test such as an objective, true-false inventory. It can be administered and scored quickly, and relatively little professional time is required to gather a mass of data.

The development of an objective test demands an independent criterion. Psychological tests have an advantage over psychiatric interviews in that the stimuli presented to the subjects and the methods of evaluation remain constant. What material will be included as stimuli, how the responses will be scored, and how these scores will be interpreted all depend on designations independent of the testing itself. There must be criterion groups involved in the development of the test material, in the test norms, and in demonstrating that the test is useful in making the decisions for which it is designed. Once a psychological test has been adequately constructed, it is an invaluable aid in comparing a particular individual with the many other people on whom the test was standardized. The test score communicates information, so that the psychologist may make use of experience (the responses) with many people with whom he has had no personal contact. This procedure also guards against the hazard of the clinician being misled by one outstandingly good or bad performance or a single unusual case. *The operational definition originally used to determine criterion groups, however, is the very problem under discussion.* Objective tests cannot solve this problem because they *follow* rather than precede such definitions.

6. *Mental health may be positive striving.* This definition implies that mental illness can be described in terms of the *absence* of mental health. Frequently this type of definition includes such terms as growth, development, maturity, responsibility, self-fulfillment, adaptation to stress, and successfully coping with life. A first problem is to determine the operational definition of these terms.

In a most elaborate attempt to delineate positive mental health, Jahoda (1958) argued that the healthy person displays active adjustment rather than passive acceptance, that he shows stable integration, and that he perceives the world and himself correctly and without being biased by his personal needs. All of these things depend upon the individual's current environment in terms of how much stress he faces or how much he can realistically strive for. On another level, the notion of striving reflects the particular bias of the middle-class Protestant ethic. *Culture-boundedness* is a major defect in this kind of definition, because behavior that is good in one country may be bad in another.

Jahoda's insistence that mental health criteria be based upon an explicit set of values has the advantage of making overt values that have been implicit. Shoben (1957) makes this clear when he states: ". . . it seems unlikely that any conception of normality can be developed apart from

defining abnormality

some general considerations that are fundamentally moral." Shoben offers the formulation that ". . . behavior is 'positive' or 'integrative' to the extent that it reflects the unique attributes of the human animal." Among these uniquely human attributes Shoben includes an enormous capacity for symbolization, a social pattern of interdependency, the ability to delay gratification in the interest of remote rewards, and a striving to act in accordance with the best principles of conduct one can conceive. One may wonder if there are not uniquely human attributes that are less admirable than those Shoben presents. One can readily conceive that some product of man's great human capacity for symbolization, such as missiles with nuclear warheads, might eventually be maladaptive on a uniquely human scale. Finally, there is the sad reality that people who display the traits of positive mental health as described above are probably so few and far between that they are the exception rather than the rule.

ADDITIONAL THEORETICAL CONSIDERATIONS

The definition of abnormality has implications for research, for future forms of treatment, and for the making of social decisions that affect the individual's very freedom. All published definitions of abnormality face one of two fundamental problems that can be stated, in perhaps oversimplified terms, as follows: either the definition identifies abnormality with a biological disorder or it involves the adoption of some set of values by the labeler. Further, there are four issues with which every approach that considers abnormality as a real entity rather than a social convention must come to terms.

Unitary or Separate Behaviors?

Mental illness may refer to a unitary trait on which every mentally ill person varies to some degree. That is, if the individual is not normal, then he can be placed in *one general* category, the mentally ill. The alternative position is that there are a variety of mental disorders that are clearly different from one another. The majority of classification systems take this latter position.

One formulation of the first position, that of a unitary trait, is that mental health or illness is composed of a number of factors and that when there are an unusual number of indications of pathology, the person may be said to be mentally ill. It may be exemplified by the following quotation:

No index has so far been proposed that will unfailingly separate normal from abnormal behavior under any and all circumstances. Furthermore, it is doubtful that such an index is possible.

In cases of sufficiently severe disturbance, any of the three fundamental criteria is likely to classify the individual as abnormal. Typically, the very disturbed individual is statistically different from his fellows, is often (but not always) upset and unhappy and does not conform. The absence of a universal, foolproof criterion is important only for borderline and questionable cases. For the most part, we may explore abnormal behavior untroubled by our inability to define abnormality precisely. [Rosen, Fox, and Gregory, 1972, p. 10.]

This definition makes use of a number of imperfect criteria to "balance each other out," and it implies a continuum. A first approach to this kind of definition is to determine the basis for the decision that unhappiness, nonconformity, and statistical rarity are attributes of mental illness. That is, the selection of specific criteria indicates a prior supposition of what mental illness "really is." For example, the early behavior therapists, like the early psychoanalysts, were unhappy with the effectiveness of their professional skills, were statistically rare, and did not conform to the prevailing treatment methods of today. It is doubtful, however, that many people would call them abnormal or mentally ill solely on this basis.

Chronic or Acute?

The second issue is whether mental illness is to be thought of as an acute reaction to specific situations or a continuing characteristic of the individual. If acute, then situational variables increase in importance; if continuing, dynamic aspects of personality are likely to be stressed. There are important consequences of both positions in the assessment and treatment of the individual. If the source of the difficulty lies in the individual's environment, the likelihood of being able to change his behavior and alleviate the problem may be greater than if the source of difficulty is an enduring characteristic within the person.

Necessarily Socially Deviant?

The third issue is whether maladaptive social behavior is a required characteristic of mental illness. If such a requirement is not made, the way is open for total societies to be designated as sick. A critical example is whether an obedient Nazi concentration-camp commander would be considered normal or abnormal. To the extent that he was responding accurately and successfully to his environment and not breaking its rules, much less coming to the professional attention of psychiatrists, he would not be labeled abnormal. Repulsive as his behavior is to mid-twentieth century Americans, such repulsion is based on a particular set of values. Although such a person may be held responsible for his acts—as Nazi war criminals were—the concept of abnormality as a special entity does not seem necessary or justified. If it is, the problem arises as to who selects the values, and this, in turn, implies that one group may select values that are applied to others. This situation of one group's values being dominant over others is the same fascistic background from which the Nazi camp commander sprang.

Values Other than Social Conformity?

A stand must be taken on a final conceptual issue: Can or should mental illness be defined on the basis of values other than social conformity? This problem also brings to mind the concentration-camp commander, but it raises the additional issue of whether the good life should not be more than conformity. To say that mental health is more than conformity is to adopt a particular set of values that calls for some special view of the healthy personality. An intuitive feel for the problem may be obtained by reference to two cases presented by Nemiah (1961, pp. 86–95). One man had a history of alcoholism and impulsive behavior. He passed a woman on a lonely road; and on a sudden impulse he grabbed her, raped her, and in the struggle strangled her to death. The second man voluntarily became the official executioner for his state. He was the person who threw the switch on 387 people, the largest number of people any executioner has killed with electricity.

Nemiah writes of the first man, "there was no premeditation; there was no thoughtful consideration of his impulse . . . no careful planning how to go about doing what he was impelled to do, no restraining himself from action until he had time to reflect on what it was that his impulse urged him to do." (p. 93.) Of the second man, Nemiah writes, ". . . the executioner went about his work carefully, slowly, methodically, and with a measure of dispassion that allowed him to do his job efficiently and skillfully. Moreover, the job of executioner became very much a part of his life and his image of himself as a person. He took pride in the official position he held. He reflected on the work he was doing; he observed carefully the effect of electrocution on the victim; he attempted to improve his techniques; he invented new methods to make the process more humane." (p. 94.) Which of these two men is the more normal?

Wegrocki believes that it is how the behavior *developed,* rather than the behavior *itself* which determines whether it should be considered normal or abnormal.

The abnormal delusion proper is, however, an attempt of the personality to deal with a conflict-producing situation, and the delusion, "like fever, becomes an attempt by nature at a cure." The patient's delusion is an internal resolution of a problem; it is his way of meeting the intolerable situation. That is why it is abnormal. It represents a spontaneous protective device of the personality, something which is not learned. [Wegrocki, 1939, p. 169.]

Elsewhere in the article, Wegrocki notes that abnormality lies in the reaction of escaping from instead of facing a conflict-producing situation. Shoben, in the article previously cited (1957), also makes explicit the value that it is better to face a problem than to escape or deny it. But the major point, in Wegrocki's words, is that "it is not the mechanism that is abnormal; it is its function which determines its abnormality." A difficulty is that since the function must be inferred, it cannot be operationally defined. In practice, a person can say that a particular behavior is abnormal and therefore must serve a particular function. This is a *post hoc, ergo propter hoc* form of reasoning: the person acted abnormally, therefore he is abnormal, and he is abnormal because he acted abnormally. Especially when a person has been taught one set of responses in his subculture and then moves to another—such as a minority or lower-class student entering a typical middle-class American public school—his behavior may *produce* conflicts rather than be the result of them.

The present authors agree with Wegrocki that if a behavior is learned, it should be considered normal. They disagree with Wegrocki that abnormality "represents a spontaneous protective device of the personality, something that is not learned." On the one hand, such a view is likely to reify the concept of personality (Krasner and Ullmann, 1973), and on the other it is difficult to conceive of any behavior arising "spontaneously."

OTHER DEFINITIONS OF ABNORMALITY

Abnormal behavior is an important and pervasive social problem. It involves, in addition to mental health professionals (psychologists, social workers, psychiatrists, psychoanalysts), many other people such as lawyers, physicians, judges, educators, ministers, and philosophers. From these diverse groups have emerged other definitions of abnormality, based on different frames of reference.

The *statistical definition* of abnormality is one which is directly implied by the word itself. The dictionary defines "abnormal" as "deviating from the norm or average." The person who is abnormal, then, is so because he is unusual in terms of frequency of occurrence in the population. The person who is most normal by a statistical definition is the person who is most like other people. A first problem with this definition can be seen by reference to people with deviantly high intelligence or, as noted above, people who are mentally healthy by definitions such as those of Jahoda (1958). Some unusual behaviors are very desirable. Second, the statistical definition comes very close to equating mental health with conformity. Considering both the social benefits of nonconformists and the negative aspects of overconformity, this definition is inadequate.

If the most normal person is the one most like other people, the statistical definition of normality implies that a person should be maladjusted *to the proper degree*. The average person is not completely free of fears. A person who had no fears whatsoever would be very rare statistically and not necessarily well adjusted. The reader may wish to think of what is involved in preparing for an exam: if he were overly worried, he might "clutch" and perform below his true capability. On the other hand, if he were not worried in the least, he might not study at all. The ideal and probably statistically most frequent student is one who is worried enough about the outcome to study and even finds the act of studying pleasant because it reduces the chance of failure. Authors who have recently struggled with the problem of positive mental health include Miller (1970), Horton (1971), and Wright (1971).

Finally, even the most socially disruptive person in a psychiatric hospital is not statistically abnormal in every aspect. In fact, such a person is very likely to understand language and respond to his culture's social rewards. *The selection of the variable on which abnormality is measured presupposes a formulation of what is crucial in determining normality.* This leads to the problems that were discussed in the definition of abnormality based on objective tests.

The *medical definition* of normality is that the person displays no symptoms and hence is not sick at all. Normality is the absence of pathology, and, conversely, pathology is defined as a disturbance in normal processes. The definition of normality and abnormality resides in the specification of disease entities.

Later in this chapter we will briefly review a set of categories of pathology devised by the American Psychiatric Association. If abnormality is the presence of a disease, the next step is the specification of the particular disease. A person is abnormal if he gives evidence of schizophrenia, or a neurosis, or the like. By implication, the person is normal if he cannot be identified as suffering from one of the psychiatric diseases. There is an implication here for treatment as well as diagnosis: if pathology is removed, normality will result. Efforts directed to behavior outside the therapy situation may be reduced because pathology resides in the individual.

The *psychoanalytic definition* of normality stems from a complicated theory which will be presented in detail in Chapter 8. At the risk of oversimplifying, it can be said that the psychoanalytic definition of normality is that the normal person's motives are conscious. "The essence of mental disturbance is precisely man's inability to face himself, to recognize the feelings and motivations that his conscious self repudiates." (Alexander and Selesnick, 1968, p. 32.) Even if consciousness of motives could be measured, few people would meet this criterion.

The *legal definition* of abnormality is both interesting and important. There are three areas of impact dealing with *competency, commitment,* and *criminal responsibility*. The distinction between the first two of these may best be summarized by a classic anecdote: A man was changing an auto tire in front of a psychiatric hospital. He tripped and the nuts rolled into a sewer. He wondered what to do until an inmate who had been watching him through the fence yelled that he should borrow a nut from each of the other three wheels. The man was surprised and said, "That's a good idea. How come you're in the hospital?" The patient drew himself up and replied, "I may be crazy, but I'm not stupid." As will be seen below, this patient may have been *committed,* but he was *competent.*

"The legal disability of incompetency is analogous to that of minority status." (Rock, Jacobson, and Janopaul, 1968, p. 242.)

A person who is legally judged *incompetent* loses the right to make contracts, vote, drive, adopt children, practice a profession, and has doubt cast upon his ability to make a will or start a divorce action. It is an interesting cultural phenomenon that marriage, unlike other contracts made when a person is legally insane, is usually held valid unless specifically set aside. If it is clear that one party was so unsound of mind, psychotic, drunk, or defective *as not to understand the nature of the contract,* the marriage can be annulled. For making wills, the person must meet three criteria: he must know he is making a will; he must know the nature and extent of his property; and he must know the natural objects of his bounty. Failure to include close relatives and warm friends may be taken to indicate that the person was not of sound mind and

defining abnormality

memory, and hence token bequests to them are advisable. If a psychiatrist is involved as a consultant, he is likely to ask the person to describe what a will is, to give an estimate of his property, and to tell who his relatives are. The psychiatrist will also note emotional reactions to these questions. The courts will usually not set aside a contract entered into prior to a judgment of incompetency if the person understood the nature and effect of the *particular* transaction. Where no advantage was taken of the person and where the contract has been executed so that the prior status quo cannot be re-established, e.g., if the person has driven a new car five hundred miles, the contract usually will stand.

From the foregoing, the reader will see that *competency* is primarily a matter of keeping the person from squandering his material goods or from being the victim of swindlers. Plato devoted space to this problem in his *Laws,* as did the Romans with their interest in property and its inheritance. It is remarkable how contemporary the Greco-Roman ideas are. (See Rosen, 1969, especially pp. 121–29.)

Commitment refers to incarceration in a psychiatric institution.

The operational purpose of a definition in commitment proceedings is to identify those individuals whose status is to be changed, specifically if their liberty is to be infringed by custody and involuntary commitment. [Rock, Jacobson, and Janopaul, 1968, p. 9].

Commitment does not necessarily mean incompetency unless the person is declared *legally insane* at the time of Commitment. The laws dealing with the processes by which a person can be committed vary with the different states. In general they follow the concept that the person must be such a danger to himself or to others that he cannot adjust in the community.

Baynes (1971) notes that, unlike criminality, the allegedly mentally ill person need not have committed any antisocial act as a prerequisite for apprehension and incarceration. The definition of mental illness is crucial, and Baynes's survey indicates that "the majority of states do not have a statutory definition of 'mental illness.'" (p. 490.) Consequently, *potential* (rather than actual) misdeeds and need for care become the definitions: "a mental disease to such an extent that a person so afflicted requires care and treatment for his own welfare or the welfare of others in the community." (p. 490.) Unfortunately, such a broad definition without specification of what "welfare" entails might then be used as the justification for removal of many if not all of the members of the population. Indeed, the *Honolulu Star Bulletin* of June 5, 1974, reports from Michigan that "the judges said the state's temporary confinement law, under which 4,000 persons were confined in fiscal 1973, is unconstitutional because 'The standard of commitment for mental illness is fatally vague and overbroad.'"

Most patients in psychiatric hospitals are not particularly dangerous. In practice, the term "dangerous" is stretched so that it seems closer to a professional judgment that the person or his family would be "better off," suffer less, or be more likely to receive needed treatment if he were in the psychiatric hospital. For example, Rock, Jacobson, and Janopaul (1968) note that: "It must be said further that the need for treatment is plain enough and strong enough to justify overruling the patient's attitude in the matter . . ." (p. 8.)

Although state laws differ, most have a variety of procedures for commitment. First, a person may voluntarily enter a hospital (commit himself). In this case he can make a written request to be released within a given period of time. Second, the person may be committed for brief and specifically limited periods of time—e.g., for emergency observation and examination, after which a report is made to a court. Commitment, unless under specific limitations, means that the person may not leave the hospital without the institution's permission. There is no time limit to the process, although the patient may petition for a writ of habeas corpus and a court hearing at any time. He may also demand that a jury of his peers, rather than the more commonly used judge and court-appointed psychiatrists, decide the issue.

A commitment is ended by a medical decision, usually that of discharge. A person may be returned to the community for an indefinite period of time and the commitment *not* broken by placing him on a temporary status which maintains him officially on the hospital's rolls.

Other than by discharge, a person, in some states, can break a commitment by escaping from the hospital and remaining in the community for a year and a day. The ability to live in the community for this length of time is considered in law a reasonable demonstration of capability.

A third legal area deals with *criminal responsibility*. When is a person so deranged that it is not fair to prosecute him for his acts? In England until 1723 the test was that the accused knew what he was doing no better than a wild beast. In 1843 a man named Daniel M'Naghten shot one of Robert Peel's secretaries whom he did not personally know. M'Naghten's trial caused a furor, and, because of it, some questions were put to the fifteen judges of England. Their replies to the questions became known as the M'Naghten Rule. The M'Naghten Rule of criminal responsibility was that at the time of the act the person had to be under such defect that he did not know what he was doing, or if he did know, did not know it was wrong. In the United States, a major step forward was taken in New Hampshire in 1869 that has been generally accepted as superseding the M'Naghten Rule. The *New Hampshire Rule* is that the person is not criminally responsible if his unlawful act was the result of mental disease or mental defect. Thus it is necessary specifically to relate the criminal act to a disease; but the person is not absolved of responsibility merely because he *has* a disease. A patient who was on trial visit, i.e., actively on the hospital rolls with a schizophrenic diagnosis, was held criminally responsible for selling marijuana because his illegal act did not grow out of his disease but rather followed the principles of free enterprise. On the other hand, a different patient who fired a shotgun at passing cars because his voices told him to was not held criminally responsible. In this case, the act was considered the direct result of a disease.

At the time of this writing (we expect continual changes as the courts grapple with the problem), the practice generally followed is that of the American Law Institute (ALI) definition: "A person is not responsible for criminal conduct if at the time of such conduct as a result of mental disease or defect he lacks substantial capacity either to appreciate the criminality of his conduct or to conform his conduct to the requirement of the law." In addition to the New Hampshire considerations, the last phase introduces the concept of an irresistible impulse.

It should be noted that legal and medical definitions may easily come into conflict (Glueck, 1966.) Theoretical orientations differ; the physician is interested in understanding and treating the person, and he views the antisocial behavior as symptomatic of an underlying illness. The lawyer is interested in the protection of people and goods, and he starts with a presumption of man as rational until proven otherwise. Legal definitions, such as knowledge of right and wrong, may not take into account scientific advances that make knowledge of right and wrong only one of many aspects of abnormality. In the authors' experience most people in psychiatric hospitals who are diagnosed as having a disease such as schizophrenia know right from wrong. Physicians dislike saying that a person is sane (a legal term) when he is ill (a medical term).

In 1954 the Group for the Advancement of Psychiatry, a body of some 150 outstanding psychiatrists and mental health professionals, advanced a definition of criminal responsibility which attempts to combine medical and legal knowledge: Legal mental illness, the Group suggests, should denote that the person required hospitalization at the time of the act. This definition has not met with the heartiest approval of the legal profession. First, there is the difficulty of operationally defining abnormality in terms of a decision to hospitalize a person. Next, the decision is made hypothetically and after an act. There is the possibility that, by this definition, being hospitalized may excuse the person from legal responsibility without further legal determination. The definition would delegate to the psychiatrist many of the duties of the legal profession. Finally, laymen may wonder why, if the person clearly needed hospitalization, he was not incarcerated prior to the act.

Competency and criminal responsibility occur together at two major but distinct points, and these should not be confused. The first is whether the individual is to be held responsible for his act; that is, a determination of his condition at the *time of the act* must be undertaken. The second is the person's condition at the *time of his trial* for the act. Legally, he must be able to understand the proceedings in order to be able to defend himself. Pfeiffer, Eisenstein, and Dabbs (1967), who studied 89 referrals from a federal court at a Public Health Service hospital, found that 88 of the prisoners received some psychiatric diagnosis (only one was "without psychiatric disorder or disease"), and that 38 percent of them were found incompetent to stand trial. Neither diagnosis of a psychotic disorder nor mental deficiency was, of itself, tantamount to incompetency to stand trial, that is, 27 percent of those diagnosed psychotic and 38 percent diagnosed mental deficient were considered fit to stand trial. Cooke (1969) surveyed patients referred by the court for study and contrasted those found competent with those found incompetent. Although those judged incompetent had significantly higher scores on some personality inventory scales, "consistent criteria are not apparent." (Cooke, 1969, p. 143.) In further work, Cooke, Johnston, and Pogany (1973) noted that proximity to evaluation facilities and knowledge concerning the use of competency evaluation laws were factors that increased the rate of referral for competency evaluation. Wenger and Fletcher (1969) found that 91 percent of people at commitment hearings without legal counsel were admitted to the hospital while only 26 percent of those with legal counsel were admitted. Kumasaka (1972) reports that since passage of the New York State Mental Hygiene Law, which provides for lawyers to help patients who contest their involuntary hospitalization on a two-physician certificate, the number of court commitments has dropped drastically. The impact of variables theoretically extraneous to the specific behavior or social decision will be returned to in Chapters 10 and 11.

A person who is not competent to stand trial may be referred for treatment so that he will be competent to be tried in the future. Persons found not guilty of a crime by reason of insanity are usually sent to a psychiatric facility for treatment. Finally, people who might benefit from treatment are also sent to hospitals. There are a number of problems, however, in this situation. One that is receiving increasing attention (Burris, 1969) involves the "right to treatment." If a person is incarcerated in order to receive treatment, but adequate treatment for his difficulty either does not exist or is so costly and rare that he does not receive it, is he being held under false pretenses or in contradiction to his constitutional rights? In *Rouse* v. *Cameron,* in 1966, the District of Columbia Circuit Court of Appeals held that mental patients committed by criminal courts had the right to adequate treatment. In *Wyatt* v. *Stickney,* in 1971, an Alabama Federal District Court extended the right to treatment to all mental patients and issued an order setting criteria for adequate treatment in terms of a humane environment, sufficient qualified staff, and individualized treatment plans. Other legal and moral issues receiving increasing attention within both the profession and the courts involve matters such as confidentiality, civil rights, and appropriate forms of treatment in the absence of fully informed consent. (Ennis and Friedman, 1973; Ennis and Siegel, 1973; Halleck, 1974; McGarry and Kaplan, 1973.)

Another problem is that no time limit can be set, or guarantee given, for the success of psychiatric treatment. This may lead to a person who has been arrested but not convicted for a relatively minor offense remaining in an institution for periods far longer than the maximum sentence he would have received for the offense if he had been found guilty. Consequently, psychiatry may be used as a form of social control (extended incarceration without legal foundation) made all the more bitter because it is officially for the person's own good (mental health) (Leifer, 1969; Szasz, 1970).

Another problem involves responsibility. If it is argued that alcoholism is a disease, is any drunk driver legally responsible for his acts? At the time of this writing, the Supreme Court has ruled that the repeated arrest of alcoholics does not constitute cruel or unusual punishment, but the trend of decisions is such that it is quite possible that by the time of publication of this material, this decision will be reversed. (Snider, 1968.) If it is, and there are neither treatments nor facilities available, one may wonder what will happen. In short, the insanity defense may be a two-edged sword. (Goldstein, 1967.)

One of the operational definitions of mental illness is that of a psychiatrist or other expert classifying a person as belonging to a specific diagnostic group. Such evaluation of people is a major social and professional function of psychiatrists and other mental health workers. The act of labeling is also the usual forerunner of the other professional functions, such as research and treatment. While later chapters will deal with data on the sociology and consistency of labeling, this section will introduce the system of labels currently in use. The labels represent the options available to a diagnostician; they also delineate the type of behavior officially considered mentally ill in our society. A review of them is therefore a necessary preparation for subsequent discussions of historical developments and theoretical formulations.

PREFATORY CONSIDERATIONS

The particular system of labels to be reviewed, the one most widely used in the United States at the time of this writing, is formalized in the *Diagnostic and Statistical Manual, Mental Disorders* developed and published by the American Psychiatric Association in 1968. This source will hereafter be referred to as DSM-II.

The development of a system of classification has been a major focus of psychiatric interest during the last century. Many different systems have been advocated, and the resulting schema are a function of theory, practice, and social pressure. DSM-I (the earlier version of the manual first published in 1952) was the result of work by many people over a number of years. In its time it represented a major revision, dictated by social circumstances, of nomenclature which had been in use since 1934.

That psychiatric intervention is a response to a social problem is illustrated in the foreword to the earlier *manual*. "The Armed Forces faced an increasing psychiatric case load as mobilization and the war went on. There was need to account accurately for all causes of morbidity, hence the need for a suitable diagnosis for every case seen by the psychiatrist, a situation not faced in civilian life. Only about 10 percent of the total cases seen fell into any of the categories ordinarily seen in public mental hospitals." (DSM-I, p. vi.)

Perhaps the key word here is "morbidity"

defining abnormality

(lack of health, or disease) which had to be "accounted for." The implication is clear that diagnosis involved labeling of illness. Once a label had been ascribed, the military authorities could make a medical decision and dispose of the case expeditiously without implying any blame or responsibility on the part of the individual so dealt with. Morbidity, operationally, was the inability to adapt to the army in a manner which was useful to that organization. The person did not perform in a manner considered desirable by the organization, and the organization decided that the cost of retraining him was not worth the outcome. The solution of labeling also implied that any failure of rapid adjustment to the service was an indication of "sickness." Finally, the categories had to place every person, i.e., "all instances of morbidity," because if a person did not have a disease he was within the limits of normality, not sick, and hence the solution of the social problem through psychiatric labeling could not have been used.

The background for DSM-II, published in 1968, was the need to bring American psychiatric practices in line with the World Health Organization International Classification of Diseases. A series of compromises resulted:

Decisions were also made regarding certain diagnoses which have not been generally accepted in U. S. psychiatry. Some of these diagnoses have been omitted here . . . No list of diagnostic terms could be completely adequate for use in all those situations and in every country and for all time . . . The committee has attempted to put down what it judges to be generally agreed upon by well informed psychiatrists today . . . The committee has attempted to select terms which it thought would least bind the judgment of the user . . . It did not try to reconcile . . . views but rather to find terms which could be used to label the disorders about which they wished to be able to debate . . . Consider, for example, the mental disorder labeled in this manual as "schizophrenia," which, in the first edition, was labeled "schizophrenic reaction." The change of label has not changed the nature of the disorder, nor will it discourage continuing debate about its nature or causes. Even if it had tried, the committee could not establish agreement about what the disorder is; it could only agree on what to call it. [DSM-II, 1968, pp. vii–ix.]

The first and major point illustrated here is that systems of categories or nosologies are *human* creations. They are devised to solve problems and may facilitate certain behaviors but also may create other difficulties. The very basis of the system is an interpersonal exchange and not an unswerving statement about nature. Every definition in the current nosology was made by people and should be in quotation marks as a statement of policy at a given time and place.

The second point is one that will be clearer after the historical survey of Chapters 6 and 7, but is noted here while this material is fresh. In the same forward as the just quoted material, there is the statement ". . . that labels of themselves condition our perceptions." (DSM-II, 1968, p. viii.) By using the term, "schizophrenic reaction," DSM-I indicated there was a category of behavior in *reaction to* situations that could be called schizophrenic. In DSM-II, the label is "schizophrenia" alone, which implies an *entity,* and this seems a genuine step backwards.

The third point may be upsetting for the reader and certainly also bothers the authors: very little of the research presented in this book used DSM-II as a frame of reference. The time required to design research, collect data, write reports, and wait for publication after manuscript acceptance means that the majority of data was collected during the era of DSM-I. Henderson and Batchelor (1962, p. 30) report that when a worker "coded 200 diagnoses both by the I.C.D. and by the A.P.A. (i.e., American Psychiatric Association's DSM-I), and then used the A.P.A. categories to translate back to the I.C.D., she found she obtained agreement not in 100 percent of cases but only in 40 percent." Although the two systems used were earlier revisions of the present ICD and DSM-II, there seems to be a reasonable basis for concern. In addition, as will be noted in the following material, not all diagnoses of schizophrenia need imply psychosis in DSM-II. It is even possible that the very fact of cooperativeness with psychological tests and experiments to some extent indicates a "schizophrenic" who is not psychotic. Different samples of "schizophrenics" may then lead to quite different data (Ullmann, 1961).

The fourth and most immediate point is how to present and define the categories. Any particular way will have some faults. The procedure used will be to outline DSM-II at this time and give detail only to the extent that the following chapters can be read meaningfully. Then, from Chapter 13 on, DSM-II will be presented in detail and some definitions from DSM-I will be used for purposes of contrast and explication.

AN OUTLINE OF CATEGORIES

DSM-II involves eleven major categories. The first is *mental retardation* or subnormal general intellectual functioning. The second large category is called *organic brain syndromes* and involves physical impairment of brain tissue. These disorders are frequently manifested by poor memory, loss of orientation for time and place, impaired judgment, and lowered intellectual capabilities such as in calculation. Emotional expressions may be shallow and rapidly changing. Organic brain syndromes may be classified on a continuum from acute (reversible, e.g., being unconscious from an anesthetic during an operation, passing out the first time from too much alcohol) to chronic (irreversible; e.g., brain damage associated with decades of overindulgence in alcohol, frequent periods of unconsciousness as in one who is "punchdrunk.") A major distinction made by DSM-II is between psychotic and nonpsychotic organic brain syndromes.

The following lengthy quotation is presented because of its controversial nature, because it is illustrative of the problems faced in constructing diagnostic system and because it presents material descriptive of psychosis, the major pattern of behavior with which abnormal behavior was concerned until the turn of the century.

Patients are described as psychotic when their mental functioning is sufficiently impaired to interfere grossly with their capacity to meet the ordinary demands of life. The impairment may result from a serious distortion in their capacity to recognize reality. Hallucinations and delusions, for example, may distort their perceptions. Alterations of mood may be so profound that the patient's capacity to respond is grossly impaired. Deficits in perception, language and memory may be so severe that the patient's capacity for mental grasp of his situation is effectively lost.

Some confusion results from the different meanings which have become attached to the word "psychosis." Some nonorganic disorders [not due to bodily change, i.e., a change of function rather than structure of the body as in the pattern of behavior called schizophrenic —EDS.], in the well-developed form in which they were first recognized, typically rendered patients psychotic. *For historical reasons, these disorders are still classified as psychoses, even though it now generally is recognized that many patients for whom these diagnoses are clinically justified are not in fact psychotic.* [italics added]. This is true particularly in the incipient or convalescent stages of the illness. To reduce confusion, when one of these disorders listed as a "psychosis" is diagnosed in a patient who is not psychotic, the qualifying phrase *not psychotic* or *not presently psychotic* should be noted and coded . . .

Example: 295.06 *Schizophrenia, simple type, not psychotic*. [DSM-II, 1968, p. 23.]

Brain syndromes are categorized as psychotic or not psychotic although the degree of impairment is also on a continuum. For example, at what point is the loss associated with senility to be considered so gross as to be psychotic? Many readers of this book will have had to study when a headache, sleep deprivation, mild alcoholic intoxication, or a fever from a cold has decreased their efficiency. This might be labeled brain syndrome without psychosis.

The third major category is composed of *psychoses not attributed to physical conditions*. The patterns of behavior may be called nonorganic or functional to distinguish them from changes in organic or bodily structure. The largest group is composed of a behavioral pattern called *schizophrenia*, which is manifested by disturbances of thinking, mood, and behavior. The person may have trouble with concept formation or appropriate emotional responsiveness. When the behavior seems an unrealistic, disturbing exaggeration of mood, the pattern is likely to be called affective disorder such as manic-depressive.

The fourth major category of DSM-II is called *neuroses*. "Anxiety is the chief characteristic of the neuroses. It may be felt and expressed directly, or it may be controlled unconsciously and automatically . . ." (DSM-II, p. 39.) The person placed here may be upset, concerned, distressed (anxiety neurosis), easily fatigued (neurasthenic neurosis), unrealistically apprehensive about specific situations (phobic neurosis), have persistent, unrealistic fears of disease (hypochondriacal neurosis), have persistent, disruptive thoughts, or feel the need to engage in actions which are unnecessary or socially unusual (obsessive-compulsive neurosis), or be usually sad and lethargic, as if he had suffered a major loss of a loved one (depressive neurosis).

In these patterns of behavior, the feeling of tension, fatigue, and arousal is relatively more explicit than in other categories of neurosis such as depersonalization neurosis, in which the person has a continuing feeling of unreality and estrangement from his own body, self, or surroundings; and hysterical neurosis, in which the person acts as if he suffered from some damage to the voluntary nervous system (conversion type of hysterical neurosis) such as loss of sensation as in blindness or loss of function as in paralysis; or his state of identity may fluctuate as with amnesia or somnambulism (dissociative type of hysterical neurosis). People in each category may display different degrees of tension or discomfort, but, in general, there are greater apparent fearful responses in the anxiety, phobic, and neurasthenic groups than in the depression, depersonalization, and hysterical groups. Unlike psychoses, people categorized as neurotics are not grossly out of contact with reality although their difficulties may be severely handicapping.

The fifth major category of DSM-II is called *personality disorders and certain other nonpsychotic mental disorders*. There seems to be a dichotomy here. Personality disorders include patterns of behavior that approach but are less severe than psychoses; that is, paranoid personality, cyclothymic personality (manic-depressive), and schizoid personality. Other personality disorders parallel neuroses, as in the hysterical and asthenic personality disorder categories. Some of the personality disorders refer to a life-long manner of interacting with other people, such as passive-aggressive or inadequate personality disorders. The following is the complete definition given in DSM-II for inadequate personality: "This behavior pattern is characterized by ineffectual responses to emotional, social, intellectual, and physical demands. While the patient seems neither physically nor mentally deficient, he does manifest inadaptability, ineptness, poor judgment, social instability, and lack of physical and emotional stamina." (DSM-II, p. 44.) The social uses to which this category may be put make it one of special importance, particularly with the definition which is as broad as it is nonspecific.

A final category within the personality

disorders is called antisocial. Here are placed people whose behavior is "basically unsocialized," who show no "loyalty to individuals, groups, or social values," and who are "grossly selfish, callous, irresponsible, impulsive, and unable to feel guilt or to learn from experience and punishment." An earlier and quite descriptive term for the people here alluded to was that of "moral imbecile."

Three other groups within the larger category of personality disorders are sexual deviation (e.g., homosexuality, fetishism, pedophilia), alcoholism, and drug dependence. These behaviors may be thought of as providing an immediate gratification at the expense of longer-term difficulties with social standards.

In general, the personality disorders are relatively new in that they permit placement of people who do not manifest the more classic patterns of psychoses, neuroses, retardation, brain syndrome, or psychosomatic disorder, and who yet act in a social manner that makes categorization institutionally useful (as in the citation from DSM-I, p. vi, quoted above).

The sixth category is called *psychophysiologic disorders* and comprises physical disorders of presumably psychogenic origin, that is, what typically are described as psychosomatic disorders. The group "is characterized by physical symptoms that are caused by emotional factors and involve a single organ system, usually under autonomic nervous system innervation." (DSM-II, p. 46.) Among the physical patterns that *may be* (but certainly are not necessarily) caused or aggravated by behavioral factors are asthma, hypertention, and peptic ulcer.

The seventh category in DSM-II is called *special symptoms*. Specific examples include some that previous nosologies categorized as hysterical (tic, some speech disturbances) or psychophysiological (some elimination and eating disturbances such as anorexia nervosa). The category is restricted to manifestations of single specific difficulties.

The eighth category in DSM-II is called *transient situational disturbances* and represents acute, reversible reactions to environmental stress. The pattern of behavior manifested may be of any degree of disruption including psychosis, but the difficulty occurs "in individuals without any apparent underlying mental disorders." (DSM-II, p. 48.) If "the symptoms persist after the stress is removed, the diagnosis of another mental disorder is indicated." (DSM-II, p. 48.) Adjustment reactions may occur at any stage of life and may be related to loss of mother, fear of abandonment, school failure, fear of combat, or forced retirement. Recognizable stress, a previous history of no unusual problems, and a cessation of problem behavior with little or no treatment other than decreased stress are considerations for placement in this category.

The ninth category of DSM-II is called *behavior disorders of childhood and adolescence* and is intended for behavior that is "more stable, internalized, and resistant to treatment than transient situational disturbances but less so than psychoses, neuroses, and personality disorders." (DSM-II, pp. 49–50.) "Characteristic manifestations include such symptoms as overactivity, inattentiveness, shyness, feeling or relection, overaggressiveness, timidity, and delinquency." (DSM-II, p. 50.) This category is halfway between transient situational disturbances and the categories of psychoses, neuroses, and personality disorders because "of the greater fluidity of all behavior at this age." (DSM-II, p. 50.) Some of the diagnostic categories may reflect brain syndrome (hyperkinetic reaction of childhood), whereas others preview schizophrenia (withdrawing reaction of childhood), neurosis (overanxious reaction of childhood), and antisocial personality disorder (unsocialized aggressive reaction of childhood).

The tenth category of DSM-II is called *conditions without manifest psychiatric disorder and nonspecific conditions.* "This category is for recording the conditions of individuals who are psychiatrically normal but who, nevertheless, have severe enough problems to warrant examination by a psychiatrist. These conditions may either become or precipitate a diagnosable mental disorder." (DSM-II, p. 51.) This is an important and fascinating category. On the one hand there is recognition that a person may have difficulties in adjustment and yet may be psychiatrically normal, while on the other hand there is implicit a concept of "no smoke without fire," and no examination by a psychiatrist without a problem.

The subcategories are marital maladjustment, social maladjustment (thrown into an unfamiliar culture or into divided loyalties to two cultures), occupational maladjustment, and dyssocial behavior. The placement of this last category, dyssocial behavior, is noteworthy, for in DSM-I it was one of the personality disorders and listed under sociopathic personality disturbance. The term was then applied to people "who manifest disregard for the usual social codes, and often come in conflict with them, as the result of having lived all their lives in an abnormal moral environment." (DSM-I, p. 38.) In short, they were normal for a culture considered "sick." The present placement indicates a recognition of the pluralistic nature of contemporary society, and although not perfect, is a step towards greater tolerance.

The eleventh and final category in DSM-II contains nondiagnostic terms for administrative use and is mentioned only for completeness.

Comments on DSM-II

Although DSM-II will be the framework of Chapters 13 through 27, and therefore be covered in greater detail, some comments are required at this time when the overview is fresh. First, DSM-II provides a few noteworthy steps forward. Aside from integration with the International Classification of Disease, the distinction between psychosis and schizophrenia, although very controversial, may go far to reduce the embarrassment of a person given a psychotic label (i.e., schizophrenia) being not insane (a legal term). Another step forward is the deletion of a distinction, which was very difficult to make, between personality pattern and personality trait disturbances. A third step forward was the removal of dyssocial behavior from personality disturbance to a condition without manifest psychiatric disorder, and the more general recognition that there may be maladjustment without psychiatric disorder. Where DSM-I sought the use of single diagnostic terms, DSM-II encourages the use of multiple psychiatric diagnoses (Spitzer and Wilson, 1968). When two diagnoses are made, the one more urgently requiring treatment is listed first, or, if this is not an issue, the more serious diagnosis is listed first.

There are a number of changes in DSM-II that are a cause for concern. One which has already been mentioned is that there are enough additions, deletions, and redefinitions to cast some doubt on the sampling of previous studies. But this problem would have had to be faced with any revision, and it would be pointless to continue in error solely to be consistent in that error.

There are some features of DSM-II that seem to point in a more conservative direction. A major one is the change from a concept of a reaction (behavior) that is psychotic or neurotic to calling the behavior psychosis or neurosis with the implication of a disease entity. Another is the return of older categories such as neurasthenia and hypochondraical neurosis. A regression of this nature is the diagnosis "explosive personality (epileptoid personality disorder)," which, on the one hand, seems to imply an underlying organic brain syndrome which should be diagnosed if present and, on the other, seems an unwarranted and unnecessary slur. (Jackson, 1970.)

Finally, some bits of lore that do not jibe with the realities of hospital and clinic, at least as the present authors have observed them, are included. For example, "Traditionally, neurotic patients, however severely handicapped by their symptoms, are not classified as psychotic because they are aware that their mental functioning is disturbed." (DSM-II, p. 39.) The vast majority of people diagnosed schizophrenic with whom we have worked have verbalized the difference between their present and former perceptions and were concerned with their disagreements with those around them. On the other hand, some people manifesting hysterical and hypochondraical behavior would resist the concept that their "mental functioning is disturbed," but rather insist that the attending physician is falling down on the job.

DSM-II as a Definition of Mental Illness and Health

The first problem with the use of DSM-II as a definition of abnormal behavior has already been covered: the distribution of people whose training is aimed towards its use is irregular. That is, all of the problems inherent in defining mental illness by the diagnosis of a psychiatrist are met here. We have also previously encountered a second problem: there is an implicit assumption in DSM-II of what a healthy person is. He is someone who meets the ordinary demands of life, who perceives accurately and is effective in situations, who does not grossly violate social conventions either with drugs and alcohol or by being selfish, callous, or aggressive. The person may be concerned, he may face stress, or he may have problems at work or in his marriage, but he does not engage in those patterns of behavior that might lead a psychiatrist to call him psychotic, neurotic, personality disorder, psychophysiologic disorder, or the like. Mental health in DSM-II is the *absence* of symptoms or patterns of behavior that are diagnosable.

Does the system include the overwhelming number of people it should and exclude the overwhelming number of people it should? There are a number of sources of data on this problem. One is the study of the consistency (reliability) with which diagnoses are made; it will be presented in Chapter 11. At this point, we may say that the reliability is better than chance for major categories, but is disturbingly low for work which has so great an impact on peoples' lives.

One source for the unreliability of diagnosis is the inexactness of the definitions: the material is too brief and key terms are not defined. A related problem is that by thinking in terms of a medical model, difficulties which are defined as being in a social matrix are ascribed to the individual without clear reference to the situations in which the behavior is emitted and evaluated.

SOME DATA

A different source of evidence on the topic is made available from the work of Temerlin (1968). His research is germane to many aspects of the sociology of mental illness and basically asked the question, what, if any, are the effects of suggestion on the making of a diagnosis.

What Temerlin did was to develop a tape of a super-normal man: a professional actor was given the role of a man who was happy and effective in his work; he established a warm, gracious, and satisfying relationship with the interviewer; he was self-confident and secure without being arrogant, competitive, or grandiose. He was identified with the parent of the same sex, was happily married and in love with his wife, and consistently enjoyed sexual intercourse. He felt that sex was fun, unrelated to anxiety, social role conflict, or status striving. He also had a good sense of humor, no hallucinations, delusions, or psychosomatic symptoms, a happy childhood, and reasonable worries like concern over Viet Nam.

There were three conditions. In Table 1, the first two groups represent the first condition, that of no suggestion as to mental health; either no suggestion at all or the

Table 1
Suggestion effects in psychiatric diagnosis.
(After Temerlin, 1968, p. 351.)
Percentages of ratings as psychotic, neurotic, or mentally healthy

GROUP	NUMBER OF RATERS	PSYCHOTIC	NEUROTIC	HEALTHY
Employment interview	24	0	29	71
No prestige suggestion	21	0	43	57
Suggestion of mental health	20	0	0	100
Suggestion of psychosis, M.D.	25	60	40	0
Suggestion of psychosis, Ph.D.	25	28	60	12
Suggestion of psychosis, trainees	45	11	78	11

designation of an employment interview. Roughly one-third of the raters indicated the man neurotic, none indicated psychosis.

In the next condition, a prestigious figure gave an "unintended" suggestion of mental health. The result was that 100 percent of the raters indicated the man was mentally healthy.

In the third and final condition, the raters were given the suggestion that the man was mentally ill. Operationally, just before the tape was played, a distinguished mental health professional remarked to the man next to him that the person on the tape was "a very interesting man because he looks neurotic, but actually is quite psychotic." For the mental health condition, the suggestion was given in the same way, notably, that it was a tape of a truly rare man, one who was normal.

The ratings were by mental health professionals: psychiatrists (M.D.s), clinical psychologists (Ph.D.s), and clinical psychology graduate students. The mental health workers of the first three groups in Table 1 were a balance of the populations in the latter three groups.

Whereas Temerlin documented suggestion effects in a tight design, Rosenhan (1973) collected field data. In order to obtain admission to psychiatric hospitals, people who were leading productive lives and had no manifest behavioral difficulties presented themselves for admission with only one behavior that was not typical of them, they heard unclear voices saying the words "empty," "hollow," and "thud." Once admitted to psychiatric hospitals, these pseudopatients ceased simulating any unusual behaviors and acted as "normally" as they could. Time before release ranged from 7 to 52 days, and during this period no staff person recognized them as false patients. Rosenhan's major thesis is that the diagnostic standards are so weak that normality and abnormality are difficult for professionals to recognize, and that the label of abnormality will color the perceptions of the person.

During the data collection, Rosenhan and his co-pseudopatients made a number of observations which are consistent with those presented throughout this volume. For example, in pursuing their research, the pseudopatients made notes. At first they did this unobtrusively, but when it seemed no one much cared, they did so openly. Such writing behavior may be usual in classrooms and laboratories; it is not on a psychiatric ward and was noted by nurses. A pseudopatient who took notes during an interview with the psychiatrist was told in a kindly fashion that he did not have to do so; the physician would remind the patient again if he forgot. Behavior that was adjustive for research workers was unusual in the hospital situation, and the staff fit such behavior into the framework provided by the diagnosis.

While no staff people seemed to suspect the pseudopatients, a number of patients did. This finding may be associated to the indoctrination of the staff in diagnostic processes, or it may be related to the small amount of time spent by psychiatrists and nurses with the patients. Not only does the diagnosis provide a biasing frame of reference, there may also be little opportunity or effort to collect conflicting evidence.

At a later time, a psychiatric staff was informed that one or more attempts to enter the hospital by pseudopatients were to be made during the following three months. Of 193 patients, 41 were alleged, with a high degree of confidence, to be pseudopatients by at least one staff member and 19, or 10 percent, were suspected by one psychiatrist and one other staff person. None of these patients were false ones. Rosenhan notes that the tendencies to designate sane people as insane may be reversed quite easily. We think the observation also touches on the problem of the reliability of psychiatric diagnosis, the need to study the professional staff as well as the people receiving treatment, the very human interpersonal interchanges involved in the labeling and treatment process, and, above all, the need to focus on actual behaviors by people.

SUMMARY

The purpose of this chapter was to define the area of study called abnormal behavior. In so doing, we presented a first overview of approaches by different investigators and professions.

There are occasions, presently called psychiatric emergencies, when a person acts in a manner that is currently considered appropriate for the intervention of a professional mental healer. Attempts to define under what conditions a person represents a psychiatric emergency, or more generally what behavior would justify calling a person either mentally healthy or mentally ill, usually end with a concept that a person is acting in a manner that is disturbing someone (including himself), and that the invocation of the label and professional healer is a solution to a problem.

The various approaches which presume that abnormal behavior can be clearly distinguished from normal behavior were reviewed. Six types of research definition were surveyed, followed by statistical, psychoanalytic, and legal definitions. Finally, the current diagnostic system of the American Psychiatric Association was introduced.

Each profession defines abnormality in terms of the problems it faces and hopes to solve. This leads to a situation in which different definitions and different consequences stem from the varying frames of reference and foci of the professions involved. Ideally, all definitions should be in agreement with each other; in practice, even the operationally defined research definitions yield unimpressive correlations. Different authors may talk about different people while using the same word, "abnormal." This in turn leads to conflicting results and confusion rather than progress in science; for the individual who suffers the social consequences of this state of affairs, the result may be tragic.

an alternative approach

2

The principal argument of this book is that abnormal behavior is no different from normal behavior in its development, its maintenance, or the manner in which it may be changed. The difference between normal and abnormal behavior is not intrinsic; rather it lies in a societal reaction. It is more useful to ask how a person develops *any* belief than how he develops a *false* belief. The principles of the development of "proper" beliefs are the same as the principles of the development of "false" beliefs. Similarly, the more fruitful question is not how a person comes to engage in deviant sexual behavior, but rather how people come to engage in any particular form of sexual behavior. Formulations of abnormal behavior should start with the conditions necessary for making an "appropriate," "good," or "successful" interpersonal response, i.e., with what is involved in responding "correctly" to stimuli.

The problem may be stated in another way. Aristotle wrote in his Ethics:

... it is possible to go too far, or not to go far enough, in respect of fear, courage, desire, anger, pity, and pleasure and pain generally, and the excess and the deficiency are alike wrong; but to experience these emotions at the right times and on the right occasions and toward the right persons and for the right causes and in the right manner is the mean or the supreme good, which is characteristic of virtue.

Every theory dealing with abnormal behavior must answer four general questions. The first is, How can one define the right times, the right places, the right people, the right reasons, and the right way of life? Second, How do people come to know (learn, recognize, act in accord with) these definitions? Third, How do some people come to act in *discord with* the times, places, people, reasons, and manners considered right by others? Finally, What may be done, practically and ethically, to change the behavior of a person so that he is on the path of "virtue," however virtue may be defined?

These four questions comprise the burden of this book. The function of the present chapter is to provide an overview of our answers to them. We are placing this material early in our exposition because it may provide a framework that will make later material relevant and meaningful. We were faced with a dilemma, however: since the material is based upon concepts of scientific method, learning, and social psychology, it might well have comprised Chapter 6 (as in the previous edition), following the material on these subjects in Chapters 3, 4, and 5. Moreover, this approach emphasizes sociological, economic, and educational concepts, so it might well have been placed subsequent to the chapter on behavior modification. Or, the chapter could represent our summary statement and hence be placed at the very end of the book. Nevertheless, our decision to place it at this point underscores our belief that the assertions made here are supported by the remainder of the book.

WHAT IS "RIGHT" BEHAVIOR AND WHO DEFINES IT?

In asking, What is "right" behavior? we must first make a decision. Is there such a thing as "right" behavior in and of itself? In dealing with bodily activity there are relatively clear standards for normal functioning. Do such criteria exist in the realm of social behavior in the way they do for physiological activity? From the review of definitions presented in Chapter 1, we may note that it is very difficult to find acts that may not be evaluated as either "right" or "wrong," depending on the social setting in which they occur. In the context of physical functioning, *who* the person is does not generally alter the evaluation of physical signs. If, on the other hand, we think of social context, a behavior such as a heterosexual union is evaluated in terms of the ages of the parties, their marital status, their feelings toward each other, their degree of privacy, their method of union, and so forth. Further, nearly every behavioral manifestation of this type has been considered correct, or at least acceptable at some time and place and by some persons and inappropriate for other times, places, and people.

Even physiological anomaly may at times be considered valuable and desirable. One classic example is the epileptic whose trance has been considered an indication of special knowledge. Another example is impotence: if the occurrence is a response to a distasteful situation, such as potential disease, paternity, eternal damnation, marriage, or morally obnoxious exploitation of another, the failure of the biological function may be a socially favorable occurrence.

If one accepts an absolute standard, that is, behavior may be "right" or "wrong" in itself, without reference to its social context, one may logically seek the sources of disruption or "pathology" in the person himself. An alternative view is that the "right" and "wrong" or "sick" and "healthy" labels for behavior represent *social evaluations.* If this is the case, the problem of what is "right" or "healthy" behavior is not solved but changed. We then must ask, (1) What are the conditions or activities that lead a person to be labelled? (2) Who does the labelling? and (3) What are the consequences of the designation for both the labeller and the labelled?

Behavior Likely to Be Called Abnormal

Most adults are physically capable of making a great many different acts at any given moment. The typical college student sitting on a hard, narrow chair in a stuffy classroom more or less listening to a droning lecturer is a good example. First, he was physically capable of cutting class and sleeping at home rather than in class. He might have spent the time talking or eating, playing frisbee on the grass, studying on his own, or making money or love. Once in class, he is physically capable of shouting obscenities, touching the person seated next to him, undressing, or walking out of the room. At any given moment, only a small fraction of the acts that a person is physically capable of making are socially appropriate. By socially appropriate is meant that the acts are welcome or at least not disturbing to the other people involved in that setting. Acts that are appropriate in one setting may be inappropriate in another time and place. The first aspect of behavior likely to be called abnormal is that it is likely to break one or more of the parameters of Aristotle's definition of virtue: it is the wrong thing, the wrong time, the wrong setting, the wrong way, or inferentially, done for the wrong reasons.

A second aspect of behavior likely to be called abnormal is that it is unpleasant enough or disturbing enough for someone to want to change it. The person who would find a change rewarding may be the person himself, a friend, spouse, parent, teacher, neighbor, or policeman. If either the people emitting the behavior or the behavior itself does not affect an individual, that individual is not likely to take steps to do something about it. The behavior of strangers may be more tolerated than the behaviors of friends or relatives because the latter have an impact where the former do not. An example may be found in large cities, where a person who is troublesome or troubled (in distress) may be ignored because the specific acts may be of no concern to an observer who does not wish to become "involved."

A third condition that is likely to increase the likelihood of the use of the "abnormal" label is that the label itself helps solve the problem raised by the aversive behavior. There are many aversive behaviors that break a specific written (criminal) law, and the very presence of the law may diminish the use of the "abnormal" label, although at times, as a compromise or for convenience, the "abnormal" label may be used. There is, however, a category of behavior that someone wishes to change that is not covered by the written law. Here, the "abnormal" or "mental illness" label provides a solution to a problem. The reports (*Time*, September 27, 1971, pp. 44–45) of the use of psychiatric clinics by Soviet authorities to deal with dissident intellectuals is a good example: "Technically, Soviet courts cannot sentence a man to prison or labor camp unless he has violated the criminal code. Health officers, however, can commit anyone to 'emergency psychiatric hospitalization' if his behavior is simply deemed abnormal." The eminent geneticist Medvedev who was critical of government actions in the scientific field was diagnosed as "split personality." The difficulty was manifested by his acts, which could be interpreted as a "poor adaptation to the social environment."

A fourth condition that increases the chance of the "abnormal" label being used is that the behavior *seems* to be senseless, self-defeating, or without favorable consequences for the individual. In behavior called abnormal, covetousness, lust, pride, and the other reasons that people recognize as sane motives for action are not immediately apparent; the average observer may say that the behavior of the person he considers abnormal seems unnecessary, unrealistic, senseless, or likely to cause pain rather than pleasure. In this situation, the "abnormal" label provides a circular explanation for the behavior: he acted the way he did because he was insane, and it is clear he was insane because of the way he acted. Aside from the solution of the social problem of what to do about the behavior itself, the use of the label "explains" it and neutralizes some of its impact. If Medvedev is a mad man, his criticisms of the system need not be taken seriously.

A fifth condition likely to increase the use of the label is that the observer has some power over the person to be labeled. This condition could also have been stated in the reverse manner: Are there conditions that are likely to decrease the application of the label of abnormality? One such condition is that the person to be labeled is in so powerful a position that he can either retaliate against the people who would label him or that he can freely ignore the annoyance of the people who find his behavior aversive. On a college campus, the difference between a professor's being a maladjusted person or a lovable eccentric may be tenure.

A sixth condition affecting the likelihood of the use of the "abnormal" label is its very availability. One of the purposes of the chapters on history in this volume is to outline the development of different concepts of abnormal behavior; with each approach there were somewhat different labels. The application of a label to a person is a human behavior that is learned and maintained by its consequences in the same manner as any other complex social behavior.

WHO DOES THE LABELING?

The current concept of the etiology of abnormality in any particular society has a major impact on who the official labelers will be in that society. If the concept involves the explanation of abnormal behavior as a result of possession by evil spirits, the labelers and healers are likely to be priests. If the concept of etiology is that of a physical defect interfering with normal perception and action, the labelers and healers are likely to be physicians.

Over time, however, societies and the problems facing professional people change. In addition, as noted by Kuhn (1970), evidence that is inconsistent with the current dominant paradigm accumulates until there is intellectual as well as social pressure for a change in models.

An example is germane: "The history of the development of social forces in Western societies shows that 'mental hospitals' and their precursors preceded the emergence of psychiatry, both as a 'scientific' discipline and as a profession." (Sharma, 1970, p. 248; Rothman, 1971.) The first hospitals in Western society were refuges for the old, the weak, the sick, the impoverished, and the orphaned, and were associated with ecclesiastical institutions as acts of religious mercy. With the decline of religious orientations, the rise of medicine, and the increasing responsibility of government for the welfare of its citizens, poor houses and retreats changed to hospitals. The use of a medical rather than an ecclesiastical or legal model in dealing with people was a humane step, but "Many of the dominant characteristics of psychiatric ideology and theory were simply rationalizations of existing conditions within mental institutions and within the society as popular attitudes." (Grob, 1967, quoted in Sharma, 1970, p. 248.) The medical approach did not grow from the data but was imported as a justification for actions already taken.

The professional labeler, then, is a person whose educational and official status legitimizes a course of action that fits the conceptual models of his society. There is a constant interaction between the tasks set by the leaders of the society, the professional person's theories, and the group of people treated.

WHAT ARE THE CONSEQUENCES OF LABELING?

The first consequence of the labeling process is that a specific problem is solved (even if a new one may be created in its stead). A way of dealing with disturbing or socially abrasive behavior is provided—particularly behavior that is not foreseen and covered by formal rules.

The process of labeling and placing behavior within the context of a theory has further effects. First, an explanation is given, which, even if it is illogical or unscientific, may be comforting to the labeler and to the labeled. The behavior, then, is not random and inexplicable but rather an example of larger concepts and processes. The use of a medical concept or label may solve immediate problems for the person who is labeled as well as for the labeler: a person with a disease is not responsible for contracting the illness and and is excused from a number of social obligations (see Chapter 5, especially regarding the role of being "sick.")

There are, however, longer-term effects of labeling that may be detrimental to both the individual and his society. Although genuine efforts have been made to help him, a person who has been hospitalized or received intensive psychological or psychiatric treatment is vulnerable in our society. He is stigmatized and may be treated with caution, concern, or avoidance by other people in terms of many jobs or interpersonal situations.[1] In addition, the very treatment given may lead to the learning of behavior that makes future adjustment more difficult. A prime example of such *iatrogenic,* or treatment-caused, effects is the result of prolonged institutionalization discussed in this book in connection with people labeled as schizophrenic.

There are two further problems generated for the society. The first is the establishment of a costly mental health industry that requires support of its personnel, buildings, bureaucracy, system of education, and so on. In a rapidly changing, pluralistic society this cost factor becomes a major consideration.

The second effect is less visible: some percentage of the unexpected, disturbing, seemingly incomprehensible behavior is socially valuable. If an innovation is presented in the right way, by the right people, and appeals to the right reasons, it may be accepted. Innovations, social movements, and behavior called abnormal share many characteristics (Ullmann, 1969).

THE DEVELOPMENT AND MAINTENANCE OF PRO-SOCIAL BEHAVIOR

In the previous section, we have discussed the conditions likely to lead someone, including the person himself, to designate actions as disturbing and worthy of change within the context of a society's professional mental healers. Following Aristotle's observations, we may set as parameters of "normal" or pro-social behavior action at the right times, the right occasions, with the right people, for the right reasons, in the right way, and in the right amount. Of the great range of behavior of which a person is physically capable, only a very select portion of acts at any given moment would qualify as "virtuous." This section describes the conditions that foster the development of pro-social behavior. This essentially requires a theory of human behavior, a task which involves a volume in itself (e.g., Krasner and Ullmann, 1973).

People are neither stimulated nor responsive in a vacuum. One person's response serves as a stimulus for another person, as well as for himself. Such stimuli may be eliciting, setting events (discriminative), or reinforcing (see Chapter 4 for an elaboration of these terms). In a larger context, humans frequently respond to their physical, social, and interpersonal environments by trying to change them. *Human behavior is always interactive.*

The Physiological Environment: Genetic Endowment

The range of physical endowment that is associated with socially acceptable behavior is either very broad or very narrow. If one considers how similar all humans are when compared with other species, the range is narrow; if one considers the differences among humans, the range is large. The individual's genetic endowment sets limits to the range of potential behaviors. A major genetic deviation will, in most cases, lead to death at an early age. A number of patterns associated with severe retardation are genetic in nature. It is generally accepted that differences in such a physical variable as height are associated, to a significant degree, with genetic characteristics. The relationship between intelligence (as measured by tests such as the Stanford-Binet) and genetic endowment is more controversial (Kamin, 1973). A matter of particularly bitter debate at this time is whether general or specific capability to deal with the environment is associated to a significant degree with different genetic inheritance. This issue has been argued within the framework of the category of schizophrenic

---

[1] That stigmatization consequent to treatment takes place (Phillips, 1963), was sharply evident in the 1972 presidential campaign, in which Thomas Eagleton was displaced as Democratic vice-presidential candidate because he had received "shock treatment" in the past for an unspecified disorder.

an alternative approach

behavior; some details of the controversy will be presented in Chapter 17.

Another example of variation of physical functioning related to genetic inheritence is illustrated by the theory advanced by Eysenck and his co-workers (Eysenck and Rachman, 1965) that because people differ in neurological structure there will be a related difference in the rate of conditioning to stimuli. Some people will condition so rapidly that they will have many extraneous conditioned responses (if negative, one might hypothesize phobias; if positive, fetishes), whereas others will condition with relative difficulty ("conscienceless" individuals called antisocial personalities, who have not learned the proscriptions of their society). Similarly, metabolic differences that are genetically associated may make more probable psychophysiologic disorders. These are interesting hypotheses for scientific investigation. What is clear, however, is that there is variation among people and that there are limits set by genetic endowment.

Many genetic differences are clearly within normal physiological limits but do lead to differences in behavior. The most salient examples at the present time are those of sex and skin color. There are differences in the ways blacks and whites, males and females are treated that are not logically or necessarily associated with their genetic endowment, but which are very real and lead to significant differences in social behavior.

There are genuine medical disorders associated with genetic differences that do not have a major impact on social behavior because of advances in treatment. Epilepsy, diabetes, and poor eyesight are examples. Few people today would argue that humans have complex patterns of behavior that are inherited or instinctive. In general, man as species is modified through learning and invention rather than through genetic evolution. The changes in the last century in man's capacity to feed himself, house himself, communicate and travel over wide distances, and control his environment are of a technological rather than genetic nature.

The Physiological Environment: Bodily Function

Information reception, processing, and emission depend upon the basic equipment, in this case the person's physique, working within acceptable limits. Extreme physiological anomaly, such as the distortion due to the mother's ingestion of the drug thalidomide, or rubella contracted by the mother during the first trimester of pregnancy, provides examples of environmental deviance that lead to alterations of physique that, in turn, are likely to limit and severely affect later behavior. There are effects on bodily functioning due to drugs such as alcohol and the debilitating effects of fever. A person suffering physiological deficits such as hunger or thirst, chronic pain as in cancer, loss of sensation as in deafness, or loss of movement as in arthritis is restricted in the acts he is capable of making. Besides the restricted ability to act, the individual's and other people's reactions to the restrictions (which are not directly germane to the behavior that the person can make) affect the individual. (See Chapter 5, especially on the making of blind men.)

If a person receives information more slowly, processes it incompletely (perhaps due to difficulty in storing it), or communicates poorly, he will act in a manner that is different from the pattern that is typical and expected in his culture. Further, an ongoing physiological need or an interfering stimuli such as poor nutrition (Eichenwald and Fry, 1969; Bergner and Susser, 1970; Kaplan, 1972) may alter his responses. Even though the behavior appears different to others, they may not necessarily evaluate it as abnormal. The person may be acting in a manner that is very acceptable to others in a person with a known physiological problem. If the existence of a medical problem is established, the tolerance accorded to a sick person is appropriately given and the professional mental healer is not called upon.

The Physiological Environment: Ecological Considerations

Pollution of air and water, foreign substances in food, increased noise levels, and decreased opportunities for rest and privacy may all affect bodily functions and, hence, responses to social stimuli. Diets and environments that cause physiological deficiency may, under certain social conditions, gradually become the norm (Wohlwill and Carson, 1972; Glass, Cohen, and Singer, 1973). Studies of human adjustment in outer space, of social isolation, of extreme climates, and of the effects of physical restriction (as in bomb shelters or submarines) indicate both the likelihood of behavioral changes as a result of extreme physical environmental conditions and also the wide range of situations within which humans maintain acceptable social behavior.

Summary of Physiological Bases of Pro-social Behavior

Human behavior is emitted by a physical body in a physical environment. Genetic and environmental factors influence behavior both by the individual and by those who respond to him. Pro-social behavior is limited by conditions which interfere with the ability to respond in typical and expected ways. But although there are differences in behavior, these behaviors are not necessarily considered abnormal in the same sense as other abnormal behavior described in this book. First, there is a considerable range of physiological endowment that is associated with normal behavior. An example is sexual behavior, in which work by Masters and Johnson (1966) indicates that there is a wide range of physiological anomaly that does not interfere with acceptable social adjustment. Second, the converse is also true: there are people whose genetic and physiological endowment, although clearly within normal limits, is a source of stigmatization from others and differential treatment. A third limitation on the effect of physiological deviance, as it applies to the topic of this volume, is that the label "genuine medical problem" has a very different impact than the label "*worthy of change by* a mental health professional." There is behavior that is considered normal and even admirable for a person with a medical defect. We will return to this when we discuss the concept of the *sick role*.

In terms of a theory of behavior, differences in physique, whether due to genetic or environmental influences, have an impact on behavior both insofar as they serve as limitations on the potential range of behavior and also as one basis for categorization of individuals. Although the majority of discussions in psychology presume an intact organism unless otherwise specified, the physical substrate of behavior and its social meaning should never be ignored.

THE BEHAVIORAL SETTING: PHYSICAL AND SOCIAL

Barker (1968), Hall (1966, 1969), Sommer (1969, 1974), Craik (1970), and Proshansky, Ittelson, and Rivlin (1970) are examples of authors who focus on the extent to which physical setting and organization of space influence behavior. A particularly interesting illustration is population density (Galle, Gove, and McPherson, 1972). Reactions to selected cues are learned as proper manners within a culture and become part of the complex but consistent patterns of behavior called social roles (see Chapter 5). An example would be personal distance, that is, how close one person comes to another. Northern Europeans are more likely to maintain a greater distance in social conversation than members of other cultures, and when they back away from a person who is uncomfortably close

an alternative approach

("pushy"), they may be perceived as indicating rejection or disdain.

Social class, geographical or national grouping, or almost any demographic sub-grouping may lead to differences in non-verbal, body language. Not only may a person be aversive to others when he does not act in the "correct" or expected manner, he may be judged "stupid." At the college level, a man who does not respond to a woman's cues of her interest in him is considered a "loser." In the psychiatric interview, a person who is not responsive to the interviewer's cues because they are part of cultural pattern of which he is not a member and hence has not learned may be called "aloof" or "socially unresponsive."

Classic examples of cues that deal with social location involve studies of seating arrangements in classrooms, libraries, and around committee tables. In the latter instance, where a person sits—at the head or side of the table—has a significant impact on his amount of speech and perceived contribution to the group's task. Sommer (1969, pp. 77–97) helped sharply increase the social interaction of older women on a psychiatric hospital ward by changing the arrangement of chairs from straight lines, shoulder to shoulder, against the wall, to an irregular pattern in the center of the room similar to a party.

Barker (1968) and his colleagues (e.g., Barker and Schoggen, 1973; Barker and Wright, 1955) carefully observed people in daily, as distinct from laboratory, contexts and documented the concept of a *behavior setting,* an ecological unit in which the discernible pattern of behavior is independent of the specific persons involved. "Correct" and expected behavior in a church service, in a classroom, or in a supermarket may be specified in general without reference to who the specific preacher, teacher, or salesperson may be, or who the specific worshipers, students, or customers may be. There are indeed differences in age, appropriate behavior, religious observance, or curriculum, but differences in the settings may account for as much, if not more, of the variance (differences among actions by people) than differences among people. Carrying the concept further, it is not only a matter of who a person is, but in what social setting he finds himself that provides a basis for evaluation of his behavior.

Social Organization

Under this title, we wish to refer to anthropological (Lowie, 1948), sociological (Cuber, 1963), and business administration (Blau and Scott, 1962; Etzioni, 1961; Golembiewski, 1962; March and Simon, 1958; Leavitt, 1964; Presthus, 1962; Thompson, 1963) variables that characterize contemporary society. As noted by McNeill (1965, especially pp. 66–72), a major breakthrough towards civilization as we know it was the development of political forms, bureaucracy, written communications, and a body of law that made it possible for large groups of people to live together. The provision and utilization of surplus food for the development of specific and special talents depends upon effective cooperation of a large number of people. Contemporary man lives in a web of organizations—people banded together for common purposes and with reciprocal obligations. Schools, churches, factories, and local, state, and federal legislatures (to say nothing of the division of labor inherent in leisure activities) make it nearly impossible for the individual to escape the organizational context.

For our purposes, it is particularly pertinent to note that the organization of people fosters certain behaviors at the expense of others. A prime example of a pattern of behavior that may be evaluated as either praiseworthy or changeworthy is that of the bureaucrat. Following Blau (1956, p. 19), there are four characteristics of bureaucracy: specialization, a hierarchy of authority, a system of rules, and impersonality. When dealing with a large number of people (or people repeatedly doing the same behavior, as in the division of labor in a factory), more units may be processed if the task is standardized and the person doing it specially trained and well-practiced. Each person's activity in his official role is checked by others. A hierarchy of authority permits a unified policy formulated centrally to be implemented throughout the system. It also means that the people closest to the actual implementation of the policy may have little or no say in its formulation. The policies aim to be fair and rational, but the scope of the system calls for rules and ways of categorizing people as cases. Written rules and recorded precedent become guides and justification for action. The goal of the system is to deal rapidly and equitably with many cases with as little favoritism or variable human judgment as possible. The result (e.g., Merton, 1957, pp. 195–206; Etzioni, 1964; Ullmann, 1967a, especially pp. 117–44) is two-fold. On the one hand the bureaucrat, in order to do his job well by the standards of his organization and immediate superior, avoids the very complexities that make for individualized response to people. Knowing too much may lead to difficulty in categorization and personal sympathy to acts not "in the book" that the bureaucrat would have to defend to his superior.

On the other hand, in order to make the cumbersome system function, dominated as it is by the rules and records of people dealing formally with each other, bureaucratic functionaries may develop out-of-channel, reciprocal-favor systems that lead to actual organizational patterns very different from the official ones. The organizational system in which a person finds himself goes far in specifying what acts are possible and what acts are likely to be rewarded or censured. In addition, the informal social structure will affect his behavior, and the range of his choices will be further restricted. The definition of "correct" behavior in this situation will depend in large measure on whether the observer is a superior, a colleague, or a client.

POLITICAL AND ECONOMIC CONSIDERATIONS

A person's opportunity to acquire the good things of life and the methods by which he may acquire them depend upon social class, general economic conditions and governmental operations (Kennedy, 1973; Hawley, 1973). Many of the concepts that we hold as self-evident aspects of the good life, both in terms of objects and activities, are relatively recent developments that are shared by only a minority of people throughout the world.

Historical Perspective

Human beings respond to only a small number of the stimuli with which they are faced. They respond in a manner not unlike the professional historian (Becker, 1935; Carr, 1961; Smith, 1964) whose decision as to what is a significant fact changes with the times in which he lives and with the tasks or decisions he faces. "All history is 'contemporary history,' declared Croce, meaning that history consists essentially in seeing the past through the eyes of the present and in the light of its problems, and that the main work of the historian is not to record, but to evaluate; for, if does not evaluate, how can he know what is worth recording?" (Carr, 1961, p. 22.) Although our past leads to our present, our present tasks alter our concepts of our past. This constant interchange of individual and environment is part of every person's daily experience; it is part of the change that is learning.

Summary of Contexts

A person lives in a physical and social environment. Knowledge of a person's age, sex, social class, education, race, marital

an alternative approach

status; his political, economic, geographical, and organizational contexts; and finally his specific current behavioral setting provide us with very strong clues as to what behavior he may be expected to make. Human learning takes place within these contexts. A person learns to make responses appropriate to the contexts in which he finds himself. To the extent that we can predict behavior from the above kinds of variables, we may have an estimate of the extent to which they place limits on the range of behaviors that are considered appropriate.

THE ROLE OF LEARNING

By the term "learning," we mean the effects of experience that takes place within the context of age, sex, race, social class, organization, physiology and the other variables we have been discussing. A person learns how to cope with his environment and how to act in a manner that is effective for one of a given age, sex, race, and so forth.

In place of the notion of natural selection based on genetic differences or instinctual patterns, humans evolve and adjust principally through the process of learning. In contrast to other species, humans are remarkable in the number and complexity of the patterns of behavior they learn. Specific learning concepts and illustrations from work with populations labeled as abnormal will be found in Chapter 4.

At this time we wish to make four interrelated general points about the contents of learning. The first is that what a person learns depends on experience within his social as well as physical environment (e.g., Petroni, 1969, regarding sick role): the experiences of a young, black female in a ghetto differ from those of a white, middle-aged college professor. Second, what a person has learned in the past alters the experiences he may gain in the future. Through learning a person's range of meaningful stimuli is altered: he not only learns specific instrumental acts, but also learns the relationship between stimuli.[2] A person learns that some stimuli are irrelevant and that others indicate opportunities to use specialized skills. Third, after physiological and demographic variables have been held constant, the differences among people are most effectively studied as differences in learning to deal with the stimuli currently present in their environment. Fourth, and crucially, *there is nothing in the learning process itself that is "right" or "wrong," "sick" or "healthy."* Learning may be evaluated as sufficient or insufficient *to a task*. The conditions likely to lead to such evaluations, that overt performance is changeworthy, have been discussed earlier (in this chapter in the section on behavior likely to be called abnormal).

A person is not a passive recipient of stimulation but actively seeks and works for certain stimulating conditions, whether these conditions be food in stomach, cessation of pain, a good grade in a college course, or a smile from a member of the opposite sex. What stimuli are likely to lead a person to act so that they are increased, decreased, maintained or ignored at any particular time or situation are in

---

[2] We have previously said that the abnormality label results in large measure from one person's behavior disturbing another's. This disturbance may be caused by upsetting the labeler's expectations as well as by directly aversive acts. "We each create our own world view out of the complex and incomplete material that is provided to us. Much of this information is provided for us by the actions of other people. We each need that created world to be a stable one, with enough order and predictability so that we can function in it. Therefore, deviance—the discovery that somebody else has an importantly different and contradictory view of the world—disconcerts us and we set out to resolve the disagreement. Because the disagreement is often rooted in social grounds rather than physical facts, its resolution inevitably involves social pressures . . ." [Darley and Darley, 1973, p. 23.]

large measure a matter of social learning. But, overall, a person reacts to his environment, responding as best he can.

CONDITIONS LEADING TO BEHAVIOR BEING EVALUATED AS CHANGEWORTHY

We may approach a person's dealing with environmental situations in the same way as we would any other skill. The process of making a "correct" response to social stimuli may be broken into a sequence: the person must receive the stimulus (attend to it and obtain information), have the skill to make the appropriate response, emit the response, and be reinforced for it. In addition, the response must be made at the right time and right place, and the individual must obtain accurate feedback about the consequences of his act.

Skills

To emit "correct" behavior, a person must be able to perform adequately. The abnormality of many people lies in one specific fact: they do not have the skill to do what is expected of them.

In any given case there may be more than one skill that requires training. It should also be clear that deficits in one area have an impact on smooth performance of other skills.

First, a person may simply not have learned the skill usually found in one with his assigned roles. If a person is presumed to have a skill he does not possess, he does not respond in the way expected of him. He is different, and this difference may be explained in terms of his being "abnormal" or "deviant." Further, not only does he not capitalize on what for other people are opportunities, but such "opportunities," because they indicate his difference, may actually become aversive. The therapist's job, then, is to teach the appropriate response. A classic example is the conditioning treatment of enuresis (bedwetting). The enuretic child has not learned to make the response of tightening the sphincter muscles in response to increased kidney pressure, and then waking up, relieving himself, and going back to sleep. If there is no physiological defect, children may be directly trained to do this.

In similar fashion, it is expected that college students will have a variety of social skills. Lillian Ross, in a book called *Reporting* has a chapter about a high school group from a small Illinois community who went to New York for a senior trip. The boys did not want to eat in a restaurant because they did not know how to order from a menu. They therefore made excuses which seemed to be irrational or neurotic in response to suggestions that they go out to eat. When it was understood that the restaurant situation raised the possibility of being thought inadequate, the boys' resistance was understandable, acceptable, and normal.

Case (1960) provides an example of how a seemingly abnormal attitude can be reinforced by keeping the person from frightening situations. He tells of a college student who had difficulty in talking to young women and so avoided the problem by saying he would talk only to nice girls—whom he defined as ones who did not smoke, wear short skirts, or use lipstick. This was more than enough to give a boy an excuse for not talking to any coed. Three points are raised by this example. First, a *skill* was not present and had to be taught. Case's approach to treatment illustrates a further basic point, that a reinforcing stimulus is required. Case suggested that the boy not talk to anyone, male or female, for a few days. This deficit had the effect of making subsequent conversation more reinforcing, and the boy progressed through a series of situations starting with talk to female clinic staff-members.

The second point is that the boy gave a "good" reason in place of the real reason. This, by definition, is the behavior Freud

an alternative approach

called rationalization. Freud formulated the behavior as the outcome of a compromise between psychic forces within the individual; it may, however, be more usefully formulated as one that is reinforced: it excused the boy from situations that were aversive to him because he would have failed in them and/or acted in a manner he or others would label "different" and "bad."

This leads to the third point illustrated. An unusual behavior, in this instance an attitude held by few people, was reinforced. The lack of skill preceded and was "more basic" than the unusual attitude.

In general, not having a required skill places the person in a situation similar to that of taking an examination for which he has not mastered the material. It is a situation the person has previously experienced as unpleasant, damaging, punishing, in short, aversive. A behavior that either terminates or avoids an aversive situation is likely to increase in frequency.

Another required ability which is a learned skill is identification of the right time and place for the performance of a skill.[3] Abnormal behavior has been described as being unexpected, unpredictable, incomprehensible, and ineffective. A person may have a skill but not emit it at the right time, i.e., when it is expected and would be reinforced. In other words, he may emit a response that is "correct" at the wrong time. He may have been taught the specific motor patterns but not how to identify the situations in which these skills are properly used. A person may have limited social skills or be competent on one particular topic; he merely stays on that topic or that skill. At minimum a person who talks about his specialty and nothing else is a bore. Not infrequently he will be thought a braggart, self-centered, or a person with a one-track mind.

Learning How and When to Label

Labeling situations properly is a necessary skill learned from an early age. The child at about two years of age who has just learned to say "daddy" receives a great amount of "oh-ahings," praise, smiles, attention, and so on after saying the word to daddy. What frequently happens is that he generalizes this behavior to situations that have some similarity to daddy but not the crucial component. The child may call "daddy" to every man he sees on the street. This is rather cute, but most mothers rapidly set about discrimination training.

The child in the foregoing illustration is responding to gross physical similarities in the situation. The mother is responding to subtler, relational, and abstract aspects of the situation. Giving the proper label, or, more generally, responding under proper control of discriminative stimuli, especially ones of an abstract-relational rather than a physical-functional nature, is a learned skill. Without such training, the person is likely to overgeneralize. Differences between situations may be quite minimal and subtle, especially to the uninitiated who do not search for or pay attention to such relevant stimuli. At another level, children may make use of rules that do not work. In terms of learning the English language, children may make "good" mistakes in new situations. A stewardess may be called "airliness," or "foot" may be given a plural form by simply adding an "s."

A person may have a specialized or seemingly idiosyncratic frame of reference. That is, he may label situations as good or bad

---

[3] Categorization and rules both for scientifically accurate categorization and observed behavior are the subject of taxonomy (Raven, Berlin, and Breedlove, 1971). It thus touches on the use of language itself, and the relationship between the person's act of labeling and his reaction to what he has labelled (Kanouse, 1971). Attribution theory, especially attributions about oneself (Ross, Rodin, and Zimbardo, 1969; Valins and Nisbett, 1971), therefore, may be relevant to the formulation of "abnormal" behavior; at a broader level, there is a study of sociologists (for recent examples, see Roman, 1971; Davis, 1972) of the use and impact of labels. The sociopsychological approach of Chapter 10 returns to these topics.

on the basis of rules or systems of labeling in a manner different from that expected by the people around him. He may do what is right and proper "in his own mind" and appear quite "different" to the people who are with him at that particular time. A college student who adheres to his mother's precepts at all times may appear strange to his college peers.

A person may fail to identify a situation "accurately" if he pays attention to stimuli that others do not consider germane. This is somewhat different from a private frame of reference. Here is an example: Two classes of students, one of which met at eleven o'clock, just before lunch, the other at one o'clock, just after lunch, were shown Rorschach (inkblot) pictures. The eleven o'clock class "saw" about twice as many food objects as the one o'clock class.

If the person has a deficit, by implication there is some stimulus in the environment which would be reinforcing, and he may very well seek it out. To this extent his sampling of the stimulus environment is biased, and he may be much more likely to identify an object as being associated with food or whatever other deficit he is under than if he did not have that deficit and was "normal." By sheer probability he may at times misidentify a situation and behave in a manner others consider inappropriate. A college student may respond to many situations as if they were sexual or potentially satisfying for his sexual needs. He may be wrong in enough cases to get the reputation of being single minded, but be right often enough to be put on a partial reinforcement schedule that is difficult to extinguish. He may frequently make sexual responses to situations that others do not consider sexual, or make sexual responses sooner or more strongly than most other people.[4] His behavior may therefore be aversive to other people and be labeled inappropriate.

Self-Labeling

A great part of a person's stimulus environment is composed of his own behavior. In part this is noticing the results of behavior and in part it is evaluating and labeling situations. One of the things people learn early in life from others such as their mothers is how to label behaviors and situations. It is possible to observe a two-and-a-half-year-old child labeling his own behavior and saying to, and about, himself, "Good boy," or "Bad boy." That this labeling of self in specific situations can lead to self-reinforcement is verifiable in laboratory studies (Bandura, 1962; Kanfer and Marston, 1963a, 1963b) with both nursery school children and college students.

The same objective situation can be labeled differently. For instance, a person who receives a C on an exam may say "good" because a C is all that is required to remain in college. On the other hand, a person may want to enter a graduate school, and label the same C bad. Grades exemplify all the effects and principles of acquired reinforcers. The person's label of the situation *summarizes* it and serves as a stimulus. These stimuli affect behavior directly, but there is an additional area of impact. The person may overgeneralize or draw an inference not warranted by the grade *per se*. He may take a "bad" grade as evidence that he is a "bad" person.[5]

A person may respond to situations labeled as bad or fearful with avoidance and may fail to learn that his labels are in

---

[4] Note the parallel to frequency, latency, and amplitude of response. Variations of behavior along these dimensions may define what other theorists call a personality trait (see Krasner and Ullmann, 1973).

[5] The Buddhist "Dhammapada, or Path of Virtue" notes on thought: "As a fletcher makes straight his arrow, a wise man makes straight his trembling and unsteady thought, which is difficult to guard, difficult to hold back . . . Whatever a hater may do to a hater, or any enemy to an enemy, a wrongly-directed mind will do him greater mischief." [Wilson, 1945, p. 118.]

error, that the situations are not harmful. Further, he may label a stimulus situation aversive and yet never have had any direct experience with it. This is exemplified by vicarious reinforcement and vicarious learning. The responses of other people usually (but certainly not always) are fair indications of proper responses to situations. Most of the readers of this book are likely to have a mild aversion toward snakes and rats, while having had little, if any, direct experience with them. These responses are likely to have been learned from other people. When confronted with these animals, the labels that have been taught are likely to be emitted and serve as stimuli for further responses.

The impact of labeling may be illustrated by a Jewish college student known to the authors. This student had been raised in an orthodox family and had been taught that it was "wrong" to eat "unclean" meat such as pork. At a college orientation dinner he ate quite a delicious cutlet and later remarked to a fellow student that it had been a very good meal. The other student said yes, he always enjoyed eating pork cutlets. The Jewish student at this point had an acute attack of nausea. There had been nothing aversive about the food itself. When it had been given a particular label, however, one associated with prior emotional responses, nausea resulted.

A person who has had direct experience with a particular stimulus may subsequently respond to an element of it as if it represented the whole prior situation. A person who has been caught in a house on fire, for example, may respond with a great deal of discomfort the next time he sees a fire, whether it is in a screened fireplace or in a leaf receptacle. To an observer, the fear or discomfort seems inappropriate to the present situation. One element of the past event, fire, is responded to in a manner appropriate to the total house-on-fire situation. Hollingworth (1930) called this situation *redintegration;* one element stands for or symbolizes the fear-provoking situation.

The person is responding to the stimulus without taking into account the current context. Fear and anticipation of aversive consequences and their physiological correlates were appropriate responses at one time to a situation in which the stimulus (fire) was a salient cue. The presence of the stimulus colors the current situation so that the entire context is responded to as if the prior situation had reoccurred.

A complementary condition is that in which one particular aspect of a situation must be present if a response is to occur. A person may make a sexual response only to redheads, the red hair being a biologically irrelevant cue that is, however, associated with prior pleasure while other hair colors are not so associated.

The Consequences of Failure to Attend

In addition to "irrational" (out of context) reactions to stimuli with aversion (phobias) or positive responses (fetishes), behavior may appear "irrational" or "inappropriate" when the person responds to stimuli others do not consider germane. Attention is an operant response of orienting to a stimulus. If such orientation is not reinforced, because differential response to the stimulus is inconsequential, the attention response will be extinguished. If this happens, there is a failure to process the information necessary to make what would usually be considered an appropriate response. Even if the individual has the skill, it does not come into play unless he has attended appropriately. Failure to respond to certain stimuli implies response to others. To the extent that the ensuing responses are not those expected by the observer, the individual seems to be irrational or idiosyncratic, or to have a thinking defect. To the extent, as noted earlier, that crucial social discriminative stimuli are relational, abstract, and relatively subtle, the person who does not pay attention to them may appear "concretistic" or "primitive." Major use of these considerations will be made in the chapters on schizophrenia.

There is also learning that involves the ignoring of stimuli as part of approved social behavior. When one is crushed against another person in a New York subway, it is inappropriate to apologize rather than to act as if the person were not there. If one ignores the unusual proximity, there is a cultural pretense that nothing unusual is happening, that one has not invaded another's space. Apologizing calls attention to the situation; if, for example, a Mid-Westerner does so to a New Yorker, the response he may obtain is enough to lead him to think all New York natives are rude. What New Yorkers may think in turn about visiting Mid-Westerners is left up to the reader's imagination.

A more complex example is provided by behavior in nudist camps. The nudist ideology maintains that nudism and sexuality are unrelated and that there is nothing shameful about exposing the body. There are, however, a number of taboos in most camps, such as no liquor, no sex talk, no body contact, no photography, and, particularly, no staring, that help maintain behavior consistent with the ideology (Weinberg, 1964).

Overt Behavior and Reinforcement

To emit a response, the person must have the necessary skill in his repertoire and must be reinforced for its emission. A skill may never have been shaped up (enuresis is an example), or it may have been extinguished, as attention responses of patients in psychiatric hospitals sometimes are. An example of the latter can be found in children who are institutionalized at a very early age. These children may go through their repertoires for evoking interactions from adults but because of the shortage in staff not be reinforced for them. They may also try other behaviors such as tantrums, crying, bouncing, and the like. Eventually they may simply sit stoically, withdrawn in a sort of "anaclitic depression" (Spitz, 1946).

Complementary to this clinical observation is the work of Brackbill (1958) illustrating how an infant's smiling response is influenced by social reactions to it. This study shows the impact of reinforcement on social behavior, differences in reinforcement schedules, and the early age at which such procedures have an effect. Eight normal children between $3\frac{1}{2}$ and $4\frac{1}{2}$ months of age were divided into two groups of four children each. For both groups there were three observation periods. In the first, operant period, the experimenter stood motionless and expressionless approximately 15 inches from the child and ascertained the rate of smiling without contingent reinforcement. During the second, conditioning period, reinforcement was meted out contingent upon the child's smiling. As soon as the child smiled, the experimenter smiled, talked softly, picked up the child and patted him, and then put him back in the crib. One group was regularly reinforced, i.e., every trial. The other group was reinforced regularly, and then successively thinned until reinforced only once for every four smiles. During the third and final period, extinction, the experimenter observed the children without reinforcing smiles, that is, reinstituted the conditions of the operant period.

The results were most interesting. During the operant period, the two groups of children did not differ, and the average rate of smiling for the two groups combined was 2.49 smiles per five-minute period. After conditioning, the average rate for the regularly reinforced group was 5.15 smiles per five-minute interval, while for the intermittent reinforcement group the averages were 6.32, 8.12, and 13.00 for the 2:1, 3:1, and 4:1 schedules, respectively. The data presented for the extinction period show that (1) the different schedules of reinforcement led to different extinction curves, and (2) the social response of smiling decreased when not reinforced. An incidental observation was that "protest" behavior such as crying and fussing was negatively correlated with smiling behavior during both conditioning and extinction periods. That is, as one behavior increased, the other decreased.[6]

The concept of reinforcement has entered each aspect of the present formulation. The development, maintenance, and alteration of behaviors all involve the scheduling of reinforcement. Many seemingly self-defeating and antisocial acts may be affected. A classic example deals with the extinction of temper tantrums. The following case was presented by Williams (1959). A 21-month-old boy had been seriously ill for much of the first 18 months of his life but his health, weight, and vigor had improved greatly during the preceding three months. The boy received the special care and attention that had previously been given him by engaging in tantrum behavior, especially at bedtimes. If the adult left the bedroom, the child would scream and fuss until the adult returned, and a parent was spending from half an hour to two hours each bedtime waiting for the child to go to sleep. In this circumstance, it was decided to remove the reinforcement: after a leisurely and relaxed bedtime preparation, the adult left the room and did not return. The length of successive tantrums are presented in Figure 1. The first extinction period showed no tantrum behavior after ten occasions; rather the child smiled and made happy sounds until he fell asleep. About a week later the child fussed and screamed when an aunt put him to bed and the aunt reinforced the behavior by returning to the room. It was necessary to extinguish the tantrum behavior again, and this is reported by the

---

[6] Similar results have been reported by Etzel and Gewirtz (1967) and Siqueland and Lipsitt (1966), Caron (1967), Rovee and Rovee (1969), Sheppard (1969), Ramey and Ourth (1971), and McKenzie and Day (1971), among others, amply indicating the early impact of operant conditioning and social reinforcement.

dotted, second extinction line of the figure. No further tantrum behavior at bedtime was reported during the next two years and no side- or after-effects were observed.

It was noted earlier in this chapter that some stimuli are responded to without regard to their contexts. A related paradigm is that of *superstitious* behavior. Behavior that is immediately followed by a positively reinforcing event is likely to be repeated under similar circumstances. Since living organisms continuously emit ongoing activity, some activities will by chance be followed by changes in the environment which had nothing to do with the behavior the organism emitted. Further, to the extent that they are reinforced every once in a while on the basis of sheer chance, these activities may be perpetuated on a partial reinforcement schedule. Students may use a favorite pen or wear a certain piece of clothing for examinations. This particular behavior may have been associated with great success at one time; it is continued even though it has no direct effect on success in exams. The fact that a long time may pass between studying (which does help exam performance) or the exam itself and the reinforcing stimulus of grades also increases the chances of the development of superstitious behavior.

A classic example of the importance of reinforcement in the development, maintenance, and cessation of a "symptom" was presented by Haughton and Ayllon (1965). A 54-year-old female patient who had been hospitalized 23 years was reported to be "idle" and to refuse to do anything on the ward except smoke. During a baseline observation period she was allowed only one cigarette after each meal. She spent 60 per cent of her waking time lying in bed. Next, a period of response shaping was inaugurated: one staff person gave her a broom, and while she held it another member of the staff gave her a cigarette. In a matter of a few days she developed a stereotyped behavior of pacing while holding the broom. The effects of various reinforcement

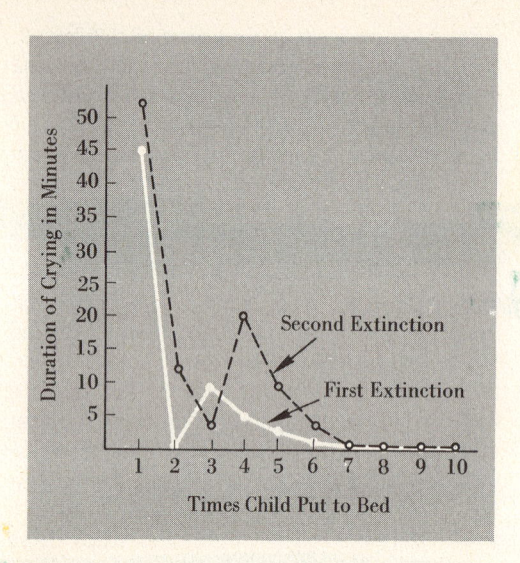

Figure 1
Length of crying in two extinction series as a function of successive occasions of being put to bed. Redrawn from Williams, 1959, p. 296.

schedules were tested during the next year of observation. Of basic import, however, was that obtaining cigarettes was contingent upon standing in an upright position holding a broom, and a great deal of the patient's time was spent in doing so.

When other patients tried to use the broom and take it away from her, she resisted firmly and sometimes aggressively. Her behavior appeared to be "compulsive" and "deviant." To put the experimentally developed behavior into proper clinical perspective, two psychiatrists were independently asked to observe and evaluate the patient from behind a one-way mirror. The first wrote, in part, ". . . it is certainly a stereotyped form of behavior such as is commonly seen in rather regressed schizophrenics and is rather analogous to the way small children or infants refuse to be parted from some favorite toy, piece of rag, etc." The second psychiatrist wrote, in part, "When regression conquers the associative process, primitive and archaic forms of thinking control the behavior.

Symbolism is a predominant mode of expression of deep-seated unfulfilled desires and instinctual impulses. . . . Her broom could be then: (1) a child that gives her love and she gives him in return her devotion; (2) a phallic symbol; (3) the sceptre of an omnipotent queen." Eventually, the researchers so thinned the reinforcement schedule that broom holding decreased. A further period of extinction was introduced to insure elimination of the broom-holding behavior.

In a two-year follow-up there was no further emission of broom-holding behavior. Was this broom holding normal or abnormal behavior? In large measure, one's answer will reflect his theoretical position on abnormal behavior and would summarize most of the material thus far presented.

The Learning of Behaviors Aversive to Others

Behaviors that are aversive to others may be learned because behaviors that would eventually have been more appropriate were not sufficiently reinforced. Under certain circumstances the child can gain the parent's attention only by strong responses such as yelling, shouting, and screaming, rather than by asking nicely. If this happens with sufficient frequency, the child may not "bother" with the reponses that have been extinguished but will emit the responses that get the results he wants.

The first aspect of this situation to note is that more appropriate behaviors were not reinforced. Behaviors that the larger culture evaluates as "good" or "correct" are maintained by reinforcement and are as likely as tantrums and bizarre broom holding to be extinguished and succeeded by alternative behaviors if they are not effectively reinforced.

The next aspect of the situation is that the reinforcement schedule may be thinned at such a rate that the aversive behavior is maintained. In a related manner, the situation may lead to inappropriate discriminative stimuli. The parents are emitting a low rate of reinforcing behavior, a procedure that would lead to extinction except that the parents do not stick to their plan. They may reach "the last straw" and "explode." What the child is reinforced (or punished) for is the behavior closest temporally to the reinforcer. This behavior may be relatively trivial. The parent is therefore likely to be reinforcing inconsequential behavior and doing so in an inconsistent manner. Under these circumstances discrimination of "good" and "bad" behavior is a difficult, if not impossible, task for the child.

If after he "explodes" the parent feels "guilty" (i.e., labels his behavior as wrong and inconsistent with the parent role), he may make amends so rapidly he will not obtain the behavior he wishes. The parent, teacher, or behavior therapist must wait until the child emits a behavior, no matter how slight, that moves in a more appropriate direction. That is, if the authority has "exploded," he makes the situation worse if he immediately makes restitution for his own "bad" behavior. Essentially he has been emitting a low rate of reinforcement and his anger may become a discriminative stimulus for positive reinforcement, i.e., the restitution. He therefore reinforces the child's provocative behavior. The sequence is: provocation—outburst—restitution. In terms of the child's behavior, what is learned is to provoke the parent. A similar model may be used to deal with some masochistic behavior—pain or degradation is followed by positive reinforcement. If the sequence is frequent enough, the "masochist" may select situations or emit behaviors likely to be the discriminative stimulus for pain. By sheer exclusion, other behaviors will not be emitted and, hence, not reinforced.

The parent must wait to make restitution until the child emits a behavior that moves in a desirable direction. *On successive occasions the child's behavior must move farther in that direction.* Maher (1966, pp. 216–18) writes very insightfully about one aspect of this situation. He notes that some people may act as if they had been reinforced for *apologizing* behavior. Punishment does not occur for the act, and reward is given for expressions of "feeling sorry." In short, the person has learned how to make verbal amends rather than to avoid emitting the behavior aversive to others. Both at a theoretical and applied level it cannot be stressed too strongly that the timing and selection of what is reinforced is as crucial as it is complex.

An example of how, despite the fact that learning principles may be valid, a behavior change program may still backfire is provided by an attempt of the senior author to stop smoking. (The junior author does not smoke, and is in no need of a behavior change program of any sort.) The technique was to be aversive conditioning, the pairing of an unpleasant stimulus with smoking. The author chose an awful stimulus to which he had never adapted: reading psychological journals. He sat in a chair, lit a cigarette, and immediately started reading the "literature." The rule was that he had to do so for a full hour after each cigarette was lit. The upshot was that the patient's rate of sitting in the chair and reading psychological journals was increased but his cigarette smoking was not particularly affected. As in the case of the female who held the broom, a strange behavior was reinforced.

Once a person has been shaped to emit behaviors that are aversive to someone else, his world is different from what it would be if he did not emit such behaviors. He is labeled and responded to in terms of that label. Because he is so labeled, what is permitted and reinforced for others is denied to him. People may indeed "be down on him" and "not treat him like other people." There is a continual interaction between the person's behavior and the environmental effects contingent on that behavior. These effects in turn feed back to him and further alter and define his environment.

Certain "abnormal" behaviors may be reinforcing in their own right, at least on a short-term basis. They are frequently sexual or addictive, and may be viewed as, first and foremost, failures to respond in manners that will be rewarding in the long as well as the short run. An example is alcoholic overindulgence to the extent that it takes the person away from an aversive situation. Another example is sexual behavior in response to disapproved stimuli that leads to orgasm but that takes the place of, and makes less likely, other, more socially approved, sexual outlets.

Through avoidance or circumstantial accident such as isolation, a person may not have gained sufficient practice in socially approved skills. He may not have learned some of the finer social skills, and this may lead to further difficulties and hence a vicious cycle. Most people have learned not only that when another person is in a good mood it is a good time to ask him for a favor, but also how to get other people in a good mood. If such skills have not been learned, the person may appear to be crude, dominant, or insensitive.

THE DEMOGRAPHIC PERSPECTIVE

To this point, we have devoted little direct attention in this section to age, sex, race, class, and other variables discussed earlier. These demographic characteristics were said to provide *limits* to behavior that might be evaluated as appropriate. They greatly influence what behaviors are to be learned.

Demographic characteristics also enter into the evaluation of behavior as changeworthy in other ways. One is that members of different groups may have difficulty understanding each other's appropriate behavior. If the appropriate standard for a white is to look directly at another person but for a black it is to look away, then a white employer may interpret the behavior of a black applicant as "evasive" or "shifty" while a black may complain of being "stared at" and made to feel "uncomfortable."

Every person, by the very nature of growing older or by marrying or taking increased employment responsibility, continuously shifts the demographic groups to which he belongs. In addition, a person may have a number of different roles at the same age—for example, at work, at play, and at home. Finally, with changes in the general culture, there are changes in what is role-appropriate behavior. This is evidenced by, among other things, the changes over a brief period of time starting in the late 1960s in what is considered appropriate, or at least permissible, on a college campus in terms of the use of previously taboo words, sexual activity, dress, and demands for shared decision making.

As Francis Bacon (1963 edition, p. 65) noted, time is the greatest innovator. It often takes as much effort to maintain the status quo, or one's position in it, as it does to develop new behavior. In Bacon's words: ". . . a forward retention of custom is as turbulent a thing as an innovation." The following quotation captures the spirit of the reluctance to give up old ways of behaving:

Latencies are behavioral sets and practices that the individual or group is unable or reluctant to abandon. Every contradiction which the social analyst studies in society is attributable to the existence of a latency, singly or in combination with other latencies. A latency is an adaptation effective in the past and persisting in present behavior tendencies even though it may not be appropriate in contemporary situations. [Bloch and Prince, 1967, p. 42.]

In a pluralistic society, members of one group may label members of another as deviant. We have previously noted that the bureaucrat, in adapting to the realities of his situation, may behave in an aversive manner to his organization's clients. At times, the very membership itself in an organization may be interpreted as evidence of deviance, such as belonging to a religious, moral, or political group that differs markedly from the norm (Smelser, 1962; Reiss, 1968).

When we discuss paranoia in Chapter 20 we will refer to the similarities between the conditions for the development of false beliefs and the development of rumor or manufactured news. At this time, the point we wish to make is that social and political conditions may foster behavior that, if taken out of the specific sociopolitical context, would be considered "deviant," "abnormal," or "changeworthy," but which are actually reasonable responses to the given conditions.

During the post–World War II period, individuals living in the Soviet Union and labeled as its intelligentsia had to know what was happening in their country in order to adjust their own personal and professional behavior. They were alert to any disparities between the official media and what eventually proved to be the "truth." They, therefore, frequently used rumors as the basis of belief and action. Up to 90 percent placed more faith in rumors than in official media (Inkeles and Bauer, 1966, p. 572).

Quite another [method of obtaining information] was through the development of subtle interpretive principles whereby the citizen attempted to discern what was *really* going on. Like all peoples whose news sources are censored and controlled, the Soviet citizen tries by inference to detect that which was withheld, or the truth that lies behind what he considers to be an untrustworthy statement. Respondents asserted frequently and spontaneously, "You had to read between the lines." The techniques they cite for reading between the lines are based on a combination of the degree of distrust for the official media and a series of implied assumptions about the nature of the Soviet system, particularly as regards its communications policy . . . The most drastic device suggested was that one should believe exactly the opposite of what the Soviet press said . . . One relatively sophisticated assumption . . . is that the Soviet government projects its own motives onto foreign governments . . . Another assumption about Soviet news policy made by our respondents was that the Soviet government would always attempt to prepare the populace in advance to accept unpleasant developments. "If there was going to be famine in the Ukraine, we always used to hear that there was hunger in Germany and Austria and that children were picking food out of garbage cans. When I saw such examples I knew that soon we would have a famine." [Inkeles and Bauer, 1966, pp. 577–78.]

The ways in which a person may realistically and rationally come to emit behavior that someone, including himself, may consider changeworthy are usually intertwined. For example, a person who has done poorly on exams and thus has found them to be a source of punishment may need to learn how to give adequate answers (e.g., study, master the prerequisites) and after so doing, reduce extraneous autonomic or conditioned emotional reactions emitted in exam situations (i.e., desensitization). Different times, places, and social-group memberships provide different opportunities and call for different types of behavior. Humans learn social as well as physiological adjustments, and the different contexts serve at times as setting stimuli and at others as reinforcing ones. We have stressed this interdependence by referring to a "sociopsychological" model and will extend our discussion of these considerations in the tenth chapter of this book.

CHANGING BEHAVIOR

It does not necessarily follow, either logically or empirically, that because a procedure is effective in rectifying a situation it indicates the etiology of that situation. Further, that a theory does not lead to effective treatment deductions does not necessarily mean that the theory is not accurate. The methodological relationship of etiology and treatment is merely one of consistency and elegance (Torrey, 1973a). In day-to-day work, however, that viewpoint that eventually leads to effective therapy is likely to be valued by practitioners.

The relationship between conditions leading to designation of behavior as changeworthy and the methods for altering behavior is a close one in the sociopsychological position. This position stems from the view that there is no behavior that is changeworthy in and of itself and from the concept that both behavior considered normal and abnormal are developed and maintained in the same ways. The concepts and procedures used in the change of any behavior apply to both changeworthy and socially appropriate behavior. As such, material on learning principles and social learning also represents material on treatment. Illustrations of behavior change will be presented throughout the book and will not detailed at this time.

There are a number of implications that may be briefly touched on at this time. The first is that the therapist has a professional role similar to that of a teacher. If a student does not do well in arithmetic, the teacher does not label that student as being all bad, nor does he place him in a category with all other people who do poorly in arithmetic. Rather, the teacher strives to find out, *for each individual*, what new experiences may best serve to bring that person to an adequate level of skill in arithmetic.

Next, the teacher takes responsibility for the student's progress. This is particularly heightened by adherence to a learning ideology: if reinforcement principles are accepted as valid, the teacher cannot blame either his students or his concepts. Rather, failure is a challenge to the teacher to check and alter his procedures. A behaviorally oriented therapist is therefore likely to blame himself rather than his client; he cannot rationalize his failures as the fault of the disease process (i.e., the individual) and abandon the person who does not respond to treatment.

SUMMARY

This chapter attempted to provide the reader with a framework for the material in the remainder of the book by outlining an approach to behavior called abnormal. Four major questions need be dealt with in any view of abnormal behavior: what behavior is considered normal or abnormal; what are the conditions leading to normal behavior; what are the conditions leading to abnormal behavior; and how may behavior designated abnormal be changed to behavior that is socially acceptable.

Because time, place, and person of both the actor and labeler are intertwined with the definition of normal or abnormal, we returned to an abstract definition of what is a "good" or "virtuous act," namely, a statement by Aristotle: ". . . excess and deficiency are alike wrong; but to experience these emotions at the right times and toward the right persons and for the right causes and in the right manner is the mean or the supreme good which is characteristic of virtue." We, therefore, approached the first two questions empirically: under what conditions or in response to what sorts of behavior will a person evaluate acts as worthy of change, and, under what conditions will an individual be likely to emit behavior considered acceptable or even worthy of maintenance and encouragement?

The critical question approached in this chapter was the third one. If normal and abnormal behavior do not differ in themselves and are developed and maintained in accord with the same principles, what are the conditions leading to behavior that in turn is likely to be considered changeworthy?

Abnormal behavior may be viewed as failure to make what is considered an appropriate response. Emphasis has been on socially normal behavior as a skill dependent upon having the expected act in one's repertoire, emitting it at the time and place

an alternative approach

where it will have reinforcing consequences, and obtaining accurate feedback about the effects of emitting it. Particular difficulties may arise when the person mislabels himself or his behavior, is under control of reinforcing stimuli different from those typically expected of one in his position, has been conditioned so that he responds to an aspect of one situation as if a different one were present in its totality (redintegration), has been extinguished for attention to cues that are typically considered relevant to the situation, responds to cues that others do not consider relevant because of particular physiological deficits or because of prior training (including superstitious behavior), has been maintained by a periodic reinforcement or self-reinforcement in behaviors that are inappropriate, or has been shaped so that he was reinforced for behaviors that others find aversive. These instances do not exhaust the possibilities, and it should be stressed that more than one of the formulations may be and probably is present in any given person's changeworthy behavior.

Within the limits of the person's physiological endowment and the manipulable resources of the environment, treatment follows an educational model. Examples of treatment and of other concepts presented in this chapter, are spread throughout the remainder of this volume.

Many of the points raised in this chapter may be illustrated by the following quotation:

I didn't set out to be a madam any more than Arthur Michael Ramsey, when he was a kid, set out to be Archbishop of Canterbury. Things just happened to both of us, I guess. At a time when most young girls decide to become schoolteachers, actresses, or lady lawyers, one doesn't, after carefully considering all the vocations open to a female, say, "That's for me; I'm going to be a madam." Madaming is the sort of thing that happens to you—like getting a battlefield commission or becoming the Dean of Women at Stanford University . . . Many are called, I always say, but few are chosen and for me it has been a steppingstone to bigger and more profitable things. (I started to say "bigger and better things," but is there really anything better, in the words of the poet, than "living in a house by the side of the road and being a friend to man"?) [Stanford, 1968, pp. 204–6.]

scientific method 3

What is known depends upon *how* it is known. If the basis of information is not clear, it is difficult to evaluate it, to integrate it meaningfully, or to use it in making decisions. Science is a discipline to improve the utilization of information gained from experience.

At a first level, there are the moral imperatives to report honestly and to see things as they actually are. It is presumed that the observer will influence his data as little as possible. While the very act of observing and experimenting may alter the data, the objective is to obtain as clear and accurate observation of germane data as possible.

Science is more than a simple collection and categorization of information. What information will be collected depends on what the experimenter thinks is an important issue on which uncertainty should be reduced. Scientists cannot and do not record and observe everything. They therefore may miss important information, because what they will investigate depends upon what they think is important. Few things are more valuable in science than good theoretical ideas that lead to obtaining data and performing experiments that are crucial. On the other hand, few things are more burdensome than theories that obscure helpful information and make presumptions which not only lead to false and erroneous observations but also keep people from testing and making new observations. For many years it was believed impossible to permanently influence abnormal behavior directly, and therefore few people tried to do so. Because no data were collected, there was no information contrary to this hypothesis.

It is not at all certain that a person exposed to a given situation will perceive it accurately. That this is so is illustrated by the following quotation:

Aristotle held that the vital principle of the embryo comes from the father alone; the role of the mother is confined to supplying the raw materials and nourishing the embryo. This doctrine was held in medieval Europe by Albertus Magnus in the 13th century and with modifications by William Harvey (1651). Some of the microscopists at the beginning of the 18th century convinced themselves that human spermatozoa contain miniature human figures complete with arms, legs, and a head, and they carefully illustrated these so-called homunculi. One of the early microscopists also found a microscopic horse in the semen of a horse and a minute fowl in the semen of a cock. [Grant, 1956.]

In similar fashion, the formulations of Galen (ca. 130–ca. 200 A.D.) were so completely accepted in the Middle Ages that early anatomists, viewing internal organs either through accidents of war or under dissection, simply did not observe or reproduce what contemporary physiologists think they "should" have seen. That is, physiological anomalies consistent with Galenic dicta were observed, but observations contrary to Galen's doctrines were rationalized as coming from "defective corpses."

DECISION MAKING

After accurate observation, the next obligation of the scientist is to make every effort to rule out alternative explanations or decisions. *Experiments are performed in order to reduce uncertainty about the world.* If they are performed in such manner that uncertainty cannot be reduced because alternative explanations cannot be ruled out, there is no clear basis for decision. The following paragraphs will discuss some of the procedures used to rule out alternative explanations.

A new drug has been developed, and a decision must be made whether it will be helpful in the treatment of some behavioral disorder. The first thing that can be done is simply to give the drug to a group of patients and see how many of them improve. If some people do improve, it might be possible to say that the drug has been helpful. But it is quite possible that a number of patients would have improved without taking the drug. What is needed is a *control group,* a group of patients who do not receive the drug. The improvement of the people in the control group will be compared with the improvement in the *experimental group* of patients who receive the drug. This strengthens the study because it provides data to rule out the alternative hypothesis that a mere passage of time was involved in the patients' improvement. But even if a superior result is found with the group receiving the drug, there would still be alternative explanations of the findings. Social scientists have gathered a great amount of information about the effect of an expectation of being helped, that is, the placebo effect. A *placebo* is either an inert substance or one whose action is so broad that it cannot be associated with a particular therapeutic effect.[1] Placebos may be sugar or gelatin made to look like the experimental drug or mild sedatives with side effects similar to the drug being tested. The object is to hold constant the effects of simply being "treated."

In the subsequent revised experiment, the experimental group will receive the drug being tested while the control group receives a placebo which looks exactly like the pill being given the experimental group. Even with this situation, which at first may appear to be well controlled, there may be an alternative explanation for favorable results. As long as the people who are giving the drug to the patient know which is the real drug and which is the placebo, the procedure is open to question. As long as the individual who administers a drug knows what the effects are supposed to be, he may communicate his expectation to the patient, often without realizing he is doing so.

The next step, then, is to make it impossible for the people who give the drug to bias the results by responding differently to the experimental group (e.g., showing interest in their improvement, paying special attention to them, asking them if they are getting better) or the control group (e.g., feeling guilty about not really helping them, being uninterested, skeptical, or even hostile to their reports of benefit). The prevention of the transmission of the experimenter's bias results in a situation that is known as a *double-blind* experiment. Both the people receiving the drug and the people giving the drug are "blind" as to who is receiving the supposedly potent drug and who is receiving the placebo.[2]

An experiment involves the observation of the effect of one variable upon another when all other variables have been held constant or randomized. In a drug-evaluation situation, the variable being investigated and experimentally manipulated is

---

[1] The reader should keep separate in his mind the physical *placebo object,* which is inert or nonspecific, and the *placebo effect,* which is a measurable change in behavior resulting not from the placebo object but from the psychological situation.

[2] This is very difficult to do in practice, and Engelhardt et al. (1969) found that physicians in a double-blind experiment guessed to which group the patients belonged. Further "When the doctor thinks the patient is on active medication, there is a higher improvement rate than when he thinks the patient is on placebo." (p. 317.)

the drug. The drug is therefore called the *independent variable*. The measure of the effect of the independent variable (drug) is called the *dependent variable*.

An example of crucial independent variables that were not held constant may be found in "tent therapy" at the start of this century (Caplan, 1969, pp. 273–83). In 1901, at Manhattan State Hospital, as a public health measure for tubercular patients, patients were housed in tents. The observed mental improvements were so rewarding that by midsummer, 1901, some nontubercular patients were also placed in tents. The patients gained in weight and social behavior. Other examples followed with good results, and patients who returned to the crowded, dirty, impersonal wards during the winter relapsed, while patients remaining in elaborate winterized tents did not. In a physiologically oriented era, fresh air, sunshine, and cleanliness were thought of as the operative factors rather than the novelty, adventure, group cohesiveness, better food, entertainment, and higher staffing that coincided with being in a tent instead of a closed ward. When tent treatment became routinized so that the patients were crowded together, staffing was poor, and special attention and patient-staff cohesiveness decreased, the effectiveness of tent treatment declined even though there remained as much sunshine and fresh air as ever.

OPERATIONAL DEFINITIONS

One reason so much time was devoted in Chapter 1 to defining abnormality is that changes in "abnormality" are dependent variables. Dependent variables in treatment studies are ways in which patients improve. As might be deduced from the first chapter, a person may improve in terms of one dependent variable but not in terms of another. The measure of improvement used to evaluate change must be operationally defined. The focus of studies of treatment is not "improvement" but a particular effect which was measured.

Generalization from empirical data is limited to the domain of things actually observed. An example might be a social scientist who wishes to find out whether Tennyson was right in saying that "it is better to have loved and lost than never to have loved at all." If he wishes to make his test scientific, he must first decide what he means by "better." Does he mean better physical health, financial position, or moral attainment? Another thing he must do is decide what he means by "love." There are many definitions of "love," some of them in conflict with others. For purposes of the present example the investigator may arbitrarily decide that the word "love" means that the person has gotten married and the word "better" refers to financial position.

What the researcher may then investigate is whether people who have gotten married and divorced are in a better financial position than people who have never gotten married. Because people who get married and divorced (have "loved" and "lost") may be different from those who never get married at all, there is a problem of sampling. If a true experiment were possible, the researcher might take a hundred men and a hundred women and randomly make half of them get married and half not get married. At the end of a set time he would have the fifty married couples divorce. The experimenter would then determine at various succeeding intervals how the financial status of the divorced people compared with that of the people who had never married. He might very well find that it is "better to have loved and lost" if the subject is getting alimony, but worse if the subject is paying it. The first point is that when a general statement is defined in terms of the manipulations and procedures involved, a very discrete, specific set of information is obtained. The data collected may be so limited to particular operations that different researchers using different definitions of the same genral term may obtain data leading to different conclusions.

This bizarre example was purposely selected to help make a second point: a person can legitimately state that he does not consider marriage to be a proper operational definition of "love" and a person's bank account to be a proper measure of "better" or "worse." This is an eminently acceptable procedure: a student or another investigator may always argue with an operational definition. But if he cannot do better or cannot show that the data collected are worse than *no* empirical evidence, he is likely to be on the short end of the argument.

An extension of the considerations dealing with operational definitions is the matter of generalization. When generalizing from a set of data, the scientist is implicitly saying that what holds for a certain limited number of observations of people holds for a greater number. In short, what is true for some members of a group is held to be true for all members of a group. It is right, proper and necessary for the student to ask whether the group of people, the specific observations, or the situation in which the observations were taken match the more general domain or population to which the results will be applied and about which decisions will be made.

The similarity between this type of evaluation of experimental data and questions about the pertinence of operational definitions can be illustrated by reference to the experiment just discussed. In the experiment, the researcher *randomly* assigned persons to the married and not-married categories and thus avoided potential sampling biases present in "real life" between those people who marry and those who remain single. In some measure, the experimenter also gained by holding constant differences in courtship and prior experiences among his married couples. To the extent, however, that selection of a marital partner in our culture deviates from random assignment, the research worker's sample differs from the group of people, the *population*, to which he wishes to apply his findings. That is, all the experimenter can decide is whether or not it was better *for the sort of people studied* to have gotten married the way they did than not at all (see Chassan, 1970). The operational definition of love was marriage, yet in the research it was a marriage contracted and terminated in an atypical manner. It is therefore very reasonable to question whether "marriage" as conducted in the research is similar enough to "marriage" as customarily contracted to justify *generalization,* or decisions, about the latter on the basis of the former.

While the concepts so far discussed about the crucial role of operational definitions in empirical science apply to physical and biological science, they have possibly an even greater place in social science. Talking about a molecule will not alter it; talking about a person may well change his environment and therefore his behavior. Words are used not only in work *about* people acting abnormally but in work *with* such people. Davidson (1958) stated the obligation beautifully: "Of all branches of helping people, psychotherapy is the one most concerned with words. Let us pause and look at our words. They are our tools. Let us keep them sharp and in good order." Insistence on knowing what a word actually signifies and the operations used to define it is a way of attaining this ideal.

In dealing with people, it is all too easy to make semantic errors. That a word "works" does not mean that what it designates exists in reality. The word "love" is a good example. A hypothetical college student might say to a coed, "If you loved me . . ." and mean, "Let's make out." The hypothetical coed might start her reply with the same words, "If you loved me . . . ," and mean, "Let's not." Different people may use the same word but mean different things. A person may use a word because it evokes a favorable response from others, but the word may still mean different things to him and the others. Even if the coed in the example had consented, she and her boy friend might still have had different things in mind.

That the word "love" is widely used does not mean that there is something that is "love" and that there is no other thing like it. Rather, using the word "love" is a behavior that people emit under varying circumstances with varying consequences, some of which are pleasant. In similar fashion, designating a person abnormal solves social dilemmas on some occasions and affects how the person giving the label treats the person so labeled. That there are social behaviors of using the word "love" or the word "abnormal" that have important consequences does not mean the words denote objective occurrences.

At first blush such an analysis of a word like "love" seems cynical and an entry into a barren, mechanistic world. This is not the case. If the word is accepted as standing for a real thing, no further questions need be asked. But if the use of the word is subjected to analysis, the person must ask by whom, under what circumstances, and with what consequences. He cannot merely say that he loves, relates, communicates, or has achieved togetherness, but rather must determine what it is to love, to relate, to communicate, or to achieve togetherness, and whether he is acting in a manner that matches his definition. He is forced to move from the image of love to its substance, and while this is a more demanding task, it is also the gateway to genuine concern for another person, whether that person is called "beloved" or "abnormal."

Insistence on operational definitions, on observation of behavior rather than theoretical abstractions, is crucial in treatment. Singer (1970, p. 390) puts the matter as follows: "Patients seem remarkably willing to forgive the inanities all too often thrown at them; they seem remarkably willing to understand that at best we know little; but they seem rightfully unwilling to forgive us our intentions of having them prove us right in our theoretical preconceptions." In short, the people we deal with want us to attend to what they do, what they are, and not something they should be that is a word, a preconception, an abstraction.

A classic example of the dominance of a theory over observation or operational definition involves the first use of electroshock therapy in which a seizure is induced. The following is from Freeman (1968, pp. 47–48):

The time had come for application to the patient. Cerletti describes his first case, a delusional and hallucinated schizophrenic man who talked only gibberish. Cautiously, an 80-volt shock was given for 1.5 seconds. The patient reacted with a jolt and momentary rigidity, but also no loss of consciousness.

"He started to sing abruptly at the top of his voice, then he quieted down. Naturally, we, who were conducting the experiment, were under great emotional strain and felt we had already taken quite a risk. Nevertheless, it was quite evident to all of us that we had been using a too low voltage. It was proposed that we should allow this patient to have some rest and repeat the experiment the next day. All at once, the patient, who evidently had been following our conversation, said clearly, and solemnly, without his usual gibberish: 'Not another one! It's murder!' I confess that such explicit admonition under such circumstances, and so emphatic and commanding, coming from a person whose enigmatic jargon had until then been very difficult to understand, shook my determination to carry on with the experiment. But it was just this fear of yielding to a superstitious notion that caused me to make up my mind. The electrodes were applied again and a 110-volt discharge was applied for 1.5 seconds.

"We observed the same instaneous, brief, generalized spasm, and soon after, the onset of the classic epileptic convulsion. We were all breathless during the tonic phase of the attack, and really overwhelmed during the apnea as we watched the cadaverous cyanosis of the patient's face; the apnea of the spontaneous epileptic convulsion is always impressive, but at that moment it seemed to all of us painfully interminable. Finally, with the first stertorous breathing and the first clonic spasm, the blood flowed better not only in the patient's vessels but also in our own. Thereupon we observed with the most intensely gratifying sensation the characteristic gradual awakening of the patient 'by steps.' He rose to sitting position and looked at us, calm and smiling, as though to inquire what we wanted of him. We asked: 'What happened to you?' He answered: 'I don't know. Maybe I was asleep.' Thus occurred the first electrically produced convulsion in man, which I at once named electroshock."

This anecdote illustrates much of what we wish to say about the relationship between patients and professionals, stimulus conditions and overt behavior, theory and practice. In the present context of insistence on observation and operational definitions, we can only ask, Was the convulsion necessary? What conditions led well-intentioned men to ignore the cry "Not another one! It's murder!" so that it haunts us to this day?

SAMPLING

An important aspect of the experimental situation deals with the *sampling* of people placed in the experimental and in the control groups. People must be selected for drug or placebo groups *randomly*. This means that every person in the population under investigation has an equal opportunity to become a member of either group. If the drug were given to a group of young patients with a high probability of improving and the placebo to a group of aged patients with a low probability of improving, differences in the dependent variable could be ascribed to the types of patients in the groups rather than to the effect of the drug itself.

The problem of sampling becomes particularly acute when the operational definition of abnormality is residence in a psychiatric hospital. Usually in seeking a physiological etiology of mental illness, a group of hospitalized psychiatric patients is compared with regard to some bodily function with a group that is "normal" by the definition of never having had a psychiatric hospitalization. Even if the subjects are matched for variables such as age, sex, education, intelligence, and social class, any difference obtained may still be an artifact of the sampling procedure. The very fact of hospitalization, rather than a particular disease, may underlie the obtained differences. Overcrowding in the vast majority of psychiatric hospitals may lead to the rapid and chronic spread of various infections of the digestive tract which in turn have a wide range of physiological effects in the functioning of organs such as the kidneys. The diet in institutions, especially ones with stringent budgets, may be low in fresh vegetables and meats and thus lead to consequent physiological effects.

Hospitalized persons may well indulge in less physical exertion than people with more typical routines of work and play. The person who is hospitalized may be frightened or outraged by his incarceration and may consequently play a dependent, inmate role. Enactment of such a social role may lead to autonomic responses which are the *effects* rather than the causes of hospitalization. Within the hospital the patient follows a schedule of eating and sleeping which is in accord with the needs of the institution's staff. That is, the patients usually are required to eat earlier than people living outside the hospital. When this is combined with the not infrequently observed disturbed, restless sleep of hospitalized psychiatric patients, group differences between inmates and "normals" in measures of biological functioning, such as those based on urine samples taken upon arising, are open to question. Finally, the hospital is presumed to be a place of treatment, and many patients in the sample, even if not currently receiving various somatic therapies such as drugs or electroshock, may well show the long-term residual effects of such treatment.

False conclusions, therefore, can be made

because of differential treatment of the sample prior to the collection of the data. This type of error is similar in form, although not in content, to the following: A person writing advertising copy for cigarettes might send a carton of his brand to every physician in town. Three days after having mailed out the cigarettes he could call up the physicians and ask, "Doctor, what cigarette are you smoking today?" Under these conditions he might find that nine out of ten physicians who smoked were smoking his brand of cigarettes on the day of the investigation. What at first would seem to be powerful results supporting the popularity of this cigarette would actually be a result of a bias in sampling.

Who will cooperate with the research may lead to a systematic difference between populations (Turner et al., 1969; Stein, 1971). Differences among populations, in turn, may lead to differences in responses due to different definitions of what is socially desirable behavior rather than differences in rates of disturbing behavior (Phillips and Clancy, 1970; Leon et al., 1970). Miller et al. (1970) provide a list of sampling problems in the field of alcoholism that indicates the extent of the problem:

1. *Varying definitions of alcoholism.* Obviously, if the definition of alcoholism were very broad, a much larger proportion of problem drinkers would be included, and some of these would differ in many respects from hard-core severely affected alcoholics.
2. *Case selection from special populations.* Many treatment programs are limited to special groups, such as war veterans, employees of a firm, subscribers to a health plan, persons able to afford private care, etc.
3. *Reputation of the treatment program.* After a treatment program becomes known for doing particularly well with a certain type of patient, it will tend to get predominantly that type of referral.
4. *Refusal of referral.* Some problem drinkers referred to a treatment program may refuse to go for evaluation, and it seems quite likely that this group differs from those who are evaluated.
5. *Rejection of applicants.* The treatment staff may select some applicants and decline others. Since this is based on some criteria, these groups are different by definition.
6. *Failure to report after acceptance into a treatment program.* Those who fail to report for a program after being accepted are likely to differ from those who do report.
7. *Exclusion from study protocol.* In most formal studies of alcoholism treatment, certain patients are excluded because of explicit requirements of the protocol; frequently this includes those patients with complicating physical illnesses, psychoses, etc.
8. *Drop-outs during treatment.* Typically some portion of accepted patients fails to complete a formal treatment program. It is possible that the "drop-outs" have somewhat different traits and attributes from the remainder.
9. *Living or moving beyond feasible follow-up distance.* Some inpatients may live at a considerable distance from the treatment institution. After completion of a treatment program, other patients gradually move out of the geographical area, making follow-up by the study team unfeasible.
10. *Deaths.* Patients who die during the follow-up period often cannot be rated in terms of drinking behavior or social adjustment, so that they tend to be dropped from the sample. Yet they are likely to differ in health and other characteristics from the survivors.
11. *Inability to trace cases.* There are almost always some ex-patients who cannot be traced, and the proportion increases with the length of the follow-up period. These persons are likely to be the nomadic, homeless, jobless ones, and their loss introduces further bias.
12. *Refusal to participate in follow-up interviews.* Some refusals are to be expected in almost all studies, even where the persons have been located. In a group of patients with alcoholism, this seems more likely to

occur among those who continue drinking. [Miller et al., 1970, pp. 98–99.]

In summary, sampling is a very crucial part of any experimental procedure, and errors in sampling illustrate that *how the data are collected* is as important as the specific data themselves.

STATISTICAL ANALYSIS

After bits of information have been collected, they need to be evaluated. The evaluation of results in an empirical, inductive science calls for a set of ideas associated with the word "statistics." The value of statistics is twofold, descriptive and inferential. First, numbers are used to *describe* results. If scientists had to talk about their data in terms of each individual case, the task of reporting would be very difficult and time-consuming. It is also very hard to keep in mind and compare more than a small number of items at any single time. There are therefore advantages to assigning some single or limited number of measures of improvement or change to each person. Further, to permit computational procedures, it is desirable that the measures be a matter of degree, i.e., scores. The modern college student is very familiar with a method of handling scores known as an average, by means of which performance in 20, 30, or 40 courses may be summarized and different students (or the same student in different semesters) may be compared. The raw information of number of hourly credits, specific courses, and grades in those courses would be so complex that often it would be difficult to compare even two people.

The scores can be used strictly for descriptive purposes. The most familiar descriptive procedure is the designation of central tendency called the average. There are other procedures that reduce masses of data to more readily understood descriptions. Perhaps one of the easiest and most direct things is to draw a picture. A picture, however, can be very misleading. As an example, the student may wish to make a graph of improvement in a particular aspect of his life during college. He can label the lines on a graph paper from 100 to 150, and mark off a period of four years on the bottom of the graph. One underweight student managed to raise his weight five pounds a year, from 100 as a freshman to 120 as a graduating senior.

Another student, also trying to gain weight, was unsuccessful and weighed 100 each year. The first student appears to have made a considerable gain. Let the reader now label his graph from 1 to 150. The difference between the two students now seems far less dramatic. Further, let the student spread out the successive years so that two inches separate each yearly weighing. Next, let him plot the same data with a quarter of an inch between each weighing. The first pictorial representation will be far less impressive in terms of steepness of increment than the second.

A different manner in which descriptions of data may be made to mislead is the use of percentages without reference to the number of cases involved. At the beginning of the twentieth century, when there was still a question whether females should be permitted to go to college, a particular college admitted women to its freshman class for the first time. At the end of the year the college administration evaluated academic ability in terms of grade-point average and reported to the alumni that of the freshmen, 50 percent of the women flunked while only 10 percent of the men failed. It could also, from the same set of data, have reported that of the freshman class, 50 men failed while only one woman failed. Both statements about the 500 men and two women would have been accurate, but the impression given by the figures and, therefore, the decisions made from them, might very well have been different.

A matter of great import for the citizen

and consumer of research is that of *base rates,* or what might have occurred had no treatment procedure been introduced. It is not correct to assume that no person will ever recover without treatment. Psychologists, for example, estimate that a neurotic's chances of getting better with no formal treatment are two to one over a two-year period (Eysenck, 1952, 1961b). Similarly, one can expect some 60 percent of schizophrenic admissions to Veterans Administration psychiatric hospitals to achieve a major remission within nine months (Ullmann, 1967a). It is, therefore, not particularly impressive when a person reports that his new form of treatment was 70 percent effective in a two-year period, because, in many instances, this improvement is essentially what would have been expected without the new treatment. Hence, one important use of a control group is to determine the base rate.

Another aspect of empirical science has to deal with matters of how far results may be taken as indicative of "truth." This procedure, called *inference,* is the second use of statistics and overlaps the area previously called generalization. In an experiment it may be found that of 100 experimental subjects receiving a drug, 80 improve and 20 remain the same. Further, among the control group only 20 people improve and 80 remain the same. This difference is a very *significant* one *statistically.* That is, *it is unlikely it could have occurred by chance.* However, there is still the possibility that the result was due to some artifact of which the experimenter was not aware and did indeed occur by chance or for some reason other than the drug. No one can say that a result did *not* occur by chance; one can only say that it is *highly unlikely* that it occurred by chance. It is very unlikely that a person who throws 20 heads in a row is using an unbiased coin—but it can and does happen. Inductive work has this limitation: one can never say something *caused* something else. One can merely say it is very improbable that something occurred by chance, and that therefore it is a more plausible decision to act as if the circumstance observed did indeed deviate from chance.

In an inductive science, predictions are made about future events. One may hypothesize that giving a particular drug will lead to a greater percentage of recovered patients than not giving the drug. When dealing with experimental data, however, one turns this particular hypothesis around to form the *null hypothesis* that the drug will have no effect different from chance. The null hypothesis may then be *rejected* if the data make it more reasonable to presume that the drug had an effect greater than that which might have frequently occurred by chance.

In short, scientists can never state that something is absolutely true; rather, they state that one thing is more probable than another and make a temporary decision. Aside from the limitations involved in drawing samples from which they *infer* to populations, there may always be some unmeasured variable underlying the result obtained. While researchers do their best to make sure that their experimental and control groups are not biased in terms of variables they know are important, and are randomly assigned in terms of all other variables, they can never be sure that there may not be some biasing effect.

The reader at this point might very well ask, "If that is the case, how can any theory ever be proved?" One cannot prove the null hypothesis in terms of saying two groups are equal. However, what one can do is *decide* among theories. Researchers can collect data that make it more probable that one theory is closer to the data than another. That is, scientists can collect data that are consistent or inconsistent with a particular theory.

One can never prove that there is no physiological difference between patients and nonpatients, but one can show that nonphysiological or behavioral techniques lead to enormously beneficial changes. If one can do this, then one is *implicitly* saying that physiological differences may well be irrelevant for treatment. It is in this manner of making a deduction from a theory, developing an operational test of that deduction, and then making a decision, that researchers choose certain lines of activity as more valuable than others.

As previously noted, when one moves from ordering a particular set of data to dealing with populations, one moves from descriptive statistics to inferential statistics. By inference is meant that data about a limited sample are used to make statements about the general population from which they were drawn.

A key concept is variation around the average rather than absolute differences between the averages of the experimental and the control groups. The importance of variation around an average is immediately apparent if the reader will think about a person who tells him the average yearly temperature in the San Francisco Bay Area is the same as the average yearly temperature in some Midwestern town. The Midwestern temperature ranges from $-20°$ to $110°$, while the San Francisco range may be from $30°$ to $90°$.

In similar fashion, knowing that two groups differ from each other by an average of ten units does not indicate whether the difference occurred by chance. If the total range of each sample is only plus or minus five units from the mean, then a difference of ten between the means would probably be significant and unlikely to have occurred by chance. If the variation around the mean of each group was plus or minus 200 units, then a difference of ten units between the means would be far less likely to be significant. However, if the means where the variation was plus and minus five were based only on three cases each, it might very well be that the future cases would vary to a far greater extent. The difference of ten, while separating the three people in one group from the three people in the other group, is relatively unstable and might not be replicated when future samples are drawn.

In similar fashion, in the second case, if the separation between the means of ten were based on millions of cases, then despite a vast amount of overlap the mean difference might be significant. This indicates that a second factor in addition to variation is needed, namely the number of cases on which the effect was observed. In general, the greater the number of cases, the smaller an absolute difference is necessary to attain statistical significance, because the difference observed is likely to be more stable. A measure that takes into account both variation of individual scores and number of cases is called the *standard deviation*.

A difference is statistically significant when the variations around the mean are such that if the experiment were repeated, the two means would still differ in the observed direction the vast majority of times. If the relationship could be expected to be repeated 95 times out of 100, the difference between the means is said to be significant at the .05 level. Similarly, if the difference could have occurred by chance only once in 100 times, it is said to be significant at the .01 level.

It is up to the individual reader and researcher to decide what is an acceptable level of statistical significance. Not only may different people come to different conclusions, but the same scientist may set different acceptable levels of significance depending upon the decision to be made. Rather than saying a great number of cases always increases confidence, one can note that if a difference based on many cases is significant only at the .05 level, one can expect a great deal of overlap. In the clinic where a general result is applied to a specific person, there would be so much overlap that errors would frequently be made in individual cases. Statistical significance deals with how often the effect would be observed upon replication. The evaluation of whether a finding is valuable depends on its statistical significance *and* the theoretical or applied use to which it will be put.

scientific method

To this point the examples have been about differences between means. It is also possible to determine the extent to which two measures vary together, that is, the *correlation* between two measures. When evaluating a correlation, the null hypothesis is that there is no systematic relationship between the variables; in short, that the correlation should be random or zero. If this were the case, then knowing the score of a person on one variable would not help to predict his score on the second variable. To the extent that a correlation deviates from zero or randomness, the ability to predict one score from the other is increased.

Correlation does not necessarily have anything to do with causation. Two things may co-vary systematically because of some third variable. An example is presented by Pokorny, Sheehan, and Atkinson (1972). In 1970, Dawson, Moore, and McGanity reported a significant relationship between the lithium concentration in the drinking waters of 27 counties in Texas and the incidence of first admissions and readmissions to Texas State Mental Hospitals. Calls for adding lithium to drinking water as a preventive measure followed. Pokorny and his coworkers took into account not only lithium concentration and incidence of hospital use but also distance of the counties (the original 27 and all 254 Texas counties) from the state hospital facilities. Admissions varied with accessibility to the hospitals. When geography was taken into account, the relationship between incidence of hospital use and lithium was random. Most of the Texas population and state psychiatric hospitals are at some distance from the relatively high-lithium Rio Grande border.

RELIABILITY AND VALIDITY

In Chapter 1 a point was made of how difficult it is to devise a definition of the concept of mental illness. It is possible, however, to develop measures of specific behaviors, and then to state *in terms of some value system* that these specific behaviors are measures of "adjustment" and that changes in them are worthwhile. These worthwhile changes are usually the dependent variables of research on treatment.

There are certain requirements of useful dependent variables. A first standard is called *reliability*. There are many forms of reliability, but all of them deal with some aspect of consistency. A dependent measure with which the student is familiar is the examination grade. If the examination is an essay-type question, there may be a problem of *rater reliability*. This is a measure of the degree to which either the same person scoring the test at different times or different people scoring the same test will assign the same scores.

If the reader thinks of the manner in which a typical essay question is scored, the possibility of inconsistent scoring is obvious. The professor takes home a stack of blue books. He presumably knew the right answers before reading the exams, and he has a dull task ahead of him. Perhaps he will permit himself a beer for every ten papers he finally gets finished. He starts at the top of the stack and works down. Usually he has a pretty good notion of what is an outstanding answer, an average answer, and an impossibly bad answer. In short, his assignment of A, C, and F is pretty clear. However, he is much less capable of knowing ahead of time what is a borderline grade, that is, a B vs. A, or B vs. C. He is likely to be influenced by momentary considerations, some of them dealing with penmanship or grammar or things unrelated to the exam. The order of the papers may have an effect. A student with a potential B paper is in luck if his paper occurs after a run of C's and D's. It looks good and he may even get an A. A student whose B paper occurs after a run of outstanding A's, however, is likely to get a C because, in contrast, his paper looks bad.

Another aspect of the situation is that as time goes on the rater is likely to become weary, indifferent, or worse, especially if he is rewarding himself with beer. He finishes grading his papers and puts them away. It is possible to ask what would happen if he regraded the papers at some later time. The student can see that there would be some variation. Some C's would go to B's, some B's go to C's, some B's would go to A's, and so forth. In short, there would be differences in the grades due to *inconsistency* in the scoring rather than to the students' test performances. The problem of *rater reliability* is faced in assigning labels to people as much as in assigning grades to exam papers.

Another form of reliability is called *test-retest reliability*. When an intelligence test is given at age eight, psychologists would like to be able to say it is a fair estimate, barring accidents and other misfortunes, of the child's capacity to be influenced by academic training at ages 10, 12, 14, 20, and so forth. In this case, it is desirable for the test categorization to be *consistent,* that is, reliable over a period of time. There are other tests for which such consistency over time would not necessarily be desirable. For example, measures of adjustment will hopefully be altered after psychological treatment. If the measure used is not sensitive to the changes in the person, the psychologist cannot hope to find differences associated with treatment. Another standard deals with the *internal consistency* of different questions on the test. Ideally, every item contributing to the test score should "pull" in the same direction to achieve a unified purpose. One way of obtaining a measure of internal consistency is to grade the test for the odd numbered items only and correlate these scores with the grades obtained from the even numbered items. The test has internal consistency to the extent that the two halves place students in similar score-positions.

The usefulness or *validity* of a test is limited by its reliability. To the extent that the measuring instrument itself leads to subject differences not associated with the variables to be measured, the chance of measuring the variable itself is reduced. *Validity* is the degree to which a measure reduces uncertainty in the making of specific decisions. A measurement of height may be highly reliable, but it has very little value as a predictor of grades in most college courses. Validity involves an association with a particular criterion or decision to be made. The criterion may be some test measure, some social behavior, or the prediction of some future event.

In all these situations there is something the test should accomplish, some use to which it is put. Tests are not valid *per se,* but valid for certain uses. For example, there is little argument that the subtests of the Wechsler-Bellevue Intelligence Tests give a useful measure of general intelligence. There is a great deal of professional controversy over whether the pattern of these subtest scores can be used to make differential diagnoses (e.g., schizophrenic versus brain injured). The same test may be valid for one task and not valid for another, and so making decisions about tests is an important area of psychological research. In many ways the word "validity" means the same as "relevance." Something that may be relevant for one task may be irrelevant for a different task or group of people.

THE USE OF THE SINGLE CASE

The preceding material has stressed the goal of reducing uncertainty in making decisions. The discussion has implied the use of groups of subjects. Such a procedure represents an ideal which, like other ideals, should be worked toward. But it also reflects one set of values to the potential exclusion of others. There are two issues which must be discussed. The first is methodological; the second is practical.

The methodological point is that groups are composed of individuals. The basic source of data in psychology ultimately is the individual and his behavior. In the study of abnormal behavior, the single case is frequently the starting point for concepts of people adjusting to a complex, uncontrolled world. As the reader will note in the chapters that follow, case histories are frequently used to *illustrate* ideas. Increasingly sophisticated own-control procedures are being devised to obtain as much information as possible from the single case. (Leitenberg, 1973). In one of the more frequently used techniques a behavior is observed and recorded under baserate conditions; then a new condition is introduced; next the original conditions are reinstated; and finally the experimental conditions are reinstituted. A number of illustrations of this sequence will be presented in the next chapter.

If an experimenter finds that a behavior which increased upon his instigating a change has decreased when he stops the change, and if he repeats this sequence a number of times, his uncertainty about the impact of the changed condition will be reduced. The reader may think of testing whether a light switch works: he flicks it on and off, on and off. Cases may also be used to challenge theories. A statement that *all* people of a given category possess certain traits requires only one exception to force reconsideration. Only one failure is enough to cast doubt on the statement "All the lights are working."

The practical point is that while their ultimate goals are the same, there is a difference between the immediate goals of clinical and experimental psychology. The aim of the experiments described above was to enable generalization to large populations. The experimentalist studies his subjects in order to move from the few to the many. The clinical worker, however, reverses this procedure. The clinician applies his knowledge of general principles to specific individuals. He moves from the many to the few. He tests himself and his theories with people who are in front of him in the present here and now. This aspect of his work attracts the clinician to single case methods.

The typical modern clinician will use both group and individual case procedures in gathering data and making his decisions. He will illustrate his theories with specific individuals, and, from his work with specific people, formulate theories that he will test with groups.

SUMMARY

This chapter has introduced a number of terms and concepts. The major point is that there are procedures for making observations public and unbiased. The student and citizen as a consumer of research should always ask questions such as: What is the operational definition? What is the control group? What is the base rate? Are there alternative explanations? Research workers welcome such questions, because *how* they obtained their information is as important to them as *what* they found. In research, the means are vital in the evaluation of the ends. These procedures are the way scientists protect patients within the hospital from wasteful, punitive, and erroneous forms of treatment. This is the scientific method, and while it has its limitations, it remains the best method yet developed by man for using experience to guide decisions. If a particular theory does not utilize data based on these procedures, it may very well be asked whether it is a reasonable basis for the treatment of human beings.

learning principles

4

This chapter and the next will present a series of concepts useful in dealing with abnormal behavior. Since the position taken in the earlier chapters is that abnormal behavior develops in the same way as any other behavior, the same concepts are used to deal with both normal and abnormal behavior.

The key throughout is the concept of *behavior,* a term described by Reese (1966) as "any observable or measurable movement of an organism, including external movements, internal movements and their effects, and glandular secretions and their effects."

When an individual has acquired a functional connection between an environmental stimulus and a response on his part, *learning* has taken place. Learning continues throughout life.

There have developed two major parallel and intertwined approaches to behavior and learning. The first is called variously Pavlovian, classical, or *respondent conditioning.* The second is called Skinnerian, instrumental, or *operant conditioning.* Skinner (1938) distinguished two kinds of behavior, respondent and operant, which are learned by classical and instrumental conditioning respectively. In Pavlovian or respondent conditioning a stimulus elicits and precedes the response.

The classic example of human respondent conditioning was offered by Watson and Rayner (1920) in an experiment with an 11-month-old child named Albert. Prior to the experiment it had been determined that certain stimuli elicited from children a fear reaction of violent start, puckered lips, trembling, or crying. One such stimulus was a sudden loud noise—for example, a hammer striking a steel bar. Other stimuli, such as a white rat, did not elicit a fear reaction. Watson and Rayner's work involved the presentation of a white rat (a neutral stimulus) followed immediately by the presentatime, the rat by itself (now a conditioned stimulus). After this sequence of events, rat followed by sound, had occurred seven times, the rat by itself (now a conditioned stimulus) elicited the fear response from Albert. Thus a stimulus which previously did not elicit the respondent behavior came to do so.

Another example of respondent conditioning is the pairing of an *unconditioned stimulus,* such as food, with a previously neutral stimulus such as a bell. If the food is presented shortly after or simultaneously with the bell, the bell alone may in time come to elicit the response of salivation. When the bell, without food, elicits salivation, the bell is called a *conditioned stimulus* and the salivation a *conditioned response.* Once formed, the conditioned response undergoes systematic changes in strength dependent upon the arrangement of the environment. If the unconditioned stimulus (e.g., food) is repeatedly omitted, the conditioned response will gradually diminish. The repeated presentation of the conditioned stimulus without the unconditioned stimulus is called *extinction.*

When a conditioned response to one stimulus has been acquired, other similar stimuli will elicit the response. This observed behavior leads to the concept of *generalization,* a reaction to new situations in accordance with their degree of similarity to prior ones. The amount of generalization decreases as the second stimulus becomes less similar to the original stimulus situation. A process complementary to generalization is *discrimination*. Conditioned discrimination is brought about through selective reinforcement and extinction. If two stimuli are similar and one is *reinforced* (followed by the unconditioned stimulus) while the other one is extinguished, discrimination will occur.

In the operant conditioning situation the sequence of the environmental stimulus and the individual's response is reversed. In this situation the subject first *emits* a response to the situation and then some environmental event occurs contingent upon the emitted behavior. Operant behavior is determined by its consequences. The term "operant" itself implies an active organism operating on its environment. If the consequences of an operant are favorable then the operant is more likely to be emitted again; that is, its frequency of occurrence will be altered in future similar situations.

In general, respondent behavior is associated with involuntary musculature, operant behavior with voluntary musculature. From birth the individual makes massive random responses, both vocal and motoric. If a stimulus following such behavior is observed to alter the rate of emission of that behavior in future similar situations, it is called a *reinforcing stimulus*. The reduction of current deprivations, such as hunger or thirst, or the termination of unpleasant or aversive conditions, such as electric shock, are effective *reinforcing stimuli*. To the extent that their pleasant nature was unlearned, they are also called *primary reinforcing stimuli*. In similar fashion, behaviors that are closely followed by or associated with termination of a pleasant situation (e.g., withdrawal of a positive reinforcing stimulus) or the start of unpleasant aversive stimuli are likely to decrease in frequency.

A frequently used mild aversive stimulus is *time-out-from-reinforcement,* in which the person is removed from a pleasant situation and placed in a dull one. The reader may think of the effect of chaperones, and, more specifically, the effect of chaperones on behavior likely to lead to their ministrations.

The range of stimuli which may be used based on this formulation seems restricted only by the acuteness of the worker's observations. In turn, such studies and their experimental follow-up indicate the range of reinforcing stimuli. Siqueland and DeLucia (1969) studied the effects of visual feedback, while Feldstein and Witryol (1971) studied the value of the reduction of uncertainty. Osborne (1969) used free time in the classroom, and Bailey and Meyerson (1969) used vibratory stimulation as a reinforcer with a profoundly retarded child. Television or music may be distorted or withdrawn (Greene and Hoats 1969; Greene, Hoats, and Hornick, 1970; Talkington and Hall, 1968; Ritschl, Mongrella, and Presbie, 1972) in an effective, response-contingent manner.

Not only the removal of an unpleasant stimulus, but the *avoidance* of such aversive stimuli may maintain behavior. Not crossing a busy intersection against the traffic light, handing in assignments on time, and remembering wedding anniversaries are examples of behaviors that may be thought of as avoiding unpleasant consequences. Because actual contingencies may change, the avoidance of a situation, or the activity engaged in to avoid it, may seem "unnecessary" and "self-defeating" to an external observer (see Sidman, 1960).

Every human activity has some *cost,* if only that of some degree of physical exertion and some choice as to how a person will spend his time. Some activities that the person would find enjoyable are not engaged in because they entail a loss of reinforcing stimuli; for example, a parent may not buy a new car because he wants to have money available for paying his offspring's tuition.

There are two important points about reinforcement that should be made explicit.

learning principles

The first is that in the daily life of human beings, many situations may be described in terms of either an increase of some pleasant stimuli or the decrease, or avoidance, of some unpleasant ones. We go to work to avoid being fired and to earn money for food. It is hard to say that we are influenced by one set of contingencies and not by another, especially when, as is usually the case, both are significantly involved. The second point is that the concept of reinforcement is an abstraction involving the relationship of stimuli and activities in general; whenever possible the specific contingencies should be spelled out. If this is done, many professional arguments are put into proper perspective.

Behavior Terminating an Aversive Stimulus

The following example from the work of Ayllon and Michael (1959) illustrates how behavior that terminates or avoids an aversive stimulus is increased and maintained. Two female patients who were on separate wards had to be spoon fed. Both were socially withdrawn but seemed to care for the neat and clean appearance of their clothing. One had been hospitalized seven months, the other for 28 years. The program involved spilling some food on them whenever they were spoon fed. This loss of personal cleanliness could be avoided by self-feeding. Further, self-feeding was to be associated with the nurse's sitting by the patient and talking with her for at least three minutes, in part so that the self-feeding would not be associated with loss of attention, in part so that "in the experience of the patient, people become nicer when she eats on her own." The program was effective with both patients. During the eight days before treatment began, the patient who had been hospitalized seven months ate five meals on her own, was spoon fed 12 meals, and refused seven meals. Her weight was 99 pounds. After seven weeks on the program, she ate 20 of 24 meals on her own, was spoon fed none, and missed four. She had gained 21 pounds.

Ayllon and Michael conclude: "Since the patient's hospital admission had been based on her refusal to eat, accompanied by statements that the food was poisoned, the success of the program led to her discharge. It is to be noted that although nothing was done to deal directly with her claims that the food was poisoned, these statements dropped out of her repertoire as she began to eat on her own."

Ayllon (1963) discusses a 47-year-old female patient diagnosed as chronic schizophrenic who had been hospitalized for nine years and whose behavior occupied a good portion of nursing staff time. A program was started whose object was to get her to stop stealing food. She was assigned to a table in the dining room where no other patients were allowed to sit. When she approached a table other than her own, or when she picked up more food than she was supposed to from the dining room counter, nurses removed her from the room. In effect, this procedure resulted in her missing a meal whenever she attempted to steal food. In two weeks, she no longer stole food. She also lost weight: at no time in nine years had she weighed less than 230 pounds; at the conclusion of treatment she weighed 180. Food stealing had made it impossible to keep her on a diet. In short, the reinforcement for stealing extra food no longer existed—the behavior now had aversive consequences.

This woman also dressed bizarrely. She wore an excessive amount of clothing: sweaters, shawls, dresses, undergarments, stockings, and sheets and towels wrapped around her body and turbanlike around her head. On occasion she wore 18 pairs of stockings. She also carried cups, a pile of extra clothes, and a large handbag. By weighing her before each meal for several weeks hospital personnel obtained an estimate of her true weight and the weight of her clothes. During treatment the condition required for reinforcment was stepping on a scale and meeting a designated weight, which was body weight plus a predetermined weight of clothing. The reinforcement was permission to go to the dining room to get a meal. When she exceeded the set weight she was told, "Sorry, you can't go in, you'll have to weigh less."

She was started with an allowance of 23 pounds of clothing, two pounds under her average. She could get down to the allowed weight by discarding clothing; if she discarded more than was required, this estimate was used for the next step. She was allowed to get on the scale, and if over the limit, take off clothes and get on again, and then go into the dining room. With gradually more stringent requirements, at the end of treatment she wore three rather than 25 pounds of clothing. She gave up carrying the cups and bundles to the scale, and she was told that she was not allowed to carry things into the dining room. The total training required 13 weeks.

At the start of the procedure she showed some "emotional behavior," crying, shouting, and throwing chairs around. These behaviors were ignored and gained her neither sympathy nor attention; they eventually dropped out. The consequences of these changes were described by Ayllon as follows:

One of the behavioral changes concomitant with the current environmental manipulation was that as the patient began dressing normally she started to participate in small social events in the hospital. This was particularly new to the patient, as she had previously remained seclusive, spending most of her time in her room. About this time the patient's parents came to visit her and insisted on taking her home for a visit. This was the first time during the patient's nine years of hospitalization that her parents had asked to take her out. They remarked that previously they had not been interested in taking her out because the patient's excessive dressing in addition to her weight made her look like a "circus freak." [Ayllon, 1963, p. 59.]

The Effects of Satiation

The operational definition of a reinforcing stimulus is one which alters the frequency of an emitted behavior. The definition is an empirical one. Repeated absence of reinforcement leads to extinction and a return of the rate of response emission to the level observed prior to institution of reinforcing stimuli contingent upon it. It should be explicit that the reinforcer is a stimulus. There are few if any objects or circumstances which in and of themselves are reinforcing.[1] Food is often talked about as a *primary reinforcer,* one which has a visceral effect that is not learned; it is therefore contrasted with money and praise as reinforcers. However, if a person is *satiated,* that is, has had a surplus of food, further food will not be reinforcing and will not alter the frequency of emission of a response.

This point is illustrated in a report by Ayllon and Michael (1959) dealing with three mental defective patients who hoarded junk such as papers, rubbish and magazines. For the five years preceding the program, the nurses had to "dejunk" one of the men several times a day. The patients' hoarding behavior was quite possibly maintained by the attention they received as well as the scarcity of printed matter on the ward. During the treatment program the ward was flooded with magazines. At the same time, usual reinforcement (attention) for hoarding was withheld. After nine weeks of flooding the ward with magazines and ignoring hoarding, none of patients hoarded any longer. This improvement was maintained for six months following the end of the treatment program.

Satiation was also successfully used with the patient who had worn a bizarre amount of clothing in a program designed to stop her hoarding of towels. During a pretreat-

---

[1] An exception might be direct electrical stimulation of certain areas of the brain.

learning principles

ment period, the towels in her room, counted three times a week, varied in number between 19 and 29. Routine removal of towels from her room was discontinued. Rather, intermittently throughout the day, someone took a towel to her room and handed it to her without comment. The first week she was given an average of seven towels a day, and by the third week this was increased to 60. When the number of towels in her room reached 625, she herself started to take them out. Thereafter, no more towels were given her. During the 12 months following, the mean number of towels in her room was 1.5 per week. Satiation aside, the pile-up of towels may have become aversive in itself. Just to keep them neat required a large expenditure of energy. Ayllon gives the following detailed description:

During the first few weeks of satiation, the patient was observed patting her cheeks with a few towels, apparently enjoying them. Later the patient was observed spending much of her time folding and stacking the approximately 600 towels in her room. A variety of remarks were made by the patient regarding receipt of towels. All verbal statements were recorded by the nurse. The following represent typical remarks made during this experiment. First week: As the nurse entered the patient's room carrying a towel, the patient would smile and say, "Oh, you found it for me thank you." Second week: When the number of towels given the patient increased rapidly, she told the nurse, "Don't give me no more towels. I've got enough." Third week: "Take them towels away. I can't sit there all night and fold towels." Fourth and fifth weeks: "Get these dirty towels out of here." Sixth week: After she started taking the towels out of her room, she remarked to the nurse, "I can't drag any more of these towels, I just can't do it." [Ayllon, 1963, p. 57.]

It should be explicit that constructs such as needs, motives, or drives are not used unless a deficit of a direct physiological nature sets the circumstance for some stimulus to have reinforcing consequences. Even in this instance, it is probably better not to infer a condition in the organism (e.g., hunger), but to talk of deficits which can be manipulated, such as no food for 20 hours. A focus on deprivations and the effect of the reinforcing stimuli helps avoid the circular reasoning involved in using needs or motives as explanations of behavior (e.g., he fought because he was hostile, and he was hostile because he fought).

The Function of Discriminative Stimuli

A *discriminative stimulus* marks the time or place when an operant will have reinforcing consequences. It does not elicit a response, elicitation being a characteristic that holds only for respondents. The green traffic light is an example of a discriminative stimulus; it does not set people going across a street in the same manner that a bright light flashed in the eye constricts the pupil. A discriminated operant is one controlled by a preceding discriminative stimulus.

The procedure, mentioned earlier in this chapter, of bringing an operant under such control is called discrimination. Whenever some particular stimulus, through association with a reinforcing stimulus, takes on discriminative stimulus properties, then other stimuli (although not directly associated with the original reinforcing stimulus) will also take on discriminative stimulus properties to the extent that they are similar to the original discriminative stimulus. This phenomenon is called *operant stimulus generalization*. Thus discriminative stimuli may become reinforcing stimuli through their association with other reinforcing stimuli. On the highways of California, for example, pedestrians are able to press a traffic button that will change the light for them. In order to obtain the discriminative stimulus, the green light, they perform operants, that is, they push buttons. Discriminative stimuli that have become reinforcing stimuli constitute the major class of reinforcing stimuli.

How a discriminative stimulus may acquire reinforcing properties is illustrated in a study by Ayllon and Haughton (1962), who worked with 32 patients who had been eating problems. Thirty had been diagnosed as schizophrenic, one as a mental defective, and one as an involutional melancholic. The median length of continuous hospitalization for the group was 20 years. The traditional treatments for eating problems—coaxing, reminding, spoon or tube feeding, and supportive electroshock—were discontinued. In order to bring eating behavior under the sole control of food, Ayllon and Haughton instructed the nurses to keep away from the patients at mealtimes. In so doing, they removed the social reinforcement, attention and sympathy, for refusal to eat. For the patient to obtain a meal, she had to walk to the dining room without coaxing, persuasion, or guidance from the nurses—and do it within half an hour of the signal that the dining room was open. After that time, the door was locked and no food was available until the next meal. The length of time the door was open was gradually reduced from half an hour to five minutes. The total process took 15 weeks, after which patients who had not been feeding problems ate 90 percent of their meals, while those who had been feeding problems ate 80 percent of their meals. This difference was not statistically significant. The signal that the dining room was open for a meal galvanized the ward: behavior which was not previously reinforced (going to the dining room door) would now be reinforced during the next five minutes. The signal that it was mealtime illustrates the function of a discriminative stimulus.

Discriminative stimuli may be developed at any stage in life. Children, who are dependent upon others for food and for termination of pain, must in large measure obtain an adult's attention as a prerequisite for obtaining their services. Attention is associated with numerous reinforcing stimuli. The adult's attention eventually is likely to be sufficient to lead to an increase of the emission of behaviors; that is, discriminative stimuli may become *acquired* or *secondary reinforcers*. Smiles, headnods, praise such as "good boy," and other indications of pleasure with the person are discriminative stimuli which mark the time and place where parents or significant others are likely to be receptive to requests and to emit behaviors that are reinforcing to the child. Staats (1970) and Clore and Byrne (1974) have further elaborated the social implications of attitude, discriminative stimuli and social reinforcement. Important demonstrations in which a contingently reinforced task acquired discriminative properties are by Redd (1972) and Zanna, Kiesler, and Pilkonis (1970).

It is important to note that discriminative stimuli and acquired reinforcers may be extinguished. Money is one of the most widely used acquired reinforcers in an adult's life, but if money failed to lead to its usual positive and pleasurable consequences, it would no longer serve as an effective discriminative stimulus. Tokens, attention, and praise require some continuing *back-up reinforcing stimulus* to maintain their effectiveness.

The following anecdotal description illustrates how undesirable or changeworthy behaviors may be maintained by reinforcement and the presence of a person who has become a discriminative stimulus:

In a certain Eastern hospital for the mentally retarded there was an unusually large number of so-called "head-bangers." The superintendent, alarmed at this state of affairs, observed conditions on the wards and found something which anybody unfamiliar with behavioral analysis could not help but approve: The nurses were most loving and kind with their patients. As soon as a patient began to hit his head against a wall, the nurse would rush to him and comfort him. In addition, to calm him down or to show her acceptance of him,

learning principles

she would give him a bit of chocolate or other candy . . . any time a nurse would appear with chocolate or other candy, patients instantly began their headbanging. [Schaefer and Martin, 1969, pp. 47–48.] [2]

FROM DISCRIMINATIVE STIMULI TO GENERALIZED REINFORCERS

Reinforcers which have achieved their reinforcing powers through their prior service as discriminative stimuli are called *acquired* or *secondary reinforcers*. Once established, a secondary reinforcer such as attention, praise, or money can increase the emission of responses other than those used during its original establishment. It therefore may be termed a *generalized reinforcer*.

Generalized reinforcers may be the most important factor in the control of behavior because they are so powerful. Ayllon and Haughton (1964) used *attention*, a generalized reinforcer, to control the verbal behavior of one of their patients. They defined attention as listening or taking an interest in the patient's verbalization. In some instances attention was backed up by the offer of a cigarette or a piece of candy. Extinction consisted of withholding social attention and the other tangible reinforcers.

Psychiatric hospital attendants became quite skillful in appearing distracted, bored, looking away, acting busy, or shifting their attention to some other event taking place on the ward. The patient, Kathy, was a 47-year-old chronic schizophrenic who had been in the hospital 16 years. Her speech centered around references to herself as "the Queen": "I'm the Queen. Why don't you give things to the Queen? The Queen wants to smoke. How's King George, have you seen him?" This had gone on for 14 years and had not been changed by a bilateral prefrontal lobotomy. Psychologists classed references to the Queen and royal family as psychotic and remarks such as "It's a nice day," "I'd like some soap," or "What time is it?" as neutral or nonpsychotic.

Observations of her speech were systematically taken and were regulated only to the extent of trying to limit each interaction to three minutes. If a mixture of psychotic and neutral talk was observed during an interaction, that interaction was put into the psychotic category. After a baseline period of observation, the attendants reinforced the psychotic talk and extinguished neutral talk. Later neutral speech was reinforced while psychotic talk was extinguished. Figure 1 illustrates the result of these environmental manipulations.

As may be noted from Figure 1, during the baseline period of observation preceding selective reinforcement, somewhat less than half the observation periods showed some talk categorized as psychotic. With reinforcement of psychotic talk and extinction of neutral or "normal" talk, the percentage of occasions on which psychotic talk was observed increased to over 80. When the contingencies were reversed, the percentage of occasions on which psychotic talk was observed fell rapidly to less than 20.

The demonstration that Kathy's verbal behavior could be controlled by the systematic application of reinforcement to specific aspects of her speech is an example of *verbal operant conditioning*. This term conveys the important concept that what an individual says, his verbalizations, can be treated as behavior and therefore follows the same behavioral principles as any other behavior (Skinner, 1957). Krasner (1958b, 1965d, 1966a) has pointed out that the considerable number of investigations of verbal operant conditioning have clearly demonstrated the responsiveness of the verbal behavior of most people to cues such as "mm-hmm" and "good" indicating attention (as a generalized reinforcer) on the part of

---

[2] Redd and Birnbrauer (1969) and Nunnally and Faw (1968) illustrated this point, of the development of discriminative stimulus values, experimentally.

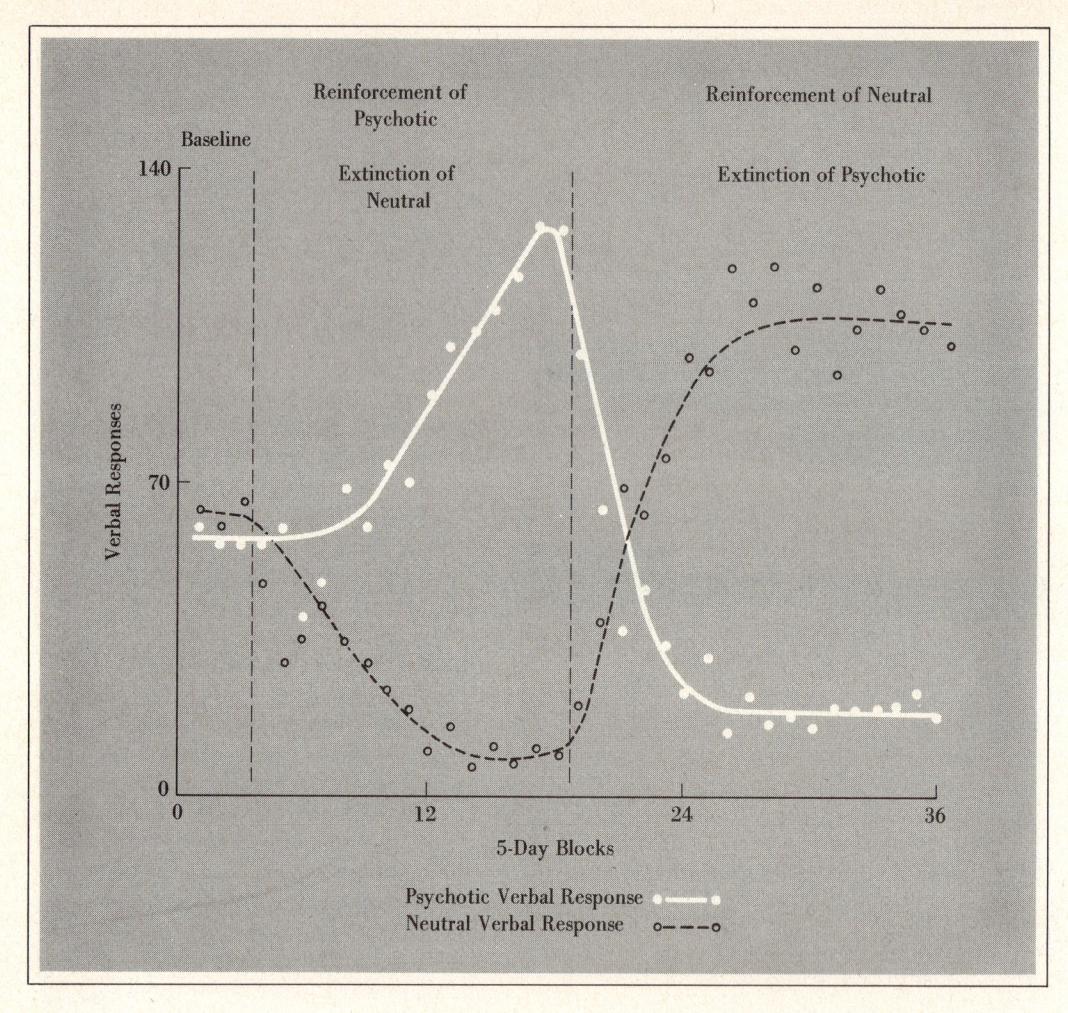

Figure 1
Redrawn from Ayllon and Haughton, 1964, p. 91.

important environmental figures. The shaping and control of what a person says is continually taking place in the reactions that verbalizations obtain from listeners.

Other examples of verbal operant conditioning appear in Chapter 18 on schizophrenia; but it is important to note here that this and similar observations indicate the relative responsiveness of the schizophrenic to his environment. This point is further emphasized in two additional cases reported by Ayllon and Haughton (1964),

similar to the one just reviewed. Suzy was a 65-year-old woman diagnosed as a chronic schizophrenic who had been in and out of hospitals during the preceding 20 years. For the three years before her transfer to the experimental ward, Suzy was described as continually complaining, tearful, depressed, whining, and crying. The following was a sample of her talk: ". . . my nerves are shot. I can't hear any more . . . for weeks I don't have any sleep and I'm scared to go to bed at night." Every once in a while Suzy

76

required spoon feeding. She had not responded to tranquilizers or other medication. The other patient was Wilma, a 57-year-old woman with a diagnosis of involutional depression. In the three years preceding her admission to the hospital she had had many somatic complaints, and when regular visits to general hospitals had failed to bring relief, she was admitted to a psychiatric hospital. Electroconvulsive therapy had had no effect on her somatic complaining.

The target behavior to be changed for both Suzy and Wilma was somatic verbalization, that is, talk about physical complaints. As in the previous illustrations, there was a schedule of three-minute contacts, and each contact was categorized as containing somatic verbalization (the target behavior) or not. The graphs of the results, shown in Figures 2 and 3, parallel each other. A baseline period of observation in which the environment was not changed occurred first.

Next, the target behavior was not reinforced (i.e., it was extinguished). This was followed by a period of time in which the reinforcing contingencies were changed and the target behavior was positively reinforced. The purpose of this procedure was to illustrate that the frequency of the target behavior was indeed a function of the environmental contingencies being manipulated. Finally, the original extinction of the target behavior was reinstated. As Figures 2 and 3 illustrate, somatic verbalizations in these women could be reduced, increased, and then once more reduced by manipulating the effect they had on other people. The authors conclude that: "Listening, paying attention to, and showing interest in somatic verbal responses increase the response whereas not listening to, 'ignoring' them, results in their virtual elimination."

Ayllon and Haughton mention that Suzy and Wilma were on the same ward. "These two patients talked to each other a great

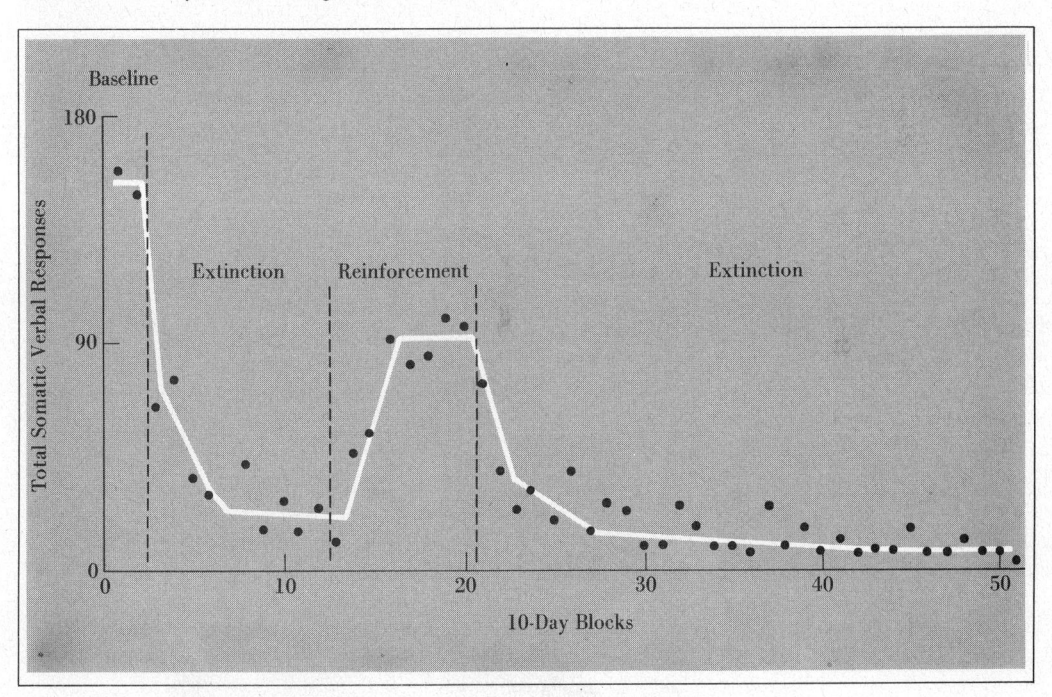

Figure 2
Redrawn from Ayllon and Haughton, 1964, p. 94.

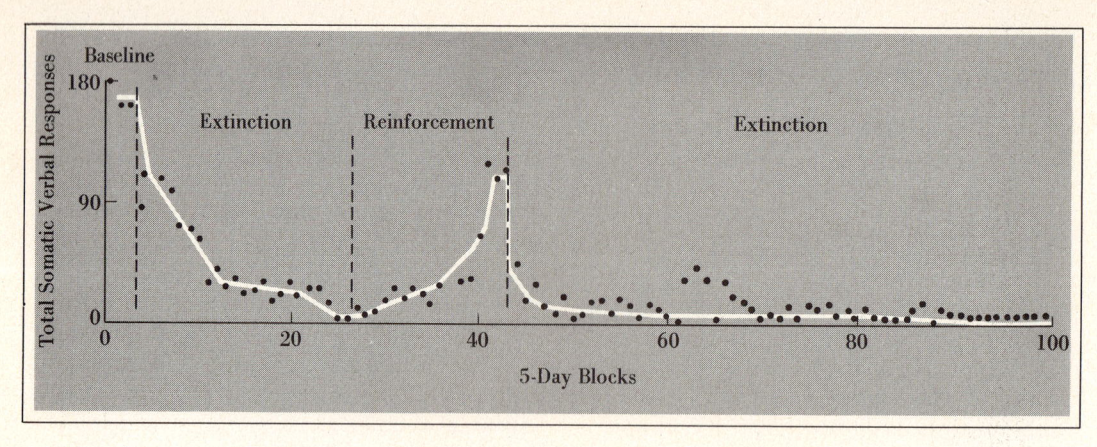

Figure 3
Redrawn from Ayllon and Haughton, 1964, p. 94.

deal, and therefore, the possibility existed for them to reinforce each other's somatic responses. This potential source of reinforcement did not appear to affect the frequency of complaints as recorded by the staff. In fact, at different points in this investigation, each patient confided to our staff that the other was not 'really sick.' "

The descriptions of Kathy, Suzy, and Wilma were presented to illustrate the use and importance of acquired or secondary reinforcers. Acquired reinforcers (as distinct from primary reinforcers) are of vital importance in the development and maintenance of behavior in our society.

There is an additional point, however, to be made at this time. Interest and attention, as examples of acquired reinforcers, are maintained primarily by their effects in the present and may be quickly extinguished. If the attendant, psychologist, or experimenter continually smiled, nodded his head, or said, "Mm-hmm" and nothing came of it, the subject (whether psychiatric hospital patient or spouse) would no longer alter his behavior contingent upon the acquired reinforcer. A person does not have a need, acquired in childhood, for attention; rather, attention (as other acquired reinforcers) marks the time and place of an operant being reinforced *now,* and if this does not occur with at least some frequency, the effectiveness of attention will eventually [3] decrease.

Because attention is a generalized reinforcer, it may maintain inappropriate as well as appropriate behavior. If such attention-gaining behavior no longer has a favorable consequence, it will be extinguished. This was illustrated by Ayllon and Michael (1959) with a hospitalized psychiatric patient who would visit the nurses' station an average of 16 times a day and disrupt the nurses' work. By ignoring the patient, the

[3] The modifier "eventually" is needed: The reader may think of the usual response when a coin is put into a Coke or cigarette machine and no goods are forthcoming. Usually there is an increase of irrelevant, *emotional* behavior which may have been infrequently reinforced in the past: the machine is kicked, hit, cursed, reasoned with, begged, etc. The start of the *process* of extinction, when the reinforcing contingencies are drastically changed, may lead to an *increase* of the target behavior. This point is important at both a theoretical and applied level. At an applied level, parents frequently become discouraged when a procedure does not work immediately. An increase at the start of an extinction procedure is something they must be counseled to expect. A more general point is that there is a technology of reinforcement that is only touched on in this book.

learning principles

nurses reduced the number of visits to an acceptable two per day. Attention-gaining responses may also be affected by making a mildly unpleasant consequence contingent on the emission of such behavior and a favorable consequence contingent upon alternative behavior. An example of such procedures is provided by Wiesen and Watson (1967) with a severely retarded 6-year-old who would grab, pull, hit, and attempt to untie the shoelaces of the nursing personnel. During a pretreatment period, such behavior was observed at the rate of over six times per minute. For 21 days, when Paul approached the resident counselors in an inappropriate manner or started to engage in disturbing attention-seeking behavior, they first said, "No," and, if this did not work, placed him out of doors for five minutes (time-out-from-reinforcement). At the same time, they reinforced his cooperative, social interactions with other children. After this treatment program, inappropriate attention responses were infrequent, as were enforced removals from the scene.

To repeat, a child does not have a "need for attention." Rather, there are learnd behaviors which are maintained because they gain attention.

Schedules of Reinforcement

The rate at which reinforcing stimuli are delivered may follow different patterns called *schedules of reinforcement*. A reinforcing stimulus can be presented either upon completion of a specific behavior or at the end of a specified time interval. Psychologists therefore talk about a *ratio of reinforcement* (e.g., one reinforcement for each act or one for every two acts) or an *interval* of reinforcement (e.g., one every ten seconds or one every minute). Further, these schedules may be fixed at every *n*th act (a *fixed ratio*) or be *variable* (randomly on a one-third or one-tenth ratio). Similarly, there may be *fixed interval* or *variable interval* schedules.[4] In general, learning is more resistant to extinction if the reinforcement is *intermittent* (for a recent example with a clinical population, see Kazdin and Polster, 1973), while the rate of emission is more constant if the schedule is variable (Weiner, 1969). A reinforcement schedule may start at a high ratio and slowly be *thinned* to a more variable and less frequent payoff. In this manner rates of reinforcement that would not have been effective earlier in a training sequence are sufficient to maintain a performance. One of the most dramatic illustrations of this is the behavior of gamblers playing slot machines.

The Shaping of Behavior

An important aspect of the application of operant principles to the modification of behavior is the method of approximations or *shaping*. In many instances there would be a long, possibly endless wait if reinforcement were restricted to the final, perfect, ultimate performance desired. In developing a performance, it is much more effective to reinforce approximations, "good mistakes," and behavior that moves closer to the ultimate performance desired. The level of the performance required prior to reinforcement may then be gradually increased. The experimenter reinforces only those responses that move in the direction of the final performance that is his goal, and he extinguishes (does not reinforce) all other responses. In shaping, the first responses reinforced in many instances only barely approximate the final desired behavior.

Isaacs, Thomas, and Goldiamond (1960) illustrate shaping in a report about a male, diagnosed as schizophrenic reaction, catatonic type, who had been mute and with-

[4] The schedule name for delivering reinforcement contingent upon the emission of certain interresponse times is the "differential reinforcement of low rates of responding." For a review of this area, see Kramer and Rilling (1970).

drawn for 19 years. He had been sitting impassively in group therapy sessions for a prolonged period of time. One day it was noted that his eyes followed a package of gum when it fell from the therapist's pocket. Thereafter the therapist worked with him individually three times a week to shape his behavior. In the first two weeks, the object was to have him focus his eyes on a stick of gum; when he did so he was given the gum. In the third and fourth weeks, the gum was not given until he made a small mouth movement and later not until he made some vocalization. By the end of the fourth week, he was making a croaking sound. During the fifth and sixth weeks, the therapist held up the gum, and when the patient emitted a vocalization (croak) the therapist said, "Say 'gum,' say 'gum.'" At the end of the sixth week (the eighteenth individual session), the patient said, "Gum, please." At the same time, he began to answer questions about his name and age. Thereafter, he responded to the therapist's questions in individual and group sessions and in the ward dayroom, but spoke to no one else.

To get the patient to talk to someone else, the therapist began to have a nurse come into the individual treatment room. The patient smiled at her, and after a month began to answer her questions. When the patient one day brought his coat to a volunteer worker on the ward (a nonverbal sign that he wanted to go out of doors), the volunteer reported the incident and was instructed to comply with the patient's request *only* as a consequence of explicit verbalizations. Similar instructions as to how to react to the patient were then given to other hospital personnel, and the patient regularly initiated verbal requests when nonverbal requests no longer effected the changes he would have found reinforcing. But, when other patients, visitors, or uninstructed personnel continued to interpret and obey nonverbal requests, he did not talk to them.

This case illustrates the procedure of shaping. The therapist reinforced with gum only those behaviors which successively moved in the direction he desired, and he did not reinforce other behaviors. It is also worth noting that after the verbal behavior, "Gum, please," had been emitted, other behaviors of a similar verbal nature were emitted, without additional step-by-step shaping. Finally, the behavior had to be generalized. This was first started with a person functionally similar to the therapist and in the particular environment in which verbal behavior itself had been reinstated. Later, the patient talked to other people but in a differential pattern. Those people who made verbalization by the patient a requirement for complying with his requests were those spoken to, while those people who reinforced the patient without requiring verbalization were not.[5]

Another technique used to develop new performances is *response chaining*, in which an increasingly long set of responses is gradually built up prior to reinforcement. First, response A must be emitted prior to reinforcement. Next, response B must be made prior to A, which precedes reinforcement, and when it is learned, behavior C is introduced. In this way an increasingly long chain of behaviors is slowly built.

Examples of the complicated chains of behavior that may be built in this manner are given by Pierrol and Sherman (1958) and by Bachrach and Karen (1963). Pierrol and Sherman trained a rat, Barnabus, to perform a complicated series of acts which ended in his pressing a bar to receive food. Barnabus was trained to go up a spiral staircase to a platform and then to run to another platform by pushing down and crossing a drawbridge. He then climbed a ladder and moved a car by a hand-over-hand

[5] The findings of this classic case have been repeated by a number of investigators with a variety of people (Neale and Liebert, 1969; Nolan and Pence, 1970; Sabatasso and Jacobson, 1970; Fineman, 1968; Fineman and Ferjo, 1969; and Hewett, 1965). Baker (1971a) reports that nine chronically mute schizophrenics reinforced for speaking improved significantly more than nine schizophrenics reinforced for silence.

pull of an attached chain. He next pedaled a car through a tunnel, climbed a flight of stairs, ran through a tube, stepped into a waiting elevator, and raised a Columbia University flag over it. This started the elevator in which Barnabus descended to the ground floor, pressed a lever, and received the food reinforcement.

Bachrach and Karen's work was with a gentleman rat called Rodent E. Lee. Rodent E. Lee climbed a circular stairway to a second landing, lowered a drawbridge to cross a room, ran a cable car down an inclined plane, climbed another set of stairs, struck two piano keys on a miniature Steinway, crawled through a wire tunnel, entered an elevator and pulled a chain which lowered him to the ground where, after striking a bar, he received a pellet of food. Each preceding act had to be emitted correctly to permit progress to the next link of the chain. The sequence of learning the links started from the last act prior to reinforcement. In chaining, shaping may be used to teach parts of the chain, such as playing the piano or running the elevator. The end product is a rodent rapidly performing a sequence of novel acts.

Prompting and Fading

Another technique for developing a seemingly new or novel performance makes use of *prompts* which are then *faded*. (Terrace, 1963; Moore and Goldiamond, 1964). The reader may be familiar with a variant of this procedure from learning to write script. The person may first trace the writing in outline form. The strength of the prompt, the printed outline of any letter, may then be reduced until it is completely absent. Frequently words may be used. For example, "The capital of Illinois is Springfield," "The capital of Illinois is Spring . . . ," "The capital of Illinois is. . . ." In practice, the procedure is much slower, more finely divided, and the proper response is followed by some reinforcing stimulus.

The following, from St. Augustine's *Confessions* (1952 edition, pp. 5, 8), illustrates random operant behavior, reinforcement, and prompting and fading that merges into modeling:

. . . for we see the like in other infants, though of myself I remember it not. Thus, little by little, I became conscious where I was; and to have a wish to express my wishes to those who could content them, and I could not . . . So I flung about at random limbs and voice, making the few signs I could . . . This I remember; and have since observed how I learned to speak. It was not that my elders taught me words (as, soon after, other learning) in any best method; but I, longing by cries and broken accents and various motions of my limbs to express my thoughts that so I might have my will . . . did myself . . . practice the sounds in my memory. When they named anything, and as they spoke they turned towards it, I saw and remembered that they called what they would point out by the name they uttered. And that they meant this thing and no other was plain from the motion of their body . . . And by constantly hearing words . . . I collected gradually for what they stood and having broken in my mouth to these signs, I thereby gave utterance to my will.

LANGUAGE AND OTHER COMPLEX OPERANT BEHAVIORS

The range of acquired reinforcers, discriminative stimuli, and complex performances is very great. Simple performances, once established, may become part of complex ones, and increasingly complex performances may be treated as units. Probably the most important human operant behavior, and certainly the one given the greatest attention in traditional therapy, is speech. All the talking in the world, no matter how true or insightful, will be useless in altering behavior unless the person responds to the words. Four conditions, however, are implicit in the understanding of language. First, the person must have *learned* the language: if this book were written in Russian, few of the readers would find it useful.

Second, the person being spoken to must *listen:* a college lecture section, especially after lunch, not infrequently provides examples of speech (by the professor) that does not alter behavior (by students on exams). If this book were written in Russian, most American readers would soon find a better use for it as a doorstop, paperweight, or birthday present for their housemother. There would be no point in spending time with it—paying attention—because such time would be meaningless, i.e., not reinforcing. A person who does not pay attention to stimuli that alter the behavior of other people is often labeled abnormal. If he has been extinguished for attending to these stimuli, however, his behavior in itself is normal, and for him to pay attention to such nonreinforcing stimuli would be abnormal.

A third requirement is that the individual be *capable* of the behavior expected or called for in response to the verbal stimuli. The two prior requirements (understanding and attention to the message) may have been met, but the person must also have the skill necessary to make the response. For example, the reader might accurately receive the message that he had to read this book in Russian and that if he did so he would be paid $100. The reader, however, might simply not have the skill to do so.

A fourth and final implicit assumption in language understanding is that if the message is correctly received and the person is capable of the act called for, he will *"want"* to perform it. The word "want" leads to the concept of motive, which, as noted earlier in this chapter, needs to be operationally defined in each case. If the person emits a behavior, an observer might infer he "wanted" to do it and, if he does not, that he did not want to. Using the concept of "wanted to" or "intended to" adds nothing beyond the actual fact that the behavior was or was not emitted under certain conditions. As noted through the foregoing material, the presumption is that if frequency of emission of a behavior has been altered, some reinforcing contingency must have occurred. It is proper then to substitute the specific reinforcing contingencies for the word "want." This not only leads to greater operational precision: it provides a step toward dealing with future behavior.

In many human situations, the circumstances are far from simple. Assume, for example, that the reader has the halting capability to read Russian that American universities call "satisfying the foreign language requirement." If the reader is now promised $100 for reading this book in Russian, and if he receives the message accurately, he may still *not* read the book in Russian. He may calculate how long the task would take him and conclude that "it just is not worth the effort." This sounds simply like he "doesn't want to." When the reinforcing contingencies are closely investigated, the observer may on occasion find what has been called a state of *conflict*. In this book the concept of conflict will be used infrequently because the term has been given so much surplus meaning that it leads to confusion.

To avoid this, proper clinical procedure is to try to specify the conflict in each instance. Conflict may be defined as a situation in which a stimulus elicits or makes likely (i.e., acts as a discriminative stimulus) two or more responses which are of relatively equal strength (likelihood of being emitted) and which are incompatible, if not mutually exclusive. In the example being discussed, much as the student might welcome $100, the task is so odious or would require so many hours that the avoidance of it is "reasonable" and/or "worthwhile" (that is, avoidance of the unpleasant situation is reinforcing). If the task would require 150 hours, the student would have to forego the other uses he could make of that time. It is possible to say the student is in conflict between approach to two positive alternatives, except that selection of one (money or activities) would mean the loss of the other. As such, this situation is similar to the vast majority of other conflict situations in that it could be called a *double approach-avoidance* situation.

It is important to note that under some conditions the student would select the $100 option even though the rate of pay was low. He might "need the money," that is, have a severe deficit such as a pressing debt and no other satisfactory way to obtain money. If he had no other uses for his time, he might also undertake the task. That is, an absence of reinforced alternatives may lead to emission of behavior that ordinarily is of low probability either for that person or for people in general.

It is important to note that failure to emit a requested or expected behavior may be due to failure to receive the message, failure to have learned the required act, or insufficient reinforcement for emission of the performance.

The Effects of Verbalization as Stimulus

Learning a language, either to receive or to send messages, is the learning of operant behavior. All the concepts previously discussed, such as shaping, discrimination, and generalization are found in its development. Grammar, and especially the learning of rules and their exceptions (e.g., irregular verbs), illustrates particularly the latter two principles. Once language has been learned, it may be modified by reinforcement of functional and/or abstract units which were not given at the time of learning. The illustrative cases of Suzy and Wilma, in this chapter, who were selectively reinforced for emission of somatic verbalizations, make this point, as do experiments on the verbal conditioning of schizophrenics for "sick talk" (Ullmann et al., 1965) or "common associations" (Ullmann, Krasner, and Edinger, 1964).

Once language has been learned, it aids in developing and guiding other behaviors. Words such as "good," "fine," "no!" or "bad" serve as acquired reinforcers. Language that is a part of the environment conveys information about the environment. Language is a prime tool for symbolization: one cue stands for some larger aspect or environmental situation. These symbols may be manipulated, as in arithmetic. The ready ability to symbolize and abstract is perhaps man's greatest biological asset, especially when the individual does not confuse the symbol with the thing symbolized.

Language and Labeling

Another area of language behavior of great importance is that of *labeling*. A person cannot and does not respond to every aspect of every situation on every occasion. Those aspects of the situation which are not pertinent to reinforcing stimuli are likely to be eventually ignored or adapted. The reader may well not know how many stairs he climbed to get to his classroom or how many windows there are on the second floor of his college's library. He has experienced these sensations many times, but they are essentially irrelevant. With learning, aspects of situations that have been germane in the past are attended to and others are ignored.

New experiences may alter what is attended to. Rapid reactions to situations call for a limited sampling of the stimuli present and for responses based on knowledge that is essentially incomplete. The situation is matched with previous ones and placed in a category. The matching, categorizing, or labeling is made on a limited number of salient similarities. Further responses are made in terms of that label. In preceding chapters, this process has been touched on in terms of people calling other people by a label such as "schizophrenic" and then acting toward them as if they were "schizophrenic." The response to a situation by labeling is a verbal behavior which serves as a discriminative stimulus for further actions for the person who emitted the stimulus. A previous example of this process involved the student who decided it was not worthwhile to read the book in Russian. The conclusion that the offer was a "bad deal" guided further behavior and served as a discriminative stimulus for the behavior of saying, "No, thanks."

Plans, strategies, problem-solving techniques, notes, and promises to oneself are all illustrations of ways in which a person may stimulate himself through language and affect his own future actions. The ability to manipulate abstractions about the future and past as well as present is, again, a great biological strength, it is also, however, an area in which one can become vulnerable. The difference between man and other primates was once oversimplified but well put by one observer of human behavior, who pointed out that many animals can signal current sexual interest but only man can make a date for next Saturday night. In this regard, words are responses by human beings that act as stimuli for further responses. Words become crucial links in behavioral chains, and as stimuli supplied by the person himself lead to the development of "self-control" (Goldiamond, 1965; Watson and Tharp, 1972; Goldfried and Merbaum, 1973; Thoreson and Mahoney, 1974).

IMITATION AND MODELING

Once basic skills have been learned, they can be used in making further learning more rapid. These skills are numerous, but the ones on which there is currently an increasing body of theoretical and applied information are *imitation* (or modeling) (Bandura, 1965a, 1969; Flanders, 1968; Peterson, 1968), *abstraction* (Bijou, 1965), and *attention*. As Bandura so accurately pointed out and carefully documented, once the person has acquired the skill of imitation, he may develop new performances rapidly. By imitation is meant that the behavior of one person leads to a similar response being made by another. The second person, in Skinner's terms (1953), has learned to match the model. Response to a model, like response to speech, presumes that the person understands the instructions, is capable of emitting the act modeled, and has a history of reinforcement so that he will indeed emit the act of imitating. This sequence, just as speech, must be acquired.

A person who has not learned to imitate may watch a model for an interminable period with no discernible alteration in behavior, a fact many speech therapists can vouch for. Baer, Peterson, and Sherman (1967) built an imitiative repertoire by programming similarity between a child and a model as discriminative for reinforcement. These investigators worked with three severely retarded but ambulatory children aged nine to twelve. The children were chosen because they lacked verbal behaviors. The experiments were conducted at mealtimes, using food as a reinforcer. The following is a detailed description of the procedure by one of the investigators:

Imitation was taught by the experimenter, who, after demonstrating a simple response, such as tapping the table, then took the child's hand, tapped it on the table, said, "Good," and gave the child a spoonful of food. After a few repetitions of this procedure, the experimenter began to fade out his participation in the child's response. For example, instead of placing the child's hand on the table he now would merely push it toward the table. This fading continued until the child performed the behavior without assistance immediately following its demonstration. In this manner the subjects were taught a number of simple imitative behaviors.

As the training progressed, the children began to demonstrate their learning by imitating new responses perfectly, following an initial demonstration. This tendency increased until the subjects were able to imitate, as soon as it was modeled, almost any simple motor response, such as putting on a hat, standing up from a sitting position, or ringing a bell. In addition, the children continued to imitate some responses even though they were never reinforced. These nonreinforced behaviors were termed "generalized imitations." Investigation showed that these generalized imitations were indirectly under the control of the reinforcement, in that they continued to be performed as long as the other imitative behaviors were reinforced; when such reinforcement was made noncontingent (given to the child regardless of performance), all imitative responses, including the generalized imitations, declined in strength. When reinforcement for some imitations was again made contingent, both generalized and reinforced imitations returned to their former high rate of performance. Thus, by making similarity of behavior between subject and models discriminative for reinforcement, a useful comprehensive set of imitative behaviors was established in previously nonimitative children. [Peterson, 1968, pp. 63–64]

This line of work has been replicated and extended by Brigham and Sherman (1968), Burgess, Burgess, and Esveldt (1970), Peterson and Whitehurst (1971), Martin (1971), Masters and Morris (1971), and Steinman and Boyce (1971). Imitation has been used in aiding social behavior in terms of altering children's fears, developing language among autistic children, and self-care behavior among retardates. Other recent uses are encouraging social interaction among retarded children (Paloutzian, Hasazi, Streifel, and Edgar, 1970) and information seeking among culturally disadvantaged school children (see Chapter 28). Having demonstrated an effect both in the laboratory and the clinic, the next step is the investigation of the conditions that affect the phenomenon. Examples of work in this area involve such variables as the complexity of the task, contingency of reinforcement, and the model (e.g., Waxler and Yarrow, 1970; Allen and Liebert, in press; Liebert, Fernandez, and Gill, 1969; Peterson et al., 1971). Ball (1970) has pointed out how similar some of these procedures are to the techniques of Itard and Seguin, nineteenth-century pioneers in work with the retarded.

Formation of Abstractions

The teaching of conceptual material such as the formation of abstraction is very similar to teaching imitation. The subject may be required to touch the one stimulus of five in a display that is most similar to a model. One specific cue, for example "largeness," or some other relationship may be exemplified. The abstraction is an aspect of the cues which is found in many situations. The correct response is one of "seeking a relation," and this relationship can be accurately identified with material that has not been previously used. In many ways abstraction is a special case of generalization. Another way of saying this is that the person is taught to respond to new situations in the same manner as he did during training.

THE TRAINING OF ATTENTION

Of great import, especially for the theoretical formulation of schizophrenia, is the act of attending. When discussing labeling, it was remarked that a person will respond to the presence or absence of some stimuli in a situation and be seemingly indifferent to others (ignore them and not alter his behavior). Some aspects of attention as a respondent may be measured at a physiological level. Attention as an operant behavior can be shaped and maintained following the principles previously described (e.g. Barnhart, 1968).

O'Leary and Becker (1967) report on training attentiveness in a classroom where one teacher dealt with 17 youngsters who were behavior problems. The investigators introduced a token reinforcement system to the whole class. Observations were focused on the eight most disruptive children. Two observers recorded behaviors labeled deviant (e.g., pushing, talking, making noise, chewing gum) every 30 seconds for an hour and a half three days a week. Behaviors manifested during the observation periods were classified as either disruptive or nondisruptive. On the first day of training the experimenter put the following words on the blackboard: "In Seat, Face Front, Raise Hand, Working, Pay Attention, Desk Clear." The experimenter then explained that tokens would be given for these behaviors and that the tokens could be exchanged for back-up reinforcers of candy, comics, perfume, etc.

The teacher rated the extent to which the child had met the criteria on the blackboard. For the first three days tokens were exchanged at the end of each period; then tokens were accumulated for two days before being cashed in; then there was a three-day period of delay, and finally a four-day delay between tokens and cash-in. The process was designed to fade out the back-up reinforcer so that more traditional secondary reinforcers of teacher praise would be acquired. In addition, group points (exchanged for popsicles) were awarded for quietness of the group during the rating period. Further techniques of verbal praise, ignoring (extinction), and time-out-from-reinforcement were used as appropriate.

During a baseline observation period the disruptive-deviant behavior ranged from 66 percent to 91 percent of the observations. The daily mean of observed deviant-disruptive behavior ranged from 3 percent to 32 percent during the time of the token training. Figure 4 shows the averages for the eight observed children for the duration of the observations including baseline, institution of token system, and the fading period of the progressive delayed cash-in. The authors concluded that, "With the introduction of the token reinforcement system a dramatic, abrupt reduction in deviant behavior occurred . . . The program was equally successful for all children observed, and repeated anecdotal evidence suggested that the children's appropriate behavior generalized to other situations."

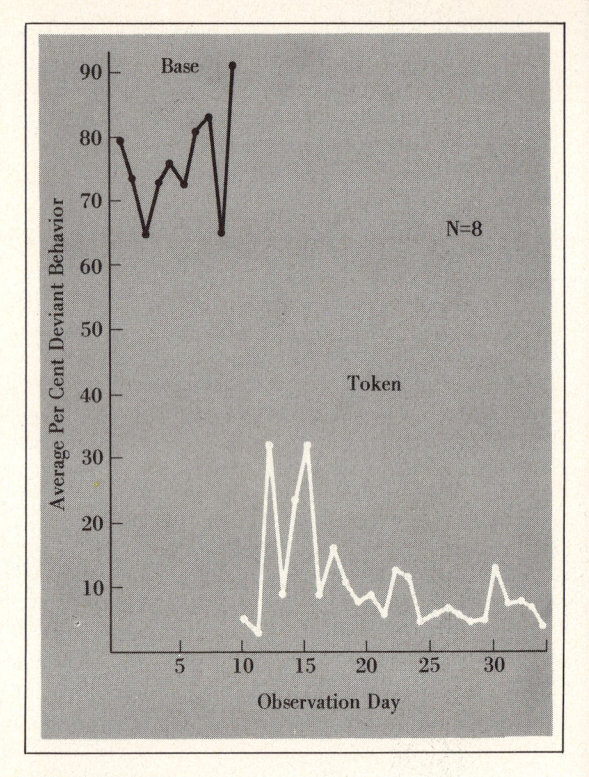

Figure 4
Redrawn from O'Leary and Becker, 1967, p. 640.

THE INTERRELATION OF OPERANT AND RESPONDENT BEHAVIOR

While up to this point operant and respondent behavior have been treated as though they were separate, in reality the two are intertwined. Operant or voluntary behaviors have respondent or autonomic consequences, and the concepts of operant and respondent conditioning serve to complement each other. Operant behaviors such

A person learns both to emit operants and the time and place in which that emission will or will not be reinforced. He learns what is *expected* of him in terms of what behaviors are likely to be positively reinforced, and, just as important, what the probable consequences are of not emitting the behavior.

Simple operants may be chained, shaped, and so overlearned that a complex behavior becomes functionally a single act or response. A response is any behavior, no matter how simple or complex, upon whose occurrence observers can agree. It may be moving a single group of muscles, or it may be the emission of a complicated grammatical and relational class of verbal behavior such as the use of first-person pronouns or emotional words. Speech is considered operant behavior. Once learned, language itself is used in further adaptive behavior. In a similar fashion, once a person has learned to imitate another person, he may progress rapidly to new performances through modeling.

The task of this chapter, then, is the delineation of a number of situations relevant to abnormal behavior which illustrate the degree to which the person is influenced by his environment in the emission of complicated patterns of behavior which other people can identify as a class of responses or as social roles. The particular topics to be discussed are those of placebo response, hypnotic behavior, sensory deprivation, and experimenter bias. In each of these situations, the person may seem to act in a manner that is discontinuous with his other social roles. In fact, these situations illustrate that altering one's behavior in response to the cues present in a current situation is synonymous with normal behavior. A person responds to situations with altered behavior to the extent that he has learned a response to these specific cues as being helpful to him. The overt behavior may seem novel or "not normal" until the regularities underlying the apparent diversity are made explicit.

ROLE ENACTMENTS

The sociological and psychological concept of *role* offers a way of organizing the consistency in behavior specific to social situations that an individual learns as a function of growing up in a particular society. A role is synonymous with a series of specific actions determined by the part a person enacts at different times.

Any given role may be viewed as a series of interrelated behaviors appropriate to a given situation and learned through past experience. A role is a category of instrumental acts (e.g., aggressive role, dominant role) reinforced in a given situation. A specific role (e.g., father, wife, teacher, patient) includes those elements of behavior which are common from one situation to another and from one individual to another.

On the basis of prior experience the individual behaves in a manner most likely to obtain reinforcement. He responds to a new situation in terms of his genetic endowment, his prior learning, his current deprivations, and the specific stimuli present (e.g., police uniforms, white coats, airplanes, young children, attractive females) which indicate that various behaviors—the specifics of which he has previously learned (e.g., aggression, deference, fear, father, Don Juan)—are likely to have reinforcing consequences. Sometimes he will respond in a manner considered inappropriate by others—because he has identified the situation inaccurately, because he has been conditioned aversively to particularly cues that are part of the situation but not necessarily crucial in defining it, because he does not have the appropriate responses (skill) in his repertoire, or because he has previously been extinguished for making the expected responses. Good judgment means selecting the right role at the right time.

The ability to identify relevant cues to react to can be greatly enhanced by training procedures.[1] Ekman (1964), for example, used photographs of people in actual stressful and cathartic situations to improve his subjects' ability to identify (discriminate) these two kinds of human interaction. Edmonson and his associates (1967) taught retarded children social cue interpretations. The therapist literally may teach the individual how to go about the search of his environment for clues as to how to judge other people's behavior. Facial expressions (Ekman and Friesen, 1971; Watson, 1972), bodily posture (Ekman and Friesen, 1967; Mehrabian, 1969), and use of space (Albert and Dabbs, 1970; Griffitt and Veitch, 1971; Frankel and Barrett, 1971; Jourard and Friedman, 1970; Mehrabian and Diamond, 1971; Pellegrini, 1971) convey meaningful information, but only if the individual has the skill to "read" correctly other people's body language or silent messages (Mehrabian, 1971; Sommer, 1969; Hall, 1966, 1969; Weitz, 1974).

[1] We have tried to limit the studies we cite to those dealing with humans, but we must note that studies of the teaching of sign language and other forms of communication to animals are useful and relevant in this area. We therefore wish to draw attention to Hinde (1972), Fouts (1973), Gardner and Gardner (1969), Premack (1971), and Sebeck (1967).

The use of space as an expression of the "proper" role in any given society is learned early (Meisels and Guarde, 1969; Berk, 1971; Aiello and Jones, 1971; Jones and Aiello, 1973; Pedersen and Shears, 1973). This becomes clinically relevant, as exemplified by Newman and Pollack (1973), who found that male high school students who were hostile toward authority, aggressive, and destructive felt discomfort due to overcloseness to others sooner than their classmates. That is, these students required larger territories or boundaries around their bodies than the comparison group. Kinzel (1970) found that the "body-buffer zone" in violent prisoners was four times as large as that for nonviolent ones. In short, there are some people one does not crowd.

Length of hair (Rosenthal and White, 1971), clothes (Gurel, Wilbur, and Gurel, 1972; Bickman, 1974), and unusual stimuli such as blood (Piliavin and Piliavin, 1972) may serve to classify people (an observer labels or stereotypes them) and lead to differential treatment in the same manner that happens in the categories of age, sex, and race. Hall (1966, 1969) has documented cross-culturally how failing to respond to stimuli that have a small magnitude but great meaning may lead to a person being considered disagreeable or ignorant (a trait name assigned to explain behavior in a manner similar to the designation "abnormal").

Clinically, a person may look for approval (Efran, 1968), communicate pleasure, displeasure, or anger (Zaidel and Mehrabian, 1969; Modigliani, 1971; Freedman et al., 1973), or interest, e.g., eye-contact or staring (Ellsworth and Carlsmith, 1968; Ellsworth, Carlsmith, and Henson, 1972). Clinically, the therapist must be alert to such behaviors; on the one hand he needs to respond to his client's actual communications, while on the other, he must be ready to identify both his client's behavior and the role-expressive behaviors expected in the client's target situations so that he may help develop effective interpersonal skills and reduce nonverbal behaviors that "turn off" other people. For example, there is an etiquette of conversation (e.g., when and how to interrupt), (Meltzer, Morris, and Hayes, 1971; Weiss, et al., 1971; Duncan, 1972). Taylor (1972) describes a class on etiquette to a Honolulu model-cities group:

> Like a little ship at sea, I dip my spoon AWAY from me! . . . "This Emily Post, one buggered-up wahine," said a large man in an orange tee shirt. . . . The purpose seems to be to make the residents of the Model Cities area more self-confident so that they may play increasingly more important roles in the community. . . . The idea of including the etiquette course was the residents' own. There isn't a board or commission in town that isn't angling for a member from Model Cities. . . .

At luncheon meetings and dinners, knowledge of proper etiquette is needed to feel comfortable and not intimidated by everyone else knowing something and perhaps looking down on one.

The impact of "acting right" is not only in terms of direct effectiveness with the other person, but also in terms of the information one gives to oneself. *A person may infer how he feels from how he acts* (Bandler, Madaras, and Bem, 1968; Warm et al., in press; Kanfer and Newman, in press). One may not only infer one's own beliefs from one's own behavior (Kiesler, Nisbett, and Zanna, 1969), but also "feelings" and other self-designations or attributions. In addition, such changes in activity lead to altered overt behavior to which other people respond. A more assertive demeanor may yield more respect from other people. The change may even be fortuitous; for example, when the senior author started wearing bifocals, his posture changed so that he would not be sighting through the spot where the two lenses touched. People responded to his posture. Many trait designations such as "warmth" or, indeed, "abnormal," are attributions based on cues which are assigned cultural meanings. In terms of treatment within the therapist role, seating during the interview (Boucher, 1972) as well as other cues (Kelly, 1972) such as leaning forward and making eye contact help communicate a positive attitude toward the client. Ullmann et al. (1968) showed that the interviewer's approaching or avoiding positive or negative self-references during an interview had an impact on later interviewee ratings on such semantic differential scales as warmth, sympathy, and competence. Bayes (1972) systematically endeavored to ascertain the behavioral cues that led other people to rate someone as warm, and found that smiling and making positive statements about others accounted for much of the differences among people. Haase and Tepper (1972) obtained similar findings with variables of eye contact, trunk lean, body orientation, and a programmed verbal empathy measure on modification of ratings of "empathy." These researches indicate that therapeutic qualities are the result not of inborn or immutable personality variables but of teachable operants.

When such elements of a social role are specified, they may then be taught, and the person who has learned may in turn become more effective, obtain greater pleasure from life, and hence increase in emission of both overt cues of warmth and in covert self-designation of being effective with and liking other people. Beyond the applied importance, this approach may be used to investigate many abstractions about which people argue much and do little. A stimulating example in this regard is work on presumed locus of control and reinforcement schedules on attributed "freedom" (Davidson and Steiner, 1971), and attributed "influence over another person" (Schopler and Layton, 1972). This line of investigation takes us into an area where social psychologists (e.g. Gergen, 1971; Kelley, 1967) may well be making a major contribution to clinical work.

Role enactments are usually dyadic (Sears, 1951), and the behavior of one person serves as stimulus for the other. The second person's behavioral responses serve as stimuli (both discriminative and reinforcing) for the first person, and so forth. Role enactments may therefore serve to define and control change in a situation.

Role enactments evoke complementary role enactments from others; a person who behaves in the "sick" role, for example, is likely to be responded to by others' enacting the role of "dealing with sick people," a role that includes behaviors likely to reinforce some aspects of the sick role and hence maintain sick behavior.

In his *Making of Blind Men* (1969), Scott contends that being blind is a learned social role. In what follows, the reader frequently may wish to replace the words "blinded person" with words like "aged," "black," "female," "young," "imprisoned," or "psychiatric patient."

Scott advances two basic theses:

The first is that many of the attitudes, behavior patterns, and qualities of character that have long been assumed to be given to blind people by their condition are, in fact, the result of ordinary processes of socialization. The second is that organized intervention programs for the blind play a major role in determining the nature of this socialization. Blindness, then, is a social role that people who have serious difficulty in seeing or who cannot see at all must learn to play. [Scott, 1969, p. 3.]

Scott points out that there are "commonsense" explanations and stereotyped expectations of the blind. Because their world is less gross, the blind are expected to be more spiritual than other people. But the blind, by the same sort of deductions, are expected to be depressed, frustrated, helpless, and docile. Sighted people learn these stereotypes and behave on the basis of them when they interact with the blind.

The first context in which a blinded person learns this view is in childhood. Here it is important to note the distinction between the congenitally blind, who are blind from birth or shortly thereafter, and the blinded, who lose their sight later, usually late in life. The vast majority of people called blind are of the blinded category; the point is that during their sighted years they learn the social role at first directed toward the blind, then towards themselves in this role.

A second context of socialization of the blind is in interaction with people who treat the blind person as helpless, docile, dependent, etc. The assumption that the person is helpless may be a self-validating hypothesis since he may be denied the opportunity to practice the skills he has and demonstrate to others and himself his competence and independence.

A third context is interaction with the social agencies created to help the blind. There are numerous agencies for the blind, so numerous, in fact, that they even compete for the limited population so that they may justify their own existence. There is a blindness "network," "system," or even "industry."

The legitimacy of this profession is in large part based upon its practitioners' claims to specialized knowledge and expertise concerning problems of blindness. Through the years, this knowledge and expertise have become increasingly formalized, so that in blindness organizations today there are a number of more or less distinctive approaches to blindness. These approaches are based on beliefs and assumptions concerning the fundamental problems experienced by people who are blind, the necessary and appropriate solutions to these problems, and the reactions of people when they first become blind and during each successive stage of their rehabilitation. These beliefs and assumptions serve to guide practitioners in dealing with clients in the clinical setting of the blindness agency. The approaches are expressed as the blindness workers' expectations of the attitudes and behavior of those they are trying to help. For blindness workers, one key indicator of the success of a rehabilitation endeavor is the degree to which the client has come to understand himself and his problems from the workers' perspective. [Scott, 1969, pp. 18–19.]

People react differently to a person considered blind than they do to one they consider sighted. But this differentiation is not made unless people perceive or label the person as blind. While this statement seems obvious, it is not. The most common definition of blind is central visual acuity of 20/200 or less in the better eye with correcting lenses. Many readers of this book who wear glasses may be like the senior author and can gain some impact of what this means by taking off their glasses. Without glasses, most of the world more than three feet away assumes the broken, hazy aspect of an impressionist painting. While definitely handicapped in comparison to others when not wearing glasses, the senior author considers himself very far from blind. There may be many severely handicapped people, therefore, who are not blind by the administrative definition, and the definition is not sensitive to how well the person actually functions.

The person must first be identified as being blind. The blind person is then assigned a new role. The label of blindness is not an attribute limited to relevant situations—for example, sensing distant physical objects—but is treated as a constant set of characteristics across most, if not all, social situations.

It is impossible for blind men to ignore these beliefs; they have no choice but to respond to them. These responses vary, but in a highly patterned way. Some blind people come to concur in the verdict that has been reached by those who see. They adopt as part of their self-concept the qualities of character, the feelings, and the behavior patterns that others insist they must have . . . Such blind men might be termed "true-believers"; they have become what others, with whom they interact, assume they must become because they are blind.

Not all blind people are true believers; there are many who explicitly, indeed insistently, reject the imputations made of them by others. They thereby manage to insulate a part of the self-concept from the assaults made on it by normals. The personal identity of such a person is not that of a blind man, but of a basically normal person who cannot see. For the blind man who responds in this way, there remains the problem that most people who see do not share the view he has reached about himself. [Scott, 1969, p. 22.]

But the world of the blinded is not merely dictated by stereotypes or attitudes. There is an effect on overt behavior, and this effect is sharpened by actual interchanges. The cues used by sighted people, such as head nods of agreement, are not effective. The blind person may turn his head away from the sighted person because his hearing is the more important channel in conversation, emitting a cue that for a sighted person would be one of disinterest. Unless experienced, the sighted person does not know how to act, especially when to help and when not to. He wants to do the right thing and not call attention to the blind person's handicap: should he help him to his chair, guide his hand to the cup of coffee or cigarette, use phrases such as "I see what you mean"? The sighted person may hesitate to respond to content with the same directness that he would when talking with a person not blind: he withholds some of his normal response lest he hurt the blind person. In short, the blind person makes the sighted constrained, uncomfortable, and even frustrated.

The blind person, in turn, not only faces this difficulty in communication, he may be placed in a position where he is dependent and compliant because he cannot return favors as easily as the sighted. The relationship may be more like a parent-child, teacher-student relationship because it is less than one between equals. From these situations, people who may be presumed to be different come to act in similar ways.

To this situation we may now add the impact of service organizations. First, it should be noted that the definition of blindness, as noted above, is not total lack of sight, and second, that there are many people who would meet the official definition who remain in the general population and, although having difficulties in seeing, are not thought of by themselves, or others, as blind. The person with severe vision problems may be referred to an agency serving the blind, be labeled blind, and then treated as if totally blind. There is a redefinition of the problem both by the person and the people serving him. This is similar to what occurs when a person enters a psychiatric hospital because of a particular behavior, is diagnosed as schizophrenic, and then treated for schizophrenia rather than the overt behavior. The situation is made more difficult because many of the techniques of the service agency were devised for people who were totally blind and are applied to people who have partial vision. For example, a person who might be able to function with enlarged print may be taught braille. Further, the presenting difficulty may have been marital, psychiatric, financial—that is specific to one area of life. Because the person happens to have visual difficulties, however, he is referred to the agency serving the blind.

A person may wish better optical aids or other specific services. The blind person believes his trouble lies in specific areas. "The personal conceptions that blinded persons have about the nature of their problems are in sharp contrasts with beliefs that workers for the blind share about the problems of blindness." (Scott, 1969, p. 77.) The service worker, on the other hand, views blindness as a total process affecting all aspects of life: "Beneath the surface of awareness lies a tremendously complicated mass of problems that must be dealt with before the surface problems can ever be successfully solved." (Scott, 1969, p. 77.) This parallels closely the approach of the traditional therapist who believes that the underlying problems must be changed before there can be behavior change. The service worker must therefore discredit the client's ideas about his own problems. The client must learn to accept the agency's formulation.

. . . in face-to-face situations, the blind person is rewarded for showing insight and subtly reprimanded for continuing to adhere to earlier notions about his problems. He is led to believe that he "really" understands past and present experiences when he couches them in terms acceptable to his therapist. If he persists in viewing his "presenting problems" as the real ones, he is labeled "unacceptable" or "uninsightful." The client is said to be "blocking" or resisting the truth. [Scott, 1969, p. 79.]

To be fully rehabilitated, with the rewards (such as progress in the program) adhering thereto, depends on accepting the agency's formulation.

Clients are rewarded for trivial things and praised for performing tasks in a mediocre fashion. This superficial and over-generous reward system makes it impossible for most clients to assess their accomplishments accurately. . . . The unstated assumption of accommodative agencies is that most of their clients will end up organizing their lives around the agency. [Scott, 1969, p. 85.]

The parallel to the custodial hospital for the psychiatric patient is striking; the person is taught to adjust to the agency, and "A blind person who has been fully socialized in the accommodative agency will be maladjusted to the larger community." (Scott, 1969, p. 86.)

We may now ask, What are the conditions leading to the adoption of the theories and practices of an accommodative agency? One aspect, similar to the development of large psychiatric hospitals, is that the accommodative agency removes the blind from the awareness of the remainder of the population. The second is that by making the difficulty severe, the dedication and expertise of the agency worker is enhanced. Blindness agencies may have a real vested interest in maintaining the stereotypes about the blind held by the general public. Public education may be more frequently directed to the availability of the agency rather than the actualities of blindedness.

Because "results" are desirable in terms

of increased accommodation, the person who is old or multiply handicapped is less likely to be served than the younger, less disabled person. This may also be due to the goal of earlier blindness workers who charted the field when fewer sick children and old people survived and blindness occurred frequently in the industrial setting.

The agency is constrained by its source of funding, and particularly when private philanthropy meets the desires and stereotypes of that source. The number of clients who meet the standard of the agency are limited, and "When an agency has the opportunity to provide services to a suitable blind person, it is reluctant to let him go completely." (Scott, 1969, p. 99.) The agency strives to keep its workload of people served high. This situation may also be observed in psychiatric hospitals in which new applications per bed (assuring an adequate average daily load) was significantly associated with measures of patient turnover and rapid release (Ullmann, 1967a).

The worker in the blindness agency is locked into the system almost as much as the blind client. Especially, if his expertise has been gained on the job in an agency, as distinct from a professional school, he is dependent on the system as it exists for his status and salary. Procedures may be continued because they fit the presumed needs of the blind, and needs may be invented to justify procedures.

In summary, ". . . there is nothing inherent in the condition of blindness that requires a person to be docile, dependent, melancholy, or helpless; nor is there anything about it that should lead him to become independent or assertive." (Scott, 1969, p. 14.) Many of the similarities among the blind stem from their treatment and not their decreased vision.

EXPECTANCY AND PERFORMANCE

Attention is focused on certain cues to the exclusion of others. People attend to, expect, anticipate, or are set for the environmental stimuli that have previously led to reinforcement. Not infrequently expectancy may be so strong that a person may misperceive objective environmental cues. Expectancy influences behavior in situations such as hypnosis, psychotherapy, placebo, and experimental research. In all these situations previously learned reinforcing contingencies are so strong that the person's behavior is influenced by his expectancy of what will occur. What an individual usually attends to are the salient, previously learned (reinforced) discriminative stimuli in any given sequence of behavior. *Expectancies, then, are a shorthand expression for the degree to which one has learned environmental contingencies.* Unfortunately, previously learned contingencies do not always correspond to those currently operating in a given situation. In other words, one may generalize inappropriately. The studies of level of aspiration (Lewin et al., 1944) deal with the development and differences between an individual's expectancies of his own performance in a given situation and the situation per se.

If a person expects contingent rewards and receives them, the confirmation of the prediction is in itself rewarding. "Being correct" in this regard is a discriminative stimulus in that being able to predict has been more frequently associated in the past with positive reinforcement than being "wrong." Occasions when one expects little and gets much are relatively infrequent and generally of such a nature as to be more positive than negative.[2]

Merton (1948) brought to prominence an important concept relevant to expectancy, that of the *self-fulfilling prophecy:* the definition of a situation (as a prophecy

---

[2] But not necessarily always more positive than negative. For example, a politician who predicts that his bailiwick will give his party a plurality of 1,000 and finds on election day that his party carried his ward by 5,000 may be in trouble. By predicting so inaccurately, he has demonstrated that he is not in touch with his people.

or as a prediction) becomes an integral part of the situation and thus affects subsequent developments. "The self-fulfilling prophecy is, in the beginning, a *false* definition of the situation evoking a new behavior which makes the originally false conception come true" (p. 195.). The behavior of labeling the situation, i.e., the "prophecy" or expectancy, is likely to alter the cues to which a person attends and responds. Because the person's behavior provides stimuli for other people, his prophecy is an aspect of the situation and alters it. Behavior leads to consequences, and as the person changes his behavior, new consequences occur, so that gradually environmental events are shaped in the direction of the expectancies. The material on the blind, just reviewed, provides an illustration.

The therapist who expects a person to be unresponsive to psychotherapy and emits cues to this effect influences his patient. When the patient does indeed respond poorly, at least in part as a result of the therapist's actions, the therapist's prediction comes true.

THE "SICK" SOCIAL ROLE

There are many roles an individual may play. Parsons (1951) refers to illness, for example, as "not merely a 'condition' but also a social role." He lists the four characteristics of the sick role in our society as: the exemption of the sick from the performance of certain of his normal social obligations; the exemption from responsibility for his own condition; the pressure of society on the individual to return to a state of health as quickly as possible; the obligation to cooperate with the people, such as physicians, who are societally sanctioned to "help" the sick person. Parsons points out that the sick role pattern was "already well established in our society before the development of modern psychopathology." One of the important contributions of Charcot and Freud was to label hysterical patients as enacting sick rather than malingering roles.

With a society, not only are the prescribed behaviors of the sick role defined but the physical location wherein the role can be enacted, the behaviors required of those reacting to the sick person, and the role behaviors of the society's sanctioned therapists are specified. Stainbrook notes how our society has transferred the locus of the sick role from the family to the centrally located hospital. "Today the modern hospital has become increasingly the social system in which the sick role as a meaningful mode of participation in society is lived out." (Stainbrook, 1959, p. 152.)

Every society recognizes (i.e., reinforces) the sick role, although what are considered "sick" behaviors may vary considerably from society to society. Implicit in the existence of a sick role is the social sanction of a complementary set of behaviors called the role of the therapist. Parsons (1951) presents four characteristics of the therapist role: the therapist assumes the obligation to do everything he can within reason to help his patient; he permits the patient to express wishes and fantasies that would not be permitted in normal social relationships; he treats the patient as if he were not a responsible adult; and "against the unconditional element of support, there is the conditional manipulation of sanctions by the therapist." As Parsons points out, these are the general features of the physician's role, and are independent of the specific technical operations of psychotherapy. The modern sick role of the "mentally ill" person and the helping role of the healer were superimposed on an existing role structure which had been developed to deal with *physical* rather than *behavioral* problems.

Effects of "Sick-role"
(Medical Model)

Examples of the thinking that enters a medical approach may be found in Kraepelin (1917, reprinted 1962), the father of contemporary diagnostic systems, when he quotes Hayner: ... "punishment would be effective only if the patient were capable of exercising his will. Since he is irrational and cannot, punishment seems unjust to him." (Kraepelin, 1962, p. 91). In short, kindly treatment is justified not for reasons of humanity or respect but because the person is not responsible. The grafting of a medical explanation onto a behavioral phenomenon is illustrated (Kraepelin, 1962, pp. 15–16) by the physician in 1845 who advocated the use of a birch rod for persistent uncleanliness (incontinence), not only because of the pain, but because of the benefit on the sphincter muscles and anus due to vigorous stimulation of the glutei.

Within the illness model behavior may be discounted, and neither the patient nor the labeler need be responsible. Second, if the person is "sick," his incarceration may be called treatment for his own good. The use of sick-role concepts permits social control over deviance without guilt over deprivation of civil liberties. (See Szasz, 1963, 1965; Leifer, 1969.)

Associated (and sometimes identical) with the therapist role is that of the *labeler*—the one who is "gatekeeper" to the sick role. When a patient presents himself to a physician, entrance into or denial of a sick role depends, in part, upon the personality, education, and experience of the physician and, in part, upon the prevailing theory of disease in the existing medical culture. Stainbrook puts this point in a historical context:

It is common knowledge that the sick-role legitimation of an individual's expression of his uneasiness may depend upon what his statement of his symptom is, to whom he makes his symptom presentation and in what social context he asserts his illness. As an example, the medical culture of a military society may deny a recognition of sickness for many evidences of behavioral and physiological adaptations to psychological stress. In World War II the Germans and Russians apparently made the sick role much less easily available for battle-stress reactions than did the American and British armies. [Stainbrook, 1959, p. 154.]

Schofield has made the cogent point that "case-finding tends frequently to result in case-making" (1964, p. 27). The investigation of the needs for treatment may define an "illness" and make it socially acceptable. Situations or problems that are bearable may bring about a socially prescribed sick-role enactment through inquiry, suggestion, or verbal operant conditioning. Many investigators have pointed out the iatrogenic phenomenon (the treatment creates problems) involved in psychotherapy in general (Frank, 1961; Schofield, 1964) and especially in hospitalized populations (Lehrman 1961; Ullmann, 1967a). The person who seeks will find, especially if the act of finding is in itself reinforcing for the observer.

OUTPATIENT PSYCHOTHERAPY

Many of the points made so far in this chapter may be illustrated in the sequence of events that are involved in receiving psychological treatment in situations other than being institutionalized (which are taken up in Chapters 10 and 18). Long before the client and the therapist work together, a great deal of screening and training has occurred that is more related to the age, sex, race, social class and social circle of the client than it is to any subsequent systematic psychological or professional activity by the therapist.

Age, class, and racial differences may be associated with the development of physical stresses and behaviors that are considered professionally changeworthy. Differences in nutrition, both before and after birth, meaningful stimulation early in life, patterns of child rearing, and the degrees to which the promises of a person's abilities, training, and expectation match the realities of his accomplishments, may lead to different rates with which groups develop life-styles and behaviors that they themselves or others consider to warrant changing. At the present time, inequities based on race and sex are particularly salient.

Irrespective of whether particular social groups are more likely than others to develop changeworthy behavior, there is a strong association between social status and recognition that the behavior should or can be changed. The very designation of a physical difficulty as an indication of sickness is a learned act. For example Koos (1954, p. 33) reports that upper-class respondents considered far more conditions appropriate for medical attention than lower-class respondents. The percentages of respondents in upper and lower classes, respectively, who recognized specified symptoms as needing medical attention were as follows: persistent backache, 53 vs. 19 percent; continued coughing, 77 vs. 23 percent; loss of weight, 80 vs. 21 percent; lump in breast, 94 vs. 44 percent; and lump in abdomen, 92 vs. 34 percent.

After a behavior causes concern or interpersonal friction, another set of behaviors, associated with social status and learning, involves what, if anything, can be done about it. At the start of the next chapter, we will touch on various theories of the etiology of behavioral difficulties. At this time, we can point out that models of man have great impact. Is the behavior a result of human nature, about which nothing can be done? Is it a result of sin? Should the person "pull himself together," possibly with the aid of a lecture from a parent, minister, coach, or boss? Should he seek help, and if he does, is a psychiatrist the person to consult?

The most extensive work on this and associated problems is Kadushin's (1969) book, *Why People Go to Psychiatrists*. Kadushin (p. 7) notes: ". . . the issue for research is what kinds of people formulate what kinds of problems—for no problem, no psychotherapist!" Kadushin studied four types of clinics in New York City, psychoanalytic, psychotherapeutic, religio-psychiatric, and hospital-based.

There is a matching of type of clinic and type of presenting problem. A crucial factor in where a person seeks help is the sort of people who are the future client's friends. Acquaintances, especially if they are psychiatrically sophisticated (what Kadushin calls members of the *Friends and Supporters of Psychotherapy*), serve to help the person define that he has a problem, that he should do something about it, reduce hesitations and reluctances about seeking help, and finally, offer specific guidance as to where to apply for treatment. Interaction with the sophisticated "Friends" also provides *expectations* about therapy, notably that the client will do most of the talking and will receive little direct advice. Further, the presenting problem becomes one that fits the model or school of the therapist to which the person is referred.

Indeed, a detailed statistical examination of changes in the way a person first conceived of his problem and the way he finally presents it to a clinic shows that applicants tend to increase their proportion of "suitable" problems, and drop their proportion of "wrong" problems. For example, applicants to analytic clinics are more likely to add sexual problems to their original set of problems and drop physical symptoms. Hospital applicants do the reverse.

Working-class persons applying to clinics do not *have* more physical problems, but they certainly *feel* that these symptoms are more valid reasons for going to see a psychiatrist than do higher-class persons. [Kadushin, 1969, pp. 106, 132, 140.]

To summarize the foregoing, there is a great deal of learning and role training before the applicant for treatment ever sees the intake worker. After formal application, there is an interaction between the professional and the patient (Goldstein, 1962, 1971) that further screens who will be accepted for individual treatment, who will remain through a course of treatment, and who will benefit therefrom.[3] The general tenor of findings is that minority and lower social-class people are less likely to be accepted for treatment; when accepted, receive fewer sessions per week; and are less likely to remain in therapy (Hollingshead and Redlich, 1958; Aronson and Overall, 1966; Hunt, 1960; Jones and Kahn, 1964; Bernstein, 1964; Myers and Schaffer, 1954; Yamamoto et al., 1967, 1968; Labreche, Turner, and Zabo, 1969; Cross et al., 1969; Rowden et al., 1970; Cohen and Richardson, 1970; Petroni and Griffin, 1970).[4]

A person with a poor educational background is unlikely to have learned the social role of the "good" psychotherapy patient in which the expected behavior reinforced involves talking about feelings, describing dreams, and emitting free associations. Thus it is unlikely that these behaviors are readily available in his repertoire. He has not been exposed to the kinds of social stimuli, books, magazines, or personal contacts that would give him an opportunity to "pick up" the appropriate skills. Instead, he is exposed to the cues of office, clinic, nurse, and doctor, and these are more likely to set the stage for the role of medical patient:

[3] Even after the person contacts a clinic, there is a strong screening effect. Eiduson (1968) notes a dropout rate of from 30 to 65 percent. Grice (1969) reports one in nine student intakes received therapy at a college clinic. Veray (1970) delineated six stages or points of attrition; and, in his data, of 1400 people who first called the clinic for psychiatric help, only 63 actually received more than seven sessions of psychotherapy.

[4] There are some reports that run counter to the trend. Kadushin (1969, pp. 121–22) did not find a strong association between social class and diagnosis and noted that, "Perhaps as a result of this literature, clinicians are becoming aware of what they feel is a class bias. Data we collected from the Religion and Psychiatry Institute in 1957, before the wide circulation of the evidence relating social class to diagnosis, showed a strong relationship between schizophrenia and low social class. In 1960 there were no such relationships." If this observation becomes generally true, it would be a heartening example that the psychotherapeutic profession, if given feedback, may correct itself.

passivity, compliance, nonresponsibility, receipt of medication, and relief of immediate symptoms. In such a situation, the patient is unlikely to do or say things warranting reinforcement, and his behavior soon becomes quite aversive to the frustrated therapist whose own behavior becomes equally aversive to the patient (Rickels and Anderson, 1967; Adams and McDonald, 1968). Further, the therapist has learned from his own previous experience, and from other therapists, *not to expect* much responsivity from such an individual whose background and values differ from his own.

The performance of a given role (i.e., role enactment) is dependent upon the availability of the necessary behaviors (knowledge of the required role), the individual's past experience with reinforcement contingencies (his "desire" to perform), and his ability to perform roles.

Summary

A role is a set of behaviors which are recognized and labeled by observers. Involved are general behaviors by different people or by the same person at different times. Detailed, idiosyncratic ways of enacting a role are of less importance (unless they are aversive) than the broader concept of role behavior as a response to situations (Barker, 1968) and relationships between people. These identifiable behaviors usually occur in response to a discriminative stimulus: the setting of time, place, and person at which certain operants have previously had reinforcing consequences. Role enactments are maintained by their environmental consequences, and this means that they must be visible, recognizable, and meaningful to observers.

Aside from consequences on observers, enacting a role has two major effects on the individual himself. The first was mentioned under the rubric of self-fulfilling prophecies. The second was touched upon and will be later elaborated in the discussion of hypnotic and placebo enactments: enacting a role has respondent (visceral) consequences. There is physiological feedback from the actions taken while enacting the role (e.g., eyestrain from reading an assignment but reduction of feelings of vulnerability because the assignment has been read).

Finally, there is an important aspect of the concept of role that must be clarified. The words "role," "role enactment," and "role-taking" may give the impression of a person consciously assuming "unreal" behavior as in a theatrical production. That is not the way the words are used here. When in the classroom, an observer would see the authors "playing" their roles of teachers. But the behavior emitted would meet all the tests of being as real as the authors' playing of their roles of parents, friends, taxpayers, and the like. Similarly, the proper behavior while listening to a college lecture is a role which is as real as the hardness of the seats in a typical lecture hall.

PLACEBO RESPONSES

The role enactment with greatest relevance for understanding what is involved in situations in which individuals receive professional assistance for their problems is that of placebo response. Placebo response may be defined as the "psychological, physiological, or psychophysiological effect of any medication or procedure given with therapeutic intent, which is independent of or minimally related to the pharmacological effect of the medication or to the specific effects of the procedure, and which operates through a psychological mechanism." (Shapiro, 1960, p. 110.) The placebo *response* must be differentiated from the *placebo* itself. Placebo responses occur as reactions to the cues of pills or other procedures that have no inherent curative properties.

"Placebo" is Latin for "I shall please." The word has a variety of usages in English including being synonymous with "vespers" for the dead," sycophancy, flattery, a "courtesy designed to soothe or gratify, a medicine used more to please than benefit a patient." Shapiro (1960), in reviewing the history of placebo in medicine, points out that despite the use by physicians for thousands of years of what are now considered useless and often dangerous medications, the prestige of physicians has always been high in most Western societies. Despite the medication, patients were helped with their symptoms and problems. In effect, the physician, by virtue of the role of healer, was able to affect favorably the behavior of other people.

Shapiro's placing of the placebo response in its historical perspective emphasizes both its importance and its neglect: "If it can be said that scientific medicine truly began only seven or eight decades ago . . . we are led to the inescapable conclusion that the history of medical treatment for the most part until relatively recently was placebos." (1959, p. 301.) "The great lesson, then, of medical history is that the placebo has always been the norm of medical practice, and it was only occasionally and at great intervals that anything really serviceable, such as the cure of scurvy by fresh fruits, was introduced into medical practice. . . . When one considers that the normative history of medical treatment, until relatively recently, has been the history of the placebo effect, one is amazed to find a veritable curtain of silence about it." (1960, p. 114.)

Those who make the greatest use of the placebo reaction often deny its existence. (For exceptions, see Carter and Allen, 1973; Fish, 1974; and Evans, 1974.) Most published works on abnormal psychology, psychiatry, and general medicine do not discuss placebo responses, and if they do, it is likely to be in terms of control groups for drug studies (see Chapter 3). Especially in psychiatric literature, there is a paucity of references to placebo (Shapiro, 1960). Several reasons seem apparent. The first is that "placebo" is often used as an epithet for the physician knowingly giving the *form* but not the *substance* of treatment. Most physicians would strongly deny that they ever deliberately give something "worthless." Shapiro (1959) reports that physicians and researchers are far more likely to find placebo effects in the work of others than in their own work. He found three times as many physicians who believed they used placebos less frequently than their colleagues as those who believed they used them more frequently.

Another reason for avoiding the topic of placebo may be the very effectiveness of the psychological variables implied in placebo responses, notably those that have been given the general label "suggestion." *The very nature of the medical model is against the placebo phenomenon being "real."* That is, treatment by suggestion is direct treatment of the behavior without reference to the presumed underlying cause. If a patient improves simply by "wanting to" or by following a psychological suggestion, this is *prima facie* evidence that he wasn't *really sick* in a physical-chemical sense.

The following quotation serves to illustrate how a placebo may set the stage for enactment of a sick as well as healthy role:

One attempt by Robins, Smith, and Lowe to confirm the Tulane findings, using comparable numbers and types of subjects and at least as rigorous controls, was quite unsuccessful. In twenty subjects, who at different times received saline or extracts of blood from normals or schizophrenics prepared according to the method for preparing taraxein [a preparation from blood of schizophrenics] there were only five instances of mental or behavioral disturbances resembling those in the original report on taraxein, and these disturbances occurred as often following the administration of saline or extracts of normal plasma as following taraxein. It is easy to dismiss the negative findings with taraxein. . . . it is considerably more difficult to dismiss the observation that a few subjects who received only saline or normal blood extract developed psychic manifestations similar to those reported from taraxein. . . . Is it possible, for example, that taraxein . . . derives its special properties from the psycho-social characteristics of the situation in which it has been tested? [Kety 1960, pp. 132–33.]

If the placebo effect is useful in the formulation of deviant behavior, a number of related questions arise. These involve the characteristics of the placebo itself, the administrator of the placebo, the reactor to the placebo, and side-effects of the placebo. The placebo serves as a discriminative stimulus because of its previous associations with curative agents. Thus, pills that are very large and imply a lot of medicine or very small and imply highly potent medicine are more effective than medium-sized pills. A hot color is advisable, while a pill that looks like aspirin has one strike against it.

"Contemporary placebo therapy seems to be consistent with the practice of the medieval physician whose concoctions were as foul-smelling and evil-tasting as possible. Apparently, treatment without specific indications should be imbued with a large element of hocus-pocus, and ideally be administered at the cost of some discomfort to the patient." (Honigfeld, 1964a.) The pill also works best when labeled the product of recent research. It is a truism that medical procedures may lose their strength after their novelty for both physicians and patients has worn off.

How a substance which is later found to be ineffective may set the stage for changed behavior is illustrated in the following news reports from *The New York Times,* which also illustrate some of the concepts in Chapter 3.

MARCH 31, 1966. A drug treatment said to erase in a few days the symptoms of schizophrenia—a devastating mental disorder for which there is yet no cure—was described at a scientific meeting . . . yesterday.

The drug, called nicotinamide adenine dinucleotide, or NAD, has been tested only since December 27 of last year, according to this report.

Yet, 13 of 17 cases of schizophrenia—one of them confined for 29 years in a mental institution and another sick for eight years—were freed from their malady within three to five days under treatment with the drug, the scientist said.

Two of the four others became much better in that time, he said, and two failed to improve for factors that were unrelated either to their illness or to the therapy.

Three other schizophrenic patients who were given the drug did not receive it long enough before the allotment for the experiment ran out, the scientist said.

When this happened, all of the patients who had become well or much improved began to relapse into their former psychotic states, providing a further indication of the drug's apparent efficacy, the scientist said. [Osmundsen, p. 41.]

* * *

June 25, 1966. A drug initially said to erase the symptoms of schizophrenia in a matter of days has been found to be no more effective than a sugar pill in subsequent tests, a psychiatrist reported yesterday.

Dr. Nathan S. Kline told the American Therapeutic Society, meeting in Chicago, that he and a group of impartial investigators had given the drug to 20 chronic schizophrenics in a carefully controlled experiment and found no drug-related improvements in the patients. . . .

Twenty male chronic schizophrenics, most of whom had received no other drug therapy for at least two months, were divided into ten carefully matched pairs, Dr. Kline said. One patient in each pair was randomly assigned to receive NAD pills and the other sugar pills prepared to resemble the drug.

In none of the tests was there any significant difference between the NAD group and the sugar pill group. . . .

Dr. Kline said that although NAD apparently was not responsible for the improvement of Dr. Hoffer's patients, something else the Canadian psychiatrist did in the course of his tests might have helped. But since Dr. Hoffer did not have a matching group of patients who did not receive the drug, he said, benefits of treatment not specifically related to the drug cannot be ruled out. [Brody, p. 11.]

The Placebo Administrator

The characteristics of the placebo administrator are also of major importance. The healer should be dignified and efficient, and should be seen in impressive surroundings. Ritualistic paraphernalia may today include a nurse, a white coat or somber business suit, learned books, a framed diploma, a pipe, mysterious charts, and, not uncommonly, a long waiting list to indicate how busy and important the physician is. Lasagna and his associates (1954) refer to these considerations as the "pharmaceutical charade," but the individual in our society has associated them with previous experiences of improvement. The function of expectancy in treatment was recognized by Osler in 1892: "Faith in the gods or in the saints cures one, faith in little pills another, hypnotic suggestion a third, faith in a plain common doctor a fourth. . . . Faith in us, faith in our drugs and methods [is] the great stock in trade of the profession . . . the touchstone of success in medicine . . . and must be considered in discussing the foundation of therapeutics . . . a most precious commodity, without which we should be very badly off."

Throughout history individuals enacting the healer role have utilized the placebo reaction effectively, often without awareness of what they were doing, although in some instances cynically exploiting the effect for the "good of the patient." The following passage, dating from A.D. 1100, illustrates that placebo reaction and healing have had a long and intimate relation:

On his way [to the patient's bedside] he will try and learn from the person who came to fetch him as much as possible of the condition of the patient in order to put himself *au courant* of the affection he will have to treat, so that if, after having examined the urine and felt the pulse, he cannot learn the nature of the illness, he can by means of the facts previously ascertained at least inspire confidence in the patient by proving to him that he has divined something of the nature of his sufferings. . . . On departing the physician promises the patient he shall recover; to those who are about the sickbed, however, he must affirm that the patient is very ill; if the patient recovers the physician's reputation will be enhanced; should he die, the physician can state that the outcome was as he predicted: [Packard, in Harington, 1922, pp. 18–20, ascribed to Archimatheus of Salerno, ca. 1100.]

The Placebo Reactor

Many studies have investigated the characteristics of persons presumably susceptible to the effects of the placebo situation, but the findings have usually been contradictory and confusing. One of the most controversial points about placebo reactors, in fact, is whether they exist at all: Honigfeld, after an exhaustive survey of the literature, concludes that "the search for the placebo-reactor would appear to be a search for a fictitious character." (1964b.) This finding would be consistent with the view that under the appropriate set of contingencies (i.e., what is reinforcing to them) most people will enact the role of placebo reactor. The problem can be put in terms of finding the environmental stimuli that make the placebo response most likely, rather than of finding who *is* or *is not* a placebo reactor.

The Placebo

In the history of medicine, thousands of nostrums now thought to be physically and chemically worthless for the ailments for which they were used have "worked," at least with some people. A partial list, and one that could be extended almost indefinitely, man's vivid imagination being what it is, could include lizard's blood, crocodile dung, hoof of ass, putrid meat, spermatic fluid of frogs, horn of deer, animal excretions, unicorn's horn (ivory from an elephant), bezoar stones (gallstones from the stomach of animals such as goats), powdered Egyptian mummy, eunuch fat, emetics, worms, and urine. Consider the treatment Charles II endured at the hands of the best physicians of his day: "A pint of blood was extracted from his right arm, and a half-pint from his left shoulder, followed by an emetic, two physics, and an enema comprising fifteen substances; the royal head was then shaved and a blister raised; then a sneezing powder, more emetics, and bleeding, soothing potions, a plaster of pitch and pigeon dung on his feet, potions containing ten different substances, chiefly herbs, finally forty drops of extract of human skull, and the application of bezoar stone; after which his majesty died." (Van Dyke, 1947; for a more complete description, see Haggard, 1929.)

Placebo Effectiveness

A number of studies have reported results of the use of placebos for purposes of control on medical and psychological problems. Diehl (1940, cited in Haas et al., 1963) made a study of cold vaccines and found that the number of yearly colds was reduced by 55 percent in the vaccine group and by 61 percent in a control group receiving placebo injections. Lasagna and his associates (1954) gave saline injections to surgical patients suffering from steady and severe wound pains and found that 30 to 40 percent reported satisfactory relief. Of the 35 papers on essential hypertension that Ayman evaluated (1933), every paper reported success, although mistletoe, diathermy, watermelon extract, and Nauheim salts were some of the therapeutic agents. In Ayman's own work, 82 percent of the patients showed definite improvement after ingesting small amounts of very dilute hydrochloric acid.

A comprehensive review of placebo literature has been presented by Haas, Fink, and Hartfelder (1963). They found that in 25 studies involving 961 patients, 28.2 percent obtained relief of pain from placebo; similarly, of 4,588 people treated for headache, 61.9 percent responded favorably to placebo; of 4,908 people treated for migraine, 32.3 percent responded favorably to placebo; of 135 people treated for neurosis, 34 percent responded favorably to placebo; and of 828 people treated for psychosis, 19 percent responded favorably to placebo. Of equal interest is that the placebo and type of distress treated interacted and led to great variations in side-effects. For example, across 14 placebo studies reviewed by Haas, Fink, and Hartfelder, the range of dizziness reported was from 0 to 66 percent, sleepiness from 0 to 50 percent, apathy from 0 to 50 percent. The side-effects in each instance were those appropriate to the illness.

Wolf and Pinsky (1954) presented illustrations of other negative side-effects of placebo, including nausea in one case and, in another, a rash that a skin consultant called a "typical dermatitis medicamentosa." The rash cleared quickly after the medication was stopped. Even more interesting is that with particular instructions or prior experience, the "medication" may have effects opposite from those that should be expected on a purely physiological level. Wolf and Wolff (1947) reported that their now famous patient Tom was repeatedly given prostigmine, which induced abdominal cramps, diarrhea, as well as hyperanemia, hypersecretion, and hypermotility of the stomach. Subsequently the same response occurred not only to tap water and lactose capsules, but also to atropine sulfate, which usually has an inhibiting effect on gastric function.

As another illustration, a pregnant patient with excessive vomiting showed the usual response of nausea and vomiting to ipecac. These manifestations were accompanied by cessation of normal gastric contractions. When ipecac was given through a tube with strong assurance that it would relieve her vomiting, gastric contractions were resumed at the same interval after ingestion of the drug, and her nausea and vomiting were relieved. (Rosenthal and Frank, 1956.) Karkalas and Lal (1970) reported that 6 of 19 patients in their placebo group showed side effects, with nausea and vomiting being most frequent.

Placebo responses may be observed in nonmedical contexts: "South Dakota ordered its communities to start fluoridating their water on July 1. So folks started calling the Sioux Falls city hall on July 1, griping about the terrible-tasting fluoridated water. They were told gently the city hadn't started fluoridation because equipment wasn't delivered yet." (Herguth, 1970.)

Placebo Reaction and Role Enactment

A study by Schachter and Singer (1962) linked role enactment, modeling, and placebo reaction. It was hypothesized that when faced with a state of physiological arousal for which he has no ready explanation, a person will label this state in terms of the information currently available to him. Schachter and Singer's experiment was cast in the framework of a study of the effects of a vitamin supplement. The subjects were asked for permission to be given a small injection of "Suproxin." The subjects then received an injection of adrenalin or a placebo, depending upon whether they were in the experimental or in the control group. Adrenalin has a well-established effect on the sympathetic nervous system: within three to five minutes following the injection "systolic blood pressure increases markedly, heart rate increases somewhat, cutaneous blood flow decreases, while muscle and cerebral blood flow increase, blood sugar and lactic acid concentration increase, and respiration rate increases slightly. As far as the subject is concerned, the major subjective symptoms are palpitation, tremor, and sometimes a feeling of flushing and accelerated breathing." The placebo consisted of a saline solution injection which should have had no physiological effect.

Some of the subjects were correctly informed of the effects of "Suproxin"; others were not told anything about its effects; and still others were misinformed: "Your feet will feel numb, you will have an itching sensation." Then each subject was placed with another subject (in reality a stooge) who purportedly had also received "Suproxin." With half of the subjects the stooge behaved euphorically, while with the other subjects he behaved angrily. The experimenters rated the subjects in terms of euphoria or anger and also obtained self-reports of mood. The results clearly indicated that, consistent with the hypothesis, subjects were more susceptible or angry when they had no explanation of their own bodily states than when they did. Of further interest was that the level of arousal, both reported and observed, was greater in the placebo condition than in the adrenalin informed condition. It seemed likely that the placebo subjects were at least as physiologically aroused as the subjects receiving adrenalin, if not more so. Thus this study demonstrated that subjects are influenced in their enactment of roles by observation of what appear to be real models and, further, that there are subjective and objective physiological consequences of such role enactments.[5]

Role Enactment and the Demand Characteristics of a Situation

The implicit and explicit cues in a given situation affect an individual's role enactments. These cues may be manipulated to obtain a target behavior. A study by Orne and Scheibe (1964) on the sensory deprivation situation has important implications for the way in which an individual's expectancies determine the cues to which he will respond. Prior to this study most investigations of sensory deprivation treated it as a "real" phenomenon. Subjects who were isolated from environmental cues, such as pilots during snowstorms or captured servicemen being "brainwashed" (see Chapter 15), behaved in "strange" ways. The problem was first taken into the laboratory at McGill University. Subjects, usually college students, were put in isolation rooms in which as much external stimulation as possible was removed. For example, subjects would wear translucent goggles over their eyes and cardboard gauntlets over their forearms and hands (Bexton, Heron, and Scott, 1954). In some studies subjects were immersed in a tank of water at body temperature (Lilly, 1956).

Another instance of isolation dealt with subjects placed in tank-type respirators where movement and external stimuli were restricted or undifferentiable (Leiderman et al., 1958). The effects on behavior obtained in all these studies were usually profound and dramatic, and included hallucinatory experiences, spatial and temporal disorientation, decrements in psychological efficiency, intensification of visual imagery, and generally marked deterioration in intellectual and emotional behavior (Solomon et al., 1961). The results were so dramatic that some theoretical formulations linked sensory deprivation phenomenon to the development of psychotic behavior.

Orne and Scheibe (1964), however, were skeptical of interpretations which ignored the demand characteristics implicit in the experimental procedure involved in isolating an individual. The concept of demand characteristics is an important one, not only for sensory deprivation studies, but for all experimental studies involving human behavior. Orne (1962) defines the *demand characteristics* of an experimental situation as the "totality of cues which convey an experimental hypothesis to the subject." The cues may include campus rumors about the research conveyed while soliciting volunteers, the experimenter, the laboratory, and the implicit and explicit communications during the experiment itself. A number of sensory deprivation studies had incorporated "panic buttons"—devices for informing the experimenter that the subject could no longer stand the situation and wanted out (Zubek et al., 1961; Vernon et al., 1961). In a study by Freedman, Grunebaum, and Greenblatt (1961) subjects had to sign a formidable and frightening form, prior to being allowed to participate in the

---

[5] For additional studies on the effects of placebos and instructions on performance see Lyerly et al. (1964); Davison and Valins (1969); Dinnerstein and Halm (1970); Goldstein, Fink, and Mettee (1972); and Mills and Mintz (1972).

study, releasing the institution and the experimenters from responsibility for negative effects. In other studies subjects underwent a careful psychiatric and physical examination to make sure they could withstand the forthcoming experimental stress. All of these procedures involved communication of the experimenter's expectation of very unusual and dramatic subject behavior.

Orne and Scheibe deliberately manipulated the environmental cues communicating the expectancy of a bizarre behavior role. Two groups were exposed to the same basic set of physical conditions. The experimental group was exposed to pre-experimental conditions designed to imply that sensory deprivation effects were expected. The control group was led to expect that nothing was to happen. Subjects volunteered (at $2 per hour) to participate in a "psychological experiment in meaning deprivation." For the experimental group the study was conducted in a psychiatric hospital with the examiner wearing a white coat. A medical history was taken; a tray of drugs and medical instruments labeled "emergency tray" was in full view. The instructions stressed the importance of reporting unusual or hallucinatory experiences. The subjects were shown a red button marked "Emergency Alarm" which they could press to get out of the situation. They were told that a physician was immediately available. The isolation room itself was well-lit, noisy, and large, and the subjects' movements were not in any way restricted. They remained in the room for three or four hours.

The control subjects were treated in the same way except that they were not exposed to the "panic" cues—emergency tray, medical interview, white coat, available physician, and panic button. Instead they were told they were a control group for a sensory deprivation study. Pre- and post-tests of intellectual efficiency were given to both groups. The two groups differed significantly on post-tests involving both intellectual tasks and clinical measures of affect. The experimental group reported a significantly greater number of sensory-deprivation type symptoms than did the control group, including perceptual aberrations ("the walls of the room are starting to waver") and intellectual dullness (inability to concentrate, the occurrence of "blank periods," unpleasant affect, anxiety, spatial disorientation, and restlessness).[6] Orne and Scheibe concluded that the subjects were responding to the demand characteristics in the situation. The authors made clear that they do not question that sensory isolation in and of itself may have drastic effects on behavior, but most studies investigating this phenomenon have not controlled for the implicit demand characteristics.

Summary

The previous discussion of roles and expectancy provides a formulation of placebo reactions. The reputation of the therapist, reports of his previous successes, and the person's previous positive experiences with therapists all enhance the expectancy of help. Further, the patient's state of pain or distress leads to an increased alertness to any environmental indications of help.

Through a process of learning, measurable changes in physiological functions become associated with role enactments and eventually become an integral part of them. A report that illustrates experimenter effects and the intertwining of operant and respondent behavior is by Chapman, Chapman, and Brelje (1969). Prior research by Hess, Seltzer, and Shlien (1965) had indicated that when observing sexually arousing pictures, people's pupils dilated. This dilation is supposedly an involuntary reaction, resulting from Pavlovian conditioning. What Chapman and his co-workers did was to present pictures with both sexually arousing and neutral

[6] For similar conceptual and empirical material see Jackson and Pollard (1962) and Jackson and Kelly (1962). For a recent survey, see Zubek (1969).

content to male undergraduates. The experiment was conducted by two different researchers, one aloof and businesslike, the other casual and outgoing. The dilation effect to sexually arousing material was obtained with the latter experimenter but not with the former. In part, at least, the subjects' relationship with the examiner and their view of what was permissible affected responses that were usually considered involuntary.

HYPNOSIS

Hypnosis is an important area of investigation historically, theoretically, and therapeutically. It enters into the study of abnormal behavior at this point for a number of reasons. First, it provides an example of a category of behavior or role enactment that is unusual, unexpected, and seemingly abnormal. The explanatory concept is called hypnosis, and the operational presumption is that something special occurs when the person enters a hypnotic *trance*. It is difficult to obtain a clear statement of what a hypnotic trance is: experts cannot reliably separate people who are in a trance (induced by a hypnotist) from people who are simulating a trance (acting as if they were in one in order to fool the experimenter). Second, if the area of hypnotic behavior can be brought within the province of normal behavior, it will provide a strong illustration of many unusual, unexpected, and startling behaviors resulting from reasonable reaction to cues. The behaviors emitted by a person enacting the hypnotic role are real, but the explanation of something special, hypnosis, may be unnecessary.

The career of Franz Anton Mesmer (1734-1815) represents the starting point of modern hypnosis. Mesmer was trained as a physician in Vienna, where he wrote his doctoral dissertation in 1776 on "The Influence of the Planets on the Human Body by means of a Magnetic Fluid." Mesmer heard of a Jesuit priest, Father Maximilian Hell, who was obtaining amazing cures of bodily pain by the use of a steel magnet, and started to use similar procedures.[7] Mesmer soon obtained some dramatic cures, especially with women who displayed convulsive disorders. A committee was appointed by the Faculty of Medicine in Vienna to investigate Mesmer's methods. The committee's conclusion was that these cures were merely based on "imagination," and as a consequence Mesmer was expelled from the local medical profession. Mesmer was confident of his new "discovery" and went to Paris, where he felt that there would be a more enlightened atmosphere for his work. He was extremely successful in his Paris clinic, but he never achieved the professional acceptance for which he so desperately strived.

Mesmer always displayed his treatment in a flamboyant manner:

Richly-stained glass shed a dim religious light on his spacious saloons, which were almost covered with mirrors. Orange-blossoms scented all the air of his corridors; incense of the most expensive kinds burned in antique vases on his chimney-pieces; aeolian harps sighed melodious music from distant chambers; while sometimes a sweet female voice, from above or below, stole softly upon the mysterious silence

---

[7] MacKay (1841; republished, 1932) cites the use of magnets by Paracelsus; the continuing use of "weapon salve" and the "powder of sympathy" (which involved stroking movements); Valentine Greatraks (flourished ca. 1660), who "imagined that he derived his powers direct from heaven, and continued to throw people into fits, and bring them to their senses again . . ." (p. 313); and Francisco Bagnone of Italy, who "had only to touch weak women with his hands, or sometimes (for the sake of working more effectively upon their fanaticism) with a relic, to make them fall into fits, and manifest all the symptoms of magnetism." (p. 316.) MacKay also cites the curative "Convulsionaries of St. Medard," who healed through what Mesmer called "crisis" (and we would call trance) in Paris at the start of the eighteenth century. The point is that Mesmer made use of elements that were already well established in the social climate of the era.

that was kept in the house, and insisted upon from all visitors. . . .

The following was the mode of operation: In the centre of the saloon was placed an oval vessel, about four feet in its longest diameter, and one foot deep. In this were laid a number of wine-bottles, filled with magnetised water, well corked-up, and disposed in radii, with their necks outwards. Water was then poured into the vessel so as just to cover the bottles, and filings of iron were thrown in occasionally to heighten the magnetic effect. The vessel was then covered with an iron cover, pierced through with many holes, and was called the *baquet*. From each hole issued a long movable rod of iron, which the patients were to apply to such parts of their bodies as were afflicted. Around this *baquet* the patients were directed to sit, holding each other by the hand, and pressing their knees together as closely as possible, to facilitate the passage of the magnetic fluid from one to the other.

Then came in the assistant magnetisers, generally strong, handsome young men, to pour into the patient from their finger-tips fresh streams of the wondrous fluid. They embraced the patient between the knees, rubbed them gently down the spine and the course of the nerves, using gentle pressure upon the breasts of the ladies, and staring them out of countenance to magnetise them by the eye! All this time the most rigorous silence was maintained, with the exception of a few wild notes on the harmonica or the piano-forte, or the melodious voice of a hidden opera-singer swelling softly at long intervals. Gradually the cheeks of the ladies began to glow, their imaginations to become inflamed and off they went, one after the other, in convulsive fits. Some of them sobbed and tore their hair, others laughed till the tears ran from their eyes, while others shrieked and screamed and yelled till they became insensible altogether.

This was the crisis of the delirium. In the midst of it, the chief actor made his appearance, waving his wand, like Prospero, to work new wonders. Dressed in a long robe of lilac-coloured silk richly embroidered with gold flowers, bearing in his hand a white magnetic rod, and with a look of dignity which would have sat well on an eastern caliph, he marched with solemn strides into the room. He awed the still sensible by his eye, and the violence of their symptoms diminished. He stroked the insensible with his hands upon the eyebrows and down the spine; traced figures upon their breast and abdomen with his long white wand, and they were restored to consciousness. They became calm, acknowledged his power, and said they felt streams of cold or burning vapour passing through their frames, according as he waved his wand or his fingers before them. [Mackey, 1841, pp. 324–25 in 1932 edition.]

This would be followed by what is called the "crisis." The crisis is of interest, among other reasons, because it illustrates fads in expected hypnotic behavior. Bailly, a historian of astronomy,

. . . has described the scenes of which he was a witness in the course of his investigation. "The sick persons, arranged in great numbers and in several rows around the *baquet,* receive the magnetism by all these means: by the iron rods which convey it to them from the *baquet*—by the cords wound round their bodies —by the connexions of the thumb, which conveys to them the magnetism of their neighbours —and by the sounds of a piano-forte, or of an agreeable voice, diffusing the magnetism in the air. The patients were also directly magnetised by means of the finger and wand of the magnetiser moved slowly before their faces, above or behind their heads, and on the diseased parts, always observing the direction of the holes. The magnetiser acts by fixing his eyes on them. But above all, they are magnetised by the application of his hands and the pressure of his fingers on the hypochondres and on the regions of the abdomen; an application often continued for a long time—sometimes for several hours.

"Meanwhile the patients in their different conditions present a very varied picture. Some are calm, tranquil, and experience no effect. Others cough, spit, feel slight pains, local or general heat, and have sweatings. Others again are agitated and tormented with convulsions. These convulsions are remarkable in regard to the number affected with them, to their duration and force. As soon as one begins to be convulsed, several others are affected. The commissioners have observed some of these convulsions last more than three hours. They are accompanied with expectorations of a muddy viscous water, brought away by violent efforts.

Sometimes streaks of blood have been observed in this fluid. These convulsions are characterised by the precipitous, involuntary motion of all the limbs, and of the whole body; by the contraction of the throat—by the leaping motions of the hypochondria and the epigastrium—by the dimness and wandering of the eyes—by piercing shrieks, tears, sobbing, and immoderate laughter. They are preceded or followed by a state of languor or reverie, a kind of depression, and sometimes drowsiness. The smallest sudden noise occasions a shuddering; and it was remarked, that the change of measure in the airs played on the piano-forte had a great influence on the patients. A quicker motion, a livelier melody, agitated them more, and renewed the vivacity of their convulsions.

"Nothing is more astonishing than the spectacle of these convulsions. One who has not seen them can form no idea of them. The spectator is as much astonished at the profound repose of one portion of the patients as at the agitation of the rest—at the various accidents which are repeated, and at the sympathies which are exhibited. Some of the patients may be seen devoting their attention exclusively to one another, rushing towards each other with open arms, smiling, soothing, and manifesting every symptom of attachment and affection. All are under the power of the magnetiser; it matters not in what state of drowsiness they may be, the sound of his voice—a look, a motion of his hand—brings them out of it. Among the patients in convulsions there are always observed a great many women and very few men." [Mackay, 1841, pp. 327–28 in 1932 edition.]

Because people obtained relief from these methods, Mesmer achieved a large and influential following, including the Marquis de Lafayette, Louis XVI, and Marie Antoinette. However, he also wanted approval from the professional and scientific men of the day as represented by the French Academy. After repeated battles a committee of prominent men was appointed in 1784 to investigate Mesmer and his techniques. This group included Benjamin Franklin, then the American ambassador to Paris, Lavoisier, the discoverer of oxygen, Bailly, and Dr. Guillotin, the physician who proposed the use of the decapitating machine. Like the earlier committee in Vienna, this committee labeled Mesmerism "imagination" and dismissed Mesmer as a fraud and charlatan. Their report has three important aspects: the first is that they could find no magnetic fluid, nothing to weigh, observe, or measure. Magnetic fluid was outside the realm of physical science. Second, they found that if they presented a magnetized object without the person's being told that it was such, there was no crisis; but if they told him that something that was actually unmagnetized was magnetized, they could obtain the crisis. In short, suggestion without magnetism led to crisis, but magnetism without suggestion did not. This is the very thing that is so important: the active ingredient was *interpersonal*—the person, the suggestion, the situation—rather than *biophysical*. The third point is that the academicians felt that the behavior during the crisis was scandalous and that the crises themselves might lead to illness.

There is in this report the most important observation on human behavior: "That which has been proved through our examination of magnetism is that *man can affect man* . . . almost at will by stimulating his imagination." (Bromberg, 1959, p. 173.) Mesmer lost the right to practice in France, died in obscurity in Switzerland in 1815, and has an enduring place in the history of psychotherapy.

Two different and opposing views as to the nature of hypnosis have been labeled by Sutcliffe (1960) as "skeptical" and "credulous." The credulous viewpoint is that there is a clear distinction between trance behavior and simulation. In the credulous view it is believed that hypnosis can produce special behavior which transcends the normal. In effect the credulous view proposes special hypnotic phenomena apparently disproportionate to the stimulation and clearly distinguishable from normal behavior. The skeptics, on the other hand, do not accept hypnotic behavior and testimony about it at face value. They consider it likely that any behavior obtainable in the "trance" state may be simulated and matched in a non-trance state.

Skeptics are apt to interpret hypnotic behavior in terms of variables such as role-taking and demand characteristics, and to consider it, for all of its apparent bizarrities, to be no different from any other normal behavior. Their evidence lies in the demonstration that all of the apparently unique behaviors observed under hypnosis are reproducible without hypnosis. Rosenhan (1967), in reviewing the literature in this field, concludes that "without exception the well-controlled experimental evidence reveals no difference between the performance of hypnotized subjects and either their own or others' waking motivated performance." Evidence from the studies of Barber (1965a), Sarbin (1965), Coe and Sarbin (1966), and Thorne (1967) confirms this observation.[8]

Styles of hypnotic induction and hypnotic trance change over time. When the literature is surveyed for common, crucial elements, very few are found. Hilgard (1965, p. 160), perhaps the most persuasive and challenging of current writers holding a credulous rather than a skeptical view, writes as follows: "Without attempting a formal definition of hypnosis, the field appears well enough specified by the increased suggestibility of the subjects following induction procedures stressing relaxation, free play of imagination, and the withdrawal of reality supports through closed eyes, narrowing of attention, and concentration on the voice of the hypnotist."

It is important to emphasize that there are *no* universal behaviors designating hypnosis. Rather, such behaviors change as a function of time and place. A hypnotized subject today behaves differently than did Mesmer's subjects. Within any given time and place, however, there is usually a clear consensus about the behaviors called for in the proper hypnotic role enactment. At present, books, movies, and television provide ample information about currently expected hypnotic role behavior.

Orne (1959) demonstrated how the role enactments of a hypnotized person are influenced by the type of information available and the authoritativeness of the source of that information. Orne lectured about and demonstrated hypnosis to two groups of students. One class demonstration involved, embedded among the usual hypnotic behaviors, a "spontaneous dominant hand catalepsy." In the literature on hypnosis, such a behavior had *never* been reported. At a later time, volunteers for hypnosis from among the students who had witnessed this demonstration preponderantly emitted "spontaneous dominant hand catalepsy" when they were hypnotized. Among the students who were in the group that did not witness the special behavior, *none* displayed it when hypnotized. Klinger (1970) and Sheehan and Bowman (1973) provide additional evidence that observing a model's responsiveness affects the observer's later responsiveness to hypnotic induction.

The evidence seems clear that all of the apparently unique and unusual behaviors associated with hypnotic performance such as stronger motor performance and heightened physiological responsiveness can be matched both by individuals simulating the hypnotic role and by persons in the normal state who have been reinforced to enact a role consistent with the demand characteristics of the situation (Krasner, Ullmann, and Fisher, 1964; Krasner, Knowles, and Ullmann, 1965). Glass and Barber (1961) have demonstrated that pla-

---

[8] It should be explicit that to say that there can be *no* difference between hypnotic and "normal" states would require proving the null hypothesis, something which (see Chapter 3) cannot be done in an inductive science. What can be done is to show, as noted in the Rosenhan quotation, that the special state, hypnosis, is not required, and is superfluous.

cebos labeled as powerful hypnotic drugs resulted in performance equivalent to that of the performance of hypnotized subjects. In another study, Barber and Hahn (1963) found that simple instructions to relax were as effective in inducing relaxation (as measured by muscle action potentials, respiration, heart rate, and skin potential) as standard hypnotic induction procedures.[9]

Sarbin's definition of *role enactment* is "the performance of patterned behaviors where the antecedent conditions include assignment to a position in the social structure." (1964b, p. 177.) In arguing that role enactment influences psychological change, Sarbin presents important data demonstrating that it also produces changes in somatic processes (1964b, 1965). Lewis and Sarbin (1943), demonstrated that hungry

[9] The two areas of hypnosis that students ask about most frequently are stage hypnosis and age regression. The interested student will enjoy Meeker and Barber's (1971) exposition of tactics used by stage hypnotists and Barber's analysis of unusual behavioral feats such as those performed by Yogis (Dahl and Barber, 1969; Barber, 1970). Studies by Staples and Wilensky (1968) and Parrish, Lundy, and Leibowitz (1968) also cast doubts on the stage effects as being due to hypnosis. A particularly interesting problem involves reports of increased hallucinations under hypnosis. Spanos and Barber (1968) note that when honest reports were demanded, nearly half the student nurses with whom they worked reported clearly hearing a suggested auditory hallucination, and nearly one-third reported seeing a suggested visual hallucination. The baseline of occurrence is higher than zero, and hypnosis did not significantly increase the rate. In later work, Spanos, McPeake, and Carter (1973) indicated how pretesting itself may influence the report of visual hallucinations. Miller, Lundy, and Galbraith (1970) dealt with the verity of visual hallucinations during hypnosis. By use of colored filters, visualized under hypnosis, these authors demonstrated that the reported hallucinated filter did not function as an actual one. This type of analysis may be applied to acupuncture. Clark and Yang (1974), for example, note that overt pain responses decreased under acupuncture but that sensory decision theory revealed no difference in discriminability, that is, no physiological change. The results depend on psychological variables and not upon a special state.

hypnotized subjects who were also good role-takers were able to inhibit gastric contractions by the imaginary eating of their normal breakfast. There have been a number of studies (Barber, 1959; Gelfand, Ullmann, and Krasner, 1963; Blitz and Dinnerstein, 1968; Satran and Goldstein, 1973); in which *pain thresholds* were raised as a result of instructions, distraction and placebos. The tolerance for real pain can be enhanced by the instructions to the individual as to what is expected of him in his role as experimental subject. Further, deliberate role enactment may be so effective that it becomes indistinguishable from "real" behavior. Orne's research (1959) demonstrated that individuals simulating hypnosis (enacting the role demands of the hypnotized subject as they had previously learned them) could *not* be differentiated from subjects who were performing the hypnotized role after having undergone traditional hypnotic induction. The role of the trance is further questioned by Gandolfo's (1971) finding that whether the suggestion was given prior to or during it made no difference.

Summary

Given the present situation and the subjects' prior experience, is hypnosis a special state or is it normal behavior? Theoretical difficulties of the credulous position have not been emphasized, e.g., the categorization of posthypnotic suggestions when hypnosis itself is a special state. Rather the evidence cited indicates that no concept of a special state is required. This does not mean that the changed behavior observed in the hypnotic (or placebo) situation is not genuine. It means that the effects can and must be explained (and later utilized) as part of normal behavior. It is also important to note that only a minority of people attain such levels of hypnotic role enactments that the striking phenomena of hypnosis are obtained. With proper shaping, an equal percentage of the population can emit these behaviors without the situation being labeled hypnotic induction.[10]

THE PSYCHOLOGICAL EXPERIMENT

Yet another way of demonstrating the effects of a role enactment upon behavior is by examining the effects upon the performance of people when they enter the role of experimenter or subject in psychological research. The experimenter role is analogous to that of other influencers of behavior: the interviewer, therapist, physician, or hypnotist. Participating in a situation labeled "research" may lead a person to behave in ways that are appropriate but discontinuous with his other activities (Krasner and Ullmann, 1973 especially pp. 202–30).

As has been noted in the previous section on hypnosis, once a subject has entered a situation with a particular label, he does his best to perform in terms of what he thinks is expected of him. Just as labeling a situation hypnosis has consequences for the kinds of behaviors the participant emits, so does labeling a situation an experiment or research. Orne (1962) found that no matter how boring, noxious, or meaningless a task he could devise, experimental subjects would continue working at it for many hours and would display little overt hostility. Rather, as indicated by their postexperimental statements, they attributed some meaning to the task and developed a rationale for their continuing it.

Milgram (1963, 1965, 1974), in a series of studies designed to test "obedience," demonstrated that subjects will obey an experimenter even to the point of inflicting painful electric shock on others. Milgram told his subjects they were to train others to perfect performances by administering increasing amounts of electric shock. Although Milgram's subjects would protest strongly against continuing the task, and some became quite disturbed at what they were doing, the majority continued to shock others up to a presumed 450-volt limitation even when seeing and hearing the obvious distress of their victims (who were really stooges). Research by Orne and Evans (1965) is a further illustration of the effect on people's behavior of participating in an "experiment."

The experimenter as well as the subject responds to these situational demands. Rosenthal and his associates (Rosenthal, 1966) have provided a series of studies dealing with the biasing influence of experimenters' beliefs in a large number of different situations. These studies have included work with human beings and with animals. In studies employing animals, for example, experimenters who were led to believe that their rats had been bred for superior learning ability obtained performances superior to those obtained by experimenters who were led to believe that their rats had been bred for inferior learning ability (Rosenthal and Fode, 1963a, 1963b; Rosenthal and Lawson, 1964). Thus, even in apparently as objective an undertaking as running experiments with laboratory animals, the bias of the experimenter may influence the results.

Another important illustration of biasing, relevant for understanding the development of deviant behavior, involves the demonstration by Rosenthal and Jacobson (1966, 1968) on the influence of bias on teachers' behavior toward children and the consequences of this bias. A nonverbal test of intelligence, disguised as a test devised to predict academic "blooming or intellectual gain," was administered to all children in an elementary school. In 18 classes of the school, 20 percent of the children were assigned to the experimental conditions by means of a table of random numbers. Teachers were told the test indicated that

---

[10] Morgan (1928) early marshaled arguments for the contention that hypnosis is based on suggestibility and that suggestibility, in turn, is a learned response to situations.

these children would show unusual intellectual gains during the academic year. The experimental treatment for these children, then, consisted only of being identified to their teacher as children who would show "unusual intelligence gains." Eight months after the experimental conditions were instituted, all children were retested with the same test, and a change score was computed for each child. The children in the experimental group whose teachers had been led to expect great intellectual gain showed a significantly greater gain on the test, a "Pygmalion effect," than did the children in the control group. The lower the grade level, the greater was the effect. For example, among the first three grades, the experimental subjects increased 24 points *in excess* of the 16 points gained by the controls. The teachers' expectations were presumably translated into behavior that led to different environments for the two groups.

Meichenbaum, Bowers, and Ross (1969), working with institutionalized adolescent female offenders repeated the Pygmalion effect and observed that some teachers increased their positive interactions with late bloomers while others decreased their negative ones with late bloomers. Rubovits and Maehr (1971) observed an increase in the teacher's request of statements from the group called "gifted," and "gifted" subjects were praised more frequently than "nongifted" ones.

Taking another step in changing "placebo" or "bias" into a direct-influence manipulation, Meichenbaum and Smart (1971), working with academically borderline freshmen students, told one group that they were "late bloomers" and compared the effect of this statement on them with two other groups. The effect was greater self-confidence, expectancy of success, and perception of course relevance as well as a relative improvement during the courses.

Bernstein (1973) and Smith, Diener, and Beaman (in press) have manipulated "demand characteristics" to favor or inhibit approach to a feared stimulus. For example, Bernstein (1970) reported that when female college students who had reported very much fear or terror in response to rats were tested on a task ostensibly designed to assess their ability to "communicate nonverbally with lower organisms," only four of 100 failed to pick up and handle a live rat. These researches, as well as careful, scholarly analyses of laboratory studies (e.g., Bernstein and Paul, 1971), as distinct from target behaviors in field settings, are important in the evaluation of data for clinical and theoretical formulations of behavior therapy. But they also indicate the strength of demand characteristics and how various aspects of the experimental situation itself may be studied (e.g., Sheehan, 1970; Bruehl and Solar, 1970; Holmes and Applebaum, 1970; Silverman, Shulman, and Wiesenthal, 1970).

A Rosenthal-type experimenter-bias effect has been noted in hypnosis (Trofer and Tart, 1964), and, most relevant for the view of hypnosis followed in this chapter, Barber, Dalal, and Calverley (1968) have indicated how small changes in questions asked of subjects and the remarks of the experimenter influence subjects' reports of what they experienced. When asked, Did you feel you could resist the suggestions?, 22 percent of the subjects stated they could not do so, while when asked, Did you feel you could not resist the suggestions?, 83 percent said they could not. We may think of the biased question as a demand characteristic. Consistent with the concept of changed behavior through role enactment, we may also note that the biased questionnaire itself may become an instrument of behavior change (Dillehay and Jernigan, 1970) in that, by the act of answering, the person has taken a public stand and may thus "commit" himself (Kiesler, 1971) to a course of action. We should note that there may well be a relation between an experimenter's background—e.g., rural/urban, native-born grandparents, etc.—and his conclusions. An example in the area of conclusions about differences in racial intelligence is presented by Sherwood and Nataupsky (1968).

SUMMARY

This chapter introduced the concept of role and role enactment, the patterning of large units of behavior resulting from learning procedures discussed in the previous chapters. It discussed a number of role enactment situations germane to abnormal behavior and its understanding: the sick role, the placebo response, sensory deprivation, hypnosis, and being involved in experimentation. In these situations, behavior is systematically influenced, and it need not be argued that the person is faking or that his behavior is unconsciously determined by intrapsychic conflicts. Rather, people respond to situations on the basis of previous experience and present expectations. Once they so respond, the very responses they make may lead to further changes of both a physiological (respondent) and a motoric (operant) nature.

approaches to abnormality
ANCIENT AND MEDIEVAL

6

The major thesis of this book is that the concept of abnormal behavior is a human creation and that models, labels, and deductions are human acts that are maintained because they solve problems. A model or paradigm will continue to be used until it breaks under the burden of inconsistent data or until a new paradigm is more effective at solving problems (Kuhn, 1970). The model of abnormal behavior a person has greatly influences what behaviors he will pay attention to and what behaviors he will consider insignificant.

It is important to note that the same is true of the writing of history (Meyerhoff, 1959; Carr, 1961). Smith, 1964; The historian selects and organizes information that he considers important, that illuminates the area of his investigation. He actively searches for and reevaluates the past largely in order to understand the present. This may be seen clearly, for example, in the plastic arts, in which there are fluctuations in the popularity and valuation of certain artists (Reitlinger, 1961; Rush, 1961) depending on the social trends of the age (Hauser, 1958, 1963), on the formulations of "tastemakers" (Lynes, 1954; Venturi, 1964), and, particularly at present, on which artists have an "impact on" other artists (Rosenberg, 1969, 1971). Artists are discovered, rediscovered, and even created. History is a continuing creation by the present. The models of abnormal behavior authors use determine the point at which they start their historical surveys and what people and events they consider salient. At present, most histories of abnormal psychology are written from the viewpoint of the medical model. Thus, they give detailed descriptions of the long struggle of medicine to gain its "rightful" dominance in the field of "sick" behavior (see Zilboorg and Henry, 1941, p. 41).

The history of abnormal psychology is related not solely, or even predominantly, to the history of medicine but rather to the history of culture, societies, theologies, philosophies, jurisprudence, politics, and the sciences.

A historical perspective has the same corrective value as cross-cultural information: it indicates that things need not necessarily be the way they are at any one time or place. Just as the great anthropologists of the 1920s and 1930s (Benedict, 1934; Boas, 1938, 1940; Linton, 1936, 1945; Lowie, 1948; Malinowski, 1926; and Mead 1935) challenged certain assumptions about "human nature," so Szasz (1961, 1971) used a historical approach to challenge the very concept of mental illness.

SOME MODELS

While elements of different models may be observed in every era, the reader may gain some orientation to the following roughly chronological material by reference to the models to be touched on. Any outline of paragraph length is destined to be arbitrary and oversimplified; nevertheless, at this point we will organize the material on the basis of presumed cause (etiology) and follow the outline suggested by Daws (1967). The earliest theories may

approaches to abnormality: ancient and medieval

be called *supernatural theories,* according to which abnormal behavior results from posession by evil spirits and treatment may be physical, such as trephining the skull (boring holes) to let the spirit out, or ritualistic (exorcism). Different theories may exist side by side; for example, in February, 1969, there were reports of the sentencing in Switzerland of two people who had killed a 17-year-old woman while attempting to beat the devil out of her (*Chicago Daily News,* February 6, 1969, p. 15; *Time,* February 7, 1969, p. 30).

A second set of theories may be called *weak-will theories.* Here the abnormal behavior is evidence of voluntary indulgence of one's baser human nature. Moral exhortation, religious stricture, and exile from the company of "decent" people may be used as treatment. Prevention might take the forms of prohibition of temptations (such as a ban on alcohol or X-rated movies until some advanced age such as 21) or a strengthening of the moral fiber by appropriately dull required courses.

The following theories are genuine medical theories. What is called abnormal behavior may be the direct or indirect result of genetic abnormality. A good example of genetic theories may be found in the area of retardation in the pattern called *Down's syndrome* or *Mongolism,* although even here, the mother's age and number of prior births (not directly genetic factors) seem associated. It is possible that intelligence, ability to deal with stress, and rapidity of conditioning are influenced by a number of genes; that people differ in this regard; and that, therefore, some people are more prone to emit behavior called abnormal than others (Eysenck and Rachman, 1965; Rosenthal, 1971).

Other physical abnormalities that may lead to behavioral difficulties are due to malnutrition on the one hand and ingestion of poisonous substances (either by the individual or by the mother during pregnancy) on the other. An example of the former is the type of retardation called *cretinism,* in which iodine is lacking; an example of the latter is the effect of the drug thalidomide when taken by the mother in the first three months of pregnancy.

Another type of physical damage is due to neurological, metabolic, or other change of physical functioning occurring through accidents (such as brain injury in traffic or war) or disease. The classic example of a true medical model is *paresis,* the effect of tertiary syphilis of the central nervous system.

Whenever there is a deviation from physiological normality, especially if it is prolonged, the person is faced with making new adjustments. Selye (1956) has discussed this matter in physiological terms. At this point we may say that disruption of normal physical functioning has been demonstrated to underlie behavioral changes in retardation and in brain syndromes. Physical changes are at least correlates of psychophysiological disorders and prolonged addictions.

Prevention and treatment for such true medical disorders may involve public health measures such as sanitation, enrichment of the diet such as the addition of vitamins or minerals to bread and water, prohibition of the use of damaging chemicals industrially such as lead in paint, increased facilities for early diagnosis and treatment (including genetic counseling), the use of specific treatments such as penicillin for syphilitic infection, and social experiences such as environmental enrichment at early ages.

Some of the very finest research workers in the field are devoted to following up and extending the true medical model. It is not a matter of whether this model is right or wrong, but under what conditions and for what behaviors, is it correct.

The *medical analogue* theories are primarily, but not wholly, derived from, or elaborations of, the work of Freud. Freud's theories will be presented in Chapter 8 and the impact of his work in Chapter 9. At this point we will note only the emphasis on biological impulses and their satisfactions in a manner similar to physical homeostasis, the concepts of set stages of psychosexual development, specific trauma such as sexual assaults or bereavements, and disorders (limited to and within the individual) involving concepts such as frustration, conflict between impulses or elements of the psyche, repression, and anxiety. Just as neurological damage may lead to decreased ability, so lack of certain psychosexual gratifications may lead to a weakened ego. Just as there are physical stresses, so frustration, conflict, and anxiety are psychological stresses. Just as prolonged physiological imbalance may lead to relatively permanent bodily changes, so frustration of psychological needs will lead to character formations. Two concepts are crucial for a set of ideas to be called a medical analogue theory: one, the concept that there is a pattern of behavior that in and of itself is normal, such as exists for physical functioning, so that a person may be called sick without reference to prior or current environmental contingencies; and two, a treatment concept that views the disturbing behavior as a symptom to be treated indirectly by reference to the "real" or underlying causes which are within the individual and associated with his personality structure.

For medical analogue theories (what Daws in 1967 called developmental, specific-trauma, frustration, conflict, and interpersonal relationship theories), prevention and treatment call for the establishment of interpersonal conditions that facilitate self-expression, insight, and improved methods of gaining satisfaction.

Two relatively new theories may follow from, or be directly opposed to, medical analogue theories: theories of society and learning formulations. Learning theoretical terms were employed by Dollard and Miller (1951) to translate psychoanalytic terms and procedures into psychological language. The result, however, was a medical analogue theory. At a societal level, crime, divorce, suicide, unemployment, institutionalization, level of education, infant mortality, racism, illegitimacy, environmental pollution, coercive rather than cohesive practices, and many other problems may be taken as a measure of the sickness or health of a society and, indirectly, as stress on individuals living within that society. It is possible to talk of societies "breaking down" (Zusman, 1969) in the same way one may talk of a person having a "nervous breakdown." Just as deviance from a presumed norm of desirable behavior is taken as evidence of abnormality in and of itself, so the criteria noted above may be taken as justification for interventions that may circumvent democratic political procedures. Finally, the manifest problem—for example, a riot—may be called symptomatic of an underlying problem, and dealing with the specific difficulty may be rejected or delayed because it is symptomatic treatment that does not get at the fundamental, underlying causes.

Alternately, societies may be viewed from a systems (Churchman, 1969), ecological (Barker, 1968), or learning (Skinner, 1971) approach. The question may then be asked: Is it by accident or design that schools, businesses, and nations order their priorities, make opportunities for different behaviors available, and pay-off different modes of adjustment? (Homans, 1961; Krasner and Ullman, 1973.) There is no such thing as a "Society," but rather there are people composing the organization, nation, or social group. These people are responsive, as individuals, to reinforcing contingencies. A view of society as focus for change, then, is an extension of the concepts introduced earlier for the development, maintenance, and change of individual behavior.

As with this last view of social theories, learning approaches may deal with manifest behavior as changeworthy rather than as symptomatic. The present volume is written from this theoretical position and no further elaboration will be given at this time.

Orientation

We have said that history is written from the viewpoint of different models. Consistent with the definition of abnormal psychology used in this book, the kinds of questions that must be asked as any era is surveyed are: Who were the sanctioned labelers of the period? What implicit models of normality were they using? What behaviors were labeled deviant? What were the techniques used to change the undesirable behavior or to move the labeled individual toward the then current norm?

"PRIMITIVE MAN"

In the long course of man's existence, he has left written records or decipherable artifacts for only a brief span of time. The tens of thousands of years prior to the Greek, Egyptian, and biblical periods are usually lumped together under the heading "primitive man." Contemporary knowledge of the structure of primitive society is conjectural and frequently based on extrapolations from observations of isolated societies that have managed to survive to the present day.

Primitive man is usually dismissed as being superstitious, spirit ridden, and animistic. For example, skulls found in Peru with small holes cut through the forehead have survived from the Stone Age. This kind of opening is now called a trephine. Because animistic beliefs are attributed to primitive man, the usual interpretation given to trephines is that the holes were used to permit evil spirits to escape from inside the skull.[1] A reasonable alternative explanation is that the holes may have been intended to relieve pressure on the brain by removing bone fragments.

[1] An operation similar to a present-day lobotomy might have occurred if a portion of the brain had to be removed because it was the home of evil spirits.

This alternative is usually not considered because it would imply too sophisticated a view of primitive man. Yet trephined skulls have been found mostly in areas where there have also been found weapons of a type that could produce skull fractures and small bone fragments.

Extrapolating from the anthropological reports of current preliterate societies, it might be argued that primitive man's sophistication in treating abnormal behavior is underestimated. Over a period of time the professional healers of any society learn the procedures which are most effective in influencing their "clients." (Torrey, 1973a) The *rationales* for their procedures differ from those of modern science, but the *procedures* themselves may be quite similar to current techniques.[2] When the shaman (priest, healer, magician) was called in to heal a sick person, he would perform a ritual attended by the patient's relatives and other onlookers. The seance was carried out in a darkened room. Among many tribes it was begun with singing and beating of drums. When an intense pitch of emotion and attention had been reached, and while the audience continued to sing and drum loudly, the shaman would have a "seizure." He would fall unconscious to the floor and would rise after a time with changed visage, and, possessed by his "spirit," carry on the drama.

The shaman or primitive therapist might

[2] For example, Hays (1964, p. 171) cites what we would call an example of aversive conditioning in the treatment of enuresis: "In parts of West Africa this is accomplished by placing a certain type of snail on the inside of the thigh, this snail staying immobile when dry but starting to move at once when wetted; the moving snail wakes the child and it is credibly reported that, as a conditioning stimulus, the sensation is hard to beat." Papageorgiou (1969, p. 117) notes a use of environmental consequences by some psychiatrically unsophisticated people in Greece: "A trough full of water is put near the bed of the patient so that, when the somnambulant gets up to walk, he treads in the water and he is awakened. This takes place several times and finally the patient is cured."

then go about his treatment as follows: First, he might provide evidence of his power by reciting how he was designated by the gods and how he had cured many other people. He might well perform some magic tricks to prove his skills. He might assign to the patient a meaningful social task which was within his power and changed his role from social outcast to social participant. A seance might be held at which the significant others of the community would confess their misdeeds toward the person being treated or make promises about their future behavior. The shaman might perform a therapeutic maneuver, such as killing the spirit symbolically, sucking it out of the person (and spitting out a bloody piece of rag he had in his mouth or removing a stone he had palmed), invoking the gods, and the like. Finally, the shaman might make a prediction or assign further socially meaningful or penitential acts.

If the person did not respond to the "demand characteristics" (see Chapter 5) of this situation, the burden of proof was on him to show that he was not impious and indeed deserving of his fate. Of great import was the fact that the form of these demand characteristics was consistent with the person's entire life style and social beliefs. In modern Africa, contemporary scientific medicine, at times, needs to be clothed in the culturally understandable content of the natives in order to be effective. Scientific medicine is as incomprehensible a magical procedure to some non-Western people as their native medical procedures would be to Americans.

The methods the shaman uses and his society accepts, develop from the concepts that his society holds on the nature of the causes and cures of disease. Thus Eskimos (from whose ritual part of the foregoing description was drawn) believed that disease was caused by one of four processes: the departure of the soul from the body; a violation of a tribal taboo; the development of a disease due to the sorcery of an enemy; or the magical intrusion of an alien object into the body. The treatment the shaman used was specific to the "cause" of the disease. If, for example, the "diagnosis" were of an "object intrusion," then the dramatic display of the intruding stone by the shaman was clear evidence to all, especially to the patient, that a "cure" had indeed been effected. (J. M. Murphy, 1964.)

INDIA

Ancient India demonstrates how the beliefs held by individuals about what is normal behavior affect and reflect the development of that society. Among the philosophical beliefs of the Hindus was that the soul transmigrated from body to body, carrying with it ancient memories. This belief had important consequences in Hindu society. One goal of any individual became that of producing sufficient bodies for previous souls to inhabit. Fertility was therefore highly valued; the more children, the more space for souls. A second method of achieving freedom of the soul for transmigration involved complete self-absorption and self-contemplation. Hence, especially among the social classes that had the leisure to do so, withdrawn behaviors, trancelike states, hallucinations, and intense self-contemplation were acceptable, even commendable behaviors. These self-absorbed individuals, "at one with the universe," saw little difference between life and death. There were socially sanctioned Hindu death cults with mass ritualistic suicides. If Hindu ritual suicides are contrasted with the suicide cults in France and Germany during the Middle Ages, it appears that in the former this behavior was considered normal, since it was an outgrowth of an accepted way of life and belief, whereas in Western lands suicide was, at best, considered sinful and qualified for labeling as psychopathological.

The literary works of ancient India such as the *Ramayana* and Vedas contain numerous references to deviant behavior. The explanations are in terms of demoniacal possession. For example, the *Ayur-Veda* offers what may well be the first classification of mental disorders. According to this document there are seven varieties of demons which, when enraged, enter the individual and produce various mental disorders. The behaviors so labeled include alcoholism, delusion (thinking oneself a god), and loss of memory.

The *Susruta,* more modern than the *Ayur-Veda,* speaks of science and theology as being one. It suggests that strong emotions may cause unusual behavior. In Hindu thought, however, all forms of life both normal and deviant were part of the oneness of nature, and thus the concept of abnormality itself was unknown.

CHINA

To readers such as the present authors the most striking aspect of ancient Chinese concepts is their similarity to Western thought. Early Chinese manuscripts (Tseng, 1973a) note five elements (wood, fire, earth, metal, and water), five climatic factors (wind, heat, humidity, dryness, and cold), and the positive and negative forces of Ying and Yang. Balance leads to harmony, while excited insanity is the result of excessive positive force, and the falling sickness (epilepsy) is the result of an excess of negative force. Following the same pattern as Western development, although usually at earlier dates, the Chinese developed concepts of psychological etiology, for example, insanity as a reaction to frustration. A quotation from Confucius (551–479 B.C.) (Tseng, 1973b, p. 192) could well summarize the position of this present volume on the nature-nurture issue: "'By nature, men are nearly alike; by practice, they get to be wide apart.' It is learning and training which leads people to become so different."

THE GREEKS

In early Greek times psychological troubles were not usually considered to be in the realm of disease and they were rarely considered the special concern of the physician. Some of the very people who today might be called abnormal were chosen to interpret the human ills of others; e.g., the priestesses at Delphi were "mentally ill," according to medical historians (see Zilboorg and Henry, 1941, pp. 37–38). Although the ancient Greeks are credited with being the first group of people to incorporate man's behavior within natural science, the evidence seems to be that this does not reflect a generally accepted point of view but rather the surviving written words of a few brilliant and unique individuals who had little influence on their society (Dodds, 1951). "'Our greatest blessings,' says Socrates in the *Phaedrus,* 'come to us by way of madness . . . provided that the madness is given us by divine gift.'" (Dodds, 1951, p. 64.) There was prophetic madness whose patron god was Apollo, ritual madness whose patron god was Dionysus, poetic madness inspired by the Muses, and erotic madness inspired by Aphrodite and Eros. In regard to this last, roughly a third of Burton's early seventeenth-century *Anatomy of Melancholy* is devoted to love melancholy.

In Greece shrines for helping the sick of all types originated through the worship of Asclepius, the god of healing. One of the most famous sanctuaries was established at Epidaurus in the 5th century B.C. Over the centuries auxiliary temples, a 12,000-seat stadium, a bathing pavilion, and two gymnasia were added. Statues of gods and famous physicians dotted the large and attractive grounds. Throughout there was an atmosphere of hopefulness and cheerfulness enhanced by tablets inscribed with detailed accounts of cures previously achieved. When the patient arrived, he had already heard tales of the marvelous cures to be obtained. His expectation of help was extremely high. Before he was permitted to approach the statue of a god, he was purified by bathing, prayer, and the burning of incense. Finally he was allowed to approach the statue of the god and touch it with the "diseased" part of his body.

The suppliant was then dressed in a white robe and put on a couch in a small room in preparation for a vision-producing sleep. During the night a priest would come and apply remedies to the diseased parts, touch the suppliant with the temple snakes, and whisper suggestions into his ear. The patient, under the influence of narcotics and the powerful suggestions, interpreted these nocturnal experiences as a visit from a god. Further, the priests would reinforce these views by interpreting the dreams as the gods giving instructions as to the proper treatment. If the patient did not have these divine communications, he was urged to make further sacrifices. If his illness did not improve, he was accused of being impious and sent elsewhere. This particular temple existed for over 800 years, and it is estimated that there were over 500 such sanctuaries in Greece.

Veith attributes the success of the temple healing to suggestion, the ritual of sham surgery, and hypnosis. "The effectiveness of these ministrations is all the more plausible because a great many of the patients appeared to have suffered from hysterical afflictions and hence were receptive to the mystical and ritualistic procedures of temple healing." (1965, p. 17.) This may be contrasted with the discussion of Mesmer in Chapter 5.

For several cogent reasons, the Greek era is generally considered the starting point of the history of abnormal psychology. Among the writings of the Greeks may be found concepts foreshadowing those of writers, investigators, and philosophers of the next 2,000 years. These writings may be cited on both sides of most issues, e.g., deviant behavior is caused by an infusion of demons and devils; or deviant behavior is a natural phenomenon understandable by rational laws.

Hippocrates (460?–377) is honored with the title "the father of medicine." He made astute *observations* about mental disorders, arguing that disorders such as epilepsy and melancholia arose from natural causes similar to those of physical diseases and that the seat of such disorders was the brain. His recommendations to his patients included marriage as a treatment for hysteria (then seen as a disorder of the uterus and consequently restricted to women) and that of a peaceful, sober, sexless, mildly athletic, vegetarian life for melancholia. He was also a classifier of mental disorders using a trichotomy of mania, melancholia, and phrenitis. His theory related the four humors (black bile, yellow bile, blood, and phlegm) to personality and mental disorders.

Hippocrates is honored in medical history because of his emphasis on *natural causes,* his acute clinical observations, his attempts at classifications and diagnosis, his focus on the role of the brain, and his psychological views. All these achievements are consistent with contemporary viewpoints.

If one seeks among the writings of the Greeks forerunners of current psychiatric and psychological thought of all shades, one can find them. For example, Hippocrates and Plato may have anticipated Freud in such things as the role of dreams. Pythagoras (6th century B.C.) may have anticipated the moral treatment of Pinel and his followers (see Chapter 7) and even some current hospital procedures in his system of recommending dietetics, music, a moral life, abstinence in some things, moderation in others, and a useful occupation.

Another reason that the Greeks represent a useful historical starting point is that, even in those times, a focal issue was the designation of the official group to label and treat abnormal behavior. In this respect, as in others, Hippocrates again represents an exception in that the physician among the Greeks was not usually the person who treated abnormal behavior. Rather, the tradition was to consider the human mind the province of philosophy, religion, or law. For many centuries this was never questioned by the medical man, and whenever medicine did try to enter this field, the theologian and philosopher violently objected. Descartes and Kant exemplify later authorities who strongly opposed medicine's interest in "psychopathology."

HELLENIC AND ROMAN PERIOD

Hellenic physicians such as Celsus (early first century A.D.), Soranus (2nd century A.D.), and Caelius Aurelianus (5th century A.D.) organized Hippocratic disease concepts into a system whereby mental disorders were classified as specific disease complexes and subdivided into acute and chronic states. These writers continued in the Hippocratic tradition insofar as classification was concerned. Their theoretical explanations, however, differed from Hippocratic ones, and resulted in therapeutic procedures that anticipated many modern techniques (Veith, 1957). Melancholia was still held to be related to black bile, and hysteria continued to be attributed to disorders of the uterus. But where Hippocrates viewed these and other conditions as caused by humoral imbalance, Soranus and Caelius believed in a pathology of solids which assumed that minute solid particles, called atoms, moved through the body and maintained health by their constant flow.

Therapeutic procedures, therefore, involved an elaborate scheme of constrictions and relaxations which called for the application of opposing forces. Recent treatment procedures involving relaxation bear some similarities to the treatments of these Hellenic physicians. For example (in "On Acute and Chronic Disease" by Caelius), relaxation was prescribed for such varied afflictions as phrenitis, lethargy, stupor, apoplexy, satyriasis, headache, epilepsy, melancholia, nocturnal emissions, and homosexuality.

The patients were kept quiet, and away from people who could excite them. In the light of current views on reinforcement procedures (Chapter 4) the following recommendation is of interest: "Have the servants, on the one hand, avoid the mistake of agreeing with everything the patient says, corroborating all his fantasies, and thus increasing his mania; and, on the other hand, have them avoid the mistake of objecting to everything he says and thus aggravating the severity of the attack. Let them rather at times lead the patient on by yielding to him and agreeing with him, and at another time indirectly correct his illusions by pointing out the truth." (Veith, 1957, p. 386.)

In the later Greek period and through the early Roman times, Hippocrates' views were in greater ascendance than in his own day. This was a period of history in which physicians achieved a prominence in the treatment of abnormal behavior that they were not again to attain until the nineteenth century. Their role was particularly important in the city that served as the base of transmission of Greek culture, Alexandria. There, physicians treated bodily dysfunctions arising from natural causes and utilized a wide variety of techniques ranging from enjoyable living arrangements, parties, dances, diet, and gymnastics to bleeding, purging, physical coercion, immersion in total darkness, and head shaving.

Galen (130–200) brought together the views of the Greco-Roman period and emphasized many ideas now considered incorrect. His work had great influence for the next 1500 years, and his views were the basis of whatever involvement the "physician" had in abnormal psychology during the Middle Ages. Little help to the patient resulted from Galen's transmission of the

Hippocratic view that melancholia was caused by thick, black bile ascending to the brain. Nor was there much benefit from Galen's own views that moisture in the body produced foolishness, that dryness produced wisdom, and that the ratio of moisture to dryness determined the condition of the patient's mind. In subsequent years, Galen's theories, rather than being abandoned, were expanded. For example, in the thirteenth century Galenic medicine, influenced by astrology, viewed epilepsy as caused by phlegm if its appearance coincided with the first quarter of the moon. The color and heat of Mars were related to the color and heat of the black bile and consequently to the severity of melancholia.

The great Roman writers Cicero (106–43) and Plutarch (46–120) concerned themselves with the art of healing the soul. Cicero said, "Diseases of the soul are both more dangerous and more numerous than those of the body," and, "Assuredly there is an art of healing the soul—I mean philosophy . . . We must use our utmost endeavor with all our resources and strength to have the power to be ourselves our own physicians." Cicero argued that emotions such as anger and fear resulted in mental disorder. He used two categories—Insania and Furor. Insania is absence of calm and poise. Furor denotes a complete breakdown of intellectual capacity, making the individual legally irresponsible. Cicero was, therefore, one of the first people to question the *legal responsibility* of the mentally ill.

Accurate observation is the first requirement of science. This is one reason why Hippocrates is honored. That Plutarch, too, could be acutely observant may be seen from this case history, in which he describes a person who is depressed as one in whom:

. . . every little evil is magnified by the scaring spectres of his anxiety. He looks on himself as a man whom the gods hate and pursue with their anger. A far worse lot is before him; he dares not employ any means of averting or of remedying the evil, lest he be found fighting against the gods. The physician, the consoling friend, are driven away. "Leave me," says the wretched man, "me the impious, the accursed, hated of the gods, to suffer my punishment." He sits out of doors, wrapped in sackcloth or in filthy rags. Ever and anon he rolls himself, naked, in the dirt confessing about this and that sin. He has eaten or drunk something wrong; he has gone some way or other which the Divine Being did not approve of. The festivals in honor of the gods give no pleasure to him, but fill him rather with fear and affright. He proves in his own case the saying of Pythagoras to be false, that we are happiest when we approach the gods, for it is just then that he is most wretched. Temples and altars are places of refuge for the persecuted; but where all others find deliverance from their fears, there this wretched man most fears and trembles. Asleep or awake, he is haunted alike by the spectres of his anxiety. Awake, he makes no use of his reason; and asleep, he enjoys no respite from his alarms. His reason always slumbers; his fears are always awake. Nowhere can he find an escape from his imaginary terrors. [Quoted in Zilboorg and Henry, 1941, p. 67.]

MIDDLE AGES

From the point of view of abnormal psychology, the major development in the Middle Ages was the dominance of the clergy in the designation and treatment of abnormal behaviors. Medicine was limited to bodily ailments. By the thirteenth century the physician and the cleric were frequently one, for nearly all physicians were also members of the clergy. The monasteries became refuges and places of confinement for the disturbed. Thus an interesting and unique combination of institutions took place, the monastery serving as church, university, and mental hospital.

At first the mentally disturbed were treated humanely. Speculation as to the causes of peculiar behavior other than divine intervention involved demonic possession and the humoral theories of ancient

approaches to abnormality: ancient and medieval

physicians. Treatment procedures involved the use of herbs, human and animal excrement, prayers, holy water, the breath or spit of priests, pilgrimages, relic handling, and amulets.

A good example of the blending of theology and the treatment of abnormal behavior, as well as of the relatively humane treatment of deviant behavior during this period, was the establishment of the Gheel colony. Gheel is near Antwerp, and from the early part of the thirteenth century retardates and psychotics were brought to the town and left in care of the townspeople. This method of boarding-out of the "insane," of family care, or home care as it is known in the United States (Ullmann and Berkman, 1959; Giovannoni and Ullmann, 1961), continues to the present day as a method of integrating mental patients with the larger community.

The treatment of hysteria is indicative of attitudes toward abnormal behavior during various periods of history. The term "hysteria" has been used as a label to cover a variety of different unusual and often bizarre behaviors (see Chapter 13). In the tenth century, as in ancient Greece, hysteria was attributed to the wandering of the uterus through the body. Its treatment is well illustrated by a tenth century manuscript of an invocation repeated many times by the treating priest, of which a part is as follows:

I conjure thee, O womb, by our Lord Jesus Christ, who walked over the sea with dry feet, who cured the sick, who expelled demons, who brought the dead back to life, by whose blood we were redeemed, by whose wound we were cured, by whose plight we were healed, by Him, I conjure thee not to harm that maid of God, N., not to occupy her head, throat, neck, chest, ears, teeth, eyes, nostrils, shoulderblades, arms, hands, heart, stomach, spleen, kidneys, back, sides, joints, navel, intestines, bladder, thighs, shins, heels, nails, but to lie down quietly in the place which God chose for thee, so that this maid of God, N., be restored to health. [Quoted in Zilboorg and Henry, 1941, pp. 131-32.]

By the thirteenth and fourteenth centuries the major and contradictory trends in society's attitudes toward abnormal behavior included a growing belief in witchcraft, a resurgent belief in man as a natural object, the re-emergence of the physician with a unique healing role in society, the growth of astrology and alchemy, and the start of society-supported hospitals, including several for people displaying bizarre behavior. Thus in this period there was considerable confusion and transition in the treatment of behavior disorders. Added to the ancient traditions were the newer approaches involving astrology, alchemy, demonology, and prayer. Remnants of the humanitarian past still remained. For example, Bartholomaeus of Salerno advised that the mentally sick be "refreshed and comforted and withdrawn from any source of dread and busy thoughts. They must be gladdened with instruments of music and some must be given occupation." (Zilboorg and Henry, 1941, p. 138)

However, the professional theories of both physicians and clergy, which were also the popular beliefs of the time, were the major determinants of treatment. Witches were blamed for impotence and loss of memory. Epileptics were advised to write out the text of the Gospel according to St. Matthew; the impotent were told to put together the halves of a nutshell; hysteria and sterility in women were relieved by fumigating the genitalia with aromatic woods.

Conditions of life were harsh and it was easier to see the work of the devil in human affairs than the work of the angels.

There are several practical implications of a Christian fundamentalist philosophy. The first is that the devil is powerful, operative, and hungry for human souls. The second is that the commodity of value is the soul, not the body. The soul is eternal, and must not be lost; the body is transient. It is the soul that differentiates man from beast, and if a man loses his soul, then there is no obligation to treat him as a man. If one looks upon mental illness as an illness of the soul, in which the body and the devil team together, then radical treatment becomes justified, should exorcism and moral treatment fail.

There is a similarity to the Age of Enlightenment, the 18th century, when the faculty of reason critically separated man from beast. If a man lost his reason, as the insane appeared to do, he was no longer treated as a man, but as a beast . . . It does not matter whether the critical faculty is soul or reason; should a man lose it, he can longer be treated as a man. The concern for the salvation of a soul was prevalent not only in regards to the insane, but in regards to all deviant behavior; wickedness and heresy were far more important deviances than insanity.

The third implication of a Christian fundamentalist philosophy is that the demarcations between religious experiences (including demonic possession) and psychologically abnormal experiences are not clearly defined. A wide spectrum of behavior that would be considered extremely pathological today was accepted as normal, if possibly peculiar, ranging from the dancing manias that affected whole towns in the 14th century (and were supported even by the townspeople and clergy who were not affected by it) to the wandering bands of Battuti, who roamed the countryside flagellating themselves and inviting the townspeople to join them; to individual experiences of a mystical or transcendental nature. The critical factor in the public's and the authority's acceptance of these deviant behaviors was not the bizarre quality of the behavior, but rather the determination of whether the behavior was in the service of Christ or in the service of Satan.

Thus, it is not true that all deviant behavior, and all insanity, was viewed as evidence of witchcraft or stemming from diabolic possession. Indeed, the tolerance for deviant behavior was greater in the Middle Ages than it is now! [Kroll, 1973, pp. 277–278.]

In the latter half of the fifteenth century and early part of the sixteenth century there occurred a number of events related to the growing belief in the existence of witchcraft which profoundly influenced the direction of abnormal psychology for hundreds of years. The most important of these events, because of its reflection of the trends of the time and its subsequent influence, was the publication in 1488 of the *Malleus malleficarum*.

This book may be characterized in many ways. It is, depending on one's point of view, a treatise on witchcraft; the classic fifteenth century abnormal psychology text; the epitome of theological values of the era; a manual for the treatment of mental disorders; or the most evil book ever written. In the fifteenth century the belief in the power of witchcraft was at its height. The period was characterized by an outpouring of strange and bizarre behaviors, many of which involved religious symbolism, hallucinations, or delusions. It was quite clear to church authorities that drastic measures were needed to combat the presumed spread of witchcraft. Pope Innocent VIII issued a bull which was in effect a declaration of war on witches. Under his aegis two Dominican monks, Sprenger and Kraemer, German inquisitors, wrote a manual on the detection and treatment of witches—*Malleus malleficarum* or *The Witch's Hammer*. This manual was the authoritative confirmation that witches did exist. It prescribed diagnostic procedures for detecting witches such as the location of peculiar body spots characterized by a lack of pain response (anesthesia which today would be characterized as hysterical).

Once an individual was diagnosed a witch or heretic, treatment was clear and logical: burning to make the body an uncomfortable home for devils, demons, and incubi. The concepts of the period may be summarized (in a passage from the *Malleus*) by the simple attribution to the devils of "six ways of injuring humanity. And one is to induce an evil love in a man for a woman, or in a woman for a man. The second is to plant hatred or jealousy in anyone. The third is to bewitch them so that a man cannot perform the genital act with a woman, or conversely a woman with a man; or by various means to procure an abortion, as has been said before. The fourth is to cause some disease in any of the human organs. The fifth, to take away life. The sixth, to deprive them of reason." (Quoted in Zilboorg and Henry, 1941, p. 158.)

The inhumanity unleashed by the *Malleus* continued well beyond the final demise of the social system which created it. The last witch was executed in England in 1722. The last witch to be officially killed in Germany was decapitated in Bavaria on March 3, 1775. The last witch was executed in Switzerland in 1782. (Nineteen witches had been executed in Salem, Massachusetts, in 1692, the last such occurrence in the American colonies.)

THE NEAR EAST

As in other fields of learning, Arabian treatment of abnormal behavior was, by current standards, more advanced than European treatment during the middle ages. Rhazes (865–925) was the most illustrious Arabian physician and is called the Persian Galen. Of interest in the present context is Rhazes' use of techniques to increase motivation. He once treated a caliph for arthritis by prescribing a hot bath. While the caliph was soaking, Rhazes threatened him with a knife and the patient got up and ran. Another physician cured a woman who suffered from such severe cramps in her joints that she could not rise, by lifting her skirt and putting her to shame. In both instances, a medical explanation involving the heating of humours, was given. Readers of dull textbooks will appreciate the following: "When the patriarch of Bokhara argued with Rhazes and could not budge the great teacher from his point, he sentenced him to be hit over the head with his own book until the book or the head broke." (Alexander and Selesnick, 1968, p. 92.)

Avicenna (980–1037), Avezoar (1113–1162), Averroes (1126–1198), and Maimonides (1135–1204) are examples of Arabian physicians who were deeply influenced by Aristotle, Hippocrates, Galen, and who combined both a religious and a humanistic orientation. Hospitals were established in major Arabian cities from the eighth century onwards, and this tradition may well be the reason for the relative superiority of Spanish refuges over French hospitals before the work of Pinel (see next chapter).

THE DISSENTERS

The Middle Ages, as in other historical periods, also gave birth to a few individuals who held views opposing those of official labelers. In many ways Juan Luis Vives (1492–1540) can be seen as a forerunner to both Freud and current behavioral psychologists. Vives is known for his astute observations of human behavior, his objective outlook, and his deep sense of social responsibility. Vives was first of all a humanist and, with his friends Sir Thomas More and Erasmus, was among the three greatest scholars of his day. Vives championed the cause of the poor and those who behaved abnormally. He wrote strong arguments against the continuing warfare in Europe. He viewed each person as having a right to enjoy the best life possible, and society as having a special responsibility to the individual.

Since there is nothing in the world more excellent than man, nor in man than his mind, particular attention should be given to the welfare of the mind; and it should be considered a highest service if we either restore the minds of others to sanity or keep them sane and rational. Hence, when a man of unsettled mind is brought to a hospital, it must be determined, first of all, whether his illness is congenital or has resulted from some misfortune, whether there is hope for his recovery or not. One ought to feel compassion for so great a disaster to the health of the human mind, and it is of utmost importance that the treatment be such that the insanity be not nourished and increased, as may result from mocking, exciting or irritating madmen. . . . [Vives, *De subven-*

tione pauperum, cited in Zilboorg and Henry, 1941, p. 187.]

In contrast to the then current emphasis on the soul as a subject of psychological consideration, Vives argued, "What the soul is, is of no concern for us to know. What its manifestations are is of great importance." ("Vives," *Encyclopedia Britannica,* 13th ed., cited in Bromberg, 1959, p. 78.) Thus a writer in the sixteenth century clearly argued that attention should be paid to behavior and not to indefinable concepts such as soul or mind. Vives also anticipated Freud in his emphasis on self-observation, introspection, and the role of feelings and emotions in human behavior.

Neither the *Malleus* nor Vives exhausted the range of views on abnormal behavior in the early sixteenth century. Two other positions were representd by Paracelsus and by Rabelais. Paracelsus (Theophrastus Bombastus von Hohenheim, 1493–1541) was a physician who reflected both traditional thinking and the struggle to move beyond such thinking. Mental illness, according to Paracelsus, was a natural disease caused by the unhealthy changes undergone at various times by the *spiritus vitae*. He rejected the theory of demonology and advanced a medical cure for abnormal behavior. Considering heat and cold causative agents, he advised that patients' toes and fingers be scarified so that fresh air might be let in to reduce the excess of heat which produced maniacal states. Considering the cause of hysteria to be sexual, Paracelsus called it *chorea lasciva*. He also believed that opinion, imagination, and ideas could be the origin of disease in children and adults.

Other physicians of the time who rank with Paracelsus were Cornelius Agrippa (1486–1535) and Johann Weyer (1515–1588). The writings and viewpoints of both were clearly skeptical of the prevailing demonology and brutality. Weyer concluded that witches were "mentally ill" and argued that the monks who tormented them should be punished. Weyer was a strong but uninfluential voice viewing abnormal behavior within a medical rather than a theological framework.

In the early sixteenth century, in addition to the official theological, humanitarian, and medical approaches to behavior, there was the satirical approach of François Rabelais (1494–1553). Rabelais, who started his career as a physician and monk and ended it as one of the great writers of all time, was an acute observer of human behavior. He noted the role of sex in both normal and disturbed behavior. He bitterly denounced religious biogtry and "monkish deviltry." He was able to do so only by couching his teachings in the context of ribald stories.

Robert Burton (1576–1640) was a clergyman and scholar rather than a physician, and his book, *Anatomy of Melancholy,* was an anthology that brought together all available knowledge of mental disorders from ancient times to his own.

Another man with a background similar to Burton was Oxford-educated Reginald Scott (1538–1599). Scott's major treatise, *The Discovery of Witchcraft,* was an outspoken denunciation of the prevailing demonological theories of mental disorders. Scott insisted upon a natural explanation for the strange experiences to which witches "confessed." He showed by logical, philosophical, and even theological arguments that these phenomena were explicable on naturalistic grounds. Scott was particularly scathing in his denunciations of the hypothetical constructs of "incubi" and "succubi" which were used to explain the techniques of Satan and his demons in eliciting bizarre behavior.

An incubus was a male demon who visited women at night, forcing them into sexual relations against their will, while a succubus was a female spirit who visited men for sexual purposes. These spirits were the cause of nightmares and other terrors of the night. The incubus, a demon with a material body, especially chose virgins and virtuous women to molest, and in so doing caused a sensation of weight on the chest, difficulty in breathing, and terror while asleep. Paracelsus had also viewed incubi as an "outgrowth of an intense and lewd imagination." Scott felt that demonic "explanations" were excuses for lechery and represented nothing more than natural phenomena such as cuckoldry or overzealous ministrations by clergy. Scott's view may be contrasted with the *Malleus*' explanation of impotence as due to "glamors." A glamor was a devil in the form of a man without his natural sex organs. The glamor would enter the intended victim without his knowledge and thus turn him into a sexless being. To regain his virility the victim had to find someone who could exorcise the demon.

THE DEVELOPMENT OF ASYLUMS

Earlier in this chapter, the combination of hospitals, universities, and monasteries during the first millennium A.D. was described. One of the first important church hospitals was St. Basil of Caesarea (founded in A.D. 369). It was a community of the sick, the aged, and the orphaned, that is, those in need of charity.[3] This pattern was observed and reacted to 1500 years later by Dorothea Dix (see Chapter 7). In 1326 a *Dollhaus* (mad house) was erected as part of the Georgehospital at Elbing (Kroll, 1973), and in 1410 in Valencia, an institution for the treatment of the mentally ill was started by a friar, Father Juan Gilabert Jofré (Rumbaut, 1972). In 1547 the monastery of St. Mary of Bethlehem in London was made into a hospital for the insane. Hogarth drew pictures of Londoners observing the inmates as a pastime, and there still is in our language the word "bedlam," a contraction stemming from the name of this hospital. The San Hipolito hospital was established in Mexico in 1565. Similar hospitals for the exclusive use of the insane were established in Paris (1641), Moscow (1765), and Vienna (1784). The treatment of the patients at these asylums can best be described as cruel and more like prison than hospital care. It was in the context of such hospital treatment that the work of Pinel and Tuke at the end of the eighteenth century took place. The next chapter takes up the history of abnormal psychology at that point.

SUMMARY

This chapter sketched some of the early formulations and treatment of abnormal behavior. It illustrated that what behaviors were considered deviant, how they were evaluated, and how they were treated changed over time and place. The major models and professions dealing with abnormal behavior have been legal, clerical, philosophical, and medical. Within each of these professions, theories and practices also changed over time. What is considered abnormal behavior is a part of and reflects the specific culture. At a meta-level, how writers and students evaluate the ideas of other people—as brilliant forerunners or as misguided wrongdoers—reflects the writers' times, models, concerns, and biases.

The individuals described in this and subsequent chapters added to human knowledge and human prejudice. Just as the word "lunatic," which refers to the theory of the influence of the moon on behavior, is still current, so the works of these men are still current. A historical survey should alert the reader to the sources of preconceptions which stand in the way of matching Hippocrates' accomplishment: to look at behavior and to see it clearly.

---

[3] Foucault (1967) implies that the leprosariums, empty because of the decrease in cases of leprosy, were turned into hospitals for the deviant, but there is a gap of two centuries that is unexplained. More germane is his noting (p. 43) that the founding in Paris of the Hospital Général was not medical but rather a quasi-judicial way of removing "undesirables" from the general population.

approaches to abnormality
MODERN

7

This chapter will deal with the historically overlapping topics of the founding of psychotherapy, moral treatment, the medical model, the behavioral approaches, and the professions that deal with unusual behaviors.

FORERUNNERS OF PSYCHOTHERAPY

The historical narrative is resumed by returning to the period following Mesmer and his introduction of the technique that was dismissed by his contemporaries as only "imagination." The rejection of Mesmer by his medical colleagues is ironical because Mesmer, like Freud (Chapters 8 and 9), made contributions to the field of psychotherapy that eventually led to medical interest in and claims of responsibility for the treatment of the neuroses.

In 1784 a pupil of Mesmer, the Marquis de Puységur, took the next major step in investigations of the hypnotic situation. Puységur was a wealthy man and a philosophically oriented philanthropist who practiced "magnetic therapy" at his large estate on soldiers, farmhands, and other "non-aristocrats." One day he stumbled upon the phenomenon which has been crucial to "hypnosis" ever since, the "sleep" that can be induced by "mesmerism." Mesmer believed that the slumbering of some of his subjects, which occurred at times during induction, was an unfortunate artifact, and sought to avoid it. Puységur noted, at first with alarm, that a young shepherd, Victor, entered a peaceful slumber under his gently stroking fingers. The boy was responsive to Puységur during this period as if he were awake and in full possession of his senses. The youth could be labeled a somnambulist, a sleep-walker. Puységur tried the same induction procedures with other people and found they were also responsive and able to talk and behave appropriately while apparently asleep. Further, these people followed (posthypnotic) suggestions made during hypnosis after being roused from the "trance." Puységur in his observations of the "sleeping" state and the lack of necessity of the dramatic "crises" which Mesmer had evoked was the major forerunner of modern hypnosis.

The story of Mesmer's earlier ostracism from medicine was repeated with John Elliotson (1791–1868) in London. Elliotson argued that mesmerism was especially useful in the treatment of hysteria and other neuroses. He pointed out that hysteria was misunderstood and treated in such a way that the disorder was often exacerbated. For example, marriage was suggested as a remedy for hysterical women on the assumption that hysteria was a sexual disease. Needless to say, disastrous results would often follow such recommendations. Elliotson argued that hysteria was not necessarily connected with the uterus nor even with females, a point made later by Freud.

Elliotson also advocated mesmerism as an anesthetic in surgical operations. In 1842 a surgeon, Dr. Ward, performed an amputation while the patient was mesmerized. Although successful, he was denounced by his colleagues as being a fraud. James Esdaile (1808–1859), also a surgeon, used mesmerism in over 250 successful operations in India. At this time, however, the chemical anesthesia came to be widely used, obviating the need for hypnosis in surgery.

James Braid (1795–1860), an English physician and surgeon, introduced the term "hypnotism" and emphasized the role of suggestion in its induction. During an experimental session, Braid was surprised to find that his subject fell into a trancelike state while looking fixedly at a bright object. He went on to demonstrate that the state of stupor could be induced by a process other than animal magnetism. He labeled this condition "hypnotism" (from Greek *hypnos*, "sleep") and used it to obtain marked improvement in a series of cases involving paralysis, migraine, rheumatism, epilepsy, deafness, and other disorders. Braid also observed that the patients were susceptible in accord with their expectation about what would happen.

The year that Braid died, a French country doctor, Ambroise-Auguste Liébault (1823–1904), began to work intensively with "mesmerism" in his general practice. Liébault, as others before him, attributed the effects of this procedure to "suggestion." So impressive was his work that he attracted a number of investigators and fellow physicians who came to learn his techniques. This group was referred to as the Nancy school because of its location in that city. The most influential of these investigators was Hippolyte Bernheim (1837–1919) who collected data on thousands of cases of the phenomenon now labeled hypnosis.

The Bernheim-Charcot Controversy

One of the most important debates of medical history was that between Bernheim and Jean-Martin Charcot (1825–1893) on the relationship between hypnosis and hysteria. Bernheim argued that hysteria and hypnosis were *both* due to suggestion and hence the phenomenon of suggestibility was not limited to hysterics and should be studied in its own right. Bernheim demonstrated that the phenomena seen in hysteria, such as paralysis, anesthesias, and deafness, could be produced by hypnosis in normal people. Conversely, these same behaviors in hysterics could be removed by hypnosis.

A different position was taken by Charcot, the head of the Salpêtrière Hospital in Paris and the most eminent neurologist of his time. Charcot was the leading figure, next to Freud, in the development of modern views on mental illness, particularly hysteria. Charcot's primary goal was to diagnose and, if possible, locate the site of a neurological disturbance. Charcot was not particularly interested in treating people and indeed he had no technique that would permit him to do so. In his focus on diagnosis, he relabeled the "hysterics" from malingerers to sick, hence changing their status and giving them a sick role (Szasz, 1961).

It was this willingness to deal with "hysterical" individuals which represented Charcot's great contribution to this field. In effect, he lent his prestige as a major medical figure to the acceptance of these individuals into the realm of medicine. Previous to Charcot, a physician who considered a hysteric as a sick person was being "fooled," and his prestige suffered accordingly. After Charcot, the diagnostician could be praised by society for his acumen in spotting and labeling the "hysteric."

Charcot was interested in both hysteria and hypnosis and considered the phenomena to be *separate* but related. He argued that both hysteria and hypnosis involved some degeneration of the nervous system. What attracted him to hypnosis, therefore, was the opportunity to study changes in the nervous system during hypnosis. Although Charcot recognized the role of suggestion, he minimized it. Here, then, was the crux of the argument between the Nancy (Bernheim) and Salpêtrière schools: hypnosis and hysteria were either psychological phenomena based on persuasion, talk, and suggestion, or they were medical phenomena based on biochemical and neurological factors.

Eventually Bernheim's view proved to have the weight of clinical and research evidence on its side, and even Charcot conceded this point.[1]

Pierre Janet (1859–1947) was a French philosopher, physician, and psychologist whose major contributions involved the psychological treatment of hysteria. Janet conceived of neurosis as a constitutional weakness of the nervous system. He thought hysteria was a result of poor heredity and degeneracy. Janet's therapeutic procedures, however, were psychological in nature and foreshadowed later work by both psychoanalysts and behavior therapists. For example, at one point Freud conceded that Janet's ideas of psychotherapy and the role of the unconscious were similar to those he and Breuer held, while Janet was to later remark that Breuer and Freud actually verified his *prior* interpretations of "subconscious fixed ideas with hystericals." (Janet, 1901, p. 290.)

In a different manner hypnosis is in many regards a forerunner of contemporary "consciousness III" (Reich, 1970). After Mesmer's death, the Societies of Harmony in major cities remained and were attractive to radically inclined intellectuals (e.g., Darnton, 1968). In 1813, Deleuze published an influential and widely read volume making major promises of increased power and awareness. Of interest in the present context is the appeal to nonrational elements:

According to M. Deleuze, any person could become a magnetiser and produce these effects, by conforming to the following conditions, and acting upon the following rules:

Forget for a while all your knowledge of physics and meta-physics.

Remove from your mind all objections that may occur.

Imagine that it is in your power to take the malady in hand, and throw it on one side.

Never reason for six weeks after you have commenced the study.

Have an active desire to do good; a firm belief in the power of magnetism, and an entire confidence in employing it. In short, repel all doubts; desire success, and act with simplicity and attention. [MacKay, 1844; 1932 edition, p. 341.]

Philosophical and Other Predecessors of Psychological Approaches

Much of the current philosophical basis of psychological therapy can be said to have been provided by Baruch Spinoza (1632–1677) and Immanuel Kant (1724–1804). Spinoza, for example, argued that "An emotion which is a passion ceases to be a passion as soon as we form a clear and distinct idea of it," and Kant wrote a tract called *The Power of the Mind, Through Simple Determination, to Become Master over Morbid Ideas.* Kant was also much interested in mental disease; his *Anthropologie* contains an extensive description and classification of mental disorders.

Johann Christian Reil (1759–1813) had taught and written extensively about psychotherapy during the late eighteenth century. Philippe Pinel (1745–1826), writing at the beginning of the nineteenth century, expressed the belief that many cases of insanity could be cured by "mildness of treatment and attention to the state of the mind exclusively," and that when "coercion" was indicated, it might be "very effectively applied without corporeal indignity." Pinel emphasized "the value of conciliatory language, kind treatment, and the revival of extinguished hopes." He also stressed "the advantage of obtaining intimate acquaintance with the character of the patient." On the other hand, to illustrate the views of the Establishment of the day, Dendy (1860) de-

---

[1] One can never prove that hypnosis is not due to neural weakness. All one can do is illustrate that every hypnotic phenomenon can be instigated without reference to trance or neurological weakness. The same point is true of later discussions of psychiatric categories: all one can do is show how certain theories are superfluous. When such demonstrations are frequent and persuasive, the contradictory theories fall into disuse, and this is what happened in the Bernheim-Charcot controversy.

scribed those who recommended the exclusive use of psychological methods, as "hoodwinked by false metaphysics." (Altschule, 1957, p. 155.)

Baron Ernst Von Feuchtersleben's (1806–1849) comments, written in 1845, constitute an important summary of mid-nineteenth century ideas about psychotherapy: "Psychical powers . . . may also be used in many cases for the purpose of cure." He recommended psychotherapy in illnesses of all types, for he believed that there was a reciprocal action between body and mind. Von Feuchtersleben considered psychotherapy especially beneficial in the treatment of what would be called psychogenic symptoms. In order to achieve a cure, it was necessary that the patient acquire complete "self-knowledge and self-control." He added: "Who in the full possession of health can boast of having attained this?" The aim of this therapy, Von Feuchtersleben said, was the restoration of the individual personality. In psychotherapy "one personality has to act upon another." The therapist is a "physician, remedy, and vehicle," all in one. The psychotic patient must be re-educated to develop social feelings. The physician must be:

. . . just, equitable, and above all, perfectly dispassionate. . . . We act according to the laws of association; that is to say, we seek to place before the patient those ideas we wish to assign, as it were, a larger place in the mind, and desire to render permanent, and which we wish to oppose, in frequent and often repeated connexion, to those ideas which are morbid. [Von Feuchtersleben, 1845, cited in Altschule, 1957, p. 156.]

Von Feuchtersleben argued that the desirable ideas must be related to an object or feeling in order to be made lasting. Bad ideas must be ignored; no attempt should be made to contradict them. One can see in these writings a prelude to recent procedures of desensitization (see Chapter 12) and extinction.

Francis Leuret (1840) was another investigator who wrote extensively about psychotherapy, and some of his basic ideas are quite modern (Wolpe and Theriant, 1971). He pointed out that it was not necessary to believe, as did many German psychiatrists of his day, that insanity is a disease of the "soul" rather than of the brain in order to practice psychotherapy. He warned that isolation from others led to deterioration of the patient's faculties. Leuret published long verbatim accounts of interviews and attempted to show that the apparent incoherence of the patient had meaning consistent with his personality.

Writing in 1917, Kraepelin (1962) frequently cites early nineteenth-century opinion about the need for education in values rather than medical treatment:

Neumann expressed his views in similar fashion: "The time has finally come for us to stop looking for the herb or salt or metal which in homeopathic or allopathic doses will cure mania, imbecility, insanity, fury or passion. They will never be found until pills are discovered which will transform a naughty child into a well-mannered child, an ignorant man into a skilled artist, a rude swain into a polished gentleman. We can rub patients with martyr's ointment until the skin peels off and turn up more martyrs than the Spanish Inquisition—and will face the fact that we are not one step closer to curing insanity. Man's psychic activities are changed, not by medicines but by habit, training, and exertion." . . . Hoffbauer looked upon the rehabilitation of a madman who had regained his sanity as a second education of the same man. "Is not the treatment of mental patients frequently comparable to education of children?" asked Heinroth. And he continued, "Every finding indicates that the comparison is apt." [pp. 69–70, 71.]

Pinel and Sonnenstein also wrote of similar concepts (Kraepelin, 1962, pp. 77–79) and Itard and Seguin, working with retardates, practiced them. (Ball, 1970) These are forerunners of behavior therapy.

MORAL TREATMENT

In 1793, Phillippe Pinel (1745–1826), recently appointed as director of the Bicêtre Hospital, received the reluctant permission of the Paris Commune to unchain the "insane" patients at the hospital. In pleading for this step, Pinel had stated that, "It is my conviction that these mentally ill are intractable only because they are deprived of fresh air and of their liberty." Once freed, there were a number of dramatic instances of changes in these unfortunate people. Pinel, in his concern for patients, studied them carefully, took notes on what he observed, and thus introduced the important procedure, a vital necessity for subsequent systematic investigation, of taking of case histories and keeping individual records.

At the same time William H. Tuke (1732–1822), an English Quaker, started the York Retreat and introduced humane treatment for mental patients in England. The work of Pinel and Tuke was reflected in the United States at the Pennsylvania Hospital by Benjamin Rush (1745–1813), who is often credited with being the "Father of American Psychiatry."[2]

Moral treatment, the label for the procedures of these individuals, represented the first effort to provide systematic and responsible care for large numbers of deviant people. The term "moral" was in this use equivalent to "emotional," "psychological," or even "behavioral." "Moral treatment was never clearly defined, possibly because its meaning was self-evident during the era in which it was used. It meant compassionate and understanding treatment of innocent sufferers. Even innocence was not a prerequisite to meriting compassion. Compassion extended to those whose mental illness was thought due to willful and excessive indulgence in the passions." (Bockoven, 1963, p. 12.)

Pinel thought his treatment appealed to the moral sense through setting an example and teaching the patient to return good for good. Under the new system, cruel punishments and almost all "shock" treatments were forbidden; cold baths and physical restraint, however, were sanctioned when necessary to subdue or punish patients.

Moral treatment strove to create a complete therapeutic environment—social, psychological, and physical. Although emphasis was placed on the relationship between physician and patient, moral treatment embraced a much larger psychological approach than individual psychotherapy. Indeed, "perhaps the greatest asset of moral treatment was the attention it gave to the value of physical setting and social influences of hospital life as curative agents." (Bockoven, 1963, p. 17.)

The term "moral" carried connotations of zeal, hope, spirit, and confidence. In moral treatment the psychiatrist talked with patients to find out their preoccupations; worked with their relatives; and made every effort to gain the confidence of the patients and fulfill their needs. Great attention was given to the physical setting of the hospital so that it would be cheerful, homelike, and not monotonous. Patients were treated so far as possible as if they "were still in the enjoyment of the healthy exercise of their mental abilities." The therapist also believed in "firmness and persistence in impressing on patients the idea that a change to more acceptable behavior was expected." (Bockoven, 1963, p. 76.)

The therapist kept in mind that even the most "insane" patients were sensitive to manifestations of interest and good will. He was warned, however, to limit the number of patients in his care to those he could

---

[2] As usual, there were many forerunners, although the credit is given to the people who make innovations visible. In this case, Spanish physicians removed the chains from their patients in 1409 and an enlightened 1774 law regarding the insane in Tuscany was implemented by Chiarugi in 1788. A better writing style and active students probably account for Pinel's greater fame. (Alexander and Selesnick, 1968, pp. 156–57).

know personally. In *Curability of Insanity*, a title reflecting the beliefs of the moral therapists, John Butler (1887) pointed out that appropriate social influence could be maintained only if hospitals were not allowed to care for more than 200 patients at one time. (Arlidge, 1859, was of the same opinion.) Butler considered monotony to be the greatest obstacle to be overcome in mental hospitals, and thus he advocated a wide variety of activities for patients.

The growth of the mental hospitals in the United States in the early part of the nineteenth century grew out of the then-current model of mental disorder and represented an attempt to change not only individual behavior but society itself. Rothman (1971) points out that in the period in which hospital building was initiated, it was believed that insanity was organic in that it involved a weakness in the brain but that the weakness was aggravated by environmental stress. The hospital superintendents, who were the leading therapists of the day, felt that the competitive stress of living in American society led to insanity. The way to treat the person was to place him in a new environment, separated from society, in which he could be retrained for a better life and returned to influence his society.

Having located the etiology of the disease in social organization, medical superintendents were confident that a setting which eliminated the irritants could restore the insane to health. The diagnosis of the causes of the disease provided the clues to a cure. . . . Rather than attempt to reorganize American society directly, they would design and oversee a distinctive environment which eliminated the tensions and the chaos. They would try to create—in a way reminiscent of the founders of utopian communities—a model society of their own, not to test a novel method for organizing production or making political decisions, but to exemplify the advantages of an orderly, regular, and disciplined routine. Here was an opportunity to meet the pressing needs of the insane, by isolating them from the dangers at loose in the community, and to further a reform program by demonstrating to the larger society the benefits of the system. Thus, medical superintendents and laymen supporters moved to create a new world for the insane, one that would not only alleviate their distress but also educate the citizens of the republic. The product of this effort was the insane asylum. [Rothman, 1971, pp. 128–29.]

Hospitals in the early nineteenth century were small and did in fact usually care for fewer than 200 patients. The superintendent and his family lived and ate with the patients, who were considered part of his family (see Charles Dickens, *Travels in America*). The patients were expected, by both fellow patients and treatment personnel, to live up to the standards provided by the staff. A healthy social role for the patients was emphasized, expected, reinforced, and, most important, actively taught.

Humanitarian treatment based on a psychological model and the expectation of improvement (Goldstein, 1962) was a major reason for the effectiveness of moral treatment. Reports that are available for this period (see Bockoven, 1963 and Dain, 1964) indicate a higher discharge rate than for previous and most subsequent periods of time.

It should be emphasized that moral treatment was *not* a single technique, but rather an approach involving every aspect of daily living being utilized by the physician for its therapeutic effect. Most of the tasks prescribed for the patients included cooperating with others, religious involvement, and doing manual or intellectual work. Moral treatment involved a way of life, a teaching program in how to make friends and develop outside interests. The goal was to help the patient enjoy life and take part in society. It should also be added that the approach was criticized by contemporaries as being naïve in that it did not remove the *cause* of the illness.

THE DECLINE OF MORAL TREATMENT

In 1841 Dorothea Dix (1802–1887) observed that many people were suffering terrible abuse in the jails and almshouses of Massachusetts. She also learned of the humane treatment patients were receiving at the three small mental hospitals in that state. From the time she learned of such suffering and its remedy, she was determined not to rest until every "insane" individual was a patient in a mental hospital. With great singleness of purpose she set out on an amazing career of reform by direct appeal to the state legislatures. She was successful in achieving the results she demanded, namely, the construction of new hospitals and the expansion of existing ones. To many people Dorothea Dix is a heroine similar to Florence Nightingale, but students of moral treatment (Dain, 1964; Bockoven, 1963) cast her in a far different role: she is credited with being one of the major reasons for the destruction of moral treatment because her emphasis on eliminating gross abuse had the effect of driving into the background any serious consideration of the requirements to be met in securing positive treatment. Dorothea Dix functioned as a self-appointed inspector of mental hospitals. Her imperious manner, rigid opinions, and attitudes of censorship introduced a new element into mental hospitals, that of petty fault-finding and punishing authority. Her great political influence gave her considerable voice in the selection of physicians for superintendents of mental hospitals. Bockoven (1963) "credits" her with being largely responsible for the emphasis that came to be placed on protecting patients against any and all mishaps and with the stagnation of hospital life which resulted from it.

During this period a new type of physician-therapist appeared, one who replaced the optimistic, enthusiastic orientation of the moral therapist with the restrictive, watchful, mishap-avoiding orientation of the administrative custodian of the insane. Interest in treatment was replaced by interest in diagnosis, legal questions of responsibility, and brain pathology.

A decade after Dorothea Dix began her campaign for building and enlarging mental hospitals, leadership in American psychiatry passed to the superintendent of the largest state hospital in America—the Utica State Hospital in New York. Dr. John P. Gray was appointed superintendent in 1854, and in 1855 he assumed editorship of *The American Journal of Insanity*. Gray insisted that insanity was *always* due to a *physical* lesion. He was the first person to introduce the microscope into American mental hospitals and to study post-mortem material in search for the etiology of mental disease. He also changed mental hospital organizations to treat the mentally ill patient as *physically* ill. He placed great emphasis on rest, diet, proper room temperature, and ventilation.

There were additional factors contributing to this shift away from moral treatment to a medical model from 1850 onward. Aside from the building of larger, centralized state hospitals resulting from the campaign of Dorothea Dix, there was an increased number of immigrants among patients. The psychiatrists had difficulty in communicating with these individuals because of differences in language, social class, and background. It was much easier to view such alien people as being sick, which would explain their deviant behavior, instead of having problems in living, which would imply, as it did to the moral therapists, that they were basically no different from their therapists.[3]

[3] The concerns and rhetoric employed in discussions about immigrant patients, such as the Irish and Italians, is strikingly similar to that about blacks a century later: "In his 1859 Annual Report, Merrick Bemis, Superintendent of Worcester State Hospital, issued an ingenious prescription for dealing with immigrant patients with bad habits: create 'separate but equal facilities.'" (Caplan, 1969, p. 75.)

The success of medicine, which had made enormous strides in the late nineteenth century in overcoming many of the major diseases afflicting humanity, led to its adoption as a model for psychiatric treatment and research. The superintendent-physicians also

> ... were anxious to protect their status as medical practitioners and to emphasize that the care of the insane required rigorous training and experience. They tried to make psychiatry a recognized, distinct specialty within medicine. ... These scientific techniques gave alienists new pride in their calling. They were now able to claim that they, like practitioners of general medicine, saw tangible, measurable traces of disease. Such advances, however, minimized interest in the observations of living patients. ... [Caplan, 1969, pp. 109–10, 135.]

Finally,

> This new psychiatric technology ... had a poor effect on the patient community. Individual care was subordinated to mass treatment of categories. ... Practitioners no longer noted idiosyncratic symptoms of a patient, but dealt with the label he had once been given. [Caplan, 1969, pp. 138.]

There was a decline in expenditures for treatment in large hospitals. State hospitals, skimping on even the basic amenities of life, were relatively inexpensive. The ordinary citizen felt relieved of his responsibilities and found it easy to be indifferent to the abnormal when they were out of sight. Increased size and reduced expenditure led to overcrowding and consequently to even further decreased effectiveness (Ullmann, 1967a). Space that had been devoted to manual therapy and recreation was increasingly used to house patients. The ratio of physicians to attendants decreased. A vicious cycle of decreased discharge rate and increased crowding ensued.

Patients with behavior problems were viewed as being afflicted in the same manner as patients with organic diseases. The patients were cast in the same role as other medically ill people, a role that required a passive, submissive, quiet, untroublesome waiting for the discovery of a cure. Remissions were looked upon with disbelief, if not downright disfavor. If no treatment was known, none could be given, and none was given. "The very idea of dead and decomposing brain cells carried with it the connotation of the patient's growing insensibility and unawareness of surroundings." (Bockoven, 1963, p. 88.) Bell (quoted in Caplan, 1969, p. 95) gave an example of this pessimism when, in 1857, he wrote: "I have come to the conclusion that, when once a man becomes insane, he is about used up for this world."

As a result of decreased expenditure and staffing, the person most intimately associated with patients became the attendant rather than the psychiatrist or "professional" person. This led to the development of the "aide culture." Unskilled and poorly paid, the aide was responsible for the care of a large number of patients. His task was to keep them clean, quiet, and peaceful rather than to help them leave the hospital. The aide reinforced those behaviors which helped him do his job and thus increased the likelihood of apathy, withdrawal, and prolonged hospitalization.

In the 1890's neuropathologists were added to the staffs of psychiatric hospitals in response to the need for neurological research. The first of the neuropathologists to devote his energies on a full-time basis to research in psychiatry was Adolf Meyer (1866–1950). Meyer organized case histories, mental and physical examinations, and special laboratory studies. He collected data in the hope of discovering the relationships between mental symptoms and pathological changes in brain cells and body chemistry. Instead of achieving this goal he found an unexpected relationship between the habit patterns of patients and their emission of abnormal behavior. From his study of patients' lives, Meyer concluded that mental illnesses were understandable as the particular reactions of the total person to his life

approaches to abnormality: modern

situation. Meyer therefore introduced a new approach to which he gave the name *psychobiology*.

Emil Kraepelin (1856–1926), a German psychiatrist, had an enormous influence on the development of psychiatry. The English translation of his *Textbook of Psychiatry* changed the system of classification of mental disorders then in use in America, and is the foundation of current official nosological systems. Kraepelin had a curious and contradictory effect on the course of psychiatry. He brought a semblance of order to the field of diagnosis and, at the same time, injected a note of somber pessimism into the matter of prognosis. He stimulated a new interest in patients' behavior at the descriptive level. Diagnosticians had to observe what the patient did and said in order to obtain material to categorize the patient. On the other hand, Kraepelin succeeded in establishing the categories as disease entities independent of the patient as a person. Furthermore, he thought the agents that caused physical disease could cause mental illnesses.

THE ORGANIC POINT OF VIEW

Since the eighteenth century there has been a steady stream of formulations of mental illness as an organic disorder. The belief was, and still is, strong that an organic cause can be found for mental illness, and, once found, will make such illnesses amenable to physical treatments such as surgery or drugs. This view is summarized in the pithy phrase: "No twisted thought without a twisted molecule. . . ." (Quoted from Gerard by Abood, 1960, p. 91.)

The discovery of the cause of general paresis and its eventual cure represents the classic success of the organic viewpoint. Here was an illustration of widespread abnormal behavior, the cause of which was eventually clearly proven to be of specific physical (organic) origin.

The first mention of the manifestation of what was to be labeled as general paralysis was reported in medical literature in 1672 by Thomas Wills. The following description by the physician, Haslam, applies to the disease as it has been since characterized:

As a rule the paralytics present disorders of motion, which are wholly independent of their mental disease. Speech is defective, the corners of the mouth are drawn down, the arms and legs are more or less deprived of their voluntary movements, and in the majority of patients, memory is materially weakened. These patients, as a rule, fail to recognize their condition so much that [though] they can scarcely keep on their legs, they still maintain they are extremely strong and capable of the greatest deeds. [Haslam, *Observations on Madness and Melancholy*, London, 1798, p. 259.]

J. E. D. Esquirol (1772–1840) in 1814 described this type of paralysis as accompanying or resulting from dementia (an overall condition of madness). This view was an expression of the general belief at that time that the paralysis was an illness *distinct* from the associated mental illness and occurred as a complication of the mental disorder. The Frenchman A. L. J. Bayle argued (in 1822) that *both* the mental and physical symptoms were an expression of a *single* disease based on a chronic inflammation of the meninges of the brain and characterized by disturbances of intellectual functions, by grandiose ideas, and by progressive muscular discoordination and enfeeblement. Further, he argued that these particular symptoms were not part of any other mental illness.

Despite what proved to be a correct identification as to the nature of general paresis (so labeled in 1862), Bayle accepted the prevailing view as to the cause of this disease. Since it was more common in males, Bayle believed that it was related to the fact that men were often subject to mental shocks, excessive drinking, and head injuries. He believed it to be purely accidental that soldiers were more often afflicted than any other class of individuals. Such individuals supposedly had become more susceptible because of the privations and excessive drinking associated with the Napoleonic Wars. Bayle also believed that there were predisposing moral causes of the disease. He related the disorder to disappointment, sorrow, violent love, profound jealousy, excessive intellectual endeavors, and passionate temperament.

Other physicians of the nineteenth century related the disease to the use of tobacco or coffee or considered it to be an accompaniment of mental excitement and overwork, or even of outstanding intellect, since the symptoms were frequently observed among government officials, military officers, artists, and musicians. Others believed that differences in climate had an influence, since the incidence of paresis was less frequent in the south of France and Italy and much more common in North Germany. Still others held that the disease was due to sexual excesses, particularly masturbation. When Esmarch and Nessen suggested in 1857 that syphilis caused paresis, Wilhelm Griesinger (1817–1868), the leading medical authority in Europe, disagreed, maintaining that the reason it affected men was because of "frequent excesses in spiritous liquors and venery" and because of "strong cigars and strong coffee."

A. Fournier, in 1875, instigated statistical studies of the incidence of illnesses which disclosed that a history of syphilis was obtained in 65 percent of the cases of general paralysis, in contrast to only 10 percent in other mental illnesses. He concluded that there was a relationship between syphilis and general paresis.

As additional data accumulated, particularly from histological studies, the involvement of the central nervous system became clearer. A conclusive experiment was conducted in 1897 by a Viennese psychiatrist, Richard von Krafft-Ebing. He inoculated with syphilitic virus nine paretic patients who had had no previous history of syphilitic infection. When none of these patients developed the secondary symptoms of syphilis, he concluded that they had been previously infected. Historically this finding was crucial to establishing the relationship of syphilis to paresis.

The cause of syphilis was sought by laboratory studies of cerebrospinal fluids and the cellular content of nerve fibers. Many investigators had found that diseases of the nervous system were accompanied by an increase in the number of nerve fiber cells. A specific test was devised by Wassermann in 1906 to determine the presence of syphilitic antibodies in blood cells. The presence of the spirochete causing syphilis (isolated in 1905 by Schaudinn and Schwann) in the bloodstream could be detected before a person "knew" he was infected. In 1913 Noguchi and Moore discovered the syphilitic spirochete in the brain of paretic patients during post-mortem examinations. This discovery brought an end to theorizing about general paralysis or paresis and was a major step toward developing a treatment procedure.

At first, treatment of general paresis was the same as for all mental disorders. Bayle, for example, recommended total abstinence from all alcoholic beverages, the use of laxatives, leeches, bleedings, and avoidance of the sun. As the relationship with syphilis began to be clearly established, the most popular medicinal agent became some form of mercury. Benjamin Rush argued that mercury acts "by abstracting morbid excitement from the brain to the mouth, by removing visceral obstructions, and by changing the cause of our patients' complaints, and fixing them wholly upon his sore mouth." (Rush, 1812, cited in Zilboorg and Henry, 1941, p. 548.)

In 1909 Paul Ehrlich introduced arsenic (Salvarsan) in the treatment of syphilitic spirochetes in the bloodstream. However, Salvarsan was not effective in killing the spirochete if it had already reached the central nervous system. It had been previously observed, usually based on chance happenings, that one serious illness would some-

approaches to abnormality: modern

times have a profound effect on another more dangerous illness. Fevers, for example, were often induced in order to fight other illness. A Viennese psychiatrist, Julius Wagner-Jauregg, suggested infecting psychotics with malaria, tuberculosis, or typhus. In 1917 he achieved considerable lasting benefit by using malaria as a treatment for paresis. In recent years penicillin has become the treatment of choice for syphilis.

The discovery of the cause of general paresis has important implications for the study of abnormal behavior. There clearly may be other diseases like paresis which are caused by physical lesions.

The Organic Viewpoint and Mental Retardation

An area in which the organic viewpoint has made important gains, and may be expected to continue to do so, is in the etiology and treatment of severe mental retardation. While retardation will be discussed in detail in Chapter 24, it may be noted at this point that the history of the care and study of the retarded parallels (although frequently 10 to 50 years later) developments in behaviors considered psychotic. The trends noted during the Middle Ages (Chapter 6) may be illustrated with this group of people. On the one hand they were tolerated and even considered the "infants of the good God." For example, the Talmud says, "From the day of the destruction of the Temple, the art of prophecy was taken away [from professionals] and given to fools," and the fifth verse of the fourth Sura of the Koran calls for the feeding, housing, and kindly treatment of those without reason. On the other hand, concepts of demonology may be seen in Luther's *Table Talks,* in which he counseled the drowning of an idiot, "a mass of flesh with no soul, corrupted and possessed by the devil."

Early efforts in rehabilitation were undertaken by Pereire (1715–1780) with deaf mutes. In 1749 he demonstrated, in Paris, a deaf mute who could read and speak. Pereire's work stimulated and influenced that of later students. Most notable among these was Itard (1774–1838), who reported his still fascinating work in attempting to train a feral child, "the wild boy of Aveyron." Seguin (1812–1880) was another major contributor who devoted himself to the education of the retarded. His work illustrated to the satisfaction of many that "idiots" could be educated.

Perhaps the most notable figure during the nineteenth century in the field of mental retardation was Johann Jacob Guggenbuhl (1816–1863). In 1838, while passing through a village in Switzerland, Guggenbuhl was stirred by a cretin mumbling the Lord's Prayer at a wayside cross. Guggenbuhl found that there existed a great number of treatises describing the symptoms and (incorrect) etiology of cretinism, but there was nothing on its treatment. In 1830 he became director of an institution for the retarded at Abendberg. His treatment of the retarded paralleled that of the moral treatment of the insane. His work was hailed throughout the world as a major reform. This proved to be both a blessing and a curse, for while Guggenbuhl was away from his institution lecturing and spreading his ideas, his own institution declined, and an investigation in 1858 found ample basis for justifiable criticism. Guggenbuhl resigned and spent the remainder of his life trying to vindicate himself. To quote Kanner (1964, p. 30): "Guggenbuhl must be acknowledged as the indisputable originator of the idea and practice of the institutional care of feebleminded individuals."

The major force in applying Guggenbuhl's advances in the United States was Samuel Gridley Howe (1801–1876). The period of Guggenbuhl and Howe might be called the moral treatment era of retardation; the emphasis was on amelioration and treatment. As with moral treatment of the insane, there was first an expansion of the *number* of institutions, and later an increase in their *size*. By 1875 there were 25 "state schools," which were analogous to centralized psychiatric hospitals. The very size of the institutions curtailed treatment and training, and the goal became custodial. Retardation, like psychosis, came to be viewed as incurable, and the resulting conditions confirmed the hypothesis.

Another parallel between psychosis and retardation was the development of a system of categorization. Until the middle of the nineteenth century, idiocy was thought of as a more or less unitary condition. The words "cretins" and "idiots" were, for example, used interchangeably. In 1887, W. W. Ireland (1832–1909) published what may be considered the first modern text in the field; it indicated 12 subdivisions such as microcephalic idiocy, cretinism, and syphilitic idiocy.

Physical Approaches to Behavior Change

In modern times, there has been developed a great range of treatment procedures to cope with various deviant behaviors. The techniques can be categorized as parallels of the major theoretical approaches, organic and psychological. If the therapist thinks of disturbed behavior in terms of maladjustment, poor interpersonal contacts, or intrapsychic conditions, then he is likely to suggest various forms of psychotherapy, psychoanalysis, behavior therapy, or environmental manipulation. If he conceptualizes his work in terms of damaged brain cells, faulty heredity, or poor physiological functioning, then he is likely to prescribe medication, surgery, shock, fever, or even sleep. It is these latter procedures that this section will describe.

Although drugs have been used throughout history in the treatment of behavioral as well as physical disorders, the current upsurge in the use of drugs started in the mid-1950's. At that time it was noted that the drug reserpine had a calming effect on hospitalized patients. Reserpine is derived from the plant rauwolfia (snake root) and had been used in India for many centuries to treat a wide range of difficulties including mental disorders. Reserpine and other drugs like it which have calming effects in individuals are classified as tranquilizers or ataractic drugs. Other drugs, called energizers, such as the monoamine oxidase inhibitors, are used to treat depression. Currently, lithium compounds are also in favor.

At first, as with other new procedures, there was considerable enthusiasm and what amounted to overoptimistic reports of the efficacy of these drugs. Then, as more careful studies were reported, a more cautious attitude evolved, because drugs seemed to lead to effects that were not much better than the effects of placebos. Despite this, the drugs have taken their place as standard treatment procedure in many hospital and out-patient situations.

The major effects of ataractic drugs may be summarized as follows:

1. Behavioral reports indicate a lessening of anxiety, aggressive behavior, and, to some extent, hallucinations and delusions. The patient taking tranquilizers becomes more docile and cooperative. All of this may be described as a general lowering of inappropriate reactivity and responsivity.

2. Many of the reported concomitants of agitated behavior, such as conflict, distortion of reality, and disturbed affect, remain unchanged.

3. Patients who are more tranquil and calm become accessible to other forms of treatment such as psychotherapy or behavior therapy.

4. When an individual becomes calmer and less agitated, he becomes less of a threat to the staff in a hospital. Nurses, aides, doctors, and family are more likely to react positively toward him, hence evoking more positive behavior on his part. In terms of hospitals this has meant more open wards and less use of physical restraints.

5. Tranquilizers may have unpleasant and undesirable side-effects such as low blood pressure, nightmares, depressions, and ulcers. There has been a continued effort by drug

companies to synthesize new drugs with fewer harmful side-effects.

6. Research on the effectiveness of these drugs was a spur to improved research design in the entire field. The area of design was discussed in Chapter 3 on research methodology, and the important effects of placebos were detailed in Chapter 5.

7. Chlorpromazine and reserpine have been used primarily with hospitalized schizophrenic patients, whereas meprobamate has been used with "anxious neurotics." The effects of drugs such as Equanil and Miltown (trade names for the generic drug meprobamate) have been debated with no real evidence that they reduce anxiety any more than other sedatives such as phenobarbital. (Greenblatt and Shader, 1971)

8. The exact way in which the tranquilizers work physiologically is largely conjectural. It is speculated that they affect subcortical brain centers and probably act on the midbrain.

The use of drugs such as antabuse for alcoholics and methadone for heroin addicts will be discussed in Chapter 22 on addictions.

Another physical form of treatment is electroconvulsive therapy (ECT). This method developed from the observation that seemingly few epileptics developed schizophrenia. At present, ECT is often considered a treatment of choice for psychotic depressives and other patients whose difficulties have a rapid, recent onset and involve agitated mood changes. There is evidence that when restricted to such a group, ECT can be very useful in hastening the time of recovery. However, as Ewalt and Farnsworth (1963, p. 199) state, "ECT is much abused, which explains the disrepute into which it has fallen in some areas, but poor judgment in the use of any treatment is to be deplored."

Why ECT should be useful, if indeed it is, is a matter of speculation. With true English restraint, Batchelor (1969, p. 322) says of ECT, "The *modus operandi* of the treatment is still conjectural." Noyes and Kolb (1963, p. 538) are Americans and put the matter more bluntly: "Not yet, however, has a theory been presented that satisfactorily explains the therapeutic action in any one of the forms of shock therapy, much less one that applies to all forms." Ewalt, Strecker, and Ebaugh (1957, p. 347) put the matter this way: "We do not know why ECT works. Apparently somehow, a combination of physiologic and psychologic reactions to the convulsive treatment produces profound changes in the ego's defense system. Whether these changes are primarily chemical, physiologic, or psychologic is by no means clear. One leans to the physiologic theories, but this is based on rationalization and not facts." The entirety of Hollister and Rosenbaum's (1970, p. 289) section on "Mode of action of ECT" runs three words: "No one knows."

In the absence of clear data, behaviorists may add their theory to the others. In part, ECT may be effective because of placebo reactions and the expectation by both patient and staff of improvement. In part, ECT may be so clearly indicative of a direct medical model that it absolves the person of responsibility for his prior behaviors and gives him an opportunity to start anew without a stigma of having previously malingered. And finally, ECT may well make the sick role uncomfortable.

A somatic therapy which continues to be utilized despite considerable controversy is psycho-surgery, in its most usual type, prefrontal lobotomy. This treatment was first conceived by Moniz in 1933 in Lisbon and first carried out under his direction by Lima in 1935 (Freeman, 1959). It was introduced to this country by Freeman and Watts in 1942.

The surgery involves the cutting of the nerve pathways between the prefrontal lobes of the brain and the thalamus. The surgical techniques may vary, as do the actual portions of the brain tissue severed or removed. The avowed rationale of the surgery, according to Moniz, is to "destroy the more or less fixed arrangement of cellular connections that exist in the brain, and particlarly those which are related to the frontal lobes" since the "fixed ideas and repetitive behavior in certain psychoses are accompanied by abnormal stabilization of cellular connections." (Freeman, 1959.) Freeman and Watts (1941) argued that the lobotomy can be used to decrease affect, particularly anxiety and tension.

These surgical procedures have been applied to individuals with a wide range of abnormal behaviors including schizophrenia, involutional psychosis, depressions of various sorts, personality disorders, and even neuroses. The results have been equivocal, and in many instances probably harmful. Barahal (1958) did a five- to ten-year follow-up on 1,000 lobotomy cases and emphasized the comparatively high rate of death, postoperative seizures, the "zombie-ism," and other undesirable behavioral characteristics. The clear inference from Becker and McFarland's lobotomy prognosis study (1955) was that the people improving after the operation were ones who were most likely to have improved without it and that it held little hope for cases with a poor prognosis.

THE BEHAVIORAL APPROACH

While many people noted the importance of learning on the development of behavior, the most direct line of development of contemporary behavioral approaches started with John Locke's (1632–1704) arguments that ideas were not inborn but came from interaction with the environment, that is, from experience.

The first major provision of a research methodology and data to spell out the effects of environmental experience was the work of Russian physiologists such as Sechenov (1829–1905), Pavlov (1849–1936), and Bekhterev (1857–1927). In Chapter 4 we reviewed some of Pavlov's work. At this point, as in Chapters 4 and 5, it is crucial to point out, as has Razran (1965) that Pavlov hypothesized a second signal system, composed of speech or verbal signals, and was not limited to an automatic or reductionist position. Outstanding among authors who have explicated this line of work are Skinner (1957) and Staats (1968, 1970). Pavlov suggested in detail *how* a general theory of behavior could be constructed in terms of *objective* physiological phenomena. He carefully explored empirical relationships, determined basic parameters, and laid the basis and terminology for literally thousands of experiments by his colleagues and their students.

J. B. Watson (1878–1958) recognized the value of the objective methods developed and used in animal psychology in exploring the nature of the learning process as a problem in the modification of behavior. Watson argued that abnormal behavior was the result of a "training" process. Watson did pioneering studies in infant conditioning and in collaboration with Rayner (Watson and Rayner, 1920) he demonstrated how a fear reaction could be developed in a young child (see Chapter 4).

The origin of present-day operant conditioning procedures may be traced, in part, to the 1898 work of E. L. Thorndike. Thorndike placed animals such as cats, dogs, and chicks in a "puzzle box" from which they could learn to escape by manipulating a door-releasing contrivance such as a latch or a lever. Once the hungry animal escaped, it obtained food. The speed of escaping increased on successive trials. From these early studies Thorndike, in 1911, formulated his "law of effect," based on his observation that when a behavior is followed by satisfying (rewarding) consequences, it is likely to be learned, and when it is followed by punishment, failure, or an annoying state of affairs, it is less likely to recur.

After Watson, the psychologist who most clearly espoused a useful form of behaviorism was E. R. Guthrie (1935, 1938, 1942). Guthrie, unlike Watson, did not start with the Pavlovian conditioned reflex as his basic paradigm of learning, but rather returned to the principles of associative learning with one law of learning as follows: "a combination of stimuli which has accompanied a movement will on its recurrence tend to be followed by that movement." (1935, p. 26.) A second statement completes his postulates about learning: "a stimulus pattern gains its full associative strength on the occasion of its first pairing with a response." (1942, p. 30.)

The following quotation illustrates the similarity of Guthrie's language and concepts to the formulation of maladaptive behavior presented in this book:

To break a habit it is first necessary to know the stimuli responsible for its release. It is then necessary to use whatever arts one has to cause the person to do something else in this situation. This is the full recipe. . . . The habit may be "sidetracked" by interrupting it in its very beginning and causing this beginning to be followed by some other action. Or the patient may, by having the action deprived of success in the sense that it removes the motivating stimulus, bring about by trial and error behavior his own substitution for the unwanted act. In all these cases we are merely insuring that a cue which was once followed by the undesirable action is *once* followed by something else. If practice of the substitution is required, this is because the undesired act had more than one cue and it is necessary to recondition all its cues. [Guthrie, 1938, pp. 386–87.]

William Burnham's 1924 volume, *The Normal Mind,* must be considered to be an important development in the growth of the behaviorial approach. Burnham anticipated many of the procedures that were to be widely used 30 years later. For example, he had a chapter specifically entitled "Inhibiting the Inhibitions" in which he argued that in treatment ". . . the essential factor . . . is the associated stimulus that inhibits the inhibitions. In other words, one brings the child definitely to face the cause of its fear, just as the horse trainer, with soothing words, leads the colt face to face with what has frightened it. Then one associates a rival stimulus with the fear inspiring object or idea. . . . by such discussion, rival stimuli would be associated, and . . . these associated ideas would inhibit the fear." (p. 149.) In this quotation, "cause" is the "fear inspiring object or idea" (stimulus) and not some "underlying cause" of which the objective stimulus is a displacement. Burnham was interested in education, mental hygiene, and training adaptive behavior so that maladaptive behavior would be less likely to occur. He presented a series of general principles which he considered to be the goals of training: the performance of social duty in a natural group; the development of integration in the face of distracting stimuli; individual responsibility in the group; and the development of conditions that give the opportunity for social success. He summarized these goals with the statement that "All this implies freedom." That is, the object is freedom to make meaningful and useful choices rather than to behave without guidance or restraint.

In the same year that Burnham's *The Normal Mind* was published, there appeared two important articles by Mary Cover Jones. The first of these (1924a) reported how a three-year-old child whose fear of a white rat had been extended to other "furry" objects, such as a rabbit, a fur coat, a feather, and cotton wool, was treated by direct conditioning, the association of a rabbit with the presence of food which the child liked. At times other children were present in the situation to foster the imitation of socially desirable responses. In a second article (1924b), Jones discussed empirical trials of a variety of techniques in the elimination of children's fears. Certain methods were quite ineffective: elimination through disuse (fears would disappear with time if the stimuli were avoided); repression (ridicule, social teasing); and verbal appeal (pleas for change). Negative adaptation (extinction), in which familiarity bred contempt, eliminated the fear, but did not re-establish a normal, interested response. A method of distraction (which merged with the method of direct reconditioning) in which the feared object was placed in the context of a desired goal was found to be fairly effective. Another useful technique was the method of direct reconditioning, the association of the feared object with a stimulus capable of arousing a pleasant reaction. Findings similar to those of Jones were reported by Jersild and Holmes (1935) and Holmes (1936). Their approach was similar to Burnham's inhibition of inhibition and to Wolpe's current concept of reciprocal inhibition (1958).

Other instances of early behavioral techniques will be briefly mentioned. In 1925, Hamilton published *An Introduction to Objective Psychopathology* that used behavioral terms as explanatory concepts. Although forms of aversion treatment for alcoholism can be found as far back as the Romans,[4] e.g., eels in the wine cup, Kantorovich (1930) presented an early contemporary approach to the conditioned aversion treatment of alcoholism (see Chapter 22). Max (1935) described an aversion treatment of an obsessional sexual difficulty (see Chapter 21); and Mowrer and Mowrer (1938) presented the crucial article in the conditioning treatment of enuresis (see Chapter 23). In all three of these approaches, a crucial element was direct training based on response contingency.

In three works (1928, 1930, 1932) Dunlap offered theory and case illustrations of the method of negative practice that has been found useful in the treatment of tics, stuttering, and nail-biting. Malleson (1959) and Yates (1958b) later extended Dunlap's techniques to some phobic and obsessive conditions. The undesirable behavior is practiced until, in Hullian terms, reactive inhibition builds up to the extent that not doing the

---

[4] Ovid, in the *Remedies of Love*, associates negative feelings with the loved object as follows:

Virtue and vice, evil and good, are siblings, or next-door neighbors,
    Easy to make mistakes, hard to tell them apart.
When you possibly can, fool yourself, ever so little,
    Call those attractions of hers defects, or possibly worse.
If she has full round breasts, call her fat as a pig. . . .
Whatever talent she lacks, coax and cajole her to use it:
    If she hasn't a voice, try to persuade her to sing;
If she trips over her feet, make her dance; if her accent's atrocious,
    Get her to talk; all thumbs? Call for the zither or lyre.

* * *

Open the windows wide, all of them, draw back the curtains,
    Let the light make clear parts that are ugly to see.
When you have come to the end, and all pleasure is over,
    When the body and mind are both exhausted and spent,
While you are bored, and you wish you had never touched any woman,
    While you haven't the least impulse to touch one again,
Then note down in your mind her every blemish of body,
    Keep your eyes on her faults, memorize every defect.
    [Humphries translation, p. 191, 193–94.]

In the same poem, Ovid proposes a satiation technique as follows:

Satisfy all your thirst, relieve the fever that burns you.
    I have nothing to say—drink from the midst of the stream,
But drink even more than the heart could possibly long for,
    Drink till your gullet is full, drink till you slobber your chin.
Keep on enjoying your girl, with nobody there to prevent you,
Let her have all your nights, let her consume all your days.
Get fed up with it all: excess puts an end to your troubles.
    Even though you believe you have had plenty, remain,
Stay till there's more than enough, till you're perfectly sure you will never
    Ask for it any more; stay till her house is a bore.
    [p. 197.]

behavior is a positively reinforcing experience (termination and/or avoidance of the aversive condition of fatigue).

Hollingworth (1930) is another investigator whose work foreshadowed current behavioral approaches. The following description of stagefright illustrates his thinking:

> On any of the three theories, the same therapy is indicated, the substitution of some other reaction for the disabling one, through re-education or new experience. If stage-fright is a direct fear phenomenon, the hopeful therapy is simply that of giving some other emotion right of way by virtue of the frequency of its appearance. Elation, enthusiasm, confidence, must be connected with the appearance of an audience. If stage-fright is the conflict of two competing tendencies, the conflict can be resolved only by strengthening the emotion which competes with the disabling tendencies. And if stage-fright be an emotional redintegration, the only way of escape is by attaching new consequents to its typical stimulus. [pp. 421–22.]

By the start of World War II, there was a considerable body of theory, practice, and research in the behavioral field. There was, however, a hiatus of a quarter century before there was widespread application of this material. There are a number of possible explanations for this "cultural lag." The majority of clinical psychologists worked in medical settings and may well have overlooked writings by Burnham, Hollingworth, Jones, Guthrie, and Jersild and Holmes, who worked in educational and research settings. Also, much of the time and energy of professional workers went into diagnostic work, which from the time of the intelligence test had been the psychologist's major contribution in the clinic. However, the increased number of clinical psychologists after World War II, the steadily increasing standards for doctoral training and research, and the growing sophistication of learning and statistical procedures led to the increased use of newer approaches. There was both an increased transfer of skills from the laboratory and an increased questioning of traditional methods. In the area of psychodiagnostics, this trend was highlighted by Meehl's book on clinical versus statistical prediction (1954), which questioned many assumptions about projective testing and personality measurement. In the area of psychotherapy perhaps the most provocative article, both as stimulant and as reflections of the growing dissatisfaction with traditional procedures, was Eysenck's unfavorable evaluation of the effectiveness of traditional psychotherapy (1952).

Attempts to link experimental and clinical psychology appeared after World War II (Dollard and Miller, 1950; Cameron and Magaret, 1951; Shaw, 1948; Shoben, 1949). These writings translated psychotherapeutic concepts into the newer and more "scientific" language of learning theory. These works led to a new way of *talking* about therapy, but they did not result in a new way of *doing* therapy.

Two books represent the application of laboratory research to the development of new methods of changing behavior. The first of these was B. F. Skinner's *Science and Human Behavior* (1953), which provided emphasis on and intellectual tools for the measurement and manipulation of molar, and hence more relevant, social behavior.

A second crucial book was Wolpe's *Psychotherapy by Reciprocal Inhibition* (1958), the first half of which included a summary of the laboratory work leading to the therapeutic techniques detailed in the latter half. Eysenck's anthology of writings on behavior therapy (1960) and the establishment of the journal *Behaviour Research and Therapy* in 1963 (Rachman, 1963a) brought together much of the material that had been widely scattered throughout the literature.

Recent investigators have supplemented the direct use of research results which has been the major factor in the marked increase in the use of behavior therapy (Krasner and Ullmann, 1965). During the 1950's, many researchers and practitioners turned their attention to studies of the change of clinically relevant human behavior. A number of anthologies (Bachrach, 1962; Berg and Bass, 1961; Biderman and Zimmer, 1961; Franks, 1964; Krasner and Ullmann, 1965; Staats, 1964; Ullmann and Krasner, 1965b; McGinnies and Ferster, 1971; Baron and Liebert, 1971; Evans and Rozelle, 1970; Toch and Smith, 1968; Ulrich, Stachnik, and Mabry, 1966, 1970) brought together a fair sampling of this material, which includes studies of attitude change, group behavior, verbal behavior in interview situations, classical conditioning, sensory deprivation, drugs, hypnosis, physiological correlates of social stimuli, modeling, role-playing, and placebo response. Psychologists who were identified as research workers turned their attention to clinical populations and problems, and the distinction between experimentalist and clinician became blurred. A psychology of social influence (Goldstein, Heller, and Sechrest, 1967; Krasner and Ullmann, 1973) developed as an area which drew support from and made contributions to many other aspects of psychology, and fostered the growth of a technology of behavior change.

THE PROFESSIONS

In earlier discussions of the people currently involved in the labeling and treatment of deviant behavior, the professions most frequently referred to are psychiatrists, psychoanalysts, clinical psychologists and social workers.

As a profession the word "psychoanalyst" refers to a person who utilizes Freud's theory and form of treatment. It should not be confused with either the word "psychologist" or "psychiatrist." A *psychiatrist* is a person who has a medical degree, an internship, and then a residency in psychiatry. A *psychologist* is a person who has earned the Ph.D., essentially a research degree. A *clinical psychologist* is a person who has a Ph.D. plus, at least, a clinical internship in the area of deviant behaviors.

In this country the vast majority of *psychoanalysts* are psychiatrists who, during their residency or shortly thereafter, studied at a psychoanalytic institute. A psychoanalyst has had a successful personal analysis, usually undergone with an outstanding "training analyst." In addition, his first cases will have been monitored and his own reactions further analyzed. A few clinical psychologists have become psychoanalysts as defined by admission to a psychoanalytic institute and completion of personal and didactic analyses. In Europe, in contrast to the United States, there are many people without doctoral degrees who are "lay analysts," a practice of which Freud approved.

Lightner Witmer (1867–1956) may be considered to be the founder of clinical psychology in the United States. He contributed a definition of the clinical psychologist, a setting in which to work, and a journal in which to publish—the major activities for a profession. In 1896 Witmer founded the first psychological clinic at the University of Pennsylvania. In a paper given that year Witmer presented what was then a new method of research and training, called the "clinical method in psychology and the diagnostic method of teaching." He described clinical psychology as derived from the results of examining many human beings one at a time, and involving an analytic method of discriminating mental abilities and defects. Witmer defined a psychological diagnosis as "an interpretation of the observed behavior of human beings." He argued that clinical psychology must develop an ordered classification of observed behavior by means of generalizations from behavior. He conceived of the psychological clinic as an institution for public service, for original research, and for training students to work with social, educational, vocational, and correctional problems.

If one substitutes the word "behavior"

for the word "mind," Witmer's definition of clinical psychology would be quite acceptable today: "For the methods of clinical psychology are necessarily involved whenever the status of an individual mind is determined by observation and experiment, and pedagogical treatment applied to effect a change, i.e., the developments of such individual mind" (1907).

G. Stanley Hall (1844–1924) influenced clinical psychologists working with disturbed behavior and psychiatry by his stimulation of Adolf Meyer's study of children. Hall's influence on clinical psychology was primarily felt through his educational endeavors, e.g., inviting Freud to lecture in this country in 1909 and training psychiatrists and psychologists such as Goddard, Terman, and Gesell.

Another development of importance for clinical psychology was the child guidance movement. William Healy, a psychiatrist, was the director of the first child guidance clinic, founded in Chicago in 1909. This clinic fostered the view that children's antisocial behavior was treatable by psychological means. In 1917 Healy and a psychologist, Augusta F. Bronner, established a clinic in Boston called the Judge Baker Foundation. This clinic and Healy and Bronner's writings became major influences in the field of juvenile delinquency.

Psychological testing played a crucial role in the development of clinical psychology. It provided a role for the psychologist that smoothed his way in the clinical setting. Francis Galton (1822–1911), a cousin of both Darwin and Huxley, is credited with establishing mental tests by his investigations of individual differences. His basic contribution was observation of behavior to make inferences about individual differences. In 1890 James McKeen Cattell (1860–1938), trained under Wundt, formalized Galton's procedures by calling them mental tests and argued strongly for standardization of procedures and establishment of norms.

With its initial emphasis on children, individual differences, and mental tests, it was natural that early clinical psychology should involve the development of intelligence tests. In Paris, the psychologist Alfred Binet (1857–1911) and the physician Théodore Simon initiated the standardized, individual test of intellectual functioning.

In 1916 Terman published the Stanford–Binet, having tested over 1,000 subjects and standardized the test for age levels three to eighteen.

An important adjunct to the individual intelligence test were group tests originally designed to screen large numbers of recruits during World War I and World War II. The Alpha Scale for literate English-speaking recruits and the Beta Scale for illiterates and non-English-speaking recruits were developed to appraise the intelligence of large numbers of men in World War I. Similar but more sophisticated tests were given on even a larger scale during World War II. During the 1930's, the continuing growth of personality and clinical psychology saw the introduction of projective techniques such as the Rorschach and the TAT (Murray, 1936).

Attempts to give charity efficiently, led in the early nineteenth century to the development of the role of "advisers" to philanthropists. "Out of this orientation, as well as the earlier investigations to determine the 'worthiness' of the poor, grew the 'case method' or casework." (Rosen, 1969, p. 311). In 1904, a full-time college curriculum was established for social workers, and in 1905 psychiatric hospitals started using trained social workers to obtain social history information along the lines suggested by Adolph Meyer. The first school of psychiatric social work was established at Smith College in 1918. Currently, social workers utilize the same range of theories, and with the exception of psychological testing and medical prescription, perform the same daily therapeutic tasks as clinical psychologists and psychiatrists.

Through private philanthropy such as the National Committee for Mental Hygiene (established in 1909 by Clifford Beers, Adolph Meyer, and William James) and through federal assistance (reflected in conferences such as the 1909 White House Conference on the Care of Dependent Children), ==interest and funding for research and treatment of people, especially children with behavioral problems, developed.== The field as it was to exist for the next half a century, was thus broadly outlined.

SUMMARY

The period between the French Revolution and World War I saw the development of the major theories and professions that characterize contemporary methods for dealing with abnormal behavior. A historical perspective indicates how formulations, treatment, and research in this field may be viewed as responses to current situations. Because of the development of anesthetics, hypnotism fell into relative obscurity at the moment it might have been widely used. Moral treatment, a hopeful and potentially major contribution during the first part of the century, literally deteriorated because of the adoption of the medical model, the building of large institutions, and the great increase in the number of patients treated in them. The achievement of moral treatment may be summarized by a quotation from Pinel (1806, cited in Bockoven, 1963, p. 34): "The successful application of moral regimen exclusively gives great weight to the supposition that, in the majority of instances, there is no organic lesion of the brain nor of the cranium." The major success of the organic approach, on the other hand, was the investigation and treatment of paresis, an advanced stage of syphilis.

Also discussed in this chapter were the major psychological and physical approaches to treating deviant behavior. Finally, the medical and professional background which set the stage for Sigmund Freud was described.

Freud and psychoanalysis

8

The person who has had the major impact upon contemporary concepts and treatment of deviant behavior has been Sigmund Freud (1856–1939). Freud can be presented in three different but overlapping contexts: as a historical figure with a great impact on his society, as the originator of a theory of personality, and as the developer of a treatment of neurosis.

Although trained as a physiologist, Freud became a practitioner of medicine because of financial pressures, specializing in the treatment of "nervous" disorders. He came into close professional contact with Josef Breuer (1842–1925), a Viennese physician who used hypnosis to help patients to talk about themselves, their problems, and any other material that came into their minds. The procedure was described as catharsis or "chimney sweeping" in that it represented a cleaning out of material that was clogging the functioning of the mind. In 1893 Freud published with Breuer the first of several papers on hysteria.

The intellectual forces at work in the Western world in the late nineteenth century had a definite impact on Freud. Charles Darwin's *The Origin of Species* (1859) viewed man as part of nature and hence an object of scientific study. The book enormously encouraged subsequent naturalistic studies of man's behavior. This was also the period in which psychology emerged as an objective science investigating the human "mind," the major landmarks being the publication of a text on psychophysics in 1860 by Gustav Fechner (1801–1887) and the founding of the first psychological laboratory by Wilhelm Wundt (1832–1920) in 1879 in Leipzig. It was also the period of growth of the life sciences such as bacteriology and genetics (Pasteur, Koch, Mendel), and it has been called the "golden age of physics," representing as it did the start of the atomic era. Of particular importance for their influence on Freud were Von Helmholtz' theory of the conservation of energy and Clark Maxwell's work on thermodynamics.

It was during this period, too, that the new medical model of abnormal behavior was coming into prominence (see the discussion of the decline of moral treatment in Chapter 7). Throughout his career Freud was attracted to and repelled by the medical model. He repeatedly expressed his annoyance with medicine as the profession to treat neuroses, arguing cogently (in, e.g., *The Question of Lay Analysis,* 1926) that psychoanalysis should not be tied to medicine, which would only hamper it as a treatment procedure.

Freud has a very richly deserved place in the history of psychology and psychiatry. It is extremely difficult to look at oneself constructively and to maintain an objective attitude about one's own problems. Only in this light can Freud's tremendous personal accomplishment be appreciated. He not only made the solitary inward journey; he developed a method others could use. This method led to a form of treatment, psychoanalysis, and a way of looking at people that has had an impact on practically every form of human behavior.

PSYCHOANALYSIS AS TREATMENT

Psychoanalysis did not spring full blown from the mind of Freud. Rather it went through a number of changes and overlapping stages in its development. In general, the procedures of each new form of the treatment were additions to the previous stage of treatment.

Although he had previously written on a number of other problems, Freud's first published works in the field of abnormal psychology were based upon his private practice as a neurologist with a small number of female Viennese upper-class women whose strange behaviors were called hysterical.

In his early work, Freud collaborated with Breuer and, influenced by Charcot, used hypnosis to treat his patients. Post-hypnotic suggestion would result in the patient's being able to move an affected limb. However, this kind of improvement did not assist the person in handling the situation that led to the "hysterical" behavior, nor did it open to the person alternative ways of gratification. Under these conditions, Freud reported some cases of initial but not lasting success. Other difficulties Freud found with hypnosis were that some people did not attain sufficiently deep hypnotic states, and that frequently the patient in the hypnotic role would indicate a lack of personal responsibility that would thwart the therapist.

Freud next proceeded to have the patient talk about the events in his past life, especially the original circumstances that presumably led to the difficulty. The person was asked to lie on a couch and to "free associate," to say whatever came to his mind. *Free association* is still the major technique in psychoanalysis. The so-called "basic rule" in psychoanalysis refers to the instruction to the patient to speak freely about *anything* that may come to mind. By such a structuring of the task for the patients, Freud facilitated their ability to talk about their difficulties. He very frequently found that the reported problem centered around sexual material, and particularly some form of trauma or seduction early in life.

One of his early theories was that hysteria was due to a sexual assault upon the individual at an early age by an older male member of the family. Freud reluctantly discarded this theory when he found, on discussion with the patient's relatives, that the sexual assaults were historically impossible because the relatives were not geographically present at the time of the supposed seductions. This led to a period of "soul searching" and deep concern on Freud's part from which emerged a revision of the theory. Freud now argued that while some of the events his patients talked about did not actually occur, they were *psychically* real. That is, even if the events had not taken place in reality, the fact that a person had such sexual fantasies served a psychodynamic purpose, and hence the fantasies themselves altered behavior.

In this early period, the goal of treatment was the release of emotions that had not been given adequate expression. The patient was encouraged to vent his feelings and consequently to obtain a *catharsis* or cleaning out of undesirable emotions. Freud found, however, that it did not seem sufficient to have people cathart, abreact, or vent their suppressed feelings. As it became clear that many people had *not* been actually traumatized in early life, a new and additional goal of treatment was to locate more subtle sources of difficulty. The patient, now a rational adult, with the aid of the analyst endeavored to gain *insight* into the relationship between his behavior and the conflicting forces within his psyche. A technique for enhancing insight was *interpretation*, the therapist's posing of his hypotheses about the person's behavior. The person, in free-associating, would come to points where he would block, where he could not talk any further, and could not make any more progress in searching his past history. This blockage was called *re-*

sistance and could be reduced by interpretation and other aspects of the therapist–patient relationship.

This series of procedures may be illustrated by the *word association test,* a projective technique (the individual projects his own personality onto the test items) devised by Jung, an early follower of Freud. In this situation the therapist requests the subject to respond with the first word that comes to his mind after hearing a word said by the therapist. There are certain expected or common associations—table–chair, house–farm, mother–father. This technique offers ways in which areas of difficulties or complexes for individuals can be hypothesized. Two indications of difficulty are unusual associations and a long pause prior to responding. The analyst has listened to many associations in his career and through their content, sequence, and blockage he develops hypotheses as to what may be the patient's complexes or areas of difficulty. With this data he is able to use his theory to formulate reasons for the patient's blockage. Essentially, the therapist tells the patient what the patient already knows, plus a little more, offering part of the next step through the interpretation. However, Freud found that simple rational knowledge of why the difficulty had developed was not sufficient. The patient would very frequently attain intellectual insight and know why he did things and yet not change his behavior.

As the patient lay on the couch with the analyst sitting behind him, he would express various kinds of feelings toward the analyst. He might accuse the analyst of lasciviousness, hostility, or indifference. The analyst, who had himself been successfully analyzed and who presumably perceived the situation more accurately than the patient, considered that these feelings were not justified by reality. They were therefore the result of the patient's present problems and his early childhood difficulties. These feelings were considered to be directed toward the therapist *as if* he were a figure in the patient's life such as his father or brother. This *transference* onto the analyst of inappropriate emotions was interpreted by the therapist in order to help the patient better understand himself and to help overcome resistance. It gave an immediacy to feeling that could not be attained through mere discussion of past history.

When the patient feels favorable emotions toward the analyst that are unrealistic, they are called *positive transference*. These can be feelings of sexual desire or of dependence. They are, however, basically unrealistic and interpreted as stemming from the patient's early childhood. If the patient expresses hostility or other negative feelings, these are called *negative transference*.

Interpretation of transference continues as a basic element of psychoanalysis. However, a number of psychoanalysts, notably Harry Stack Sullivan, Karen Horney, and, in particular, Franz Alexander, found it possible in certain situations to interpret the *relationship* which the person *currently* had with other people, including the analyst. That is, rather than saying that the person was establishing a relationship based on childhood needs, how he acted with the analyst in the therapy hour was a reality which itself could be interpreted and "worked with."

The analyst would face the patient with reality and respond to him in a direct and realistic manner. He provided the patient with the valuable experience of an individual (1) who was both interested in the patient and professionally trained; (2) who was capable of responding to the patient's needs without interference from his own emotional requirements; (3) who would respond realistically and appropriately to the patient's behavior; and (4) who could when necessary point out accurately, that is, interpret, how the patient was relating to another person. The analyst provided a new experience or emotional re-education (Alexander and French, 1946, pp. 18–19).

To summarize the aspects of psychoanalytic treatment covered so far, there are four separate but interrelated techniques: *catharsis, insight, transference interpretation,* and *emotional re-education.* A person in a face-to-face interpersonal relationship in psychoanalysis may develop strong feelings, may show anger, may emit an emotional outburst, may have inappropriate feelings toward the analyst, and from the analyst's mature responses may learn new and more effective modes of adjustment.

The psychoanalyst's view of his therapeutic role stemmed from his theory of personality: the source of the difficulty lay within the patient and was unconscious. The very phenomena of the psychoanalytic situation itself, such as resistance and transference, were manifestations of intrapsychic conflicts in the same manner as more typically labeled symptoms. The analyst served as midwife to a process and, like a midwife, aided by removing obstacles without being responsible for the difficulties. The first hypothesis about the patient's behavior was that it was determined by and related to his problem. The analyst could then label the patient's behavior as indicative of intrapsychic conflicts and have a source of explanations of observed phenomena. On the other hand, the analyst traditionally was nonjudgmental and nonpunitive in the typical social meaning of that concept. To the extent that the person's behavior was caused by unconscious processes, the patient was not responsible for it and deserved tolerance. "Case histories have no villains, only victims." (attributed to Freud by Wolman, 1968, p. 170).

Finally, the analyst eschewed normal social contact with the patient. This took the form of avoiding the patient at social gatherings, and until recently, of not performing professional behaviors such as prescribing medication. The reason was that the analyst's "real" behaviors might lead to a vitiation of the transference: it would be difficult to separate the fantasied or projected analyst from the real one.

Waelder presents a most succinct statement of the relation between psychoanalysis as a theory and as a treatment procedure:

Psychoanalytic therapy stands and falls with the psychoanalytic theory of the neuroses. If this theory is correct, the psychoanalytic treatment appears as the only causal treatment, so far developed, of the neuroses, which treats the condition by trying to remove its cause; and if the theory should prove to be wholly or partially incorrect, the psychoanalytic treatment would lose its *raison d'être*, and whatever results have been achieved by its application would have to be explained as incidental, due to some other factors. [Waelder, 1960, p. 212.]

Waelder then proceeds to describe the goal of the psychoanalytic treatment as that of undoing the repressions and restoring to consciousness the full inner conflicts. These formerly repressed drives are put in contact with the rest of the personality and "all tendencies can vie with each other on the market place of consciousness and the solution of the conflict may be worked out, not immediately but with time. . . . Undoing repressions and making conscious the unconscious does therefore establish the situation which would have prevailed had repression not interfered." (p. 213.) The bringing back of a situation which previously had been avoided must inevitably bring a form of suffering with it. Freud (1933) described this by saying that "analysis transforms neurotic suffering into everyday misery."

PSYCHOANALYSIS AS THEORY

While there were many psychoanalysts who deviated from Freud's theoretical formulations and applications (Jung, Rank, Adler, and Sullivan, for example), the major cause of Freud's rejecting them was not deviation in *practice* but deviation from a major theoretical orientation, that of a basic biological drive. In Freud's theory, a person is viewed as having a limited amount of psychic energy, called *libido*, and certain inborn biological needs which are tension-arousing. Pleasure is the reduction of these biological tensions. While the amount of libido varies from person to person, in each person it is fixed much as there is a fixed amount of water in a reservoir. At birth a person is thought to have only strivings toward biological gratification (*pleasure principle*) centered on the mouth in sucking and eating. This first stage of pleasure through the mouth is called the *oral stage*.

One of the person's first experiences of meeting social demands is during toilet training. There is biological gratification in the release of tension through excretion. This in Freudian terms is called the *anal stage*. In this period the person begins to develop the *reality principle*, a recognition of the limitations on the pleasure principle due to punishment for inappropriate behavior by other, more powerful people. There are certain things which he wants to happen which do not occur and certain objects (people) he cannot control completely. From birth onward, the person gradually learns to make a distinction between himself and others. This distinction between his internal and external environments is the basic step in the development of the *ego*. It is clear that behavior indicative of the pleasure principle and of the reality principle may come into conflict. Innate biological, *id* impulses are placed under societal constraints. It is this gradual control of the biological by the social which may be seen as the core of Freud and other biologically oriented personality theorists (see Hollingworth, 1930, pp. 45–51, and Allport, 1937, pp. 114–21).

The next major locus of biological gratifications, according to Freudian theory, is centered on the penis, during the so-called *phallic* and *genital stages*. Concomitant with the phallic stage is a working through of the boy's relationship with his parents. Because the mother has been the major source of biological pleasures, the boy is thought of as wishing to obtain sole possession of her. However, he learns that the father has prior rights to the mother and he becomes jealous of the father. At a certain point the boy's masturbatory activity and his competition with the father interact. It is implied to the boy that if he does not stop playing with the penis he is likely to lose it. When the boy finds out that little girls have apparently lost their penises he becomes terrified. To protect himself the boy solves the threatening situation by giving up the mother and identifying with the father. That is, he resolves the *Oedipus complex*, his desire for his mother and wish for his father's death. He accepts as right and best for himself *his* view of the father's morality. This primitive morality, the basis of the *superego*, is the all-or-none, absolute, childish view of adult morals held by the five-year-old. It is not a rational conscience but primarily an unconscious, very stringent, puritanical view of moral behavior. At this point Freud presumes that the child gives up all sexual strivings until puberty, when the sexual drive again becomes strong. This period from the resolution of the Oedipus complex to puberty is called the *latency* period.

The development of conscience in girls, who do not have the possibility of being threatened by penis loss, is less clear. Since girls do not have a penis to lose, many Freudians have said that they cannot have a genuine castration anxiety and hence will not introject the adult conscience properly. Other analysts have said that the girl blames the mother for her lack of a penis and wishes to have the father give her a child to make up for her physiological lack.

At puberty, and assuming continuing favorable psychosexual conditions, the person will reach the *genital* stage. This is the final psychosexual stage of development and represents normality. In this stage, as all others, biological impulses require tension reduction (pleasure principle) and are modified by societal constraints (reality principle). The biological tension may be reduced through socially acceptable behavior that is an indirect or partial gratification. This procedure is called *sublimation,* the discharge of biological tension in socially useful or acceptable acts.

Individual differences, both normal and pathological, arise from the vicissitudes of psychosexual development. As indicated earlier, expressions of biological impulses are constrained by societal dictates. The behaviors and constraints represented by the id, the ego, and the superego, may conflict with each other. The normal succession of development to more mature goals may be disrupted by punishment, moral aversion, lack of available goal objects, or trauma. In the Freudian model normal behavior is the natural state and deviation from normal requires an explanation. Thus if the biological impulse which requires gratification is blocked for any reason, the need for its expression and gratification still continues.

For example, the impulse may be a socially unacceptable sexual desire (id impulse), the direct expression of which would elicit punishment as it conflicts with reality. The result of this conflict is that a pressure for expression builds up like flood waters on a dam and is held back only through the expenditure of psychic energy (libido). The pressure may be reduced by giving partial, altered, disguised, and more socially acceptable expression to the impulse in a manner similar to draining some water from an overflowing reservoir. The manner of expression may be disguised, hence symbolic, and the resulting behavior may be indicative or *symptomatic* of the underlying impulse. The particular form of expression selected is the one that will give the greatest gratification with the least threat. The specific overt behavior may be used to reduce more than one impulse at a time. The behavior is called *overdetermined* because it stems not only from the *present* reality situation but also from various *unconscious* forces. The energy used to repress an unacceptable impulse is not available for use in some other area of adjustment. The human being comprises an intrapsychic economy the parameters of which are unacceptable impulses and limited libido.

Among the impulses which need gratification are those associated with the oral, anal, and phallic stages previously discussed. If gratification of these impulses is not sufficient at the proper time in childhood, it is hypothesized that the person will continue to seek gratification for them in distorted form throughout his life. The person should not, on the other hand, receive overgratification at any level lest he not proceed in the normal manner. Finally, an experience, whether extremely gratifying or fear provoking, may also lead to difficulties. All three of these contingencies can lead to *fixation* at a particular stage, that is, an apparent continuation of the gratification-seeking appropriate to an earlier stage of psychosexual development. In addition, if a person has obtained gratification at one stage and is unable to be gratified (meets overwhelming stress) at the next, he is likely to *regress* and behave (seek his gratifications) in a manner appropriate to the earlier stage.

Adult *character* structure or *individual differences* are linked to differential ways of seeking gratification and distorted means of expression. The *traits* to be discussed are considered within the normal range unless they are so extreme as to lead to further stress and maladjustment. What is most important is that the form of character development in an individual illustrates and prepares the way for the Freudian view of the development of abnormal behavior. The *oral character* (an individual fixated at the oral stage) is viewed as passive, dependent on others, and preoccupied with food or other activities of the mouth such as drinking, smoking, or kissing. Early overindulgence may lead to feelings of optimism and self-assurance, while early deprivation is said to lead to pessimism and sadism. Traits associated with the *anal character* focus around elimination and retention. An example of the latter is the oft-mentioned triad of frugality, obstinacy, and orderliness arising from overly severe toilet training or, by *reaction formation,* to a laxness in such training or a revolt against such training. Sloppiness and irregularity can be "associated" with presumed lax toilet training, vanity and exhibitionism with "fixation" at an early phallic stage. All differences in personality traits are associated by Freudians with the psychosexual stages, and idiosyncratic behaviors may lead to inferences about their causes.

If expression, even in distorted form, is too threatening, the person will react inappropriately to stimuli associated with his difficulty. It is therefore possible for an extremely independent person to be *really* defending against desires to be nurtured.

If a person has not been gratified appropriately, a certain amount of his limited supply of libido is depleted in the defense against inappropriate impulses. He therefore has less energy left for more difficult tasks and a backlog of inappropriate, overdetermined characteristics that make difficulties more likely at each successive stage. A person may seem to be adjusting well but actually be using such a great amount of libido to keep the unsatisfied needs in check that it is likely that he will eventually break down under stress at a later stage. This breakdown is associated with *anxiety.*

Freudian theory involves several types of anxiety. First, there is real or *objective anxiety,* in which the source of danger (loss of gratification) is external to the individual. Second, there is *moral anxiety,* which involves a threat from the superego for doing or thinking something contrary to the person's moral standards. Of greatest importance is *neurotic anxiety,* which involves id impulses which are unacceptable to the ego and which cannot be dealt with effectively by repression or distortion. There are three types of neurotic anxiety. In *free-floating* anxiety the person is constantly apprehensive. The *phobic* form of anxiety derives from the same source as free-floating anxiety but is characterized by specific, limited, irrational fears. In *panic* the id impulses are likely to start breaking through, and threatening material previously held in check may be unleashed. This kind of anxiety is analogous to a dam breaking. Defenses crumble, libido is withdrawn from other, less basic uses (i.e., there is *ego decompensation*), and further threatening material is unloosed. The extreme occurs when there is an absence of ego defense and hence a direct expression of impulses. To understand how this may occur, it is necessary to look at the situation in which there is partial gratification of impulses, the ego-defense mechanisms.

A paradigmatic example of how the pressure may be reduced is through slips of the tongue, which reveal needs or suppressed impulses. For example, a minister, instead of saying he is tired of giving his sermon to weary benches, might say he is tired of giving sermons to beery wenches. Accidents or forgetting are similarly viewed. If one forgets a person's name it is presumed to be a hostile act indicating dislike of him. If the date of an exam is forgotten, it is presumed to be because it is threatening.

Dreaming is a key behavior in psychoanalytic fomulations. Dreaming is presumed to protect the person so that he can continue to sleep. In sleep, however, controls are relaxed, and repressed material in the unconscious threatens to slip out. The *censor* distorts what takes place so that the person will not be awakened. Therefore, dreams are symbolic in nature. There is a distinction between the *manifest* content, the specific dream that actually is dreamed, and the *latent* content of the dream, which is what the dream really means. For example, a person may dream of having a Cadillac. This is the manifest content. An analysis of the dream might reveal that the car represents a desire for status, superiority, and power. The latent content of the dream of a Cadillac is the desire to overcome inferiority feelings, a notion which has to be distorted.

Another example of partial release is seen in *humor.* The Freudian conception is

Freud and psychoanalysis

that through a joke the person is able to express something which had been repressed. The libido released because it is no longer needed to hold back the impulse is then manifested in laughter. Jokes are likely to be hostile or sexual in content, because these are the major repressed impulses in our society.

Slips, forgetting, dreams, and jokes are normal ways of reducing the pressure involved in the conflict between individual impulse and societal restrictions. In all of these pressure is reduced by giving it an indirect form of expression. Slips, dreams, and jokes illustrate the supposedly unconscious sources of behavior and the indirect gratification that lies at the root of *symptoms*. These phenomena, as well as posthypnotic suggestions, were prime sources of evidence for the concept of the *unconscious*, a theoretical construct referring to motivations that are forcefully held from consciousness. Like the id, ego, and superego, the unconscious has no physical location in the body. However, in psychoanalytic theory repressed impulses and events are conventionally placed in the unconscious, and it is theorized that they continue actively to seek expression.

Impulses which the ego cannot handle except by repression never-the-less retain their dynamic drive and tension. They continue to lead a subterranean life. . . . Deep-seated drives and urges are not destroyed by repression; on the contrary, although automatically restrained, they remain unchanged in quality and intensity. These drives and urges are, in fact, unmodified in any respect save that the individual is not consciously aware of the disowned strivings. Though frustrated, they constantly seek satisfaction. [Kolb, 1968, p. 63.]

The psychoanalytic unconscious is dynamic and ahistorical. The frustrations of yesteryear remain undiminished and strongly demand satisfaction.

The *defense mechanisms* are ways of reducing tension. If a person cannot do something directly, he may make do with a substitute *(displacement)*. Displacement may be thought of as on gradients of similarity and fear. If a person fears something greatly, then the object on which he will displace his emotion will probably be more dissimilar than if he is less frightened. For instance, if a child is angry with his mother, he may aggress against the nursery-school teacher, and if greatly afraid, he may displace the impulse onto other children or even dolls. At times the fear may be presumed to be so great that the person shows it by not showing it at all. Anna Freud (1946) cites a case in *The Ego and Mechanisms of Defense* in which it was said that a little girl was so severely afraid of castration that in a year and a half of analysis she never showed any indications of it.

The mechanism of *rationalization* is basically presenting a good reason to justify an action when the real reason is unacceptable. If a student is so far behind in his work that the very sight of the books is distasteful, he may go to a movie. However, it is unacceptable just to leave the books; an acceptable reason is that the student needs the rest and will study better after the movie.

Another mechanism is that of *projection;* if a person's impulses are unacceptable, he may "project" them onto other. For a person to say "I hate someone" is unacceptable. However, if the other individual is seen as threatening him in the first place, it becomes acceptable to hate him. In the defense mechanism of *identification* the person derives some gratification through seeing another person obtain such gratification. This is vicarious pleasure, hero-worship, or name dropping. On a college campus, identification is "we" when referring to the football team.

In *reaction formation* the individual does the opposite of the repressed impulse. A person who is sloppy in a chemistry laboratory may overreact and counter his impulses by being overly neat. In *dissociation* the person performs with "logic-tight" inconsistency. The person who preaches the Golden

Rule on Sunday may also be a tough businessman on the other days of the week. He keeps the two areas apart. *Compensation* is a form of substitution. It need not be the opposite of the impulse, as in reaction formation, or even displacement to a different object. For example, the person may wish to be dominant; if he cannot dominate in one area, he may proceed to become proficient in a different one. Thus, although he does not attain his original goal of dominance in a field such as athletics, he may obtain satisfaction in a different area, such as in scholarship. *Repression* is the mechanism by which the impulse is guarded against unconsciously. Repression and its analogue, *suppression,* where the impulse is consciously put out of mind, are very expensive in terms of the intrapsychic economy.

In Freudian theory there is only one mechanism associated with adult, societally approved satisfaction. This mechanism, *sublimation,* is used to explain all the forward progress of civilization; it has already been discussed in this chapter. In sublimation, as in other defenses, impulses are satisfied symbolically. For example, it is presumed that scientists are essentially voyeurs and wish to discover or witness the "primal scene," i.e., parents having intercourse.

At times it is difficult to separate the different defense mechanisms that may be present. For example, is the privately appointed book censor who reads in order to locate erotic stimuli illustrating a defense mechanism called *repetition compulsion,* is he *rationalizing,* is he showing *reaction formation,* or is he performing a social service and showing *sublimation?* Because of his effect on others, the censor might very well be *compensating.* On the other hand, he might be *projecting* his lasciviousness on authors who are merely being realistic. He might be *undoing* by atoning for the sinful acts of his youth. The censor might be *introjecting* the standards of society to bolster his own ego structure, or he might be *displacing* his fears of hostile impulses by an irrational aversion to sexual material.

It must be emphasized that emitting the behavior described by defense mechanisms is normal. The point at which such behaviors should cause concern is when they do more harm than good. The action taken to gain some gratification or avoid some unpleasantness may in itself be maladaptive by leading to new difficulties.

SUMMARY

The psychoanalytic theory may be summarized by noting that it provides a method for explaining all adult behavior. Because of the basic assumptions of biological needs in conflict with social restrictions, the explanation is one that requires indirect treatment of the underlying conflicts rather than direct manipulation of overt behaviors.

In this chapter psychoanalysis has been presented as a historical development and *method* of investigation advanced by Freud, as a form of *treatment,* and as a *theory* of human behavior. While the three are interrelated, they should not be confused because they have had important separate, albeit overlapping, consequences.

the conceptual impact of Freud
SYMPTOM, PERSONALITY, AND ANXIETY

9

Freud's work influenced almost every aspect of psychological treatment, and his formulations continue to have major impact on the field. Central to Freud's contribution is the change from a descriptive psychiatry to a dynamic or analytic framework which seeks for psychological as well as physiological explanations. Although his model is a medical analogue, in terms of the formulation of symptomatic behavior, Freud made a major contribution in moving the focus of investigation from physical forces to psychological variables. In work influenced by Freud there are three interrelated concepts: *symptom, personality,* and *anxiety*. This chapter will be devoted to a discussion of these three terms and will endeavor to alert the student to the background, implications, and problems involved in these concepts in contemporary professional writings.

SYMPTOM

Given the theory of symptom formation proposed by Freud, the strategy of therapy is to treat the cause (intrapsychic dynamics). Therapy therefore becomes expressive, indirect, or evocative. That is, if the symptom is a compromise between internal forces, the manifest behavior cannot be altered effectively or permanently by direct treatment because change can only be mediated by affecting intrapsychic forces. According to psychoanalytic theory a person needs to work on his underlying problems and conflicts and gain insight into them before he achieves permanent cure.

The extent to which Freud's concepts were adopted professionally may be illustrated by citing how psychoanalytically influenced psychologists formulate the notion of symptom.

Thorpe and Katz (1948, pp. 161–62) follow Fenichel (1945, p. 20) closely and contend that "Mental symptoms *are signs of disorder or maladjustment* that must be studied and evaluated to determine the reason for their presence; they are *not the disorder* to be labeled and treated." These two psychologists continue by saying that "All mental symptoms not of organic origin are significant and meaningful. In the main, they are evidences of psychological danger, or repression, or of threats to the individual's sense of personal worth or feeling of security. . . . It has been deduced from clinical evidence that the symptoms exhibited by a given patient are *the most 'economical' mechanisms available under the circumstances* and they are probably the least harmful that he could have adopted." The concept of intrapsychic economy is similar to that of overdetermined behavior. The reasoning is as follows: The patient in all likelihood has more than one conflict or unexpressed, unacceptable impulse. The symptom then may give partial gratification to more than one problem on the basis that as much gratification of unacceptable material will be obtained at as little "cost" in disruptive, abnormal, or symptomatic behavior as possible. This concept is of importance because it leads not only to the deduction of symptom substitution, as discussed in the following material, but also the deduction that *the new symptomatic behavior should be more disruptive or unacceptable because it replaces the previous, "most economical mechanism."*

Similar formulations may be found in Hutt and Gibby (1957, pp. 78–79), Cameron (1963, p. 452), Stern (1964, pp. 35–36), Coleman (1964, p. 225), Wolman (1968, p. 24), Batchelor (1969, p. 125), Kolb (1968, pp. 61–64 and 87–88). A final example is from Singer (1970, p. 92):

The reason symptomatic cures are deemed undesirable lies in the fact that the disappearance of the symptom, no matter how pleasing to all parties concerned, is ultimately a sign that the communicative process has become somewhat reduced, making further explorations more difficult, unless, of course, the disappearance of the symptom is based upon thorough insight and subsequent resolution of the communicated conflict.

In short, according to these views, the underlying cause must be treated or new maladaptive behavior will be emitted. That is, if the symptom is taken away, the "purpose served" by the symptom will necessarily lead to the development of new maladaptive behavior. This hypothesis is called *symptom substitution*. It is one of the few unequivocal hypotheses in the Freudian system.

This line of thought was cast in learning terms by Dollard and Miller (1950) in a section headed "increased drive from interfering with symptom." Dollard and Miller write, "According to our hypothesis, a learned symptom must produce a certain amount of reduction in the state of high drive motivating it. Therefore, interfering with the symptom by any of the foregoing methods will be expected to throw the patient back into a state of high drive and conflict." (p. 385.)

By "foregoing methods," these authors refer to incompatible responses, hypnosis, punishment, and "transference cures." The formulation by Dollard and Miller demonstrates that if one accepts a drive theory and a notion of intrapsychic anxiety (as a drive and prime cause of symptoms), then one is actually returning to a Freudian-type model.[1] Within such a model, the indirect Freudian type of therapy would be a necessary and preferable form of treatment. In fact, direct approaches to symptoms would be considered harmful to the patient, since success in symptom removal would only result in replacement by an even more undesirable symptom. If, on the other hand, there is no evidence for symptom substitution, then there is a great deal of wasted therapeutic effort, and indirect forms of treatment and the formulations supporting them become unnecessary and even undesirable.

The first argument against the hypothesis of symptom substitution is that there is little or no evidence for it. To quote Yates (1958a): "Considering the significant role such a distinction has played in clinical psychology, experimental demonstration of its existence is singularly lacking." Failure to obtain evidence for a theory does not necessarily invalidate it, since the null hypothesis can never be proved. Belief in the notion of symptom substitution, however, has significant social and scientific consequences. If a theory is completely accepted, no conflicting data will be collected. Yates noted that while there was considerable evidence for the value of a symptomatic treatment such as the conditioning approach to enuresis (e.g., H. G. Jones, 1960b), this technique was rarely used in the British Isles because of the acceptance of the concept of symptom substitution.

Since the time of Yates' article there has been a steady accumulation of evidence that symptom substitution rarely if ever occurs. That is, new maladaptive behavior of any sort is very rarely if ever observed following direct, behavioral treatment. Investigators of this area have reported estimates of such occurrence as ranging from zero to (at most) 5 percent (Rachman, 1963b). It appears

---

[1] This is illustrated particularly well by Allport (1937, p. 114–21) in his discussion of biological theories of personality.

clear, then, that *symptom substitution is the exception and not the rule.*

There are also more parsimonious explanations of maladaptive behaviors following treatment than symptom substitution. If, after treatment, a person emits a different maladaptive behavior or the same one again, there are alternative explanations which do not require concepts of underlying cause, repression, symbolization, indirect gratification, and the like. First, in the very nature of life, there may be what can be called *resensitization*. There is nothing that precludes a person from undergoing new and trying experiences. A person may be in an auto accident, and may become quite fearful and upset each time thereafter when he is required to enter an automobile. The problem may reach such proportions that behavioral treatment (e.g., desensitization; see Kushner, 1965a, and Wolpe, 1962, for examples) is given and the person makes a relaxed rather than tense response to entering automobiles. Unfortunately, there is nothing in this world that can guarantee that this person will not be involved in another auto accident. And if he is, and once again develops this fear, it is not necessary to hypothesize symptom substitution.

Second, the maladaptive behavior worked with may be one of a number of maladaptive patterns of response in the subject's repertoire. *Particularly if extinction is used,* it is quite possible that *there will be a succession of maladaptive behaviors.* That is, the therapist programs the environment so that the maladaptive behavior is not reinforced. In a similar manner, early in his career, Freud gave posthypnotic suggestions that the person would be able to move a paralyzed limb. In these circumstances *only half the job has been done.* The frequency of emission of one response to the situation has been decreased, and other responses the person is capable of making are more likely to be emitted (Sajwaj, Twardosz, and Burke, 1972). There is absolutely nothing to guarantee that these alternative behaviors will be adjustive. It would even be considered likely that given the history of reinforcement which led the person to perform a particular maladaptive behavior, other types of maladaptive behavior would be emitted, particularly if the prior behavior had some positive effect on the environment (e.g., gained sympathy) or had been reinforcing itself (e.g., alcohol).

After treatment by extinction, hypnotic suggestion or punishment, if a new adjustive behavior is not also developed, different maladjustive behaviors may occur, but there is no need to call them symptom substitution.

It has been argued that direct alteration of behavior is merely the treatment of symptoms. This is a misunderstanding, because *the emphasis in treatment should be on the development of skills or new responses to stimuli.* An example of this would be a person who develops a rash prior to exams. Behavioral treatment would not deal with the rash but with the situation with which the rash was associated, that is, exams.

Third, *if all the stimuli to which the inappropriate response was made are not dealt with,* the inappropriate response may recur in the presence of the stimuli to which new responses were not developed. For example, a person may give up smoking and think he has the problem licked. He then enters an unusual situation, a long ride across the country with two noisy children. If he has not practiced the elimination of smoking in this situation, he may well smoke again.

Fourth, the *change in the person creates a change in the environment*. Usually changes toward more adaptive behavior are welcomed and reinforced by significant others. The change in the person is likely to lead to a change in the environment such that the new behavior is maintained because it is more acceptable and more pleasant for others. However, there are situations in which a person's change to what is generally considered more adaptive behavior may be aversive or frustrating to some other person. For example if a husband after therapy asserts himself and sticks up for his legitimate human rights, the wife may feel that treatment has done him more harm than good. If a patient is being compensated during the period of his "illness" and his wife has been receiving funds that she would ordinarily not receive, a change for the better in the patient's behavior leading to a reduction in compensation may not be welcomed or reinforced by the wife.

Aside from the effect of new behavior on other people, there is an effect from observing one's own behavior. There is the simple but crucial fact that one can be different. This is a matter of being able to control one's own behavior, being able to make new responses, and having a choice of alternative behaviors.

Finally, *the new behavior may be inconsistent with maladaptive behaviors which are not in themselves the direct focus of treatment.* There is a limited amount of time in the day and a limited number of social interactions in which maladaptive responses might be made. By sheer chance, the more frequently a person acts in an adaptive manner, the less frequently he will act in a maladaptive way. A person should not be viewed as *incapable* of making a particular response, but rather he should be seen as not emitting that response *at a given time* because he is emitting an alternative response. This is most important in depression, in which the person has previously manifested interpersonal skills but now does not talk, is withdrawn, and does not smile. The ability to talk, interact, and smile is present, but the acts are not emitted. When a person first enacts a new role, he may not do so with perfect smoothness. There may at times be gaucheness and overreaction. Such behaviors following treatment seem more accurately formulated as aspects of the learning process than as symptom substitution.

To repeat, under scrupulous examination, at most one out of 20 cases where direct treatment has been used shows some later behavioral difficulty. Symptom substitution may therefore be said to be the exception rather than the rule. In fact, we should expect and do find a generalization of positive behavior, that is, the opposite of symptom substitution (Suinn, 1968; Lanyon, Manosevitz, and Imber, 1968). From the immediately foregoing paragraphs symptom substitution is an explanation that seems unnecessary at best and, when it leads to avoidance of use of more effective methods, may do an injustice to people seeking help.

In summary, the psychoanalytic formulation of symptoms is that they serve as partial and symbolic gratifications of underlying intrapsychic conflicts. This theory has important effects on treatment; if the theory is true, symptom substitution will occur. The weight of empirical evidence is against this theory, and an analysis of the situation indicates that in the rare instances when new maladaptive behavior is manifested after direct treatment, there are many alternative and more parsimonious explanations than the one deduced from psychoanalysis.

ANXIETY AND SYMPTOM

"Anxiety is the chief characteristic of the neuroses. It may be felt and expressed directly, or it may be controlled unconsciously and automatically by conversion, displacement, and various other psychological mechanisms." (DSM-II, p. 39.) Further, in the definition of hysterical neurosis (DSM-II, p. 39) we find that "Symptoms . . . are symbolic of the underlying conflict." More detail is provided by DSM-I, which defines "anxiety" in psychoneurotic disorders as a "danger signal felt and perceived by the conscious portion of the personality"; anxiety is produced by "a threat from within the personality (e.g., by supercharged repressed emotions . . .)." The very definitions presume Freud's theory: that is, the explanation is part of the description. The definitions use terms such as "unconsciously," "supercharged, repressed emotions," "automatically controlled," and "anxiety." The extent to which Freudian theory has become a part of the definition of abnormal behavior provides evidence for the degree to which these concepts have been accepted within the current psychiatric model.

The definitions of types of neurosis in DSM-I show how the Freudian formulation of mental illness is extended to the definition of the subcategories. For example, dissociative reaction is defined as follows: "The repressed impulse giving rise to the anxiety may be discharged by, or deflected into, various symptomatic expressions, such as depersonalization, dissociated personality, stupor, fugue, amnesia, dream state, somnambulism, etc." (p. 32.) For conversion reaction, "Instead of being experienced consciously (either diffusely or displaced, as in phobias) the impulse causing the anxiety is 'converted' into functional symptoms in organs or parts of the body, usually those that are mainly under voluntary control. The symptoms serve to lessen conscious (felt) anxiety and ordinarily are symbolic of the underlying mental conflict." For phobic reaction, "the anxiety of these patients becomes detached from a specific idea, object, or situation in the daily life and is displaced to some symbolic idea or situation in the form of a specific neurotic fear."

The term "anxiety" is used in a variety of ways that are confusing and even contradictory: anxiety is *detached*, it is *displaced*, yet it is also defined as *a danger signal* (felt and perceived by the *conscious* portion of the personality).

Finally, DSM-I uses a key term, "personality," which supplements "anxiety" and which can be illustrated with the definition of psychotic reactions: "From this grouping, a psychotic reaction may be defined as one in which the personality, in its struggle for adjustment to internal and external stresses, utilizes severe affective disturbances, profound autism and withdrawal from reality, and/or formation of delusions or hallucinations." (pp. 11–12.) In this definition personality is *reified* so that it *struggles* to adjust and *utilizes* certain behaviors. Once an abstract concept becomes alive and is given human qualities, then it loses all semblance of objectivity and becomes so broad that it is meaningless.

PERSONALITY

A comment frequently made in reaction to descriptions of behavioral techniques is, "Yes, you can change behavior, but do you *really* change the person?" This question reflects the presumption that there is a "real" person or personality underlying overt behavior, something that must be changed and of which manifest behavior is merely symptomatic, symbolic, or expressive. There is an implication that what is "inside" and "way down deep" is "realer" than that which is manifest and observed. One way of responding to such questions is to ask how a scientific observer can know when a person "really" changes. What is the "real" person? How can this person be known other than through his behavior? The position taken in this book affirms that all that can be known about a person depends on the data provided by his behavior. By the definition of "behavior" given in Chapter 4 this means a limitation to things which can be quantified and therefore to operational definitions.

To avoid arriving at a situation where a concept, personality, is reified so that it *struggles* to adjust and *utilizes* defenses, there must be constant reference to the data on which statements are based. If this is not done, meaningless words may be used to gloss over important and fruitful problems. "Personality" has many meanings and has been used in many ways. Allport (1937), for example, reviewed 50 different definitions. An analysis of the uses of the word "personality" must involve the concepts of stimulus, response, and the variables mediating between the stimulus and the response. For example, personality may be conceived of as a *stimulus* to other people: an individual may be responded to by other people as pleasing or unpleasing, as dominant or aggressive. This definition of "personality" involves how an individual affects other people, that is, their behavior in response to him.

Personality may also be conceived of as a set of *responses*. The evaluation of these responses involves generalization from one sample of behavior to another. A person who responds more frequently, more rapidly, or more strongly in a particular way, for example with hostility, is said to be a hostile person, to have a trait of hostility. With this concept, as with personality as stimulus, the responses of others are of critical importance. In both instances, personality as social stimulus or as response, labeling behavior rather than dealing with it offers little gain and is a major source for potential error. Aside from the error of overgeneralization, there is the temptation to use the *description* of a behavior as an *explanation* of behavior.

At an empirical level, evidence for general traits across different situations is at best scarce (Mischel, 1968, especially pp. 1–148; Krasner and Ullmann, 1973). In fact, as Mischel (p. 176) points out, if behavior did not change with situations, human survival based on adaptability would be difficult. Rodin (1972) found typical behavior descriptions to yield considerably more information than trait descriptions, while Larsen et al. (1972) found, as had Bernstein (1973, cited in Chapter 5) that experimental conditions (situations) were far better predictors of overt behavior than personality descriptors.

Finally, personality may be viewed as a *mediating* variable leading to individual differences in responses to identical stimuli. This places the primary locus of individual behavior on "the dynamic organization within the individual of those psychological systems that determine his unique adjustment to his environment" (Allport, 1937). Such a view leads to many inferences and conjectures about behavior but few observations beyond those obtained without this concept. The broader the content of such personality systems, the less exact are the deductions and measurements that can be based on them.

An individual may well think of his own behavior and note that he probably acts more introverted in situations with which he is less familiar, less sure of himself, or where there are people whose leadership he respects, than he does in situations where he has greater knowledge, greater skill, greater authority, or is recognized by other people as an expert and is asked to take a more active, outgoing role. The situation thus has a great deal to do with the responses that will be emitted and labeled. It is less productive to talk about a general characteristic such as a person's social adequacy than it is to talk about his inadequacy in examination situations, in meeting members of the opposite sex, in dealing with authority figures, in working by himself, in working with other people, and so forth. At best there are low positive correlations when predictions of a general nature are made from one situation to another. The magnitude of the correlations increase as the situations become more similar to each other. As situations increase in similarity, the research worker bases his predictions increasingly on observed behavior, and an intervening concept of personality becomes steadily less useful and less necessary.

There is great difficulty in presuming that a blocked striving will continue to exert influence and endeavor to escape the unconscious, disguise its manifestations, and create symptoms. That is, it is difficult to see how a failure of satisfaction at one age leads *directly* to striving, conflict, and symptoms at a later age. It is hard to understand how suppressed desires associated with an early and overvigorous toilet training continue to be active in the "unconscious." What is more readily understandable is that behaviors developed at that time were reinforced and thus were more frequently emitted. It also seems reasonable that the sort of person who would harshly toilet-train the child would also harshly train the child in other behaviors. It seems more parsimonious to think of an ongoing environment than a continuation of a "dynamic" need. The resulting behavior may be observed in adulthood, but the stimuli reinforcing it are not partial gratification of intrapsychic impulses but rather the reinforcement the person as an adult obtains for being orderly, neat, rigid, pedantic, and rule-abiding.

A concept integral to psychoanalytic formulations of personality is that of conscious–unconscious. A problem with this concept is that if a behavior is not overtly manifested, it may be said to be repressed. It is therefore difficult to make predictions about the overt behavior and to evaluate in a unidirectional manner the behavior that is emitted.

What is the evidence for the existence of the unconscious? Hypnosis was discussed in Chapter 5, and posthypnotic suggestions were one of the major arguments for an unconscious. But, as argued in Chapter 5, hypnotic behavior is essentially a matter of playing a social role. It is reasonable to ask what theory of either neurology or unconscious would permit the subject to be capable of verbalizing a command (under hypnosis he is "aware" of the request) and not capable of doing so a minute later (when the "trance" itself has been terminated). This latter situation can be reversed by again placing the subject "under hypnosis." An "idea" will be "conscious" when the stimuli appropriate to its emission are present.

Another source of evidence for the unconscious rests with the psychoanalytic interpretation of slips of the tongue and accidents. The interpretations placed on such behavior by Freud are not the only possible ones. It is possible that such behavior arises through competing responses and stimulus or response generalization. Each of the examples cited by Freud in his *Psychopathology of Everyday Life* might be given an equally probable and more parsimonious alternative explanation. For example, Freud reported "accidentally" knocking down a statue on his desk due to displacement of hostility. All that is required is the additional information of a picture of Freud at his desk (e.g., Edmund Engelman's photograph in Jones' *Biography*, 1955, vol. 2, pp. 400–401) showing his precariously perched collection of statues, and a hypothesis that Freud was often angry. Unconscious motivation need not enter into the analysis of the situation.[2]

Because dreams involve the subject's reports rather than the dreams themselves, a naturalistic approach to this area is more difficult (Kleitman, 1963; Dement, 1960, 1964, 1965.)

The concept of repression need not enter into an explanation of what one finds humorous. Numerous studies have reported that humor is associated with habitual overt behavior (Byrne, 1955; Ullmann and Lim, 1962; Keith-Lee and Spiegel, 1966) and strength of drive (Strickland, 1959). Doris and Fierman (1955), O'Connell (1960), and Hetherington and Wray (1964) found complex interactions between environment and humor.

Berkowitz (1970) demonstrated that rather than having a cathartic effect and reducing aggressive responses, aggressive humor may have a modeling effect and increase aggressive responses. Davis and Farina (1970) showed how the appreciation of humor may have a direct communication function. Male undergraduates were given cartoons to rate by an attractive woman who explained that she was working for the English department on a cartoon anthology. In the nonarousal condition, the experimenter's manner and dress were proper, polite, and formal; in the arousal condition her manner was flirtatious, and her dress

[2] For an example of recent scientific investigation of the behavior called "repression," see Holmes (1970, 1972) and Holmes and Schallow (1969).

maximized her considerable sexual attractiveness. Subjects in these two conditions were further randomly assigned to a communication condition in which their responses were made to the experimenter and to a noncommunication condition in which subjects responded on an answer form while the experimenter was busy at a different task. The appreciation of sexual over nonsexual cartoons was significantly greater for the aroused than the nonaroused subjects, and within the communication condition the sexual cartoons were described as significantly funnier by the aroused than by the nonaroused subjects. Rather than assuming that the subjects were necessarily aroused, we might simply note that cues were present making one set of responses more likely than another (e.g., the Chapman, Chapman, and Brelje, 1969, work cited in Chapter 5). This type of formulation is in line with work by Nosanchuk and Lightstone (1974) who used "canned" (recorded) laughter to demonstrate the effects of group cues on humor appreciation.

Laird (1974) brings together the concepts of self-attribution and effect of one's own role-expressive behavior (see Chapter 5) in the study of humor. Briefly, subjects were induced to smile or frown, and they reported cartoons viewed while they were smiling to be more humorous than cartoons viewed when they were frowning.

Young and Frye (1966) illustrated the role of social learning and demand characteristics in the response to humorous stimuli. In one of three experiments reported by Young and Frye, the subjects (S's) were 64 males who heard a tape of ten jokes each from four categories—humor, wit, nonsense, and sex—and were asked to indicate the degree to which they liked each joke. The experimenter observed each subject and tallied the number of times he laughed out loud. The subjects were divided into four equal groups. In the first group only 16 males were present (*control* condition). In the three other groups, just as the experiment was to begin "a young, very attractive female" confederate experimenter (CE) came into the room and said she was sorry for being late. The experimenter told her that she was scheduled for the next hour, but CE replied that she had another appointment at that time and would be grateful if she could participate in the research at that time. The experimenter reluctantly agreed. Under all the remaining conditions, CE laughed at 20 of the 40 jokes. In the *laugh-sex* condition, she laughed at all ten sex jokes and ten randomly selected others; in the *neutral* condition she made no overt response to the sex jokes and laughed at 20 of the other jokes; finally, in the *embarrassed* condition, CE laughed at 20 of the nonsex jokes, but gasped, hid her face, turned away from the group, and generally showed embarrassment at the sex jokes.

There was no statistically significant difference between the humor preference ratings in the control and neutral conditions, and it is possible, therefore, to infer that CE's presence itself was not a major factor in altering humor preference behavior. In the laugh-sex condition, the sex jokes were rated as significantly more liked than in the neutral and control conditions, and in the embarrassed condition, the sex jokes were rated as significantly less liked than in the neutral and control conditions. "The changes in overt laughing were particularly striking, e.g., only two S's of one group laughed at five jokes under the embarrassing condition, but all S's laughed and/or made comments on at least 60 percent of the jokes under the condition of CE's laughing."

Summarizing this study and the ones previously cited, it is possible to suggest that rather than being a function of repressed wishes, laughter and the appreciation of humor are a function of situational stimuli and habitual patterns of response. The approach here illustrated with humor, which draws on the concepts introduced in Chapters 4 and 5, may provide a method for investigating the areas of human behavior discussed by Freud. Adherence to scientific method and a behavior influence model seems to offer a method that is both simpler in its formulation and richer in its results.

ANXIETY

The word anxiety was hardly used in standard medical and psychological textbooks until the late 1930's. It was a result of Freud's writings about Angst, translated as anxiety, that the term now has wide currency." (Sarbin, 1964a, p. 634.) The central place anxiety has in the explanation of symptoms is one of the major effects Freud had on the field. The degree to which this has taken place may be ascertained from the quotations from DSM-I and from the material on symptom formation cited earlier in this chapter. In essence, a person does something symptomatic in order to reduce anxiety. The word "anxiety" may become, like the words "mental illness," a panchreston (Szasz, 1957): a word that explains all and hence nothing.

What is meant by anxiety? To quote English and English (1958, p. 35): "When a term is frequently employed in behavioristic learning theory, in psychoanalysis, and in nearly every field of psychology between them, the variety and shadings of meaning become very troublesome. *Anxiety* must be read with great vigilance for the author's meaning or, more often than not, his several meanings." While Cattell and Scheier (1961) isolated some 120 different procedures for assessing anxiety, the basic operational definitions seem to arise from physiological behavior, overt behavior, and self-reports. Sarbin (1964a, p. 630) summarizes this matter: "That there is no unequivocal definition of anxiety can be readily demonstrated. A perusal of textbooks, journal articles, dictionaries, and other sources gives a confused picture. Some of the definitions are expressed in terms of overt behavior, such as tremor, stuttering, and coughing; some in terms of complex conduct such as avoidance, defense and denial; some in terms of antecedent events such as aversive stimuli and memories of traumatic events; some in terms of physiological responses such as heart rate, GSR [galvanic skin response] and respiratory rate; and some in terms that have no existent referents, such as apprehension, dispositions, emotional states, states of mind, psychic states, affects and feelings."

To this résumé should be added two definitions of anxiety previously presented: the first is that of DSM-I (p. 31): "Anxiety in psychoneurotic disorders is a danger signal felt and perceived by the conscious portion of the personality. It is produced by a threat from within the personality. . . ." This definition includes concepts of the cause of anxiety rather than a description of anxiety itself. The second additional definition involves a concept of the operation of anxiety: ". . . a learned symptom must produce a certain amount of reduction in the state of high drive motivating it. Therefore, interfering with the symptom by any of the foregoing [direct] methods will be expected to throw the patient back into a state of high drive and conflict." (Dollard and Miller, 1950, p. 385.) The "drive" in psychoanalysis is the reduction of conflict and anxiety. Symptoms are taken as evidence for anxiety regardless of the absence or presence of "anxious behavior." Not only is anxiety troublesome in terms of the domains of description, it may also be used to refer to domains of explanation.

A first important issue is whether the different measures of anxiety are related; specifically whether physiological, behavioral, and self-report measures show positive correlations. A great deal of work is summarized by Maher when he writes (1966, p. 187): "Anxiety is best regarded as a construct or inferred state. . . . Measures of anxiety in the three categories [verbal report, overt (motor) behavior, and physiological measurement] have not generally produced high correlations with each other, and many problems exist with regard to their reliability. At the present time there is no strong evidence to warrant an empirical distinction between anxiety and any more general conception of increased drive or arousal. Measures of one are highly congruent with measures of the other, and the behavioral consequences of one are much the same as those of the other." Having written this, Maher illustrates in the immediately subsequent sentence the current status of the field by writing: "Many kinds of pathological behavior may be regarded as anxiety-reduction techniques—that is to say, they are patterns of response that have developed because they have been reinforced by anxiety reduction." Scientifically this is an uncomfortable situation: something that is inferred from unsatisfactory measures is used to explain abnormal behavior.

There is no gainsaying that escape or avoidance of unpleasant situations is reinforcing. The obvious deduction, which will be followed throughout this book, was stated by Sarbin (1964a, p. 631) as follows: "The behavior that follows aversive stimuli can be described satisfactorily without posing anxiety as an intervening variable." Put differently, rather than using the word "anxiety," one should specify the situation itself. This may be particularly important with regard to physiological indices of anxiety: to the extent that they overlap greatly, and may even be identical with measures of arousal, there is nothing in them *per se* that makes them pleasant rather than unpleasant. Rather, hearkening back to the work by Schachter and Singer presented in Chapter 5, the labeling of the arousing situation as unpleasant may be crucial in the person reporting that he is "anxious." The *label* of the situation as well as the situation itself or physiological responses to it seems necessary.

Is there an alternative to the concept of anxiety to explain continuing maladaptive behavior? It should first be noted that both maladaptive and adaptive behavior may be continued long after the situations in which they were originally developed have changed. The behavior is maintained by different reinforcing consequences. Examples are the effect of money and the emission of acts such as reading, which once were terminally reinforced and now are instrumental and parts of larger social roles.

Just as some behaviors may become discriminative stimuli for pleasant situations, so environmental events may become discriminative stimuli for unpleasant events. The person may strive for his boss's attention or his friend's smile, and be upset when he is ineffective in getting them. His activities may also have an effect on his body. This is clearest where a desire for athletic skill leads to a change in musculature, because of the actions (practice) that follow. In a similar manner, the temporal sequence involved in anxiety is hard to separate: does the person manifest the physiological changes associated with the concept "anxiety" and then make the overt role behaviors labeled as anxious, or do the role behaviors, including the act of labeling, lead to responses that heighten physiological indices of anxiety?

A final problem with the concept of anxiety, found also with definitions of mental health and mental illness, was touched on above: the empirical intercorrelations between different definitions of anxiety (e.g., among behavioral, physiological, and self-report measures) of the same person at the same time are unfortunately low. Further, the correlations between the same measures of anxiety taken at different times and in different situations are also of a low order. At a research level, this means that two investigators with different operational definitions of anxiety may arrive at conflicting results because they are talking about different things while using the same words. At minimum the operations must be specified each time the concept of "anxiety" is used. Once having done so, there is little gained from the use of the word.

ON PSYCHOANALYSIS AS AN INTELLECTUAL SYSTEM

Freud provides an explanation for almost all human enterprises. The range of the applications of psychoanalytic theory is enormous. Every idiosyncratic act may be explained within his system. For example, cigarette smoking seems an obvious manner of gratifying oral impulses. It may, however, be anal: a person deposits wastes in a receptacle and excretes (exhales smoke). Furthermore, the part of the cigarette from which the ashes grow is called the butt. The logic of such extrapolations is that excretions involve the depositing of wastes; smoking involves the depositing of wastes; therefore smoking and excretion are related, i.e., smoking is excretion. This form of logic is called assertion of the predicate. A psychoanalyst would not necessarily be dismayed by this exposition. He would argue that the logic of the unconscious is indeed primitive and that the previous exposition is merely further evidence of this fact. Most scientists are less than comfortable with such an exposition and would prefer empirical evidence—reliable data that could not be explicated by alternative hypotheses.

Freudian theory does not lend itself to external checks, since the very absence of a behavior may be taken as evidence for the strength of the repression, hence the strength of the "need" or "anxiety." An overt behavior may well indicate its opposite through reaction formation. To the extent that external observation cannot alter the decisions about the hypotheses, the theory is a closed system. Further, the system has in it an explanation of its critics. The very asperity of their criticism is an indication of how true and apt the theory is of its critics. In earlier days, the particular novelty of the theory was its view of sexual behavior, and a critic was, by definition, sexually frustrated, if not worse. This approach leads to arguments about critics as people (*ad hominem*) as distinct from counter-arguments to the ideas (*ad verbum*).

A good example is how critics of psychoanalytic treatment are dealt with. They are asked if they have had personal analysis. If they answer that they have not, they are discounted as not really knowing what they are talking about any more than a person who has not had a religious experience can know what is meant by the word. If a critic responds that he has indeed had a personal analysis, his very criticism indicates that his analysis was a failure and that he is probably manifesting his unworked-through negative transference. The only person who may talk about the theory is the one who agrees with it. In short, only believers are considered to be in a position to discuss the theory or practice of psychoanalysis.

Why, then, has psychoanalysis flourished? One explanation is implicit in the foregoing paragraphs: the system offers a reason for and hence (presumably) an understanding of a great many phenomena and, as a closed system, is relatively impervious to criticism by having an explanation for the very act of criticism.

As a technique, psychoanalysis may be no more effective than no treatment at all (Eysenck, 1952; Rachman, 1971). The base rate of recovery from neurosis is not zero but closer to two out of three in two years and nine out of ten in a five-year period. Because psychoanalysis focuses on childhood material and "sick" behavior, there may be social reinforcement of the emission of upset talk and behavior through the attention of the therapist. Also, in an unsystematic manner, the discussion may lead to some extinction (stimuli not followed by unpleasantness) or even reconditioning (stimuli associated with the therapeutically calm milieu). The therapist's interpretations may at times provide formulas that lead the person to make altered and hence reinforced responses in the extratherapy situation. In short, from the patient's point of view, psychoanalytic therapy may be continued, even as shamanism, because there are successes. These successes are not founded on a theory for which there is experimental evidence, nor is practice derived from such evidence. The procedures may be effective despite rather than because of the therapist's rationale.

SUMMARY

In this chapter three concepts that are widely used in abnormal psychology and that were greatly influenced if not developed by Freud were discussed. These concepts were symptom, personality, and anxiety. The place of these concepts in current diagnosis illustrate Freud's continuing impact. The point of the chapter was not to present an attack on Freud, but rather to investigate the key concepts that are applied to individuals in the clinical situation. Both at a theoretical and applied level these concepts are open to severe questioning. The present chapter suggested that what is actually denoted be substituted in each case for the words "symptom," "anxiety," and "personality."

social and societal contexts

10

In order for a human activity to be designated as abnormal, a social situation must be involved. The Prologue and first chapter of this book noted the mutual interdependence of people and the importance of their being able to predict each other's behavior. This position has a number of implications: in the Prologue, *deviance* was defined as failure to act in accordance with the wishes and expectations of others,[1] and *abnormality* as the type of deviance that sanctioned the professional attention of people such as psychologists and psychiatrists. This led to the observation that what was expected and what was deviant depended on variables of time, place, and person.[2] An understanding of abnormality

---

[1] What appears at first to be an obvious exception is the behavior of a person already designated as abnormal. As will be seen in Chapter 18, this is not necessarily an exception because the "sick role" is one that is learned. A person who does not play it properly may be punished, and one who plays it correctly may be reinforced. A notable book indicating that hospitalized people could and do play the role is by Braginsky, Braginsky, and Ring (1969). Kiev (1969, p. 111) summarizes the point: "The concept of a culturally recognized and accepted way of 'going crazy' best explains the relationship among these various behavioral patterns."

[2] Or more accurately, the person's status, a concept Linton describes: "The place in a particular system which a certain individual occupies at a particular time will be referred to as his *status* with respect to that system. . . . The second term, *role*, will be used to designate the sum total of the culture patterns associated with a particular status. It thus includes the attitudes, values and behavior ascribed by the society to any and all persons occupying this status. It can even be extended to include the legitimate expectations of such persons with respect to the behavior toward them of persons in other statuses within the same system." (1945, pp. 76–77.)

must therefore take into account the sociological context of the act and its evaluation, and that is the task to which this chapter is addressed.

LABELING AS BEHAVIOR

Given the considerations of time, place, and person it is impossible to designate either a particular act or a particular actor as abnormal *per se*. This was the burden of the presentation of Chapter 1, where it was noted that no fully satisfactory operational definition of abnormality has been devised. It was also noted that different professional groups or situations called forth special definitions of abnormality. Labeling behavior is a social act and, like any other social act, is one that is developed and maintained by reinforcing contingencies.

This point has been aptly expressed by Pronko (1963, p. 34): "Classification is, first of all, a human activity. It always involves a person observing phenomena in which he can perceive similarities and differences. There is always another essential but easily overlooked point: the observer has a *purpose* or *aim* in ordering those same data." Chapter 1 also outlined the diagnostic labels. Further discussion of the diagnostic process will occur in the next chapter, which deals with steps in the diagnostic act. The present chapter is more involved with what Pronko calls the "purpose" or "aim" of the act.

The Labeler's Problem

An important analysis of the diagnostic act has been made by Scheff (1966a, pp. 105-27). Consider the physician's situation of having to decide whether to hospitalize a person or not. There are essentially two natural verifications of his decision: the person was indeed sick, or the person was not sick. It is possible to make a fourfold table in the manner of Figure 1.

Following the letter designation of cells in Figure 1, it is possible to evaluate the various outcomes for physical ills. If, as in A, the patient is indeed sick and the physician has hospitalized him, the physician has done the proper thing and his judgment has been verified. If, as in C, the physician hospitalizes the person and it is found that the person was not ill, the physician has not lost a great deal: he has practiced sound, conservative medicine, and, if anything, the patient will be grateful to him for his concern and care. If, as in D, the physician does not hospitalize and the person is indeed not ill, the physician has not made any visible professional gain and has had to reject the patient's complaints. If, finally, as in B, the physician does not hospitalize the patient and it is found that there was indeed an illness justifying hospitalization, the physician is a bad diagnostician and has poorly served both the patient and his profession. Because there is no stigma attached to being physically ill, because a careful physical checkup takes only a few days, and because there is relatively little expense, the medical patient has little to lose by being hospitalized. When in doubt, the physician does the rational thing; he hospitalizes the patient.

The situation is different for the person in the case of psychiatric hospitalization. While there is a strong carry-over of the concept "When in doubt, hospitalize," psychiatric hospitalization may lead to increased rather than decreased behavioral problems. These problems may occur through the training received in the hospital milieu (Sommer and Osmond, 1961; Barton, 1959; Wing, 1962; Price and Denner, 1973); and the stigma attached to having been a patient in a psychiatric hospital (Lamy, 1966; Spitzer and Denzin, 1968). Additional problems are raised by the greater length of psychiatric hospitalization. In short, the individual has much more to lose by psychiatric hospitalization than by hospitalization for a physical ailment.

Two additional pieces of information offered by Scheff on diagnostic practices are worth noting. That the trend for physicians dealing with physical illness is to err in a "conservative" (sick) direction may be noted in Garland's (1959) study of 14,867 X-ray films for signs of tuberculosis. There were 1,216 positive (sick) readings that turned out to be clinically negative (i.e., false

Figure 1

	Physician's Decision	
Case Outcome	Hospitalize	Do Not Hospitalize
Sick	A	B
Not Sick	C	D

alarms) and only 24 negative (not sick) readings that later turned out to be clinically active. The bias to call a film "sick" or pathological was 50 times greater than the bias in the direction of health. Because the cost to the patient of extra clinical tests is slight compared to the cost of untreated tuberculosis, this type of bias is socially acceptable. A similar result was reported by Bakwin (1956) in a study of the advisability of tonsillectomy for 1,000 school children. Of these children, 611 had their tonsils removed. The remaining 389 children were then examined by other physicians and 174 were selected for tonsillectomy. This left a group of 215 children, and when another group of physicians examined them, 99 were adjudged in need of tonsillectomy. Still another group of physicians examined the remaining children, and nearly half were again judged to be in need of the operation.

Shifting to the psychiatric situation, Scheff (1966a, pp. 130–32) reports on ratings of patients by 25 psychiatrists admitting patients to a state psychiatric hospital. The ostensible reasons for admitting patients to such a hospital are to protect the patient and to protect other members of society. Of 164 involuntarily confined patients, 102 or 63 percent were rated as neither dangerous to others nor severely mentally impaired (i.e., needing protection for themselves). Mechanic (1962) writes: "In the two mental hospitals studied over a period of three months, the investigator never observed a case where the psychiatrist advised the patient that he did not need treatment. Rather, all persons who appeared at the hospital were absorbed into the patient population regardless of their ability to function adequately outside the hospital." Kutner (1962), Miller and Schwartz (1966) and Maisel (1973) made similar observations. Haney and Michielutte (1968) report that the availability of facilities was an important factor in adjudication of incompetency, and that for the individual case, there were higher percentages of incompetency judgments when the person was older and when the petition had been initiated by a community agency rather than the family. Scheff reports on observations of court proceedings as follows:

Our observations of 116 judicial hearings raised the question of the adequacy of the psychiatric examination. Eighty-six of the hearings failed to establish that the patients were "mentally ill" (according to the criteria stated by the judges in interviews). Indeed, the behavior and responses of 48 of the patients at the hearings seemed completely unexceptionable. Yet the psychiatric examiners had not recommended the release of a single one of these patients. Examining the court records of 80 additional cases, we found still not a single recommendation for release. [1966a, p. 139.]

The Social Function of Labeling

It has been pointed out that psychiatric diagnosis is a social act made in the light of prior training that is manifested by biases toward the conservative or "sick" decision. The next question is why such behavior is maintained, or to put the issue bluntly, what are the conditions that lead social agencies to pay psychiatrists for such behavior? What function is served by such diagnoses?

A person who acts in a manner that is unexpected *in an area in which someone else has a stake* poses a problem for the other person. This problem can be solved in a number of ways, *one* of which is to call the person mentally ill. Szasz (1966b, pp. 150, 153) points out that terms like "waiter," "stenographer," and "judge" not only classify occupations but also define role expectations. He then offers an example: "The waiter refuses to wait on tables. He sits in the back of the cafe and scribbles endlessly on scraps of paper. When asked what he is doing, he either scowls condescendingly and refuses to answer, or confides to friends that he is writing a treatise on philosophy that will save the world. He is taken to a mental hospital by the police." First of all, the man raised a problem, but it might have been solved by coercing him to wait on tables or by firing him. He might have been begged by his wife and children who depended on his wages. Calling the police and having the man taken to the psychiatric hospital was but one possible solution.

The second aspect of this example is that the act of calling the police and the steps in the sequence of hospitalization represent human behaviors. The acts must be in the individual's repertoire and must, whether learned through direct or vicarious reinforcement, be matched to a particular situation. In short, the situation must be labeled by the cafe owner as one fitting the category "Call the cops to take the guy to the loony bin." As with any other act, if prior experiences in similar situations have not worked out well—for example, led to endless red tape and court appearances—the cafe owner would not emit the acts. If, however, through his reading of the mass media or prior personal experience, the cafe owner has learned that this is the effective and correct act, he will perform it.

We must now digress. The police, when they arrive, also demonstrate the effects of their prior learning, the contingencies on them, and their response to the present situation in which they find themselves. From direct observation, Bittner (1967) found that law officers were reluctant to initiate psychiatric hospitalization on their own responsibility. One reason for this was that they might be incorrect and face later embarrassment and legal action. Second, police see many people who might be called "sick," and if they lowered their own standards of a psychiatric emergency, they would flood themselves and hospitals with extra work. Third, officers believe that while they must work with such people, it is not a proper law enforcement task. Fourth, taking a person to the psychiatric service is likely to be a long and tedious process in which they must wait at the admitting office and, at times, be questioned in a manner that casts doubt on their own judgment.

There are five frequently overlapping conditions under which the police will take the person to a psychiatric setting. The first is a suicide attempt. The second is very serious or blatant behavior such as radically incongruous affect, seizures, or odd postures indicating that the person cannot take care of himself. As will be noted below, if someone else is willing to take care of the person, the officers are not likely to take him for psychiatric admission. The third circumstance is severe agitation, especially if there is a nontrivial threat of violence. This is especially true if the person is unresponsive to efforts to calm him. An example of a trivial threat would be a feeble and senile old woman assaulting a strong, healthy son. A fourth circumstance is a person who is a public nuisance and who cannot be calmed or induced to leave the scene. The fifth circumstance is when the complaint comes from someone who stands in a responsible relation to the person, such as a physician or employer.

If the police do not arrest the person, they may help people (such as the family or physician) who will take responsibility to move the person to an institution. Second, and most often, they will help return a person to his usual environment or caretakers, thus transferring responsibility. For example, police transportation, communication, and information resources may be used to return a senile or retarded person to his family. Third, the officer, may give "first aid" in order to calm the person. He does so, if possible, by removing the person, from the context in which he was found because it may be a cause for his agitation and in order to establish boundaries for control and to reduce the complexity of the situation. Further, the person is treated in a routine, matter-of-fact manner, as if it were a typical incident. That is, a delusion is not challenged, but rather questions asked as

social and societal contexts

they would be when a criminal case is to be built.

The task of the police is not only to enforce the law but also to keep the peace. They must make choices, and their acts depend upon the realities of the immediate situation and their own priorities. What the police do and do not respond to provides one type of definition of deviant behavior.

A third issue touched on by the example of the waiter is that he broke no specific written rule. He committed no criminal act. The situation is similar to that of the *Shaw* case in England. Shaw published a *Ladies Directory* which contained paid advertisements by women whose monetary approach to sex was at variance with official moral expectations. There was involved an alleged conspiracy to corrupt public morals: an offense that broke no statute. The judges in the House of Lords permitted the charge to stand, and one of the judges advanced the view that:

> ... the Court of King's Bench was *custos morum* of the people and had superintendency of offences *contra bonos mores*. ... there is in that Court a residual power, where no statute has yet intervened to supersede the common law, to superintend those offences which are prejudicial to the common welfare. Such occasions will be rare, for Parliament has not been slow to legislate when attention has been sufficiently aroused. But gaps remain and will always remain, since no one can foresee every way in which the wickedness of man may disrupt the order of society. [Hart, 1966, p. 9.]

The use of psychiatric intervention may permit controls to be extended in much the same way as illustrated by the Court of King's Bench: where no written rules exist, social control may be effected through psychiatric intervention. The particular value that is sacrificed is that offenses should be carefully defined so that an individual may know beforehand what acts are criminal and what are not.

Public Information and Labeling

The second point derived from the example of the waiter who wrote rather than served at table was that calling the police was a learned response to the situation. This point in turn leads to two considerations. The first is that such an act is the right, the proper, the humane thing to do. In general (Nunnally, 1961), the opinion of the public about mental illness is not very different from that of experts in the field such as psychiatrists and psychologists. However, the attitudes of the public (as measured by semantic differential scales) are in general far more negative toward the mental patient than those of professionals. Giovannoni and Ullmann (1963) found that hospitalized psychiatric patients gave responses very similar to those obtained by Nunnally. Manis, Houts, and Blake (1963) also found that psychiatric and nonpsychiatric patients held similar views about mental illness, and Mayo, Havelock, and Simpson (1971) found that psychiatric patients rated the concept "mental patient" lower than they rated themselves. In short, there is a widespread and shared unfavorable conception of the characteristics of the mental patient and his role.

It is generally viewed as good and desirable that the public share the views of mental health experts, notably that mental illness is like any other illness and should be treated by a physician. Woodward (1951) reports on data gathered by the procedures of a Roper survey. Woodward writes. "The first major conclusion that emerges from an analysis of the study results is that people (at least in Louisville) are definitely moving toward a humanitarian and scientific point of view toward mental illness . . . that mental illness is a sickness that should evoke sympathetic understanding and . . . requires some form of professional treatment."

Two brief case histories were presented,

and respondents were given a list from which they could select what would be the best thing to do. The assumptions of the investigators are clear from Woodward's statement about the subject of one of the case histories: "The lady described in the question . . . is a paranoid type clearly in need of professional treatment." The question was as follows: "Mrs. B had always been a little suspicious and inclined to take the worst view of things, but she had led a fairly happy married life until she began to accuse her husband of not loving her any more. When she saw him speak politely to an attractive widow next door, Mrs. B waited until he had left, got hold of his gun, and then went over and threatened to kill the widow. Mrs. B's husband hadn't done anything wrong and doesn't know what to do about her." Of the total sample, 26 percent thought it would be best for her minister to talk with her, 21 percent thought her husband should give her a good talking-to and see if she came to her senses, 21 percent said the family doctor should be called and give a sedative to calm her down, 13 percent thought the husband should stay home and prove to Mrs. B he loved her, 7 percent said Mrs. B should be taken to a mental hospital where she could be treated and not do anyone any harm, 1 percent said the police should be called to lock her up immediately, and 11 percent of the respondents "did not know" or "did not like any of these alternatives."

A second matter derived from the waiter incident needs further comment; it is exemplified by the cafe owner's calling the police. This involves the designation of abnormal behavior by nonprofessionals. It is a crucial problem in epidemiological studies. Zubin puts the matter as follows:

The detection, rather than diagnosis, of mental disorders is made largely by laymen—the patient himself, his family, friends, neighbors, the community and its public officials, such as policemen, sheriffs, etc. . . . Thus, at least the initial detection of mental illness is based largely on those aspects of the patient's behavior which deviate from expected social and cultural norms. As a result, sociocultural forces tend to bias the apparent prevalence of mental illness. [1966, p. 47.]

The two important points, that mass media disseminate information about the roles of both the abnormal person and his significant others, and that the vast majority of actions leading to people's being called to the attention of professional workers are initiated by laymen, are brought together in a statement by Jerome Frank:

An interesting, if somewhat unfortunate, consequence of the fact that social attitudes play such a big role in the definition of mental illness is that mental health education may be a two-edged sword. By teaching people to regard certain types of distress or behavioral oddities as illnesses rather than as normal reactions to life's stresses, harmless eccentricities, or moral weaknesses, it may cause alarm and increase the demand for psychotherapy. This may explain the curious fact that the use of psychotherapy tends to keep pace with its availability. The greater the number of treatment facilities and the more widely they are known, the larger the number of persons seeking their services. Psychotherapy is the only form of treatment which, at least to some extent, appears to create the illness it treats. It can never suffer the unfortunate fate of Victor Borge's physician uncle who became despondent on realizing that he had discovered a cure for which there was no disease. [Frank, 1961, pp. 6–7.]

SOCIAL EVENTS LEADING TO THE LABEL "ABNORMAL"

Up to this point the discussion of the implications of the definition of mental illness has centered on the referral situation and its social function. This section will examine the specific cultural and class variables likely to lead to the person's being labeled abnormal.

Cross-cultural Considerations

Benedict (1934) noted that "localized social norms" among "simpler" people offered an

social and societal contexts

opportunity to test cultural concepts which might have been considered as universal and inevitable if only standardized Western European people were available for study. One of her most striking findings was that many people who would be considered abnormal in our culture would fit into other cultures with ease and honor. Benedict points out the valued place of cataleptic and trancelike states in the role of the shaman in diverse cultures. She cites work by Fortune (1932) describing a Melanesian culture in which the major theme was a belief that other people were trying to harm the individual. Belief in the malevolence of others was omnipresent. A flavor of this belief may be gathered by the fact that the polite phrase at the acceptance of a gift was, "And if you now poison me, how shall I repay you this present?"

Benedict writes, "Now in this society where no one may work with another and no one may share with another, Fortune describes the individual who was regarded by all his fellows as crazy. He was not one of those who periodically ran amok and, beside himself and frothing at the mouth, fell with a knife upon anyone he could reach. Such behavior they did not regard as putting anyone outside the pale. They did not even put the individuals who were known to be liable to these attacks under any kind of control. They merely fled when they saw the attack coming and kept out of the way. 'He would be all right tomorrow.' But there was one man of sunny, kindly disposition who liked work and liked to be helpful. The compulsion was too strong for him to repress it in favor of the opposite tendencies of his culture. Men and women never spoke of him without laughing; he was silly and simple and definitely crazy. Nevertheless, to the ethnologist used to a culture that has, in Christianity, made his type the model of all virtue, he seemed a pleasant fellow."

Reports such as this one, particularly as they involve aggression against one's fellows, from cultures such as the Kwakiutl (Benedict, 1934) and the Mundugumor (Mead, 1935) have a major and continuing place in theoretical formulations of abnormal behavior. Compared to normal people in these cultures, Mrs. B, who threatened the attractive widow next door, is a gentle type. Yet, Mrs. B "is a paranoid type clearly in need of professional treatment." Such comparisons question the very nature of the concept of abnormality. Benedict (1934) wrote: "Most of those organizations of personality that seem to us most incontrovertibly abnormal have been used by different civilizations in the very foundations of their institutional life. . . . We recognize that morality differs in every society, and is a convenient term for socially approved habits. . . . The concept of the normal is properly a variant of the concept of the good. It is that which society has approved. A normal action is one that falls well within the limits of expected behavior for a particular society."

SPECIFIC PATTERNS. Among the more interesting items of anthropological work is the description of "ethnic" psychoses: *amok,* a homicidal rampage; *piblokto,* an endemic convulsive disorder among the polar Eskimos; *guria* is a shaking syndrome observed in New Guinea; *windigo,* psychosis among the Algonquin Indian hunters, in which the starved man becomes convinced he is in the power of a supernatural monster with an insatiable craving for human flesh; *ufufunyane,* noted among South African tribes such as the Zulus and Zhosa, which consists of attacks of shouting and sobbing, sometimes accompanied by abdominal pains and loss of consciousness and sight, attributed to the operation of magical love potions administered by rejected lovers. Among Siberian groups, especially women, there at times appears a copying mania called *amurakh; menerik* is similar but there is wilder screaming and dancing, often ending in an epileptiform seizure. *Kere,* observed among the people of the Malayan archipelago and South China, is an acute anxiety reaction in which the person (usually but not always male) fears that his sex organ will shrink and disappear into his abdomen. *Latah,* usually seen in middle-aged Malaysian women, has a number of indicants: following commands automatically, repetitive imitation, and most interestingly, in contrast to Gilles de la Tourette syndrome, saying an obscenity after being startled. As Guthrie (1973) remarks: "That it never occurs when they are alone may help to explain the disorder." (p. 9.) In *juramentado,* a Muslim Filipino from the islands near Borneo, after going through various rituals, takes his dagger and tries to kill as many Christians as possible in the belief that he will be repaid in the hereafter. *Susto* or *espanto,* a fear state attributed to loss of soul, is associated with many correlates of physiological arousal, and is observed in the Spanish-speaking New World, including the Southwestern United States. Good sources for this topic may be found in Wittkower (1969), Kiev (1972), and Yap (1969). It requires quite a bit of compromise with the definitions used in the United States to place these behaviors in the diagnostic system presented in Chapter 1 of this book.

Cross-cultural Incidence of Mental Disorders

As indicated in Chapter 1, the availability of professional resources is a major determinant of the incidence of mental disorder. Further, as noted in Chapter 5, especially in reference to the example from Koos (1954), the recognition that a difficulty calls for a physician's attention is associated with social status and community customs (Linn, 1968). Zola (1966) points out that the decision to seek aid is often unrelated to seriousness and discomfort, and hence a selective process associated with culture is operating—for example, different standards of normal behavior (Michael, 1967b). A class bias may exist in the very nature of the class being powerful enough to create labels (Thio, 1973). Differences in the incidence of psychiatric disorders among social groups may be a result of these selective processes rather than a result of true rates or of actual behavior. Such considerations make it difficult to determine whether one society or one period of history is especially conducive to mental disorders. Goldhamer and Marshall (1949) reviewed hospital records in Massachusetts from 1840 onwards to determine the effect of cultural changes on the frequency of mental disorders. Their conclusion was that other than an increase in people over age 50, made possible by increases in life expectancy, admission rates remained stable throughout the various changing periods of history surveyed. In fact, if incidence is measured by hospitalization, it is now decreasing. In 1955, when the United States' population was 166 million, 560,000 people were in state and country mental hospitals. In 1970, with a population of 205 million, the number was 350,000. This was the fifteenth consecutive year of decrease (Coleman and Broen, 1972, p. 19) and indicates the role of treatment and social policy on incidence.

There formerly was a popular notion that there were no instances of mental illness among the relatively isolated, closely knit Hutterites. Eaton and Weil (1955), on close investigation, found that roughly one in 43 of the Hutterites displayed symptoms of mental disorder or had recovered from such symptoms. While the rate is far lower than the estimates made by studies of prevalence in other groups (which will be noted below), it is not, as had been rumored, zero. What was perhaps most useful to the Hutterite who was "mentally ill" was to be encouraged to participate in the normal life of the family and community, and most were able to do some useful work. The person was neither rejected nor cast away into a state hospital. It would seem that the favorable "mental health" record of the Hutterites was as much dependent upon what the group did when a person took the role of the mentally ill as it was that the society did not recognize or permit such a role or was so "healthy" that no one ever emitted such behaviors.

Lambo has observed:

> Our clinical work in Nigeria shows that the diagnostic criteria and assessment of prognostic possibilities which hold in Western culture are equally applicable to the Nigerian patients who have been in contact with this culture. However, this does not seem to hold for patients whose social and cultural background is as different from a Western background as that of the non-literate African. In this group schizophrenic symptomatology in the main shows a considerable degree of diversity, polymorphism and affective swings. [1965, p. 70.]

Complexity of culture may be considered as a situation in which alternative behaviors are likely to be available, and when the traditional or normal acts are extinguished, new available role enactments are emitted. This is considerably different from a notion that cultural complexity in and of itself leads to stress.

Beyond the problems of diagnostic reliability, to be discussed in the next chapter, the role of the physician himself must be brought into consideration in evaluating the social implications of the diagnostic situation. Lin (1965, p. 22) noted: "It seems to me that the education and training background of the psychiatrist is more decisive than cultural variations in the identification of symptom-complexes."

Loudon (1965), reviewing his work in South Wales, notes the important role of the general practitioner in the referral-labeling process. The general practitioner's attitudes toward the psychiatric specialist influenced public concepts about psychiatrists in general and types of symptoms about which psychiatrists should be consulted. Further, Loudon suggests that variations between socioeconomic segments of the population affect the general practitioner's concepts of both prevalence of psychiatric problems and appropriate referrals. Awareness of the individual's social characteristics may have as much influence on the physician as the purely clinical picture.

The physician is not alone in the diagnostic interchange, and Rubin (1965, p. 355) comments that in order to interact with the psychiatrist-anthropologist, the native must assign a role to him. The anthropologist may, therefore, first be categorized as, for instance, a Voodoo priest; after this has been done, the people have a role available for interaction with him, but it is as they would interact with a Voodoo priest rather than as they would interact with a "scientist" or *our* type of psychiatrist, neither of which they have conceptualized.

Murphy and Leighton (1965) point out that the non-Western groups may describe a wide range of behaviors that would fall in the province of psychiatrists, but they do not necessarily use the same concepts employed in our culture. Similarly, Leighton points out that (1) behaviors may be agreed upon, but (2) conceptualizations (and hence, eventual evaluations) may differ:

> An intriguing fact here is that there is no word for depression in Yoruba. When we described individual symptoms—crying spells, feeling blue, loss of appetite, waking early in the morning and so on—these were immediately recognized by the Yoruba, although the whole constellation of symptoms still did not form a syndrome in their minds; to us the various features all fitted together, but it had not occurred to our informants that they made a pattern. On the other hand, there was one disorder, puzzling to us, that was frequently reported, both by the native healers who were our key source of information and also by certain members of our sample who were questioned about their previous illnesses. They would quite often say that they suffered from *inorun*, which was translated to us as heavenly fire. *Inorun* quite clearly is a syndrome in their minds, although I still cannot make it form a pattern in mine. (1965, p. 83.)

Epidemiological Studies

These conceptual difficulties are crucial in epidemiological studies: studies "of the health condition of a population in relation to any conceivable factors existing in or affecting that population which may influence the health state or affect its distribution in that population." (Lemkau and Crocetti, 1967, p. 225). "Epidemiologists try to find populations with differing rates of illness and then try to compare their respective environments in the hope of discovering possible causes of disease." (Arthur 1971, p. 12.) The approach is essentially correlational and not causal; if we found a higher rate of psychosis among students who had failed than passed a course, we could not say whether the psychosis led to poor grades or whether the poor grades were a stress producing psychosis.

While diagnostic and sampling procedures vary from one study to another, the rates of mental illness found on such surveys of the general population have been alarmingly high, albeit quite variable (see Arthur, 1971, table 4, p. 61). A quotation from Alexander Leighton, who has been as responsible as any other person for serious work in this field, provides a summary:

In this connexion, some figures may be quoted. In a rural district in North America, one of our studies has shown that at least 29 percent of the adult population have psychiatric symptoms and are impaired by these to a significant degree (D. C. Leighton et al., 1963a, b). A similar study in Manhattan (Srole et al., 1962) yields a figure of 23 percent. Another sampling study (not yet published) of a small commune in France shows 26 percent affected. The investigation of the entire population of two rural parishes in Sweden (Essen-Moller, 1956; Hagnell, 1964) indicates that 25 percent have psychiatric difficulties. Studies in other areas are comparable. Research work conducted by professor Lambo and myself (A. H. Leighton et al., 1963a, b) in the Western region of Nigeria points to 16 percent of the adults in rural villages and 17 percent of the adults in a segment of a city having psychiatric symptoms to a significant degree. . . . As soon as one begins to look at subdivisions of these populations, marked differences on a considerable range appear. Thus, in some communities in the North American rural area, 72 percent of the population were estimated to have a significant degree of disorder. In Nigeria, the range was from 6 to 50 percent. [1965, pp. 219–20.]

The work by Srole et al. (1962) is the most widely cited one in this area and deserves some description. A part of Manhattan's East Side including 174,000 people was selected as the area to be studied. Blocks, homes in the blocks, and people in the homes were randomly sampled. People over 60 and transients were systematically excluded, and of 1,911 people drawn, 1,660 answered a rather long, structured questionnaire about their past and present physical and mental symptoms. *Symptoms were categorized as absent, mild, moderate, and serious, and interference with life adjustment as none, some, great, and incapacitating.* The basic data were collected by trained nonmedical professionals and then evaluated by psychiatric clinicians. Sources of unreliability (see Chapter 3) may arise from data gathering or interviewer methods, from variability of the interviewee, and the method of evaluation by the psychiatric clinician. The bias toward diagnosing illness noted earlier in this chapter could operate, and, in fact, rater reliability was far and away greatest in the area of incapacity of functioning. Socioeconomic status was estimated from father's education and occupation, and it was found that the percentage of people rated "healthy" declined and the percentage of people rated "impaired" rose as socioeconomic status declined. In addiction, as age increased, rated incapacity increased. But the most generally interesting finding was that fewer than one in four people were "well" and close to one in five were "incapacitated."[3]

[3] Similar results are reported in Plunkett and Gordon (1960), Pasamanick (1961), and Phillips (1966); Gillis, Lewis, and Slabbert (1968) reported lower rate (11.8 percent) and three times the rate in persons of the lowest class compared to those in the highest. Gunderson, Arthur, and Richardson (1968) found that the admission rate for enlisted Navy men was twice that of petty officers, and that

Given these various conceptual difficulties (Dohrenwend and Dohrenwend, 1969), we may well refer to an excellent summary by Draguns and Phillips (1972) on the general findings of cross-cultural studies:

What information exists is in the form of bicultural comparisons, and it justifies the conclusion that cultural effects on the manifestations of psychopathology are extremely difficult to eliminate. Such effects remain potent despite the imposition of a variety of controls in the form of restriction to a single diagnostic group (Kimura, 1965, 1967; Opler and Singer, 1959; Schooler and Caudill, 1964), multidimensional social and diagnostic matching (Draguns et al., 1971; Fabrega et al., 1967; Fundia et al., 1971), using identical observers for both groups of the comparison (Kimura, 1965; Jakovljevic, 1963; Nachshon et al., in press, Draguns, Leaman and Rosenfeld, 1971; Skea et al., 1969), or relying on native observers at both sites of the investigation (Draguns et al., 1971; Fundia et al., 1971; Sechrest, 1969). Moreover, cultural effects have survived the application of computerized techniques of diagnosis (Spitzer and Endicott, 1969), resulting in the exclusion of observer bias from diagnostic judgment (Cooper et al., 1969). Differences have been repeatedly reported in the form of symptoms (Draguns et al., 1971; Enright and Jaeckle, 1963; Fabrega et al., 1967; Fundia et al., 1971; Sechrest, 1969), symptom dominance patterns (Draguns et al., 1971; Fundia et al., 1971), and diagnostic entities (Bourne, 1970; Cooper et al., 1969; Jakovljevic, 1963; Saenger, 1968). These results from bicultural comparisons are paralleled by the findings of the two worldwide studies of the distribution and manifestation of depression and schizophrenia throughout the world (Murphy et al., 1963, 1967). These inquiries yielded the impression of a relatively greater prevalence of depression in Western and European countries and of schizophrenia in some of the countries in eastern and southern Asia. Moreover, the symptom patterns, though overlapping, were not identical. The primary manifestations of depression, for example, insomnia and loss of interest in social environment, were encountered virtually throughout the world with only small variations of frequency. There were, however, both culture-specific additions and omissions beyond that pattern; religious preoccupations and theatrical grief were quite uncharacteristic of the Japanese depressives, and loss of appetite and cyclical mood swings were uncommon in India. Cross-culturally valid relationships also emerged in these two surveys, pointing, among other things, to the worldwide tendency for higher rates of depression in upper socioeconomic strata, in cohesive social structures, and among women.

Ecological and Social Class Studies of Mental Disorders

Two areas of investigation that have yielded interesting results are those of geographical location and social class. The former has been called ecological study. The seminal work in this area was by Robert Faris, and the single most important publication is that of Faris and Dunham (1939). The technique uses admission to psychiatric institutions as an index of mental health, a definition which, while open to question (see Chapter 1 of this book), is both reliable and culturally relevant. It was found by these authors, and frequently substantiated thereafter, that a

---

for petty officers it was twice that of officers. This was particularly true for the neurotic and personality-disorder categories. Goldberg and Blackwell (1970), drawing cases from a general medical practice, and using a stricter diagnostic criterion, report two interesting findings. First, "conspicuous psychiatric morbidity" of a surburban general practice was found to be 20 percent. . . . Second, at follow-up six months later, two-thirds of the patients were functioning in the normal range. This latter finding bears on epidemiological studies, on the one hand, but also on the stability of behavioral problems over time as affected by the presence or absence of labeling or other professional intervention.

An excellent critical review of epidemiology is that of Mishler and Scotch (1963). A related topic is the degree to which general medical patients may manifest symptoms justifying psychiatric referral. Stoeckle, Zola, and Davidson (1964), who provide an excellent review and new data, might set the figure as high as between 50 and 80 percent. Similar additional reports are by Silbert (1964), and Denney et al. (1966), who, like Zusman (1967), make the point that the practitioner in physical medicine requires training in identifying psychiatric disorders. An outstanding reference on social class and psychological problems is by Dohrenwend and Dohrenwend (1969).

disproportionate number of schizophrenics entered hospitals from "disorganized" or socially "heterogenous" areas (e.g., Levy and Rowitz, 1971). Faris argued that where social contacts are "adequate" and the person is neither sheltered nor ostracized from the mainstream of his culture, schizophrenia is rare, and where it does arise, the response to it by the individual's social milieu is generally therapeutic. The basic datum, of increased rates of schizophrenics admitted to hospitals from deteriorating sections of a city and a decrease of rate of admissions as distance of residence increases from this center, has been replicated; these studies have been reviewd by Faris (1944) and by Dunham (1955, 1966).

Associated with ecological research are studies of the association of social class with mental illness. As noted in the discussion of the work by Srole et al. (1962) on the prevalence of mental illness to the point of impairment in Manhattan, lower social class was associated with higher percentages of impairment and lower percentages of people evaluated as "well." While there have been exceptions to this rule (Kleiner and Parker, 1963), in broad outline it has been substantiated by a number of independent investigators.

The study that is deservedly the most widely cited in this area is by Hollingshead and Redlich (1953). The first step taken in this project was to delineate the social class structure of the population (New Haven, Connecticut, and surrounding towns). Five classes were defined: Class I were essentially wealthy, high-social-prestige business and professional men; Class II, managers and lesser ranking professionals; Class III, small proprietors, white collar workers, and skilled laborers; Class IV, semiskilled workers; and Class V, factory laborers and unskilled laborers. While the occupation of those being studied was highlighted, factors such as education and place of residence were also taken into consideration. Next, a psychiatric census was taken to ascertain which residents were receiving psychiatric care on a given day, December 1, 1950. A control group was established by taking a 5 percent sample of community households from the *City Directory*. The psychiatric and normal samples were categorized on the basis of the social class system described above. A highly significant association was found between social class and being under psychiatric care. A smaller percentage of the higher classes (I-IV) were under psychiatric care than would have been expected by the frequency of such people in the population, and a far greater number of the people under psychiatric care came from the lowest social class (V) than would have been expected by chance. Class V comprised 17.8 percent of the general population but accounted for 36.8 percent of the people under psychiatric care.

The diagnosis of the person under psychiatric care was also significantly associated with his social class. The upper classes (I and II) were likely to be diagnosed as neurotic, while people from the lower classes (IV and V) were likely to be diagnosed psychotic. The respective percentages of each class diagnosed neurotic and psychotic were as follows: I: 53 percent neurotic and 47 percent psychotic: II: 67 percent neurotic and 33 percent psychotic; III: 44 percent neurotic and 56 percent psychotic; IV: 23 percent neurotic and 77 percent psychotic; V: 8 percent neurotic and 92 percent psychotic. Finally, the type of therapy given members of the social classes differed, the upper classes being more likely to receive psychotherapy, the lower classes being more likely to receive physical treatments such as shock or no specific treatment other than custody.

Two obvious social variables which deserve mention, if only in passing, are sex and race. Different rates of sexual incidence for varying diagnoses have been frequently noted (Rose and Stub, 1955; Garai, 1970; Pokorny and Overall, 1970). While these differences are striking, at present little practical or theoretical use has been made of them other than in psychoanalytic and political theories (Chesler, 1972). An illustration of how such differences may be used is indicated by Frumkin (1955), who presented correlations among income, occupational prestige, and rates of first admission to psychiatric hospitals separately for men and women. The correlation between income and prestige was .90 and .74 respectively for men and women; that between rate of admission and prestige was .81 and .53; and that between rate of admission and income was .71 and .15. The association of occupational prestige and income is greater for males than females. These data indicate that it would probably be wiser to look for the correlates of variables such as occupational status than to stop with the sociological variable itself. Tuckman and Kleiner (1962) illustrate this point, using an index of discrepancy between education as an indicator of aspiration and occupation as an indicator of achievement. Rates of admission to hospitals for schizophrenia were more accurately predicted by such an index than by measures of social status alone.

Kleiner, Tuckman, and Lavell (1960) replicated the broad findings of the New Haven study (Hollingshead and Redlich, 1953) in Philadelphia, but also reported differences between males and females, whites and nonwhites. The schizophrenic diagnosis was applied to one in three white persons, while it was given to one in two nonwhites. This finding was true for both males and females. It was also of interest that across nine diagnostic categories, for males and females separately (i.e., 18 comparisons), in every case nonwhites were younger at the time of first admission than whites of the same sex and diagnosis.

Before leaving this topic, it is worth noting that the belief that a *drift* toward lower socioeconomic status is positively associated with mental illness, either as a cause or as an effect, is not borne out by the data (Kleiner and Parker, 1963; Turner and Wagenfeld, 1967). Nor is there an increase in mental illnesses, such as psychosis, found among those individuals who have risen in socioeconomic status.[4]

LEARNING TO BE NORMALLY ABNORMAL

The act of diagnosing someone is a social act, involving the material on which this decision is based, the pressures on the professional person making the diagnosis, and a special set of concepts. Sociologists and anthropologists have sought to determine whether there are specific types of social situations likely to lead to a greater number of people acting in an abnormal manner. In essence the question is whether there are conditions under which the professional group will apply the label more frequently. General practitioners, mass media, and other social influences work to delineate *when* a person is to be labeled abnormal and *how* he is to be handled.

If abnormal behavior is defined as deviance (rule and/or expectation breaking) that sanctions psychiatric intervention, then the obvious place to start a discussion of abnormality is not with the people who break the rules, but with the rules themselves and the ways in which they are learned.[5]

---

[4] Kleiner and Parker (1963) provide an excellent review of the area, as does Scott (1958b). Additional examples of work in this area relate to the reciprocal relationship of the patient's social class and the psychiatrist's response (Myers and Roberts, 1959; Moore, Benedek, and Wallace, 1963; Aronson and Overall, 1966; and Michael, 1967). Vail, Lucera, and Boen (1966), surveying 123 variables across 87 counties, "demonstrated that half the variance in state hospital load was associated with socioeconomic variables. Poor counties showed a higher incidence and prevalence of major mental illness than did wealthier counties." Examples of other variables are work on dwelling-unit density (Kahn and Perlin, 1967; Galle, Gove, and McPherson, 1972) and ethnic discrimination (Wignall and Koppin, 1967).

[5] Rules develop in much the same way as the concept of abnormality advocated in this volume: "Law . . . begins when someone takes to doing

Rules

The first thing about rules is that they are constantly changing. Opportunities for behavior that previously did not exist now do, and some behaviors that only a short time ago were frowned upon are today considered normal. In our society the area of sexual expression is the most notable example. There are many ways of focusing on social change, but the following law passed by the British Parliament in 1770 dramatically points up the difference in social rules then and now. "All women, of whatever age, rank, profession or degree, whether virgins, maids or widows, that shall impose upon, seduce or betray into matrimony any of his Majesty's subjects, by scents, paints, cosmetics, washes, artificial teeth, false hair, iron stave hoops, high-heeled shoes, bolstered hips or padded bosoms shall incur the penalty of the law enforced against witchcraft and like misdemeanors, and upon conviction, that marriage shall stand null and void."

Another example of changes in rules, this one in the area of religion, deals with how a small New England private school gained the reputation of "godless Harvard." ". . . the very limits of religious irresponsibility were not reached until 1760, when the Harvard faculty granted permission to Anglican students to attend Christ Church, Cambridge, instead of the Congregational meetinghouse." (Rudolph, 1965, p. 17.)

The second thing about rules is that there are many of them. At a formal, legal level, the complexity of written rules is basic to the existence of professions such as law and accounting. Because there are so many of them, rules may conflict. In Chapter 2 it was noted that a person might act in a manner that was unexpected and upsetting to those around him if he guided his behavior by discriminative stimuli that were culturally or geographically distant and not shared by those immediately present. Proper behavior for a fraternity brother may lead to role enactments that are not expected from a good churchgoing son who is also a gentleman and a serious student.[6]

At times academic advisers help cut red tape and break rules so that the very purpose of the institution responsible for the rules may be served. Such nonconformity in the service of the organization is perhaps characteristic of much of bureaucratic society, and is certainly a necessary feature of large psychiatric hospitals see Ullmann, 1967a). Conflicts among rules are made more likely by the varied nature of our society. The cultural richness and pluralism of America and its relative degree of opportunity for upward mobility increase the opportunity for the individual to be faced with choices in terms of religion, occupation, and personal conduct. There is even the choice to reject the dominant value structure of the society, as manifested by the counter-culture.

Conversely, the symbols of having made a choice may in and of themselves lead to aversive consequences. There are periodic reports of court battles over whether high school students should cut their hair. The ultimate of such pressures is exemplified by an Iowa court's decision (reported in *Time,* February 25, 1966, pp. 45–48) to refuse permission for a son to return to a father who was a political liberal, a reader of works on Zen Buddhism, and a writer-photographer without concern for formal religious training, so that his son could be raised by more conventional grandparents.

It is practically impossible to obey all the rules. Again, the area of sex is one that most readily offers illustrations. There is the repeated observation, based on work such as

---

something someone else does not like." (K. Llewellyn, cited in Mayer, 1967, p. ix.) For a more formal analysis of rules, see Scandura (1970).

[6] This example touches on two points which are integrated into the following material: first there may be "role conflict." The second is that a person will not break rules unless there is opportunity to attain goals through "illegitimate means" (Cloward, 1959).

the Kinsey report, that in their sexual behavior at least 95 percent of the American population have broken some written rule at some time or other. Wallerstein and Wyle (1947) report 99 percent of respondents from the general population admitted to having committed one or more offenses serious enough to draw a maximum sentence of not less than a year. For example, among men, 84 percent had committed malicious mischief, 85 percent disorderly conduct, and 89 percent larceny. Of the men, 57 percent admitted to tax evasion, and 40 percent of women admitted to this offense. Among the woman 81 percent admitted to malicious mischief, 76 percent to disorderly conduct, and 83 percent to larceny. Approximately three-fourths of both men and women admitted to indecency.

Perfect adherence to rules is rarely found. If a policeman enforced all the minor violations he noticed in his rounds, he would spend so much time testifying in court that he would not be able to fulfill his function of protection against and detection of major crimes. Further, rigorous and complete enforcement of the laws would fill beyond capacity the community's psychiatric hospitals and jails. Finally, complete enforcement of rules would probably bring a reaction that would lead to the termination of many rules and aversive consequences to the promulgators.

If all rules cannot be enforced, there are two important considerations. The first is that breaking the rule is not sufficient for the label of deviant or abnormal. It can well be argued that being caught and publicly labeled is an integral and possibly even necessary step in a career of deviance.

The second consideration is that justice in the form of apprehension and public labeling is unevenly administered. Many breaches of rules are overlooked or minimally punished because they are not "worth the trouble" of enforcing.

Associated with the unenforceability of all rules is the concept that rules may be so breached that their violation is itself institutionalized. Rule following, like any other behavior, must be worthwhile. If the cost of breaking a rule is less than the cost of following it, the rule is likely to be broken. Lemert (1967, p. 11) makes this point in terms of compliance with weight regulations by trucks on northern California highways. If the cost of two trips is greater than the cost of a single trip plus fine, the law is likely to be broken, and fines for violations will be accepted as a normal cost of business. This is accepted by state officials to the extent that trucking companies are sent monthly statements of fines due.

The fact that change in the expectations of individuals is controlled by subsequent reinforcement is illustrated on a communitywide scale by two parallel studies. Leighton (1965, pp. 231–32) tells hows a power company built a dam and provided employment over three years for a poverty-stricken community. The people discovered credit and appliances, particularly television, which introduced them to general American values. "The breadwinners also discovered something else about television sets; if they did not retain their jobs and pay premiums on the sets, somebody came along and took them away. They were thus trapped into working steadily. One result of this was that the men from this community, who had previously had a reputation for being poor employees, gradually developed the opposite kind of reputation." The parallel instance is where employment ceases. Cottrell (1951) relates how a shift to the use of diesel engines disrupted the economy of a town. The lower classes, lacking a major investment, could move to other places, but the more settled, propertied classes shifted toward radicalism and ideological rebellion.

Another illustration of these concepts was presented by Rosenthal (1954), who described the abandonment of the traditional Jewish pattern by young lower-class people in a small Polish town between the two World Wars. The main determinant of status for the total group lay in learning, charity, and good deeds. Being able to play this role depended in turn on wealth and leisure, and young people in the lower class were at a severe disadvantage. Since they could not compete in a way of life in which the central values were difficult if not impossible to attain, they were more likely to forsake the way of life altogether.

Rules, informal expectations, and written laws are discriminative stimuli. That is, they indicate the conditions under which certain behaviors will have reinforcing consequences. With association, either simultaneous or chained, they become acquired reinforcers. But as such, they may be extinguished. An overwhelming inflation such as that in Germany during the 1920's is an example of one of Western civilization's most widely used secondary reinforcers becoming invalid for an entire population.

Rules will be adhered to only if adherence is worthwhile. Lemert (1967, p. 15), for example, notes that the Naval supply section in San Francisco observed weight distribution guidelines on axles of trucks in a manner not done by private concerns. The private firms could write off trucks as depreciated equipment, while the Navy could not do this and had a low budget for maintenance. Thus the latter were involved in a situation in which there was reinforcement for rule adherence which was not true for the former.

Another example of this is King's (1956, p. 116) quotation of a manifesto by an American Indian tribe that was backsliding in terms of the rules laid down by missionary workers: "No more blanket, no more hallelujah!"

Riots in ghettos display similar principles. If a person has studied and followed the rules properly and then cannot find a job, he may question the entire procedure. As one young man said, "I put my faith in the Man and he didn't come through." A riot is an alternative behavior to playing by the rules. In addition, some riots have obtained short-run benefits that should have been forthcoming without the riots but were not.

A third point about rules is that frequently virtue is its own reward, there being no other. The likelihood of reinforcement for rule-following behavior is not certain. While the mass media glorify the self-made man, and while the religious ethos of the country is one of self-responsibility and opportunity limited only by personal effort (Fromm, 1941, 1947; Tawney, 1926), the facts of life are that room at the top is restricted rather than unlimited. The majority of the large organizations in which Americans increasingly live, work, worship, and play are pyramidal, so that the farther one rises, the fewer are the positions available above him. Aside from limitations in opportunity, there are limitations in ability which have little if anything to do with effort. There is frequently a gap between aspiration (what one labels as the good life) and accomplishment. In the United States today mass media such as television provide models of the good life (e.g., appliances) which are frequently unattainable by the general public.

A fourth feature of rules is that they are made by people in power, that is, by people who are in positions to dispense reinforcers. To make a formal rule, especially a written one such as a law, is a major enterprise on the part of many people. By implication there are conditions that those in power wish to perpetuate and other conditions, acts by people (usually specific individuals), that they wish to minimize. The English law against the use of deceit by women in the attraction of men was made by men.

In terms of unwritten rules, there must be a standard of what is expected and proper behavior. As noted in the review of prevalence studies earlier in the chapter, there are many individuals in the population who might be termed mentally ill but who manage to make some sort of socially appropriate adjustment. The societal agent who imposes rules is likely to be a member of the class currently holding power. If a person has not been taught the rules of a particular group, he will be considered strange by members of it. On the one hand, he may have had, at best, minimal exposure to such rules, or having had such exposure, little opportunity or reinforcement for following such rules. It is in this regard that it is reasonable that lower socioeconomic classes should have higher rates of both prevalence and incidence of severe "abnormalities." In similar fashion, it is reasonable that the better organized the person's social group and the more reinforcing contact he has with other people, the lower will be the rates of incidence and prevalence of mental illness. Finally, the closer the person is in socioeconomic, educational, and common value system to the societally sanctioned labeler, the more likely it is that his behavior will be *understandable* to the labeler and hence not as readily diagnosed as mentally ill.[7]

Rule Learning, Rule Following, and Abnormality

If one can formulate the development of a "normal" person, be he student or professor, one will have a description and set of principles for dealing with any learned bizarre behavior. Timothy Leary made this point cogently when he said there is nothing so far out as a square.

Rules, as discriminative stimuli, are both learned and unlearned; and the unlearning of one set of rules implies a new set of rules

---

[7] Education, religion, and race are examples of variables that may affect relative frequency of self-referral (Scheff, 1966b) or utilization of a clinic (Rabkin and Lytle, 1966; Kasl and Schlingensliepen, 1970). Educational differences within professions may also affect frequency of referral (Bentz, 1967), as do school size and attitudes of the principal toward psychological services (Robbins, Mercer, and Meyers, 1967). Different professions among mental health workers use different ways of persuading people to seek assistance (Toban, 1970), and these modes may then be investigated (Colson, 1973; Fischer and Turner, 1970).

rather than no rules. Such change is necessary as people grow from children to parents and employees, and the same concepts hold for people who receive abnormal labels and those who through treatment receive labels called normal. Toch (1965) provides a model in terms of social movements:

Usually, the hold of the movement is thus weakened *gradually*. First a few outposts are sacrificed; doubts about minor matters come to the fore; other "weaknesses" are perceived; and eventually, the bonds linking member to movement become sufficiently tenuous to snap under stress. [Toch, 1965, p. 165] The convert is a *disillusioned* person, and disillusionment is a slow, surreptitious type of change. It begins with undercover reservations to the effort of remaining loyal. It represents a cumulative record of the costs of adaptation. Whether it dies in its suppressed state or becomes publicized in awareness depends on the number and the import of disillusioning experiences that are encountered. . . . a person will tend to become disillusioned if he becomes actively involved in life situations for which he has been ill-prepared by socialization. [1965, p. 128.]

For example, to become a marijuana smoker, first of all a person must be in a geographical, temporal, and social environment where marijuana is available. A student who had lived in a protected environment in which marijuana was not available and who had therefore followed other patterns may, upon entering college, find that his previous patterns of social behavior, such as dependence on parents and teachers, serious and dedicated memorization of textbooks, and the like, are no longer rewarded as they were in high school. He may be extinguished for square behaviors and go to pot. After having the role available, he must smoke (enact the role). And even that is not enough; he must learn to smoke marijuana properly in order to get the effect. Next he must identify the effect of the drug, and finally he must label the changes (note the Schachter and Singer, 1962 work cited in Chapter 5) as being good and pleasurable. These considerations represent successive stages, and failure to enact or be reinforced for any stage is likely to lead to a decrease of the behavior.

This model is directly applicable to the use of alcohol or indulgence in sexual intercourse and involves *reduction of ties to a prior evaluative system and of aversive consequences for deviation from it*. Such a stepwise progression was called shaping in Chapter 4, but it may also be called a *career*. To become a physician a person must get into college, take pre-med courses, then move through medical school and internship. Failure (cessation of reinforcement) at any point will terminate the career.

At the point of being extinguished or, in Toch's terms, disillusioned, the person may emit many different behaviors. The ones that are reinforced are likely to increase in emission, while those not reinforced are likely to decrease. Once again the important element making for the stability of a pattern of behavior, whether labeled normal or abnormal, is reinforcement. The fact that prevalence rates (the number of people who might be labeled) are so much higher than incidence rates (the number of people who are actually labeled, hospitalized, and treated) is taken by Scheff (1966a) to be indicative of the fugacious nature of much "mental illness." From this datum, the great amount of "residual deviance," the difference between prevalence and incidence, and, more generally, the near universal presence of some deviant (rule-breaking) behavior, Scheff, like a number of other sociologists, points out that it is the act of *being labeled* that stabilizes the mentally ill role. This important step will be discussed next.

Labeling: A Further Step in Being Normally Abnormal

In *As I Lay Dying*, William Faulkner spoke of the effects of labeling a person sane or crazy:

Sometimes I ain't so sho who's got ere a right to say when a man is crazy and when he ain't. Sometimes I think it ain't none of us pure crazy and ain't none of us pure sane until the balance of us folks talks him that-a-way. It's like it ain't so much what a fellow does, but it's the way the majority of folks is looking at him when he does it. [p. 510.]

It has been stressed that failure to learn socially approved habits or the extinction of such behavior is one condition leading to the emission of acts that will be labeled abnormal. Benedict (1934) talks of those individuals who are liable to serious disturbances because "their habits are culturally unsupported." Benedict (1934) also pointed out that the particular forms of behavior to which unstable individuals of any group are liable are many of them matters of cultural patterning like any other behavior and even in trance the individual holds strictly to the rules and expectations of his culture, and his experience is as locally patterned as a marriage rite or an economic exchange.

Being labeled in itself has an enormous effect. The crux of the matter conceptually is that while some specific aspect of the person's *behavior* leads to labeling, in practice it is the total *person* who is labeled and who is then reacted to in terms of his label. This difference in behavior of other people toward him makes a great difference in the acts he can and will continue to emit.

In addition to labeling other people, a person also labels himself. A person's actions may be at odds with his beliefs about how he should act, a situation called cognitive dissonance by Festinger (1957), inconsistency by Lecky (1945), and incongruity leading to an increase of unassimilated precepts by McReynolds (1960). Whatever the term, the person is vulnerable to being found out or being called upon to play roles that are inconsistent with each other, that is, situations which have been called conflictual. Given this background, the person may emit behavior in order to make his behavior more consistent. The most likely action is to alter one's concepts of proper behavior. In addition, many behaviors labeled improper may be considered so on irrational grounds so that having acted in an improper way, the person may relabel the act as "not so bad." An example which comes to mind is cutting classes, a matter that in grade school is the grave sin called truancy but in college is normal, mature, independent behavior.

Probably the majority of people who commit deviant acts and are not publicly labeled show the effect in greater tolerance of others. Some people, however, do not make use of this alternative: they may refer themselves for treatment, make restitution anonymously, or avoid assiduously the conditions that led to their deviance. To therapists, the most tragic response to deviance is the one in which a person labels himself and acts in accordance with the most negative stereotypes and false information present in our culture. A prime example of this with college students occurs when a person labels himself a homosexual and by no longer dating women confirms his diagnosis (this is an example of the self-validating hypothesis) or when a woman labels herself a nymphomaniac and stops being discriminating. In this latter case feelings of disgust and frustration may lead to a further high turnover of lovers and added confirmation of the label.

The examples just cited lead to the concept of *secondary deviance*. Lemert (1951, 1967) summarizes this concept as follows:

Primary deviation is assumed to arise in a wide variety of social, cultural, and psychological contexts, and at best has only marginal implications for the psychic structure of the individual; it does not lead to symbolic reorganization at the level of self-regarding attitudes and social roles. Secondary deviation is deviant behavior, or social roles based upon it, which becomes means of defense, attack, or adaptation to the overt and covert problems created by the societal reaction to primary deviation. [1967, p. 17.]

Bearing in mind that societal reaction may be applied by the person himself, the key concept is that the act itself probably does not have as long-term consequences as do reactions to the act. Rather than taking the view that deviant acts precede their social control, it is possible to take the position that in a society where there are many value systems and where reinforcing stimuli are neither equitably nor rationally distributed, the breaking of some rules occurs through chance, ignorance, or extinction of rule-following behavior. The acts will not particularly affect the individual until his life is changed as a consequence of the enforcement of the rules. From this point on, the person's behavior is altered either through new sources of reinforcement or through exclusion from previous sources of reinforcement. Further behavior may then be the result of reactions to the deviance rather than the deviant behavior itself.

While such a process can occur without public condemnation, it is easiest to demonstrate in instances where there has been public labeling. In this case it is the public labeling of the act rather than the act itself that is the crucial event in the shaping of succeeding behavior.

The most obvious aspect of public labeling is punishment. Incarceration, whether in a prison or a psychiatric hospital, limits the person's range of social contacts and occupational activities. Entrance into an institution may involve depersonalization and other degrading circumstances—for example, being assigned a number in place of a name (see Goffman, 1961). The public labeling may stigmatize the person, that is, mark him as defective, degenerate, or otherwise infamous. He is then treated in terms of the label. All the negative concepts, many of them demonstrably erroneous, held about members of the class are ascribed to the labeled individual. The result, on the one hand, is that he may not be able to obtain a job commensurate with his abilities, may not be trusted, and may be put under special observation on the job, while, on the other hand, he is placed in a position where major interpersonal satisfactions such as friendship and acceptance are found only with social outcasts like himself.

A prime example of such a situation is that of the drug addict, who is believed to be untrustworthy, impulsive, and criminal. Drug addicts have a special language and culture. In major part this is due to the illegal act typically involved in obtaining drugs: friendship is knowing where to make a connection. In part this is also due to the reaction of society to the addict. In the United States, physicians who are addicts and obtain drugs without criminal connections do not develop the secondary characteristics of the addict culture. The same finding is true of the general population in the United Kingdom, where addicts may obtain their supplies through legitimate (and far less expensive) channels. In the United States, supplies for a heroin habit are expensive and call for frequent, large expenditures. The addict, especially if deprived of legitimate employment, is forced to crime to raise money. An addict's characteristic behavior ("personality") seems more likely to be the *effect* of the addiction rather than a predisposing or causative element.

The point illustrated by reference to the addict is that characteristics associated with perpetrators of deviant behavior may be secondary to the act. How the person labeled as abnormal is treated after he has been labeled may lead to uniformities of behavior based on uniformities of reinforcing contingencies. "The ultimate example of these [additional rules placed on labeled deviants] is found in prisons. In a list of forty punishable rule violations held to in one state prison only six corresponded to what would be misdemeanors or felonies outside of the prison" (Lemert, 1967, p. 61). In similar fashion, men released from prison may have their parole revoked if they drink, get married without permission, leave the vicinity without permission, or have intercourse with someone other than their wives. In this case, the very onerousness of the rules makes compliance less likely.

Implicit in the definition of abnormality and the deductions from it discussed in this chapter is the concept that normality is a social evaluation. This evaluation depends on the standpoint of the observer, and this standpoint, in turn, has been learned and continues to be maintained by reinforcement. The view, then, is that there is not one single, universal standard of normality, but rather normality within groups. There are different sorts of normal, conventional insiders and different sorts of deviants or outsiders. The member of a small religious sect may see the majority of other people as sinners; the marijuana user may see himself as cool, and nonusers as squares; the sexually liberated may see the conventional person as a prude if not downright sad. An article on Weight-Watchers, Inc. (*Time*, April 7, 1967, p. 54) makes the point: ". . . people who are not fat are known as 'civilians' to the members with weight problems."

Once a person has been "converted" and has joined a group or received a new label, the same variables that led him to defect from the larger, modal social group are involved if he is to be reconverted. Operationally, the behavior of people in the two groups is not altered by the same reinforcing stimuli. Much of the unpredictability of the deviant or outsider is that he does not act the way he should, that is, the way the labeler himself acts or would want others to act. There are few things more difficult to accept and more upsetting for a person than for another not to respond to the stimuli he emits, especially when they are intended as kindnesses. The first person's well-practiced operant behavior is literally being extinguished when a second person does not respond "correctly." Its social functions aside, the act of labeling some people as abnormal confirms the correctness of the labeler's values and the adequacy of his repertoire. This may be particularly vital to some psychologists and psychiatrists: a person who is not responsive to them must be mad.

A prime example of the furor over people who will not respond to the dominant culture's values is the counter-culture movement. Against the typical ethic of work, acquisitiveness, delay of gratification, and personal self-discipline, this group poses the values of sensory experience and an emphasis on inner rather than outer experience. Very explicitly, the hippie "drops out," that is, will not follow the accepted pattern of normality. The hippie minority poses the question of whether it is necessarily good to accumulate worldly possessions and status, especially if these are acquired at the expense of other people or of one's own inner peace.

A good picture of socialization to a different norm is Shaw's monograph *The Jack-Roller* (1930). Jackrolling is taking a drunk's money after luring him to some deserted spot by some inducement such as the offer of homosexual practices. Shaw's jackroller learned as proper behavior what the dominant culture would consider deviant:

One day my stepmother told William to take me to the railroad yard to break into box-cars. [The subject was six at the time.] William always led the way and made the plans. He would open the cars, and I would crawl in and hand out the merchandise. In the cars were foodstuffs, exactly the things my mother wanted. We filled our cart, which we had made for this purpose, and proceeded toward home. After we arrived home with our ill-gotten goods, my stepmother would meet us and pat me on the back and say I was a good boy and that I would be rewarded. [p. 53.]

Whenever the boys got together they talked about robbing and made more plans for stealing. I hardly knew any boys who did not go robbing. . . . Fellows who had "done time" were big shots and looked up to and gave the little fellows tips on how to get by and pull off big jobs. [p. 54.]

[At age 15] I was looked up to as the hero of the quartet because I had done 56 months in St. Charles, more than all the others put together. They naturally thought I was one who had a vast experience and was regarded as one might regard the big social hit of society. [p. 96.]

A final quotation from Shaw serves two purposes: first, to indicate that an outsider may have a clear set of values about which he feels as strongly and righteously as the insiders do about theirs; and second, to show that this set of values may be in direct opposition to the dominant culture's set of values and may make difficult the altering of the outsider's behavior.

I believe that any game should be played according to the rules of the game. Violators of rules should be punished. Crime is a game, and therefore as a rat violates the rules or code by informing the "dicks" and the "screws," he should be punished when caught, just like other criminals are punished. I think everyone will agree with me in my feelings about these low rats. All prisoners who are worthy of the name will agree with me. [p. 112.]

Having been labeled abnormal may lead to reinforcement for the emission of behaviors consistent with the label but not necessarily part of the behavior that originally led to the labeling. The jackroller's pride in his prison record and attitude toward informers are examples. Often having been labeled a deviant may make normal behavior illegitimate and lead to further rule-breaking as a safeguard against being caught. The abnormal label then places the person under a new set of rules: the convict must lead a more restricted life than the nonconvict; the hospitalized patient may be ignored because he is mentally unbalanced.

Once a person assumes a role, there are additional elements of behavior that are typically considered part of the role. People respond to him in a particular manner, and if he does not react as expected, that is, does not respond to the cues given to him, others are upset with him and do not reinforce him. This pattern was observed with the blinded (Chapter 5). Another example is provided by Erikson (1957) who noted that a group of hospitalized psychiatric patients organized and produced dramatic plays before outside audiences with a skill that surprised professional drama critics: "At a prizewinning performance in a neighboring city, some of the audience were and remained under the impression that the players were members of the medical staff rather than patients in the institution." Yet one of the patients, after doing a very fine job in the play, returned to the patients' dormitory and tried to set fire to it. Erikson uses this as an example of role-expressive behavior: To obtain the benefits of being a patient within the social usage of the medical model, the patient must present himself (and his "illness") in the manner recognized by the culture. The public idea of the mentally ill includes a breakdown in intellect, irrational behavior, and an inability to control one's impulses. The person who does well in an activity such as a public performance may thus raise questions about his sanity.

Falsely enacting the sick role is called malingering. Cohen (1966, p. 15) notes that such behavior is considered very bad: "Indeed, he is now guilty of a type of deviance that is everywhere regarded with a special odium. He has claimed an identity that he does not really have. . . . To make such a false claim is to force other people to take up and play the correlative roles, to subject themselves to a certain discipline, to go through elaborate and sometimes stressful motions that turn out to be meaningless and 'don't count.' It is a flagrant violation of trust." The patient who performed in the play was in the difficult position of having to look incompetent to justify his release from normal social responsibilities.

In summary, being labeled as deviant or abnormal has consequences in terms of further behavior. These consequences change reinforcing contingencies, and the general pattern is toward shaping action in the direction of the pattern of behavior appropriate to the label.

LEARNING TO BE A BUGHOUSER

Throughout previous sections of this chapter it has been noted that a pattern of abnormality is a learned social act dependent upon the responses of other people to the signals emitted by the "abnormal" individual. Consistent with these considerations is the notion that people who themselves do not break the rules may support the deviant. Tannenbaum (1938) made this point in regard to lawbreaking deviants, that is, criminals. He noted that monetary "backers," lawyers, bondsmen, dishonest police, and crooked politicians have supported the criminal element.

It is possible to go further and note that law enforcement and rehabilitation agencies literally depend on apprehended criminals as much as schoolteachers depend upon students. To quote Tannenbaum (1938, p. 63): "It is not too much to say that the development of the criminal career as here described is possible only because there are more or less well-organized and recognized agencies that live off, and depend upon, the profit-making opportunities which the criminal supplies."

The gatekeeper to the role of abnormality, the person who legitimizes the role and over time teaches the public its changing characteristics, is the mental health professional. Aside from the formal educational requirements, it is proper to ask what are the conditions which shape *him,* for an understanding of the mental health worker will aid in understanding the psychiatric patient.

There are few data on the conditions that lead to the selection of a career in mental health. The most pertinent material lies in research on the performance of residents in psychiatry (Holt and Luborsky, 1958) and medical specialists (Strong and Tucker, 1952). Because the people tested in these studies were well along in their careers, it is impossible to give the reasons they chose the profession they did.

There are three aspects of the shaping

of a recruit to the mental health profession (for clinical examples, see Cohen, 1966, especially 104–5; Viscott, 1973; Blum and Rosenberg, 1968). The first is that the situation is ambiguous; this volume has indicated that there is controversy in the field. Crutchfield (1955), among others, indicated that people are more easily influenced on matters of opinion whose validity derives from a social frame of reference than on matters of fact.

Next, conformity is more likely if the task is difficult for the person, that is, if the person does not know what to do or how to do it. If external cues or alternative information is withheld, the person cannot match his behavior to any but the available models, and this also leads to conformity.

Finally, the greater the prestige of the models or leaders, the more likely the person will be to conform. To such generalizations from social psychology should be added the fact that continuing reinforcement plays a vital role, both as avoidance of unpleasant situations such as censure and as maximization of praise and advances in status and salary.

The second aspect of the training situation is the bureaucratic nature of the institutions in which professional training takes place. Blau (1956) has noted that the four basic characteristics of bureaucratic organization are specialization of function, hierarchical status, rules, and impersonality.

Ideally, each person reports only to his immediate superior. In a large psychiatric hospital this has the effect that the people most intimately involved with patients, trainees and attendants, being on the lowset level of the hierarchy, report to people whose job is to supervise them rather than interact with patients. The effects are to denigrate interacting with patients; advancement and authority are negatively associated with interaction with patients. The supervisor makes his decisions on the basis of acts that he can see, acts that are *visible,* and these are rarely interactions with patients.

On the one hand this leads to a bias of activities that the supervisee will engage in with patients. Henry (1964) made this point when he quoted a psychiatric nurse: "When you go off duty, they don't know whether you have spent time with the patients, but they do know whether you have written in the chart." The visible and reinforced activity is not interaction with patients, but records that the supervisor can check. Interaction with the supervisor rather than with patients is the major supervisee activity about which the supervisor knows. To the extent that the supervisor is separated from the patients, his knowledge about them is general. The interaction with the supervisor then becomes theoretical rather than practical, and consistency with the supervisor's views rather than the reality of service is what is likely to be reinforced. A social worker once muttered as she was on her way to a supervisory conference, "Well, I'm going in and vague it up." [8]

Because every new situation cannot be taken up, rules to cover situations must be developed. The rules may proliferate so that few people know them all, but they exist and can be applied when it serves someone's ends. The safest thing is to abide by rules that are generalizations (Etzioni, 1964, p. 12).

Cases are matched to rules, and when the fit is clear enough, the rules provide the decision. The individual merits of the case are a source of confusion. The bureaucrat may be curt, not because he is basically an anal-sadistic person à la Freud, but because the more he hears, the more he is put in a situation where his role as an effective employee is put in opposition to his role as a pleasant human being. If he makes an exception, he is faced with the problem of explaining to his supervisor how he, the

---

[8] Gerber (1967) found that those practitioners who were closer to the ward setting were better able to differentiate psychotic variables than those practitioners who were farther away from the ward setting.

employee, came to do something different from what the supervisor would have done.

Other lines of investigations support this point. Ekman (1961) relates how when psychiatric screening was ordered for all first courtmartial offenders in two regiments, there was a sharp drop in courts-martial in these regiments. This drop was not matched in two control regiments in which this procedure had not been instituted. When the new procedure was terminated, the rate of courts-martial increased in the experimental regiments and became similar to that of the control regiments. In short, to the extent that psychiatric intervention in military procedures was aversive, when courts-martial became a discriminative stimulus for such intervention, the calling of courtsmartial decreased.

A second source of data is by Butterfield, Barnett, and Bensberg (1966), who found that turnover rate of attendants at institutions for the retarded was in large measure accounted for by the economic climate of the counties in which the institutions were located.

A third area deals with prescription of medication. Klerman et al. (1960) reported a significant positive correlation between ethnocentrism of resident psychiatrists and their prescription of drugs. Mendel (1967) noted that experienced therapists used fewer tranquilizing drugs to manage hospitalized psychotic patients. Because of lower staffing, patients admitted on weekends had a greater chance of receiving medication. A rule was made that no patient admitted to the ward was to receive a tranquilizer during the first 12 hours of hospitalization. Prior to this rule, 82 percent of all schizophrenics admitted to the ward were placed on tranquilizers at some time during a seven-day stay. After the change, only 27 percent received such medication during their stay. The number of patients discharged with a prescription for medication decreased from 85 percent to 6 percent. *To recapitulate, responses of the professional personnel are influenced by administrative and economic variables and not solely by the behavior of the patient.*

A third and final general comment about the training situation in the hospital is the widespread adoption of the medical model by the staff. This is reflected in the very use of the word "hospital," the historical development of hospitals after the era of moral treatment, and the training of treatment staff as medical and "paramedical" specialists. In physical medicine the body is conceptually a complicated biochemical apparatus, and the person is the rather boring address of an interesting malfunction. Specialization may be appropriate to physical medicine as is large hospital size which makes possible enough cases to support such specialization. While not an ideal situation for the individual who is also a patient, specialized techniques of physical medicine may be successfully separated from each other: X-ray, dentistry, surgery, and the like. This fragmentation fits neatly with bureaucracy, where the line of authority is easiest when drawn by profession and specialty rather than by the total functional task, the person and his social environment.

A psychoanalytic variant of the medical model also has impact on the staff and particularly the trainee. As noted in Chapters 8 and 9, all behavior may be related within psychoanalytic theory to deprivations and defenses. If a person does something that is not "right" as defined by the professional supervisor, it is appropriate to ask why he did so. Since the supervisor has power, the answer is some flaw in the supervisee's personality. The recruit is faced with a situation in which his supervisor may evaluate his behavior as a manifestation of personality difficulty rather than as mature ideation which deserves answers based on evidence. Once labeled as a person "having authority problems," whatever the trainee says may be evaluated in terms of his motivations rather than the truth or falsity of the specific verbalization. Stanton and Schwartz (1954, p. 205) make this point when they write that ". . . modern psychiatrists and psychologists make up one of the few groups in history where *ad hominem* argument may be treated with greater respect than an argument confined to the subject matter under discussion."

Under these conditions, the trainee learns to fit in and act as his mentors think he should. Advancement is usually given to those who are liked by (Holt and Luborsky, 1958) and are like (Ullmann, 1967a, pp. 136–41) the supervisor. In this manner there is a reduction of information contrary to the supervisor's views. An extreme example of this may be seen in Frank's review of the training of the psychoanalyst (1961, pp. 116–34).

Among the aspects of the therapist role the student learns are the jargon and the approach to patients.[9] He may believe that the problem is insufficient "giving" on the part of others and therefore "give" in an endlessly loving manner, or he may ask what the patients are getting out of the interchange and make his own responses differentially favorable depending on the sort of behavior the patient emits. The trainee comes to the clinic setting relatively naïve, but he is trained so that he is quite different from either the way he previously was or the way normal people, including himself, act with other normal people. A person who puts up with taunting, testing behavior in the manner of the ideal "clinician" (Cohen, 1966; Viscott, 1973), if he were not doing so in the context of mid-twentieth century psychotherapy, would be considered either a saint or a masochist.

[9] It has long been noted that differences between professions, such as teachers compared to mental health practitioners, will lead to different evaluations of the seriousness of problem behaviors (Wickman, 1929; Stouffer, 1952, 1956; Ziv, 1970). Needless to say, differences exist between children of different ages and teachers (Mutimer and Rosemier, 1967). Similar findings have been reported in the psychiatric setting (Dietze, 1966; Goldschmid and Domino, 1967; Bozarth and Daly, 1969; Gerber, 1967; Lorei, 1970; Mackey, 1969; Spiegel, Kieth-Spiegel, and Grayson, 1967; Rosenthal et al., 1970) with differences between professional groups reflecting their different responsibilities.

Yet this behavior is what is reinforced professionally, even if there is a paucity of empirical evidence to support its value to the patient and hence to the society that the institution supports.

People are trained to act "professionally," and the resulting decisions affect other peoples' lives. The referral among professional people offers an opportunity to study the many variables other than "disease" or overt behavior that affect the decisions. Rogawski and Edmundson (1971) followed up patients that had been referred from an admitting-evaluation unit to psychiatric clinics or other social agency. Other than previous hospital contact, no patient-related data significantly predicted who would "complete" the referral or could not be seen. Daytime referrals were completed in 49.2 percent of the cases, while night or weekend referrals were completed in 25.5 percent. If the therapist called the agency, the referral was completed in 55.6 percent of the cases, if the patient was to call, in 30.6 percent. In turn, what the person is told, e.g., whether to expect a "warm" or "cold" therapist, has an impact on his response (Greenberg, Goldstein, and Perry, 1970).

Mendel and Rapport (1969) studied decisions for admissions about 269 consecutive individuals. If a person had been previously hospitalized, he was more likely (77 percent) to be hospitalized than if he had not (34 percent). Social workers tended to hospitalize a smaller percentage than psychologists or psychiatrists, who in turn hospitalized fewer than psychiatric residents. With experience, the rate of hospitalization decreased. Of the people seen during regular working hours, 32 percent were hospitalized, while of those seen after hours and weekends, 61 percent were hospitalized. Who saw the person and when made a large difference, while "the direct observation of decisions . . . showed that the patient population hospitalized was indistinguishable from the patient population not hospitalized on the basis of severity of symptoms."

(p. 325.) While the decision makers thought they were deciding on the basis of severity of symptoms, they also said that they would not have hospitalized 84 percent of the people they did if the social situation had been different, i.e., if there had been someone to take responsibility.

In similar work, Appell and Tisdall (1968) devised a checklist of criteria for admission to an institution for the retarded. The cases admitted averaged 41.7 IQ, those not admitted, 38.2 IQ; therefore, IQ was not a major factor in admission. A broken home, poor living conditions, financial pressure, and causing community problems such that there were pressures to admit the person were significantly associated with admission. For example, 62 percent of the admitted had inadequate living conditions, while only 22 percent of the nonadmitted were so described. Eighty-five percent of the admitted came under community pressure, whereas such pressure was present in only 34 percent of the nonadmitted. In short, there seemed to be a problem for which the institution was a solution.

A number of workers report that males are admitted more frequently than females to institutions for the retarded, (Olsen, 1967; Singer and Osborn, 1970) and this is probably due to the greater and more visible demands on the male role. Shellhaas and Nihira (1969, 1970) found that getting in trouble with the law, inadequate housing, and antisocial behavior such as aggression, prostitution, and school disruption were associated with referral to an institution.

Fontana, Gessner, and Lorr (1968) investigated psychiatrists' and social workers' criteria for treatment recommendations. Social workers had an emphasis on rational and immediate expectations of the patients, while psychiatrists centered more on underlying illnesses and psychodynamics. Weissman (1969) also found differences among psychiatrists, psychologists, and social workers, and noted that team members can agree on more criteria relating to rejection of a case for treatment than they can for acceptance. Polak (1970) contrasted the goals of patients, therapists, and members of the general community and found that the staff goals centered on changing intrapsychic experience and the patients' behavior within the hospital, whereas patients were oriented to extra-hospital adjustment and the people with whom they were to live in the future. Patterns of communication among staff members, especially during staff conferences (Schacht and Blacker, 1969; Blacker and Schacht, 1970), and administrative patterns (Beck et al., 1967) have also yielded important results. *The crucial point is that the professional person is as much an actor in the drama of "mental illness" as the patient, and both learn and continue to play their roles as a result of social-influence variables* (Krasner and Ullmann, 1973).

The trainee learns to conform, where "Conforming behavior is regarded as behavior reflecting the *successful* influence of other persons" and deviant behavior is regarded as 'behavior reflecting the *rejected* influence of other persons" (Bass, 1961, pp. 38, 40).

SUMMARY

Starting from the definition of abnormal behavior as that type of deviance or rule- and expectation-breaking which sanctions the intervention of the mental health professional, the pressures on the labeler were investigated. The social function of labeling was described: calling a person mentally ill is a way of solving a social problem. The concept of abnormality is particularly useful in instances where people are distressed by behavior that is upsetting but not specifically criminal. Successful use of the solution of labeling someone as needing a "helping" professional is a learned behavior, and presumes that the laymen who are case finders and initiators of the labeling cycle have some concepts of the mentally ill role.

The behaviors that will lead people to

designate someone as mentally ill vary with time, place, and person. This insight is one of the major contributions of cross-cultural psychiatry. Within a given culture, such as ours, there is evidence from epidemiological studies that the rate of people emitting behavior that might possibly be labeled abnormal (prevalence) is far higher than the rate of people hospitalized or treated for such behavior (incidence). The label itself is applied with discretion within the culture, again probably in terms of solving a social problem rather than in terms of the classic abnormal pattern *per se*.

Race, sex, location of home, and social class are among the variables associated with differential rates of hospitalization. One possible unifying theme is that among racial minorities, lower classes, and people living in slum areas there is less social reinforcement, less opportunity to emit and be reinforced for the behaviors considered desirable by white, middle-class standards. Rather than being reinforced, a person who finds his vocational opportunities not commensurate with his educational abilities will be extinguished for trying. Such a person may be thought of as acting in a manner analogous to a person who becomes disillusioned and joins a new social movement. The pattern of behavior in the prior role has not been reinforced, and the aversive consequences of deviation from such standards are therefore reduced. At the same time, the new identity may be entered into gradually in the step-by-step sequence of a career or of shaping. Such a process is more likely when there are changing rules, numerous rules, rules that may well conflict and cannot all be either obeyed or equally enforced, and rules that are made by and for the benefit of special groups.

Having either labeled himself or been publicly stigmatized, a person is affected by the fact of his designation. This process follows the concept of self-fulfilling prophecy. People act toward the person labeled as abnormal not only in terms of the person and his behavior as they are, but also in terms of concepts about the category of persons into which he has been placed. The person may therefore be subjected to extremely stringent rules that militate further against normal patterns for acquiring reinforcement; or he may be more likely to engage in acts consistent with the new role he has adopted or to which he has been assigned. Examples of how this may occur were presented in terms of smoking marijuana, being blinded, becoming a jackroller, and becoming a clinician.

behavioral evaluation
DIAGNOSIS AND ASSESSMENT
11

Professional workers have four major funcsions: evaluation, treatment, research, and training. Evaluation plays an important role in the other three areas since it is vital to treatment decisions, the description of groupings in research, measuring the effects of independent variables, and the training of persons who are encouraged to recognize and refer cases, such as ministers and policemen as well as people such as teachers and parents who are taught to monitor and alter their own behaviors and those of others. Within a sociopsychological framework assessment centers on overt behavior and stems from behavioral, educational, and learning concepts. Diagnostic work, which we will take up first, is more likely to stem from medical procedures and dynamic personality theory.

The traditional methods of examination include laboratory tests, the taking of social history, ward observations, psychological tests, and, above all, a psychiatric interview or mental-status examination. The task of the *diagnostician* is to match the individual with a category or syndrome. A psychiatric syndrome is a group of symptoms that together are characteristic of a specific condition, disease, or the like. The first question, then, is how consistently do different diagnosticians place the same people in the same categories? Using a term introduced in Chapter 3, we ask, What is the *rater reliability* of psychiatric diagnoses?

RELIABILITY OF PSYCHIATRIC DIAGNOSIS

Because a psychiatric diagnosis is a social act, the behavior of the labeler is as much a matter of concern as the behavior of the labeled. Schmidt and Fonda (1956) studied all the 426 patients admitted to a state hospital during a six-month period. Each patient was independently diagnosed by (1) one of a group of eight psychiatric residents, and then (2) one of three chief psychiatrists. There are 91 labels in DSM-I, of which only 40 were actually used.[1] These are called *subtypes,* e.g., paranoid type of schizophrenic reaction, obsessive-compulsive reaction (subtype) of psychoneurotic dis-

[1] At the time of this writing, studies using DSM-II have not yet appeared in the literature, although the reduced definitional material in the new *Manual* does not lead us to expect a dramatic increase in rater reliability. Interest has shifted to the conditions under which certain people receive different labels. An example of this type of work is the study by Temerlin on suggestion effects in psychiatric labeling, discussed in Chapter 1. Another trend is the investigation of behavioral or administrative criteria: who will be accepted for individual psychotherapy; who will be institutionalized; who will be released, rather than what the person is called. Arthur (1969) calls this a decision-making model.

A further trend is an increasingly fine mathematical analysis of what the diagnostician actually, rather than theoretically, responds to is exemplified by the work of Goldberg (1965, 1968, 1970), Miller and Tripodi (1967), and Wiggins, Hoffman, and Taber (1969). Still another trend is the introduction of computer technology, as in Stoebel and Glueck's (1970) work. A final trend is represented in the latter part of the present chapter, which follows a behavioral approach in which the focus is on overt behavior, the preceding stimulus, and succeeding consequences. Among germinal articles in this approach are ones by Skinner (1966), Bijou (1966), Bijou and Peterson (1971), Ferster (1965), Bricker 1970), Greenspoon and Gersten (1967), Nurnberger and Zimmerman (1970), Wolff and Merrens (1974), and Kanfer and Saslow (1965, 1969). Measurement is far from dead (Cronbach, 1970; Lanyon and Goodstein, 1971; Nunnally, 1970), but it is changing.

order. The subtypes were then grouped into eleven classes of *disorder,* such as schizophrenia, psychoneurosis, mental deficiency; and the eleven disorders were grouped into three major categories: organic, psychotic, and characterological. This last group included psychoneurosis and personality disorders, while the first (organic) category included mental deficiency. The major category used by the chief psychiatrists had been correctly anticipated by the residents in 92 percent of the organic cases, 80 percent of the psychotic cases, and 71 percent of the characterological cases.

In general, as the category became more specific, the discriminations became more difficult, the frequency of cases smaller, and the reliability lower. Table 1 presents material for the eleven disorders. Overall, in 55 percent of the cases the residents chose the one category in eleven which the chief psychiatrist had chosen. The rate of agreement dwindled as the categorization became more specific. Agreement about the diagnosis of a specific subtype of a disorder occurred in only about half the cases and was almost absent in cases involving the personality and psychoneurotic disorders.

The study by Schmidt and Fonda could be criticized on the basis of the lack of experience of the residents, the use of hospitalized patients (all presumably severely ill and hence restricting the range of scores), and potential patient changes in the time between the assessments by the resident and staff psychiatrists. An article by Beck et al.

Table 1
Proportions of official diagnoses correctly anticipated in the residents' tentative diagnoses

CLASSIFICATION	OFFICIAL DIAGNOSIS: CHIEF PSYCHIATRIST	MAJOR CATEGORY N	%	SPECIFIC N	SUBTYPE %
Organic	193	178	92	142	74 *
Acute brain syndrome	66			45	68
Chronic brain syndrome	115			92	80
Mental deficiency	12			5	42
Psychotic	161	128	80	75	47 *
Involutional	14			8	57
Affective	20			7	35
Schizophrenic	118			60	51
Unclassified	9			0	0
Characterological	72	51	71	17	24 *
Neurosis	25			4	16
Personality pattern	12			1	8
Personality trait	16			1	6
Sociopathic	19			11	58
Total	426	426	357	84	234	55

* Total in category.
Source: Schmidt and Fonda, 1956.

(1962) persents data relevant to these criticisms.

Four experienced, board-level psychiatrists (i.e., accredited specialists) who were on the faculty of a medical school paired up to interview successively (about five minutes apart) 153 outpatients. Prior to interviewing, the psychiatrists conferred with each other and reached agreement on diagnostic criteria. They made a set of guidelines beyond that of DSM-I. In short, these workers were very skilled, specially prepared, and careful. With 153 patients each diagnosed by two psychiatrists, there are 306 "calls" or "diagnoses."

Table 2 presents the most gratifying

Table 2
Percentage of agreement among psychiatrists for six diagnostic categories

CATEGORY	N CALLS	% AGREEMENT
Neurotic depression	92	63
Anxiety reaction	58	55
Sociopath	11	54
Schizophrenic reaction	60	53
Involutional melancholia	10	40
Personality trait disturbance	26	38

Source: Beck et al., 1962.

study in the literature in terms of degree of agreement for subtypes of disorder, but considerable disagreement still exists. Additional information obtained by Beck et al. (1962) involved a rating by the psychiatrists of their certainty about the diagnoses. When *both* psychiatrists were certain, they agreed in 81 percent of the cases; when *both* were uncertain, they agreed in 25 percent of the cases; all other combinations of certainty, e.g., one certain and the other fairly certain, yielded 47 percent to 50 percent agreement. Finally, there was an agreement rate of 70 percent for the three categories, psychotic, neurotic, and character disorder.

Ward et al. (1962) followed up the work of Beck et al. (1962) by using a portion of the 153 cases reported by Beck et al. The objective was to determine why the psychiatrists had disagreed. The authors found three sources of error. First, in 5 percent of cases the primary reason for disagreement was inconsistency on the part of patients, who gave different material to the different interviewers. The second primary reason was inconsistency on the part of the diagnostician: he used different interview techniques, weighted symptoms differently, or made different interpretations of the same interview data. This reason accounted for 32.5 percent of the disagreements. Inadequacies of the diagnostic system's categories accounted for the remaining 62.5 percent of primary reasons for disagreement: impractically fine distinction required; forced choice of predominant major category, e.g., between psychoneurotic disorder and personality disorder when evidence of both entries was present; an uncertainty about criteria stemming from insufficient clarification in definitions of the nosological system. Of troubles with unclear definitions, 80 percent centered around attempts to distinguish between chronic undifferentiated schizophrenia and nonpsychotic disorders. Sheperd et al. (1968) found variations in (1) observations, (2) inferences from such observations, and (3) categorizations of observations as sources of difficulty.

Sandifer, Pettus, and Quade (1964) collected data at three hospitals. The evaluators attended the typical hospital diagnostic conferences at which were presented the results of the patient's physical, laboratory, and mental status exams, and his pre-hospital and current hospital adjustment. The patient was then interviewed by one psychiatrist in the presence of other psychiatrists who had an opportunity to ask questions. All the patients were first admissions between 15 and 29 years of age who had been admitted to the hospitals one to three weeks prior to the diagnostic conference. The authors excluded "inebriate" commitments. Ten diagnosticians were at each conference (a total of 14 participated). "These diagnosticians were the senior physicians charged with the responsibility of rendering the official diagnoses for their respective hospitals." They held the same status as the "chief psychiatrists" of the Schmidt and Fonda study. The labeling system used was the 12 major diagnostic categories of the National Institutes of Health Public Mental Hospital Report. There were 91 patients who were seen in this manner. Table 3 presents this material

Table 3
Percentage of agreement among psychiatrists for twelve different categories

CATEGORY	N CALLS	% AGREEMENT
All categories	910	57
Schizophrenia	170	74
Mental deficiency	40	73
Personality disorder	205	66
Chronic brain syndrome	56	66
Psychoneurosis	223	56
Acute brain syndrome	40	46
Psychophysiologic reaction	25	40
Manic depressive	45	36
Involutional psychotic	59	26
Psychotic depressive	33	22
Psychotic reaction, other	4	17
Paranoid reaction	10	13

Source: Sandifer et al., 1964.

in terms of the 12 categories, the frequency of "calls" (i.e., with 91 cases and ten diagnosticians there are 910 calls), and percentage of agreement.

The results presented in Table 3 indicate that, for example, if one psychiatrist diagnosed psychophysiologic reaction, chances were that another psychiatrist gave a different diagnosis 60 percent of the time. Sandifer et al. collected data on confidence of diagnosis, and obtained results similar to those of Beck et al.: (1) in the vast majority of cases the psychiatrists were confident of their diagnoses, and (2) high certainty increased reliability from an overall of 57 percent to 65 percent agreement, low certainty decreased reliability from an overall 57 percent to 45 percent.

Sandifer and his co-workers (Sandifer, Hordern, Timbury and Green, 1968) used films to repeat the work just described with diagnosticians in London and Glasgow. Whereas American (North Carolina) diagnosticians agreed with each other 58 percent of the time, agreement was 49 percent and 44 percent among London and Glasgow diagnosticians, respectively. The London group agreed 64 percent of the time among themselves, and the figure was 73 percent for the Glasgow group, but only 48 percent between London and Glasgow. The point is that each area may build up its own norms that differ somewhat from other training and treatment groups.

Kadushin (1969, pp. 110–29) indicates how this training may occur:

Because psychiatric theory and concepts are not well agreed upon, the rules by which diagnosticians move from the manifest responses of patients to their underlying psychiatric diagnoses are incoherently or poorly specified. Therefore, the social situation of clinics becomes more important in determining diagnosis than the characteristics of applicants. The divergent theories of the various clinics also account for much of the differences among them in diagnosis. Each clinic's position is fixed in the process of routinizing the complex scientific vocabulary of diagnosis. Through social interaction, each clinic develops its own set of norms for the application of diagnostic terminology, for each seems to have a favorite diagnostic category. Finally, administrative reasons force many clinicians who would not otherwise do so to make diagnoses. Consequently, the diagnoses themselves seem to follow a clinic's administrative exigencies. [p. 111.]

Fabrega and Wallace (1968) add to this idea with data, using the 22-item questionnaire of the Midtown Study described in Chapter 10. Groups of Mexican and American psychiatric and nonpsychiatric physicians were asked to evaluate the psychiatric relevance (e.g., Is psychiatric consultation called for?) of pathological responses to each question. All four groups were in accord that the two most serious responses were feeling apart when among friends and wondering if anything was worthwhile. There was general agreement that items such as feeling hot all over or having a fullness in the head or nose were of the least psychiatric significance. When there were significant differences (6 of 22 times for Mexican and 9 of 22 times for American) between psychiatric and nonpsychiatric physicians, the trend was for psychiatrists to consider a symptom more serious than nonpsychiatrists. In 3 of the 22 instances, American physicians considered symptoms more serious than did the Mexican physicians.

Finally, we should not forget that, as pointed out in Chapters 6 and 7, on history, the theories and diagnostic practices of the profession have changed radically over time (Schimel et al., 1973).

Consistency over Time and Place

We have so far discussed rater reliability, that is, the consistency with which labels are assigned by different professionals. A different matter is the consistency of behavior or of labeling of that behavior *over different times and places*. There are three areas in which this matter is crucial. The first is a test of theories. If unlabeled problem behavior is transitory while such behavior when labeled is increasingly stable, then the sociopsychological approach of authors such as Becker (1963), Scheff (1966a), Lemert (1967), Schur (1971), and the present authors would be strengthened, in contrast to a medical model or analogue in which the "disease" or underlying cause is within the individual and isolated from society and current situation.

The second area involves professional-intervention approaches. A community mental health approach (discussed in Chapter 29) has as one form of intervention early detection of problems or of people who are likely to develop behavior problems (i.e., high risk cases). Tagging a person as likely to have problems and providing him with special treatment runs the risk of a reverse "Pygmalion" effect (see Chapter 5), a self-fulfilling prophecy of difficulty.

The third area stems from the sociopsychological approach and clinical observation: people respond to situations, and when situations change, people change. Examples of this will follow, particularly in Chapter 18, when we deal with impression management by hospitalized psychiatric patients (Braginsky, Braginsky, and Ring, 1969). At this point we can note that when supposedly chronic schizophrenics are taken on trips to town, they act far more "normal" or "like other people" than they do back in the institution—an observation that the reader might have predicted on the basis of the work on demand characteristics presented in Chapter 5. The ability to respond, and to extinguish "good" behavior when not reinforced, may be illustrated by an incident in which the senior author displayed his chronic incompetence. He was a consultant and sitting at the nurses' station of a ward for chronic schizophrenics. A patient whose most visible behavioral problems were rocking and pulling her hair (to the extent that she was bald in patches) looked up from her crouched position and said, "Hello, Dr. Ullmann." Dr. Ullmann must have looked confused at this unexpected behavior and failed to reply. The woman then said, "Your picture is on the wall." Dr. Ullmann said, "Oh." The woman gave him up as a bad job and went back to rocking and hair pulling. The ward was one in which, to orient the residents, photos of all the staff were posted. The woman had recognized Ullmann, made a socially appropriate gesture, correctly interpreted his confusion, gave him an explanation, and then gave him up as a lost cause. This kind of appropriate responsiveness of people to changing situations is contradictory to a stable disease model. A related observation is by Del Castillo (1970), who reported that patients manifested more psychotic symptoms when interviews were held in their mother-tongues than when they were conducted in what was to them a foreign language (i.e., English), while Marcos et al. (1973) report the reverse. The point, however is illustrated by both studies: factors irrelevant to a "disease" affect the observations.

Clarizio (1968) noted that save for aggressive rule breaking, most children's behavioral problems seemed to resolve themselves with increasing age. A different way of stating this is that if rater bias (knowledge of later difficulty) [2] is controlled, when the life histories of adults called "normal" and "abnormal" are compared, both have evidences of earlier problem behaviors and "traumatic histories."

An observation of treated people having greater social problems later in life is by Robbins (1966). The presumed need for treatment and effects of labeling are confounded, but either the treatment was a dismal failure (e.g., only one-sixth later had good work history) or the labeling and treatment process had a severely adverse effect. One cannot say with any certainty, but, to quote Scheff and Sundstrom (1970), who presented the best review of the topic available at the time of this writing, "Although the studies are crude and inconclusive, the existing weight of evidence may be interpreted as supporting labeling rather than psychiatric theory." (p. 37.)

We may go one step further; if behavior is a function of situation, and if the situation is stable, the behavior is likely to be maintained. As noted in Chapter 18, training to adjust to the treatment situation may, itself, provide regularities in behavior that are not associated with a "disease."

Other empirical studies on the reliability of psychiatric diagnosis are consistent with the material presented here: Ash, 1949; Babigian et al., 1965; Doering and Raymong, 1934; Mehlman, 1952; Kreitman, 1961; Kreitman et al., 1961; Raines and Rohrer, 1955; Seeman, 1953; Stoller and Gertsman, 1963; Nathan et al., 1969; Ullmann and Gurel, 1962; Zubin, 1966; Gauron and Dickenson, 1969, Ley, 1972; Jakubaschk and Werner, 1974; Agnew and Bannister, 1973.

Evaluation

The reliability of psychiatric diagnosis presents an interesting example of how a set of data may lead to alternative conclusions. For example, Quay (1963a), in introducing the Schmidt and Fonda (1956) study in a collection of readings, wrote as follows: "The study by Schmidt and Fonda demonstrates a lack of agreement among psychiatric diagnosticians, particularly when they are asked to classify patients into narrow subcategories rather than into the broader groupings of the major disorders." Schmidt and Fonda (1956) conclude their article as follows: "It is concluded that satisfactory reliability has been demonstrated for some of the psychiatric diagnoses, but that this carries no implication regarding their semantic validity or usefulness."

Buss (1966, p. 41) writes: "Summarizing, we may conclude that psychoses, taken generically, can be diagnosed with considerable reliability. There is some evidence that one psychosis, schizophrenia, can be diagnosed reliably (74 percent agreement reported by Sandifer et al., 1964). Thus the commonly held belief in the unreliability of psychiatric diagnoses is incorrect or at best only partly correct." Sandifer et al., on the other hand, start the discussion of their results as follows: "The initial finding of this study was additional information that the reliability of psychiatric diagnosis is

---

[2] An experiment illustrating this effect with eventual suicides is reported by Hood (1970).

not generally satisfactory for scientific purposes if only one opinion is used."

The reader is also presented with a clear illustration of the fact that no single level of statistical significance can be used without interpretation relevant to the decision to be made. The degree of agreement in the four studies reviewed is generally greater than would have been expected on the basis of chance. But the reader should still ask whether this degree of agreement is sufficient for the type of decisions involved. For example, the number of cases in which there was disagreement on the diagnosis of schizophrenia ranged from 10 percent to 40 percent. Can an error once in ten times be accepted? *The evaluation must be influenced by the use to which the decision is put.* If there is a research study, the particular subjects involved will not be greatly influenced, although overgeneralization of poor results may delay use of a valuable technique or, as more frequently occurs, lead to the widespread use of an ineffective technique. A 10 percent error of classification may not do irreparable harm in research, although the chance of significant and useful research results when there is a 40 percent error of classification is probably slight. When dealing with the individual case, one must again ask what degree of error is tolerable. If diagnosis makes a treatment difference, then how frequently can diagnostic disagreement (unreliability) be permitted? There are no guidelines, but generally clinicians believe that the level of reliability required for ethical usage in individual cases should be far higher than that required for research purposes. How much higher depends on the extent to which the label will lead to differences in the person's treatment.

EMPIRICAL APPROACHES TO DIAGNOSIS

The task that Kraepelin set himself was to bring order into the welter of behavior considered abnormal. His model of abnormality was that of diseases with symptoms. If enough symptoms appeared together, a syndrome could be labeled. Ideally, there would be few categories with little if any overlap.

Zigler and Phillips (1961) reviewed the case records of 793 hospitalized patients who had been referred for psychological appraisal. As may be seen from Table 4 there were four major groups of patients and 35 symptoms. As with the majority of statistical approaches to symptomatology, the very rare symptoms, those occurring in less than 5 percent of the cases, were excluded from the analysis. The data in Table 4 are the frequency with which the admitting psychiatrist or referring agency noted the symptom as present.

Perusal of Table 4 is rewarding for many reasons. First, it offers some notion of the task faced by Kraepelin and by more recent practitioners of factor analytic techniques, statistical methods designed to determine "what goes with what." Factor analytic procedures use a wide range of test, behavioral, or interview ratings. Every measure is correlated with every other measure, and the correlations are organized to determine the fewest clusters of correlations that will account for the greatest amount of the differences between the measures of the people. Factor analyses by authors such as Wittenborn, Holzberg, and Simon (1953), Lorr, Klett, and McNair (1963), Lorr and Klett 1969), Eysenck (1961a) and Hautaluoma (1971) indicate that the behavior of patients given the same diagnostic label is not homogeneous, but rather comprises different subclusters; that some of these behaviors are contradictory with each other so that the presence of one would empirically reduce the probability of the manifestation of the other; and that there is a wide spread of high scores on certain clusters across patients given different diagnostic labels.

Inspection of Table 4 indicates directly two major and interrelated points. Given 35 symptoms and four diagnostic groups,

Table 4
Percentage of individuals in total sample and in each diagnostic category manifesting each symptom

SYMPTOM	TOTAL HOSPITAL (N = 793)	MANIC-DEPRESSIVE (N = 75)	PSYCHO-NEUROTIC (N = 152)	CHARACTER DISORDER (N = 279)	SCHIZO-PHRENIC (N = 287)
Depressed	38	64	58	31	28
Tense	37	32	46	33	36
Suspiciousness	35	25	16	17	65
Drinking	19	17	14	32	8
Hallucinations	19	11	4	12	35
Suicidal attempt	16	24	19	15	12
Suicidal ideas	15	29	23	15	8
Bodily complaints	15	21	21	5	19
Emotional outburst	14	17	12	18	9
Withdrawn	14	4	12	7	25
Perplexed	14	9	9	8	24
Assaultive	12	5	6	18	5
Self-depreciatory	12	16	16	8	13
Threatens assault	10	4	11	14	7
Sexual preoccupation	10	9	9	6	14
Maniacal outburst	9	11	6	7	12
Bizarre ideas	9	11	1	2	20
Robbery	8	0	3	18	3
Apathetic	8	8	8	4	11
Irresponsible behavior	7	3	7	9	7
Headaches	6	7	10	4	5
Perversions (except homosexuality)	5	0	5	10	2
Euphoria	5	17	2	2	5
Fears own hostile impulses	5	4	9	5	2
Mood swings	5	9	5	4	4
Insomnia	5	11	7	3	5
Psychosomatic disorders	4	7	6	3	5
Does not eat	4	9	4	2	4
Lying	3	0	1	7	0
Homosexuality	3	3	3	8	2
Rape	3	0	3	8	1
Obsessions	3	8	3	1	4
Depersonalization	3	4	1	0	6
Feels perverted	3	0	3	1	5
Phobias	2	4	5	0	2

Source: Zigler and Phillips, 1961.

there are 140 entries. In only three of these entries is the percentage over 50 percent. Two of these three entries are the manifestation of depression; depression occurs frequently in both a form of psychosis and in psychoneurosis. There are ten entries between 30 percent and 65 percent. Being tense ocurs in at least a third of all four of the diagnostic groups. The other high-frequency symptoms are depression and drinking in the character disorders and hallucinations in the schizophrenic patients. Even though rare symptoms were previously discarded from consideration, in 93 percent of the cells the frequency of presence of a symptom is less than 30 percent. In other words, the chances are better than two to one that a person given the diagnostic label will not manifest a particular symptom. The first point, then, is that the symptoms are not as frequent or consistent within categories as would be gathered from standard textbook definitions.

Related to this point is the column on the far left, the percentage with which the symptoms were manifested for the entire sample of 793 patients. The interesting feature is that the frequency of the symptoms is so relatively low that one might expect a great deal of overlap with the nonhospitalized "normal" population. For example, as lecturers to college classes, the present authors would be delighted if only 8 percent of their students were apathetic. For the total sample, phobias (irrational fears), headaches, insomnia, and psychosomatic disorders occur less than once in 20 times among the hospitalized population. Such a base rate would be below that estimated for the general population. Usually any incident of homosexuality, even if isolated and unrepeated, is reported in a psychiatric record. The rate of 3 percent for homosexuality is far below the Kinsey, Pomeroy, and Martin (1948) estimate that from 18 to 42 percent of the male population have had some homosexual experience to orgasm after age 16, and that from 5 to 22 percent of the adult male population is exclusively or almost exclusively homosexual. Finally, one may well wonder if more or less than 10 percent of college students are preoccupied by sex.

The low frequencies of symptoms reported by Zigler and Phillips are all the more impressive when one bears in mind the nature of admission interviews and court commitment procedures outlined in the previous chapter. The interviewing psychiatrist is continually searching for the pathology that will justify the safest course of action, that is, hospitalization. To quote from Scheff:

Finally, the interpretations of some of the evidence as showing mental illness seemed capricious. Thus one of the patients, when asked, "In what ways are a banana, an orange, and an apple alike?" answered, "They are all something to eat." This answer was used by the examiner in explaining his recommendation to commit. The observer had noted that the patient's behavior and responses seemed appropriate and asked why the recommendation to commit had been made. The doctor stated that her behavior had been bizarre (possibly referring to her alleged promiscuity), her affect inappropriate ("When she talked about being pregnant, it was without feeling,") and with regard to the question above: "She wasn't able to say a banana and an orange were fruit. She couldn't take it one step further, she had to say it was something to eat." In other words, this psychiatrist was suggesting that in her thinking the patient manifested concreteness, which is held to be a symptom of mental illness. Yet in her other answers to classification questions, and to proverb interpretations, concreteness was not apparent, suggesting that the examiner's application of the test was arbitrary. In another case, the physician stated that he thought the patient was suspicious and distrustful, because he had asked about the possibility of being represented by counsel at the judicial hearing. [1966a, pp. 146–47.]

Similar examples of taking a small, relatively atypical, and inconsequential bit of behavior and magnifying it into an example of disorientation, distrust, or disorganization of thinking may be found in transcripts of courtroom proceedings presented by Szasz (1965a).

A final point exemplified by reference to Table 4 is the overlap of symptoms. No symptom is found exclusively in one category and not another. For example, manifestations of suspiciousness and hallucinations, the hallmarks of paranoid schizophrenia, are found at times in categories other than schizophrenia. Thus, there may be agreement on the "facts" of behavior and yet a basis for disagreements about diagnostic categorization. The situation permits personal, educational, sociological and theoretical pressures to act on the psychiatrists and to be manifest in their diagnostic behavior (Arthur and Gunderson, 1966; Gauron and Dickenson, 1966a, b; Ellis and Sells, 1964; Lakin and Lieberman, 1965; Jones and Kahn, 1966; Grosz and Grossman, 1964, 1968; Lowinger and Dobie, 1968; Sandifer, Hordern, and Green, 1970; Routh and King, 1972). Pasamanick, Dinitz, and Lefton (1959) in discussing their data make this point very clearly:

. . . despite protestations that their point of reference is always the individual, clinicians in fact may be so committed to a particular school of thought, that the patient's diagnosis and treatment is largely predetermined. Clinicians, as indicated by these data, may be selectively perceiving and emphasizing only those characteristics and attributes of other patients which are relevant to their own preconceived systems of thought. As a consequence, they may be overlooking other patient characteristics which would be considered crucial by colleagues who are otherwise committed. This makes it possible for one psychiatrist to diagnose nearly all of his patients as schizophrenic while an equally competent clinician diagnoses a comparable group of patients as psychoneurotics.

Among the preconceived ideas in the realm of psychiatric diagnosis are the major concepts that are usually offered as separating the three principal classes of functional disorders, psychosis, neurosis, and personality disorder. As noted in the review of this system in Chapter 1, the chief characteristic of psychoneurotic disorders is anxiety, while the personality disorders are characterized by minimal subjective anxiety. Psychotic disorders are supposed to be characterized by failure to test and evaluate external reality, which is specifically manifested in schizophrenic reactions by disturbances in concept formation and intellectual functions.

Ullmann and Hunrichs (1958) tested for the presence of these characteristics in a group of consecutive admissions to a psychiatric hospital. They found no significant differences between the three diagnostic categories in terms of three measures of anxiety and four concept-formation tasks. Ullmann and Hunrichs found that on these psychological measures the patients diagnosed as personality disorder were, if anything, more anxious than the patients diagnosed as neurotic. These findings were similar to those obtained by Zimet and Brackbill 1956) using samples of patients diagnosed at a general medical rather than in a psychiatric hospital.

Many of the points raised are recapitulated in a major study by Nathan et al. (1968), in which a flow chart was devised to help draw labels from observed behaviors. If the person manifested any one of the first five cues, he was called psychotic. Table 5 indicates that, with few false positives, a strong separation may be made between the psychotic and neurotic categories Nathan et al. do not give exact figures on either number of false positives and negatives, but do state that 90 percent of psychotic patients were labeled accurately. The pattern, anxiety in the absence of any of the first five behaviors pathognomic of psychosis, correctly identified 64 percent of the neurotics and mislabeled as neurotic 5 percent of the psychotics. The differentiation between neurotic and personality disorder was poor, and half the people called personality disorder were categorized psychotic or neurotic by this system. Finally, people

Table 5
Symptoms and diagnostic divisions

MANIFESTS	PERCENTAGE OF 220 PSYCHOTIC	165 NEUROTIC	160 PERSONALITY DISORDER	60 ABS
Hallucinations	49	0	1	30
Delusions	75	1	3	35
Lack of Reality Testing	73	1	2	45
Autism	36	0	0	20
Loose Associations	38	0	1	35
Anxiety	39	57	41	60
Compulsions, Phobic or Conversion Behavior	15	12	9	15
Depression	37	86	62	38
Depression—Inappropriate	17	24	22	18
Depression—Appropriate	11	51	29	13
Admit Illness	25	63	38	35
Not Admit Illness	19	8	11	12
Pronounced Emotions	53	49	47	35
Pronounced Emotions—Appropriate	7	29	23	13
Pronounced Emotions—Inappropriate	40	14	11	15
Secondary Gain	1	29	32	13

Source: After Nathan et al., 1968

placed in the acute brain syndrome category were not computed at all. The results are essentially similar with the Schmidt and Fonda findings about the major categories: material in the Nathan et al. (1968) tables indicates that finer categorization such as type of psychosis would probably yield less agreement.

PSYCHOLOGICAL TESTS

A psychological test is a sample of behavior collected and interpreted in a manner to permit reduction of uncertainty in making a decision. As the reader will remember from Chapter 3, this is the essential definition of an experiment, and indeed the same principles and care that were discussed in terms of experimentation apply to psychological testing.

At their best, psychological tests offer a number of advantages. To the extent that the test material is constant, differences among individuals are not due to differences in interview stimuli. The limitation on this, as noted by authors such as Masling (1960), Klein and Temerlin (1969), Lee and Temerlin (1970), Levy and Kahn (1970) is that the test situation is not restricted to test materials, but includes the psychological situation of the person taking the test and the behavior of the test administrator. This is similar to the experimenter effect mentioned in Chapter 5 and in articles by McGuigan (1963), Kintz et al. (1965), Rosenthal (1967), and Sattler (1970).

Given this view of the psychological test as a human transaction, we should expect all the influences observed in human interactions in general to be present. This indeed is the case. For example, Marwit (1969), Ganzer et al. (1970), and Rosenthal and Hertz (1972), showed modeling effects in the

Rorschach situation, Trachtman (1971) found a bias against lower-socioeconomic-status subjects, Hersen and Greaves (1971) provide evidence of the effect of verbal reinforcement on Rorschach responses, while Stewart and Patterson (1973) do the same for the TAT. Social and monetary reinforcement have an impact on performance of intellectual tasks of the type used to make school and vocational placement (Baumeister and Ward, 1967; Wright, 1968; Miller, 1969; Kubany and Sloggett, 1971; Edlund, 1972; Ayllon and Kelly, 1972). Sex of the subject and interpreter may make a significant difference in ratings of severity (Lewittes, Moselle, and Simmons, 1973), as does political orientation as in the case of a conservative male examiner evaluating a politically active liberal woman (Abramowitz et al., 1973).

If the testing situation is standard, norms may be developed. Once quantification is possible, one individual's score may be compared with the scores of many people. Not only does quantification provide a more reliable method of comparison, it also permits the individual clinician to use information collected by other people.

When giving a standardized intelligence test such as the Wechsler–Bellevue or the Stanford–Binet, the clinical psychologist makes use of literally thousands of cases he has never seen from the test's standardization and subsequent research on it. Without statistical methods the individual clinician could not have kept clearly in mind this number of cases, nor could he have remained free from the bias of the outstanding or unusual case.

Psychological tests may be relatively easier to administer, score, and interpret than a psychiatric interview. For example, a psychometrician or other specialist can administer and interpret individual and group intelligence tests such as those with which the reader may be familiar from college entrance exams or screening at the draft board. Once properly developed and standardized, an objective psychological test may be administered by a person who has minimal training; it may be scored by machine and interpreted (e.g., a decision can be made to accept or reject the testee or to give more tests) by references to numerical norms. For all these reasons, psychological tests are very appealing and have played a great role in the professional history of clinical psychology.

There are problems, however, in the use of psychological tests. A test represents a sample of behavior. The psychologist who wishes to base a decision on a test must have a theory and evidence to guide him in what behavior to select and how to move from his test data to the behavioral decision. Different theories will lead to different procedures.

Projective Tests

The projective tests for the most part illustrate a theory and process of generalization based on psychoanalytic concepts. In a projective test a standard stimulus such as an inkblot (in the Rorschach Test) or an untitled picture (in the Thematic Apperception Test) is presented to the subject, whose task is to say what the inkblot looks like or to make up a story about the picture. Such procedures have long been known at an intuitive level; Shakespeare has Hamlet and Polonius discuss what can be seen in clouds. In the projective approach a stimulus situation which does not have a clearly defined socially learned response is presented. The person makes a response, and since *he* made it, it must be indicative of *his* personality and *his* needs. This presumption is consonant with psychoanalytic theory, and it is not surprising that early projective techniques were developed by psychoanalysts. For example, the word association test was devised by Jung. Given a large number of words, say, 100, hypotheses could be drawn that the group of words to which there were bizarre or blocked associations formed a "complex." As long as this remained a hypothesis subject to further data collection, the situation was scientifically tenable. A danger, even at this level, however, was that the clinician would search for material to substantiate his hypothesis; that is, he would be more sensitive to and biased in the direction of his hypothesis and therefore less responsive to alternative hypotheses.

The current status of projective techniques is a matter of dispute among psychologists. Psychoanalytically oriented psychologists and psychiatrists are more likely to have faith in them than experimentally oriented psychologists. A typical quotation is from Noyes and Kolb (1963, p. 495): "The Rorschach is the projective test most likely to reveal nuclear conflicts, basic anxieties, and the level of emotional maturation. The validity and meaningfulness of projective test results are dependent on the skill, experience, and the personality of the psychologist." The first sentence of this quotation indicates one reason why some psychologists are reluctant to use projective tests: some psychologists do not posit underlying conflicts, basic anxieties, or psychosexual theories of emotional development. The second sentence in this quotation touches on issues of reliability. Different examiners are not consistent in their interpretations of projective test protocols, and, as hinted at by Noyes and Kolb, it is hard at times to know whether the psychologist or the patient is being revealed.

Standardized Tests

The development of intelligence tests indicates how tests are always based upon explicit and implicit assumptions about the nature of the behavior being studied. An early definition of intelligence used by Binet included the tendency to take and maintain a definite direction, the capacity to make adaptations for the purpose of attaining the desired end, and the power to be self-critical. In addition, it was presumed that the domain of discourse was intellectual rather than, for instance, physical. Eventually, the basic factor in intelligence, as the tests were developed by Binet and Simon and by Terman and Merrill, was the ability to deal with abstractions.

Some additional assumptions about intelligence were made. One was that its measurement should as far as possible be uninfluenced by the person's prior learning or experience. Operationally, this meant that items selected would entail material that was either so novel or so common that the effect of an individual's previous experience would be sharply curtailed. These concepts guided the development of a large pool of items that were then subjected to further screening.

In order to screen items, an assumption about criteria had to be made. This assumption was that, at least until the individual reached his mid-teens, intelligence was something that increased with age. This assumption led to the criterion that, with increasing age, a given task should be passed by increasingly high percentages of children. The Binet intelligence scales are basically age-scales: because of the manner in which they were developed, they compare the individual with other children and tell whether he is ahead of, behind, or roughly equal with other children his age. They do that and nothing more. The scales use a concept of mental age: the child is functioning (as measured by the test) at the level of the average child of a certain age. Comparing his mental age (M.A.: his score on the test) with his chronological age (C.A.) permits a statement of how many years or months he is ahead of or behind average children. Because bright children will gain "time" as years pass, W. Stern introduced the concept of an intelligence quotient, IQ, defined as M.A. divided by C.A. multiplied by 100. This score is relatively stable over time in terms of not being influenced by increasing number of years; e.g., from age 4 to age 12, a child might move from being one year advanced to being three years advanced, but still have an IQ of 125.

The test author can make additional assumptions. For example, if it is assumed that there is no difference in intelligence between the sexes, materials that differentiate boys from girls will be eliminated from the item pool. At a later date, using a test so constructed, one cannot properly say that the sexes are of equal intelligence.

Once the test is constructed, carefully selected groups of subjects (in terms of socioeconomic status, geographical distribution, and the like) should be tested to establish norms. A good test manual permits the test to be administered in exactly the same manner whether the examiner is in Australia or Brooklyn. Scoring standards also are clear enough so that rater reliability is as near perfect as possible. Finally, the test is validated in terms of what decisions or predictions it can help make. The intelligence tests have proved useful for predicting response to academic training. They may, however, at advanced stages of college and graduate work delineate a necessary but not a sufficient condition for academic achievement: that is, a minimum amount of intelligence, steadily increasing as years of education increase, is needed. Without it, achievement is very difficult if not impossible. However, having such a minimum is no guarantee of success. While in this case there may be few false negatives (lacking in intelligence but getting good grades) there may be many false positives (has high intelligence but does not get good grades). Other factors, such as special abilities, study habits, and reinforcement for academic achievement enter the picture.

Personality Inventories

The personality inventory was originally used as a group screening device in the first World War. Such a test, as devised by Woodworth, was simply a list of questions that psychiatrists frequently asked. The inventory was and is a standardized interview, and a person with a large number of pathological items is a candidate for more intensive individual examination.

Various refinements that have been made in inventories can be exemplified by the MMPI (Minnesota Multiphasic Personality Inventory). Items were first selected from clinical records and screened to provide those which differentiated such psychiatric populations as hysterics, psychopaths, paranoids, and schizophrenics from normal people. It should be explicit that psychiatrists designated the criterion groups. "Actually, what most inventories are trying to do is to *predict the diagnostic behavior of psychiatrists,* and not to establish new meanings for the terms used" (Gough, 1955, p. 278). Next, items that differentiated the criterion groups better than chance were saved and combined into scales.

Once in the pool, any item that differentiates the criterion groups by better than chance is saved. It is a completely empirical procedure, and the content of the item is of relatively little interest. This is an important point, because a frequent criticism of psychological inventories is based on picking out a particular item and ridiculing it. The item is there, not because of its content, but because it is carrying its own weight in the overall task of the test.

Second, the "normals" are not completely separated from a criterion group by any one item. The concept of statistical normality is well illustrated by some of the scales of the MMPI where too *low* a score alerts the clinician to needed further work. For example, a person who denied all anxiety would be statistically deviant and therefore subject to further screening.

The matter of denial leads to a discussion of faking. People may tend to fake in a socially desirable direction and deny abnormality when they do not wish psychiatric treatment or when a test is used for employee selection. They may on occasion also fake in a socially undesirable direction—for example, at the point of induction into the armed forces or when they wish compensation or dispensation from responsibility. Work with the MMPI illustrates a number of techniques to mitigate the effects of faking. The first method is to include a number of items that indicate, if too many are answered in a particular direction, that the person is too good to be true. This essentially takes into account that the vast majority of human beings do have some mildly bad features: they may gossip, swear, or tell polite lies. A person who denied all such foibles would either be faking "good" or be a very statistically rare individual.

Another device is the inclusion of some items that are answered in an unfavorable direction only once in 20 times or even less frequently. If 60 such items are used, it is within chance limits for a normal person to answer three to five in the unusual direction. If the person answers very many more in the bizarre direction, he is either faking "bad" or in truth is very rare.

Another technique is to locate by statistical procedures those items and answers which indicate that the person is suppressing reports of difficulties that are actually present. In some regards, the reader may think of this as a scale to locate the characteristics of a criterion group of false negatives. Another possible procedure is to have large groups of normal people, such as people in the army or in labor unions, fill out the inventory. Some of these people may be asked to fill it out "honestly" while others may be asked to make believe they were "mentally ill." The extent that the popular conceptions of mental illness do not coincide with actual behavior of psychiatric patients permits the collection of items that are answered in a particular manner by people faking mental illness but not by people who are so designated by psychiatrists. In some respects, such a scale is an empirical collection of false common beliefs.

What the personality inventory provides is a series of situations (questions) that match the subject's behavior (answers) to those of one group or another (hysteric or nonhysteric, paranoid or nonparanoid, faking "bad" or not faking "bad").

A test, particularly a personality inventory, is frequently a matter of the individual's reporting how he is likely to respond. This report may be accurate, and thus individuals high on a test score such as dominance may be more likely to act in a manner that is "dominant" than people with low scores on this scale. To the extent, however, that the test samples responses to general rather than specific situations, the predictions will be weak, and to the extent that the situations to be predicted depart from the criteria for item selection, the predictions may approach chance. Frank (1969) summarizes a large literature: "The review of these studies seems to reveal that when the behavioral and test correlates of psychiatric diagnosis are analyzed, one finds little or no consistency in the dependent variable (in this instance, social or test behavior when the independent variable, the criterion for selection, is psychiatric diagnosis." (p. 164.) Potkay (1973), reviewing 30 studies, found that personal history data ". . . is at least, if not more, effective than projective and objective test sources of information."

SOME THINGS TO CONSIDER

We have emphasized scientific method as an aid in decision making. Psychological tests should be used with the same rigor as any other method of collecting data scientifically. After matters of reliability have been assessed, there remains the most crucial issue of all, that of *validity or relevance* in making decisions. Tests are used for both selection and placement, whether it be for treatment or employment. In the realm of employment, the Supreme Court decision of *Griggs* vs. *Duke Power Co.* indicated that legally, as well as scientifically, tests must be related to the job. Test scores may be in error because the person taking the test is not skilled at test-taking or because the test situation itself is frightening or distasteful. Of greater import, the test may be presumed but not demonstrated to be relevant to success on the job; our society values intelligence and good mental health (whatever these may be), but it is likely that there are industrial tasks for which high intelligence is not relevant or may be even a disadvantage.

Similarly, there are research and scholarly occupations for which a degree of indifference to the opinions of others is an asset rather than a liability. If the range of scores is restricted, if clear criteria cannot be established, if the relationship of test to criteria is complex rather than simple and linear, and if the test has not been validated on the population from which the test-taker belongs, great care must be exercised in evaluating test scores (Goslin, 1968). The best practice is to revalidate, that is, collect data, store but not use it, and survey at a later date how much, if any, improvement there would have been in the decisions had the tests been used.

Other Considerations

There is a cost of professional time and effort to testing. If the decision is already made, testing adds nothing to the decision. If psychotherapy would be prescribed for every person, a test indicating whether therapy is advisable would be superfluous. Aside from the need to evaluate the worth of the screening compared to the value of the same resource used in some other way (e.g., treatment, training, research), the issue as just put raises the matter of *base rates*.

There are statements that have no semantic validity, that is, that may be true of everybody or true of nobody and thus cannot be checked as differentiating. Such statements may seem penetrating and true (Merrens and Richards, 1970; Snyder and Larson, 1972; Weisberg, 1970; Dmitruk, Collins, and Clinger, 1973): they are illustrated in the demonstration of the *Barnum effect*. This occurs when a class is handed back individual personality analyses after taking a personality test. After each student has said how good the interpretation is, one student reads his or her evaluation aloud, and all find that they have been given the same write-up.

Base rates enter evaluation procedures in another manner. We may be correct 99 percent of the time and yet have done very little. For example, if we said that none of the students in our classes in abnormal psychology are schizophrenic, retarded, brain-injured, or liable to commit suicide in the next 12 months, we would probably be 99 percent correct. In the absence of valid information, the safest bet is *what is most probable*. The bet that any individual will commit suicide in the next twelve months is not 50–50, but rather one in ten thousand. The prediction of infrequently occurring events is particularly difficult. If we derive "signs" from the protocols of 50 people who committed suicide compared to 50 people who did not, even if we attain signs far better than chance, we will have to move from a situation in which we move from 50–50 to one in 10,000. This is likely to increase our rate of false positives (people called suicidal who will not commit suicide). We may then ask whether suicide precautions are justified for 100 people, only one of whom, we know not which, is a true positive (actually suicidal). If suicide precautions mean hospitalization because the person is in a danger to himself, we may ask how many people we should stigmatize and deprive of liberty to save one person.

If there is no stigma or great cost to a false positive, and we have a surplus of candidates (such as the situation of selection by the draft during peacetime), the problem is reduced. However, there remains an ethical problem: for every person we reject, we make more likely that *some other person* will be accepted (e.g., drafted).

How Were the Data Collected?

Many studies reported in the literature contrast two groups—for example, 50 people who had made serious suicide attempts and 50 people who had not. In such studies, it is impossible to say whether differences are causes or effects of the labeling processes. For example, are differences between hospitalized schizophrenics and other groups the *cause* of the hospitalization or the *result* of the treatment they receive in the hospital? Are the differences between suicide attempters related to the cause of the attempt or are they the results of attention, embarrassment, or other effects of having made the attempt?

Illusory Correlation

Clinicians frequently use "signs" that have little if any empirical validity. The question may be asked, as it was by Chapman and Chapman (1967; replicated by Chapman and Chapman, 1969; Starr and Katkin, 1969; Golding and Rorer, 1971), How do outstanding professional people such as clinical psychologists come to believe in what is not empirically true?

The details of the careful procedures in this area cannot be given here, but the basic procedure is to present the subject with clinical material, such as a drawing by a "patient" (draw-a-person test) and to give two "characteristics" of the person who supposedly made the response. A list of characteristics and a list of clinical (draw-a-person) signs are made up, and characteristics and signs are so varied that every characteristic is paired with every sign an equal number of times. Undergraduates are then exposed to the associations. The purely rational outcome, since signs and characteristics are random and balanced, would be for no clustering or bias by the subjects when they are later asked to give the characteristic associated with a sign. This is not what is observed; rather, there is a strong matching of a sign as indicative of a characteristic that is far beyond the expectations of chance. The previously naïve subjects give the same association of signs and characteristics found in the clinical psychology literature. For example, a large head is associated with intelligence, atypically drawn eyes with suspicion, broad shoulders with manliness, and elaborated sexual areas with impotence. What is the basis for this strong association despite the random pairing during training? If one makes the assumption that projective drawing is valid, then these pairings are ones that make both semantic and "common" sense in our culture at this time, so that it is possible to hypothesize that characteristics would be associated to drawing "signs" without any exposure at all. This is indeed the case (Chapman and Chapman, 1967).

The psychological tester is human. He is trained to a task by consequences, and these may be administrative rather than scientific. Above all, he brings a linguistic and cultural background to his task, and this background may mislead and hinder him in giving the service he wishes to provide.

DATA FOR BEHAVIORAL DECISIONS

Data are gathered in order to make decisions. The first step for the psychologist is to specify what decision he wants to make. Only after he has decided what he wants to find out will he have a guide to what data are relevant. While this may seem obvious, a clinical psychologist frequently accepts referrals that ask vague questions unrelated to a decision; for example, "What are the personality dynamics?" Once the question is clear, the psychologist has a basis for selecting relevant information; i.e., the question itself may provide a lead to what behavior should be sampled, or, if a test is to be devised, what criteria should be selected for item screening and later validation.

A second general principle is that the data should require as little generalization as possible from the situation in which data are collected to the situation of the decision. If a psychologist is interested in deciding whether to undertake therapy, his diagnostic questions may blend with the therapy itself. In part, the best decisions about the chances of modifying a person's behavior may come from limited samplings of the results of such modification procedures. Similarly, if the focus is on behavior, then measures of the frequency of the target behaviors (those to be changed and those to be developed) will be used as part of therapy to decide whether the procedures are being successful and, when successful, the point at which treatment should be terminated (Cautela, 1968; Gottman and Leiblum, 1974).

In a diagnostic procedure for behavioral modification, the therapist asks a limited number of general questions. Most of these questions center around the word "what." He will ask *what* is the person doing or not doing that leads to the referral and brings him to the attention of the therapist. This is the question, by definition, of what is "abnormal" behavior. The behavior therapist must make a value judgment whether a behavior should be changed (see Ullmann, 1969a). As long as there is no implicit distinction between normal and abnormal in the behavior itself, the therapist is responsible for the decision to alter the behavior in a way he is not if the behavior is, by definition, "sick." The behavior therapist must therefore decide if the behavior may be ethically subject to modification: is it in the service of *both* the patient and the significant others in his environment for a change to be made? The diagnostic decision may be (1) that the behavior being emitted is not of a nature requiring change, (2) that it would not be in the service of either person or significant others to change it, or (3) that no behavioral modification program could be devised to change it. In these circumstances, the diagnostic decision is not to undertake treatment.

Once the target behavior has been decided upon, the next question is *what* are the conditions under which the behavior is emitted. It is presumed that a behavior that occurs frequently or strongly enough to lead to a referral must be in response to some stimulus situation. This may be a matter of finding out what link in the prerequisites for the approved social act has not been learned or reinforced. Data as to when the abnormal actions occur are collected through observation and informants. Adults who have referred themselves may themselves be the observers or informants.

The next question usually deals with the effect of the abnormal behavior. *What* happens after the person has acted in the "abnormal" manner? As the reader would predict from Chapter 4, psychologists are particularly interested in the reinforcing stimuli that may be contingent upon the "abnormal" act. They are also interested in what does *not* happen—in terms of *what* situations are avoided and *what* acts are not emitted. Frequently, but not always, a description of the first manifestations of the undesired behaviors is helpful. This is not because some historical event must be worked through or that some conflict in the past must be brought to consciousness. It is rather a way of focusing on the history of reinforcement for a given behavior. Through this question psychologists may obtain clues to the reinforcement pattern and learn about the generalization of the behavior and changes in the reinforcing stimuli maintaining it. From the questions of what behavior, what social situations, and what consequences psychologists determine the target for behavior modification.

The next steps seek to determine *what* techniques and *what* procedures will be likely to be helpful. If the behavior is currently maintained by a response-contingent reinforcement, the next question asks in *what* ways the environment can be altered so that the reinforcing stimulus is not contingent upon the "abnormal" behavior but instead is contingent upon some alternative, more socially desirable action. There are two lines of questions. The first concerns *what* stimuli are positive reinforcers for the subject. At times reinforcers may have to be developed: in the chapter on children's behavioral difficulties (Chapter 23) there will be examples of the use of food deprivation to increase the reinforcing characteristic of food and the use of shock to provide the reinforcement of escape or termination of an aversive stimulus. The second question is associated with the starting point of diagnostic procedures. It asks *what* ideally the person would be doing in reaction to the stimulus situation that is now the setting for maladaptive behavior: *what* behavior should take the place of the abnormal behavior, *what* should be taught. Once this stage has been reached, there is a matching of target behavior to technique.

Two points are explicit. There is a continual emphasis on the question of "what," and there is a continual emphasis on measurement. The two procedures come together in the rubric that definitions should be operational. Given the influence of Freud, much previous diagnostic work, particularly projective techniques and psychiatric interviews with adults, centered on the question "why." Presuming unconscious motivation or disease processes, overt behavior was, by definition, only a surface manifestation, a symptom. The underlying cause, the *why*, was the focus of diagnostic work. The answers to *why* questions are frequently beyond behavioral specification, testing, and direct modification. The question *What happens when he acts?* may seem to the reader to be semantically similar to the question *Why does he act?* but this is so only if the reader has the frame of reference that a person acts because of reinforcing contingencies.

What questions are much more likely to lead to behavioral answers than *why* questions. However, a long series of questions may be needed to find the specific behaviors and situations that are to be targets. A psychologist may ask a patient who has read Freud, "What would you like different?" and the patient will answer, "I want to have greater ego-strength." The behavioral psychologist does not argue about whether there is such a thing as "ego-strength," but asks, "What would you be doing differently if your ego were strengthened?"

Once the target behavior has been decided upon and a number of hypotheses have been developed about the situations and reinforcing contingencies, the hypotheses are tested. For example, if the psychologist hypothesizes that a child has tantrums because they are followed by attention, the parents may be asked to (1) withhold attention during tantrum behavior and (2) make as certain as possible that *legitimate* demands for attention are met rapidly when the child acts in an appropriate manner. It is important to note that this in no way implies that the child has a "need" for attention and therefore will get better if simply given adequate amounts of attention. Attention should be given contingent upon some particular response whose frequency of emission it is desirable to increase. It is more efficient, therefore, to choose the response to be reinforced than to leave to chance what will be reinforced.

It is worth noting that the step of placing the person into some diagnostic category was not taken in this example. Nothing would have been gained by it.

SUMMARY

Abnormality may be operationally defined by psychiatric labeling and by scores on psychological tests. Psychiatric labeling has been found to be frequently inconsistent. Disagreements stem in good measure from the difference between textbook descriptions of psychiatric syndromes and the behavior actually emitted by patients. A diagnosis may be a self-fulfilling prophecy and the label may alter the behavior of professionals as well as laymen toward the labeled person.

While psychological tests have many advantages, they are all only as useful as their standardization and validation. Three types of psychological tests were discussed: projective tests, such as the Rorschach, ability tests such as the Binet measures of intelligence, and questionnaires such as the Minnesota Multiphasic Personality Inventory. A psychological test should be treated as a miniature experiment designed to help arrive at a decision. The same thoughtfulness and care that characterizes research should characterize psychological testing, particularly when decisions based on tests may gravely influence human lives.

In a final section the behavioral approach to assessment was presented. The crucial questions are of a *what* nature rather than a *why* nature. The stress is on observable behavior, research procedures, and quantification. The experimental procedures presented in Chapter 3 are directly applicable. If practicing psychologists are to justify their social role on the basis of their training in a scientific discipline, it could not be otherwise.

behavior modification

12

The previous chapters have focused on methods of formulating and measuring changeworthy behavior. This chapter deals with the question, What can be done to help people? The chapter will survey various forms of psychological treatment and the rationale for them. Part 2 of the book, which follows, will be devoted to describing specific clinical manifestations and how they may be treated.

In dealing with processes of changing human behavior, four concepts must be discussed and differentiated: social influence, behavior modification, evocative psychotherapy, and behavior therapy.

CONCEPTS OF BEHAVIORAL CHANGE

One person may program the environment, including his own behavior, to affect a second person's behavior. Because other people are a major source of acquired reinforcers, this is probably the largest general category of behavior in which socialized human beings engage.

Behavior influence is a term that includes situations in which one human being exerts some degree of control over another. Formal school education would fall in this category, as would environmental design, monetary policy, advertising, psychological experiments, and sensory deprivation (Krasner and Ullmann, 1973). Behavior influence refers to the process of change itself, not to an evaluation of the social desirability of the behavior being changed.

Behavior modification, on the other hand, primarily involves the changing of behaviors that have been labeled socially deviant. In effect, behavior modification involves altering the actions of individuals who have been brought within the labeling system in the manner described in Chapters 1, 2, 10 and 11.

The term *behavior modification* may be applied to many different techniques used with a broad spectrum of problems by people of varying professional and nonprofessional affiliation, including parents and teachers. For example, a volume on research in behavior modification (Krasner and Ullmann, 1965) dealt with shaping, modeling, verbal conditioning, computer simulation, and hypnosis, among other techniques. The people influenced by these procedures ranged from retardates to college students, from schizophrenics to normal children. In similar fashion, a book on clinical applications of behavior modification (Ullmann and Krasner, 1965b) reported the efforts not only of psychologists and psychiatrists, but also of classroom teachers, parents, nurses, and peers.

Within the realm of behavior modification there are two conceptually different approaches. Treatment deducible from the sociopsychological model that aims to alter a person's behavior directly through application of general psychological principles will be called *behavior therapy*. Treatment deducible from a medical or psychoanalytic model that aims to alter a person's behavior indirectly by first altering intrapsychic organizations will be called *evocative psychotherapy*. The term "evocative" is used in the dictionary sense of "evoke" —"to call up or produce (memories, feelings, etc.); ... cause to appear; summon; ... to produce or suggest through artistry and imagination a vivid impression of reality ..." (Random House Unabridged). In these techniques, the therapist does *not deliberately* apply response-contingent reinforcement in the manner of behavior therapists.

Both evocative psychotherapy and behavior therapy are forms of behavior modification, which in turn is one type of behavior influence.

FROM FREUD TO ROGERS

More than anyone else, Freud is the progenitor of evocative psychotherapies. Freud asked his patients to do something which was then almost completely unique: to talk freely. He listened and made inferences, often excellent ones, about cause-and-effect relationships in the patient's life. Freud accepted the patient's verbal behavior as representing a valid sample of his actual and symbolic (fantasy) life. As noted in Chapter 5, however, a key concept in evaluating the psychotherapeutic interview centers around the biasing effects of the examiner-interviewer (Rosenthal, 1966; Schofield, 1964), and it might well be asked which came first, the overt life behavior or Freud's theoretical interpretation (Wolpe and Rachman, 1960).

The American psychiatrist Harry Stack Sullivan (1892–1949) moved psychotherapy forward by calling the therapist a "participant observer," a view that approximates the behavioral role of an active, biasing, influencing therapist. Sullivan (1953, 1954, 1956) formulated the therapeutic situation as a type of communication between two people. He emphasized to a greater extent than Freud not only what a person said, but *how* he said it, that is, gestural behavior, rate of speech, intonations, and silences. For Sullivan the interviewer-therapist was an expert in interpersonal relationships and consequently one who used his knowledge in helping patients become more effective in their own lives.

Sullivan conceived of behavior as response patterns that elicited specific reactions from other. If the source of disturbed behavior lay in these habitual response patterns, then treatment involved the therapist's using his own behavior to correct them. Or, to use behavioral terms, the therapist served as a model and a social reinforcer shaping "desirable" behaviors.

Sullivan analyzed the interview in terms of the ways in which interpersonal communications were mediated, namely, verbally and nonverbally. Speech, or verbal behavior, was the vehicle of communication of self-reaction and of psychotherapy. Sullivan's view is consistent with analyses of situations that categorize behaviors in terms of their social consequences. As a "participant observer," Sullivan used his own behavior as both antecedent to the patient's behavior and as a consequence for it. Thus he conceived of the patient as responding to social situations rather than to internal wishes, drives, or impulses, and responding to the therapist as he would to other persons. The therapist took advantage of the fact that treatment was not a unique situation but prototypical of other interpersonal relationships. He then deliberately modified specific patient behaviors, and his objective determined the techniques he used.

Sullivan also advocated a general tension-reduction theory of learning which included concepts of anxiety gradients, rewards and punishments affecting likelihood of response, and a trial-and-error modeling procedure. Central to the learning process in Sullivan's theories was the therapist's awareness of his own role in the interaction. The therapist must know his stimulus value for patients, how he affects others, and in general the specifics of how he facilitates or retards behavior.

With regard to the features just described, Sullivan was a predecessor of behavior therapy: he emphasized an active, contingent, controlled, and controlling role for the therapist. Essentially a social therapist seeing the locus of change as external to the individual, he viewed the therapist as a scientist who was devoted to investigation of the process of change. Sullivan attempted to objectify therapy; his insistence on empirical observation stimulated research.

Carl Rogers was responsible for the recording of therapy interviews for research and training purposes. He was the first to publish (1942) a verbatim transcript of an entire psychotherapy session. This event opened the way to naturalistic observation of what actually happened in psychotherapy and the field of endeavor called content analysis. Rogers offers both a comprehensive theory of personality and a theoretical framework for bringing about change in human behavior. The two are closely interrelated; for the techniques of the therapist follow from the theoretical rationale. A number of concepts (1951, 1959, 1961) are basic to Rogers' approach, which is considered primarily phenomenological or subjective; that is, an individual's behavior can only be understood in terms of his subjective experiences. Rogers emphasizes the affective and internal responses of the individual, who is seen as actively attending to and reaching out to his environment.

Rogers assumes almost as a matter of faith that man is innately good. It is unfortunate experiences which have created his current problems. Further, Rogers assumes that behavior is goal directed and purposive. That is, the individual is not a passive recipient of his environment, but continually seeks to affect his environment in such a way as to maintain self-consistency and to enhance himself.

Rogers deserves credit for performing and stimulating research that demonstrated a clear relationship between therapist behaviors and patient responses. For example, Snyder (1954) published a list of "tactics" used by Rogerian therapists that included "clarification of feeling, restatement of content, simple acceptance, structuring, interpretation, nondirective leads, direct questions, approval, and encouragement." Therapists' verbalizations may be observed, categorized, and counted. Further, each kind of verbal behavior may have different effects on the client's responses, and such hypotheses may be tested empirically.

A second major contribution by Rogers was his emphasis on the therapist's value orientation. Rogers is a great humanist, and believes that the way to preserve the integrity of the individual is for the therapist to use a "nondirective" attitude. The therapist must not interfere with or direct the patient. He should avoid giving information or advice, asking direct questions, and offering interpretations, reassurance, or persuasion. Classically, in client-centered therapy, change originates within the individual who has a basic need to "actualize," experience, and grow. The therapist fosters growth by acceptance, warmth, and permissiveness. Rogers' views on this matter differ from those presented in this book by not making therapist behavior contingent on patient behavior. In effect, Rogers contends the psychology of social influence should not be applied to therapy, for to influence is to "destroy." Although one can select passages from his writings (1961) in which it appears that he is reluctantly moving in the direction of acknowledging influence elements in therapeutic procedures, his arguments in his debates with Skinner (Rogers and Skinner, 1956) still stand as perhaps the clearest expression of the "nondirective" approach to behavior modification.

The technical breakthrough of the Rogerians in recording complete psychotherapy sessions and the consequent use of transcripts made possible an analysis of the *content* of a therapy session. Investigators studied the "natural" interaction during psychotherapy and tried to determine what, if any, lawful relationships were demonstrated. The result was a large number of studies analyzing (structure, grammar, themes, feeling) the therapy interview (Auld and Murray, 1955; Gottschalk, Springer, and Gleser, 1961; Leary and Gill, 1959; Mahl, 1956, 1959; Mowrer, 1953; Murray, 1956; Phillips, 1956; Saslow and Matarazzo, 1959; Strupp, 1958; Marsden, 1965; and Truax, 1966a, 1968). In this type of research, there is no attempt to manipulate variables or interfere in any way with the "natural process" of therapy (as conceived of by the therapist). These studies represent a way of identifying variables important in the psychotherapy situation such as "warmth of relationship" (Raush and Bordin, 1957; Bordin, 1959); depth of interpretation (Harway et al., 1955; Speisman, 1959); degree of interviewer's "commitment"; therapist empathy; and "unconditional positive regard" (Truax, 1963, 1966b). Another related area of investigation is that of the relationship between the verbal behavior of the interviewer or therapist and psychophysiological changes in one or both of the participants, usually the interviewee (Grace, Wolf, and Wolff, 1951; Wolf and Wolff, 1947; DiMascio, Boyd, and Greenblatt, 1957; Lacey, 1959). This work demonstrates that verbal behavior involves more than mere words, but has measurable physiological effects on the individual.

A number of similarities characterize the various evocative procedures, from Freud to Rogers. The motivating force for the difficulty lies within the individual. The disturbance may be called a conflict, a drive, or an unrealized potential. If the locus of the difficulty is internal, then the task of the therapist is to provide the conditions that bring about changes in these internal processes and thereafter in observable behavior. These setting conditions may include: specific suggestions from the therapist as to patient behavior ("Just say the first thing that comes into your mind"; "Tell me about your father"); indirect cues as to the areas of the patient's life relevant to the therapy situation ("You must have had a difficult childhood"); interpretation of the patient's verbalization or behavior ("With all these present difficulties with authority figures you must have really hated your father"; "The constant quarreling with your wife is caused by the resentment originally directed toward your mother"); reflection of the *real* feeling of a patient ("You must have been very angry when your boss told you that"); and, perhaps most important of all, the attitudes and feelings of the therapist about his patient (warmth, acceptance, unconditional positive regard).

DISSATISFACTION WITH EVOCATIVE THERAPY

Freud, Sullivan, Rogers, and many other contributors developed techniques of whose efficacy professional helpers became increasingly convinced. Yet there were many severe criticisms of the evocative psychotherapist. Basic questions may be asked about the efficacy of psychotherapy (see "Outcome Studies," below). Further, psychotherapy is an expensive and time-consuming procedure. The time estimates, influenced by classical psychoanalysis, were conceived of in terms of years rather than months. Another time factor was the waste inherent in the large numbers of people who dropped out of therapy before they or the therapist considered them "cured" (Brandt, 1965).

Group Treatment

Group therapy was used in 1903 by Pratt in his work with tuberculosis patients (Ruitenbeek, 1970), by Adler in work with parents and children in 1921 (Dreikurs, 1959), and by Moreno in 1914 in a way strongly foreshadowing current encounter groups (Schloss, Siroka, and Siroka, 1971). It was not until after World War II, however, that group treatment took its place among the leading psychotherapeutic procedures. At first group therapy was considered to be an inadequate alternative to individual therapy, necessitated by a shortage of therapists. However, it soon became obvious that putting a group of individuals together to discuss their problems and to interact could be useful in bringing about behavioral changes. Group therapy became more than a substitute for individual therapy.

Groups have been used within the context of psychotherapy (Yalom, 1970), behavior therapy, and encounter-sensitivity. Within the behavioral context, systematic desensitization (Paul and Shannon, 1966; Meichenbaum, Gilmore, and Fedoravicius, 1971), procedures for teaching self-control procedures (Wollersheim, 1970; Ober, 1968), and a modified form of rational-emotive treatment (Meichenbaum, Gilmore, and Fedoravicius, 1971) have been used with groups of people. Liberman (1971), D'Zurilla (1966), Wiggins and Salzberg (1966), and Hauserman, Zweback, and Plotkin (1972) provide examples of use of behavioral procedures such as response contingent reinforcement to increase favorable target behaviors in group situations. Plotkin's article is especially interesting because of its inclusion of a reversal of contingencies and because the sample, "silent" institutionalized adolescents, was particularly difficult. Not only did contingent reinforcement increase appropriate verbalizations, but "once the rate of initiations increased, group peer pressure used social reinforcement to bring about a decrease in silly, off-topic verbalizations and a subsequent increase of initiations which were appropriate and relevant to the interests of the group." (p. 90.)

Of particular interest because of its recency, its wide publicity, and the nature of acts occurring within its context is the group activity called *sensitivity* training or *encounter* grouping. It may be viewed as a religious exercise, a form of entertainment, a social movement(Krasner and Ullmann, 1973, especially pp. 444–62), or a behavior-change medium.

Encounter and sensitivity groups were influenced by work in the industrial setting (Roethlisberger and Dickson, 1939) in terms of production and morale, and by social psychology (Lewin, 1947), which studied group-decision processes. According to the tradition, it was discovered by accident that the discussion of what had transpired in the group was even more useful than the group activity being discussed. Leaderless group discussion and feedback became a major vehicle for work with teachers and industrial managers and was emphasized at the National Training Laboratory (NTL). Other influences came from work with psychiatric groups, notably Moreno (1953), with his psychodrama innovations, Jones' therapeutic community in England (1953), as well as more typical group psychotherapists (Slavson, 1950; Powdermaker and Frank, 1953).

An important book, both for technique and theory, called *Gestalt Psychology* (Perls, Hefferline, and Goodman, 1951), introduced an alternative name. The rationale for the activities includes the work of Freud and Rogers, but also reflects the concerns of the times; these involved the breakdown of the family and church, the segmentation of work and its separation from place of residence, and the stereotyping of life and decreased closeness of most interpersonal relationships in large urban communities. While Jung had emphasized positive potentialities in his system, authors such as Maslow (1968) and Bugental (1966) wove these into a psychological school. May (1961) redefined anxiety in terms of a scheme inspired by philosophers who were phenomenological and *existential*. This last word became, like gestalt, an alternative label for the more general movement. Finally, while community feeling had declined, basic needs for food, shelter, security, and consumer goods had been satisfied for a large portion of the population that was both educated and resistive to the increasingly abstract roles their jobs required. In this economic and social climate, a "counter-culture" (Rozak, 1969; Reich, 1970) developed which supported and enhanced the trend. Eastern mysticism, meditation, massage, sensual experiences of all sorts, regressive games, and altered states of consciousness through drugs have been added at various times and places such as Esalen.

The fundamental concepts of encounter-sensitivity groups is Freudian: first, there is an emphasis on energy (libido) and freeing it through lifting of repression by symbolic but active expression (catharsis), and an emphasis that sensual and socially unusual behaviors are more important and "realer" than activities not "repressed" and under social control. Some examples may make this point:

In an encounter group we find the energies within us and around us, experiencing them, and begin to learn to control them, rather than denying or repressing them. From this point of view, any technique is appropriate if it enables us to contact without the defense limiting our energy in a particular area, or helps us to contact the energy itself so that we can experience it and learn to live with it like an unruly animal whose existence we have denied, but who appears, nevertheless, when we finally accept the possibility of its existence. [Mann, 1970, p. xiii.]

The encounter situation does include behaviors not usual for the relatively highly educated, usually white and professional or middle-class people who currently form the majority of the encounter-group population. In fact, one of the attractions of the encounter is that behavior not permissible in everyday typical situations is accepted and even encouraged.

The group situation has two emphases: (*a*) total candor in expression and (*b*) experience that is bodily or sensation-oriented. The unifying theme is "feeling" rather than "ideation." Some observations by Howard (1970) focus on the specific kinds of acceptable and desirable group behavior: (Quoting Charles Seashore of NTL:) "You have to learn oblique intervention, too, and develop a repertoire of fantasies, analogies and games to provide people with ways to experience directly things that aren't intellectual." (p. 41.) (Quoting Schutz:) "The further you go toward violence, sexuality, and loneliness . . . the better trainer you are, almost linearly." (p. 42.) "At these workshops . . . everyone is obliged to confess publicly to his mate three secrets which might seriously jeopardize the relationship." (pp. 65–66.)

"Tell her" said Lloyd. "You're punishing me for no reason! I'd like to tear your hair out by the roots!"

Bindrim leapt across the room and grabbed from a box a Sears, Roebuck catalogue, which he thrust at Lloyd.

"Here's her hair," he said. "Go ahead! Tear it out!"

Lloyd did so, ravaging the catalogue into a mass of ragged confetti. But he still looked frustrated.

"Your face looks as if you'd like to bite somebody," Bindrim said. "Would you?"

"Yes," said Lloyd. "My father." This time Bindrim gave him a raw potato. Lloyd gagged as he bit into it, but seemed to feel better. To every workshop Bindrim brings a kit of such supplies: potatoes to bite, catalogues and phone books to rip, magazines to roll up and use as clubs, pieces of snappable wood to fracture, pillows to punch and nippled plastic baby bottles to bite or sometimes to fill with warm milk.

"Different people," he said, "express anger differently. There are whippers, biters, slappers, stranglers, and throwers. The idea is to regress, if possible, to the trauma that caused the distortion." [pp. 94–95.]

The thrust of the counter-culture and encounter-sensitivity movement is towards sensuality and away from intellectual control. Back (1972) puts it this way:

Sensitivity training is a procedure that uses group action as an end in itself. The principle of feedback is of primary concern in sensitivity group meetings. Second, taboos of ordinary society are reversed: frankness substitutes for tact, self-expression for manners, nonverbal techniques for language, and immediacy for responsibility. . . . A third feature which may seem contradictory is the strong commitment of the sensitivity training movement to the justification of its procedure through scientific method alone and not through religious or ideological commitments. Emerging from these three characteristics of sensitivity groups is a fourth, general one, the overarching stress on the value of change, a change whose direction is not necessarily determined. [p. 31.]

The implication of this attitude is a complete denial . . . of the importance of abstraction and symbolism. The cult of the experience is justified by deprecating symbolic statements, especially higher abstractions, and extolling strong sensual experiences, especially the more direct ones. This value shift is carried out in three ways: from symbols to concrete expression, from intellect to emotions, and from the mind to the body. [p. 79.]

Reich (1970, p. 278): "Consciousness III is deeply suspicious of logic, rationality, analysis, and of principles."

This stance stems from a number of sources. The first is the psychoanalytic theory, especially libido, defenses, and the unconscious (see Chapter 8), but here, as pointed out by Maliver (1973, especially Chapter 8), without typical safeguards for clients. One reason is that psychotherapists have responsibilities to clients and may not advertise. The encounter-sensitivity circle very frequently engages in public, advertised unscreened meetings. The people so doing may not call themselves therapists, even though they use therapeutic theories and procedures and make claims for personality changes that the purchaser thinks of as therapeutic. Second, many encounter-sensitivity practitioners adhere to an antiscientific rationale in order to avoid scientific validation. The rationale given is that science in itself is inhumane. May (1961) poses as a principle that science must fit or be "relevant" to the topic investigated, and that measurement and specification segments the human, and hence is not germane. Second, it is asserted that the simple can be understood or explained only in terms of the more complex; thus there can be no reduction of complexity or explanation on a biochemical, physiological or observed behavioral basis. A third principle May supports is that he studies only "two-persons-existing-in-a-world," and, therefore, he cannot separate the acts and thoughts of one person from the other to study sequences of behavior (antecedents and consequents, effects of environmental manipulation, etc.) of one person in terms of responses of the other. May also limits his data to the two-person unit in the immediate experience, that is, the consulting room.

Combining May's theories with other writings, we can summarize: a person is a set of potentialities; adjustment to life limits and threatens the person; to the extent the person alters or limits himself in the face of these pressures, he is less real or genuine; the ultimate of lack of genuineness is death, and everyone is presumed to fear death; when a person acts in a manner towards genuineness, he is taking a risk, and it is easier to conform rather than risk, even though conformity leads to non-genuineness and death-in-life; anxiety is the state of the person in his struggle against the forces that would destroy his being, i.e., make him conform; the struggle leads to the overt change worthy behaviors, "psychoses" or "neuroses"; the therapist provides a genuine experience, that of himself, but it is for the person to be responsible, to choose new patterns of behavior, for if the therapist directly teaches or helps the client, the person would be engaging in a new conformity; a good therapist, by definition, is not responsible.

A person may enjoy the dramatic, unusual, and sensual aspects of an encounter group, and may, as with a placebo, feel better for the experience. What evidence exists (see Maliver, 1973, especially Chapter 6) indicates that there is a serious chance for difficulties to occur (Gottschalk, 1966; Yalom and Lieberman, 1971; Lieberman,

Yalom, and Miles, 1971), especially when the style of the leader is aggressive, demanding, and authoritarian. The beneficial results wear off over time, and more nonparticipating controls (six to eight months later) have improved, and fewer have made negative changes, than participants.

One problem faced by encounter-sensitivity as currently practiced is that of reentry to the ongoing, work-a-day world. The practices and values of encounter-sensitivity are likely to be counter-productive in many job and marital situations.

In encounter-sensitivity, as with hypnosis, people do things that are unusual and unexpected; a large group may jump, shout, touch, and undress at the commands of the leader—an observation of value when we discuss hysterical epidemics (see Chapter 13). "An air of competitive showmanship" may take over and "subtle kudos were awarded to whoever could tell the most vivid or unusual story." (Maliver, 1973, p. 32). ". . . in the typical group, the pressure to experience awareness is enormous, and the urge to fake it is almost irresistible. Most group members have been coached by friends and promotional brochures; they believe that a peak experience is not only desirable but necessary if one is to have fullest happiness and mental health." (Blanchard, 1970.) The group may be the most tyrannical and coercive force met with and those who insist on their theories, which rule out follow-up, validation, and responsibility, the most self-centered and inhumane of people.

Psychotherapy as a Process of Control of Behavior

Most therapists are uncomfortable in a role labeled as a "controller" or "manipulator" of behavior. The evidence, however, is that this is an accurate description of the therapist's role. For example, Sheehan (1953) and Graham (1960) both report studies in which personality attributes of benefited patients changed significantly in the direction of the therapist's own personality. Rosenthal (1955) found that "improved" patients changed their "moral" values in the direction of the therapist's values. Palmore, Lennard, and Hendin (1959) report increasing similarity in verbal behavior between patients and therapists as therapy proceeds. Stekel (1951) points out that the patients' dreams always confirm the theoretical formulations of their therapists. Heine (1953) reports a study of three different approaches to therapy in which the patients' subjective reports of the changes that took place within themselves did not differ, while there were sharp differences along "school" (therapist) lines as to the theoretical explanation of these changes by the patients. Whitehorn (1959) points out that successful psychotherapy involves leadership "toward the therapist's conception of what constitutes value in life." The evidence is strong that the therapist by virtue of his role can and does influence and control the behavior and values of the human beings who come to him for help.[1]

Skinner and Rogers (Rogers and Skinner, 1956), representing different extremes on this issue, have debated both the presence and desirability of control in psychotherapy. The therapist may misuse his

[1] "Radical therapy" (Radical Therapist Collective, 1971) considers treatment aimed at adjustment to an ongoing social system as necessarily reactionary. The motto is that therapy means change, not adjustment, and that the change should be in the social and political structures of society, not within the individual. "They view the capitalistic society as the sole cause of the troubles of the emotionally disturbed poor, blacks, women, and homosexuals." (Ruitenbeek, 1972, pp. 4–5). An extreme, which extends the medical analogue and may have implications of devaluing the very people it is designed to help, is a suggestion (Diamond, 1973) that social factors such as poverty and discrimination be considered by criminal laws in the same way in which "mental illness" is used in determining criminal responsibility. While the present volume has pointed out the sociological aspects of diagnostic labeling and its potential political impacts (see also Halleck, 1972), it avoids both therapeutic nihilism and the use of labeling to attain a particular political end.

control. The counter-control, which discourages the misuse of power, is represented by the ethical standards and practices of the various organized professions to which the therapist belongs. Skinner proposes that it is this danger of misuse which explains the popularity of theories of psychotherapy that deny that human behavior can be controlled.[2] Refusal to accept the responsibility of control is merely to leave control in other hands.[3] Skinner does not agree with Rogers that the individual always holds within himself the solution to his problems. If individuals were the product of training and education that have effectively supplied the kinds of solutions Rogers advocates, then it would be unlikely that the individual would be in therapy. But if, as is more likely, the individual was the product of excessive or damaging kinds of control or deprivation, he would not have learned appropriate behavior.

Ellis gives a cogent discussion of controls in psychotherapy in a defense of his specialized behavioral approach called Rational-Emotive Therapy:

> Those who allege that RT (rational-emotive therapy) is too authoritarian and controlling do not seem to face that virtually *all* psychotherapies, including the nondirective, passive, client-centered, and existentialist techniques, are actually distinctly authoritative and controlling. The therapist, because of his training and experience, is invariably some kind of authority in his field. . . . Even if he does not look upon himself in this manner, the members of his clientele almost invariably do. [1962, p. 364.]

Ellis points out that even the nondirective therapist is taking a role because he thinks it will be effective, and "the real question is not whether the therapist is authoritative and controlling but in what manner he exerts his authority and control."

Irrespective of the therapist's avowed orientation, the process of psychotherapy is one of doing something to change the client. In behavior therapy there is explicit specification of what the practitioner does to help the person, a specification that may be nonexistent in evocative psychotherapy and distorted by some encounter therapists.[4]

Behavior therapy starts with the kinds of assessment procedures described in the last section of Chapter 11. As part of these procedures the working behavior therapist is likely to look for the answer to three questions: (1) what behaviors should be increased or decreased; (2) what contingencies currently support the subject's behavior (either to maintain his undesirable behavior or to reduce the likelihood of his performing a more adaptive response); and (3) what skills may be taught or stimuli manipulated to alter the subject's behavior. The next section deals with methods by which this goal may be achieved.

---

[2] An example of denial is the explicit statement, "Humanistic psychology tries to tell it not like it is, but like it ought to be." (Matson, 1973, p. 11).

[3] Scientific investigation does not create behavioral control; it reveals it so that it may be studied, harnessed, and put to use in an open manner that is of service to people within the social group.

[4] "He [Esalen leader, Brown] stated the usual warning and added: 'This is a very subtle ground rule, because it means that whatever you do, or whatever happens to you in terms of your experience here, is really your responsibility. If you do something it is your responsibility; if you don't do something, it's also your responsibility.'

"Brown went on to suggest that each person in the group introduce himself to another in what he called 'a special way'—namely to introduce himself by bragging about something. When my turn came, I gave my name and indicated that I didn't feel like bragging. Even though I was exercising the permission explicitly granted by Brown not five minutes before, other members of the group quickly reacted with questions like, 'Aren't you going to tell us *anything* about yourself?' and 'Why don't you share yourself with us?'

"Morris Parloff, writing in the *International Journal of Group Psychotherapy* in 1970, commented, 'The mere announcement that participants are free to decide participation is no assurance that the rights of the nonconformist will be protected. Free choice can only be exercised when the individual is not threatened by humiliation, reprisal, rejection, or ridicule.'" (Maliver, 1973, pp. 46–47).

METHOD OF CHANGE: BEHAVIOR THERAPY

While there are many *techniques*, there are few *general principles* involved in behavior therapy. In terms of techniques, Bandura (1961) organized his review of the field of behavior therapy around the topics of extinction, discrimination learning, methods of reward, punishment, and social imitation. Grossberg (1964) organized his review around the topics of aversion, negative practice, positive conditioning, reinforcement withdrawal, and desensitization. Kalish (1965) stressed classical conditioning and argued that the various techniques reduced to extinction and conditioning. Kanfer (1973) discussed four basic learning models: classical conditioning, operant conditioning, observational learning, and self-regulation. Although the techniques are important, none of them, as such, define behavior therapy. Rather, behavior therapy can be summarized as involving many procedures that utilize *systematic environmental contingencies to alter directly the subject's reactions to situations*.

There are two points crucial in this description. The first is the systematic nature of the arrangement of the stimulus environment. The second is that reaction to situations, *not* the specific response *in vacuo*, is the focus of treatment. It has been mistakenly said that behavior therapy involves "symptomatic treatment" in terms of a treatment limited to responses. As was noted in Chapter 8, the therapist who "removes" a particular behavior without helping to replace it with some more adjustive response to the situation in which the former behavior was emitted is doing only half his professional job. In behavior therapy the patient is taught to make new and socially more appropriate responses in place of his previous reactions. The former behavior is not "removed"; it is replaced. The object is to obtain behavior in response to stimuli which is incompatible with and more desirable than the previous behavior.

In helping to develop this new kind of response, two important aspects of an individual's life are being affected. First, his stimulus value for others is changed. They will now react differently to him, and usually welcome and help maintain the new behavior. Second, he is now able to exert some control over his environment and his own behavior.

In order to achieve these objectives, the behavior therapist utilizes a series of techniques. Some of these techniques are briefly described below. Further descriptions and illustrations are presented in the subsequent chapters within the context of specific problems. Among recent volumes presenting further material are ones by Mikulas (1972), Thomas (1974), Schwitzgebel and Kolb (1974) and Rimm and Masters (1974).

The Training of Assertive Responses

Assertion may be defined as insistence on one's legitimate rights. If one does not do so, the result is that not only is the person exploited but also he labels himself as "weak" or "incompetent."

The first step, as in all forms of behavioral intervention, is one of assessment: "Whatever the nature of the problem (circumscribed, pervasive, avoidant, or maladaptive), the person is functionally unassertive for at least one of three reasons: (1) a genuine skill deficit—not knowing how to be appropriately assertive, (2) inadequate stimulus discrimination—not knowing the circumstances under which assertion is appropriate, or (3) a fear of irrational or rational consequences, which may be self-generated, of being assertive. It is crucial for the clinician to determine which of these functional reasons is or are the case, because each of them requires different therapeutic interventions." (MacDonald, 1974).

In assertive training the therapist sets up for the person a series of tasks that progressively approximate the eventual socially appropriate and effective behavior. The behavior therapist uses his relationship with the individual to help him try out a new adaptive response. The therapist may do this by reasoning (Ellis, 1962) or by assigning specific tasks. Role-playing may be used, both within the therapy situation (Wolpe, 1954, 1958; Wolpe and Lazarus, 1966) and outside it (Kelly, 1955). Role playing may provide a source of information about how other people view situations (Clore and Jeffery, 1972) or a chance to observe themselves (Kopel and Arkowitz, 1974), as well as a more general opportunity to practice new behaviors. Another frequently used procedure for teaching assertive behavior is modeling (Hersen et al., 1973; Kazdin, in press).

Wagner (1968) reinforced anger expressiveness directly, while Lomont et al. (1969) compared group assertion training with more traditional insight therapy involving exploration and interpretation of feelings. Assertion therapy consisted of the systematic practice of behaviors which help people deal with social situations. Role playing was the major vehicle, but the people were also told that their difficulties stemmed from anxiety in dealing with others and these particular procedures would assist them in this area. The assertion group showed changes on the posttests, while the insight group did not.

McFall and his co-workers (McFall and Marston, 1970; McFall and Lillesand, 1971) directly trained appropriate assertion responses including refusal of unreasonable requests. The work is notable for the care taken in developing situations, the spelling out of procedures, and the experimental design. Modeling and coaching of both overt acts and the responses the person makes for himself, (specifying the tasks, providing them gradually, and giving feedback both by compliments and by suggestions for improvement) may also be part of the procedure, as well as recording and evaluating the frequency and quality of one's acts outside the direct treatment session (Rehm and Marston, 1968).

Serber (1972) deals with nonverbal behaviors such as loudness of voice, fluency of spoken words, eye contact, facial expression, bodily expression, and distance from the person with whom one is interacting. Eisler, Miller, and Hersen (1973) investigated components of assertive behavior that included duration of looking, smiles, duration of replies, quickness of replies, loudness and fluency of speech, and content of speech such as compliance, requests for new behavior, and expression of feeling. The situation is clearly defined, there is concentration upon a limited and learnable task, and there is feedback, including audiovisual recording, for the client to review. What has been learned about nonverbal role-expressive behavior (see Chapter 5) can and should be systematically applied. Generalization from favorable experiences may occur. By this procedure the individual can enter into and make adaptive responses in progressively more difficult situations. As in all behavior-change procedures, the person acts differently, and people, in turn, respond differently to him. This may well lead to further favorable changes in self-concept.

The Use of Sexual Responses

One frequent problem presented by individuals involves anticipated aversive consequences (anxiety as defined by Wolpe) associated with sexual responses. Whether anxiety and sexual responses are incompatible, as Wolpe theorizes, is a moot point. In terms of behavior therapy, sexual feelings may be used systematically. Examples are Davison's (1968a) case of elimination of a sadistic fantasy (Chapter 21), the treatment of impotence, (Masters and Johnson, 1970), and homosexuality (Davison and Liebert, 1972; Marquis, 1970). The pleasurable stimuli are used to gradually associate new and culturally appropriate responses to situations in which ineffective behavior was previously emitted.

The Development of Relaxation Responses

Jacobson hypothesized that a state of muscle relaxation was incompatible with anxiety, defined as muscle tension, and introduced a method for obtaining muscular relaxation. Jacobson (1938) and Haugen, Dixon, and Dickel (1958) taught people to practice such techniques in progressively more general and more difficult life situations. Wolpe (1954, 1958) made a major contribution when he systematically paired muscular relaxation with visualized scenes and objects to which inappropriate "anxiety" responses had been made. Paul (1966) provided a relaxation procedure which can be taught in half an hour.

In *systematic desensitization* a person is taught to relax, and this state of relaxation is associated with the visualization of potentially threatening situations. The situations are arranged in a series, or "hierarchy," which moves from the least to the most threatening situation. As each situation in the hierarchy is successively associated with the response of relaxation, by generalization all other items in the hierarchy are affected and the person progresses to items that originally were difficult. Generalization to the extratherapy situation parallels progress on the visualized hierarchy (Rachman, 1966a).

The Use of Conditioned Avoidance Responses

Wolpe (1954) describes three techniques used in conditioning avoidance responses: a dominant motor response, "anxiety-relief" responses, and pairing undesirable behavior with aversive stimuli. The first of these, conditioned inhibition of anxiety through a dominant motor response, is based on the experimental finding by Mowrer and Viek (1948) that when animals were repeatedly exposed to a continuous mild electric shock, those who learned a definite motor response in relation to termination of shock developed less anxiety than those who were not able to learn such a response.

This finding also parallels the observation that Pavlovian experimental neurosis is likely to be induced in animals whose movements are restricted. Wolpe (1954), in an illustration of this technique, describes the case of a woman who was afraid of falling. The therapist instructed her to imagine a mild fall. When she had the image clearly, an electric current was passed into her forearm which ceased upon her making a brisk forearm movement. After a number of trials, this movement became an immediate response to shock, and the patient reported the idea of falling to be less unpleasant. She was able to attempt an actual fall and then proceeded to more difficult tasks.

The second of these techniques involves "anxiety-relief" responses, and is based on the concept that if an uncomfortable stimulus is administered to a person for several seconds and then is stopped upon a clearly designated signal, that signal becomes associated with the bodily correlates following cessation of the aversive stimulus. This procedure follows the development of secondary reinforcers described in Chapter 4.

The third use of conditioned avoidance responses involves overcoming an undesirable approach response to a stimulus by pairing such a stimulus with an aversive one. Eventually the individual reacts with avoidance to the stimulus that had previously elicited a strong approach response. This procedure is illustrated in Chapter 22 on work with alcoholics and in Chapter 21 on sexual difficulties.

Aversive stimuli may include unpleasant tastes, (for instance, lemon juice given to infants) (Sajwaj, Libet, and Agras, in press), distortion of television (Greene and Hoats, 1969), or hot and smoky air (poetic justice) in the treatment of cigarette smokers (Grimaldi and Lichtenstein, 1969). Aversive stimuli should not be abusive; rather, aversive stimuli are most effective when they have clear attentional value, are contingent on a target activity, provide information, and signal that an alternative behavior, of which the subject is capable, will be more effective.

The use of aversive stimulation requires the greatest care and professional skill because of the nature of the stimulus used, the complexities involved, and the chance of misuse (Marks, 1968; Rachman and Teasdale, 1969; Hallam and Rachman, 1972; Lovibond, 1970). If possible, alternative methods are and should be used.

Evocative Therapy as a Behavioral Technique

The procedures of evocative therapy may illustrate either extinction (making the maladaptive responses in the presence of a person who does not reinforce them) or reconditioning, the discussion of the threatening stimuli in the presence of the calm, relaxing (and relaxed) therapist. The difference between behavior therapy and evocative therapy lies in the use, or lack thereof, of concepts such as insight and the systematic nature of the behavior therapist's use of conversation to *recondition* rather than to *uncover*. This implies that the person's level of discomfort must be kept low so that the likelihood of the production of a new response is greater than is its redintegrated threat. During evocative therapy, the therapist may *selectively reinforce* (or shape) the verbalizations that are new and more effective.

The therapist exhibits differential interest, sympathy, and praise to different types of behavior. Once new behavior has occurred, it is reinforced with meaningful responses. Talk of feelings, formulation of the etiology of problems, analysis of interpersonal relationships, and healthy remarks may all be reinforced by the therapist and lead to the patient's having a feeling of improvement. This in turn may alter the clients perceptions of and responses to social situations and hence how others react to him.

Although complete acceptance and permissiveness may be a therapist behavior that the patient expects and finds helpful in the establishment of rapport, it is in the long run a relatively inefficient technique of behavior change. If one accepts everything and reacts to all behaviors in the same way, one deprives the person of an opportunity to discriminate between his adaptive and maladaptive behaviors.

Garfield and Bergin (1971) studied the relationship of "accurate empathy," "warmth," and "genuineness" to outcome in psychotherapy and found no significant relationships between these therapeutic conditions and an array of outcome measures. The therapist would probably do best to use these pleasant conditions contingently rather than unconditionally.

Response Modeling

Once the person has learned to imitate another person, new behaviors may be facilitated by observing another person (Bandura, 1971). The behavior of others may serve as discriminative stimuli for the subject, indicating that something is permissible or not, or as models to match, providing new information as to how to deal with situations. Finally, as pointed out by Bandura (1969), there may be vicarious acquisitions and extinction of autonomic responses. There is clinical evidence for the strength, both useful and dangerous, of social imitation. A child who is not afraid of a stimulus may, when paired with a child who is afraid of it, develop the latter's fear. Jones (1924b) presents an illustration, as does Sherman (1965), of this effect of modeling. The Bandura, Blanchard, and Ritter (1969) work cited later in this chapter represents one of the most vivid examples of the use of response modeling. Much of the work on altruism, the development of impulse control, and conception and question-asking behavior cited in Chapter 28 makes use of modeling. Heller (1969), Stewart (1969), and Ullmann (1969b) discuss the use of models in outpatient psychotherapy.

Modeling may be used effectively to train staff in their interaction with patients (Wallace et al., 1973). Such procedures are important for their impact on improving treatment, but even more so for major policy decisions as to what and how change agents can be taught to be effective.

The Use of Negative Practice

The therapeutic use of negative practice was the contribution of Dunlap (1932). Yates (1958b) presented a more concise formulation of the procedure and related it to Hullian reactive inhibition. If an individual repeatedly practices a tic, stammer, or other undesirable habit in massed trials, the reactive inhibition or fatigue associated with having made the response will lead to making the response become painful. Under these conditions *not* emitting the response will avoid the aversive situation (e.g., the effects of fatigue) and hence be effectively reinforced.

Extinction of a Response

Behavior (whether called normal or abnormal) is maintained by reinforcement. When the reinforcing stimuli that currently maintain the behavior are removed, the person's response to a situation is likely to change and the maladaptive behavior is likely to decrease in frequency. New alternative behaviors are then, if only by chance, more likely to be emitted. Extinction of a behavior can best be illustrated when the subject makes a major physical effort, such as a temper tantrum, and is "ignored." An example of extinction of a child's temper tantrum was noted in the cases by Williams (Chapter 2), and other instances have been reported by Wolf, Risley, and Mees (1964) and Zimmerman and Zimmerman (1962).

Positive Reinforcement of Selected Responses

This is perhaps the most basic technique of behavior modification. It takes various forms, including many of the specific techniques previously discussed in Chapter 4. For example, reinforcement may be given for progressively more difficult performances (shaping), as in Isaacs, Thomas, and Goldiamond's (1960) work with a mute catatonic. Krumboltz and Thoresen (1964) offer another illustration of this technique, which involved the systematic reinforcement of information-seeking responses during an interview. The investigators defined reinforcement as any verbal or nonverbal response by a counselor which indicated approval. They found that this kind of systematic reinforcement of client statements during an interview resulted in a significant increase in the clients' voluntarily engaging in a number of information-seeking behaviors in real life after leaving the interview (as compared with a control group not receiving systematic reinforcement).

Stimulus Deprivation and Satiation

The effectiveness of a presumed reinforcing stimulus in affecting a given behavior may be manipulated by depriving the individual of that stimulus for a period of time, or providing such an abundance of the stimulus that the reinforcing value of the stimulus is reduced. Both procedures were illustrated in Chapter 4.

Self-modification

In dealing with abuse of drugs, change of certain sexual acts, eating, smoking, and very particularly (in Chapter 28) with positive or socially welcome unusual behaviors, we will discuss self-modification. A person can and does arrange his environment to maximize his own effectiveness—for example, dressing and acting in ways to maximize, as far as he can determine, the favorable responses of others. Thus, people can serve as their own behavior modifiers: scheduling themselves, making contracts with themselves, and then reinforcing themselves either explicitly or symbolically. Goldfried and Merbaum (1973) have collected a number of classic articles in this area, while Watson and Tharp (1972) presented an integrated program for self-modification that was applied and revised from use with college students. Aside from the merits of the work itself, it has importance as helping to define the concept of self and as one illustration of how behavior influence may, when clearly explicated, be put to use by people for their own benefit.

Cognitions: Talking to Oneself

One of the major developments in behavior therapy during the last five years,[5] covered in some measure in Chapter 28, is the training of the person to evaluate this own performance and bring the things he says to himself under his own control (Meichenbaum, 1973). There may be redirection of attention so that the individual does not focus on potential hazards (Meichenbaum, 1972); rearrangement of thoughts following the Premack principle (Ullmann, 1969c); thought-stopping, in which the patient makes an aversive, loud, disruptive, "Stop!" response contingent on the disruptive thought (Stern, 1970; Wolpe, 1971; Kumar and Wilkinson, 1971; Rimm, 1973); or contingent, symbolic unpleasant stimuli as in covert sensitization (Cautela, 1967, 1970a, b). Masters (1970) points out that how one looks at an event, whether good behavior is a matter of being controlled or of controlling others for a reinforcing stimulus,

has an effect on overt behavior. World War II German propaganda used words such as "defensive success," "successful disengagement," "elastic defense," "mobile defense," "withdrawing maneuver," "unencircling maneuver," "according to plan," "shortening of the front." "systematic evacuation," "without enemy pressure," "undisturbed by the enemy," and "withdrawal to the enemy's surprise" after "the destruction of all important establishments" to designate retreat. (Choukas, 1965, p. 125.)

As Meichenbaum (1973) points out, verbal operant conditioning indicates that the therapist may bring client verbalizations under control, and, therefore, the next obvious step is to teach the client, using the same behavioral principles, what to say to himself. A thought is an operant, and should be amenable to operant conditioning. (Ullmann, 1970). In turn, the client may gain control of the therapist by the same verbal operant conditioning principles (Lauver, Kelley, and Froehle, 1971).

A person may record other people's behaviors and their antecedents and consequents and alter his behavior as a result (Libb, House, and Green, 1973). It is reasonable to ask what the effects would be of a person charting his own behavior, a procedure that is an integral part of self-modification. The result (Kazdin, 1974) may well be therapeutic in itself. The person may find himself gathering data rather than making diffuse responses to situations. Further, the very act of charting may reduce the activity; for example, a person may reinforce himself for a decreasing line of cigarettes smoked or increasing numbers of hours studied.

In similar fashion, people may contract with each other as to the various costs or benefits of certain acts (Bardill, 1972; Stuart, 1971, 1972). Such contingency contracting is fundamental to token economies in the home, classroom, and hospital ward. Again, if a person can do something with another person, it is possible for him to do so with himself.

---

[5] In the first century A.D., Epictetus said, "Men are disturbed not by things, but by the views which they take of them," and Buddha, who died circa 480 B.C. said, "All that we are is the result of our thoughts; it is founded on our thoughts; made up of our thoughts." (Ross, 1966, p. 114.)

Other Techniques

New methods of modifying behavior are constantly being introduced. Among such techniques are the use of teaching machines, greater use of the reinforcing properties of group membership, the more frequent use of intermittent reinforcement, the training of parents in behavior-modification techniques, and the development of total programs in which reinforcement is in the form of tokens. Therapy, however, does not rest on specific methods of application or techniques, but rather on the planned, explicit manipulation of differences in the environment contingent upon the person's responses to stimuli. The possibilities for new approaches are limited only by the creativity of experimental psychologists and the ingenuity of clinical workers.

THE IMPLICIT DEMAND CHARACTERISTICS IN BEHAVIOR MODIFICATION

Social influence variables are a significant aspect in all the techniques just described. While the techniques are methods of influence themselves, they take place in a larger context.

There have been a number of attempts to describe what is common to psychotherapists across different schools of treatment and different social groups. Torrey (1973a) offers four components of psychotherapy. The first, which he calls the principle of Rumpelstiltskin, is that the therapists are able to name what is wrong with their patients, and the very act of naming is therapeutic. The second is that therapists use their personal qualities to help their patients, although the traits involved vary from one culture to another. The third is that patients' expectancies are mobilized, as in our discussion of placebos in Chapter 5. Associated with increasing patients' expectancies of change are any special training the therapist might have, or an impressive office locale. The fourth and final component of psychotherapy according to Torrey is that there be a technique. The technique is consistent with the values of the culture; for example, it claims scientific status in Western groups, but it may be religious in orientation among other groups. By implication, how the technique is administered, according to Torrey, is more important than what it is.

Frank (1971) offers six features common to all psychotherapies. The first is "an intense, emotionally charged, confiding relationship with a helping person, often with the participation of a group." (p. 355). The second is a rationale that includes an explanation of the cause of the distress and a method of relieving it. The third is provision of new information concerning the nature and sources of the patient's problem and possible alternative ways of dealing with them. The fourth is strengthening the patient's expectations of help through the personal qualities of the therapist, enhanced by his status in society and the setting in which he works. The fifth is the provision of success experiences that heighten the patient's hopes and sense of competence. The sixth shared feature "is facilitation of emotional arousal, which seems to be a prerequisite to attitudinal and behavioral changes." (p. 357)

Explicit in Frank's work (Frank, 1972) and implicit in Torrey's is that behavioral problems are due to a general demoralization and are not specific in terms of responses to situations. Behavior therapists would agree strongly with Frank's second, third, and fifth features. The training of peers, parents, attendants, teachers, and the like, to provide educational experiences within the home, classroom, or ward, argues in some measure against the fourth feature. Further, Wilkins (1973) questions the validity of the concept of expectancy of therapeutic gain as explanatory. When possible, however, behaviorists prepare the clients so that they will attend to and make use of the experiences prescribed for them. The first and sixth features are open to dispute, especially as techniques are demonstrated to be specifiable, teachable, and effective.

To indicate where there is agreement, in systematic desensitization, which Paul and Bernstein (1974) aptly call a "package of therapeutic procedures," there is a period of explanation during which the person is given a rationale for what is about to happen. His role and that of the therapist is made explicit and may be enhanced by pretreatment information (Goldstein, 1968; Greenberg, 1969). In institutional work such as that of Ayllon and Azrin (1965) and Atthowe and Krasner (1968), the reinforcing contingencies of a token economy (see Chapter 20) are posted on the walls of the ward. In giving the individual an explanation of what is about to happen and what is happening to him, one implicitly and explicitly tells him that there are reinforcing contingencies over which he can obtain some control.

There are important social influence effects associated with a procedure such as relaxation. The subject is following instructions given by the therapist. When being taught relaxation, he is instructed to pay special attention to a particular aspect of the environment, his own body and the germane changes that occur when there is a sharp decrease of tension. A series of physiological responses takes place which he can "feel" and for which he has been provided the labels "good," "valuable," and "relaxed." Additionally, these relaxation responses are likely to have been associated with previous pleasant experiences (e.g., going to sleep). As in the Schachter and Singer (1962) experiment detailed in Chapter 5, the changed sensations to which the person's attention is directed are labeled by the therapist as good, pleasant, and necessary. On the one hand, the observed changes validate the therapist's predictions, while on the other the subject is demonstrably responsible for his current state. He is given strong evidence that through his own behavior he can change his environment, namely, at this point, his "feelings." Further, any move in this direction is reinforced by the therapist's approval.

The next ingredient in systematic desensitization is the linkage of relaxation with a progressive visualization of the threatening stimuli. These stimuli are introduced as parts of the new relaxed role which the subject has just been taught. When the person starts to become "tense," there are indications that he has difficulty assimilating this element into his new role. The process can be conceptualized in terms of Guthrie's (1935) view that the individual tends to repeat what he did previously, and the last response was a relaxed rather than an uncomfortable reaction. This position may also be formulated by noting that one may well overcome fears if the frightening object or situation can be examined without the previous extraneous feeling of uneasiness. For example, a person with a fear of climbing stairs might be encouraged to look at stairs, their lines, shape, and color, while being told very firmly and authoritatively that he would not be allowed to climb them. That is, the stimuli and the previous response to them would be separated so that a different response to stairs would be present and experienced. In terms of the concept of redintegration, the person is encouraged to place the cue in its fuller, realistic context. Wine (1971) applies such an analysis to test anxiety.

On a more general level, the person is provided stimuli (or feedback) from that part of the environment which is himself. He obtains a new, more objective view of himself by monitoring himself. This might be described by words such as an altered self-concept or, more simply, as a new role. Whatever the terms, the person finds that he can "be" different (behave differently), and the therapist demonstrates this to him immediately and directly. *Insight may then follow rather than precede the changed behavior.* Leitenberg et al. (1971) make this point in relation to a physiological measure, heart-rate, as well as self-verbalizations. The person can better tell what he had been doing, because he is in a position to contrast his past behavior with his present activities. The behavioral procedure then becomes a major technique for obtaining a new and different view of one, and is not merely a technique limited to changing isolated bits of behavior.

The views expressed in the foregoing section are open to debate. Lang, Melamed, and Hart (1970); Cotler (1970), Krapfl and Nawas (1969) and Baker, Cohen, and Saunders (1973) are examples of the use of desensitization delivered by a machine, and Kahn and Baker (1968) and Phillips, Johnson, and Geyer (1972) of a do-it-yourself at home procedure. While delivery of desensitization itself may be automated, the total situation as experienced by the subject must be considered.

The therapist has a "theory" that helps him respond rapidly to patient behavior. What is helpful or important is decided upon by the professional person. Thus, patient behavior may be shaped by the therapist, who may compliment his patient for "working" or making progress by saying the right thing. In a less direct manner, the therapist may guide the patient's verbal behavior by interest, friendliness, or other nonverbal cues described and utilized in verbal operant conditioning (Krasner, 1958a, b, 1962b, 1966a).[6]

---

[6] An example is research on increasing affective self-references through verbal operant conditioning (Aiken and Parker, 1965; Merbaum and Southwell, 1965; Dicken and Fordham, 1967; Ince, 1968a; Kahn, 1967; Phelan, Tang and Hekmat, 1967; Hekmat and Lee, 1970; Hekmat and Theiss, 1971), expressions of dependency (Schuldt, 1966), and scores on personality tests (Harmatz, 1967). Hekmat (1971) repeated and extended work by Adams, Butler, and Noblin (1962) when he contrasted the effects of reflections and interpretations as reinforcement for increasing affective self-references. Recently interest has centered on self-disclosure; Jourard and Jaffee (1970) and Sarason, Ganzer, and Singer (1972) have shown the effect of modeling on this target behavior.

Words or covert oral behavior (McGuigan, 1970) may become targets for reconditioning in

Whether because of his theory or his personal feelings of comfort on hearing certain material, the evocative therapist trains the patient to emit selected "correct" responses. Roback (1974) reviewed the literature and research on insight and found that one major stumbling block was the absence of a definition of the concept. A psychoanalyst, Marmor, has given a description of the end result of the social influence process which can serve as a summary statement:

Each school gives its own particular brand of insight. Who shall say whose are the correct insights? The fact is that patients treated by analysts of all these schools may not only respond favorably, but also believe strongly in the insights which they have been given. Even admittedly "inexact" interpretations have been noted to be of therapeutic value. Moreover, the problem is even more complicated than this; for, depending upon the point of view of the analyst, the patients of each school seem to bring up precisely the kind of phenomenological data which confirms the theories and interpretations of their analysts. Thus each theory tends to be self-validating. . . . What we call insight is essentially the conceptual framework by means of which a therapist establishes or attempts to establish a logical relationship between events, feelings or experiences that seem unrelated in the mind of the patient. In terms of the analyst's objectives, insights constitute the rationale by which the patient is persuaded to accept the model of more "mature" or "healthy" behavior which analysts of all schools, implicitly or explicitly, hold out to him. Now since interactions that put the patient's material within one frame of reference seem to be just as effective for the patient as interpretations that put it within another frame of reference, it is logical to conclude that the specific insight given *cannot* be the only or

---

order to alter sequences of behavior. DiCaprio (1970) used satiation procedures such as repetition, visual fixation, and auditory exposure to bring to a neutral level language symbols, while Hekmat and Vanian (1971) paired the word "snake" with pleasant associates such as the words "beautiful gift."

Behavior Change and Attitude Change

Are there changes in measurable aspects of attitude or affect once behavior itself is changed? One of the points made in Chapter 5 was that when a social act changes, affect and attitudes may also change. Festinger (1964) and Wicker (1969) has reported that there is very little experimental evidence that changes in attitudes brought about by the usual kinds of "persuasive communications" used by social psychologists result in consequent observable changes in behavior. Bem (1967), in reviewing studies on the relationship between attitudes, beliefs, and behavior, found that attitude changes *follow* rather than precede behavioral changes. "The self-descriptive statements that typically comprise the operational definitions of 'beliefs' and 'attitudes' are found to be the dependent variables of the relationship and are under the partial functional control of the behaviors that precede them."

Bandura, Blanchard, and Ritter (1969) carried out a study designed to compare the efficacy of various behavioral approaches to modifying behavior, to test relative effects over a period of time, and to test generalization effects. Their experiment permitted them to relate the effects of behavior change to subsequent attitudinal changes. Bandura et al. compared the effectiveness of three behavioral techniques in changing snake phobias. It is important to emphasize that the 32 subjects were all suffering from a *real* problem that was affecting their daily functioning. These were individuals from the community who answered a newspaper advertisement offering to help them with snake phobia. The subjects included persons who were unable to go hunting, hiking, and camping for fear of snakes: real estate salesmen who encountered snakes in showing homes in a beautiful but snake-ridden part of town; individuals anticipating Peace Corps assignments in foreign countries; a museum official who was fearful of the snake room in his museum; schoolteachers whose children would bring in pet snakes for fondling; and a woman whose neighbor kept a boa constrictor, resulting in a near heart attack on her part and a physician's recommendation that she seek a cure for her response to snakes.

The subjects were pretested with attitude scales and a fear-survey schedule which contained an inventory of stimuli to which people might be frightened and an indication of the intensity of their fear reaction to these items. They were then tested on a snake-avoidance scale, which involved specific approach–avoidance behavior vis-à-vis a live snake. They were accepted for the remainder of the study only if they failed to pass an item in the scale involving the lifting of the snake in his cage. The subjects were then assigned to one of four conditions: (1) exposure to a hierarchy of items related to snake phobia in a Wolpean systematic desensitization procedure; (2) an automated modeling procedure in which the subject was given training in relaxation and then was shown a film depicting children and adults playing with snakes; (3) a live modeling and guided participation procedure in which the subject first watched through a one-way mirror as the therapist played with the snake; then entered the room and, through gradual steps, touched the snake and eventually held it. In each instance the therapist would model the snake handling and indicate to the subject that he could imitate him when he felt comfortable enough. As the subject increased snake-handling behavior, the therapist gradually faded out his activity; (4) a control group which was pretested and retested but received no intervening treatment.

Each of the three experimental groups received ten treatment sessions. At the completion of treatment each of the subjects was retested with the same attitude scale, fear-survey schedule, and the behavioral task of confrontation with a real snake. In addition to test generalization effects, the confrontation task was repeated with a rat snake of a different color and appearance from the king snake used in the pretest and during treatment.

The results of the study were clear and unequivocal. The live modeling and guided participation procedure was significantly more effective than either the film model or desensitization procedures, both of which were significantly better than no treatment. In fact, each of the subjects in the live model procedure reached the last item in the confrontation task and was able to sit in a chair with his hands at his side and allow the snake to be placed in his lap and crawl on him for 30 seconds.

The investigators next took an unusual and important step. In each instance in which a subject in the desensitization and film model procedures was not "cured," i.e., was unable to achieve the final task, they trained him by means of the live model and guided participation task. By doing this they achieved 100 percent "cures," i.e., in every instance the subject was able to allow the snake to crawl on him for 30 seconds.

Of equal importance to the theoretical issues involved, the investigators found significant subsequent change in attitudes about snakes that was related to the changed behavior. Modeling procedures effected attitude change more than did desensitization procedures. Further, the range and intensity of general fears decreased more sharply in the two modeling groups than in the desensitization and control groups.

The investigators concluded that a powerful treatment procedure is strong enough to eliminate possible therapist differences (they used two experimenters of different sex) even though most of the subjects had expressed an initial conviction that the treatment procedures would not help them. A six-month follow-up indicated that all subjects (including the controls who had been subsequently brought to the point of terminal behavior by the live modeling method) reported that the fear of snakes continued to be absent as evidenced by specific incidents of contact with snakes.

This study illustrates several of the important points about behavior modification procedures.

1. Procedures involving techniques that elicit overt behavior from the subject are most effective. In this instance, although no specific social reinforcement was given by the experimenter for the subject's handling the snake, it may be surmised that the subjects reacted to their own specific bits of behavior with self-reinforcement.
2. Behavior change has important consequences for subsequent attitudes. Attitudes about concepts such as snakes change *after* behavior toward the snakes has changed.
3. The change in this behavior, the fear of snakes, was brought about without any reference to the possible origins of snake phobia. Whether the fear of snakes was learned by traumatic incident, whether it was picked up from parental attitudes, whether it was inherent, or whether it was symbolic of sexual difficulties was irrelevant to successful treatment.
4. Although behavior was treated directly without any effort to "get at" underlying causes, there was no evidence of symptom substitution.

EVALUATIONS OF PSYCHOTHERAPY EFFECTIVENESS

As pointed out earlier, one of the reasons for the development of behavior therapy was disillusionment with the effectiveness of evocative psychotherapy. Evaluations by Eysenck (1952, 1961b) are typical. Based on a review of outcome studies, Eysenck concluded that:

... all methods of psychotherapy fail to improve on the recovery rate obtained through ordinary life experiences and nonspecific treatment. What is even more conclusive, we have found that short methods of treatment based on an alternative hypothesis are significantly more successful in treating neurotic disorders than is psychotherapy of the psychoanalytic type. This alternative method is based on a point of view which regards neurotic disorders as conditioned responses or learnt habits which are non-adaptive, but which are persistent because they are constantly receiving reinforcement. Like all other habits they are subject to extinction according to rules elaborated by modern learning theory and sufficiently well understood to make possible deductions which can be tested experimentally.

Eysenck's data, Saenger (1970), Schorer et al. (1968), and Rachman (1971) on the same subject, and Levitt's (1957, 1963) data on children indicate that within two years two-thirds of all neuroses are likely to "remit" (improve) without professional intervention. But this does not mean that improvement just "happens" by luck, chance, or unknown forces. The environment is never static. Jersild and Holmes (1935) reported the methods used by parents to combat their children's fears (see Chapter 2). Stevenson (1961) gleaned the literature for examples of "spontaneous" remissions. A spontaneous remission implies that there is a disease that has run its course and that the patient is restored to his former (healthy) status without external intervention. The illness apparently "just goes away." The operational definition of spontaneous remission is "change with no professional intervention." Through parents, friends, and circumstances the person comes into contact with new stimuli and makes new responses. Further, a person may eventually be unable to avoid stimuli, and this may set the stage for extinction. He may be presented the stimuli in a slow progression and in a new and pleasanter context—in effect, desensitization in practice (see Chapter 14). In short, *behavior modification as teaching and learning is part of the normal environment.*[7]

One of the objectives of therapy research, then, is to attempt to demonstrate that the process of therapy does change behavior more effectively than no professional treatment during the same period of time. This may be in terms of a faster recovery or a higher percentage of people recovering or both. Next, placebo effects must be taken into account to indicate whether it is the contact with the healer alone or what the healer does that is the helping factor. Studies investigating the outcome of therapy, therefore, must use experimental designs that test the effectiveness of specific procedures against other procedures or no treatment at all (see Chapter 3).

Cross (1964) reviewed evaluation studies of traditional psychotherapy that used control groups. He found only nine such studies in existence, six of which were interpreted as showing a positive effect of therapy. However, Cross cautioned that the treatment in these studies was, for the most part, quite brief or superficial; measurement techniques were of questionable or unproven validity; and, in some studies (Rogers and Dymond, 1954), the method of control itself was questionable. Cross concluded that "while psychotherapy is probably the most popular single area of specialization within psychology (not to mention psychiatry) its efficacy has not been scientifically demonstrated beyond reasonable doubt. Still opinion is strong among psychotherapists that they help their patients." (1964, p. 416.) Fiske et al. (1970) reiterated Cross's point about psychotherapy research: "We have little systematic experimental knowledge of psychotherapy, of its effectiveness, and of the factors facilitating its effects." (p. 727.)

Luborsky et al. (1971) surveyed the fac-

---

[7] Schorer (1970, p. 160) noted: "Improvement is attributed by treated patients to improved understanding, and by the untreated to the practice of self-help."

tors influencing the outcome of psychotherapy from 166 quantitative studies. The largest number of significant factors dealt with the type of patient, and relatively few with the therapist or treatment. There was little in the way of what the therapist did, i.e. different procedures, that had an impact. The patient variables which were related to improvement were being better adjusted to begin with, being more motivated, more intelligent, and having higher social achievements. Other than being anxious, the patient with the most favorable prognosis for improvement was the one who needed treatment least. Combined with the absence of significant treatment factors, the survey is an indictment of evocative forms of treatment. In an independent survey (not cited by Luborsky et al., 1971), Goldman and Mendelsohn (1969) also found that psychotherapists felt they worked best with a patient who exhibits little disturbance. These authors noted that social adjustment seemed the most generally favored criterion for evaluating outcome.

Studies investigating the effects of psychotherapy by follow-up of the behavior of subjects over a period of time usually run into methodological difficulties. Paul (1967b) points out the problems that have hampered follow-up studies: differing pre- and post-treatment methods of assessment (Sinett, Stimpert, and Straight, 1965); the use of assessment procedures of questionable validity and reliability (Cooper, Gelder, and Marks, 1965; Schmidt, Castell, and Brown, 1965); the failure to use an appropriate no-treatment control group in assessing behavior change in the absence of treatment (Fiske and Goodman, 1965; Rogers and Dymond, 1954); the uncontrolled nature of what has happened to the subjects (e.g., more treatment for some) in the interim period between termination and the follow-up (Braceland, 1966); the attrition of the sample through loss of contact with many of the subjects (Fairweather and Simon, 1963); the possible differences that may exist between those individuals who return for a follow-up and those who do not. These considerations, and other methodological problems in measuring the effects of treatment procedures, caused Colby (1964) to summarize the "outcome of psychotherapy" situation with the phrase "utter chaos."

Experimental Evidence of the
Effectiveness of Systematic Desensitization

A clear experimental approach to the comparative effectiveness of differing treatment methods is offered by Paul (1966), who investigated various procedures for alleviating "maladaptive anxiety." The subjects were students who were manifesting "performance anxiety." A specific measurable behavior was selected as the criterion of effectiveness for comparing different treatment procedures. The behavior was "anxiety," but with clear-cut operational definitions. The situation responded to by students with "anxious" behavior was giving a talk to a group of strangers, including psychologists who were evaluating them. The pre- to post-measures included self-report and physiological measures of anxiety as well as overt behavior in the form of a "timed-behavioral checklist for performance anxiety." This last measure consisted of 20 observable "symptoms" of anxiety, such as pacing, swaying, feet shuffling, knees trembling, extraneous arm and hand movements, arms rigid, face flushed, heavy breathing, perspiration or quivering voice, the presence or absence of which were recorded by four trained observers during the first four minutes of a speech presentation.

The subjects were then assigned to one of four groups: (1) insight-oriented psychotherapy; (2) systematic desensitization; (3) attention-placebo; (4) no-treatment control. In addition, there was a fifth no-contact control. Five experienced therapists ("dynamic, and insight oriented" in background) worked individually with three subjects in each of the three treatment groups for five hours over a period of six weeks. On completion of treatment, the people in the three treatment and the no-treatment control groups again presented a speech, and measures of self-report and physiological and behavioral anxiety were obtained.

The first treatment group, "insight-oriented psychotherapy," involved the interview approach typically utilized by the experienced therapists in their daily work. Anxiety reduction was attempted through helping the client gain "insight" and self-understanding of the historical and current interpersonal aspects of his problem.

The second group received systematic desensitization in the manner described earlier in this chapter. This new procedure was taught to the therapists, who had had no previous experience with it.

The third group received an "attention placebo." The aim of this condition was to determine the extent of improvement attained by nonspecific social influence treatments such as the subjects' expectation of relief, and the attention, warmth, suggestion, faith, and interest of the therapist. This group was given a "fast-acting tranquilizer" which worked while they were occupied with a "stressful task." The rationale given the subjects was that they were being trained to perform nonanxiously while under stress and that their bodies would develop a tolerance for stress which would carry over to other stressful situations such as making a speech. The "fast-acting tranquilizer" was actually chemically inert.

Two control groups were used: the no-treatment controls were administered all the pre- and post-measures, but received no treatment, and the no-contact controls, who were never seen by the experimenter, received no treatment and were unaware they were part of the study. These latter subjects took a limited self-report test as part of testing during regular classroom hours.

The results indicated that on almost every measure the desensitization group improved significantly more than the other two treatment groups, psychotherapy and attention placebo. These two groups, in turn, improved significantly more than the no-treatment group. For example, on the behavior check list (of overt "anxiety" behavior) 100 percent of the desensitization group improved, as against 60 percent of the insight group, 73 percent of the attention-placebo group, and 24 percent of the no-treatment control group. Comparative figures of "improved" or "much improved," based on change in all three measures used, were: desensitization, 100 percent; insight, 47 percent; attention placebo, 47 percent; and no-treatment control, 17 percent. Further, these effects were maintained on a six-week and two-year (Paul, 1967a) follow-up. There was no evidence of symptom substitution either immediately after the study or on the two-year follow-up. An interesting and important finding (confirming the importance of expectation and the social-psychological nature of experiments as touched on in Chapter 5) was that the no-treatment controls who were part of the study improved somewhat and in some cases significantly more than the no-contact controls.

Paul concluded that (1) working with people in a psychotherapeutic setting does produce greater reductions of anxiety than no treatment; (2) in the absence of treatment for anxiety, one semester of attendance in a speech course does not result in significant reduction in interpersonal performance anxiety; (3) the nonspecific effects of relationship, attention suggestion, and expectation of benefit produce as much measurable anxiety reduction as gaining "insight" and increased self-understanding; (4) treatment based on psychological principles, specifically systematic desensitization was the most effective way to treat anxiety of a social–evaluative nature. Kondas (1967) and Woy and Efran (1972) are examples of replication of Paul's findings.

SUMMARY

This chapter discussed various approaches to the modification of behavior. The contributions of Sullivan, Rogers, and encounter therapists were introduced. Behavior modification involves the application of a broad range of psychological principles to changeworthy behavior. Behavior therapy was compared with evocative psychotherapy in terms of rational and procedure.

All therapies have major common elements. Behavior therapy is not one specific technique, but rather the direct training of individuals in ways to alter their behavior. Behavior therapy involves the application of the appropriate techniques to a particular individual at a particular time. It is characterized by deductions from a psychological model, deliberate use of social influence, direct treatment, focus on current events maintaining behavior, and active therapist behavior. Behavior therapy may be summarized as the programming of situations and contingencies to alter an individual's response to enivronmental stimuli. Because behavior therapy is a form of teaching, the behavior therapist is far from cold or "mechanical," and his student is anything but passive.

Enduring issues in all therapies—responsibility, the role of insight, attitude change preceding or following behavior change, and use of theory in practice—were discussed. Behavior modification, including both evocative therapy and behavior therapy, is currently in a period of new ideas and tumultuous debate—a period that is confusing, exciting, challenging, and hopeful.

neurosis I
MAJOR ROLE-PLAYING COMPONENTS
13

This chapter starts a review of behavior labeled abnormal. For a first definition of the sample of behaviors to be discussed, we will use the diagnostic systems of the American Psychiatric Association. We will refer to both DSM-I and DSM-II. While DSM-II is the system currently used, DSM-I frequently provides a more detailed definition and, given the publication lag, was the system in use at the time of much of the literature on which this volume draws.

Throughout the following chapters, we will first give the category and its DSM definition. We will then specify the behaviors under discussion, how they may develop, and how they may be changed. We will thus integrate treatment with description. Since we will cover as many different treatment techniques as we can, new procedures will be introduced for various behaviors. It is crucial, however, that the reader not think that each treatment procedure is specific to a category of behavior. In the very fundamental aspect of considering people rather than abstract categories, each person is assessed individually and the method that is most appropriate is used.

We have chosen to start with the category of neurosis because of its important historical role and the amount of material written about it by both psychoanalysts and behaviorists.

DSM-II: DEFINITIONS AND GENERAL COMMENTS

"Anxiety is the chief characteristic of the neuroses. It may be felt and expressed directly, or it may be controlled unconsciously and automatically by conversion, displacement, and various other psychological mechanisms. Generally, these mechanisms produce symptoms experienced as subjective distress from which the patient desires relief.

"The neuroses, as contrasted to the psychoses, manifest neither gross distortion or misinterpretation of external reality, nor gross personality disorganization. . . .

"Traditionally, neurotic patients, however severely handicapped by their symptoms, are not classified as psychotic because they are aware that their mental functioning is disturbed." [DSM-II, 1968, p. 39.]

A number of features of this definition require comment. First, the category was changed from "psychoneurotic disorders" in DSM-I to "neuroses," and the subcategories from "reactions" (e.g., phobic reaction) to "neuroses" (e.g., phobic neuroses") in order to remain neutral in the debate as to whether the etiology was organic-genetic as opposed to functional-psychoanalytic. The definition, however, with its use of concepts of unconscious and automatic mechanisms such as conversion, displacement, and the like, adopts the psychoanalytic view.

A second general point is that while "anxiety is the chief characteristic," anxiety is not defined. DSM-I (1952, pp. 31–32) did provide such a definition:

Anxiety in psychoneurotic disorders is a danger signal felt and perceived by the conscious portion of the personality. It is produced by a threat from within the personality (e.g., by supercharged repressed emotions, including such aggressive impulses as hostility and resentment), with or without stimulation from such external situations as loss of love, loss of prestige, threat of injury.

For a further discussion of the unconscious, repression, anxiety, and personality in the Freudian theory, see Chapter 9.

A last point deals with the differentiation of neuroses from psychoses. While the definition of psychoses has been made more restrictive in DSM-II (see Chapter 1, Overview of Categories), the majority of people who are hospitalized and called psychotic are aware that their mental functioning is, if not actually disturbed, at least considered disturbed. On the other hand, people categorized as severely neurotic respond in terms of fears that are not considered appropriate to the present situation and therefore misinterpret reality. Further, attention to selected aspects of the environment, those which fit and make more sensible their previously determined course of behavior, may also lead to dogmatic, difficult-to-change concepts that the naïve observer considers unrealistic. The statement in DSM-II as to the differentiation of neurosis from psychosis is therefore oversimplified.

The subcategories of neuroses in DSM-II are called anxiety, hysterical, phobic, obsessive-compulsive, depressive, neurasthenic, depersonalization, and hypochondriacal. If a person shows a combination of patterns, that is, mixed neurosis, he is diagnosed according to the preponderant symptom. There is no mention of how one determines which behavior pattern is predominant, and this may reduce the reliability of diagnosis.

General Approach

In Chapter 4, we described how learning has been roughly divided into operant and respondent types, although the two are intertwined and occur at the same time or in sequence—for example, a person performing voluntary acts to avoid involuntary autonomic responses. Because we must present the material in some sequence, and *not* because the distinctions are absolute, the neuroses will be divided into groups on the basis of the importance of social role and operant learning. We will start with hysterical and depressive behavior in this chapter, and in the next focus on phobic and obsessive-compulsive behavior, in which one may more frequently observe respondent behavior. However, even in these behaviors, respondents may occur when the person does not have the operants to deal effectively with a situation, and operants may occur to avoid respondents. The distinction is pedagogical and organizational rather than empirical.

HYSTERICAL NEUROSIS

DSM-I offered the two separate subcategories of "conversion reaction" and "dissociative reaction," while DSM-II categorizes both as "types" or further subdivisions of hysterical neurosis. Because of the strong role-playing components in both conversion and dissociation, we (Ullmann and Krasner, 1969, p. 273) and authors such as West (1967, p. 890) consider this an advance. Historically, the two labels have been difficult to separate; Puységur, Charcot, and Freud used behaviors during hypnosis as a model for both hysterical and dissociative reactions (see Chapters 5 and 8), and Janet's concept of dissociation played a role in his formulation of both categories. The major reason for placing the two categories together, however, is that the actual behaviors emitted by people so labeled are strikingly similar: they involve the voluntary musculature and may be formulated as role enactments that have been modeled or shaped and that are maintained by reinforcement.

Hysterical Behavior: Definitions

DSM-II defines hysterical neurosis as "characterized by an involuntary psychogenic loss or disorder of function. Symptoms characteristically begin and end suddenly in emotionally charged situations and are symbolic of the underlying conflicts." (DSM-II, p. 39.) DSM-II proceeds to divide the hysterical neurosis into *conversion* and *dissociative* types.

In the conversion type, the special senses or voluntary nervous system are affected, causing such symptoms as blindness, deafness, anosmia (loss of sense of smell—ED.), anaestehesias, paresthesias (abnormal sensations such as itching—ED.), paralyses, ataxias (loss of muscular coordination—ED.), akinesias (impaired voluntary movement—ED.), and dyskinesias (difficulty in performing voluntary movements—ED.). Often the patient shows an inappropriate lack of concern or *belle indifférence* about these symptoms which may actually provide him secondary gain[1] by winning him sympathy or relieving him of unpleasant responsibilities. [DSM-II, pp. 39–40.]

The conversion type of neurosis is distinguished from psychophysiological difficulties in that the former involves the voluntary nervous system whereas the latter involves the autonomic nervous system. It also differs from malingering "which is done consciously" (DSM-II, p. 40), and from neurological lesions, that is, true biophysiological or medical disorders that lead to loss of function.[2]

[1] The words "secondary gain" refer to a psychoanalytic formulation in which the primary gain is the reduction of intrapsychic conflict and/or anxiety. Once the impulses have achieved indirect, symbolic gratification—that is, the "symptom" has been developed—the new (symptomatic) behavior alters the environment. If the person, excused from certain duties, is the object of sympathy and the like, these results are called "secondary gain" because they are pleasant but were not primary in the formation of the symptom.

[2] In DSM-I, tic, stuttering, Ganser syndrome, and craft palsies such as writer's cramp were considered conversion reactions; in DSM-II, they are placed elsewhere: the first two as special symptoms, the third as a transient situational disturbance, an adjustment reaction of adult life, and the fourth, variously, in one of the two foregoing categories, or as a psychophysiologic, musculoskeletal disorder.

The formal, DSM-II definition of the *dissociative type* of hysterical neurosis notes that "alterations may occur in the patient's state of consciousness or in his identity, to produce such symptoms as amnesia, somnambulism, fugue, and multiple personality." *Hysterical neurosis* involves the voluntary nervous system but the difficulty is supposedly "involuntary." People emitting hysterical behavior manifest no physiological or anatomical changes that would explain their disfunctions. However, these people "cannot" move various limbs, "cannot" feel various sensations such as pain, and "cannot" see, hear, or speak. On examination, it is determined that not only is there no physical cause but also the pattern of symptoms is such as to be "physiological nonsense." Physical structures do not parallel the loss of physical function these people manifest. Individuals may manifest various anesthetic "bands," not unlike sweat bands, bracelets, or belts. Such phenomena simply do not make any sense in terms of the distribution of nerve endings. Similarly, a person may have a paralysis of the hand terminating sharply and completely at the wrist or an arm paralysis terminating sharply and completely at the shoulder.[3]

Ganser syndrome is manifested when a person acts in an extravagantly bizarre manner, like the stereotype of a psychotic rather than the clinical actuality. It usually occurs when an individual is imprisoned for a crime or awaiting the death sentence. The person may give incorrect but approximate answers to questions; for example, six times six is 37, Columbus discovered America in 1491. Psychotics either do not respond or answer questions dealing with nonthreatening, over-learned material correctly. Ganser syndrome is rare but challenging since it pushes the limits of the distinction between malingering and "true" mental illness. It seems, in this case, that having a recognized label, such as Ganser syndrome, makes the difference.

[3] A major effort to increase the precision of the label hysteria is by Woodruff, Guze, and their colleagues. The three basic criteria they offer are: (1) The person must demonstrate a dramatic or complicated medical history beginning before age 35; (2) the person must admit to 25 symptoms in nine of ten special review-of-symptom areas; and (3) no other diagnosis can be made to explain the

Here, then, is a conceptual problem. Are these people faking? If one says, "No, they are not faking," then how can one explain their behavior? A possible explanation is that there is a disease or, analogous to a disease, an underlying conflict. Freud, whose theory is in the current definition, carried this further. The person is not malingering because the symptom is the resolution of an *unconscious* conflict over which he has no control.[4]

In *dissociative neurosis,* by tradition, "The four classical dissociative reactions are fugue, amnesia, somnambulism, and multiple personality." (West, 1697, p. 885.) *Fugue* is the leaving of one's present life situation and the establishment of a somewhat different mode of life in another locale; the person manifesting a fugue reaction is *amnesic* for his prior mode of life, that is, he does not remember it. *Somnambulism* is sleepwalking and *multiple personality* is the enactment of two or more relatively independent or inconsistent social roles (in other terms, the development of two or more independent personality systems, which are inferred from the behavior).

With the exception of sleepwalking, the manifestations of dissociative reaction are relatively rare. Abse (1966) found 200 documented cases in the psychiatric literature. Sleepwalking is currently being studied by investigators interested in the more general problem of sleep itself (Luce and Segal, 1966). Gastaut and Broughton (1964) offer data that it is not dreaming but deeper stages of sleep in which such nighttime motor behavior occurs, while Broughton (1968) pinpoints confusional states of arousal rather than dreaming sleep as the most likely time for somnambulism and nightmares. There is ample evidence (Luce and Segal, 1966, pp. 134–35) that the sleepwalker, contrary to tradition, may well hurt himself. Many cases of sleepwalking may be closely associated with neurological abnormalities and may not be dissociative reactions in the context of psychogenic disorders.

In the roles taken in both fugue and multiple personality, individuals behave with relative appropriateness and do not manifest psychotic symptoms. Many students have difficulty with the notion that a form of dissociative neurosis (e.g., multiple personality) is a neurosis, while the literal definition of schizophrenia, a psychosis, is split personality. The key distinction is that none of the roles played in dissociative neuroses are psychotic and that the major mechanisms presumed to be involved, repression and dissociation, are neurotic.[5]

One way to deal conceptually with dissociative behaviors, as with conversion, is to say that the person is malingering or faking. Another possibility, as with hysteria, is to say that the other "personality" represents repressed impulses that strive for expression: for example given fixation or repression, a weakened ego, and intrapsychic conflicts, situational stimuli may arouse (or re-arouse) anxieties. The person,

---

symptoms. (Woodruff, 1967; Guze, 1967.) This procedure may have usefulness for prediction and prevalence studies (e.g., Farley, Woodruff, and Guze, 1968; Woodruff, Clayton, and Guze, 1969), but it may also be confusing when some people who show the behaviors discussed under the traditional label do not meet the criteria.

[4] Freud's early theories of hysteria involved ideas and feelings that were unacceptable to the individual and hence split off from the mainstream of consciousness to spare him the pain of recognizing his less than perfectly honorable tendencies. Further early work led Freud to hypothesize that every hysterical woman had been sexually molested as a child, usually by the father or a close relative. When further observations conflicted with this theory, Freud was led to formulate his previous observations as indicative of the strength of fantasies. In the resulting formulation, hysteria was conceived of "as a specific clinical entity arising from specific sexual conflicts originating in the oedipal period of psychosexual adjustment." (Nemiah, 1967a, p. 875.)

[5] For treatment of "multiple personality" in a man also called schizophrenic, see Kohlenberg (1973) who used differential reinforcement to manipulate rate of behavior in the manifestation of each personality.

no longer able to control previously repressed impulses, acts on them. In this formulation, as with conversion, the behavior is unconsciously determined. To quote Noyes and Kolb (1963, p. 429), "In the fugue the patient indulges in acts or fantasies that are in conflict with his superego, and the function of the fugue is to permit the carrying out of these acts or fantasies."

A Behavioral Reformulation

Hysteria represents a set of behaviors that have been described since the time of the ancient Greeks and Egyptians (Veith, 1965). "Hysteria" derives from the Greek word for uterus. "There were suggestions that deprivations of sexual relations led to a drying up of the uterus which, as it lost weight, would rise up and wander through the body in search of moisture and humidity, thereby causing various symptoms depending on where the organ settled." (Small, 1969.) The manner in which hysteria is formulated and treated reflects the models of the era, which may be demonological or medical (Veith, 1965; McCulloch, 1969; Cleghorn, 1969a).

Hysterical behaviors are often quite restricted. Ironside and Batchelor (1945) noted that the hysterical visual symptoms of pilots were closely related to performance duties. Night fliers more often developed failing day vision. The traditional example of the restrictive nature of hysterical responses are what have been called the craft palsies. For example, violinists may develop paralysis in bowing their instruments but be able to make normal use of the same muscle groups in nonmusical activities such as playing tennis.

Another aspect of hysteria is that the manifestations vary among historical periods and within given times and places, and depend to some extent upon the medical sophistication, or lack thereof, of the people. For example, Proctor (1958) found that out of 191 consecutive cases diagnosed at the University of North Carolina Medical School Psychiatric Unit, 25 cases, or 13 per cent, were hysterical. Not only was this an extraordinarily high percentage, but the cases were more florid than those usually observed at present in the United States. Proctor looked at his case records and found that some of his patients came from the back country or "tobacco road" areas of the South characterized by religious fanaticism, rigid upbringing of children, and great restrictiveness in pleasure. In short, Proctor had drawn his classical, but no longer common, forms of hysteria from a group that was different from and, in many ways, decades behind the knowledge of the larger society. Observations by Weinstein, Eck, and Lyerly (1969) in Appalachia support Proctor and emphasize the cultural and communication aspects of the behavior. Similarly, the hysterical behaviors labeled shell shock in World War I were rarely seen in World War II and Korea, but Cardin and Schramel (1966) report a possible increase in Viet Nam.

This pattern of observing a model and attending to bodily sensations that are usually ignored may well underlie other "epidemics" of hysterical behavior (Schuler and Parenton, 1943; Hendriksen and Oeding, 1940; Johnson, 1945; Huxley, 1952; Jacobs, 1965; Kerchoff, Back and Miller, 1965; Knight, Friedman, and Sulianti, 1965). In the situations described in these works there were common elements such as vivid, sensationalistic publicity indicating that something important and threatening was happening, or closeness of the victims as fellow members in a factory, convent, or school.

An example of epidemic hysteria follows:

Two years before the outbreak described in the present study, one of the girls in the school became pregnant. She and a fellow-student (the admitted father of her child) were sent to the State Correctional School. Prior to the onset of the present outbreak in the school, a rumor circulated that one or two of the girls were pregnant, and that these girls would be sent to the Correctional School. There had been considerable sexual promiscuity among the students. Some of this, for example, took place at school during lunch time in the photography darkroom. A 14-year-old crippled girl with a very low mental age had had intercourse with more than 30 boys. Another girl, age 15, was found to be pregnant and was requested to leave school. The word circulated that all the girls would be given pregnancy tests, and anxiety swept through the school. The attacks began shortly thereafter. . . .

. . . (following a choir concert) A 13-year-old girl became dizzy, passed out, and was taken home in an unconscious condition. . . . The following day at school, a close friend (age 13) who had witnessed the attack in church had a "blackout spell . . . On March 6, another girl had an attack at school, and two days later a different girl had an attack. By the 22nd of March eight girls were having the blackout spells and by April 3 over 20 girls and one boy were affected. . . . On a few occasions there were as many as seven students having attacks simultaneously.

The students discovered early in the outbreak that those students who were especially influenced and likely to have attacks were those who touched, supported or carried to the lounge some girl who had had a "blackout spell." Thus, they concluded that having an attack was a highly individual thing and would involve only certain ones. On some level they recognized the sexual implications. This became clear when the one male student had a "blackout spell" and the comment swept through the school, "Will he have a boy or girl?" [Knight, Friedman, and Sulianti, 1965, pp. 858–59, 861.]

Kerchoff and Back (1969), discussing a different epidemic episode, provide the following ideas, which are all the more impressive since they fit so well the foregoing quotation:

In cases of hysterical contagion, a number of individuals interact in a common setting (such as school or factory) in an atmosphere of unresolved tension. A belief in the threat adds yet another source of tension—fear . . . Something dramatic happens for which there is no immediate explanation. A person gets sick or goes beserk . . . For the source of threat to be accepted, however, it must have some cultural legitimacy. [Kerchoff and Back, 1969, p. 46.]

A Sociopsychological Formulation of Hysteria

Disturbance of any voluntary activity, whether motor or a report of sensory experience, may be called hysterical. Sydenham, in the late seventeenth century, noted that such phenomena could mimic almost all known diseases (Nemiah, 1967a, p. 871). When the role enactment leads to activities having involuntary nervous system correlates, temperature, respiratory, and digestive changes may also occur.

The basic step is to ascertain what behavior is actually being emitted by the person called hysterical. The person has not really "lost" any motor function such as the ability to walk, or sensory function such as the ability to feel pain or use his eyesight. Rather *the person emits behavior matching his concept of a person who has a disease that affects his motor or sensory abilities.* For example, a person may not use visual cues of which he is physically capable, and he may make greater use of nonvisual cues.

There are, then, two separate questions that need to be answered. The first is whether people are capable of such behavior. If this is answered affirmatively, the second question deals with the specification of the conditions under which people will emit it.

Chapter 5 discussed situations such as placebo, hypnosis, and experimenter bias in which people were neither faking nor unconsciously motivated, but rather responding in socially appropriate ways to the stimuli presented to them. For example, the people who in the Orne and Scheibe (1964) experiment reported "sensory deprivation" effects after being exposed to a number of cues (a medical check-up, signing a waiver, a panic button) could not easily be said to be either faking or unconsciously motivated. A person who spontaneously developed "dominant-hand catalepsy" after observing this phenomenon might well be neither faking nor unconsciously motivated, but rather acting in the manner considered appropriate to the social situation. Of most immediate relevance to hysteria are placebo effects. Considering the Schachter and Singer experiment presented in Chapter 5, a person who has been given a placebo and then emits behavior similar to that of a stooge need not be either faking or unconsciously motivated.

Clinical observations of placebo effects are even more directly applicable to hysterical behavior. It would be difficult to say that a person who is given a placebo after an operation and reports relief from pain is either faking or unconsciously motivated. Rather, such a person is likely to attend to stimuli different from those of a person who has not been given "medication." The person who has had an operation and has been given a placebo is under strong social pressure: on the one hand, he has had previous experiences in which medication has been followed by relief, and, on the other, for him to report a failure in his physician's power to alleviate pain might be frightening since it would cast some doubt on the wisdom and ability of the physician who operated on him. In answer to the first question posed, then, some people can indeed emit behaviors that match the role of loss of motor ability or loss of sensation.

The second question is a specification of the conditions likely to lead to the emission of such behavior. Following the concepts presented in Chapter 10, people responding in the culturally expected or normal nonhysterical manner would have been extinguished or be low in receipt of effective reinforcing stimuli compared to enactment of the behavior categorized as hysterical. Under some conditions "hysterical" behaviors are culturally expected. For example, a person studying diligently may not "hear" his roommate's typewriter if by this is meant that his behavior is not altered by that source of stimulation. Many adolescent and pre-adolescent Americans seem to require a radio tuned to hideous sounds in order to study. Although these children are not much more abnormal than most others of their age, they seem to hear neither their radios nor their fathers' pleas.

Both the development and the treatment of hysterical behaviors, like hypnotic ones, usually call for shaping into the role (chapters 5 and 10). First a person has had prior experience (as actor or audience) with the role. That is, he knows the "lines." Usually people who emit behavior labeled hysterical have either themselves had physiological difficulties of that nature (Fallik and Sigal, 1971) or have observed relatives who had such difficulties. Ziegler, Imboden, and Meyer (1960) note that the ability to simulate symptoms is positively correlated with degree of medical sophistication. Next, the role enactment is reinforced. The person must live in a culture in which the "sick" behavior is accepted. These various generalizations are illustrated by a case of hysterical blindness reported by Brady and Lind (1961). The patient was a 40-year-old veteran. He had two maternal aunts who were totally blind during their last years. He served in the army for three years, and while in England he developed dendritic keratitis of the right eye following a tonsillectomy. Corneal scarring resulted, and the visual acuity of his right eye was reduced to 20/80. Shortly after this he was given a medical discharge from the army and a small pension because of the loss of vision. After release from service the patient held a succession of semiskilled jobs but remained at none for more than a year. He seemed to tolerate responsibility poorly and was very sensitive to criticism. During the twelve years following discharge there were three minor recurrences of his eye infection for which he was treated in hospitals. After each occurrence he applied for additional pension but was refused because there had been no additional loss of vision.

Prior to entering the service the patient had married. "From his description of his married life, one gets the picture of almost constant harassment from his wife and mother-in-law. Nonetheless, he speaks of his wife only in the most endearing terms."

Three days before Christmas, twelve years after leaving the service, while shopping with his wife and mother-in-law he suddenly became totally blind in both eyes. "His wife and mother-in-law were being more demanding than usual, requiring him to work nights and weekends at various chores under their foremanship. One immediate consequence of his blindness was, then, partial escape from this situation."

It is interesting, in the light of Proctor's findings cited above, that the family sought aid from a Fundamentalist minister before taking the man to a hospital. During the following two years the patient received various treatments, including drugs, psychotherapy, and sodium pentothal interviews. Although a diagnosis of hysterical blindness was made, the patient was enrolled in a course of training for the blind and was awarded a special pension for his total disability. In addition he received financial assistance from the community for his children and some money from his relatives.

The clinical picture had much in common with many other people called hysterical: "... the patient did not seem greatly alarmed by his loss of sight, but instead had an attitude of patient forebearance." Nemiah (1961) uses the phrase "hobbling hero" to describe this behavior by a paralyzed man. More generally, this acceptance of "fate" has been called *la belle indifférence*.

The treatment technique used by Brady and Lind was the reinforcement of the patient's use of a visual cue by making approval, avoidance of criticism, and privileges such as trips to the hospital's canteen contingent upon such behavior. The patient was given two sessions a day, five days a week, in which his task was to press a button at 18- to 21-second intervals. A response (button press) 18 to 21 seconds after his previous response (button press) would be reinforced. Errors marked the start of the next 18- to 21-second period, and hence delayed reinforcement. A light went on during the three-second period when a button press would be reinforced. Use of the visual cue permitted a relatively easy way to attain a very high rate of reinforcement. Brady and Lind wrote their first report after the patient had "regained" and used visual cues for thirteen months, read newspapers, and was gainfully employed.[6]

The major interest in the case is the illustration of some of the precursors of the hysterical role. The man had seen blind people and had himself an eye ailment and experienced the benefit of treatment and pension. He had relatively little to lose and much to gain by playing the sick, "blind" role rather than the healthy, "normal" role.

Once the person has made the act, and performed the new role, he cannot easily shift back to his prior role. Playing the role is maintained by immediate benefits such as avoiding unpleasant situations; once emitted, the behavior may also be maintained as avoidance. The person may continue to play the role because not doing so would cast doubt on his prior behavior in that role. This is one reason why a placebo technique may be effective: it gives the person an "out," saves face, and avoids many of the aversive consequences of "giving up" the "sick" behavior

In short, the role behavior called hysterical is the emission of the behavior *like* that of a person who has lost some voluntary function. The words "acting" and "role" imply to many people a concept of "put-on" or "not real." This is unfortunate, because the role enactments of the person labeled hysterical are as real as the role enactments

---

[6] Discussion of the determinants of behavior of this case and the treatment procedure may be found in Grosz and Zimmerman (1965, 1970), Zimmerman and Grosz (1966), and Miller (1968). Stolz and Wolf (1969) report the impact of response contingent reinforcement on a supposedly "blind" adolescent retardate, and thus provide a replication.

of the reader of this book as student, parent, lover, employee, and the like. Each behavior is in response to a situation, and all behaviors emitted are equally real. The "real–unreal" distinction usually pertains to the attributed motivation of the behavior.

To malinger, according to the dictionary, is to fake an illness in order to avoid work. The problem then seems simple: if a person "consciously" takes the role with full awareness of the reinforcing contingencies, he is a malingerer; if he does so "unconsciously" he is sick and hysteric. As previously noted, this distinction cannot serve for phenomena such as hypnosis, placebo, and experimental demand characteristics. Rather, the person responds to situations in terms of his history of reinforcement.

In clinical practice there are a number of rules of thumb for differentiating hysteria from malingering. One of these is that supposedly the hysteric displays no anxiety, having solved his problem and gotten out of the situation. In this regard he is not unlike many men who had been scared during combat but who, after being wounded, even severely wounded, felt remarkably well and displayed far less tension than they had previously. A man with a bullet hole is not considered either a malingerer or a hysteric, but in terms of reinforcing principles the situation is the same. He has a valid medical excuse to retire from danger. Clinically, the hysteric is reported to display *la belle indifférence*; that is, he does not seem upset. The hysteric gladly, voluminously, and endlessly welcomes an opportunity to talk about his symptoms, his physical complaint, and what it is doing to him. The malingerer is likely to perceive an interview with a physician as a challenge and a threat and therefore to be far more guarded. Other descriptions of the hysteric may be used *to see if the picture tallies with the role as it is defined by the professional labeler*. In some measure these subsidiary patterns may be due to the role-playing ability of the "hysteric" in contrast to the "malingerer." The behavioral distinctions boil down to the hysteric's playing a role that is accepted by the labeler.[7]

The behavioral view avoids the dichotomies of sick-healthy, conscious-unconscious, aware-unaware, and faking-real. The focus is the behavior, and the person is treated humanely and realistically as being shaped and reinforced by environmental circumstances. It should not be necessary to require the excuse of illness before treating a person humanely.

CLINICAL OBSERVATIONS AND TREATMENT OF HYSTERIA

The earliest recorded treatment of hysterical behavior is presented by a tablet erected in a Greek temple. A man who was paralyzed in his legs came to the temple with his life savings. He had sat down with his bag of money in front of him when suddenly a young man (possibly a temple acolyte under orders of the priests) dashed along, picked up the bag of money, and ran away. The crippled man got to his feet and gave chase. He was cured and erected a plaque to the god whose timely intervention made it possible for him to give chase. A similar situation is reported by Noyes

[7] Spiro (1968) writes that "Malingering should be only diagnosed in the absence of psychiatric illness and the presence of behavior appropriately adaptive to a clear-cut long-term goal." (p. 569.) Spiro then discusses people who purposely distort their medical histories, produce misleading physical findings, and falsify laboratory findings through self-inflicted wounds. They may subject themselves to painful diagnostic and treatment procedures, which in turn may lead to permanent physical changes and problems. The pattern is rare and Spiro noted 38 cases in the medical literature. Such "Hospital Hoboes," "Hospital Addicts," or people displaying Munchaussen's syndrome, because of severity, duration over time, and consistency with a labeler's categories, like the Ganser syndrome, are considered as not malingering.

and Kolb (1963, p. 433): "One patient who developed hysterical mutism in prison dreamed that the institution for mental diseases to which he had been transferred was on fire, whereupon he screamed and thereafter talked normally."

The placebo reaction was mentioned as a model for the development of behavior which might be labeled hysterical. The following is a description of a form of placebo used deliberately as a treatment by a Soviet physician:

We use a form of indirect suggestion psychotherapy to remove the fixated symptoms of hysteria, otherwise unyielding to ordinary methods. A week before treatment starts, the patient is informed at considerable length that his illness is functional in character, distinguished by conversion phenomena. The patient is assured, however, that he is to be treated in a manner that will be of considerable help. After spending several days in expectation of the "medication" intended to remove the symptoms of his ailment, the patient is conducted to the treatment room and invited to lie down on a couch. He is then informed that the "medication" will be poured slowly on a special mask and assimilated by his organism by means of breathing in the evaporated drug. He is further assured that the substance brings no unpleasant reaction whatsoever, such as nausea, or headache. These remarks help considerably to avoid any possible complication arising in auto-suggestion. The patient is then told, in a manner well-adjusted to the level of his education, that he will feel much better, that the symptoms of his disease are a product of cortical inhibition and that the drug being a powerful stimulating substance, is intended to remove the inhibition. It is explained, for instance, that the patient's hyperkinesis is determined by excitation of brain cells, and that the drug, by calming the nervous system, puts them back into a normal state.

Immediately after this, a registered nurse begins to pour, drop by drop, some aromatic liquid, such as menthol dissolved in alcohol, on the mask already on the patient's face. The whole procedure of treatment takes no more than ten minutes. In the meantime, a discussion is conducted with some other physician concerning the effectiveness of the treatment, with which the latter concurs. They point out that the drug has an excellent effect on the nervous system and is capable of removing many pathological manifestations. No remarks are addressed directly to the patient; from the very beginning of the treatment he remains a passive listener to the conversation conducted only between the two physicians: the conversation is actually a question of indirect suggestion.

This method of treatment has been used by us for a great variety of symptoms, including hysterical contracture, hyperkinesis, partial paralysis, astasia-abasia [inability to stand or walk without legs wobbling or collapsing, although the patient has normal control while sitting or lying down], mutism and persistent vomiting. [Schreiber, 1962, pp. 85–86.]

Schreiber goes on to ask (p. 88): "An important question of principle must not be disregarded in connection with this method of indirect suggestion therapy. To what extent is medical ethics compatible with the use of an indifferent substance while it is supposed to be a valuable medication?

"In each concrete case, the physician must decide for himself as to the method of treatment. In indirect suggestion therapy, the physician's words are of great and real benefit to the patient. Is it right to abstain from uttering them? Is it right to leave the patient sick when he can be cured?"

A common form of behavior therapy, shaping, is illustrated in the treatment of aphonia (the person does not talk in a normal voice) by Bangs and Freidinger (1949). A 13-year-old girl had been aphonic for seven years. There were no ostensible precipitating causes, and during this period of time, from six to thirteen, she had talked briefly once while recovering from anesthesia for a tonsillectomy and she had laughed aloud after chiropractic therapy. There had been only slight improvement of speech under hypnosis and there had been no carryover after termination of the trance. Bangs and Freidinger report that the greatest difficulty was keeping the girl interested and reinforced. They used praise such as telling her how ingenious she was. They started by asking her to breathe deeply. This is something which is an "easy" thing to do, and which does not seem relevant or particularly threatening in terms of being aphonic.

For the girl not to have cooperated with the breathing exercises would have been for her to deny her role of being sick and cooperative with the physicians' suggestions. The therapists next asked the girl to move from breathing exercises to exhaling and humming. The girl was asked to make a humming sound. From humming, the girl was asked to hum consonants, especially sounds such as "m." After consonants, the assignments went to words, then to reading, and then conversation. Each successive step was small and not to have taken it would have been a violation of the sick role and contradictory to her previous behaviors. "The entire therapy covered a period of ten and a half weeks. Follow-up interviews revealed no new conversion symptoms, and two years following discharge the patient was still maintaining vocalization."

A similar example of shaping is provided by Walton and Black (1959). In addition this case illustrates three major points. First, as in the Bangs and Freidinger case, there was no evidence of symptom substitution. Second, the behavior had been chronic and had lasted seven years. Third, because of the great amount of treatment which had been unsuccessful, there was some indication that the behavioral approach was more than a placebo. The patient was a female, in her mid-twenties, from a broken home, whose mother was a thief if not worse. She had had a minor throat operation at age seventeen and shortly thereafter lost her voice. At the time of treatment, she had been aphonic for seven years and completely mute for two. She had had no remission after intensive psychotherapy, hypnosis, insulin, ether and methedrin abreaction, narcoanalysis, and LSD. Avoiding the home situation and possibly the undesirable attentions from her mother's male friends might have reinforced being sick. The behavior was further maintained by the interest and attention of professional people.

The treatment used involved shaping and reactive inhibition. The woman was not particularly "intellectual." She was asked to read for fifteen minutes from an uninteresting volume. She first had to mouth the words with no sound. Next she was asked to whisper the words. At each step, if she did not read loudly enough, she was asked to read more. That is, reading loudly enough now led to an immediate reinforcement, the termination of a dull task. Once she was reading at a certain volume, the number of people present was increased and there was reading of plays with other people. There was generalization to the ward. The authors describe the result as follows: "She talked to patients and staff alike without fatigue and without any limits to the amounts she spoke." The woman was seen periodically after discharge, and was found not only to be earning her own living but to have improved further in regard to speech. On the job she was observed shouting. In addition, during the next twenty months, she met two stressful interpersonal situations without relapse or new difficulties.[8]

[8] At times it is hard to decide whether an elective mute person—one who has good ability at language but a very low rate of talk—is to be categorized as psychotic or hysteric. Good further examples to the ones detailed above are by Wulbert et al. (1973), Norman and Broman (1970), Neale and Liebert (1969), and Reid et al. (1967). The point is that the type of intervention here described has been effectively used in a variety of settings and the results replicated by different people. Falling between the shaping of the mute catatonic by Isaacs, Thomas, and Goldiamond (1960) described in Chapter 4 are the treatment of children who may not have the social skills (Blake and Moss, 1967) or the incentive (Calhoun and Koenig, 1973) to speak. The formulation of the behavior and treatment in these cases may draw heavily on work dealing with "performance anxiety" (e.g., the work by Paul on public speaking presented in Chapter

The complex, sequential and multitechnique approach of most clinical work is illustrated by Meichenbaum (1966a). Mr. S was a 43-year-old man with a high school education whose difficulty was an inability to keep his eyes open. This behavior, which had become severe during the previous six weeks, occurred most frequently at home and occasionally at work. During the preceding two years, however, Mr. S had sought help from various opticians and a chiropractor. Mr. S thought his problem physical; difficulties in his life, however, centered around friction with his mother and wife. The first therapeutic tactic involved general bodily relaxation. Mr. S was seen for an hour a day for two weeks; during this time he was encouraged to take deep breaths, inhaling and exhaling slowly. He was told that this would relax his body and as he exhaled, his eyes would open. After this period, Mr. S was more relaxed, managed to keep his eyes open 75 percent of the time, and was able to leave the hospital. During the next month, Mr. S was seen eight times as an outpatient. The therapeutic tactic at this point involved the pairing of relaxation with visualization of opening his eyes in the mornings. After this period, Mr. S was able to return to work. Mr. S reported that he continued to close his eyes when confronted with an important decision or when his wife, mother, or employer tried to dominate him. In order to replace passive behavior with more realistic, assertive behavior, role-playing was undertaken. Mr. S was seen once a week for three additional months. He and the therapist rehearsed responses to situations in which Mr. S would present his wife, mother, and employer with his own ideas and beliefs.

Three months after the last of these sessions, Mr. S had obtained a better job and had resolved with his wife a problem about the religious training of their son which had been a major issue. What is a "symptom" according to a sociopsychological model depends on the observer; the therapist reported no evidence of symptom substitution. The wife, however, who was pleased about her husband's ability to keep his eyes open and return to work, "was mildly upset by her husband's recently acquired assertive behavior, e.g., he expressed his ideas and feelings more forcefully and on one occasion raised his voice to her." From the wife's point of view, this may well have been symptom substitution.[9]

A Reformulation of
Dissociative Behavior

A sociopsychological approach to dissociative behavior is similar to the one used in hysteria. Hypnosis again provides an analogue to the behavior under discussion. As the reader will recall, Puységur was working with a peasant boy who, under the conditions of the hypnotist's repetitious stroking, instructions, and calm voice, went to sleep. The boy opened his eyes and moved around, but his attention still seemed focused. In short, he acted like a somnambulist. It is from this incident that a great deal of work, including that of Charcot and Janet, developed.

As detailed in Chapter 5, hypnosis may be conceived of as appropriate role-playing rather than some special state discontinuous with "normal" behavior. As with hypnosis, not to accept such a formulation would pose a complex physiological problem: it would be necessary to explain how a person

---

12) or, more generally, the avoidance behaviors leading to the designation of phobia discussed in the next chapter.

[9] Additional illustrations of behavioral formulation and treatment of hysterical behaviors may be obtained from Clark (1963b), Malmo, Davis, and Barza (1952), Sears and Cohen (1933), Beyme (1964), and Brierley (1967); Liebson (1969), Parry-Jones, Santer-Wetstrate, and Crawley (1970), and Keehn, Kuechler, and Wilkinson (1973). Additionally, Hersen et al. (1972) reported on the effects of social reinforcement on walking behavior, and Bhattacharyya and Singh (1971) reported on the effects of aversive stimuli on hysterical "fits."

so massively brain injured as to forget his name can during a fugue enact social roles that include supporting himself for months; and, if he is brain injured, how he can forget and then remember such a great quantity of material. Similarly, the individual with multiple personality may shift from one personality to another rapidly. At times one "personality" may be aware of another. This is analogous to posthypnotic suggestion, and both phenomena seem parsimoniously and effectively dealt with as role-playing.

There is a limit to one's attention span, and response is usually made to only a limited number of the cues in the situation. Almost by definition normal people are, to some extent, dissociated. The appropriate roles of a college student in the classroom, at a dance, a football game, or working after school are all different. In each situation the person wears different clothes, responds to different cues, emits different behaviors. A student in a large lecture raises his hand before he speaks, calls the other person "sir," and thereafter provides learned references, arguments, and observations. The student would be well advised not to act this way on a date or in his fraternity house. The language used in the locker room is seldom emitted in the presence of one's mother. *It is a matter of normality to play different roles.* When responding appropriately, the person attends to some cues and not to others, and emits some acts in his repertoire and not others. It may frequently happen that aspects of one role may be extremely disruptive during other role enactments. Professors having to grade exams do better to think of maintaining the Standards of the University and the Profession than of their training, which teaches them to "love thy neighbor as thyself," "to suffer little children," and that though they have the gift of prophecy and understand all mysteries and all knowledge, without charity they are nothing.

In addition to enacting different roles and yet reacting within broad, socially normal limits within each role, there is in the textbook view of dissociative behavior the implication that the person is not conscious of his other behavior patterns. The limitations of attention span, noted in preceding paragraphs, provide a theoretical basis for such a phenomenon. Hypnosis offers an example devoid of concepts of either faking or unconscious intrapsychic conflicts. Weitzenhoffer (1953, p. 99) strongly suggests that hypnotic rapport is a form of restricted awareness associated hypersuggestibility to some or all the stimuli in the range of awareness and that, conversely, when properly established, the hypnotic situation can limit an individual's awareness to the point of excluding certain stimuli from it. In more general terms, certain stimuli are no longer meaningful and are no more attended to than the number of individual steps in a staircase, while other stimuli, to which the individual did not previously react overtly, are functionally effective. The person manifesting behavior labeled fugue or multiple personality may be considered to have altered his allegiance in the manner of a convert to a new social movement whose selective attention and inattention are a function of altered reinforcing contingencies.

Illustrative Cases

Mr. X, reported in Dorcus and Shaffer (1945, pp. 376–377), was a 35-year-old businessman who left home on a business trip. Efforts to locate him were unsuccessful until three days later, when he was found in a town two hundred miles away. He was able to recall the details of his fugue, and this is what happened: He reported having had an affair with a married woman and feared exposure by her husband. Two days before the fugue, an anonymous letter advised him that he was in danger. Just before his departure for a business meeting, he was puzzled by a phone call that someone had apparently initiated without completing. Next, when he was driving downtown, he noticed that the driver of the car directly behind him was the husband of his lady friend. The three-day fugue ensued.

In another case a businessman who had been a pillar of his community manifested a fifteen-month fugue state. He had not liked his home situation and had become discontented with his marriage. Under hypnosis he "learned" that during the fugue he had worked as a laborer at a chemical plant. It was the same job he had held summers when he had worked his way through college, and, as in those days, he "led a frivolous, unrestrained, bohemian life," frequenting bars and cocktail lounges. Some of these incidents were such that, as a Sunday school superintendent, he felt called upon to blush.

Another famous case of fugue is that of Rou, described by Janet (1920, pp. 51–53). Rou was a 17-year-old grocer's boy who lived with his mother in Paris. He was mild-mannered, nervous, passive, and unambitious. On occasion after work, Rou would visit a nearby tavern where sailors made him tipsy and told him fantastic stories of their travels. Rou manifested brief fugues, especially after drinking. On one occasion, however, he was missed and not heard from for several months. During this time he worked his way down to the south of France doing odd jobs such as pulling a barge.

People do not just get up and go. In the cases just cited, the men involved were in situations in which there were few reinforcing stimuli, that is, few reasons for them to remain. They had, at minimum, little to lose in emitting the behavior labeled as a fugue. On the other hand, they had something to gain by so doing—for example, avoiding potential violence, leading a bohemian existence, or being adventurous. As with hysteria, there are probably personal experiences and models for the fugue behavior. Noyes and Kolb (1963, p. 249) offer one hypothesis for short-term fugue behavior: "The model for a number of fugue states apparently has been supplied by a previous head injury with a resulting amnesia, or amnesic states induced through alcohol, or identification with others who suffered dissociative reactions." In the cases cited, the people had heard tales (vicarious learning) or previously played the roles.

An instructive case is supplied by Walton (1961b). A 35-year-old architectural assistant was referred for treatment because he had somnambulistic episodes during which he tried to do his wife bodily harm. He was not "aware" of this behavior, although in the more violent instances he had tried to strangle his wife, whose struggles were sufficient to awaken him. This behavior had occurred nearly every night for the previous six months. On psychological examination it was found that the patient was shy and inhibited, especially in regard to his mother, who was domineering, authoritarian, rigid, and interfered with his marriage. In the patient's eyes, the wife at that time had a number of characteristics in common with the mother—notably, neurotic behavior and endeavors to force him to do things to which he objected.

The case was formulated in learning terms as one due to stimulus generalization from the mother to the wife. It was hypothesized that during sleep there was a reduction of expectation of aversive consequences for aggressive behavior as well as the decreased avoidance associated with generalization from the primary conditioned stimulus (mother) to the wife. The man was instructed in both the rationale and specific instances of being more assertive with his mother. There was only one therapeutic interview with the psychologist.

After two weeks the wife reported a decrease in her husband's somnambulism. Two months later the patient wrote saying he had not had any "nightmares" (his euphemism) for the last five or six weeks. Two years after the only professional treatment session, the patient and wife reported that there had been no further somnambulistic episodes. The marriage was better than ever, and the patient had achieved a number of gains, among which was treating his mother with firmness when the situation required it. In short, on two-year follow-up, there was no return of the target (somnambulistic) behavior and no symptom substitution.

Aside from exemplifying direct treatment of a neurotic behavior, this case illustrates the formulation of dissociative behavior in learning terms and the use of assertive responses. It should be emphasized that great clinical skill was needed in pinpointing the difficulty.[10] Above all, it is worth noting that rather than focusing on somnambulism itself, the therapist instructed the patient in a more adequate reaction to a difficult social situation.[11]

In summary, dissociative behaviors may be formulated in a manner similar to hysterical behaviors: both involve operant behavior which has been shaped, modeled and reinforced into a pattern, which while normal in development and maintenance, is inappropriate socially and designated as suitable for alteration by societally approved professionals. With both hysterical and dissociative behavior, a learning formulation seems more satisfactory than positing either unconscious motivation or malingering.

DEPRESSIVE NEUROSIS

Depressive behavior plays a role not only among the psychoneuroses but also among the psychoses such as the schizo-affective type of schizophrenia, the de-

---

[10] It is possible to hypothesize far less success if, for instance, the relationship with the wife rather than the mother had been the focus of suggested behavioral changes, although some might have been obtained through generalization from wife back to mother.

[11] Clement (1970), who had parents fully awaken a child when the somnambulistic episode started, also dealt with discrimination between angry feelings and hostile acts. Congdon, Hain, and Stevenson (1972) provide a case of multiple personality in which approriate assertion and attitudes towards sex made the extra "personality" unnecessary.

---

pressed type of manic-depressive psychosis, and involutional melancholia. Bizarre behavior to the point of gross distortion of reality and inability to care for oneself in addition to the depressed behavior would lead to a psychotic diagnosis. While the experience of depression seems a common one—for example, Brand (1972) used the term "the age of melancholy"—Silverman (1968) reports that, at a diagnosable level, epidemiological studies indicate a prevalence at any given time of only one per thousand for depressive psychosis and two or three times that number for neurotic depression. Mendels (1970, p. 1) estimates that "about five out of every 100 adults become significantly depressed at some time in their lives."

In DSM-II (1968, p. 40), depressive neurosis "is manifested by an excessive reaction of depression due to an internal conflict or to an identifiable event such as the loss of a love object or cherished possession." The DSM-I definition is as follows:

The anxiety in this reaction is allayed, and hence partially relieved, by depression and self-depreciation. The reaction is precipitated by a current situation, frequently by some loss sustained by the patient, and often is associated with the feeling of guilt for past failures or deeds. The degree of the reaction in such cases is dependent upon the intensity of the patient's ambivalent feeling toward his loss (love, possession) as well as upon the realistic circumstances of the loss. [DSM-I, pp. 33–34.]

Depressive behavior associated with loss of job, home, or loved ones is usually considered within the range of normal behavior. Kiloh (1968, p. 813) writes: "Depression, like anxiety, is a universal experience, and we regard it as abnormal only if it appears without reason or if it seems excessive in its degree or duration in relation to the provocation." The concept of ambivalence and guilt is part of the DSM-I definition itself. That is, the definition considers normal some depressed responses to loss of loved ones or important life goals. The inappropriate behavior, in the current system of categorization, presumes that, unconsciously, the person really wanted to lose the object or harm the lost person. This he cannot admit and, therefore, his reaction is an overreaction. He must not only cope with the loss, but theoretically must deal with the unacceptable thought that at some level he welcomes this loss.

Behaviorally, it is necessary to start by asking what behaviors lead an observer to apply the label of depression. Depression has been called a "constellation" (Wolpe, 1971) and "a whole family of disorders" (Seligman, 1973). Given the unreliability of psychiatric diagnosis, the following description overlaps with that of psychotic depressions, and, in fact, much of the general description in this area (Beck, 1967; Mendels, 1970; Kiloh, 1968; Paykel, 1971) does not make the distinction as clearly as one might wish. One set of behaviors may be called *underactivity*. There is a slowness of movement and speech, and every voluntary act seems, both to the observer and subject, to require great effort. A second set of behaviors deals with *expression*. Nothing seems worthwhile or interesting. The person expects failure and rejects future plans and efforts to cheer him up. There may be much self-blame and feelings of sinfulness, worthlessness, and powerlessness. The person is sad; he may weep, moan, wring his hands, eat little, sleep poorly, sigh frequently. In addition, he may emit verbal behavior of sad affect and disinterest to stimuli that the majority of people find pleasant or interesting. His outlook is limited, unchanging, and bleak both as to his abilities and what options are present.

It is the frequency of overt behaviors that is the focus of any sociopsychological formulation. In depression, the focus is on a decrease of active, environment-manipulating behaviors and an increase in certain role enactments, both verbal and gestural, indicative of helplessness and hopelessness. Ferster (1973) notes that the person probably still has the behaviors in his repertoire and may emit them at a low rate, but that "the current conditions do not support the activities of which he is potentially capable." (p. 861.) The problem then becomes the specification of the conditions. Ferster stresses avoidance of aversive stimuli and loss of jobs or companions that supported or made meaningful the emitted acts.

Seligman (1973) takes as his focus learned helplessness which presumes a history of learning a strategy or approach to problems; learned helplessness fits into a reaction to a loss paradigm when the person or circumstance presumed necessary for avoidance of punishment or obtaining gratification is removed. A more prolonged set of circumstances is indicated by Bandura (1969, p. 37) when he writes:

Many of the people who seek treatment are neither incompetent or anxiously inhibited, but they experience a great deal of personal distress stemming from excessively high standards for self-evaluation, often supported by unfavorable comparisons with models noted for their extraordinary achievements. This process typically gives rise to depressive reactions, to feelings of worthlessness and lack of purposefulness, and to lessened disposition to perform because of negative self-generated consequences.

In this situation, the person provides the aversive stimulus noted in Ferster's remarks; the critical event may be failure to live up to personal standards as demands increase with increasing age. High personal standards, when excessive and unrealistic, also lead to extinction: no act is worthy of reinforcement. Wolpe (1971) poses three clinical contexts for reactive depression: prolongation of normal reaction to loss; a consequence of severe and prolonged anxiety; and failure in interpersonal relations due to the inhibiting result of that anxiety.

A somewhat different emphasis is provided by Lewinsohn and Atwood (1969), who pose, as the assumptions of their approach,

(a) a reduced rate of positive reinforcement is a critical antecedent condition for the occurence of depressed behaviors; (b) social interactions provide contingencies which strengthen and maintain depressive behaviors. The latter are seen as part of a vicious circle in which the depressive behaviors serve to maintain the individual's impoverished social relations and the latter serve to prolong his depression. [p. 166.]

Liberman and Raskin (1972) utilize both respondent and operant concepts: "The onset of depressive behaviors may be viewed as a respondent to the reduction of environmental reinforcers (e.g., loss of loved one). The maintenance of depressive behaviors, once they appear, may be viewed as a process of operant conditioning whereby attention from significant others serves as reinforcement for the symptoms." (p. 42.) The slowing down of the emission of the behavior (psychomotor retardation) may occur because major discriminative stimuli under which behavior was emitted are no longer present. The person must learn new patterns of behavior: to do this he undergoes a period of trial and error, a period during which he learns new schedules, new operants, and new discriminative stimuli. During this period he must also "unlearn," that is, learn to emit behavior different from that which was previously appropriate. In the period of mourning a person frequently comes in contact with stimuli that were associated with the lost object. He may respond with behavior that was appropriate prior to the loss.

A certain amount of playing the depressed role is culturally appropriate (Averill, 1968; Volkan, 1970). A person who suffers the loss of a major source of positive reinforcement and does not display some of the behavior called depressed would be considered unusual, unexpected, bizarre, and even psychotic. As with so many other "abnormal" behaviors, the issue becomes an evaluation of whether the behavior is appropriate in either intensity or duration. Cameron and Magaret (1951, p. 316) make the point: "We reserve the diagnosis of *depressive disorder* for behavior that resembles that of the grief-stricken person, but in which the excitants are not identified, or seem not to deserve so intense a reaction. . . ."

The treatment of depression is essentially one of helping the individual establish new behaviors that will be reinforced. How this is done is a matter of both operant and respondent conditioning. The person, if he is in a situation where it is appropriate to be depressed, will receive condolence, attention, sympathy, and other social support. As a result, the response of others to depression may maintain it. The person may be reinforced for his emission of depressive behaviors or he can be reinforced for emission of behaviors antithetical to the depressed role. In terms of playing the depressed role, the formulation of treatment is close to that outlined for hysteria. At times, however, the treatment also resembles that for obsessive-compulsives and phobics, who must be taught to emit new behaviors so that they will no longer avoid situations. In both instances, consistent with the theoretical concepts reviewed above, social skills are crucial (Libet and Lewinsohn, 1973).

Given the orientation that the requirements of each case must be analyzed rather than treating a category of depression, a variety of techniques for altering the behaviors that lead to the label of "depression" have appeared in the behavioral literature. Todd (1972), for example, made use of the Premack principle so that a client had to read positive statements about herself prior to smoking a cigarette. Within the week, not only did the depression "lift," the number of positive statements the client would make about herself increased. Jackson (1972) reports on a client who seems to fit the problem of self-evaluation noted by Bandura in the quotation in this section. The treatment involved the client setting down ahead of time what she intended to accomplish when doing a task and then matching the goal to the result.

The combination of monitoring self-reinforcement led to a realistic evaluation of her acts, which, in turn, increased self-reinforcements and decreased depressive behaviors. Seitz (1971) employed four techniques during eight sessions, including "Premacking" and assertion training.

Tharp, Watson, and Kaya (1973) relate the application of self-modification procedures by four undergraduate women to depressed feelings. Self-observation, making an effectively competing response to previously "self-hassling" stimuli, and increasing "honest" statements through reinforcement were among the strategies. Aside from the immediate target behaviors dealt with, these procedures emphasize the active, effective role the person can play and hence are antithetical to denigrating self-statements or learned helplessness. The person becomes an effective agent changing his own behavior or that of significant others (Lewinsohn and Shaw, 1969).

Specifying the situations and reactions that calls for change to reduce the "depressive" behavior may require field observation (Lewinsohn and Shaffer, 1971). For example, Lewinsohn and Atwood (1969) report on a woman who initiated conversation at home to an unresponsive and essentially extinguishing family. On other occasions, behaviors consistent with the role of being "depressed," such as a negative self-evaluation, may be made the direct target. The style of speech—for example, slow with flat affect (Weintraub and Aronson, 1967; Rice, Abroms, and Saxman, 1969) may be altered directly. Robinson and Lewinsohn (1973) report on the beneficial effects of speeding up the speech rate of a "depressed" (and to conversationalists quite likely depressing) man. Appropriate assertive behavior (see Chapter 12) and effective social skills—for example, activity level, variety of friends, rate of positive reactions emitted, and speed of response (Lewinsohn and Graf, 1973; Libet and Lewinsohn, 1973)—counter the feedback of "depression" to the person as well as significant others. Activity that is meaningful, as in token economy, may well be antithetical to depression (Hersen et al., 1973). Reisinger (1972), working within a token economy, "charged" the person for crying and paid her for smiles. The study included alterations of the contingencies to document their impact and a 14-month follow-up to illustrate the maintenance of new behavior after discharge.

SUMMARY

This volume's coverage of specific behaviors called abnormal began with a discussion of the category called hysteria. Hysteria is of particular interest because of its historical importance and because it offers a major test of theoretical formulations.

The present discussion takes the view that these behaviors result from neither unconscious motivations nor conscious malingering. Rather a person is categorized as enacting the hysterical role when he behaves in a manner that is so classified by societal labelers. The behaviors that cue the diagnostician are learned. Conversion, dissociative, and depressive behavior are conceived of as normal acts, analogous to hypnotic and placebo responses, which are appropriate to given antecedent and current conditions and need not be considered manifestations either of faking or of unconscious needs. This chapter has described instances of these behaviors and a variety of direct interventions which resulted in amelioration without evidence of symptom substitution. For both the "normal" and "abnormal" roles, the person needs to learn the culturally meaningful acts and be supported in them. A change in established roles requires experience of increased pleasantness with alternative behaviors, and these, in turn, require a learning process. The goal is a person who deals with his environment in a way that is effective and welcome to himself and others: as effective behavior increases, both his concept of himself and the concept held by others improves in a favorable manner.

neurosis II
TENSIONAL COMPONENTS
14

In the last chapter we dealt with behaviors called neurotic which, at least in our view, involved a major element of role playing and the shaping of operants. The patterns we will deal with in this chapter have a more directly observable respondent tension, or an avoidance component. Further, we may divide the behaviors into those that seem pervasive, such as neurasthenia or anxiety neurosis, and those that may be more limited in their manifestations, such as hypochrondriasis, depersonalization, craft palsies (neurosis, other), some obsessive-compulsive behaviors, and those that are more specific to particular situations such as phobia. As we progress, however, the reader will realize that these distinctions quickly break down and are useful only for pedagogical purposes.

PHOBIC BEHAVIOR

DSM-II (p. 40) notes that phobic neurosis "is characterized by intense fear of an object or situation which the patient consciously recognizes as no real danger to him. His apprehension may be experienced as faintness, fatigue, palpitations, perspiration, nausea, tremor, and even panic. Phobias are generally attributed to fears displaced to the phobic object or situation from some other object of which the patient is unaware." DSM-I (p. 33) sharpens the psychoanalytic notion of displacement so that the object or situation feared is symbolic, and adds the behavioral observation that "the patient attempts to control his anxiety by avoiding the phobic object or situation."

General Discussion

What is signified by the word "phobic"? There are specific relationships, objects, and situations to which the person responds with feelings of discomfort, inability, and anticipation of aversive consequences. These situations are not ones an "objective" observer would consider fear-provoking, and the person himself is very likely to report that his responses are "wrong" or "irritational." If such reactions are not socially debilitating, however, they are not considered phobias. For example, dislike of snakes is relatively common, and as many as 2 percent of college students may respond very emotionally to snakes or even to pictures of them. Another relatively common fear is of rats. Interestingly enough, the same person who can be very upset by a mouse or rat may think other rodents such as squirrels are cute. Similarly, the college student who will engage in deep kissing may hesitate to use his beloved's toothbrush. Such behaviors are not considered phobic. In fact, fear of snakes, spiders, or rats may even be culturally role-appropriate behavior. *To be considered phobic* the fear must be evaluated as *disproportionate* to the situation and socially *disturbing* by some observer, including the person himself. That is, the response deviates from what is expected in the culture and is disruptive. A person who has an aversion to certain foods or who has other specific dislikes which do not interfere with either his life or that of other people will not be considered phobic because nobody is inconvenienced to the point of making a change worthwhile.

Agras, Sylvester, and Oliveau (1969) found the prevalence of mild phobias in the general population to be 74.7 per 1000 persons, and of severely disabling phobias to be 2.2 per 1000. "Severe disability was defined as absence from work for an employed person, and inability to manage the common household tasks for a housewife." (p. 153.)

Three matters of general comment are essential: first, the behavior that comes to be called a phobia indicates that the person has made a culturally inappropriate response, either by avoiding the situation if he can, or by a disorganized, ineffective, subjectively unpleasant behavior if he cannot; second, the use of anxiety as an explanatory concept is likely to obscure rather than clarify the problem if an operational definition of anxiety is not provided and rigidly adhered to.

Third, in the DSM definition it is presumed that there is an underlying cause and that the observed avoidance of a particular idea, object, or situation is a *displacement*. By definition a displacement is the "shift of emotion or symbolic meaning from a person or object toward which it was originally directed to another person or object. Often displacement involves difficult emotions, such as hostility and anxiety. A common subject for cartoons is the meek office clerk who has been refused a raise by his domineering boss. Instead of expressing his hostility toward his employer—which would be dangerous—he goes home and snaps irritably at his wife because dinner is a few minutes late." (Coleman, 1972, p. 129.) Another definition of displacement (Nemiah, 1961, p. 309) is "a defense mechanism characterized by (1) the shifting of emotions or fantasies from the object to which they were originally attached to a substitute; (2) the shifting of the psychic energies from one form of expression to another."

Given the definition of a phobia as a displacement, there are two related effects: the first is that a phobia, so defined, cannot be altered by direct retraining procedures, or if such are used, symptom substitution (see Chapter 9) should result; and, second, again by definition, if direct retraining procedures are effective and no symptom substitution results, the original abnormal behavior was not a "true" phobia. This point of view, expressed by Frazier and Carr (1967),[1] exemplifies what is meant by a closed system.

REFORMULATION OF PHOBIC BEHAVIOR

The sociopsychological approach harks back to a specification of what the target behavior is: a person avoids a situation or is uncomfortable in it. We need, therefore, to delineate situations in which people do not engage in acts or are very tense when they do. In reading the following, please remember this distinction: between (1) being able to do something and not doing it, and (2) not being able to do something and therefore not doing it.

In Chapters 2, 4, and 10 the point was made that the person must be *capable* of emitting a required act or else his response to situations that have been punishing or have been so labeled is to avoid them. At a college level, instructors and courses associ-

---

[1] "In the person who develops a phobic reaction, it can be assumed that under extreme anxiety such differentiation becomes defective and that a regressive identification with the feared object or situation takes place. It can also be assumed that the original identification was characterized by ambivalence, since the phobia generally evolves around things or situations that either directly or symbolically represent a source of earlier satisfaction and attraction as well as of threat, in fantasy if not actuality. Like any neurotic symptom, every phobia can be viewed as representing a compromise between wish (temptation, gratification) and prohibition (threat, fear). For example, heights (and falling from them) literally and figuratively represent fears common to both child and adult, but they also represent powerful pleasures of flight and abandon that under certain conditions are found to be most enjoyable: playing, falling, and jumping games, diving, skiing, sailing, and falling in the moral sense (that is, sinning)." (Frazier and Carr, 1967, p. 903.)

ated with the word "statistics" frequently are avoided. This may be due in part to modeling, but basically it is a matter of a situation's having been given a negative label and then having been responded to in terms of that label. Direct experience may lead to avoidant behavior. *If the person does not have the requisite act in his repertoire,* he will fail in the situation, and this failure will lead to the situation's being designated as unpleasant and to be avoided if at all possible.

Readers of this book are likely to have a passing experience with exams, some of which they had studied for and some on which they lucked out. With exams, a person may be frightened, and may not be innately capable: abilities, appropriate studying, and even rational behavior on the part of exam makers and evaluators play a role.

If the situation cannot be avoided, disruption of an effective reaction may lead to failure to emit the normally expected behavior. The person may be capable of making the expected or normal response but following the models of Chapters 2, 4, and 10, *he misidentifies the situation;* he does not recognize the discriminative stimuli typical in the culture. Watson and Rayner's (1920) case of Albert's fear of a rodent, mentioned in Chapter 4, is a good example. Prior to conditioning, Albert was "normal": he cooed, gurgled, reached for or ignored the animal. After conditioning, he tensed, screamed, and became upset when the animal was presented. Looking at the effects of the pairing of sudden loud noise and animal, it is possible to say that Albert acted to the previously neutral animal as if sudden loud noise was an element of the animal. To the extent that a sudden loud noise was temporally an aspect of presentation of the animal, this was a valid aspect of the situation for Albert. For an objective observer such as the experimenter or the reader, it is not a "true" statement of the situation.

What a person does has an effect on himself and what he does has an effect on others. In terms of the latter, *the consequences of being frightened and avoiding situations are varied, but not infrequently the response of others to such behavior is acceptance and sympathy.* That is, a functional analysis indicates that the person is reinforced by favorable consequences and permission to leave an unpleasant situation because it "makes him uptight" (anxious). These behaviors have been touched on at various times previously in this volume. It need only be repeated that there may be reinforcement of phobic behaviors in a manner similar to the immediate gains noted in the manifestation of hysterical behavior.

What a person does also has an effect on himself. The feedback provided by role enactments was noted in the latter sections of Chapter 4. Labeling situations is an operant behavior (Homme, 1966).

A person can avoid a situation he labels as punishing; *the avoidance of the presumed punishment leads to the maintenance of the behavior* (Solomon and Wynne, 1953, 1954). *The response to the situation, however, further confirms the label the person gives himself.* A student who continually avoids statistics and other mathematics courses confirms to himself by his own behavior that he is a person who "can't" take statistics courses. In addition, the avoidance results in restricting the student's choice to courses for which statistics is not a requirement. The person has moved from avoiding a limited situation to becoming the sort of person who avoids a *class* of situations and who eventually may act in terms of this self-identity. Behaviorally, this is what Adlerians mean by the concept of a "guiding fiction."

A person may report without much emotion that he is scared of some situation; but then he may become greatly upset as a reaction to his being afraid. Another way of saying this is that a person may not be avoiding a situation in terms of that situation itself, but rather in terms of *what he expects he will do in that situation.* The distinction may be clearer if one thinks that a person may avoid a situation which calls for assertiveness not because he is upset or incapable of being assertive but because he wishes to avoid the presumed consequences of being assertive. A person may not fear being aggressive but rather the *consequences* of being aggressive.

It is in these terms that the diagnostic approach of behavior therapy asks many *what* questions. As noted in Chapter 11, in evaluating a situation the behavior therapist shifts from traditional *why* questions to *what* questions. He must ask what is the person doing. He must ask under what condition the particular behaviors are emitted. He must ask what are the effects of the acts, what changes occur after they are emitted. He must ask what other behaviors the person might emit. He asks this last question in terms of what actions may have been ex-extinguished, what situations are being avoided, and what reinforcers can be applied, by the therapist, by the patient, and by interested significant others such as attendants, teachers, parents, and friends. Historical information enters frequently in terms of what the conditions were under which the phobic behavior was first emitted. This is not a matter of interest in working through historical suppressions but rather an attempt to gain information regarding what specific cues are being responded to with the behavior to be changed.

The present formulation has not made much use of the Pavlovian model (see Chapter 4). Another formulation of phobias by Eysenck and Rachman depends to a greater extent on a respondent conditioning model, makes use of a concept of drive, and follows a Hullian rather than a Skinnerian model. Eysenck and Rachman (1965, pp. 81–82) summarize their concepts as follows:

1. Phobias are learned responses.
2. Stimuli develop phobic [-producing] qualities when they are associated temporally and spatially with a fear-producing state of affairs.
3. Neutral stimuli that are of relevance in the fear-producing situation and/or make an impact on the person in the situation are more likely to develop phobic qualities than weak or irrelevant stimuli.
4. Repetition of association between the fear situation and the new phobic stimuli will strengthen the phobia.
5. Associations between high-intensity fear situations and neutral stimuli are more likely to produce phobic reactions.
6. Generalization from the original phobic stimulus to stimuli of a similar nature will occur.
7. Noxious experiences that occur under conditions of excessive confinement are more likely to produce phobic reactions.
8. Neutral stimuli that are associated with a noxious experience(s) may develop (secondary) motivating properties. This acquired drive is termed the fear-drive.
9. Responses (such as avoidance) that reduce the fear-drive are reinforced.

The quoted views of Eysenck and Rachman come from a context in which two additional concepts are implicit. The first, is the hypothesis that individuals differ on a genetic basis in their conditionability and that people with difficulties labeled phobic, anxiety, and obsessive-compulsive reactions are more readily conditioned than people manifesting hysterical and antisocial difficulties. Eysenck and his co-workers specify introverts as the type of people most likely to develop surplus conditioned responses. Items 3, 4, 5, and 7 in the quotation above further specify the conditions most likely to lead to phobic responses. Second, Eysenck and Rachman posit two types of learning difficulties. The first is a learning of *irrelevant* (phobic) reactions. The second is the learning of an immediately reinforced response (e.g., orgasm), to *inappropriate* stimulus situations (e.g., homosexuality, fetishism, and transvestism).

The Eysenck-Rachman model follows in its first stages that of Pavlovian or classical conditioning. Eysenck and Rachman correctly use the term "a fear-producing *state of affairs*," because aversive consequences may be taught vicariously (Berger, 1962;

Bandura, 1965b; Bandura and Rosenthal, 1966; Kanfer, 1965b) and because it is difficult to specify conditions, particularly after infancy, which are universally fear-producing. The closest one can come to universal aversive stimuli are severe pain or severe deprivation of physiological necessities. Very quickly in a person's life, especially in our culture, secondary or acquired reinforcers assume a major role in learning.

Points 8 and 9 of the Eysenck and Rachman quotation indicate that avoidance of the phobic response-producing situation is reinforcing. The behavior is maintained by escape and avoidance from presumed aversive consequences. The aversive consequences in turn, as noted, are likely to be acquired rather than necessarily primary reinforcers. The reduction of the threat of failure may reinforce the studying of inherently boring material. This is a socially appropriate response, and many phobic responses may be treated by helping the person to acquire a needed skill. A person who avoids members of the opposite sex because of repeated failure may well need to be taught social skills necessary for success (for example, dancing, grooming, and the like) as well as the more specific retraining of prior responses of avoidance or physiological discomfort. The reasons given, or other maneuvers that are developed, to justify avoidant behavior may also be disruptive. In line with this, a second point to make explicit is that *the paradigm of phobic responses may be applied to a wide range of situations in which failure to react effectively* leads to the situation becoming unpleasant, "fear-producing," and avoided.

To recapitulate, a person may respond to a particular aspect of a situation in a manner appropriate in a prior and different context. He may also not have requisite skills and thus learn to avoid a situation. Finally, he may learn to avoid situations through modeling. Explicitly, no matter how the behavior was learned, the treatment is one of *direct retraining*.

The therapeutic task therefore is twofold. The first is to help the person to make a new, different, and more adaptive response and thereby not withdraw or escape from the situation. The operant behavior is changed by removing the reinforcing stimuli that maintained avoidance behavior. The person may gain experience with the stimuli and learn that the stimulus situation is not what he thought it to be. The goal is for him to come in contact with the situation and remain in it without aversive consequences, or, even better, deal effectively and enjoyably with it. By definition, the former is extinction: exposure to the conditioned stimulus without presentation of the unconditioned stimulus so that aversive consequences are not forthcoming. The latter is reconditioning.

The major therapeutic problem is to have the subject enter the situation. Forcing a person into an aversive situation may in itself be aversive so that respondents labeled as unpleasant are contiguous with the stimulus. These unpleasant stimuli are due to the treatment, not the stimulus, but their effect follows the conditioning paradigm of pairing unpleasantness with the conditioned stimulus. The strategy, therefore, is to have the person approach the stimulus *slowly* so that each increasing approach toward the stimulus is made with an affect different from and contradictory to the avoidant (phobic) response. That is, there is retraining beyond simple extinction. The goal is for the subject to emit a new, contradictory response to the stimulus in place of the prior inappropriate response. Throughout retraining procedures, therefore, there is a need to agree on behaviors for the person to emit and to maintain such behaviors at a stronger level than the inappropriate or avoidance responses they are to replace.

ILLUSTRATIONS OF TREATMENT PROCEDURES

The following illustrative cases will be concerned with adults. Chapter 23 will present similar material with children.

Desensitization in Practice

In this situation, the therapist provides actual materials in such a progression that they lead to emission of appropriate responses. Freeman and Kendrick (1960) describe a mother of two children, whose cat phobia, which she had had since age four, had become socially crippling in the past two years. Retraining started with having her feel the textures of different materials, working from velvet up to a glove made of rabbit fur. She next looked at pictures of cats and stroked toy kittens. At the end of the session, she took these objects home and placed them around her house. Finally, she was given a baby kitten, which she raised to a grown cat. Within a month of starting treatment she had taken a kitten home, and a month after that she touched a full-grown cat without the psychologist's being present.

On follow-up she was found to have been free of phobic responses for eight months and to have had only one bad experience in which she realized that she was afraid of a specific cat and not of cats in general. Rather than symptom substitution, which would have been expected if the cat phobia were a displacement, other symptoms or socially undesirable behavior not directly treated dropped out. The woman was able to go into her garden, she stopped biting her nails, and was able to perform more appropriate behaviors in her home. Such *in vivo* training may be used alone or in addition to systematic desensitization (Garfield et al., 1967; Murphy, 1963; Gentry, 1970; Bernstein and Beatty, 1971) or as part of the procedure of modeling with guided participation in which the therapist first does a task and then the subject does the same and is rewarded for so doing.

Use of Rapport

Another illustrative case (Meyer, 1957) is one in which the therapist used himself and his relationship with the patient to replace a fearful response with a contradictory feeling of security. A 48-year-old married woman had "blackouts" which were suspected of being caused by temporal lobe epilepsy. The blackouts had started 20 years before. At age 44 the woman started to have peculiar and horrible feelings based upon a fear of falling. She became afraid to go out of her home without friends, and later became too fearful to go out at all. She resigned her job and stopped caring for her home. The rationale of the treatment was explained and discussed with her. During this time, the therapist endeavored to establish good rapport. The therapist deliberately intruded himself as part of the various environmental situations during treatment and, by establishing an effective relationship, he became a reassuring stimulus tending to reduce fear. The therapist first took the woman to the roof of the hospital where there were walls but no ceiling. Then he took her to the hospital garden, where he left her and made her try to find him. That is, she took a walk and was reinforced for it by finding the therapist. Then she went for more extensive walks with the therapist and other staff members whom she knew. She next went outside the hospital grounds, increasing the length of her travels. Then she went by herself to meet the staff, to ride on buses, and to go on shopping expeditions. In short, she was given a series of tasks of increasing difficulty in real life with the relationship to the examiner acting as a stimulus to differentiate these situations. The therapist first acted as a discriminative stimulus for security and then later became a secondary reinforcing stimulus making the effort of moving in the streets worthwhile. These experiences led to a remission of the phobia.

"Anxiety-Relief" Responses

Meyer (1957) also reports on a 42-year-old married man who had blackouts, excessive tensions, and various fears, mainly of crowded places. At age 22, while in the service, he had fainting attacks while on parade. He became tense and panicky in crowded places. After age 38 control became more tenuous, and the inappropriate behavior seemed to generalize more readily to previously neutral situations. Phenobarbital administered by his physician had not been useful. No specific stimulus was encountered, and desensitization based on relaxation techniques failed because the man could not evoke increased distress by thinking about difficult situations.

As noted in Chapter 4, termination of an aversive stimulus situation is reinforcing. Therefore, the man was brought in contact with an electrical current and when the current became unbearable, he was told to say aloud "calm yourself." This led to the shock being terminated. The words "calm yourself" became a conditioned stimulus for termination of something unpleasant, including the physiological correlates of the shock. The man was taught to make this response and thereafter practiced it in increasingly difficult situations. For example, he was taken by the experimenter to an empty movie house, and later to crowded ones. Additional material on the anxiety-relief technique is presented by Wolpe (1958, pp. 180–181), Wolpe and Lazarus (1966, pp. 149–151), Thorpe et al. (1964), Solyom and Miller (1967), and Solyom et al. (1972).

Systematic Desensitization

Systematic desensitization was used in the study by Paul (1966) discussed in Chapter 12. As the reader will remember, the person is taught to relax his muscles and, while calm, visualizes situations in an increasing hierarchy of difficulty. The person visualizes each situation for a set time, and if he becomes the least bit tense he immediately signals the therapist, stops the image, and returns to relaxing.

Paul (1968a, b) has presented an extensive review of the literature on systematic desensitization. The professional reader interested in clinical applications is referred to the over 50 illustrative case articles listed by Paul (1968a). Paul (1968b) reviews 20 reports in which control procedures were used. To quote his conclusion: "The findings were overwhelmingly positive, and for the first time in the history of psychological treatments, a specific therapeutic package was found to reliably produce therapeutic benefits for clients across a broad range of distressing problems where anxiety is of fundamental importance. 'Relapse' and 'symptom substitution' were notably lacking, although the majority of authors were attuned to these problems."

The strategy has been to develop effective therapeutic packages and then to analyze the components to determine what is necessary, what is sufficient, and what may be eliminated without decrease in efficiency. Because this work is frequently done by laboratory analog, using animals such as snakes, rodents and spiders, conflicting results may be obtained. At the present time, many, but not all, of Wolpe's concepts have been confirmed (Van Egeren, Feather, and Hein, 1971). It is clear that social and operant as well as respondent variables are involved (Wilkins, 1971) in these packages. These variables increase in relevance as one moves from problems where the person has the needed act in his repertoire to problems where the person needs to learn how to act in the situation before he can so do without discomfort.

Group Therapy by Desensitization

Paul and Shannon (1966) extended Paul's (1966) work (reviewed in Chapter 12) by working with groups of five students. In addition to dealing with a speech situation, as done in work with individuals previously cited, during the latter part of the series of ten sessions, a hierarchy was devised dealing with examinations. Aside from the benefits obtained on measures of comfort in speech situations, the individuals in the group treatment improved their academic grades to a significantly greater extent than a matched, no-treatment control group. Some discussion occurred in the Paul and Shannon therapy groups, in part around hierarchy construction, in part as discriminating important cues in the situation. Katahn, Strenger, and Cherry (1966) more directly combined advice and discussion with desensitization, as did Cohen (1969), McManus (1971), and Meichenbaum, Gilmore, and Fedoravicius (1971). Donner (1970) found automated desensitization effective, although the therapist present was an aid, while Allen (1973) demonstrated the usefulness of automated relaxation with study counseling. Meichenbaum (1972) focussed on the "cognitive" aspects of counseling, the identification of stimuli leading to "test-anxiety" responses and methods of coping actively with such stimuli.

There is a large literature on test anxiety (Allen 1972). It is important as a target in itself, but it also attracts research workers because it provides a large population of people interested in participating in the behavior-change procedures. Further, there are three criteria: reported test discomfort; behavior in a model test (with the advantage that everyone takes the same exam, but with the disadvantage that it is an analog and not the real thing that has implication for graduation and later job placement); and student grade-point average in college courses. This latter criterion is the pay-off for most students and faculty; and since it is the result of continued effort and is distant from research, it is less biased by the subject's desire to please the research worker.

Johnson and Sechrest (1968) reported that desensitization had a greater effect on test anxiety than relaxation alone (which did not differ from a control group). This finding is similar to that by Davison (1968b) with snakes. From the many researches available, we have focused upon the ones that included grade average, since from both research (Garlington and Cotler, 1968) and observation one may find that test anxiety is not necessarily highly related to test performance (grades). There are people who do well despite being tense, and there are some people who are relaxed and receive poor grades.

The areas of examinations involves not only acts in a person's repertoire, but also the need for the development of acts such as studying and mastery of material. The next step in this area is work with groups who are less interested in academic success, that is, drop-outs and borderline students, frequently from impoverished areas.

Lazarus (1961) worked with people whose behavioral difficulties were more representative of the types met in clinical settings. Included were 35 middle-class people, 11 of whom were acrophobics (dread of high places), 15 claustrophobics, 5 impotent men, and 4 other phobics. The basic design was to compare the efficacy of systematic desensitization with more traditional dynamic or insight-oriented group therapy. In operation there were three groups: 18 of the people were treated by systematic desensitization (relaxation and paired relevant visualization). The remaining 17 were treated under two conditions: 9 by traditional or interpretive group therapy alone, the other 8 by such conventional therapy, plus for the last quarter of each session, relaxation training without pairing.

This last procedure was used to offer some evidence that the effective agent in desensitization was not merely the relaxation technique. People were randomly assigned to treatments with as close matching as possible of individuals with similar behavioral difficulties in the three conditions. A desensitization hierarchy was constructed, and the group members read the items in the hierarchy off cards: this made it possible for people in the same group to be desensitized along different hierarchies.

Before and after treatment, behavior as well as self-report measures were sought. Only those people whose difficulties imposed a severe limitation on their social mobility or jeopardized their interpersonal relationships were admitted to the study. People who were acrophobic were required to climb a metal fire escape; claustrophobics were placed in a room with walls that were moved in on them. After therapy, to be considered a sucess the acrophobics had to climb the fire escape to a height of 50 feet and go to a roof garden eight stories above the street and count the number of passing cars for two minutes. Claustrophobics had to sit for five minutes in the cubicle with the walls inches from them.

A person's report of improvement, increased ability to acept his difficulty, or achievement of "personality reintegration" without behavioral change was not considered a success. Of the people treated with systematic desensitization, 13 of 18 recovered, while in the same number of sessions, none of the 9 people in the interpretive treatment group recovered and 2 of the 8 people in the interpretation plus relaxation group recovered. The difference in recovery rate was statistically significant. Further, when the 15 people in the latter two groups who had not recovered were treated by group desensitization, 10 recovered.[2] A finding similar to this latter one is reported by Gelder and Marks (1968).

Modeling

A model may serve as a discriminative stimulus, a stimulus incompatible with other more distressing stimuli, or as an indicant of potentially reinforced operants. Perhaps the first clinical demonstration of this procedure was with children (Jones, 1924b). An experiment by Bandura, Blanchard, and Ritter (1967) was presented in Chapter 12, and a further experimental demonstration of this technique (Bandura and Menlove,

[2] One might say that repeatedly labeling a situation as frightening and avoiding it is obsessive-compulsive rather than phobic behavior. Given the similarity between the two diagnostic categories, one might expect that systematic densensitization has been used in the treatment of obsessive-compulsive behavior: Walton and Mather (1963) and Haslam (1965a) are examples.

1968) will be found in Chapter 23 dealing with children.

It is also possible to hypothesize that modeling of a person with whom one has a continuing relationship has a reciprocal effect: modeling may reduce unrealistic avoidance behavior and hence be reinforcing; because the consequence is reinforcing, such modeling of and identification with another person is likely to increase. Of prime importance, modeling provides information on how to act in the situation, what a person should do to be effective.

Contact Desensitization

Contact desensitization makes use of rapport, modeling by the therapist, gradual steps by the client, and reinforcement of progress by the therapist and the client himself. Ritter (1969a, 1969b) presents evidence for the importance of the various aspects of this package and its efficiency, using people who were afraid of heights (acrophobic). Schaap and Dana (1968) also worked with this target behavior and found self-applied systematic desensitization to be feasible.

Operant Procedures

If the object is to have a person engage in acts of which he is capable but avoids, the analysis must include the gains he obtains for not doing the act (i.e., what aversive or presumably aversive consequence is escaped or avoided, what positive benefits, such as attention, does he get for not engaging in the act), and what does a person need to know to engage effectively in the act. Teaching the person to emit the behavior may include various techniques noted above—for example, prompting and fading of the prompt by the experimenter and positive consequences for engaging in the act. Agras and his coworkers (Agras, Leitenberg, Barlow, and Thomson, 1969) illustrated these points by shaping walking behavior in a person who would be categorized as hysterical, and a person afraid of enclosed places (claustrophobic), using therapist (rapport) as reinforcement. Agras, Leitenberg, and Barlow (1968) also reported on work with three agoraphobics (persons who have a fear of open space) in which increasing distance covered cued the therapists' social reinforcement. Both researches are notable for the use of single-subject designs in which the conditions of reinforcement were demonstrated to affect the behavior. Birk (1968) also reports on a man who had been unable to work or leave home without discomfort for 17 years. The analysis revealed severe social deprivation due to his isolation, a lack of knowledge of how to work or be away from home, and absence of anyone ever having reinforced him for not retreating. Social reinforcement was aimed not only at distances but at independent behavior, and resulted in success, including work, friends, and taking trips.

Reactive Inhibition and Implosion

Malleson (1959) presented an analysis of phobia in which he noted that one source of reinforcement for a phobic response was release from and avoidance of the situation. He reported a case in which a student had to take and pass a crucial exam two days later. Typical procedures of sedation did not work, and there was not sufficient time for conventional psychotherapeutic techniques. The student was therefore made to sit up in bed and to feel his fear as fully as possible. He was asked to tell of the awful consequences of failing. At first he sobbed and trembled, but after half an hour he became calm. Every time he felt a small wave of alarm, he was told *not* to push it aside but to experience it fully, profoundly, and vividly, to enhance it, and to augment it. If he did not spontaneously report such upsetting stimuli, he was told, every 20 or 30 minutes, to make a special effort to do so.

After a while, the student seemed almost unable to feel frightened: "He had, as it were, exhausted the affect in the whole situation." Malleson hypothesized that in addition to the removal of the reinforcing consequence of successful flight, this procedure led to the build-up of fatigue or reactive inhibition in a manner analogous to the massing of practice in the treatment of tics (see Chapter 12). It might be added that there certainly is pairing of the anticipated aversive situation with no immediate aversive consequences (extinction) and possibly also with the favorable stimulus of doing something about the situation (enacting a more adult, competent role), the expectation of improvement (placebo effect), and the presence of the interested and sympathetic experimenter.

Much of this procedure may be viewed as a sharpening of advice given by Dale Carnegie (1948, p. 12) for a person to analyze a catastrophic situation, figure out what the worst thing that could happen might be, accept such an event as a starting point, and then devote time and energy to improve upon the worst (which had already been accepted).

While not identical in either theoretical formulation or clinical practice, Malleson's reactive inhibition technique is similar to other techniques, one of which is Stampfl's implosive therapy (Stampfl and Levis, 1967). Hogan and Kirchner report on an experimental test of implosive therapy that used as the dependent variable avoidance behavior of rats.

The experimental group began with scenes such as imagining their touching a rat, having a rat nibble at their finger, or feeling one run across their hand. Then the rat might bite them on the arm. The Ss might next experience the rat running rapidly over their body. The rodent could pierce them viciously in the neck, swish its tail in their face, or claw about in their hair. It might even devour their eyes.

The Ss might be told to open their mouths. Suddenly, the rodent jumped in, and they swallowed it. The animal then destroyed various internal organs of their bodies. Perhaps Ss might be locked in a room full of rats, or a man-sized disease-ridden, slimy, gray sewer rat might attack them. The possibilities are innumerable. . . . The therapist knew what scenes generated the most anxiety, and he elaborated upon them. [Hogan and Kirchner, 1967, pp. 107–8.]

Wolpin and Raines (1966) used a similar technique and found it effective, while Rachman (1966a), Willis and Edwards (1969), and DeMoor (1970) and Mealiea and Nawas (1971), on the other hand, did not find it effective. Prevention of the avoidance response has also been called "Flooding." (Baum, 1970.)

Although it is seemingly directly opposite in procedure to systematic desensitization, the implosive process is similar in (1) applying learning concepts and (2) directly altering behavior. It should be explicit that with implosive therapy, as with all other therapeutic procedures, a great measure of clinical skill is required. Perhaps the most important element in the situation is the need to establish trust and confidence in the therapist so that the experience is associated with the avoided object and not with the therapist. Great skill is also required to have the treated person cooperate so that he remains in the situation and vividly visualizes the scenes until extinction occurs. If extinction does not take place, resensitization is a distinct possibility. Morganstern (1973) reviewing work on implosive therapy, "concluded that there is, at present, no convincing evidence of the effectiveness of implosion or flooding with human subjects. . . ." (p. 318.)

A General Comment:
Behavior Therapy and Seduction

In the authors' classes at about this point a glow of understanding lights up the face of some student (for some reason, it is always a male), and he blusters out, "It's just like seduction!" Exactly true. Seduction has as its synonym "lure," and the definition is to persuade, to lead, to entice, to win over. A seducer is one who persuades another to a course of action that presumably would not have been taken otherwise. Folowing the outline of the sociopsychological model, the seducer reduces the cues making the status quo reinforcing and increases the positive reinforcement gained from some alternative behavior. He reduces avoidance of the new act, usually by gradual presentation of a hierarchy of situations. (Overly rapid movement along such a hierarchy without proper persuasion is not seduction.) Seducers are known to pair themselves with pleasant stimuli; each new step is a reasonable outgrowth of former acts, and each step makes more likely further acts. The therapist is changing behavior, and it follows that he will use the same principles as any other person altering behavior.

OBSESSIVE-COMPULSIVE BEHAVIOR

DSM-II (p. 40) defines obsessive-compulsive neurosis as

characterized by the persistent intrusion of unwanted thoughts, urges, or actions that the patient is unable to stop. The thoughts may consist of single words or ideas, ruminations, or trains of thoughts often perceived by the patient as nonsensical. The actions vary from simple movements to complex rituals such as repeated handwashing. Anxiety and distress are often present either if the patient is prevented from completing his compulsive ritual or if he is concerned about being unable to control himself.

DSM-I (p. 33) added an emphasis on anxiety being associated with the unwanted ideas and linked the behavior more explicitly to a psychoanalytic formulation by referring to the person as seeing the ideas and behavior as unreasonable but being "compelled to carry out his rituals."

General Discussion

A person may well have repetitious and uncomfortable thoughts until he has performed a specific act, whether the act be socially appropriate or inappropriate. Students, for example, often think about studying for exams; but only if they themselves or others consider the thought inappropriate or the act disruptive is the term "obsessive-compulsive" used. As with phobic reactions, someone must be inconvenienced by the behavior to the point of being reinforced for endeavors to change it.

There are many behaviors in our culture that are traditional rather than rational but that a person would be uncomfortable in not performing. A man's wearing a dress shirt, tie, and jacket is an example. Other behaviors that are unwanted or seemingly irrelevant are not stepping on cracks, not walking under ladders, and avoiding the paths of black cats. A person who engages in such superstitions might be mildly ridiculed but is not considered obsessive-compulsive. However, where a behavior appropriate to a given situation is *not* made, and where instead some other behavior is emitted which seems to be all the person can do at that point, the interpretation is made that the person is "compelled" to emit "unwanted" behavior, and hence is called obsessive-compulsive.

The theoretical difference between an obsession and a compulsion is that an obsession is an unwanted *thought,* while a compulsion is an "impulse" or "urge" to commit an *act* which when emitted would be called "compulsive." There is an implied distinction between thinking and acting. Both, however, are operant behaviors. Attending and labeling are the major elements of "thinking" and are aspects of most overt role enactments. Thoughts that are not operants imply a dualism of mind and body. The distinction between obsessions and compulsions is not particularly helpful in either research or therapy. Empirically, many people with obsessions have compulsions and vice versa. For these reasons obsessions and compulsions are properly linked together in a single conceptual category.

The range of obsessive-compulsive acts is limited only by the range of human behavior. To quote Nemiah (1967b, p. 914): "The phenomena may be manifested psychically or behaviorally; they may be experienced as ideas or as impulses; they may refer to events anticipated in the future or actions already completed; they may express desires and wishes or protective measures against such desires; they may be simple, uncomplicated acts and ideas or elaborate, ritualized patterns of thinking and behavior; their meaning may be obvious to the most unsophisticated observer, or they may be the end result of highly complicated psychological condensations and distortions that yield their secret only to the skilled investigator." Nemiah also notes: "When the obsessive-compulsive phenomena are psychic, no one would know that there was anything unusual going on in the patient unless he chose to divulge his purely private experiences." (p. 916.) [3]

A Reformulation

Obsessions and compulsions may be formulated in a manner analogous to phobias; both are learned, coping responses to situations. The basic *what* questions noted above are asked. A first observation is that the person may not emit the culturally expected act because he has not mastered the required responses. In a "Peanuts" panel, Linus tells of a beautiful girl; he was tongue-tied when he met her, so he did the only thing he could—he hit her. (It might be added that if she reinforced such behavior with smiles, attention, and respect, Linus might have been on his way to a stable pattern of sadistic heterosexual response maintained by aperiodic reinforcement.)

Obsessive-compulsive acts may be reinforced by keeping the person from certain situations. For example, in college it is socially acceptable to leave or avoid social

---

[3] For a distillate of the psychoanalytic formulation of obsessive-compulsive reaction, Nemiah (1967b, p. 923) is recommended.

situations in order to study. We have dealt with compulsive studying by finding out what was avoided, in this case members of the opposite sex, and then teaching ways of dealing pleasantly with these people. It is hard to say whether we were dealing with such a compulsion or with a phobia of opposite sex peers; we think we were just teaching people how to deal with situations so they no longer had to be avoided.

Some compulsions may quite technically be superstitious behavior; a behavior that was fortuitously followed by favorable consequences is repeated and the person is uncomfortable and unsure if he cannot emit the act. One of the senior author's best students was a woman who during examinations manifested trichotillomania (hair-pulling). It is related that as a schoolboy Sir Walter Scott was always second best in recitations to a boy who twisted his coat button while answering questions. Sir Walter one day cut the button off his rival's coat and became first in the class.

Many of the obsessions involve "uncontrollable impulses." For example, many unmarried college students suffer deprivations in the area of sex. They are likely to respond to a wide range of stimuli as relevant to a sexual dimension. Because they pay undue attention to this dimension, they may be said, compared to older married people, to be obsessed with sex.

Unreasonably high standards are frequently associated with obsessive-compulsive responses. Such standards may be reinforced as a socially acceptable excuse from activities. For example, men may have to meet such high standards to suit her that a particular woman may never date.

A matter touched on in Chapter 2 was differing frames of reference in judging behavior. A scientist may be working for a very select group of fellow scientists and may literally take decades to prepare his work. On the other hand, a student may have great difficulty completing a term paper or some other performance that has to be evaluated within a relatively short period of time. He can avoid the evaluation by not finishing or not turning in his work, regardless of the quality he has achieved in it. By chewing endlessly, the person need never swallow.[4]

In short, obsessive-compulsive behavior is a response to a situation that is evaluated by others as socially inadequate. The behavior may result from failure to learn a correct response or focusing on aspects of the situation other people deem unexpected and incorrect.[5] The formulation of obsessive-compulsive behavior is identical to that given for phobic behavior; the difference is that in the obsessive behavior the targets originally deemed changeworthy are repetitious thoughts and acts, while in phobic problems the target is avoidant behavior.

Behavioral Treatment of Obsessive-Compulsive Acts

Two direct deductions can be made from the foregoing material. The first is that the psychological situation in which the behavior is emitted is a better focus for treatment than the obsessive or compulsive behavior per se. If obsessive-compulsive behaviors are reactions to social situations, then the most direct form of treatment is the teaching of new ways to deal with those situations. This formulation is directly analogous to the treatment of phobias. *Any treatment of phobic behavior described in the previous chapter may be used in the treatment of obsessive-compulsive responses and vice versa.*

Both the development and treatment of compulsive behaviors may be illustrated by the same anecdote of a reinforced behavior becoming a stable role:

I have asked thousands of businessmen to smile at someone every hour of the day for a week and then to come to class and talk about the

[4] But Roper, Rachman, and Hodgson (1973) note that there is a decrease in tension when obsessive checking is over, and this immediately contingent consequence may reinforce the checking.
[5] For consistent, albeit not identical, theoretical analyses, see Rachman (1971) and Mather (1970).

results. How has it worked? Let's see . . . here is a letter from William B. Steinhardt, a member of the New York Curb Exchange. His case isn't isolated. In fact, it is typical of hundreds of others. "I have been married for over 18 years," writes Mr. Steinhardt, "and in all that time I have seldom smiled at my wife or spoken two dozen words to her from the time I got up until I was ready to leave for business. I was one of the worst grouches who ever walked down Broadway. Since you asked me to make a talk about my experience with smiles, I thought I would try it for a week. So the next morning, while combing my hair, I looked at my glum mug in the mirror and said to myself, "Bill, you have to wipe that scowl off that sour puss of yours today. You are going to smile. You are going to begin right now." As I sat down to breakfast, I greeted my wife with a "Good morning, my dear," and smiled as I said it. You warned that she might be surprised, well you underestimated her reaction. She was bewildered. She was shocked. . . . I soon found that everybody was smiling back at me. I treat those who come to me with complaints or grievances in a cheerful manner. I smile as I listen to them and I find that adjustments are accomplished much easier. I find that smiles are bringing me dollars, many dollars every day." [Carnegie, 1936, pp. 70–71.]

From the description it might be said that Mr. Steinhardt was on his way to becoming a compulsive smiler.

As a deduction from the view that "thoughts" are operants, Ullmann (1970) treated thoughts that disruptively intruded into a studying behavior by an application of the Premack principle (high frequency behaviors may be used to reinforce low frequency behaviors). The thoughts were more frequently occurring natural events than studying; hence permission to think the thoughts was made contingent upon completion of a small portion of studying. The amount to be studied prior to permission to think the thoughts was gradually increased. Instead of "fighting" the disruptive thoughts, they were used as reinforcing stimuli.

Mahoney (1971) tells of a 22-year-old man who experienced "pervasive and uncontrollable" thoughts that he was brain damaged, persecuted, and "odd." A variety of techniques were used, one being wearing a heavy rubber band and snapping it whenever the thoughts occurred, that is applying a mildly aversive stimulus. Of greater interest, was an effort to increase positive self-thoughts to replace the self-depreciatory ones. Cards with positive thoughts written out were attached to the client's cigarette pack; smoking was the reward for reading the positive material. The smoking and cards were then faded out as positive thoughts became spontaneous and satisfying in themselves. Aside from effective treatment of the obsessional material, the client obtained a job and overcame a mild depression. In addition to the clinical importance of this study, it indicates how "thoughts" may be treated as acts.

Yen (1971) used a technique of response cost called the "red-tape" method. An 18-year-old male who excessively checked items in the home, up to 25 different instances per evening, had to first write down the results of his checking and later, not only the results, but also what he had expected and what he would have done had things been amiss. Checking behavior stabilized between one and two times per evening.

Handwashing is considered a classic compulsive behavior; Bailey and Atchinson (1969) report how this behavior was reduced in a deaf-mute who was in the hospital for treatment of "epilepsy with a psychotic reaction." Observations were made on a variable interval schedule and if the person was *not* washing, he was reinforced with both attention and physical objects. A particularly strong reinforcer was given when four observations in a row showed nonwashing behavior. Wolpe (1964) and Rackensperger and Feinberg (1972) used systematic desensitization to reduce concern about dirt on hands.

Another classic compulsive behavior is repeated, purposeless stealing, that is, kleptomania. Kellam (1969) successfully used aversive stimuli to a film of shoplifting acts, Marzagão (1972) developed a hierarchy to desensitize the person to the social situations that led to anxiety and preceded the act of stealing, while Kraft (1970a) had the person first send money equal to the value of the object that had been purloined and then visit the store without shoplifting.

Rachman and his colleagues (Rachman, Hodgson, and Marks, 1971; Rachman, Hodgson, and Marzillier, 1970; Hodgson, Rachman, and Marks, 1972) make use of modeling and flooding (response prevention); Rainey (1972) and Boulougouris and Bassiakos (1973) report further on flooding methods, while Yamagami (1971) and Campbell (1973) made use of thought-stopping (see Chapter 12).

Additional illustrative cases are by Weiner (1967), Hersen (1968), Wisocki (1970), Bevan (1960), Haslam (1965a), Walton (1960a), Lazarus (1958), Tanner (1971), Taylor (1963). Meyer (1973), who reports on delay therapy, (in which one programs increasing duration between impulse and its gratification) writes accurately: "The range of obsessions and their consummatory compulsion behaviors are limited only by the imagination of the patient. The actual subset of the techniques should likewise be limited only by the ingenuity of the therapist." (p. 709.)

The over-riding points we can make from the methods that have been tried successfully in the clinic are: (1) direct treatment, (2) through a wide variety of procedures, both across cases and, more frequently than not, within the same case, so that (3) the person learns that he can be different and (4) the value of such new behavior. The value of experiencing change and new behavior by oneself has been well put by the noted psychoanalysts Alexander and French (1946):

Like the adage, nothing succeeds like success, there is no more powerful therapeutic factor than the performance of activities which were formerly neurotically impaired or inhibited. No insight, no emotional discharge, no recollection can be as reassuring as accomplishment in the actual life situation in which the individual failed. Thus the ego regains that confidence which is the fundamental condition, the prerequisite, of mental health. Every success encourages new trials, and decreases inferiority feelings, resentments, and their sequelae—fear, guilt, and resulting inhibitions. Successful attempts at productive work, love, self-assertion, or competition will change the vicious cycle to a benign one; as they are repeated, they become habitual and thus eventually bring about a complete change in the personality. [p. 40.]

DIFFUSE ANXIOUS BEHAVIOR

Phobic, obsessive-compulsive, and hysterical behaviors have been presumed to be ways of dealing with the discomfort produced by stimuli with which the individual cannot adequately deal. Supposedly, the discomfort is intrapsychic and not based on external, daily situations because that kind of uneasiness would have to be considered realistic. *Anxiety neurosis*, then, is defined in DSM-II as "characterized by anxious over-concern extending to panic and frequently associated with somatic symptoms. Unlike *Phobic neurosis,* anxiety may occur under any circumstance and is not restricted to specific situations or objects. This disorder must be distinguished from normal, apprehension or fear, which occurs in realistically dangerous situations." (DSM-II, p. 39.)

General Discussion

The DSM definitions of the neuroses previously given presented anxiety as an unpleasant state that was avoided or reduced by the symptomatic behavior. In anxiety neuroses presumably no such "defenses" exist, or, if they exist, they are diffuse and ineffective. The definition given above is purely descriptive and says anxiety is present. It notes that anxiety is "not restricted to definite situations or objects." This is a difficult concept for a psychologist, since it implies a response without a stimulus. Therefore, the first approach behaviorists take in dealing with anxiety states is to look for situations in which "anxiety" responses are emitted. That is, the behavior therapist may well treat an "anxiety reaction" as a complex phobic response.

The person may have developed phobic responses to many stimuli or to widely pervasive stimuli (Wolpe, 1964). Further, both stimuli and responses, may generalize. For example, a person may find a particular professor aversive and generalize this successively to the building he works in, to his field of specialization, to his university. The effective stimuli may be complex and diffuse —for example, some people are afraid of "largeness." It may be that the effective stimulus is a state within the person such as being tired or overworked or the like which has been associated with unpleasant events. Every time the person has a particular physiological state or a particular social relationship, he may redintegrate previous aversive situations. One of the behavior therapist's tasks is the difficult one of identifying the crucial situational dimensions. In this way, many "complex" anxiety reactions are found to be "simple." That is, by making the assumption that the origin of anxiety reactions is no different from that of phobias, many anxiety reactions are reduced to phobias and treated by methods such as systematic desensitization.

As noted previously, there are many behaviors leading to the label of anxiety— sweating, rapid heart beating, desire to urinate, shallow breathing, feelings of being choked, pupillary dilations, flushing of the face, tremulousness, dizziness, faintness and the like. The person acting the "anxious" role gets feedback, and therefore it is frequently hard to distinguish operant activity leading to respondents and respondents leading to operant behavior. Noyes and Kolb (1963, p. 395) make an interesting comment along these lines: "Hyperventilation is the common physiological means by which the subjective disturbance noted in the usual acute anxiety attack takes place."

A fearful response is likely to evoke various behaviors from other people. Such behaviors frequently are of sympathy and thus serve to reinforce the person in his anxious role behavior and make it more likely for him to continue. Some of our remarks on depression are relevant here.

Treatment techniques have made use of various forms of medication (tranquilizers and carbon-dioxide therapy) to reduce the physiological feedback. A behavioristic use of such medication has as its aim the development of new responses or the provision of a response-contingent environmental change. That is, the drugs will be given only in particular times and places so that the medication plays the same role as muscle relaxation.

The techniques used in dealing with phobias and obsessions can be used with anxiety responses as here formulated. If the person's own labeling and overt behavior provides stimuli that are responded to, then role-retraining is a major technique. A frequent role enactment requiring retraining has been labeled *assertiveness*. Standing up for one's *legitimate* rights is what is here meant by assertiveness. It does not mean asserting one's illegitimate rights, because the probabilities are that if one does so one will be punished. People in general are decent and rational, and if a person performs a legitimate act he is likely to be reinforced for doing so. If he does not perform a reasonable act, the feedback of not doing so, of foregoing legitimate reinforcement, may further add to his concept of himself as inadequate.

Training in assertion is along a hierarchy similar in design and conceptualization to that used in systematic desensitization. For example, in cases of extreme shyness toward members of the opposite sex, a college student might first be told that once a day he must smile at a member of the opposite sex. He is allowed to smile from 50 paces, but he should look at women and actually make the response. Smiling behavior is not likely to be punished. The distance of the smiling behavior may be gradually shortened. Next the person may be encouraged to take gradually closer geographical positions to members of the opposite sex. He may be encouraged to sit at the same table in the cafeteria. Hopefully, some interaction will take place by chance. He may be coached by his therapist in making innocuous social remarks. At various points, members of the class of females, such as psychology trainees or secretaries, may be introduced in the therapy situation.

In a different manner, he may be encouraged and coached both within the therapy hour and beyond it in emission of behaviors that are part of the assertive role (Wolpe, 1958, pp. 114–30; Wolpe and Lazarus, 1966, pp. 38–53; Rehm and Marston, 1968; McFall and Marston, 1970; McFall and Twentyman, 1973.) Such behaviors might be an increased emission of sentences beginning with "I," the increased use of words that express feeling, and the direct expression of his own feelings, his likes, and his dislikes (Perls, Hefferline, and Goodman, 1951; Salter, 1961). There may be role-playing of the situation with the therapist, who sometimes takes the role of a key environmental figure, sometimes the role of the patient. Seeing the therapist enact an assertive role may provide a model. The person playing himself as the therapist acts the part of the authority figure may give the therapist material to discuss and the client an opportunity to try out alternative responses. Systematic desensitization may be used conjointly for hierarchies of emitting new responses and visualizing what would happen with increasing assertion. That is, the therapist not only tries to build up a repertoire of responses, he also works to increase the probability that such responses will be made in situations outside therapy.

Albert Ellis (1962) has noted that a person may maintain behaviors by labeling himself or conceptualizing situations in an irritational or inaccurate manner. Ellis lists a number of irrational ideas that are frequent within contemporary American culture. If a person holds the following ideas, there may be many situations in which he cannot live up to his premises, to which he therefore will respond poorly, and in which he will evaluate himself as inadequate:

The idea that it is a dire necessity for an adult human being to be loved or approved by virtually every significant other person in his community. [p. 61.]

The idea that one should be thoroughly competent, adequate, and achieving in all possible respects if one is to consider oneself worthwhile. [p. 63.]

The idea that if something is or may be dangerous or fearsome, one should be terribly concerned about it and should keep dwelling on the possibility of its occurring. [p. 75.]

The idea that there is invariably a right, precise, and perfect solution to human problems and that it is catastrophic if this perfect solution is not found. [p. 86.]

Essentially Ellis endeavors to change the responses a person makes by modeling and shaping more rational self-evaluative statements. The therapist may punish the emission of irrational labels by arguing against them, by showing that they are foolish, and in other ways making the verbalization of these ideas itself a characteristic of being "bad." At the same time, the therapist reinforces the emission of different evaluations of situations.

Therapists such as Salter, Ellis, and Kelly all assign specific tasks. Their therapeutic maneuvers are oriented toward the emission by the patient of the behavior. Psychological skill is involved in making sure, as far as possible, of success in these external situations, and, if it is possible, providing some protection or face-saving device for the individual against those circumstances in which the therapist's suggestions do not work out.

Just as maladaptive behavior may generalize because it is reinforced, so it may be presumed that adaptive behavior will also

neuroses II: tensional components

generalize because it is reinforced. The importance of changed behavior in extratherapy situations was previously made through a quotation (Alexander and French, 1946, p. 40). It bears repeating, this time from Lief's (1967, p. 870) review of anxiety reactions: "Regardless of the form of treatment, the patient must practice new forms of behavior. Unless his changes in attitude are translated into behavior and are constantly practiced until they become automatic, as in learning any new skill, such as golf, tennis, dancing, or typing, treatment will have little value. A great deal of evidence supports the view that if a person changes his behavior (perhaps by external pressures) before he changes his attitude, his attitudes will also change, until they are in line with his new behavior. . . . In this fashion the patient can modify his environment or change his responses so that old stressful stimuli no longer evoke anxiety and discomfort." This is the goal; the remainder is a matter of technique.

HYPOCHONDRIACAL BEHAVIOR

This pattern of behavior ". . . is dominated by a preoccupation with the body and its functions and with fear of presumed diseases of various organs. Though the fears are not of delusional quality as in psychotic depression, they persist despite reassurance. The condition differs from hysterical neurosis in that there are no actual losses or distortions of function." (DSM-II, p. 41)

General Remarks

While the label "hypochondriac" is widely used in popular conversation, the pattern of concern, complaining, and generalized poor health used as an excuse to avoid social situations or control significant others was not included as a separate category in DSM-I. Burton (reprint, 1927, pp. 350–52), in the *Anatomy of Melancholy,* has a subsection on "windy hypochondriacal melancholy" in which he writes ". . . and therefore Crato boldly avers that, in this diversity of symptoms which commonly accompany this disease, *no physician can truly say what part is affected.*" (p. 350; Burton's italics.) And, as far as medical knowledge is concerned, no part is affected, although the person continues to complain, worry, be sensitive to all bodily sensations, and restrict his social life and that of those around him.

The distinction between hysteria and hypochondriacal behavior is well put in the DSM-II definition; we would note that Munchausen's syndrome, mentioned in the last chapter, has elements in common with both patterns.

Bianchi (1973) noted unnecessary operations, psychogenic pain, somatic preoccupation, and female gender as representative of hypochondriasis. The generalized weakness and concern may also make differentiation from neurasthenia difficult, while the repeated "thought" is similar to obsession.

Behavioral formulations and treatment of this condition are similar to other problems discussed in this chapter, especially anxious, depressed, and obsessive behavior. Examples are Gentry (1970a), desensitization of a fear of cancer, Furst and Cooper's (1970) report on the concerns people have about heart attacks, and Rifkin (1968) reports on desensitization of five cases of such fears, technically called *cardiac neurosis.* In a larger scheme, the somatic complaining is the subject of a functional analysis of behavior similar to that detailed in Chapter 27 on existential verbalizations.

DEPERSONALIZATION BEHAVIOR

Traditionally, *depersonalization* has been discussed in reference to people called schizophrenic and as one of the effects of drugs. It was not one of the neuroses listed in DSM-I. DSM-II defines *depersonalization neurosis* as follows: "This syndrome is dominated by a feeling of unreality and of estrangement from the self, body, or surroundings. This diagnosis should not be used if the condition is part of some other mental disorder such as an acute situational reaction. A brief experience of depersonalization is not necessarily a symptom of illness." (DSM-II, p. 41.)

General Comments

Experiences of depersonalization are very common. Dixon (1963) and Roberts (1960) report that a high percentage of normal people, including college students, report having had such experiences of vagueness, detachment, or observing themselves as if outside of themselves. In addition, fatigue, drugs, lack of sleep, or sensory deprivation may lead to these same experiences (Stedman, 1970). The reader may wish to try the following: repeat for two minutes a phrase, for example, "a rose is a rose is a rose . . ." After awhile, attention may drift and the reader may have the feeling of being an observer to the person producing the "is a rose, is a rose, is a rose." That will be roses but not neuroses. The last sentence of the definition quoted above is both true and important: to be changeworthy depersonalization must be recurrent, intrusive, and disruptive.

NEURASTHENIC BEHAVIOR

Neurasthenia, the third and last of the neuroses new to DSM-II "is characterized by complaints of chronic weakness, easy fatigability (*sic.!*), and sometimes exhaustion. Unlike in hysterical neurosis, the patient's complaints are genuinely distressing to him and there is no evidence of secondary gain. It differs from *anxiety neurosis* and from *psychophysiologic disorders* in the nature of the predominant complaint. It differs from *depressive neurosis* in the moderateness of the depression and the chronicity of its course. (In DSM-I, this condition was called 'Psychophysiologic nervous system reaction.')" (DSM-II, pp. 40–41).

The DSM-I definition of psychophysiologic nervous system reaction (DSM-I, p. 31) is as follows: "This category includes psychophysiologic asthenic reaction, [weakness, lack of strength] in which generalized fatigue is the predominating complaint. There may be associated visceral complaints. This term includes many cases formerly called 'neurasthenia.' In some instances, an asthenic reaction may represent a conversion reaction; if so, it will be so classified with asthenia as a manifestation. In other instances it may be a manifestation of anxiety reaction and should be recorded as such."

General Comments

The "predominant complaint" is weakness; if it were fear of illness or becoming sick, we would use the label "hypochondriasis," and if it were fear, tension, worry, or the like, the label "anxiety neurosis" would be applicable. The reader may wish to think of the degree of arousal experienced before an exam or an important interview. If this arousal were to persist for days or weeks, a feeling of exhaustion would be a genuine result. It is in this regard that the patterns called anxiety overlap with neurasthenia. In the same fashion, there is a lassitude, lack of operant output in depression, and the person may report inability to function due to weakness. Hence depression and neurasthenia also overlap in their manifestation.

It is important, ethically, scientifically, and therapeutically, to make sure that no physical illness is present when dealing with an individual who reports any bodily complaints. Slade (1968) points out that workers on a heart disease epidemiology study equated neurasthenia to neurocirculatory asthenia (weakness) and found that 20.8 percent of the sample between the ages of 30 and 60 could be so classified.

Beard in 1869 (Slade, 1968) or Van Deusen, two months earlier (Chatel and

Peele, 1970), are given credit for the first clinical descriptions under modern usage of the term neurasthenia. These writings gave a clinical description and application to the earlier concepts that many difficulties were due to nervous system irritation and exhaustion. Since it was more acceptable to be called neurasthenic (a medical term similar to contemporary use of the phrase "nervous breakdown") than insane, it was used so widely as to become the "garbage can of medicine." (Chatel and Peele, 1970, p. 1404.) The giant in the area is the late nineteenth-century formulator of the "rest cure," S. Weir Mitchell. Here is part of one of his clinical descriptions:

"Some years ago, I saw a woman . . . a pallid, feeble creature . . . everything wearied her—to walk, to drive, to sew. She was the woman with a back, and a shawl on her shoulders, and a sofa for a home, and hysterics for a diversion. She tired out the doctors, and exhausted drug shops and spas, and travel, and outlived a nurse or two . . . She was five feet four, and weighed 94 pounds, and had as much figure as a hat rack, and no more bosom than the average chicken of a boarding house table." (Quoted in Chatel and Peele, 1970, p. 1407).

Chatel and Peele comment that the scope of neurasthenia was like an accordion, stretching and contracting; a beautiful way of expressing the rise and fall of fads: "With the development of other neuroses, the bellows had little air, and the accordion was silent in the psychiatric literature from about 1910 to 1930." (p. 1405)

Further, ". . . we surveyed Saint Elizabeth's Hospital's [one of the largest psychiatric institutions in the United States—ed.] use of the diagnosis 'neurasthenia.' From 1855 to 1901, the term was never used. From 1902 onward it has never been used more than four times in any one year, and during many years it has not been used at all. Nor did we find any 'hidden' under the label 'neurophysiological reaction.' Of the 102,000 admissions to Saint Elizabeth's Hospital in the past 114 years, we would estimate that the term has been used fewer than 50 times." (Chatel and Peele, 1970, p. 1408). It will be interesting to see if there is an increase in the use of the term now that it is included in DSM-II. In the meantime, there is a dearth of literature to draw on. As a product of prolonged arousal or as an analogue of hypochondriasis, neurasthenic behavior seems, at this point of time, properly formulated and treated along the general lines previously discussed.

OTHER NEUROSES

The DSM-II (p. 41) definition of this category is that it "includes specific psychoneurotic disorders not classified elsewhere such as 'writers cramp' and other occupational neuroses." If there is a mixture of neurotic patterns, the diagnostic categorization is made on the basis of the one that predominates.

Discussion

The worker makes use of the general definition of neurosis and then uses the category, "other," for the explicit pattern. The present authors think that the category of special symptoms, to be discussed in the next chapter, is more accurate and serves the client better by providing a less upsetting label.

Liversedge and Sylvester (1955) conceive of writer's cramp as conditioned responses which are then reinforced by avoidance or escape from a situation. Their technique involved immediate aversive feedback for the disruptive behavior. If a person could not write because of a tremor, he was made to place a stylus in successively smaller holes of a metal plate. Contact with the side of the plate because of the tremor led to a shock to the palm of the nonwriting hand. If the person's difficulty involved spasms, he was asked to trace a zig-zag pattern with a stylus. If he touched the sides of the pattern, he received a shock. If his symptom was a claw-like clutching, a rubber pad was fixed to the palm of his hand, and any inappropriately great pressure led to a mild shock. In three sessions of twenty minutes each, a complete cure was achieved with a man who exhibited these last symptoms. In later work Sylvester and Liversedge (1960) report 39 cases, all of whom obtained some improvement. The authors consider that they obtained major improvement with 29 of the 39 cases within three to six weeks of treatment. On follow-up, the majority of the people who had been treated were found to be engaged in writing four to six hours per day. There was no evidence of symptom substitution. Liversedge and Sylvester note that as their experience in designing equipment increased, so did their rate of patient improvement. This raises a point common to all behavior therapies: a technology is involved. The present book can merely abstract and outline the procedures. Application of such procedures calls for intensive specialized training.

SUMMARY

This chapter dealt with those patterns of behavior called neurotic not covered in Chapter 13. These are phobias, obsessions and compulsions, anxiety reactions, and three new subcategories: hypochondriasis, neurasthenia, and depersonalization. Each of these sets of behaviors was approached from the sociopsychological framework outlined in earlier chapters. There was an illustration of treatment procedures involving behavioral techniques such as desensitization, the development of anxiety-relief responses, modeling, role-taking, reactive inhibition, and implosion. All of these methods deal directly with behavior. Even those situations in which the stimuli to which the individual reacts are obscure (as in anxiety reaction) are reducible to the same framework as those in which the stimuli seem clearer (as in phobias). In all of the treatment procedures cited, changes in the target behavior are related to other positive changes in the individual's life and do not result in symptom substitution.

Psychoanalysis of stutterers reveals the anal-sadistic universe of wishes as the basis of symptoms. For them, the function of speech regularly has an anal-sadistic significance. Speaking means, first, the utterance of obscene, especially anal, words and second, an aggressive act directly against the listener. . . .

The same motives which in childhood were directed against pleasurable playing with feces make their appearance again in the form of inhibitions or prohibitions of the pleasure of playing with words. The expulsion and retention of feces, and actually the retention of words, just as previously the retention of feces, may either be the reassurance against possible loss or a pleasurable auto-erotic activity. One may speak in stuttering, of a displacement upwards of the functions of the anal sphincters. . . . [1945, pp. 311–12.]

The present authors view stuttering as learned behavior and, in the absence of definite physical disability, as a behavior that may be directly retrained by a variety of techniques. The vast majority of human beings display some disfluencies in their speech. At the time they are learning speech, these may be particularly frequent. What seems vital is a differential response to the speech disfluency (Kasprisin–Burrelli, Egolf and Shames, 1972).

Evidence for this view comes from three major sources. The first is cross-cultural. Stewart (1971) examined the universality of stuttering as a problem in human communication by reviewing studies done in different cultural groups. His major finding was that stuttering did not occur in groups that did not have a term for it in their language and that recognized the nature of the process of child development and growth. Johnson (1965) has noted that labeling the child as a "stutterer" resulted in changed behavior toward the child, which in turn reinforced the speech difficulty.

A second source of data comes from "spontaneous recoveries." Many people who had a definite problem in stuttering during school years recover without professional intervention (Martyn and Sheehan, 1968; Sheehan and Martyn, 1970; Cooper, 1972). After the early teen period, this effect is absent.

The third source of data comes from direct manipulation of speech fluency. The reader may note the frequency of hesitations, gaps, grunts, and other breaks in the speech of typical college lecturers. There is ample disfluent behavior in normal speech to provide an operant that can be shaped by response-contingent reinforcement. This was done by Flanagan, Goldiamond, and Azrin (1959), who required normally fluent subjects to read from printed pages and recorded nonfluencies until a stable rate was established. A persistent shock was then introduced. Its cessation for a limited period was made contingent upon nonfluency. Stuttering was instated and then eliminated (eventual extinction when shock was disconnected) through this response-contingent procedure.

Sheehan (1951) pointed out that there is a positive reinforcement following stuttering, namely, the next fluently spoken word and the ability to continue. He therefore had as his experimental condition the repetition of the stuttered word until it was properly spoken, thus interfering with the reinforcement of stuttering by "going on to the next word." Not being able to continue to the next word, in turn, is a time-out from positive reinforcement, and when made response contingent (when the person stuttered he was not permitted to continue to hold attention as is the case in daily situations) stuttering decreased (Haroldson, Martin, and Starr, 1968; Martin and Haroldson, 1969; Egolf, Shames and Seltzer, 1971). That is, the reinforcing consequence noted by Sheehan was removed. Additional study of reinforcement contingencies are presented by Moore and Ritterman (1973) Daly and Frick (1970) and Egolf et al. (1972). Bar (1971) and Russell, Clark, and Van Sommers (1968) make the important point, implicit in many of the studies cited in this section, that the target, to be reinforced by positive consequences, is fluent speech.

A person may anticipate aversive consequences and may therefore be "anxious," or, in turn, because the person is dysfluent, he may be "anxious." Sheehan, Hadley, and Gould (1967) observed more stuttering when adult stutterers read passages to authority figures than when they read to peers. Adams (1969), after reviewing the literature, found that emotion-arousing stimulation impaired stutterers' performances. If one can pinpoint a problem area, then methods that reduce tension, such as systematic desensitization (Brutten and Shoemaker, 1967; Rosenthal, 1968; and Lanyon, 1969), become relevant and useful. Wahler et al. (1970) found that when child management problems decreased, stuttering was reduced.

An important technique and concept is that of distraction (Biggs and Sheehan, 1969), psychologically, or auditory interference (Webster and Lubker, 1968), physiologically. This concept is explicit in the Cherry-Sayers technique in which feedback is a crucial element. After conducting a series of laboratory studies which could serve as a model for the effective use of experimental findings in treatment, Cherry and Sayers (1956) argued that stammering is a perceptual rather than a motor disturbance. By having the person *shadow* speech he hears, that is, repeat *exactly* what he hears, lagging behind a reader by two syllables, the therapist diverts the person's attention from his own speech. Under these conditions, fluent speech is developed as a habit. Cherry and Sayers present ten cases, seven of which were successful. These cases illustrate the use of the technique with children as young as two-and-a-half years and with adults who had been nonfluent over 50 years. After training in the procedure of shadowing, it is possible for the subject, if he falls back into poor habits, to practice by himself and shadow a tape recording of someone else reading. Kondas (1967) has reported successful extension to work with children.

The Cherry-Sayers technique may be utilized within the context of other behavior therapies. Walton and Black (1958) report the case of a man whose stammer became markedly worse when he used a telephone. The treatment proceeded from reading two words behind the psychologist, then shadowing in this manner over the telephone, then relaying a message over the phone, then talking to people known to him, and finally talking over the telephone to people unknown to him. In another case (Walton and Mather, 1963) a 40-year-old married male was symptom free in the therapy situation after the use of the Cherry-Sayers method, but required systematic desensitization of a hierarchy of giving his superiors precise information before he was free of stammering in the extra-therapeutic environment.

In a further procedure to promote fluent speech in the extra-therapy situation, Meyer and Mair (1963) introduced a metronomic device similar in appearance to a hearing aid to pace speech. This device was integrated by Brady (1968; 1969; 1971; Berman and Brady, 1973) with other procedures into a very effective treatment package. In independent work, Azrin and his colleagues (Azrin, Jones, and Flye, 1968; Jones and Azrin, 1969) also developed the use of a portable metronome to aid in the synchronization of speech. Other helpful instruments, *which must be used within the context of a larger program and are aides but not treatment in themselves,* involve a portable masking noise (Perkins and Curlee, 1969) and the sound of a waterfall activated by the person speaking and ceasing when he listens (reported in *Time,* August 24, 1970, p. 42).

Yet another technique was introduced by Goldiamond (1965b) and extended by Curlee and Perkins (1969) and Ingham and Andrews (1973). The basic aspect of this procedure is the disruption of patterns of speech by delayed auditory feedback. The person, in order to monitor his own speech, slows down his verbal output and the resulting fluent speech is then shaped to a normal rate of emission.

From the foregoing it is possible to conclude that nonfluent speech may be treated by: aversive stimuli; positive reinforcement for fluency; extinction; deprivation to increase the reinforcement of fluent speech; negative practice; distraction and embedding in positive contexts; disruption of feedback; and systematic desensitization. In clinical practice, it is usual that some combination of these direct behavioral techniques will be used.

Learning Disturbance

A major institution for socialization in our culture is the school. A person learns skills basic to earning a living and being an effective citizen—for example, reading, computation, and writing. Difficulties may be the result of sensory or motor handicaps, specific brain injuries, retardation, and different cultural values and experiences. Problems may also involve responses to a school situation for which the person is unprepared and hence unable to deal with in a manner that is satisfying to either himself or to others who are significant to him, such as teachers. At this point we must simply draw a line due to limitations of space in this book, time in the reader's life, and competence on the part of the present authors. We recommend texts such as those by Telford and Sawrey (1972) and Cruickshank (1971).

Sleep Problems

Judging from the amount of medication sold, with and without prescription, insomnia seems to be a major problem for contemporary Americans (Dement, 1972; Kales and Kales, 1970). We will merely note some success by relaxation instructions (Weil and Goldfried, 1973; Kahn, Baker, and Weiss, 1968; Borkovec and Fowles, 1973; Geer and Katkin, 1966) and classical conditioning techniques (Poser, Fenton, and Scotton, 1965; Evans and Bond, 1969). Somnambulism was touched on in Chapter 13, and the effects of sleep deprivation will be touched on later in this chapter. Research on nightmares (Hersen, 1972) and dream content (Walker and Johnson, 1974) occupies many psychologists but is plagued by methodological problems.

One of the most interesting lines of current research makes use of attribution theory, or how the person labels himself (see Chapters 2 and 10). Storms and Nisbett (1970) gave insomniac people a placebo a few minutes before going to bed and told one group that it would cause arousal and the other group that it would cause decreased arousal (relaxation). The people in the supposed arousal condition got to sleep more quickly than they had on nights without pills because they attributed their arousal to the pills rather than themselves, while the supposed relaxation subjects got to sleep less quickly because they attributed their sleeplessness to unusually intense arousal that kept them awake after taking the pills.

Davision, Tsujimoto, and Glaros (1973) gave subjects a strong sleep medication and self-relaxation instructions. After treatment, half the subjects were told that they had been given the correct amount of the drug while the others were told they had been given too weak a dosage. All subjects were told to discontinue the drug but continue with the relaxation. Therapeutic gain was maintained better by those who had been told that they had received too weak a prescription, presumably because they attributed their improvement to themselves rather than the medicine.

Tic and Other Psychomotor Problems

A tic is an intermittent twitching or jerking of voluntary muscles. One common behavioral approach used in the treatment of tics is based on Dunlap's (1930) negative practice, although refinements of both the theory and the technique within the conceptual system of Clark L. Hull have led many therapists to use the term "reactive inhibition." Operationally, the person is asked to practice the unwanted behavior, the tic. By massing practice, fatigue is built up and the act of emitting the tic becomes painful and aversive. Conversely, not emitting the tic is reinforced through avoidance of fatigue. Further, the tic is emitted in the absence of the stimuli in the presence of which it is usually emitted. As such, there may be extinction through omission of the behavior without the presence of the "unconditioned stimulus."

In a different manner, Barrett (1962) controlled tics through differential favorable and unfavorable consequences contingent upon the emission of tics. She set up a program in which emission of tics interrupted music the individual wished to hear. Yates (1958b), Jones (1960a), and Nicassio et al. (1972) have reported on the use of reactive inhibition, and Walton (1961a) and Ernst (cited in Jones, 1960a, p. 257) have found it useful with 11- and 13-year-old subjects respectively. Rafi (1962) reports successful treatment of two cases, one by the reactive inhibition technique, the other by a more classic Pavlovian method. Frederick (1971) used both massed practice and systematic desensitization in treating a tic. Spasmodic torticollis, a contraction of the neck muscles causing head-turning and strange postures, has been responsive to operant training (Agras and Marshall, 1965; Brierely, 1967; Bernhardt, Hersen, and Barlow, 1972). Hollingworth reports a case where simple feedback was sufficient:

The method was simple enough. The patient wore spectacles. Whenever he had occasion to sit quietly, as in reading, a lead pencil was laid across the frame of the spectacles so that it lightly came in contact with the upper surface of the eyelids. This constant stimulus or load adequately inhibited the wink as long as the pencil remained in position. The boy then practiced lifting the eyelids and closing them at will, thus moving the pencil up and down. Developing voluntary control of a muscle means establishing some subtle inner cue as its effective stimulus. As this occurred, the stimulus to the previous "automatic" movement lost its effectiveness and the tic disappeared. [1930, p. 249.]

GILLES DE LA TOURETTE. A pattern of behavior that has muscular manifestations (such as those involved in tics) and verbal manifestations (such as those involved in stuttering) is called *Gilles de la Tourette syndrome.* There is an overreaction to sudden stimuli with a startle response and the emission of a grunt which over time usually shapes into an obscenity. In his original work de la Tourette drew heavily upon observations made by Dr. George M. Beard in the 1870's of 50 cases of French Canadians in Maine who jumped violently in response to sudden noise. This observation raised worldwide interest.

Clark (1966) reports on the treatment of three cases of Gilles de la Tourette syndrome. His method was based on the process of reactive inhibition as used with tics. He was successful with two of the three cases. The third case terminated treatment after ten sessions although at the time some progress had been made.

Miller (1970) treated a child who made barking noises by a combination of procedures: a quiet warning by a parent early in the emission of the behavior (before it became disruptive) and then time out from supper table, television, or other present activity to his bedroom where as much noise as he wished was permissible. In addition, there was reward for not emitting the target behavior. A major feature of a complicated case treated by Thomas, Abrams, and Johnson (1971) was self-monitoring, while Tophoff (1973) used mass practice, relaxation, and assertive training, and Lahey, McNees, and McNees (1973) used mass practice followed by a time out from reinforcement procedure.

Rosen and Wesner (1973) successfully treated a case of Tourette's syndrome with a strategy of teaching a substitute, less disruptive behavior. Another feature was using classmates to provide peer pressure by reinforcing them for time the subject's behavior was under control. Of particular importance in this work was the introduction of various conditions which demonstrated the operant nature of the problem. These studies are worth contrasting with that of Shapiro et al. (1973) who claim Tourette's syndrome is an organic impairment of the brain and suggest the use of drugs.

Other Target Behaviors

It is possible to make a nearly endless list of operant acts that people wish to change in others. Because of the amount of behavior taught in each culture and the relative power of parents and their offspring, many of these behaviors are associated with children and retardation, such as control of destructive behavior, self-feeding, grooming, and responsiveness to other people. Nail-biting (Bucher, 1968; McNamara, 1972), thumb-sucking (Skiba, Pettigrew, and Alden, 1971), and bruxism (tooth-grinding) (Heller and Strang, 1973), among others, have been treated by behavioral methods. These examples also have in common that they may be formulated psychoanalytically as oral equivalents, and diagnostically as compulsions or addictions, in a manner similar to smoking (Chapter 27) or overeating (see this chapter).

Feeding Problems

Anorexia nervosa involves severe malnutrition in an individual with no disease or organic pathology. Sours (1968) notes a mortality rate of from 5 to 15 percent. The individual simply rejects food. The term itself is defined by Bliss and Branch (1960, p. 24) as "a malnutrition due to deficient diet, in which the caloric restriction is entirely psychological and is not related directly to economic status or the availability of food." Bliss and Branch investigated 22 cases of anorexia nervosa (19 women and 3 men), with special emphasis on determining possible causes of the disorder. The major feature that seemed to characterize their patients was their enormous diversity in background and psychological makeup. Even the behaviors involved in losing weight were different. Some would refuse to eat; others would eat enormously and then vomit. This diversity so impressed Bliss and Branch that they concluded that anorexia nervosa was not a single disorder but covered many different and diverse disorders.[1] Sours (1968) also concluded that there was little to justify its classification as a specific nosological entity.

Perhaps the most useful way of conceptualizing anorexia is to view noneating behavior as an operant maintained by environmental consequences. The behavior of refusing to eat, irrespective of how it is developed, is maintained by the reactions of individuals to it. An illustration of this viewpoint is presented by Bachrach, Erwin, and Mohr (1965), who were called in to work with a woman whose weight had dropped from 120 pounds to 47 pounds and who seemed close to death.

The first thing done was to observe and analyze the patient's immediate environment. She was in an attractive hospital room with pictures on the wall, flowers, and a view of the grounds through her window. She had access to visitors, a radio, books, records, television, and magazines. People would visit her, read to her, and put on the TV for her. It was obvious that she enjoyed these activities and enjoyed her visitors. The experimenters considered that these stimuli could be positively reinforcing. She was removed from her pleasant hospital room and transferred to

---

[1] It may be noted that DSM-I listed it as an example of psychophysiological reactions, while many authors view it as a hysterical disorder.

a private room in the psychiatric ward which was furnished only with a bed, a night stand, a chair, and a sink.

The investigators obtained the cooperation of the patient's family and the hospital administration, particularly the nurses. Their initial program involved the total cessation of any visits from outsiders, medical staff, or training faculty. The nurses kept contact with the patient to the barest minimum and entered her room only to change her linen and to bring her water and meals. The patient was told that each of the three members of the investigating team, a resident, a psychologist, and a medical student, would eat one meal a day with her. When the patient lifted her fork to move toward spearing a piece of food, the experimenter would talk to her about something in which she might have an interest. The required response was then successively raised to lifting the food toward her mouth, chewing, and so forth. Initially, any part of the meal that was consumed would be the basis for an additional reinforcement, e.g., radio, TV set, or phonograph brought in by the nurse at a signal from the experimenter. More and more of the meal had to be consumed in order to be reinforced, until she was eventually required to eat everything on the plate.

The meals were slowly increased in caloric value, and her weight began to rise. There was a generalization of reinforcers from the experimenters' eating with her to a broader class of reinforcing events such as having a patient of her own choice eat with her in her room, or eating in the solarium with other patients. Later on she was taken for walks around the hospital grounds by a student nurse or a patient she selected. Her family and other visitors were also provided in increasing frequency as her eating and weight rose. All such reinforcements—visitors, walks, mail, setting and shampooing of hair—were postponed until after mealtime so that they would constitute the reinforcement for eating behavior.

At one point during her hospital stay, when she weighed 63 pounds, there was no further evidence of gaining weight. What had happened was that she was vomiting the food she did eat. It was decided to make all of the above reinforcements available, but contingent upon only a *gain in weight*, and not simply upon eating behavior. She was weighed every day at three o'clock, and the major class of reinforcements was made contingent upon the scale reading.

Six weeks after the experiment began the patient was discharged from the hospital, having gained 14 pounds while on the ward. In order to generalize the methods established under the controlled conditions of the hospital to the outside world, the experimenters enlisted the aid of the patient's family. They were instructed to avoid reinforcement of complaints, not to make an issue of eating, to reinforce weight maintenance verbally, to give her no special diet, to refrain from weighing her at home (the weighing in was to occur only on her periodic visits to the hospital), to discuss only pleasant topics at mealtimes, never to allow her to eat alone, to follow a rigid schedule for meals with an alarm clock at each meal, to use a purple tablecloth initially as a discriminative stimulus for mealtime table behavior, and to encourage her to dine out with others under enjoyable conditions.

Her weight continued to increase, and about a year later she was readmitted to the hospital to be tested again under controlled conditions for another six weeks. Upon her final discharge she weighed 88 pounds. She was followed for another year and a half, and reports indicated that her eating behavior and activity level continued high. Her weight stabilized in the 80's. She took a number of training courses as a nurse, her level of social interaction was high, and she was given a responsible nursing position. Similar successful uses of response-contingent reinforcement are reported by Leitenberg, Agras, and Thomson (1968); Stumphauzer (1969); Azerrad and Stafford (1969); Blinder, Freeman, and Stankard (1970); Scrignar (1971); Bianco

(1972); Elkin et al. (1973); and Lobb and Schaefer (1971).

One of the important points in presenting this case and listing its replications, is that the therapists at no time went into the possible etiology of the refusal to eat, or explored the usual kinds of personality dynamics. They did not argue against the notion of Nemiah (1950, 1961), among others, that the anorexic has a conflict over sexuality which is expressed in disturbed eating and which is interpreted psychodynamically as fear of oral impregnation. Rather, Bachrach et al. demonstrated that by focusing directly on the behavior, lack of eating, and by manipulating the reinforcements, it was possible to increase the patient's weight, with consequent results on how others reacted to her and how she saw her own role. As she became more effective, others reinforced this more effective role.

Hallsten (1965) reports on the treatment of a 12-year-old girl who was placed in a state psychiatric hospital because of anorexia nervosa. Three years before, at 90 pounds, she had been obese and had been called "Fatty." A bright girl, at nine she undertook a study of nutrition, made up a 1,000 calorie diet, and at the time of admission, was 25 pounds under her age-height-appropriate weight and had twice been in general hospitals because of her eating behavior.

Hallsten's report is of particular interest because the girl, Ann, did not gain weight during the first period of hospitalization while various drugs and threats were used. To teach Ann the elements of systematic desensitization, she was first treated for her fear of storms. During this period, her weight did not change. However, starting with the first session of desensitization on a hierarchy dealing with eating, her eating behavior and weight improved. Hospitalization and irrelevant densitization did not lead to a change, while desensitization on a relevant hierarchy did. The hierarchy included material on becoming fatter, a necessary procedure, for as she gained weight, her peers teased her, and she had to approach the situation from which she had previously "escaped." Ann's weight stabilized at an appropriate level. Schnurer, Rubin, and Roy (1973) report a similar treatment.

A person who ingests but vomits prior to digestion also may be called anorexic. Lang (1965a) reports his work with a 22-year-old nurse who had not been eating, had been vomiting, and had lost 20 pounds in the previous six months. Lang's approach was to reduce anxiety by increasing behaviors incompatible with it in key situations involving travel, reaction to criticism, and the classroom. As the patient's anxiety and discomfort decreased and she obtained positive responses from others, she began to eat, regained most of her weight, and only "rarely had problems in eating." At the end of a one-year follow-up she had maintained her gains and was enjoying life. Burgess (1969) presented a similar case. Alford, Blanchard, and Buckley (1972) used extinction to reduce vomiting as did Wolf et al. (1965) with a child whose vomiting had previously led to escape from the classroom. Smeets (1970) and Komechak (1971) have successfully used extinction to reduce vomiting in retarded people, while White and Taylor (1967), Luckey, Watson, and Musick (1968), and Kohlenberg (1970) used noxious stimuli to reduce vomiting and ruminations. Epstein and Hersen (1974) paid a man for each day his gagging decreased. Stoffelmayr (1970) and Mogan and O'Brien (1972) also report successful treatment of vomiting and retching responses by behavioral procedures.

A case that introduces a number of very important points is reported by Lang and Melamed (1969). A 9-month-old infant's life was seriously in danger because from his fifth month on, he would vomit the food he had ingested. He also re-chewed and ruminated. The behavior was quite possibly originally associated with thumb-sucking and gagging therefrom, but the behavior occured at the time of treatment, preceded by gagging without thumb-sucking (it could be, and at times had been, restrained). Aside from physical restraints, a wide gamut of surgical, pharmacological, dietary, and psychotherapeutic (i.e., one-to-one mothering) procedures had been tried. Using nurses' observation and electrical activity of the muscles involved in gagging, shock was administered at the start of each episode of vomiting. Shock was for one second with one-second interpulse time until vomiting ceased. After the first day of treatment, few shocks had to be administered. The child gained weight and, according to his pediatrician, on follow-up, was active, alert, and attentive. No evidence of symptom substitution was observed, but rather positive social behavior increased. Similar interventions in life-threatening situations are reported by Watkins (1972) who dealt with a severely retarded 14-year-old male who weighed 45 pounds, and Sajwaj, Libet, and Agras (in press) who treated a 6-month-old infant by squirting lemon juice in her mouth when rumination or its precursors were detected.

A point that should be raised involves the justification for the use of a noxious stimulus. Under what conditions is the use of aversive stimulation justified? Under what conditions would it be unjustified not to use it? We will return to this issue in Chapter 29.

Enuresis and Encopresis

We will discuss bowel and bladder control in Chapter 23, devoted to children.

Cephalagia

Cephalagia means headache and is frequently an important indication of genuine physiological disorder as in organic brain syndrome. Tension can lead to headaches, and if after careful medical examination tension is found to be the cause, behavioral and biofeedback methods may be of genuine assistance (Budzynski, Stoyva, and Adler, 1970; Leaf and Gaarder, 1971; Tasto and Hinkle, 1973).

Overeating

Operationally, anorexia nervosa is not eating enough and overeating is eating too much. For this reason, we will deal with overeating at this point although it has been placed by various authorities among the compulsions and addictions. We have written at length on overeating elsewhere (Krasner and Ullmann, 1973, pp. 309–25) and refer the reader to that effort for a summary of psychoanalytic and behavioral theories and a composite of self-control procedures used by behavior therapists.

In an increasingly sedentary society, it is easy to eat too much. The person who becomes overweight is denigrated and discriminated against (Mayer, 1968, pp. 84–91; *Time*, January 14, 1974, p. 8). While there have been important reports that treat weight reduction within the anxiety-compulsion paradigm (e.g., Bornstein and Sipprelle, 1973), self-control, environmental redesign, and social consequences seem to the present authors to be preferable approaches. The elements of self-control have been described by Ferster, Nurnberger and Levitt (1962); Goldiamond (1965b), Homme (1965), Mann (1972), Upper and Newton (1971), and Stuart (1967; 1971), as well as in the following citations. Solid experiments have been reported by Horan and Johnson (1971), Harmatz and Lapuc (1968), Harris (1969), Wollersheim (1970), Hagen (1970), Penick et al. (1971), and Mahoney, Moura, and Wade (1973), all using control groups and indicating the efficacy of behavioral techniques involving self-control.

The self-control procedures involved knowledge of ultimate aversive consequences, recording, training in the act of eating, control of the eating situation and getting supplies, self-reinforcement, and contingent social consequences.

GENERAL COMMENTS

With this background, we may return to the behavior formulation of the category of special symptoms. The reader will have noted that, in each case, the behavior was a response to a situation. Further, the components of an adequate response were taken into account as well as the pattern emitted currently. It is important to note that a great variety of approaches and specific treatment techniques are effective. Aside from the general therapeutic aspects of all influence procedures (as noted, for example, by Frank, 1965—see Chapter 12), the individual is given new information about his own behavior. Indeed, feedback about the person's acts may come from within his body as well as from sources or people external to it.

The difficulties may be part of larger patterns of changeworthy behavior, but this does not imply any causal relationship. A person with a tension headache is likely to become less patient and less tolerant of distractions. There may be a correlation between the two events, but the causality, if any, may be the reverse. We will return to this in our discussion of psychophysiological disorders. The point here is that behaviors may be dealt with one at a time even when a multitude of changeworthy behaviors are manifested at the same time. Frequently, indeed, change in one leads to favorable change in another.

TRANSIENT SITUATIONAL DISTURBANCE

At some time in life, every person acts in a manner that seems to those around him to be irrational, self-defeating, and different from both the way he himself typically acts and the way a person is expected to act. Students with three final exams on the same day, people who have lost jobs, or youths who have been served notices by their draft boards have all been known to be abrupt, impolite, or even anxious, depressed, and disorganized. To quote DSM-II (p. 48),

This major category is reserved for more or less transient disorders of any severity (including those of psychotic proportions) that occur in individuals without any apparent underlying mental disorders and that represent an acute reaction to overwhelming environmental stress. A diagnosis in this category should specify the cause and manifestations of the disturbance so far as possible. If the patient has good adaptive capacity, his symptoms usually recede as the stress diminishes. If, however, the symptoms persist after the stress is removed, the diagnosis of another mental disorder is indicated.

The subcategories are by age, that is, adjustment reaction of infancy, of childhood, of adolescence, of adult life, and of late life. For example, an adjustment reaction of adult life would be "A Ganser syndrome associated with death sentence and manifested by incorrect but approximate answers to questions" (DSM-II, p. 49).

An important feature of the definition to which attention must be given is the concept of an "overwhelming" situation. Three things must be noted. The first is that an overwhelming situation is one that people in general, and psychiatrists in particular, would consider hard and difficult to cope with. If the labeler considers the stimuli to be adequate to justify the behavior (operationally, might he, the labeler, have emitted undesirable behavior in such a situation?), he is more likely to call it an overwhelming situation. This is a not unusual frame of reference: it implies that to understand all is to forgive all. An example of this distinction comes from Maher:

When a patient is responding to stimuli which are not present to observers, he may be regarded as having lost contact with reality. Reality, in this case, is defined by the consensus of other observers present. . . . Sensory deprivation as well as certain drug and fatigue effects may induce behavior indicative of hallucinations; we tend to reject them as signs of psychosis mainly because we are able to assign another antecedent to them. [1966, p. 6.]

A second feature of an "overwhelming" situation is that it overwhelms a particular individual. This is alluded to as adjustive capacity, which might, in a psychoanalytic model, be considered an enduring trait of the individual resulting from his level of psychosexual development. The present authors think it is preferable to define the situation in terms of the likelihood of the person's emitting a response satisfactory to himself and to others. The greater the range of situations in which the person will emit such responses the greater, it might be said, is his adjustive capacity. If adjustive capacity is defined as a high probability of a socially effective response, an "overwhelming" situation is one to which the person does not emit such a response.

The third feature of an "overwhelming" situation is the need to specify, if possible, what sorts of situations are likely to be so categorized. One way to approach this is to canvass the DSM-II situations in which the diagnosis is likely to be made. Separation from mother, birth of a sibling, school failure, unwanted pregnancy, combat, death sentence, and enforced retirement are examples. A situation may be said to be overwhelming when it is so rare or so difficult that the person has not been taught how to deal with it. More generally, a situation is "overwhelming" when few, if any, responses the person could conceivably make are likely to be satisfying. As such, the person's adjustive capacity is one side of the situation, and an abrupt change of reinforcing contingencies is the other. Basic training in the army may be viewed as such a situation (Bourne, 1967).

Continual effort is being made to operationalize the concept of stress as it applies to human behavioral difficulties. Dohrenwend (1973a) notes that there are two, not completely separated, conceptions of stressfulness, namely, undesirability and life change. Dohrenwend (1973b) notes that people of lower social status are exposed to more stressful life events, which may be one reason for the greater number of behavioral problems among such people. Myers et al. (1972) report that the greater the net change in life events over a two-year period, the greater the change in mental status, with an increase in life events being associated with a worsening and a decrease in life events, an improvement in mental status. Vinokur and Selzer (1973) provide data that undesirable life events, but not desirable ones (for example, a job promotion), were related to stress or emotional disturbance. While various lists of events are used (for example, Holmes and Rahe, 1967), the inventories generally include material on such matters as marital status, family composition, physical health, employment, education, and place of residence.

A very major point is whether the changed life events are causes or effects of the individual's actions. While the usual view is that they are causal, Fontana et al. (1972) raise some interesting questions. After noting that a dramatic rise in changed life events during the preceding year was found for patients who were hospitalized as compared to a nonhospitalized group, these authors found that most of the events in the patients' lives occurred as a result of some action on the part of the patients themselves rather than having been imposed on them by circumstances beyond their control. Also, most of these events were involved with problems prompting hospitalization, and the frequency of various events differed among patients according to the patients' preferred explanations for their troubles.

The difficulties and the results of the difficulties cannot be separated. For example, as a person drinks more and is more often openly hostile, his employment or marital adjustment may change in an undesirable manner, leading to occasions for increased drinking and/or more open hostility. Fontana et al. ask whether the individual himself may not manipulate stressful events as an aspect of his style of coping with life.

A last point raised by the DSM-II definition is that the outcome of treatment indicates whether or not a person has suffered a transient situational disturbance. If the person improves rapidly, or with a minimum amount of treatment, he is called a transient situational personality disorder. If the person does *not* improve, by definition it was not because the therapy was poor but because the behavior was the manifestation of some "deeper," more severe ailment and hence another label should have been assigned.

General Discussion

An example of the complex relationship between situation and "transient" response is one with which the reader may be familiar: that of studying under great pressure. The person is placed in a situation that has been a discriminative stimulus for a high probability of aversive feedback in the past. That is, he is vulnerable, for he must make responses but has difficulty in emitting them. This situation in itself is aversive. The stimuli that make up the situation and the labeling of the person by himself as being in such a situation may feed back at both an operant and respondent level, redintegrating prior uncomfortable situations.

Another example involves driving on slippery city streets, or foggy roads, or roads with poor shoulders and worse drivers. The person is driving on a long trip; under these circumstances extreme conscientiousness and meticulousness is demanded. The likelihood of having an accident leads to a great expenditure of energy; literally, the person is working fairly steadily to avoid punishment. A small amount of risk that is not too prolonged may be experienced as a challenge and may be mildly stimulating. Some people may later be surprised how well they worked at the task, how well they drove. The difficulty, however, may become greater or more prolonged. Further, the danger is not definite in its location; that is, there is no way of controlling the other bad drivers. Over a period of time there may be genuine physiological changes and fatigue. Attention becomes focused on possible sources of danger, and spontaneity may be lost.

Certain features of behavior may become exaggerated; a person may become a clutch-rider, or may have his foot steadily on the brake. He keeps being set for danger and exaggerates precautionary behavior. He responds more and more exclusively to limited cues in the situation. As time progresses, or danger mounts, the continued focusing of attention may become increasingly difficult; and the person may become less capable simply through fatigue. His thoughts may be incessantly occupied with the danger he faces, and he has difficulty in inhibiting bodily responses. Some of these are respondents and physiological correlates of anticipation of aversive consequences: that is, perspiration, tremor, restlessness, fast-beating heart, and quickened breathing. Thought and judgment may deteriorate, actions may become erratic or uncoordinated; new acts may be started before others are completed.

The person is so set to respond to elements without their proper context that he may not properly evaluate a stimulus before initiating a response to it. He may emit parts of two inconsistent operant behaviors at the same time. He may start oversteering, may start moving from side to side on the road, may brake too rapidly, or may start braking when indeed there was no point to braking the car. He is erratic; he may react to his own behavior by increased feelings of discomfort. He is indeed driving poorly, and he should recognize this. Not only does he act in a certain way, but he gets feedback from these acts. He may have a feeling of being overburdened, incompetent, vulnerable, and very likely to have a severe accident. In an extreme state the entire situation may resemble a nightmare in which he is rushing wildly about.

The end product of such situations in human beings resembles the behavior of laboratory animals who have undergone the development of experimental neurosis. The person must respond, but he cannot distinguish between the correct and incorrect response. The discrimination is too difficult for him. In situations such as these the animals display a wide range of unexpected, seemingly unreasonable behavior, including loss of ability to make discriminations they previously were able to make.

Panic as a Paradigm of the Transient Situational Disturbances

Schultz (1964, pp. 6–8) has distinguished two aspects of the definition of panic behavior: (1) There is overt "fleeing" behavior (this distinguishes the definition from economic panics) which leads to the destruction of the group; (2) the "fleeing" behavior must be nonadaptive for the physical survival of the group members. There is the implication that if the fleeing behavior is adaptive, the situation is not one of panic. One of the conditions most likely to lead to panic behavior is the prior destruction of the psychological group. "The three essential components of our definition of panic thus become fear, flight, and limited access to escape routes." (Schultz, 1964, p. 8.) The usual reinforcing contingencies that militate against both flight and the treatment of other people as obstacles are withdrawn. The situation may be so novel that there are no standard and previously practiced methods for dealing with it. Panic may occur when "a highly cherished value is threatened and when no reduction or elimination of threat is apparent." (Schultz, 1964, p. 17.) In behavioral terms, there is an aversive situation in which no satisfactory behavior seems possible; the perceived reward situation is such that typical cooperation between people breaks down and flight appears the only adaptive response.

In flight the person becomes deprived of his previous methods of dealing with situations and must emit new procedures (1) at which he may be unskilled, (2) which may seem good ideas because of some unessential similarity to previous solutions, or (3) which may even be poor solutions, i.e., low on anyone's repertoire, but simply the best behavior available under the circumstances. Again, feedback may add to the stressfulness of the situation: "Human beings usually become panicked in situations which have previously been linguistically defined as fearful or terrifying." (Lindesmith and Strauss, 1949, p. 332.)

A social learning analysis of panic focuses on the observations that "panic develops only when possible avenues for escape become evident." (Foreman, 1953.) Under these circumstances there is potential reinforcement, a discriminative stimulus, for the "panic" behavior. In both the laboratory (Mintz, 1951) and observed (submarine and mine) disasters where there is no possible exit from the situation, panics do not develop.

Aside from any properties of the situation itself, the *behavior of others* in the situation may increase the chance of panic behavior, when there is disregard of normal social patterns. To quote Mintz (1951): "But, if the cooperative pattern of behavior is disturbed, the usual advice, 'Keep your head, don't push, wait for your turn, and you will be safe,' ceases to be valid." That is, the typical social contract learned previously and implicit in most "normal" situations is no longer operative and, hence, no longer observed. The pushing of the people illustrates that the contract has been abrogated (Kelley et al., 1965). The pushing individuals threaten the person, and his strict adherence to prior rules becomes a threat to his life. Schultz (1964, p. 62) makes the point that of seven panic incidents observed during World War II, all had the same origin: the sight of a few members of the group in full and unexplained flight to the rear.

The present analysis permits a discussion of what is meant by impulsive behavior. Quarantelli (1954) puts it this way: "Thus panic is marked by loss of self control. . . ." and Foreman (1953): "Panic is extremely impulsive action." What seems to be the case, operationally, is that stimulus contingencies that typically and previously controlled behavior are no longer effective. Panic behavior is impulsive or uncontrolled only in that an observer has difficulty determining the stimuli to which the person is reacting. The label "impulsive" is likely to be used when, as in panic and in schizophrenia (as will be seen in Chapter 18), the expected discriminative stimuli are not attended to. In such instances the person's behavior is idiosyncratic, which means it is relatively less predictable from the patterns of other people. However, the person is still responding to stimuli. The concept "impulsive" or "uncontrolled" is a function of the observers' deficit, not of the behavior itself.

In short, panic behavior may occur when previous patterns of behavior are not operative and the restrictions against alternative behavior have been reduced. The behavior may be seemingly self-defeating and incomprehensible to an "objective" observer, but the situation is one in which any possible solution may be tried.

CIVILIAN DISASTER

The most notable rapid alteration of reinforcing stimuli occurs in the case of fires, floods, and earthquakes (Coblentz, 1950; Barton, 1969). In these cases one's life may be directly threatened and one's work or place of employment may be lost. On a more long-term basis, disasters may occur in the form of an industry shutting down, depriving a person of employment, status, and dignity, or in the form of urban renewal and consequent enforced relocation.

In the first stages of the so-called shock reaction, the individual does not know what to do. He may look stunned, dazed, or apathetic, and he will do whatever he is told. He may wander around aimlessly until someone guides him or reorients him. This may be followed by a stage in which he willingly seeks and takes directions and seems passive. The person tries to perform his tasks. He may be inefficient even in performing well-practiced routines. There may also be a stage in which he talks endlessly about the situation or asserts himself, criticizes the people in charge, and essentially formulates the meaning of the incident for himself.

Much depends on what happens at this stage; for instance, whether there is reinforcement in terms of potential compensations or avoidance of duties. If his endless repetition and recounting of the situation is positively reinforced rather than met matter-of-factly, the person may be shaped to an enduring pattern of behavior, one which is more difficult to deal with at a later date because it will have had a history of widespread reinforcement. The endless talking may be of value if paired with relaxation responses (e.g., desensitization), and the expression of criticism may be a form of assertive therapy.

A civilian catastrophe of a different nature has been found with families from neighborhoods who have been forced to move because of urban renewal. Even though these people have been relocated in new and superior homes, some of them have suffered depressions lasting from six months to two years. Previous patterns of behavior and specific people who had been reinforcing were lost. The individuals who had had many friends and neighbors, and who could spend their lives with people with similar interests and patterns of behavior, found that suddenly all this had changed. They were put in situations different from any they had ever experienced before. There may, in this situation, be "culture shock." That is, the person does not know how to act, and may even go about reinstituting conditions that are evaluated as undesirable but are the ones to which he had been previously accustomed. Not knowing how to act, and therefore not acting, may lead to a diagnosis of depression.[2]

WAR NEUROSIS

War neurosis is typically experienced by persons who have spent periods of up to several months in a danger zone, who have been pinned down by severe shell fire for two or three days, or who have seen a buddy who has been a source of reinforcement killed and who may therefore experience conflict between relief at not having been killed and guilt over that feeling of relief. Various types of reinforcing stimuli maintain a person in his social role of good soldier. High ideals seem to be less enduring, and less effective, than hatred of the enemy, which in turn is less effective than a short-term military objective, which is less effective and more likely to be given up than the reinforcement that comes from pride (ability to label one self in positive terms), which in turn is less effective than loyalty toward and maintenance of appropriate role behavior in the group. This hierarchy seems ordered by immediacy and explicitness of the locus of reinforcing stimuli. The death of a buddy may be the most disruptive of all, since it deprives the person of his most important immediate reinforcing stimulus.

In both World Wars and the Korean War the most effective form of remediation was an expectancy, firmly communicated to the soldier, that he should and would return to duty. The further he was removed from combat, the more difficult treatment became. On the one hand, the soldier was reinforced for a sick role, and

[2] A similar situation occurs when an individual retires from the military and faces a life situation in which many new role behaviors are required. See McNeil and Giffen (1967).

on the other hand that role was so validated by medical procedures that giving it up became more difficult. The favored treatment was to provide the soldier with warm food, medication, sleep, and physical recuperation. As soon as possible, he was returned to the highest level of duty feasible. (Brill, 1967.)

In general, between 80 and 90 percent of men can be returned to duty, and only 10 percent of these will break a second time. The program of prevention involves the development of attitudes and conditions which maintain group stability and positive reinforcement. That is, the amount of positive reinforcement reciprocally received in the immediate military group is increased so that violation of group norms becomes less likely. Second, there is early recognition and prompt management of maladaptive behavior. If it is at all possible, the person is removed from the stressful situation as rapidly as feasible. Finally, there is prompt and complete treatment within the military situation to avoid having the soldier discharged as ill, labeled as such, and given compensation (Bloch, 1969).

The most frequently occurring type of war neurosis to be treated is one in which the soldier has had a traumatic experience and now emits either diffuse fearful responses or is amnesic for the total situation. It is usually presumed, however, that he, at some level, remembers this material and spends a great deal of energy repressing it. Treatment typically involves either hypnosis or a drug such as sodium pentothal or sodium amytal, under which the person discusses and relives the traumatic situation. This kind of treatment is similar theoretically and clinically to catharsis (Chapter 8).

This treatment may be reformulated behaviorally by noting that the person is brought into contact with the situation while relaxed by the drug and protected by the therapist. If this is the case, then an alternative possibility for treatment is directly behavioral and follows the desensitization paradigm. Two reports provide illustrations of such treatment programs of combat problems.

The first, by Pascal (1947), describes 12 cases, ten of whom improved dramatically in an average of seven sessions. The two failures were caused by transfer by the army of the therapist in one case and of the patient in the other. This means that Pascal reported ten successes out of ten in an average of seven sessions. The procedure was to relax the soldier and then to have him talk about his experiences while relaxed. The therapist would suggest the scene sketchily on the basis of the information received in the interview.

The relaxation was induced by hyperventilation and associated muscle relaxation rather than by hypnosis or drugs. The therapist had the men imagine that they were in the traumatic situation. His theory was that he wanted to obtain recall of repressed material and, hence, abreaction. He argued that (1) what causes repression is anxiety; (2) relaxation reduces anxiety; therefore (3) it will reduce repression. Pascal was using a neo-Freudian medical model, but operationally he was obtaining relaxation and then pairing relevant material with the relaxed state. The success, ten out of ten, is as great as any reported with the use of drugs or hypnosis. It is impossible to say on the basis of this report which theory was correct, that of reducing repression and bringing material to consciousness or that of reconditioning.

Another study of combat problems is by Saul, Rome, and Leuser (1946). These authors observed the similarity between training for combat and training police horses for traffic duty. The horses had to be taught not to respond with startle patterns to noises or sudden stimuli. This was accomplished by gradually exposing the horses to the target situations. These authors therefore used gradual exposure to films of naval combat with war neurosis patients. The authors describe work with 14 patients, with whom they obtained marked success in 13 cases in an average of 12 fifteen-minute showings. They utilized three major principles of therapy. First, the patient's confidence had to be developed and maintained by having a staff member, whom he knew was interested in him, present in the situation. The group of patients viewing the movies was kept small, and more than 6 were never present at any one time.

The second principle in the therapy was that of gradualness. The showings of the movies started in the morning with the shades up and door open. The patient could stand at the door and peek into the room. He was allowed to walk out whenever he wanted to. He was encouraged to talk and to criticize the action as an expert. At first there were no sound effects. They were later gradually introduced. At times the patient himself had control of the level of sound amplification. After the patients became bored with scenes that had previously terrified them, they were shown pictures of hand-to-hand combat. They were also encouraged to see newsreels, movies, and similar events that they previously had avoided. Combined with gradualness, the third principle was that the patient was able to control the strength of the stimuli. Care was taken throughout the treatment that the protection given to the patient was far stronger than the emotional behavior the stimuli might provoke.

The successful treatment of 13 out of 14 cases in an average of three hours, based on the efforts of an enlisted man using a projector, again compares quite favorably with other procedures. It is also worth noting that both articles described procedures that took place geographically quite distant from the combat lines and thus probably dealt with more difficult cases.

PRISONERS OF WAR

Another situation which may be included among those leading to transient behavioral disturbances is that of being in a prisoner-of-war camp. Such a situation is in and of itself enormously stressful. The individual finds himself cut off from all of his usual sources of support and in an adverse physical and psychological situation. There is a special subtype of prisoner-of-war situation which has aroused considerable attention in recent years. This is one in which the captors deliberately manipulate the living conditions to bring about a change in the behavior of the prisoner. That is, the captors utilize the environment to obtain a confession from the prisoner, to enlist his assistance in their propaganda program, to alter his identification with his own country's goals, or to become more sympathetic to their long-range aims. This type of milieu control is popularly called brainwashing. Other terms that have been used to describe these techniques include "thought reform," "thought control," and "political conditioning."

The term "brainwashing" has become part of the American vocabulary since the process was described by George Orwell in his novel *1984*. The phrase designated an environmental control so absolute that its effects were the same as if one took out a person's brain and literally washed it clear of all thoughts considered undesirable by the authorities. Brainwashing as a political and social means of influence came into prominence during the Korean War, when large numbers of American prisoners fell into the hands of the Chinese. (Kinkead, 1959.) Special psychiatric teams interviewed all returning prisoners in Korea over a period of several months. As a result, a picture of the techniques employed emerged. (Lifton, 1954; Segal, 1954; Strassman, Thaler, and Schein, 1956.)

The behavior of the prisoners when they were eventually released and found themselves in the safety of an American hospital setting was characterized by apathy, detachment, loss of spontaneity, tenseness, suspiciousness, confusion, and ambivalence, both to their former captors and to their current saviors. In many ways this behavior was similar to that of individuals who have undergone a major catastrophe such as a fire or earthquake. This "zombie-like" reaction "wore off" to some extent after about a week. However, reports of feelings of alienation from others, apprehensiveness, confusion, and outbursts of hostility still characterized the repatriates' behavior for a considerable period of time. Subsequent reports indicate that most of the returning prisoners were eventually able to effect an adequate adjustment to American society.

Farber, Harlow, and West (1957) offered the conditions of DDD—Debility-Dependency-Dread—as being the basic ingredients of the thought-reform process. They point out that the conditions of DDD lead to increased susceptibility to conditioning. The Chinese used DDD on an intermittent reinforcement schedule. The first objective was to control prisoner expectancy. When captured, the prisoner was frightened and apprehensive and expected to be executed or severely tortured. He was physically weak, and dependent upon his captor for his very life. Instead of torture, the prisoner more often than not encountered a friendly captor who would offer him a cigarette and welcome him as a friend. Throughout the subsequent imprisonment there would be an alternation of friendship and harshness. As the prisoner found himself unable to predict what he might expect from his captor, he became more responsive to reinforcing stimuli and even more susceptible to the captor's influence.

Lifton (1956, 1957a, b) describes the systematic use of "milieu control," which involved the control and manipulation of all communication and sensory stimulation and compares it to the effects of sensory deprivation (Lilly, 1956). In both instances the subject is unable to check on what is reality. Having no other source of verification or information, he has no alternative but to accept the communications which come to him. Control of input of stimuli in the POW camp affected the kinds of letters that were allowed to reach the prisoners (bills, "Dear John" letters), newspapers, books, radio broadcasts, and lectures. Any information contrary to the attitudes to be developed was withheld from the prisoners. In some instances sensory input was severely limited by placing the prisoners (usually Air Force officers) in physical isolation. In a very large percentage of instances confessions of germ warfare followed soon after such physical isolation and deliberate sensory deprivation.

Among the prisoners handled on a group basis, techniques apparently similar to those found in conventional group therapy were used. The prisoners were encouraged to verbalize hostility and to examine both their political beliefs and their personal responses to imprisonment. Self-examination and confession by prisoners were amply rewarded. Typically there was group pressure to engage in this activity. The entire company would not be permitted to eat or to participate in an enjoyable activity until everyone had engaged in some sort of self-expression. It did not matter at the beginning how superficial such self-examination was as long as the person engaged in it. Therefore, not only did the prisoner have to choose to do something trivial and be reinforced, but he also had the pressure that failure to participate delayed reinforcement for his fellow prisoners. Once an activity was engaged in, its reprehensibleness was reduced. The prisoner's beliefs and his overt behavior were at variance, and it is usually easier in that situation to alter one's beliefs. (Festinger, 1957.)

There is great pressure in our society in general and specifically in a military situation to be loyal to one's comrades. However, disloyalty did not lead to severe punishment of the person informed upon, but rather very mild remonstration. The immediate reinforcement for the informer and the lack of violent negative effects on the informed on were such that one in ten prisoners of war did play the informer role at some time. In this situation it quickly developed that no prisoner knew who was an informer and who was not, who could be trusted and who could not. As a result, group feeling was destroyed.

The same techniques were far more intensively applied by the Chinese to their own political prisoners (Lifton, 1961). The Communist instructors would have prisoners ascribe the causes of their misfortune to the former regime. They would "dig up the roots." The prisoners were encouraged to become part of the forces of the revolution, the "one heart" movement. Communist soldiers stressed morality and dedication through personal example. Such examples were contrary to what had been observed in the anti-Communist ranks. There was encouragement of the expression of grievances against non-Communist groups, and the Communist goals were presented as highly desirable.

There was heavy reliance on group discussion, creating an atmosphere in which students had to commit themselves and subject themselves to detailed scrutiny and analysis. There was use of criticism and self-criticism to stimulate self-examination and permit group members to compete with each other in self-exposure and mutual exposure. The aim of this procedure was the denigration and hence destruction of all emotional ties with the past. There was systematic rewarding by group members and authorities for self-exposure, confession, and self-criticism, thus setting the tone that any man was redeemable if he was willing to allow "reactionary tendencies" to be exorcised. There was also mutual surveillance in which if person A failed to report person B and some other person reported B, A would then become suspect. "As this process takes hold, one may expect that individuals increasingly lose their ability to identify what others really believe, because it becomes increasingly difficult to check the accuracy of their perception. To the extent that the government succeeds in creating an image of the world as a place in which what a person says publicly is taken to be equivalent to what he believes privately, it undermines the individual's confidence in the belief that he and others have of a private world or makes him forget how to go about looking for it." (Schein, Schneier, and Barker, 1961, p. 77.)

The evidence provided the prisoner in terms of propaganda, his own behavior, his current situation, and the reinforcement for taking an alternative point of view all led to an "unfreezing" of his previously held opinions and beliefs. The crucial turning point was to "take the Communist point of view," that is, to permit himself to see things from the Communists' assumptions and position. Once this assumption was made, everything fell into place and there existed both an explanation of why things had happened and a method of ending the aversive stimulation.

The major stresses operating to unfreeze, confess, and take the Communists' point of view were the prisoner's fear for himself or for others, his desire to comply with the wishes of others, his desire to relieve the pressure from his cellmate who viewed him as a traitor, a saboteur, and the like, the desire to end pain, to achieve a relationship with cellmates, to adapt and achieve a sense of reality, to settle his case and be released, and to just end the whole situation.

To counter these immediate concerns there were only nonmaterial distant concepts that were not being maintained in the face of the attitudes of his captors, the reality of his situation, and the behavior of his cellmates. These vaguer concepts included fear of going against his own values, fear of inconsistency with his self-image, probable loss of integrity, inability to be intellectually dishonest, fear of violating reference-group norms, fear of future consequences, unwillingness to be coerced, fear of punishment for a false confession, and the like. Therefore, confession was an immediate solution to real problems, whereas not to confess was maintained by inoperative distant values. Once a person accepted the Communist line, these threats were relieved, and his behavior of confessing was thoroughly reinforced to the point where it became ritualized and easier to believe in than not believe in.

It should be pointed out that there was considerable difference in susceptibility to these thought-reform influences among American POW's. To begin with, there was a screening process by the captors to segregate "natural" leaders (estimated at about 5 percent) from the remainder, on whom the more intensive efforts were tried. The "thought-reform" techniques were considered least effective among those individuals with strong religious beliefs and with those who were usually disciplinary problems under the best of circumstances.

Most, if not all, behavior, feelings, and attitudes returned to "normal" when the prisoners were removed from the camps and returned to their previous home environments. The situation now called for different behaviors, and most were able to "readjust."

The "brainwashing" situation has been described in detail to demonstrate the following points: (1) The same kind of sociopsychological analysis in terms of expectancy, role, reinforcement, and stimulus control that is made of psychoses and neuroses can be made of a transient situational disorder such as that involved in a prisoner-of-war camp. (2) The techniques of thought reform with their emphasis on milieu manipulation, behavior change, and restructuring of feelings and attitudes are similar to those of behavior modification. In both situations the interviewer is convinced that what he is doing is for the best interests of the influenced person (see Frank, 1961, on training psychoanalysts). (3) Although the individual can to some extent be trained to resist the influence of the thought reformer, by his expectancies, by firm convictions, or by reinforcing "negativism," the most effective procedure is removal from the overwhelming situation. (4) The situational development of altered beliefs is germane to the development of other false beliefs, that is, to paranoia (see Chapter 20).

A NOTE ON SLEEP DEPRIVATION

One of the most interesting areas involving transient reactions currently being investigated is that of sleep (see especially Luce and Segal, 1966). In some civilian disasters and combat experiences, the stressful situation itself leads to a severe lack of sleep, while in many other rigorous situations sleep is disturbed. Difficulties in sleep are reported by patients admitted to psychiatric hospitals for a wide variety of diagnoses (although it is hard to tell whether such difficulties are greater than those of the nonhospitalized population and even how well *reports* of sleep difficulties are consistent with *actual* sleep difficulties).

There are many reports of hallucinations and paranoid ideation being emitted by ostensibly normal people after prolonged sleep deprivation (see Brauschi and West, 1959). For example (*Champaign-Urbana Courier,* October 22, 1967) a marathon for the world's record for continuous piano playing was held in Saybrook, Illinois. The winner was Mrs. Stephens, an organist at the Saybrook Christian Church, who played for 74 hours. "Several of the contestants reported having hallucinations during the contest. 'I did have an hallucination while I was playing,' Mrs. Stephens said. 'All the people were covered with red hair.'" The direct effects of sleep deprivation are conceptually and clinically more akin to toxic than to functional psychosis. However, shortness of temper, startle response, inability to concentrate, as well as suspiciousness and hallucinatory behavior may provide additional difficulties for the person to overcome. That is, sleep deprivation may be both a cause and a result of "overwhelming" situations.

SUMMARY

This chapter reviewed the categories of transient situational disturbances and special symptoms. A sociopsychological formulation was presented. This formulation, like the general model in Chapter 10, highlighted the lessening of adherence to previous standards and the consequent emission of new behavior. The chapter specifically dealt with panic behavior and behavior associated with civilian and military stresses. No difference was discerned in terms of behavior or its development between transient situational disturbances and other categories such as the neuroses. Rather, a social evaluation of the prior situations and the later recovery are major elements in the diagnosis. The special symptoms were similarly formulated and the variety of effective and direct procedures were reviewed. It can be hypothesized that, if effectively treated, all functional disorders may be viewed as transient maladjustments.

psycho-physiological disorders

16

DSM-II characterizes psychophysiologic disorders by "physical symptoms that are caused by emotional factors and involve a single organ system, usually under autonomic nervous system innervation. The physiological changes involved are those that normally accompany certain emotional states, but in these disorders the changes are more intense and sustained. The individual may not be consciously aware of his emotional state." (p. 46.)

Nine specific subcategories are listed in DSM-II—each referring to a different organ system in which psychophysiological disorders occur. (a) Skin (e.g., neurodermatosis, pruritis); (b) musculoskeletal (e.g., backache, muscle cramps, tension headaches); (c) respiratory (e.g., bronchial asthma, sighing, hiccups); (d) cardiovascular (e.g., paroxysmal tachycardia, hypertension, vascular spasms, and migraine); (e) hemic and lymphatic; (f) gastro-intestinal (e.g., peptic ulcer, chronic gastritis, ulcerative or mucous colitis, constipation, hyperacidity, "heartburn," "irritable colon"); (g) genito-urinary (e.g., disturbances in menstruation and micturition, dyspareuna and impotence); (h) endocrine; and (i) organs of special sense.

DSM-I noted that conversion reactions seem to alleviate "anxiety," whereas the psychophysiological reactions do not. The psychophysiologic disorders have a "physiological rather than symbolic origin of symptoms." Finally, the kinds of structural changes involved in psychophysiologic disorders may actually threaten the patient's life, whereas conversion reactions rarely do. The psychophysiologic disorders are differentiated from anxiety reactions in that the former involve but a single organ system in contrast to the more pervasive involvement of the latter.

The word "psychosomatic" has two uses. The first is that an individual's physical state and his behavior influence each other. The second is the denotation of a category of physical illness related to emotional factors. To avoid confusion, the DSM-I uses "psychosomatic" for the former meaning and "psychophysiologic" for the latter.

An extension of psychosomatic medicine in the direction of incorporating environmental and ecological variables has developed (Lipowski, 1973). The emphasis is on investigating the relationship between in formation or stimulus overload and the individual's psychophysiological functions.

HISTORY OF THE CONCEPT

Prior to the nineteenth century there were many anecdotal accounts of the relationship between "thinking" or "feeling" on the one hand and disease on the other.

The belief was widely held by nineteenth-century investigators who sought to unite psychology and medicine that bodily disease could be induced from various emotions or "states of mind." The physiologists of the nineteenth and early twentieth centuries, with their concepts of irritability and irritation, argued that sensations below the conscious threshold could trigger various parts of the nervous system (see Stainbrook, 1952).

There was a period in the 1940's and

1950's when the term "psychosomatic" was extremely popular. Usage of the term grew to the point where it encompassed so many disorders that it became almost meaningless. Alexander and French (1948) used the term broadly to denote disorders in which there was a close relationship between discrete bodily response and interpersonal behavior.

A recent major focus of interest in psychosomatic disorders has been on the possibility of using instrumental learning concepts and techniques in understanding the etiology, maintenance, and modification of psychosomatic symptoms. Miller (1969) summarized it as follows: ". . . evidence of the instrumental learning of visceral responses removes the main basis for assuming that the psychosomatic symptoms that involve the autonomic nervous system are fundamentally different from those functional symptoms, such as hysterical ones, that involve the cerebrospinal system. . . ."

"In considering the possibility of alleviating psychosomatic symptoms directly by reducing their frequency through operant feedback procedures, the assumption is made that the symptom may be dealt with directly through visceral retraining, a kind of autonomic behavior therapy." (Shapiro and Schwartz, 1972, pp. 174–75.)

The list of functions so far shown to be modified operant-feedback methods in man include electrodermal activity; heart-rate speeding, slowing, and stabilization; systolic and diastolic blood pressure; gross muscle potentials; single motor unit activity; alpha, beta, and theta rhythms of the EEG; evoked cortical responses; skin temperature; peripheral vasomotor activity; and salivation.[1]

The biofeedback technique in human studies involves giving the individual information about changes in a particular function such as heartrate or blood pressure or muscle potential and rewarding him for a response of a particular amplitude or direction.

The selection of physiologic response characteristics for modification, whether amplitude, waveform, latency, or direction, depends on the imagination and ingenuity of the investigator, the capability of instrumentation to identify the response of interest and provide a feedback display, and the relevance of the response—theoretical, clinical, or otherwise. It is well known that operant conditioning techniques have been used to produce variations in fine control and regulation of ongoing skeletal motor behaviors. Used in conjunction with feedback methods, similar fine control would seem feasible in the case of visceral and neural processes. [Shapiro and Schwartz, 1973, p. 172.]

CAUTIONS IN THE USE OF THE CONCEPT

Beyond the usual considerations in the use of diagnostic concepts, there are some special ones related to psychosomatics. First, there has been a tendency to label as psychosomatic anyone with an ulcer, asthma, or high blood pressure. To say that *at times* "emotional" (or, preferably, behavioral) factors may play a part in the development or maintenance of such physical difficulties is very different from saying they *always* do. The uncritical use of the word "psychosomatic" and the implication of a need for psychotherapy is logically similar to saying that since some boys currently wear their hair long anyone with long hair is a boy. Further, physical difficulties may lead to behavioral problems and, even if stronger correlates existed than have so far been found, cause and effect would be far from well-established.

The tissue damage observed in patients with psychophysiologic disorders is genuine. As a professional in contact with individuals with these problems, the psychologist must

---

[1] Reviews of studies with humans are found in Budzynski and Stoyva (1972), Katkin and Murray (1968), and Katkin (1971). Selected papers have been reprinted in Barber (1970), Kamiya et al. (1971), and Shapiro et al. (1973). These collections also include related papers on hypnosis, meditation, yoga, drugs and altered states of consciousness, and cognitive control of internal and emotional states.

work closely with a physician. No greater disservice can be done than to label the patient's suffering "psychosomatic" and thus not bring to bear the best available medical attention. Further, the evidence for effective clinical treatment is such that behavioral factors usually do not play a role which may be called "causative" and thus lead to a diagnosis within the strict definition of the term. Where with most other patterns of abnormal behavior the psychological model seems a more parsimonious approach, the opposite is true with psychophysiological reactions: this is a group of disorders in which the biophysiological approach seems the first, most appropriate model, and only after careful study should the behavioral model be tried in clinical practice.

THE INTERNAL AND EXTERNAL ENVIRONMENT

Dealing with the area of psychophysiological reactions raises the question of the relationship between the *behavioral* environment and the *internal physical one*. To what degree may internal, supposedly involuntary functions be influenced by life experiences such as conditioning? As noted earlier in the summary of placebo and hypnosis work, this occurs to a great extent. Two further lines of investigation are the effects of feedback of physiological functioning on the individual and the establishment of internal conditioned responses.

The vast majority of human acts have observable motor aspects and measurable physiological components. When a person enacts a social role involving aggressive, hostile, calm, angry, or loving behavior, there are measurable concomitants in heart rate, blood pressure, psychogalvanic reflex, and respiration rate. The following quotation from Haggard gives vivid illustrations of this relationship between social role and physiological concomitants:

The chill of disease is the same as the chill which comes with stronger fear; in both cases "goose flesh" results as the minute cutaneous muscles cause the hairs to stand on end in an effort to diminish the loss of heat from the body. In man the erection of the hairs is less evident than it is in animals such as the cat; man instead of bristling has goose flesh. In fever the heart beats rapidly; by counting the pulse the physician can estimate the severity of the fever. The heart also beats rapidly in emotion.

Paralysis of a limb may be a sign of serious disease, but a man may be paralyzed with fear and he may be struck dumb and blind with terror. Diarrhea also is a symptom of disease, but it is likewise often a complication of emotion. King James I of England was prone to diarrhea from the emotion aroused by distressing matters of state. The excessive secretion of saliva, called salivation, may occur in disease, while in fever the mouth may dry out and become parched. The saliva is also secreted excessively when a savory food is merely thought of; and the mouth dries out with fear. This last is shown by the glass of water put before the public speaker; he drinks before he speaks because he is frightened and afterward because he has dried his mouth by talking. The dry mouth of fear was one of the early legal tests, a form of "ordeal." The mouth of the defendant was filled with flour; if he was innocent and felt no fear, his saliva flowed and he was able to swallow the flour; if he was guilty his fear kept his mouth dry and he choked. Vomiting may come from illness and it may also come from fear or the smell of some disgusting substance. The pressure of the blood in the artery rises slowly as the kidneys harden with age, but it also rises even from the emotion caused by having a physician apply the apparatus to determine its height. The blood of a man with diabetes contains an abnormal amount of sugar and some of it finds its way into his urine; strong emotions suffered in restraint may temporarily cause both of these symptoms, as in the football substitute sitting on the side lines or the student faced with a difficult examination.

Most of the symptoms of disease can be counterfeited by the influence of the nervous system upon bodily functions. Mental irritation or depression can produce dyspepsia, jaundice, or a general decline. Fright may produce palpitation of the heart, and heart failure has resulted from business reverses.

Pain, which is the supreme subjective phenomenon of disease, is almost wholly mental. A man during rage feels no pain from injury until after his anger has cooled; the same man waiting in the anteroom of the dentist may suffer agony in anticipation. The early Christians, while being burned alive, signaled to their friends who waited for the ordeal, by raising their seared arms in the flames to signify that they felt no pain. Religious enthusiasm was their anesthetic. . . . [1929, pp. 297–98.]

THEORIES OF ORIGIN OF PSYCHOPHYSIOLOGICAL DISORDERS

The major theories of the development of psychophysiological disorders have speculated on the effects of constitutional weakness, of heredity, of previous illness and accidents in an individual's life, of the presence of illness in relatives of the patient, of the symbolic meaning to the patient of the organ system affected, of the nature of current emotional stress or conflict, of the secondary gain brought about by the symptom "selected," and of previous conditioning (Kaplan and Kaplan, 1959; Sternbach, 1971; Mendelson, Hirsch and Webber, 1956).

Hereditary

As in other disorders, hereditary factors are difficult to demonstrate. Rosen and Gregory (1965) report that brothers of ulcer patients are about twice as likely to have ulcers as comparable members of the general population. Similar results have been reported for asthma, migraine, and hypertension. However, this observation could as well be attributed to common factors in learning and experience as to genetic factors.

Somatic Weakness

There is a view that the physical disorder occurs in a body organ which is weakened, compared with other organs, by poor genetic endowment or prior illness. Thus, there would be no direct connection in meaning between any psychological stress and the specific organ affected, but rather a chance relationship, with the weakest physical link breaking first. Rees (1964) reported that 80 percent of a sample of asthmatics had had a history of previous respiratory infection. The theory of the site of breakdown being determined by "weakness" is difficult to test and borders on *ex post facto* reasoning; the organ broke down, therefore it was weak.

Stress Theory

One of the important biological theories explaining the origin of psychophysiological disorders is the stress theory of Hans Selye (1956). Selye argues that the body reacts to a stressful or threatening situation in terms of a complete mobilization of physiological resources. If the stress is too prolonged, the emergency resources become exhausted and physiological symptoms appear. These symptoms are called "diseases of adaptation." The "essential alarm reaction" of the individual to environmental stress illustrates such symptoms. One of the disadvantages of Selye's theory is that it does not predict why one individual develops an adaptation syndrome and another does not.

Inherited Autonomic Patterns

One theory of the development of psychophysiological disorders argues for a basic (inherited or acquired) difference between individuals in autonomic reactivity. Lacey and his group (Lacey, Bateman, and Van-Lehn, 1953) demonstrated that, at least insofar as college students are concerned, there is a stable, consistent, and idiosyncratic pattern of autonomic activity. If an individual's characteristic pattern of reaction to stress involves rise in blood pressure, it is likely to be repeated from stress to stress regardless of the specifics of the situation. Malmo and Shagass (1949) demonstrated a difference in reactivity between patients with cardiovascular symptoms and those with headaches. The former were more likely to react to stress with cardiovascular response than with muscle tension, whereas this pattern was reversed with the headache patients. These views are consistent with the psychological and conditioning theories presented next, and combined with them begin to offer a meaningful explanation.

Psychological Theories

The various psychological theories of the origin of psychophysiological disorders can be put into two categories. The first are theories that relate behavior to specific function in a manner consistent in most instances with the present volume's behavioral approach. In contrast are those theories that argue for interpreting psychophysiological disorders as symbolic or as regression to an earlier level of psychosexual functioning.

Observations from psychoanalysis of people with psychophysiological reactions (Weiss and English, 1943; Dunbar, 1954) led to the formulation of specific personality patterns as causal for specific physiological disorders. For example, early studies of duodenal ulcer patients (Alexander, 1934; Brush, 1939; Ruesch, 1948) used such terms as "go-getter," "energetic," "striving," "strongly ambitious," "hard-driving," and "self-assertive" in describing their ulcer patients. On the other hand, Krasner (1953) and Modell and Potter (1949), basing their results on psychological tests, found duodenal ulcer patients to be passive and dependent. This difference in personality description was found to be related to the differences in the socioeconomic status of the subjects. In similar fashion, Kapp, Rosenbaum, and Romano (1946) reported that their private-practice ulcer patients were assertive, while a group of patients whom they examined in a charity ward were passive, nonassertive, and dependent.

Other theorists describe ulcer patients as being "really" passive and dependent. In similar fashion, hypertensive patients are presumed to have suppressed anger due to dominant mothers; migraine headache due to traits of ambition, hostility, envy, and perfectionism; asthma due to a suppressed cry for the mother; and so forth. Page (1971, pp. 390–91) notes, "Attempts to relate selectivity of psychosomatic symptoms to personality variables have been unsuccessful. In comparison with the greater population, persons with psychosomatic disorders may show greater dependence-independence conflicts, greater repressed hostility, and higher levels of anxiety, but experimental findings do not support the hypothesis that certain personality characteristics are directly correlated with particular psychosomatic disorders (Buss, 1966)."

In contrast to the psychoanalytic conceptualization, there are multifacet theories explaining the current development of the organic symptom as related to the effects of a current emotional concomitant of behavior. For example, there have been a series of studies which have found that anger and hostility were responsible for excessive stomach motility and ulcer formation. These studies were conducted during psychiatric interviews and involved observation of the stomach through a gastric fistula (Wolf and Wolff, 1947).

Wolf and Wolff's subject Tom was unusual in that, because of an operation which literally placed a window over his stomach, his gastric functioning could be directly observed. Actual changes in the mucous membrane could be observed while Tom experienced various emotions. Increased gastric activity occurred when Tom was angry, when he was fired from a job for alleged incompetence, and when he resented an individual who was dominating his life. Thus, emotions may affect gastrointestinal functions.

Taking this viewpoint one step further the argument would be that prolonged experience in any one role which elicits continual anger and frustration would lead to physical damage. The argument would run that various stress situations arouse emotional tensions. The continued physiological components of the emotion may eventually lead to structural damage. Hokanson and Burgess (1964) put subjects in highly frustrating situations, and measured their physiological functioning with tests of systolic blood pressure and heart rate. After the frustrating situation the subjects who had had an opportunity to display actual physical or verbal aggression against their frustrator returned significantly more quickly to normal heart rate and blood pressure than those who were permitted no aggression or at best fantasy aggression.

A variation of the personality-correlate theory of psychophysiological disorders is the view that there is a specific "attitude" or a specific "conflict" involved which is directly related to the specific disorder. Grace and Graham (1952) argue that particular attitudes determine the kind of psychosomatic symptom that may develop in a given patient. To test this theory, Graham and his associates induced specific attitudes by hypnosis and investigated the correlates of attitudes upon autonomic patterns.

Platonov (1959) concluded that verbal suggestion can influence the activity of the heart, the state of the cardiovascular system, and changes in the vasomotor system. Other Russian investigators have demonstrated that a person could accelerate his heart rate without changing his respiration; the thought of stimulation of the skin by a mustard plaster caused rise in blood pressure. Further, Russian scientists have been able to demonstrate conditioned heart reflexes. In one study a rise in blood pressure in response to a bell was subsequently obtained in response to the word "bell" when uttered not only by the experimenter but when uttered by the subject as well.

Physical concomitants of the behavior that is an integral part of the role, if they are intense, prolonged, or continuous enough, may (1) be elicited by a wide variety of stimuli and (2) lead to tissue damage so that (3) feedback of physiological effects acts as a further stimulus.

Conditioning

A number of investigators have approached the problem of the origin of psychophysiological disorders through the concepts of classical conditioning. This approach derives from Pavlov, whose book *Work of the Digestive Glands* in 1879 emphasized that the activity of the main digestive organs such as the liver, pancreas, and gastric glands can be influenced through the nervous system. The basis of this influence is the neural connection between the internal organs and the cerebral cortex which transmits information in both directions. It has since been repeatedly demonstrated that physiological functioning (e.g., cardiovascular, gastrointestinal) can be, respondently or classically, conditioned (Cannon, 1929; Gantt, 1964; Lacey, 1956; Liddell, 1956; Mahl, 1949; Malmo, 1950).

Only more recently, however, have there begun to be developed studies demonstrating that autonomic responses can be strengthened by the presentation of reinforcement *after* their emission, that is, as operants. Evidence (Engel and Hansen, 1966; Engel and Chism, 1967; Hnatiow and Lang, 1965; Kimmel, 1967; Kimmel and Hill, 1960; Kimmel and Kimmel, 1963; Mandler, Preven, and Kuhlman, 1962; Razran, 1961; Miller and DiCara, 1967; Benson et al., 1971; Brener and Kleinman, 1970; DiCara and Miller, 1968; Kamiya et al., 1971; Katkin and Murray, 1968; Miller, 1969; Schwartz, Shapiro, and Tursky, 1971; and Schwartz, 1972) suggests that autonomic responses can be conditioned instrumentally.

Lang, Stroufe, and Hastings (1967) have demonstrated the remarkable control that an individual can attain over his heart rate when heart beat is viewed as an operant response. Their subjects used equipment that measured heart rate. The task of the subject was to maintain his own heart rate, within certain limits, as measured on the dial. When subjects received visual feedback on each trial as to how successful they were, they literally were able to maintain their heart-rate response so that it was within the prescribed limits (in contrast to a control group that did not receive feedback). Subjects were also able to control their heart rate on instruction. It was not clear to the investigators what physiological mechanism was used to control heart rate, although it was clear that respiration, an obvious choice, was not the mechanism used. Shearn (1962) reported similar results in which delay of shock was made contingent on accelerated heart rate.

Ascough and Sipprelle (1968) also demonstrated that spontaneous increase *and* decrease in heart rate can be brought under control of operant verbal conditioning. Their results showed significant conditioning effects, with increasing differences from the original baseline over a group of sessions even when possible mediating responses were taken into account. As with the Lang study, the possibility of respiratory changes being responsible for changes in heart rate was ruled out. Scott et al. (1973), using television-viewing and money as reinforcing stimuli, provide a demonstration of how such results may be applied clinically, while Elder et al. (1973) provide similar material in the area of blood pressure for essential hypertension patients.

Another example of viewing psychophysiological functioning as operant behavior is a study by Crider, Shapiro, and Tursky (1966). They demonstrated that contingent stimulation of spontaneous electrodermal fluctuations increased in frequency of occurrence relative to noncontingent stimulation. Their instructions to subjects were to "think emotional thoughts." After being strapped to imposing looking equipment, subjects were told that the equipment was measuring their thought processes. When the recordings measured "emotional thinking," they would hear a tone. Each tone was worth five cents. The criterion for receiving reinforcement was the production of a skin potential response of at least .5 m.v. amplitude. The ability to obtain such conditioning was likened to obtaining a conditioned orienting reflex (Sokolov, 1963).

Crider, Shapiro, and Tursky concluded that as conditioning progresses other relatively minor covert responses also tend to evoke electrodermal activity. Operant reinforcement of electrodermal activity may result in a modified feedback loop in which covert response-produced stimuli feed into motor centers of the brain eliciting an electrodermal response followed by a reinforcing stimulus. Reinforcement in turn serves to enhance the reactivity of these centers to other formerly subthreshold peripheral inputs. These results are similar to other reports of successful operant conditioning of electrodermal responses with contingent stimulation techniques with human subjects (Fowler and Kimmel, 1962; R. J. Johnson, 1963; Kimmel and Kimmel, 1963).

Shapiro and Schwartz (1972) offer a comprehensive review of the relationship between conditioning procedures and changes in autonomic functioning. They point out that conditioned changes in visceral responses are not necessarily correlated with overall changes in autonomic arousal. Physiological functions, which appear to be correlated with each other, can actually be dissociated from one another by means of the techniques of feedback and operant conditioning. Shapiro et al. (1969) offered an example of this which derived from their series of studies on blood pressure and heart rate. In the first experiment, normal (nonhypertensive) subjects were given feedback and reward for increasing or decreasing systolic blood pressure while heart rate was simultaneously monitored. Significant differences in pressure changes were obtained between increase and decrease subjects without corresponding differences in heart rate.

The authors then replicated this result in a second sample of subjects. A similar experiment was performed, except that this time feedback and reward were given for increasing or decreasing heart rate while systolic blood presure was simultaneously monitored. This time heart rate was conditioned without corresponding changes in blood pressure. They concluded that conditioned changes in blood pressure were not dependent on heart rate, and vice versa, hence emphasizing the specificities within autonomic functioning.

Subjects rewarded for simultaneous increases in heart rate and systolic blood pressure showed comparable increases in both, and those rewarded for simultaneous decreases showed sizable decreases in both. Similarly, the effectiveness of the operant procedures is even more striking given the finding that differentiation of heart rate and systolic blood pressure (both moving in opposite directions) is also possible, though constrained by a number of biologic factors. [Shapiro and Schwartz, 1973, p. 174.]

Words may serve as stimuli. Protopopov (1921, cited by Platonov, 1959, p. 22) demonstrated that a verbal stimulus may facilitate and accelerate the formation of a new conditioned reflex if the *name* of the stimulus is added to the new conditioned stimulus. Thus, the word that signifies the name of the given object, and is a well-established natural conditioned stimulus, may greatly reinforce the new condition reflex. Cooper (1959) has illustrated this thesis in the area of social prejudice, and Craig (1968) and Craig and Lowery (1969) illustrated vicarious autonomic arousal. The most complete theory of meaning, conditioning, attitude, reinforcement, and discrimination is by Staats (1970).

Following Pavlov, the word takes on powerful signaling properties. Owing to the entire preceding life of the human adult, a word is connected with all the external and internal stimuli coming to the cerebral hemisphere, signals all of them, replaces all of them and can, therefore, evoke all the actions and reactions of the organism which these stimuli produce. In short, a word is a real conditioned stimulus for people.

An important phase for the Russian investigators of the physiological effects of "the word" was the demonstration that conditioning of reflexes or functions takes place to the *meaning* of the word, not to its sound. That is, if the conditioned response is elicited by the sight of the word "hare," it would also be elicited by the word "rabbit" but not by the word "hair." Another illustration of this procedure of "semantic conditioning" (Razran, 1961) is the conditioning of a GSR reaction to the word "break." The subject is then exposed to additional words to determine his reaction. Will the GSR response be elicited by "brake" or by "damage"? The evidence is that the response will be elicited by the word that is semantically similar rather than the word that is sonorically similar.

Interoceptive conditioning provides a further step in the control of internal behavior. Razran (1961) cites the many studies which demonstrate that the entire spectrum of autonomic reactions may be brought under control by pairing a verbalized exteroceptive conditioned stimulus with an interoceptive unconditioned stimulus. There are many illustrations of studies that have experimentally developed an association between an external behavior such as withdrawing a foot from a shock grid and an internal response of the autonomic system, e.g., "an urge to urinate." For example, an individual can learn to associate the somatic sensation expected of him when the dial of a measuring device reaches a certain critical point. Studies using false feedback indicate that the subject "experiences" the expected sensation even though there is no objective physiological reason to do so.

Of particular theoretical and clinical import is the degree to which cortical activity can be influenced through conditioning. Wyrwicka, Sterman, and Clemente (1962) stimulated the basal forebrain synchronizing area of the cat to induce the behavioral and electroencephalographic (EEG) manifestations of sleep. By pairing such stimulation with tone, the tone eventually led to the emission of sleep patterns. Granda and Hammack (1961) effectively used operant conditioning techniques to produce organized behavior during sleep as defined by EEG records. Stevens (1962) trained ten epileptic subjects to press a lever to avoid a mildly painful shock each time paroxysmal epileptiform activity occurred in their own EEG's. All subjects learned to avoid the shock as long as they could gain EEG information. One subject was able to respond to the purely subjective effect of his own paroxysmal activity within the limits of the experiment.

One of the most important factors in assessing psychophysiological disorders is to determine the relation between internal events and external behavior. There has been repeated evidence that emotional states or role enactments are accompanied by physiological changes. More recently studies have been reported which point to the fact that internal events may facilitate the manifestation of external behavior depending upon the meaning attached to the internal physiological cues. This can best be illustrated by the Schachter and Singer study (1962) described in Chapter 5. In that study the experimenters manipulated the meaning attributable to the epinephrine-induced states by the use of models. In effect, the external clues as to the meaning of the internal cues influence subsequent behavior.

Reasoning from the findings of Schachter and his associates (Latane and Schachter, 1962; Schachter and Wheeler, 1962; Schachter, 1964; Singer, 1963), Valins (1966, 1967) investigated whether the way an individual labels emotional stimuli is affected by the information he receives concerning his own internal reaction to those stimuli. Valins worked with college male subjects and showed them ten slides of semi-nude females (culled from *Playboy*). One group of subjects "heard" their heart rates increase markedly to five of the slides and not change to the other five. The heart rate feedback was predetermined by the experimenter, was not a function of the "real" heart rate reaction, and was explained to the subject with a convincing experimental explanation as to why he was "hearing" his heart rate. A second group of subjects heard a marked decrease in the bogus heart rate to the same selected five slides and no change to the other five. In comparison with the slides to which the subjects did not hear a change in the bogus heart rate, the slides to which they heard a marked change, *whether increased or decreased,* were rated significantly more attractive during the experiment, during a follow-up interview, and as choice for a reward to take away with them. Thus, the significant factor in the individual's behavior was what he *thought* were his reactions.

HYPNOSIS AND PHYSIOLOGICAL CHANGE

Chapter 5 noted that role enactments during hypnosis had physiological concomitants. The role of the hypnotized subject is one that has sensory, circulatory, gastrointestinal, and cutaneous correlates related to the subtleties of the verbal suggestions involved. Further, and of even greater importance, similar physiological effects can be produced by symbolic stimulation without "hypnosis" (Barber, 1961b). All of the physiological effects that can be induced in some persons with hypnosis can also be induced in some persons without hypnosis.

Klemme (1963) found that suggestions to accelerate and decelerate the heart produced noticeable effects in the majority of his subjects under both waking and hypnosis situations. In a study on the effects of pain, both hypnotic analgesia (insensitivity to pain) and waking-imagined analgesia instructions were effective in attenuating pain reactivity as indicated by subjective reports and reduction in respiratory irregularities and forehead muscle tension (Barber and Hahn, 1964).

Barber, after an exhaustive survey of the field of hypnosis and physiology, concludes that "it is difficult if not impossible to find a physiological index which differentiates 'the hypnotic state' from 'the normal waking state.' . . . physiological functions vary in the same way during 'hypnosis' as they do during 'waking' behavior" (1961b, pp. 410-411). A further review (Barber, 1965b) substantiates this point. There does not appear to be any evidence that hypnotized individuals differ from other people in any measurable physiological or neurological functioning (see Rosenhan, 1967, quoted in Chapter 5). Thus, *although a great range of physiological changes may occur during hypnosis, under proper conditions these same changes may occur through nonhypnotized role-playing.*

An example of this linkage between hypnotic role enactments and the development of specific psychophysiological disorders comes from studies demonstrating the effects that "words" may have on the digestive and gastrointestinal systems. For example, hunger pangs can be reduced by having the subject, while under hypnosis, imagine eating food. In these studies the digestive tract secretions varied according to the imagined meal; e.g., imagery of a juicy steak produce secretions different from and far pleasanter than the sour taste produced by the imagined eating of a lemon.

An important question is whether there is a meaningful correlation between molar human behavior and physiological measures. The GSR has been a widely used physiological measurement because it is relatively easy to obtain and because it is presumably related to various definitions of anxiety (see Chapter 9).

Dittes (1957a, b) demonstrated that the verbalizations of patients in psychotherapy are accompanied by changes in galvanic skin responses. He found (1957a) that statements by a therapy patient acknowledging personal sexual behavior or even desires were frequently accompanied during the early hours of therapy with galvanic skin responses. During later therapy hours the GSR deflections became gradually lessened. He concluded that the GSR is associated with feelings such as fear or embarrassment in the interpersonal relationship with the therapist. As therapy progresses, such responses decrease, and this has an effect on physiological functioning.

Gordon, Martin, and Lundy (1959), on the other hand, found that GSR deflection increased during experimental psychotherapy sessions when subjects were asked to "think about" or "talk about" conflicts with parents. The apparent differences between these two studies may be understood in terms of the context and of the expectations of the participants; the former study took place in the context of "psychotherapy," the latter in the context of "research." Both studies do emphasize that there is an association between GSR and the content of verbalization.

A Summary Statement

There is an interdependent relationship between a person's enactment of roles and his autonomic responses. Such autonomic responses may result from direct, classical conditioning or may be the result of the actions the person has emitted. Further, they may serve as cues for further operant behaviors. The person's social environment may have an influence, at times a major one, on his internal physical environment and hence may play an important contributory role to physical deviations from normality. The research reviewed in the previous paragraphs indicates some of the evidence for these statements, which summarize the approach called psychosomatic to the specific ailments called psychophysiological disorders.

The interconnection of operant and respondent behavior is the crucial point of this chapter and may best be illustrated by instances in which it is difficult, if not impossible, to determine whether a person's problem is a function of operant or respondent conditioning.

One clinical manifestation of this problem is the decision whether a pattern of behavior should be labeled hysterical or psychophysiological. A prime example is the following case report:

After June Clark, 17, had sneezed every few seconds of her waking day for five months, experts in half a dozen medical specialties were stymied. Nothing helped, not even a trip to the dry air of Phoenix. . . . Psychologist Malcolm Kushner of Coral Gables VA Hospital volunteered to make an electrical attack on June's sneezing. . . .

Dr. Kushner used a relatively simple, low-powered electric-shock device, activated by sound—the sound of June's sneezes. Electrodes were attached to her forearm for 30 minutes, and every time she sneezed she got a mild electric shock. After a ten-minute break, the electrodes were put on the other arm. In little more than four hours, June's sneezes, which had been reverberating every 40 seconds, stopped. Since then, she has had only a few ordinary sneezes, none of the dry, racking kind that had been draining her strength for so long. "We hope the absence of sneezes will last," said Dr. Kushner cautiously. "So do I," snapped June. "I never want to see that machine again." [*Time,* June 17, 1966, p. 72.]

Another example in which it is difficult to determine whether the problem is operant or respondent, hysterical or psychophysiological, is vomiting. A person may develop a gagging, nauseated response through classical conditioning or as a response to situations that are followed by reinforcement (see Chapter 15). Aversive conditioning, similar to the work of Kushner in the immediately preceding paragraph, has also been successful with chronic cough (Alexander et al., 1973) and rumination behavior of retarded individuals (White and Taylor, 1967). Wolf et al. (1965) report work with Laura, a nine-year-old retarded girl who was permitted to leave the classroom and return to the dormitory when she had vomited on her dress. The maximum number of instances of vomiting on a single day was 21. The treatment program involved shaping desirable classroom behavior with praise and candy, ceasing such reinforcement when she vomited (time out from reinforcement), and keeping Laura in the classroom until the end of the period (extinction). The rate of vomiting declined to zero in an orderly manner over a period of 30 class days.

CLINICAL APPLICATIONS

"In the past decade, we have witnessed a major breakthrough in research on the behavioral regulation of visceral and neural processes." With that unusually strong assertion, Shapiro and Schwartz (1972) start their thorough review of the field of biofeedback and visceral learning. The developments involve a reversal of the previously held assumption among investigators that visceral and neural processes were not subject to voluntary regulation as are skeletal muscles. The evidence is accumulating that these processes are indeed controllable. Specific illustrations of treatment procedures appear in this section.

Skin Problems

An example of the treatment of neurodermatitis within a behavior-modification framework is the following case presented by Walton (1960d). A 20-year-old woman had a long-standing neurodermatitis at the nape of her neck which was apparently associated with her scratching. She had received a variety of somatic treatments from two general practitioners and a skin specialist over a two-year period. Both the patient and her mother had been relegated to an inferior position in the family, and her brother received a disproportionate amount of attention and the family budget for his education. The dermatitis, which may well have originated because of physical considerations, led to change in this status, with greater attention and concern being paid the patient. It was, therefore, suggested by the therapist that the patient should receive no reward for her condition. The members of the family were told to ignore the condition, and her fiancé, who used to apply ointment to her neck, was told to desist from his labors of love. Over a period of two months the frequency of the scratching decreased until it stopped altogether. There was an improvement in the skin, and by three months the skin condition had disappeared. On four-year follow-up there was found to be no symptom substitution either of skin condition or other psychiatric difficulty.

This case illustrates the difference in conceptualization between the evocative and operant approach in that it focuses on attention as a generalized reinforcer. The principles utilized are very similar to those used by Ayllon in modifying schizophrenics' behavior, as described in Chapter 4. Allen and Harris (1966) present a similar case—withhold reinforcement for scratching and reinforce other desirable behavior—where the mother was trained to work with her five-year-old child.

Ratliff and Stein (1968) report the use of aversive stimulation with a 22-year-old, single, male college student suffering from neurodermatitis. An electric shock was administered in nine one-hour sessions whenever the man scratched any part of his body. The shock was terminated after the scratching was stopped and the subject said aloud, "Don't scratch." To establish a permanent therapeutic effect, the conditioning procedure was coupled with a relaxation technique in which the man controlled the tone of various muscle groups. A six-month follow-up study revealed a complete suppression of scratching.

Watson, Tharp, and Krisberg (1972) present a different form of self-modification, in which a woman was taught to substitute stroking and then patting for damaging scratching. While her boyfriend provided reinforcement for progress, the client also provided herself with reinforcement for carrying out the program.

Bronchial Asthma

A number of investigators have conceptualized bronchial asthma as a conditioned response (Franks and Leigh, 1959). Turnbull (1962) demonstrated that "asthma-like" reactions can be learned by animals during conditioning procedures. The experimenter can shape breathing behavior by reinforcement to the point where respiratory patterns are elicited that closely approximate asthmatic breathing. Using conditioning to painful stimuli, Gantt (1944) induced changes in breathing in dogs; Lidell (1951) produced similar effects of raucous breathing in goats and sheep. Ottenberg et al. (1958) sensitized guinea pigs to egg white administered by aerosol spray and produced asthma-like attacks. Generalization was demonstrated when the guinea pigs responded "asthmatically" to the aerosol *apparatus* without the spray and finally even to the pen. Masserman and Pechtel (1953) conditioned asthmatic breathing in "neurotic" monkeys.

Dekker and Groen (1956) conditioned bronchial asthmatic response to the inhalation of allergens in a human being. Dekker et al. (1957) proceeded to demonstrate generalization in that patients who had had asthmatic reactions to allergens would also develop attacks when a neutral solvent was used. Eventally an asthmatic response was elicited by the mouthpiece of the inhaler apparatus alone. Luparello et al. (1968) indicated the strong effects of suggestion in up to half the subjects when they thought a placebo was an allergen.

Bykov (1957) demonstrated that autonomic responses may be conditioned to a fantasied stimulus. For example, if a person is requested to imagine that he is responding to a command such as "Get ready for for work," his pulse rate and respiration will increase. Thus, if a response can be conditioned to fantasy, it can be deconditioned by imagining the conditioned stimulus and applying the concept of stimulus generalization. This is essentially Wolpe's (1958) method in systematic desensitization.

Moore (1965) tested this procedure in a controlled study. Twelve asthmatic patients (six adults and six children) were treated either by relaxation in a systematic desensitization paradigm, relaxation with suggestion, or relaxation alone. The patients served as their own controls. Systematic desensitization was found to have the greatest effect on *respiratory* functions; the other two procedures did not differ from each other in effectiveness, although all three produced equal amounts of *subjective* improvement.

Walton (1960c) describes a case of bronchial asthma treated by behavior therapy. The patient was a male in his mid-thirties, who had been suffering from asthmatic attacks for seven years. He showed poor social skills and vacillated in making decisions required by his job. His asthmatic attacks would occur on encountering visitors to his factory from whom he had to secure orders. There was a series of other specific situations, primarily involving his job, during which asthmatic attacks would occur. Because his attacks seemed to be related to his relations with other people, the therapist trained him in assertive behavior. At the end of eight treatment sessions he was able to deal with people whom he had previously avoided. His social relations improved, and he remained free of asthmatic attacks.

Both Gardner (1968) and Miklich (1973) report operant reinforcement of relaxation (slow-down) for a six-year-old hyperkinetic boy and subsequent training to reduce the severity of asthmatic attacks. Neisworth and Moore (1972) also used operant techniques applied by the mother of a seven-year-old boy to reduce bedtime asthmatic attacks, and Creer (1970) obtained useful effects with a time-out-from-positive-reinforcement procedure.

Although it deals with breathing rather than asthma per se, an article by Wright et al. (1969) may be taken as a paradigm of operant involvement in psychophysiologic difficulties—not unlike the Lang and Melamed study (1969) cited in Chapter 15. Wright et al. report on successful work with two eight-month-old infants who had to have tubes placed to by-pass the throats. They were physiologically very capable of normal breathing but did not do so when the tubes were removed. The first step was to find what was pleasurable to the children, such as rough-housing and tender-loving social contact. Three times a day the tube was occluded and the child was given the maximum amount of pleasure. As with the case of the anorexic treated by Bachrach, Erwin and Moore cited in Chapter 15, at other times, the children were isolated from toys and social contacts. By the end of the first week, both had progressed to the point where they were able to eat and drink during the periods of occlusion, and by the twentieth day, each of the three periods lasted five hours. The tubes were removed since they were no longer required.

Gastrointestinal Reactions

There are many gastrointestinal disorders, such as various forms of colitis, gastritis, chronic diarrhea, and other problems of digestion and elimination.

Peptic ulcer is the generic name for the development of lesions in either the lining of the stomach or of the duodenum. The lesions are due to an excessive flow of acid secretion which acts upon the lining of the stomach or duodenum, resulting in wounds which may bleed excessively. The problem is to determine what, besides food being digested, stimulates the flow of these juices. The evidence seems quite clear that emotional factors may be an important consideration in the overproduction of acid secretion.

The following case (Wolpe, 1958, pp. 148-152) illustrates an approach to the alleviation of the chronic stress associated with a passive social role. The patient was a 46-year-old single dressmaker. A year before treatment she started having epigastric pain which was removed by medication, but she still had radiological evidence of an active ulcer. She felt nauseated at any sign of the slightest interpersonal stress, which was quite frequent. She was seen by the therapist for 25 sessions altogether, with an 18-month follow-up. Although training in assertion was not successful, she was successfully trained in relaxation in conjunction with systematic desensitization on a hierarchy of her sensitivity to people. Because of her strong reaction to people shouting, an additional hierachy was used, with items ranging from men across the road engaged in an argument to people punching each other with the patient as the only witness. The effects were on her external behavior as well as on the "ulcers." She was able to take a trip and to talk freely to others in the hotel where she stayed; she saw an hour-long fight outside her workroom and was unruffled. Her mother had a heart attack, and the patient gave her a pill and calmly went back to sleep. After treatment and the 18-month follow-up, there was improvement in personal functioning, cessation of the stomach symptoms, and the disappearance of any radiological evidence of the ulcer.

In short, while there may be various background factors, the behavioral formulation is that there are environmental stimuli which lead to subjective reactions. Among these reactions are the playing of specific roles that have somatic correlates.

Genito-urinary Reactions

DSM-II gives as examples of the problems in this area elimination, menstruation (see Mullen, 1968) and sexual function (e.g., impotence). We will deal with the latter in Chapter 21.

Jones (1956) describes work with a 23-year-old single woman whose frequent urges to urinate made her employment as a dancer impossible. Psychotherapy and general hospital treatment were ineffective in helping her. Jones then used a technique developed by Bykov. He placed a manometer before her, indicating to her the amount of fluid in her bladder. This reading could be altered without her knowledge. Since the urge to urinate occurs at a definite pressure for each individual, she rapidly developed a connection between the manometer reading and the urge to urinate. By determining the feedback reading to be given to her, it was possible to increase the bladder volume prior to urination. Five sessions at two-day intervals were used to train her to accept a greater bladder volume prior to a subjective urinary urge. In addition, Jones helped her overcome her fears of interpersonal contacts, which had grown out of her urinary problem, by developing a series of graded tasks that involved her preparing for and participating in a dance recital. She was able to make increasingly longer excursions away from the hospital room and to have increased contact with other people. Jones reported that 15 months after her discharge from the hospital she was still free of the urinary problems, had not developed any new symptoms, and had married with apparent success. Taylor (1972) reports reduction of excessive frequency of urination by systematic desensitization of daily activity situations. Parallel reports dealing with diarrhea are presented by Hedberg (1973) and Cohen and Reed (1968).

Quarti and Renaud (1964) describe a conditioning technique for the treatment of constipation. They administered a laxative and then paired the subsequent bowel movement with electrical stimulation from a "belt" placed on each side of the lumbar spine. Because defecation is accompanied by a massive reflex of the colon, the time and place of defecation paired the electrical stimulus with this reflex. Quarti and Renaud gradually reduced the amount of the laxative and used only the electrical stimulation in a particular time and place. Eventually, the appropriate time and place were sufficient to elicit defecation without the electrical stimulation. In a similar area, excessive urinary retention was treated successfully by Lamontagne and Marks (1973) by prolonged exposure to the situation in a paradigm similar to flooding for phobias, and by Cooper (1965) by higher-order Pavlovian conditioning.

Hypertension

One of the major new developments involves the application of the instrumental conditioning literature to the control of high blood pressure. The approach involves the treating of the blood pressure response as an operant and determining the most effective way of manipulating it. Elder et al. (1973) demonstrated that patients could be conditioned to lower blood pressure by 20 to 30 percent over a period as brief as four days by providing an external signal and verbal praise contingent upon each reduction in diastolic pressure that met a pre-set criterion.

Shapiro et al. (1969) studied seven patients with essential hypertension. The patients were first adapted to the laboratory by attending five to sixteen control sessions during which pressures were recorded but no feedback was given. In the following one-hour sessions, feedback was given to patients on each heart beat during which their systolic pressure fell below criterion levels. Patients were given eight to thirty-four daily conditioning sessions. With reductions in pressure from the final five control sessions to the final five conditioning sessions, five of the seven patients showed positive response to the procedure.

Engel (1968, 1973, 1974) pioneered in research on the operant control of cardiac arrhythmias. Eight patients with premature ventricular contractions were given feedback information about beat-to-beat changes in heart rate (Weiss and Engel, 1971). A number of different training conditions were employed, such as heart-rate speeding, heart-rate slowing, alternation of speeding and slowing, and maintenance of heart rate within a certain range. Whenever the patient's heart rate was in accord with the particular schedule, a light was turned on to indicate success and a meter accumulated the total time of success. Variations in procedure were determined by individual patient's requirements.

Headaches

Budzynski and Stoyva (1969; Budzynski et al., 1973) have developed an instrument for producing deep muscle relaxation by means of analog information biofeedback. In their procedure, electromyogram (EMG) electrodes are placed over the frontalis muscle, and the feedback is in the form of a high-pitched tone for high levels of EMG activity. As the muscle tension decreases, the tone lowers in pitch. To keep the tone low, the individual has to relax the muscle. As he improves, the gain or sensitivity of the feedback system is increased, and he is required to maintain still lower tension in order to keep the tone low in frequency. As patients advance through the program, there is a heightened awareness of maladaptive rising tension, an increasing ability to reduce such tension, and a decreasing tendency to overreact to stress. Fichtler and Zimmerman (1973) report benefit for tension headache from exposure to tape recorded relaxation, and references to migraine headache will be found in Chapter 25.

Based on the observation that certain yogis tend to emit extensive alpha with no alpha blocking and show decreased reactivity to being stuck by a pin while meditating, Gannon and Sternbach (1971) attempted to treat a patient (studied for 70 sessions) with recurrent headaches through alpha training. Their results suggest that some reduction of pain did occur. These data are consistent with scattered reports of the effects of yoga and meditation, but controlled studies of the effects of alpha-training—or meditation itself—are lacking. Whether or not transcendental meditation leads to more rapid alpha, and is clinically beneficial, is still unknown.

SUMMARY

The term "psychosomatics" is best saved for a philosophy of medicine and human beings that emphasizes the interdependence of physical and behavioral functions. Psychophysiological reactions are specific tissue disorders in which behavioral or emotional factors play a significant role. Great care must be taken in practice that disorders appropriately following a biochemical medical model not be classified as psychophysiological ones.

The psychophysiological disorders highlight the area of research dealing with the effect of behavior on physiological functioning. Such effects have been demonstrated for both operant and respondent conditioning. Enacting a role leads to altered physiological functioning. Two roles in which this may be clearly seen are those of hypnotic and placebo responses. Further work with animals and human beings provides additional evidence that a person's behavior alters his internal physical environment as well as his external social environment.

Some of the theories used to formulate psychophysiological reactions were reviewed. Behavioral treatment was illustrated by a number of cases. Not only specific responses but also the situations to which they were made must be taken into account.

In few other areas is there so much new theory, data, excitement, and hope. The student, however, should not confuse the promise of the laboratory with the reality of the clinic. The next decade must be addressed to this task.

schizophrenic behavior
A DESCRIPTION

17

In this chapter and the next we will discuss a category of behaviors that are given the label of "psychoses." DSM-II describes two major groupings within the psychoses: the "organic brain syndromes" (see Chapter 25) and the "functional psychoses."

Patients are described as psychotic when their mental functioning is sufficiently impaired to interfere grossly with their capacity to meet the ordinary demands of life. The impairment may result from a serious distortion in their capacity to recognize reality. Hallucinations and delusions, for example, may distort their perceptions. Alterations of mood may be so profound that the patient's capacity to respond appropriately is grossly impaired. Deficits in perception, language and memory may be so severe that the patient's capacity for mental grasp of his situation is effectively lost. [p. 23]

A major problem with diagnostic work is that no one is psychotic all the time. Rather, there are reactions to certain situations that lead to the designation of "psychosis." DSM-II (p. 23) states it "is recognized that many patients for whom these diagnoses are clinically justified are not in fact psychotic." One may even categorize a person "schizophrenia, simple type, not psychotic."

GENERAL DISCUSSION

O'Kelly and Muckler (1955, p. 262) say: "Psychotic behavior is characterized by a disruption of the integrated adaptation to stress at all life levels." O'Kelly and Muckler, however (pp. 275, 283, 291), then proceed to present a number of cases of people called schizophrenic who maintained a high level of adjustment. One case was a college student who first came to the attention of the student health service because he had told his roommates that he had worked out a way to make love to girls any place in the world by means of a system of thought control. The student, however, had been doing adequately in his more formal college work.

Another case presented by O'Kelly and Muckler was a university student who had made a good record for three years in college, not only in his studies but also in his social relations. He was arrested for starting a fight with an employee at a local store. The young man was interviewed and it was discovered that he had been actively delusional since his freshman year. He had kept a diary detailing his preoccupation with the persecutory forces in his environment.

As one walks across the grounds of a small, treatment-oriented psychiatric hospital, which look more like a college campus than anything else, people can be seen walking or sitting under the trees. While some few may talk to themselves or move in a manneristic way, the biggest difference between the patients and people on their way to class is that college students seem to rush around, knowing where they are going (which may or may not be true). On the other hand, there seems to be a slow, quiet indifference in the people one sees as he walks across the hospital grounds or sits in the hospital canteen and bowling alley.

Similarly, on most wards, as compared

to college dormitory common rooms, the difference is evidenced by a lack of purpose and by interpersonal isolation. At times there is some banter, but it is slow and not general. The usual contemporary psychiatric ward is similar to the lobbies of Skid Row hotels where the drifters sit watching television or to the despondent isolation of an impersonal bar where each man sits alone thinking his own thoughts. The typical psychiatric hospital and ward are not snake pits, bedlams, or the collection of strangely acting people portrayed in the mass media. In fact, one of the most poignant experiences the senior author ever had was sitting in the day room of a psychiatric ward with the men watching a TV rerun of a movie in which Bob Hope was faking insanity to escape the villain. One scene portrayed Hope in an insane asylum where the inmates dressed and acted bizarrely and expressed delusions such as believing they were Napoleon. There sat a group of men in a genuine psychiatric ward behaving appropriately, seriously watching a portrayal of something beyond the experience of any of them. One could only wonder who was crazy, the men on the ward watching the film or the people in Hollywood who made it.

Patients in psychiatric hospitals are anything but "out of it." When the senior author played bridge on a psychiatric ward, he found the table play to be excellent, although the bidding was somewhat assertive, that is, like that of some of his colleagues on the psychology faculty. Perhaps the experience that most clearly brought home to him how important and pervasive attitudes toward psychiatric patients are occurred one hot June afternoon when he was driving into a psychiatric hospital to which he was a consultant. Looking over to a rise of the grounds he saw a man who seemingly was alone and boxing the air and otherwise gesturing violently. The writer said to himself, "My God, I haven't seen mannerisms like that for years." The car moved along, and he then saw that the man was a member of the staff giving a talk to a group of patients who sat quietly on the downward slope at the top of which the staff man was standing.

A similar incident, in reverse, occurred to the junior author. An important behavior on which considerable emphasis is placed in a token economy program (Atthowe and Krasner, 1968, described in Chapter 18) because of the more favorable behavior it evokes from others is neatness of dress. One day, after being away from the ward for some time, the writer saw a well-dressed, distinguished-looking, gray-haired gentleman standing on the ward. The immediate reaction was, "This must be a new psychiatrist on the ward and no one even told me!" The second reaction was to recognize the gentleman as one of the older ward inhabitants now in dress indistinguishable from that of any "normal" person. We cite these experiences to point to the impact of the hospital atmosphere on even those most sophisticated of observers, the present authors.

It is widely believed by the public that psychotic patients are violent and exercise little control over their impulses. This frightens people and may lead to a reduction in the opporunity for psychotics to obtain gratification through usual channels and, hence, (as noted in Chapter 10), to be reinforced for socially approved modes of behavior. Across the entire population of patients, however, antisocial aggressive acts are *less frequent* than in the normal population. For patients in the hospital, this point, as well as the importance of the staff person's attitude, is made by Dr. Walter Barton: "A frightened but docile person who is accosted in a hostile and aggressive manner can be turned into a barricaded battler. . . . But the reverse is equally true. Most disturbed people who are already standing their ground and making threats can be quickly rendered cooperative by someone who is trained and who knows what he is doing. It is mainly a matter of bringing in a staff person well experienced with patients who can give a show of confidence and transmit the expectations that the patient will behave well." (Quoted in Glasscote et al., 1966, p. 30)

With respect to ex-patients, the same point is made by Scheff (1966a, p. 72), who notes that newspaper reports invariably call attention to a history of psychiatric hospitalization in malefactors (often in an attention-grabbing headline starting with "ex-mental patient") but not when they are reporting socially approved acts. Such reports by communication media lead to biased views and perpetuation of stereotyped beliefs. "Actually it has been demonstrated that the incidence of crimes of violence (or of any crime) is much lower among former mental patients than in the general population," Scheff continues, citing four studies to buttress the point.

Additional information is presented by Giovannoni and Gurel (1967), who compared the troubles with the law of a group of male veterans, under 60, diagnosed schizophrenic, and those of the general population (which includes women, children, and aged males). It would seem fair to say that ex-mental patients are clearly no worse than the general population, particularly if the comparison groups are of their own age and sex.

Although labeled psychotic, many of the patients can and do function in the real world. Estimates of the number of patients who are capable of such functioning range up to 85 percent of the hospitalized population. This point was made by Cooper and Early (1961), who surveyed 1,012 patients, of whom 85.2 percent had been continuously hospitalized for over two years. In terms of behavior, 84.4 percent were *not* in need of custodial care, and only 36.7 percent were not doing some socially useful work in the hospital. Cooper and Early cite other studies that obtained similar findings:

A large proportion of all patients under care in mental hospitals show no serious disturbance of behavior, and their retention is determined largely by social factors. Cross et al. (1957) surveyed the chronic population of a large mental hospital, and found that although most of the patients had been under care continuously for ten years or more, only a very small proportion required constant vigilance, while about two thirds needed only "routine" care. The degree of supervision accorded seemed to depend as much on ward tradition and administrative policy as on the patient's mental disturbance. Garratt et al. (1958), from a study of the Birmingham mental hospitals, found that of a large number of patients reviewed, 75% needed only limited hospital facilities, while 12% needed no hospital facilities whatever, and remained in the hospital for entirely social reasons. Furthermore, of the large group requiring only limited hospital facilities, 86% were fully ambulant, and 49% needed no nursing supervision in the hospital.

In summary, the study of abnormality involves, by definition, deviant behavior. The syndromes are more interesting and more easily grasped if the deviance is emphasized. But such an emphasis ignores the reality that most of the behavior of the overwhelming proportion of hospitalized patients is neither disruptive nor particularly different from that of "normals." The belief that hospitalized psychotics are dangerous, bizarre, and wild is not only false, it is harmful.

In the past several years, there has been a sharp change in the attitudes of *some* professionals toward the hospitalized psychiatric patient. In part, growing out of the push for basic human rights in the 1960's, and, in part, out of a shift in formulations away from the "disease" model, different issues are arising. What are the legal rights of a hospitalized individual? What are the basic human needs of any people? These questions and their answers involve a merging of legal, moral, political, social and medical issues.

A DESCRIPTION OF SCHIZOPHRENIA

Freedman, Kaplan, and Saddock write (1972) that there are "an estimated 320,000 hospitalized schizophrenic patients in the United States today. When undiagnosed, untreated, and ambulatory cases are added to this number, the total rises to nearly 600,000. Schizophrenics now occupy close to two-thirds of our mental hospital beds and more than a quarter of all hospital beds." (p. 217.) People called schizophrenic are often hospitalized during late adolescence and early adulthood and, given improvements in general medicine, have a life span that permits them to remain hospitalized 40 or 50 years. The reader may contrast the time element involved in schizophrenia with a more common medical situation, that of childbirth. In childbirth the typical hospital stay is three or four days and therefore each year one bed may serve a hundred different patients.

The following discussion will use the term *schizophrenic,* without quotation marks and without modifying phrases, to refer to a group of people commonly so labeled. For the reasons cited in the prologue it is necessary to present the textbook pictures of these individuals, but it should be explicit that very few textbook schizophrenics exist. The problem is made more difficult because there is even debate about what constitute the fundamental behaviors characteristic of schizophrenia. Buss (1966, p. 187) put the matter this way: "The number of symptoms that have been labeled schizophrenic is so large as to bewilder the student." Noyes and Kolb (1963, p. 325) write: "Although it is relatively easy to describe some of the more striking psychopathology of the schizophrenic reactions, no definition of this mental illness has yet received universal assent." Batchelor (1969, p. 259) reports that "The main groups are reasonably distinctive, but even these are not clear-cut, there are admixtures and transitions, and one could if one wished form almost as many groups as there are affected individuals." The same author notes that "the detailed symptomatology is extraordinarily varied." (p. 260.)

DSM-II describes schizophrenia as follows:

This large category includes a group of disorders manifested by characteristic disturbances of thinking, mood, and behavior. Disturbances in thinking are marked by alterations of concept formation which may lead to misinterpretation of reality and sometimes to delusions and hallucinations, which frequently appear psychologically self-protective. Corollary mood changes include ambivalent, constricted, and inappropriate emotional responsiveness and loss of empathy with others. Behavior may be withdrawn, regressive, and bizarre. [p. 33.]

The quotation just cited touches on the major defining characteristics of schizophrenia: disturbances in reality relationships, unusual behaviors, impaired intellectual performance, disorganized thinking, and reduced or inappropriate expression of emotions. The speech attributed to schizophrenics is jumpy, poorly connected, with one concept following another in a manner that the observer cannot understand. The typical description is that the person does not make clear the *associations* or links between ideas; he seems to fail to take the viewpoint of the listener and talks in a manner not uncommon in free associations during psychoanalytic therapy, in the dreams of normal people, and in college lecturers.

The basic definition of schizophrenia also includes *affective* disturbances, that is, feelings or emotions that are inappropriate to the situation. At times there appears to be a split between the ideas the person discusses—his parents' death, his wife's desertion, the loss of his job—and the bland way he talks about such events. The person may appear apathetic, indifferent, or even gigglingly gay as he talks about what should be tragically upsetting material. He may at times also seem to be pulled in different directions, a situation that is called *ambivalence.*

The basic definition further notes that the person is likely to withdraw from reality. It is difficult, at a descriptive level, to say whether such a retreat is the *cause* of being out of touch with reality and consequently results in an inappropriate response to reality, or whether it is an *effect* of not receiving adequate reinforcement due to other difficulties. In either case, the typical textbook description of schizophrenia includes a concept of autism, which means that there is a tendency for one's thinking and perceiving to be regulated unduly by personal wishes rather than by objective reality. There may also be a correlated overemphasis by the person on his fantasy life.

Association, affect, ambivalence, and autism are called "Bleuler's four A's" because he thought them to be the fundamental symptoms of schizophrenia. To quote Buss (1966, p. 187), however, "The last two are rejected as being fundamental by most authorities, and there is some doubt about the first two."

Schneider's first-order symptoms include the hearing of one's thought, auditory hallucinations, somatic hallucinations, the experience of having one's thoughts controlled and of spreading of one's thoughts to others, delusions, and the experience of being controlled or influenced from the outside. Schizophrenia could also be diagnosed on the basis of second-order symptoms along with an otherwise typical clinical appearance. Second-order symptoms include other forms of hallucinations, perplexity, depressive and euphoric disorders of affect, and emotional blunting. Bleuler also referred to secondary symptoms such as hallucinations, delusions, and illusions. [Freedman, Kaplan and Saddock, 1972, pp. 228–29.]

Batchelor (1969, p. 260) writes: "A most prominent symptom is failure of affect, or emotional blunting, showing itself in apathy and indifference.... Another impressive feature is the disharmony between the mood and the thought. It is this more than anything else that distinguishes schizophrenia from other types of mental disorder."

The patient does not seem to appreciate joy, sorrow, or fear; his attitude seems one of indifference to his condition, and "I don't care" or "I don't know" is a frequently repeated phrase. The person may be said to be withdrawn, indifferent, and unresponsive to the stimuli in his environment—in short, apathetic. What is an adequate stimulus for the "normal" person is either disregarded or responded to in an inappropriate manner. As noted in Chapter 10, a deviant person is one who does not respond to the same stimuli as members of the dominant group, and a conformist is one who shows the successful influence of another. In short, seemingly inappropriate response to what the culture presumes to be adequate stimuli may appear to be a fundamental characteristic.

The major symptom of schizophrenia is usually given in terms of association. Landis and Bolles (1950, p. 158), for instance, say the following: "The thought disorder, [Bleuler] believed, consisted in a loss of coherence in the normal associations between ideas. The stream of thought was only partially guided by one or another central idea, such as a normal person would use in his thinking. Because of this, words of similar sound, alliteration, generalizations, nonsense words, and the like enter into their thought process making it illogical, odd, and incomprehensible."

Meehl (1962) and Braatz (1970) talk of *cognitive slippage* and Buss (1966) of *interference* as the important characteristics of schizophrenia. Buss (1966, pp. 298–302) notes that there are two variants of interference theory. The first one emphasizes the tendency of schizophrenics to include irrelevancies in their concepts. The person attends to too many aspects of the situation and hence is likely to respond to some that are irrelevant. The second variant emphasizes attention. Normal people supposedly can "filter out" irrelevant elements while schizophrenics cannot. Payne, Mattussek, and George (1959, quoted in Buss, 1966, p. 301) describe it this way: "It is as if some 'filter mechanism' cuts out or inhibits the stimuli, both internal and external, which are irrelevant to the task at hand, to allow the most efficient 'processing' of incoming information."

The intellectual "deficit" supposed to be manifested by schizophrenics should affect performance on tests such as the Wechsler–Bellevue. Ullmann and Hunrichs (1958) and Salzman et al. (1966) did not find this to be true. Kendig and Richmond (1940) tested 500 schizophrenics and several other groups for purposes of comparison. On the whole, the patients tested were below normal. Inspection of their performances, however, revealed that the weakness was manifested in tasks demanding *sustained attention or sustained effort*. Apart from this weakness there were no other particular mental functions that showed impairment, and there was no evidence of general deterioration.

In terms of specific behaviors, there may be disturbances of language and thought in which the person coins new words (neologisms); moves from word to word, or idea to idea, without filling in the intervening gaps for the listener (scattering); misidentifies himself or others (depersonalization); displays an indifference to what the culture considers logical; and pursues seemingly irrelevant details so that his talk is tangential and irrelevant. Although not restricted to schizophrenia only (Goodwin, Alderson, and Rosenthal, 1971), the person may *hallucinate*, that is, report experiences when no identifiable overt stimuli for them are present. He may hear voices or see things that the observer does not see or hear. Finally, the patient may report *delusions*, that is, false beliefs. The type of thinking ascribed to schizophrenics may appear to be like that of children or adults discussing politics, love, and the family budget (Glasner, 1966).

Normal children who have not yet learned the rules of speech typical for their culture may make mistakes. They will overgeneralize; things which, according to adults, "normally" do not go together are put together. Rather than a logical ordering, there may be combinations based on some physical or functional similarity. Associations that follow each other because of similarity of sound are called *clang* associations. In some measure poetry is related to this kind of thinking. For example, if the lines "Oh, my luve's like a red, red rose/ That's newly sprung in June" were evaluated in the harsh light of adult logic, Burns would seem to be saying that his girl friend is long and thin and has a big red head and that he must be careful about how he grabs her or he will be stuck. A child may generalize inappropriately from one rule to another. The daughter of one of the authors at age six started making up stories about a little girl who lived in Saville. Her parents did not understand how she had arrived at the name of this town until one day, collecting the mail they noticed that the post office had a large sign, "Savoy, Ill." "Saville" was a contraction, and one that became apparent and understandable. Without such understanding, the town of Saville had seemed a *neologism. Much of schizophrenic ideation is not a deficit in the patient but a deficit in the listener.* If the listener were capable of filling in the gaps, he would "understand" the patient.

Some schizophrenics giggle, grimace, assume strange postures, or perform repetitive rituals and strange movements. They may be extremely agitated, pace, and move their arms, or they may be almost immobile and actively resist movement. They may be mute and assume a posture such as huddling in a fetal position. Other motor symptoms shown by the schizophrenic may be an automatic obedience to commands, letting the psychiatric staff mold his body into strange postures which he then maintains (*waxy flexibility*). He may repeat what is said to him (*echolalia*) or mimic what others do (*echopraxia*). There may be a disregard for conventional behavior ranging from slovenly personal habits to public masturbation. In general, any behavior of which a human being is capable may, when emitted inappropriately, i.e., not under the control of culturally acceptable discriminative stimuli, be called schizophrenic.

TYPES OF SCHIZOPHRENIA

There are ten subtypes of schizophrenia. It must be noted that the reliability of labeling them is low, in part because of the presence of indicators of more than one type of schizophrenia in the behavior of many patients, in part because the pattern of behavior emitted by a given patient may change over time. For example, a person may well change from schizophrenia paranoid type to schizophrenia hebephrenic type as, over time, a delusional system which was originally relatively discrete and systematized becomes pervasive, fragmented, and unsystematized. In addition, with increasing age, the effects of continued institutionalization become manifest.

The first four types of schizophrenia are the "classic" ones: simple, hebephrenic, catatonic, and paranoid.

Schizophrenia, simple type is defined (DSM-II, p. 33) as follows:

This psychosis is characterized chiefly by a slow and insidious reduction of external attachments and interests and by apathy and indifference leading to impoverishment of interpersonal relations, mental deterioration, and adjustment on a lower level of functioning. In general, the condition is less dramatically psychotic than are the hebephrenic, catatonic, and paranoid types of schizophrenia.

The simple type of schizophrenic has typically been considered a drifter and a person likely to take a job which would neither be a challenge nor demand much interpersonal contact. Groups such as vagabonds, hoboes, prostitutes, or those making a marginal adjustment in solitary occupations have traditionally been thought of as being composed of a high percentage of simple types of schizophrenia. Under hospitalization and close questioning, delusions and hallucinations are sometimes elicited. The person seems to withdraw and become indifferent to stimuli that are usually considered reinforcing, and his style of life is one of minimal interpersonal involvement.

The simple type of schizophrenic has further been described as lacking mature heterosexual adjustment, normal aggressiveness, and a normal degree of extraversion; he seems uninterested and even irritable when his friends try to arouse him from his apathy. He may perform odd jobs, endure pain, discomfort, hunger, filth, danger, and social disgrace with a seeming lack of emotional reaction. Formal testing usually reveals little intellectual defect, although the patient may be discovered to hold highly original and illogical ideas on many subjects.

Schizophrenia, hebephrenic type is defined (DSM-II, p. 33) as follows:

This psychosis is characterized by disorganized thinking, shallow and inappropriate affect, unpredictable giggling, silly and regressive behavior and mannerisms, and frequent hypochondriacal complaints. Delusions and hallucinations, if present, are transient and not well organized.

The person displays a deteriorated sloppy manner of dress. Grimacing, giggling mannerisms are made in response to emotionally serious topics. Delusions (false beliefs) are held in an unsystematized fashion, and the person may seem to totally disregard logic or arguments of fact. The somatic delusions frequently are of organs of the body rotting or being absent. These delusions may be not unlike television commercials in which a person with a headache has a rope (and nothing else) in his head which tightens until a pill leaves it limp.

The hebephrenic is silly, absurd, and irritable; he laughs, cries, and is constantly changeable; his moods seem unrelated to the environment. Speech, thought, and action may be incoherent, or at other times bizarre. He smiles and grimaces for no apparent reasons; he is manneristic, posturing, and performs various rituals. His hallucinations and delusions are bizarre, unsystematized, transient, childish, and "regressive." The delusions do not fit together, do not form a system; one delusion may follow another, and be contradictory to it. The hebephrenic seems to emit whatever response will serve the immediate situation. Hallucinations are frequent and are responded to without apparent distress. One of the writers once asked a hebephrenic why he was giggling. The man said it was because of the voices. The writer asked if this was upsetting and was told, "No, they've been there so long they keep me company. They amuse me by the silly things they tell me." The silly, non-upsetting things in this instance were accusations of engaging in homosexual practices.

Schizophrenia, paranoid type is defined (DSM-II, p. 34) as follows:

This type of schizophrenia is characterized primarily by the presence of persecutory or grandiose delusions, often associated with hallucinations. Excessive religiosity is sometimes seen. The patient's attitude is frequently hostile and aggressive, and his behavior tends to be consistent with his delusions. In general the disorder does not manifest the gross personality disorganization of the hebephrenic and catatonic types, perhaps because the patient uses the mechanism of projection, which ascribes to others characteristics he cannot accept in himself. Three subtypes of the disorder may sometimes be differentiated, depending on the predominant symptoms: hostile, grandiose, and hallucinatory.

If the person has a fairly coherent somatic delusion, he is paranoid; if the delusion is extraordinarily bizarre or unsystematized, he is hebephrenic.

In the early stages, the well-systematized paranoid may seem very little different from a person who is a member of some exotic or fringe group. He may believe he has special information which explains events (such as his failures) that would otherwise be confusing to him. Having a definite viewpoint, he seeks further evidence to buttress his belief structure. This is entirely appropriate behavior, and psychologists have been known to do the same. The difference between the scientists and the paranoid arises, if it does, in the quantity and quality of evidence that can be marshaled to support the belief. The paranoid may distort his data to fit his needs. As time goes on, the delusion, while still systematized, may become elaborated and include many types of data. The evidence may come from inconsistent sources and may be distorted, such as quotations that are misinterpreted or taken out of context. There may be anger at anyone questioning him too closely. The paranoid, with his special knowledge, may be supercilious and aloof. He may explain his troubles as a persecution due to his importance or grandeur. He frequently has hallucinations. Compared to other types of schizophrenics, he is likely to remain intellectually responsive, to be alert, and, when not involved with material relevant to his delusions, quite friendly. If pushed, however, the paranoid schizophrenic is more likely to respond with aggression than other types of schizophrenics, who are more likely to withdraw.

Schizophrenia, catatonic type is defined (DSM-II, pp. 33–34) as follows:

It is frequently possible and useful to distinguish two subtypes of catatonic schizophrenia. One is marked by excessive and sometimes violent motor activity and excitement and the other by generalized inhibition manifested by stupor, mutism, negativism, or waxy flexibility. In time, some cases deteriorate to a vegetative state.

Thus, there are two forms of the catatonic type of schizophrenia: the *agitated* and the *stuporous*. The stuporous catatonic may be extremely negativistic and show great muscular rigidity. When asked to do anything, he may do the opposite. For a person routinely to do the opposite of what he is asked is good evidence that he understands clearly what he was asked to do. The stuporous type of patient may assume a posture and hold it for long periods of time. Under some conditions he may be molded into and maintain bizarre postures, such as being seated with one arm held up and one leg stuck out (waxy flexibility). He may be mute and seemingly indifferent to what goes on around him, but, when he recovers he will remember incidents in which he was mistreated and which he deeply resented.

The agitated catatonic may show unorganized and aggressive motor activity that seems without purpose, stereotyped, and limited in space. He may strike out unpredictably against himself or others, or he may show elaborate mannerisms. He paces, and while sometimes mute and expressionless, at other times he speaks as if under great pressure.

Other Types of Schizophrenia

The simple, hebephrenic, paranoid, and catatonic types of schizophrenia are the classic types. There are in the American Psychiatric Association *Manual* five additional types of schizophrenia plus a category for "other unspecified types."

An *acute schizophrenic episode* is defined (DSM-II p. 34) as follows:

This diagnosis does not apply to acute episodes of schizophrenic disorders described elsewhere. This condition is distinguished by the acute onset of schizophrenic symptoms, often associated with confusion, perplexity, ideas of reference, emotional turmoil, dream-like dissociation, and excitement, depression, or fear. The acute onset distinguishes this condition from simple schizophrenia. In time these patients may take on the characteristics of catatonic, hebephrenic or paranoid schizophrenia, in which case their diagnosis should be changed accordingly. In many cases, the patient recovers within weeks, but sometimes his disorganization becomes progressive. More frequently remission is followed by recurrence. (In DSM-I, this condition was listed as "Schizophrenia, acute undifferentiated type.")

Many important topics are touched on in this definition. The word "acute" refers to sharp, severe, and sudden, in contrast to chronic or ongoing. Placement in the category, unlike the previous types of schizophrenia described, depends on case-history material. Those patients who display a variety of symptoms, any one of which might have led to a diagnosis of one of the four classic types, are placed in this category and in the chronic undifferentiated type of schizophrenia. As such, the acute and chronic undifferentiated types make officially available a method for dealing with nontextbook cases. Of great importance is the concept that the pattern of symptoms may change over time in the direction of a "definable" (classic) reaction type. On the one hand this indicates, as noted earlier, that the symptomatology changes over time, and on the other that there may be shaping contingent on the attention paid to certain symptoms by the staff.

Schizophrenia, chronic undifferentiated type is defined (DSM-II, p. 35) as follows:

This category is for patients who show mixed schizophrenic symptoms and who present definite schizophrenic thought, affect, and behavior not classifiable under other types of schizophrenia.

The word "chronic" is used as the opposite of "acute" and indicates a habitual pattern of long duration or frequent recurrence. Again, the category serves to place people who manifest the general characteristics of schizophrenia and yet do not clearly fit one of the four major patterns. Since this category was included in the nosological system, more and more use has been made of it because it permits the diagnostician to hedge his bets.

schizophrenic behavior: a description

The person who is hospitalized may well be behaving no differently than he did when he managed to adjust outside the hospital. People may make "borderline" adjustments such that under careful scrutiny or increased stress they are considered either to be schizophrenics or very likely to act in a schizophrenic manner at some future date. Additionally, a person may act in a manner that a psychiatrist would call schizophrenic and, yet, as pointed out in Chapters 1 and 10 may not be brought by laymen to the psychiatrist's attention.

The following example is taken from an article by Smith, Pumphrey, and Hall (1963): "A male patient hit his mother periodically, talked in a loud and hostile manner to the voices, used profane language, and masturbated openly at home for one year. The decision to seek hospitalization occurred promptly when he carved obscenities on the new grand piano. The mother acted because she was afraid that her spouse, the patient's stepfather, would leave her, since the piano was a status symbol and the carving would present tangible evidence to the neighbors that the family was indecent." In another case (Glasscote et al., 1966, p. 18) a woman who refused to wear clothing had been allowed to stay home for a number of months, but was brought to the hospital after the first time she answered the door. The patient's behavior had not changed appreciably, but the family's evaluation of it as a potential threat to them had.

After the fact of psychiatric intervention, previous behaviors which were not considered significant at the time may be reinterpreted. In the example from Smith et al. (1963) just cited, the man's use of profanity was noted, although cussing is not a particularly rare behavior among American males.

Schizophrenia, schizo-affective type is defined (DSM-II, p. 35) as follows:

This category is for patients showing a mixture of schizophrenic symptoms and pronounced elation or depression. Within this category, it may be useful to distinguish excited from depressed types.

In short, this is a category for placing patients who are not clearly manic-depressive because of the nature of their ideation and at the same time are not clearly schizophrenic because of the presence of strong affect.

Schizophrenia, childhood type is used to classify schizophrenic-like behavior occurring before puberty. The age of the patient may make his overt behaviors quite different from those of an adult schizophrenic. A discussion of the behavior and treatment of children called schizophrenic or autistic will be presented in Chapter 23.

Schizophrenia, residual type is defined (DSM-II, pp. 34–35) as follows:

This category is for patients showing signs of schizophrenia but who, following a psychiatric schizophrenic episode, are no longer psychotic.

This category highlights one of the major differences between the medical and psychological approaches because, by definition, people placed in it are capable of getting along in a community. The "residual" disturbances of thinking, feeling, and/or behavior are not pathological in themselves but are so in the light of the person's history of a psychotic episode. This implies that a person may not recover from schizophrenia even though he adjusts in the community. The person who displays the exact same behavior but who has not been hospitalized or had an overt labeled schizophrenic episode does not meet this definition. He has to be categorized elsewhere (e.g., schizoid personality), if at all.

Schizophrenia, latent type is a category reserved for patients having clear symptoms of schizophrenia but no history of a psychotic episode. Disorders sometimes designated as incipient, prepsychotic, pseudoneurotic, pseudopsychopathic, or borderline schizophrenia are categorized here.

FACTOR ANALYSIS OF "SYMPTOMATIC" BEHAVIOR

In the previous pages, the range of symptoms has been approached through a review of the types of schizophrenia. A different approach arises from attempts to organize the symptoms by use of statistical techniques. In addition to providing a systematic overview, factor analytic studies focus on discrete, definable behaviors. The following material stems from one such study, that of Lorr, Klett, and McNair (1963), who identify ten clusters of psychotic behavior.

The first is *excitement*, including increased motor activity, elevated mood, and lack of restraint. The individual may show hurried speech, dramatize himself or his symptoms, be loud and boisterous, overactive and restless, talk excessively, and try to dominate the psychiatric interview.

A second factor is *paranoid projection*. Here are found hostile, persecutory, controlling ideas and behavior. The individual may be preoccupied with delusions and believe that other people conspire against him (delusions of persecution) or talk about him (delusions of reference), or that other people or external forces such as radiowaves control his actions (delusions of influence).

In the next grouping of symptoms, *hostile belligerence*, the person is hostile, bitter, and resentful; he tends to blame other people for his problems, is suspicious of other people, and expresses an attitude of disdain. He may be characterized as sullen, irritable, grouchy, resentful, and excessively complaining and fault-finding.

A fourth group is called *perceptual distortion*. Here the person hears voices that accuse him, blame him, threaten him with punishment, or exhort him to action. He may see visions or have false perceptions of touch, taste, or smell.

Fifth, the person may show what is called *anxious intropunitiveness* and blame or condemn himself and be fearful about specific matters in the future. He is self-depreciative, expresses feelings of guilt, may have suicidal thoughts or unwanted ideas, feel himself unworthy or sinful, and, in general, feel depressed.

A sixth cluster of symptoms involves *psychomotor retardation* and apathy. The person manifests slowed speech, slowed movement, and indifference about the future. He may have a fixed facial expression, a deficiency for recent memory, be slovenly in personal grooming and at times ignore or fail to answer questions.

In a seventh grouping of symptoms may be found *motor disturbances*. Interestingly enough, muteness and waxy flexibility are rarely observed today. People in this group exhibit peculiar rigid postures, inappropriate grinning and giggling, peculiar grimaces, and repetitive gestures.

The next grouping is called *conceptual disorganization* and is probably a central factor in most syndromes of psychosis. Here are placed the behaviors of giving answers that are irrelevant and incoherent. Other indications are the use of neologisms, the inappropriate repetition of certain words or phrases, and the tendency to drift off the subject (tangential speech).[1] In an interview there may be vague answers, poor judgment (as evaluated by the examiner), rambling and tangential speech (which touches on a relevant topic but then moves in an unexpected, different direction), poverty of thought (indicated by repetitiveness, confu-

---

[1] If ever there was a good example that one behavior out of context does not make a psychosis, *drifting off the topic* is it. The authors do not know any college professor who does not seem tangential. Such tangential speech is in reality the professor's sudden penetrating insight which integrates previously disparate entities. Even as psychiatrists may not be able to follow the intellectual productions of psychotics, students may not properly appreciate professors. The difference is that psychiatrists have power over patients, but, thank goodness, it is the professors who have power over students.

sion, incoherence, and incongruity of thought and feeling), and implausible or bizarre ideation.

The ninth group of symptoms is called *disorientation,* in which the patient may not know he is in the hospital, where the hospital is located, the name of anyone else in the hospital, the season of the year, the calendar year, or his own age.

The final cluster is called *grandiose expansiveness.* The patient's behaviors are the exhibition of an attitude of superiority, belief in possessing unusual power, being a well-known personality, having a divine mission, or hearing voices that praise him.

ADDITIONAL DIMENSIONS IN THE STUDY OF SCHIZOPHRENIA

The observation that there is great heterogeneity in the behaviors of schizophrenics has led many authors, notably Adolph Meyer, to think of schizophrenia as a *group* of reactions rather than as a single unitary disease.

Variation *within* criterion groups (for example, schizophrenics vs. neurotics, or schizophrenics receiving a specific treatment vs. a control group of schizophrenics not receiving such a treatment) reduces the chances of obtaining significant differences between the groups. Four variables are useful for reducing differences among patients called schizophrenic: (1) the process-reactive dimension, (2) the length of hospitalization, (3) the presence or absence of paranoia, and (4) the presence or absence of "anxiety." Patients in a group where these variables have been held constant are likely to be much more similar in their response to a situation than if these variables had not been taken into account.

The Process-Reactive Dimension

Elements of a process-reactive dimension may be found throughout the history of schizophrenia (e.g., Cancro and Pruyser, 1970). As was noted in Chapter 6, Pinel at the start of the nineteenth century inaugurated the keeping of case records so that material dealing with the progress as well as the status of abnormal behavior became available to investigators. In 1849 John Connolly observed that young persons sometimes fell into a state of melancholia in which they seemed to lose interest in their previous pursuits and seemed intellectually and emotionally deadened. In 1860 Morel first used the term "dementia praecox" in describing a boy who had been bright and alert, but who progressively grew more apathetic, disinterested, and interpersonally ineffective. In 1871 Hecker first described hebephrenia; and in 1874 Kahlbaum first described catatonia. It was in 1896 that Kraepelin hypothesized that a common denominator existed for behaviors such as those described by Morel, Hecker, and Kahlbaum, and applied the term "dementia praecox." In 1906 Adolph Meyer proposed that these behaviors were due to *reactions* to difficulties in adaptation rather than the results of a progressive neural deterioration.

In 1911 Bleuler coined the term "schizophrenia" (a concept based on the lack of integration between thought, feeling, and activity). Bleuler was successful in his debate with Kraepelin because he demonstrated that there were cases that did not display inevitable deterioration but rather recovered.

Observations accumulated on the differences between those patients who recovered and those who did not. The areas of clinical symptoms, prior social adjustment, psychological test performances, constitutional factors, and physiological responses were all investigated. A landmark in this work was accomplished by Wittman (1941), who developed a scale based on the rating of 30 variables drawn from the literature. Wittman's scale predicted response to therapy with close to 90 percent accuracy, while psychiatric predictions were essentially chance. Statistical analyses of Wittman's approach by Becker (1959) and Lorr, Wittman, and Schanberger (1951) led to a reduction of the number of scales used.

An alternative method was developed by Phillips (1953), and an elaborate theory dealing with level of psychological development was presented by Kantor, Wallner, and Winder (1953) and Kantor and Winder (1959). These methods depended on quite elaborate and time-consuming rating procedures involving clinical records, psychiatric interviews, or both. Difficulties in different materials available and in rater reliability also led to problems.

Ullmann and Giovannoni (1964) presented a true-false inventory scale which the patient could himself fill out and which, therefore, provided a considerable saving in time and effort for the research worker. Reviews of the many uses to which the concept has been put may be found in Herron (1962), Higgins (1964), and Higgins and Peterson (1966). Typical of research are reports by Stephens, Astrup, and Mangrum (1966, 1967).

The basic concept involved is that there is a continuum of those schizophrenics who remit (improve or "recover") and those who do not. Some authors, particularly early ones, considered that patients who remitted might be reacting to difficulties in their lives (hence the term "reactive"), while those who did not remit were manifesting a true physiological illness (hence "process," from the presumed physiological process).

A number of additional labels differentiating the two "types" of schizophrenia have been used. These labels indicate what the particular authors using them think the key elements are. The process schizophrenic has at times been called a "shut-in" personality, one who early in life withdraws from social contacts. The process schizophrenic has also been called a "poor premorbid," by which is meant that his adjustment prior to hospitalization was below average.

Among the items differentiating the process and reactive poles of the dimension in Ullmann and Giovannoni's self-report scale are the following: the process schizophrenic has not been married, has never worked at one job for two years, has had no academic or vocational training after high school, was not a member of a gang or group of friends in high school, did not date steadily as a teenager, did not like physical education, has never been deeply in love with someone and told them about it, has not held jobs where people are expected to stay a long time, has never paid towards buying a house, and has had no sudden change in life (such as marriage, birth of a baby, death, loss of a loved one or job) prior to entering the hospital. Other cues sometimes used are that the process schizophrenic, compared to the reactive, will display gradual onset of the behavior, will show flattened affect, marked impairment of abstract thinking, and little change to physiological stresses.

The major criterion for the validation of a process-reactive measure is predication of release from the psychiatric hospital, and, in this regard, marital status is probably the single best predictor (Ullmann, 1967a). Among the numerous studies indicating that this dimension effectively predicts release from the hospital are those by Chapman, Day, and Burstein (1961), Chase and Silverman (1943), and Meichenbaum (1966a). King (1958) provides an example of the differential autonomic responsivity of process and reactive schizophrenics; Garmezy and Rodnick (1959) provide an example of differential learning between the two groups; and Becker (1956), Levine (1959), Steffy and Becker (1961), Zimet and Fine (1959), and Ullmann and Eck (1965) illustrate the significant association between the process-reactive continuum and the degree of thinking disorder. By taking into account the process-reactive dimension, more homogeneous groups can be determined and a source of subject variation can be either reduced or specified.

Other Dimensions

In Chapter 10, it was noted that a diagnosis alters how others respond to the person and hence influences the person's behavior. An outstanding example of this is residence in a psychiatric hospital. Through prolonged exposure to the hospital situation, the person may learn new patterns of adjustment. Short-term and long-term schizophrenics may therefore respond very differently to the same treatment situations.

An example of what is involved is an experiment by McInnis and Ullmann (1967). The subjects were 80 male schizophrenics under 55 years of age. Half the subjects had been currently hospitalized 6 months or less (average 3.2 months) while the other half had a current hospitalization of at least 36 months (average 168.5 months). The 40 short-term patients were randomly assigned to a probability learning task in which half received a reward each time they were correct while the other half were given a reward at the start and saw it reduced each time they were incorrect. The same random assignment to gain of positive reinforcement or loss of reinforcement was carried out with the long-term patients. In the probability learning task, a person can maximize reinforcement by choosing the more frequently occurring stimulus when one stimulus appears 75 percent of the time and the other 25 percent of the time. The data in Table 1 refer to the number of times the more frequently occurring stimulus was chosen during trials 101 through 200.[2]

The data presented in this table illustrate two points. The first is that for both reinforcement conditions, the short-term patients were more responsive than the long-term patients. Of greater interest, however, is the second point: the short-term patients were significantly more responsive to the condition of *gaining* than avoiding loss of reward, while the reverse was true to a significant extent for the long-term patients. If one simply asks, "Are schizophrenics more responsive to maximizing reward or avoiding punishment?" (summing the two columns) the present data would say "neither." However, when subjects' length of hospitalization is taken into account, the answer is that some schizophrenics are more responsive to the former, some to the latter. The length-of-hospitalization variable, even as the judicious use of the process-reactive dimension, leads to significant relationships that would not be obtained if one worked with generalizations about "all" schizophrenics.

Two other dimensions of great interest in current research will be briefly mentioned. The first is the dimension of paranoid-nonparanoid. Articles by Winder (1952) and Silverman (1964) provide examples of how different patterns of clinical behavior are manifested by paranoids and nonparanoids on psychological dimensions, especially perceptual ones.

The final variable is that of "anxiety." This dimension is usually defined operationally by responses to true-false questionnaires. The difficulties with the concept of anxiety were discussed in Chapter 9 of this

Table 1

Number of choices of the more frequent stimulus during second 100 trials in a probability learning situation for 4 groups of 20 hospitalized schizophrenics

	AVOID LOSS OF REWARD	GAIN REWARD
Short term	82.90	89.45
Long term	76.20	66.20

Source: McInnis and Ullmann, 1967.

[2] Prior work (Ullmann and Straughan, 1959) indicates that in the absence of an extrinsic reinforcer, schizophrenics behave like the normal adults of Estes and Straughan (1954). The present task has the advantages of being one that schizophrenics understand and enjoy, and in which a large number of trials may be rapidly observed. The results are consistent with other researches, e.g., McCarthy (1964), Atkinson and Robinson (1961), and Ullmann and Forsyth (1959).

book. As will be noted in the next section, for some theorists anxiety is a crucial variable, and therefore should be taken into account in empirical work.

ATTEMPTS TO GENERALIZE ABOUT SCHIZOPHRENIA

This section will approach the issues of what is schizophrenia and what are its crucial aspects by reviewing a variety of descriptive and etiological theories about it. The theories of schizophrenia may be roughly categorized as *cognitive, regressive, biological,* and *behavioristic*. As will be noted, the theories blend into each other.

Earlier in this chapter, a major cognitive approach was touched on through reference to *interference* theory. The core element of schizophrenia is presumed to be some defect, possibly habitual but probably physiological in nature, such that the schizophrenic cannot separate out key stimuli in a manner that permits normal individuals to select and respond only to relevant aspects of their environment and to ignore extraneous cues. Buss (1966, pp. 286–308) outlines conditions leading to interference. If the person manifests interference, he is at a disadvantage in coping with the world, and therefore withdrawal, suspiciousness, and indifference may follow.

A basically cognitive theory of motivation has been advanced by McReynolds, who sees the individual as (1) obtaining and receiving stimulation from the environment and (2) assimilating and integrating these stimuli with his previous experiences. If the new experiences do not fit or are incongruous with previous experiences, there is an increase in anxiety. McReynolds writes (1960, p. 263): "It can be presumed that the reactions to a large quantity of unassimilated percepts are primarily of two kinds: first, attempts to keep the quantity of unassimilated material from getting even greater; and second, attempts to bring about assimilation of the unassimilated percepts."

The first kind of reaction leads to selective avoidance, withdrawal, and apathy; the second leads to delusions and thinking disorders. Increasing consistent experiences and rationalizing incongruent ones may lead to a narrowing of attention or a loosening of standards of acceptable evidence, and hence to apparent delusions and disorganization of thinking.

Cameron (1947) and Cameron and Magaret (1951) present a biosocial approach to schizophrenia which shows the influence of Adolph Meyer. The central concept leading to disorganization of thinking and other pathological behaviors is described by Cameron (p. 450) as follows: "In schizophrenic disorganization, as our clinical cases will illustrate, the patient's role-taking becomes desocialized. It moves away from its social derivation in directions that are determined by private fantasy, and includes responses in shared social situations which have validity only in a fantasy context (*overinclusion*), until eventually it no longer corresponds to the socially determined role-taking of other persons in the same culture."

Cameron and Magaret (1951, p. 459) list the conditions favoring disorganization as (1) interruption of ongoing activity (frustration); (2) environmental change (alteration in a previously supporting environment); (3) preoccupation (domination by a single theme to the exclusion of virtually all else); (4) emotional excitement (arousal of anger or fear, which destroys fine coordination, increases the magnitude of errors, and exaggerates muscular tension); (5) ineffectual role-taking (through lack of training or adverse circumstances, such that the person cannot or does not take the perspective of the other person [see Cameron, 1947, p. 93]); (6) situational complexity (new or conflicting demands); and (7) cerebral incompetence (such as fever or brain injury, which would be more likely diagnosed brain injury than schizophrenia). Schizophrenia, involving defective role-taking and disorganization of thinking, represents a reaction to situations that are difficult or stressful. The symptoms of schizophrenia, in turn, may create still greater difficulty for the individual as his decreased capabilities lead to further involvement with fantasy as opposed to reality.

Salzinger (1971) offers a hypothesis about schizophrenic behavior which attempts to take into account genetic aspects as well as the fact that behavior is modifiable throughout one's lifetime. His view is that "the behavior of schizophrenic patients is more often controlled by stimuli which are immediate in their spatial and temporal environment than is that of normals." (p. 601.)

A Genetic View

Perhaps the most appealing presentation of a physiological theory of schizophrenia was made by Meehl (1962). As noted in passing earlier in this chapter, Meehl considers "cognitive slippage" to be the fundamental symptomatic behavior of schizophrenia. The slippage is caused by some physiological dysfunction. Studies of twins are taken as indications that the difficulty is inherited.

Many studies (Essen-Möller, 1941; Kallmann, 1946, 1953; Shields and Slater, 1961) have reported that as consanguinity increases, the chances of schizophrenia increase. The typical research approach is to find a person who is hospitalized, diagnosed schizophrenic, and who has a twin; the chances of the twin being schizophrenic are far greater than that found in the general population and are far greater if the siblings are identical (*monozygotic*) than if they are fraternal (*dizygotic*). It is necessary, in order to separate the effects of heredity from environment, to compare monozygotic and dizygotic twins separated at birth with those reared together.

Although this claim is made by a number of studies, Jackson (1960, p. 40) reviewed the literature and concluded:

. . . let it be said here regarding twins who are alleged to have been reared apart and who both developed schizophrenia, that an exhaustive search of American and European literature of the past forty years has uncovered only two such cases. . . . These two cases, considering the incidence of schizophrenia, could have occurred on a chance basis. . . . Kallmann in his 1946 paper designated a category among identical twins of "separated" and "non-separated." However, his terms refer only to *separation five years prior to the psychosis.* Because his age group ranged from 15 to 44 years, and because his average age is stated to be 33 years (p. 317), it is obvious that the twins were not apart during their formative years.

It should also be noted that being reared by different people (e.g., aunt rather than mother) does not mean a different environment.

Two other arguments against the apparent conclusions of the genetic studies should be noted. The first is that many of the reported concordance indices are greater than the reliability of the diagnosis of schizophrenia itself. In addition to problems in the diagnostic criterion there are technical difficulties in determining whether twins are identical or fraternal at the time they are adults. The second concern with the genetic approach arises from work such as that of Tienari (1963), who started with a sample of twins and found 16 pairs in which one was schizophrenic and the other was not (i.e., zero concordance). Results in a similar vein were obtained by Kringlen (1964, 1966), Pollin et al. (1966), and Rosenthal (1959, 1962). Pollin et al. (1969) point out that 85 percent of monozygotic twins in their sample were discordant for schizophrenia.

Meehl (1962) calls the *neural integrative defect,* that which is inherited, *schizotaxia.* Social learning imposes on a person so endowed a personality organization which Meehl calls *schizotypic.* "Only a subset of schizotypic personalities decompensate into clinical schizophrenia. It seems likely that the most important causal influence pushing the schizotype toward schizophrenic decompensation is the schizophrenogenic mother." In short, heredity is considered a necessary but not a sufficient cause of schizophrenia. According to Meehl, if the heredity is not schizotaxic, regardless of stress schizotypy and later schizophrenia will not develop.

Erlenmeyer-Kimling (1972), a proponent of a genetic viewpoint, contends that of the several directions now being taken in contemporary genetic research on schizophrenia, three seem to be the most promising for the eventual disentanglement of gene-environment interactions. These approaches have developed from the traditional family-study methods used in earlier genetic investigations.

One of the current approaches involves adoption studies in which it is possible to separate the effects of the biological and the psychological transmission of psychopathology. This approach overcomes one of the most serious criticisms that has persistently dogged previous work on the genetic etiology of schizophrenia. The pioneering study of this type was conducted a few years ago by Leonard Heston (1966) . . .[3]

. . . A second line of research, which so far has received too little attention, involves the investigation of biological (e.g., biochemical, immunological, etc.) responses in first-degree relatives of schizophrenic probands. Basically, the point here is to attempt to distinguish between those biological characteristics found in schizophrenic patients that are *products* of the disease process and those that may be associated with hereditary factors *underlying* the disease . . .[4]

---

[3] A closer look at Heston's study is required: of 74 children born to mothers who were diagnosed schizophrenic and patients at a state hospital and who were separated from their mothers at birth, sixteen subjects were dropped, and the remaining 58 were matched from the same foundling homes. When follow-up was undertaken, 5 more subjects were lost. At follow-up, all of the investigations and interviews were conducted by the author, who was not blind as to the subjects' groups. Written dossiers, including the interview by the author, were rated by two psychiatrists who did not know the subjects' groups and by the author who did. Information was incomplete on 25 people, but these people were not discarded. Differences in score assignment were discussed by the author and the raters in conference. With these procedures, 5 of the 47 people in the experimental group were found to be schizophrenic (and 42 not), while none of the controls were so found. Retardation was more frequent in the experimental group (4 cases versus 0) and sociopathic personality (9 cases versus 2). There was no attempt to correlate other sociocultural measures such as military service, schooling, social class, etc. There was no account taken of prenatal diet and care (state hospital food, the effect of medication on the foetus, etc.). There was no evidence that either the foster parents or the placement personnel were blind as to the children's histories. If one cannot explain the rate of retardation otherwise, one might even hypothesize that the mothers' diagnoses were severely confounded for there is little evidence supporting a notion that retardation or sociopathy is genetically linked to schizophrenia. Finally, Heston notes that his figures are consistent with reports of rates for single parents who are schizophrenic; one may wonder who were the men who fathered children of hospitalized schizophrenic women? Kety et al. (1971) surveyed adoptions in Copenhagen between 1924 and 1948 and found 5483 adoptions to persons not biologically related. Of these, 507 had been hospitalized, and of this group, 33 were agreed upon as index cases (note the extreme sample selection). The number of relatives of the index and control cases who had been hospitalized were determined. It is important to note that no one who had ever had any psychiatric history whatsover was used as a control. For the index cases, 13 of 150 relatives had some incidence on the "schizophrenic spectrum" while the rate was 3 out of 156 relatives for the controls. The appropriate test, that of the number of index cases versus the number of control cases is not given. The effect, at best, is a very weak one, and given methodological problems, may well be artifactual.

[4] This presumes that a relevant physiological variable has been discovered. There are numerous biochemical hypotheses that are promulgated with great fanfare. In fact, as Farina (1972) points out, there are so many that they tend to conflict and invalidate each other. Further, ". . . when other researchers test the hypotheses, and especially if better controls are instituted, the results are typically negative." (Farina, 1972, p. 7.) From the many examples possible, we may cite Brown, Quarrington, and Stancer (1969) on glucose tolerance; Pivnicki and Christie (1968) on body build; Pue, Hoare, and Adamson (1969) on "pink" spot; Keup, Seto, and Gonda (1970) on "gray" spot (eating bananas made a big difference, however); and Griswold, Pace, and Grunbaum (1969), who found physiological indicators of the stress response to be present only when the patient was hyperactive. The null hypoth-

schizophrenic behavior: a description

The third and final direction that is being taken in contemporary research on schizophrenia entails the observation of subjects who are considered, by some criterion, to have a potentially high risk of manifesting schizophrenia, but who have not yet done so at the time of initial observation. Measures are obtained on these high-risk subjects *before* overt onset of disturbed functioning, and the evolution of the illness can then be traced in those subjects who do later break down. High-risk research is intended to separate significant manifestations—behavioral, physiological, etc.—that characterize preschizophrenic individuals from those signs in schizophrenic patients that may simply be the consequences of the illness." [Erlenmeyer-Kimling, 1972, pp. 364–65]

These studies have thus far concentrated on the children of schizophrenic parents. In Mednick and Schulzinger's (1968) long-term research, the subjects are preadolescent and teen-aged offspring of schizophrenic mothers. These subjects and their matched controls are being followed up so that the occurrence of "mental" breakdown, of varying degrees of severity, can be ascertained. The data now becoming available point to associations between breakdown and specific response patterns, especially certain psychophysiological patterns, that were seen when the subjects were tested as youngsters in 1962.

Several similar programs of prospective research have been initiated (cf. Anthony, 1968; Erlenmeyer-Kimling, 1968; Garmezy, 1969; Rosenthal, 1971; Sameroff and Zax, 1973). All have in common one basic question: Who in a high-risk group will later become schizophrenic? If 10 percent of children with one affected parent and 40 percent of those with two affected parents eventually evidence schizophrenic behavior, this means that 90 percent and 60 percent, respectively, of the two groups did *not* show the behavior. Some of these latter children will perhaps exhibit other "deviancies"; but the rest will become healthy, "normal" adults. What is it that distinguishes the children who will later be labeled as deviant from those who will not be despite their all having had earlier experiences with equally poor life circumstances?

... At present, there are no systematic means for identifying those individuals who are likely to experience a later psychiatric breakdown. Certainly there are no empirically based methods of intervention for the purpose of preventing—or at minimum, decelerating—the development of psychopathology. In prospective research, it is hypothesized that indicators of vulnerability are to be found at relatively early ages and that they show themselves as emerging difficulties in areas continuous with the behavioral deficiencies observed in adult schizophrenia. It is expected, therefore, that the pinpointing of these precursory signs of developing disabilities in mental life, through investigations of known high-risk groups, will constitute the first step toward implementation of mass-screening methods and the establishment of valid approaches to environmental intervention. [Erlenmeyer-Kimling, 1972, pp. 368–69]

Recent twin studies have tended to diminish previously estimated concordance rates for schizophrenia (Hoffer and Pollin, 1970; Mosher and Gunderson, 1973), and Campion and Tucker (1973) point out physiological and developmental differences in monozygotic twins that are rarely acknowledged in existing twin studies. "Most geneticists now believe that schizophrenia, per se, is not inherited. Rather, it is a *predisposition* to schizophrenia (or, perhaps, to psychopathology in general) which is transmitted genetically." (Mosher and Gunderson, 1973, p. 21.)

It should be explicit that no trait or predisposition can be shown to be influenced genetically until the trait or predisposition is defined, and this remains to be done. Further studies of monozygotic twins discordant for schizophrenia point out the "complexities" in this area, that is, environmen-

---

esis cannot be proved, but the strategy of demonstrating genetic effects by biochemical measurements prior to validating such techniques does seem rather risky.

tal factors that reduce the concordance indices (Pollin et al., 1966; Hoaken, 1969; Guggenheim et al., 1969).

Other Theories

There have been numerous *biochemical theories of schizophrenia*. The present volume will make no attempt to review this material. Attention is called here to Chapter 5, in which two instances of biochemical theories were illustrated. The first of these dealt with an adverse placebo effect in which a saline (salt water) injection was as effective as a supposedly schizophrenia-inducing compound; the second was the effect of NAD, the original administration of which by an interested psychiatrist led to remarkable results but which, on a later controlled study, was found to be no more effective than a sugar pill. Some of the difficulties in biochemical research on schizophrenia were touched on in Chapter 3 under problems of control groups. While neither a genetic nor a biochemical basis for schizophrenia can be ruled out (nor, if it were found, would it alter the necessity for judicious application of behavioral principles in rehabilitation), the present evidence for such an etiology seems more hopeful than factual.

A *regressive* theory of schizophrenia means that the person acts in a childlike manner, and hence is *fixated* at an early level of development. The disorganization of thinking may then be called primary process, id-like thinking about what would be pleasant, as distinct from secondary process, ego-like thinking concerned with the evaluation of consequences. Arieti (1955), in particular, places the difficulty of the schizophrenic in terms of faulty logic, notably the assertion of the predicate (A is Y; B is Y; therefore A is B; for example, schizophrenics, in some ways, act like children; children act like children; therefore schizophrenics are children). Later Arieti (1967, p. 453) wrote, "Preschizophrenic panic occurs when the archaic infantile thought process and its original content are reactivated by later conceptual conclusions, with a resulting unacceptable image of the self."

Buss (1966, pp. 237–63) presents an excellent evaluative review of regressive theories, and Maher (1966, pp. 425–31) marshals empirical evidence against a defect in formal logic as being uniquely indicative of schizophrenia. Both authors point out the cultural relativism involved in regressive theories. Buss (1966, p. 261) notes that the person need not necessarily be repeating outgrown modes of behavior; he may merely be acting in a manner judged immature by his culture. Maher (1966, p. 428) points out that formal laws of logic deal with the relations between propositions. They need have no more to do with the thinking of normal adults than ideal dental therapeutics have to do with how the majority of people take care of their teeth.

Aside from the views of the authors mentioned, there are other approaches associated with the regressive theory. The one touched on in the quotation from Meehl (1962) is that of a schizophrenogenic mother. The hypothesis is that the mothers of schizophrenics differ from the mothers of normal males in how they reared their children. The typical manner of investigating this concept (e.g., Mark, 1953) is to present a series of attitude statements to mothers of men who are hospitalized for schizophrenia and a matched group of mothers of men hospitalized for some other, nonpsychiatric, medical reason. The experience of having raised such an individual may lead to differences in the two groups of mothers as an effect rather than as a cause of the son's current behavior. Further, such studies fail to replicate each other's findings. For example, the study by Mark was substantiated neither by Freedman and Grayson (1955) nor by Jackson et al. (1958).

Frank (1965) critically reviews the literature on the role of the family in the development of psychopathology and concludes that research over a period of 40 years has failed to demonstrate that there are particular modes of child-rearing likely to be antecedent to schizophrenia or neurosis.

Another theoretical view of schizophrenia is that there is some *defect in motivation*. The motivational theorists, as distinguished from behavioral and/or sociopsychological theorists, make use of an internal state of affairs, notably anxiety. In this regard, the present authors make a distinction, not made by Buss (1966), between *drive* or internal motivation, and *reinforcement* or external response-contingent changes in the environment.

The clinical observation from which the motivational approach starts is that schizophrenics do not respond appropriately, i.e., with interest and approach, to the same stimuli as do "normal" people. In many experiments contrasting schizophrenics and "normals," the schizophrenics do less well, and this difference may be due to a lack of "motivation."

If lack of motivation is the key difficulty, then the obvious experimental treatment would be to increase motivation. Motivational theorists attempt to do this. A first way is by urging or coaxing, but this is relatively ineffective as a treatment for a number of reasons. The patient is not responding to the same values as do comparison groups of "normals." For example, if social withdrawal is a major behavior that leads to a diagnosis of schizophrenia, it seems worthless to use mild social pressure to "motivate" the patient. Further, the reinforcing stimulus is frequently given before rather than after the patient's emission of the act in these experiments.

A gratuitous assumption by authors dealing with those theories is that if lack of motivation is the key to schizophrenia, then schizophrenics should not only improve under conditions of differential "motivation," but should improve significantly more than the "normals." It seems remarkable that a number of experiments have found patients responsive at all to the sort of urging which is effective with college students. When a mild noxious stimulus is used, and especially when the patient cannot avoid it, and receives feedback about his performance after each trial (Losen, 1961; Atkinson and Robinson, 1961), some favorable effects have been obtained with schizophrenics. Avoidance of an annoying noise has been found effective in a number of experiments (Pascal and Swensen, 1952; Grisell and Rosenbaum, 1963; King, 1962; Lang, 1959; Rosenbaum, Grisell, and MacKavey, 1957; Cavanaugh, 1958; Brown, 1961), as has a mild electric shock (Cohen, 1956).

A number of motivational theories find the central problem of schizophrenia to be a matter of too much motivation, notably too high a drive. Here anxiety is considered the drive. The work of McReynolds previously cited is an example. McReynolds equated an excessive number of unassimilated percepts as a condition of anxiety. To reduce anxiety, the person acts in a way to reduce new percepts. Other authors (Rodnick and Garmezy, 1957) carry this further in making a fear of social censure, especially in process (poor premorbid) schizophrenics, a key factor.

A special variant of these theories is one by Mednick (1958), who equates high anxiety with high drive and hence overgeneralization to stimuli. Such overgeneralization is used to explain disorganization of thinking. The evidence for overgeneralization by schizophrenics is at best equivocal (Buss and Daniell, 1967). Observation indicates that while clinically the acute schizophrenic may seem anxious, the chronic schizophrenic does not. Mednick therefore hypothesizes that thinking irrelevant thoughts (caused in the manner noted above) is so effective that anxiety is reduced below that of normal people.

Impression Management

The next three types of theory, impression management, sociology, and linguistic analysis, have important implications for the sociopsychological theory of schizophrenia (see next chapter). Impression management counters the view that schizophrenics' behavior is characterized by deficits—that is, implicitly, a schizophrenic for whatever reason has had some loss of ability or deficit (Hunt and Cofer, 1944) to perform the various tasks of life. Instead, the person may have control over these "deficits" and perform in relationship to his current life and hospital goals. Braginsky and Braginsky (1967, 1969) initiated a line of investigation designed to test whether hospitalized schizophrenic patients could manage the impressions they give to others. If, for example, a patient were on an open ward and it is assumed that he wants to stay there to avoid being sent to a closed ward, could he offer a better impression of his behavior to avoid being sent to a closed ward? The evidence in a number of studies strongly suggests that to a significant extent schizophrenics can manage the impressions they make on others (Fontana and Klein, 1968; Fontana, et al., 1968; Fontana and Gessner, 1969; Price, 1972, 1973; Kelly, Farina, and Mosher, 1971).

Ideological-Sociological Theories

Still another way of presenting the concept of schizophrenia is to put it in the context of ideology. Scheff (1970) refers to the concept of schizophrenia as "the leading edge of an ideology embedded in the historical and cultural present of the white middle class of Western societies. The concept of illness and its associated vocabulary—symptoms, therapies, patients, and physicians—reify and legitimatize the prevailing public order at the expense of other possible worlds."

The so-called symptoms of mental illness, in contrast to, for example, pneumonia or syphillis, are not culture-free but rather are offenses against the norms or the implicit understanding inherent in a specific culture as to what is appropriate behavior.

As an alternative to the medical illness model, Scheff offers the sociological labeling theory (Becker, 1963; Krauss, 1968). The labeling theory of deviance is based upon a series of hypotheses. Residual rule-breaking may arise from many diverse sources, including those that are organic, psychological, or situational. In comparison with treated mental illness, the unrecorded residual rule-breaking is very common, is usually denied, and is of transitory significance.

In many instances the deviant accepts his public labeling. Further, as pointed out in Chapters 2 and 10, the label alters the behavior of the person so categorized as well as those with whom he interacts.

In a more traditional vein, Dunham (1971) offers the field of sociological psychiatry in contrast to the fields of biological psychiatry and analytical psychiatry. In doing so, he runs into the usual problem of diagnoses, which he tries to resolve by using the terms "hard" and "soft" diagnoses of schizophrenia.

Under the soft category are included psychoanalytic theory, learning theory, socialization theory, and anomie theory. Dunham describes the soft diagnosis as "humanistic, imaginative, sympathetic, and most readable." (p. 207.) It also gives lip service to genetic possibilities. "The central aspect of the 'soft' diagnosis is that it depends primarily upon psychic and behavioral data that are abstracted from the patient and conceptualized into an explanation for his peculiarities of expression and behavior."

The hard diagnosis, on the other hand, is based on biological and neurological evidence. It emphasizes genetics and views schizophrenia as an hereditary disease.

The 1939 Faris and Dunham study (see Chapter 10) was a landmark in the sense of sociologists moving into a medical area. As Dunham put it, "it was a study conducted by sociologists and thus tended to emphasize that mental illness was a relevant area for sociological investigation . . . It set the stage for at least two decades of debate between psychiatrists and sociologists with respect to the interpretation of findings." (p. 208)

Despite the introduction of the sociologists into this "game," the major point is that they were playing by the rules of the medical people by accepting the disease model.

Of particular interest is the fact that the sociological approach introduced new problems and questions:

> These obstacles centered around the issue of adequate coverage, thus pointing to the nonhospitalized cases, the problem of psychiatric diagnosis, the amount of geographical and vertical mobility within the urban community, the gap between onset and beginning of treatment, the differential use of psychiatric facilities, the multiplication of psychiatric facilities, the tremendous age span of psychiatric cases, and, finally, the controversy as to whether incidence or prevalence rates would be a superior measure in the epidemiological study of mental illness." [p. 208]

Linguistic Analysis

An approach to conceptualizing schizophrenia that complements our social-psychological one is the historical, linguistic and metaphorical approach of Sarbin (1971).

> The widely held belief in the existence of a disease entity called schizophrenia is no longer supportable. . . . The burden of my argument rests on the acceptance of two propositions—both of which can be supported with plentiful documentation. (1) That the official position is that schizophrenia belongs to a class of illnesses called mental illness, and (2) that a person who is a candidate for the diagnosis of schizophrenia comes to the attention of the diagnoser as the result of overt conduct that violates certain propriety norms.
>
> When these two statements are placed side by side, a dissonance emerges: for many centuries, illness has been conceptualized as a conjunction: a self-report of bodily disturbance, such as an itch, plus observable bodily symptoms, such as a rash or a swelling. To understand how norm-violating conduct, say, talking to non-existent persons (which does not include a complaint like itches or bodily symptoms like rashes), was assimilated to the traditional conception of illness requires a brief excursion into the history of medical psychology. [p. 4]
>
> The major transformation occurs when the *as if* distinction of metaphors is dropped:
>
> In the case of illness as a metaphor for conditions not meeting the usual criteria of illness, the dropping of the "as if" was facilitated by the practitioners of physic, forerunners to modern-day physicians. It was awkward for them to talk about two kinds of illness, "real" illness and "as if" illness. When Galenic classifications were reintroduced, the "as if" was dropped. Thus, post-Renaissance physicians could concern themselves with illness as traditionally understood and also with norm violations as illness. A review of the 16th and 17th century treatises on "physic" reveals clearly that the honored theory of Galen was the standard for diagnosis and treatment. The diagnostic problem was how to construct inferences about balancing or tempering the humors inside the organism.
>
> The prestige of the new science helped in establishing the model of Galen for both kinds of "illness"—those with bodily complaints and observable symptoms, and those without bodily complaints but with unacceptable behavior being substituted for bodily symptoms. Thus, the public report of strange imaginings, on the one hand and fever, on the other, were treated as belonging to the same class, that is, symptoms. [p. 7]
>
> The practice of medicine came to include not only every physiological condition but also all behavior:
>
> Now, any item of conduct—laughing, crying, threatening, spitting, the reporting of imaginings, the expression of unpopular beliefs, wearing unconventional clothing, resisting authority and denouncing myths—could be called symptoms of underlying internal pathology. . . . The history of psychology shows repeatedly that its metaphors or hypothetical constructs tend to become myths. The auxiliary grammatical device, the "as if," is dropped, and the deformed sentence renders the construction as literal

truth.... Behavior that would mystify us and ordinarily lead to psychiatric diagnosing can instead be seen as unconventional, non-conforming, or even creative efforts of a person to make sense out of a complex, probabilistic and changing world. [pp. 15, 35] [5]

Finally, we must note the "blaming-the-victim" approach to schizophrenia emphasized by Ryan (1971). This ideological view conceives of the schizophrenic as a victim of social and economic influences in the same manner as blacks, addicts, women, and the poor. The person is blamed for his disability by the consequences of the label and further by the manner in which solutions are sought for social problems.

The social problem of mental disease has been viewed as a collection of individual cases of deviance, persons who—through unusual hereditary taint, or exceptional distortion of character—have become unfit for normal activities. The solution to these problems was to segregate the deviants, to protect them, to give them *asylum* from the life of the community for which they were no longer competent. This has been the dominant style in American social welfare and health activities, then: to treat what we call social problems, such as poverty, disease, and mental illness, in terms of the individual deviance of the special, unusual groups of persons who had those problems. [Ryan, 1971, p. 15]

IS THE CONCEPT SCHIZOPHRENIA VIABLE?

The material on description in this chapter was prefaced with the observation that textbook schizophrenics were the exception rather than the rule. We then reviewed the material in current textbooks and presented the most popular theories about schizophrenia. After having made the reader suffer, we now ask a key question: How useful or practical is the concept of schizophrenia itself, and, hence, the theories that presume that a schizophrenic disease or deficit exists.

One approach to this question is to ask how reliable the DSM-II types of schizophrenia are and how well they cover the people to whom the label is applied. Blashfield (1973) found the interrater agreement to be quite poor: "The median intraclass correlation is .1063. The low value indicated that less than 1 percent of the total response variance in all the data was accounted for by agreement between the judges. Even for the most reliable diagnosis—paranoid schizophrenia—interrater reliability accounted for less than 10 percent of the variance." (p. 385). Another way of putting this is that Blashfield's data indicate that judges agreed in their primary diagnoses only one out of four times. Blashfield found that the degree of coverage was inversely proportional to reliability. Only when reliability was low, was the coverage adequate: In short, DSM-II types of schizophrenia did not function adequately as a form of nomenclature.

Another approach is to determine the sources of variance for the use of a concept. Fitzgibbons and Shearn (1972) collected data from mental health professionals about schizophrenia and found that type of professional discipline accounted for a significant portion of the variance in etiological factors; theoretical orientation of the judges was related to opinions about the nature of schizophrena and questions of prognosis; and place of employment was related to opinions about etiology and phenomenology: "The findings are interpreted as casting doubt on the remaining usefulness of the term 'schizophrenia.'" (p. 288).

Another line of research deals with the question whether schizophrenia is universal, that is observed across cultures. Murphy, et al. (1963) sent a questionnaire to 120 individuals or psychiatric centers across the world, of which 40 in 27 countries replied. The results showed that the "dis-

---

[5] This last concept, combined with elements of psychoanalytic regressive and existential ideology is essentially Laing's (1964, 1967) approach to schizophrenia.

tribution of schizophrenic symptoms appears to vary in association with social, cultural, observational, and conceptual factors" (p. 248). Murphy et al. write: "The main significance of our findings at this stage is that doubt has been thrown on the picture which Euro-American psychiatry has built up of the schizophrenic process. For instance, considering the high percentages of the simplex and catatonic sub-types of schizophrenia reported for certain Asian samples . . . and the low percentages of the paranoid sub-type, it might be questioned whether the delusional systems which are the most familiar feature of chronic schizophrenia in Euro-American hospitals are an essential part of the disease process. Might they not be culturally conditioned attempts by the personality to 'make sense' of that process, attempts which Eastern cultures inspire to a much lesser degree?" (pp. 248-49).

In a recent review of this topic, Torrey (1973) summarizes the situation as follows:

In fact, however, there is no evidence upon which to base a belief in the universality of schizophrenia. The studies which have been used to support this belief are found, on careful examination, not necessarily to point in this direction at all. If anything, they may lead to the opposite conclusion: Schizophrenia may *not* be a universal disorder. [p. 53]

Torrey then reanalyzes the studies that have already been published in this area. Of particular interest is his noting that until the 1940's, the universality of schizophrenia was still an open question subject to debate. The study most responsible for the closing of the debate was the 1954 review by Benedict and Jacks, "Mental Illness in Primitive Societies." Since its publication, most subsequent textbooks cite it as proof of the universality of schizophrenia. Torrey's criticisms of the Benedict and Jacks studies are that the so-called primitive societies cited were not really primitive, and that three of these studies were based on reports of hospitalized cases of schizophrenia (hospitalization being itself an indicant of civilization). Moreover, many of these so-called primitive societies, at the time of being studied, were considered to be in the process of acculturation (being influenced by Western civilization).

Torrey (p. 56) put this material within a behavior-influence context by concluding that, "Once an idea becomes part of a textbook, it develops a life of its own and is seldom questioned. This is what has occurred with the idea that schizophrenia is universal."

This questioning of the concept of schizophrenia, its identifiability and universality, sets the stage for the next chapter. There is no doubt that the term is used by professional people with consequences to those who receive the label. Our task in Chapter 18 will be to describe conditions that lead the professionals to give the label, and the consequences, to the individual in terms of how his life and behavior is altered. After we are clear on what is meant by the word schizophrenia, we may be in a better position to assist people so designated.

SUMMARY

In this chapter the concept of psychosis in general and schizophrenia in particular has been reviewed. The aim was to define what is meant by the word "schizophrenic" and to indicate some of the approaches to delimiting the behaviors involved and the variety of explanations offered by theoreticians and research investigators.

the socio-psychological formulation and treatment of schizophrenia

18

In the previous chapter the behaviors likely to lead to the label of schizophrenia were discussed. These behaviors include, first, apparent disorganization of thinking in which the person's response is not the "good," "abstract," "appropriate" one expected of people in his particular culture, and second, an indifference, apathy, or withdrawal from efforts to maximize the sort of stimuli that other people in the culture considered positively reinforcing. The behavior of the schizophrenic, like that of other people called abnormal is unexpected and seemingly inexplicable. Most notably, the schizophrenic seems to be hurting himself by not taking advantage of his opportunities to obtain the good things of life. The issue, then, is how to formulate as the result of social reinforcement behaviors that seem to be the antithesis of normality.

BACKGROUND

All too often textbooks make psychology appear rational, obvious, and deductive. Psychology, however, especially clinical and abnormal psychology, involves people.

When the senior author was an undergraduate, as part of the course in abnormal psychology, he participated in a tour of the wards of a large state psychiatric hospital. Walking through the wards at that time was a depressing experience: literally over a hundred men might crouch in fetal positions along the walls of a "dayroom." The tour guide, the hospital's superintendent, noticed that one man in a fetal posture had his back perilously close to the radiator and simply said to him, "There's an empty chair over there and I think you'd be more comfortable in it." The man scrambled up, got in the chair, and resumed his motionless, curled up, bizarre posture symbolic of "deep regression to the womb." He was certainly aware of and responsive to the stimuli in his environment, as demonstrated by his carrying out a suggestion immediately and accurately. His reaction was inconsistent with a concept of pervasive illness and withdrawal into autism. The only way to assimilate such a performance into a disease concept is to say that the responsiveness itself is a sign of the illness and to call it automatic obedience.

Calfee describes the test-taking performance of a subject diagnosed as schizophrenia, catatonic type:

He walked in with the characteristic robot-like quality associated with catatonia. His face was devoid of all expression whatsoever. He seemed like an automated machine. It was difficult to believe he had even heard the instructions let alone understood them. He was scheduled to begin with the sentence building task. When asked if he had any questions about the procedure, a full minute and a half elapsed before he responded with a flat, emotionless "no." The experimenter was resigned to a very difficult and lengthy session. From the first moment of the task proper, however, a remarkable change took place. The subject responded promptly to each card, with excellent sentences, demonstrating an unusual command of both grammar and vocabulary with no untoward hesitancies in his presentations and with a natural tonal quality to his voice. Rather than experiencing a lengthy tortuous session as anticipated after his entrance, he gave one of the most satisfactory performances in terms of originality of composition and comprehension of the task. He also completed the 200 trials in less than the average time. As soon as the responses to the final card had been recorded, the subject's demonstrated competence vanished and the zombie-like quality reappeared. The mechanized man marched himself stiffly out of the experimental room. The performance task session proceeded in a similar manner of contrast between his "normal" behavior, and his task-oriented behavior. It is no longer possible for this experimenter to believe in schizophrenia as an entity. The subject could, and did, drop the behavioral symptoms for which he was labeled when confronted with a task situation. [1965, pp. 46–47.]

Another incident illustrating the situational nature of catatonic behavior occurred when one of the authors worked as a co-therapist with a group of catatonic patients. Two perfectly normal psychologists selected a group of eight "classic" catatonic schizophrenics. These eight patients were led or dragged daily to the group meeting room. The therapists would start the sessions by carefully explaining to the patients that this was their hour and advising them to use it wisely. This was followed by considerable silence which was acceptable to everyone, since both patients and therapists had plenty of time.

After three months the therapists realized that something significant was happening in these sessions. Their behavior in the group had become indistinguishable from that of the patients. They would enter the room with the patients, sit down, move into the classic fetal position, head bowed, and quietly spend the hour immersed in their own pleasant or unpleasant fantasies. To preserve the mental health of the therapists, it was necessary to change techniques. The therapists began to be very active and talk about each of the patients. Within a few weeks it became clear that the therapists' comments and interpretations were "received" by the patients. For example, one patient, egged on by the therapist to the point where he had to reply, burst out with a verbatim restatement of what the therapist had said a month earlier.

Two conclusions can be drawn from these incidents: catatonic behavior can be learned if it is reinforced (i.e., appropriate), and the person called catatonic has not withdrawn from contact with the world but rather is unresponsive to some stimuli. The therapist must find the stimuli to which the patient will respond.

Additional observations leading to a sociopsychological viewpoint come from studies of the effect of placebos. Illustrations in Chapter 5 indicated how a placebo may lead to assumption of a psychotic role, and, how responsive chronic schizophrenics may be to expectations of improved behavior.

Another source of the sociopsychological model is the repeated clinical observation that patients emit startlingly different behaviors under different social situations. Bizarre behaviors present for years typically are not manifested on trips to town or when dressed up for activities such as a dance with volunteers. Within the hospital, an interview with the ward physician is a time to emit complaints and sick behavior, while less of this behavior, both verbal and motoric, is observed in "free" situations in the ward dayroom and even less in directly productive activities such as occupational, physical, and athletic therapies.

Zarlock (1966) formalized these observations in a study of the behavior of 30 schizophrenic patients observed in four environmental conditions: recreational, occupational, social, and medical. Recordings were made of their language and role behavior within each of these environmental conditions. Table 1 presents the data on three groups of ten men each. As the reader may note, a hundred times the amount of pathological speech was observed in the "medical" setting as was seen in the "recreational" one. Zarlock also notes that the participants in the study demonstrated "a

Table 1
Number of verbal responses indicating pathology made by three groups of schizophrenic patients

Groups	A	B	C	TOTAL	MEAN *
Recreational	2	0	1	3	.1
Occupational	3	5	4	12	.4
Social	5	2	5	12	.4
Medical	112	97	115	324	10.8

* Mean: The average number of verbal responses made in each session.
Source: Zarlock, 1966.

flexibility of role behavior and adopted appropriate roles in different environmental conditions."

Braginsky, Grosse, and Ring (1966) performed an experiment to illustrate the responsiveness of hospitalized psychiatric patients to social circumstances, that is, impression management as introduced in Chapter 17. Subjects were 20 "old-timers" and 20 "short-timers." Half of each of these groups took a "Mental Illness Test" while the other half took the same material under the title of a "Self-Insight Test." In the former, the instructions read, "We have found that the more items answered True by a patient the more severely ill a patient is and the greater are his chances of remaining in the hospital for a long period of time." For the Self-Insight Test, the instructions read, "We have found that the more items answered True by a patient the more he knows about himself, the less severely ill he is and the greater are his chances of remaining in the hospital for a short period of time." It was hypothesized that "old-timers" would wish to remain in the hospital more than the short-timers, who were considered as more desirous of leaving the hospital. Table 2 presents some of the findings. The crucial point is that *both* old-timers and short-timers engaged in impression-management, that is, their

Table 2
Average number of true responses endorsed by old- and short-timers

GROUPS	MENTAL ILLNESS TEST	SELF-INSIGHT TEST
Old-timers	18.80	9.70
Short-timers	13.00	18.80

Source: Braginsky et al., 1966.

responses were in the direction which would serve to enhance what were to them reinforcing conditions. Braginsky and Braginsky (1967) and Kelly, Farina, and Mosher (1971) illustrate the same effect in which behavior in a psychiatric interview provided the dependent measure, while Ishiyama and Brown (1966) and Grayson and Olinger (1957) provide additional data indicating that hospitalized psychiatric patients' psychological test behavior may be manipulated. Towbin (1969) and Fontana and Corey (1970) show how treatment programs emphasizing patient responsibility must take into account impression management by the staff as well as the patients.

Another source of data leading to the sociopsychological approach and the treatment of the person as essentially normal stems from the success of moral treatment in the early nineteenth century (see Chapter 7). In addition, the difference between the behaviors observed between 1800 and 1865 and those observed from 1865 to 1945 indicates the effect of the environment on people considered in need of hospitalization.

Data from anthropological studies (e.g., Torrey, 1973b) make the same point. Torrey (pp. 123–24) cites a study which compared Ayurvedic treatment with Western psychiatric methods at a hospital in India. While 85 percent of the people were improved with Western methods, 75 percent were improved with the Ayurvedic procedure. The results are indicative of the importance of psychosocial rather than physiological variables.

The impact of administrative changes is consistent with a psychosocial rather than disease model. For instance, Lafave et al. (1967) report a decrease of the population of a psychiatric hospital from 1519 to 421, although the number of other psychiatric beds in the region rose by only 40. The large psychiatric hospital was phased out and a regional system used in its place. Langsley, Machotke, and Flomenhaft (1971) report how 300 patients, requiring immediate hospitalization, were randomly assigned to outpatient family-crisis therapy or admitted to the psychiatric hospital. At 6- and 18-months follow-ups, the people not admitted were adjusting as well as those admitted, and fewer had required later hospitalization and overall required less than half the total number of hospital days of those people admitted.

In Chapter 10, it was noted that calling a person abnormal is a solution to social problems which must be learned and which is applied with varying degrees of frequency. The great number of people residing in the community who are supposedly incapacitated because of psychiatric difficulties (see studies of prevalence in Chapter 10) indicate that it takes more than simply the presence of a psychiatric abnormality to lead to the attention of mental health professionals. To these considerations may be added the work of Thomas Szasz on the logic of mental illness as a concept, and studies (see Chapter 11) on the reliability (or lack of it) of psychiatric diagnosis. In summary, personal experience, observation of patients, historical background, empirical studies, and critical evaluation of theory provide the background for the development of an alternative approach to schizophrenia, the sociopsychological model presented in this chapter.

To recapitulate the conceptualization presented in Chapters 2 and 10, adherence to the official or dominant rules of a society is learned. If the rules are not thoroughly learned, or if, as is more likely, an opposing set of rules is learned, the result may be abnormal behavior, as that of the jackroller. The person may be extinguished for conformity to rules through lack of reinforcement. A nonconformist is one for whom such influence is not effective. He may not receive reinforcement or, particularly after conversion to a new set of standards, the reinforcers typical for the society are no longer effective in altering, shaping, or maintaining his behavior. Changes in reinforcers occur with changes in status such as moves from student to alumnus, from child to adult, or from employee to boss. In each case the behaviors that were previously reinforced no longer pay off, and different behaviors are necessary. Failure to emit these new behaviors and continued emission of the previous behaviors disturb other people. The person is no longer reinforced for behaviors that previously were successful. No more expressive phrase is available for this situation than "the honeymoon is over."

The requirements for emission of a "normal act" are to have the act in the repertoire, to learn the appropriate times and places (discriminative stimuli) for its emission, to attend to the environment, especially the discriminative stimuli, to emit the act, and to be reinforced for its emission.

A FORMULATION OF SCHIZOPHRENIA

The crucial element in formulating schizophrenic behavior within a sociopsychological model is the failure of reinforcement for a sequence of behavior. The effect is that discriminative stimuli no longer mark the times and places where certain behaviors will have reinforcing consequences. More simply, the operant of paying attention to cues that others attend to is no longer emitted. Attention is viewed as an operant behavior, *not* as a function of the mind genetically determined or varying with cognitive qualities. As anyone who has ever sat through a college lecture knows, attention responses require effort. When they do not pay off, they decrease in emission.

There are two aspects of this extinction of the attention response to particular social cues. If the person no longer attends to the discriminative stimuli (acquired reinforcers) common to people in the core culture, the influence of this group is reduced and the likelihood that he will become a rule breaker is increased. Further, the person's "mind" is not a blank, but rather other cues are attended to. At times this may lead to new socially valuable behavior. More usually, however, the person may appear to others as "abstracted," "tangential," or "irrelevant." A person attending to cues different from those presumed of one in his status may be suddenly called upon to respond to cues to which he has not attended.

A not uncommon example is a question asked of a college student whose mind has been on more enjoyable things than the lecture. The response made under these circumstances is likely to seem "illogical," "childish," and "concrete" rather than the abstract, insightful verbalization expected of him. The listener who knows and expects the right answer may not understand the student's answer. In short, the person who was not paying attention may display poor social judgment (not respond to the cues emitted by others which indicate the nature of the situation) and may display disorganization of thinking (concrete, irrelevant, bizarre associations which the listener cannot follow). *The crucial behavior, from which other indications of schizophrenia may be deduced, lies in the extinction of attention to social stimuli to which "normal" people respond.*

There is agreement by all observers that attention is "disturbed," but the present authors make this point central to their theoretical formulation. A quotation from Noyes and Kolb (1963, p. 336) summarizes the situation: "This lack of attention and of concentration gives rise to the misleading impression that the patient is intellectually impaired, whereas he is intellectually inert."

Another standard psychiatric text makes a similar observation about attention (Batchelor, 1969, pp. 260–61): "The apathy and lack of interest are usually so marked that active attention to any specific problem is fleeting. . . . The general intellectual faculties are unimpaired, and the remembrance and grasp of school knowledge are not interfered with. Any apparent intellectual deterioration arises from lack of attention and concentration."

The laboratory approach to attention has been twofold. In the work of Lindsley (1956), "psychotic episodes" are defined as ones in which the rate of response is disrupted *as if* the person were responding to nonrelevant stimuli. That is, the person is not attending to the stimuli the experimenter considers relevant (see also Nathan et al., 1964). Another empirical approach deals with attention, or "set," as measured by reaction time (see Maher, 1966, pp. 371–77; Silverman, 1964). This research generally indicates (Maher, 1966, p. 434) that "the mechanisms responsible for the direction and maintenance of attention in the normal individual seem clearly to be disrupted in many schizophrenic patients."

However, Rosenbaum (1967) and Maher (1966, p. 376) also point out that "when the response serves to terminate noxious physical stimulation (electric shock, unpleasant noise) subjects improve. Schizophrenics produce responses similar to those of normals." While the null hypothesis can never be proved, and hence a physical basis can never be ruled out, it seems plausible that differences in reinforcing contingencies may account for differences in attentiveness between schizophrenics and normals.

There are two ways in which observed laboratory differences in attention may be viewed. The first deals with the social situation and the implicit demands of the experiment (see Orne, 1962). Let the reader presume that he is sitting in the dayroom of a ward on which he is a patient. He is lonely, confused, and powerless. Along comes a young psychologist and asks him to press keys as fast as possible in response to a stimulus. He may wonder what the psychologist is after and what effect it will have on his case. This is a quite different situation from the reader being asked to help a fellow collegian out with a psychological experiment which presumably has scientific merit. This difference in social context must be considered in evaluating any consequent differences in performance.

A second approach to the motivational issue is to hypothesize that the schizophrenic is responding to internal, idiosyncratic, autistic stimuli and hence that his perception of the experimenter's stimuli is "interfered" with. The experimenter has little reinforcing value (until he provides it, either in terms of human relationship or noxious stimuli to avoid), and hence other (more important) matters will be attended to. If an experimenter thinks that just because his apparatus and instructions are the same, his experimental conditions are identical for college students and hospitalized schizophrenics, he is naïve.

Is it possible to deduce the development of the other behaviors considered schizophrenic from a lack of attention? Although most of what has been presented thus far would argue against formulating a list of specific schizophrenic behaviors, for purposes of discussion the symptoms listed by Noyes and Kolb (1963) in their section entitled "Psychopathology" (pp. 332–42) provide a starting point. They argue that disharmonies of thought and action are usually manifested in a blandness of affect. The person does not seem to care, i.e., is not attentive (shaped by) reinforcers effective with others. He attends to alternative cues because the culturally presumed ones have been extinguished. This may, therefore, lead to the appearance of being preoccupied, aloof, and failing to empathize with (i.e., identify accurately and then reflect the appropriate mood of) others. If others have let him down and he no longer is attentive to them, he may act in a manner indicative to others of emotional withdrawal (unresponsive, uninfluenced by them in the way they wish). Attentiveness to stimuli required at work and attention to the reinforcing stimuli provided by completed work may shift so that the work itself deteriorates.

At this point, a vicious cycle may be instituted. Performing in an unexpected and unsatisfactory manner may lead to a further decrease of emission and hence reinforcement for conforming behavior. The person may appear lazy in the eyes of others. He may become the object of increased disciplinary action and react with additional feelings of alienation. He may believe that others do not appreciate him and are out to "get" him. He may try various ways of returning to acceptable behavior. Not infrequently an appeal to the medical model through somatic complaining is noticed. When ordinary symptoms do not serve to bring him within the typical scope of medicine, bizarre somatic complaints may develop. The person may become indifferent to the typical demands of society and become as lax in his personal habits of dress and grooming as men on a camping trip. Another way back to "normality" is to attempt to think the situation through and find an explanation for it. This may take the form of finding a plotter behind it all, development of elaborate and untalented philosophical schemes, or of detailed and not always aesthetic works of art.

Poverty of affect is a lack of responsiveness to stimuli not dissimilar in formulation to the apathy seen in depressives or transient situational maladjustments where there has been a rapid alteration and decrease of positive reinforcement. Disharmony may be directly deduced from failure to attend to cues (discriminative stimuli) for the correct emotion. It should be kept in mind that inappropriate affect is a label applied by a professional when a person does not react in the way the professional thinks he should; that is, when he misses the professional worker's cues. Further, by being indifferent the person avoids situations. If he makes no commitments of an emotional sort, he will not be hurt when someone does not keep his word or live up to expectations.

The patient may at times seem as if he knows the words but not the music. This may be called *depersonalization*, a feeling of vagueness, unreality, or detachment. The person is no longer directly under control of the reinforcers and, further, may have suffered from the decreased sensory and interpersonal stimulation of the psychiatric hospital.

Earlier, the relation of lack of attentiveness to bizarre ideation was noted. Such lack of attentiveness can lead to erratic or bizarre associations. For example, Blumberg and Giller (1965) found evidence of distractibility or "primary process" thinking for all their diagnostic groups and concluded that such "cognitive errors are not unique to schizophrenia." The schizophrenic attends to stimuli the professional interviewer considers irrelevant. Further, he has been extinguished for discriminative stimuli, among which are the other person's understanding and caring. Cameron's (1947) concept of the importance of taking the other person's view is relevant in such a situation; since looking at the situation from the vantage point of the other person has not been very useful, doing so is decreased. Rather, behaviors that previously "worked" and seemed to satisfy similar interviewers will be repeated. Set phrases, neologisms, "word salad," and over-elaborate stilted speech may all be emitted. If, as with grooming, things make no difference, language will deteriorate.

Just as the path of least resistance for the patient is to say anything that satisfies, so there may at times be automatic obedience and automatic negativism. These words in their technical sense refer to the patient's seeming to systematically do either whatever is asked of him or none of the things asked of him. Taking a strategy and sticking to it has two advantages: first, if the person is making minimal discriminations about his environment, one way of playing it cool is to do what he is told. The other aspect is that he has a ready-made response, and the bothersome process of attending and decoding, which has not had great success, can be short-circuited.

Finally there are the behaviors of *reports* of delusions and of hallucinations that, together with disorganization of thinking, usually lead to the clinical diagnosis of schizophrenia. A delusion is a false belief. The development of beliefs that one is the recipient of special attention or of persecution has been touched on earlier in this section. As a person converts from one reference group to another, he finds that one set of beliefs has not borne fruit, whereas a second set may solve problems and lead to reinforcement. The examples in Chapter 4 of verbal conditioning of delusions of grandeur and somatic complaining are indications of how a false belief, just as a "true" one, has a reciprocal relationship with the environment.

Hallucinations may be approached in a number of ways within the present formulation. The person may learn of hallucinations as part of the enactment of the psychiatric patient role from reading the mass media, observation of others, and the questions of psychiatric examiners. He may have had experiences which lie on the continuum toward hallucination: illusions, dreams, sleep deprivation, and drugs may all provide a background. He has some indication of the sensations to attend to and to label (see Chapter 10 for a description of how one learns to smoke and enjoy marijuana).

As the person evidences extinction for attention to stimuli usually meaningful in his society, he decreases his chances for positive reinforcement. At a certain point stimuli, both from within and without, have equal import and may seem equally "real" (worth attending to) or equally unreal (the state called depersonalization). McReynolds (1960) suggests that a low rate of sensory input, whether due to the environment or the person's difficulty in assimilating percepts, will lead to a situation in which the distinction between the real and the unreal is hard to maintain, and which, perhaps analogously to sensory deprivation phenomena, leads to hallucinations. Hallucinations might even be maintained for the stimulation they provide. The person under conditions of deprivation of typical reinforcements may have sharp, continuing deficits, notably in our society in the area of sex. He may focus attention on a love-object and may find stimuli associated with it to be prepotent for their connection with reinforcement or potential reinforcement. An object which is physically present is misperceived, that is, perceived differently from reality. The step between misapprehensions of external stimuli (illusions) and misapprehension of internal stimuli is a relatively small one.

Sarbin (1967), following his metaphorical-semantic approach (see prior chapter), traces the history of the concept of hallucination and points out the cultural background in which the word "hallucination" was first used in English (in 1572). At that time it meant a ghost or spirit walking by night; its Latin root meant "idle talk" or "wandering of the mind." It was used synonymously with "illusion." In short, the jump made by the individual was also made linguistically over time: from an external stimulus to an internal one, from a stimulus that was *like* to a stimulus that was indeed internal.

A situation that may lead an external observer to hypothesize the presence of hallucinations may be called intense behavior rehearsal. Most people have experienced the situation of going over what they should have said or what they will say in an important situation. The behavior rehearsal may become very real; this is especially true in a situation in which there has been a reduction of competing external stimuli. It is hard to say how frequent such vivid internal dialogues are, but at least one college professor is known to the authors whose involvement with his lectures is such that he has raised eyebrows as he mutters words or smiles foolishly to himself as he walks to class rehearsing his day's performance. If this professor were a patient walking across the grounds of a psychiatric hospital, an observer might infer from his mutterings and grimacing that he was hallucinating. Because of his status as a college professor, only the automobile drivers are worried, and their diagnosis of him ranges from mental deficiency to potential suicide.

McGuigan (1966) offers evidence that auditory hallucinations represent a talking to oneself. Using an event recorder attached to the larynx, McGuigan found that covert oral behavior (chin and tongue movement, breathing, whispering) increased just before the report of auditory hallucinations. Measures of nonoral behavior were not associated with the hallucinatory reports. In effect, the "voices" this individual heard were his own. McGuigan concludes that if this finding were generally found to be true, it would open the way to controlling "hallucinations" through standard operant conditioning procedures and biofeedback equipment.

In this section, a picture was drawn of behaviors called schizophrenic being deducible from an extinction of responses, notably attention to stimuli which culturally are considered important. Throughout an attempt has been made to demonstrate that neither the conditions nor the behaviors are unique to people labeled schizophrenic, but rather that this is a formulation of how the frequency of such behaviors may come to be increased. Of equal import is that the behavior of a person who is called a schizophrenic is very far from being totally extinguished.

Rather there are situations and specific conditions under which he fails to emit the response (or makes an alternative one), but these situations may be very limited. The ability to be attentive is not lost. That is, the act may not be emitted, but it is in the patient's repertoire and available under the right conditions. Investigators as different as Lindsley (1960) and Batchelor (1969, p. 273) agree on this point. The former writes, "Most patients are hospitalized because the time of occurrence of their infrequent psychotic episodes cannot be predicted." The latter author cites Freeman, Cameron, and McGhie (1958) to the effect that "the ego is never completely lost even in the most demented patient." In his remarks on treatment Batchelor notes that schizophrenics are accessible and capable of forming emotional bonds and that the therapist should build upon strengths, "re-educating, encouraging, advising, praising, rewarding; directing the patient persistently towards normal ways of thinking and acting. This sort of supportive therapy is relevant in every case." (1969, p. 285.)

The extinction of attention is quite restricted, although, over time, especially in a psychiatric hospital, it may generalize to other behaviors. Also, particularly in a hospital, there is learning of additional role enactments or secondary deviations that are *iatrogenic* (engendered by the treatment). On the positive side are experiments on the successful direct improvement of attending behaviors (Wagner, 1968; Meichenbaum and Cameron, 1973).

The purpose of this section has been to illustrate the role of extinction attention in the formulation of the class of abnormal behavior called schizophrenic. In large measure this is an amplification of Chapters 2 and 10. It also leads to a direct hypothesis about treatment—that systematically applied positive reinforcement for active, attentive involvement with the stimuli considered culturally important may well lead to diminution of the maladaptive behavior.

GETTING TO THE HOSPITAL

Playing the role of being "mentally ill" is a social transaction in which expectation and reinforcement are reciprocally involved in shaping consequent behavior. In Chapter 10, and in earlier sections in this chapter, it was noted that when alternative roles or ways of obtaining reinforcement have been extinguished, the mentally ill role may be a solution available to the person or his significant others (Polak, 1967).

The mentally ill role may be taken with varying degrees of self-cueing or self-labeling. Both in general terms and in its specific enactments, the role is known to the person from his exposure to the mass media and observation of other persons labeled mentally ill. Further, there are behaviors emitted by "normals" that an expert may label "schizophrenic." (Tucker, Harrow, and Hoffman, 1969). Just as in hysteria and in hypnosis, a working knowledge of the role is readily available. In the face of extinction of other responses to the environment, or encouragement for the "sick" role, the subject will emit the mentally ill role (Levitz and Ullmann, 1969). If he emits it in an environment that pays attention to his behavior, recognizes it "correctly," and makes the "appropriate" response to it, he will maintain it.

At an immediate, as distinct from long-term, level, there are strong positive consequences for playing the role. A student may think of a situation in which he has three final exams the next day. He realizes that after passing them he will have to leave the college campus, his friends, and his familiar mode of life to labor and pay taxes. At this point the mentally ill role might offer more favorable consequences than the normal role. As has been pointed out previously, if the person has been adequately reinforced in the past for conforming to the core culture, then he will be unlikely to give it up even if it has unpleasant aspects. But if the dominant, conforming pattern has not been satisfying either personally or intellectually, the person may well resort to a different short-term solution.

Enacting a deviant role need not be a "conscious" choice. Two things are required. First, the person must fail to conform, and, second, he must be brought to the attention of a socially sanctioned labeler. Deviant behavior itself is common. Scheff (1966a), for example, refers to such behavior as residual deviance. He notes that epidemiological studies of mental health (see Chapter 10) find from eight to twenty "mentally ill" people for each individual hospitalized or treated.

Little is known about which particular individuals emitting mentally ill role behaviors will be officially labeled. Mishler and Waxler (1963), Moore et al. (1962), and Wilson et al. (1964) indicate that there are choice points and that there are many people who might have been hospitalized by some labeler's decision.[1] If such people are not hospitalized, many manage to adjust adequately in the community.[2]

Who in particular will be hospitalized cannot at present be specified from behavior only. The number of people who display the same behavior and who are not hospitalized argues strongly that it is not disturbed behavior itself, but behavior disturbing to others, that is crucial in the social

[1] See also Clausen and Yarrow (1955), Denzin and Spitzer (1966), Linn (1961), and Hammer (1963).

[2] Another source of data supporting this statement is that the patient's psychiatric condition on discharge does not predict subsequent readmission (Odegard, 1961; Jones and Sidebotham, 1962; Ellsworth et al., 1967).

sequence leading to hospitalization. What can be said at present is that there is a baserate in the population of behaviors which could be called schizophrenic by a mental health professional and that this baserate may be higher in lower socioeconomic classes (Kohn, 1973) and other groups who are not under the control of the stimuli to which the dominant cultural group attend.

SCHIZOPHRENIA AND THE HOSPITAL

The vast majority of what is known about the schizophrenic role and its shaping occurs in the social context of professional interviews and psychiatric hospitals. In part this is because schizophrenia is usually operationally defined in terms of a psychiatric diagnosis and/or of confinement to a psychiatric hospital. The official definitions of psychosis and schizophrenia are such that it would be unexpected for a person so diagnosed to be adjusting without disruption outside the psychiatric hospital.

The other major reason why so little is known about the shaping of the schizophrenic outside the hospital environment is that it is in the hospital that the professional person interacts with the schizophrenic. It is in this environment that he organizes his observations and responds to patients.

The organization of the hospital and professional care follow temporal lines from diagnosis through admission wards to continued treatment wards. Behavior is shaped through various stages, each stage facilitating and making possible the next (i.e., a career). The professional's expectations of "appropriate" patient behavior may selectively reinforce "schizophrenia." *To the extent that consistencies exist in the behavior of schizophrenics, these behaviors may be reasonable responses to the environment rather than a function of the nature of the person.*

The mental health professional has the

task of diagnosing the patient so that further action, release or hospitalization, is justified. Just as differential responsiveness alters the verbal behavior of delusional patients (see, e.g., Chapter 4), so the diagnostician's differential interest will focus attention on those symptoms which are significant to his system of classification and by inattention will tend to extinguish those complaints, unexpected behaviors, and disruptions which are not "significant" to his way of thinking. Balint makes the point that even in physical medicine the questioning and interest of the physician may train the patient (e.g., 1957, pp. 18, 43, 216) to tailor his symptom picture to the one the physician expects. The physician cannot be too careful about his facial expression and offhand remarks, because these remain with the patient, who ponders them carefully, since they deal with matters of life and death. As Henderson (1935) noted, the physician can never impart all his knowledge to the layman, and his comments are to some degree ambiguous and open to various interpretations. In large measure, the doctor-patient interaction fits the conditions likely to heighten conformity (see Chapter 10). Lehrman (1961) reports that the physician may bully and pout until the patient gives the information the psychiatrist needs to make his decision. The patient not only has the cues provided by his own prior exposure to concepts of mental illness; he is taught directly by his psychiatrist.

This form of influence carries over to the treatment situation (Frank, 1961). In the mental hospital, gaining insight and acting in a manner consistent with the role of "improving patient" will be explicitly reinforced by the professional therapist. If the patient fits the role with which the physician is comfortable, the physician will reinforce him with "individualistic" rather than bureaucratic or mechanical treatment. Loeb (1957) indicates how fitting the expected pattern is rewarding for both the patient and the therapist:

However, the patient, too, can modify this role by participating in the diagnostic culture. If he can talk about himself, his fellow patients, and the staff in terms of their "individual dynamics" he is thought to be an especially good patient, he shows insight, and he tends to get along well. In other words, the therapist can relate to him in a way that goes beyond the superordination–subordination relationship involved in the doctor-mental patient dyad. They can interact as individuals.

The position of the patient admitted to a psychiatric hospital and placed on a psychiatric ward has received considerable attention. Notable among authors is Goffman (1961), who points out that the patient is deprived of those personal cues which might help him maintain his precious identity (his clothes, his status in the world outside the hospital) and is "degraded" in a manner similar to recruits to other total organizations such as the army, monastic orders, and prisons. Again, the effect of total institutions on individual behavior may be viewed in the context of the conditions that heighten conformity and lead to changed belief.

To what demands will the person placed on the ward conform? What reinforcing stimuli will be contingent on what responses? These questions view the patient's behavior as meaningful and not as symptomatic of an illness.

The major feature of training in the hospital involves the personnel who are spatially and temporally closest to the patient, the attendants or aides. As the psychiatric hospital became larger and more oriented toward a disease concept (see Chapter 7), the role of the psychiatric patient became increasingly parallel to that of the medical patient. This role called for the individual to be clean, quiet, passive, and to wait uncomplainingly for the discoveries that would lead to his cure. The patient was not responsible for his acts; while this absolved him from blame (one of the positive consequences of taking the mental patient role), it also meant that he could not be trusted with matches for his cigarettes, laces for his shoes, or freedom of movement in and out of the ward. As the number of patients per physician increased and the physician assumed a more medical than personal role, the importance of the attendant increased. The attendant was poorly paid, poorly educated, and looked down upon by people both in the hospital and in the community (presumably not only for his social status but for the mistaken, widespread belief that long exposure to the mentally ill denotes some morbidity in the person).[3]

The results for which the attendant was reinforced were the safe, quiet, and proper behavior of patients. Treatment was a medical problem and not the concern of the aide. By analogy, the attendant was a babysitter and not a teacher. It should be kept in mind, too, that the attendant was responsible for large numbers of patients and had to organize and control them in some manner. Even today, it is not unusual for one attendant to be responsible for the behavior of a ward numbering 30 to 100 people. The solution to this problem—called the *aide culture*—used excellent principles for a goal which, unfortunately, was not the avowed social purpose of the hospital: *the aim of the aide culture was the comfort and successful adjustment of the aide rather than the ultimate reintegration of the patient in the extrahospital community.*

The patient ". . . is taught, first of all,

[3] A more sophisticated hypothesis is that the groups who carry out the shameful, morally dirty work considered necessary in a society become outgroups. Rainwater points out that, at present, teachers, welfare workers, and policemen dealing with minorities may become such outgroups in order to gloss over what is actually being done. ". . . a new dimension is added, a dimension of silence and ignorance about exactly what these functionaries are expected to do, and how in fact they do carry out society's covert orders to control and cool out those who must be excluded from ordinary society." (1967, p. 2.) The concept seems eminently applicable to the mental hospital attendant.

how to behave in his new role as a hospital patient." (Bloom, 1963, p. 191.) The person who does the majority of the teaching in terms of dispensing reinforcement is the attendant. "The attendants govern both the patient's position in the patient's social system and his relations to the physician. They do this not in terms of the individual patient's psychiatric condition or his needs but rather in terms of the requirements of their own social system. . . . Adjustment is a critical problem for the average patient, since his contact with other personnel in the system besides the attendant and other patients amounts only to a small fraction of the time through the year. Even this small amount is usually mediated through the attendant, who often interprets the patient to the ward physician, the social worker, or the occupational and recreational therapists." (Belknap, 1956, p. 65.)

The manner in which the attendant reinforces the patient is as follows (see Belknap, 1956, pp. 130–175; Dunham and Weinberg, 1960, pp. 123–128): he can dispense positive reinforcing stimuli such as assignment to the more desirable jobs, sleeping in better rooms with fewer and less disturbed patients, minor luxuries such as coffee on the ward, access to some privacy, opportunity to bathe and change clothes more often than the required minimum, attention to requests such as a needed light for a cigarette. Of great importance is the attendant's own behavior toward the patient as a model for the other patients on the ward. If the attendant is courteous and humane, the patient is likely to be treated in this way by other patients. On the other hand, the attendant has a number of aversive stimuli which he can dispense. He can belittle the patient, be impatient with him, or ignore him and thus model for others how to treat the patient. He may withdraw any privileges over which he has control.

Of particular importance is the fact that the time of the "treatment" staff, the psychiatrist, psychologist, and social worker, is at an enormous premium. The psychiatrist, who is medically responsible for the patient and who makes administrative decisions, has little contact with the patient. He must depend upon the report of the attendant, who can either "put in a good word" for the patient or who can put the patient's behavior in a negative light. Because the majority of patients average less than ten minutes a month with the ward physician, the aide has enormous power as a "gatekeeper" and channel of information. He can, and frequently does, guide therapy by reporting that a patient is improving or becoming more disturbed. The attendant learns to phrase behavior that annoys him in psychiatric jargon. The ultimate reinforcing stimuli are positive (privileges to go on the grounds alone, transfer to a ward specializing in discharge) and aversive (placement on a list for electroconvulsive therapy, transfer to a less hopeful ward). In short, most of the things beyond sheer physical survival that make life hopeful and human are under the control of or strongly influenced by the attendant. In the authors' experience in psychiatric hospitals, physical abuse of patients is rare: the aide has little need for it in order to control the patient.

Given that the aide has reinforcing stimuli to dispense, under what conditions and for what behaviors does he "pay off"? The reader may wonder what he would do if faced with the task of keeping some 30 to 100 people clean, quiet, and calmly waiting for a psychiatric Godot. The solution taken by the attendant involves dividing the patients into three groups: those who help, those who cause no trouble, and those who are a problem. The patients who help are reinforced positively; they clean up after other patients, mop floors and make beds, warn the aide if someone seems to be becoming agitated, and, in a pinch, protect the aide and help out in subduing a violent patient. The nontroublesome patients form an intermediate stratum. The troublemakers are the object of punishing attention. Over time, a patient may move from one group to another.

The ward environment is devoid of personal possessions, recent newspapers and magazines, and the vast majority of typical sources of leisure time stimulation. Possession of reading material and playing cards is a privilege that can be offered by the attendant. To guard against furniture being picked up and thrown, the chairs are likely to be made of heavy, unattractive wood. To avoid sexual misdemeanors, in terms of a very rigid moralistic public institution code, privacy in the dormitory and lavatory may be denied. The patient must sit in the dayroom with its dull, drab walls. While television has provided a source of stimulation not known before, and hence probably represents a great boon, if the patient does not like a program there is no way to avoid it or the endless noise of the audio.

Approach and self-assertive responses which we consider normal and even therapeutic (see Chapter 12) tend to be extinguished.[4] A person who insisted on seeing a physician to complain would be considered a troublemaker. A classic illustration is the case of Clifford Beers, whose experiences, recounted in *A Mind that Found Itself*, were instrumental in the establishment of the mental hygiene movement. To quote Bloom's (1963, p. 191) résumé: "What Beers describes as therapeutic progress, however, was not so interpreted by the staff of the several hospitals in which he was a patient. Rather, his change from a stuporous but quiet patient into an articulate, energetic, and assertive one was interpreted as an increase of disturbance. Similar experiences

---

[4] In this regard, Ullmann (1958) observed a decrease in self-assertion (increased dependency and submissiveness) for retested, hospitalized patients. Reimanis, Krugman, and Lasky (1965) noted that low-compliance subjects were younger and had been in the institution a shorter period of time, and Cull (1971) found that schizophrenics (who had been hospitalized continuously for at least six months) made more conforming responses than "normals."

are described by virtually all the published autobiographical patient writings."

The patient is taught to avoid causing trouble for the aide. The pattern eventually developed is similar to the disinvolvement, or "playing it cool," observed with prisoners of war (e.g., Strassman, Thaler, and Schein, 1956). This point is emphasized by observations made in a state psychiatric hospital. Dunham and Weinberg (1960, p. 48) cite a patient's comment: "As soon as you start holding your own and trying to stand up for yourself, the attendants say you are disturbed and want to put you on ward 7" (for acutely agitated patients). Dunham and Weinberg elaborate this point as follows:

Adherence to the routine means protection; deviation involves risks and penalties. New experiences and new events are a source of interest and excitement; but any impending change beyond their control arouses insecurities and apprehensions. . . . Length of stay itself has a positive value by making the outside community recede in the distance. . . . One factor is the patient's skewed sense of time. On the one hand, the hospital monotony leaves a "sameness" that stirs few feelings. On the other hand, the patient's few emotional experiences are so vividly recalled that they seem to have a continual recency. [pp. 123–28.]

The result is that there are few activities that are both normal and encouraged. A passive, inert, undaring, unspontaneous apathy marks the long-term or continued-treatment patient. In Dunham and Weinberg's (1960, p. 120) words: "They had little, if anything, to do except sit continually on hard chairs and provide a minimum of difficulty for the attendant." Much of the experience of the next 100 years was forecast by Arlidge at the time of the breakdown of moral treatment:

In a colossal refuge for the insane, a patient may be said to lose his individuality, and to become a member of a machine so put together as to move with precise regularity and invariable routine;—a triumph of skill adapted to show how such unpromising materials as crazy men and women may be drilled into order and guided by rule, but not an apparatus calculated to restore their pristine conditions and their independent self-governing existence. In all cases admitting of recovery, or of material amelioration, a gigantic asylum is a gigantic evil, and, figuratively speaking, a manufactory of chronic insanity. [1859, p. 102.]

It need only be added that Arlidge noted with horror the growth of hospitals into "lunatic colonies of eight or nine hundred, or even a thousand or more inhabitants." (p. 102). As contrast, Ullmann (1967a), working with what is probably the finest system of psychiatric hospitals in the world, defined a small hospital as one with 1,200 patients.

DEDUCTIONS FROM THE HOSPITAL SITUATION

The previous paragraphs have described the social environment of the hospital. The large size of the hospital, its bureaucratic structure, and the training in conformity will all have an effect on patient behavior. This section will (1) try to make explicit how key behaviors indicative of schizophrenia are shaped in the hospital, and (2) provide empirical information indicating the appropriateness of the sociopsychological model applied to schizophrenia. (Later sections of this chapter will deal with experiments that manipulate key symptoms in a response-contingent manner and with the application of sociopsychological concepts in the form of treatment called "token economy.")

The Hospital and Schizophrenic Behaviors

A behavior from which other indications of schizophrenia may be deduced is attention. The situation for the adult psychiatric patient is similar (though not identical) to that of children reared in institutions. Yarrow (1961), reviewing studies of institutionalization of children, noted that the institutional environment was relatively lacking in sensory stimulation and was colorless and drab. The emotional environment was described as bland and lacking variation of feeling tone, the infant being exposed to neither strongly positive nor strongly negative affective stimulation.[5] The low ratio of staff to inmates led to little mothering contact.

Of most direct relevance, there tended to be little recognition by adults for the child's positive achievements and little, and at best inconsistent, reinforcement for positive learning of desirable social responses. Frequent results of early and prolonged institutionalization were a decrease in measurable intellectual ability over time, inadequate social responsiveness, a lack of attachment to others, inadequate social discrimination as evidenced by different responses to strangers and to familiar caretakers, and a lack of differential emotional expression and response. Both the adult and the child are in situations which very directly fail to reinforce behaviors that would be appropriate and expected outside the institution. Approaching or reaching out to others may be extinguished because of lack of staff. If not extinguished, such behavior is inconsistently reinforced so that adequate training is not provided.[6]

The psychiatric patient, as noted in the previous section, is taught to avoid trouble. Withdrawal from social contact is encouraged. There is little practice in emitting the social responses likely to change others, because the people in authority are unlikely to change.

While a few small, private, and expensive psychiatric hospitals may provide personal attention, these "lodges" and "institutes" are likely to be heavily psychoanalytic, and behavior is treated as meaningful only in the context of the patient's intrapsychic dynamics. His behavior may be accepted, but it is given little import in altering other people. There is no realistic impact to the patient of himself as agent: he is presumed irresponsible. The result is that there is little reinforcement for being attentive to cues and emitting differential responses.

The extinction of attentive responses has two effects. The first is that the sources of meaningful stimulation for other people do not serve the same function for the hospitalized psychiatric patient. This adds to his sensory impoverishment. Attentiveness

---

[5] In a bureaucracy, involvement and personal attention run counter to equality of treatment based on overt formalized criteria.

[6] The adverse effects of institutionalization have also been found with retardates (Kugel and Reque, 1961; Lyle, 1959, 1960; Kaufman, 1953, 1967; Centerwell and Centerwell, 1960; Stevenson and Fabel, 1961; Zigler, 1967; Butterfield and Zigler, 1970). Chambers (1965, p. 36) concludes his work on conditioning of psychotics with the following statement: "The conditioning data failed to confirm the hypothesized effects of psychosis but indicated that institutionalization was an important factor influencing performance, irrespective of whether S was psychotic." Jankowski, Grzesiuk, and Markiewicz (1970) came to the same conclusion, and Silverman, Berg, and Kantor (1966) found that significant differences existed in the perceptual performances of early-term and long-term prison inmates, and that these differences were comparable to those found within acute and chronic schizophrenics. Wynne (1963) reports similar data for verbal behavior. Gelfand, Gelfand, and Dobson (1967); Warren and Mondy (1971); Allen, Clinsky, and Veit (in press); and Buehler, Patterson, and Furniss (1966) provide observations that institutional settings typically provide reinforcement contingent upon inappropriate rather than prosocial behavior. On the other hand, the adverse effects of the institutional environment may be counteracted (Dreiblatt and Weatherly, 1965; Vogel, Kun, and Meshorer, 1967) by judicious human contact. Characteristics of hospitals such as small size and high staffing (Ullmann, 1967; Lasky and Dowling, 1971; Linn, 1970) have been found to be associated with high turnover and rapid release of patients; Blackburn (1972) reports that staff in hospitals with high turnover tend to take more risks in releasing maginally adaptive patients; and Linn (1970), Ellsworth et al. (1971), and Palmer and McGuire (1973) report that negative characteristics may be attributed to efficient units: that is, aesthetic surroundings such as window curtains which make a ward *pleasant* may not make it *effective*.

to external stimuli is a major element in being able to separate outer from personal reality. Without reinforcement for scanning the situation, hallucinatory and illusory behavior may be increased.

The second aspect is that behavior labeled as thinking disorder may be increased. There is little reinforcement for logical as opposed to illogical thought. When responses are demanded by the environment, usually any ideational or verbal response will be acceptable. Efforts at thought or speech in the societally expected mode are not systematically reinforced. The associations may then be made on a physical or functional rather than abstract-logical basis, a situation consistent with Salzinger's position noted in the previous chapter.

In the previous chapter, mention was made of speech taken as indicative of "cognitive slippage," or ideation likely to be labeled schizophrenic. An example of such speech was offered by one of the senior author's children when she noticed a teenager blushing. She said, "Suzy is a rose, but I'm a lady." Coming without any particular antecedents, this is a comment that seems highly idiosyncratic, difficult to understand, and patently inappropriate. On the other hand, Suzy was red (or at least her face was), roses are red, and therefore Suzy was a rose. In similar fashion, ladies keep their cool, the author's daughter was not blushing, and therefore *she* was a lady. Both statements may be called *assert ons of the predicate*. A generalization is made on the basis of one aspect of the stimuli rather than on an adult, logical, abstract basis.

Bridger spells out how generalizations on the basis of physical and functional similarities, rather than on logical or abstract bases, may describe the verbal patterns of schizophrenic "ideation":

My basic hypothesis is that as the level of human mental functioning becomes more primitive and less symbolic, it corresponds more closely to the phenomena of animal conditioning, first signal system activity. The following processes describe the kinds of associations or stimulus substitutions seen in first signal system activity.

1. *Primary stimulus generalization*. Things become associated because of physical similarity, i.e., if a square paired with shock produces a fear response, a rectangle will also produce the same fear response.

2. *Generalization based upon temporal or spatial contiguity*. Wickens has shown that if a light is followed by a buzzer which is in turn followed by shock, the light and buzzer come to signalize not only shock but each other.

3. *Stimulus generalization based upon identity of affect or activity*. If a light is paired with shock and produces both fear and avoidance behavior and a buzzer paired with shock produces only fear, the buzzer alone will later produce avoidance behavior similar to that elicited by the light. The avoidance response is generalized from the light to the buzzer because of the identity of the affect, fear.

4. *Generalization based upon identity of function*. Animals know objects only in terms of their direct experience. A dog repeatedly fed on a chair responds to the chair only as a place to be fed, not as an object independent of this experience. This is analogous to Von Domarus' principle of the equivalence of objects through identity of predicate. Objects are then associated according to the function they serve. [1964, pp. 188–89.]

If, instead of making his associations logically and abstractly, a person made them on the basis of the sound of the words (clang associations, puns) or the temporal, emotional, and functional contiguity of the objects denoted, his speech would appear, to the adult standards of Western civilization, to be bizarre, childish, and so deviant (in terms of expected rules of speech) as to be "sick." Such responses are, however, easier to make than logical ones, and, without reinforcement, evidence for the achievement of logical discourse is not emitted.

In short, the situation of the psychiatric hospital, particularly in the "back" wards of the large public hospital under the control of the aide culture, is likely to extinguish normal behavior and to reinforce meek, uninvolved, withdrawn, inert compliance. Attentive responses, differentiation of environmental stimuli, active approach, and logical-abstract thought may all be extinguished because such responses have no significant consequences. Thus observed, consistency among labeled schizophrenics may be heightened and sharpened by the form of treatment and may be the result, not the cause, of hospitalization.

Effects of Hospital Practices

Manis, Houts, and Blake (1963) reported on the manner in which indoctrination of the patient in the attitudes of the staff takes place. These authors found that psychiatric hospitalization is generally accompanied by a change in the patient's beliefs about mental illness in a direction toward those held by the staff; and those patients whose beliefs were most strikingly influenced by the staff tended to respond most favorably to treatment.

Almond, Keniston, and Boltax (1969a), working in a university hospital therapeutic community, made the same point: "... the vast majority of patients change toward the prescribed value system of the ward community" (p. 351), which in this instance was of social openness and ward involvement as value aspects of the "patient role based on identification with the staff" (p. 351). Almond, Keniston, and Boltax (1969b) noted that the adoption of these values was complex, and "patients' first-week behavioral response to the intense socialization pressures of the unit studied predict discharge level of acceptance of milieu values." (p. 442.) Notions of what a *therapeutic community* is vary (Zeitlyn, 1967), but in general they follow the concepts of Jones (1953) and Wilmer (1958) in their attempts to democratize the institution in order to ward off patient dependency and eventual chronicity.

The aim of the organization is to make certain that a patient's every social contact and his every treatment experience are synergistically applied toward realistic, specific treatment goals. These goals are learning to control or set limits on the main kinds of pathological behavior (destructiveness, disorganization, deviancy, dysphoria, and dependency), and to develop basic psychological skills (orientation, assertion, occupation, and recreation). [Abroms, 1969, p. 560.]

Abroms cites in particular community-based meetings that encourage participation and interpersonal conflict-resolution. Almond, Keniston, and Boltax (1968) offered as value scales the goals of "be a member," "be open," "take responsibility," "have faith in the ward," "view family realistically," and "face problems directly." Rabiner, Gomez, and Gralnick (1964) note open channels of communications, broadened decision-making, expectation of socially acceptable behavior, increasing interaction, emphasis on group process, and patient responsibility for daily activities.

These objectives and procedures may be found in both behavioral and psychoanalytically oriented organizations. In the latter, many encounter-sensitivity procedures and psychoanalytic interpretations of underlying motivations may occur. Spadoni and Smith (1969), reporting on a therapeutic community of this type in which the outcome of treatment of acute schizophrenic patients suffering their first "decompensation" was very poor (less than half, six months later, had been discharged to the community), write:

One possible detrimental factor in the unit was the staff's not responding to the patient's overt verbalizations but instead of responding to what was felt to be the covert message. If a patient stated, "I hear my mother's voice," a staff member might reply, "Why are you afraid of me?" This type of interchange occurred throughout the day and produced considerable confusion and resentment in patients. They frequently complained that they did not understand what the staff was saying and accused them of double-talk and "trying to read minds." [p. 550.]

On the other hand, Heap et al. (1970) using a behavioral approach within the broader milieu therapy outline and with patients whose average length of hospitalization was 5.6 years and average IQ was 85, reported favorable results, particularly compared to a control group. This procedure will be returned to later in this chapter, the point here being to separate out the goals from the procedures used to attain such goals.

Kennard (1957) reports a situation in which, because of physical remodeling of the wards, there were shifts in the location of both patients and staff and a resultant change in the disposition of patients. Kennard writes, "The conclusion seems inescapable that the difference in results is not due to the current psychiatric condition of the patient, but is due to the presence of staff which is able to sift through the patients and work with those who were accessible to existing forms of therapy." In a hospital where few patients had the privilege of going alone on the grounds, 254 beds previously reserved for tuberculosis patients were made available for psychiatric patients. Within two months, Kennard reports, 254 patients from locked wards were found and transferred to the open (unlocked) wards. Again, Kennard concludes that it was the availability of the space rather than the pattern of psychiatric symptoms that was primarily responsible for the granting of the new freedom.

In similar fashion, Barrett, Kuriansky, and Gurland (1972) followed up patients released as an emergency measure during a strike at a psychiatric hospital. Over a quarter of the chronic patients who would not ordinarily have been released were in the community at four-week and six-month follow-up. The patients who remained out of the hospital did not differ from those who returned in terms of "psychopathology" but did have some useful function in the families with whom they went to live and did not interfere with the family routines.

Riggs (1970) reports improvement due to a change in wards. Sommer and Ross (1958), Ittelson, Proshansky, and Rivlin (1970), and Holahan and Saegert (1973) report on how remodeling a ward can increase socializing among patients. The impact of environmental design supports a sociopsychological rather than intrapersonal or disease model of schizophrenia.

In Chapter 5 the effects of drugs which themselves were inert or nonspecific were discussed in terms of both the production and elimination of indications for the schizophrenic label. Kamman et al. (1954), after surveying 90 treatment articles, pointed out that while there were great variations in technique, theory, and qualifications of therapists, almost *anything* that has been tried at one time or another has benefited some schizophrenics. The effects are probably in terms of the expectation and reinforcement for improvement on the part of the staff, and the clear designation of "healthy" behavior as appropriate, Freeman (1958, p. 499), in a review of reports on the effect of tranquilizers in the treatment of schizophrenia, expresses this point as follows:

It is undoubtedly true that some proportion of the improvement from the drugs is due to the increased interest and attention of the hospital personnel. The double-blind studies have all indicated that 20 to 30 per cent of the placebo-treated patients show some degree of improvement.... Another advantage of the drug treatment is the elevation of morale of the hospital personnel, especially those dealing directly with chronic patients. There is definitely less of a hopeless attitude toward such patients, and the greater interaction between the patient and the personnel is undoubtedly a pronounced factor in contributing to the lesser tension of the patients. It may well be that this is the most important benefit of the drugs....

From a behavioral or sociopsychological view, it seems poor practice to give a drug and then let the patient sit as if the drug would cure the disorder by itself. Any benefit of the drug, such as increased relaxation, will be associated with the environment: if the environment is a restricted, atypical one such as the psychiatric hospital, the person is not likely to increase his emission of prosocial behaviors useful outside the hospital. He may adjust better to the hospital milieu in a manner similar to the goals of the aide culture, but adjustment to the extrahospital situation is not something innate or inborn.

It is assumed that the patient will neither leave the hospital nor be eligible for an equalitarian relationship with the staff member. When under the conditions of overcrowding outlined above, a promising candidate is sought for discharge, the stable caste relationship on the ward is interrupted and a new type of relationship emerges. If a patient is considered for discharge, an implicit hypothesis about him is formed among the staff members: "This person is able to carry on an acceptable social life in the outside world." One way of testing this hypothesis is to interact with this person as if he were a normal individual and to notice how he responds. . . . What starts as an experiment has unintended consequences. The staff member's initiation of normal social interaction brings into play a whole network of expectations which often bring the patient into closer conformity with socially acceptable conduct. [Cumming and Cumming, 1957, pp. 68–69.]

The key issue is whether conditions can be developed in which both staff and patients are reinforced for acting toward each other as normal people. Only in this way can behaviors be shaped that not only will lead to an easier time for the hospital staff but that will carry over to the community. In part, placebo effects indicate what might be done.

It seems fair to hypothesize that many of the most severe behaviors attributed to the "disease" called schizophrenia are caused by its treatment, and that many consistencies are the consistencies of the treatment rather than of something originally in the patient. The burden of what has preceded is that there may be self-validating hypotheses held by the staff, and that these hypotheses may work toward either the patient's benefit or toward his continued emission of behavior indicative of schizophrenia. In both cases, however, the patient is reacting in a way that is learned as an adjustment to the staff and hospital conditions. To the extent that this is true, it may be said that there is no worse place for a crazy man than the madhouse; it may also be said that maybe there are no crazy patients, but rather there are crazy treatments.

BEYOND THE HOSPITAL

The editors of the *Schizophrenia Bulletin* noted that "many psychiatrists now believe that most chronically hospitalized patients—the withdrawn, uncommunicative, emotionless persons who perpetually reside on the back wards of mental hospitals—are actually victims of the treatment they receive." (p. 4, fall 1972.)

Although the mental hospital plays a major role in the social process called schizophrenia, it is only a part of the broader system of a mental illness profession, which in turn serves as a form of social control (see Chapters 1, 2, and 10). In 1927 Burrow wrote, "And so the real disorder, after all, is not dementia praecox but psychiatry." (pg. 137.) Zarlock (1972) puts the matter this way: ". . . schizophrenia is a cultural phenomenon which emerges from a social and evolutionary process. Without the presence of social sophistication, a clinical profession could not exist, standard biases of perception could not be sustained, and the phenomenon of schizophrenia could not become manifest." (p. 835.) Zusman (1967) makes the point that as theories and treatment facilities change, the behavior of psychiatric patients changes. For example, in the early eighteenth century, "Conolly was able to abolish restraint completely at Manwell and found, as he had predicted in advance, that rather than becoming dangerous and uncontrollable, his patients developed more self-control." (p. 218.)

There are research workers, therapists, hospital staff such as psychiatrists, nurses, aides, hospital and clinic administrators, other hospital staff such as secretaries, custodians, dietitians, and other personnel, research assistants, book writers on abnormal psychology, book publishers, teachers of abnormal psychology, filmmakers (e.g., a directory of films on schizophrenia in the fall 1972 *Schizophrenia Bulletin* lists over 200 entries), the pharmaceutical industry, and so forth. Each of these groups has vested interests in the maintenance of their concepts of schizophrenia and mental illness. These many people must be taken into account in the alteration of the concepts of the treatment and modification of "schizophrenic" behavior. Further, the elimination or reduction of "schizophrenia" will have implications for many people's livelihood.

The "schizophrenia" and the mental health industry maintain each other. Just as crime cannot be understood without the reference to law and law enforcement, investigation of schizophrenia must take into account the mental health industry. Most research and treatment of schizophrenia has foundered because of a failure to take cognizance of this relationship. Work on training aides and parents within the token economies discussed toward the end of this chapter is one step in this direction. Challenges to a disease model of schizophrenia through texts aimed at the college students who are the source for new members of the mental health industry are another.

EXPERIMENTS IN THE SOCIOPSYCHOLOGICAL MODEL

If the patient in a psychiatric hospital is responsive to a wide range of social stimuli such as placebo and therapeutic community, a crucial question is whether certain environmental manipulations are more effective than others. The sociopsychological model would lead to the hypothesis that response-contingent reinforcement should be such a manipulation. Further, the dependent variable in such experiments should be the key behaviors considered indicative of schizophrenia. If such behaviors are amenable to direct manipulation, the experiments in turn bolster the sociopsychological approach and provide data inconsistent with physiological or intrapsychic formulations of schizophrenia.

The key behavioral indicants for the label of schizophrenia are (1) disorganization of thinking, (2) apathy, (3) social withdrawal, and (4) verbalizations that are bizarre or aversive to listeners. The following experiments involve random assignment of patients to various groups which are treated differently in terms of a specified independent variable.

Disorganization of Thinking

There are a number of ways in which disorganization of thinking has been measured. Two popular methods are word associations and interpretation of proverbs. Becker (1956) devised and validated a highly reliable method for identifying the intellectual level of the interpretation of proverbs. Kaufman (1960) extended Becker's work by increasing the number of proverbs and devising alternate forms of the test. In both Becker's and Little's (1966) work, the proverb test was found to be significantly correlated with a measure of the process-reactive distinction.

Little (1966) indicated how the atmosphere created by the experimenter may alter the patient's "disorganization of thinking." Little administered one of the forms of the Kaufman proverbs on Day 1 of the experiment. On Day 2, the patients were assigned to either a positive, negative, or control group. The positive and negative groups received a standard psychiatric interview. In the positive group, the interviewer made comments such as "Fine," "Very good," "I see," "How interesting," "I understand," and so forth. In the negative condition the interviewer made comments such as "Can you do better?," "Are you sure of that?," "Would you hurry?," and, in general, was businesslike, brusque, clipped, and sarcastic. The control group did not undergo an interview. The second form of the proverbs test was then administered. The positive interaction group improved an average of 8.08 units and the negative interaction group decreased an average of 4.71 units. Both these scores were significantly different from the control group, which improved an average of 2.29 units. The control group took into account increased familiarity with the experimenter and practice effects. Not only did the patients improve in their emission of appropriate, abstract responses after a positive interaction, but they also decreased in this behavior after a negative interaction.

Meichenbaum (1966a) specifically reinforced the abstract interpretation of proverbs. Patients were randomly assigned to four experimental conditions. All subjects were seen for an hour on each of two consecutive days. On the first day a number of pre-experimental measures were collected. On the second day, the crucial experimental treatments were administered during a test of proverb interpretation. All subjects first interpreted 12 proverbs as a baseline measure. There followed 36 additional proverbs, the last 12 of which (numbers 37 through 48 inclusive) constituted the test measure to be compared to the baseline. From the thirteenth proverb onwards the members of a first group, the *contingent positive* group, were reinforced with an "Mmmh-hmm," a smile, a head nod, and an encouraging "Good" whenever they gave an appropriate and abstract interpretation of a proverb.

A second group, *noncontingent positive* reinforcement, received the same response at the same time as subjects in the first, contingent positive, group, but was reinforced regardless of the quality of the response. A third group was a *contingent negative group;* whenever its members gave a vague, false, literal, or absurd response, the experimenter emitted a frown, an "Uh-uh," shook his head "No" and said, discouragingly, "Poor." The final group was a *control* group in which the experimenter remained neutral throughout the test.

The mean changes from baseline (first 12) to test measure (last 12) proverbs was an increase of 8.28 for the contingent positive group and .69 for the noncontingent positive group, and a decrease of .22 for the contingent negative and 1.84 for the control group. The gain of the contingent positive group was significantly different from the other three groups, which, in turn, did not differ from each other. A Similarities Test, a measure of ability at abstractions found in the Wechsler Scales of Intelligence, was administered before and after the experimental treatments. The contingent positive group gained an average of 2.19 units on this test, while the other groups changed −.50 (noncontingent positive), −.69 (contingent negative), and .06 (control). The contingent positive group differed significantly in this change from the other groups.

Studies using word associations serve as additional examples of the direct manipulation of measures of disorganized thinking in an experimental setting (Ullmann, Krasner, and Edinger, 1964; True, 1966; Panek, 1967; Thompson, 1967).

Apathy

Lack of interest in the environment is probably the major treatment problem when working with chronic schizophrenic patients. Emotional blandness and lack of affect (and hence "inappropriate" affect) may be deduced as further correlates of apathy. There are two major areas in which the behavioral correlates of apathy may be manipulated: verbal behavior and nonverbal motor activity.

Noyes and Kolb (1963, pp. 332–34) use terms such as "poverty of feeling" and "loss of colorfulness of personality." The patient's speech seems devoid of those words which provide the flavor of the human condition. Clinically, the ability to emit affect self-references, that is, feelings about oneself, has a long history of being an important objective of psychotherapy and a correlate of mental health. Ullmann (1957a) indicated that the emission of greater affect in a semi-structured psychological test was significantly related to adequacy of interpersonal relations in group therapy meetings. In further work with the Thematic Apperception Test (Ullmann, 1957b, 1958; Ullmann and McFarland, 1957; Gurel and Ullmann, 1958) a definition of emotional words was developed and investigated.

Given a clinically relevant variable, the next problem is to manipulate it. Krasner (1958a) applied Skinnerian concepts, as reviewed in Chapter 4, to the verbal behavior of hospitalized schizophrenics. A series of researches by Ullmann and Krasner combined the variable of emotional words with the verbal operant-conditioning procedure of response-contingent cues when the subject emitted an emotional word. The number of emotional words used by patients could be increased (Weiss, Krasner, and Ullmann, 1963; Ullmann, Krasner, and Sherman, 1963) for the same verbal class and in the same manner as observed in other studies with college students (Weiss, Krasner, and Ullmann, 1960; Ekman, Krasner, and Ullmann, 1963) and medical students (Krasner, Ullmann, Weiss, and Collins, 1961). Surveying these and other studies, it was noted that with the introduction of reinforcement after a nonreinforcement baseline period, the emotional words emitted by the subjects became not only more frequent, but also more pleasant (Ullmann, Krasner, and Gelfand, 1963). A related finding by Ullmann, Weiss, and Krasner (1963) was that such increased emotional expressiveness decreased a form of unresponsiveness to stimuli, perceptual defensiveness (Shannon, 1962), especially among people who were "inhibitors" as measured by an inventory scale (Ullmann, 1962).

Salzinger and Pisoni (1958, 1961) and Salzinger, Portnoy, and Feldman (1964) report similar results with conditioning affect self-references in schizophrenics. These two sets of researches, taken together, demonstrate that schizophrenics' affective speech may be increased within the context of situations that are clinically relevant to the patient: "personality" tests and quasidiagnostic interviews. Other examples of verbal conditioning have occurred in various clinical contexts (Dinoff et al., 1960; Rickard, Dignam, and Horner, 1960; Ayllon and Haughton, 1962, presented in Chapter 4; and Adams et al., 1962, who showed how spurious psychoanalytic interpretation served as reinforcing stimuli for schizophrenics' verbal behavior). In further studies, Wolff (1971) used verbal satiation; Wincze, Leitenberg, and Agras (1972) used token reinforcement and feedback; Liberman et al. (1973) used social reinforcement for rational talk and termination (time-out) for delusional speech; and Patterson and Teigen (1973) taught giving factual rather than delusional answers. These articles lay the foundation for more ambitious procedures to train effectiveness of speech. While not directly aimed at delusional speech, Hartlage (1970) compared the effect of 22 student nurses, each dealing with a matched pair of patients. With one patient, the nurses reinforced adaptive responses, while with the other statements were interpreted and insight and transference encouraged. The patients in the first group improved significantly more on a measure of overall adjustment, notably in communication and interpersonal relations.

The second aspect of apathy deals with motor rather than verbal behavior. Schaefer and Martin (1966) note that the overt behavioral pattern of apathy is a limited response to the environment. As the environment changes, the patient does not. "It is often said that such patients never do anything. But this is clearly not true, since the patient emits the behaviors which his limited repertoire contains quite frequently and continuously. In effect, the patient's behavior affords no reinforcement for responses made by therapists. As he ignores attempts at verbal interaction, he practices the most effective form of extinction imaginable." (1966, p. 1147.)

Schaefer and Martin recorded patients' behavior at half-hour intervals. A nurse would check what the patient was doing on three scales: *mutually exclusive behaviors*—walking, running, standing, sitting, lying down; *concomitant behaviors*—talking, singing, playing music, painting, reading, listening to others, listening to radio, watching TV, group activity; *idiosyncratic behaviors*—rocking, pacing, chattering. From a review of clinical records to designate "withdrawn," "apathetic," or "disinterested" patients, it was found that the absence of concomitant behaviors was an excellent measure of what was generally called apathy. Having a behavioral target (i.e., an operational definition of apathy), the next step was to see if this behavior could be influenced.

The work took place within the framework of a token economy in which tokens, plus verbal praise and, at times, more direct reinforcers (cigarettes which tokens could buy), were used. They were given by the staff for three major areas of behavior: *personal hygiene,* because sloppiness is often taken as an indication that the patient does not care; *social interactions* such as polite "Good mornings" and socially valid questions, because failure to emit such behaviors indicates social withdrawal and disinterest; *adequate working performance* such as emptying waste baskets, because the person who does a good job on such tasks indicates that he cares.

The sample was composed of 40 patients whose medical records indicated apathy and who resided on wards for hospital-habituated chronic schizophrenics. By the toss of a coin, half were placed in the experimental group and half in a control group which received routine ward treatment procedures.

The patients were checked on the three scales detailed above for five consecutive working days, every half hour from six in the morning until nine at night. The reinforcement procedure was started, and at the end of each month, the patients were again observed every half hour during a five-day working week. The controls improved a slight and statistically insignificant amount, while the experimental group improved a significant amount.

Grooming (Mertens and Fuller, 1963), independence (Mikulic, 1971), activity (Mitchell and Stoffelmayr, 1973), and work (Esser, 1967), as well as social responses (Kale et al., 1968; O'Brien, Azrin, and Henson, 1969; Milby, 1970) may all be treated directly, and while valuable as targets in themselves, are also beneficial as feedback to the individual himself in that they are role expressive of social competence rather than dependence.

Social Withdrawal

Social withdrawal, as noted above, is associated with apathy (unresponsiveness to cues that commonly are effective discriminative stimuli for "normal" people). A classic experiment was conducted by King, Armitage, and Tilton (1960). The therapeutic *sequence* started from responses the patient was already making and, by easy transitions, moved from simple to more difficult task situations. Finally, the therapist set the atmosphere and had the responsibility of evaluating whether the patient was ready for the next stage. Patients who had undergone considerable therapy in their average of nine years of hospitalization and had shown no major changes during the last two years were randomly assigned to four groups. They were diagnosed schizophrenic and behaviorally showed low physical and verbal activity. "Mute," "apathetic," and "extremely poor prognosis" would be appropriate words to describe the sample. There were 12 patients in each of four groups. A *recreation therapy* group met for three to five hours a week; a *verbal ther-*

apy group received individual attention with a therapist who tried to establish communication on any basis. With mute patients, this condition was a therapist monologue with hopeful pauses. A third group was a *control* group which received no treatment or attention beyond that common to the ward. The fourth group, the *operant-interpersonal* group, will be called the experimental group in the present résumé. This group was seen three times a week for 20 to 30 minutes for 15 weeks. Cigarettes, candy, and color slides were used as reinforcing stimuli.

There were three phases of the study: simple operant behavior, simple and complex problem-solving, and cooperative problem-solving. In the first phase the therapist described the machine which called for the pulling of a lever to obtain a reinforcing stimulus. The therapist gave a demonstration and, if needed, placed the patient's hand on the lever, pushed it down, unwrapped the candy, and put it in his mouth. The patients were taught to pull the lever. When this behavior was established, the reinforcement schedule was thinned. In the second phase the lever could be moved toward and away from the patient and to the right or left. In this manner increasingly difficult problems or sequences of lever movements were introduced.

The therapist slowly introduced verbal behavior into the situation by prompts or directions toward the formulation of the problem. Slowly, personal questions ("What did you have for breakfast?") were introduced. In the third phase the therapist and the patient worked together as a team, one making the first move, then the other, and so on. Task-oriented verbal interactions were encouraged ("Who does what next?"). In the next part of this phase two patients worked together while the experimenter and six other patients stood around and watched. Every patient had the opportunity of working with every other patient. Occasionally the therapist would take a turn and make a mistake so that the patients would talk to him about the error of his ways. In short, by using a task-oriented situation in which speech was worthwhile, a simple situation was built into a complex, cooperative one.

King and his co-workers collected a considerable number of measures of adjustment before and after therapy. All indicated the greater effectiveness of the operant-interpersonal method: "The operant-interpersonal method was more effective than all the control methods in promoting clinical improvement, based on both ward observations and interview assessments. Comparisons on the following variables also yielded differences in favor of the operant-interpersonal method: level of verbalization, motivation to leave the ward, resistance to therapy, more interest in occupational therapy, decreased enuresis, and transfers to better wards. The patients undergoing verbal therapy became worse in some ways (e.g., verbal withdrawal)." (p. 286.)

With a less regressed patient population verbal conditioning of emotional words in an individual setting was found to be associated with increased adequacy of behavior in therapy groups (Ullmann, Krasner, and Collins, 1961; Ullmann, Krasner, and Ekman, 1961). Ravensborg (1972) and DiScipio, Glickman, and Hollander (1973) are examples of the use of the operant approach to increase interpersonal awareness and social interaction among patients called schizophrenic. In an elaborate experiment, Gutride, Goldstein, and Hunter (1973) evaluated the impact of *structured learning therapy* (Goldstein, 1973) (modeling plus role playing plus social reinforcement) on various measures of social interaction among psychiatric patients. Structured learning therapy yielded significant improvements on four of seven measures. A psychotherapy group appeared to have had no effect on social interactions, although a finer analysis showed that under some conditions psychotherapy may have had an adverse effect.

Bizarre or Aversive Verbalization

There are two ways in which verbal behavior may be indicative of schizophrenia. The first has to do with when a person will *not* talk; this annoys or upsets another person, who may call the first person schizophrenic. As noted by Schaefer and Martin (1966), the observer is extinguished by the nonspeaking patient. It would not be correct to say that the patient does not communicate, for he certainly communicates something about the reinforcing properties of the person he does not talk to. In addition to material already cited, Sherman (1965), Wilson and Walters (1966), Schwartz and Hawkins (1967), and Kassorla (1968) present case material on the use of imitation in the treatment of people with a very low rate of speech. In addition, systematic desensitization has been used (Cowden and Ford, 1962; Zeisset, 1968, Slade, 1972) with people who have trouble talking to others or become tense in particularly difficult situations. Weidner (1969) reports that after desensitization, a patient spent increased amounts of time outside the hospital, which he had avoided for six years because he thought the CIA would kill him.

A problem different from not enough talk is talk that is grouchy, griping, or grotesque. Ullmann et al. (1965) performed the following experiment: each of five experimenters saw 12 patients, four each in three conditions. The situation was a twenty-minute semistructured clinical interview. After a baseline period, during which the interviewer made no response save to ask questions, the experimental conditions were instituted. In one group, whenever the subject emitted "healthy talk" the examiner would smile, nod his head, and show approval. In the second group, the experimenter did the same thing whenever the patient emitted "sick talk." Healthy talk, in contrast to sick talk, was the verbalization of comfort rather than discomfort, liking or approach behavior as distinct from disliking and avoidance behavior, good physical and mental health as distinct from poor physical and mental health, personal assets rather than personal liabilities, presence rather than absence of motivation, plans and realistic nonpathological statements as distinct from bizarre ideation, and optimism, well-being, self-esteem, contentment, enthusiasm, and favorable perceptions of others rather than negative self-references, discontent, upset, and anxiety.

A third group was a control group in which, to approximate the number of experimenter-emitted reinforcing stimuli without biasing the patient in either a sick talk or healthy talk direction, the experimenter emitted his approving behaviors whenever the patient used a plural noun. The group reinforced for healthy talk decreased in the percentage of sick talk (sick talk divided by sick talk plus healthy talk), while the group reinforced for sick talk and the control group reinforced for plural nouns showed a tendency approaching statistical significance to increase in the percentage of emitted sick talk. The differences among the groups were significant.

An interesting side finding was that the reinforcement of plural nouns had much the same effect as the reinforcement of sick talk. If the reader will try selectively reinforcing a friend for the emission of plural nouns, he may agree with the after-the-fact hypothesis (requiring further validation) that such behavior on the part of an interviewer is strange and unexpected. It would be consistent with the sociopsychological model if patients became "sicker" when the interviewer acted in a socially unusual and "sick" manner—not unlike the observation by Spadoni and Smith (1967) about their therapeutic communities, quoted in this chapter.

Further work, using a definition of "sick talk" more restricted to bizarre verbalization and involving interviews on ten successive days, has been completed by Meichenbaum (1969). This work provided an elaborate series of checks on the transfer of improved verbal behavior, after selective reinforcement, to other tasks and people. The very elaborateness of the work makes it impossible to do it justice in the present context, but the point is that the type of work done by Ullmann et al. (1965) can be and has been repeated by an independent worker.

A Word About Experiments

The experimental method is Western man's prime way of learning about his world. However, the method is only as valuable as the material to which it is applied. The preceding experiments dealt with behaviors that have direct clinical relevance; they may be contrasted with experiments on reaction time, scanning picture tubes, or other dependent variables which are inferentially related to those indicants likely to be labeled schizophrenic. Another way of stating this concept is that complex equipment and a room marked "laboratory" do not make meaningful experimentation. They may even militate against it. The first task for the experimenter is to make the response meaningful and worth emitting for the subject. Considerable planning and practice enter into such efforts, and the findings are a function of the experimenter's preparation, not an automatic, invariable result.

Experimenters need training as much as, if not more than, patients do. To gain the cooperation of a hospitalized psychiatric patient requires a tactfulness of approach. The experiment starts when the experimenter is trained in how to look at and formulate the psychiatric patient. Another way of phrasing this is the warning that unsophisticated applications at either a clinical or experimental level will be likely to obtain the results they deserve.

Many of the experiments reviewed in this section made use of verbal conditioning, a procedure in which a relatively trivial reinforcing stimulus (usually a smile, a nod of the head, and/or an "Mmh-hmm") is emit-

ted contingent upon the subject's behavior. The very fact that such a small environmental change is effective seems inconsistent with a picture of the schizophrenic as withdrawn and socially unresponsive. The easiest analogy to the schizophrenic is that of a rejected lover: only a rejected lover on the rebound is more responsive than a schizophrenic to human kindness, patience, and personal interest. But like a rejected lover, few people are more sensitive to rebuff and more wary of commitment than a schizophrenic. With tact, sensitivity, and genuine respect for the person as an individual, there is little that is not possible; without these, little can be accomplished.

In verbal conditioning experiments more than in most situations, the experimenter is the instrument, the source of reinforcing stimuli. As work proceeded in the series of efforts touched on above, it became clear that there were few "problem" patients but many problems with experiments that had sought the trappings of scientific rigor at the expense of subject rapport. If what has been done with a smile, a head nod, and a grunt is fact, and the replications indicate it is, then what can be done with stronger and more continuing reinforcing stimuli?

APPLICATIONS OF CONCEPTS: TREATMENT

Nydegger (1972) used verbal conditioning to affect hallucinatory behavior with a 20-year-old male diagnosed as paranoid schizophrenic who had reported auditory and visual hallucinations and a very rigid religious delusional system.

To deal with this a verbal conditioning paradigm was used. I explained to S that his "voices" were really just thoughts for which he was unwilling to take responsibility, and in the future he should say "thoughts" instead of "voices." When S and I were talking (apparently reinforcing for him) and he said "voices" I would look away, check my watch, begin to leave, and do other things associated with breaking contact. When he spoke about "thoughts," "decisions" or anything involving personal responsibility I would maintain eye contact, smile, nod my head and say "mm-hmm." The rest of the staff were also informed of these contingencies and were encouraged to do the same, and most of them did.

. . . The delusional system, which was also functional in removing him from conflict, responded to verbal conditioning and assertive training. After 2 months of treatment the hallucinations and delusions ceased to be reported or observed. The patient has had no recurrence of psychotic symptoms for 2½ years.

. . . While the result of the treatment indicated impressively that behavior labeled psychotic can be modified, it is interesting to record the reactions of some members of the staff. They asserted that the patient had not been purged of his hallucinations, but had merely been taught not to speak of them. Thus it could not be said that he was not hallucinating. When I asked the critics how they knew that S had hallucinated in the first place, they promptly reeled off these behavioral indicators: he talks to himself; "listens" to things no one else hears; withdraws to isolated corners; and says that he hallucinates. I then pointed out that all of these indicators were observable behavior—a point which they reluctantly conceded. I then asserted that since none of the indicative behaviors existed any longer, it could be maintained that S no longer hallucinated. [pp. 225–27.]

Haynes and Geddy (1973) successfully used time out from reinforcement to decrease hallucinations while Slade (1972) used desensitization for stimuli likely to lead to hallucinatory behavior. Reasoning that if auditory hallucinations are a result of one's own subvocal verbalizations, and that these may be interfered with by other use of vocal musculature, Erikson and Gustafson (1972) used humming and gargling to help the person "stop the voices."

Richardson, Karkalas, and Lal (1972) decreased hallucinations of "electricity" by contingently removing privileges; the specificity of the contingency was illustrated in that auditory hallucinations for which no treatment was given did not change. Bucher and Fabricatore (1970) report a patient who kept records of disturbing hallucinations, and using a portable machine, gave himself contingent shocks until the auditory voices declined to zero. Rutner and Bugle (1969) successfully used self-monitoring; further, social reinforcement was given for reported reductions in hallucinatory behavior. After 16 days of treatment, no reports of hallucinations occurred for six months, and other aspects of the patient's behavior also improved. In an experiment not as intensive as case work, Weingaertner (1971) obtained the fascinating result that after two weeks, groups using a self-shock apparatus, a placebo, or nothing (control group), all three groups improved. These results, combined with the wide range of behavioral techniques, indicate that hallucinations are amenable to social-influence procedures. Rather than any particular single technique, the procedure used should fit the specific individual in treatment, and under these conditions, benefit beyond that attainable by general interest and expectation should be obtained. But Weingaertner's data show that these social variables, in themselves, are strong ones and should be used to decrease rather than reinforce hallucinatory behavior.

Baker (1971) offers an interesting study of how operant conditioning was used to reinstate verbalization in mute schizophrenics in which eighteen schizophrenic patients who had been mute from three to 37 years were selected by means of a speech test. Nine of these were positively reinforced for speaking and nine were reinforced for staying silent. After 25 sessions, the speech-reinforced group had improved significantly more than the silence-reinforced group.

Another way of conceptualizing the task of helping the schizophrenic to improve his behavior is to systematically manipulate environmental events, which can be done in a variety of ways. Meichenbaum and Cameron (1973) first modeled a task, talking aloud while the subject observed; then the subject performed the same task while the experimenter instructed the subject aloud; next the subject was asked to perform the task again while instructing himself aloud; then the subject performed the task while whispering to himself (lip movements), and finally the subject performed the task convertly (without lip movements).

The training thus focuses on the specific details of how and what to do. A major aspect of this training was to teach when to use the task-relevant self-instructions. The schizophrenics were in effect trained to monitor their own behavior and to become sensitive to the facial and behavioral interpersonal cues with which others respond to "schizophrenic behavior." These cues then became discriminative stimuli to emit task-relevant self-instructions and appropriate behaviors "The schizophrenic was trained to 'listen to himself,' to monitor his own thinking, and if his cognitions were maladaptive, to produce incompatible self-statements and behaviors. The focus of therapy shifted from manipulating external environmental consequences to directly influencing how the client perceives, evaluates, and reacts to the environment." (p. 531.)

There have been a further series of utilizations of behavioral techniques, primarily operant, in modifying specific aspects of schizophrenic behavior. Magaro and Staples (1972) have used schizophrenic patients as therapists for other patients. Muzekari and Kamis (1973) used videotape feedback and modeling to influence task-oriented verbal behavior of schizophrenics. Similar successful studies have been reported by Matefy (1972), Baker (1971), Shean (1973), Dowd and Abelson (1973), and McFall and Lillesand (1971).

Family Treatment

Treatment of the schizophrenic in the context of his family has grown and flourished since its inception in the 1950's. Massie and Beels (1972) have reviewed the outcome of the family treatment approach to schizophrenia (e.g., the work of MacGregor et al., 1964; Friedman et al., 1965; Jackson and Wheatland, 1961; Bowen, 1960; Esterson, Cooper, and Laing, 1964) and have concluded that such studies are ". . . relatively limited and inadequate in scope. Numbers of families treated by different family techniques are too few, follow-up periods are not long enough, and research is not adequately controlled . . . nonetheless, family techniques do give indications of effectiveness of treating schizophrenia." (p. 35) Feinsilver and Gunderson (1972), in reviewing a series of such studies, conclude that studies of psychotherapy (including direct analysis, psychoanalysis, client-centered therapy) ". . . have neither proved psychotherapy ineffective nor proved any strong evidence of its helpfulness." (p. 21.)

The training of parents, teachers, and siblings in the application of behavioral procedures may be found throughout this book, especially in Chapters 12, 23, and 28.

TOKEN ECONOMIES

If the concepts of the sociopsychological model are accepted, it seems reasonable to treat hospitalized psychiatric patients not as diseased but as normal people capable of appropriate actions if adequate consequences for actions are provided. This in large measure was the philosophy of the era of moral treatment: "The moral therapist acted toward his patients as though they were mentally well. He believed that kindness and forbearance were essential in dealing with them. He also believed in firmness and persistence in impressing on patients the idea that a change to more acceptable behavior was expected." (Bockoven, 1963, p. 76.)

Dunham and Weinberg (1960) point out that in the aide culture the attendants respond to the patients much in the same way they would respond to normal persons in a situation in which they, the aides, were dominant. The implication Dunham and Weinberg give is that this is not good because the patients are "sick." The prime reason the present authors disavow the aide culture is that its purpose is to benefit the attendants and not the patients, who are best served by treatment that leads to a life outside the hospital. But the very success of the aide culture in attaining behavior change should lead psychologists to study what is being done, to take the effective elements and use them in a manner that is humane and directed to the service of the patient.

The aide culture makes use of a number of realistic and immediate reinforcers to shape behavior. The situation in which a person is expected to act in a manner acceptable to another in order to obtain a particular favorable response from that person is the common one for social interaction. Essentially adults are paid to work and in turn use their money to obtain a variety of reinforcing stimuli. As time progresses, people are paid on longer fixed-interval schedules and are paid for larger units of behavior. A process of shaping the behavior and thinning the reinforcement schedule is followed. What is also implied is that the program for learning is individually tailored. Finally, there is relatively little coercion or direct supervisory control in the final stages; if a parent, boss, group member, or aide is required as a stimulus setting the time and place where the person will perform, then there is less likelihood for the person to emit the acts when the discriminative stimulus of the authority figure is not present.

The token economy programs represent a recent development in institutional treatment of long-term patients. The token programs can be seen as an extension of the sociopsychological principles, discussed in earlier chapters, to large-scale living units (Krasner, 1968a).

The composition of a token economy is defined by at least three aspects. First, there is the designation by the institutional staff of certain specific patient behaviors as good, desirable, and reinforceable. Second, there is a medium of exchange, an object that stands for something else. It may be plastic rectangles shaped like credit cards, small metallic coins, poker chips, marks on a piece of paper, or even green stamps. Third, there is a way of utilizing the tokens, the *back-up* reinforcers themselves. These "good things" may range from food to being allowed to sit peacefully in a chair.

The approach to the patients involves the development of behaviors that will lead to reinforcement from others and enhance the skills necessary for him to take a responsible social role in the institution and eventually to live successfully outside the hospital.

Ayllon and Azrin (1965) report the results of a token economy in a psychiatric hospital ward. The behaviors selected for reinforcement included such things as serving meals, cleaning floors, sorting laundry, washing dishes, and self-grooming. Reinforcement consisted of the opportunity to engage in activities that had a high level of occurrence when freely allowed. The reinforcers selected were part of the naturalistic context. One of the widely held beliefs about schizophrenic patients is that few stimuli are effective reinforcers for them. Ayllon and Azrin made no a priori decisions about what might be an effective reinforcer. Instead, their approach involved the observation of patients' behavior to discover what patients actually did. They applied the general principle expressed by Premack (1959) that any behavior with a high frequency of occurrence can be used as a reinforcer. Thus, the reinforcers included such things as paying rent for a room; selecting the people to eat with; passes; a chance to speak to the ward physician, chaplain, or psychologist; TV; candy; cigarettes; and other amenities of life. Tokens serve as acquired reinforcers that bridge the delay between behavior and an ultimate reinforcement. The investigators placed particular emphasis on the objective definition and quantification of the responses and reinforcers and upon programming and recording procedures.

Ayllon and Azrin report a series of six experiments in each of which they demonstrated that target behavior systematically changed as a function of the token reinforcement. One experiment is typical of their procedures. The response they were interested in consisted of off-ward work assignments. Patients selected the one they preferred from a list of available jobs paying tokens. After ten days they were told that although they could continue working on their job there would be no tokens for doing it. Of the eight patients involved, seven immediately selected another job that had previously been nonpreferred. The eighth patient switched a few days later. In the third phase of the experiment the contingencies were reversed and the preferred jobs led to tokens. All eight patients switched back to the previously preferred original jobs.

The results of the six experiments demonstrated that the reinforcement procedure was effective in maintaining desired performance. In each experiment, the performance fell to a near-zero level when the established response reinforcement relation was discontinued. On the other hand, reintroduction of the reinforcement procedure restored performance almost immediately and maintained it at a high level.

Ayllon and Azrin's token economy was set up on a ward in a midwestern state hospital with a population of long-term female patients. Another token economy program (Atthowe and Krasner, 1968; Krasner, 1965a, 1966b) was set up in a western Veterans Administration hospital with a group of male patients averaging 58 years of age and a median length of hospitalization of 24 years. Most of these patients had been labeled chronic schizophrenics. As a group, their behavior was apathetic and indifferent, manifested by inactivity, dependency, and social isolation. The procedures used were similar to those developed by Ayllon and Azrin. However, one of the major differences was in the amount of total control exerted by the experimenters. The Atthowe and Krasner program was designed to be used on an open ward in which patients could come and go, if, of course, they had the right number of tokens for the gatekeeper. There was a considerable amount of possible off-ward behavior. The token economy had to compete with the outside money economy. Many kinds of economic problems had to be faced. To cope with these problems, special procedures had to be developed such as a banking system to foster savings, a monthly discount rate to cut down hoarding, and variously colored tokens to prevent stealing.

Prior to the introduction of tokens, most patients refused to go to any of the activities available to them and showed little interest in their environment. They sat or slept on the ward during the day. Among the new, reinforced behaviors were enacting the role of responsible people who are adept at self-grooming, keeping their living facilities clean, dressing neatly, holding a job, and interacting with other people. Responsibility also involved being affected by normal social reinforcement. Thus, each time tokens were given, they were paired with verbalizations such as "Good," "I'm pleased," or "Fine job," and an explicit statement as to the contingencies involved—e.g., "You received three tokens because you got a good rating from your job supervisor."

The token-economy program was a significant success as measured by changes in specified behavior, observers' ratings, and reactions of hospital staff. The greatest changes were in the appearance and atmosphere of the ward. The changes in specified behaviors, such as attendance at group activity, were a function of the number of tokens (value) given for the activity. Group attendance increased as more tokens were given for it, and then decreased as the payoff returned to its previous value.

Finally, the token program had an enormous effect on the attitudes of staff throughout the hospital. The staff found that they could have a therapeutic effect on patient behavior. Staff morale increased, and working on the token ward became a matter of prestige. In the hospital where the Atthowe and Krasner program was under way, additional wards adopted similar token economies as a way of life because of their apparent usefulness in changing patient behavior.

Winkler (1968a) reports the result of a token-economy program in a closed female ward with patients averaging 49 years of age and twelve years hospitalization in a hospital in New South Wales, Australia. The patients' behavior was characterized by an excessive amount of violence and screaming as well as apathy and general lack of response to the ward environment. Winkler also reported a significant improvement in staff morale as indicated by a drop in absenteeism. In the four months after the program began absenteeism was 24 percent below that for the four months before the program began, while, in a comparable ward, absenteeism over the same period dropped only 3 percent.

Without exception, Winkler reports that every type of behavior that was reinforced improved. In addition, behaviors not specifically in the program, such as violence and loud noise, decreased. Winkler also carried out a number of studies designed to determine whether the patients' behavior was really under the control of the tokens. In one experiment, tokens for shoe cleaning were stopped for three weeks and then reintroduced. There was an immediate decrease of this behavior with a discontinuation of tokens and an immediate increase upon their reintroduction. Similar results occurred with other behaviors.

Winkler (1968b) reports on the third phase of his program, which was concerned with the effects on behavior of the relationships between the number of tokens in the patients' possession, the system's economic balance, and amount of reinforcement (wages). Winkler makes a major contribution in bringing together economic theory and a closed system in which variables such as earning and prices can be experimentally manipulated.

This first economic experiment indicated a close relationship between savings and token-earning behavior. Behavior under a low savings condition was better than behavior under a high savings one and reduction in savings improved behavior. The improvement in behavior when the economic balance was altered in favor of income, and the change in behavior during economic disequilibrium, suggest that the economic balance does not affect behavior directly but through the way it affects savings.

Another variation of experimental design in token programs has been reported by Lloyd and Garlington (1968). Seven types of behavior of 13 chronic schizophrenic female patients were rated during four experimental phases. During conditions 1 and 3, the patients were given a token allowance in the morning on a noncontingent basis. During conditions 2 and 4, tokens were paid on a contingent basis, that is, the patients received tokens commensurate with the ratings of their behavior (e.g., neatness, eating habits, and bed-making). These ratings were higher during conditions 2 and 4 than during conditions 1 and 3 The authors concluded that *contingent* tokens were controlling the behavior of the patients.

The goal of the research investigator using a token economy is to demonstrate, first, significant behavioral change, and second, that the change is a function of the specific techniques involved in the token program.

The token-economy program, insofar as research procedures are concerned, may be divided into the following categories:

(a) *Programs that are primarily demonstrational projects.* No attempt is made to control variables. Although change may be observed, it is difficult to attribute it to the contingencies of receipt of tokens and their back-up reinforcers, per se.

(b) *Programs using base rate and own-controls* (see Chapter 3). Measurement is taken of the operant rate of patient behaviors for a specific perod of time. The token program is introduced and the same behaviors are measured. In some instances the token contingencies may be removed while the behavior continues to be measured. Then the token contingencies are reintroduced. The work of Ayllon and Azrin (1965) and Arann and Horner (1972) provide illustrations as do many of the programs in this category (Lloyd and Abel, 1970; Shean and Zeidberg, 1971; Steffy et al., 1969; Suchotliff et al., 1970; Upper, 1971; Fernandez, Fischer, and Ryan, 1973; Henderson and Scoles, 1970; and Gorham et al., 1970).

(c) *The effectiveness of the token economy procedure is tested by the use of control groups, which receive either no specific treatment or a different treatment.* Studies by Marks, Shalock, and Sonoda (1968); Gripp and Magaro (1971); Olsen and Greenberg (1972); Maley, Feldman, and Ruskin (1973); Birky, Chambliss, and Wasden (1971) illustrate this approach.

In a token-control comparison study Heap et al. (1970) used token economy procedures to attain the goals promulgated by therapeutic communities. For example, in the ward government (a usual aspect of therapeutic community), the positions were paid for an clearly defined in terms of *tasks* rather than personality or encountering tactics. In small group meetings, attendants elicited and reinforced situation-appropriate verbalizations and interactions rather than insight or depth interpretations. Further, inappropriate behavior was ignored (extinguished). These latter procedures are similar to those covered earlier under verbal conditioning—e.g., Hartlage's (1970) study. The following material, reported in percentages, for the experimental and control wards respectively, give hospital outcome: remain on ward after six months, 13 percent, 68 percent; assigned to custodial ward, 24 percent, 4 percent; absent without permission, 2.6 percent, 6 percent; assigned to advanced ward, 14.4 percent, 0 percent; furloughed or discharged, 45 percent, 18 percent; returned for further treatment, 0 percent, 4 percent (recomputed from Heap et al., 1970, Table 2, p. 352.)

(d) *Performance in the token economy program is related to performance in another learning task.* Panek (1967) worked with 32 chronic schizophrenics (from the Atthowe-Krasner ward). He conditioned common word associations (from the Kent-Rosanoff and Russell-Jenkins lists) with positive and negative contingencies of verbal and token reinforcement. The study then compared success in associate learning with total number of ward token transactions. This latter figure was taken as a measure of the responsivity to reinforcement—that is, the patient who *earned* the most tokens and *spent* the most tokens was considered most *responsive* to the token program. The results showed significant increase of common word associations under either positive (saying "right" and giving a fractional ward token) or negative (saying "wrong" and taking away a fractional ward token) reinforcement, but no significant differences under the two contingencies. Most important, learning-rate rankings were significantly correlated with rankings of total token usage.

The Token Economy and Staff Training

One of the key variables in the success of token economy programs is the training and morale of the staff. This is typified by the report of McReynolds and Coleman (1972) on the impact of a token program on the *staff* as well as on the patients. An evaluation of the effects of their token program with regressed "back ward" patients after one year revealed substantial gains in patient eating, grooming, and dressing behavior and involvement in activities on and off the ward. In addition, measures of staff attitudes toward patients indicated significant gains in staff "expectations" about the treatability of patients and the degree of the latter's psychological deficit. The emphasis on the relationship between the staff and patients is summarized as follows:

Favorable changes in both on ward and off ward staff attitudes toward patients as a result of a year's involvement in the token program is an encouraging, if not especially surprising, finding. Also impressive to the present observers, though difficult to measure systematically, are the qualitative changes in patient-staff interactions evident in the increased frequency of mutual smiles and other verbal and nonverbal communications of concern. Such changes in staff attitudes and behavior appear to relate to a number of aspects of their involvement in the token economy. First, training seminars and lectures were carefully focused to influence staff thinking about the treatment and treatability of patients. As such the training procedures themselves represent an attitude change procedure. More importantly, however, the effects of the reinforcement procedures were readily and repeatedly observed by staff. The limited but meaningful nature of initial target behavior made it easy for ward staff to judge the effects of the token reinforcement procedures. That is, the proof of the treatability of the patients and the efficacy of the token reinforcement was obvious to each staff member. Also important in this "see-for-yourself" aspect of token economy is the focus on appropriate patient behavior as part of the reinforcement procedures as opposed to the usual crisis-only policy of attending only to those patients who are disturbing other patients, staff or ward tranquility. Thus, token reinforcement procedures produced a significant change in the input of information on typical patient behavior received by staff, information capable of reversing the latters' opinion and atttiudes about patient capabilities. Lastly, the reinforcement in the form of praise and attention given to the token ward from both inside and outside the hospital served to further identification with the token program and engender feeling of pride in both their role as *treatment* personnel and their patients as legitimate, worthwhile therapy candidates. [p. 33.]

The reader will remember our remarks earlier in this chapter on the task assigned the aide and the subsequent development of the aide culture. Cleland and Peck (1967) make the point that being an aide may be unstimulating and devoid of significant social interactions—in fact, a situation not unlike that of the patient. Harmatz (1973) observed that a great deal of the ward personnel's time was spent in activity away from patients and in tasks that were visible to superiors such as housekeeping and paperwork. In Footnote 6 of this chapter, we cited reference material indicating that the aide was likely to use social reinforcement in a manner that was inefficient and not to the benefit of the patient. Hollander and Plutchik (1972) reinforced aides with trading stamps for each task completed. Contact with the patients increased, and then decreased when the reinforcement contingency was removed. Hollander, Plutchik, and Horner (1973) showed the important association of attendant behavior under reinforcement to patient behavior and called the result a "piggyback effect." This type of procedure and staff training by modeling as introduced by Wallace et al. (1973), increases staff-patient interaction in a manner that is meaningful to both parties.

In an extension of the training model, Ludwig, Marx, and Hill (1971) used a "double conditioning" treatment paradigm in which patients acted as behavior therapists for fellow chronic schizophrenics. An experimental program was initiated in a state hospital. The nursing and the aide staff were trained in the basic principles of operant conditioning via movies, video tapes, readings, and seminars. These staff members then served as trainers of the trainers.

Twenty-seven **patients**, who carried the

diagnosis of chronic schizophrenia and were regarded as treatment failures of traditional psychiatric therapies, were divided into nine trios. Two members of each trio were assigned to serve as "guardian therapists" for the third who was the more regressed "charge" patient. The treatment model involved:

... the training of these patients through operant conditioning procedures to act in turn as behavioral therapists for fellow chronic schizophrenics.... A standardized hierarchy of response levels, ranging from simple eye contact to complex forms of social behavior, was constructed for all charge patients. Daily 45-minute behavior therapy (BT) sessions were held in which the guardians together with two staff systematically administered both social (e.g., praise) and primary reinforcements (e.g., ice cream, soda, cigarettes, chocolate, etc.) to the charge patient to induce him to progress to advanced levels in the response hierarchy. An arbitrary figure of 80 per cent correct responses constituted the criterion used to gauge when it was appropriate to thin out the differential reinforcement rate, as well as when to proceed to the next higher level in the hierarchy.

Each of the BT sessions was divided into 3-minute time blocks with guardians alternating turns in conditioning their charge. As guardian patients worked, they were given considerable praise, encouragement and instruction from assigned staff. At the end of each time block, they would be given one coupon for effort and one for performance if they earned it. These coupons (secondary reinforcers) were negotiable for assorted "goodies" and "treats." [p. 31.]

Similar work with retardates has been reported by Kazdin (1971), Whalen, and Henker (1969, 1971), Craighead and Mercatoris (1973), and Craighead, Mercatoris, and Bellak (in press).

The Token Economy—Evaluations

Liberman (1972) summarizes his extensive review of the utilization of behavior modification technology with schizophrenics by indicating that they have been:

applied to a wide variety of schizophrenic behaviors, including social interaction, delusions, hallucinations, self-help and grooming skills, and instrumental work behavior. The token economy, a systematic and consistent use of reinforcement principles to patients' behaviors in a ward milieu, has been shown to be effective in increasing the adaptive repertoire of institutionalized schizophrenics. Behavioral interventions are effective, even when phenothiazine medication is withdrawn from chronic psychotics, reflecting the interactions between environmental control, behavior, and drugs. In an environment where contingencies of reinforcement are consistently applied toward improving patient's behavior, the major tranquilizers appear to be less critically necessary than in a milieu where custodial care is provided.

Generalization of treatment effects to new situations such as the community, has not yet been shown to occur regularly as a result of behavior modification efforts. However, there are methods available to enhance generalization or transfer of training, and the next decade will probably show progress in this direction. (p. 47.)

In an evaluative review of approximately 100 different token-economy programs with such populations as hospitalized adults, mental retardates, children in classrooms, delinquents, and various community centers, Kazdin and Bootzin (1972) concluded that "A wide variety of behaviors can be changed in many different populations of subjects using conditioned reinforcers." (p. 367.) However, they felt that three areas needed further investigation, namely those involving generalization, the failure to bring more complex behaviors such as language within the context of the token systems, and the fact that all studies report that there are some subjects whose behavior is not altered. "The stability of changes effected, and the generalization of improvements to nontreatment settings, if demonstrated, will strengthen the thrust of the trend to establish token economies in numerous treatment, rehabilitation, and educational settings." (p. 367). Carlson, Hersen, and Eisler (1972) and Kazdin (in press) reach similar conclusions on both the success attained so far by token economies and the need for new data, such as experiments comparing token economies to other treatments.

SUMMARY

The sociopsychological approach to the behavior called schizophrenic started with the observation that when situations called for appropriate behavior and the emission of such behavior was made worthwhile, people diagnosed as schizophrenics acted in an appropriate manner. It was further noted that the prevalence of behavior that might be labeled schizophrenic was far higher than the incidence of labeled schizophrenics. Sociological factors are required in addition to the emission of specific behaviors before a person is diagnosed and placed in a psychiatric hospital. The short-term advantages of enacting the schizophrenic role were described. Further, it was pointed out that the role is taught in psychiatric interviews, by modeling, and by the situation of the large psychiatric hospital. Evidence for the sociopsychological viewpoint comes from experiments in which the core behavioral indicants of schizophrenia serve as dependent variables (disorganization of thinking, social withdrawal, apathy, inappropriate or aversive affect) and are significantly affected by direct environmental manipulations such as verbal operant conditioning. Another line of evidence for the sociopsychological model comes from the application of experimental studies to specific cases and to the development of token economies.

extreme affective behavior

19

After schizophrenia, the second major grouping listed by DSM-II in the category of "psychosis not attributed to physical conditions listed previously" is that of "major affective disorders" or "affective psychoses." These disorders are characterized by a "single disorder of mood, either extreme depression or elation, that dominates the mental life of the patient and is responsible for whatever loss of contact he has with his environment." (p. 35.)

The affective disorders have four subcategories—involutional melancholia; manic-depressive illness, manic type; manic-depressive illness, depressed type; and manic-depressive illness, circular type.

Manic-depressive "illness" is characterized by "severe mood swings and a tendency to remission and recurrence. Patients may be given this diagnosis in the absence of a previous history of affective psychosis if there is no obvious precipitating event." (p. 36.)

The manic type of this disorder consists exclusively of manic episodes characterized by "excessive elation, irritability, talkativeness, flight of ideas, and accelerated speech and motor activity." (p. 34.)

The depressed type consists exclusively of depressive episodes characterized by "severely depressed mood and by mental and motor retardation progressing occasionally to stupor. Uneasiness, apprehension, perplexity and agitation may also be present." (p. 36.) The major differentiation of this category from the "psychotic depressive reaction" (described below) is that the latter is more readily attributed to an event or experienced stress which may have precipitated it.

The circular type of manic-depressive "illness" is characterized by "at least one attack of both a depressive episode *and* a manic episode."

Finally, the category of "psychotic depressive reaction," listed as an "other psychosis," must be noted. This label describes "a depressive mood attributable to some experience." (p. 38.) This is considered to occur in an individual who does not have a history of repeated depressions or cyclothymic mood swings. The major differentiation between the psychotic and the neurotic depression (see Chapter 13) depends on whether "the reaction impairs reality testing or functional adequacy" to the point where the individual can be considered to be psychotic. The word "depression," at one and the same time, may serve as a "disease," a psychiatric entity, a psychological reaction type, a "symptom" of several psychological problems, or a description of a behavioral deficit.

Historical Background

Among the ancients, "mania" was the label for all behaviors characterized by unusual excitement, and "melancholia" (black bile), was used for all individuals with abnormal depression. Hippocrates described mania and melancholia in the fourth century B.C. By the first century A.D. Aretaeus, representing the thinking of many writers of his time, said that melancholia "is a lowness of the spirits without fever; and it appears to me that melancholy is the commencement and a part of mania." (Cameron, 1944, p. 873.)

By the sixteenth century mania and melancholia were generally considered to be one disorder and included many behaviors not now usually considered to be characteristic of the diagnosis. In 1684 a French physician named Bonet first put the two names together to form a single disorder called manic-depression insanity. It was the French psychiatrist Falret in 1851 who described the behaviors as cyclical and who had a major influence on Kraepelin's theories. Kraepelin (1923)[1] formalized the belief of his day by categorizing all severe depressions and all elated excitement as manifestations of a single phasic disease process. This has been the generally accepted view until the present. Psychoanalysts have accepted Kraepelin's position. Radó, for example, asserts (1928) that "The manic condition succeeds the phase of self-punishment (depression) with the same regularity with which formerly in the biological process, the bliss of satiety succeeded to hunger."

Abraham (1911), a pupil of Freud, introduced manic-depressive psychosis into psychoanalysis by comparing melancholic depression with normal grief. Where the normal mourner was interested in the lost person, the depressed individual was seen as tormented by feelings of guilt because of "unconscious hostility" toward the lost person. Freud in his paper "Mourning and Melancholia" (1917) accepted Abraham's formulations and pointed out that in melancholia there is an internal loss because the lost person had been "incorporated."

Alexander's (1948) view of melancholia as an exaggerated form of mourning may be considered as typical of psychoanalytic views. The libido is withdrawn from the outside world because of the individual's ambivalence toward the lost loved one and the latent hostility is turned back onto the person himself. The loved one can no longer be hated, and this feeling, enhanced by guilt, is turned inward and exacerbates the suffering.

The social context of the onset of manic-depressive disorders, irrespective of any possible genetic (Winokur et al., 1971; Winokur, 1970; Fieve, 1972) or biochemical involvement, is stressed by most investigators (Schwab, 1971; Schwab et al., 1968; Paykel and Weissmann, 1973; Klerman, 1971).

Marsella, Kinzie, and Gordon (1971) selected a group of 196 subjects from 508 students enrolled at the University of Hawaii. These subjects all had a score of at least 50 on a depression scale (Zung, 1965), which, according to criterion group norms, placed them at "clinically significant levels of depression." The subjects were Americans of Japanese, Chinese, or Caucasian ancestry, and factor analysis revealed different patterns of depression for each ethnic group. The high rate of scores indicative of depression in the Marsella, Kinzie, and Gordon (1971) study, close to 40 percent, is consistent with the 24 percent in the Midtown study (see Chapter 10) and points up a great methodological problem in this area, the very definition of the problem. The present chapter focuses on people who have been hospitalized, while Chapter 13 dealt primarily with those who were not—but, as the sophisticated reader will recognize, this distinction is a poor one at best.

MANIC BEHAVIOR

Three subcategories or stages are usually employed in describing behavior labeled as manic, they are: hypomania, acute mania, and delirious mania. The *hypomanic* individual is characterized by overactivity, flightiness, and elation. It is often hard to differentiate hypomanic behavior from highly competent active, ag-

---

[1] Kraepelin first used the term "manic-depressive insanity" in the sixth edition of his *Textbook of Psychiatry* (1899) and did not fully expand the concept to that of a single disease until his eighth edition (1923).

gressive, and sociable behavior. When an individual has enormous confidence in himself, undertakes many new projects, sleeps infrequently, keeps many engagements, talks incessantly, telephones, writes, makes appointments, and generally seems involved with the world in every conceivable way, is he hypomanic or simply a hard-working, constructive individual? The differential considerations are effectiveness, consistency, and rationality. Hypomanic behaviors are characterized by literally "much ado about nothing"; little is actually accomplished, friends become annoyed or exasperated, and the behavior is excessive, whether it be in areas of alcohol, sex, talk, or money. There is a seemingly forced life-of-the-party gaiety that may be annoying to others, since it seems unreal and not appropriate to the social situation.

The *acute* manic individual can no longer pass as having socially acceptable behavior. The elation and activity are more pronounced. He may talk loudly and be extremely boisterous and overbearing. He fluctuates rapidly between being angry, gay, irritable, and violent. He may attack people physically, verbally, or, at rare times, sexually. He may break furniture. His sequence of ideas may seem irrational because one idea follows another so rapidly that a listener has trouble understanding him and thus may find him incoherent. The acute manic is steadily active, unable to remain quiet and to listen or take into account other people's ideas or feelings. The pressure of speech and activity may be so extreme that the observer feels the person is trying to drown out or avoid unpleasant stimuli.

The *delirious manic* comes closest to the classic description of a raving maniac. He is in an extreme state of hyperactivity, is disoriented as to time and place, may hallucinate, be unresponsive to pain, and pace and scream until he becomes utterly exhausted. A person may gradually progress from hypomania to delirious mania over time, or the delirious mania may, in rare instances, be emitted without a "warm-up" period.

DEPRESSIVE BEHAVIOR

The behavior that is characteristic of the depressive may also be categorized into three steps of severity: simple depression, acute depression, and acute stupor. In all three the major characteristics are sad affect, psychomotor retardation, and apparent difficulty in thinking.

The *simple depressive* is characterized by a general slowing of activities. He seems to have lost all enthusiasm or zest for living. He may sit and stare. He may fail to eat. He feels sinful, guilty, and worthless. He is able to recognize the changes in his behavior and is well oriented. He may report many vague bodily complaints such as headaches, inability to sleep, and loss of appetite. Often there is preoccupation with suicidal thoughts. The distinction between simple depression and reactive depression is difficult to make. The criteria take into account the antecedent situations in terms of stress and the "reality" or "appropriateness" of the response.

In *acute depression* psychomotor retardation is more pronounced. There is no evidence of spontaneity. Unrealistic bodily complaints (hypochondriacal ideas) may extend into delusional systems involving belief that the body is falling apart or that there is punishment for previous sex practices. The individual reports feeling hopeless and helpless. He sighs, looks desolate, and nothing seems to attract his interest.

In *depressive stupor* the individual becomes almost completely unresponsive, withdrawn, and inactive. He is bedridden. He has to be fed, washed, and bathed. Vivid and upsetting hallucinations may occur.

Plutarch's description of the behavior of depressed individuals, quoted in Chapter 7, is still accurate. The reader might well turn back to it at this point.

Factor analysis has been valuable in specifying the behaviors leading to the label of depression. Grinker et al. (1961) report the results of a factor analysis of material on 96 patients admitted for hospitalization with a diagnosis of "depression" (which included both neurotic and psychotic depressions). Their results can be reported first in terms of five sets of factors that involved descriptions of the *feelings* and *concerns* of the patients as they verbalized them. These were categorized as follows:

1. A factor describing characteristics of hopelessness, helplessness, failure, sadness, unworthiness, guilt, and internal suffering. There is no appeal to the outside world; no conviction that receiving anything from the environment would change how the patient feels. There is self-concept of "badness."
2. A factor describing characteristics of concern over material loss and an inner conviction that this feeling state (and the illness) could be changed if only the outside world would provide something.
3. A factor describing characteristics of guilt over wrong-doing by the patient, wishes to make restitution, and a feeling that the illness was brought on by the patient himself and is deserved.
4. A factor describing characteristics of "free anxiety."
5. A factor describing characteristics of envy, loneliness, martyred affliction, secondary gain, and gratification from the illness, and attempts, by provoking guilt, to force the world into making redress.

A second set of factors, derived from *observation* of the depressed patients, was based on a behavior checklist and resulted in ten behavioral factors comprising:

1. Characteristics of isolation, withdrawal, and apathy.
2. Characteristics of retardation, slowing of thought processes and speech, and little regard for personal appearance.
3. Characteristics of general retardation in behavior and gait, but less isolated and withdrawn than factor 1.
4. Characteristics of angry, provocative, complaining behavior.
5. Presence of somatic complaints, including dizzy spells and constipation.
6. Characteristics which sound like an "organic" syndrome: impairment of memory, confusion, inability to concentrate, and limited and repetitive thought content.
7. Characteristics of agitation, tremulousness, and restlessness.
8. Characteristics of rigidity and psychomotor retardation.
9. Presence of somatic symptoms such as dry skin and hair, along with minor abnormalities detectable on physical examination.
10. Characteristics of ingratiating behavior: attempting to help patients and staff, and expressing appreciation for the interest of the staff and the facilities of the hospital.

There were no significant correlations between the two sets of factors from the two trait lists. Grinker et al. developed four factor patterns by combining the factors of both trait lists as follows:

a. Feelings: dismal, hopeless, loss of self-esteem, slight guilt feelings.
   Behavior: isolated, withdrawn, apathetic, speech and thinking slowed, with some cognitive disturbances.
b. Feelings: hopeless with low self-esteem, considerable guilt feelings, high anxiety.
   Behavior: agitation and clinging demands for attention.
c. Feelings: abandonment and loss of love.
   Behavior: agitated, demanding, hypochondriacal.
d. Feelings: gloom, hopelessness, and anxiety.
   Behavior: demanding, angry, provocative.

In addition to the work of Grinker and his group, there have been other studies using factor analysis of depressive behaviors. Mendels (1970) reviews these studies for communality of findings. These studies report agreement on characterizing patients with endogenous (nonreactive) depression as being retarded, lacking in reactivity to environmental changes, showing a loss of interest in life, having bodily symptoms, lacking a precipitating stress, and having middle-of-night insomnia. In contrast to the person with clearly reactive depressions, the individual labeled as depressed endogenously was more likely to be older, to have a history of previous episodes, to show weight loss, to have early-morning awakening, to show self-reproach or guilt, to have suicidal thoughts or attempts, to be clear of "hysterical" symptoms, and to perceive his depression as qualitatively different from ordinary sadness or downcast spirits.

Thus, the factor analytic studies as well as the multitude of observations of depressed individuals indicate that depression comprises very specific behaviors, not the kind of totality often attributed to it. Seitz (1970) found intercorrelations between psychological tests of depression but not between such measures and psychiatric ratings. Weckowicz, Cropley, and Muir (1971), Paykel (1971), and Kendell (1969) are among authors who have found the factorial structure of depressive symptoms to be complex, hard to replicate, and less than satisfactory. Kendell (1969, p. 215) summarizes the situation: "So far these statistical techniques have not fulfilled the hopes that were placed in them, partly because of their inherent limitations, possibly also because the clearly defined entities we are searching for do not exist."

Friedman (1964) reports a study that questions the notion that the severely depressed patient's gross social impairment also affects his cognitive-perceptual functioning. Friedman selected a group of 55 patients of diagnostically "pure" depression: manic-depressive psychosis, depressed phase; agitated depression; and involutional psychosis. He did not include cases in which depression was associated with neuroses or schizophrenia. Friedman found that his 55 depressed patients when matched for age, sex, education, and intelligence with 65 normals were able to perform as well as the normals on a series of cognitive, perceptual, and psychomotor tests. This was despite the fact that they rated themselves significantly lower in their abilities.

Friedman concluded that the actual ability and performance during severe depression is not consistent with the patient's unrealistically low image of himself. His experience of helplessness is a subjective report rather than an objective reality. Friedman noted that the patient's response to most of the tasks was that of protest that he was too tired and incapable of performing. "If the examiner pleasantly ignored this or sympathized, and then proceeded with the test instructions, the patient would practically always cooperate and would appear to become quite involved and motivated to do well." (p. 243.) This is an excellent illustration of not maintaining the patient's complaining behavior by accepting it, but rather ignoring such verbalization and presenting the depressive with an alternative role involving accomplishment.

INVOLUTIONAL MELANCHOLIA

Involutional melancholia is a "disorder occurring in the involutional period and characterized by worry, anxiety, agitation, and severe insomnia. Feelings of guilt and somatic preoccupations are frequently present and may be of delusional proportions." (DSM-II, p. 36.)

Involutional melancholia is thus, to a large extent, diagnosed by exclusion. That is, it is distinguishable from the manic-depressive category by an absence of previous episodes. It differs from schizophrenia in that inappropriate mood characterizes the impairment of reality. Finally, it is not a psychotic-depressive reaction in that the depression is not a reaction to a specific life experience. "Opinion is divided as to whether this psychosis can be distinguished from the other affective disorders. It is therefore recommended that involutional patients not be given this diagnosis unless all other affective disorders have been ruled out." (p. 36.)

The term "involutional melancholia" is one that originally attributed depressions to changes in menopausal women. Evidence has not supported a biological (metabolic) causation. Rather it seems clear that social and emotional factors that may be associated with middle age are more important. The age range for involutional diagnoses has been from 35 to 65. These diagnoses are often rationalized at the lower age end as indicating an individual "approaching the menopause," at the other extreme as being the "delayed effect of the menopause." [2]

Nor is the presence or absence of previous depressive behavior a discriminating criterion. Usually the fact that an individual has not received a specific label previously in his life means that circumstances were not sufficient to bring the behavior to the attention of the labelers, or that reinforcing contingencies (stress or lack of it) were such as not to evoke the behavior. Whatever the case, the historical aspect of the involutional categorization does not appear to be a reliable or useful criterion.

Factor analytic studies fail to demonstrate clear-cut, unique behavior patterns for the involutional. Wittenborn and Baily (1952) investigated 20 patients diagnosed as involutional depressives. They factor-analyzed ratings of the patients on a set of 55 symptom rating scales. They found *no* general factor to indicate a consistent similarity among these patients. That is, the diagnosis of involutional psychosis had no consistent descriptive implications from patient to patient. The authors concluded that there is "no descriptive merit in the diagnosis of involutional psychosis even when supplemented with a secondary diagnosis."

A SOCIOPSYCHOLOGICAL FORMULATION

Severe depression does seem to occur with greater frequency in the middle years. This observation would gibe with economic, social, and physical changes in reinforcing stimuli. As individuals grow older and less able to perform physically, as reflexes slow down, as eyesight becomes less acute, as hearing decreases, as minor physical disabilities become more serious, these may elicit emotional reactions related to feelings of inadequacy and incompetence. Older people may have trouble finding suitable employment. Children may leave home and end the *raison d'être* of some marriages. In contemporary American society there is an emphasis on youth—witness the plethora of magazine articles and books claiming that life really does not end at 40 and that the individuals may have a few more useful years. There is an enormous barrage of commercials telling women how to keep a youthful appearance and delay the ravages of middle age.

The remarks made on depressive neurosis in Chapter 13 are pertinent here. Following the sociopsychological formulations used throughout this book, the patterns of behavior the person has learned no longer provide reinforcing consequences.[3] The person then emits alternative behaviors. Our culture recognizes a pattern of behavior designated as the depressed role. Because most people respond with kindness to the cues called depressed behavior, there well may be immediate reinforcement for emitting such behavior. The depressed role is

---

[2] Friedman (1964) found that his diagnostically pure depressed patients were almost exclusively over 40 and, in passing, questioned whether psychotic depression is not a condition almost exclusively of middle and old age. Winokur (1973) writes "From the current data menopause does not seem to be an important factor in precipitating an episode of affective disorder" (p. 93). Discussing a different source of life change, Bargilai and Davies (1972) found a post-partum depression in 2.7/1000 deliveries. The meaning of birth, motherhood, and the child was more important than the stress of parturition itself.

[3] Burton, in his *Anatomy of Melancholy* (1927 ed., p. 532), for example, noted, "A man dies as often as he loses his friends."

likely to become chronic when the person does not find alternative situations, acts, and objects for his affection. If depressed role enactments continue, most other people will become less responsive.[4] The effect over time is toward placing the person on an intermittent reinforcement schedule resistant to extinction. The specific enactment (e.g., depressed rather than schizophrenic behavior) is a function of the individual's prior circumstances such as what types of behavior he has observed. It is also a function of the types of behavior others around him recognize as calling forth complementary role enactments from them.

Some of the circumstances which may precede depression are universal. People die in all societies, loved ones change; life can become less pleasant and less meaningful for many realistic reasons. How the individual "handles" these realistic difficulties is determined by the availability of social roles. For example, faced with such dilemmas, one individual may resort to the role of an over-conscientious and hard worker; another may attempt self destruction; and a third may emit role behaviors of the "depressed person."

It was formerly thought that depression was rare among the people of "simpler civilizations." This concept was based in part on the idea that a more advanced civilization was required to institutionalize rituals and roles for realistic situations such as the death of a loved one, e.g., the role of the bereaved. The elaborate funeral rituals found in California (Bowman, 1959; Mitford, 1963; Waugh, 1948) exemplify what can happen in an advanced Western society.

However, anthropological studies such as that of Field (1960) in Ghana demonstrated that depressed role behaviors are frequent

---

[4] And Burton (idem, p. 535) also wrote, "Tis unbecoming idly to mourn the dead . . . we should not dwell too long upon our passions, to be desperately sad, immoderate grievers, to let them tyranize, there's an art of not being too unhappy, a medium to be kept: We do not . . . forbid men to grieve, but to grieve overmuch."

---

in disintegrating, individually anarchistic societies, no matter how primitive. He cites an example of a societally sanctioned social role of depression available to women in the Ashanti religion. "Depressed" women in large numbers travel to religious shrines and hurl wild accusations of witchcraft against themselves. Field interprets this to mean that the self-accusation of witchcraft provides justification for feelings of failure and worthlessness. The Ashanti woman raises a large family with great care, is an excellent housekeeper and a good businesswoman. When she grows older, however, her husband often takes a younger bride to whom he gives his affection and possessions. This turnabout is appropriate in the culture, and there is little the wife can do about it. Her previous behaviors are no longer reinforced. A new role may now be enacted: the self-abnegation involved in confessing that she has been a witch all along. In effect she is saying that she has become useless because she has always been evil and consequently deserves her present fate of being hated and rejected. She is then ready to be cured and to step into her next role, that of discarded wife.

In our society, unfortunately, there is emphasis that failure is due to the individual himself. Under these conditions, and without alternative specification of what to do, the depressive role may be enacted. The social paradox involved in observing depression is emphasized by Beck (1967) in pointing out the "astonishing contrast between the depressed person's image of himself and the objective facts. A wealthy man moans that he doesn't have the financial resources to feed his children. A widely acclaimed beauty begs for plastic surgery in the belief that she is ugly. An eminent physicist berates himself 'for being stupid.'" (p. 3.)

Interpreting depression in terms of social determinants, Becker points out that "In our culture we are familiar with the person who lives his life for the wishes of his parents and becomes depressed when they die and he has reached the age of 40 or 50. He has lost the only audience for whom the plot in which he was performing was valid. He is left in the hopeless despair of the actor who knows only one set of lines and loses the one audience who wants to hear it." (1964, p. 127.)

Volkart (1957) points out how our society trains people to "love, honor and obey" only a few others. When death or some other circumstance leaves the loyal person without his major source of reinforcement and he seeks professional help, "the psychiatrist is apt to hold a microscope to his body chemistry or measure his saliva." Volkart puts the problem as follows: "Any culture which, in the name of mental health, encourages extreme and exclusive emotional investments by one person in a selected few others, but which does not provide suitable outlets and alternatives for the inevitable bereavement, is simply altering the conditions of, and perhaps postponing, sound mental health. It may, in the vernacular, be building persons up for a big letdown by exacerbating vulnerability." (Volkart, 1957, p. 304.) Becker summarizes the view of a society which fosters a restricted range of interpersonal reinforcement and labels as ill any realistic reaction to societal events as follows:

In other words, in our culture we champion limited horizons—a limited range of objects—and call people "mentally ill" when they suffer its effects. We make no provision for sustaining meaning when the bottom drops out of someone's life. When a woman's children marry, when the mirror begins to reflect the gradual and irrevocable loss of her charm, her performance as a responsible person, culturally desirable, is over. She may find herself left with no part to play, as early as her late 30's—worth nothing to justify and sustain her identity. Since this utter subversion of meaning usually coincides with menopause, psychiatry has labeled the depression that may occur "involutional depression." Medical psychiatry has only recently come to focus on social role; clinically, it was easier to imagine that the depression is somehow due to bodily changes. Or, the psychoanalytic theory might see this as a pampered self-pity over the imagined loss of sexual capacity, over the inevitable diminution of instinctual vigor. [1964, p. 128.]

One of the most interesting phenomena in the field of abnormal behavior in recent years has been a marked decrease in the giving of the manic-depressive label to individuals. This decrease is attested to from reports based on first admissions to hospitals all over the United States. For example, the incidence of first hospital admissions of manic-depressive psychoses in New York State decreased from 13.5 percent of all admissions in 1928 to 3.8 percent in 1947. (Arieti, 1959.)

That manic-depressive psychosis labels are generally being replaced by schizophrenia seems quite clear. The explanation is not as clear. A possible one is that the theoretical orientation of the labelers may change, so that different behaviors may be deemed relevant and a new set of labels may become popular. This possibility is far from new and exemplifies the problems of psychiatric diagnosis.

Shakow (1968, p. 120), talking of the late 1920's, reports:

We were impressed . . . with the differences between the classification of the Boston State Hospital and those made at Worcester. Of the 57 cases diagnosed dementia praecox at the Boston Psychopathic Hospital, the Boston State Hospital called only 12 per cent dementia praecox, whereas of the 72 diagnosed dementia praecox at Boston Psychopathic Hospital, at Worcester we called 37 per cent dementia praecox. On the other hand, of the 134 cases diagnosed by the Boston Psychopathic Hospital as manic-depressive the Boston State Hospital placed over 28 per cent in this category, whereas of the 20 sent to Worcester State Hospital so diagnosed, only 10 per cent were called manic-depressive. The wide variation between these two diagnostic categories made at the two hospitals—1 to 3 and 3 to 1—were, in part, an outgrowth of the psychiatric orientations of their respective superintendents. Dr. May of Boston State Hospital . . . was strongly influenced by Kraepelin's theory of dementia praecox and therefore included in this category only those cases who had a poor prognosis. The attitude of Dr. Bryan at the Worcester State Hospital was, conversely, more progressive. He recognized, for instance, the catatonic subtype as a division of dementia praecox having a generally good prognosis. At the Boston State Hospital, under the influence of Dr. May, this type was, on the contrary, often labeled "manic-depressive." The professional attitudes of these men were reflected in the different number of patients at the two institutions falling into each of these groups.

It is also conceivable that the actual incidence of manic-depressive behaviors has decreased. If this is so, the reason may lie in sociocultural changes during this period. One interesting hypothesis is offered by Arieti (1959), who relates manic-depressive behaviors to Reisman, Glazer, and Denny's (1950) notion of inner-directed personality (one with deeply felt concepts of responsibility, duty, guilt, and punishment) and the frequency of such people in contemporary culture. Arieti argues that as the inner-directed personality became less frequent, the associated manic-depressive behaviors became less frequent. Eaton and Weil's (1955) study of the Hutterites may be cited as additional evidence for this relationship. The Hutterites are a group of people of German ancestry who settled in the mountain states of the U.S. and in Canada. Their life, very much concerned with religion, fits most of the criteria for an inner-directed society. Eaton and Weil labeled 39 of the 8,542 Hutterites as manic-depressives and only 9 as schizophrenic. The incidence of manic-depressive behaviors far outweighs schizophrenia, the reverse of the ratio generally found in the United States. Linsky (1969) related rate of depression across communities to *aspirations* blocked by low opportunity rather than low opportunity alone.

A major effort to integrate clinical, experimental, genetic, biochemical, and neurophysiological data is offered by Akiskal and McKinney (1973). They argue that depression in animals is sufficiently analogous to human depression that studies of depression in animals can be generalized to human behavior. They note that animal models simulate some of the central features of clinical depression such as helplessness and object loss. After reviewing a wide number of studies, including investigations based on humans and primates (e.g., Harlow) by investigators ranging from Spitz and Bowlby to Beck, Seligman, and Lewinsohn, Akiskal and McKinney arrive at the following conclusion aimed at a integrative, unifying hypothesis:

In summary, chronic aversive stimulation, loss of reinforcement, and loss of control over reinforcement are overlapping concepts that describe a state of hopelessness and helplessness deriving from interpersonal relations. A variety of techniques, deriving from both classical and instrumental conditioning, could be utilized to alleviate such depressive states, but apparently these techniques are useful in the milder, so-called neurotic, depressions and that more severe depressions usually require antidepressant drugs or electroconvulsive therapy. . . . There are two possible explanations for this phenomenon: (i) no matter what interpersonal factors elicit or maintain depressive behaviors, once these behaviors assume severe proportions they become biologically autonomous—the stage of melancholia . . . and, consequently, require somatic therapies; (ii) severe depressions have underlying biochemical predispositions and, therefore, would not respond to any appreciable degree to verbal therapy.

The advantage of such an approach is that it covers all current sets of hypotheses as to the nature and treatment of depression, including some which may be erroneous.

TREATMENT OF DEPRESSION

The foregoing material suggests the treatment of changing depressed role enactments by not responding to them and by firmly and consistently providing opportunities and reinforcement for behaviors.

The following case description illustrates how the apparently most "depressed" of individuals may be responsive to being placed in a social role "demanding" behavior other than that characteristic of the depressed role:

> Let me describe a personal experience I had with Alfred Adler, as another example of this relationship. I had a depressed senile patient in a sanitarium near Vienna. At that time, we had no shock treatments and the depressed, melancholic patients remained in their condition. There was nothing one could do for them. I wanted to get a particular man out of the hospital with a person to take care of him, but the family was opposed to it, so I called Adler for a consultation. He came, and I remember it well—the patient was sitting in front of him, and the residents, the psychiatrists, the nurses, in a big circle around him—and Adler began to interview the man, asking his name, and how he felt. The patient in his very slow way began to answer. Adler didn't wait for the answer, but went on to the next question, and the patient began again to answer very slowly. Again, Adler was not long in asking him a third question. I became quite embarrassed. After all, this was my teacher—I was proud of him. I thought, "Doesn't this man know how to conduct a psychiatric interview? How can he have an interview with a depressed melancholic patient if he doesn't wait to hear what he has to say?" But Adler kept on like that, and you can imagine that nothing came out of the patient because after two or three words, Adler would ask the next question. I couldn't understand what he was doing, when suddenly the patient, who wanted to say something, began to talk fast. Nobody had thought about the possibility that the melancholic patient could talk fast if he really wanted to. But, that was Adler . . . the fundamental belief that it was up to the patient to do things. . . . [Dreikurs, 1961, pp. 85–86.]

Current treatment procedures for the affective disorders include various drug, shock, and milieu psychotherapies. As appropriate, tranquilizers (for "mania") and energizers, e.g., Tofranil (for depression), are used with varying degrees of success. There seems to be considerable agreement among therapists that electroshock (EST) is the "treatment of choice" with depressed patients. Although there is no acceptable rationale as to why it works, there is evidence that it does work. For example, studies of depressed patients receiving EST report improvement rates 80 percent (Kalinowsky and Hoch, 1946, 1961), 97 percent (improved or "recovered," Thomas, 1954), and 65 percent (about the same percentage as a control group but improving approximately 60 percent faster) (Huston and Locher, 1948).

At present, one drug, lithium carbonate, has emerged as a major factor in the treatment of manic depressive behaviors. The early studies which appear to demonstrate the usefulness of this drug were subsequently severely criticized on methodological grounds (Blackwell and Shepard, 1968). In 1968 the Veterans Administration and the National Institute of Mental Health organized a multihospital collaborative project on lithium carbonate therapy of affective disorders. Prien et al. (1973) report the results of this study. They found that:

> In an 18 hospital study, 205 patients hospitalized with a diagnosis of manic-depressive illness, manic type, were treated upon discharge with lithium carbonate or placebo for a two-year period. Lithium carbonate was significantly more effective than placebo in preventing relapses (i.e., affective episodes severe enough to require hospitalization or use of nonstudy drugs.) The difference in treatment outcome between lithium carbonate and placebo was due mainly to the lower incidence of manic relapses on lithium carbonate. Patients on lithium carbonate also had a lower incidence of depressive relapses than patients on placebo but the limited incidence of severe depression in this sample makes it difficult to draw any conclusions regarding the prophylactic efficacy of lithium carbonate in depressive illness. The results from this trial coupled with those from other studies indicate that lithium carbonate combined with regular clinical appraisals is a safe and effective

treatment for preventing relapse in manic-depressive illness. [p. 337.]

The authors note that their study as well as the four other studies (Baastrup, 1964; Coppen et al., 1971; Fieve, 1972; and Hullen et al., 1972) all found lithium to be more effective than a placebo. "Whether it is more effective than other psychopharmacologic treatments remains to be answered." (p. 341.)

Thus far no specific therapeutic technique has been developed by the behavior therapist for the treatment of depression. Rather, the specific behaviors which may be subsumed under depression are approached individually and, as illustrated in Chapter 13, are treated in terms of the realities of the specific case. This is very consistent with the theory and practice of Lewinsohn and his colleagues (e.g., Lewinsohn, Weinstein, and Alper, 1970) who emphasize overcoming lack of social skills that result in reduced social support. (See also Lewinsohn, Lobitz, and Wilson, 1973; Todd, 1972; Reisinger, 1972; Moss and Boren, 1972; Wolpe, 1970; Lewinsohn and Atwood, 1969; Seitz, 1971a, 1971b; and Sims and Lazarus, 1973.)

SUMMARY

This chapter has focused upon the affective reactions, particularly mania and depression. We have offered a history of the development of the concepts and their social usage. A major problem in this area, for both the professional and the general public is to be able to distinguish the various labels of "depression" from each other. We have also described some of the theories as to the causes of depression. As with all other disorders, the specifics of treatment follow from the model of causation. The evidence for the exclusive usefulness of any one model, be it genetic, biochemical, psychoanalytic, behavioral, or social, is presently not very powerful. We are still in the early stages of understanding severely depressed behavior and quite possibly even agreeing as to what its characteristics are.

personality disorders with particular reference to paranoid behavior

20

Every adjective—beautiful, psychotic, intelligent, suspicious—implies a continuum from much to little. This chapter will be devoted to a category, personality disorder, that may best be considered as a middle ground between the clear and "obvious" behavioral patterns previously described and variation within "normal" and socially acceptable limits. The subcategories of paranoid, cyclothymic, inadequate, and schizoid personality are akin to psychotic behaviors; obsessive-compulsive, hysterical, and asthenic personality are akin to neurotic behaviors; explosive, antisocial, and passive-aggressive personality introduce patterns of behavior that categorize individuals who pose problems for themselves or others, but who do not conform to the major categories of psychosis, neurosis, brain injury, retardation, etc.

DSM-II (pp. 41–42) notes that "This group of disorders is characterized by deeply ingrained maladaptive patterns of behavior that are perceptibly different in quality from psychotic and neurotic symptoms. Generally, these are life-long patterns, often recognizable by the time of adolescence or earlier."

There have been major changes in this category from DSM-I, which defined personality disorders as follows: "These disorders are characterized by developmental defects or pathological trends in the personality structure, with minimal subjective anxiety, and little or no sense of distress. In most instances, the disorder is manifested by a lifelong pattern of action or behavior, rather than by mental or emotional symptoms." (p. 34.) DSM-I divided the personality disorders into three major subgroups with special-symptom reactions ("This category is useful in occasional situations where a specific symptom is the single outstanding expression of the psychopathology." (DSM-I, p. 39)) (see Chapter 15) as an "additional grouping for flexibility in diagnosis." (DSM-I, p. 34.)

The three main divisions of personality disorders in DSM-I were personality pattern disturbance, personality trait disturbance, and sociopathic personality disturbance. "The personality pattern disturbances are considered deep-seated disturbances, with little room for regression [other than to psychosis—ed.]. Personality trait disturbances and sociopathic personality disturbances under stress may, at times, regress to a lower level of personality organization and function without development of psychosis." (DSM-I, pp. 34–35.) What this lower level is was not specified.

The DSM-I personality pattern disturbances were four in number—inadequate, schizoid, cyclothymic, and paranoid. They are borderline to psychosis and "can rarely if ever be altered in their inherent structures by any form of therapy." (DSM-I, p. 35.)

The second main grouping in DSM-I was personality trait disturbance, which applied "to individuals who are unable to maintain their emotional equilibrium and independence under minor or major stress because of disturbances in emotional development." (DSM-I, p. 36.) Neurotic features such as anxiety, conversion, and phobia should be relatively insignificant and basic personality maldevelopment (undefined) is the major feature—presumably, fixations and/or regression to preoedipal psychosexual levels. There were three specified trait disturbances, compulsive personality, emotionally unstable personality, and passive-aggressive personality. The latter two are of particular interest since they may shed light, respectively, on explosive and passive-aggressive personality as used in DSM-II.

The third main division of personality disorders in DSM-I was that of sociopathic personality disturbance: "Individuals to be placed in this category are ill primarily in terms of society and conformity with the prevailing cultural milieu, and not only in terms of personal discomfort and relations with other individuals." (DSM-I, p. 38.) The subcategories included antisocial reaction, dyssocial reaction, sexual deviation, and addiction. In DSM-II, only the first remains as a personality disorder, per se, the second, dyssocial, being now considered a "condition without manifest psychiatric disorder," and the last two being given separate status as "certain other nonpsychotic mental disorders."

Discussion

A first aspect of the DSM-II definition of personality disorders is that the patterns are "deeply ingrained" and of long duration. DSM-I, following psychoanalytic formulations, indicates that they are due to personality development and structure.

A second aspect noted by DSM-II is that the patterns of behavior of these people are "perceptibly different" from neurosis, psychosis, etc. It does not, however, indicate in what way they are different. DSM-I gives an answer: where anxiety and subjective distress are key elements, particularly in neurosis, they are supposedly absent in the personality disorders. (We say "supposedly" since psychological test measures do not uphold the assertion—see, for example, Zimet and Brackbill, 1956; Ullmann and Hunrichs, 1958.) The concept of a character disorder, associated with a pregenital psychosexual developmental stage—for example, anal personality (see Chapter 8 on psychoanalysis)—developed in response to clinical observation of people who entered analysis but did not display classic neurotic features such as anxiety, and were difficult to change. In a sociological context, DSM-I grew out of the military experience in the Second World War, in which there was a need to account for (i.e., label) for all cases, but in which traditional categories covered only 10 percent of the instances (DSM-I, p. vi).

PARANOID BEHAVIOR

Among the subcategories of personality disorder is paranoid personality. We will devote the major portion of this chapter to this topic because the concept of paranoia has received considerable clinical and theoretical consideration, and may be taken as an example of different theoretical approaches.

The term "paranoia" comes from Greek, meaning beside or beyond reason. This accurately touches the major behavior involved: a false belief not susceptible to logical argument. The word has been used at least since the second century A.D. Although Lewis (1970) notes that paranoia was not a technical term from the time of the Greeks till the eighteenth century, in 1621 Burton wrote in the *The Anatomy of Melancholy:*

. . . he thinks every man observes him, aims at him, derides him, owes him malice. Most part *they are afraid they are bewitched, possessed, or poisoned by their enemies,* and sometimes they suspect their nearest friends . . . *Suspicion* and *jealousy* are general symptoms: they are commonly distrustful, timorous, apt to mistake, and amplify, testy, pettish, peevish, and ready to snarl upon every small occasion, with their greatest friends, and without a cause, given or not given, it will be to their offense. If they speak in jest, he takes it in good earnest. If they be not saluted, invited, consulted with, called to counsel, etc., or that any respect, small compliment, or ceremony be omitted, they think themselves neglected and contemned: for a time that tortures them. If two talk together, discourse, whisper, jest, or tell a tale in general, he thinks presently they mean him, applies all to himself. Or if they talk with him, he is ready to misconstrue every word they speak, and interpret it to the worst; he cannot endure any man to look steadily on him, speak to him almost, laugh, jest, or be familiar, or hem or point, cough, or spit, or make a noise sometimes, etc. He thinks they laugh or point at him, or do it in disgrace of him, circumvent him, contemn him . . . He works upon it, and long after this false conceit of an abuse troubles him. [Burton, 1927 edition, pp. 332–33.]

Paranoid behavior, like depression, is a major element in a number of diagnostic categories: the paranoid type of schizophrenic, the categories of psychosis called paranoid states (i.e., paranoia and involutional paranoid state), and the nonpsychotic paranoid personality. Clinical observation indicates that paranoid behavior may occur in cases with brain damage such as paresis and senility, and may, as all other patterns of abnormal behavior, be observed in transient situational maladjustments.

The behaviors likely to be designated paranoid range from sensitiveness to slights; cautiousness; rigid adherence to rules; social isolation; overcriticism of others; and self-righteousness; to overt delusions of persecution, influence, grandiosity, and reference. The delusion of *persecution* is usually considered the prototypical behavior. The person believes that other people are trying to destroy him; they may endeavor to *influence* him, either through bizarre means such as radio waves and night-time attacks or by keeping information from him and spreading malicious gossip about him. A reason for such influence on the part of others is their jealousy of him; hence, by implication, he is particularly important. This is the delusion of *grandiosity*. To the extent that the person called paranoid has "insight" into the workings of other people that the remainder of the population does not have, he is superior: like the college professor, he knows something other people do not and are not intelligent enough to grasp. The person may be on the alert for attacks and thus misinterpret aspects of his environment. He may manifest delusions of *reference* and give a personal meaning to events that are fortuitous or do not particularly apply to him.

Other behaviors which have been noted in connection with the label "paranoid" but which have not been assigned as central a position as the delusions just mentioned are unusual beliefs dealing with religion, politics, legal processes, and sex. Eventually, any aspect of social life may be the focus of beliefs considered exaggerated if not downright false: there are health nuts, academic-freedom nuts, and even some people who think psychology is interesting.

PARANOID STATES

The paranoid states are categorized in DSM-II (p. 37) as "psychoses": "These are psychotic disorders in which a delusion, generally persecutory or grandiose, is the essential abnormality. Disturbances in mood, behavior and thinking (including hallucinations) are derived from this delusion. This distinguishes paranoid states from the affective psychoses and schizophrenias, in which mood and thought disorders, respectively, are the central abnormalities." DSM-I (p. 28) noted that these patterns are "ordinarily without hallucinations. The emotional responses and behavior are consistent with the ideas held. Intelligence is well preserved."

Paranoia is defined in DSM-II (p. 38) as follows: "This extremely rare condition is characterized by gradual development of an intricate, complex, and elaborate paranoid system based on and often proceeding logically from misinterpretation of an actual event. Frequently the patient considers himself endowed with unique and superior ability. In spite of a chronic course, the condition does not seem to interfere with the rest of the patient's thinking and personality." The definition of this category is nearly identical with that of DSM-I. DSM-I, however, had a second category, that of paranoid state, likely to be of relatively short duration, in which the systematization observed in paranoia was lacking, while the fragmentation and deterioration observed with people called schizophrenic was also lacking. DSM-II does not have this category but has one called involutional paranoid state, "characterized by delusion formation with onset in the involutional period" but "absence of conspicuous thought disorders typical of schizophrenia." (DSM-II, p. 38.) Finally, DSM-II has a category of *other paranoid state* "for paranoid psychotic reactions not classified earlier." (DSM-II, p. 38.) The nonpsychotic *paranoid personality* is "characterized by hypersensitivity, rigidity, unwarranted suspicion, jealousy, envy, excessive self-importance, and a tendency to blame others and ascribe evil motives to them. These characteristics often interfere with the patient's ability to maintain satisfactory interpersonal relations. Of course, the presence of suspicion of itself does not justify this diagnosis, since the suspicion may be warranted in some instances." (DSM-II, p. 42.)

The only symptom in this category is that of paranoia, specifically a delusion or false belief. Although the individual is psychotic, the behaviors which would lead to a schizophrenic diagnosis are not manifest. The *paranoid states* are distinguished from schizophrenia by the narrowness of their distortions of reality and by the absence of other psychotic symptoms. As the reader will remember, psychoses involve gross impairment of the "capacity to meet the ordinary demands of life." (DSM-II, p. 23.)

It is difficult to conceive of a psychotic, especially one with delusions, who would not manifest some aspect of schizophrenia. Clinically, such cases are extremely difficult to find. Sullivan (1956) puts it this way:

Yet the fact is that every person who gets lost in the schizophrenic morasses has paranoid feelings and can be led to express paranoid content at times; and, on the other hand, every paranoid person that I have encountered has in his history a period of schizophrenic content . . . But how few people ever approach the absolute pole of pure paranoia may be suggested by the fact that out of, I suppose, fully three thousand veteran cases with which I had some contact in one of the hospitals where I have worked, only one even raised the diagnostic problem of whether he might be a pure paranoid.

Lewis (1970, p. 5), discussing the "paranoia question," writes that, "In a carefully reasoned paper in 1912, he (Kraepelin) considered whether, in view of its shabby record, paranoia had better be dropped altogether as a legitimate category."

FORMULATIONS OF PARANOIA

There have been three pivotal formulations of paranoia: those of Freud (1915, 1922), Cameron (1959, 1967), and Lemert (1962). Each has had important consequences for the conceptualization and treatment of paranoia.

Freud's Formulation

Freud made two contributions. The first was a formulation of paranoid behaviors in terms of a *defense mechanism* that is ascribed to normal people and, in exaggerated form, to neurotics and psychotics. This mechanism is *projection*, the attribution of one's own unacceptable traits to another person. The second aspect of Freud's work on paranoia was the hypothesis, since questioned by psychoanalysts as well as other workers, that paranoid projection necessarily involves unacceptable and unsublimated homosexual impulses. Freud's major formulation of paranoia occurred in his analysis of an autobiography written by Daniel Paul Schreber, *Memoirs of My Nervous Illness*. "Although Freud had no contact with Schreber, who was the patient of the famous neurologist Flechsig, he studied Schreber's autobiography and made a masterful analysis of its paranoid contents. Freud's conclusions from this study and from his own and his colleagues' experiences was that paranoid reactions and homosexuality were inseparable." (Cameron, 1967, p. 667.) Aside from failure of clinical evidence to support Freud's hypothesis, Freud has been criticized because Schreber was quite overtly schizophrenic and thus far from a "pure" paranoid.

Freud did report on paranoid patients with whom he had direct contact. In a 1922 essay on "certain neurotic mechanisms in jealousy, paranoia and homosexuality," Freud wrote: "When I saw him he was still subject only to clearly defined attacks, which lasted for several days and, curiously enough, regularly appeared on the day following an act of intercourse [with his wife] which was, incidentally, satisfying to both of them. The inference is justified that after every satiation of the heterosexual libido the homosexual component, likewise stimulated by the act, forced for itself an outlet in the attack of jealousy." (p. 235.)

The use of the term "homosexual" to describe a man who obtains heterosexual gratification with his wife and with other women and who has emitted no overt adult homosexual act differs from contemporary usage such as that of Kinsey (see Chapter 21). It might be possible to hypothesize, both generally and from the few details Freud presents, that the man was attracted to his wife and was upset when she emitted in the presence of other men those cues which successfully aroused him.

Freud continues (p. 235): "His abnormality really reduced itself to this, that he watched his wife's unconscious mind much more closely and then regarded it as far more important than anyone else would have thought of doing." The same observation might be applied to the behavior of Freud vis-à-vis his patient. In similar fashion, in his 1915 paper "A case of paranoia running counter to the psychoanalytical theory of the disease" (pp. 150–61), one may observe a normal man (Freud) searching for information which will maintain a specialized view of the world. The two points to be made by these references are that the data on which Freud based his theory are skimpy and that much of the behavior of the paranoid lies well within the realm of normal, appropriate, and socially acceptable activity.

Cameron's Formulation

Cameron's concept of the paranoid pseudocommunity represents a major step forward in the formulation of paranoid behavior. Cameron hypothesizes the existence of a threat or stress and a great likelihood that the person involved has had a lifelong pattern of finding fault with everyone but himself. It is difficult to reason with such a person, who finds himself isolated and estranged at the very moment when he most needs someone to confide in and to give him a more balanced view of a situation. Having no one whom he can trust, he may withdraw socially and emotionally. Rather than change his false beliefs and his mode of approach to situations, he reconstructs the realities around him to fit his views. He is therefore not subjected to contradictory information which a close friend might provide. Because his own behavior may increase the threat, the person is indeed in a difficult situation; and as people in difficult, threatening situations often do, he becomes watchful, uneasy, puzzled, and, by searching for it, finds further confirmatory evidence of threat.

Delusions of reference, the belief that others are paying special attention to him, laughing at him, or disturbing his work and home situation, develop as minor everyday frustrations are reinterpreted. The individual may become actively suspicious and seek causes for his difficult interpersonal situation. If he tells someone else about his ideas, he is likely to find that the other person disagrees with him. He may interpret such behavior as meaning that other people do not understand him or even that they are part of the general conspiracy of people and events against him.

The person may question why this should occur. Many puzzles are solved when a false belief makes sense of the prior confused situation. The false belief helps assimilate many experiences which were previously contradictory. It does so, however, at the expense of accuracy and long-term interpersonal adjustment. Given the power and effectiveness of the organizing belief, there develops a further belief in a group of "them" who plot against the person. Because "they" do not really exist in the manner the paranoid believes, he is living in a "pseudo-community." The belief is considered false because it is based on evidence that seems inadequate, contradictory, and invalid to the normal person or the assessing mental health professional.

The paranoid's activities are ones which would be considered rational for any person who actually was threatened or persecuted. Running throughout Cameron's formulation is the thread of the person's increasing isolation from others, both as an effect and as a further cause for an inability to see things from other people's point of view. There is a reasonable and inexorable progression in the development of the behavior, a progression which when sublime is called Greek drama and when mundane is called shaping.

Lemert's Formulation

A further step forward in the formulation of paranoid behavior was made by Lemert (1962), who argued that the individual's suspiciousness might be a *realistic* response to the situation. Rather than saying that the paranoid construes the world as if the "others" were against him, Lemert introduces evidence that the world may indeed be against the individual. The feelings that he is being watched, that he is being specially treated, that other people are against him *may be true.* Whether it is because the individual is difficult to get along with, differs from others in some manner, or is placed by chance in a situation where reinforcement contingencies are sparse or suddenly altered, he may emit behaviors which are aversive to others. He may seem abrupt, lacking in sensitivity, and overly aggressive. These behaviors may be realistic responses made in order to obtain clear overt responses from others and hence establish what the situation really is. For example, many paranoids are litigious and seek public trials or written documentation so that they can hold other people to their words at later times. If a person needs to find solid evidence that others are trying subtly to exclude him or to deprive him of his job, this sort of behavior is eminently realistic.

Lemert thus shifts the spotlight away from the individual in isolation to an investigation of *both* the paranoid and the other people around him. Lemert indicates that calling a person paranoid (or mentally ill) permits others to disregard their social obligations to him, to isolate him from the mainstream of information and responsibility, or to remove him from the scene by psychiatric hospitalization. The question remains, however, why people should pick on one particular individual. Lemert hypothesizes that there are frequently genuine issues centering around differences of opinion. In such situations, or in situations involving a sudden change in the environment caused by the death of relatives, loss of position, loss of professional certification, failure to be promoted, age, or physiological life-cycle changes, there may indeed occur threats to the person's status which he endeavors to ameliorate in the only ways he knows. Unfortunately, he may do so in a manner disruptive to others.

Lemert has a phrase which excellently describes the pressures on the individual. He says that the paranoid often may have the feeling of having the status of a *stranger on trial* in each new group he enters. That is, he seems to have been deprived of his prior sources of reinforcement and modes of adaptation and thus feels he must prove himself in each new situation. Such an individual may be very difficult for others to adjust to. He may act in a manner contrary to the way they accept as appropriate. The observers then may employ different methods to avoid taking him or their obligations to him seriously. They may develop what is, in fact, a pseudo-community as they are falsely polite or cooperative.

In a formal organization the individual may indeed be watched by others, who develop a network around him, making sure that they gather together when he is not present, shift the conversation when he approaches, start collecting evidence against him, or withhold information from him. In some instances, as Lemert points out, the individual may be placed under actual surveillance, and people, on police initiative or on their own, may watch his home, seeking new signs of deviation. There is a crystallization of the rationale for official action as the people in power positions observe the watched individual and seek further data to maintain or to document their viewpoint.[1]

Lemert portrays the individual called paranoid as one who indeed *is excluded* by others. If he has difficulty taking the viewpoint of the others, it is because others are indeed against him and have isolated him.

---

[1] In formal outline, this procedure is no different from the method by which a scientist develops his theories. He collects data, thinks about them, and develops various explanations to fit the facts. Eventually he develops hypotheses that integrate his information. He may then proceed to search the literature for further information consistent with his hypothesis, and look for reasons why information that does not fit with his theory is incorrect, inappropriate, or spurious. Finally, he may devise experiments to create additional information.

The concepts and formulations presented by Lemert are beautifully illustrated in a volume by Mrs. E. P. W. Packard (1875) called *Modern Persecution*. From 1861 through 1863, Mrs. Packard was a patient at an Illinois state psychiatric hospital. She was at first treated with great consideration and personal closeness by the superintendent of the asylum, Dr. McFarland. Her treatment, as she describes it, would be considered today as within the best traditions of the then declining moral treatment. After she had been in the hospital a number of months and been treated as a favorite and in a humane way for that era, she wrote Dr. McFarland a "reproof" for his abuse of patients. This reproof was 17 printed pages long. The quotations are presented here to ask the reader whether a woman who is a patient in a mental hospital and writes the superintendent (whom she reports as having treated her very well) in the following manner is paranoid or not.

The office of a Reprover is put upon me; and this to me, the hardest of all crosses, I bear for Christ's sake. Christ is now my only Master, and His will, not my own, is now my only choice. Oh! my Master, help me to do this duty under Thy special guidance and dictation. In Christ's own expressive language, I say, "Come let us reason together!" . . . Yes, in our insane asylums may be found the only real *sane* beings in the world, who, like the righteous of Sodom, are to become the world's saviors. . . . I have proof from a personal observation of your own actions . . . that you, sir, have exhibited more evidence of insanity on your part, than I have seen on any person since I entered this institution! and I think your insanity deserves and merits, imprisonment for life, in a state of extreme torture. . . . You have merited the reputation of a *Nero*, and that reputation you will have, unless you repent. . . . I feel called of God, and I shall obey this call, to expose your character by exposing your actions, to the light of 1861, unless you repent. I have ability—I have influence—I have friends—I have money—I have God's promised aid . . . to aid me in doing this. . . . And what is worse for you, sir, is the fact this is known—and known by those who are determined . . . to have your character exposed and your insanity punished. . . . I am also a monument for the age—a standing miracle, almost—of the power of faith to shield one from insanity. . . . Besides, Dr. McFarland, there are others in this institution, that have now become invulnerable. . . . They are protected by a spiritual power that is invincible, and all your skillfully worked machinery for making maniacs, cannot make maniacs of them. As your friend, I advise you to beware! There are more for us, than there are against us. You are the weaker party. . . . Remember, Dr. McFarland, this is your last chance. The fatal dyke is but a few moments ahead of you. Repentance or exposure! [Packard, 1875, pp. 120–37.]

Dr. McFarland had Mrs. Packard transferred to a more disturbed ward, and Mrs. Packard wondered if her reproof had offended him.

Knowing only the foregoing segment, most readers would agree that Mrs. Packard displayed poor judgment and false beliefs, including touches of delusions of persecution and grandeur.

Mrs. Packard's book was written a dozen years after her release from the hospital. One cannot say at that point whether she was abnormal as a result of her hospitalization or had been abnormal before being hospitalized. The entire tenor of the book is that Mrs. Packard is perfect and utterly loving. She is always right; she is always on a higher plane. She has excellent ability to reason logically, to take another person's statements out of context, and to make them appear illogical. She makes very acute and accurate observations on the treatment of mental patients at a period when moral treatment was changing to large institutional treatment. Even in 1875, when she was writing, there are elements of what might be called assertion of the predicate and grandiosity. In her dedication she lists her children and then writes, "Yes, it is for you, my jewels, I have lived—it is for you I have suffered the agonies of Gethsemane's garden—it is for you I have hung on this cross of crucifixion; and have been entombed three years in a living cemetery; and Oh! it is for your sakes that I hope to rise again, to find my maternal joys immortalized." (p. v.) In addition: "Yes, the mother has died. But she has risen again—the mother of her country—and her sons and daughters are—*The American Republic.*" (p. vi.)

Mrs. Packard was a minister's daughter who married a minister who had been her father's assistant. Both men were dominant and patriarchal. After some twenty years of marriage and six children, she developed theological views at variance with those of her husband. "In short, from my present standpoint, I cannot but believe that the doctrine of total depravity conflicts with the dictates of reason, common sense and the Bible. And the only offense my persecutors claim I have committed, is, that I have dared to be true to these my honest convictions, and to give utterance to these views in a Bible-class in Mateno, Kankakee County, Illinois." (pp. 33–34.)

Mrs. Packard's theological views would be accepted today as reasonable and not even particularly liberal. However, they did conflict with those of her husband and, given the milieu of an Illinois rural town in 1860, they were a source of great interest in the community. Attendance at the Bible class she taught increased, and there was some danger of the congregation splitting or, at least, of her husband losing his job. "These questions troubled both our teacher, Deacon Smith, and their pastor. They could not answer them satisfactorily to themselves or to the class; and it was to extricate themselves from this unpleasant dilemma that they at once agreed that this question was the result of a diseased brain, from whence it had emanated, and therefore it was unworthy of their consideration! Thus their reputation for intelligence and ability was placed beyond question, and the infallibility of their creed remained inviolate! And their *'poor afflicted Christian sister'* must be kindly cared for within the massive walls of a prison lest the diseased brain communicate its contagion to other brains, and then what will become of our creed! for we cannot afford to follow the example of this 'Man of God,' and sacrifice our wives and mothers to save our creed!" (p. xvii.)

In short, for whatever reason, difficulties with her husband, a more humane and liberal interpretation of the Bible, a desire for notoriety, or even a desire to embarrass her husband who might have been flirting with a younger member of the congregation, Mrs. Packard proceeded to discuss and give vent to ideas that were disturbing to her husband and disruptive of the congregation.

During the ensuing period, Mrs. Packard noticed meetings being held which she thought were concerned with her. These ideas might have been delusions of reference. However, it is safe to presume that pressure was put on her husband and that he discussed with others what to do ". . . in most earnest conversation, which was always carried on in a whisper whenever I was in hearing distance, and my presence seemed always to evoke manifestations of guilt on their part. I think the theme of conversation at these clandestine interviews was, my abduction and how it should be secured." (p. 44.)

It would seem reasonable that Mrs. Packard's behavior had led to what Lemert would call *exclusion*. In trying to deal with Mrs. Packard's disruptive behavior, it is reasonable to assume there were discussions about her, observations of her, and the devising of plans to which she was not privy. Mrs. Packard was taken to the state hospital at Jacksonville, Illinois. Her removal from her home, placement on the train, and the ensuing trip were, to say the least, dramatic. She refused to walk, since that might be interpreted as compliance with her husband's ideas. She had to be carried. A maximum of embarrassment to her husband was a not unforeseen result.

Mrs. Packard prayed in front of the sheriff for divine forgiveness for Mr. Packard; she writes, "In fact, if I know anything of my own heart, I do know that it did not cherish a single feeling of resentment towards him." Despite this disclaimer, Mrs. Packard's denigration of her husband is so complete that it is great literature.

The Illinois legal system at that time did not recognize a married woman as a separate entity. Once a woman was married, she was a dependent of her husband. As a result, a husband could place his wife in the state hospital. All that was required was the acceptance of the patient by the superintendent of the hospital. There was not the recourse to a legal body that would have been required for a male or for an unmarried woman. This law was eventually changed, a step for which Mrs. Packard was in part responsible.[2]

[2] Deutsch (1937, p. 307) writes of Mrs. Packard: "Her allegations created a national sensation and resulted in a wave of sentiment in favor of legislation providing better safeguards for persons 'accused' of insanity." A bill to this effect passed the Illinois legislature in 1867. Mrs. Packard lectured throughout the country, and her books sold well. It is possible that such vindication might have provided a realistic basis for some allegations that, in her 1875 volume, touch on grandiosity. The professional reader may also wish to contrast the following quotation with concepts such as those espoused by Szasz (1963, 1965a) and by the present authors: ". . . in 1865, she presented two bills for the consideration of a legislative committee. The first read: 'No person shall be regarded or treated as an insane person or a monomaniac simply for the expression of opinions, no matter how absurd these opinions may appear.' This bill, she explained with much reason, was intended to protect reformers and progressive thinkers from being adjudged insane merely because their ideals might seem too 'queer' to their more backward contemporaries. He second bill read as follows: 'No person shall be imprisoned and treated as an insane person except for *irregularities* of conduct, such as indicate that the individual is so lost to reason as to render him an unaccountable moral agent.' By these bills she hoped to establish general *behavior* rather than particular *opinions* as a criterion for determining insanity." (Deutsch, 1937, p. 424.) It was noted in Chapter 7 that each era reinterprets the past: Deutsch, writing in 1937, has glowing things to say about Dorothea Dix (see Chapter 8) and generally unfavorable things about the impact of Mrs. Packard, while the present authors reverse the procedure.

With this additional background, the reader may again want to consider whether Mrs. Packard should be categorized as paranoid or as normal. Her history illustrates various aspects of the situation described by Lemert. She was excluded by others who planned her final disposition. Her cause, both theological and legal, was just if one accepts the standards current a century later. Whether the cause or the effect of her experiences, however, the book written a dozen years later provides ample indications of unusual thinking. If the reader is not sure whether Mrs. Packard was paranoid or not, we have succeeded in illustrating the point we wished to make.

A SOCIOPSYCHOLOGICAL FORMULATION

The question that follows from formulations of paranoid reactions such as those of Cameron and Lemert is how an individual comes to hold a false belief or, eventually, any belief at all. The viewpoint manifested throughout this book is that there is no such thing as abnormal behavior per se, but rather that all behavior is understandable and appropriate given the person's history and current circumstances.

All that is known of a person's beliefs are his actions, i.e., what he says and what he does, both of which are operant behaviors. Therefore, the problem becomes to determine how a person develops behaviors which later disturb observers who are in positions of power to reward or punish.

The individual is always responding to his environment. His responses alter the behavior of other people; and because he has behaved and been reinforced in a particular manner, his own behavior is also altered. When a person's behavior is reinforced, his selection of stimuli from the environment is altered. He pays attention to what has been useful to him in the past. As a result of his experience he becomes sensitive to particular stimuli within the environment. An instance is the sensitivity of a mother to the crying of a child. Frequently she will respond to auditory cues which nonparents in the same room do not "hear."

One empirical example is found in studies noting a relatively greater likelihood of people diagnosed as paranoid reporting threatening material than reporting neutral material (Ullmann, 1958, 1962; Shannon, 1962). The problem, then, is a delineation of conditions under which a person is particularly sensitive to stimuli that others label as threatening.

Paranoia may be approached in terms of information and its evaluation. Isolation, difficulty in taking another person's viewpoint, and Cameron's pseudo-community may all be considered disruptions in information-gathering: the paranoid person traditionally has been considered one who thinks straight about a biased sample of information.

Frequently the person called paranoid displays an "exquisite" sensitivity, mulls over small details, and assigns meaning to them from which he draws inferences. The Russian biologist Zhores Medvedev was hospitalized for psychiatric observation against his will in the spring of 1970. The incident drew national and international attention and he was released. Writing about the experience, (Medvedev and Medvedev, 1972), he and his brother show great "sensitivity": the question is whether this sensitivity is warranted, and what other paths were open to them.

But it turned out that nobody from Kaluga had made inquiries about my son at his school. And so the whole thing began to look very odd. Why had it been arranged through the Chairman of the City Soviet and not directly through the school? Why were they so adamant about seeing the father and not the mother? And why not send for our son as well, who was after all already seventeen? . . .

"Excuse my curiosity," he went on, "but how is your brother's son doing at school? Twins often have similar problems with their children, you know."

These questions made it *completely obvious* [italics added] that the stranger was no educationalist but a psychiatrist who was cautiously trying to explore my family background. . . .

There could be no better bonus for Lysenko and his friends than the accusation that Zhores was mentally unbalanced. Perhaps the Lysenkoists had used their great influence in the Agricultural Section of the Central Committee to mount the whole operation; perhaps it was they who had arranged the details with the Kaluga authorities . . . I decided to accept this supposition as a working hypothesis and act accordingly. My companions agreed with me. [Medvedev and Medvedev, 1972, pp. 14, 18, 52,]

The core behavior of paranoia is the expression of beliefs that are considered so improbable as to be false. In day-to-day living, people do not check every story; rather, they make decisions that something is so unlikely that it is reasonable to presume that it is false. In other words, they act like scientists rejecting the null hypothesis (see Chapter 3).

For example, quite a few citizens in the general population did not believe in the landing on the moon by United States astronauts, even though the event was presented live on television. "According to the poll, a small percentage of every population area —including 18 percent of Mobile, Alabama —is convinced that Apollos 11 and 12 were monstrous hoaxes perpetrated on the U.S. citizenry by the government and its media." (Mueller, 1970.) Another example of rejection of the improbable is provided by material excerpted and commented on by Szasz (1963, pp. 166–68) from *The New York Times* of September 28, 1962:

"After four years at the Matteawan State Hospital for the Criminal Insane, 39-year-old Victor Rosario became a free man yesterday, largely because he finally got someone to look into a fantastic story that he had tenaciously insisted was true.

"The core of the story was that his wife's love had been stolen by another man who drew blood from his arms and drank it in beer to prove his vigor. Mr. Rosario told this story to everyone, including at least eleven psychiatrists, but not until a woman lawyer verified it did anyone believe him. Yesterday charges of assault that had been brought against him in 1958 were dismissed in Bronx Criminal Court.

"In 1957 Mr. Rosario had been placidly married for almost eight years. He and his wife, Caen, had two children, Martha and Victor, now 9 and 7 years old respectively. Then Mr. Rosario introduced a male boarder into their home at 725 Fox Street, the Bronx. It was this man who won Mrs. Rosario's affection. The wife, from whom Mr. Rosario is separated, signed a sworn affidavit in June stating that this was true.

"Mr. Rosario, a waiter and longshoreman, ordered the boarder to leave. He refused and the two men lived in the apartment in considerable tension until Mr. Rosario left.

"He returned later, however, in a jealous rage and allegedly struck and kicked his wife and threatened her with a bailing hook. She called the police, who said they arrested him on June 22, 1958.

"Mr. Rosario was charged with simple assault, resisting arrest, and illegally using a weapon. *He was sent to Bellevue Hospital for observation and was committed to Matteawan on October 14, 1958, on the testimony of two psychiatrists.* They said that he appeared to be a paranoiac and was incapable of understanding the charges against him.

"Matteawan is a large and formidable-looking institution in the Hudson Valley hills at Beacon, about 60 miles north of the city. There Mr. Rosario worked in the kitchen cleaning silverware and paring vegetables, and he began his long campaign to free himself.

"He had come to New York in 1946 from Puerto Rico and his English was very limited, but he labored painstakingly with a dictionary and wrote to a great many Government figures, to friends and lawyers. *He also drew up six writs of habeas corpus, all of which were dismissed by State Supreme Court in Dutchess County or were ignored.*

"Mr. Rosario told everyone who interviewed him the story of the drawn blood. 'The doctors told me that if I forgot that story, they might let me go, but the truth is the truth no matter what anyone says,' he said yesterday. So he never changed his story.

"Last November he wrote the first of several appeals to Mrs. Sara Halbert of Zapata and

Halbert, a New York City law firm. He was told that a relative would have to confer with Mrs. Halbert. At length two cousins flew up from Puerto Rico and prevailed upon the lawyer to visit Mr. Rosario.

"After a second visit, Mrs. Halbert went to Mr. Rosario's wife. She confirmed his story and signed the affidavit, asserting that the boarder had taken the blood in beer and had written on a wall in letters of blood.

"Mrs. Halbert said she presented the affidavit to Dr. Cecil Johnston, director of the hospital on Aug. 27. She asked that Mr. Rosario be released immediately. *The following day, four psychiatrists interviewed him, and he was shortly declared fit to return to the Bronx to face trial.*

"Dr. Johnston said by telephone yesterday that more than the affidavit had entered into the decision, but he acknowledged that the new information had caused the staff to look on the patient in a little different manner. He said Mr. Rosario had been interviewed on seventeen occasions by nine psychiatrists in four years.

"Mrs. Halbert moved in court yesterday that the case be dismissed. The motion was granted by Judge Ambrose J. Haddock, after Assistant District Attorney Joseph Tiger had agreed." [Italics added by Szasz] [p. 168.]

The "delusion" did not instigate hospitalization but rather justified it. Mrs. Rosario asked for help when physically threatened, but Mr. Rosario's beliefs justified the diagnosis of paranoia, which in turn permitted psychiatric hospitalization.

Social psychology is the area of behavioral science in which the greatest effort has been made to delineate, experiment with, and understand the development of beliefs, opinions, attitudes, and the like. One potential source of hypotheses stems from Staats' theory (1970), which starts with classical conditioning of words and their designates so that a conditioned response, either favorable or unfavorable, is made to elements of that class in new situations. Another area that seems very promising is attribution theory (Kelley, 1967) and the study of conditions under which the person labels himself or others. Bem (1965, 1967) exemplifies contributions on the point that a person may be influenced by observing his own behavior in the same manner as when he observes others; and Kiesler (1971) provides research in the area of commitment.

Another area of social psychology and sociology is that of propaganda and rumor. Both carry the connotation of being false, although this need not necessarily be the case, as in "news leaks" and "institutional" advertising. Much of what we have discussed so far may be mirrored by the following quotation: "For the most part, we do not first see, and then define, we define first and then see." (Lippmann, in Choukas, 1965, p. 105.)

There are other snares that may trap the mind in its effort to reduce reality to workable pictures. "Most of us," wrote the editors of the *Propaganda Analysis Bulletin,* "try to make the world intelligible to ourselves by eliminating details which do not fit into the picture we find easiest to comprehend." They then proceeded to show how "the successful propagandist keys his propaganda to this psychological process of simplification "by eliminating all 'ifs,' 'buts,' and 'ands.'" For it is the simple image that is most likely to become stable, to be accepted uncritically, and retained immutable long after the object or person it originally mirrored disappears from the scene or is changed. [Choukas, 1965, p. 103.]

Then, there is a different type of effect, a tangential one, which may be felt by the individual as a result of persistent propaganda activity. A person may not succumb to direct manipulative effects; he may, however, become so obsessed by the fear of such a possibility or so overwhelmed by the notion of propaganda's omnipotence that he, too, may lose his mental balance and be unable to perceive reality in a normal manner. Linebarger has even a name for such a person—the "propaganda addict." "The propaganda addict," he says, "takes everything with a ton of salt; what he does believe is lost in what he doesn't believe. The ordinary controls of civilized life—regard for truth, regard for law, respect for neighbors, obedience to good manners, love of God—cease to operate effectively because the propaganda-dizzy man sees in everything its propaganda content and nothing else. Everything, from a girl dancing on a stage to an ecclesiastic officiating in a cathedral, is either *for* him or *against* him. Nothing is innocent; nothing is pleasurable; everything is connected with his diseased apprehension of power. [Linebarger, 1948, p. 78, in Choukas, 1965, p. 258.]

Shibutani (1966) refers to rumor as improvised news and notes that a crisis is defined by people not being able to work together because they cannot predict each other or events. Rumor fills this need, as the false belief of paranoia provides a way of anticipating what others do.

TREATMENT OF PARANOID BEHAVIOR

Following the sociopsychological formulation, behavior labeled paranoid is learned as a response to situations which extinguish appropriate responses and shape the person toward the target (paranoid) behavior. Treatment is directed, as with other behaviors, toward the emission of an alternative and more socially appropriate act. An example of a behavioral program which altered a paranoid delusion was presented in Chapter 4 in the case of a positive reinforcing stimulus generated by avoidance of an aversive situation. The woman who would not feed herself did so when such activity avoided food-spilling on her clothes. The delusion that her food was poisoned "spontaneously" dropped out.

A further illustration of how paranoia may be treated in the present conceptual framework is provided by Davison (1966). Upon admission to the hospital, Mr. B was diagnosed paranoid schizophrenic by one psychiatrist and paranoid state by another. His history was as follows: After a medical discharge from the military for an eye imbalance, he had frequently encountered difficulties arising from actions and schemes that had "a paranoid flavor." His current admission to the hospital was at his wife's insistence, and Mr. B structured his concern as finding out about twitches over his right eye, heart, and solar plexus. His problems seemed to have started four years earlier after the suicide of his only brother. At that time he became preoccupied with "pressure points" over his right eye, which he interpreted as being caused by a spirit that helped him make decisions. Tranquilizers and surgery had been of little help. The behavior therapist interviewed Mr. B and asked him to describe tension-producing situations likely to lead to "pressure points." Mr. B was taught relaxation procedures and how to apply them in his daily life. During therapy, which comprised eight sessions in a nine-week period, the therapist introduced games that would increase tension and hence provide additional, on-the-spot training in relaxing under pressure After the first month, Mr. B's speech changed: he talked of "sensations" rather than "pressure points." The therapist taught him better ways to label his own behavior. He began to assert himself at home, and his marriage improved.

Discussing treatment of paranoids, Batchelor (1969, p. 306) writes: "It is very seldom that such cases ever make an adequate, or satisfactory, adjustment irrespective of any form of treatment which may be employed." Noyes and Kolb (1963, p. 376) write: "It is doubtful if a case of traditional paranoia ever recovers." Cameron (1967, p. 673) writes: "Classical full blown paranoia is by definition incurable." Kaplan and Sadock (1971, p. 528) write. "Classical paranoia is incurable and virtually untreatable."

In contrast to this pessimistic view, the behavioral formulation leads to treating paranoid ideation in a manner similar to other behaviors: to withdraw reinforcement for the socially disturbing operants and to shape alternative reactions to social situations that, if possible, are incompatible with the disturbing beliefs.

OTHER PERSONALITY DISORDERS

Our previous general remarks on, and our approach to, paranoid behavior applies to the other subcategories of personality disorder. We will review the DSM-II definitions briefly.

Cyclothymic personality, also known as affective personality, "is manifested by recurring and alternating periods of depression and elation. Periods of elation may be marked by ambition, warmth, enthusiasm, optimism, and high energy. Periods of depression may be marked by worry, pessimism, low energy, and a sense of futility. These mood variations are not readily attributable to external circumstances." (DSM-II, p. 42.) As with other personality disorders, it is hard at times to distinguish the typical adult from the one to be labeled cyclothymic. For example, the authors would like to think that they act in the manner described for periods of elation. They, unfortunately, recognize that most of the time they act in a manner more consistent with the description of periods of depression.

Schizoid personality refers to a pattern manifested by "shyness, oversensitivity, seclusiveness, avoidance of close competitive relationships, and often eccentricity. Autistic thinking without loss of capacity to recognize reality is common, as is daydreaming and the inability to express hostility and ordinary aggressive feelings. These patients react to disturbing experiences and conflicts with apparent detachment." (DSM-II, p. 42.) Again, the reader may wish to think of the studious college professor who spends considerable periods of time in lonely and esoteric pursuits and whose sense of time, priorities, or personal maturity seems to leave him with a calm akin to indifference regarding some areas of daily concern, while capable of great excitement over concepts, principles, or intellectual controversies of an abstract and not apparently immediate nature.

Inadequate personality is a pattern "characterized by ineffectual responses to emotional, social, intellectual, and physical demands. While the patient seems neither physically nor mentally deficient, he does manifest inadaptibility, ineptness, poor judgment, social instability, and lack of physical and emotional stamina." (DSM-II, p. 44.) The nature of the judgments required to delineate what is meant by these defining characteristics is such that the category may be widely used.

Obsessive compulsive personality seems to define an ideal employee from one view and a "workaholic" from another. It is "characterized by excessive concern with conformity and adherence to standards of conscience. Consequently, individuals in this group may be rigid, over-inhibited, over-conscientious, over-dutiful, and unable to relax easily." (DSM-II, p. 43.) The diagnostic task calls for distinction between this category and obsessive-compulsive neurosis. Similarly, the next two categories require the difficult distinction between them and hysterical and neurasthenic neuroses.

Hysterical personality or histrionic personality disorder is "characterized by excitability, emotional instability, over-reactivity, and self-dramatization. This self-dramatization is always attention-seeking and often seductive, whether or not the patient is aware of its purpose. These personalities are also immature, self-centered, often vain, and usually dependent on others." (DSM-II, p. 43.) Cleghorn (1969a, 1969b, p. 558) lists seven traits gleaned from the literature: egocentricity, exhibitionism, emotionality (of a shallow, flighty sort, cf., Lorenz, 1955), dependency, sexual provocativeness, fear of sexuality, and suggestibility. The fifth and sixth traits, provocativeness and fear of sex, are not necessarily inconsistent if one considers a teasing, mock-theatrical playing at the role.

Jordan and Kempler (1970) and O'Neil and Kempler (1969) have provided laboratory evidence consistent with an approach-avoidance conflict in the sexual area.

Asthenic personality "is characterized by easy fatigability, low energy level, lack of enthusiasm, marked incapacity for enjoyment, and oversensitivity to physical and emotional stress." (DSM-II, p. 43.) Aside from the difficulties in differentiating the category from neurasthenic neurosis, it is similar to inadequate personality and some depressions.

Explosive personality is also known as "epileptoid personality disorder" because of an unfortunate historical misunderstanding. "This behavior pattern is characterized by gross outbursts of rage or of verbal or physical aggressiveness. These outbursts are strikingly different from the patient's usual behavior, and he may be regretful and repentant for them. These patients are generally considered excitable, aggressive, and over-responsive to environmental pressures. It is the intensity of the outbursts and the individual's inability to control them which distinguishes this group." (DSM-II, p. 42.) In DSM-I, the personality disorder category included a personality trait disturbance called "emotionally unstable personality," in which "the individual reacts with excitability and ineffectiveness when confronted with minor stress. His judgment may be undependable under stress, and his relationship to other people is continuously fraught with fluctuating emotional attitudes, because of strong and poorly controlled hostility, guilt, and anxiety." (p. 36.) The category may also include the DSM-I grouping called passive-aggressive personality, aggressive type. It provides a diagnostic label for people who are difficult to deal with. In a behavioral model, an inability to control impulses should be considered, as a lack of knowledge of how to respond effectively to certain situations.

Passive-aggressive personality "is characterized by both passivity and aggressiveness. The aggressiveness may be expressed passively, for example by obstructionism, pouting, procrastination, intentional inefficiency, or stubbornness. This behavior commonly reflects hostility which the individual feels he dare not express openly. Often the behavior is one expression of the patient's resentment at failing to find gratification in a relationship with an individual or institution upon which he is over-dependent." (DSM-II, pp. 43–44.) DSM-I also included a passive-dependent type characterized by helplessness, indecisiveness, and a tendency to cling to others.

A key concept is that the person is at fault; it is he who is over-dependent and therefore angry when his presumably unreasonable demands are not met. It is hard to distinguish between behavior that is within the limits normal for a population and behavior that is extreme enough to warrant the passive-aggressive label. At times, however, the availability of the category has great administrative usefulness.

While each case must first be evaluated, the modeling of assertive behavior (see Chapter 12) seems very useful in this area (for example, Katz, 1971; Goldstein et al., 1973).

Other categories in personality disorders and certain nonpsychotic mental disorders, as noted above, include antisocial personality and the separate entities of sexual deviations, alcoholism, and drug dependence. The next chapters will deal with these topics.

A Note on Labeling by Experts

The closeness of these patterns of behavior to what is socially acceptable, the difficulty in distinguishing between people acting in this manner from the general population, and the obvious administrative utility of the diagnosis make the personality disorders a category warranting concern. The potentials for misuse of the diagnostic system are greatest when the behaviors are least clearly distinguishable from generally acceptable behavior. The existence and availability of a label very often releases the institution from a sense of responsibility. The Medvedevs (1972) provide an illustration: "My wife and friends said that they, after all, had known me for many years and had never noticed the slightest trace of abnormal behaviour, but he argued with them, alleging that only an experienced psychiatrist can detect the 'early stages' of mental illness." (p. 102.)

SUMMARY

This chapter dealt primarily with personality disorders, especially paranoid behavior. Descriptions, theories, and clinical practice were touched on. It was suggested that false beliefs must be studied in the same way as true beliefs.

The personality disorders are particularly challenging because the behaviors are so hard to distinguish from behavior within "normal" limits.

sexual behavior

21

Sexual behaviors that were viewed as difficulties were categorized by DSM-I within the larger group of personality disorders and, within personality disorders, in the subcategory of sociopathic personality disturbances. DSM-I (pp. 38–39) defined sexual deviation as follows: "This diagnosis is reserved for deviant sexuality which is not symptomatic of extensive syndromes, such as schizophrenic and obsessional reactions. This term includes most of the cases formerly classed as 'psychopathic personality with pathologic sexuality.' The diagnosis will specify the type of the pathological behavior, such as homosexuality, transvestism, pedophilia, fetishism, and sexual sadism (including rape, sexual assault, mutilation)."

In DSM-II, the category of personality disorders and certain nonpsychotic mental disorders includes four major subcategories: personality disorders, sexual deviations, alcoholism, and drug dependence. The definition of the subcategory sexual deviations is given as follows:

This category is for individuals whose sexual interests are directed primarily toward objects other than people of the opposite sex, toward sexual acts not usually associated with coitus, or toward coitus performed under bizarre circumstances as in necrophilia [with cadavers—ED.], pedophilia [with children—ED.], sexual sadism [giving pain—ED.] and fetishism [unusual arousal by an irrelevant condition or object, e.g., specific garments, hair color, etc.—ED.]. Even though many find their practices distasteful, they remain unable to substitute normal sexual behavior for them. The diagnosis is not appropriate for individuals who perform deviant sexual acts because normal sexual objects are not available to them. [DSM-II, p 44.]

A major event, both for the people involved and as an indication of the sociological nature of diagnostic formulations, occurred in December, 1973, when the American Psychiatric Association, by a vote of 13 to 0, with two abstentions, ruled to remove homosexuality from its list of mental disorders. The trustees did not declare homosexuality normal as its task force on nomenclature had recommended; rather, they inserted a new category called "sexual orientation disturbance" for those people who wanted to change their orientation or sought a different adjustment.

As noted above, disturbing sexual behavior may occur with other abnormal behaviors. If a person does not pay attention to the same stimuli as other people, appears "psychotic," and is consequently isolated from members of the opposite sex (as in a hospital), it is easy to understand how he might have difficulty establishing adequate interpersonal relations.

In addition, certain specific sexual difficulties, notably orgasmic dysfunction (previously called frigidity) and impotence, may also be classified as psychophysiological disorder, genitourinary disorder.

A further complication is that difficulties in the sexual area may result in other problem behaviors. Given the views of deviant sexual behaviors held by our culture and the emphasis placed on appropriate sexual behavior as a measure of personal attractiveness and social competence, other forms of abnormal behavior might very well be an effect of a type of sexual adjustment rather than a cause. Considering that a recurrent source of pleasure places a person in situations in which he may be severely punished if caught, it is understandable that a person emitting statistically rare or "deviant behavior" may feel worthless or insecure.

A related point should be made explicit: to say that there are people who emit homosexual, sadistic, or other socially disavowed behavior is very different from saying there are homosexuals, sadists, or deviants. The difference may at first glance seem trivial and semantic, and the reader may say, "I can define a homosexual: he's a person who emits homosexual behavior." The difference between saying a person is a homosexual and saying a person emits homosexual behavior is that the former places him in a delineated category, with the resulting social consequences (see Chapters 2 and 10) of such categorization. The homosexuality is, then, the result of "the sort of person he is," and many negative social characteristics are attributed to him. Aside from these effects at an explanatory and social level, there is a crucial effect at a treatment level. In therapy, the consequences of the former approach ("He's a homosexual") will be to focus on changing the "underlying personality," while that of the latter ("He emits homosexual acts") will be to focus on the behavior.

The matter of treatment raises a very important issue. Clinical psychologists and psychiatrists have been among the foremost authors and experts in the field of sexual behavior. If one stops to think about this situation, there are elements of absurdity to it. In the very nature of being under treatment, someone, usually the person himself, is expressing disruption, disappointment, and dissatisfaction with the behavior. As a result, the sample of people on whom practitioners have gathered information is an atypical one. A psychoanalyst is frequently quoted as saying that he has never seen a well-adjusted homosexual. As therapists, the present authors can say they have never seen a happy, well-adjusted heterosexual in therapy. If they did, they would be admitting that they treated people who did not need it. Given this situation, being a mental health practitioner does not make a person an expert on sexual behavior. Ideas about sexual behavior must come from the study of sociology, anthropology, social history, physiology, and comparative psychology as well as from clinical practice.

To return to the definition of sexual deviation given by DSM-II, we may note both a positive change and a hidden assumption. The recognition that social conditions affect the evaluation of the specific act may be seen as an advantage in conceptualizing sexual disorders. The unavailability of "normal sexual objects" leads to a concept of a "situational" (as opposed to a "fundamental" or "characterological") problem.

The hidden assumption in the DSM-II diagnosis is in the phrase, "They remain unable" and in the words "appropriate" and "normal." The word "unable," here, does not refer to availability as discussed in the previous paragraph, but to intrapsychic force in a manner similar to the notion that a hysteric "cannot" function in the way he is capable of physiologically. It follows from this assumption that treatment is aimed primarily at the intrapsychic structure and only indirectly at the behavior. Further, words such as "normal," "usual," and "appropriate" imply a general (rather than a shifting, relativistic) standard of normality. Implicit in the DSM-II definition is that the standard is heterosexual coitus, in the correct manner, with the correct person, under correct circumstances, and for the correct reasons.

DEFINITIONS OF SEXUAL NORMALITY

Nowhere is the role of social evaluation in the definition of abnormal behavior clearer than in the realm of sexual activity. All living things, if the species is to continue, must reproduce. At a *biological level* normality might be defined as whatever the organism is capable of doing. Varieties of "deviant" behavior such as an animal doing acts appropriate for the other sex or selecting an "inappropriate" object such as a member of its own sex are observed with rodents and primates. The point is that if "natural" and "normal" involve doing what mammals do, then many of the behaviors that often enter into legal definitions as "unnatural" are observed in other species and are "natural."

There has been a great emphasis on genital sexuality, specifically on that type of union which leads to reproduction. Work such as that by Masters and Johnson (1966) indicates that in terms of satisfaction there is no physiological basis for such a notion as the criterion of normality. Masters and Johnson (1970, p. 10) make an additional, important observation: "Sexual functioning is a natural physiological process, yet it has a unique facility that no other natural physiological process, such as respiratory, bladder, or bowel function, can imitate. Sexual responsivity can be delayed indefinitely or functionally denied for a lifetime. No other basic physiological process can claim such malleability of physical expression." Sexual behavior in humans is a very social act and its very definition, as well as its expression, displays great variation among people of the same society as well as among different times in an individual's life.

At a species level, normality might be defined as that behavior which extends or increases the chances of survival of the species. However, the human species is threatened by a population explosion. One might therefore say that reproduction should be presumed to be abnormal. Further, sexual gratification and reproduction are increasingly separated. Even without contraceptive devices, only a small percentage of sexual contacts between human adults of opposite sex leads to reproduction. There are both satisfying sexual contacts without reproduction and, given orgasmic dysfunction ("frigidity"), frequent instances of reproduction without satisfaction. Therefore, definitions of normality in terms of orgasmic capability, observed mammalian behavior, or continuation of the species are at variance with behavior considered socially acceptable in our culture at this time.

As noted in Chapter 8, psychoanalytic theory presumes progress through oral, anal, phallic, and genital stages of psychosexual development. With this background, orgasm through union with the genitalia of a member of the opposite sex is an indication of maturity,[1] and other behaviors may be considered symptomatic of fixations at earlier psychosexual stages. Such pregenital gratifications are acceptable in psychoanalytic theory as sublimations if they occur prior to heterosexual genital union, but not if they lead to orgasm or take the place of heterosexual union.

Ford and Beach (1951) make use of the Yale Cross-Cultural Index to illustrate deviations from this view in societies other than those of contemporary Western culture. Similar data is provided by Forberg's (1965) survey of the literature of the Greco-Roman classical authors and Edwardes' (1959) survey of the Near Eastern and African literatures. The range of behaviors considered appropriate cross-culturally is essentially the total range of observed sexual responses. In similar fashion, the range of behaviors considered deviant and the sexual stimuli reacted to with repugnance also vary across and within cultures; for example, deep kissing, a favorite pastime of college students, is considered "dirty" by many American prostitutes.

Rather than an individual limited to a single set of stimuli and a single stereotyped response, one should expect a progressive and changing range of stimuli to which adults react. In this regard, the work of Kinsey and his associates gives evidence that, indeed, there are typically a variety of sexual modes and stimuli for sexual behav-

---

[1] Freud made a distinction between vaginal and clitoral orgasm; this distinction is as erroneous physiologically as it has been psychologically harmful to those women who have taken it seriously.

iors emitted by supposedly normal individuals. Kinsey's work has been severely criticized, as have most other researches on sexual behavior in human beings, particularly those dealing with behavior in our culture. The use of works such as those by Kinsey, Pomeroy, and Martin (1948), Masters and Johnson (1966), and Ford and Beach (1951) deserves some comment.

The reader in his daily life must frequently face the task of making decisions about what behaviors are appropriate. Clinical psychologists are often asked to evaluate and help people who are having difficulties in the area of sexual behavior (by implication, to change them) and hence must also make decisions about the desirability of certain behaviors as compared to others. Such professional decisions might be made on the basis of personal experience, essentially saying that what the authors personally do and believe is right and proper. The difficulty with this approach is that there could be as many standards as there are clinical psychologists.

Normality might be considered in terms of *legal definitions*. However, it is noteworthy that whenever legal definitions are surveyed, it is found that an act which might not even be considered a misdemeanor in one state might lead to 20 years in prison in another state. The psychologist as a scientist and practitioner is uncomfortable when his definition changes by crossing a state line. Another difficulty with legal definitions is that there have been estimates that the number of adults who at some time in their lives have committed sexual transgressions ranges to 95 percent (e.g., Kinsey et al., 1948, p. 392).

There are also *religious definitions*, which are reflected in the legal code, but different religious sects have different conceptions of appropriate behavior. Thus religious definitions are not too useful as general guidelines.

One can make a distinction between the variable of *morality-immorality* and that of *decency-indecency*. It seems that the sexual codes enforced on college campuses today are more likely to deal with the latter than the former. According to legal and religious standards it is immoral to have intercourse with anyone besides one's spouse. Having intercourse with one's spouse is not *immoral*. Having intercourse with one's spouse in the middle of the campus at high noon is *indecent*.

The next alternative is a *statistical* definition, and it is the one frequently used by therapists. Even though it has enormous scientific and ethical difficulties, the therapist makes the best first estimate he can of *typical* behavior for a person at the age, sex, and socioeconomic status of his client. In this instance normality is behaving like most of the people in that particular person's subgroup. After this estimate, he will probably seek to avoid any immediate rupture with religious, legal, or moral standards of conduct. In addition, as will be noted in Chapter 29, the psychologist has a responsibility not only to his client but also to the people with whom his client interacts.

How does the therapist know what is the typical behavior of a person of a given age, sex, and socioeconomic status? He must determine these before he can start offering alternatives and discussing with the patient what the therapeutic contract will be. As noted earlier, the psychologist's own observations are likely to have been biased by the very nature of the population he serves. Therefore, psychologists must make use of surveys, although they may not be perfect. The choice is between no information and less than perfect information.

Hunt (1974) reports the results of a national questionnaire of an adult (over 17) sample of 982 men and 1,044 women (whose race, marital status, age, education, occupation, and geographic location was approximately proportionate to those of the entire American population) in 24 cities. The results were compared with the findings that Kinsey made around a quarter of a century earlier. Among the conclusions of this summary were: premarital sex has become more acceptable and widespread; the use of prostitutes by young single males has sharply decreased; couples in general, young and old, married and unmarried, have considerably increased the variety of techniques and frequency of coital relationships; rates of orgasm for females have increased; homosexual behavior has not increased in incidence although it has increased in visibility. Hunt concludes that "sexual liberalism is the emergent ideal that the great majority of young Americans—and a fair number of older ones—are trying to live up to." (p. 207.) Among the more general views on the social implications of changing sexual behaviors is Hunt's observation that "there has been no chaotic and anarchic dissolution of standards but, rather, a major shift towards somewhat different, highly organized standards that remain integrated with existing social values and with the institution of love, marriage, and the family." (p. 207.)

All such survey material is dependent upon the method of data collection. Typically the people upon whom data are based are volunteers, and their reports must be considered from this perspective. In the Masters and Johnson (1966) work on physiological aspects of sexual behavior, about 750 men and women performed various sexual acts while behavioral and psychophysiological measures were obtained. One may question the appropriateness of generalization to the total population from the people who volunteered and were accepted for this project. However, there is no other source of equivalent data, and a person arguing that sexual responses at a physiological level are not similar in nonvolunteers bears the burden of proof. Again the reader must decide whether he would wish to be counseled by a person making use of such data or by a person who relied on his limited personal opinions or observations.

The trend in our society during the last hundred years has been toward greater recognition of the sexual rights of women. The trend in marriage manuals has moved from first condoning to then advocating a variety of behaviors which a hundred years ago would have been considered "wicked." [2]

Some indication of the changes of the last 100 years may be obtained from a volume published in 1870 by Fowler: [3]

Women were thus counseled by Fowler: "Love-making girls, do you at all realize what you are doing? When you kiss, and allow yourself to be kissed 'with an appetite,' to fondle and be fondled, hug and be hugged, you are thereby actually perpetrating mental sexual intercourse. . . . So flagrant a violation of her laws Nature must punish. Young folks, as you set by moral purity and virtue, how *dare* you reciprocate love till you have acquired a right to by betrothal?" (pp. 531–32.) From Fowler's section on "liberties during courtship kill love." we learn: "All liberties during courtship kill spiritual love. Let any and every woman, of any experience whatever, attest that every iota of sexual freedom she ever allowed any man to take with her deadened his love for her. . . . And the more familiarity she allowed, the more he despised her ever afterwards. Even if the familiarity did not extend to intercourse, still it deadened his love in exact proportion thereto; and if it did thus extend, killed it." (pp. 544–45.)

Reviewing the sources of current definitions of normal sexual behavior, it seems that legal, religious, and psychoanalytic definitions are dogmatic and do not parallel observed behavior sufficiently to warrant their use at a professional level. Biological, statistical, and administrative definitions may be descriptive of current behavior and potentialities, but they do not provide clear

---

[2] If the present authors have a view on such matters, it is that to tell people they *must* do something in an intimate relationship is as bad as to tell them that they must *not* do the same thing.

[3] We thank the noted scholar and sexologist, Mike Ullmann, for calling this volume to our attention. For additional material in this area, the student may wish to consult Veith (1970) or Breasted (1971).

A SOCIOPSYCHOLOGICAL APPROACH

As with the other behaviors discussed throughout this book, rather than try to define what is normal and what is not one may ask how anybody comes to like or value anything. Rather than ask how perverted or deviant behavior develops, the question is how any behavior is learned.

As one moves up the phylogenetic scale, the role of instinctual patterns and hormonal control diminishes to such an extent that even in cases of extreme physiological anomalies, social training takes precedence over many physiological limitations. Beach (1969, p. 34) makes the point in these words: "The marked freedom of erotic responsiveness from hormonal control in our species is, I believe, a direct consequence of the extreme dependence of human behavior upon the complex and intricately organized neocortex." Other material on this topic is reviewed by Rosenberg and Sutton-Smith (1972, especially pp. 33–34), Money (1970), and Money and Ehrhardt (1973).

Hormonal, genetic, and physiological deviation theories are contraindicated by current research. For example, after reviewing genetic and hormonal theories of homosexuality, Buss flatly concludes that "none of the biological hypotheses has received support, and they have been discarded by most investigators." (1966, p. 461.)

The child from birth is capable of pleasurable stimulation of a genital nature. If there is a pleasurable stimulus, any behavior or stimulus immediately preceding or contiguous with it may come to have sexual meaning. The individual may (1) seek to increase its frequency in his environment and (2) not respond to other stimuli, either because of simple statistical probability (there is a limited amount of time and energy) or by restricting his attention.

This process of the social learning of sexual behavior, developing from man's biological origins, is described by Kinsey et al. as follows:

Learning and conditioning in connection with human sexual behavior involve the same sorts of processes as learning and conditioning in other types of behavior. But man, because of his highly developed forebrain, may be more conditionable than any of the other mammals. . . .

The sexual capacities which an individual inherits at birth appear to be nothing more than the necessary anatomy and the physiologic capacity to respond to a sufficient physical or psychologic stimulus. All human females and males who are not too greatly incapacitated physically appear to be born with such capacities. . . .

But apart from these inherent capacities, most other aspects of human sexual behavior appear to be the product of learning and conditioning. From the time it is born, and probably before it is born, the infant comes into contact with some of the elements that enter into its later sexual experience. From its first physical contacts with other objects, and particularly from its contacts with other human bodies, the child learns that there are satisfactions which may be obtained through tactile stimulation. . . .

The type of person who first introduces an individual to particular types of socio-sexual activities may have a great deal to do with his or her subsequent attitudes, his or her interest in continuing such activity, and his or her dissatisfactions with other types of activity. Above all, experience develops a certain amount of technical facility, and an individual *learns* how to masturbate and *learns* how to utilize particular techniques in petting, in coitus, or in homosexual or other relations. . . .

As a result of its experience, an animal acquires certain patterns of behavior which lead it to react positively to certain sorts of stimuli, and to react negatively to other sorts of stimuli. . . .

An individual may come to prefer particular types of individuals as sexual partners; may prefer tall persons or short persons; may prefer blondes or brunettes; may prefer sexual partners who are much younger or much older, or of his or her own age, may develop an incapacity to respond to any except a single sexual partner, or a preference for variety in sexual experience; may prefer a heterosexual or a homosexual pattern of behavior; may prefer masturbation to the pursuit of socio-sexual contacts; may prefer a considerable amount of petting prior to actual coitus, or immediate coitus without preliminary play; may find satisfaction or be offended by the use of certain genital, oral, or anal techniques; may come to desire a variety of positions in coitus, or the more or less exclusive use of a single position; may choose a farm animal instead of a human partner for sexual relationships. All of these choices and reactions to particular stimuli may seem reasonable enough and more or less inevitable to the person who is involved, even though some of them may seem un-understandable, unnatural, and abnormal to the individual who has not been conditioned by the same sort of experience. . . .

. . . The prominence given to classification of behavior as normal or abnormal, and the long list of special terms used for classifying such behavior, usually represent moralistic classifications rather than any scientific attempt to discover the origins of such behavior, or to determine their real social significance. [1953, pp. 644–46.]

The sociopsychological model includes but goes beyond Kinsey's formulation, notably in an emphasis on operant as well as respondent conditioning. The reduction of sexual tension, by orgasm, is pleasurable and hence is a primary reinforcing stimulus. *Respondent* conditioning occurs in that stimuli which were previously neutral may be so associated with sexual responses that they themselves lead to the emission of various sexual responses. In similar fashion, a sexual act may be paired with an aversive stimulus with the result that the response to the sexual stimulus may be that appropriate to the aversive stimulus, i.e., fear and repugnance.

Operant conditioning plays a crucial role in human sexual behavior. The range of potentially adequate biological stimuli and acts is greater than that selected by a particular culture as appropriate. A person may be shaped to repeat a particular pattern of sexual responses either with an appropriate or an inappropriate sexual object. Modeling and language greatly extend the range of behaviors to which the human being may be exposed and the feedback he obtains (or presents to himself) about his sexual activity.

Various systems for categorizing sexual behaviors have been proposed, but none is completely satisfactory. A major reason is that the same act may be emitted under different conditions and different antecedent conditions may lead to emission of the same specific act. A second reason is that the same individual may, and usually does, emit a variety of acts. A person may engage in occasional homosexual acts, may be sadistic in such relations, and may reach orgasm by masturbation when so doing. As with other human behavior, sexual acts do not fall into neat, mutually exclusive categories.

It should be explicit that the sexual act requires practice to be emitted smoothly and with optimum effectiveness. Of even greater import, operants that are not specifically sexual are required to emit socially acceptable sexual behavior. In a college community, for example, it is necessary to select an appropriate person, make a date, and be capable of shaping a prospective partner to the desired time, place, and activity. Perfect biological normality without accompanying social skill may lead to an unsatisfactory sexual adjustment.

An example of a behavior in which nonsexual operants have been ineffective in setting a socially appropriate basis for sexual behavior is that of rape. There are three categories of rape: the seduction of minors (statutory rape); a form of fetishistic behavior (sexual gratification occurring only when the partner is unwilling or damaged in some way); and, most frequently, one of a number of modes of sexual gratification in which a partner is not a willing participant. Most rapists are in their early twenties, and about half are married and living with their wives at the time of the act

(FBI, 1963). Gebhard et al. note about rapists that "their heterosexual adjustment is quantitatively well above average." Further, some appear "to be statistically normal individuals who simply misjudged the situation." (1965).

The comments above illustrate that there are two aspects of the emission of normal sexual behavior. *There is behavior in response to a sexual situation; there are, in addition, behaviors required to arrive at that situation*. While these latter are not typically the focus of discussions of sex theory, they are as crucial an element in therapy as the specific sexual responses themselves. Gagnon and Simon (1969) make this point as follows:

Language has its greatest power with reference to sex, for not only is it the mechanism by which the biological events are given meaning, but it is also the mechanism by which the biological events are potentiated. Unless two people recognize a sexual situation, there will not be the potentiation of the physiological concomitants that Masters and Johnson have demonstrated as necessary in the production of sexual excitement and the orgasmic cycle. The social meaning given to the physical acts releases biological events. [1969, p. 47.]

The general formulation may now be made by return to the paradigm presented in Chapters 2 and 4: the successful social act presumes that (1) certain messages are attended to; (2) they are correctly decoded; (3) the person is capable of acting on them; and (4) the gain from the required enactment is greater than either the cost of emitting it or the gain from possible alternative enactments. Another way of introducing the same model is to refer to the development of the career of the marijuana smoker presented in Chapter 10. The steps to heterosexuality may well parallel those to marijuana smoking: a loosening of ties to prior standards (usually associated with changes in locale and status, e.g., marriage), a shaping geographically and emotionally to a group with a new point of view, a gradual introduction to the techniques, and a labeling of resulting sensations. The commission of the act itself may lead to further changes both in the person's labeling of himself and in his group identification.

The reader may wish to contrast the manner in which normal sexual behavior is taught with the way in which other important behaviors, such as reading, are taught. Children see their parents reading; they are read to, and letters are pointed out to them. They are vastly praised for reading. They are encouraged to talk about what they have read, and they listen to their parents discuss what they have read. They are taught reading in schools, and they are encouraged to use the local library.

There would seem to be general agreement, at least within the mental health professions, that sexual activity should be openly discussed and that it should be regarded as normal and pleasurable. There is a preponderance of professional opinion that there should be as little constraint as possible over the behavior of consenting adults in private (e.g., Hart, 1966; Schur, 1965a; GAP, 1966b). By implication, it is a matter of concern when one person's sexual behavior causes another undue harm or emotional upset.

The sexual act is *role expressive*. It is more than physiological release: witness the difference in feelings about oneself, whether of guilt or competence, attendant upon gratification through masturbation or heterosexual intercourse. "Real" men or women document their competence or attractiveness to others through certain, specific acts. One may document being a "good" person by many sexual encounters and conquests or by fidelity and chastity. In both instances, the sexual activity is part of and expressive of a larger, interrelated group of acts called a role (see Chapter 5).

While all behavior is equally "learned" and hence equally "normal," to the extent that an individual shares the attitudes of his culture he may be adversely affected when he engages in proscribed behavior. If he is to do so, he should not do so as a result of avoidance of unrealistically threatening stimuli or because he does not have the skills that make alternatives available. That is, he should have control or choice over his behavior to the extent of working for positive reinforcement instead of avoiding aversive stimulation. Operationally this means that the practicing psychologist will strive to increase the range of potential acts the client can make without causing pain to himself or other people. In a positive sense, people should learn how to attain respectful interactions with others. Such considerations, however, do not specify what acts will be permitted and what acts will not be permitted.

The specific acts may be designated by the society, although the official morality may not be practiced by a majority of people. It should be noted that one of the rarest of sexual adjustments found in nature is encouraged in Western civilization: chastity. Customs have changed so that kissing and mild caressing are countenanced by most college officials. Theoretically, after such modest pleasures, a person is ready for marriage. After marriage, people ideally are fully and ecstatically responsive to their spouses and never again responsive to any other stimuli.[4] If one can explain how a person makes this type of specialized adjustment, one is well on the way to having a developed model of general sexual behavior.

General Comments

When a person deviates from a modal social value, he may begin to question himself, not only on the specific act, but also as to what such a deviation may imply about his more general adequacy. Through our quotations from Fowler (1870), we have

---

[4] According to Kinsey et al. (1953), a fourth of the married women and half of the married men had engaged in at least one incident of extramarital coitus by age 40.

sampled, all too briefly, the general tenor of restrictiveness that has existed in the area of sexual behavior. Despite some lessening in this regard in recent times, compared to other cultures, ours is still repressive, especially at an official or public level (Ford and Beach, 1951; Edwardes and Masters, 1962). An example that gives a flavor of the kind of background that may lead to behaviors that are deemed changeworthy comes from the late Victorian era.

"An early and primitive example of a device using aversive stimulation to control sexual behavior was a male chastity belt patented in 1897. The apparatus consisted of an aperture with a series of barbed points through which the appropriate organ would pass. Expansion of the organ would result in contact with these points causing pain, thus 'preventing self-abuse' and diverting thoughts from 'running in lascivious channels.'" (Schwitzgebel, 1968, p. 449.) Another example stems from the negative attitude toward masturbation. A French physician, Tissot, in 1774, gave a medical rationale for proscribing this activity. The dean of American psychology, introducer of Freud and Jung to America, G. Stanley Hall, wrote in his 1907 monumental work on adolescence:

The onanistic psychosis seems especially to predispose to convulsive disorders like epilepsy, to which it is so akin, but weakness of memory and attention, paranoia, agitation, cachexia [general ill health with emaciation—ED.] . . . dwarfing or hypertrophy of the organs themselves. . . . One of the most direct moral effects is lying, secretiveness, and hypocrisy which conceals or denies a whole area of interests very real to the subject, and this is closely connected with cowardice, timidity, egoism, and frivolity. . . . The masturbator's heart, so often discussed, is weak like his voice. . . . There are early physical signs of decrepitude and senescence, grey hairs, and especially baldness, a stooping and enfeebled gait, the impulsive and narrow egoism which always goes with overindulgence. . . . [pp. 443–44.]

Anthropologists and sociologists provide

evidence that similar concepts continue to the present time. For example, Messenger (1971), writing about an Irish folk community, notes: "There is much evidence to indicate that the female orgasm is unknown—or at least doubted, or considered a deviant response." (p. 44.) And (relevant also to our discussion of pornography in Chapter 27) "Returned 'Yanks' have been denounced from the pulpit for describing American sexual practices to island youths, and such 'pornographic' magazines as *Time* and *Life*, mailed by kin from abroad, have aroused curates to spirited sermons and instruction." (p. 14.) Another example from contemporary Western civilization comes from Rainwater (1971): "Specifically noted in each of these four cultures [of poverty—ED.] was the dictum, 'Sex is a man's pleasure and a woman's duty.' Sexual relations exist for the pleasure of the man; enjoyment for the woman is either optional or disapproved. . . . In Tepoztlan, . . . women who are passionate and 'need' men are referred to as loca (crazy). . . ." (p. 189.) Rainwater provides a table (p. 195) indicating that as social class increases, the frequency of enjoyment of sexual relations by wives increases.

Strictures against sexual expression have had two effects on individuals in the society. The first is that the individual may have difficulty in learning how and when to engage in sexual behavior and may even develop an aversion to sexual activity. The second effect is that feelings such as fear of discovery, or guilt over exploiting another, or anger over being exploited interfere with the development and maintenance of a centering of attention ("sensate focus," to use Masters and Johnson's 1970 term) on the physical stimuli present in the environment.

One may think of covert sensitization, in which a person focuses on aversive stimuli; the sexual arousal is the stimulus immediately preceding unpleasant and fear-provoking ideas, and this may not only interfere with sensate focus, it may decrease the very opportunities for such. A limerick (quoted in Katchadourian and Lunde, 1972, p. 471) summarizes this point:

There was a young lady named Wilde
Who kept herself quite undefiled
by thinking of Jesus
And social diseases
And the fear of having a child.

Indeed, one of the first things a behavioral therapist will do in treatment of difficulties between a heterosexual couple is to ascertain both the general and specific stimuli that may be interfering with sexual enjoyment. Sometimes a very simple answer is found. An example is a newspaper report (*Honolulu Star-Bulletin and Advertiser*, p. D-6, April 8, 1973) that: "Dr. Ralph L. Krisppy said recently a study of 27 women between the ages of 18 and 30 showed that 17 of them had become sexually frigid since their husbands grew beards. He said that some of the women claimed their husbands' beards tickled so much they could not concentrate." Before the male reader takes to the razor blade, the bearded senior author of this volume suggests a rereading of Chapter 3 on scientific method. But the newspaper story makes a point which has been repeated clinically by Schimel (1971). With great wisdom, Schimel writes: "For me all such sexual complaints as 'impotence,' 'frigidity,' 'premature ejaculation,' and so forth are undefinable abstractions until I know with great specificity to what behaviors the patient is attaching these words and in what contexts they occur." (p. 24.) Schimel presents a number of cases, the following being typical:

A 41-year-old male complained of loss of erection during intercourse, a constant state of tension, duodenal ulcer, irritability, and temper outbursts which were endangering his business prospects as well as his marital adjustment.

He was proud of his wife's great sexual responsiveness, which included shouting at the moment of orgasm. The shouting, as well as her clawing, sobbing, etc., pleased him and convinced him she was very responsive sexually. However, it caused him acute embarrassment, particularly because of their children or the presence of guests in the house. It was suggested to the wife that the screaming on orgasm was unnecessary and that it might give the children some unhealthy ideas about sexual activities. She desisted. The husband reported considerable relief. [p. 29.]

Fear of harming or being harmed, of pregnancy, discovery, venereal disease, moral retribution, abandonment, and the like frequently interfere with sensate focus. Things people say to themselves—more generally called attitudes, expectations, or the like—are the focus of early therapeutic interviews. Misinformation requires correction, and the therapist's calm acceptance and relaxed questioning is itself therapeutic and a form of modeling. Very frequently the frustrations found in other parts of a relationship interfere with the sexual relationship and the sexual problem becomes one that is more generally interpersonal or marital (e.g., Stuart, 1969). The sexual difficulty may be an early indicator of an interpersonal problem that brings the couple for counseling, and the gratifications of sexual activity may lead otherwise unwilling partners to try new patterns of non-sexual interaction. Sexual behavior is role-expressive and does not occur in a purely biological vacuum; treatment must take this into account.

Our goal is not to increase or decrease any specific activity, but to provide the person with such skills that he or she is realistically capable of making a choice. Knowing how to be an attractive person and practicing such behavior without undue and irrelevant tension, is frequently the immediate focus of treatment rather than any specific sexual activity. If the target is heterosexual activity, there must be a partner, and finding and developing a comfortable relationship for both people requires social skills.

It is within this context that factors such as how to dress, where to circulate, how to talk; how to interpret small gestures, hints, and invitations; how to offer gently, and how to accept rejection without overgeneralizing to all people on all occasions, become the burden of much of the treatment. From our own clinical work and from the reports of our colleagues we would conclude that it is not any particular mode of dress or physical attractant that is crucial, but rather it is the demonstration of interest in the other person as an individual. The key advice may be: relate, don't overwhelm or impress. In summary, before an individual will alter a pattern of behavior, he must be able to do so realistically. This often requires training in skills that are typically considered social rather than sexual.

Problems and Solutions

We are now ready to sample some of the more typical problems encountered in therapeutic practice. We cannot cover all areas; for example, we will only mention in passing transsexuals (those who wish and/or receive a change of sexual physique consistent with their psychological identity), although this is a topic of strong current interest (Stoller, 1968; Driscoll, 1971). Further, what is considered changeworthy indicates the concerns of the culture at a given moment, and our society is changing rapidly. Perhaps the strongest example of such change is in the area of abortion; when writing the first edition of this volume, it would have been worth a professor's job to provide the type of information which a few years later was advertised in the campus newspaper.

Impotence in the male is inability to attain sexual gratification because of loss of erection either through *ejaculatio praecox*, in which orgasm is reached immediately prior to or very soon after insertion, or an inability to attain erection at all. The psychoanalytic formulation will not be reviewed for all of the following behaviors, but it will be for impotence in order to give some indication of such thinking in the area of sexual behavior.

Fenichel gives a typical psychoanalytic formulation of these behaviors:

Essentially, impotence and frigidity are not returns of the repressed from the repression but clinical manifestations and bulwarks of the defense itself. Unconsciously the person believes that sexual activity is dangerous, and the defensive force that therefore demands avoidance of the sexual act is sustained and assured by physical interference with the physical reflexes. Impotence is a physical alteration arising from a defensive action by the ego which prevents the carrying out of an instinctual activity regarded as dangerous. . . . As a rule, the basic danger implied is castration, the unconscious idea being that the penis might be injured in the vagina. Fear over loss of love plays a smaller part as a cause of impotence. Fear of one's own excitation, however, may complicate the castration anxiety. The reason these dangers are believed to be connected with sexual intercourse is obvious: the fear was once connected with infantile sexual aims; these infantile sexual aims were warded off and thus have been preserved in the unconscious; they come up again whenever sexual excitement is experienced. Since the preservation of infantile sexual aims is one of the characteristic traits of neurosis, disturbances of potency are found as accompanying manifestations of all neuroses.

The nuclear complex of infantile sexuality is the Oedipus complex. In the simplest and most typical cases, impotence is based on a persistence of an unconscious sensual attachment to the mother. Superficially no sexual attachment is completely attractive because the partner is never the mother; in a deeper layer, every sexual attachment has to be inhibited, because every partner represents the mother. [1945, p. 170.]

By this theory the treatment of impotence must entail a complete analysis of the Oedipus complex and a reworking of the intrapsychic economy. In contrast, the behavioral formulation of impotence is similar to that of a phobia. The person makes a fearful rather than an appropriate (sexual) response to the situation. The therapeutic goal, therefore, is to teach him how to make the nonfearful, appropriate sexual response that will be reinforcing.

Kraines (1948), a student of Adolph Meyer, made the following suggestion: "In addition, in cases of impotence if the patient is forbidden to have sex relations for a week (assuming as it were that his impotence will disappear) while indulging in much sex play, it will be found that freedom from the necessity of having sex relations combined with the stimulation of the sex play, will tend to make the patient so potent and eager as to make him disregard the command to wait for a week."

Two things are to be noted in this approach. The patient is counseled to avoid further failure experiences. At the same time, he is asked to enter the situation. The pleasurable stimulation in the absence of the failure experience will lead to a reconditioning and direction of attention to the pleasurable aspects of the situation. Following Wolpe's (1958) and Masters's and Johnson's (1970) suggestions, the person progresses to more intimate acts only when he has a strong urge to do so, and when he is not in the least tense. The first indication of discomfort or decrease of desire signals the need to drop back and retrace one's steps. This procedure is quite similar to desensitization in practice, that is, progressive exposure to the feared object. To this technique may be added systematic desensitization with relaxation and visualization of a hierarchy dealing with the sexual act (Razani, 1972).

There are two elements which the therapist must deal with in the treatment of impotence. Impotence may be initially manifested for many reasons: the male is fatigued, the situation lacks privacy, the male bethinks himself of disease, paternity, eternal damnation, or some antithetical, nonsexual stimulus. An unusual but paradigmatic instance is reported by Wolpe and Lazarus (1966, p. 103): ". . . a 36-year-old man who was sexually adequate until two years previously when he suffered a mild coronary thrombosis while engaged in sexual intercourse, and thereafter experienced trepidation at the thought of sexual indulgence. . . ."

A second problem arises *after* the first instance of impotence. The male anticipates failure or at least devotes some of his attention to this possibility. This possibility is threatening in a society which places considerable emphasis on sexual activity as a mark of manliness. The very worry about failure makes it more likely.

Primary impotence is defined by a situation in which the individual has never achieved erection sufficient for sexual intromission (whether heterosexual or homosexual). By this definition, erection for purposes of masturbation does not preclude the category of primary impotence. When the man has had at least one success but fails on 25 percent or more of the occasions, he is considered treatment-worthy, that is, *secondary* impotence. It is worth noting that in only 7 of 213 cases seen by Masters and Johnson was a physical difficulty associated with secondary impotence. Whereas ". . . an immature or even negatively disposed sexual value system" (p. 143) was most often associated with primary impotence, premature ejaculation and alcoholic overindulgence were the most frequent conditions for the first instances of secondary impotence.

When does a man ejaculate prematurely? Various absolute lengths of time have been propounded—for example, 30 seconds after insertion, two minutes, and so forth. Masters and Johnson, in keeping with their interpersonal orientation, offer as definition that the partner is not being satisfied at least half the time.

Specific techniques may be added to the general procedures. For premature ejaculation the procedure developed by Semans (1956) and elaborated by Masters and Johnson (1970) may be included. This involves aborting the ejaculation by pressure on the penis, followed by return to foreplay or reinsertion. Insertion itself includes gradual increase in the male's activity; an early phase involves insertion without movement so that the man may experience and grow accustomed to the stimuli present.

Once an erection is attained through petting and maintained for a period of time, the man may think of some irrelevant topic so he will lose the erection. This seems paradoxical, but it helps illustrate the part he plays in the activity, and it also permits him to re-attain the erection. This provides more than one learning trial per sexual encounter and teaches that loss of erection does not mean cessation of the activity.

The first point demonstrated by these details is that treatment is direct relearning. The second is the complex, social, sequential nature of the sexual act; it is a total interpersonal act. In this regard, Masters and Johnson (1970) make remarks that are particularly valuable: "No man can will an erection. . . . Whenever any individual evaluates his sexual performance or that of his partner during an active sexual encounter, he is removing sex from its natural context." (p. 196) "Quiet, nondemanding stroking . . . provides opportunity to give and receive sensate pleasure, but of greater importance, *opportunity to think and feel sexually without orientation to performance.*" (pp. 201–202.) To summarize, probably the best advice is to love the other person; the moment a person uses another to prove something, he courts failure.

Masters's and Johnson's (1970, p. 367, Table 2) basic success is 80 percent. Wolpe (1958) reports on the treatment of seven cases of impotence, five of them successful. Other successful cases have been reported by Lazarus and Rachman (1960), Lazarus (1965a), Kushner (1965b), Dengrove (1967), Apter (1961), and Kraft and Al-Issa (1968). Friedman (1968) used a drug to obtain relaxation and was successful with eight of ten erective problems and with three of six ejaculatory problems. Lobitz and LoPiccolo (1972) used a broader range of behavioral techniques and report success in six of six premature ejaculation cases and four of six erectile failure cases. The major point in

Ejaculatory Incompetence

While relatively rare, ejaculatory incompetence is important because it is a male analogue to orgasmic dysfunction of the female. Masters and Johnson (1970) report 100 percent success with the 17 cases they treated. The male attains and maintains erection; the changeworthy behavior is that he does not attain orgasm or ejaculate intravaginally. Aside from mutual pleasuring and other general approaches, when ejaculation is inevitable, the male inserts. After a number of such experiences, insertion may occur at lower levels of excitation and longer intravaginal time may follow.

Orgasmic dysfunction, formerly improperly called frigidity is failure on the part of the woman to achieve orgasm. A first step requires providing accurate information (Wolpe, 1971; Masters and Johnson, 1970). Lazarus (1963) reported on 16 cases using systematic desensitization, in nine of which he obtained success in an average of 28 sessions. It is also interesting to note that he was capable of identifying his failures in 15 or fewer sessions, so that the waste of time, money, and effort by both patient and therapist was avoided. Supporting results were reported by Madsen and Ullmann (1967), who had the husband of the woman being treated take an active part in the therapy situation. Aside from discussion of the situation and attempts to ameliorate problems such as fear of pregnancy, the treatment of orgasmic dysfunction in the Lazarus and the Madsen and Ullmann studies follows the paradigm of treatment for phobia. A hierarchy of progressive sexual intimacy is developed. The patient is taught to relax, and the situations are presented to her. In the Madsen and Ullmann procedure the husband is the person who presents the stimuli and who, under the guidance of the therapist, paces the wife in terms of both what and when to visualize. (For a further discussion, see Krasner and Ullmann, 1973, pp. 289–93.)

Brady (1966, 1967), Chapman (1968), Masters and Johnson (1970), Kraft and Al-Issa (1967a), Haslam (1965b), and Wincze (1971) also report successful behavioral treatment of this behavior. In an excellent article, Lobitz and LoPiccolo (1972) report 13 successes out of 13 cases for primary female orgasmic dysfunction and three of nine successes with secondary orgasmic dysfunction.

While not limited to orgasmic dysfunction, a major research by Obler (1973) is best placed here. Obler used three groups: a behavioral one, a traditional (neopsychoanalytic), and a control to deal with various sexual problems. His major measure was a percentage of success per sexual experience. Of the behavioral group, 80 percent were sexually functional a year and a half after the end of treatment, while few if any of the people in the other two groups were. During the period of treatment, the behavior therapy group had an average success rate of 42 percent for women and 45 percent for men, while the comparable figures for the traditional and control groups were three percent and two percent for women and three percent and two percent for men, respectively. The number of sexual experiences was largest in the behavioral treatment group. The behavioral treatment involved principally desensitization, but also incorporated assertive confidence training.

Unusual Stimuli

The foregoing material dealt with difficulties within heterosexual relatonships, which are usually self-referred and compose the most frequent sexual behaviors worked with by clinical psychologists. While subtle interpersonal and social pressures may well operate, no major ethical problems are usually raised. The material has centered on the direct training and re-education in sexual ideas and practices. Heterosexual male and female problems such as impotence and orgasmic dysfunction are frequently categorized as physiopsychological disorders of the genitourinary tract rather than "sexual deviations." We now turn to behaviors that are typically placed in the category "sexual deviation," which involves acts, objects, or setting events that are currently socially frowned upon. Here, very major and appropriate ethical concerns can be and have been raised (Weinberg, 1972; Gochros, 1972; Yoell et al., 1971).

Fetishism may be thought of as sexual behavior under control of an inappropriate discriminative stimulus. To quote Henderson and Batchelor (1962, p. 200): "In all such cases the normal sexual act may not reach attainment in the absence of some accustomed stimulus. A particular scent, hair, fur, silk underwear, slippers, high-heeled shoes, garters, handkerchiefs, may all be necessary accompaniments. It is only when the particular fetish becomes completely detached from the person, and is itself utilized as the sexual object that we regard the condition as pathological." This definition, while more liberal than most in the literature, still implies that there is some absolute norm of appropriate behavior.

If one takes the strictly biological orientation that the person is capable of a wide range of responses including homosexual ones, then "normal" heterosexual behavior might be described as fetishistic. Further, socially acceptable behavior typically is not only limited to members of the opposite sex but to members of the opposite sex of an age approximately that of the person and often to the person's spouse. Each culture develops norms of sexual attractiveness, and if the person is attracted by a particular hair color, bust development, length of lip, or pattern of scars, he might again theoretically be called a fetishist. Rachman (1966a) has demonstrated this concept in an experimental analogue.

Fetishism becomes changeworthy when the object leads to a sexual response of a "compulsive" nature at an inappropriate time and place.

Raymond (1956) reports on the treatment of a 33-year-old married man who had been referred for prefrontal leucotomy after he had attacked a perambulator. This was the twelfth such attack known to the police. He had had impulses to damage handbags and perambulators since age ten, and estimated that he had made such attacks an average of two or three times a week. He had received many hours of analytical therapy and had been able to trace back the history of his abnormality and to see the significance and sexual symbolism of perambulators and handbags. However, the attacks had continued. The treatment was explained to the patient, who was dubious but ready to try anything. A collection of handbags, perambulators, and colored illustrations was obtained. These were shown to the patient after he had received an injection of apomorphine and just before nausea was produced.

The treatment was given every two hours, day and night; at night, amphetamine was used to keep the patient awake. After a week, the patient was allowed to go home for eight days. He returned, and reported "jubilantly" that for the first time he had been able to have intercourse with his wife without using fantasies of handbags or perambulators. The same treatment was continued. In addition, the patient was asked to write about the objects, which he did in great detail. After five days he said that the mere sight of the objects made him sick. At this, he was confined to bed and handbags and perambulators were piled around him.

The treatment continued at irregular intervals. On the ninth day he broke down and sobbed until the objects were removed. He handed over, on his own, a set of film negatives of perambulators. He left the hospital and six months later was readmitted for a booster course of treatment (which he felt he did not need): a colored movie film was made of women carrying handbags and pushing perambulators. The film was started each time just before the onset of nausea. A follow-up 19 months later showed that in addition to no overt behavior or trouble with the police, the patient no longer required the fantasies for successful intercourse. He progressed on his job, and no other symptoms replaced the fetish.

Other papers reporting successful treatment of fetishism using an aversion technique are by Raymond (cited in Rachman, 1961), Thorpe et al. (1964, case no. 5), McGuire and Vallance (1964), Kushner (1965b), Marks, Rachman, and Gelder (1965), Bond and Evans (1967), Raymond and O'Keeffe (1965), Marks and Gelder (1967), Marks, Gelder, and Bancroft (1970), Fookes (1969), and Haslam and Rachman (1972).

Fetishism may be considered a paradigm for *transvestism, sadism,* and *masochism,* in which sexual arousal and gratification are restricted to or made more likely by, respectively, wearing clothing of the opposite sex, inflicting pain, and receiving pain. In these situations the person has come to associate a particular stimulus with sexual activity and gratification. The stimulus may be an object or a characteristic of a person such as in fetishism. It may, however, also be social role such as dominance in sadism or submission in masochism. If a male, for example, does not know the socially appropriate manner of approaching, wooing, and winning a member of the opposite sex, he may generalize from other situations and behaviors in which he has been successful. He may, therefore, act in a brash, aggressive, rough manner, and, in a majority of cases, he will be rejected. However, if these behaviors are followed by acquiescence on the part of some other person at times and if they lead to orgasm on his part, they may be repeated. They work, and in terms of that individual's history of reinforcement they are normal, reasonable behaviors. They become disturbing only to the extent that they interfere with further adjustment such as reducing the number of people who will respond positively to him. The partner in a sexual act may shape the other person by being responsive only to certain activities.

A case illustrative of role dominance and sexual gratification is reported by Thompson:

I once saw a young woman (in a court setting) who had her husband arrested after ten years of marriage. During the diagnostic interview, she told me of ten years of frequent, severe beatings by her husband which included his having her strip down while he burned her on the chest with a cigarette. When asked if she had called the police she replied, "No, they'd never believe me, he's too good a liar," despite the fact that she had two welts on her chest at that very moment. She also said that her husband would arouse her sexually by playing with her breasts, but "he'd do it just to be mean because he'd never have intercourse with me after he got me excited."

Why then had she had her husband arrested? Because two months ago he had left her for another woman. [1965, p. 24.]

A second formulation of the development of masochism, sadism, and other forms of sexual behavior involving specific times and places may be given in terms of the reinforcement which results from avoiding a stimulus that has been aversive on a previous occasion. Such behavior may be learned through vicarious reinforcement as well as through more direct experience with that stimulus. An example is homosexual behavior that is antithetical to and avoids contact with members of the opposite sex. In such cases the male stimulus marks the time and place where it will be "safe" to emit the sexual act. Third, fetishistic acts will develop for lack of a repertoire, making success under other conditions unlikely. Examples are people who are potent only with minors (pedophilia) or prostitutes.

Transvestism denotes that the individual, as part of the behaviors leading to sexual gratification, dresses in the clothes of members of the opposite sex. Many of the foregoing ideas are brought together in a formulation by Buckner (1970). A first step in becoming a transvestite is association of some item of feminine apparel with sexual gratification between ages five and 14. At adolescence, the second step is difficulty in heterosexual relationships, such as fear of rejection or feelings of physical or personal inadequacy. A third step is when homosexual outlets are also blocked, either through socialized aversion or lack of opportunity. The fourth step is elaboration of masturbation fantasies and development of contacts with the transvestite culture and literature. The fifth and final step involves the fixing of the gratification pattern in an identity of a transvestite or at least on the occasion of cross-dressing.

When self-referred, successful treatment of transvestism by behavioral techniques has been reported by Dengrove (1967), Thorpe et al. (1964, case no. 4), Clark (1963a, 1965), Morgenstern, Pearce, and Davies (1963), Barker et al. (1961), Cooper (1963), Blakemore et al. (1965a, b), and Fookes (1968). Gersham (1970) used a variety of behavioral procedures, and Moss, Rada, and Appel (1970) added environmental control, notably the wife refusing to support the husband's cross-dressing but being receptive to sexual activity without transvestism. Similar direct procedures have been used with pedophilia (Rosenthal, in press), exhibitionism (Abel, Levis, and Clancy, 1970; MacCulloch, Williams, and Birtles, 1971).

Lavin et al. (1961) report on a 22-year-old married truck driver who had had a recurrent desire to dress in female clothing since age eight and had derived erotic satisfaction from it since age 15. While transvestism had continued during service in the Royal Air Force and after marriage, his sexual relationships with his wife were good. Lavin et al. noted that the conditioned stimulus must be prepared to correspond to the patient's behavioral difficulty and must not include anything without significance for the behavior under modification. The patient was excited by dressing in female clothes and viewing himself in the mirror. Twelve 35 mm. transparencies were taken of the patient in various stages of female dress, and a tape recording was made of the patient reading from a script describing his putting on various garments. This procedure was designed to strengthen the conditioned stimulus and to insure the presence of the stimulus even when the patient's eyes were closed. Aversion therapy was continued every two hours for six days and six nights. The unconditioned stimulus was nausea, produced by apomorphine. As soon as the injection began to take effect, a slide was projected onto a screen and the tape recording was played back. The stimulus was terminated after the patient started vomiting. The patient and his wife were interviewed three times during the six months following treatment, and each time they stated that recovery was complete. Six months after completion of therapy, the patient reported the continued absence of transvestism. Lavin et al. conclude that "The prediction of symptom substitution inherent in a psychoanalytic theory has not so far been borne out."

In Chapter 10 it was noted that there are some behaviors which are expressive of a role and other behaviors which are correlates thereof (i.e., secondary deviance). A hypothesis germane to some masochistic and homosexual behaviors is that the person is uncomfortable in emitting the typical role-expressive behavior.[5] If this is so, training in how to make assertive responses in the extratherapy situation and in the use of systematic desensitization within the therapy situation may be beneficial. Dengrove (1967) reports the treatment of a man who was "excessively inhibited at his job" and a transvestite. It was noted that "just seeing an attractively dressed woman would trigger off his transvestism." Treatment was directed, through use of systematic desensi-

---

[5] The demand for legitimate human rights is particularly pertinent for women (Jakubowski-Spector, 1973; MacDonald, in press).

tization, toward his feeling of inability to equal his father's success, and hence building up his own confidence and self-esteem. Eventually he was able to visualize female attire and still remain relaxed.

Exhibitionism refers to intentional exposure of sex organs under inappropriate conditions. The typical exhibitionist is a shy person who behaves as if he had difficulties in approaching women. He may well gain considerable gratification from the reaction of shock his display creates. Over a period of time, the pairing of sexual release with exhibition may lead to the various situations in which exhibiting behavior comes by itself to have strong stimulus control not unlike that of a fetish object. Treatment is usually directed along more than a single dimension and is likely to include systematic desensitization for the situations which previously had typically led to exhibiting behavior and encouragement of and tutoring in more assertive social behavior. Cases treated in this manner have been reported by Bond and Hutchinson (1960), Dengrove (1967), Ritchie (1968), Witzig (1968), Abel et al. (1970), Kushner and Sadler (1966), Wickramasekera (1968), Barnett (1972), and Lutzker (1973).

Voyeurism refers to sexual gratification attained while secretively looking at sexual stimuli. Wolpe (1958) reports decrease of voyeuristic behavior after assertive training and systematic desensitization for discomfort in interpersonal situations. Madsen (in a personal communication) similarly reports successful treatment of voyeuristic behavior. Gaupp, Stern, and Ratliff (1971) used aversion relief, while Jackson (1969) shaped the behavior via masturbation to pictures.

Masochism refers to sexual excitement in conjunction with being subjected to pain. *Sadism* is sexual excitement attendant upon the infliction of pain on another person. Davison (1968a) reports on the treatment of a 21-year-old college senior who reported he had not had "normal" fantasies since age 11. While he masturbated about five times a week, he had exclusively sadistic fantasies centering around torturing women. He declared that he was never aroused by any other image and had only twice kissed girls. Treatment had two aspects. The first was the pairing of sexual arousal with culturally appropriate stimuli. The student was instructed to look at *Playboy* pictures while masturbating in his room. Sadistic fantasies were, at first, used to attain erection. During the following weeks, the stimuli to be attended to while masturbating were slowly changed from viewing to imagining, and from idealizations to more immediate, real, and available social stimuli. At each step of the procedure, the backup stimulus to attain erection was shifted to the previously learned stimulus. A second aspect of treatment was the use of an aversive thought attendant upon undesired behavior (i.e., sadistic fantasy). This procedure was started in the third treatment session: when a sadistic fantasy would come to his mind the student was to think of engaging in coprophilic acts ("steaming urine with reeking fecal boli bobbing on top which he drank"). Total treatment sessions were six in number. The sadistic fantasies did not recur, and typical college dating was encouraged. A similar successful treatment of sadistic fantasies has been reported by Mees (1966).

Homosexuality refers to sexual desire or behavior directed toward a member of one's own sex. It is crucial in dealing with homosexuality to make it clear that a great range of behaviors may be labeled homosexual both in terms of the kinds of behavior as well as the relative frequency of such behaviors (Humphreys, 1970). If account is not taken of these differences within a group manifesting a particular behavior, grave difficulties result for both research and therapy. The frequency of male homosexual behavior reported by Kinsey et al. (1948), although consistent with other studies in the field, surprised many people. Kinsey found that approximately one in six males had had some homosexual contact after age 16.

It is important to note that the degree of homosexual involvement compared to heterosexual involvement is not an all-or-none phenomenon. Kinsey and his coworkers used a seven-point scale in their survey. The scale points and the frequencies obtained for different groups of females and males are shown in Table 1. The percentages are cumulative. The table has the advantage of indicating that the figures are estimates. In studies on the incidence of homosexuality and the outcome of treatment, the Kinsey rating of the subjects is a crucial item of information, a Kinsey "6" being presumed to be more difficult to treat successfully than a Kinsey "2" or "3." An important semantic and theoretical issue is whether a Kinsey "1" or "2" should be called a homosexual. Logically it seems as unreasonable to label a person a homosexual because of behavior at step 2 as it would be to label him a heterosexual because of behavior of low frequency at steps 4 and 5.[6]

A second matter in which there is a great range is in the type of activity in the homosexual act. Hooker (1962) reports on these differences in the "homosexual community," and Reiss (1964) similarly reports on the activity of adolescent boys in Chicago who, in order to earn money, permit males to perform oral homosexual acts on them. The boys are achieving orgasm in the presence of another of the same sex. However, they do not consider themselves homosexual because they are doing it for money, achieve sexual gratification at times with members of the opposite sex, and give up the activity when they are old enough to make money in other ways. Neither they nor their peer group consider the acts homosexual.

Other types of homosexual behavior include the male obtaining gratification only in an *active* role either through oral or anal contact with the partner and the male only *permitting* such acts to be performed upon him. There are many males who perform both roles.

The behavioral characteristics of effeminacy and transvestism are not necessarily indicative of homosexuality. Placing a person in a category leads to ascribing to him many characteristics which he may not exhibit in his actual behavior. The effects of being placed in the category (see Chapter 10) may lead to regularities of behavior, but these regularities are *effects* of the categorization rather than *causes* of homosexual acts.[7]

The rate of female homosexual behavior is lower, and there is greater tolerance of physical contact between women (e.g., embracing in public). Quite possibly men, who usually are society's lawmakers, are less threatened by female than male homosexuality.[8]

There have been relatively few reports of treatment of female homosexuality; Blitch and Haynes (1972) emphasize a wide range of techniques (systematic desensitization, role-playing, use of masturbation fantasies). From our own work, we would stress that the first step is development of good interpersonal relationships, with both women

[6] The concept of homosexual behavior as a symptom of a severe emotional behavior leads to treatment deductions: see Bieber (1967), Socarides (1968), Morganthaler (1968), and Ovesey and Gaylin (1965). Data on overt homosexuals who are not in treatment (e.g., Loney, 1971, 1972; Wilson and Greene, 1971; Siegelman, 1972; Thompson, McCandless, and Strickland, 1971; Hooker, 1957) indicate that overt homosexuality need not be associated with "severe emotional disorder," and feelings of guilt, isolation, and constriction of opportunity when they do occur may be a result of societal prejudice rather than a necessary aspect of homosexuality.

[7] One may speculate on the matter endlessly. For example, homosexual women may reproduce, while impotent and homosexual males may not. Brown (1952) noted that crossculturally, 68 percent of societies measured punished male homosexuality while only 33 percent of societies punished female homosexuality.

[8] The homosexual community is seeking to obtain legitimate human and civil rights. Among recent books in this area are ones by Humphreys (1970), Sagarin (1969), and Teal (1971).

Table 1
Kinsey scale points for heterosexual-homosexual experience

SCALE POINT		FEMALES	MALES
0:	Entirely heterosexual experience		
	Single	61–72%	53–78%
	Married	89–90%	90–92%
	Previously married	75–80%	......
1–6:	At least some homosexual experience	11–20%	18–42%
2–6:	More than incidental homosexual experience	6–14%	13–38%
3–6:	Homosexual as much or more than heterosexual	4–11%	9–32%
4–6:	Mostly homosexual experience	3–8%	7–26%
5–6:	Almost exclusive homosexual experience	2–6%	5–22%
6:	Exclusively homosexual experience	1–3%	3–16%

Source: Kinsey et al., 1953, p. 488.

and men. As such, we are likely to focus on sticking up for one's legitimate rights, being able to express one's feelings and having them respected. After a good relationship has been established with a male, the treatment is similar to that for orgasmic dysfunction.

To the extent that sexual arousal and satisfaction occur in the presence of stimuli considered inappropriate, homosexual behavior may be dealt with in the paradigm presented for fetishism. Indeed, the treatment of homosexuality parallels in many instances that of the fetishistic behaviors, which in turn greatly overlap the formulation and treatment of phobias and compulsions. There are two aspects of treatment which would be derived from the theoretical model presented in previous chapters: a socially disturbing behavior is reduced, and an alternative set of behaviors is encouraged. The optimal way to achieve reduction of disturbing behavior is to teach the substitution of a more socially effective reaction to the situations in which the unwanted target behavior has been emitted. However, on occasion, aversive stimuli may be employed. Examples of pairing the inappropriate stimulus with aversive rather than sexually gratifying experiences have been presented in the previous section of this chapter dealing with fetishism and transvestism. Aversive stimuli may also be used to provide reinforcement when the appropriate act serves to terminate or avoid such stimuli (Thorpe et al., 1964).

This procedure may be called anticipatory avoidance, and the most complete, sophisticated, and documented work in the area is in Feldman and MacCulloch (1971). These authors obtained a 60 percent improvement rate. Feldman and MacCulloch (1964, 1965) adapted an anticipatory avoidance technique to the clinical situation in the following way:

The homosexual patient views a male slide which is back-projected onto a screen. He is instructed to leave on a picture for as long as he finds it attractive. After the slide has been on the screen for 8 seconds, the patient receives a shock if he has not by then removed it by means of a switch with which he is provided. If he does switch off within the 8 second period he avoids the shock. Once the patient is avoiding regularly he is placed on a standardized reinforcement schedule which consists of three types of trials randomly interspersed. The first type consists of reinforced trials (the patient's attempt to switch off succeeds immediately). The second consists of delay trials (the patient's attempt to switch off is held up for varying intervals of time within the 8 second period.) He does, however, eventually succeed in avoiding. Finally, one-third of all trials are non-reinforced (the patient does receive a shock irrespective of his attempts to switch off). In addition, on two-fifths of the trials, selected at random, a female slide is projected onto the screen contiguous with the offset of the male slide, and is left on for about 10 seconds. This is then removed by the therapist and the patient can, if he wishes, request that it be returned. However, his request is met in an entirely random manner. A further feature is the use of hierarchies of male and female slides. The patient places the slides in their order of attractiveness for him so that the treatment starts with the least atracive male slide being paired with the most attractive female slide; the two hierarchies then being moved along simultaneously. [Feldman, 1966, p. 172.]

Of 26 patients treated in this manner, 18, or 69 percent, had shown complete absence of homosexual practices together with an almost complete absence of homosexual fantasy. Follow-up ranged from three months to two years. Two-thirds of the sample were Kinsey scale 5 or 6 and none had less than a Kinsey rating of 3.

Aversive stimuli may be used to build up anxiety-relief and anticipatory avoidance responses (Schmidt et al., 1965; Larson, 1970; MacCulloch, Birtles and Feldman, 1971). Aversive stimuli that can be used include apomorphine (to induce vomiting), electric stimuli, a noxious smell (Colson, 1972), and, as referred to earlier in regard to sadistic fantasies, a rehearsal procedure to focus attention on the ultimate aversive consequences of the act, or an upsetting, disgusting aspect of the situation (Gold and Neufeld, 1965; Curtis and Presly, 1972; Kendrick and McCullough, 1972; Maletzky, 1973). Serber (1970) discusses shame aversion therapy, a technique in which the person who is ashamed or self-conscious of the act (transvestism, voyeurism, exhibitionism) performs the act in front of observers for a quarter to half an hour. Reitz and Keil (1971) report successful use of this procedure with an exhibitionist. The aversive stimulus may be presented at the very first impulse toward the inappropriate act, or it may be paired with an element of the object. The programming of the aversive stimulus may be on a fixed ratio or a variable one. It must be emphasized that there is a complex technology involved in these matters and that aversive conditioning is not a matter for simple-minded, amateur application (Feldman, 1966).

Concurrent with decreasing emission of one set of responses is the encouragement of the emission of an alternative set of behaviors.

An important technique, which resembles aspects of work by Davison (1968a) and Marquis (1970), and the Masters and Johnson procedure with ejaculatory incompetence, involves the person gaining arousal by imagining a homosexual stimulus and masturbating. At the point of orgasmic inevitability, the person focuses on a heterosexual symbol such as a photograph in order to pair orgasm with heterosexual stimuli. Once established, the point of attention to the heterosexual stimulus may be moved to points of lesser arousal or the heterosexual stimulus may be gradually changed to types that were previously even less arousing than the first used. Clinically, a crucial point occurs when the client first becomes aroused by a heterosexual rather than homosexual symbol; a matter of great encouragement, this indicates that change is indeed possible. Other techniques to achieve change may include: coaching in the proper way to make dates and to encourage members of the opposite sex; the use of systematic desensitization to members of the opposite sex; (e.g., Levin et al., 1968; Huff, 1970; DiScipio, 1968; Kraft, 1967; Lamberd, 1969); fading from homosexual to heterosexual stimuli (Barlow and Agras, 1973); the training of expressive role behaviors such as appropriate assertion; the divulging of accurate information about sex; and the discussion of attitudes toward sexual stimuli. In terms of the last technique, the concepts and approaches of Ellis (1962) are a valuable contribution. All too often people will label their own sexual behavior as indicative of illness. These labeling reactions become effective stimuli and may lead to further failure to emit socially appropriate behavior.

An approach emphasized by Ellis is to ask the person to view rationally the consequences of various acts. This might be put as the person's role-playing or rehearsing future behavior. The question frequently is to decide what the effects of a particular behavior might be. For example, would it be so devastating to the individual if a woman did not wish to accept an invitation for a date? The therapist then provides a model of the appropriate reactions for the client: he might point out that it would not be as pleasant as being accepted but that it is after all only one woman and one occasion; why not ask another? At worst all that has happened is that one has had a human experience. The experience is devastating only when the client overgeneralizes to the point of using it as (incorrect) evidence that he is worthless.

It is along these lines that the very model adhered to in the behavioral approach to sexual difficulties may have therapeutic benefit in itself. The person seeking help reports that he has emitted homosexual behavior under certain circumstances. The therapist may investigate with him these circumstances and alternative appropriate behaviors. The person is considered to be a normal person rather than one with symptoms of "a severe emotional disorder." His strengths and his socially appropriate responses in his work, for example, are pointed out. The very genuine respect the therapist has for him may lead to a change in self-labeling and make more likely the emission of the new behavior which is the goal of treatment. The successful emission of different behavior, in turn, is the strongest possible evidence that indeed he is *not* sick and can look forward to further successes. The focus throughout treatment is on *what* can be done. This leads to a rapid grappling with the problems involved in emitting new behaviors, and here, the therapist, using a combination of the procedures discussed in this section (e.g., Hanson and Abesso, 1972), can be of real assistance.

Freund (1960) found for a group of 28 men who did not enter therapy under external pressure (that is, because of police referral), 39.3 percent obtained a nonhomosexual adaptation lasting several years, and another 17.9 percent obtained a short-term heterosexual adjustment lasting several months. In short, approximately 57 percent obtained benefit. Freund merely claimed that his procedures required far less time and therapist effort than typical psychoanalytic efforts in order to achieve equal benefit. Compared with the reports of Bieber et al. (1962), Curran and Parr (1957), and Woodward (1958) on their treatment with traditional therapy of more prognostically favorable homosexuals, procedures such as those of Freund and Feldman and MacCulloch seem to be anywhere from two to five times as effective and to match results achieved by Ellis (1956).

Other reports of the use of aversive stimuli in the treatment of homosexual behavior have come from Max (1935) and James (1962). An interesting use of aversive stimuli was that of Fisher (reported in a personal communication), who developed a transistorized pocket shock apparatus that the person could use to apply an aversive stimulus to himself in extratherapy life situations contingent upon the first noticeable inclination to engage in homosexual behavior. Aside from the obvious advantages of generalization, such a procedure may abort an act by use of an aversive stimulus while approach responses are relatively low.

Stevenson and Wolpe (1960) present three successful cases in which the essential element was teaching the men to be more assertive and to perform acts that are associated in our culture with the masculine role. Similar techniques and successes have been reported by Ellis (1965), Salter (1961), and Edwards (1972).

The following case is cited by Stevenson (1961; based on a case of Wolberg, 1954):

A young student was raised by an ill-tempered and shrewish mother, whose behavior so alienated the patient from women that he considered himself at the time of entering therapy doomed to homosexuality. He had almost no social relationships with girls, and they had never got beyond the slightest physical contact. He seemed to select girls who were as inhibited sexually as himself. Not long after he began treatment he moved from one boarding house to another. Soon afterwards, an attractive girl moved into the next room of the boarding house. They became acquainted and the friendship grew. They discovered that when they unlocked the connecting door between their rooms they could be together more often. The girl was outgoing and warmly affectionate. She was also experienced in the ways of sex and almost before the patient knew it, she had enticed him (or seduced him) so that he was soon enjoying sexual intercourse while entirely forgetting his fears of being a homosexual. They were eventually married.

This case and the larger article by Stevenson from which it came, as well as articles by Wolpe (1961), Lesse (1964), Eysenck (1959), and Rachman (1971) raise an important issue: that of "spontaneous remission," a term that has been used to describe the recovery of a patient without professional assistance. To the behavioral scientist, there is no such thing as a spontaneous remission, unless one wants to use that term to designate changed circumstances about which the professional person is ignorant. Learning always continues in the individual's interpersonal environment. Friends, parents, and simple force of circumstance may lead to new learning, particularly of new contexts and outcomes for previously avoided situations. Such changes are not "spontaneous remissions" but new learning; they follow the same principles of learning as those of behavior development and behavior change by professional therapists. This may be summarized simply by reiterating that people must learn sexual behaviors.

ETHICAL CONSIDERATIONS

Sexual standards change. Sexual practices which may be statistically rare still are in the domain of interpersonal behavior, and if they occur between consenting adults in private are increasingly viewed as not the appropriate concern of the law. When *may*, and, when *should*, the agents of society intervene?

Of crucial importance is the fact that the procedures just described require the active cooperation of the person being treated. Freund (1960) found almost no success with men who had been coerced into treatment. The informed consent of the person is a therapeutic as well as an ethical necessity.

Cross-dressing, acts between consenting adults in private which do not do irreversible harm, and experiments in new lifestyles do not in themselves constitute changeworthy behavior. But the person who wishes to alter his behavior, be it cross-dressing or same-sex relationships, should be permitted that choice.

Among behaviors that seem worth changing, or in which society does seem to have a legitimate interest, are ones that impinge upon other people who do not consent (e.g., rape) or who are incapable of protecting themselves (e.g., incest and pedophilia). Of greater ethical difficulty is the welfare of the very young, very old, and retarded. An example is provided by Anant (1968a) of a 20-year-old woman with an IQ of 59. "Whenever she went out to work on some job, in a cafeteria, etc., she would seduce the first available customer and disappear with him, with the result that no establishment was prepared to hire her any longer." She was faced with continued institutionalization. Should she have been dissuaded from a source of pleasure? By current standards, her sexual activity needed to be placed under stimulus control: of time and place, and most important, of a developed relationship. The technique Anant used was covert sensitization in which the woman visualized unpleasant aversive consequences stemming from the behavior to be changed: She was told about pregnancy, venereal disease, and "murder at the hands of a sex fiend":

Imagine that you meet a stranger in a bar where you are working. You agree to go out with him after your work. He drives you to a deserted place, far removed from the main road. There, he has sexual relations with you in a very aggressive way. You become a little bit scared. After the intercourse, he takes out a rope from the car and, before you realize what he is doing, he ties your hands and feet. Then he gags you and tells you that he would kill you. You are very much scared. You can't even scream for help. Now, he takes a knife out of his pocket and opens it. It is a very big and shining knife. He approaches you with the knife. You are scared like hell, but are quite helpless. You start feeling sorry you came with him. . . .

Olson and Kelley (1969) used an aversive stimulus to reduce masturbatory activity that was worrying a 23-year-old, unmarried male. At what point is masturbation change-worthy? Considerations might include the locale of the acts and whether they were so frequent they interfered with other activities such as reading an abnormal psychology text. But, if the person concerned about masturbation masturbates in private with a frequency within limits typical for unmarried male college students, and participates fully and effectively in other life experiences, should his desire to change be encouraged or should his views on the matter be altered? The latter is not his request; can a therapist "know better?"

At times a person may be having difficulties in pursuit of a behavior considered unconventional; for example, a man may become impotent in the homosexual act. The point is illustrated by a case from Oswald (1962) which also illustrates the development of a fetish. The man was a 32-year-old soldier who was sexually aroused by tying himself up in shiny black rubber. This had started when in his youth a group of boys had overpowered him, put a sheet over his head, and masturbated him. He came for treatment because recently, after tying himself up, he had had difficulty in releasing himself from the rubber sheets, hood, and ropes. The therapist might as easily reduce the irrelevant anxiety caused by this one experience through use of systematic desensitization as he might use aversive stimuli to reduce the desire to engage in the fetishistic activity at all. In this case, the man's wishes coincided with conventional standards, but what if he had requested assistance for the opposite?

A final example of the types of problems encountered in this area stemmed from the senior author's participation in a symposium in which an existentially oriented therapist, who knew about and eventually used direct behavioral approaches successfully, told of a year's treatment of an impotent male prior to trying the effective procedures which then did work very rapidly. The question is whether it is ethical to wait so long. This may be what the husband wished, but what were the wife's choices in the interim? When the activity is a mutual interpersonal activity, the therapist must consider not only his immediate client but also the other people who are significantly affected. And there are times, as in this example, when not acting is as ethically problematical as any application of a specific treatment.

SUMMARY

More clearly than most other behaviors, sexual activity illustrates the importance of social evaluation and labeling. This chapter discussed some of the pressures on the therapist in evaluating whether a behavior should be changed. At the present time, there are no clear standards, much less research, on which to base such decisions. One notion, however, is that an activity may be questioned if it interferes with or takes the place of a form of behavior that is *presumed* to be more mature, satisfying, rewarding, or socially acceptable. Masturbatory behavior may be questioned if it replaces heterosexual behavior in marriage, but not if it is the most acceptable outlet available to a person in prisons, military settings, or prior to marriage.

A sexual activity should probably not be changed by a technique such as aversive conditioning unless (1) a better activity is unavailable, (2) one can teach and reinforce such an alternative outlet, and (3) failing the above, the present behavior is so socially reprehensible that its pursuit leads to increasingly negative social consequences. Each behavior must be judged by its appropriateness to the individual in terms of his age, socioeconomic status, available acceptable outlets, and consequences to other people. One must not apply any morality, particularly his own, unless he can provide a specific helping function to the client. However, a therapist is a representative of society, and, if he takes a salary from an institution, a representative of an organization as well. A therapist must come to terms with the morality of his institution. If he cannot, he is well-advised to seek a different employer or clinical setting.

At the level of citizenship it is proper and even obligatory to attempt to decrease the gap between official morality and actual behavior. But above all other considerations there is the requirement of respect for the person who emits behavior of which he is biologically capable but which is deviant in terms of a social evaluation in a particular time and place. Given these considerations, sexual behaviors were formulated as learned responses, and methods for new learning were described.

addictive behavior

22

DSM-II places *alcoholism* and *drug dependence*, like "sexual deviations," in the category of personality disorders and certain other nonpsychotic mental disorders. DSM-I used the label "addiction" as a generic term that included both "alcoholism" and "drug addiction" but offered no definition of the term. DSM-II uses "addiction" as synonymous with "dependent on" alcohol or drugs.

DEFINING ADDICTION

The specification of who should be termed addicted raises great difficulties. One problem is the very notion of addiction. There are concepts of *physiological addiction, psychological dependency, abuse, likelihood* of abuse, and the social and physiological *consequences* of prior indulgence.

Physiological addiction has as its criteria *habituation* as we use it[1] and *abstinence* (withdrawal) *syndrome*. Habituation refers to the bodily adaptation to a physiological condition (drugs, alcohol) that results in progressively greater amounts being tolerated and therefore progressively greater doses being required to attain effects. Abstinence or withdrawal syndrome refers to the consequences of sudden decrease of ingestion of the drug. Ewing (1967, p. 1007) notes that in 75 percent of people regularly taking eight or more tablets of meprobamate (Miltown, Equanil), the abstinence reaction will involve insomnia, tremor, muscle twitching, anxiety, weakness, and nausea. More severe reactions occur with the withdrawal of, say, morphine; they may include restlessness, yawning, hypertension, sweating, and cramps. In the case of barbiturate withdrawal, delirium tremens, convulsions, confusion, and hallucinations occur. Physical addiction genuinely follows a medical model: the responses observed are the result of biochemical adjustments. Medical attention and procedures are required in the management of the patient. The psychologists's professional role occurs *after* physiological responses are brought within normal range of functioning. The behaviors which led to the physiological condition (or more specifically, substitution of new behaviors for them) are the proper sphere for the behavioral scientist.

Psychological dependency refers to use of a foreign substance (drug, alcohol) as a typical response to a variety of situations. The situation may be one of physical addiction the response to which is reinforced by the termination of the abstinence syndrome, or it may be one in which the individual periodically uses alcohol or drugs to reduce discomfort in interpersonal situations. The person emits the response of using the substance in a stereotyped manner that is analogous to behavior emitted by people labeled compulsive. While psychological dependency and physiological addiction are *not* mutually exclusive, there

---

[1] Jones, Shainberg, and Byer (1969, p. 4) illustrate differences in usages of terms in that their "habituation" is close to our use of "dependence": "If the psychic influence is strong, individuals may become habituated to almost anything." According to these authors a placebo required to sleep is an example of habituation.

are frequent instances (the use of marijuana is an example) in which a person may act in a manner that is called psychologically dependent while *not* being physically addicted.

The term *abuse* is a social evaluation. The person engages in the act in a way that is improper and harmful to himself. While acting in an improper and ultimately self-defeating manner does not rule out either physical addiction or psychological dependency, the term "abuse" may also be applied to people who engage in the activity without developing either addictive or dependent responses. The social evaluation enters crucially into the limits of tolerated behavior: the limits for a Midwestern minister and a Madison Avenue executive are different.

Jones, Shainberg, and Byer (1969, p. 5) define an abusive dose as "the amount needed to produce the side effects and actions desired by an individual abusing a drug." Further, "when a drug is self-administered in toxic dosages and damages an individual, a society, or both, the drug is being abused." (p. 11.)

The criterion of *likelihood of becoming addicted,* or more accurately, likelihood of abusing, becoming psychologically dependent upon, or physically addicted, has reference to both past and future events. There are progressive stages which increase the likelihood of behavior in the next step. The person is shaped into a career of addiction. It is a general belief among professionals that the earlier in a career a person receives treatment, the easier and more successful treatment will be (Holden, 1973; Sobell, Schaeffer, and Mills, 1972). A person who shows evidences of embarking on a pattern leading to addictive behavior may well be counseled to seek professional help in altering his behavior. An example of the concept of likelihood may be observed in Alcoholics Anonymous, in which a person who has not had an alcoholic drink for ten years will introduce himself as an "alcoholic," but one "who is not drinking today." The concept seems paradoxical but is maintained because it indicates the prediction of adverse behavior upon resumption of drinking.

As with all other categories of abnormal behavior, there is a matter of secondary deviation, the effects of having engaged in and been designated as an alcoholic or drug addict. Further, in addictive behaviors, notably alcoholism, there may be irreversible physiological consequences of the activity as well as social consequences. On a physiological level, the person may be diagnosed as manifesting a chronic brain syndrome or as having permanent damage to internal organs such as the liver. At a social level, the person may have alienated his friends, employer, and spouse. Even though he may not be currently drinking to an excessive degree, particularly as compared with others of his social status, the person may still be designated and treated as an alcoholic by some friends and social agencies because of his reputation.

ALCOHOLISM

DSM-II defines alcoholism as follows: "This category is for patients whose alcohol intake is great enough to damage their physical health or their personal or social functioning, or when it has become a prerequisite to normal functioning. If the alcoholism is due to another mental disorder, both diagnoses should be made." (p. 45.)

The general category is then divided into three subcategories. First, the classification of "episodic excessive drinking" is made: "If alcoholism is present and the individual becomes intoxicated as frequently as four times a year." ("Intoxication" is defined as "a state in which the individual's coordination or speech is definitely impaired or his behavior is clearly altered.") Second, the label "habitual excessive drinking" is given to individuals "who are alcoholic and who either become intoxicated more than 12 times a year or are recognizably under the influence of alcohol more than once a week, even though not intoxicated." (p. 45.) Finally there is the subcategory of "alcohol addiction." This is based on evidence (direct or presumptive) that the patient is dependent upon alcohol. The best direct evidence is the appearance of "withdrawal symptoms." The fact that an individual is unable to go a single day without a drink is considered to be "presumptive evidence." A further presumption of addiction to alcohol is heavy drinking for three months or more.

The more severe effects of alcohol are categorized under the "psychoses associated with organic brain syndromes" as "alcoholic psychoses." The difficulties associated with alcoholic psychoses are "delirium tremens," "Korsakov's psychosis," "other alcoholic hallucinosis," "alcohol paranoid state," "acute alcohol intoxication," "alcoholic deterioration," and "pathological intoxication." Delirium tremens and Korsakov's psychosis will be described in detail below.

The use of alcohol to affect man's behavior extends back to the earliest recorded history and exists in all parts of the earth. It has been estimated that as many as 80 million people in the United States drink alcoholic beverages and that 4.5 to 5 million may be considered, by some definitions, to be alcoholic (Chafetz, 1967, p. 1014).[2] The Social Research Group of George Washington University in a survey of the drinking habits of adult Americans reported (*Time*, December 29, 1967, p. 15) that about 6.8 million people drink enough to be classified as "problem drinkers."

At present, alcoholism is considered the fourth most prevalent "disease" in the United States. Approximately 200,000 new cases are identified each year, and alcoholics constitute up to 50 percent of first admissions to mental hospitals. At least half of the 50,000 traffic deaths and the 1.9 million disabling traffic injuries each year are associated with alcohol.

Implicit in the categorization of a person as "alcoholic" is that the individual, by virtue of his drinking behavior, acts in a disturbing manner. The target behavior is variously characterized by inability to control one's drinking habits, impairment of perceptual and intellectual functioning, antagonism toward other individuals, and general inability to function on a job, at home, and in social situations. The categorization of "alcoholic" may be made on several different and contradictory criteria: the physiological effects of drinking; the inability to stop drinking; the amount drunk; and the social consequences of drinking.

The World Health Organization's (1955) definition of an alcoholic is as follows: "Alcoholics are those excessive drinkers whose dependence on alcohol has attained such a degree that they show a noticeable mental disturbance or an interference with their mental and bodily health, their interpersonal relations and their smooth social and economic functioning; or who show the prodromal signs of such developments. They therefore require treatment." (Kessel and Walton, 1965, p. 18.)

In short, they drink too much.

Various indices of the effects of alcohol are used to ascertain the frequency of alcoholism: death due to cirrhosis of the liver; admission for alcoholic psychosis; house-to-house check (e.g., in Washington Heights, New York, where the rate of drinking problems was determined to be 3 per 100 for males, 1 per 100 females). The incidence by different measures varies across countries and across time periods. The clearest example of social effects, because the countries and methods of measurements are held constant, is by sex ratios: in the United States the ratio of male to female alcoholics is 7:1; in Norway, 23:1; in Switzerland, 12:1; in England, 2:1.

---

[2] A review of the literature and an insight into the problems involved may be obtained from Lipscomb (1966), Blum and Blum (1967), and Chafetz (1971).

Patterns of Drinking

Jellinek (1960) describes at least four different patterns of drinking behavior which to a large extent represent cultural and social differences. *Alpha alcoholism* is characterized by the use of alcohol as a means of alleviating bodily or emotional pain. "The drinking is 'undisciplined' in the sense that it contravenes such rules as society tacitly agrees upon such as time, occasion, locale, amount and effect of drinking, but does not lead to 'loss of control' or 'inability to abstain' " (p. 36). The major consequences of this drinking pattern are disturbed interpersonal relationships. There are no signs that the alcoholism becomes progressive even though it may cover a span of many years.

Beta alcoholism is characterized by physical complications such as gastritis or cirrhosis of the liver, which may occur with or without physical addiction or psychological dependence on alcohol. Nutritional damage is a major effect, as is a lessened life span and low vocational productivity.

The pattern producing the greatest damage is labeled *gamma alcoholism* by Jellinek. This is characterized by a large increase in tissue tolerance for alcohol. Thus larger and larger amounts have to be consumed to have an effect. It is in this pattern that the classic behaviors involving withdrawal symptoms, "craving" (physical dependence), and loss of control appear. The social consequences of excessive drinking are greatest in this category.

Delta alcoholism also has the characteristics of increased tolerance for alcohol and withdrawal symptoms resulting from cellular metabolism. The major difference between delta and gamma alcoholism is the delta alcoholic's inability to abstain from drinking for even a short period of time, although he is able to control the amount of intake at any given time. There are social and cultural differences between these two patterns: gamma alcoholism predominates in the United States and Canada; the delta type predominates in wine-drinking countries such as France.

There are many specific additional behaviors involved in alcoholism, especially of the gamma type. Most of these develop as a consequence of and concomitant with the drinking behavior. These include: starting the day with a drink; laying in additional supplies of alcohol to avoid shortages; hiding bottles in obscure places; struggling to maintain employment; rationalizing drinking; trying to compensate for poor social behavior with gifts to one's family; avoiding discussing drinking behavior; surreptitious drinking; and blaming others such as family members for the drinking. The most critical behaviors pointing to the final loss of control include morning drinking, increasing consumption, extreme or socially unacceptable behavior, blackouts, and amnesia. A major point in the progression from drinker to alcoholic is when the alcohol itself becomes a stress instead of an aid to decreasing tension.

Kessel and Walton (1965) approach the behaviors involved in alcoholism by dividing them into three phases characterized by the following behaviors: *excessive drinking* —more time spent in social drinking, drinking more nights of the week, sneaking drinks, adopting strategies to get more drinks, guilt over drinking, feeling that drink has become a necessity; *alcohol addiction*—greater frequency of amnesias, compulsive drinking, drop in work efficiency, absenteeism, getting drunk in the daytime, compensatory bragging, financial extravagance, deceiving one's family, forcing one's spouse to take over more responsibilities, self-deception, morbid jealousy, getting drunk on week ends, loss of job, breakup of family, neglect of meals; *chronic alcoholism* —continuous drinking, frequent confused thinking, use of cheap wines, and delirium tremens.

Effects of Alcohol

One of the most important consequences of alcoholism is malnutrition. Alcohol provides calories, and the alcoholic eats less, because he has less appetite or because he has less money to buy food. The malnutrition is expressed particularly in lack of Vitamin B, which is a prime cause of Korsakov's psychosis and Wernicke's syndrome (see below).

Alcohol is a depressant which brings about a lessening of self-criticism and inhibition. The person is less likely to assess risks. This may reduce avoidance responses and hence, under certain conditions, make consumption of alcohol a socially useful behavior. A. D. Ullman (1952) considers the only advantage of alcohol to be tension reduction. "The first thing to be depressed is the power of restraint. . . . The solitary become gregarious, shy men loquacious and the fearful foolhardy. Self-critical men can treat themselves kindly, sexually inhibited men dare to be amorous." (Kessel and Walton, 1965, p. 26.)

In popular fiction and the movies alcoholism is often depicted as accompanied by delirium tremens or DT's. There is agreement today that DT's occurs only in certain prolonged drinkers who have had a sudden drop in the alcoholic level of their blood. Why this occurs with one person and not another is not known. In general, DT's will eventually occur in approximately 5 percent of alcoholics. Without the best medical care it may be fatal in up to 25 percent of cases, while with medication and, particularly, a supportive social environment, Simpson et al. (1968) found no significant withdrawal effects for 1654 admissions, much less, full-blown delirium tremens or death. DSM-II describes delirium tremens as "a variety of acute brain syndrome characterized by delirium, coarse tremors, and frightening visual hallucinations usually becoming more intense in the dark." (p. 25.) Gross et al. (1972), however, noted great problems in categorizing the withdrawal symptoms, and Singer and Wong (1973) highlight cultural effects when they note that one-third of 100 consecutive admissions for alcoholism and alcoholic psychoses in Hong Kong reported a hallucination of a character with the head of a cow and the face of a horse, the traditional guard at the gate of hell.

From *Huckleberry Finn* comes an excellent description of DT's:

I don't know how long I was asleep, but all of a sudden there was an awful scream and I was up. There was Pap looking wild, and skipping around every which way and yelling about snakes. He said they was crawling up his legs; and then he would give a jump and scream, and say one had bit him on the cheek—but I couldn't see no snakes. He started round and round the cabin, hollering, "Take him off! take him off; he's biting me on the neck!" I never see a man look so wild in the eyes. Pretty soon he was all fagged out, and fell down panting; then he rolled over and over wonderful fast, kicking things every which way, and striking and grabbing at the air with his hands, and screaming and saying there was devils a-hold of him. He wore out by and by, and laid still awhile, moaning. Then he laid stiller, and didn't make a sound. I could hear the owls and wolves away off in the woods, and it seemed terrible still. He was laying over by the corner. By and by he raised up part way and listened, with his head to one side. He says, very low: "Tramp—tramp—tramp; that's the dead; tramp—tramp—tramp; they're coming after me but I won't go. Oh, they're here! don't touch me—don't! hands off—they're cold; let go. Oh, let a poor devil alone." Then he went down on all fours and crawled off, begging them to let him alone, and he rolled himself up in his blanket and wallowed in under the old pine table, still a-begging; and then he went to crying. I could hear him through the blanket.

Accompanying alcoholic hallucinosis may be auditory and visual hallucinations, disorientation, acute fear, suggestibility, and tremors.

Korsakov's psychosis is the best illustration of an acute psychotic reaction due to excessive alcohol. This series of behaviors was first described in 1887 by the Russian psychiatrist for whom it is named. The behaviors include a memory defect for recent events, confabulation (filling in memory gaps with reminiscences and distortions), and disorientation for time and place. It is now believed that a deficiency of Vitamin B and other dietary inadequacies are the primary cause of these behaviors. Clinically the psychosis develops in the course of chronic alcoholism, usually following an attack of delirium tremens. Usually a vitamin-rich diet enables the patient to return to more adequate physical health.

Another serious physical condition resulting from excessive alcohol is *Wernicke's encephalopathy*, which involves great difficulty in concentrating and slowness in answering questions. It frequently involves a memory loss, paralysis of some eyeball movements, and disturbance in gait and balance. The condition is associated with pathology in the base of the brain and is due to deficiency of Vitamin B.

History of Alcohol

Alcohol in some form is known to practically every society. Alcohol made its first appearance in Mesopotamia about 5,000 years ago (Rouéché, 1960).

The Egyptians were noted for drunkenness at their large banquets. The Jews, having been exposed to Egyptian culture, denounced drunkenness in the Old Testament but still held drinking in esteem and even prescribed it. The Book of Proverbs suggests, "Give strong drink unto him that is ready to perish and wine to those that be of heavy heart." The Greeks and Romans also made extensive use of alcohol, primarily beer and wine. It was not until A.D. 800 that an Arabian alchemist developed the process of distillation which increased the range and potency of beverages. By the thirteenth century there developed in Europe a universal panacea, a distillation of wine, aqua vitae, which promised a prolonged life and youth everlasting. This aqua vitae (water of life) was used as a medicine to cure all ills, including baldness, toothache, and bad breath. Aqua vitae is now known as brandy, deriving from the Dutch word "brandewijn" meaning burnt or distilled wine.

An important element in the history of the social impact of alcohol is the manner in which a given society conceptualizes and explains drinking behavior. Linsky (1971) reports the results of an historical analysis of "the image of the alcoholic" as viewed by popular magazines in the first seven decades of this century. The shifts in the causal attributions of excessive drinking were related to the theories of behavior, both popular and "scientific," current in the given period:

The changes in public view of alcoholism during the twentieth century provide a graphic illustration of how a form of deviance may be rapidly redefined. . . . For the first three decades of the twentieth century the causal agent was seen as clearly outside of the alcoholic, resting in environmental forces. A decisive change occurred by the forties when the focus shifted to factors inside the alcoholic, principally psychological. Since the forties there appears to be a moderate trend away from strictly internal explanation, with articles often citing both internal and external factors. . . . Attribution of moral blame to the agent causing alcoholism has declined steadily over the last seven decades. [pp. 573–74.] [3]

These changes in popular beliefs about the causes and nature of alcoholism reflect broader beliefs about the nature of man and what is normal and abnormal behavior. In this sense the views about alcoholsm are similar to those about all other forms of deviance (see Chapters 2 and 10). Popular belief systems are closely related to those of professionals in any given period, and these

[3] An example: "The liquor traffic is the most fiendish, corrupt and hell-soaked institution that ever crawled out of the slime of the eternal pit. . . . It takes the kind, loving husband and father, smothers every spark of love in his bosom, and transforms him into a heartless wretch, and makes him steal the shoes from his starving babe's feet to find the price for a glass of liquor. It takes your sweet innocent daughter, robs her of her virtue, and transforms her into a brazen, wanton harlot." (Quoted in Ray, 1972, p. 83.)

models of explanation are then related to and interact with the "treatment" procedures that are undertaken by the professionals.[4]

Theories of Alcoholism

In the 1830's, two physicians, Dr. Samuel Woodward and Dr. Eli Todd, suggested that there be special institutions where inebriates could be helped. The implication was that this particular deviance could be classified neither with criminal behavior nor with mental disorders. In the mid-1880's, about a dozen institutions for inebriates came into existence. The managers of these hospitals for inebriates founded a society and a journal which continually emphasized that inebriety was a disease.

The medical world of the nineteenth century in general harshly condemned the alcoholic and viewed inebriates as "vicious" rather than as diseased. This difference in theoretical view has continued to the present day. Jellinek (1960), reviewing the various psychological formulations of alcoholism, summarized them in three broad categories. First, there is the view that alcoholism is a psychological illness; second, there is the view that it is the symptom of some other more basic psychological disorder; and third, there is the view that completely rejects the notion of an illness. Jellinek points out that most conceptualizations in all three categories are no more than slogans. There are, for example, mere assertions that alcoholism is a disease; Wexberg (1951) expresses it this way: "In no other area of research and social or medical endeavor have slogans so extensively replaced theoretical insight as a basis for therapeutic action, as in alcoholism. The emotional impact of the statement, 'alcoholism is a sickness,' is such that very few people care to stop to think what it actually means."

[4] Siegler, Osmond, and Newell (1968) review eight such models.

Learning Formulations of Alcoholism

There have been several alternative approaches to explaining alcoholism in terms of learning theory. One such approach represents an application of the Dollard-Miller-Hullian drive model (as opposed to a response reinforcement model, e.g., Kepner, 1964; Keehn, 1969, 1970), which uses the idea of anxiety reduction to explain the excessive ingestion of alcohol. For example, Conger (1956) argues that the drinking response becomes habitual because it leads to a reduction in drive (anxiety). To the extent that alcohol reduces tensions, worry, and "anxiety," it serves as a source of reward to the individual.

Conger attempts to explain excessive drinking, not necessarily addiction, by arguing that "if we assume that drinking is learned because it is reinforced, one apparent exception is offered by the man whose drinking is, at least socially, more punishing than rewarding. The man who is alienating his boss, his wife, and his friends hardly seems to be socially rewarded for drinking. However, two factors should be considered here. One is the immediacy of reinforcement. Immediate reinforcements are more effective than delayed ones. This learning principle is called the gradient of reinforcement. It may be that, according to this principle, the immediate reduction in anxiety more than compensates for the punitive attitude of the man's wife the next morning. The other factor is the amount of drive and conflict. The personal anxiety-reducing effects of alcohol may, if the anxiety is great enough, constitute greater reinforcement than the competing social punishment."

The drive-reduction, goal-gradient formulations of alcoholism may be inadequate: experimental evidence has questioned Miller's gradient model of conflict (Maher, 1966, pp. 149–50). The major problem, however, is what will be treated, the drive or the behavior.

A SOCIOPSYCHOLOGICAL FORMULATION

Alcoholic overindulgence depends upon a specific operant behavior: the ingestion of alcoholic beverages (symbolically, "elbow-bending"). The behavior becomes a matter of concern to others, and hence the amount consumed and the specific physiological effects are of secondary concern to the target behavior of drinking under conditions considered inappropriate. This circumstance may be stated more positively—that is, it is a matter of consuming alcohol rather than emitting some other behavior. Following the formulations presented in Chapters 10 and 12, then, the first step in both the conceptualization and treatment of alcoholic over-indulgence is to determine what the appropriate alternative behaviors are and under what conditions they may be emitted. In terms of the model used throughout this book (e.g., Chapter 2) the person must be trained and capable in the emission of certain acts, must emit them, and must be reinforced for their emission.

In dealing with alcoholic overindulgence the first step is to define situations in which drinking occurs. The second step is to define the conditions which make for socially acceptable and unacceptable drinking. The third step is to specify conditions leading to increase of socially acceptable behavior.

As previously noted, knowledge of alcohol is universal. There are certain primitive cultures, and within Western societies certain subgroups, in which alcoholic overindulgence is relatively rare. For example, in the United States, people whose ancestors emigrated from Northern Europe have far higher rates of alcoholism than people whose forebears emigrated from Southern Europe. Jewish, Italian, and Chinese Americans are groups with notably low rates of alcoholic overindulgence. The common thread in these groups is a clear designation of the appropriate ceremonial, nutritional, or festive uses of alcohol. Use of alcohol outside these limits, any kind of overindulgence, is frowned upon. In contrast, groups such as Irish and English Americans may have a pattern in which alcohol is not part of daily life or family ritual but in which it is appropriate to overindulge on occasion. For the former groups, overindulgence requires a breaking with a life pattern.

Larsen and Abu-Laban (1968) relate drinking behavior patterns to norms of groups from which the individual receives guidance, and MacAndrew and Edgerton (1970) note how the specifics of being drunk vary from group to group and are learned aspects of the culture rather than a form of disinhibition or shedding of culture.

In an experiment which, with the work on controlled drinking to be discussed below, has great importance in arguing against the concept that one drink will lead to a craving for more alcohol and loss of control by the alcoholic, Engle and Williams (1972) gave a strongly flavored vitamin drink with no alcohol in it to one group of alcoholics, and the same drink with an ounce of vodka in it to another. In each group, half the subjects were told they were drinking some alcohol. Subjects who were given the mixture and were told it was alcohol reported stronger craving than subjects who had not been told. The "craving" seemed to be related to information rather than chemical or physiological factors.

There are social pressures to indulge in alcohol. Kessel and Walton (1965, p. 11) make the point this way: "Though we frown on drunkards we are suspicious of teetotallers. Over a glass we enjoy old friends and make new ones, proclaim our loyalties, discuss affairs, negotiate and seal bargains." Whether at the bar that is the poor man's club or at the business cocktail party, alcohol is a part of the life of most adult Americans. Drinking alcohol in moderation not only is associated with pleasant social circumstances, it may be pleasant in itself. As noted previously, it may reduce self-criticism or sensitivity to the criticism of others. The person may emit operants which he would not otherwise emit and may be rewarded for his behavior. This has been expressed in a number of ways, the most elegant, perhaps, being the operational definition of the superego as that part of the mind that is soluble in alcohol.

In more stately prose, Batchelor (1969, p. 53) refers to alcohol as follows: " 'It brings its votary from the chill periphery of things to the radiant core,' reducing feelings of shyness and loneliness, and is highly effective (if only transiently so) in relieving tensions and easing guilt, drowning the nagging voices of duty and conscience: so that it is not surprising that so many abuse it." In addition to the effects of alcohol itself, the sociopsychological model presumes that the person learns that alcohol sets the time and place where certain acts which he could not or would not otherwise emit will be reinforcing. In other words, a person may be capable of a particular social behavior but, for whatever reason, emit it only under the discriminative stimulus of drinking alcohol.

Alcohol may have a further effect: it may provide an excuse for activity which would otherwise be socially unacceptable. This aspect of drinking has been noted in phrases such as *"In vino veritas"* and "it's the alcohol talking." That is, in our culture, at least, alcohol provides an excuse to act in a particular manner, not unlike the use of placebo or hypnosis. The person may try out new behaviors, because, given an alcoholic intake, he is not completely responsible. In short, there is ample opportunity to emit the operant of drinking and be reinforced for behaviors emitted under the influence of alcohol, so that alcoholic indulgence becomes an acquired reinforcer. In addition, there are a number of reinforced roles made possible only by alcohol. Eric Berne (1964) calls some of these roles "games."

The experience of indulgence in alcohol may negate attitudinal patterns contradictory to such indulgence and overindulgence. The person is extinguished for or at least provided with data contradictory to severe avoidance of alcohol. He is geographically and temporally placed to observe people who indulge and to find that the effects are not so outrageously bad as he presumed. The progressive use of alcohol brings with it the effects of overindulgence itself. These are in part physiological in terms of liver damage and malnutrition; in part generalization of drinking behavior to additional situations; and in part social as increased drinking decreases the opportunities for other forms of social reinforcement either at work or in marriage. For example, a loss of a desired promotion will be an occasion for drinking, and this, in turn, may further reduce vocational effectiveness.

If this model is correct, then the focus of treatment is twofold: the reduction of drinking and the increase of socially appropriate alternative activities. The psychologist must ask what responses the person should make to those stimuli which previously were associated with drinking.

TREATMENT OF ALCOHOLISM

Because alcoholism is widespread and disturbing, nearly every known method of treatment has been applied to it. These methods include medication, social control, psychotherapy, hypnosis, desensitization, aversion therapy, operant conditioning, and the group approach of Alcoholics Anonymous (A.A.).

A long-term study by Gerard, Saenger, and Wile (1962) questions the effectiveness of the usual psychotherapeutic approaches for changing alcoholics' drinking behavior. A random sample of 400 patients from state-supported alcoholic clinics was studied. Based on follow-up studies over a number of years, 18 percent were abstinent at least one year prior to follow-up, 14 percent still used alcohol but no longer considered themselves to have a drinking problem, 41 percent still used alcohol and were unchanged, and 17 percent were dead. The authors estimate that of the 18 percent still abstinent, 10 percent were able to sustain their improvement independently. The rest relied upon some institutionalized support such as A.A. The reasons given for abstinence were both negative and positive, that is, fear of death, arrest, liver damage, and the positive reactions they were getting from others who liked them sober. These figures are consistent with those of Kurland (1968), who reports 15.5 percent of former patients making a good to excellent adjustment, and Rohan (1970), who reports roughly one-third of those patients who responded to a follow-up questionnaire to have remained sober.

Levinson and Sereny (1969) compared a psychologically oriented ("insight") therapy with a recreational treatment and found four of 26 people in the former group improved while nine of 27 in the latter group improved. Clancy, Vanderhoof, and Campbell (1967) had four groups: (1) a single session of aversive conditioning using apnea (temporary suspension of respiration) induced by the drug succinylcholine; (2) a placebo identical to the first group; (3) routine group and drug treatment; and (4) a no-treatment group. One year later, the respective percentages showing substantial improvement were 88 percent, 70 percent, 66 percent and 45 percent, and the average months abstinent were respectively 7.4, 5.4, 4.6 and 2.2. The point is that there are some people who improve with little or no treatment and that routine treatment and certain drugs such as hallucinogens do little better (Bowen, Soskin, and Chotlos, 1970; Faillace, Vourlekis, and Szara, 1970) than this base rate.

Behavioral Approaches

The behavioral formulation of the treatment of alcoholic indulgence is analogous to the behavioral treatment of any other set of problem behaviors which have major disruptive social and physiological consequences. A first step in treatment, therefore, is a rapid cessation or significant decrease of the drinking behavior itself. A second, and just as important, task in treatment is the establishment of reinforcement for sobriety.

Drinking Behavior

A major contribution of the behavioral approach to alcoholism is in its reconceptualization of the problem into the assessment of measurable behavior. How frequent is drinking, under what circumstances is it done, and where and what are the consequences in terms of reactions from others?

How is such information to be obtained? There are reports of techniques of enhancing the likelihood of accurate self-reports, such as the study by Miller (1972), who instructed his patient to record on an index card the number of alcoholic beverages consumed daily.

Sobell and Sobell (1973) devised a more complex self-monitoring technique, in which information such as the type of drink, percentage of alcoholic content, date and time ordered, number of sips, total amount consumed, and the location of drinking is recorded on an "Alcohol Intake Sheet." Record keeping is useful not only for eventual behavior modification, but also for the self-control techniques it introduces. Other report techniques include reports of friends and relatives of the individual with an alcohol problem and the use of various blood or breath tests that give clues as to alcohol level in the blood.[5] Finally, there is the obvious record of the consequences of severe drinking, namely, employment levels, arrests for intoxication, and hospitalizations for problems related to alcohol.

[5] Lovell (1972) discusses the complexities of the interaction of scientific, measurement, and judicial problems raised by the use of breath tests.

Investigators have developed a series of measures for studying drinking behavior under controlled laboratory condition. In one such set of laboratory analogue tasks alcohol is used as a reinforcement for a specific behavioral response. The alcohol may be made contingent upon performance of a simple motor task or of complex, self-help behaviors in a hospital setting. For example, Miller et al. (1974) studied the effect of social stress on operant drinking among ten "alcoholics" (as evidenced by a medical diagnosis, arrests and hospitalizations due to alcohol, and a mean length of problem drinking of 19 years) and ten "social drinkers" (with no evidence of alcohol abuse).

In this study, drinking was measured by ten minutes of operant responding, during which each lever press earned alcohol reinforcement on a fixed ratio schedule. During the stress conditions, the subjects were exposed to simulated interpersonal encounters requiring assertive behavior. For example, they were exposed to a social situation and asked to respond as they would in their own life situation. In one situation the subject takes his car to the service station to have a new tire put on. When he returns for the car he is told that two tires were put on and that the car was given a major tuneup costing $150. Similar stressful scenes were presented to both groups. Alcoholics significantly increased their operant responding to attain alcohol following stressful situations, while social drinkers did not. Measures of autonomic responsivity indicated that both groups were equally stressed. Thus, although the situations used were equally stressful for both, the alcoholics resorted to drinking significantly more than social drinkers.

The authors speculate that a significant part of the chain of alcohol abuse may not be stress itself but the cue of heightened emotional arousal. Either positive or negative arousal may serve as a cue for excessive drinking. This could explain why many alcoholics report that drinking episodes frequently occur not only in the presence of stress but also under conditions that are highly pleasurable. Other investigators who have studied the relationship between stress, arousal, and drinking include Allman, Taylor and Nathan (1972), and Higgins and Marlatt (1973).

Mello and Mendelsohn (1965) introduced a procedure by which lever-pressing responses were reinforced with alcohol which was automatically dispensed into a shot glass in front of the subject. They worked with two hospitalized alcoholics who were reinforced with either 10 cc. of bourbon or ten cents in cash contingent upon their changing the color of lights by pressing a response key. In later variations of this experimental approach, subjects could earn points which could be traded for alcohol (Mello and Mendelsohn, 1971; Nathan et al., 1970; Nathan and O'Brien, 1971). Miller, Hersen, and Eisler (1973) used this general procedure to study the complex interaction between instruction, agreement, and contracts as it influences operant drinking of chronic alcoholics.

Finally, Powell et al. (1973) found that drinking experience is a better predictor of tolerance to alcohol than personality tests. This type of data is consistent with a behavioral rather than a psychonalytic approach.

Specific Social-Learning

Treatment of drinking problems by social learning or behavioral approaches (see Chapter 12) have multiplied enormously in recent years as a viable alternative to the traditional methods.

Miller and Barlow (1973) offer a review and analysis of these approaches, which are categorized under four major procedures: aversion, relaxation, operant conditioning, and "controlled" drinking.

Aversion Procedures

The aversion therapies involve associating unpleasant stimuli with drinking patterns and with the environmental cues which evoke drinking behavior. The three major types of aversion therapies are those involving chemicals, electric shock, and verbalizations. The Romans introduced one of the first pairings of alcohol and an aversive stimulus when they placed an eel in a wine cup and made the patient drink. A widely used current form of aversive conditioning follows the pattern developed by Lemere and his co-workers (Lemere et al., 1942). Examples of the procedure were given in the previous chapter. Nausea and vomiting are produced by intramuscular injection of emetine hydrochloride. Immediately prior to the nausea, the patient is given alcoholic drinks, so that the smell, taste, and sight of liquor become associated with the nausea (Franks, 1966).

Lemere and Voegtlin (1950) evaluate 13 years of treatment using the drug *emetine:* of 4100 patients, approximately 50 percent achieved total abstinence.

Cessation of drinking may be sufficient to regain previously lost sources of social reinforcement as well as avoidance of unpleasant physiological and legal consequences. The sociopsychological model presumes that the rate of 50 percent abstinence after aversive conditioning is along lines which make abstinence rewarding. While aperiodic reinforcement, booster courses, and other innovations may well increase the rate of abstinence, efforts should be made to increase socially useful behaviors in response to situations which previously led to indulgence in alcohol. To this end Narrol (1967) has described a token economy for the rehabilitation of alcoholics similar to that used by Ayllon and Azrin (1965) and Liebson et al. (1971) (see Chapter 18). Blake (1965, 1967) combined aversion therapy (using electrical stimuli rather than emetics) with training in relaxation responses.

Another approach involves the use of a drug such as Antabuse (disulfiram) (e.g., Haynes, 1973), which causes the individual to become violently ill if he drinks alcohol. Antabuse interferes with the normal oxidation of alcohol and causes an increase of acetaldehyde in the body. If the patient drinks alcohol within 24 or more hours after a dose of Antabuse, acetaldehyde poisoning develops. This reaction is characterized by flushed face, headache, palpitations, dizziness, nausea, vomiting, hypertension, apprehension and great difficulty in breathing. The person receiving Antabuse therapy is receiving a genuine physiological treatment. Psychological principles are involved: the effects of Antabuse may be demonstrated to the person and hence provide a single strong aversive experience. Because one cannot drink alcohol for 24 to 72 hours after ingestion of Antabuse, the decision to be abstinent is made prior to and outside the situation that has a high chance of leading to drinking behavior.

Other techniques have been developed to pair a response of discomfort with alcohol. Gordova and Kovalev (1961) used hypnosis instead of apomorphine with patients whose drinking had led to digestive deterioration which contraindicated the use of the emetic. The procedure was to have the patient visualize being in a bar, drinking, and becoming violently ill. The sessions were conducted twice weekly in groups of four or five persons, and altogether each patient received five to twelve such sessions. Gordova and Kovalev report that 55 percent of cases in which there was adequate follow-up were abstinent for at least a year. Anant (1967, 1968b, 1968c) and Cautela (1967) focused their patients' attention by use of deep relaxation, and then followed with a sequence of scenes of aversive consequences. Anant reports success in 25 cases, while Ashem and Donner (1968) report an experiment with statistically significant effects for such covert sensitization.

Aversive conditioning adds an immediate

experience to the ultimate aversive consequences of drinking. These latter—loss of friends, jobs, status, and the like—should become part of treatment, and indeed have been used by investigators such as Mertens and Fuller (1964a, b).

Mills et al. (1971) found that avoidance-conditioning techniques worked successfully to shape the acquisition of a socially acceptable drinking response repertoire over as few as 12 conditioning sessions. A more extensive and comprehensive behavioral treatment program for alcoholics has been used by Sobell and Sobell (1972a, 1972b). In that study, avoidance conditioning to shape appropriate drinking behavior was combined with procedures to analyze setting events for the drinking of individual subjects, and to train those subjects in alternative, more appropriate responses to those situations.

Desensitization of Drinking Behavior

As in most other disorders and problem behaviors, systematic desensitization has been used with alcoholics. Kraft (1969, 1971) and Kraft and Al-Issa (1967) report a series of case studies in which the alcoholic clients were desensitized to lessen anxiety in situations associated with excessive alcoholic intake. The hierarchies developed involved the exposure to social settings with more and more people. All of the eight subjects treated by this method were reported to be improved to the point that they could drink moderately in social situations.

Operant and Controlled Drinking Approaches

There are a number of different procedures utilized with alcoholics within the operant approach. The rationale for these may be summarized by the Sobell and Sobell (1973) observation: "A behavior therapy for alcoholism was designed on the rationale that alcoholic drinking is a discriminated operant response. Treatment emphasized determining setting events for each subject's drinking and training equally effective alternative responses to those situations." (p. 49.) Sobell and Sobell worked with 70 male hospitalized alcoholics assigned to a treatment goal of either nondrinking or controlled drinking. The nondrinkers were shaped to total abstinence while the controlled drinkers practiced appropriate drinking behavior. Follow-up measuring drinking and other behaviors found that experimental subjects functioned significantly better after discharge than control subjects, regardless of treatment goal. Successful experimental subjects could apply treatment principles to setting events not considered during treatment, suggesting the occurrence of role-learning. Results are discussed as evidence that some "alcoholics" can acquire and maintain controlled drinking behaviors.

In another study demonstrating the possibility of training alcoholics for controlled drinking, Sobell, Schaefer, and Mills (1972) systematically observed alcoholic behavior such as "drink preference, sip magnitude, amount of time to consume drinks and amount of time between sips," Twenty-three normal drinkers and 26 hospital-admitted alcoholics were observed as they consumed up to 16 ounces of 86-proof liquor or its equivalent in an experimental bar-and-lounge environment. The alcoholics in this study ordered more drinks, preferred straight drinks, took larger sips and drank faster, but took a longer time between sips than did the "normal" drinkers. The authors argue that it is the ability to make such detailed observations that offers opportunity to train alcoholics to become controlled drinkers as an alternative to abstinence. Various operant-conditioning principles may provide tools for shaping the desired behavior or making the alcoholic pattern more like the nonabusive drinker's.

Lovibond and Caddy (1970) devised an important new way of producing moderate drinking behavior. Outpatient alcoholics were trained to discriminate their own blood-alcohol concentration. Subjects were instructed to drink pure alcohol in fruit juice until their blood-alcohol level reached a certain specific percent. Electric shock was made contingent upon blood-alcohol concentrations above that level. A control group received noncontingent shock. Follow-up data indicated that 21 of the 26 in the experimental group were drinking in a controlled fashion, whereas the control group subjects were drinking significantly more than the criterion level even during the treatment sessions.

The operant approach has also extended beyond the hospital and clinic into influencing the community environment so as to decrease the likelihood of drink-provoking and maintaining stimuli. Sulzer (1965) obtained the cooperation of friends and the wife of an alcoholic. Peer companionship and the attention of the wife were made contingent upon nonalcoholic drinking behavior. For example, the friends would leave if the client were to order an alcoholic drink but would remain if a nonalcoholic beverage were ordered.

Observation of and the assistance of wives has characterized a series of subsequent studies involving behavior in the community. Hersen, Miller, and Eisler (1973) report a descriptive analysis of the nonverbal interactions between four alcoholics and their wives. They found that the wives paid significantly more attention to the husbands during discussion of their alcoholic behavior. They speculate that this attention may serve as a positive reinforcer for the husband.

Wives were trained in the use of standard behavior-modification techniques to change family interactions (Cheek et al., 1971). They applied the procedures (mostly based on principles of contingent reinforcement) to their husbands' behavior which was most disruptive of the family, such as aggressiveness and failure to accept responsibility. An important element in the program was training the wives in relaxation and systematic desensitization to help deal with marital tensions. Most of the wives who completed the program reported some moderate success in improving family communication and decreasing the tensions. Behavioral contracting was used in a case reported by Miller (1972) in which a wife assisted her alcoholic husband and daily records were kept of drinking behavior, which decreased rapidly.

Hunt and Azrin (1973) report another illustration of the community-operant approach which rearranged the vocational, family, and social reinforcers of the alcoholic such that time out from these reinforcers would occur if he began to drink. Emphasis in this program was on training the alcoholic and his family in very specific ways of handling legal, financial, vocational, and interpersonal problems.

A comprehensive evaluation of the effectiveness of the behavioral approaches, particularly the operant, in modifying alcoholic behavior is not yet available because of the recency of their development and application to this problem area. Their major impact thus far is to help reconceptualize the problems of the alcoholic into the specifics of drinking and other associated cues and behavior—a process which opens the way to modification and evaluation of change. The emphasis has been on a movement away from the use of isolated techniques such as aversion conditioning and specific desensitization to a broader use of environmental-influence procedures which focus on training the individual and his family in ways of controlling the reinforcement contingencies in his own life. Further, the success of controlled drinking provides a challenge to some long-held stereotypes of alcoholism and its treatment (for example, that the alcoholic cannot stop after one drink due to some unique biological characteristic) (Pattison, 1968; Verden and Shatterly, 1971; Sobell, Sobell, and Christelman, 1972; Bigelow et al., 1972; Cohen, Liebson, and Faillace, 1972, 1973; Gottheil et al., 1973).

Social-Group Approaches

One approach to alcoholism represents a combination of group therapy and religious elements to provide social reinforcement for abstinence from alcohol. This is Alcoholics Anonymous, founded in 1935 by two recovered alcoholics, Dr. Bob and Bill W. A.A. represents a social movement which has spread throughout the country. The weekly meetings of A.A. groups involve the participation of all present in discussion, concern for each other, and general social fellowship. Fellow members are always available in an individual crisis to help prevent resort to drink. A.A. extends beyond the individual to encompass his whole family through the mechanism of women's auxiliaries and teenage children's groups.

New role behavior is expected of the individual. There is available strong and rapid social reinforcement for behavior such as sobriety, confession of previous misdeeds, helping others stay sober, working in a family context, and being a responsible individual. Alcoholism is handled within a social context using modeling and focusing on the aversive consequences of alcoholism, the social isolation and rejection which noxious drinking behaviors evoke from others. In addition, the person learns to control his own behavior and is encouraged to enact a meaningful role in helping others. There is considerable selectivity in those who gain help from A.A. With those who actively participate, A.A. claims about 75 percent succeed in maintaining abstinence, although this figure may include several relapses for any individual.

Summary

Alcoholic overindulgence is viewed as an operant behavior that is shaped and maintained by its consequences. It follows the sociopsychological model and is treated in a manner similar to behaviors labeled sexually deviant and obsessive-compulsive. Because there are physiological and social effects of alcoholic overindulgence that are destructive to the individual and potentially for others (e.g., drunken driving), a first step in dealing with alcoholic overindulgence is toward abstinence or significant reduction of drinking. Aversive conditioning seems to lead to a significant gain in this regard, roughly 50 percent abstinent for six or more months, within relatively few treatment sessions. Abstinence itself is likely to lead to increased social reinforcement and avoidance of aversive consequences. The gain made through aversive conditioning is therefore maintained by ongoing social interactions. While improvements in aversive conditioning such as the use of additional techniques and stimuli, booster courses, aperiodic reinforcement, and the like, are foreseen, the next major step in the treatment of alcoholic overindulgence is probably in the realm of teaching social roles that will provide reward for operants antithetical to alcoholic overindulgence. Controlled drinking is a major new development in this area and has many implications for both theory and treatment.

DRUG ADDICTION

This section will deal with the abuse of chemical substances other than alcohol. Prolonged, repetitive, and excessive use of many physical substances may lead to the label of addiction. For example, smoking and obesity may lead to physical changes which are disturbing to some persons and hence may lead to pressure for change. As noted in the model presented in Chapters 2 and 10, labeling the behavior as an illness leads to the use of one form of social control: it is considered correct to enact public health measures for the person's own good.

The distinction between addiction, dependency, and abuse made at the beginning of the chapter is of direct relevance to any evaluation of the effects of drugs. There are a number of different ways of classifying the various drugs involved, primarily in terms of their effects. Some drugs such as heroin appear to result in physiological *addiction*; that is, the body "craves" greater and greater amounts in order to achieve the effects associated with the drug. Other drugs such as marijuana are not physically addictive, but the pleasure a person receives from them and whatever effects he has learned to associate with them are strong enough to maintain repeated usage.

The DSM-II category of drug dependence applies to those individuals who are "dependent on drugs other than alcohol, tobacco, and ordinary caffeine-containing beverages. . . . The diagnosis requires evidence of habitual use or a clear sense of need for the drug. Withdrawal symptoms are not the only evidence of dependence; while always present when opium derivatives are withdrawn, they may be entirely absent when cocaine or marihuana are withdrawn." (p. 45.)

Drug dependence is then divided into eight categories in terms of drugs to which one can become addicted. These are: (1) opium and its derivatives (2) synthetic analgesics with morphine-like effects (3) barbiturates (4) other hypnotics and sedatives or tranquilizers (5) cocaine (6) Cannabis sativa (hashish, marijuana) (7) other psycho-stimulants (amphetamines, etc.) (8) hallucinogens.

Drug Usage

Although there is a great amount of publicity about the use of drugs, the extent of drug addiction, dependency, and abuse in the United States is known only in very general terms.

According to the report issued by the White House Special Action Office for Drug Abuse, heroin addiction in the United States doubled between 1965 and 1969. However, the report said that data from 28,713 patients admitted to federal drug-treatment programs between June 1969 and March 1973 show a reversal in the trend toward more addicts. The report attributes the decrease in the rate of heroin addiction to a number of factors, including the availability of more treatment facilities, increased law enforcement efforts, and people getting the word that "heroin is bad news."

Using what it calls "capture-recapture method," the Federal Bureau of Narcotics and Dangerous Drugs concluded in 1971: " '. . . It is virtually certain that the number of addicts in 1969 falls somewhere between 285,000 and 345,000. The best estimate of the number of addicts for that year is 315,000.' The estimate of the National Institute of Mental Health in 1971, based on a wide range of data, was 250,000 addicts. In this report, we use both the bureau and NIMH estimates in placing the number of addicts at between 250,000 and 315,000 in 1971." (Brecher, 1972, p. 62.)

Accurate estimates of the use of marijuana and hallucinogens such as LSD are even more difficult because of the relative ease of obtaining these drugs, the lesser likelihood of their usage coming to the attention of legal or medical authorities, and the spread of their usage in the past few years. LSD usage is probably tapering off from its peak in late 1966 and early 1967. Some surveys report that at various colleges up to 10 percent of the students may have tried LSD at least once during the height of its popularity and up to half of all college students have experimented with marijuana.

HISTORICAL BACKGROUND

To understand addiction it is necessary to be aware of the complex interplay between numerous influences—sociological, legal, cultural, pharmacological, medical, racial, political, moral—and the impact of mass communications. As Brecher (1972) indicates, the effects of any drug or alcohol depend on "Who is taking the drug, in what dosage, by what route of administration, and under what circumstances . . . even the simplest drugs have a wide range of effects—depending not only on their chemistry but on the ways in which they are used, the laws that govern their use, the user's attitudes and expectations, society's attitudes and expectations, and countless other factors." (p. xi.) Swanson (1972) notes that there are four major theoretical models for drug abuse: legal-political, medical-psychiatric, socio-cultural, and mystical-religious.

Drug addiction has a long history in the United States; Musto (1973) refers to it as "the American disease." In 1806, Sertürner published his work on the isolation of the active ingredient in opium, and in 1853, Wood perfected the hypodermic syringe. In the wars during the 1860's, morphine was used to ease pain, and because of its constipating effect, to treat dysentery. Brecher (1972) describes nineteenth-century America as a "dope fiend's paradise." Opium was on sale legally at low prices, and various other opiates were available through physicians, drug stores, grocery and general stores, and the mail. According to estimates, up to 1 percent of the population was addicted to opium (Ray, 1972, p. 187), but "it was not a major social problem." (See also Kramer, 1971, and Swatos, 1972.)

Although some states outlawed it earlier, Congress did not ban the cultivation of opium poppies until 1942. However, in 1909 smoking opium was prohibited in the United States. A major factor in its prohibition at that point was its association in the popular literature with the Chinese, who were actively persecuted, particularly on the West Coast.

Although legal in the nineteenth century, the use of opiates was considered as disreputable as drinking alcohol.

Opiate use was also frowned upon in some circles as *immoral*, a vice akin to dancing, smoking, theater-going, gambling, or sexual promiscuity. But while deemed immoral, it is important to note that opiate use in the 19th Century was not subject to the moral sanctions current today. Employees were not fired for addiction. Wives did not divorce their addicted husbands, or husbands their addicted wives; children were not taken from their homes and lodged in foster homes or institutions because one or both parents were addicted. Addicts continued to participate fully in the life of the community. . . . Thus, the 19th Century avoided one of the most disastrous effects of current narcotics laws and attitudes—the rise of a deviant addict subculture, cut off from respectable society and without a "road back" to respectability. [Brecher, 1972, pp. 6–7.]

Illustrating changes in belief and influence on legislation, Musto writes: "By 1914, prominent newpapers, physicians, pharmacists, and congressmen believed opiates and cocaine predisposed habitués toward insanity and crime. They were widely seen as substances associated with foreigners or alien subgroups. Cocaine raised the specter of the wild Negro, opium the devious Chinese, morphine the tramps in the slums; it was feared that use of all these drugs was spreading into the 'higher classes' " (p. 65).

Patent elixirs were used indiscriminately to relieve everything from headaches to diarrhea. This was the period of wonder-working medications such as Mrs. Winslow's Soothing Syrup, Dr. Cole's Catarrh Cure, McMumm's Elixir of Opium, and Perkins' Diarrhea Mixture, containing among its ingredients as much as 10 percent narcotic content in opium, morphine, codeine, or cocaine. One of the problems at the time was that physicians did not recognize the addictive nature of many of these drugs. For example, heroin, discovered in 1898, was found to relieve the withdrawal symptoms of morphine. Hence it was first believed to be a cure for morphine addiction and was substituted for morphine in cough medicines and tonics.

Years after its use became widespread, medical journals carried articles stressing its nonaddicting properties. [Nyswander, 1965, p. 22; see also Freud's cocaine episode in Jones, 1953.] It is important at this juncture to realize that the drug addict before 1914 had little or no involvement with criminal activity. He carried on his job, maintained his home and family life. His illness did not inflict injury on anyone other than himself. He considered himself and was considered by others to be grappling with a definite and difficult problem, and he expected to obtain treatment in a legitimate manner. [Nyswander, 1965, p. 23.]

The question of whether addiction is a disease became crucial during 1919 and 1920 in the United States and followed the Supreme Court declaration that maintenance of addiction without a cause such as intractable pain was illegal. But if addiction was a bona fide disease, perhaps addicts could be legally maintained after all. Leading physicians, who in the past had sought stringent anti-narcotic laws and had also declared addiction a disease, now averred that it was not a disease at all, at least not an *organic* disease requiring doses of narcotics. Withdrawal symptoms and signs for which they had once recommended intricate physiological therapies were now said to be "purely functional manifestations and have no physical basis." This conclusion came while the medical profession was split and each side bitterly accused the other of a conspiracy to either foster dope fiends or to jail sick patients. . . . Just as the belief that addiction was a disease drew upon the new studies in immunology in the late 19th Century, so the decision in 1920 that addiction was functional came when the new psychology —psychoanalysis—could be invoked as an explanation of dysfunction and as a source of effective therapy . . . Later, in the 1920's, the belief in the organic reality of withdrawal, even if not understood, was again asserted by many in the medical profession, but it was still linked to psychological disorder . . . "normal" persons did not choose to become addicted; therefore, the addict by choice was a "psychopath." Addiction was only one aspect of the psychopath's life which included other criminal activity and social ineptness. [Musto, 1973, pp. 82–84.]

With the passage of the Harrison Narcotics Act in 1914 the attitudes toward drug addiction changed. Through this Act, later acts, and court interpretations of them, the sale and dispensation of narcotic drugs became a federal offense (Ray, 1972, 17–34; Kramer, 1972). Thus it became impossible for drug addicts to get their supplies from legitimate sources. The role of addict became the role of criminal. The Harrison Narcotics Act, being basically a revenue code, placed enforcement in the hands of the Bureau of Internal Revenue. "Severe enforcement procedures were put into effect. Many physicians were imprisoned for ministering to their patients, and overnight a million victims of a horrifying illness were transformed into criminals. When the legislators and enforcement officers ignored the terrible needs imposed on the addict by his disease, his one alternative was to turn to the underworld for relief." (Nyswander, 1965, p. 24.) After this, out of fear of prosecution, no legitimate physician would run the risk of prescribing narcotics for an addict.

Musto summarizes the political-historical approach to addiction as follows:

American concern with narcotics is more than a medical or legal problem, it is in the fullest sense a political problem. The energy that has given impetus to drug control and prohibition came from profound tensions among socioeconomic groups, ethnic minorities, and generations, as well as the psychological attraction of certain drugs. The form of this control has been shaped by the gradual evolution of constitutional law and the lessening limitation of federal police powers. The bad results of drug use and the number of drug users have often been exaggerated for partisan advantage. Public demand for action against drug abuse has led to regulative decisions that lack a true regard for the reality of drug use. Relations with foreign nations, often the source of the drugs, have been a theme in the domestic scene from the beginning of the American antinarcotic movement. . . .

The most passionate support for legal prohibition of narcotics has been associated with fear of a given drug's effect on a specified minority. Certain drugs were dreaded because they seemed to undermine essential social restrictions which kept these groups under control: cocaine was supposed to enable Blacks to withstand bullets which would kill persons and to stimulate sexual assault. Fear that smoking opium facilitated sexual contact between Chinese and White Americans was also a factor in its total prohibition. Chicanos in the Southwest were belived to be incited to violence by smoking marihuana. Heroin was linked in the 1920's with a turbulent age-group: adolescents in reckless and promiscuous urban gangs, alcohol was associated with immigrants crowding into large and corrupt cities. In each instance, use of a particular drug was attributed to an identifiable and threatening minority group. [p. 244–45.]

In 1973, the National Commission on Marijuana and Drug Abuse issued a report which called for a treatment approach to narcotics addiction rather than punishment and stigmatizing only those habits which threaten society. The final report urged the legalization of the possession of marijuana, which it said was not habit-forming and did not promote crime by those who used it.[6]

The treatment of narcotic addicts in the United States is often contrasted with that in Great Britain. In 1920 England passed the Dangerous Drug Act, which placed stringent controls on the import, manufacture, sale, and possession of narcotic drugs. The ruling principle of the English program is that narcotics may legally be administered to addicts after prolonged attempt at cure if "the drug cannot be safely discontinued entirely, on account of the severity of the withdrawal symptoms produced" or if the patient "while capable of leading a useful and relatively normal life when a certain minimum dose is regularly administered, becomes incapable of this when the drug is entirely discontinued." There is no compulsory treatment in Great Britain, nor do any state institutions specialize in the treatment of addicts.

Schur (1965b), who surveyed the British and the American systems, writes of the British program: "This entire approach has worked remarkably well. Not only has the estimated number of addicts remained extremely low, it has actually decreased. . . . All the evidence indicates that there are very few addicts other than those receiving their supplies through legal channels. No sizeable underworld drug traffic exists. The addict furnishes no economic incentive for contraband peddling, and needn't become a thief or prostitute to pay for drugs. . . . it would seem that by refusing to treat the addict as a criminal, Britain has kept him from becoming one." (p. 153.) Schur concludes that "all available evidence indicates that it is not addiction itself, but the punitive approach to addiction which produces antisocial behavior in addicts."

In 1968 a new set of regulations in England resulted in the development of specific treatment centers for addicts. These were mainly outpatient treatment clinics with treatment programs varying from unit to unit. There has been a general trend to substitute methadone for heroin. The number of addicts in England has been quite small. For example, the total number of individuals treated in 1970 in England was about 1,200, which has become a fairly stable figure (Department of Health and Social Security, 1971). (See also Hawks, 1971; and Bewley et al., 1972, for critical reviews of the drug situation in England.)

After a detailed review of the approach used in England to cope with its drug problems, Judson (1973) concludes:

Does the British approach work? The clinics are impressive, for their measurable statistics and for the relationship and mood of their staffs and their clients. . . . What the United States has done is to push these people, the addicts, outside of any such social control, while what the English have done—or, at least, begun to do within the framework of the clinics—is to establish viable social rituals for narcotics. . . .

THE EFFECTS OF SPECIFIC DRUGS

What are the physical effects of addiction? The answer to this is far more difficult than might be expected. The following quo-

---

[6] Adler (1970) puts the drug abuse of the 1960's into the context of a social movement. Szasz (1972), Feldman (1968), and Becker (1967), also emphasize the relationship between drug usage and social and political context. A different context, in an overmedicated and self-medicating society (Muller, 1972) is the role of the pharmaceutical industry (Ognibene, 1973).

tation is from a 1962 Supreme Court Decision (*Robinson* v. *California,* 370–U.S. 660) cited by Brecher (1972, p. 21):

> To be a confirmed drug addict is to be one of the walking dead. . . . The teeth have rotted out, the appetite is lost, and the stomach and intestines don't function properly. The gall bladder becomes inflamed; eyes and skin turn a bilious yellow; in some cases membranes of the nose turn a flaming red; the partition separating the nostrils is eaten away—breathing is difficult. Oxygen in the blood decreases; bronchitis and tuberculosis develop. Good traits of character disappear and bad ones emerge. Sex organs become affected. Veins collapse and livid purplish scars remain. Boils and abscesses plague the skin; gnawing pain racks the body. Nerves snap; vicious twitching develops. Imaginary and fantastic fears blight the mind and sometimes complete insanity results. Often times, too, death comes—much too early in life. . . . Such is the torment of being a drug addict; such is the plague of being one of the walking dead.

The effects of the specific drugs, to be described below, are perhaps not quite as dramatic as indicated in this court decision.

Heroin and Morphine

Opiates, or opium derivatives, primarily heroin and morphine, are the major category of physiologically addictive drugs. They are introduced into the body by smoking, eating, or by hypodermic injection. Their immediate effects include euphoria, drowsiness, relief of pain, reveries, and lack of coordination. Both act to depress the functions of the central nervous system. Morphine acts more slowly and less intensely than heroin. The pleasant effects last for about four hours. A negative phase follows and, unless the addict receives another dose within the next several hours (up to 12 or more), he may begin to experience withdrawal effects. The nature or even the occurrence of withdrawal symptoms is not always predictable, and it would seem that to some extent at least they are a function of the individual's expectation. The reports of the experience of the Synanon group include instances of addicts not experiencing withdrawal symptoms in situations where such symptoms are not expected.

The social consequences of addiction for the individual go beyond the physiological effects. Malnutrition caused by loss of appetite, the danger of tetanus or hepatitis from unsterile needles, the loss of sexual interest, the development of bronchitis and other respiratory difficulties, the lessened response to pain, the centering of life around the drugs, the need to steal in order to maintain the habit, the association with underworld figures, the eventual entanglement with legal authorities and likely jailing because of illegal possession of narcotics, and, finally, the social ostracism that goes with criminal behavior are all likely aversive consequences of opiate addiction. But the point to be emphasized is that many effects attributable to the opiates such as the above-mentioned are consequences of drug-taking in a social context, not of the drugs themselves.

Heroin, morphine, and opium are termed addictive for two major reasons. First, users of the drugs gradually develop a tolerance for them, necessitating increasing amounts to obtain the feeling of euphoria, relaxation, pain relief, or pleasant reverie. Second, if the drugs are not continued, in many instances the individual begins to experience the extremely unpleasant sensations (sweating, restlessness, depression, irritability, increased heavy breathing) of withdrawal. In some instances the withdrawal effects may be so severe, involving hallucinations, manic activities, tremors, and cardiovascular involvement, that death may occur. These effects, if not treated with drugs, may last up to a week.

Barbiturates

The barbiturates (e.g., phenobarbital, nembutal, seconal, amytal) are the second most common category of drug to cause physical addiction. The most common form of usage is the sleeping pill. Barbiturates act as depressants and induce muscle relaxation. Unlike the opiate user, the barbiturate-indulging individual can maintain himself on a minimum dosage, usually to help him sleep. Excessive use, hence abuse, comes when the dosage is increased because of greater tolerance, resulting in irritability, weight loss, impaired thinking, and possible brain damage. Withdrawal symptoms may be as severe as those of the opiates, if not more so, resulting in convulsions and delirium. Large doses are fatal, as evidenced by the attribution of over 1,500 suicides a year to barbiturates (Lyons, 1968).

Amphetamines

The amphetamines (e.g., benzedrine, dexedrine, methedrine) are a group of drugs, developed fairly recently, which serve as stimulants and arouse feelings of euphoria. They help depressed people feel more alive and are used by tired people to feel more alert. They can readily be used to excess.

The individual may become frenetic in his behavior. A large dose can result in hallucinations and psychotic-like delusions of persecution. Batchelor (1969) refers to the effects as "intoxication" rather than "addiction." Addicts may use the amphetamines to supplement their other drugs, but the amphetamines are not physically addictive in and of themselves.

Cocaine

Cocaine, a stimulant extracted from the leaves of the coca plant, has been used for centuries as a local anesthetic. It is ingested either by sniffing, injecting, or swallowing. The immediate effects are a euphoric state, which may, however, be preceded by headaches or dizziness. As a stimulant cocaine may induce and accentuate sleeplessness and sexual excitement. An overdose can result in a toxic psychosis. Cocaine is a good illustration of a drug that is not addictive in a physiological sense (e.g., there are no withdrawal effects) but that leads to psychological dependence. The World Health Organization and United States federal law both classify cocaine as a narcotic or addictive drug, although technically it is not. A 1971 report indicates that cocaine usage has emerged as a problem after nearly 40 years.

Marijuana

Marijuana has a wide range of possible behavioral effects. It is also by far the most controversial of the substances described in this chapter.

Despite its widespread use there exists very little clear-cut scientific data as to its effects. Marijuana can serve as a stimulant, a depressant, or a hallucinogen. It can be smoked, swallowed, or sniffed. It can produce relaxation, euphoria, decreased efficiency, and distorted time perception.

At this time the evidence does not point to marijuana as being physically addictive, but there is some indication it may reduce cellular resistance to illness. Current controversies revolve about questions as to whether it results in psychological dependence, whether it leads to the taking of clearly addictive drugs such as heroin, and just how widespread its usage is, especially on college campuses. In all of these controversies there is considerable heat but very little light.

The development of marijuana smoking careers and the social learning involved were described in Chapter 10. Much of this can be summarized by the following passage from Becker (1963, p. 53): "Marijuana-produced sensations are not automatically or necessarily pleasurable. The taste for such experience is a socially acquired one, not different in kind from acquired tastes for oysters or dry martinis."

In recent years there has been a considerable growth of investigation into the effects of marijuana usage (Goode, 1969; Grinspoon, 1971; Hasleton, 1972; Linn, 1971; Snyder, 1971; LaDriere and Szcepkowski,

1972; McGlothlin, Arnold, and Rowan, 1970; Mirin et al., 1970; and Pillart, 1970).

An important example of such research was by Weil, Zinberg, and Nelson (1968), who gave marijuana of two strengths and a placebo cigarette (with stalks to mimic odor) to naïve and chronic users. "It proved extremely difficult to find marijuana-naïve persons in the student population of Boston, and nearly two months of interviewing were required to obtain nine men." (p. 1236.) The naïve subjects were taught how to inhale effectively for marijuana smoking, and of the people screened, while all were confirmed tobacco smokers, five developed nicotine reactions when they smoked regular cigarettes in the required fashion. These effects were more spectacular than any observed from marijuana smoking.

The experiment was conducted in a neutral setting. With the large dose, all chronic marijuana users became high, but only one of the nine naïve subjects had a definite marijuana reaction, and he was the one who had expressed a desire to get high. Both groups increased in heart rate as a result of marijuana. On psychomotor tests, the trend was for chronic users to improve slightly, naïve subjects to deteriorate. Lemberger et al. (1970) offer data for what might be one explanation (other than psychological factors and the ability to discriminate and play a marijuana role) for the greater perception of being high among chronic users: using radioactive tracers, it was found that the active ingredient in marijuana may take up to eight days to be excreted. If this is the case, the frequent, heavy user may have a large build-up. While such material is hypothetical, it may still serve as a useful warning.

The Hallucinogenic Drugs

There is one group of drugs the effects of which are similar and which in some studies are treated interchangeably. These are mescaline ("cactus," "peyote"), LSD, and psilocybin ("mushrooms"). LSD is the chemical shorthand for d-lysergic acid diethylamide and is one of the most powerful drugs yet developed to produce hallucinogenic responses. A dose of as little as a quarter-millionth of an ounce may produce effects that can last for hours. An equivalent dose of LSD is 100 times more powerful than psilocybin and about 7,000 times more powerful than mescaline (Lyons, 1968).

Among the typical reactions to LSD are hallucinations, distortion of perception, exhilaration, excitation, and, possibly, panic and psychotic-like bizarre behaviors. There are some clearly observable physical effects of LSD. The drug causes pimples, stronger tendon reflexes such as knee jerk, and enlarged pupils. Nausea and muscle pain are also sometimes reported, and the drug may lower the threshold for vision and hearing. One interesting effect is the experiencing of one sense in terms of another, called *synesthesia*.

The effects of LSD, perhaps to a greater extent than those of any of the other drugs described, depend on the social circumstances in which it is taken. Unger (1963) suggests that the characteristic effects which persist for a relatively long period are to be attributed not to the action of LSD itself but to some as yet unidentified aspect of the chain of events triggered by drug administration. Certain recurring characteristics in the subjective reports of the drug takers seem to be independent of personality, setting, or expectation. These are unusual visual experiences, a feeling of detachment, and a retrospective testimonial as to the impressiveness of the experience.

It is quite clear that the setting and the expectations of both the administrator and the user of the drug are the major influences in the reports and experiences of the subjects (Blum et al., 1964). Unger, in reviewing the literature, finds that:

Whenever psychoanalytically oriented therapists have employed LSD, practically without exception the patient relives childhood memories. The interesting point is that this phenomenon has practically *never* been noted in the experimental literature [1963, p. 284.]

When the effects of LSD were first reported, there was considerable excitement because it was thought that here was a drug that produced effects similar to those of schizophrenia. In fact, LSD and other drugs similar to it were labeled psychomimetic or psychosis-mimicking. However, it is now obvious that LSD's effects are in many ways dissimilar to functional psychoses. For example, many of the perceptual effects differ; the LSD user reports intense color, visual illusions, and visual hallucinations, whereas the schizophrenic does not. Nor does the schizophrenic display the euphoria of the LSD user or his desire to communicate about his experiences. Bizarre, manneristic behaviors are common in schizophrenia, rare in LSD users; schizophrenics speech may be marked by bodily preoccupations while the LSD user is interested in new sensations.

In a review of the literature on research on LSD, McWilliams and Tuttle (1973) conclude that "the danger of long-lasting psychological damage is low when the drug is used by emotionally stable individuals in securely controlled settings." (p. 241.) On the other hand, adverse reactions have occurred most frequently among people who were not emotionally stable, in crisis situations or unsettling environments, and who took the drug in unsupervised settings. Psychotic episodes and suicidal behavior, although rare, have occurred in such circumstances. However, the authors emphasize that "research on LSD, particularly its long-term psychological effects is very poor. Most studies are based on subjective case reports, surveys, or use very weak experimental controls. The lack of comparable control groups and base-rate statistics for nondrug therapies makes interpretation of studies with patients very difficult." (p. 349.) (Other reports on LSD and hallucinogens are given by Blacker et al., 1968; Freedman, 1968; Houston, 1969; Impier et al., 1968; Johnson, 1969; and Smart, 1969, 1970, among literally dozens of such reports.)

TREATMENT

There is a growing number of illustrations of the use of behavior-therapy techniques in the treatment of drug abuse. On a conceptual level, Cahoon and Crosby (1972) suggest that learning variables may underlie some instances of chronic drug use. Wikler (1971) presents a "conditioning" interpretation of drug abuse. Saper (1971) offers learning alternatives to the use of addictive drugs. Aversion therapy has been utilized for heroin addicts (Thomason and Rathod, 1968; Liberman, 1968; Leser, 1967; and Raymond, 1964).

Spevack, Pihl, and Rowan (1973) report on the use of aversion conditioning and systematic desensitization with two different drug-related problems. Three habitual amphetamine users were administered painful electric shocks contingent on thoughts directed to the process and act of injecting amphetamines. Systematic desensitization was used to treat a series of phobias that developed subsequent to adverse LSD reactions.

Other investigators have utilized: covert conditioning techniques (Wisocki, 1973); token economies and "operant reinforcement systems" (O'Brien, Raynes, and Patch, 1971); "micro-economy" (another term for a token economy) (Miles et al., 1972); contingency contracting (Boudin, 1972); induced anxiety (Boer and Sipprelle, 1969); and systematic desensitization (Kraft, 1969, 1970b). In such studies, the same basic principles are utilized as in work with people who overindulge in alcohol or food.

A widely publicized approach, *Synanon*, founded in 1958 by Charles E. Dederich, resembles Alcoholics Anonymous. This group attempts to provide a climate consisting of a family structure of a nineteenth-century family set-up of the type that produced inner-directed personalities.

The key element in this program for addicts is the "Synanon," which is a form of group psychotherapy. This group is run by an individual who is a recovered addict, and who uses his own experiences as a yardstick in his work with the group. He may employ a variety of techniques such as ridicule and hostile attack to stimulate the group members.

Synanon's approach to bringing about change is to work directly on the offending behavior, the use of the addictive drug (Yablonsky, 1965). Synanon then endeavors to create a new and different role for the person. It proceeds to reinforce, with social approval, the newer and more desirable behaviors. In many ways this program is similar to moral treatment as described in Chapter 7.

There is an interesting similarity between the point of view of the initiators of Synanon and some of the viewpoints of the behavioral approach. (See Karen and Bower for a behavioral analysis of Synanon, 1968). However, Synanon's dogmatic, autocratic, and frequently debasing methods, e.g. its "haircut" technique, may work against benefit to the participant.

By the mid-1960's, . . . even Synanon itself conceded that its program had with few exceptions failed to turn out abstinent alumni. Members apparently cured beyond any possibility of relapse promptly relapsed when they left the sheltering confines of Synanon or of other therapeutic communities to which they had transferred. Dederich himself estimated in 1971 that the relapse rate among Synanon graduates was in the neighborhood of 90 percent. . . .

Synanon, to its credit, now recognizes its inability to graduate "cured" heroin addicts. It no longer presents itself as solely or even primarily a treatment center for heroin addicts, and it no longer claims that it can graduate successful ex-addicts. Rather, it presents itself as a way of life, admits nonaddicts, and states that the goal is to remain in Synanon forever. Other therapeutic communities, too, are increasingly presenting themselves as a way of life rather than a cure for heroin addiction. [Brecher, 1972, p. 82.]

Another recent and highly controversial approach toward heroin addition has been to maintain the addict on another drug, *methadone hydrochloride,* which is as addictive as heroin but permits the addict to function socially more adequately than when he is on heroin. Dole and Nyswander (1965) developed this treatment accidentally while working with a group of heroin "mainliners" (people who inject the drug intravenously). A daily oral high-dosage administration of methadone seemed to block the urge to return to heroin which characterizes its user after withdrawal effects have subsided. By the use of the alternative drug the patients were generally able to return to the community, become self-supporting, but were still drug-addicted.

The advantages of methadone are that it eliminates the physiological craving for heroin, it maintains an even "high," allowing an addict to function in society, and it can be taken orally. It is less expensive than heroin, since it can be decriminalized. Methadone was widely hailed as an effective strategy against heroin addiction (Dole, 1971). Babst, Chambers, and Warner (1971) note that the best group for use of methadone was one composed of people who had been abusers for 5 years or less and did not use different drugs or alcohol at the same time, while the group that did poorest on methadone were people who had abused drugs for 12 to 15 years and had had 7 or more convictions. However, there is now considerable controversy (e.g., Renner and Rubin, 1973 versus O'Malley, Anderson, and Lazare, 1972) about the efficacy of methadone maintenance and the use of one addictive drug as a substitute for another. Further, methadone, which is rapidly becoming a black-market product (Arehart, 1972), is both a "solution" and a problem (Bazell, 1973).

In one of the strongest criticisms of the use of methadone, Lennard et al. (1972) argue that the use of methadone on a large scale "supports, and indeed reinforces a drug-oriented approach to the solution of social and personal problems. . . . When it is advocated or required as the treatment for *all* addicts, the methadone solution forces a technological management approach that is in opposition to efforts to replace a reliance on drugs with a reliance on persons and creative social arrangements." (p. 176.)

In any case, the search for drugs that block the effects of heroin will continue (Hammond, 1971; Maugh, 1972).

SUMMARY

The two major types of addiction discussed were the use of alcohol and of drugs. To understand this area it is necessary to distinguish between the concepts of *physiological* addiction, psychological *dependency*, *abuse*, and the *likelihood* of abuse. The prevalence of, description of, and the personal and social consequences of excessive drinking were discussed. It was emphasized that there are various patterns of drinking, each with somewhat different social effects. The various phases of alcohol consumption may terminate in chronic alcoholic addiction with attendant severe physical damage and possible organic disorders such as Korsakov's psychosis. The history of alcohol and various theories as to the causes of alcoholism were presented. Within the sociopsychological formulation, various treatment procedures were described, including those of aversive conditioning, environmental manipulation, and controlled drinking. The major emphasis in treatment is twofold: the decrease of the drinking behavior and the substitution of socially appropriate behavior.

Drug addiction was presented in terms of the social and personal incidence of its occurrence, its historical context, and the major types of addictive drugs and their effects. There is a close treatment analogue between drugs and alcohol in that both involve the need to stop one behavior and substitute another that is more acceptable personally and socially. Further, both reflect medical, cultural, and political models of what is socially and personally appropriate.

children's behavior

23

Of all the areas covered in this text, ideas about children's behavior have changed most within the last decade. In almost all the traditional behaviors which are considered under the rubric of children's disorders—autism, retardation, schizophrenia, conduct problems, classroom disruption, learning disability—there are controversies and new approaches. In addition, there has been a growth in the studies of important aspects of children's behaviors such as the impact of TV, the social meaning of the IQ; the learning of sexual stereotypes in elementary classrooms and their impact on notions of proper adult roles; changing conceptions of the nature and function of the classroom; the evaluation and the impact of special programs such as Head Start and Follow Through on children's behavior; the effects of poverty on children; the growth of the child advocacy movement and concern for the rights of children; the growth of behavioral programs in the classroom, first as remedial and subsequently as common practice in teacher training; and concepts of the classroom as a planned environment and testing ground for future social organization.

Children may be viewed as a group under societal pressure in much the same way as the blind, the aged, and the female. There is a change from viewing societal expectations and practices as "right and natural" to determining what is actually happening and how the current situation came about. A category such as minority status or child is not an explanation of behavior but an observation of contingencies.

Changeworthy Behavior

Just as even the healthiest child is subject to an occasional cold, sore throat, or bruise, so does every child in the course of his first decade and a half, at times, act in a way that might be placed under the heading of behavior disorders or within the province of child psychiatry. An example of how any behavior may be considered a symptom may be obtained from the "Sympton List" of a proposed classification of children's disorders (GAP, 1966a, p. 276). Among other disturbances listed are incessant talk, interjectional speech (interrupting), loud talking, punning, and whispering.

Batchelor (1969, p. 474) points out the other side of this situation by noting that most children overcome their problems with little or no professional intervention: "Indeed, while giving proper weight to the immense effect of the child's environment in producing psychological disturbances in him, it is necessary to remember that all children are subjected to innumerable traumata, and the wonder is, not how many nervous and unstable children there are, but what a large proportion grow to be reasonably normal men and women."

This concept is of great importance: without professional intervention and labelling, most children's behavioral difficulties ameliorate. This may be a function of changes in parents' rearing strategies, new opportunities as classroom teachers and schools change, or the changes in bodily growth and social opportunities for the child as years go by. The majority of studies showing disappointing change over time are ones of traditional psychotherapy, which may well maintain disturbing behaviors rather than alter the child's behavior or that of his significant others. Clarizio (1968) and Scheff and Sundstrom (1970) document this point, which has major social implications for procedures that "red-tag" children early in their lives as a form of "prevention."

HISTORICAL DEVELOPMENT

Child psychiatry is a relatively recent development. If a person is a psychiatrist, he is likely, as Noyes and Kolb (1963, p. 482) do, to attribute the first organized psychiatric study of childhood maladjustments to Healy in Chicago in 1909. If he is a psychologist, he is likely to give credit to Witmer at the University of Pennsylvania in 1896. If he is a Freudian, he will note that Freud published his three contributions to the theory of sex in 1905 and that one of these was an article on childhood sexuality. Psychoanalytic thinking was first applied to children by Freud himself in the famous case of little Hans.[1] In the latter half of the nineteenth century, Darwin collected material on children and children's emotions, G. Stanley Hall questioned adults about their childhood experiences, and a child welfare movement, with particular devotion to the family developed. (Rosen, 1969, pp. 288–303). Two major social reforms, the development of child labor laws, and compulsory education also were intimately involved, as causes and effects, of the development of the period of childhood as we know it today. Finally, it should be remembered that protection of children from destructive abuse by parents is a product of the late 1870's and the model was prevention of cruelty to animals.

[1] Wolpe and Rachman's (1960) discussion of this case is classic and strongly recommended.

Some feeling for the state of child psychiatry at the turn of the century may be gained from Berkley's (1900) lecture delivered at Johns Hopkins University in 1899.

The faulty, high-pressure, educational methods now in vogue in our ordinary schools are responsible for a large number of the mental breakdowns noticed between the ages of ten and twelve years, as well as later. Although the actual growth of the cerebrum at this period is quite advanced, and the size of the head approaches that of the adult, the tissues themselves are far from mature, and are totally unable to cope with the undue stimulation and pressure which false educational methods lay upon them. But when, as too frequently happens, no proper steps are taken to insure to the children a sufficient quantity of fresh air and outdoor exercise, which might go far to counterbalance the continued draft upon the activity and stability of the brain tissues, the strain becomes too great to be withstood, and neurasthenia, melancholia, or even a permanent dementia, is the result. The pity is all the greater when we consider that many of these children whose nervous systems are wrecked by faulty education, although possessing an inherited taint, might have grown up to be useful men and women....

Masturbation in early life is another factor in the production of alienation. Few healthy children at the age of six or seven years are given to this practice, but the contrary must be affirmed for those of neurotic parentage. The drain upon the imperfectly developed system, the moral effect, the efforts at concealment, all conduce to nervous outbreaks and mental debility. One child (J. S.), who began the secret vice at age four years, indulged in heterosexual intercourse from her ninth year, and graduated at puberty as a paranoiac with hallucinations principally of a sexual character. Of course no system of moral education would have prevailed with this pronounced degenerate, and fortunately such instances are rare. [pp. 554, 555.] [2]

[2] The concept of a drain on energy or overly great stimulation (literally blowing the child's mind) is an illustration of how a medical reason was found to uphold a moral stricture—a situation similar to the use of psychiatric categorization as a form of social control. In fact, the current use of the concept of "adjustment" is similar to the

Berkley's therapeutics are little different from Roman psychiatry: moderate diet and healthy living. "The diet of nerve weaklings should be given the most careful attention. It should be unstimulating, but at the same time nutritious and fattening. A layer of fat beneath the skin is a resource of untold value in times of stress, since it supplies a food reserve upon which to draw." (p. 565.) Berkley also believed that insufficient chewing of certain foods, especially cereal containing "brain and nerve builders, may be in a measure responsible for the increasing tendency to nervous breakdowns in the present generation." (p. 566.) Such work may be contrasted with Burton (1927 edition, pp. 284–85) some two and a half centuries earlier:

. . . if a man escape a bad nurse, he may be undone by evil bringing up . . . bad parents, stepmothers, tutors, masters, teachers, too rigorous, too severe, too remiss or indulgent on the other side, are often fountains and furtherers of this disease. Parents, and such as have the tuition and oversight of children, offend many times in that they are too stern, always threatening, chiding, brawling, whipping, or striking; by means of which their poor children are so disheartened and cowed, that they never after have any courage, a merry hour in their lives, or take pleasure in anything. . . . Some fright their children with beggars, bugbears, and hobgoblins, if they cry, or be otherwise unruly . . . these things ought not at all, or to be sparingly done, and upon just occasion. Tyrannical, impatient, hare-brain Schoolmasters, dry-as-dusts . . . are in this kind as bad as hangmen and executioners, they make many children endure a martyrdom all the while they are at school . . . chiding, railing, frowning, lashing, tasking, keeping, that they are broken in spirit, moped many times, weary of their lives, and think no slavery in the world (as once I did myself) like to that of a Grammar Scholar. . . . Others again, in that opposite extreme, do as great harm by their too much remissness; they give them no bringing up, no calling to busy themselves about, or to live in, teach them no trade, or set them in any good course. . . .

A rapid growth in child psychiatry took place after the First World War when the National Committee for Mental Hygiene, supported by the Commonwealth Fund, sponsored child guidance clinics and provided fellowships for the study of child psychiatry. In addition to the work of educators such as Montessori and Pestalozzi, clinical child psychology was benefited by successes in intelligence testing, such as the work of Goddard in 1905 and Terman and Merrill in 1917. "It was not until 1926 that Homburger wrote the first treatise on the psychopathology of childhood that can be said to be informed by a concern for the child as a person, and it was not until 1935 that Kanner published the first American textbook with the title *Child Psychiatry*." (Eisenberg, 1969, p. 389.) It was also Kanner (1943) who reported the group of behaviors now called early infantile autism.

Kanner combines the very best features of scholarship and the psychobiological tradition of Adolph Meyer. Kanner himself (1962) traces the history of child psychiatry and remarks: "The great Esquirol reported in 1838 the cases of three 'little homicidal monomaniacs.' Of an eleven-year-old girl who pushed two infants into a well, he had nothing more to say than that she 'was known for her evil habits.'" This quotation, aside from its intrinsic charm, indicates how early efforts to deal with children were in terms of a theory of little adults.

PROBLEMS OF DESCRIPTION

It is customary to include under the heading of children's behavior disorders a vast range of major and minor deviations from vaguely defined and variously considered norms of general maturation and specific performances. Textbooks . . . are therefore organized collections of a multitude of diverse disturbances.

---

former use of "healthy.' Comfort (1969) elaborates on these points and has an excellent review (pp. 69–113) on the history of medical strictures against masturbation.

children's behavior

... Just as pediatric literature occupies itself with every known departure from ideal physical health at an early age, so do the discussions of abnormal child psychology comprise every known problem of overt and implicit behavior in the first years of life [such as] fever, delirium, nail biting, stuttering, schizophrenia.... [Kanner, 1944.]

In order to standardize the collection of statistics, Kanner suggests that the domain of child psychiatry should be considered the first thirteen or fourteen years of life. That is, the very word "child" in child psychiatry may be the subject of debate.[3]

Within the diagnostic groupings of DSM-II a child may be mentally retarded, may be suffering from an organic brain syndrome, or may be categorized as schizophrenia, childhood type. The vast majority of difficulties, however, are categorized as special symptoms (e.g., speech disturbance, tic, enuresis; see Chapter 15), transient situational disturbances; adjustment reactions of infancy, childhood, or adolescence; or behavior disorders of childhood and adolescence. Specific subcategories of this last group are hyperkinetic reaction, withdrawing reaction, overanxious reaction, runaway reaction, unsocialized aggressive reaction, and group delinquent reaction, all with the modifier "of childhood" or "of adolescence," depending on the person's age.

DSM-II states that *hyperkinetic reaction* is characterized by overactivity, restlessness, distractability, short attention span; *withdrawing reaction* is characterized by seclusiveness, sensitivity, shyness, timidity, general inability to form close interpersonal relationships; *overanxious reaction* is characterized by chronic anxiety, excessive and unrealistic fears, sleeplessness, nightmares, exaggerated autonomic responses, and the person tends to be immature, self-conscious, grossly lacking in self-confidence, conforming, inhibited, dutiful, approval-seeking, and apprehensive in new situations and unfamiliar surroundings; *runaway reaction* is characterized by "escape from threatening situations by running away from home for a day or more without permission. Typically they are immature and timid, and feel rejected at home, inadequate and friendless. They often steal furtively." (DSM-II, p. 50.); *unsocialized aggressive reaction* is characterized by overt or covert hostile disobedience, quarrelsomeness, physical and verbal aggressiveness, vengefulness, destructiveness, temper tantrums, solitary stealing, lying, and hostile teasing of other children. "These patients usually have no consistent parental acceptance and discipline." (DSM-II, p. 51.) *Group delinquent reaction* is characterized by values, behavior, and skills of a delinquent peer group or gang to whom they are loyal and with whom they characteristically skip school, and stay out late at night. "The condition is more common in boys than girls. When group delinquency occurs with girls it usually involves sexual delinquency, although shoplifting is common." (DSM-II, p. 51.)

In practice, Rosen, Barn, and Cramer (1964) note that in a study of 1,200 psychiatric clinics, 32 percent of the children seen went entirely undiagnosed and another 30 percent were diagnosed simply as "adjustment reaction" without further specification. Dreger et al. (1964), after finding that approximately 40 percent of the children diagnosed at 17 reporting clinics were categorized as adjustment reactions of childhood, wrote: "Looked at realistically, what this means is that after the elaborate diagnostic procedures used in most clinics are completed, the child is placed in a category, which says exactly what we knew about him in the first place, that he has a problem."

The results of factor analysis of children's behavioral difficulties agree in the major factors: conduct problems, personality problems, immaturity, and socialized

---

[3] This problem continues: for example, the proposed classification of childhood disorders (GAP, 1966a) has strong implications that adolescents are included. This proposal includes abortion, frigidity, impotence, ovulation pain, and nocturnal emissions in its symptom list (pp. 283–84).

delinquency (Quay, 1972). Sines et al. (1969) used 70 statements, which mothers of boys at clinics checked as present or absent in the last six months. Six dimensions were identified: aggression, inhibition, activity level, sleep disturbance, somatization, and sociability. Miller (1967a) also used parents of male children being seen at clinics, and the resulting dimensions [Miller, 1967b] were infantile aggression, hyperactivity, antisocial behavior, social withdrawal, anxiety, sleep disturbance, learning disability, and immaturity. Miller et al. (1967) applied these scales to a general population of children and found that girls in general were checked on fewer items, and that while "normal" children manifested a few of the items in every dimension, they rarely showed a large number of behaviors related to any one type of dimension (as did the "disturbed" or clinic children).

A study using teachers rather than parents to rate six-to-eight-year-old children by Dielman, Cattell, and Lepper (1971) obtained eight variables: hyperactivity, disciplinary problems, sluggishness, paranoiac tendencies, social withdrawal, acting out, speech problems, and antisocial tendencies. Because many of these dimensions overlap previous work, but also because of the severe sound of some of the labels, the highest loading items in each may be given: *hyperactivity*—extremely excitable, excessively high pitched or loud voice; *disciplinary problems*—negative attitude, uncooperative in group situations; *sluggishness*—short attention span, inattentive, lazy; *paranoiac tendencies*—greediness, jealousy, suspicion; *social withdrawal*—unexplained sadness, social reserve, easily embarrassed; *acting-out*—profane language, destructive of others' property; *speech problem*—stuttering; *antisocial tendencies*—belongs to a gang.

Wysocki and Wysocki (1970) very cogently added information about age, intelligence, physical handicaps, and change of residence or broken home to their factorial study, and found that these variables, especially intelligence, loaded highly on the dimensions and accounted for important differences not previously explained. Such work can only be encouraged, for other demographic characteristics, such as socioeconomic status, tap both values of the parents and expectations of teachers.

A final important variant of the factorial approach is by Wolff (1971), who used 100 children referred to a clinic and a comparison group matched for age, sex, socioeconomic status and attending the same school. Wolff found four factors which overlap previous work: aggressive acting-out, inhibited behavior, antisocial behavior, and toilet functions. Two additional types of information are presented by Wolff: frequency in the normal (nonclinic) population and differentiation of clinic from nonclinic population. Among behaviors occurring rarely (10 percent or less among controls), those that distinguished the two groups were lying, stealing, destructiveness, bed-wetting and fighting, while nightmares, sleepwalking, psychosomatic illnesses, constipation, and stammering did not.

Among moderately frequent items (11 percent to 25 percent among controls), those that distinguished the two groups were being high-strung, disobedient, poor attention, over active, sad in mood, and withdrawn. Those items that did not distinguish the groups were being reckless, timid, overly concerned with death, having physical complaints, overeating, and having a speech defect other than stammering. Among items that occurred in 25 percent or more of the control (normal) children, those that distinguished between the groups were anxiety, temper tantrums, poor relationship with siblings, and being oversubmissive with other children. Items that did not separate the groups were nail-biting, nose-picking, object-sucking, night (as distinct from sleep) walking, demanding company at night, food fads, excessive modesty, shyness, and undue avoidance of fighting.

This material illustrates a number of points:

1. Nonclinic children may display at least some of the same behaviors as clinic children.
2. Many of the problems are ones that are difficulties for significant others, such as parents and teachers, in terms of adult standards.
3. What is put into a factor analysis determines what comes out, and this point, in turn, is dependent upon number 2.

The evaluative aspect of all behavior problems is heightened with children. The referral is usually made by an adult. The child is abnormal by the definition used in this book, that is, he fails to meet someone's expectation of appropriate behavior, and this leads to action by an adult such as a parent, teacher, or parole officer to change his behavior. A strong, albeit indirect piece of evidence in this regard is by Dalton (1970), who reported that "of 100 children's emergency admissions to a hospital nearly half (49 percent) were admitted during the mother's paramenstruum. There was a statistically significant association between mother's menstruation and the child's admission for both accidents and illnesses. The eldest child in the family appeared to be most affected." (p. 27.) The question may be when can the parent cope rather than when is the child in need.

For pedagogical purposes at present, it seems best (1) to cluster target behaviors, and (2) when treating each individual, to use the methods most appropriate to that child and his interpersonal situation. The following material is separated into (1) personal problems and phobias, essentially the overanxious and withdrawn reactions of DSM-II or the personality problems of the factor analytic work just discussed; (2) conduct problems or the unsocialized aggressive and hyperkinetic reactions; (3) bowel and bladder control, because of their great historical import, the amount of data available, and their psychoanalytic implications; and (4) severely withdrawn, maladaptive, "psychotic" behavior. Two recent topics, minimal brain injury and the battered child, will be touched on separately.

FEARFUL BEHAVIOR

Watson and Rayner (1920) established a conditioned emotional response to a furry rodent in an eight-month-old child. Presentation of the animal, which had previously been a neutral stimulus, was paired with a sudden loud noise. A few such experiences were sufficient for the sight of the animal alone to lead to the child's emission of crying and other indications of distress. The child's behavior was "phobic"—an irrational and unusual fear—or an understandable and appropriate response, depending on one's theory and knowledge of prior reinforcement.[4]

Jones (1924a), in another classic report, described the termination of a phobia of a rabbit. Explanations, verbal encouragement, belittling, and disuse by avoidance of the stimulus were of little or no avail. The two most useful methods were modeling (presentation of the animal in the presence of a number of peers who enjoyed playing with it) and pairing gradually closer proximity of the animal with food.

Other people during the 1920's reported the direct instigation of phobias (Moss, 1924) and behavioral forms of treatment (Burnham, 1924). Jersild and Holmes (1935), as a by-product of work on children's fears, listed how parents dealt with their children's fears. They found that verbal explanation and reassurance, the most frequent procedure, was relatively ineffective if not supported by some additional technique. A demonstration by an adult of the

[4] Wallin (1939) secured written material on early difficulties of adjustment from college graduates and undergraduates. Many of these retrospective reports illustrate "adverse emotional conditioning" in accord with the paradigm advanced by Watson and Rayner.

thing feared was somewhat effective.[5] Coercion and ridicule, removing the feared object (the method of disuse), and ignoring the children's fears [6] were ineffective techniques. Two procedures were effective. The first was a graded presentation of the fear stimulus introducing the child to it by degrees. It was both frequently used and very successful. "Following are instances in which the method was used successfully: in dealing with the child who was afraid of the flow of water from faucets, the mother made it a policy to get him accustomed to a small flow of water, she then gradually increased the flow; to overcome fear of alarm clocks, the parents used a clock with a softer ring, and then introduced a louder clock; mother herself begins to cut the child's hair in the barber shop . . . while he grows accustomed to the chair and the surroundings, and then the barber finishes the job; to cope with fear of the dark, [the] child was first given a very dim light in his room and then subsequently this light was withdrawn." (Jersild and Holmes, 1935, p. 87.)

The second method of overcoming fears consisted of "definite attempts to promote skill in dealing with the feared stimulus." Jersild and Holmes describe the treatment as follows: "One child was much afraid of an imaginary dog. . . . [The mother] entered into make-believe play with the child and brought the imaginary dog into the play. . . . One mother made a dark, much-feared closet a center of games with her child, thereby leading the child to explore the closet, to incorporate it into her own activities. One mother encouraged her child's interest in doing small errands . . . by sending her occasionally on errands into a much-feared room. . . . in many instances skills were first cultivated with a less intense stimulus; thus, the child is taught how to push the vacuum cleaner when it was silent, to operate the levers of a tractor when it is quiet." (pp. 88–90.)

Holmes (1936) observed that 14 out of 20 nursery school children were afraid to enter a dark room to retrieve a ball. The children were then exposed to the situation in gradually increasing exposures. After a few practice sessions, 13 of the 14 initially frightened children went into the room without hesitation and recovered the ball.

The first point to be made is that parents can and in fact do perform many of the functions of behavior therapists. Second, the fears (or "phobias") reported by Jersild and Holmes were never brought to a professional mental healer and therefore might be called "spontaneous remissions." However, there is nothing spontaneous about the changes which illustrate the general principles of learning. Given these examples, what do behavior therapists have to offer parents? First, the behavior therapist may help formulate the problem and treatment in such a way that the parents can understand the treatment and participate in it. The behavior therapist encourages parents to persist. This is important because nonprofessionals are likely to give up too soon. They want a technique to work fast and often tell a therapist that a procedure he suggests has been tried and failed. Closer questioning usually reveals that the procedure was tried once or briefly. When working with individuals, smooth learning curves are the exception, the rule being jagged ups and downs around a general movement toward the goal. Second, through asking questions of what the target behavior is, what maintains it, and what environmental stimuli may be altered, the behavior therapist works with the parents on strategies and trains them in the tactics of behavior modification.

---

[5] A lack of repetition and technical skill might explain the relative failure of this technique.

[6] This is very important: in everyday practice, extinction is a reasonable procedure if the child makes a massive operant expenditure. Sailor et al. (1968) with a retardate, and Carlson et al. (1968) with an autistic child, successfully dealt with tantrums by extinction supplemented with positive reinforcement procedures. Many parents do not have the patience to present the requisite number of trials.

Training Parents

The parent is used in the same manner as the ward staff in psychiatric hospitals, the teacher in school settings, or the partner in the treatment of sexual difficulties. In this manner behavior modification is carried on directly in the situation in which the target behavior is to be changed. The parents are programmed to identify antecedent conditions and respond systematically to target behaviors. Another way of saying this is that the problem of generalization from professional treatment to the "real life" target situation is attenuated.

Hawkins et al. (1966) extend the treatment of the child and programming of the mother to the home. These authors, before describing their work, make the following valid points: "Traditional types of therapy have a number of deficiencies. First, the child's behavior is seldom observed by the therapist, leaving definition of the problem and description of the child's behavior totally up to the parent. Second, the behavior of the parent toward the child is seldom observed. Thus considerable reliance is placed on the verbal report of the parent and child and on the imagination of the therapist. Third, when 'practical suggestions' are made by the therapist, they may be so general or technical that it is difficult for the parent to translate them into specific behavior. Fourth, since no objective record is kept of behavior changes over short intervals (e.g., minutes, hours, days), it is difficult to judge the effectiveness of the treatment." (pp. 99-100.)

Hawkins et al. (1966) report on a child who was brought to the clinic because he was difficult to manage. At ages three and four and a half, he had been evaluated at a clinic for retarded children and obtained Stanford-Binet scores of 72 and 80 respectively. He was described as having borderline intelligence, as being hyperactive, and possibly brain-damaged. Treatment was conducted in the home and involved five phases: a first baseline period where observations of the mother-child interactions were made; the first experimental period where the mother was trained as will be described below; a second baseline period where the experimenters merely observed and the mother was told to interact with the child, Peter, in the manner she had before; a second experimental period similar to the first experimental period; and a follow-up 24 days after the last experimental period.

One of the first major tasks of the behavior therapist is to ascertain what specific activities defined the disruptive target behaviors to be altered. A large portion of Peter's objectionable behavior was composed of (1) biting his shirt or arm, (2) sticking out his tongue, (3) kicking or hitting himself, others, or objects, (4) calling someone or something a derogatory name, (5) removing or threatening to remove his clothing, (6) saying "No!" loudly and vigorously, (7) threatening to damage objects or persons, (8) throwing objects, and (9) pushing his sister. The frequency of these behaviors was recorded for successive ten-second intervals during each hour session. The time that Peter spent in a time-out room during the training periods did not count toward the hour of treatment-session time.

After recording and observing the mother and child for 16 baseline sessions (phase one), the mother was informed of the nine objectionable behaviors. She was shown three signals that were to be made by the experimenter to indicate how she was to respond to Peter. At signal A she was to tell Peter to stop whatever objectionable behavior he was emitting. At signal B she was to immediately place him in his room and lock the door. At signal C she was to immediately give him praise, attention, and affectionate physical contact. During the experimental sessions every time Peter emitted an objectionable behavior signal A was first given; if Peter did not stop or soon repeated the objectionable behavior, signal B was given; occasionally, when the

477

psychologist noticed that Peter was playing in a particularly desirable manner, signal C was given.

These response-contingent behaviors may be contrasted with the previous responses by Peter's mother: when Peter behaved objectionably, she would often try to explain to him why he should not act thus; or she would try to interest him in some new activity by offering toys or food.[7] Peter was occasionally punished by the withdrawal of a misused toy or other object, but he was often able to persuade his mother to return the item almost immediately. He was also punished by being placed in a high-chair and being forced to remain there for short periods of time. Considerable tantrum behavior usually followed such disciplinary measures and was quite effective in maintaining the mother's attention, largely in the form of verbal persuasion and argument.

When placed in the time-out room, which was as devoid of toys and other pleasant, distracting stimuli as possible, Peter had to remain there a minimum of five minutes and be quiet for at least a short period before he was let out. The reinforcement, being let out, was contingent upon desirable (quiet) behavior, *not* on continued tantrum behavior; too short a period might lead to a game of being picked up and being given attention and the like on the way to and from the time-out room. In short, as with other behavior therapy techniques, there is a technology which depends upon a determination of what the subject is to be taught.

When, after 6 experimental treatment sessions, Peter's emission of objectionable behaviors appeared stable, the contingencies were returned to baseline; i.e., the mother was told to do as she did before and the experimenter observed but did not cue her. After this second baseline period of 14 sessions, the second experimental period of 6 sessions occurred, and then 24 days later, during which time Peter's mother was free to use any techniques she chose, 3 post-session checks were made. Figure 1 presents the results graphically. After experimental sessions, the rate of objectionable behavior was approximately one-sixth of what it had been during the baseline period.

The early work of Wahler et al. (1965, 1966) is similar, save that the mother-child interactions took place in a clinic rather than a home setting. The mother and child were observed interacting in a playroom. Three types of behavior had to be defined and their baserate recorded: the child's behaviors indicative of the type that caused problems in the extratherapy environment, the child's behavior that was socially acceptable and incompatible with the undesirable target behavior, and the mother's differential response-contingent reactions to the child. By discussion before and after treatment sessions and by means of lights, the mother was helped in discriminating the target behaviors and her emission of appropriate responses to them. During the sessions the lights were initially used to signal what responses the mother should make.

A succeeding step was for the mother to discriminate the child's behavior without cues from the experimenter. The lights were then used to signal correct and incorrect responses, hence providing immediate evaluative feedback about her responses.[8]

Wahler et al. present material dealing with the differential reinforcement of chil-

---

[7] As Hawkins et al. (1966) note, such a procedure follows the concept of "distraction" or "redirection" advocated by many child-centered nursery school practitioners, but is likely operationally to be the positive reinforcement of behaviors the person wishes to change.

[8] Such stimuli are operationally reinforcing stimuli. That this is so indicates a point too frequently overlooked in traditional therapies in which the mother undergoes therapy for *her* problems at the same time that her child is treated for his. Behavior therapy assumes, correctly in the vast majority of cases, that parents are rational people with the long-term welfare of their children at heart.

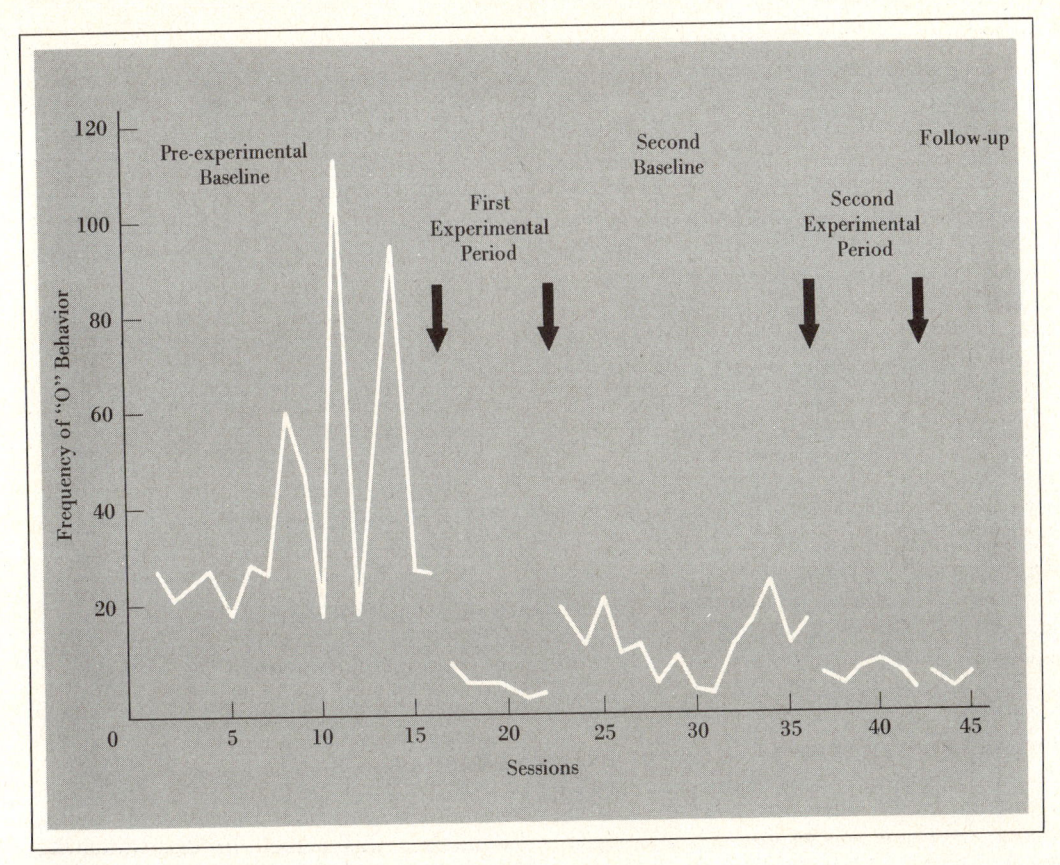

Figure 1
Number of 10-second intervals, per 1-hour session, in which O (objectionable) behavior occurred. Redrawn from Hawkins et al., 1966, p. 105.

dren's commanding vs. cooperative behavior. By taking measures of both the mother's and the child's behavior, some graphic indication of the degree to which the mother may alter her behavior and its effect can be obtained. Danny was a six-year-old boy who "virtually determined his own bedtime, foods he would eat, when the parents would play with him, and other household activities. . . . His parents reported they were simply 'unable' to refuse his demands, and they had rarely attempted to ignore or punish him. On the few occasions when they had refused him, they quickly relented when he began to shout or cry." When the mother was responsive to cooperative behavior and ignored commanding behavior, the commanding responses remained almost stable in terms of increase of accumulated frequency while the cooperative responses rose sharply. When there was a reversal of contingency in which commanding behaviors were reinforced, commanding behaviors rose.

Russo (1964) and Straughan (1964) provide examples of cases in which the parents observed (modeled) the therapist at work with the child. In the Straughan study the parents then conducted the therapy sessions at home. The procedure is most explicitly illustrated by work with a case of stuttering (Rickard and Mundy, 1965). A nine-year-old boy had been intermittently receiving speech therapy for the previous two years. A shaping procedure was used. In successive phases, the child had to read phrases, then sentences, then paragraphs, and finally had to make conversation to receive reinforcement (principally tokens for which toys could be bought). Aside from the steady improvement under this method of successively better performances at more difficult tasks, the important feature of this work was that after the early sessions the mother acted first as a silent participant at the treatment sessions, then as the therapist, and finally as a silent observer as the father, who had been observing the sessions, undertook the therapist role. Among other behavior therapy procedures, training parents has been an integral part of the treatment of destructive behavior (O'Leary, O'Leary, and Becker, 1967), excessive scratching (Allen and Harris, 1966), and autistic children (Walder, 1966; Wetzel et al., 1966; Nordquist and Wahler, 1973; Browning, 1971). One of the major findings by Lovaas et al. (1973) was that autistic children whose parents were trained to carry out behavior therapy continued to improve during the follow-up period.

There has been a burgeoning of reports of the training of parents. For example, both Ford (1974) and O'Dell (1974) review more than 70 reports on parent-training programs offered by behavior therapists in the late 1960's and early 1970's. The recipient of the training is generally the mother; infrequently the father alone is the recipient, but a growing number of studies train both parents together with the teacher (e.g., Meerbaum, 1973; Patterson, 1972), and programs for training groups of parents are being developed (Kemp, 1972; Ullmann and Kemp, 1973). Much of the training itself takes place in the context of the clinic or counseling center, while a smaller amount of the training takes place in the home itself. Two programs report training parents in three settings: the home, the clinic, and one other setting such as the school. (Patterson and Brodsky, 1966; Wahler and Erikson, 1969). It is reasonable to assume that training in a number of settings should facilitate the maintenance and generalization of improved behavior. In addition, the home may be the locus of reinforcement for changed behavior in the school setting (Bailey, Wolf, and Phillips, 1970).

Many parental-training programs use instructions and/or informal modeling or cueing as training procedures. Recently, however, there has been an increasing tendency for programs to include a multiplicity of techniques, such as active participation experiences, the use and understanding of systematic contingencies, video tape feedback, role training, daily feedback, group discussion, programmed texts, contracts, films, and post-training counseling (Berkowitz and Graziano, 1972; Johnson and Katz, 1973; Reisinger, 1972; Patterson, 1972; Walter and Gilmore, 1973; Toepfer et al., 1972; Walder et al., 1971; Hall, 1970, 1972).

Most of the parent-training programs focus on teaching only a limited number of specific procedures rather than training the parents in the broader skills of conceptualizing and functionally analyzing their living situation. Few of the investigators have systematically observed the parent behavior or that of the siblings, peers, or teachers of the particular child involved.

The vast majority of the studies of the training of parents have been optimistic about utilizing this technique in producing improved behavior in children. The training of parents and other environmental figures represents a major and logical extension of the sociopsychological model. It permits work with target behaviors and populations that the traditional therapist previously avoided (lower socioeconomic status, aggressive acts, and severe problems such as retardation and autism). Such work requires time for the development and validation of teaching material (Patterson, Cobb, and Ray, 1973), but it provides a strategy for prevention through the teaching of skills prior to crises, which leads to community programs (see Chapters 28 and 29).

On Punishment and Parental Attitudes

The use of aversive stimuli is a departure from the traditional professional approaches to child training in general and therapy in particular. There are three major lines of argument against the use of punishment. The first is the concept that behavioral difficulties are a result of an underlying conflict or defect in psychosexual adjustment. This line of reasoning, which has been called the medical model in this book, justifies a procedure such as regressive shock with some children while deploring the use of shock in a much milder, less frequent, but response-contingent manner as in work by Tate and Baroff (1966) and Lovaas et al. (1965) discussed in this chapter.

A second line of argument is one generated by psychologists whose work has been crucial to behavior therapy. Skinner (1938) and Estes (1944) presented data indicating that in the long run punishment did not decrease the emission of a response but rather was only temporarily effective. In the intervening quarter of a century data accumulated that this view was incomplete (see Solomon, 1964; Church, 1963). Of immediate import, for example, was that the intensity of the punishment, the timing of the punishment, and the opportunity for the punished organism to make an alternative response were among a host of other crucial conditions affecting the results of punishment.

The third line of reasoning is that coercion, especially the infliction of pain, is contrary to the values of our culture. This view has been reflected by Skinner himself (e.g., *Walden Two*, 1948) as well as in nondirective and psychoanalytic works. Where Skinner argued that punishment was ineffective, the latter argued that it might be traumatic. All schools agreed that punishment should not be used.

Solomon (1964) defines punishment as "a noxious stimulus, one which will support, by its termination or omission, the growth of new escape or avoidance responses. It is one which the subject will reject, if given a choice between the punishment stimulus and no stimulus at all." Time out from reinforcement has been shown to have these properties (Leitenberg, 1965).

While a review of the complexities of punishment, particularly if subhuman studies were included, is far beyond the scope of this book, some generalizations are important. First, punishment may lead to arousal, temporary suppression, partial suppression, or complete suppression, depending on its intensity. In general, the aversive stimulus should be sufficiently intense, and care should be taken that the subject does not habituate or get used to the aversive stimulus. Next, it seems far better to make aversive stimulation contingent upon early acts in a sequence rather than upon consummatory responses. This statement is based in part on the notion that the therapist is interested in training a particular mode of activity (e.g., heterosexuality rather than homosexuality) rather than decreasing a particular mode of biological gratification (sexual climax). The timing of punishment is crucial in such training procedures, and, in general, the earlier in the inappropriate chain the aversive stimulus is applied, the better. Timing is important in general, for, as seen in Chapter 2, if timing is improper, punishment may become a discriminative stimulus for positive reinforcement.

With aversive stimuli as with positive reinforcement, the therapist must use the very greatest care to determine what he is reinforcing. For purposes of both therapists and parents, a concept of vital importance is that *if one instrumental act is punished, an alternative operant must be available and positively reinforced.* This concept was demonstrated by Holz, Azrin, and Ayllon (1963), who conditioned mental patients to respond at a high rate. An attempt was then made to eliminate the response by means of a mild punishment. When only one response was available for obtaining the reinforcement, the mild punishment (a time out from reinforcement) was not effective. When an alternative response was available for obtaining the reinforcement, the mild punishment was completely effective.

Punishment may suppress a behavior; punishment may serve as a discriminative stimulus; punishment may permit the reinforcement of particular behaviors; and punishment may serve in the development of secondary reinforcers. Improperly applied, however, punishment may serve in all these capacities to teach the person responses that were not intended. If punishment is improperly applied the individual may learn to avoid rather than approach the acts and people the therapist or parent wants approached. *It is not a matter of punishing or, similarly, reinforcing or not reinforcing a child, but of what is positively reinforced and what is punished.*

Put differently, Kogan and Wimberger (1971) report that comparison (nonclinic) mothers tended to exercise their control over their children by telling them *what* to do, while mothers of children seen at clinics controlled their children by not accepting what the children had already done.

Parental Attitudes

Parental attitudes, which have been the subject of relatively intensive study, may be approached in the light of the foregoing material. An attitude has been defined (Hilgard, 1962) as "an orientation toward or away from some object, concept, or situation." Attitudes are usually measured by responses to a questionnaire. The concepts of attitudes and personality traits are difficult to distinguish. Hilgard (1962), for example, defines a trait as "a persisting characteristic or dimension of personality according to which an individual can be rated or measured." The similarity is also noted by the definitions presented by English and English (1958, p. 50 and p. 560); an attitude is defined as "an enduring, learned predisposition to behave in a consistent way toward a given class of objects" while a trait is defined as "any enduring or persisting character or characteristic of a person by means of which he can be distinguished from another."

The point of this digression is that many of the difficulties and criticisms raised in Chapter 9 on the topic of personality apply to the realm of attitudes. A second theoretical issue is that the relation between attitude and behavior is tenuous, and it is more likely that a change in behavior will lead to a change in "cognition" than that changed "cognitions" will lead to changed behaviors (see, for example, Festinger, 1964). In this regard, responses by parents to questions about their opinions as to how to raise children may be biased in that the opinions they express may be as much a result of their experiences with their children as that their children's behavior is the result of the opinions.

There are additional complexities in work with parent attitudes. Becker (1964, p. 202), after a review of empirical studies, makes the point as follows: "It is apparent that the consequences of disciplinary practices cannot be fully understood except in the context of the warmth of the parent-child relation, the prior history of disciplinary practices and emotional relations, and role-structure of the family, and the social and economic conditions under which a particular family unit is living." At one level, expressed attitudes toward child-rearing are associated with cultural variables, and at another level a mother who is warm and firm with her child is quite different from a mother whose firm disciplinary attitudes are associated with dislike for her child. Frank (1965), after reviewing 40 years of work, came to the conclusion that "No factors were found in the parent-child interaction of schizophrenics, neurotics or those with behavior disorders which could be identified as unique to them or which could distinguish one group from the other, or any of the groups from the families of the controls."

Associated with parental attitudes are two other areas of research. Both center on the child's early experience in global rather than specific and continuing patterns of experience, and both imply some sort of trauma that must be overcome. The first is that of a broken home and the second is psychoanalytic theory itself.

The incidence of broken homes among groups of "normals" used as controls for studies of pathological groups has been estimated as between 12 and 30 percent. Oltman, McGarry, and Friedman (1952) found that the incidence of broken homes and parental deprivation in the families of schizophrenics (34 percent) was not very different from that found in the families of hospital employees (32 percent).

An example of a test of psychoanalytic hypotheses in this area is a study by Sewell (1952), who obtained detailed information on the child-training experience of 162 farm children of "old American" stock. Through selection of children, cultural, occupational, and socioeconomic influences were held constant. Only children from unbroken homes and five to six years of age were selected in order to hold constant the effects of age and school experience. Personality tests, ratings, and overt social behavior were compared to manner and frequency of nursing, weaning, bowel and bladder training (early vs. late, degree of punishment), and sleep security. Of 460 chi-squares (a statistical procedure for determining the association between two measures) only 18 were significant at or beyond the level to be expected by chance once in 20 times. By chance, 23 associations should have been statistically significant. Further, of the 460 associations computed, 215 were in the direction predicted by psychoanalytic theory, while 245 were in the direction opposite to psychoanalytic predictions.

The present authors agree with Holmes when he wrote:

> Still other parents, usually of the upper classes, will spend incredible lengths of time trying to surmount the angry, stubborn wails of their three-year-old with endlessly patient explanations of why he should not play with matches. The three-year-old will regard being sent to his room as far more realistic than a mountain of logic. Even a spanking would be better than all that talk. At the extreme end of the benevolence-malevolence continuum is the exhaustively overindulgent, overprotective parent who, by withholding all visible forms of punishment or discipline, inflicts the cruelest punishment of all. He teaches his child nothing about reality. [1964, p. 15.]

The Battered Child

In 1962, Kempe et al. wrote an article on physical abuse of children by parents and defined a syndrome. In the decade following, professional people, having had their attention called to the phenomenon, produced considerable material (Bakan, 1971; Gil, 1970; Fontana, 1971); the popular press took up the area for feature articles, and groups such as Parents Anonymous were formed (Taylor, 1972). A literature on these parents has developed which has vast methodological limitations (Spinetta and Rigler, 1972). The general pattern so far observed is that of a parent who is lonely, isolated, dependent, and impulsive. Of particular import, these parents did not know how to deal with the situation they found themselves in as parents. The method of choice for both prevention and treatment is not the denigration of parents or the treatment of their underlying hostilities, but training them in better ways to deal with the responsibilities of being parents. To tell a person that if he is good and loving his offspring will be so, probably increases tension and the likelihood of destructive behavior rather than the effective behavior.

Summary

The behavioral approach stresses the training of parents both as prevention and as part of treatment. The behavioral approach aims for an increase in effectiveness and an increase in feelings of humanness and competence rather than guilt, frustration, and dependency. In this context, questions of what do parents do and when do they do it are the focus, rather than whether the parents present themselves as "warm" or "cold," "permissive" or "restrictive."

Some Behavioral Techniques

Whether applied by parent or professional therapist, the same principles and (with necessary modifications) techniques illustrated with adults may be used with children.

Extinction was previously illustrated in the control of a child's temper tantrums (Williams, 1959; see Chapter 2). An illustration from clinical practice is provided by an example from Batchelor (1969):

> Simon J., aged 5, was brought by his mother on account of a "nervous habit" of a curious kind. On going to bed he would put his arms up to and around his head (without actually touching it) and rock his head and arm at increasing speed until he was "hysterical," to use the mother's phrase. By this she meant that he seemed not to be able to hear when at the height of the habit, and could only be stopped by placing one's hand on him. . . . The mother was advised that the habit could not hurt him physically unless he banged himself against some hard object, and it was pointed out that the physical damage would be limited to that. . . . She was advised to talk to him about it and to give him a small diary, asking him to keep it himself and to put a cross against the days when he managed not to do it, and to give him little rewards for slight improvement. . . . Three months later the habit was reported to have ceased. [pp. 495–96.]

Phillips (1956, 1960, 1961) presents some additional detail on procedures which are similar to the Batchelor case in both content and spirit. Phillips (1956, p. 47) notes that his *assertion-structured therapy* led to 53 of 59 patients entering therapy and 51 of these 53 obtaining benefit in an average of fewer than eight sessions. In contrast, at the same clinic and with no noticeable bias of assignment, of 190 cases initially interviewed, 103 were judged unsuitable for treatment by psychoanalytically oriented therapists, 42 refused therapy themselves, and the remaining 45 completed a course of psychoanalytically oriented therapy averaging 17 sessions. For approximately 75 percent of these 45 cases, benefit was reported.

In discussing his techniques, Phillips (1960) comments that: "The parent is given 'common sense' explanations of what the child's behavior means ('He's trying to get by with this and he probably thinks you won't stop him.' 'He's had luck with this approach before, so why won't he try it again?' 'If you become more definite and consistent, this will help the child know where he stands with you.')" Also, "Stress is placed on 'keeping structure,' that is, on setting limits on behavior and specific aims for achievement. This allows the parent and the child to develop a success pattern in daily relationships rather than being bogged down with failures and impasses." In addition, "homework, household chores and a fairly set (but not rigid) routine is emphasized. Children misbehave, it is hypothesized, largely out of having too loose a structure of requirements and relationships."

Desensitization in practice (see Chapter 14) may also be used with children. As noted in reference to Jersild and Holmes (1935) the child is gradually introduced to the feared stimulus. Bentler (1962) used this procedure with a twelve-month-old girl with a fear of water. In similar fashion, Eysenck and Rachman (1965, pp. 209–10) present the case of a nine-year-old boy who had a bee phobia of three years' duration that interfered with his activities because he was afraid to go out of the house. The procedure began with exposure of small photographs of bees and then went on to the following phases: large photographs, colored photographs, dead bee in bottle at far end of room, dead bee on coat, gradually increasing manipulations of dead bees, and so forth. In addition, the boy's parents were encouraged to take him on brief, controlled visits to a natural history museum. The boy made gradual and systematic progress, and after eight sessions he and his mother both reported that he was "very much improved, he no longer has a physical reaction; he used to go white, sweaty, cold and trembling and his legs were like jelly. He can play alone in the garden quite comfortably." A follow-up after three months showed no recurrence of the phobia.

A stimulus leading to inappropriate fearful responses may be paired with relaxation. Lazarus (1960) reports the use of *systematic desensitization*, in which relaxation was paired with a visualized hierarchy by a 9½-year-old girl who suffered night terrors and severe abdominal pains (which the physician had labeled as psychosomatic). Additional maladaptive behaviors reported were bedwetting and fear of separation from the mother. Immediately prior to the child's difficulties a school friend had fallen into a pond and drowned, her next-door playmate had died of meningitis, and the girl had witnessed a motor accident in which a man had died. In five sessions spaced over ten consecutive days, the girl was desensitized for a hierarchy involving increasing periods of separation from her mother. The child's difficulties "dissipated," and at a 15-month follow-up she "had maintained an eminently satisfactory level of adjustment."

Drugs may also be used to produce relaxation. Lazarus (1960) describes the case of a 3½-year-old boy who had displayed a severe "phobia" of dogs since he had been bitten by one six months before. The fear had generalized to cats and birds, and so he was afraid to go out of doors. A puppy introduced into the home was ineffective: he became "hysterical" at the sight of it. In this case, a satisfactory level of sedation was attained, and in this condition the child was introduced to various animals. Progress was in terms of gradually reducing the level of sedation rather than the strength of the presented stimulus. Treatment required five weeks, and a follow-up a year later indicated the child had not relapsed in any respect.

Frequently children, especially boys, have difficulty learning to relax. Taking a leaf from the Jersild and Holmes (1935) work, mentioned above, the feared stimulus may be placed within an activity which the child likes. If the procedure is properly (gradually) paced, the pleasant features of the situation counter the unpleasant ones.

Lazarus and Abramovitz (1962) have applied this idea in their technique called *emotive imagery*. Children visualize elaborate fantasy situations involving their favorite heroes, activities, or desired goals, and aspects of the difficult stimulus are gradually woven into the fantasy. Lazarus and Abramovitz report the use of this technique with nine phobic children whose ages ranged from seven to fourteen. Seven of the children recovered in an average of 3.3 sessions, and follow-up inquiries revealed no relapses or symptom substitution.

An indication of the use of a combined operant approach and parental training is the case of a seven-year-old boy who was resistant to going to school and who at home did not move away from geographical proximity to his mother (Patterson, 1965a). Two therapy tactics were used. First, there was *shaping*, in which doll play of a structured nature was used. Whenever either the child dolls played away from the parent dolls or whenever in the discussion of the doll play the child himself made a statement of greater independence, he received a piece of candy. Over a period of time the threshold of behaviors leading to candy was gradually increased. The play sessions lasted roughly half of each therapy hour. During the remainder of the session, the mother was coached in the child's presence to reinforce desirable behavior at home. Whenever the child would play outside the house or emit more appropriate "brave" behavior in terms of geographical mobility and independence, he was to receive a reward. Also, his bravery was to be reported to his father at the evening meal. The treatment required 23 sessions. "On a follow-up of Karl's classroom adjustment three months after termination of treatment, the school reported dramatic improvement in his general adjustment as well as no further evidence of fearfulness." (Patterson, 1965a, p. 283.) Clement and Milne (1967), Clement (1968); Clement, Fazzone, and Goldstein (1970) present experimental support for the use of token reinforcement to increase verbalization and social play during group therapy sessions.

The use of the dolls in this last case differs from that of indirect or expressive therapy.[9] In behavior therapy the doll play situation is a method of obtaining behavior which may be shaped. The child is reinforced for the behaviors that will be desirable in the extratherapy situation; he may be hypothesized to be practicing them and increasing the likelihood of their emission.

An interesting and instructive experimental study is by Cassell (1965). Children between the ages of three and eleven who were in the hospital for cardiac catheterization were randomly assigned, 20 to an experimental group, 20 to a control group. They were treated in the same way, save that the children in the experimental group received the following puppet therapy: The day before cardiac catheterization at the hospital, the therapist first handled the doctor-puppet while the child worked with the patient-puppet, and many of the cardiac catheterization procedures (sedation injection, arm and leg restraint, electrode implantation, stitches to wound, etc.) were rehearsed. Following this, the roles were reversed: the child played the physician, the therapist the child. Additional explanations and opportunity for the child to familiarize himself with the aspects of the procedure were provided. The children who received the puppet experience were significantly less disturbed during the cardiac catheterization procedure than the control group children. The day following the cardiac catheterization, another puppet therapy session was held. The experimental group children expressed to their parents a significantly greater willingness to return to the hospital than the control group children. An interesting note on the specificity of such procedures is that the two groups did not differ significantly on ratings of ward behaviors during hospitalization or general emotional behavior at home following hospitalization.

In the group, the child may be posed with interpersonal problems with which he has difficulties. These may be presented in increasing order of difficulty for him, and both he and other group members may be presented the situations as problems to be solved. Effective and more socially acceptable alternatives may then be reinforced. Elements of this procedure may be found in Patterson's (1965) work, in Gittelman's (1965) work on *behavior rehearsal*, and Clement's (1968) use of tangible reinforcers in child group therapy. The procedure also bears similarities to Meichenbaum's work (to be described in Chapter 28) in training impulsive children to talk to themselves, and derives some theoretical support from

---

[9] Consistent with the medical analogue, traditional or evocative therapy relies on concepts of an underlying cause, fixation, and the like. Play therapy is viewed as providing material for interpretation in a manner similar to adult free-association. Two volumes which present reviews of this approach are by Kessler (1966) and Hammer and Kaplan (1967). An example of psychodynamic thinking in child therapy is provided by Ginott (1972, p. 46): "Sexually inadequate boys may especially benefit from fire play. The symbolic meaning of the activity is not lost on these children. Like music, it talks to the unconscious. They encounter an adult male who allows them to use a big match with a red top that lights up when rubbed. Dramatically, many boys choose to light the match on the zipper of their fly. Symbolically, they are granted potency, and they sense it."

Shure's, Spivack's, and Jaeger's (1971) finding of a relationship between the child's ability to conceptualize alternative solutions to real-life problems and teacher ratings of classroom behavior.

Modeling

Alteration of behavior after viewing others (*imitation, modeling,* or *vicarious reinforcement*) has been referred to in the treatment of adults (see Chapters 12, 14 and 18). The following experiment, which is itself a model of experimental design, was performed by Bandura, Grusec, and Menlove (1967). Children from three nursery schools, 24 boys and 24 girls three to five years of age, were first given a standardized graded sequence of 14 performance tasks in which they were asked to engage in increasingly close interactions with a dog. The children were to walk up to a playpen and look at the dog, touch the dog, pet the dog, walk the dog on a leash, remove the leash, turn the dog over to scratch its stomach, climb into the pen with the dog, feed the dog, and remain alone in the room in the pen with the dog. Based on this pretest, the children were divided into groups of high, middle, and low avoidance behavior with the dog. There were four treatment conditions. In the first, the *modeling-positive context,* the children observed a "fearless peer model" play with the dog in the context of a highly enjoyable party atmosphere. There were eight ten-minute treatment sessions conducted on four consecutive days. Each session, attended by four children, involved a party with hats, treats, prizes, stories, balloons, and similar pleasant stimuli. In the midst of the party, the dog was placed in the pen and for three minutes a four-year-old boy, "fearless peer," entered and played with the dog. He engaged in progressively bold displays of contact with the dog. Pretest findings had shown that when the modeled displays were too fear-provoking, children actively avoided looking at the performances.

A second group of children was placed in the *modeling-neutral context.* The same model displayed the same sequence of approaches and interaction with the dog, but the party context was omitted. During the eight sessions the children were merely seated at a table to observe the performance. This condition served to give information as to how important the pleasant context was. An *exposure-positive condition* included the parties and the presence of the dog, but the fearless peer did not perform. This provided information as to the role of the model. In a fourth and final control condition, the children participated in the parties, but neither the dog nor the fearless peer was present.

On the day following the last treatment session, the children were retested on the sequence of performance tasks they had undergone prior to treatment. Different rooms were used for treatment and assessment procedures. The adult administering the test had little knowledge of the conditions to which the children had been assigned. Finally, a different dog was introduced, and half the children were tested first with the original experimental dog and then with the unfamiliar dog; for the remaining children, this order was reversed. The average approach scores to the two dogs were virtually identical, and further work indicated that the two dogs had acted nearly identically compared with each other and across experimental conditions. These various procedures were all designed to eliminate alternative explanations of the obtained findings in a manner described in Chapter 3 of this book.

Finally, a month later, the children were again tested with both animals. The basic results are presented visually in Figure 2. Results with the two modeling conditions differed significantly from results with the two nonmodeling conditions, but one modeling condition (or nonmodeling condition) did not differ significantly from the other. Put in a different manner, after treatment 67 percent of the children in the modeling

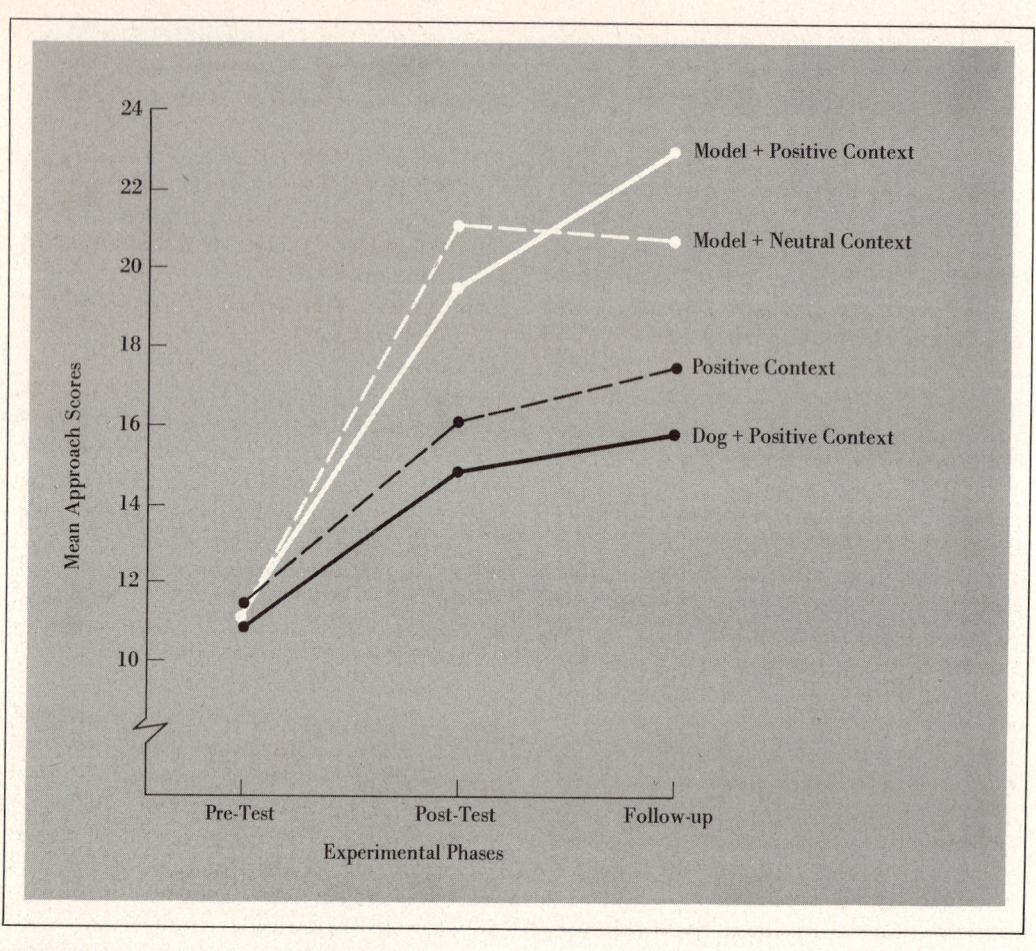

Figure 2
Mean approach scores achieved by children in each of the treatment conditions on the three different periods of assessment. Redrawn from Bandura et al., 1967, p. 21.

treatments remained alone in the room in the playpen with the dog, while only 33 percent of the nonmodeling treatment children did so. Another matter of interest was that of the children who were most avoidant on the pretest, 55 percent in the two modeling conditions attained this level following the treatment sessions, while only 13 percent in the two nonmodeling conditions did so. These differences, observed at the time of the post-test, were maintained on follow-up testing. In short, this work demonstrates that modeling may be an excellent tool for the treatment of children's fears.

Summary

This section has discussed a variety of children's behaviors that are considered suitable for change. One focus has been on the role of the parent, just as in the next section the focus will be on the role of the teacher. As noted, a behavioral formulation stresses training in the situation where change is desired, and hence the therapy and "reality" milieus are brought as close together as possible. In a behavioral formulation, the training of the significant other in discriminating and differentially reinforcing both desirable and undesirable target behaviors is of major importance. A second focus of this section was the alteration of "fearful" or "neurotic" behaviors. It was noted how therapeutic tactics parallel to those used with adults, may be employed with children.

"CONDUCT PROBLEMS"

As noted in prior chapters, a behavior may follow the same paradigm as "neurotic behaviors" and yet receive a different label from professional observers. One difference between "neurotic" behavior and "conduct" problems is an apparent variable of activity toward or away from situations and people. For example, Batchelor (1969, p. 491) in referring to such behaviors as truancy, lying, stealing, cruelty, and temper outbursts, says, "These are positive acts. . . ."

Conduct problems involve behaviors that are "more understandable" than personality difficulties, if "understandable" refers to immediacy of reinforcement. It seems easier to understand the advantages to a child who lies, cheats, steals, or is disruptive in the classroom than to understand the advantages to a child who fears and avoids stimuli that others deal with effectively and with pleasure. Rosen, Fox and Gregory (1972, p. 385) remark, as have many others, that "Most parents regard as a problem only those behaviors that pose threats to them, and, as a result, the quietly disturbed tend to be ignored or tacitly encouraged." In short, a dichotomy has developed between avoidant behaviors and undesirable forms of approach behaviors.

Certain "bad" behaviors feel good. This concept can be refined, and in fact has been, as the *Premack principle*. The following material, from Homme et al. (1963), illustrates not only this principle but also the use of behaviors to develop prosocial behaviors that in other contexts would be called symptomatic of conduct problems.

Premack's principle (Premack, 1959) can be stated as follows: if behavior B is of higher probability than behavior A, then behavior A can be made more probable by making behavior B contingent upon it. For example, if going to the beach is more likely than studying, the rate of studying can be increased by making going to the beach contingent on having studied. Homme et al. (1963) worked with three-year-old nursery school children. The children paid scant attention to verbal requests (operationally, their behavior did not change after such instructions). They would continue their activities: run, scream, push chairs, and so forth. These latter behaviors may be called high probability behaviors (type B in the Premack formulation). Prosocial behaviors of doing what the teacher wanted, such as sitting quietly on the chair, could be increased if emission of such behavior by the child was followed by permission to emit a type B behavior. "For example, sitting quietly in a chair and looking at the blackboard would be intermittently followed by the sound of the bell, with the instruction: 'Run and scream.' The Ss [subjects] would then leap to their feet and run around the room screaming. At another signal they would stop. At this time they would get another signal and an instruction to engage in some other behavior which, on a quasi-random schedule, might be one of high or low probability. At a later stage, Ss earned tokens for low probability behaviors which could be later used to 'buy' the opportunity for high probability activities." (Homme et al., 1963, p. 544.)

In a few days the children were very responsive to the teacher's requests—so "compliant," in fact, that a naïve observer might have thought that extensive punishment had been used to train them. Among the high probability behaviors used were throwing a plastic cup, kicking a waste basket, and pushing the experimenter around the room in his caster-equipped chair. The effect may have been due in part to the fact that the adults were able to predict high probability behaviors that the children had not yet emitted on their own, and in part to the "quasi-random" scheduling of either high or low probability behaviors. Wasik (1970) extended this line of work with a four-phase demonstration with 20 children in a school for "culturally deprived children."

In diagnosis, theoretical formulation, and treatment, the conduct disorders follow the general outline of abnormal behavior advanced throughout this book.

A case presented by Batchelor illustrates the point that prosocial behavior must lead to reinforcement or alternative behaviors will be emitted.

> Stealing as rebellion was well shown by a boy of 13 who was brought by his mother, who was in great distress. He was the eldest child and only boy in the family, and had been the apple of his parents' eye, but two years previously he had begun to steal anything of value that he could find lying about the house. He stole his mother's money, his father's cigars and his sister's sweets. He was incorrigible; no punishment was of any avail. This hardened young delinquent, when interviewed, rapidly dissolved into tears. It came out bit by bit that after dayschool, which ended about four o'clock, he was expected by his mother to do two hours' lessons; thereafter to practice the violin (which he loathed) for half an hour, and after that to help his mother in the garden. If any leisure remained before bedtime he was allowed to play with his sister in the garden; the village boys were considered "too rough." Nominally he had ample pocket-money for one of his years—8d a week—but 4d of this he gave (under duress) to foreign missions, and the other 4d he placed in his bank against the purchase of Christmas and birthday presents for the rest of the family. A reasonable rearrangement of pocket-money and of other conditions of his life led to an immediate cessation of stealing. [1969, p. 492.]

The general therapeutic strategy is to decrease the emission of the disruptive ("symptomatic") behavior and to increase the emission of alternative prosocial behavior in response to previously difficult situations. One direct technique is that of *extinction*. Extinction has been used successfully to decrease disruptive classroom behavior (Zimmerman and Zimmerman, 1962); it will be illustrated in the succeeding material. As stressed earlier in this chapter, when used without other techniques, extinction is neither a smooth nor immediate "cure." Parents and teachers initiating an extinction program must stick to their guns. A sentence in a case presented by Batchelor (1969, p. 493) reflects an all too frequent situation in which parents endeavoring to extinguish a behavior provide aperiodic reinforcement for obstinate behavior: "Threats were tried, but Gladys screamed if deprived of her weekly penny, and found that by this means she could always get it back."

A technique used with adults and described in Chapters 14 and 21 was the development of *anxiety-relief* responses. The following case (Lazarus, 1960) illustrates this procedure as well as that of *aversive conditioning*. In the former, the stimulus to be conditioned (as positive anxiety-relief) is followed by shock termination, where in aversive conditioning it is followed by shock instigation.

A ten-year-old boy woke up every night between one and two and climbed into his mother's bed. Bribes, threats, rewards in the morning, and one night of attempted extinction (he cried for four hours before his parents, exhausted, gave in) all did no good. Formal therapy lasted one interview. After interviewing and finding that the boy expressed a desire to stop this behavior, an electric shock apparatus was placed on the boy's arm. When the boy obtained a clear image of his mother's bed, he signaled and the electric shock went on. When the stimulus became unbearable, after an average of three and a half seconds, he said aloud, "my bed," and the shock was turned off.

The boy received 14 trials during a ten-minute period. Mother's bed became associated with pain and his own bed with cessation of an aversive stimulus.

The boy and his family came in the next week and the boy proudly reported that he had stayed in his own bed every night. He had awakened the first five nights but had turned over and gone back to sleep. He slept through the other nights. His brothers and sisters felt much more favorably toward him, the father took an active interest in the child now that "he had the makings of a man" (and let the father get his sleep), and the father spontaneously brought home a pet for him. The mother reported that the change in the family was nothing short of "miraculous."

A common conduct difficulty is aggression and/or hostility. Traditional formulations have centered around some defect of inhibition or guilt or some increase in drive. The latter formulation is the most famous one: frustration leads to aggression (Dollard et al., 1939). One alternative view has been advanced by Bandura and Walters (1959), who view aggressive behavior as normal behavior which has been given a negative evaluation by some person in authority, i.e., behavior which a labeler would like to have changed. The reader may wish to stop, as behavioral scientists have come to do more frequently, and ask himself what he means by aggressive and/or hostile behavior. Given provocation, behavior which would otherwise be antisocial is considered not only appropriate but also so expected that its failure to be emitted at times is called passivity, dependence, or some other label indicating that a change would be legitimate. Patterson, Littman, and Bricker (1967) consider aggressive behaviors as part of the larger category of assertive behavior, and hypothesize that favorable responses by peers will maintain such behavior. If aggressive behavior is followed by aversive consequences, either the behavior will decrease or the victim be changed. Observations over nine months supported this view and, in turn, lead to the concept that one method of combatting aggression is by teaching legitimate assertion to former "victims." Results consistent with this view have been reported by Perry and Perry (1974). A further study by Walters and Brown (1964) may illustrate these considerations.

An aggressive response "involves both a value judgment and the identification of a response sequence as possessing characteristics that are likely to inflict pain, damage, or loss on others. . . . the possession of high intensity is one such characteristic." (Walters and Brown, 1964, p. 376.) Walters and Brown point out that a child who gently tugs at his mother's apron is likely to be called dependent, but if he tugs violently he is likely to be called aggressive. Walters and Brown report work on this topic. The key subjects were 16 second-grade boys. Each boy was trained in two conditions, one in which he was reinforced for high magnitude responses, one for low magnitude responses. Whether he was trained first for high or low magnitude responses was a matter of random assignment for a statistical procedure called counterbalancing. Each training session was followed by a "testing" session on the same day.

In the training session the apparatus consisted of a large plastic clown toy (a Bobo doll) that had been fitted with equipment to measure the strength with which the boy hit it. When the clown was struck, his eyes and a flower in his buttonhole lit up. For further reinforcement marbles were dispensed by a remote control button when the experimenter wished. The child was introduced to the apparatus by being told that the game was played by hitting Bobo in the stomach. The child was to keep any marbles he won. He was given two minutes of warmup, during which time marbles were given every 30 seconds. After this there was a two-minute rest period during which the equipment was calibrated. The 10 most intense responses or least intense responses (blows to Bobo) were ascertained. During the period that followed, reinforcement occurred only when the blows were more intense or less intense than these limits. After each boy had received 15 reinforced responses under these conditions, he was given his marbles and returned to his classroom. A second training session, in which the reinforced response was reversed, was given two weeks later.

During the testing session, each trained boy was paired with a second-grade boy who had not undergone training. Testing sessions were divided into three parts. In the first part the children played "Cover the Cross" for three minutes. The object of this game is to be the person standing on the cross when the referee yells "Stop!" The second part of the testing sessions involved free play together by the boys. The third part involved the game of "Scalp" in which the players try to remove adhesive tape (the scalp) from each other's arms without losing their own. If a scalp was removed in less than two minutes, another round of "Scalp" was played so that the duration of observations would be equal.

Two observers who had no knowledge of the purpose of the experiment and of the conditions under which the boys had been trained were located behind a one-way screen. The raters noted the number of 20-second intervals during which there was an instance of aggression (butting, kneeing, elbowing, kicking, punching, pulling, pushing, hand twisting, and sitting on the other's back). The second testing session was the same as the first.

In an additional experiment Walters and Brown trained children to make high- and low-intensity responses when pressing a lever. For this work kindergarten and first-grade boys were used, so that the subjects were different in the two experiments.

With both groups of boys, the results were similar. Boys were significantly more aggressive (as operationally defined by the rating of aggressive behavior during the testing session) following high intensity training than during testing sessions following low intensity training. Which training, high or low intensity, came first did not make a statistically significant difference.

An experiment such as this one by Walters and Brown and ones by Nelson, Gelfand, and Hartmann (1969), and Katz (1971) may serve to test not only concepts of aggression but also concepts of abnormality. Are children who emit physically aggressive behavior after modeling or high intensity training "normal" or "abnormal"? Is it more accurate to talk of aggressive drives and impulses or to talk in terms of the results of prior training?

If aggression is viewed as a result of training, it may be modified directly without recourse to underlying causes. An illustration of such a procedure in a nursery school setting is provided by Brown and Elliot (1965). The goal of this work was to control the aggressive behavior of the boys in an entire nursery school class by removing positive generalized reinforcement (attention) for aggressive acts, while giving attention to cooperative acts.

There were 27 three- and four-year-old boys. Two observers (two in order to check reliability) made ratings of the occurrence of physical (pushes, pulls, holds, hits, strikes, annoys, interferes, etc.) and verbal (threatens, disparages) aggression. A *pre-treatment* baseline was established by one week of observation. The *first treatment* period lasted two weeks, with observations and ratings being made during the second week. The teachers were then told that the experiment was over and that they could act without the constraints of the experimental procedure. Three weeks after this another set of ratings was taken for a *first follow-up* period. Two weeks after this follow-up, treatment was reinstated for two weeks and a *second treatment* observation was made during the second week.

The treatment condition involved giving as much attention as possible to cooperative, nonaggressive behavior. If necessary, dangerous encounters (with hammers, for example) were broken up with no recrimination and as little fuss as possible. Table 1 presents the average daily number of physical, verbal, and total aggressive responses for the four observation phases just discussed.

Table 1
Average number of responses in various categories of aggression

PHASES	PHYSICAL	VERBAL	TOTAL
Pre-treatment	41.2	22.8	64.0
First treatment	26.0	17.4	43.4
Follow-up	37.8	13.8	51.6
Second treatment	21.0	4.6	25.6

Source: Brown and Elliot, 1965, p. 106.

The authors write (p. 107): "The teachers, incidentally, were skeptical of the success of the method when it was first proposed, though they came ultimately to be convinced of it. What made its success dramatic to them was the effect upon two very aggressive boys, both of whom became friendly and cooperative to a degree not thought possible." It is interesting that while the decrease in verbal aggression was maintained, physical aggression returned part way to its pretreatment level prior to reinstitution of the treatment conditions. Something that is successful is reinforcing to teachers, parents, and other treatment figures and will continue to be used unless it is "costly" (see Chapter 10, and Chapter 4 on conflict). Physical aggression may be harder for teachers to ignore than verbal aggression: "The more raucous scenes were tense, with the teachers waiting, alert and ready for the first bit of calm and cooperative behavior to appear and allow them to administer attention." In summary, the teachers as well as the children learn new behaviors.

There are individual cases of regressed crawling (Harris et al., 1964), social isolation (Allen et al., 1965), crying (Hart et al., 1964), lack of vigorous physical activity (Johnston et al., 1966), and negative response to peers (Scott, Burton, and Yarrow, 1967) that parallel in design (observation, treatment, prior conditions, and final treatment) the work on an entire class reported by Brown and Elliot. Clinical work on disruptive and aggressive behaviors is exemplified by Gentry (1970) in the laboratory; Goodlet, Goodlet, and Dredge (1970) in the school; and Bernal et al. (1968) in the home.

Many of the concepts discussed in Chapters 4, 5, and the present one are illustrated by a case presented by Burchard and Tyler (1965). Donny, a 13½-year-old boy, had been institutionalized since age nine when his mother was unable to handle his stealing, destructiveness, firesetting, and cruelty to small children and domestic animals. Diagnostic labels ranged from schizophrenia to psychopathic personality, and despite various treatments Donny's behavior worsened. One form of treatment tried for two years was regressive shock therapy,[10] in which Donny was "regressed" to the point of taking a bottle from his therapist and sitting on his lap receiving long periods of physical contact. After two years of regressive therapy other methods of treatment were tried and were also found to be ineffective. During the year prior to Burchard and Tyler's therapeutic intervention, Donny had been confined to an isolation room on more than 40 occasions for a total of 200 days. His most serious offenses included glue-sniffing, breaking and entering, vandalism, and inflicting damage on himself and others.

Burchard and Tyler noted that increased staff attention seemed to be the consequence of misbehaving. Although he was placed in the isolation room, the staff would visit with Donny and bring him treats. While he spent

[10] The concept of regressive shock is to disrupt the organism to the point of a very low biological state and then provide the mothering relationship in actual oral and anal training which the patient supposedly had failed to receive from his parents.

more time in isolation than any other boy, he also received more attention than any other boy. During the five months of treatment, Donny was taken off all tranquilizing medication and special forms of psychotherapy. Whenever he displayed any unacceptable behavior, he was immediately placed in isolation in a matter-of-fact manner. A radio immediately above the room was placed at moderate volume so that Donny could not communicate with other boys who previously had given him praise and sympathy when he was in isolation. For each hour Donny remained out of isolation he received a token reinforcement with which he would buy such things as cigarettes,[11] soda, trips to town, movies, and the like. Over time, in Donny's case after two months, the token and isolation-room schedules were altered. As will be noted below, the reinforcement schedule also changed as Donny's behavior was shaped.

There was a consistent decline in unacceptable behavior. In terms of being placed in isolation, there was a decline over five months of 33 percent. Of greater significance was that the seriousness of the offenses decreased. During the first month Donny's offenses included glue-sniffing, fighting, and stealing. During the last month Donny's most serious offenses were fighting, running in the cottage (ward), disruptive behavior in the school and cottage, and insolence to the cottage staff. The staff also commented that as the study progressed they had raised their previous standards of acceptable behavior to include behaviors that were previously unpunished—for example, running in the cottage.

Additional case reports of such treatment programs may be found in the psychological literature. Boardman (1962) reports on the treatment of Rusty, a boy who was truant and destructive. The key therapeutic procedure was making Rusty face the aversive consequences of his behavior, for example, by locking him out of the house when he wandered off. Treatment of compulsive stealing was reported by Wetzel (1966). In this case a strong relation between the patient, Mike, and the cook in the institution was developed. Mike's daily visits to the cook were curtailed when he stole (a time-out-from positive reinforcement), and he received both praise and material reinforcement when he resisted temptation and did not steal. Case reports by authors such as Patterson et al. (1965), Patterson and Brodsky (1966), Wahler (1967), Pihl (1967), White (1959), and Davison (1969) provide details for the student and break ground for later workers on a larger, classroom-size scale such as Becker, Madsen, Arnold, and Thomas (1967), Quay, Sprague, Werry, and McQueen (1967), and, as previously noted, O'Leary and Becker (1967). A particularly impressive report is by Doubros and Daniels (1966), who successfully brought under control the hyperactive behavior of six mentally retarded children through differential reinforcement and fading procedures. Martin et al. (1968) report on training autistic children in kindergarten-class behavior.

This section has discussed behavior in which children act in an antisocial manner. The formulation of these "conduct" problems has been the same as the formulation of "neurotic" disturbances: the behavior develops as a result of prior and continuing reinforcement and is treated by reinforcing alternative and incompatible behaviors. The case examples illustrate these procedures. It should be noted that specific applications vary with the realities of situations rather than with some theoretical scheme. That is, the principles remain stable, but the implementation can and should vary.

Following the more general model previously presented, antisocial behaviors, even as other difficulties, may be seen to arise from a lack of skills leading to a failure to emit and be reinforced for culturally ex-

---

[11] It is an interesting comment on values that giving cigarettes is an acceptable and widespread procedure in institutions of this type, whether as the lesser of two evils or as an acceptance of the mores of the inmates.

pected behavior. This problem may also be approached directly. It brings the treatment of abnormal behavior into the province of education. While this topic will be touched on in the next chapter on retardation, it is important to note that while a child may at times lag in school because of nonacademic behavioral difficulties, it is just as likely that behavioral or "emotional" problems may be preceded by failure and consequent lack of reinforcement in academic areas. While at times correction of one area of difficulty is associated with improvement in the other, this correlation should not be taken for granted. School is the child's work; a psychologist who deals with nonacademic problems and does not heed academic difficulties is not doing his whole job, and as a consequence may obtain less than the fully gratifying results he expects.[12]

CLASSROOM BEHAVIOR

One of the important recent developments in work with children has been the use of modification techniques in the classroom. Two major anthologies of work in this area are by O'Leary and O'Leary (1972) and by Klein, Hapkiewicz, and Rosen (1973). Becker (1973), reviewing the application of behavior principles in classrooms,

[12] If one accepts the sociopsychological model, then treatment aimed at developing a socially useful response in school-age children must make use of the body of knowledge of educational psychology. This task is unfortunately beyond the limits of the present volume, but the authors do wish to note the great strides recently made in programmed learning, especially for retardates (Greene, 1967), and other applications of reinforcement principles to academic settings. They also wish to note that while the present book focuses on the use of learning principles with socially disturbing target behaviors, the same principles can and have been used to foster cooperation (Azrin and Lindsley, 1956), "generosity" (Wiesen et al., 1967), sharing behavior (Doland and Adelberg, 1967), reading (Staats, 1965; Staats and Butterfield, 1965; Hewett, Mayhew, and Rabb, 1967; Whitlock, 1966), writing (Parson, 1964), speech (Sapon, 1967), studying (Miller, 1964), and school work in general (Tyler, 1967).

points out that most of the so-called innovative ideas which have been generally accepted in educational settings ". . . have been known and used by many psychologists and educators for forty years or more." (p. 77.)

The two factors that prevented the more widespread application of these ideas were the adoption of the intrapsychic, "disease" model in the classroom and the lack of strong research demonstrating the efficacy of specific procedures. A child's inability to learn was attributed by psychologists to some undesirable characteristic of the child such as his low IQ, his home background, an emotional disturbance, or a lack of readiness to learn (or read). All learning failures could be attributed to some handicap or learning disability on the part of the child, *not* the teacher.

The primary shift is to the concept of a learning environment planned by a teacher who considers himself or herself responsible for setting up the conditions for student learning. A major thrust of investigators, influenced by social learning concepts, has involved not only classroom applications but also the training of teachers (McDonald, 1973). Beyond the use of behavior modification in the classroom are broader concepts about the role of the teacher as an integrator of the environment and a facilitator of learning (Krasner and Krasner, 1972). (See Chapter 28 for further discussion of changing children's behavior in the classroom.)

HYPERACTIVITY

Hyperactivity is one of the major problems involving the behavior of children, yet it is still far from clear just what behaviors are involved in this label. Many children who come to the attention of teachers, school psychologists, or child-guidance workers are described as "hyperactive." Among the overt behaviors are exaggerated muscular activity (hyperkinesis), low frustration tolerance, poor motor coordination, short attention span, and low school achievement presumably due to excessive movement and lack of attention interfering with the learning process. This general type of hyperactivity is called "hyperkinetic reaction" in DSM-II, in contrast to no mention in DSM-I. Does this mention in DSM-II indicate the development of a new disease, the awareness and greater alertness of the professional to a disorder not previously of major concern, or the advent of a treatment method (drugs) for which practitioners sought more and more behaviors as being applicable? Wender (1971) has estimated the prevalence of hyperactivity in the general child population to be in the range of 5 to 10 percent. Huessey, Marshall, and Gendron (1973) show that hyperkinesis is not a stable pattern over time.

A highly controversial concept, that of "minimal brain dysfunction," has begun to be widely used among diagnosticians of children's disorders (Clements, 1966; Gunderson, 1971; Wender, 1971; Silver, 1971). The inference is made that children who misbehave, particularly if they are hyperactive, have some sort of neurological damage or defect, i.e., minimal brain dysfunction, often of a "subclinical" variety. However, the site of such damage has not been localized, nor is there strong evidence that the diagnosis has been a particularly useful predictor of academic achievement (Edwards, Alley, and Synder, 1971). Further, the term "hyperactive behavior" has been used to describe partially a wide range of other disorders with children, such as depression, schizophrenia, and demonstrated brain damage.

The clearest statement on the reality of minimal brain dysfunction, however, has come from Dr. Francis Crinella, a grantee of the Office of Education. He said that minimal brain dysfunction "has become one of our most fashionable forms of consensual ignorance." No simple medical examination or even an electro-encephalogram can disclose the presence of the disorder; "soft" neurological signs seem to be the only physical manifestation. [Witter, 1971, p. 31.]

Broadhead (1973) presents some data that indicate that minimal brain injured may be an alternative when authorities do not wish to use the more derogating designation of borderline retardation. Among children of the same IQ range, the parents of the children called minimally brain injured were of higher education, occupation, and social position than those of children called educable mentally retarded.

The treatment of children who have received the label of "hyperactive" has been a source of further controversy in both psychology and pediatrics (Sroufe and Stewart, 1973). Drug therapy, particularly stimulants such as the amphetamines, have become the popular form of treatment including up to 10 percent of all students in some school districts (Sroufe, 1972).

Investigators (Freedman et al., 1971; Wender, 1971; Fish, 1971) report that the stimulant drugs have been "beneficial" in one-half to two-thirds of the cases in which they have been used. However, the use of drugs with children brings up questions as to the conditions, goals, and effects of such treatment. Critics of drug usage contend that diagnostic categories such as minimal brain dysfunctions are so vague and unspecific that many children who receive the label are actually reacting to specific environmental stimuli (uninspiring curriculum, ghetto schools, crowded classrooms, etc.) (Battle and Lacey, 1972). Thus the drugs are used (in much the same way as tranquilizers in mental hospitals) for management in the classroom or home.

Twitchell (1971, p. 135) states the matter as follows:

I cannot accept Wender's cavalier approach to drug treatment. He urges a trial of medication "in all children whom the diagnosis of MBD [Minimal Brain Damage] is suspected." Suspected by whom—the teacher, the parent, the guidance counselor? And Wender's concept of MBD is extremely broad. Would all children with some learning difficulty or all neurotic adolescents have a trial of amphetamines? If generally adopted, such a policy would not only enlarge the over-medicated society but also might well compound the problem of addiction by making these drugs still more readily available.

The label plus the drug treatment brings the child into the mentally ill or sick category and the social and self-labeling that follow (see Chapters 2 and 10). The use of drugs enhances the belief in the efficacy of outside agents rather than attribution of change to one's own efforts (an important element in the development of self-control in children and responsibility in teachers).

The controversy about the existence of the minimal brain syndrome is intensified by the results of Routh and Roberts (1972), who did a factor analysis of 16 measures and ratings for a sample of 89 children attending a child development clinic. The measures included most of the variables mentioned most frequently used as indications of hyperactivity. They found only a few instances of significant relationships, especially when age and IQ were statistically controlled. They concluded that they had failed to find evidence for minimal brain damage as being a behavioral "syndrome."

Treatment

A particularly important illustrative case was presented by Patterson (1965b). Earl was a nine-year-old boy in the second grade. He was referred to the university clinic because of marked hyperactive behavior and academic retardation. He was described as being in almost continuous motion in the classroom and impossible to control unless he was in the immediate physical presence of the teacher. He was easily distracted, would work on his lessons for short periods of time or not at all, and leave his desk and wander around the room. He was destructive to the other children in the classroom and although he relieved their boredom, by and large they avoided him.

Previous to his adoption at age three, Earl had been treated with extreme brutality by his natural parents and later by his grandparents. His medical records showed a skull fracture which he received at less than one year of age, and at age four he was referred for neurological examination because of recurring convulsions and motor incoordination.

The therapeutic procedure began when the boy was observed for a period of time. Most of his hyperactivity was categorized as talking, pushing, hitting, pinching, looking about the room, looking out the window, moving out of his location, tapping, squirming, handling objects, and the like. Conditioning sessions followed a baseline observation period. The procedure brought fellow classmates into the situation. They were told that Earl had trouble learning things and one reason he was not learning was that he moved around and did not pay attention. Every time a light which was placed on his desk would flash, Earl had earned a penny or a piece of candy. This occurred for every ten-second period during which Earl had been attentive. The counter attached to the light would keep score. At the end of a period, the pennies and candies which Earl had earned would be divided among all of the class.

In short, the program was such that Earl received a feedback (a flash of light and the counter) reinforcement for himself plus support or even social pressure from his peers. That is, Earl's good behavior became meaningful not only to himself but also to those around him, who no longer reinforced him with laughter or social approval for his disruptive behavior. Quite the contrary—they reinforced his good behavior. Under the training program, there was a sharp decrease in disruptive responses.

A telephone call to Earl's parents four months after the study indicated that the teachers in school reported him to be much "quieter." For the first time, other children came to his home to play and he was making progress in a remedial reading program.

Although there have been several studies of the use of behavioral techniques on hyperactive behavior (e.g., Krop, 1971; Whitman, Caponigri, and Mercurio, 1971; Twardost and Sajwaj, 1972; Knowles, Prutsman, and Raduege, 1968; and Cermak, Stein, and Abelson, 1973), there has yet been no systematic comparison of behavioral technique with drug treatment. Christensen and Sprague (1973) superimposed the use of operant-conditioning procedures on drug treatment (Ritalin) and found that a combination of the two was more effective than medication alone. However, this study was carried out in a laboratory situation rather than in a classroom.

A number of studies have followed the lead of Patterson (1965b) in his use of a group reward program for a hyperactive child, in which the rewards from his peers were made contingent upon his behavior. Several have offered variations in which a certain level of performance by the entire group was required in order for each individual to get a reward (Barrish, Saunders, and Wolf, 1969; Graubard, 1969). Conversely, there was the technique of group reward based upon the performance of the individual target child (Evans and Oswalt, 1968; Rosenbaum, O'Leary, and Jacob, 1973). Jacob, O'Leary, and Price (1974) concluded that the changes they obtained in using a behavioral program (involving daily rewards) were at least comparable to the best improvements reportedly obtained in drug studies, and that "thus the behavioral program offers an alternative to drug treatment of hyperactive children."

Work such as that by Sykes, Douglas, and Morgenstern (1973) indicates that hyperactive subjects are no different from normal controls in their ability to direct their attention for brief periods. The task becomes to sustain attention. Put differently, in an important article by Alabiso (1972), attention inhibits or is incompatible with hyperactive behavior, and the therapeutic strategy then is to develop ways to maintain attention.

TOILET TRAINING

A section is devoted to this topic for a number of reasons. The first is historical. One of the earliest large-scale studies of the direct retraining of children's behavior was made by Mowrer and Mowrer (1938) on bed-wetting or, as it will be called from here on, *enuresis*. Second, there have been many replications of Mowrer's and Mowrer's work so that there are probably more data on this topic than on any one children's problem. An additional reason is that toilet training has an important place in psychoanalytic theory.

Mowrer and Mowrer used observations from pediatric hospital situations. As early as 1909, an electrical pad was devised which, when moistened, closed a circuit and rang a bell. A nurse came and awoke and changed the child. Under these conditions, it was reported that a number of children no longer wet their beds. Mowrer and Mowrer improved this device and added a number of important therapeutic elements. One was that the child was told to drink a normal amount of water before bedtime, and when he had not wet the bed for a week, he was asked to take an extra glass of water prior to bedtime. The aim was to *teach* a correct response instead of simply to avoid a difficulty. This procedure is currently called "over-learning," and is one method for reducing relapse rate (Young and Morgan, 1972a). Young and Morgan (1972b) report a 10 percent relapse rate by this method, compared to a 29 percent rate without it.

Mowrer and Mowrer (1938) reported 100 percent success with a series of thirty children. They also reported that instead of symptom substitution there was, if anything, an improvement in the general psychological health and self-evaluation of the treated children. This finding has been noted also by Morgan and Witmer (1938), Davidson and Douglass (1950), Geppert (1953), Baller and Shalock (1956), Gillison and Skinner (1958), Wickes (1958), and Lovibond (1963a, b). The reader may wish to consider how a person feels when he or she has overcome enuresis; Shader (1968), for example, presents such a case for a 20-year-old college student. One should expect general improvement rather than symptom substitutions. In a more systematic, experimental fashion, a general improvement was the finding of Baker (1969), who observed significant improvement on several independent measures of adjustment.

De Leon and Mandell (1966) studied 87 children of both sexes, from age 5½ to 14, referred to a community mental health center with a diagnosis of functional enuresis. Records were taken by the mother for approximately two weeks after initial contact with the clinic. The children were then assigned to groups similar in age and sex. The first group was the *conditioning group* in which a signal alarm device and sleeping pad were installed in the home. The second group was called a *psychotherapy-counseling group,* which met once a week twelve times for forty-minute sessions with the child and twenty minutes of counseling with the mother. Finally, there was a *control group:* following the initial clinic visit, these children received no treatment, but data were collected nightly for 90 days.

The term "cure" was operationally defined as 13 consecutive dry nights. The results showed that in the conditioning group, of the children who completed treatment 44 of 51, or 86.3 percent, were cured with the training device; while 2 of 11, or 18.2 percent, and 2 of 18, or 11.1 percent, of the children were cured in the psychotherapy and control groups respectively. The average time to reach cure for the conditioning group was 54.5 days; for the psychotherapy group it was 103.5 days; and for the control group it was 84 days. A big problem in this area is that of relapse. In the conditioning group there were 79.6 percent instances of relapse; in the psychotherapy group 100 percent of those cured relapsed; and in the control group, one out of the two, or 50 percent relapsed. The mean number of days until relapse following the 13 consecutive dry nights for the conditioning group was 88.7 days; while for the psychotherapy group it was 1.5 days; and for the control group, 1.0 day after having attained the criterion of 13 successive nights. There were significant differences not only in percentage of relapses and length of time to relapse, but also in fewer wet nights when there were relapses.

Therefore, in terms of percent of children helped, speed, length of time to relapse, severity of relapse, to say nothing of the more general savings in professional time and energy, the conditioning method was superior. Werry (1966, p. 228) summarizes a similar study as follows: "The conditioning apparatus proved significantly superior to both no treatment and brief psychotherapy, these latter two being indistinguishable statistically from each other in effect."

The first and, to the reader of this book (see Chapter 4), the obvious additional technique to reduce relapse is the use of intermittent reinforcement. Lovibond (1964, personal communication cited in Eysenck and Rachman, 1965, p. 197) reported that the relapse rate could be cut from one in three to one in five (which is more typical than the 79 percent reported by DeLeon and Mandell) by use of intermittent reinforcement. Turner, Young, and Rachman (1970) supported the intermittent-reinforcement procedure. Finley et al. (1973) strongly supported intermittent reinforcement over continuous reinforcement and the efficacy of both techniques over a placebo group.

The procedures so far discussed follow a Pavlovian model. To this, recent work has introduced operant techniques (Kimmel and Kimmel, 1970; Paschalit, Kimmel and Kimmel, 1972; Miller, 1973; Samaan, 1972; Stedman, 1972), which include prompting, fading of prompts, immediate social and extrinsic reinforcement, and shaping of increased degrees of control. Various technical innovations, particularly for work with retardates (Azrin, Bugle, and O'Brien, 1971) may alert the staff (parents) or aid in discrimination (Wagenen et al., 1969).

The general sociopsychological paradigm sets the goal of therapy as an acceptable response to a situation rather than solely the elimination of an objectionable response. Neale (1963) followed this paradigm in the instance of *encopresis* or bowel incontinence. It is interesting that in training children in our culture, the stress is all on not soiling, on holding back, on *not* performing an act, rather than the performance of the act at the socially appropriate time and place. A child who holds back overly long will lose the internal feedback of cues of the necessity to move his bowels. At a certain point, without any feedback whatsoever, the muscular process of digestion will lead to soiling. Neale's approach, therefore, was that of placing children in the proper place four times a day and reinforcing them with praise and candy for the appropriate behavior. There was no punishment for soiling. Although genitourinary and eliminatory behavior was discussed in the section dealing with involuntary musculature (psychophysiological reactions, Chapter 16), there is crucial involvement of voluntary muscle contractions inaugurated by the subject. Neale reports success with this procedure in three out of four extremely severe cases of encopresis. Similar procedures and success have been reported by Edelman (1971), Pedrini and Pedrini (1971), and Young and Goldsmith (1972), while the focal procedures used by Conger (1970) and Balson (1973) involved extinction by stopping attention for soiling. Ferinden and Handel (1970) made washing out the soiled clothes and making up time lost from the classroom the consequence for encopresis.

Peterson and London (1965) report how a severely encopretic child was treated by a twofold approach. When the child avoided bowel movements for a long period of time (constipation), the bowel movement was very painful when it did occur. This further reinforced avoidance of bowel movements and established a vicious circle. The first step in treatment was the induction of relaxation by a quasi-hypnotic procedure. While the child was relaxed it was suggested to him that bowel movements would not be painful. Following this, when the child did move his bowels appropriately, he was reinforced with social praise and candy. Success was noted, and no symptom substitution observed. Lal and Lindsley (1968) treated constipation successfully by making caresses and water play contingent upon the bowel movement, while Tomlinson (1970) used bubble gum, and Perzan, Boulanger, and Fischer (1972) used both repetitive suggestions and material reinforcers.

Marshall (1966) used reinforcement procedures of the type described by Neale with an autistic child, and cases of the training of "normal" children by rewarding them for asking to be allowed to go to the bathroom and/or completing the act successfully [13] have been reported by Keehn (1964), Pumroy and Pumroy (1965), and Madsen (1965).

In work with retardates, toilet training is a socially meaningful self-help goal. Authors reporting success with the application of learning principles to the toilet training of severe retardates are Dayan (1964); Hundziak, Maurer, and Watson (1965); Giles and Wolf (1966); Wagenen et al. (1969); Azrin and Foxx (1971), Mahoney, Wagenen, and Meyerson (1971).

Summary

This section may be summarized by making a number of points: (1) Theoretical notions may block empirical progress. An effective technique for the treatment of enuresis was available for many years and was not used.

[13] The worker must be careful not to reinforce only the asking. Further, appropriate elimination should become an instrumental act that is part of a larger social role—for example, a mature person who can go to school. If this is not done, and if the only way to obtain the reinforcer is through elimination, inappropriately high frequency may result (see Chapter 16 on overly frequent urination).

Werry (1966) surveyed 72 staff pediatricians at the Montreal Children's Hospital and found that although all of them had heard of the technique, only one-third had ever had any experience with it, "and this experience was in most cases marginal." (2) The procedure is one of selecting a target behavior and teaching a prosocial response incompatible with it. (3) There is a complex technology of behavior modification that needs to be learned and that will be improved through refined analyses of situations and applications of procedures such as intermittent reinforcement and operant as well as respondent procedures.

AUTISM AND CHILDHOOD SCHIZOPHRENIA

As we have indicated throughout, differences in diagnostic categories are not clear-cut. Difficulties in labeling are particularly confusing in the area of severe disorders occurring in childhood. Parents seeking help for their child go from one professional setting to another without much assistance and may find the same child labeled as schizophrenic, autistic, brain-damaged, or mentally retarded. DeMyer et al. (1971) evaluated 44 children on five of the most frequently used scales. While correlations between the scales were significant in most cases, they showed an overlap of 35 percent at best.

The category of "schizophrenia, childhood type" is defined in DSM-II as "for cases in which schizophrenic symptoms appear before puberty. The condition may be manifested by autistic, atypical, and withdrawn behavior; failure to develop identity separate from the mother's; and general unevenness, gross immaturity, and inadequacy in development. These developmental defects may result in mental retardation which should also be diagnosed." (p. 35.) There is no diagnostic category for childhood autism per se.

Kanner (1943) was the first to distinguish between schizophrenia and autism, primarily by contrasting children who had withdrawn from social relationships (schizophrenia), with those who had never been able to establish such relationships (autism), and failure to use language for communicative purposes (schizophrenia) with a pressure to maintain sameness (autism). This distinction is not necessarily clear and remains highly controversial among professionals in this field. Autism is relatively rare. Case reports on the backgrounds of autistic children indicate that although the children come from all kinds of ethnic and socioeconomic backgrounds, the occupational and educational status of their parents is usually at least average or above. (Ritvo and Ornitz, 1970; Treffert, 1970.) Following Werry (1972, p. 187), we may estimate the prevalence of all childhood psychosis as between 7 and 20 per 100,000, but it should also be noted that prevalence may be affected by the number of child psychiatrists in a given locale (Nicol and MacKay, 1968).

Among the symptoms of childhood schizophrenia are seclusiveness, loss of interest in surroundings, disturbances in emotional response to people, emotional blunting, reversion to "primitive" types of behavior, negativism, mannerisms, sensitivity to criticism, physical inactivity, repetitive movements, and idiosyncratic speech and thinking. The child may be apathetic or uncontrollably destructive to himself, to objects, or to others. Rosen, Fox, and Gregory (1972, p. 395) summarize the problems of distinguishing between autism and schizophrenic reaction, childhood type, as follows: "Because no clear syndrome is implicit in it, the definition has been variously elaborated by a number of investigators." The discriminating item is the concept that the schizophrenic reaction, childhood type, is a regression from some higher stage of development, while the child who is diagnosed "early infantile autism" has manifested tendencies to withdraw since the first year of life. This would indicate that early infantile autism may be somatogenic, and Rimland (1964) has marshaled evidence that this may well be the case. However, to quote Rosen, Fox, and Gregory again (1972, p. 396): "Early infantile autism is so similar to childhood schizophrenia in its manifestations that sometimes the two disorders cannot be differentiated except on the basis of historical data." Masters and Miller (1970) conclude that early infantile autism has not yet been demonstrated to be unitary behavior disorder, and Douglas and Sanders (1968) observed that Rimland's checklist validly distinguished between retarded children and 13 called infantile autism, although none of them reached the cutoff point established by Rimland for that diagnosis.

Three final comments are in order. The first is that hallucinations and delusions are rarely reported, and to this extent the picture is different from that of many adult schizophrenics. The second is that, as Kanner (1957, p. 737) pointed out, the term may be used so freely to designate any severe emotional disturbance that it may lose its meaning, a theme repeated by Rutter (1972). The third is that prognosis is poor but not hopeless. Kanner, Rodriguez, and Ashenden (1972) presented 9 cases (of 96) who as adults had made a good adjustment. Bender (1973) reports that about one-third of the people who had been diagnosed as schizophrenic as children had made a satisfactory adjustment in the community as adults. Figures from DeMyer et al. (1973) indicate 1 to 2 percent recovered to normality and 5 to 15 percent as "borderline." It should be noted that severity at intake, quality of treatment, and length of follow-up and stringency of criteria vary among different studies.

It is interesting to note that Kanner described parents of autistic children as follows: "In the whole group there are few really warmhearted fathers and mothers. For the most part the antecedents and collaterals are persons strongly preoccupied with abstraction of a scientific, literary, or artistic nature and limited in genuine contact with people. Even some of the happiest marriages are rather cold and formal affairs." (1957, p. 742.) If Kanner's picture is accurate, it seems reasonable to hypothesize that a lack of reinforcement for approach to adults as discriminative stimuli for pleasant consequences may be involved. It is hard, however, to say which comes first, the child's withdrawal or the adult's.

Kanner (1957, p. 739) notes that "Almost every mother recalled her astonishment at the child's failure to assume the usual anticipatory posture to being picked up." While there may be retrospective falsification in such reports, it is likely that the mothers may have tried many techniques to obtain positive responses, and the fluctuation from one procedure to another may have further confused the child and set up a vicious circle of maternal discouragement, leading to inconsistent reinforcement, leading to decrease response by the child and further maternal discouragement.

In autism as in schizophrenia a label may obscure the wide diversity of behaviors.

... almost all that has been written about autistic children has been based on the assumption that there is an underlying entity or a disease and that the behaviors one observes are expressive or symptomatic of this disease. It has always been thought that if this underlying process were changed, then the whole set of behaviors would also change. Much of this search into autism has been characterized by repeated attempts to determine (and continuous disagreements about) exactly what behavioral grouping should constitute the diagnosis of autism. ... Perhaps it was a mistake to invest so much research on the guess that all these behaviors pointed to *one* underlying distinct process called autism. It is, for example, quite possible that the different behaviors are related to several different kinds of antecedent conditions. [Lovaas and Koegel, 1973, p. 233.]

Based on this view, Lovaas and his co-investigators developed procedures to help these children overcome specific undesirable behaviors and to develop alternative ones. Although the focus is on changing specific behaviors, there clearly are interrelationships between response classes.

Behavioral Approaches to Autism

The first specific attempt to conceptualize the behavoir of autistic children within an environmental-learning framework was that of Ferster (1961). This was followed by a set of experiments in which autistic children were exposed to simplified but controlled environments in which they could engage in simple behaviors such as lever-pulling for reinforcers that were functional to them. (Ferster and DeMeyer, 1961.) This was the first demonstration that behavior of autistic children could be brought under control of explicit environmental changes. The general approach in this work was to select a simple response such as pressing a key and sustaining the behavior by positive reinforcement. Three children who were severely disturbed and diagnosed (childhood) schizophrenia and who had no known brain dysfunction were placed in a room in which there were various coin-operated machines dispensing candy and trinkets. The children progressed from simple key-pressing to matching-to-sample. Instead of pressing the key for tokens, the child was first taught to respond to a sample appearing in the center window of a display panel. Touching the sample drew the child's attention to it, on the one hand, and produced a second frame on the other.

The sample appeared in the center window with a matching figure to either the left or right and a nonmatching figure in the remaining position. If the child touched the matching figure, a token was delivered; if he touched the nonmatching figure, the machine went "dead" for a period of time; that is, there was time out from reinforcement. Once the child accurately matched simple figures (for example, colored dots), the complexity of the material was gradually increased. Very high levels of accuracy and, hence, inferentially, attention to intellectually demanding tasks were obtained.

If a single case of behavior modification of a child called schizophrenic has become classic, it is the case of Dicky (Wolf, Risley, and Mees, 1964). Dicky was a 3½-year-old boy who had developed cataracts in the lenses of both eyes when he was nine months old. At that time severe temper tantrums and sleep problems also developed. During his second year Dicky underwent various eye operations which made it necessary that he wear glasses, but for more than a year his parents failed to have him wear them. At the time Dicky was first seen he had been variously diagnosed as retarded, brain injured, psychotic, and having hyperthyroidism and phenylpyruvic oligophrenia. It was predicted that Dicky would become blind in six months if he did not start wearing glasses. At that time, in addition to the other difficulties he manifested, Dicky did not eat normally, had temper tantrums which included self-destructive acts such as head-banging, face-slapping, hair-pulling, and face-scratching, and did not sleep unless one or both of his parents stayed by his bed.

Tantrums were dealt with in a manner similar to that discussed earlier in this chapter in regard to the work by Burchard and Tyler with Donny. Dicky was placed in a room until he quieted down and had been calm a minimum amount of time. As with Donny, as time progressed the tantrum behavior that resulted in his being matter-of-factly placed in the isolation or time-out room was expanded to include all "atavistic" or undesirable tantrum behavior. Bedtime problems were dealt with by the same technique: a bedtime tantrum did not result in attention. Because words like "No!" and "Stop that!" had been backed up with aversive consequences (the time-out room), such words were adequate to help change Dicky's eating behavior. The new bedtime and tantrum behaviors were fostered in the home by having Dicky's parents model the therapists on the ward and at home.

The problem of getting Dicky to wear

his glasses was approached through shaping. For five weeks Dicky was given candy as a reinforcing stimulus for handling his glasses in an effort to approximate the act of wearing them. When progress proved discouraging, he was deprived first of breakfast and then of lunch. He became noticeably more interested in the reinforcer and more cooperative. At the end of 30 minutes of shaping under the condition of a strong reinforcer, Dicky was placing the glasses properly and looking at objects. After this, progress was rapid. After glasses-wearing had been established by use of food, weaker reinforcers such as the attendant's saying "Put on your glasses and let's go for a walk" were adequate. If Dicky removed his glasses during pleasurable occasions such as meals, walks, automobile rides, and outdoor play, the activity was terminated.

The investigators also used bites of food as rewards for Dicky's imitation of the attendant's labeling of pictures. After Dicky imitated, the pictures were presented without the attendant's prompting. Food was needed at the start of the procedure, but adult attention and praise were effective in maintaining and expanding Dicky's appropriate use of speech. At the time of writing (1964), when Dicky was five, he initiated requests and comments and used personal pronouns correctly. He was reported as continuing to wear his glasses, manifesting neither tantrums nor sleeping problems, increasing his verbal skills, and being "a new source of joy to members of his family." Wolf et al. (1967) report on further work with Dicky in a nursery school setting. Among the problems dealt with were toilet training and social interactions. At the time of this latter report, Dicky was able to attend public school.

In a subsequent report on Dicky, there is evidence that he is performing well in regular classrooms (Needelman and Sulzbacher, 1972). "Dicky's steady progress has brought him to the point where he is regarded by his current teacher as a kind and considerate student, well-liked by his classmates, a student who works quietly, pays attention in class, and takes pride in his work. His reading level is appropriate for his grade." (p. 7).

Some remnants of "his autistic behavior," such as rocking in his seat or hand-flapping, continue. However, his teacher and his classmates either do not notice or attribute this behavior to his visual handicap. The current observers of Dicky's behavior report that there is no evidence of substituted deviant behavior for those behaviors which were the object of his early treatment. "However, Dicky has been extremely fortunate in having had exemplary teachers who have used classroom procedures compatible with those which were initially so successful." (p. 9.)

Various aspects of Dicky's treatment have been repeated and elaborated by other workers, especially Nordquist and Wahler (1973). Operant techniques have been used in the development of speech in autistic children by Hewett (1965), Schell, Stark, and Giddan (1967), Commons, Paul, and Fargo (1966), Dameron (1965), Lovaas et al. (1965, 1966), Wolf et al. (1967), Nelson and Evans (1968), Fineman (1968), Fineman and Ferjo (1969), Shaw (1969), Bartlett et al. (1971), and Tramontana and Stimbert (1970), and in "mute" children by Kerr, Myerson, and Michael (1965), Salzinger et al. (1965), Hingtgen and Coulter (1967), Stark, Meisel, and Wright (1969), and Stark (1972). Operant procedures have been used to redirect attention (Marr, Miller, and Straub, 1966, Churchill and Bryson, 1972) and to deal with stuttering by schizophrenic children (Browning, 1967).

Brawley et al. (1969) treated a seven-year-old boy, Steve, who had been diagnosed as autistic five years before. On the hospital ward Steve rarely used speech, spent long periods of time lying on couches and staring at the wall, rarely handled toys, slapped himself forcefully on the head, emitted bizarre body and hand movements, and licked the wall. Appropriate behavior was designated as speaking comprehensibly, using objects as they were intended, and following requests; inappropriate behaviors were hurting himself, speaking incomprehensibly, social withdrawal, and tantrums. Originally, the staff gave far more attention to inappropriate than appropriate behavior, but under a therapeutic regimen, food and social reinforcement were made contingent on appropriate actions. Following such procedures, comprehensible speech increased from 2 percent to 46 percent of the time, while withdrawn and bizarre verbalizations decreased to essentially zero emission. What makes this report and the work of McConnell (1969) and Bartlett et al. (1971) particularly interesting is that in order to illustrate the role of the reinforcement contingency in the changed behavior, part of the program was reversed. Appropriate verbalization sharply decreased under this condition. Finally, the reinforcement of appropriate behavior was again instituted, and Steve's emission of appropriate speech once again increased. This type of work extends and documents the verbal conditioning discussed in Chapter 4.

Graziano and Kean (1967) taught four autistic children, ages five through nine, to be comfortable, calm, settled, and relaxed. These authors report that decreased excitement observed during the training in relaxation generalized to the remainder of the day.

As noted in this and other chapters, modeling may also be an effective method of treatment. The process of imitation, however, must be learned. Metz (1965) developed generalized imitation in two young children called schizophrenic. The children were deprived of breakfast in order to make lunch a more effective reinforcing stimulus. There were six periods: (1) pretesting, (2) preliminary training, (3) early testing, (4) intensive training, (5) later testing, and (6) post-testing.

The first pretesting period established a baseline of imitative responses in which one person, the model, made a response, and the second, imitating person made use of the model's activity as a discriminative stimulus to emit that behavior. In the second, preliminary training period, the child was oriented to the procedure, and "Good" and tokens were established as reinforcing stimuli. In this period, regardless of the child's response the therapist said "Good," handed him a token, and showed him how to use it to obtain food. Gradually the number of tokens needed was increased.

The next task was to use passive demonstration (i.e., prompting by physically guiding the child and then reinforcing him) and shaping to build a repertoire of three pairs of tasks. Prompts were then faded. In the third period, the early testing period, ten new tasks to be imitated were interspersed with the six learned in the prior period (to guarantee some success and lunch for the child). When the child imitated these new tasks, he was reinforced. Four nonreinforced tasks were also interspersed. Periods of intensive training, repeated later training, and post-testing (with new tasks, and "Good" but not food or token reinforcement) followed. Imitation of both rewarded and nonrewarded tasks increased. In short, imitation may be taught to children called schizophrenic. In a later article, Metz (1966) discusses his general program and work with nine autistic children.

Results similar to those of Metz were reported by Lovaas et al. (1966b) and Hingtgen, Coulter, and Churchill (1967) for teaching imitative speech to mute schizophrenic children. Lovaas et al. (1967) report on the establishment of imitation in 11 schizophrenic children and the use of this skill in establishing personal hygiene, drawing, and other socially desirable behaviors. Baer, Peterson, and Sherman (1967) taught imitation and used this accomplishment to teach initial verbal behavior to retarded children. Hartung (1970) brought the various procedures together in the systematic outline of a program.

A classic illustration of the development of imitation and its application in further treatment was reported by Risley and Wolf

(1967). These authors established functional (normal) speech with four children whose use of words had previously been *echolalic*, that is, an immediate repetition of the words spoken by another person. It may appear paradoxical, but the first step in training echolalic children was the establishment of imitation. The key, however, is that the child reliably imitate the therapist, i.e., have his verbal behavior brought under control. When this is done, the second step is to teach naming behavior: the response to a stimulus is imitated. The therapist then fades out his prompts and the child is naming objects appropriately. Phrases and appropriate conversational requests and responses are the next steps in this program. Along the way, food is used as a reinforcing stimulus. When food is given, it is paired with the word "Good."

The scheduling of the food reinforcer may be shifted from every occasion to an intermittent schedule, and the secondary reinforcer (praise) may be introduced. Eventually, the speech is effective in obtaining compliance from adults through appropriate requests. Appropriate speech is thus maintained as it is with "normal" people: it works to make life pleasanter. The other procedures mentioned in this section are used: undesirable behavior such as tantrums is reduced by the therapist's refusing to respond to it (extinction) and delaying further reinforcing activities for a period of time (time out from reinforcement; a mildly aversive stimulus). The likelihood of generalization is increased by the active cooperation of parents and other interested adults.

Compliance with adult requests is, like imitation, an important response for adjustment in childhood. This area was touched on briefly in the reference to Davison's work training college undergraduates and is the subject of a demonstration film by Davison and Krasner (1964) which shows the function of response-contingent reinforcement in work with autistic children. A number of clinical examples are provided by Ferster and Simons (1966); Brown, Pace, and Becker (1969); Craighead, O'Leary, and Allen (1973); and Ayllon and Skuban (1973).

Cowan, Hoddinott, and Wright (1965) worked with 12 autistic children. In the first part of their work the children were asked to select objects of a shape or color requested by the experimenter. In order to keep the child interested, after the completion of every response the child received a piece of popcorn, whether he had selected the correct color or not. Two children obtained perfect scores while the other ten children gave fewer correct responses than would have been expected by chance. There were no systematic errors (e.g., selecting green all the time instead of red); this finding was strong evidence of the children's going out of their way *not* to comply, that is, negativism. This first finding also indicated that the children were capable of form and shape discriminations, for only in this manner could they have selected fewer correct objects than by chance.

In the second part of their report, Cowan et al. worked with the ten children who had been negativistic (given fewer correct responses than expected by chance). The only difference in this part of the work was that children were given popcorn only after they had been correct (selected the object requested by the experimenter). Four of the ten children showed significant compliance within 60 trials under this regimen and perfect compliance when transferred to a new concept for which they had not been trained with the popcorn reinforcer. The remaining six children continued to make fewer correct responses through 120 trials than they would have made if they had randomly guessed. This work used a mild reinforcing stimulus and a relatively brief procedure, but even within these limits it was clear that workers in the field must make a distinction between responses the child cannot make and responses he is unwilling to make.

Another kind of behavior touched on in the case of Dicky was self-destructive behavior.[14] Self-destructive behavior is disturbing and unexpected. Tate and Baroff (1966) report on the use of two behavioral techniques to decrease self-injurious behavior in a blind nine-year-old boy who banged hs head forcefully against floors, walls, and other hard objects, slapped his face with his hands, punched his face with his fists, hit his shoulder with his chin, and kicked himself. The boy, Sam, was usually restrained (tied up) in bed. It was noticed that he enjoyed physical contact. In a first study, observations were made during 20 daily 20-minute sessions. There were five control sessions during which self-injurious responses were ignored, then five experimental sessions during which self-injurious responses were punished, then five additional control sessions, and finally five additional experimental sessions. Figure 3 gives a picture of the procedure and the results. During control sessions Sam walked around the institution with two experimenters who held his hands and ignored self-injurious responses. During experimental sessions, when Sam hit himself the experimenters jerked their hands free so that Sam had no physical contact with them. This "punishment," a time out from reinforcement for three seconds, was made without comment, and contact was re-established after three seconds.

The median rate of self-injurious responses (SIR's) was 6.6 per minute during the first control period, fell to a median of .1 per minute during the first experimental period, rose to 3.3 during the second control period, and was 1.0 during the final experimental period. An interesting observation, which has also been found by other workers (Risley, 1964; Lovaas et al., 1965) was that Sam's social behavior was more acceptable and alert on experimental days than on control period days. On control days, Sam typically whined, cried, hesitated in his walk, and seemed unresponsive to his environment. On experimental days there was no crying, he smiled more, and appeared more responsive to his environment.

Two days after the last experimental session described above, Tate and Baroff (1966) instigated a second procedure. In this case, a painful electric shock was made contingent upon self-injurious behavior. Sam was first untied and allowed a period of free responding. During this 24-minute baseline period there were 120 instances of self-injurious behavior. Sam was then told that if he continued to hit himself, he would be shocked and the shock would hurt. Thereafter, no further comments were made, and when Sam hurt himself, he received a half-second shock. During the following 90 minutes only five self-injurious responses were emitted. The authors talked to Sam and praised all noninjurious responses. During succeeding days, Sam was given greater physical freedom (i.e., removed from restraint). The rate of self-injurious behavior steadily decreased, and at the time of the report had not been observed at all for 20 consecutive days. In the interim, Sam became steadily more responsive. Clinging to people and posturing also ceased.

Perhaps the most important continuing work in this area has been that of Ivar Lovaas and his co-workers. This chapter will cover in detail only one article by this group. Lovaas, Schaeffer, and Simmons (1965) had three goals in this particular study: to teach children to comply with a request, to decrease self-stimulatory and self-destructive behavior, and to pair the word "No" with a shock and test its acquisition of behavior-suppressing properties, i.e., its establishment as a secondary reinforcer. While the first two goals overlap with work cited previously in this section, the third goal is a line of research which, like obedience to commands and acquisi-

---

[14] For an additional illustrative case of direct treatment of head-bumping see Mogel and Schiff (1967). Self-injurious and self-mutilating behavior is discussed further in chapter 27.

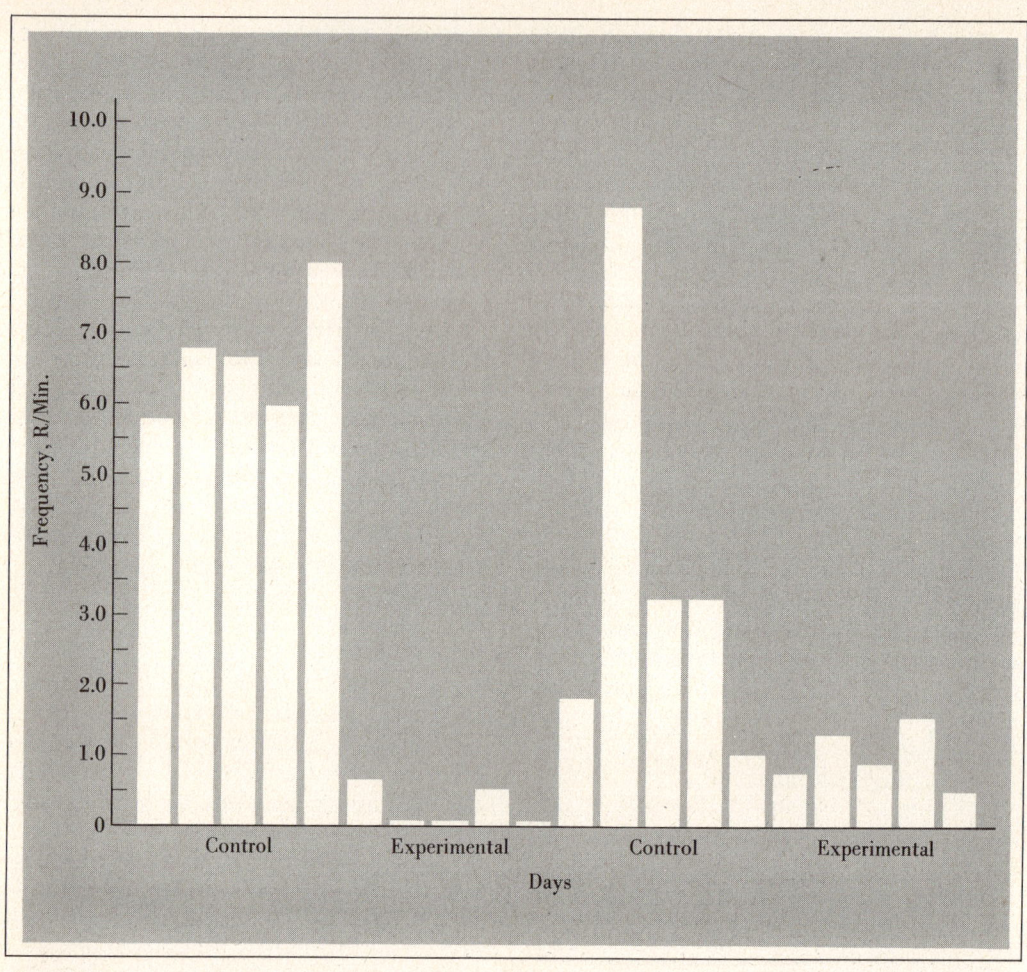

Figure 3
Effect of the punishment procedure of Study I on the daily average frequency of SIR's. On experimental days SIR's were followed by withdrawal of human physical contact after a minimum interval of 3 sec. On control days the SIR's were ignored. Redrawn from Tate and Baroff, 1966, p. 283.

tion of imitation, aims at a type of behavior that is more general and crucial in the treatment of autistic children. The subjects of the study were two five-year-old identical twins who were diagnosed schizophrenic, evidenced no social responsiveness, did not speak or recognize each other or adults, were not toilet trained, and handled objects in a stereotyped manner. These children spent up to three-fourths of their time in rocking and other self-stimulatory behavior. They also engaged in temper tantrums and hit themselves. They had been previously treated with intensive traditional psychotherapy in a residential treatment setting.

children's behavior

The children were seen individually in a room whose floors had been wired so that a shock could be delivered to their feet. During two pre-shock 20-minute sessions, the experimenters said to the children "Come here" about 200 times and recorded the effect of this social stimulus. There were two phases to the first set of three shock sessions. At first, a shock went on, and ended when the child approached an experimenter to the request "Come here." If the child did not move in the experimenter's direction in three seconds, he was prompted (moved) to do so. In this instance, the children could *escape* shock by making the social response. In the remaining sessions, the children could *avoid* the shock by making the social response: if after five seconds the child had not moved toward the experimenter, the shock was turned on. Over time, the distance between the child and experimenter was increased and the prompts were faded. Shock was also turned on if the child at any time engaged in self-stimulatory or tantrum behavior. Simultaneous with the onset of shock, the experimenter would say "No" and thereby pair the word "No" with shock. The three shock sessions were followed by eleven "extinction" (no shock) sessions over a ten-month

Figure 4
Proportion of self-stimulation and tantrums (pathological behaviors) and physical contact (social behavior).
Redrawn from Lovaas, Schaeffer, and Simmons, 1965, p. 103.

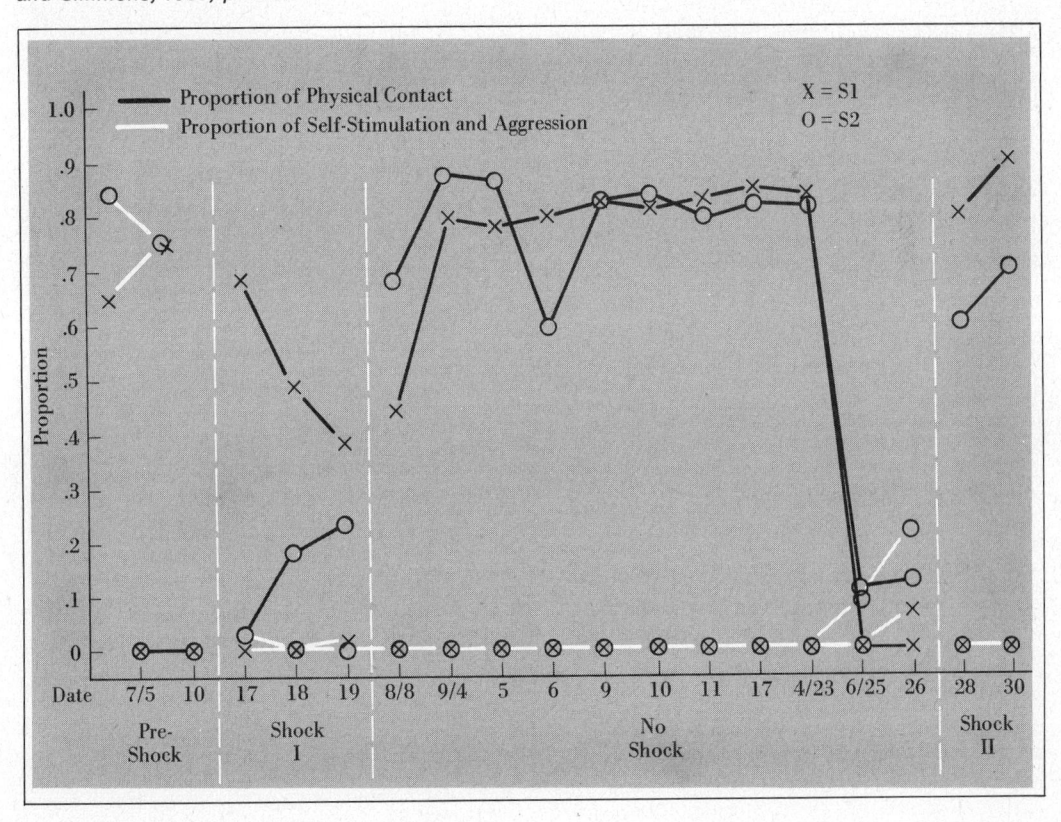

period: in the latter the situations and procedures were the same as described above save that neither shock nor the command "No" was used by the experimenter. In a second shock phase there were three additional sessions. In the first of these the child was brought into the experimental room and given a two-second shock not contingent upon any behavior by either the child or the experimenter. *This was the only shock given.* In all other aspects, these sessions were similar to the preceding extinction sessions.

Figure 4 shows the results for the four stages. Different points, "X" and "O," are used for each twin (an X in an O indicates that both were at the same level); the broken line indicates that the emission of self-stimulatory and aggressive behavior was very high during the pre-shock sessions and dropped out almost completely and permanently after instigation of response-contingent shock. The rate of physical contact increased markedly and remained high for nine months. The single noncontingent shock in the training situation seems to have reinstated the prior training. Lovaas et al. (1965) also noted that "social behaviors replaced the pathological behaviors."

The results of the acquisition of "No" as an effective reinforcer are presented in Figure 5. The task was to press a lever for a candy reinforcer. After 12 preshock trials on this apparatus, a stable rate of response was observed, and, as may be noted from the figure, the word "No" had no effect on lever-pressing. After the shock sessions, the word "No" had a very noticeable effect on lever-pressing. Similar generalization, observed in ward settings, was the subject of additional studies. Again, as with the observations of Tate and Baroff with Sam, it was noted (Lovaas et al., 1965, p. 103): "In particular, they seemed more alert, affectionate, and seeking of E's [the experimenter's] company. And surprisingly, during successful shock avoidance they appeared happy."

Few studies, such as Ney (1967), compare

Figure 5
Lever-pressing for candy as cumulative response curves: effect of "no" on lever-pressings by S1 before and after "no" was paired with shock.
Redrawn from Lovaas, Schaeffer, and Simmons, 1965, p. 103.

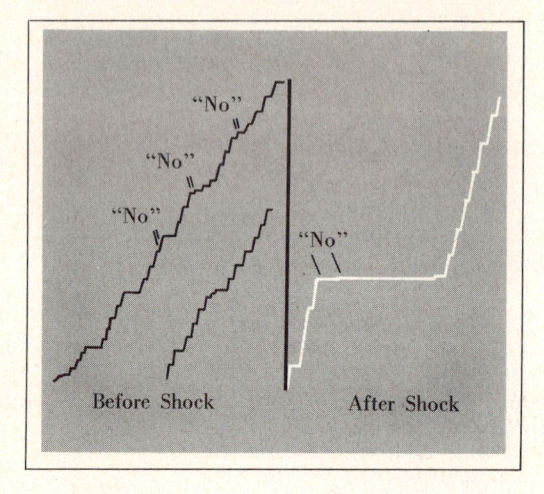

two different methods of treatment; Ney, Palvesky, and Markely (1971) report the results of a study designed to examine the relative effectiveness of operant conditioning and play therapy in improving the communication and social functioning of psychotic children. They used a group of ten "schizophrenic" boys, 3 to 15 years of age, who received 50 sessions of operant conditioning followed by 50 sessions of play therapy over a period of three months. A matched group of ten boys had the same treatments but in reverse order. Both groups showed gains in mental age, as measured by intelligence tests, and in amount of speech. However, the improvement was greater after operant conditioning than after play therapy. The authors conclude that

Our study indicates that operant conditioning is more effective than play therapy in the treatment of schizophrenic children. It is suggested that operant conditioning may reverse the child's early learning in which social reinforcers by parents were perceived negatively rather than positively, or were not perceived at all. Since schizophrenic or autistic children appear to possess the basic elements of speech, they may give up their determination to be anticommunicative and start talking (even before speech is reinforced) after their motivational difficulties are resolved. [p. 347.]

Summary

This section has presented work with autistic or schizophrenic children. The typical view has been that these children have a very poor prognosis. The behavioral approach is to analyze the current performances and to supply response-contingent reinforcement in an effort to develop skills that had been either extinguished or never learned. The results, as noted above, have been encouraging. "Symptoms" such as self-injurious and self-stimulatory behavior may be decreased (Foxx and Azrin, 1973), and socially useful general responses such as imitation and compliance to adults may be increased. While some physical defect cannot be ruled out, the concepts of autism or schizophrenia, which are poorly defined at best, seem to be of little relevance for treatment. As with the difficulties discussed previously in this chapter, a behavioral analysis focusing on responses to situations rather than diagnoses leads to similar general principles of treatment and more encouraging results.

SUMMARY

This chapter discussed children's behavioral problems. The application of behavior therapy procedures with children is relatively recent. The problems of diagnosis and treatment, however, are similar to those found with adults. A behavioral approach to children's disorders leads to the same principles of evaluation and treatment found with adults. In terms of the evaluative principles, little seems to be gained by formal diagnostic categorization. In terms of treatment, the major difference between work with children and adults is that through use of parents and teachers the environment of a child may be more easily controlled than that of an adult outpatient. Examples of a variety of treatment techniques were presented, and while it was frequently made explicit that behavioral treatment involves a technology not possible to describe completely in the limits of this volume, it was stated that a key concept was counting actual events and applying response-contingent reinforcement. This was of particular importance in dealing with punishment and with the place of parental attitudes. In terms of the latter, it was noted that what the parent did and when he did it were probably far more useful foci of study than how he felt about such acts in the abstract.

retardation
24

"Mental retardation may be viewed as a medical, psychological, or educational problem, but in the final analysis, it is primarily a social problem. Throughout history, the attitude toward the mentally retarded reflected the general social attitudes of a given people or a given culture." (Freedman, Kaplan, and Sadock, 1972.) While this observation could be made about all the categories we have discussed, it is especially poignant in the instance of mental retardation.

The behaviors included in this chapter are labeled "mental retardation" in DSM-II (pp. 14–22). (DSM-I used the words "mental deficiency") and refers to "subnormal general intellectual functioning which originates during the developmental period and is associated with impairment of either learning and social adjustment or maturation or both."

The definition of retardation is also linked with the concept of intelligence and its measurement. This diagnostic classification defines categories of retardation for those with an IQ of 85 or below. The categories of mental retardation are: borderline —IQ of 68 to 85; mild—IQ 52 to 67; moderate—IQ 36 to 51; severe—IQ 20 to 35; profound—IQ under 20.

These classifications are based on the statistical distribution of levels of intellectual functioning for the general population based on tests of intelligence. Based on the assumption that intelligence is normally distributed, the range of intelligence given for each of the above classifications corresponds to one standard deviation.

To avoid the simplistic view that retardation is measured solely by performance on intelligence tests, DSM-II notes, "It is recognized that the intelligence quotient should not be the only criterion used in making a diagnosis of mental retardation or in evaluating its severity. It should serve only to help in making a clinical judgment of the patient's adaptive behavioral capacity. This judgment should also be based on an evaluation of the patient's developmental history and present functioning, including academic and vocational achievement, motor skills, and social and emotional maturity." (p. 14.)

This chapter focuses on the factors that influence this judgment, the process of making this judgment, and the consequences of this judgment as well as on treatment.

CLINICAL SUBCATEGORIES

DSM-II recognizes nine subcategories of mental retardation. One subcategory is the result of cerebral damage "from intracranial infections, serums, drugs, or toxic agents." (p. 15.) Examples include cogenital rubella, congenital syphilis, and encephalopathy. There are many ways in which the fetus may be damaged, including a variety of diseases that the mother can contract such as meningitis or influenza.

A second subcategory of retardation includes the effects of a trauma or of a physical agent. This may involve injury at birth due to difficulties of labor or injury after birth including a fractured skull or prolonged unconsciousness.

3. A third subcategory involves retardation directly due to metabolic, nutritional, or growth dysfunction—"Including disorders of lipid, carbohydrate and protein metabolism, and deficiencies of nutrition." (p. 17.) A number of diseases are involved: *Tay-Sach's* disease, for example, is caused by a single recessive gene which may result in gradual deterioration, blindness, and death before age three. *Niemann-Pick's* disease involves enlargement of the liver and spleen, with results similar to those of Tay-Sach's disease. *Phenylketonuria* is a metabolic disorder genetically transmitted as a simple recessive gene.

4. A fourth subcategory involves all conditions associated with neoplasms or growths except those that are secondary to trauma or infection.

5. A fifth subcategory includes retardation associated with chromosomal abnormalities. The most common of these is *Langdon-Down* disease or *Mongolism*. The degree of retardation ranges from moderate to severe. "Other congenital defects are frequently present and the intellectual development decelerates with time." (DSM-II, p. 20.)

6. A sixth subcategory is of most significance to us because of its linkage with social and environmental factors. Included within this category are the "many cases of mental retardation with no clinical or historical evidence of organic disease or pathology but for which there is some history of psycho-social deprivation." (DSM-II, p. 21.) There are two further subcategories within this group, that of "cultural-familial" retardation and that "associated with environmental deprivation." The former requires that there be evidence of retardation in at least one of the parents and in one or more siblings. Related retardation is usually mild. The category of environmental deprivation is based on the assumption that an individual who is deprived of normal environmental stimulation in infancy may be unable to acquire the knowledge and skills necessary for normal functioning. "This type of deprivation may result from severe sensory impairment, even in an environment otherwise rich in stimulation. More rarely it may result from severe environmental limitations or atypical cultural milieus. The degree of retardation is always marginal or mild." (DSM-II, pp. 21–22.)

The final three subcategories are of retardation "associated with prematurity," "following major psychiatric disorder," and "associated with diseases and conditions due to unknown prenatal influence."

The Diagnosis of Retardation

Three concepts are involved in the diagnosis of retardation. The first is that the difficulty has existed either from birth or shortly thereafter. Difficulties that arise later in life and lead to a decrease in tested and functioning intelligence are categorized primarily as brain syndromes.

The second general concept is that the intelligence quotient plays a role in the diagnosis. The upper boundary of IQ 85 in the definition "borderline retardation" is important. This means that in terms of the test score in the definition, roughly one-sixth of the population can be called borderline and two and a half percent of the population, mild mental retardation.

The third concept is that how the person manages to function in society is crucial. A person who is managing to adjust in society, who supports himself, stays out of trouble with the law, does not squander his money, and is not overly dependent on direction from others, demonstrates capacity that should take precedence over any measurement on a psychological test. In summary, there are three factors in the definition of retardation: the duration of the defect, the intelligence quotient, and the social adjustment.

Throne's (1970) view of the relationship between intelligence test scores and performance is related to a view of the potentialities of people called retarded.

"Standardized intelligence test scores are transmuted frequential expectancies or estimates of intelligent or related performance under average circumstances. They are prognostications of a subject's ability to learn under the average circumstances which presumably prevail in typical home and academic settings. Such scores constitute extrapolations twice removed from *in situ* behavioral events. They are second-order theoretical values derived from first-order theoretical values (raw performance scores *on tests*); they do not reflect *in situ* performance even under average circumstances.

... But another index of intelligence may be obtained without the restrictions imposed by standardized tests. Alteration of the environmental circumstances under which a subject functions intelligently (however functioning intelligence is defined) can yield improved intelligent functioning in those circumstances. To be sure, predictions to other behavioral classes (intelligent or otherwise) may be made on the basis of these findings.

... He [the behavior modifier] exchanges an assessment strategy debarring intervention for one requiring that intervention be employed. *He assesses intelligent behavior through its improvement.* Insofar as he determines the consequential variables functionally responsible for behavior, he provides a sufficient basis for interpreting the results produced. [p. 1–2, 8.]

Under this view, the concept of retardation as a comparison point, being on the lower end of a continuum of performance, loses its traditional meaning. The behavior modifiers stress individual performance, and the concept of baseline utilizes one's own performance as the yardstick of comparison.

Put differently, operationally, intelligence is whatever a test measures when it is used as the definition of intelligence. It is, therefore, necessary to know the method used to define intelligence when the test was developed and validated. In general terms, current intelligence tests measure, to a great extent, the ability to reason abstractly: the ability to manipulate symbols and to benefit from training in symbol manipulation. This sample of behavior is then used to predict a different one.

The intelligence test measures intelligent behavior, and this, in turn, involves (1) a definition of what intelligent behavior is, and (2) a performance by the person taking the test. To the extent that the standard test assumes a white, middle-class background, it is biased against blacks and Chicanos, particularly those of school age; and this is the kind of test administered by schools. Many minority members pass social behavioral tests while doing poorly on intelligence tests (Mercer, 1972). Further, "After a person is graduated from high school, the *retarded* label does not stick, unless he is among the more intellectually and physically sub-normal adults; only one-fifth of our cases were over 20." (Mercer, 1972, p. 44.)

Perhaps the best way to grasp the impact of our society's emphasis on the ability to reason abstractly is to review some of the points raised by Dexter (1964). Dexter starts by asking the reader to consider gawkiness as a cardinal social defect and imagine a society which stresses grace and style in movement in the same way our society stresses intellectual skill. In order to read, write, and run complicated machines, physical grace would be required because engineers and businessmen would assume that normal people are graceful. The schools would stress movement, dancing, and rhythmics, and there would be tests of manifest grace, grace aptitude, chronological grace, and the like. The children who were below average in grace would be the butt of jokes, social rejects, and isolates. To enter college, a person would have to have a high grace quotient, G.Q.

In our society the laws for making contracts, instructions for putting things together, and rational purchases all presume verbal skill and an ability at abstract thinking. Persons with low ability in this regard are placed in special classes or made to feel inferior and a drag in normal classrooms. They are sometimes politely called exceptional children. The retarded are denied employment and have their legal rights infringed upon on a number of issues on which intellectual ability may be irrelevant, just as a "gawky" person might be kept from being a professor or something else for which grace is unimportant. For example, intelligence tests may be used as general screening devices in government and industry, where they often have no validity for the specific job being considered. In this regard, intelligence test scores may be as irrelevant to a position as sex and race of the applicant.

Studies of children who had been diagnosed as mentally retarded during school years have found many of them at work and leading independent lives (Kennedy, 1948; Collmann and Newlyn, 1957; Ferguson and Kerr, 1958; Muench, 1944; Porter and Milazzo, 1958; Saenger, 1957; Baller, Charles, and Miller, 1967; Kokaska, 1968). Charles (1957), for example, studied 127 persons who had been members of the special class for the mentally retarded in Lincoln, Nebraska, in 1936. He found 80 percent of them employable and usually employed and 80 percent married. About half of the males, however, had been prosecuted for some violation of law, although violence was seldom involved. Few of the females had court records. Charles thought that the violations, most of which were for drunkenness, were as characteristic of the low socioeconomic class of these persons as of their low IQs. Strickland and Arrell (1967) also report that 80 percent of retarded youths found jobs for which they had been trained, while Jackson (1968) puts the percentage of vocationally "unadjusted" at 32 percent. Cameron and Titus (1973) report that life satisfaction of retardates (average IQ, 71; age, 13) is comparable to that of normals (average IQ, 98; age 14), as based on class observations and teacher and parent ratings.

Bijou, Ainsworth, and Stockey (1943) traced 101 retarded women who had been released from a training school. After eight years, 70 of the women were rated as average or better in adjustment; 73 were married, and the women were, in general, self-supporting both socially and economically. Keane (1972) followed up 198 graduates of a residential school for the retarded and found 45 percent employed, 13 percent in sheltered workshops, 12 percent in day schools, 22 percent in institutions, 3 percent dead and 3 percent unemployed.

Dexter (1964) makes an interesting point. He asks what would happen if the majority of the population were retarded. Probably, there would be adjustments such as having large colonies where people would work in groups with one or two people of higher intelligence available for emergencies. The routines would be within the scope of high- and middle-grade retarded—that is, people who are stable and much better trained than seven-year-olds. Instructions would have to be given slowly, contracts simplified, and machines less demanding on the operators; but only the unusual or emergent situation would require the presence of the supervisor of superior intelligence or accomplishment.

Finally, Braginsky and Braginsky (1972) randomly assigned 23 boys and 7 girls in a small private school for the mentally retarded to take an individual intelligence test under one of three conditions related to selection for an undesirable new program. In the first two conditions, the subjects were told either that "kids who do poorly on the test" or "kids who do well on the test" would be selected for the program. In the control condition the subjects took the test under conventional instructions. The test scores varied as a function of the two experimental conditions (a significant increase among those told that to do "poorly" would result in selection, a significant decrease among those told that doing "well" would be selected), thus supporting the argument that retardates are capable of using "impression management" to gain control over what happens to them. (See Chapters 17 and 18 for similar work with schizophrenics.)

Physiological Defects

The normal distribution curve is bell-shaped, with the highest frequencies at average. There is a steady decrease in frequency as one moves toward either end, so that the most extreme cases, either high or low, are theoretically the least frequent. If intelligence were purely a matter of multiple genetic endowment, there would be little, if any, deviation from an ideal bell-shaped curve. However, at the extreme retarded end of the distribution one finds an excess of cases over what would be expected by chance. In the population of the United States one would expect 50 people with IQ's of 0 to 20, but the actual incidence is estimated as 92,750 or close to 200,000 percent of what would be expected by chance. The excess for the range IQ 20 to 50 is only 125 percent, and for IQ 50 to 70 only 1 percent (Robinson and Robinson, 1965, p. 42).

Making an enormous oversimplification, one may account for the disproportionate number of profoundly retarded (IQ 20 and under) on the basis of physiological anomalies. In similar fashion, one may account for the normal distribution (expected statistical estimate matching obtained prevalence) from IQ 50 up along lines of genetic endowment and cultural deprivation of stimulation. One may therefore posit two general etiologies of mental retardation. Following this distinction for didactic purposes, the first cluster to be described deals with explicit physiological anomalies. These cases are genuinely within the province of the medical model in terms of etiology. The psychologist plays a role in diagnosis and, when the physiological anomaly has been treated, in rehabilitation.

It should also be noted that in the physiological difficulties which will be briefly outlined below there recently have been great strides made in diagnosis, remediation, and eventual prevention.

An example of a syndrome caused by a chromosomal aberration is *Mongolism* or *Down's Syndrome* or *trisomy-21 anomaly*. From 10 to 20 percent of moderately and severely retarded children are Mongoloid, and their birth rate is approximately one in six to nine hundred live births. The syndrome of Mongolism is of historical interest since it was one of the first to be isolated from the general rubric of all retardation being called cretinism. This was accomplished by Down in 1866. Aside from intellectual impairment, the symptoms are a small skull; underdeveloped nasal bones resulting in a flat bridge; shallow, egg-shaped eye sockets with eyes often slanting in appearance; small chin and ears; a large fissured tongue protruding from a small mouth; short, broad neck with loose skin at sides; short, broad, flat, square hands and feet; disproportionate shortness of the fifth finger; and sparse, fine, straight hair.

Mongolism is of great interest because for many years it was noted to occur in certain families more frequently than would have been expected by chance, and, very importantly, it was found that the likelihood of a child's being Mongoloid increased with the age of the mother and the number of children to which she had given birth. Therefore, some glandular imbalance was frequently hypothesized. However, in 1959, Lejeune, Gauthier, and Turpin found 47 chromosomes in several Mongoloid cases, and subsequent studies have shown that approximately 95 percent of Mongoloids have 47 chromosomes instead of the normal complement of 46. Typically, Mongoloids are trisomic for chromosome 21, although this trisomy may possibly occur with chromosome 22. Syndromes associated with specific defective genes are rare, but examples are found such as tuberous sclerosis (Bourneville's disease), neurofibromatosis (von Recklinghausen's disease), and cerebral angiomatosis (Sturge–Weber–Dimitri's disease).

Difficulties may occur because of metabolic and storage disorders. One example is galactosemia, a congenital disorder in which there is an absence of the enzyme required to metabolize galactose, a carbohydrate constituent of milk. The transmission of the clinical syndrome is a recessive gene and low tolerance for galactose. Early removal of milk from the diet results in disappearance of the symptom.

A similar disorder is phenylketonuria (PKU), which accounts for perhaps 1 percent of older retardates in institutions and for about one case per ten thousand live births. In PKU there is a block in the metabolic transformation into tyrosine of the protein substance phenylalanine which is present in most foods. The incomplete metabolites are released into the body. These are injurious to the brain and result in retardation. The disorder may be diagnosed from the age of a few weeks onward by very simple tests for the presence of phenylpyruvic acid in the urine. Therefore, a number of states now provide support for massive screening programs which are simple and inexpensive enough that the discovery of even a few cases in early infancy repays the effort involved. Treatment consists of feeding the child a diet consisting primarily of a mixture of nutritive substances in which there is no more than the essential amount of phenylalanine.

The physical environment starts at the moment of fertilization. Defects may develop during the prenatal period and, owing to diet, after birth. Of great social import is that proper maternal diet is a factor in carrying the child for a full nine months' pregnancy. Premature babies have not only a greater likelihood of dying but, if surviving, have a lower chance of attaining their complete potential intellectual endowment. Appropriate medical care both before and after birth may therefore help reduce the frequency of retardation.

Acute maternal infections may affect later intellectual attainment. Most common is *rubella* or *German measles*. If the mother contracts German measles during the first three months of pregnancy, there is a significant chance that the child will be retarded. Current research indicates that 47 percent of infants born to mothers infected in the first month of pregnancy are abnormal, 22 percent of mothers infected in the second month, and 7 percent in the third month. A rubella vaccine was licensed in 1969 and, it is hoped, will decrease this source of retardation.

A second illustration involves syphilis. In the past this was a major cause of congenital mental deficiency, but its incidence today is fortunately reduced through compulsory blood tests and effective antibiotic therapy.

The use of drugs either prenatally or during birth may have unfortunate effects on the child. A major example was thalidomide.

During the process of birth itself the child may be injured. This may be due to lack of oxygen or to unfortunate techniques on the part of the physician. Infections, tumors, and all the other ills which may injure the brain may affect the child. Young children bite and taste indiscriminately. Most states have laws prohibiting the use of lead paint on cribs. The poisons found in family medicine cabinets should be carefully stored and locked.

Cretinism is particularly important historically. As the reader will remember from the survey in Chapter 7, up to one hundred years ago all retardates were called cretins. In 1891, Dr. George Murray published his discovery that the injection of thyroid gland extract was beneficial in cases resulting from a thyroid deficiency in later life and characterized by mental dullness. This discovery led in turn to a treatment with thyroid extract for children and eventually to public health measures which insured adequate iodine in the ordinary diet. Today, cretinism probably accounts for less than 5 percent of the institutionalized mentally retarded population. In cretinism, the thyroid gland, which plays an important role in regulating the speed of virtually all cellular processes in the body, is probably defective at birth. A high incidence of endemic cretinism is common in mountainous regions because of an unusually low concentration of iodine in the soil, water, and air.

Other physical difficulties which may be associated with mental deficiency are congenital abnormality of the skull and brain: microcephaly is characterized by an abnormally small skull; in hydrocephaly there is a skull malformation which makes the individual appear to have too large a head (usually because of prenatal factors, birth trauma, or postnatal injury which affects the amount of fluid within the skull). There are other neurological disorders, notable among which are cerebral palsy and infections of the brain such as those that occur after meningitis and encephalitis.

This section has dealt with genetic factors, metabolic disorders, infections, toxic agents, traumas, and the like; in short, difficulties with distinct physiological etiologies and true medical, chemical-physical disorders. This group represents probably the most severe 25 percent of cases in the category of retardation (Zigler, 1967).

CULTURAL-FAMILIAL RETARDATION

The majority of retardates, approximately 75 percent, do *not* reveal any known physiological syndrome. It may be hypothesized that the familial or unknown etiology group differs in some manner from the group with physiological defect. "The retardate having an extremely low IQ (below 40) is almost invariably of the physiologically defective type. Familial retardates, on the other hand, are almost invariably mildly retarded, usually with IQs above 50." (Zigler, 1967, p. 292.)

It is reasonable to assume that neurological capabilities, and hence the *limits* of intelligence, are determined in large measure by many genes. It should not be forgotten, however, that the person with an IQ that places him in the lowest 2 or 3 percent of the normal distribution is as much a part of that distribution as the person who is in the top 2 or 3 percent of the population. There are theories, reviewed by Zigler (1967), of an underlying defect, without as yet physiological specification, to account for membership in the lower 2 to 3 percent of the population. The weight of empirical data, however, supports a view that this group is within, and an integral part of, the normal distribution of genetic endowment, and this chapter will proceed on such an assumption.

The life-experiences of the child who is intellectually slow may be such that he is less reinforced (one might say extinguished) for "experience-producing drives" (Hayes, 1962; Hunt, 1961). That is, intellectual stimulation is a reinforcing circumstance for the majority of people, especially the college-trained people who are the model of the core culture. In culturally deprived segments of the population (i.e., in families which for genetic or economic reasons do not share to as great an extent the core culture), there may be failure to provide or to be responsive to such stimulation. Further, intellectual stimulation and novel sensorimotor experiences may themselves be the setting for aversive environmental occurrences. In a manner analogous to that with the antisocial personality, there may be for the retarded an attenuation of the range of reinforcing stimuli typically acquired in the society.

The presumption implicit in the use of terms such as "core culture" and "society" is that there is a pattern of life which represents the model of appropriate behavior. Mercer (1965) provides empirical evidence on this particular point and the sociopsychological model in general. Mercer reasoned that educational and intellectual achievement are more valued by the core, middle-class culture than by the lower socioeconomic classes which are more distant from and share less in the attainments of the core culture. If this is so, people with lesser educational attainment and capability (i.e., retardates) would be more likely to be considered "deviant" in middle-class families than in lower-class families. With this background, all the patients released from a hospital for the mentally retarded over a three-year period who had not been readmitted were matched by age, sex, IQ, ethnic background, and year of admission with patients remaining in the hospital. Of the released patients, 36.5 percent of the heads of household had socioeconomic indices above the median; for the patients remaining in the hospital the percentage was 61.4 percent.

The lower-class families were far more optimistic about the chances of their children's making adult social adjustments than were the upper classes. It is interesting that for high-status persons, medical people were the single most important group in placing the child in the hospital, while for the lower-status people it was police and welfare agencies. That is, physicians are sought out by families in the high-status group to initiate the placement process more frequently than by the low-status group, for whom the process was initiated by others such as police and welfare workers.

Crucial to an understanding of retardation as a social event is an awareness of the attitudes held by various segments of society toward the "retarded." Retardation is not an entity unto itself but rather occurs in a social context which includes the reactions of others both to the label and to the behaviors associated with the label.

The pediatricians most frequently are considered to be the first group of professionals to become aware of and to label retardation (Harth, 1973). They are particularly involved in helping parents make decisions about institutionalization or home care. The studies of the attitudes and beliefs of pediatricians indicate that they "had limited knowledge, training and interest in the area of mental retardation . . . medical education programs are generally deficient with regards to mental retardation." (Harth, 1973, p. 151.) This observation helps explain the "shopping" behavior noted by Anderson (1971) of the parents of retarded children. The evidence seems to indicate that special-class teachers of retardates may be underestimating the ability of their students. Dunn (1968) reported that the academic achievement of retarded students was lower in special classes than in regular classes.

There have been findings that the severely retarded child appears to be the least preferred type of "exceptional child" to be worked with by professionals (Warren and Turner, 1966). Studies of the attitudes of the employees in institutions for retardates indicate a wide and conflicting behavior, ranging from warmth and kindness to utter brutality. Bozarth and Daly (1969) found that work supervisors had more favorable perceptions than child-case aides whose perceptions, in turn, were more favorable than those of education and activity employees.

The educational attainments of the retarded in the Mercer (1965) low-status group were less different from those of their parents and siblings than were those of the high-status group. Lessened general attainment and increased dependency on others, including welfare organizations, was more acceptable in the low-status than in the high-status groups. In short, the retarded person was less likely to be considered deviant in the low-status group than in the high-status group because he was less different. To cite one mother: "'There is nothing wrong with Benny. He just can't read or write.' Since the mother spoke only broken English, had no formal schooling, and could not read or write, Benny did not appear deviant to her." (Mercer, 1965, p. 33.) Consistent with this is the work of Appell and Tisdall (1968) [cited in Chapter 10], showing that living conditions and community problems rather than IQ distinguished retardates who were institutionalized from those who were not.

A Social View of Retardation

A major approach to conceptualization of retardation is by Braginsky and Braginsky (1971), who argue that so-called retardates are in fact undifferentiated from their unlabeled peers and do well on psychological dimensions relevant for adaptation. In short, retardates are differentiated on sociopolitical dimensions as the result of identifiable familial, educational, legal, and bureaucratic occurrences.

We found that mental institutions function primarily as catchment areas which facilitate the "social sanitation" process of society. The concept of mental illness, when applied to the inmates of these institutions, was devoid of meaning, obfuscating and distorting completely the behavior of the patients. The reason for their incarceration was that they either could not or did not want to function in the mainstream of society. They were marginal members of the community—surplus people. Thus, mental hospitals as well as the mental health professionals help to keep society's "house in order" by removing from the mainstream its human debris. [p. vi.]

Within that context, the Braginskys express their view of retardation as follows: "In short, we suspected that the diagnosis of cultural-familial (or educable, origin unknown, and so on) *mental retardation* was to the child what the diagnosis of *mental illness* (functional psychosis) was to the adult: a myth which conveniently and effectively serves society, enabling it to misconstrue completely the nature of its needed reforms." (p. vi.)

The Braginskys focus on the multitude of children labeled as mildly retarded or cultural-familial or retardation of unknown origin. These are contrasted with the more severely impaired, whose retardation is due to brain damage or genetic defects.

The Braginskys argue that despite the multitude of observations and definitions tracing back to the ancient Greeks, there still is no generally accepted definition of retardation. This lack of clarity as to what "it" is has not prevented the categorization of millions of persons. For example, the President's Panel on Mental Retardation (1962) ranked retardation fourth in prevalence as a "disease" entity. The panel then makes clear that they are using the term "mental retardation" as a hypothetical construct that links many antecedent conditions with behavioral outcomes such as low intelligence. The Braginskys point out that the key to understanding the traditional approach to mental retardation lies in the panel's conclusion that the one "key common characteristic found in all cases is *inadequately developed intelligence*." However, there are other experts who argue that even with an adequate intelligence-test score they may still be mentally retarded by the criterion of being socially inadequate.

The Braginskys view retardation as a *metaphor* in a manner similar to Sarbin's work on psychosis (see Chapter 17).

The term mental retardation is simply a metaphor chosen to connote certain assumed qualities of putative, invisible mental processes. More specifically, it is inferred that it appears *as if* retarded mental processes underlie particular behaviors. Or, we infer that behavior appears *as if* it were retarded. Too often, the *as if* conditions are forgotten and we are left with "mentally retarded behavior." As a consequence, retardation becomes accepted as a concrete disease state instead of the metaphor that it is. [p. 15–16.]

Retardation—The Braginskys' Alternative Paradigm

The Braginskys present their case for an alternative paradigm. Their approach is to view retardation as a "Hansel and Gretel" metaphor.

While the metaphor of mental retardation focuses upon assumed inner defects, the Hansel and Gretel metaphor makes no assumptions concerning the inner nature of man, but focuses instead upon observable social events. According to this metaphor, given certain social conditions, anyone could become a Hansel or Gretel—anyone could become an institutionalized mental retardate.... The most obvious and most potent condition is that the child is unloved and unwanted by the family or its surrogates (foster or stepparents)....

The fragmentation of family life often echoes the relationship between the family and society in general. That is, these families tend to be marginal, living on the outskirts of the mainstream. Society's response to these families constitutes the final step in the transformation process. Welfare agencies, social workers, institutions for the retarded, and the supporting cast of social servants finally label and incarcerate the unwanted child. Surely, rejection alone is not sufficient to warrant the title of retardation. Society's contribution is to finalize the transformation by turning the unwanted child into the mentally defective child.... The most consistent and unambiguous finding after a century of research concerning the institutionalized members of our society (such as mental patients, retardates, and prisoners) is that almost all come from the lower class. This does not mean that poverty alone can account for the putative personal defects or the incarceration of individuals, but it appears to be a necessary condition.... By "negative visibility" we mean that certain people behave in such a way as to violate, threaten, or disrupt the values and propriety norms of the mainstream of society. For instance, a person who breaks laws or acts in a bizarre and frightening fashion becomes visible in a highly negative way. [pp. 160–61.]

The Braginskys stress the parents' role in the transformation of the child to a retardate. They hypothesize that families beset by economic problems and not adhering to the cultural values such as "Love thy children" are apt to see their child as an additional burden. They argue that most of the parents from whom retardates emerge come from "surplus populations" (Farber, 1968). As they use the term, it refers to people who are of "no use to the productive capacity of a society." Farber estimates as much as 25 percent of the American population may belong in the category of surplus population, which includes the technologically unemployed, the rural poor, migratory workers, the unskilled workers, the aged, and the physically disabled.

The conclusions and suggestions of the Braginskys as to the direction of treatment of retardates is the development of "cooperative retreats," not only for the retarded but as a replacement for the mental hospital, the training school, and the home for the aged. These retreats would provide a permanent refuge for those who cannot or do not want to "make it" in our complex society.

A BEHAVIORAL VIEW OF RETARDATION

Retarded behavior may be formulated in still another manner, one which lends itself readily to fruitful research and treatment. For its development and implementation with retarded children and with behavioral problems of childhood, this approach owes its greatest debt to Sidney W. Bijou. The following illustrates how a behavioral psychologist approaches retardation:

Retardation, from a behavior analysis view, is conceived to be a description of a person's behavior which, like all other behavior, is a function of his genetic and personal history. The specific behaviors said to define retardation, or "inadequate adaptive" behavior, are of major concern not as indicators of pathology, but as the basis for planning a teaching program, remedial or compensatory.

It is undeniable that the biological factors listed in the AMA formulation, insofar as they are observable, are among the conditions that may produce retarded behavior. However, they must be viewed functionally, that is, as (a) *limiting the person's response equipment* (sensory, motor, and the neurological connecting system) so that he cannot respond normally, and (b) *providing an abnormal internal environment* (some of the usual stimuli are absent or they occur with unusual intensities and durations), thereby generating abnormal reactions. Hence, the important thing about biological factors for a functional analysis is that they may reduce the response potential of the person and may distort his internal environment.

Sociocultural factors also contribute to retardation. In more general terms than those in the AMA formulation, sociocultural factors are considered as the institutional practices of the culture, together with the unique behaviors of parents, peers, teachers, and others in direct interaction with the child in the form of child-rearing practices, teacher-pupil-school relationships, and so forth. Sociocultural factors must also be viewed functionally. For example, child-rearing practices which produce strong anxiety and aversive reactions may hinder the normal development of the child. Furthermore, the physical environment, consisting of the natural and man-made objects of the culture, is included in the sociocultural category. Hence prolonged absences of the usual objects in the cultures constitute restrictions in opportunities for the child to develop normal behavioral repertoires. [Bijou, 1973, pp. 262–63.]

It is right and proper to ask if there are patterns of learning that have led to a limited behavioral repertoire. On the basis of such an analysis, testable programs may be developed to determine whether new experiences may lead to the generation of useful behavior not previously learned. *The focus of interest is shifted from a search for "intelligence" to a search for the conditions of "intelligent behavior."* This may be put differently: "Adaptive behavior refers to a matching between the resources of an individual and the demands of his environment. A person can be neither adaptive nor maladaptive in a vacuum. He is only adaptive or maladaptive in relation to the demands of the particular social system in which he is a member. Accurate descriptions of environmental demands made on the retardate is an essential prerequisite for the assessment of adaptive behavior and for the development of sound rehabilitation programs." (Nihira, 1973, p. 111.)

Such thinking brings the actions of the people involved with the "retarded" person into the definition; that is, are their demands made in such a way that *they* are acting intelligently? Further, it leads to broadening the base of rehabilitation to such matters as design of the social and physical environment (industrial psychologists' work on man-machine systems provides paradigms) and the use of nonprofessional people such as parents (Edlund, 1971) and other retardates (Criaghead and Mercatoris, 1973).

There are a number of avenues which can lead to atypical learning. The child may be relatively unresponsive ("not as fast" as the adult expects). If the adult pays little attention to the child, the intellectual situations required for developing the expected repertoire of responses will not be presented. In school, for example, the retarded child may be a "drag." The teacher may call on him out of "fairness," accept a poor answer without comment, and, having done her duty, move to her brighter students. There may literally be no training in discriminating adequate from poor responses and hence an indifference to material which is meaningful to brighter children (for some results and a way of obtaining data in this area, see Paris and Cairns, 1972).

The retarded child may, therefore, not possess many skills, not because he is intellectually incapable of them but because he has not had adequate experience with them. Work such as that by Dennis and Najarian (1957), Sayegh and Dennis (1965), Steinman (1968), Ross (1969), and Paloutzian et al. (1970) illustrates how supplementary experiences can result in rapid increases in behavioral development on the part of environmentally retarded infants. Other ways in which desirable behaviors fail to be developed or in which undesirable behaviors are increased in emission parallel the formulations given in Chapters 2, 10, and 23 of this volume: there may be extinction through lack of reinforcement, noncontingent reinforcement, reinforcement for inappropriate behaviors, or punishment so severe that there is generalization of response suppression to behaviors not intended by the punisher.

If such a formulation is correct, or even partially correct, great benefit to both the retardate and society may accrue from programs designed to provide improved learning experiences. The next section details such procedures.

BEHAVIORAL TREATMENT OF THE RETARDED

Whether his difficulty is physiological or environmental or both the retarded individual is responsive to the environment. This point is attested to by the establishment of conditioned responses in the most severely retarded of all subjects, the vegetative idiot who emits almost no responses. Fuller (1949), Rice and McDaniel (1966), Rice et al. (1967), Hopkins (1968), Piper and MacKinnon (1969); Lloyd, Russell, and Garmize (1970); Husted, Wallin, and Wooden (1971); and Brownfield and Keehan (1966) have reported success in the operant conditioning of very profoundly retarded subjects. The point to be made is that a defect, even the most severe, does not rule out response to the environment and the alteration of behavior through training.

Self-help Behavior

Both for the saving in staff time and energy and for the human dignity involved, basic self-help skills are of major importance. Examples of instruction in feeding and dressing have been provided by Bensberg, Colwell, and Cassel (1965) Whitney and Barnard (1966), Peterson (1967), Roos (1965), Karen and Maxwell (1967), Thompson, et al. (1970), Groves and Carroccio (1971), Martin et al. (1971), and Lemke and Mitchell (1972). An example of this type of work is provided by Minge and Ball (1967), who devised a detailed, step-by-step program for shaping up dressing behavior. The steps included behaviors such as attending, coming to the technicians, sitting down, remaining seated, and removing and putting on various articles of clothing. Six girls with an average IQ of 16, none of whom were toilet trained, used words to communicate, or made any effort at dressing themselves, were studied. Food was used as the reinforcing stimulus. Training occurred twice a day for 15 minutes. At the beginning, gestures, tugs, and other prompts were given in addition to a verbal request. Over time, to obtain the reinforcing stimulus, the subjects had to respond correctly to reduced prompts. The program was followed for two months, and significant progress was noted both in absolute terms and in terms of gains relative to a matched group of retardates who were not given such training.

Another example of a self-help procedure is the teaching of self-feeding skills (O'Brien, Bugle, and Azrin, 1972; O'Brien and Azrin, 1972). Berkowitz, Sherry, and Davis (1971) describe a program involving the training of profoundly retarded boys who had never spoon-fed themselves. The self-feeding task was divided into seven discrete steps, with each succeeding step requiring the individual to perform more of the self-feeding process. All of the boys learned to perform the self-feeding tasks within 2 to 60 days, and 10 of the 14 boys in the study were still feeding themselves 41 months later. Zeiler and Jervey (1968) also demonstrate how self-feeding can be taught to a profoundly retarded person; with self-feeding and the giving of food contingent upon appropriate behavior, other positive changes, especially in destructive and disruptive behavior, were manifested.

The use of training apparatuses for the severely retarded child is illustrated by the Azrin, Bugle, and O'Brien (1971) study. They describe a training procedure for eliminating daytime incontinence that provides an immediate signal when the child voids so that the trainer can react immediately.

The range of behavior taught is essentially a catalog of the acts a person needs to master to function socially. These may be an increase in instruction-following (Zimmerman, Zimmerman, and Russell, 1969; Whitman, Zakaras, and Chardos, 1971), reduction of stereotypes (Flavell, 1973; Guess and Rutherford, 1967; Mulhern and Baumeister, 1969), "rocking" (Baumeister and Forehand, 1971), screaming (Reiss and Redd, 1970; Hamilton and Standahl, 1969), crawling (O'Brien, Azrin, and Bugle, 1972), or bizarre gestures (Weisberg, Passman, and Russell, 1973), and increasing exercise (Sechrest, 1968). Stephan, Stephano, and Talkington (1973) used modeling to teach retarded women how to use the telephone. For major reviews of this area, see Watson (1967, 1973); Baker and Ward (1971); Bijou (1968); Gardner (1971, a and b); Weisberg (1971); and Drash (1972).

Speech

It was noted in the previous section that the behavioral difficulties of the retardate may well develop as a consequence of learning-histories similar to those of nonretarded children who manifest disturbing behavior. In studies by Cook and Adams (1966), Drash and Leibowitz (1973); Straughan, Potter, and Hamilton (1965); Hamilton and Stephens (1967), McClure (1968), Talkington and Hall (1968), MacCubrey (1971), Barton (1970), and Kerr, Meyerson, and Michael (1965) examples are provided of speech-deficient (mute, bizarre, or unintelligible) children who responded to direct retraining in which speech activity had meaningful consequences. Talkington, Hall, and Altman (1973) showed the benefit of peer modeling in training communication skills. Because the procedures overlap greatly those described in work with autistic children in Chapter 23, further detail will not be presented here.

Work

Less severely retarded than people who require training in speech and self-help are persons who benefit from vocational training. Kliebhan (1966), Evans and Spradlin (1966), Kraus (1971), Kazdin (1973), and Logan et al. (1971) are recent authors who point out that in a workshop situation, retardates are responsive to expectancies, modeling, monetary rewards, and interpersonal atmospheres.

Classroom Behavior

Our society's major focus on retardation occurs around the classroom situation and the acquisition of responses taught therein. This area may be approached from three directions, although all three are intertwined in actual training situations.

The first problem is that the student must emit certain prosocial behaviors as a necessary, albeit not sufficient, condition for education. These behaviors may be called attention, self-control, and/or cooperation. Their development with nonretarded children was noted in the previous chapter in reference to work by Patterson (1965b), Quay et al. (1967), Doubros and Daniels (1966), Becker et al. (1967), and O'Leary and Becker (1967). Disruptive behavior at mealtimes by profoundly retarded children (IQ less than 20) has been the subject of work by Edwards and Lilly (1966), and there have been reports of work with aggressive and destructive behaviors of retardates as well (Hamilton, Stephens, and Allen, 1967; Mazik and McNamara, 1967).

Birnbrauer (1967) describes the application of behavioral concepts to a classroom of 20 boys with IQ less than 44. The teacher used tangible reinforcers, then token reinforcers, and finally symbolic and social reinforcement. Time out from reinforcement such as removal from the chance to earn tokens in the classroom was also used. Doubros (1966) reports on individual therapy situations to ameliorate disruptive behavior in retarded children, while Santostefano and Stayton (1967) trained mothers, who in turn trained their children, to deploy attention selectively, actively, and appropriately.

If the child has been prepared for the classroom situation, the next matter is the operation of the classroom itself. Birnbrauer et al. (1965a, b) describe a classroom in which irrelevant or disruptive behavior is extinguished and appropriate behaviors or approximations thereto are reinforced. Content material consists of copying tracings, which are then faded. Perhaps the overriding factor of importance is that being right or wrong has immediate and meaningful consequences: on such responses depend tokens which can later be turned in for tangible reinforcement.

The final matter of import is the succession of intellectual tasks. If the key factor involved in differential intellectual endowment is ease or rapidity of response to instruction, a crucial beneficial operation would involve programming intellectual experience at a rate geared to the student. Such a rate must not be too slow for the superior student lest he become bored; for the retardate, it must not be so fast that he experiences failure. The problem may well be one of improper pacing by the teacher rather than a defect in the child. Indeed, the preparation of teaching materials in sequences that provide small enough steps, frequent enough repetitions, and immediate consequential feedback seems a crucial task. Bijou (1965) presents material on the development of a program for a crucial variable, conceptualizing behavior, with normal, and retarded children.

The techniques and theory of the behavioral approach overlap with and mutually reinforce findings with nonretarded groups, and the results themselves are encouraging. As pointed out in the previous section, the focus is on increasing intelligent behavior rather than on finding a defect. In this regard, also, the approach reflects the same general principles illustrated throughout this volume. (See also Bijou et al. 1969; Drash, 1972; Mackay and Sidman, 1968; and Sidman and Stoddard, 1966.)

TOKEN-ECONOMY WORK WITH RETARDATES

The principles and techniques of the application of operant conditioning procedures in a token economy were described in Chapter 18 in regard to adult hospitalized schizophrenic patients. The same principles and procedures apply to recent token-economy work with retardates. The emphasis in these programs is a part of the development of social, educational, and vocational skills with individuals who ordinarily might have been considered untreatable.

Girardeau and Spradlin (1964; see also Spradlin and Girardeau, 1966) report one of the first successful applications of a token-economy program with retardates. The following is a description of their program, which in principle and technique is prototypical of other similar programs:

A beginning effort has been made at Parsons State Hospital and Training Center in the development of a comprehensive program designed to train moderately retarded children to live adequately in their home community (Girardeau & Spradlin, 1964). A cottage of 28 adolescent girls (IQ range = 20-50) was selected and two 21-year-old girls were hired as additional personnel. After a gross evaluation period, bronze tokens approximately the size of a half-dollar were established as generalized conditioned reinforcers by allowing the girls to trade them for candy, fruit, cosmetics, soda pop, lace underwear and numerous other articles. In addition to purchasing items with the tokens, there were rental materials available, such as watches, record players and records, bicycles, and transistor radios.

After about 10 days a shaping procedure was introduced, i.e., the girls were required to make slight improvements in their behavior before tokens were given to them. One of the most immediate problems was that of devising constructive activities for these girls. Pets (goldfish, parakeet, turtles) were introduced on the cottage, and the girls were taught how to care for pets. The rewarding of self-care activities was a major part of the program for the first year but many other activities were included in the program. The activities listed in Table 1 are illustrative of the variety of skills which are being developed. The elimination of undesirable behavior is being accomplished primarily by using an extinction procedure (e.g., totally ignoring tantrum behavior) and by rewarding behavior which is incompatible with the undesirable or maladaptive behavior. When it has been necessary to reduce the frequency of behavior quickly, a combination of mild punishment (time out from earning tokens) of the undesirable behavior and reward for other desirable behavior has been used. Gross observations indicate that desirable behavior is increasing in frequency and that undesirable behavior is decreasing in frequency. [Spradlin and Girardeau, 1966, pp. 287–88.]

Baldwin (1967) reports the results of an investigation of the effects of various reinforcers on the development of social skills in a retarded population. He was also interested in whether IQ or chronological age were significant variables in responsiveness to these reinforcers. His population consisted of 72 boys and 24 girls from ages 6 to 12 and IQs 30 to 70. All were institutionalized as retardates. Children of comparable characteristics were utilized on each of the four wards. The four treatment conditions were: (1) a token economy (see Chapter 18); (2) a social reinforcement group (social reinforcers primarily comprised verbal and motoric indications of approval); (3) immediate food reinforcement; and (4) a con-

Table 1

A sample of the behaviors which are rewarded and approximate reward amounts

BEHAVIOR	APPROXIMATE REWARD AMOUNT
Making up bed	1 token
Dressing for meal	2 tokens
Brushing teeth	2 tokens
Taking shower properly	2 tokens
Helping clean cottage	Quite variable
Setting hair	4 tokens
Straightening bed drawer	2 tokens
Trimming and filing nails	2 tokens
Combing hair	1 token
Washing hair	2 tokens
Group play (30 min.)	5 tokens
Coloring	Quite variable
Work placement in institution	10 tokens/day
Cleaning goldfish bowl	5 tokens
Feeding goldfish	1 token
Cleaning bird cage	5 tokens
School readiness tasks	Quite variable
Being on time at work or speech therapy	4 tokens
Shining shoes	5 tokens
General proper use of leisure time (20-min. period)	4 tokens

Source: Spradlin and Girardeau, 1966.

trol ward receiving no special treatment. The behaviors measured were social skills. The results indicated that the token program was significantly more effective than the other programs for older children, whereas food reinforcement was significantly more effective with the youngest children. Baldwin's results are important because they demonstrate differential age responsivity to the concreteness of reinforcement. As might be expected, a younger child is more amenable to the effect of tangible reinforcers than is an older child. A certain amount of socialization is necessary for the individual to learn that he can delay gratification. In their general responsiveness to reinforcement, retardates are similar to normal children. It is of interest that in Baldwin's study differences in IQ were irrelevant in the children's responsiveness.

Roos and Oliver (1969) report a study of the effectiveness of operant conditioning procedures using two control groups. They worked with twenty "severely retarded" institutionalized young children. Their experimental group involved training procedures based on both primary and social reinforcers. One control group, labeled placebo, used techniques of special education classes but not systematic operant training. A third group of children received traditional hospital care. Results indicated that the experimental group using the operant training procedures showed significantly greater increment in the development of self-help skills than the other two groups. The greatest gains by the experimental group were made during the first six months. This finding suggests that, as with other groups, operant procedures worked so rapidly that they presented a difficult task to the staff, that of the continuing development of new procedures and tasks to maintain momentum.

One of the most important elements in the usefulness of a token-economy program is the effect that it has upon the behavior of the attendants. It is enormously encouraging to an individual working in an institution to see that his behavior is instrumental in helping develop special skills in the people he is working with. As an illustration of this point, Baldwin (1967) reports the finding that attendants trained in token-economy techniques with retarded children in one ward emit significantly more positive patient-oriented responses and less "custodial" behavior when working in other wards than attendants without such training.

The token-economy technique has been extended to work with "antisocial" retardates (Burchard, 1967); with adolescent female retardates (Lent, 1965; Pietsch, Morrow, and Schlesinger, 1967); with classrooms as described in the previous section (Birnbrauer et al., 1965a, b; Birnbrauer, 1967; Wolf, Giles, and Hall, 1968); and with the profoundly retarded (Comtois and Holland, 1966; Girardeau, 1971; Baker, 1973; and Nawas and Braun, 1970 a, b, and c).

SUMMARY

The designation of mental retardation must take into consideration not only the individual's intelligence test scores but his social adjustment as well. Various criteria of retardation involving different levels of performance were described. Perhaps the most salient feature in this area is the emphasis society places upon the kinds of intellectual skills involved in intelligence tests, such as ability with verbalization and abstract thinking. The lack of these skills is the kind of behavioral deficit which makes an individual likely to be labeled retarded and, depending upon the socioeconomic class into which he is born, to be stigmatized or institutionalized.

There are also a number of clearly physiological diseases involving genetic chromosomal defects, birth injuries, metabolic dysfunction, or infections during pregnancy which are associated with the most severely disabled group of individuals categorized as mentally retarded. In the treatment procedures described, emphasis was on the development of self-help and social behaviors. Current behavioral approaches emphasize the use of retraining procedures in the areas of speech, work, and the classroom. Direct retraining is used to foster skills that make for independent, dignified living.

Current research indicates the need to go beyond the intelligence test as a measure of ability and to take into account social class, race, and ethnic origin so that the person's social adjustment and skills are evaluated in terms of his own culture rather than a standard that is inappropriate and eventually damaging to all concerned.

brain syndromes and geriatrics

25

This chapter will discuss a group of disorders that involve defects of the cerebral cortex and the central nervous system with *consequent effects* upon behavior of which old age is an example. The disorders are characterized as acute or chronic, depending upon the reversibility of the damage and, with or without psychosis, depending upon the behavioral impairment observed. The brain disorders are characterized by (1) impairment of orientation; (2) impairment of memory; (3) impairment of all intellectual functions (comprehension, calculation, knowledge, learning, etc); (4) impairment of judgment; (5) lability and shallowness of affect.

The brain disorders, involving as they do damage to organic tissue, are also classifiable as mild, moderate, or severe, depending on the amount of tissue damage and the individual's response to this stress. Brain disorders, just like colds or broken bones, may occur in people manifesting other abnormal behavior patterns such as psychosis, neurosis, and personality disorders. The consequences of brain damage may result in severely maladaptive behavior as a reaction to the stress of the changes associated with the disease as well as through direct loss of intellectual functions.

CLASSIFICATION OF BRAIN SYNDROMES

This section will list the various organic brain syndromes presented in DSM-II. This information will indicate the range of illness; however, as will be noted in subsequent sections, the relationship between amount of tissue damage and subsequent behavior is neither simple nor clear.

Acute brain disorders may result from insults to the organism such as infections (meningitis, pneumonia), ingestion of toxic substances (drugs, poisons, alcohol), trauma (head injury due to accidents, war, surgery), circulatory disturbance (arterial hypertension, cerebral embolism), convulsive disorder, metabolic disturbance, or cancer. In short, any deviation from normal (nonpathological) tissue functioning may affect a person's behavior. The disorder is acute if it is of relatively brief duration and reversible.

Chronic brain disorders result from more or less irreversible, diffuse impairment of cerebral tissue function. While the underlying illness may respond to treatment, as in syphilis, there remains always a certain irreducible minimum of brain tissue destruction that cannot be reversed, even though the loss of function may be almost imperceptible clinically.

Chronic brain syndromes may result from infection (syphilis), poisons (arsenic, illuminating gas, drugs, alcohol), trauma (accidents, war, etc.), chronic, progressive disease (cerebral arteriosclerosis), circulatory disturbance, convulsive disorders, aging, poor nutrition, cancer, and genetic defect. Many of the causes are the same as noted for acute brain syndromes, the distinction being reversibility.

There is also a category of chronic brain disorders that is associated with diseases of unknown causes. These include diseases such as multiple sclerosis, Huntington's chorea, Pick's disease, and other disorders of a probable hereditary nature, some of which will be described in the next section.

SOME SPECIFIC ORGANIC DISEASES

There are several disorders which are clearly degenerative diseases of the nervous system. Although the origins of these diseases are unknown, their effects in terms of brain damage are clear. These diseases are comparatively rare.

Huntington's Chorea

Huntington's chorea appears to be genetically determined. The disease usually becomes manifest when the patient is in his late thirties, and the average length of life after onset varies between 10 and 20 years. The behavioral and physical symptoms involve progressive deterioration. Peculiar behavior may occur years before the physical symptoms appear in drastic form. The behavioral manifestations include slovenliness in dress, carelessness of social conventions such as obscenity and spitting, violence, depression, irritability, poor memory, euphoria, poor judgment, delusions, and suicidal ideas. Later, hallucinations and silly delusions may develop. The physical symptoms include continuous movements of the head, trunk, and limbs, uncontrollable movements involving all limbs, and speech becoming hesitant and stumbling with clicking sounds. The patient walks with a bizarre, jerking, and irregular gait. Finally he becomes physically helpless, with severe, uncontrollable movements and intellectual deterioration.

Alzheimer's Disease

Alzheimer's disease is a rare brain disease which may appear when the individual is in his forties or fifties. The symptoms occur subtly at first and may manifest themselves in the individual's having difficulty in concentration, appearing absentminded, and being irritable. Difficulties in attention, concentration, and comprehension seriously interfere with the person's ability to perform ordinary daily tasks. At this point the individual reacts to his own incapacity by blaming others, and ideas of reference, suspicion, and persecution are expressed. Gradually the individual forgets both remote and recent events, and eventually he becomes disoriented as to time and place, bedridden, and vegetative. The disease progresses to death in an average of about four years.

Pick's Disease

Arnold Pick, a Prague physician, in 1892 described a degenerative disease of the nervous system involving a circumscribed atrophy of the frontal and temporal lobes. This disease is likely to occur in individuals between the ages of 45 and 60. The symptom picture in its early stages is similar to that of Alzheimer's disease. The first signs are inability to pay attention and concentrate, leading to forgetfulness and apparent lack of interest. The individual becomes perplexed and confused, and his incompetency evokes great concern from others. Gradually he becomes unable to perform the simplest of tasks or to care for himself. He becomes disoriented, and his speech becomes stereotyped. Eventually he becomes completely vegetative.

"Clinically it is extremely difficult—and sometimes impossible—to differentiate Pick's disease from Alzheimer's. They occur at the same age period, run more or less identical course, and exhibit similar phenomena." (Henderson and Batchelor, 1962, p. 402.) The cause of Pick's disease is unknown, but what evidence there is would point to a genetic etiology.

Parkinson's Disease

The term "Parkinson" is used in two ways: to designate a specific neurological disease

brain syndromes and geriatrics

characterized by severe muscular tremors; and to designate the tremors themselves which may occur consequent to various brain disorders such as encephalitis and tumors. Parkinson's disease is a good illustration of how the psychological reaction to physical incapacity and deformity may become more incapacitating than the physical manifestations themselves. The individual reacts to his neurological abnormality by withdrawing from contact with others, becoming apathetic and indifferent, and failing to concentrate.

The attributed causes of Parkinson's disease include heredity, viruses, and deficient brain metabolism. Treatment procedures include drugs and surgery. A more optimistic attitude toward its treatment is now current.

Epidemic Encephalitis

Epidemic encephalitis was first described in 1917 and was attributed to a virus causing an inflammation of brain tissue. There were a considerable number of cases following the first World War until about 1925. Since then it has been rare in Western countries, although it still occurs with considerable frequency in parts of Asia and Africa. The acute symptoms include fever, delirium, and stupor. The stupor itself is unusual in that the patient can be aroused from sleep for brief intervals, during which he can answer questions. The early symptoms may also take the form of extreme psychomotor excitement. The individual may become restless, irritable, and agitated. The aftereffects of an attack of encephalitis may not be impairing in and of themselves. However, as in other brain disorders, the individual may react to his altered abilities with any of the psychotic and neurotic manifestations, particularly with depression, anxiety, apathy, and withdrawal. Treatment involves antibiotics together with psychotherapy and vocational retraining.

The description of these disorders points up two important considerations which apply to all brain disorders. First, the early manifestations of neural degeneration may be very similar to behaviors found in neurotic and psychotic behavior. As has been emphasized with psychophysiological disorders (Chapter 16), it is extremely important that an assessment of problem behavior include the likelihood of the presence of physical disease. Second, after the physical illness has been stabilized, if that is possible, the individual must learn to adjust to his decreased physical and intellectual abilities. In this regard there are effects of physical disease which are not directly physiological in nature. These latter difficulties are as much in the proper realm of the educator and psychologist as is the training of the retardate (see Chapter 24). The goal is to achieve as much as possible within the limits set by the person's capabilities.

EFFECTS OF REMOVAL OF BRAIN TISSUE

Implicit in the standard classification of the categories of the brain disorders is the assumption that injury to any part of the brain has some consequence on subsequent behavior. Yet this relationship may be more complex than at first seems apparent. Pronko reviews the case material involving removal of various parts of the brain and comes to the following conclusions:

Removal of the (1) right frontal lobe (2) left frontal lobe (3) both frontal lobes (4) entire right cerebrum or (5) entire left cerebrum may leave no apparent behavioral consequences or it may lead to improvement in general behavior and/or intelligence test performance or decreased efficiency in behavior performance.

Removal of pathological tissue regardless of location in the brain may lead to (1) no apparent harmful effects (2) postoperative improvement of behavior and IQ or (3) *restitution* of behavior lost prior to operation. [1963, p. 63.]

Austin and Grant (1955), reviewing previous studies, gathered 40 cases involving the removal of one cerebral hemisphere. Among the cases were four involving *total* removal of the right cerebral hemisphere because of malignant brain tumor. The surgeons were surprised at the considerable return of motor and verbal functions in all four patients.

Hebb (1939) reports on four cases of surgical removal of the left hemisphere. The patients Hebb described did not show any deterioration and in fact demonstrated apparent intellectual improvement. Hebb concluded that the left hemisphere was no more important than the right unless speech fibers were involved. He also argued that psychological defects which follow removal of brain tissue may be due to the presence of pathological tissue rather than to tissue destruction alone. Hebb (1945) further noted two reasons for the difference in reports of the effects of removal of brain tissue; the first is inexactness in locating the specific site of the damaged tissue, and the second is the fact that a small but diffuse area of pathological tissue remaining after an operation may have a greater effect on producing deviant behavior than the clean-cut removal of a much larger area of tissue.

An important consideration in viewing the effects of physiological damage is that the behavioral effects may well be due to the reaction of the individual rather than the damage itself. When an individual suddenly finds himself unable to perform the tasks of which he had previously been capable, he finds himself under stress in the manner described for transient situational disorders (Chapter 15). In effect, the results are much the same as when the sources of reinforcement for the individual are withdrawn or suddenly altered. In the depressive reactions, the loss may involve the death of a loved individual; in brain damage the loss involves the ability to perform adequately. The behavioral consequences of brain damage therefore vary considerably depending upon the individual's learned methods for dealing with novel situations and demands on himself.

It seems clear, from the investigations of several writers (Freeman, 1959; Bowman and Blau, 1943; Ruesch, Harris, and Bowman, 1945; Pronko, 1963), that change in behavior following brain injury is not necessarily related to the injury itself. Rather, what is involved is the meaning of the injury to the patient and his reaction to the injury. The fact that a behavior becomes salient and reacted to after a brain injury does not mean that the injury "caused" the behavior. Many of the behaviors described in patients when they come in contact with an investigator following a head injury may be the same behavior characteristics they exhibited prior to their injuries. This is directly analogous to the consideration in Chapter 10 that many people adjusting in the community would be called schizophrenic if they were brought to the attention of a psychiatrist. If brain injury brings a person to the attention of a psychiatrist and the person acts in a peculiar manner, it does not mean that the brain injury *caused* the peculiar behavior." (1963, p. 58.)

One of the most important studies relating to brain function and behavior has been the investigation of man's "split brain" (Gazzaniga, 1967). Sperry (1964) had previously demonstrated that surgery had been successful in controlling epileptic seizures by an operation involving the cutting of the corpus callosum, the tissue that connects the two cerebral hemispheres. The expectation for this surgery was that the seizures would be controlled in one hemisphere. What happened instead was that total elimination of seizures resulted for *both* hemispheres.

Following these findings, Gazzaniga reported on the results of ten such split-brain operations. He found that "one of the most striking observations was that the operation produced no noticeable change in the patient's temperament, personality, or general intelligence" (1967, p. 24).

ASSESSMENT OF BRAIN DAMAGE

Clinical psychologists have used psychological tests to assess the effects of damage to cortical tissue. The problems involved in this area include all of the problems inherent in psychological testing (Chapter 11) as well as additional problems created by the nature of brain damage. To illustrate the amount of energy which has been put into this area, Yates (1966), reviewing the psychological literature for the years 1960–1964 only in the general area of the effects of brain damage in children and adults, found over 700 references involving psychological testing.

Yates argued that there are three major false assumptions in the construction and application of tests to assess the effects of brain damage which primarily use the difference in performance between brain-damaged individuals and control subjects as the criteria for selection of discriminating items. These assumptions provide important information about the presumed relationship between brain damage and behavior. First, there is the assumption that brain damage may be treated as a unitary concept and that the criterion group of brain-damaged individuals may be composed of all individuals known to be brain damaged from whatever cause.

This assumption is untrue because the effects of brain damage, according to Yates, must be regarded from a hierarchical viewpoint. "That is, brain damage will produce in any given individual (a) a general deterioration in all aspects of functioning; but will also produce (b) differential (group) effects, depending upon the location, extent, etc., of the damage; and will produce (c) highly specific effects if it occurs in certain highly specified areas of the brain. In any individual case, it is essential to consider the evidence carefully from all three of these angles." (p. 112.) Thus, any one test of brain damage would be unlikely to be useful. The effects of brain damage are manifested in different ways according to which of the hierarchical levels is tapped by a particular test.

The second assumption against which Yates argues is that a test of brain damage which has been validated on clearly demonstrable brain-damaged groups may be properly used for clinical diagnostic purposes. Yates' objection to this assumption is that in validating a particular test only clear-cut, independently diagnosed cases are included in the brain-damaged group. In clinical practice, on the other hand, the test is primarily used to select those individuals who do not have clear-cut neurological evidence of brain damage. These are not the same sorts of individuals as used in the criterion group.

The third assumption against which Yates argues is very relevant to the evidence about brain damage previously cited in this chapter. "This is the naïve belief held by many clinicians constructing tests of brain damage that the neurological criteria of brain damage are essentially more valid than psychological criteria." (p. 113.) When contrasted with other material cited above, Yates' work illustrates further the controversial nature of the field at both the theoretical and empirical levels.

Gurland (1973) carries this line of reasoning further with particular reference to the aged. The line between expected effects of aging and special or "psychopathological processes" is an indistinct one. In terms of cognitive impairment, Eisdorfer (1973, p. 71) notes that "There is now reason to question the accuracy of many of our beliefs concerning the aged as well as the simpleminded notion of a necessary age-linked decrement in all functions with age past maturity."

More sophisticated approaches consider the relevance of the material on the test to the person and the motivation of the subjects, their state of general physical health, and their ongoing levels of intellectual stimulation. Gurland also points out that self-reports of loss of function, such as poorer memory, may reflect self-fulfilling and self-reported declines, and may not be mirrored on psychological tests. Depression is common among the aged, but it may be a function of loss of friends through death, loss of social function through retirement, and social isolation. Social isolation, in turn, may be a result of difficulty in movement and decreased expendable income (Loether, 1967). Institutionalization, as in the area of retardation, may be a social solution rather than a result of deterioration per se; up to 50 percent of the people over 60 who are institutionalized might well live outside the institution if accommodations could be found (Dubey, 1968; Cohen and Kraft, 1968; Loether, 1967, p. 28), and "many old people living in the community have the same symptoms as those living in institutions." (Gurland, 1973, p. 349.) Decreased energy involves a comparison with other people, a reason for action, and considerations of general physical well-being.

The aging process illustrates the interaction of physical, social, and conceptual-measurement problems. Given the problems in a diagnostic cutting point (i.e., demarcation of "pathology" from nonpathology), Gurland (1973, p. 368) suggests: "Decisions about treatment and prevention could now more fruitfully depend upon pragmatic considerations such as the natural history of a given behavior, whether it is distressing or disabling to the patient or to others, and whether there is an effective way to modify it." In short, one must move from a medical to a social decision model.

TREATMENT OF AN ILLUSTRATIVE PROBLEM BEHAVIOR

The treatment of the organic brain disorders is medical in nature and involves the use of drugs or surgery, depending upon the specific disease. The contribution of psychological approaches is to help the individual learn to deal with situations to the best of his ability.

The behavioral approach to individuals with organic brain damage is much the same as for other previously described diagnostic categories. That is, the question is not what is the label but rather what are the problem behaviors. For example, Rohan and Provost (1966) report the application of operant conditioning procedures to a 40-year-old blind, brain-damaged patient who had not been able to feed himself for the past five years. Many attempts to train him to eat by himself failed. The training program involved the use of rewards contingent upon the occurrence of emission of a component of self-feeding. The response components of eating ranged from the gross response of sitting at a table to finer movements such as holding a utensil and placing food in his mouth.

Initially a reward (food being placed in his mouth) would occur for simply sitting at a table. On later trials more components of the eating act, such as sitting at the table and reaching for a spoon, had to occur before a reward was received. The patient was placed on a food-deprivation schedule so that food was obtained only in the training situation. In addition to these operant procedures, a further procedure used was the gradual introduction of the noises of the dining room which had been aversive to the patient. This was done by playing a tape recording of the dining room sounds at successively louder levels. These procedures resulted in the patient's feeding himself in the dining room within two weeks after the start of training. At a five-month follow-up the patient's eating behavior had been maintained.

Similar cases illustrating at a clinical level how learning-based techniques may be used to ameliorate various "organic" deficits are increasing in frequency. These cases include work by Stary, Barankova, and Obrda (1968) on spasmodic paralysis; Otis, Morcombe, and Pittman (1970) on memory in Korsakoff's syndrome; Hall and Broden (1967), on muscle coordination activities in brain-injured children; Goodkin (1969) on aphasic speech; Brookshire (1970) on crying in a multiple sclerosis patient; and a range of retraining activities (Salzinger, Feldman, and Portnoy, 1970; Taylor and Persons, 1970; and Fowler, Fordyce, and Berni, 1969).

BEING OLD IN A YOUNG WORLD: SENILITY—MAYBE

"The problem of the aged may be catalogued in terms of money, health and psychological dislocation." (Bevan, 1972.) "While the percentage of the population aged 65 and over rose steadily from 2.7% in 1860 to 9.1% in 1970, the proportion of the aged males who were gainfully employed in the labor market dropped from 68% in 1890 to 26% in 1969. . . ." (Zubin, 1973, p. 3.) Because of changes in life expectancy and patterns of birthrates, the proportion of the population that is aged and retired will continue to increase.

Aging has been thought of in itself as a reduction of physical and psychological capacity that leads to behavioral problems; in short, as a chronic brain syndrome.

There are a number of associated questions. The first is whether there are effects of being aged that are primarily social and secondarily physical. Second, do the aged differ, and if they do, can their problems be ameliorated?

One of the largest surveys (Andelman, 1972) found that workers over age 65 did their work as well if not better than younger workers. Political action groups, such as the "Gray Panthers," are being formed to help the aged find alternatives to a bingo and shuffleboard style of life (Kottke, 1970; Sanders, 1970; Greenhouse, 1971). Among the political objectives are improved facilities, health care, mass transportation, nursing-home supervision, and supervised commitment procedures so that the aged will not be institutionalized at the whim of their younger relatives. Long-term planning calls for grocery and other stores and amenities near residences so that transportation problems should not arise.

The standard age of 65 for purposes of social security is a product of a time of depression (in the 1930's) when jobs were a highly prized commodity. The average level of physical well-being of older people has changed in the last 40 years, as has in many instances the nature of work; these changes make it possible for an older person to remain productive, using his knowledge rather than his muscles. At the same time, particularly at the time of this writing, an inflationary trend places the person having a reduced, fixed income in a frightening position; one in four of the aged in the United States lives in poverty. (UPI, November 26, 1971; Scott, 1972). Social security payments limit the amount of a person's earnings before he will be penalized, yet the purchasing power of the dollar declines.

Even before age 65, because of the overhead estimated for retirement, finding work becomes increasingly difficult for older people, and movement from one organization to another without highly specialized skills, increasingly less likely. The jobless rate of males 45 years and over increases rapidly; one in every five jobless workers is over 45 (UPI, November 26, 1971). At present, the image in advertising, television, and mass media is towards a youth culture, and the middle-aged man is faced with either changing his life-style, from clothes and haircut to concepts of interpersonal response, or being considered dated. He has spent his life acting and working in a manner that is looked down upon, and the promised fruits of his daily efforts are despised by his children, ridiculed by the public, and eroded by inflation, taxation, and government programs that seem to help everybody but him. His energy is depleted, his youthful dreams gone, but his burden of work remains (Skerly, 1973). An extreme example of prejudice against the aged is that of a college professor whose thesis is "The old, having no future, are dangerously free from the consequences of their own political acts, and it makes no sense to allow the vote to someone who is actually unlikely to survive and pay the bills for (what) he may help select." (Tiede, 1970, p. 19.)

With the children raised, no longer in the swing and gossip of the daily work, and with the increasing frequency of death of life-time companions, there is a restriction socially as well as economically. The point of these comments is that the social and economic variables create a stress (change, loss of reinforcement) associated with increasing age, and it is in this context that physical deterioration must be evaluated. The enforced limitation of activity may enhance physical deterioration (MacDonald 1973).

Being old is defined within a socio-political context (Rome, 1972). A prime characteristic of the role at present (Phillips, 1962) is being unemployed, and not age in years. In addition, once a person is unemployed, he may well place a different meaning on illnesses: he no longer considers them interruptions in his work pattern that are to be reversed, but rather features of himself to be accepted and even ones justifying his current unemployment.

The role includes dressing more conservatively, confining one's friendships to members of one's own age bracket, being in poor health, being unemployed and financially dependent, and generally being in a markedly different and predominantly negative period of life.

The essentially aversive nature of this role is reflected in the resistance to accepting it. Kastenbaum and Durkee (1964) found that people over seventy consistently classify themselves as middle-aged. Similarly, Phillips (1962), using a sample of 346 people aged 60 or older all of whom lived in the community, found that 61 percent classified themselves as middle-aged (compared with only 15 percent who classified themselves as old), that 67 percent thought that other people thought they were middle-aged, and that 62 percent reported that they felt younger than most people their age.

Simmons (1964) working cross-culturally, found that prestige of the aged in a given society was strongly associated with the importance of the societal functions they performed. The decreased function of the aged in our society may be due to the rapid development of technology and information, which has decreased the value of individually accumulated wisdom.

Carp (1969) notes that senility "is a particularly ill-defined term. It has no scientific meaning but a vague and perjorative one. Unlike 'senile brain disease,' it has no clear physiological referents." (p. 203.) The typical traits of senility are depression, anxiety, and rigidity, each of which may be observed in populations of all ages. What Carp did was to use a senility index to compare a group of normal, not institutionalized older people with young college students. The older group (ages 52 to 92; average age, 72) numbered 295; the college students numbered 270 (ages 17 to 25); (average age 20). A high score meant senile. The college students averaged 31.2; the older people 14.6. The results were statistically and socially significant: the younger people were more senile. This was replicated by a pilot study in which 41 college students rated their roomates and an old person with whom they were acquainted: the averages were 28.9 and 19.2 respectively.

If we follow Carp's line of thinking, we may ask whether the effects of age may be reversed or obviated by psychological means. Kahana and Kahana (1970) randomly assigned aged psychiatric male patients to age-integrated and age-segregated wards. The people placed in the age-integrated wards showed greater improvements and responsivness on mental-status exams three weeks later than those placed in the age-segregated wards. Nash and Zimring (1969) found that a placebo alone was not effective, but both subjective evaluations of gain and objective measurements of improved short-term memory showed that improvement was greater for those people (average age 82) who expected benefit.

"Senile Dementia"

In evaluating senile dementia, as with other types of brain disorders, it must be noted that there is no clear-cut relationship between the pathological anatomy of brains and senile behavior. Rothschild (1945) argued that senile psychosis could not be directly attributed to the damaged tissue, but to "the person's capacity to compensate for the damage."

Gallinek (1948), using autopsy reports and observations of behavior prior to death, noted that an individual's behavior could be markedly "senile" when only relatively minor organic damage had occurred. Conversely, major anatomical impairment was found in indiviuals with *no* observable behavior pathology. Gallinek's findings were confirmed in a later study by Ehrenberg and Gullingsrud (1955).

Raskin and Ehrenberg (1956) did a post-mortem study of 270 patients ranging from 60 to 97 years of age and found that the presence of arteriosclerosis and brain damage was much more frequent in normal individuals than had been previously suspected. They concluded that there was no significant correlation between brain damage and behavior and considered that sudden upheavals in the life of an individual were more likely to account for the psychoses of old age than were anatomical changes. Gal (1959) also did a post-mortem study of 104 patients, aged 65 to 94, and confirmed even more dramatically these earlier findings of a lack of correlation between brain damage and behavior.

Further evidence for the possibility of behavior change in older individuals has been a series of reports of successful psychotherapy, both individual and group, with individuals ranging from 65 to 95 years of age (Bowman and Engle, 1960).

Williams and Jaco (1958) found marked social, cultural, and economic factors in the incidence of senile psychosis. In a survey made in Texas, these authors found that the rate of senile psychosis was highest for Anglo-Americans, intermediate for blacks, and quite low for Spanish-Americans. They related this finding to the difference in attitudes toward the aged in American society (in which old age is strongly rejected) and in Latin-American society (in which old age is a period of dignity and usefulness). The American family and economic system place the aged in a role of "obsolescence," making them feel a burden rather than a value to younger people.

Volpe and Kastenbaum (1967) worked with aged men who seemed so physically and emotionally incapacitated that they required around-the-clock nursing care. The mean age of these individuals was 78. The nursing and the medical notes described them as "agitated, hostile and incontinent." The patients had a record of tearing off their clothes and striking out at each other, and they seemed to show no concern about what was going on around them. They could perform no services for themselves. The investigators introduced some simple innovations on the ward. They provided a record player, a decorated bulletin board, games, and cards; they dressed the patients in white shirts and ties; and they served beer in 12-ounce bottles, with crackers and cheese, at 2:00 P.M. each day. Within one month the behavior of the patients had changed markedly. The amount of medication given dropped sharply, as did incontinence and jacket restraint. Social responsivity, as indicated by the request for and participation in dances and parties, increased. The improved social functioning was also associated with marked improvement in mental orientation. Chien (1971) and Becker and Cesar (1973) confirmed these results. Other procedures with the aged are illustrated by Cautela (1969), Loew and Silverstone (1971), and MacDonald and Butler (1974).

The authors attribute these dramatic changes and improvement to the fact that the specific innovations "served to facilitate *expectancies of mutual gratification* on the part of patients and staff members." In effect, the demand characteristics of the ward had been changed from a medical to a social situation (Kastenbaum, 1965). The people were now treated as responsible individuals in much the same way that patients were cared for in the era of moral treatment (Chapter 7) and that they are treated today in token economy programs (Chapter 18). As the expectancy of what people are capable of doing increases, more "normal" behaviors occur and are reinforced. If such great changes can be brought about so quickly by relatively simple changes in the environment, then it is clear that the traditional concepts of what is involved in senility may be seriously questioned.

EPILEPSY

The term "epilepsy" is used to designate a group of convulsive behaviors related to a disorder in the central nervous system. Many of the etiological agents underlying chronic brain syndromes can and do cause convulsions. Convulsions may occur in the presence of syphilis, intoxication, trauma, cerebral arteriosclerosis, and intracranial neoplasm. When the convulsions are symptomatic of such other etiological agents, the chronic brain syndrome is classified under the headings for those particular disturbances. The usual case that is put in this category is the epileptic who shows a gradual development of mental dullness, slowness of associative thinking, impairment of memory and other intellectual functions, and apathy.

Julius Caesar, Mohammed, and Napoleon are among the many famous people who have suffered epileptic seizures. Epilepsy, which has the longest history of any physical disorder (Hoch and Knight, 1947), was believed to result from the visit of a god to the body; hence the references to it as the "sacred disease." The exact incidence of epilepsy in the United States today can only be roughly estimated. Coleman (1972) presents an estimate of the number of persons "subject to epileptic seizures" as between two and three million. Epilepsy is usually classified in terms of four main types: grand mal, petit mal, Jacksonian, and psychomotor.

Grand mal epilepsy, or the "great illness," is the most dramatic of the epileptic types. There are considered to be four phases. First is the *aura*, which may not always be present. This is a signal such as dizziness or an unusual sensory experience such as a flash of light, an odor, or a buzzing or ringing in the ears prior to a seizure. The next phase, the *tonic* stage, comprises brief rigid muscular tension which may last for one or two minutes and includes a sharp intake of breath. In the next, the *clonic* stage, the muscles contract and relax rhythmically, leading to violent contortions. There may be jerking movements with the head striking the ground, legs spasmodically jerking up and down, arms thrusting outward with the jaw opening and closing, and a bubbly foam appearing in the mouth. In the final stage, the *coma*, the patient becomes unconscious, the muscles relax gradually, and the patient may slowly return to normal. His first reactions on awakening are bewilderment, confusion, and exhaustion.

The *petit mal*, or "small illness," seizure is much less dramatic. It is milder and briefer and involves little or no loss of consciousness. The patient may stop what he is doing and stare vacantly about him and then resume his work. There may be brief spasmodic muscular twitches of various parts of the body. In many instances, this type of seizure is not readily obvious

brain syndromes and geriatrics

to others, and sometimes the patient himself is not aware of his behavior.

The *Jacksonian seizure* is similar to grand mal. The seizure starts in one part of the body, such as a finger or hand, and spreads to the arm or leg or one side of the body. These seizures are usually attributed to a localized, specific brain lesion, the removal of which frequently brings about recovery.

In *psychomotor epilepsy* the patient loses consciousness and, while unconscious, performs some organized behavior. This behavior is usually a routine task, but it may be an antisocial, unusual, or even violent behavior. For example, Van Gogh's cutting off of his ear was considered to have occurred during an attack of psychomotor epilepsy. Despite the few instances of violence and antisocial behavior during epileptic attacks, most psychomotor epileptics are not considered dangerous to others. Turner and Merlis (1962) found that only 5 out of 337 epileptics had committed illegal acts during seizures.

Medication such as dilantin and phenobarbital, has been very effective in the reduction of epileptic seizures.

In some instances of epilepsy, it is quite difficult to specify the stimulus that elicits the seizure. In other instances, it is quite clear what the precipitating factor is and the stimulus can be manipulated to induce convulsions. One of the most interesting illustrations of this is of epileptic reactions which have been conditioned to musical stimuli. Daly and Barry (1957) reviewed almost a hundred years of musicogenic epilepsy. Examples included individuals who had seizures when playing the piano, when listening to a brass or a wind instrument play bass notes, or when listening to specific types of classical music or to specific notes on instruments such as a piano or organ. One patient had seizures when listening to the music of the popular songs "Green Eyes" and "Amapola." The authors point out that neither neurological examinations nor X-rays revealed any abnormal condition in the brain.

Mawdsley and Manc (1961) report a patient who had a grand mal seizure while adjusting a TV set as the screen began to flicker. Pronko (1963) describes the television set as a source eliciting epileptic behavior. Roman slave traders utilized the same principle by rotating a potter's wheel in front of the eyes of slaves and watching their reaction before purchasing them so that they could rule out their being epileptic.

To the extent that environmental conditions and the person's response to them may increase the neurological response manifested by epileptic seizure, the psychologist may have a role to play in the treatment of some cases of epilepsy. He may investigate conditions leading to EEG changes. If stimuli have been fortuitously conditioned to seizure, counter-conditioning may be of value.

Efron (1956, 1957) reports the application of a Pavlovian type of conditioning procedure to arrest seizures of a woman with temporal lobe epilepsy. For 26 years the woman had been suffering from attacks which involved olfactory and auditory hallucinations and adversive head movements preceding the climax of the grand mal seizure. No arrested seizures had ever occurred; once the first part of the aura began, a stereotyped fit seemed inevitable. Efron (1956) found that the application of a specific sensory stimulus, an unpleasant odor, during the first stage of the attack was able to stop further development of the aura and to prevent the occurrence of the tonic and clonic phases. The patient was able to stop seizures when they were about to occur by inhaling from a vial the odors of various aromatic oils.

In terms of treatment procedures, Efron (1957) first arrested the seizures in this patient by simultaneously presenting two stimuli to the subject. The first was a concentrated odor of jasmine which had been effective in arresting her seizures. The second stimulus was an inexpensive silvered bracelet. The patient was instructed to stare intently for 15 to 30 seconds at the bracelet while sniffing the vial of essence of jasmine. Five different persons exposed her to the sight of the bracelet and to the odor of jasmine during the eight-day period so that the response would not depend on the presence of any particular person. Also, the double stimulation was performed in various locations around the hospital to avoid unrelated conditioning to specific aspects in her environment. At the end of eight days of conditioning the bracelet alone was presented to the patient, and she "experienced" the odor of the concentrated jasmine in a vivid fashion.

During the sessions a spontaneous seizure occurred, and it was arrested by the patient's staring at the bracelet for a few seconds. After this success the patient was permitted to go home with only the bracelet to control the seizure. The anticonvulsive medication had previously been discontinued. At one point it was found that merely thinking intently about the bracelet proved sufficient to inhibit the seizure. Further formal conditioning was not necessary, since each arrested seizure appeared to serve as a reinforcement. An eight-month follow-up indicated that she had remained seizure-free and she was able to resume a full-time singing career. Robinson and Robinson (1965, p. 121), Pinto (1972), Sterman and Friar (1972), Gardner (1967), Forster (1969), and Parrino (1971) present material that buttresses this report.

In a paper reminiscent of Lang and Melamed (1969), Wright (1973) used aversive stimuli to reduce the self-induced seizures of a five-year-old retardate. Scholander (1972) found a reduction in seizures after successful treatment of a painful "compulsive" twisting of the head. Among the more hopeful new procedures currently being developed are applications of biofeedback (Trotter, 1973).

Among other behaviors associated, rightly or wrongly, with brain injury, useful interventions have been reported in the areas of vertigo (Fowler et al., 1971), migraine headache (Lutker, 1971; Mitchell, 1971a, 1971b), and various speech and motor problems (Ince, 1968a; Goodkin, 1969b; McReynolds, 1969; and Salzinger, Feldman, and Portnoy, 1970). The points raised by these articles are that change-worthy behaviors by brain-injured people may not be *directly* associated with the brain dysfunction, and even if they are, the resulting behavior may have been increased in frequency or extent by environmental reactions to it. As such, the direct re-educational efforts of behavioral treatment have a genuine role in medical rehabilitation.

SUMMARY

This chapter has described some of the brain syndromes, situations in which disruptive behavior occurs as a direct or indirect result of a deviation from physiological health. These disorders are dealt with appropriately within a medical model: treatment is directed first toward the correction of underlying physiological conditions. After physical treatment has taken place, the psychologist has an important role in training the individual to make the most of his abilities, even if these abilities are genuinely reduced. In this regard, the theoretical situation is analogous to transient situational maladjustments (Chapter 15) in which there has been a dramatic change in range of reinforcing stimuli. In terms of specific therapies, the state of affairs is analogous to the educational procedures discussed in the previous chapter on retardation. In some situations, however, a physiological difference leads to a change in social role, either through general expectations or personal ascription. In such instances, as with older age, the problem is social and behavioral and should be treated in these rather than in medical contexts.

ptq
conflict with the prevailing society

ANTISOCIAL AND DYSSOCIAL BEHAVIOR

26

DSM-I had a subcategory of personality disorders called sociopathic personality disturbance in which individuals were placed who were "ill primarily in terms of society and of conformity with the prevailing cultural milieu." In addition to sexual deviation and addiction, the subcategories of sociopathic personality in DSM-I were antisocial and dyssocial reaction. Antisocial reactions are labeled *antisocial personality* in DSM-II, placed within the larger category of personality disorders, and defined as follows:

This term is reserved for individuals who are basically unsocialized and whose behavior pattern brings them repeatedly into conflict with society. They are incapable of significant loyalty to individuals, groups or social values. They are grossly selfish, callous, irresponsible, impulsive, and unable to feel guilt or to learn from experience and punishment. Frustration tolerance is low. They tend to blame others or offer plausible rationalizations for their behavior. [DSM-II, p. 43].

One of the more progressive steps in DSM-II is that what were called dyssocial reactions (and placed within personality disorders) in DSM-I are now categorized as dyssocial behavior and placed in the category of conditions "without manifest psychiatric disorder." The DSM-I definition was of "individuals who manifest disregard for the usual social codes, and often come tion and addiction, the subcategories of having lived all their lives in an abnormal moral environment. They may be capable of strong loyalties. These individuals typically do not show significant personality deviations other than those implied by adherence to the values or code of their own predatory, criminal, or other social group." (DSM-I, p. 38.) DSM-II gives as examples "racketeers, dishonest gamblers, prostitutes, and dope peddlers." (DSM-II, p. 52) While the unfortunate moralistic flavor remains, the step forward is that a person may be normal in terms of a restricted social group while at the same time at odds with a larger, dominant one, and still may not necessarily be considered "psychiatrically impaired" or as having a personality disorder.

The problem touched on by the antisocial label is that there are people who act in a manner that is socially disturbing. Their behaviors do not fall into recognizable patterns of psychosis, neurosis, or psychophysiological disorders; there are no abrupt, immediately apparent, overwhelming environmental stresses as in transient situational maladjustment. And there is no evidence of either mental retardation or brain injury. Yet the people act in an incomprehensible manner: if they break laws it is in such a repetitive, almost self-defeating, foolish manner that it seems unlikely that they act as a result of having compared the risk of being caught with the gain that could result if they were not caught. Having given up concepts of demonology, how is one to understand such people? The behavior these people manifest is considered poor social judgment but is *not* psychotic. The diagnostic concept, the group of people denoted, and the social puzzle will become clearer through the following historical survey of the term "psychopath."

THE HISTORY OF A LABEL

Although the behaviors described within the current category of antisocial personality have been a part of the human scene since ancient times, the concept of "psychopath" as a psychiatric classification began with Pinel's diagnosis of a patient as suffering from *manie sans délire* (McCord and McCord, 1964). Despite coming from a wealthy, noble family and having been given everything he wanted, this patient could never satisfy his desires. He was aroused to fury at any obstacle in his way and kicked a dog to death, whipped a horse, and threw a peasant woman into a well.

Other labels important to the understanding of modern viewpoints on psychopathy were those of "moral insanity" and "moral derangement." The former term was introduced in 1835 by Pritchard and referred to an individual who was without "insane illusion or hallucination" and whose condition did not affect the "intellect or knowing and reasoning facilities." Such a person was one in whom "the moral and active principles of the mind are strongly perverted or depraved." Rush (1812) defined "moral derangement" as a state "when the will becomes the involuntary vehicle of vicious actions through the instrumentality of the passions." He included among "the morbid operations of the will" the behaviors of murder, theft, lying, and drinking. Rush refers to such individuals as having "derangement of the moral faculties," which he thought of as innate; he considered the condition to be due to "an original defective organization in those parts of the body which are occupied by the moral faculties of the mind." (Lowrey, 1944.) Ray (1838) classified moral insanity in the category of affective mania. Ray felt that these people would commit crimes for reasons inexplicable to themselves and others. He attributed such events to the working of a blind, instinctive, and irresistible impulse.

The views of Pinel, Rush, Pritchard, and Ray evoked considerable controversy because the implication of their argument was that socially disturbing behaviors of an extreme nature, including crime, were actually a form of insanity and, as such, came within the province of medicine. The counter arguments described these behaviors as "sinful" or "evil," but *not* as "sick." It was argued that the act of describing such undesirable action as "illness" destroyed the grounds for human responsibility. This dispute reached a peak in the trial of Guiteau, the assassin of President Garfield. Defense psychiatrists argued that Guiteau was morally insane and thus not responsible for his behavior. The prosecution produced psychiatrists who argued that Guiteau was sane since he knew the difference between right and wrong. The jury upheld the latter group, and Guiteau was executed.

The professional concept of psychopathy began to move slowly in the direction of the belief that these behaviors were due to *innate,* inherited causes. In 1888, Koch contributed the term "psychopathic inferiority," implying a constitutional predisposition to such behavior. Tredgold (1915, p. 321) argued that the "moral defective" was really feebleminded: ". . . my experience is that most persistent criminals are the offspring of a decidedly neurotic or mentally abnormal stock, and that they possess many characteristics identical with those occurring in ordinary aments."

Fernald (1908) presented the other side of the coin with the belief that every imbecile is a potential criminal needing only a particular environment and opportunity to express his criminal tendency. Thus, in contrast to the earlier ideas, the tendency became that of equating immoral behavior with stupid behavior. This view culminated in the British Mental Deficiencies Act of 1913 in which moral imbeciles were defined as "persons who from an early age display some permanent mental defect coupled with strong vicious criminal propensities on which punishment has had little or no deterrent effect."

The approach linking psychopathy with innate characteristics culminated in the Italian school of criminology led by Lombroso (1911). It was claimed that the criminal was a born "type" who had clear "stigmatizing" facial features which were signs of degeneracy and discernibly different from those of normal people. Among the signs of the degenerate criminal were a cleft palate, a low forehead, unusual shaped head or nose, protruding ears, high cheekbones, and a scanty beard. These features were a direct throwback to the savage caveman. Lest the reader's mirror cause him too much anxiety, it must be clearly stated that, Hollywood type-casting notwithstanding, this theory has been almost universally abandoned.

The next important development was the introduction of more careful gathering of data about these people. Bernard Glueck, a psychiatrist at Sing Sing prison in the early 1920's, labeled approximately 20 percent of the inmates as constitutional psychopaths and found that these were the individuals who also had the greatest recidivism, drunkenness, and addiction.

In 1924 Bolsi reported the observation that encephalitis (a brain inflammation) can result in psychopathic symptoms in individuals who had previously been "normal." The consequences of Bolsi's findings in the behavior of the professional investigators were equivalent to those that followed the demonstration that syphilis caused paresis. The organically minded investigators hailed this as evidence that malfunction of the brain accounted for psychopathic behavior, which, *if true*, would have eventually solved the puzzling problem.

In the 1930's and 1940's the influence of psychoanalysis began to be manifested in the field of psychopathy. For example, Alexander and Staub (1929) hypothesized that the criminal was unconsciously motivated by a desire for punishment and argued that the psychopath was fixated at the phallic stage of development.

DESCRIPTION AND THEORIES OF PSYCHOPATHY [1]

The behaviors which may result in a person's being designated as an antisocial personality are listed below. As is true in other categories, not *all* these behaviors are characteristic of any *one* individual; rather, they are representative of general types of behaviors. Further, many people who act in this manner may not come to the attention of authorities; that is, there is a great amount of residual deviance (see the references to Wallerstein and Wyle, 1947, and Empey and Erickson, 1966, in Chapter 10). First of all the individual must perform an act or series of acts that brings him to the attention of the authorities. Often this is a behavior designated as criminal by the legal code or as morally wrong in terms of custom. As the representative of authority learns more about the behavior of the offending individual, some or all of the following characteristics frequently emerge:

1. The individual does not play by the usual rules of society. He generally does not seem responsive to the kinds of reinforcements that are effective with most people.

2. He talks a good game. There is a façade of competency or maturity. He is often charming and verbalizes the right things, the things others want to hear. His behavior, however, is at marked variance with his verbalization. There is an inconsistency between words and actions, and between words at various times.

3. He may perform illegal or unusual behaviors characterized by "impulsiveness." He is likely to react to stimuli in the immediate situation without regard for the consequences of his behavior for himself or for others, consequences which may seem apparent to an observer, but not to him.

4. He may repeatedly commit crimes in-

---

[1] Given the confusion of terminology, the words "sociopath," "psychopath," and "antisocial" as used in this section reflect their interchangeable nature in the literature under discussion.

546

volving pettiness and deceit, such as fraud, forgery, and "con-man" behavior.

5. He may be a chronic liar, but his lies are often difficult to spot because of the sincerity with which he emits them. It is only after considerable contact that the untruthfulness of many of his statements becomes obvious. He will often express regret or sorrow, but this is an example of saying the thing most calculated to placate others. But there seems to be no "real self-blame" or "insight."

6. He usually does not display anxiety or guilt about his behavior.

7. He does not seem to learn from experience. He will repeatedly emit a behavior that seems self-defeating or simply stupid. Even if caught and punished for the behavior, he may repeat the stupidity.

8. He is likely to be uninfluenced by any form of authority and discipline. Although he may be intelligent, he usually will not go very far in formal schooling since he is likely to get into difficulty with school authorities.

9. He seems unable to sustain any close interpersonal relationship. He uses other persons as objects rather than as individuals. He dehumanizes others; he cannot empathize with, identify with, or take the view of other human beings. He is likely to disappoint anyone who has prolonged contact with him, such as family or friends. He usually will change jobs frequently, desert his family, borrow money and fail to pay it back, and yet continually ask for another chance and usually get it because of his verbal assurances of repentance.

10. He seems unable to wait, to forego present pleasures for future gratifications. Consequently there is little successful long-term planning or achievement of long-range goals.

Not everyone who is labeled an antisocial personality manifests all these behaviors, and all the behaviors may be emitted to some degree by people not labeled as psychopathic. For example, a businessman who is loyal to his family's welfare or to his company may have to engage in one or more of the foregoing ten types of acts.

The problem of categorization in this area is complicated by the conflicting views of the relation of antisocial personality to the concept of anxiety. There has been previous discussion (Chapter 9) of the limited usefulness of the concept of anxiety, but assuming for the moment that the concept *is* measurable, are antisocial personalities deviant in regard to anxiety? The lack of anxiety is taken to be one of the characteristics clearly distinguishing the personality disorders in general from the psychoneuroses. However, observers (from Alexander and Staub, 1929) have noted individuals called antisocial or psychopathic who are "anxious." To resolve this dilemma with any kind of consistency, the notion developed of two types of psychopath, the true or primary psychopath and the secondary, neurotic psychopath. In some regard this is implicitly recognized in DSM-I when it is noted that "sociopathic reactions are very often symptomatic" of various other disorders.

Cleckley (1964), Karpman (1941), and Lykken (1957) all argue for a designation of the category "primary sociopathy or primary psychopath" characterized as being: "a) clearly defective as compared to normals in their ability to develop (i.e., condition) anxiety, in the sense of an anticipatory emotional response to warning signals previously associated with nocioceptive stimulation. Persons with such a defect would also be expected to show b) abnormally little manifest anxiety in life situations normally conducive to this response, and to be c) relatively incapable of avoidance learning under circumstances where such learning can only be effected through the mediation of the anxiety response" (Lykken, 1957).

Lykken also reports a study in which he compared these two types of psychopaths with normal subjects on galvanic skin response (GSR) conditioning and avoidance learning. The task involved the measurement of GSR in anticipation of electric shock. Lykken found that anxiety was highest in the normals and lowest in the primary sociopaths, and the order of conditioning and avoidance learning differed in the same magnitude. Other similar studies using GSR as the measure of anxiety (Hare, 1965, 1970; Schmauk, 1970; Sutker, 1970) have tended to support and refine this difference in conditionability between psychopaths and normals. Since many theorists argue that some anxiety is necessary for an individual to learn a new task, the absence of anxiety is taken as an explanation of the sociopath's failure to learn by experience and his repeated behaviors leading to social punishment.

As to the conditions or causes which have led to the socially deviant behavior of the psychopath, theories have run the gamut from heredity through physiology to the family, social, and cultural environment.

Heredity and the Sociopath

The historical material presented earlier in this chapter indicated how closely the term "psychopath" has been tied to the notion of an inborn lack of moral sense. The investigation for hereditary factors in psychopathy runs into the same kinds of methodological problems as do all studies involving the effects of heredity and environment. McCord and McCord, after reviewing relevant studies, conclude "that the research on the constitutional or genetic basis of psychopathy is inconclusive and contradictory. . . . Heredity cannot yet be excluded as a causal factor. With more adequate delineation, with more rigidly controlled experiments, and with more sensitive measurement, an hereditary link may possibly be established. Given our current knowledge, however, the extravagant claims of the geneticists must be questioned." (1960, pp. 60–61.)

In the last decade, a great deal of investigation has centered on an extra Y (XYY) on the 47th chromosome.[2] Best estimates are that between .10 percent and .40 percent of the normal population has this anomaly, which has been observed, in many but not all studies, to occur with roughly 2 percent frequency in penal-mental institutions (Hook, 1973). That there is some association between the chromosomal anomaly and institutionalization seems to be the burden of evidence, although Fox (1971) presents strong counter-arguments and, explicitly, "persons with an extra Y chromosome will constitute but an insignificant portion of the perpetrators of violent crimes" (Jarvik, Klodin, and Matsuyama, 1973, p. 679), while many nonviolent XYY men exist in the general community. Tallness, poor skin, and borderline intelligence, as well as "episodic aggressiveness" have been associated with XYY, but Owen (1972) writes: "No consistent personality or behavioral constellation has been successfully predicted from the XYY complement." (p. 209.)

The XYY effect has ethical and legal ramifications; for example, is the anomaly a defense in murder because there may be a physical substrate, i.e., disease? There is no direct link to antisocial behavior, although some evidence may be forthcoming in the next decade. Jarvik, Klodin, and Matsuyama (1973) consider the genetic effect to be of interest as a tool for theory development: "The XYY genotype may be seen as highlighting the association between maleness and violence." The present authors, still a bit embarrassed by their words on genetic damage and LSD in the first edition of this book (Ullmann and Krasner, 1969), are inclined to be conservative; they also think that with increased equality of treatment, women are likely to increase in male virtues such as violence, crime, ulcers, and suicide.

---

[2] Polani (1969) and Price (1969) review other chromosomal abnormalities, the most notable being Klinefelter's syndrome (47, XXY), which occurs in .2 percent of live births and is associated with shyness, childishness, lack of drive, small testicles, little facial hair, and some intellectual impairment.

Brain Function and Sociopathy

The only current evidence that might support a belief in the constitutional nature of psychopathy is the finding that some psychopaths have abnormal EEG's. This finding, however, has been equivocal. Many sociopaths have normal EEG's, and it is not clear that the percentage of abnormal EEG's among sociopaths is any greater than among other groups such as psychotics or neurotics.

Two key concepts are exemplified in this argument. The first is that of the baserate of the sign, in this case the abnormal EEG. Ostrow and Ostrow (1946) collected the EEG's of 440 convicts. From these, they designated as their psychopathic group 69 men who were very impulsive, unable to accept social limitations, and had severe difficulties in empathy. Of this group, 50 percent had abnormal EEG's. Among comparison groups, Ostrow and Ostrow report that 56 percent of homosexuals, 98 percent of epileptics, 80 percent of schizophrenics, and 65 percent of conscientious objectors had abnormal EEG's. The second problem is the effect of baserate when a finding is applied to the entire population. This has been discussed as the problem of false positives and false negatives. It may be stated that not all psychopaths have abnormal EEG's nor do all law-abiding citizens have normal EEG's. Since there are far more people in the latter group than the former, the number of misdiagnoses indicates that abnormal EEG's are certainly not a sufficient cause for antisocial behavior and probably not even a necessary one.

Robins' summary statement reflects the opinion of the present authors (and Loomis, Bohnert, and Huncke, 1967): "Despite numerous electroencephalographic (EEG) studies indicating varying but high rates of abnormality in adult criminals, there is no proof that brain damage or abnormality as reflected in the EEG is a necessary precondition for the development of antisocial reaction." (1967, pp. 955–56.) Hare (1970, p. 36) finds the best current hypothesis in the field to be a possible "lowered state of cortical excitability and the attenuation of sensory input, particularly input that would ordinarily have disturbing consequences." This latter view focuses research on the nature of stimuli and away from physique *per se*.

Family Relations of the Sociopath

Early investigators such as Partridge (1928), Knight (1933), and Haller (1942) all considered rejection, usually by mothers, as a causative factor in the development of psychopathy. Another group of investigators (Szurek, 1942; Linder, 1944; Greenacre, 1945; Bowlby, 1952) also emphasized rejection, but by the father. In one of the more comprehensive studies of criminal behavior, McCord, McCord, and Zola (1959) found a strong link between the emergence of psychopathic behavior and emotional deprivation as indicated by parental conflict, cruelty, erratic punishment, and neglect.

Bender (1947) concluded that all psychopathic children have experienced emotional deprivation and neglect, particularly in the first three years of life. Bender's formulation is that the child who has little opportunity to learn socially desirable behavior from adult models and who does not experience the adult as a socially reinforcing object is likely to display subsequently nonsocial or antisocial behavior. Bowlby et al. (1956) investigated cases of early deprivation and concluded that children who are isolated at a very young age are unable to relate to others in adult situations. Most reports of "feral children" raised in isolation (Davis, 1940) or in deprived institutional atmospheres (Freud and Burlingham, 1944) propose a definite relationship between isolation and lack of response to human beings.

McCord and McCord (1964) come to the conclusion that there are three causal patterns in the development of psychopathy. The first is severe rejection itself. The second is mild rejection combined with damage to the brain (possibly the hypothalamus). The third is mild rejection, even in the absence of neural disorder, if the environment fails to provide behaviors alternative to psychopathic ones. While this type of work is persuasive, one must note that, as with the EEG, there is a baserate of deprivation among normals and that research from studies meeting minimal standards of comparison have been uniformly disappointing (Frank, 1965).

Role-Taking and Sociopathy

Gough (1948) presented a view of psychopathy based upon role-taking theory. He defined a deficiency in role-playing as the incapacity to look upon oneself as an object or to identify with another's point of view. The psychopath presumably cannot foretell the consequences of his behavior because he is unable to look at his own behavior from another's point of view. The social emotions of embarrassment, loyalty, or gregariousness are not experienced by the psychopath. Being deficient in the ability to take the role of others, he is surprised and resentful when others disapprove of his behavior. The psychopath is unable to form deep attachments because he cannot identify with other people.

The Sociopath and Conditionability

Eysenck (1957) presents a theory of the origin of sociopathic behavior which is based upon learning theory. He postulates two inherent and basic variables: introversion–extraversion and neuroticism. The individual who is high on extraversion and low on neuroticism (anxiety) would condition slowly, and would build up reactive inhibition quickly and dissipate it slowly. Eysenck relates socialization to the ability to be conditioned, from which it would follow that the sociopath, unable to be conditioned properly, would be less likely to become socialized. Eysenck also has a category of secondary psychopath which represents a combination of high neuroticism (anxiety) and high extraversion.

Another source of experimental evidence on the responsivity of sociopaths comes from verbal conditioning studies. If sociopaths have a learning deficit, then it is reasonable to assume that they should react less strongly to the kinds of stimuli that evoke emotional reactions in others. Johns and Quay (1962, p. 217) express this point: "The psychopath can thus be said to be one who knows the words but not the music." Yet the experimental evidence in the verbal conditioning studies is contradictory as to the responsiveness of sociopaths to social reinforcement (Johns and Quay, 1962; Quay and Hunt, 1965; Persons and Persons, 1965; Bernard and Eisenman, 1967). It is clear from these studies that it cannot be said that the sociopath can or cannot be conditioned. Rather, conditionability of the sociopath, as with any other group of individuals, is a function of the many variables present in conditioning studies. (See Weiss, Krasner, and Ullmann, 1960, for a study illustrating how situational variables in a conditioning study may be manipulated.)

Stimulation-Seeking and the Sociopath

An important conceptualization of the nature of psychopathic personality is the stimulation-seeking theory advanced by Quay (1965), which in many ways complements both Eysenck's theory and the social learning viewpoint to be presented below. Quay observes that the impulsivity of the sociopath can be interpreted as the "lack of even minimal tolerance for sameness. . . . The basic hypothesis is that psychopathic behavior represents an extreme of stimulation-seeking behavior and that the psychopath's primary abnormality lies in the realm of basal reactivity and/or adaptation to sensory inputs of all types." (1965, p. 180.)

Quay argues that if the psychopath has a lessened basal reactivity or an increased rate of adaptation, then he must frequently find himself in a condition of stimulus deprivation. This state of affairs is highly unpleasant, and the psychopath seeks new stimulation. In a highly organized and restrictive society this stimulation often involves breaking some kind of legal or moral code.

Strong support for Quay's theory was provided by Skrzypek (1967). Skrzypek selected 33 "psychopathic" and 33 "neurotic" delinquents by use of ratings of overt behaviors made on a checklist (Quay, 1964; Peterson, 1961). The groups did not differ as to age, IQ, length of stay in the institution at which the study was made, or number of school grades completed. The flavor of the concept of primary ("true") and secondary ("neurotic") psychopathy may be gained by contrasting the following two sets of behaviors. The unsocialized or psychopathic delinquents were high on the following characteristics: restless, attention-seeking, disruptive, boisterous, short attention span, inattentive to what others say, fighting, temper tantrums, lazy on assigned tasks, irresponsible, undependable, disobedient, uncooperative, distractible, negativistice, impertinent, profane, and irritable. The disturbed, neurotic, or anxious delinquents were characterized, on the other hand, by higher ratings on the following characteristics: doesn't know how to have fun, self-conscious, feelings of inferiority, preoccupied, shy, socially withdrawn, lacks self-confidence, easily flustered, generally fearful, daydreaming, tense, depressed, lethargic, and easily startled. After a period of perceptual isolation, "psychopathic" delinquents increased their preference for novel stimuli, while "anxious" delinquents increased in self-rated anxiety and decreased in preference of complex figures. In Skrzypek's work, on pre-test measures of (self-rated) anxiety, the "psychopathic" delinquents were very significantly lower than the "neurotic" delinquents; high self-rated anxiety was very highly related to low novelty preference (−.84), low "psychopathic" behavior rating (−.86), and high "neurotic" behavior rating (.83).

A SOCIOPSYCHOLOGICAL FORMULATION OF ANTISOCIAL (PSYCHOPATHIC) BEHAVIOR

The behavior to be conceptualized in the sociopsychological formulation is that of a person who shows poor social judgment, who frequently breaks rules and promises, who seems unaffected by stimuli that control the behavior of most other people in his society. Specifically, other people do not seem to act as acquired reinforcers for him.[3] In this sense, there is no real distinction between the psychopath and the schizophrenic; both are not under the control of typical social stimuli. Both emit behavior that disturbs other people, in part, because it is so unexpected. The similarity between the psychopath and schizophrenic has been pointed out by a number of authors, most notably Cleckley (1964), who emphasized the semantic dementia of the psychopath; that is, his words or promises are meaningless. Cleckley terms the apparent nonpsychotic behavior of the psychopath as merely "the mask of sanity" which hides the true psychotic nature of the disorder.

The poor judgment of the psychopath, however, takes the form of antisocial, impulsive behavior. Such behavior seems short-sighted, childish, and self-defeating. An important point, as relevant to the psychopath as to the schizophrenic, is that in the vast majority of his behaviors the persons appears normal, i.e., acts in an expected, undisturbing manner. Perhaps the easiest way to illustrate this is to let the reader note that a person cannot "break

[3] McCord and McCord (1964) describe the "warped capacity for love" on the part of the psychopath. "Either because he is incapable of forming them, or because his experience has not shown him how to form them, the psychopath wards off close attachments." (p. 16.)

a promise" unless someone trusts him, and cannot be a forger, embezzler, or cash checks without sufficient funds without having been trusted.

A typical pattern of behavior for the psychopath is to hold a job, to do well, and, after the novelty and challenge have gone, to emit a disturbing behavior such as telling off the boss, not reporting for work, or embezzling. The act is perceived as impulsive; to cite a common quip, the lid is off the id. The person acts in a manner that many other people have at times wished to but refrained from for fear of the easily foreseen consequences. It is this behavior of failing to evaluate consequences that leads some experts to say that psychopathy involves a deficit of "anxiety."

From the general sociopsychological formulation (Chapters 2 and 10) it follows that the psychopath has either been insufficiently trained in the crucial steps in the procedure of emitting a social response or else has been trained in a manner different from that typical in the core culture. Several kinds of observations on psychopathy seem to offer leads in this direction. One group of observations would point to the view that the "wrong" things were reinforced.

Buss (1966) argues that two kinds of parental models foster the development of psychopathy. First is the parent who is cold and distant to the child. Buss argues that the child imitates the parent and becomes cold and distant in his own relationships. He learns the formal attributes of social situations without ever becoming involved with them. The second parental model comprises inconsistencies of rewards and punishments which make it difficult for the child to learn a definite role model, with the result that a consistent self-concept does not develop. The parents reward both "superficial conformity" and "underhanded nonconformity." Because the parent behaves arbitrarily and inconsistently, punishment is the result, but it is unpredictable. Therefore, the child learns how to avoid blame and punishment rather than how to differentiate right from wrong. A frequently observed behavior is that of a child either lying to avoid punishment or making superficial responses such as, "I'm sorry and I won't do it again." The child has then been rewarded for escaping punishment without feeling guilt.

Maher (1966) offers a variation of this theory. He points out that the sociopath is not behaving as a result of any defect at all but rather as the end result of "a particular set of learning experiences which happen to equip him poorly for adult responsibility." In effect one may hypothesize that the child must learn to emit the responses called "being lovable." If he emits these "lovable" or "ingratiating" responses, he is likely to avoid unpleasant consequences and later increase positive responses. The psychopath may (Maher, 1966) be a person who has been reinforced for emitting such acts at the wrong time; that is, when they help him avoid the consequences of his acts. Therefore, he has learned to apologize but not to avoid that for which he must apologize. Hare (1970, p. 109) presents evidence for a direct modeling hypothesis: ". . . it appears that one of the best predictors of adult psychopathy is having a father who was himself psychopathic, alcoholic, or antisocial" and who may himself show poor impulse control.

Observations such as those of Buss and Maher are particularly helpful in conceptualizing the psychopathic behavior of middle-class children.

The present authors would go a step further in arguing that the psychopath frequently finds himself in a situation in which his behavior is treated as if it were *inconsequential*. The effects of his behavior are unpredictable for him, and hence he has difficulty learning about himself. Where such training in eliciting feedback is provided—in making amends, in being charming—the person later to be called psychopathic learns very well indeed.

A related point is that if what he does is considered inconsequential, then there may be no reason for him to attend to certain social stimuli. In this sense the psychopath may have found himself frequently in a situation similar to that of the schizophrenic, for whom there also may have been no "payoff" for attending to certain socially defined stimuli.

Given this formulation, there is a different schedule of reinforcement for the psychopath. The unexpected behavior that wrecks success may be related to the lack of adequate feedback of behavior to the individual. The psychopath appears stimulus-deprived (Quay, 1965) because he has been (and is) deprived of major sources of stimuli. What would be adequate to shape most people in the society is not sufficient to maintain conforming behavior. The result is extinction rather than reinforcement. As noted in Chapter 15, "impulsiveness" is behavior that an observer (usually middle-class) does not consider situation-appropriate. The person acts impulsively because the amount of effective reinforcing stimuli is insufficient to maintain his current behavior. That is, the job others consider "good" is "not good enough," and the consequences of losing it then are trivial.

A different set of circumstances may also lead to similar behavior. Case histories of people later called psychopaths who came from broken and/or extreme lower-class homes frequently indicate that they had been recipients of very severe physical punishment. The child had learned, quite rationally, that people are anything but positive reinforcers. Staying away from others and avoiding trouble would thus be very reasonable behavior. It is also likely that inconsistency, that is, punishment based on the adults' shifting moods rather than on the child's objective behavior, is involved. The result is twofold. First, the child's behavior is inconsequential; it seems that no matter what he does, if he interacts with people he will be punished. In this regard extreme punishment and extreme indulgence have similar eventual consequences. Second, whereas the inconsistent *overindulged* pattern leads to reinforcement of escape through apology and ingratiation, the inconsistent *brutally punished* pattern leads to avoidance by physical distance. Again the behavioral results are identical: when one's own behavior fails to serve as a meaningful stimulus for others, the consequences for the person are much the same whether the others have been seemingly too kind or too mean.

Other people do not become effective secondary reinforcing stimuli for this individual. This is important because the vast majority of actions by others that are typically reinforcing are acquired or secondary reinforcing stimuli. The person called a psychopath is, if anything, more skilled than average in emitting behavior that will influence others to act in a manner that is explicitly reinforcing. He is able to sell himself to others, and the payment they make by not punishing him or by giving him a good job is indeed reinforcing. Other people, then, seem to serve as secondary reinforcing stimuli. The distinction here is between the seducer and the genuine lover.

The psychopath may indeed sell himself well and apparently be influenced (i.e., reinforced in the sense that his behavior is altered) by the extrinsic reinforcement of the other person's compliance. In fact, he may be even more effective as salesman or seducer than the average person because he is not paying attention to the other person's welfare: he is less likely to avoid lying to the other person and to worry about the ultimate aversive consequences for the other person.

In a heterosexual interpersonal relationship the psychopath can display a great deal of energy and enthusiasm at the beginning of a relationship just as he does at the start of a job or when "turning over a new leaf." However, curiosity ("Can't I do it?"

"What will it be like?") is soon satisfied. Where other people mature in their relationships in terms of the development of the other person's happiness as a reinforcing stimulus, the psychopath soon is satiated: there is a surplus of the reinforcing stimulus, there is nothing new. Not unlike the Madison Avenue stereotype, the psychopath asks, "What have you done for me recently?" He (or she, for women have been known to act in this manner) then breaks the relationship, usually by transferring his attention and favors to another. The psychopath is surprised when the other person is disturbed or hurt. He frequently expresses puzzlement that the other person is so immature, weak, or dependent as to be depressed: it was fun, it's over now, why is she bugging me and trying to make me feel bad?

It is in this regard that Quay's formulation of the psychopath as a stimulus-seeker fits with the sociopsychological formulation: the psychopath does indeed act as if rapidly satiated or as if new stimuli are continually required to maintain desired levels of behavior. This is not necessarily physiological in etiology, and it may be hypothesized that a host of stimuli based on his own and others' behavior are simply not effective for the psychopath. To the psychopath relationships are only skin-deep, love is a frenzy, and the object of work is to attain a status, not any intrinsic accomplishment and satisfaction. There is indeed deprivation of experience and an emphasis on sensory newness, turmoil, and large muscle activity. The psychopath experiences these; he does not experience the subtler, less direct, but more humanizing long-term aspects of the interpersonal environment. The pattern of behavior may in the long run lead not only to overt stimulus seeking, but (as noted in Chapter 16 on the physiological effects of role-playing, and in Chapter 18 on the effects of institutionalization) to differences in perceptual and somatic input and processing.

If this formulation is correct, then treatment should involve making the person's behavior *meaningful*. This indication indeed seems the common thread in the reports of effective treatment of the psychopath. Case reports by people with philosophies as divergent as Aichorn (1935), Makarenko (1936), Maxwell Jones (1953), and Cohen and Filipczak (1971) illustrate this.

The present formulation (and the majority of writing in this field) has so far overlooked the "neurotic" delinquent (the second group described in Skrzypek's 1967 work). The people in this group commit violations of the social and legal code which are similar to those of the "primary" or "true" psychopathic person just described. It is possible to hypothesize that they may be reacting to situations in a manner similar to that of some people variously labeled hysteric, schizophrenic, and, particularly, obsessive. That is, the core difficulty may well have been failure in training in the emission of the socially expected and desirable act. The socially disruptive behavior may be a response which is immediately reinforced either by short-term gain or as an escape or avoidance of a situation. The formulation of compulsive behavior may be appropriate here (see Chapter 14), and treatment should focus more on the development of appropriate operant behavior than on the sources of appropriate reinforcing stimuli (as with the "true psychopathic" group).

In summary, there is probably no entity called antisocial personality into which an individual can be fitted. It is only possible to describe the behaviors that are disturbing to a society and that therefore lead to labels. Whereas most individuals have experienced in their early environment a set of circumstances which have led to the development of their own and other people's behavior as secondary reinforcers, there are some individuals whose early environment militated against the full development of this source of meaningful stimuli.

DYSSOCIAL ACTIONS

The dyssocial category is a label used for individuals with no obvious pathology other than trouble with a specific set of rules. These people may be excellent fathers and husbands with deep loyalty to their families, friends, and "organizations." (See, for example, Jones, 1967, pp. 30–33.) Their behavior is not sick, it is *illegal*. The reader may wish to consider how his behavior would be viewed by Shaw's *Jack-roller* in Chapter 10.

The legal definition of criminal behavior may change from age to age: trading in alcohol in 1923 was a crime; in 1933 it was not. For example, Martin and Fitzpatrick (1964, p. 26) note that, "In the United States in 1931, three-fourths of all inmates of Federal and State prisons had been sentenced for committing acts that fifteen years earlier would not have been considered crimes." There are rules of the game or social norms at any given time in history. Sociologists classify norms into four major types—folkways, mores, customary law, and enacted law. *Folkways* are social rules enhanced by informal social controls such as gossip, ridicule, or ostracism. *Mores* are rules whose violation calls for strong moral indignation. *Customary law* involves those norms enforced by the community as a whole or by the community's formally chosen representatives. *Enacted law* designates the rules or norms that are formally instituted by a king or a legislative body. In the United States, the enacted law comprises the state and federal constitutional provisions. Customary law consists of maxims, principles, and customs of long usage developed in England over the course of centuries and then transplanted to America. These legal rules, known as the common law in the Anglo-Saxon legal system, are enforced by the courts in spite of the fact that they have not been decreed by a governmental body. Despite the growth of enacted law, the common law continues to provide norms backed by the power of the state for the control of social behavior (Sykes, 1956).

In Chapter 10 we noted the choices the police had when dealing with disruptive behavior associated with "mental disorder." The same holds for delinquents (Piliavin and Briar, 1964; Piliavin and Wertham, 1967). We must do the same, in far greater detail, in the area of dyssocial behavior. There must be an act that is illegal, opportunity to engage in it, observation of the act, and a judicial and an enforcement system. To be more explicit:

To illustrate the process of labeling an individual as a delinquent, let us examine the hypothetical case of a teen-age boy involved in a street fight between two groups of adolescents. When he has been picked up by a policeman and his name recorded, three decisions have already been made: first, he has committed an offense; second, the offense warranted intervention; and third, it was necessary to record his name. A further series of decisions, which may be called administrative, follow. The process of recording the event requires that a name be given to the delinquent act. The names from which the choice is made come from a list of actions the community has previously specified as violations of the law. Such a list includes a wide variety of actions, from ball playing on the streets to homicide, but in our example the boy might be charged with assault, disorderly conduct, fighting, or curfew violation. When a name has been chosen for the offense, the policeman fills out a card with the juvenile's name, age, offense, and other identifying data. He must then decide whether he should release the juvenile or cite him to Juvenile Court. If he cites him to Juvenile Court, the court must make still more decisions. First, there must be an investigation, which determines whether a petition will be filed, making the case an "official" one, or whether it will be handled as an "unofficial" case. Next there are all the steps leading to a decision as to whether the boy will be held in custody, made a ward of the court, placed on probation, or released. [Eisner, 1969, P. 14].

Studies of delinquency and crime must therefore take into account the various acts and actors involved, (such as gangs and police) as well as laws and offenses themselves. The judicial system, for example, needs to be studied, for as Jones (1967, p. 9) notes, "The courts are the gateway to the penal system." The label of delinquency or criminal behavior partakes of secondary deviance; it has consequences far beyond the first act or primary deviant behavior. Aside from differential treatment (as in job-seeking) and increased risk of harsher punishment for further acts, one outcome of the judicial system may be imprisonment. In the institution, a new set of behaviors is learned, just as in psychiatric hospitals. Much criminal behavior may be iatrogenic, that is, a result of the treatment. Notable in this regard is training in the values, acts, and opportunities of the subculture of the prison population. Studies on the effects of institutional incarceration (prisonization) include: Clemmer (1968), Hazelrig (1968), Johnston, Savitz, and Wolfgang (1962), and Sykes (1969).

The sociopsychological formulation of behavior labeled dyssocial is the same as that applied to any normal behavior. Membership in Students for a Democratic Society or the Ku Klux Klan, patterns of earning money, or ways of relating to authority are all learned. Such behavior is proper or improper depending on the view of the observer, and is maintained and altered by reinforcing contingencies. If the person is not extinguished for the "deviant" social mode and given opportunity to emit and be reinforced for socially appropriate behavior, he will continue in his mode of adjustment. It is not a matter of "knowing" what is "good" but of how "good" is defined. There are supports for antiauthoritarian behavior in the deviant group: the wrongness (the label leading to avoidance) is nullified and social support is given for the anti-middle class act. Dyssocial behavior, then, is a prime example of the present sociopsychological formulation. If dyssocial behavior is sick, then any learned behavior may be called sick.

JUVENILE DELINQUENCY

The incidence of delinquency is difficult to estimate because the definition depends on legal procedures, and most states differ as to what constitutes a juvenile offender. Also, not all offenders are treated in a similar manner. There are social class differences in the detection of and disposition of the juvenile. Differential police coverage, decisions to make a case official, and legal counsel affect the statistics. A key behavior in identifying delinquency is being caught. A series of investigators (Porterfield, 1946; Murphy, Shirley, and Witmer, 1946; Miller, 1962; Reiss and Rhodes, 1961; Nye, Short, and Olsen, 1958; Akers, 1964; Gibson, 1967; Crane, 1958) have found strong evidence of hidden delinquency: for example, college students may admit to having committed acts during their high school years that, if discovered *at the time,* would have resulted in their having been classified as delinquent. Hidden delinquency is of major theoretical and policy importance because, with "white-collar crime" (crime committed in government, business, and professional settings by persons acting in their occupational roles), [Sutherland, 1949; Geis, 1968], it indicates that law-breaking is neither a lower-class, economic-deprivation behavior nor solely the result of unsocialized, uneducated, "impulsive" people.

It is important to note that there are various types of crime; for example, Martin and Fitzpatrick (1964) distinguish between white-collar crime, organized crime, and traditional crime such as assault, theft, rape, and so forth, while Ferdinand (1966) and Clinard and Quinney (1967) relate types of crime to social-class styles and opportunities. The important matter is that we think of acts in terms of responses to situations rather than lump all acts into a single category called crime or delinquency. If we do not make such distinctions, the very heterogeneity of the acts (as well as differences in family relationship, intellectual achievement, etc.) classified as equal leads to oversimplifications; and such, unfortunately, seems to be the current status of the field, despite efforts to the contrary (Stein, Sarbin, and Kulik, 1971).

The theories in the field range on a continuum from the sociological-epidemiological to the intraindividual psychodynamics which seem almost totally isolated from the cultural milieu within which acts take place (Cavan 1964; Giallombardo, 1966). Martin and Fitzpatrick (1964) divide theories into those that emphasize social defects, those that emphasize defects in the immediate operating milieu, those that are family-centered, and those that are individual-centered. It seems to us that data from the former types of theories are necessary before material gathered in the framework of the latter are meaningful.

A first major approach, then, is epidemiological: what are the correlates that increase the likelihood of a person being labeled delinquent? Being male, from an unstable home, of lower socioeconomic status, residing in an area marked by low owner-occupancy and overcrowding, and being 16 to 17 years of age are the features that seem most predictive of a person's attaining delinquent status. The label of delinquent is not necessarily related to severity of law-breaking: it may be given when the person's name is recorded by authorities for preventive measures ("to understand, help, and protect the child") or for acts that would not be criminal for an adult (e.g., curfew violation). Eisner (1969) found that while nationally only 4 percent of all children between 10 and 17 years of age are stopped by the police in a year, the rate for black, male, 17-year-olds (his highest "risk" group) was 57.5 percent, half of which resulted in juvenile court cases. It is interesting that one parent in the home was more highly associated with juvenile court appearance rates than either two parents or no parent in the home. In one geographical area of San Francisco, Eisner found the delinquency rate (interactions where at least name was taken) to be 74.4 percent for 17-year-old black males, and in another 71.1 percent, while one census area had no recorded delinquency, that is, 0.0 percent.

Within this context, delinquency as defined by Eisner is statistically normal in certain census tracts and not in others. Different values, different opportunities to gain satisfactions in a manner defined as legitimate by the larger society, and conflicts between different generations and ethnic groups may all enter into the statistics. Finally, the delinquent act may be supported by peers, either as models or for the personal status gained from the act, beyond the monetary values gained. This leads to theories emphasizing "defects" in the immediate milieu, as, for example, the easier access to buyers of stolen goods in some neighborhoods in contrast to others. The important point is that the situation is not one devoid of standards, but one of a social system different from, yet influenced by (as a reaction to), the larger dominant social group. In Martin and Fitzpatrick's words, "It is both motivated and goal-directed activity which is explicable *not* as deviation from the norms of the established adult world (as represented by parents, church, and school), but as conformity to the prevailing social standards of the particular peer groups which the adolescent uses as his chief reference groups. . . ." (p. 88.)

When dealing at a family level of theory, it is possible to point out many potential conditions for later delinquent behavior. For example, parents may have difficulties of their own such as anxiety, addiction, unemployment; they may be irresponsible either in their own lives or by exploiting their children for personal social motives—by using the child against the spouse or to act out vicariously against the school; parents may be unstable, nonsupporting, or display a pattern of immediate unrestrained gratification; parents may be hostile to the children in such a manner that unsocialized behavior is a reasonable, self-protective response. The catalog of potential parental misbehaviors is long and far from exhausted here.

There are many illustrations of the argument that delinquent behavior is reinforced and maintained within family and peer groups. Shaw and McKay (1942) report that most delinquents come from homes in which parents and siblings were delinquent. Glueck and Glueck (1950) report that 84 percent of the delinquents in Massachusetts reformatories came from homes in which there were criminals.

However, the complexities of the home environment for the delinquent go beyond the mere presence and encouragement of criminal behavior. It has frequently been reported that a majority of institutionalized delinquents come from broken homes. It is not the broken home per se that causes difficulty for the youth, but the fact that broken homes result in many more adult figures coming into his life. It may be argued that the presence of many parental figures in the home increases the likelihood of noninterest or rejection by some, if not all, of them, which leads, in turn, to inconsistency of reinforcement and a lack of the necessary consistent model of socialized behavior.

A good illustration of the relation between the availability of role models and subsequent delinquent behavior is given by McCord and McCord (1958). A five-year observation of 253 boys and their families from a lower-class urban area in the Cambridge–Somerville vicinity of Massachusetts was followed up by a study 20 years later of those who became delinquent. The environmental combination that was most likely to lead to delinquent behavior was the presence of a criminal role model in the father and the absence of maternal warmth. On the other hand, consistent discipline and love from at least one parent to a large extent counteracted the father's criminal role model. It may be argued that rejection is likely to reduce reinforcement of prosocial behaviors, and the presence of the criminal role model gives the *information* as to one alternative form of behavior, namely crime.

Further evidence along this line comes from studies by Bandura and Walters (1959) of 26 aggressive delinquent boys. These authors found a pattern of father rejection plus inconsistent handling by both parents. The fathers frequently used physically punitive methods of discipline. Thus there was a combination of rejection, hostility, and a lack of clear socially approved guidelines as to what kind of behavior would receive parental reinforcement.

This pattern of father rejection of the delinquent was also found by Andry (1960). Various kinds of sociopathic behavior in the fathers of delinquent boys, such as alcoholism, brutality, nonsupport, and frequent absence from home have been reported repeatedly (Glueck and Glueck, 1962).

Of major importance in the development of delinquent behavior are opportunity, peer models, and immediate reinforcement for delinquent behavior. This is exemplified by the role of gangs in fostering delinquent behavior. Vedder (1963) describes three different types of gang activities. One he calls "criminal," where the activities of the gang are directed toward illegal ways of obtaining money. A second represents "conflict," in which violence is used to gain status. A third is "retreatist," in which drugs and promiscuous sex are stressed. An additional category with high delinquency potential is the large, amorphous group of youths, frequently school dropouts, who spend their time in a loose-knit streetcorner, drive-in, or bowling alley society. The evidence seems to indicate that most gangs are not delinquent. It is clear that the gangs supply the kinds of social approval, peer reinforcement, status, meaning, and value system that are not obtained from the home, school, or other typical socially approved organizations. The gang becomes the principal agent of socialization for many teenagers. The acts reinforced are not necessarily the ones considered desirable by the dominant adult middle-class culture.

If the development of delinquent and/or criminal behavior is viewed in social reinforcement and modeling terms, then what is the data concerning the role of the parents or other adults in the delinquent's early life in the family? Peterson and Becker summarize the many studies on family interaction and delinquency by stressing the difference in child rearing resulting from differences in social-class value emphasis. It is the middle class that defines laws and designates behaviors to be classified as delinquent. "Emphasis on toughness, worldly smartness, and independence from authority is sometimes coupled with a de-emphasis of achievement, consideration for others, and self-control among members of the lower class. In terms of behavior theory, this means that models for behavior of the kind that are 'tough,' 'smart' and so on are plentifully available, and social reinforcement for such behavior is frequent, immediate and strong." (1965, p. 92.) Further, peer groups as well as parents may reinforce the kind of behavior likely to eventuate in a label of delinquency.

Despite the many significant social class variables, the fact remains that many lower-class children do not behave in a manner leading to the label "delinquent" and many middle-class children do.

As has been described, some investigations place etiological significance on the father's behavior (Bandura and Walters, 1959); others place more on that of the mother (McCord, McCord, and Zola, 1959). Peterson and Becker conclude, "The development of stable behavior tendencies depends on the intensity and consistency with which emotionally effective rewards and punishments are administered. Excessively harsh treatment, especially if unaccompanied by generally affectionate acceptance, ordinarily arouses resentment, and this reduces the effectiveness of discipline. Excessive leniency is tantamount to neglect. The regulatory emotional expectancies are never established." (1965, p. 94.) Thus the general picture in delinquent families is of parents whose discipline is either severe or lax or, most likely, an inconsistent alternation between the two.

The argument is often presented that delinquent behavior is an expression of a youth's frustration with his poor living conditions, poor economic situation, or poor family relationships. In effect, it has become a socially accepted myth that such frustration tends to lead to and even justify aggression. However, recent studies (see remarks on aggression in Chapter 23) indicate that aggressive behavior is likely to occur as a function of reinforcement of such aggression.

Treatment of Delinquency

An illustration of treatment of delinquent behavior is the program in effect at Camp Butner, North Carolina, as described by Burchard (1967). Burchard conceptualized antisocial behavior as behavior which is "acquired, maintained and modified by the same principles as other learned behavior." Therefore, he argued that an individual "can learn constructive, socially acceptable behavior by being placed in an environment where the behavioral consequences are programmed according to the principles of operant conditioning. Instead of administering an excess of reinforcement or punishment on an indiscriminate, non-contingent basis, behavior should be punished or reinforced systematically on a response-contingent basis. This has been the objective of the Intensive Training Program." The result was an experimental residential program of behavior modification for mildly retarded delinquent adolescents.

Burchard utilized techniques based on the principles of "reinforcement, punishment, and programmed instruction." It was a standardized program, involving mostly nonprofessional people, and developed to teach the delinquent individuals the practical skills essential for adjusting adequately to the community and for eliminating or markedly reducing forms of antisocial behavior. As in other operant programs, the procedures involved the definition of the behaviors to be reinforced, selection of an effective reinforcer, and programming the reinforcement contingencies. The two criteria for the selection of the behaviors to be reinforced were, first, behaviors that produce a physical and identifiable change in the environment that can be reliably observed and reinforced, and, second, behaviors which provide the individual with a behavioral repertoire that will lead to reinforcement in a community environment. Behaviors selected were those involved in maintaining a job, staying in school, budgeting money, buying and caring for clothes, buying food and meals, and cooperating with peers and adults.

Within this context Burchard completed a series of specific illustrative experiments. He selected a specific behavior such as sitting at a desk during workshop and school time. The design of the experiment was based on "an A-B-A type of analysis": reinforcement was contingent on the response during the first phase, noncontingent during the second phase, and then contingent again during the third phase. Each phase lasted five consecutive days. The resident received five tokens for accumulating time while sitting at his desk and also for doing specific schools tasks. In the second five days he received an equivalent number of tokens, but noncontingently. In the third five-day period the contingent reinforcement was resumed. There was an immediate decline in performance during the noncontingent phase and a reinstatement of performance under reinforcement during the third phase.

Another illustration of applications of behavioral principles to modifying the behavior of juvenile delinquents is Project CASE (Contingencies Applicable for Special Education) at the National Training School for Boys (Cohen et al., 1966). The target behavior shaped was academic work in the form of programmed instruction. If the student completed a unit of the program with a score of at least 90 percent, he was eligible to take an examination on which he could earn reinforcement in the form of points each worth one cent. These points could be used to buy Cokes, potato chips, Sears Roebuck items, or entrance into a lounge where his friends were; to register for a new program; to rent books; or to get time in the library or a private "office" with a telephone. The only way the student could obtain points was by emitting the desired behavior, namely studying.

The study by Cohen et al. also illustrated that the systematic contingent application of reinforcement was most effective when it took place within an environment programmed so that the likelihood of desirable behavior was enhanced and undesirable behavior decreased. Thus the investigators built a special environment, including classrooms, study booths, control rooms, library, store and lounge. Cohen et al. also used the principle of gradually incorporating newer and more relevant payoffs. The students gradually switched from working for Cokes to working for the more educationally relevant behavior of library time or new programs.

The results on the 16 students in the project indicated that the program was successful in generating desirable educational activities. There were also other favorable changes in behavior. In four and one half months there were *no* discipline problems, and the boys did not in any way destroy or deface the facilities. The social behavior of the delinquent boys matched that of nondelinquents. Similar work and results have been reported by Clements and McKee (1968), Boren and Coleman (1970b), Fineman (1968), Tyler and Brown (1967, 1968), Colman and Baker (1969), Bednar et al. (1970), Karacki and Levinson (1970), Lawson et al. (1971), Jesness and DeRisi (1973), and Mann and Moss (1973).

Achievement Place is a community-based family-style rehabilitation program for delinquent boys run in a token-economy fashion. Reports make use of reversals of reinforcement contingencies to demonstrate the impact of manipulations on target behavior and fading to indicate methods for reducing overt contingencies while maintaining gains made during training. These procedures stimulate generalization of results to principles and vice versa. Among the target behaviors so studied are the strength of home-based reinforcement for school work, and target behaviors such as aggressiveness (or physical disruptiveness) (Bostow and Bailey, 1969; Horton, 1970; Vukelich and Hake, 1971; Kaufman and O'Leary, 1972; Webster and Azrin, 1973), cleanliness, punctuality, and grammatical speech (Phillips et al., 1971, 1973; Bailey, Wolf, and Phillips, 1970; Phillips, 1968).

Among the most interesting reports from Achievement Place are ones that touch on topics which will be discussed in chapters 28 and 29 of this volume. One topic is peers as therapists: In this instance (Bailey et al., 1971) the peers used modelling, social reinforcement, contingent points, and feeding to correct emission of sounds such as "th" and "ing." Fixsen, Phillips, and Wolf (1973) report on self-government and the discussion of rules and their enforcement with trials. Aside from the general success of the venture, the response contingency aspects are noteworthy; for example, when points were earned for calling trials, trials increased and more trivial violations were reported.

Another approach toward the modification of delinquent behavior is that developed by the Schwitzgebel brothers and their co-workers (Schwitzgebel, 1960, 1961, 1963, 1964, 1967; Schwitzgebel and Kolb, 1964; Schwitzgebel, Schwitzgebel, Pahnke, and Hurd, 1964) based on the earlier work of Slack (1960). This group of investigators developed a pioneering approach to the delinquent involving a functional analysis of behavior. The adolescents working within the project had been labeled delinquents by a court. The laboratory for the project was set up in a large storefront on a streetcorner in a respectable business district, and the project received the name of "Street Corner Research." The experimental group comprised 30 males employed by the project for six months or longer. Of these people 25 had appeared in courts and 20 had spent six months or more in correctional institutions. At the time of the project they averaged 18 years of age and had an average of $9\frac{1}{2}$ years of education. A control group was formed by matching each member of the experimental group with a male offender chosen from police records.

The techniques used with the experimental group of delinquents involved a four step sequence:

1. Defining in measurable units the final, desired behavior as specifically as possible.
2. Determining the available reinforcers that were most likely to be effective.
3. Determining the subject's repertoire of present and previous behavior.
4. Applying the reinforcers according to an explicit theoretical model and modifying application according to results (feedback).

The initial goal of the project was to get the adolescent into the laboratory. The experimenters accomplished this by going into the community and offering to hire people with delinquent records as subjects in a study of delinquency. Subjects were paid for their participation, which initially involved talking to a tape recorder about their experiences as a delinquent. For those who initially did not report to the laboratory, gradual shaping procedures were used in which the subjects were given cigarettes or food as over a period of time they came closer to the laboratory. They received different sums of money depending on how close they approximated the agreed-upon time of arrival at the laboratory. A number of interviewers gradually built up a close relationship with the subjects. The interviews included philosophic discussions, moral guidance, or "psychoanalysis." The boys were paid for specific jobs in the laboratory, such as soldering. Then gradually jobs were obtained outside the laboratory in the community.

A follow-up study of the first 20 subjects in this program (Schwitzgebel, 1964) three years after termination of employment in the program showed that the number of arrests and months of incarceration of the employees was about half that of a matched control group. Within the overall program Schwitzgebel (1967) reports the results of seven controlled studies which demonstrate the points previously made about the effects of reinforcement contingent on the behavior of delinquents.

Schwitzgebel matched two groups of his delinquent employees and treated them differentially during the course of 20 tape-recorded interviews on four classes of operants: hostile statements, positive statements, prompt arrival at work, and general employability. Hostile statements were followed by mild aversive consequences (inattention and mild verbal disagreement) while the other target operants were followed by a positive consequence (verbal praise or a small gift such as cigarettes, candy, or cash). The results in both a laboratory and a natural setting (restaurant) indicated that there was a significant increase in the frequency of the three target behaviors that were followed by positive consequences. The hostile statements, however, which were followed by "punishment," did not significantly decrease.

Procedures of direct training in effective social skills (Roos, 1968) have been extended in the area of juvenile delinquency, in a manner similar to work with other target behaviors, to include the use of peer models (Sarason, 1968; Stumphauzer, 1972) and the family and home members (Stuart, 1971; Patterson, Cobb, and Ray, 1973). Not only are these methods more readily taught, more hopeful, and more effective than procedures stemming from a medical model or "sick" personality framework, they suggest methods for training in schools and homes that may reduce the number and severity of different problem behaviors. They remove blame from the "victim" and give methods and responsibilities to teachers, parents, and rehabilitation personnel.

Prevention of Delinquency

The goal of preventive measures is to develop such skills that people will be able to negotiate the social system in a manner that is satisfactory to both themselves and to others. In developing a technology to accomplish this goal, it is probably most efficient in the long run to work with individual cases, classrooms, and wards, rather than promulgate system-wide policies. Further, these first steps help train the people who will instruct others so that policy change can be successfully implemented.

Wahler and Erickson (1969) and Tharp and Wetzel (1969) offer examples of the training of members of the community to provide behavior modification guidance to their fellows. This model was applied by MacDonald, Gallimore, and MacDonald (1970), using a local parent as the mediator, who worked with students on the target behavior of attendance. For 20 students on the contingency contracting scheme, attendance reached 90 percent while the 15 students seen by a contact counselor using the method in which she was experienced averaged 65 percent attendance, which was similar to their starting rate.

Long and Williams (1973) investigated various reinforcing stimuli and contingencies with inner-city junior high school students and noted the effectiveness of free time (rather than feedback by tokens) as a reinforcer. Clark, Lachowicz, and Wolf (1968) hired school dropouts and paid them for workbook items successfully completed, while Staats et al. (1967) used nonprofessionals providing extrinsic reinforcement to improve reading skills. Wasik et al. (1969), Hart and Risley (1968), and Reynolds and

Risely (1968) provide case histories of behavior modification with culturally deprived childrens' speech and classroom behavior.

Examples of "larger" problems dealt with in a sociopsychological model may be cited briefly. Hauserman, Walen, and Behling (1973) reinforced sitting with a new friend in the cafeteria and noted significant generalization to integration of students during the play period. Miller and Miller (1970) increased the number of welfare recipients attending self-help meetings from an average of 3 to 15 by reinforcement procedures and noted that participation in other activities was related to such attendance. Jones and Azrin (1973), noting the "word-of-mouth" nature of much hiring, effectively used an information-reward system to have community members report otherwise unpublicized job openings. The information-reward system led to ten times as many job leads and eight times as many placements as a no-reward advertisement. Additional material of this nature will be presented in Chapters 28 and 29.

SUMMARY

This chapter discussed antisocial personality, dyssocial behavior, and people whose behavior comes into conflict with the rules of the dominant social group.

Historically the psychopathic label has been applied to people who act in a socially disturbing way. Further, these behaviors are usually not characteristic patterns of other psychiatric categories, nor is there evidence of brain injury or retardation.

The behaviors of the antisocial person were described, and various explanatory theories were presented. There are individuals whose history of reinforcement decreased the effectiveness of other people's behavior as secondary reinforcers.

In addition, culturally approved behavior must be learned and maintained by ongoing reinforcement. A formulation of juvenile delinquency and illustrations of behavioral interventions were presented. The procedures point to methods for prevention as well as treatment.

placing limits on personal behavior

OTHER CHANGEWORTHY BEHAVIORS

27

Pornography and obscenity, smoking, gambling, suicide, and "existential" problems are examples of behaviors which are not directly included in DSM-II but which are treated in the literature and in clinical practice, and are considered changeworthy by large numbers of people. The selection of the specific topics is idiosyncratic, but, in combination, they illustrate social concerns that are currently within the province of "mental healers."

These behaviors are redefined to be consistent with the approaches of the professions to which they are usually assigned. There are community (suicide), legal (pornography), private enterprise (gambling), and philosophical and religious (existential problems) models. The interplay of social structure, political concern, legal maneuver, economic background, and personality theory is seen in one form or another with each of these topics. Beyond this interplay, the topics illustrate the use of concepts of abnormality to supplement written law for behaviors that disturb someone so that attempts to change or limit activities can be initiated. These behaviors all raise the broad value question of the point at which a social organization may intervene in the acts of its members.

In this chapter, we start with the social regulation of stimuli which the individual may well encounter in his environment. As a useful illustration of material that is the object of both a legal and a medical model, there is the question of pornography and obscenity. We then move on to existential problems.

The third major category is suicide. Does a person have a right to decide the termination of his own life and the fate of his body or not? The "not" is the almost universal reverence for human life; does the saving of life justify interference? If we say yes, then why not interfere with other forms of self-destruction, such as drinking alcohol, smoking, overeating, or gambling against overwhelming odds? And if we can interfere for the sake of life, might we not as well dictate style of life or the conditions under which life is to be started and to be lived? These questions would lead us back to the issues involved in existential problems and, eventually, lead us to the issues of obscenity. Hence, the chapter is intended as question-raising social criticism. In this respect, all the study of abnormal behavior can be considered social commentary.

PORNOGRAPHY AND OBSCENITY

If we think of our concerns in terms of social control, a number of questions are raised: Is an act harmful to the individual or to others? If it is harmful to others, what limits are to be imposed in defining and limiting the act? And how, in general, does the act harm?

These questions are raised by pornography—here defined as representation through word or picture of sexual acts. The current Supreme Court position is that it is constitutional for states and localities to ban any work which, taken as a whole, appeals to the prurient interest in sex, or which portrays sexual conduct in a patently offensive way, and which, taken as a whole, does not have serious literary, artistic, political, or scientific value. There are three tests: appeal to prurient interest; offensiveness; and artistic, scientific, literary, political merit. This last is a change from a prior standard, that of the production being utterly without redeeming social merit. Another major change, not stressed in previous court decisions, was that of the use of community standards as criteria.

Offensiveness eventually refers to standards of conduct accepted in a specific community; however, community standards change, and it is possible that two communities in the same state have different standards; a state court is then faced with conflicting standards within its domain. Further, what constitutes the geographic limits of "community" is not clear. In cities like New York and Honolulu, the "adult" movie houses cluster in specific downtown areas and by their existence reflect the standards of that square block of the community.

The question as to how standards may be determined was discussed in Chapter 21 in regard to treatment of sexual behavior. One might note the differences between religious, educational, economic, racial, political, ethnic, age, and sex categories. Further, is an acceptable community standard what people say is the best way to act, the way they behave in public or in private, or the way they will permit others to act even though they may disapprove?

Social merit, whatever the needed percentage of the total production, is difficult to define because at any point of time, activities that do not conform may be considered without social merit. A psychoanalyst might consider it a service to the community to protect it from the present volume, which certainly has no artistic, literary, or political merit.

But our interest is most attuned to *prurient interest,* which is appealed to by pornography. "Prurient," according to the Random House Dictionary, refers to lustful or lascivious thoughts or desires. There is an implication that such thoughts are restlessly craving, like an itch that may not be scratched. On the one hand, this is the Judeo-Christian belief that one should not covet or sin even in thought; while on the other, it is psychoanalytic: that added stimulation may weaken defenses against a proscribed (repressed) act.

Poteete (1970, p. 59), introducing an article by Kant and Goldstein (1970), quotes from a 1917 book, "One-half the youths in our prisons and houses of correction started on their evil careers by reading bad books. . . . These books are the nicotine and alcohol of literature; they poison and burn . . . the head and heart as surely as their cousins do the stomach."

A similar approach to the evil of books is evidenced in the report of the burning of "obscene" books (e.g., Kurt Vonnegut's *Slaughterhouse Five*) in a South Dakota town in 1973 because of the presence of a number of "bad" words. The local school board ordered that the lockers of the high school students be searched to be sure that all copies of the books were found and destroyed.

One question, then, is, Who uses pornography and with what effects? Kant and Goldstein (1970) matched sex offenders, users of pornography, and "normals." They found that "the normal adults in our sample reported more experience with pornography as teenagers than any deviant group we studied and, as adults, they continue to see more erotica than sex offenders do. . . . The child molesters had seen less pornography of every kind than our normal group did. Only 62 percent of these sex offenders who prefer immature partners had seen representations of heterosexual intercourse, while 85 percent of the control group had encountered this kind of pornography as teenagers." (Kant and Goldstein, p. 59.) That pornography is related to sexual crime is debatable from the above data on the one hand, and from the experience of countries that have liberalized their laws. The fact that sex crimes decreased in Denmark after such liberalization, however, is but very partial evidence since such liberalization was in the context of other legal changes.

The Commission on Obscenity and Pornography found that patrons of adult bookstores and movies may be characterized as preponderantly white, middle-class, middle-aged, married males. Roughly four-fifths of adult males and females have been exposed to pornographic stimuli during their teens as part of the general exchange of sex information that ordinarily occurs among adolescent peers. Such exchange is social rather than necessarily sexual, and is consistent with exposure to pornographic stimuli being, if anything, more frequent among the "normal" than the people who are socially isolated, who avoid sexual topics, and who more frequently later have sexual difficulties.

When observing sexual stimuli, roughly four-fifths of both males and females do show mild arousal responses. The effect may be an increase in the person's preponderant method of sexual satisfaction; for example, people whose usual method of gratification is heterosexual intercourse may increase their rate of heterosexual intercourse, while those without partners are likely to increase frequency of masturbation during the 24 hours following exposure to pornography. When compared with a group that did not observe pornographic stimuli, during the following weeks, there was no significant difference in innovation or other rare sexual patterns in a group that frequently observed such stimuli. A control group is crucial because during a period of weeks and months, some adults, with or without benefit of pornographic stimuli, will engage in activities that are novel for them.

Thus, while there may be arousal from observing sexual stimuli, it is of the persons' typical mode of adjustment, and, secondly, what is arousing is limited in large measure to that pattern. This may well be why Kinsey believed that women were less responsive to pornographic stimuli; the effect may not have been in women but in stimuli which in that era were devised for men and hence not relevant to women. Stoller (1970) makes the same point in terms of the erotica of transvestites—it is boring to those who do not share the preference.

In short, from what research exists, the effects of pornographic stimuli appear to be trivial and thus point to a limitation of the effects of modeling. It is clear that with humans, in most situations, it is not a matter of "monkey see, monkey do." A number of points need to be kept in mind; the first is that pornographic stimuli usually deal with terminal behaviors and do not illustrate the *social* acts necessary prior to the terminal ones. Second, if the modeling stimuli, as any material on a hierarchy, are too strong or rapid, the effect is one of turning away. Third, pornographic material may satiate as its novelty is reduced (e.g., Sherr, 1971). Finally, there are consistencies, both in the stimuli and in the context in which they are observed, which make unusual behaviors unlikely; for example, sexuality is rarely portrayed unless the audience is pre-selected.

Cursing and Wall-Writing

Time magazine of May 21, 1973 (p. 103) reported that the Georgia Supreme Court upheld a rule against the use of obscene, vulgar, or profane language in the presence of a person under 14 years of age. Laws against use of certain words in public have been upheld in Utah (*Time*, September 28, 1970, p. 63) but not Maryland (*Time*, May 16, 1969, p. 72), where, in the seventeenth century, punishment included a hole bored through the tongue.

But people do use strong language (Sagarin, 1962; Montagu, 1967). From the *Chicago Daily News*, May 13, 1969: "Dr. Paul Cameron of Wayne State U. hid tape recorders here and there to discover how much cursing Detroiters do. Some of his more printable findings: Two of the 20 most-used words in Detroit are unprintable.

The fifth most popular word in Detroit during nonwork hours is 'damn.' ... Secretaries cuss less than 1 percent of the time, but poolplayers cuss 30 percent of the time." (p. 13.)

And from Iversen (1965) we learn:

Indeed, Yankee oaths were so numerous and pungent that General George Washington was obliged to issue a personal communique on the subject in 1779:

"Many and pointed orders have been issued against that unmeaning and abominable custom of swearing, notwithstanding which, with much regret, the General observes that it prevails, if possible, more than ever. ... For the sake, therefore, of religion, decency, and order, the General hopes and trusts that the officers of every rank will use their influence and authority to check a vice which is as unprofitable as it is wicked and shameful." [p. 163.]

"According to the earwitness account of General Charles Scott, however, Washington swore one day at Monmouth, "... until the leaves shook on the trees ... on that day, he swore like an angel from heaven." (pp. 163–64.)

A psychoanalytically oriented formulation of "dirty words" is offered by Hartogs (1968): "... all forms of obscenity have one thing in common: they are a mask of fear. They camouflage a reality too unbearable without the release obtained through the therapeutic four-letter word. Obscenity flings contempt at whatever enslaves us. It covers up our doubt and insecurity and 'solves' our problems through symbolic aggression." (pp. 18–19.) "One of the main functions of obscenity in American life is to serve as an outlet for the intolerable tension created within the personality by the opposing cultural polarities of Puritan conformity and the freewheeling search for the self." (p. 24.)

But cursing, even though "strong" language, is still language. We may therefore attempt an analysis along verbal operant conditioning lines which would include modeling. Of greatest interest would be the reinforcement for the act of saying the word. One source of reinforcement is the effect of cursing on others: it may make them take our words more seriously as the "strong" language serves to underline our thoughts. As role-expressive behavior, it may also serve to define the speaker. This may be as a virile, unafraid person whose language is an indication of defiance; or as an angry person ready to disavow inhibitions or conformities in order to have his way; or as a person who uses the language, as slang is at times used, to determine whether the listener will understand (an indication of the listener's social group or likely further reaction) or be shocked. In this latter case swearing is used to probe another person. A different set of reinforcers arise due to timing: if I drop my chalk during a lecture, I say "damn" (or at least think it). My discomfiture is short-lived, and what happens immediately after the word, in terms of timing and *not* cause and effect, is a release. The situation is really not that bad. Swearing may be superstitious behavior. And if the class laughs, it is likely to reinforce swearing temporarily rather than chalk-dropping.

Wall-writing may be a grab for immortality, a form of self-advertisement, a method of communicating to an audience that cannot answer, a political act (both for the message and the defiance involved in the writing itself), or, as some psychoanalysts would have it, a symptom of anal fixation revealed in the pleasure of smearing and dirtying. It is an act that is generally frowned upon: although grafitti is commonly observed, few people have observed a toilet-writer in action or will admit to such an act (Mockbridge, 1969, p. 11, 38, 69–70). Rhyne and Ullmann (1972) chose the men's room at the student union of a Middle Western university to determine the effect of a notice that had not been scrawled on, versus one that had, in attracting wall-writing behavior. In this study, the model of a person having written, did not affect the rate of people adding their messages. The study did provide a base rate for wall-writing by that population and locale: the rate was one in twenty people.

GAMBLING

Gambling might as easily have been included under the obsessive-compulsive behaviors or addictions. Along with smoking, it illustrates a behavior which, if taken to an extreme, may become a hazard to the person's social adjustment and may cause both him and his significant others grave concern. Gambling and smoking are self-inflicted harms and thus may be placed with suicide and self-injurious behavior. The reason for discussing gambling at this point is that at present in the United States it is legally regulated behavior and is the object of self-help, coordinated by such groups as Gamblers Anonymous (Bycel, 1971), and professional intervention (Goorney, 1968; Seager, 1970; Cotler, 1971).

Various theories have been offered for the development of gambling behavior. Among psychoanalytic explanations are orality, denial of the reality principle (and hence omnipotence), slow suicide, and vent of aggression. Associated with the latter: "Freud related gambling to the gambler's real fear of castration—and accounted for the addiction as a repetition of the compulsion to masturbate." (Adler and Goleman, 1969, pg. 733.) Other theories include concepts of masochism and a desire for increased stimulation. Adler and Goleman (1969) consider gambling and alcoholism to be functional equivalents and offer the weak evidence that across 117 cultures, the two were significantly *not* associated with each other; that is, if gambling is prevalent, there will be little drinking and vice versa.

The basic defining behavior for gambling is risking something valuable on an event of uncertain outcome determined, at least in part, by chance. Among the behaviors that lead to the designation of changeworthy gambling is that the topic consumes an inordinate amount of the person's time, he invests and loses more than he can afford, he does not seem to learn from experience, and he is less likely to stop when losing than when ahead. Bolen and Boyd (1968) make this latter feature a crucial one in their formulation: the unconscious motivation is related to losing, while the "normal" gambler is interested in diversion, relaxation, and winning, and hence will stop to limit his losses.

Various efforts have been made to relate gambling to psychopathic deviate (antisocial personality) since both groups seem unrealistically impulsive and fail to learn from experience, but the results have not been encouraging (Snortum, 1968). Such efforts also face the problem of the behavior being described being the result rather than the cause of the gambling.

A different approach is to provide different types of tasks experimentally to determine whether certain schedules of reinforcement or other conditions lead to different rates of gambling or strategies of choice (e.g., Rachlin and Frankel, 1969). Among the most advanced of these studies is one by Levitz (1971), who experimentally manipulated winning or losing money on a gambling task and (false) "information" about how well the person was doing relative to other people on the task. After the induction of these six experimental conditions (win-lose crossed with doing better, equal, or worse than others), the people were allowed to bet or not on 51 succeeding trials in which the odds were steadily against them. Early winning and having received the information that they had done better than others both led to significantly more choices to gamble. These people also reported greater confidence in their selections and thought of the outcomes as more related to skill than chance. A final interesting finding was that speed of making choices when gambling was the best predictor of later persistence in the second phase of the study. While a limited analogue, this study indicated that prior conditions may be fruitfully investigated for impact on rate of later choices of an "irrational," risky nature.

SMOKING CIGARETTES

Smoking has been found by the surgeon general to be injurious to one's health, and the consumer is so warned on the package and in magazine advertisements. The use of television is denied to cigarette manufacturers while politicians may request equal time. Smokers are segregated and seated to the rear of airplanes (where it is likely to be bumpier). Even confirmed smokers, such as the senior author, will agree that the smoke itself is not particularly pleasant and the habit is expensive and dirty. The first question, then, is What are the conditions that lead to and maintain smoking activity?

To the extent that smoking is irrational (an addiction, compulsion, or other bad name) and self-destructive, the Freudians hypothesize an underlying cause, most frequently oral (although the production of wastes growing from a butt that are placed in a receptacle has distinctly anal connotations, and cigars and extra-long cigarettes that may be waved around have exhibitionistic, phallic connotations). Tomkins (1966) brings the oral concept together with a quasi-Pavlovian model and writes: "Sucking or smoking, therefore, is innately capable of reducing the negative affect of distress and of evoking the positive affect of enjoyment." (p. 18.) Nesbitt (1973) documented physiological arousal as an effect of nicotine and found that people obtaining nicotine through smoking were less emotional than when smoking nonnicotine cigarettes. A major effort at discovering personality variables associated with smoking (Coan, 1973) reported that smokers tended to be more extraverted, more distress prone, more liberal, more open to experience, and more inclined to favor spontaneity than nonsmokers.

This work is also notable for endeavoring to separate out a pattern of adjustive smoking associated with pleasure, tension-relief, and positive relationship to the environment from a maladjustive pattern associated with tension, ingrained habit, and seemingly addictive behavior.

Given the widespread nature of smoking behavior, the health hazard, and the easy quantification of the target behavior, there has been a great deal of effort at reducing smoking. As of this writing, the results have been disappointing (Keutzer, Lichtenstein, and Mees, 1968; Bernstein, 1969, 1970; Hunt and Matarazzo, 1973) and, in general, have not been significantly better, especially on follow-up, than placebo procedures which involved a decision to cease combined with another person's monitoring of that commitment. In addition, the general population of smokers may no more be sampled by these experiments than is the general population of homosexuals by those who seek professional help. Finally, there are problems of dropout from treatment, which in some studies run as high as 80 percent.

Among the behavioral treatments that have been tried with cigarette smoking are aversive and cognitive procedures (Steffy, Meichenbaum, and Best, 1970); aversive procedures (Ober, 1968; Whitman, 1972; Chapman, Smith, and Layton, 1971); stimulus saturation (Marrone, Merksamer, and Salzberg, 1970; Resnick, 1968); graduated reduction (Levinson et al., 1971); role playing (Mann and Janis, 1968; Platt, Krassen, and Mausner, 1969; Mausner and Platt, 1971); deposit contracts (Winett, 1971); and various combination (Best and Steffy, 1971; Sachs, Bean, and Morrow, 1970; Keutzer, 1968; Wagner and Bragg, 1972).

The present authors' prejudice favors a method of self-monitoring, self-control through response cost for smoking and reward for not, and planned alternative acts to replace lighting up (e.g., McFall, 1970;

Roberts, 1969; Nolan, 1968; Upper and Meredith, 1970), but compelling data are not available to make such a plan anything but a preference (Young, 1973). The problem seems to be in the great number of situations in which the confirmed smoker lights up, in the relatively delayed and small cost of the habit, and, possibly, in the immediate positive benefits, whether physiological or social (doing something, emiting a role-expressive behavior).

EXISTENTIAL PROBLEMS: A BEHAVIORAL APPROACH

In Chapter 12, existential problems were touched on in relation to encounter-sensitivity methods. The present material has, as its first purpose, an illustration of the behavioral approach to supposedly complex behavior (Ullmann, 1973). Second, many professional and educated people talk as if existential problems exist. It is interesting to discuss a category which is of recent origin and not recognized in either DSM-I or DSM-II.

As with other labels of human activity, the behavioral approach starts with an insistence on defining the topic. More specifically, under what conditions will the label "existential problem" be used by clients and therapists? When therapists are asked this question, the usual answer starts with the words, "The client says that . . ." The behavior presented to the therapist by the client is likely to be self-labeling. The client makes a generalization about himself: he is alienated, disillusioned, bored by it all, or confused and uncertain about life, death, and who he is. Such labeling is a learned act and is subject to the concepts of social learning. Secondary behaviors are mild depression, apparent absence of classic diagnostic patterns (e.g. psychosis), failure to live up to what is socially defined as full capacity, and failure to be treated successfully by traditional (psychoanalytic) methods.

The most complete and formal description of existential neurosis within a nonbehavioral model is by Maddi (1967), who discusses a set of symptoms, a stress, and a premorbid personality, the latter two leading to the first. In terms of symptoms, Maddi writes:

The cognitive component of the existential neurosis is meaningless, or chronic inability to believe in the truth, importance, usefulness, or interest value of any of the things one is engaged in or can imagine doing. The most characteristic features of affective tone are blandness and boredom, punctuated by periods of depression which become less frequent as the disorder is prolonged. As to the realm of action, activity level may be low to moderate, but more important than amount of activity is the introspective and objectivity observable fact that activities are not chosen. There is little selectivity, it being immaterial to the person what if any activities he pursues. [p. 313.]

"The symptoms of the neurosis," Maddi writes, "all point to a rather comprehensive psychological death, where there is no longer even anguish or anger to remind the person that he is a person." The premorbid personality is characterised by fragmentation and concretism and a self-identity (labeling?) as no more than a player of social roles and an embodiment of biological needs. The precipitating stresses are ones that disconfirm this identity (or make it ineffective), such as imminent death and gross disruption of the social order. Maddi includes a long description of an ideal personality, which he says has theoretical import, although it "is usually a null class" (p. 312), and which may be attained by proper child rearing. Although totally lacking in empirical documentation or operational definitions, and utilizing a medical analogue (e.g., disorder), Maddi's article is recommended as one of the clearest statements of the existential position by a person who identifies with that view.

The sociopsychological model indicates that the act (or role) must be available, must be recognized by others, and must be responded to in a manner that will maintain it. The point is that whether one is working at a theoretical or therapeutic level, one should not accept the statement, "Existential problems are." Rather, one must ask, "Existential problems are *what?*"

The orientation towards operational definitions has an effect of specifying therapeutic strategy. The behaviorist additionally asks questions such as what is maintaining the target behavior and what alternative acts by the person would contradict the label. But above all, the behaviorist does not stop with the presentation of the label. If, for example, a student said that he had trouble studying, the therapist would start work by provisionally saying the person had a studying problem. He would then seek for conditions which would develop and maintain successful studying behavior. If, on the other hand, a student says that he does not find studying to be *worthwhile,* one might say the person has an existential problem and deal with "worthwhileness" as a philosophical entity. The behaviorist in the same situation would consider the person as having a studying problem, and one that was, at least as a start, partially defined. The task would be to find reinforcing stimuli that the student might apply effectively.

Aside from practical therapy tactics, the approach used has implications for the therapist and his values as much as for the client. The therapist may legitimize a set of acts for the subject. With the so-called existential problems more than with most other difficulties in living, the therapist acts as a gatekeeper. Aside from such considerations as time and money, the role of being in therapy has consequences for the client. There are times when the most "therapeutic" thing a psychologist can do is to reject the applicant for therapy.

As noted above, the person presents himself (or complains) as follows: "nothing grabs me"; "nothing turns me on"; "I don't know what I want to do"; "I don't know who I am"; "I don't feel real"; "I'm not living"; "I want to be genuine"; "I want to feel close"; "I feel alienated." We may ask ourselves, To what conditions would verbalizations of this type be a reasonable response? A set of conditions leading to the verbalization of "existential problems" may show, under closer scrutiny, that the difficulties are not in any sense existential. In these cases, the "existential" verbalizations are the result of a lack of skill, knowledge, or the like. A person may say that he does not know what to do with his life and he may mean what he says. *There are a group of problems that are vocational selection problems.* A young adult in our society, especially if he is of a social class that aims for a job requiring a long period of preparation, makes a choice that is almost as important as that of a mate. He may know his future spouse more intimately than he does any field of work. The therapy question becomes one of how to decide whether the problem is vocational rather than existential. As in many other cases, a good starting point is to ask under what circumstances would the person not have the problem, that is, what should change. If the answer is choice of a job, vocational counseling and samples of work such as may be found in Krumboltz and Thoresen (1969, pp. 293–96) is particularly useful. The consequent career goal may make studies "relevant."

A person may feel aimless, helpless, or even alienated when he does not do well at his desired work. While the person may have general capacities such as those measured by intelligence tests that indicate he should do the work with ease and even pleasure, he may not achieve in a manner commensurate with his ability. A lack of skills may lead to an avoidance of the situations in which he is incompetent. After a series of unpleasant experiences, the person may become anxious at the thought of the situations, that is, in anticipation of aversive consequences. The paradigm for phobias is appropriate in this instance: the person must have capacity, must practice (i.e., for exams, must study), and, if the case calls for it, be desensitized for the situation. In the present context, the existential statements may be accurate reports of the consequences of having a studying problem. In addition, *the existential verbalizations may be a way of negating the importance of the failure*. The existential verbalizations are maintained because they help the person avoid, escape, or minimize an unpleasant situation.

There are a number of generalizations that follow from these observations. The therapist seeks for specific activities and may well deal with existential verbalizations by providing necessary information or skills. Again, the question arises as to how to decide what to do. In one sense, the therapist must be able to ascertain what "normal" adjustment is for a person of a particular age, sex, and social class. In addition to typical procedures for ascertaining deficits in activities, needed skills, and inappropriate avoidance of situations, interviews may be devoted to determining whether the person has a satisfactory vocational plan, a good relationship with members of both the same and the opposite sex, and, while remaining out of trouble with the law, some pleasurable avocational activities. By such interviewing, a target behavior may be found that indicates that the problem is not what is typically considered existential. An example would be a feeling of "loneliness" that was associated with a lack of friends. Rather than dealing with "feelings of isolation" as inherent in the nature of man, the therapist's task may be to reduce behaviors that are aversive to others or avoidance of interpersonal situations while increasing the person's social skills. Many problems of alienation may be realistic behavioral difficulties in making and keeping friends. *As the problem becomes more clearly specified, its "existential" nature diminishes.* (for case examples, see Nawas 1971; Ullmann, 1972, and Wanderer, 1972) When the behavioral therapist is successful under these conditions—and he very frequently is—existential therapists may claim he did not treat "real" existential problems.

There are a number of people who emit existential verbalizations who meet the criteria for minimal normal adjustment and possession of requisite skills. There is one group of such people whose behavior clearly should not be changed by therapists. These are people, usually college students or recent graduates, for whom the existential verbalization is role-expressive. Existential complaints may be as appropriate as other fashionable roles. The person is adjusting well and his complaints provide the aura of being an intellectual, serious, or creative person. The verbalizations may serve as adequate reasons for pleasurable interludes such as sensitivity groups and conversations with the opposite sex. The "existential problem" is a useful activity, and if such verbalizations are skillfully used to attain social success, they seem as appropriate as bowling, dancing, or holding one's liquor. The key diagnostic question centers on the consequences of the verbalizations. If the function is social and there are no major areas of interpersonal or vocational deficit, it would seem to be a disservice to alter the verbalization.

There is a group of people who do not seem to have major deficits in social or intellectual skills but who fail to a considerable degree to live up to their potential or the opportunities available to them. Very frequently this group seems to be part of the contemporary college student population, although the vague, irksome dissatisfaction may be found frequently in people in the symbol manipulation professions. Here the complaints are of life not being what it should be or not being sufficiently satisfying despite external indications of success. While other people would indeed be grateful to possess their type of work and rewards, these individuals say that daily living is an increasing and, at times, insurmountable effort.

At first sight, there is a paradox: although the external reinforcers seem plentiful and strong enough for most people, they are inadequate for these people. Two formulations fit the conditions leading to the observed behavior. The first is satiation: in the circumstance of a surplus of a reinforcing stimulus, the reinforcer no longer functions as such. In this regard, existential problems are a correlate of an affluent society. Since what one wants is synonymous with what one finds reinforcing, the diagnostic investigation may well start with "What do you want?" Generalizations such as "good, warm, genuine relations" may lead to specifics so that the problem can be formulated within the models cited above. But if no specific change in acts, relations, or outcomes can be obtained, the investigation may well start with a search for a reinforcing stimulus, and more specifically a way of countering satiation. On occasion a deprivation may have to be self-induced. The person may delay providing himself with a reinforcing event until he has performed an act that he currently finds less rewarding. The Premack principle may be helpful in locating reinforcing stimuli: acts that are frequently emitted are made contingent on the behavior that is not as frequently emitted as desirable. The extreme to which one may have to go is illustrated by a student who was requested to drink coffee and not permit himself to urinate until certain segments of his assignment had been completed.[1]

Associated with the problem of satiation is one of expectation. Many people seem to take a passive role in their own lives in a manner experienced with LSD and television.[2] There seems to be a notion that there is something that will "grab them" and "turn them on" and that it is the therapists' duty to find it for them. It is conceivable that parents and high school teachers have fostered this role as an acceptable one, and the result is a learned helplessness similar to that outlined by Seligman (1973, especially p. 46). In addition, many students have been on a very high ratio of reinforcement. The college situation, as distinct from the high school, introduces achievement through independence rather than through conformity. The length of time between effort and payoff increases abruptly when one enters college: exams are fewer and prompts are not given with the frequency found in high school. Another way of saying this is that the typical college is impersonal: fewer people stand over the student and fewer teachers care if he succeeds or fails. Skills in consistent studying and self-reinforcement are

---

[1] In the first quarter of the seventeenth century, Burton (1927 ed., pp. 212–13) described the elements of satiation and need for activity as well as the picture of many people presenting existential problems: "This much I dare boldly say, he or she that is idle, be they of what condition they will, never so rich, so well allied, fortunate, happy, let them have all things in abundance, and felicity, that heart can wish and desire, all contentment; so long as he or she or they are idle, they shall never be pleased, never well in body and mind, but weary still, sickly still, vexed still, loathing still, weeping, sighing, grieving, suspecting, offended with the world, with every object, wishing themselves gone or dead, or else carried away with some foolish fantasy or other. . . . When you shall hear and see so many discontented persons in all places where you come, some many several grievances, unnecessary complaints, fear, suspicions, the best means to redress is to set them awork, so to busy their minds; for the truth is, they are idle. Well they may build castles in the air for a time, and soothe up themselves with phantastical and pleasant humours, but in the end they will prove as bitter as gall, they shall be still I say discontent, suspicious, fearful, jealous, sad, fretting, and vexing of themselves; so long as they be idle, it is impossible to please them. . . . An idle person, (as he follows it) knows not when he is well, what he would have, or whither he would go. He is tired out with everything, displeased with all, weary of his life: neither well at home nor abroad, he wanders, and lives beside himself."

[2] Space permits us only to refer the reader to efforts such as those by Tart (1972) and Ornstein (1973) to place altered states of consciousness within a more general intellectual purview.

presumed. Finally, greater investment of effort must be made before the material, which does increase in difficulty, is reinforcing in its own right.

It seems reasonable to say that colleges might test students' study skills and help them in this regard if they have not learned how to learn. The problem for the therapist working with a particular individual, however, is to find ways to help him bridge the early periods of learning before the material has become meaningful and intrinsically interesting. Again, the burden of treatment shifts to overt targets by this formulation. Further, training in self-control and self-reinforcement may have an effect on the more general strategy of learned helplessness.

While related to the passive role that permits criticism without active effort, a second set of conditions (in addition to satiation) may make for a reduction in the rate of reinforcement for ongoing activities. This is a matter of overly high expectations of either others or oneself (Bandura 1969, p. 37). When standards are unrealistically high, the chance of satisfaction is reduced, and a person may experience a mild depression (see Chapter 13). In Pindar's words:

> *She was in love with what was not there;*
> *it has happened to many.*
> *There is a mortal breed most full of futility.*
> *In contempt of what is at hand, they strain*
> *into the future, hunting impossibilities*
> *on the wings of ineffectual hopes.*
> [3rd Pythian ode, Lattimore, ed., 1947, p. 52.]

While the behavior therapist cannot provide ultimate answers to the client's value questions, he can aid in the search for such answers. He can break the search procedure into small, comprehensible, and encompassable steps, and he can act as a source of feedback for actions taken. The therapist may be a model or prompt; he may fade himself out and serve as a reinforcer of client-initiated acts (Ullmann, 1969c). The object is to teach the person ways to help himself and to ensure through proper programming that progress is made and is satisfying. In more typical existential language, the goal is to teach the client that his own being is defined by his efforts at becoming.

SUICIDE

The estimated rate of deaths by suicide in the United States is usually given as 11 per 100,000 per year. With a population of approximately 200,000,000 this means 22,000 suicides a year. Suicide is more frequent than homicide (Stengel, 1964, p. 49). For every "successful" suicide there are eight attempts which fail.

Other data indicate that half of all suicides are under 45 years of age; a disproportionately high rate of divorced people commit suicide; professional people such as physicians and lawyers have the highest incidence among occupations,[3] although all vocations are represented; women make more unsuccessful attempts than men, but kill themselves at a lower rate than men (e.g., Shneidman, Farberow, and Litman, 1968, p. 205); most suicides come from urban areas; suicide is likely to increase with increasing age, especially among men; suicide is considerably more frequent in some countries (e.g., Hungary, West Germany) than others (e.g., Ireland); is increased in likelihood by heavy use of alcohol, coming from a broken home, having a "mental" disorder or physical illness; and is lessened in likelihood among blacks and religiously devout people. While only a minority of people leave notes, a majority, estimated at up to 80 percent (e.g., Rude-

---

[3] Four of the 52 deceased artists in a Metropolitan Museum of Art exhibit on American Painting in the twentieth century had, according to their biographies (Geldzahler, 1965), committed suicide, and one other artist had died in a one-car auto accident which might have been suicidal; much in the way of intellectual stimulation, untestable hypotheses, and professional publication may be drawn from such data.

stam, 1971), have given warnings of suicidal thoughts.[4]

Most suicide-risk scales make use of data of this nature. Which person of a group whose members are suicidal is most likely to kill himself is a different question, requiring data from a population different from the general one. Having a plan, having the means, and having made a prior attempt (Eisenthal, Farberow, and Shneidman, 1966; Tuckman, Youngman, and Kreizman, 1968) are usually indications of increased risk. Attempts to develop such scales (Tuckman and Youngman, 1968; Devries, 1968; Lester, 1970; and Miskimins and Wilson, 1969) remain in their early stages.

Research Problems

Shneidman and Farberow (1957a) point out that the word "suicide" is used indiscriminately to cover a number of different categories of behavior, making any single clear definition very difficult. Calling an individual "suicidal" may mean that he has committed or attempted or threatened suicide, or that he is depressed and may have ideas of suicide, or that he is generally behaving in a self-destructive way. There are also conflicting descriptions of characteristics of suicidal behavior. The "causes" of suicide are usually determined after the act and are therefore assumptions. For example, if an elderly person commits suicide, usually the cause is attributed to health or financial conditions, whereas in a younger individual the same behavior may be attributed to interpersonal or intrapersonal conflicts.

Categories of Suicide

One type of definition of suicide involves a *post hoc* (after the fact) determination; that is, the individual is labeled as "suicidal" *after* he has committed suicide. It is sometimes difficult, however, to determine whether the individual actually killed himself. To be termed a suicide in the medical-legal sense the individual must have played a major role in bringing about his own death and there must have been an *intention* to die.

There are *empirical* definitions which label an individual as "suicidal" if he has certain sets of symptoms or behaviors or a "personality" that has been found to have preceded suicidal behavior in others. Thus one may be called suicidal if he behaves the way some people who committed suicide behaved prior to the act.

The psychiatric definition relates suicide to certain symptoms, primarily those of depression. Guze and Robins (1970) estimated that the likelihood of death by suicide is 30 times greater for people who have had "primary affective disorders" (of psychotic magnitude) than for the general population. The trouble is that although some of the many depressed people attempt or commit suicide, many suicides are not linked to depression. Further, the most dangerous time for suicide is not at the height of depression but rather at the time the individual is recovering from his depression.

Theories of Suicide

Among the many theoretical approaches to suicide (See Lester and Lester, 1971, especially pages 116–26) two major ones are by Durkheim, a French sociologist, and by Freud. Durkheim theorized that suicide

---

[4] Any statement may be challenged because of the relative rarity of the suicidal act in the general population (i.e., one per ten thousand per year) and the complexity of variables of age, sex, religion, social class, race, etc. which must be taken into account. As such, Lester (1970b, 1971) has challenged the social disorganization relationship to suicide and shown how different sampling may lead to a positive, negative, or random relationship between suicide and homicide. It also seems to stretch the data, from a small and (almost by definition) unusual sample of people, to generalize about cultures on the basis of suicides, and, perhaps to a lesser extent, about suicide on the basis of differences in cultures in which suicides are but a very small minority (Hippler, 1969; Krauss, and Krauss, 1968; Krauss and Tesser, 1971).

could be understood in terms of man's relation to his society and hence is a sociological phenomenon. Durkheim differentiated three types of suicide. The first was labeled *altruistic* suicide, in which the customs of a society facilitate or even demand the act. The Indian practice of suttee, in which the widow would cast herself upon the funeral pyre of her husband, and the Japanese practice of hara-kiri are illustrations of such suicides.

Second is *egoistic* suicide, in which the individual fails to identify with the institutions of his society and assumes individual responsibility or blame for bad behavior. The third type is *anomic* suicide, in which an individual's adjustment to society is disrupted, usually by separation from a key figure in his life. The anomic suicide may be said not to share the values supposedly common to his society; hence, he may be said to be alienated.

All three of these types of suicide are essentially oriented to society. Freud, on the other hand, viewed the causes of suicide as being primarily intrapsychic. He argued that suicide is the result of original feelings of love directed toward an internalized love object turning to anger or hostility as a consequence of frustration. Because the love object has become internalized, or a part of oneself, the aggressive feelings are directed toward the self.

Neither explanation seems adequate. Successful self-destruction may be based on an individual's estimate of his current life situation in which he believes that there is no adequate source of reinforcement available to him. In this regard there are strong similarities between suicide and panic responses (see Chapter 15). Suicide may involve a real or anticipated loss of job, health, friends, or relatives. Frequently, and most sadly, the individual's labeling of his life situation is objectively wrong. Alvarez talks of "the imperviousness to everything outside the closed world of self-destruction." (1973, p. 117.)

Alvarez quotes Camus: "What is called a reason for living is also an excellent reason for dying." (p. 88.) Stengel (1964, pp. 67–69) makes the point through the observations of a scholar from another planet: there are some people who hurt themselves very seriously, to the point that one in eight or nine die. Most of the people who do so give a clear warning. Whether the outcome is fatal or not, people are very concerned and upset. In short, Stengel argues that we must look to reactions of the environment and consider suicide not in terms of attempted death, but as an act having impact on the environment. While this need not be true for all cases—for example, the suicide which is a "logical" escape from unremitting physical pain of terminal illness—suicide and attempted suicide may well be an effort, to use Alvarez's words, "to break through the patterns . . . which they have unwittingly imposed on their lives." (p. 126.) A suicidal gesture may be a grand, last gamble for a new deal. Many suicides, then, are not determined to die, but rather to *live differently;* the act often is a flirting with unknown quantities of poison or other risks, by people who "in committing a suicidal act are just as muddled as they are whenever they do anything of importance under emotional stress." (Stengel, 1964, p. 71.) Stengel (p. 73) also noted that of 500 attempted suicides studied by Swedish investigators, only 4 percent could be regarded as well planned, but only 7 percent were relatively harmless. Suicide may be affected by models and opportunity:

. . . for example, the maidens of Miletos who, according to Plutarch, rushed to hang themselves until one of the city elders suggested shaming their bodies by carrying them through the market place—whereupon vanity, if not sanity, prevailed; or the fifteen wounded soldiers in Les Invalides Hospital in Paris who hanged themselves from the same hook in 1772—the epidemic stopped when the hook was removed; or the thousands of Russian peasants who burned themselves to death in the seventeenth century in the belief that the Antichrist was coming; or the hundreds of Japanese who threw themselves into the crater of Mihara-Yama from 1933 until access to the mountain was closed in 1935; or all those Chicagoans who jumped off "Suicide Bridge" until the authorities, in despair, finally tore the thing down. [Alvarez, 1973, pp. 104–5.)]

At the time of this writing, there is an argument (Fosburgh, 1973) over whether a wall restraining suicides should be put on the Golden Gate Bridge, from which 500 people have jumped. The wall would block the view of the multitude crossing the bridge, and it would probably make suicide by jumping from the bridge more difficult and less likely. It would decrease the option of the general population both to look and to jump.

The potential of limiting a civil liberty in order to reduce the suicide rate is illustrated in a study of the suicide rate during the 268-day newspaper strike in Detroit (Motto, 1970). If newspaper stories of suicide encourage the act, then suicide rates should have decreased; while the evidence was far from conclusive, there did seem to be good evidence for a significant decrease in the young female group. Blumenthal and Bergner (1973) report results supporting this finding based on a New York City newspaper strike. If this is so, should certain news stories be decreased as a public health measure? In some regards, this concept is present in limitations on pornography.

Shneidman and Farberow (1957b) analyzed suicide notes as clues to understanding suicidal behavior. They studied over 800 notes left by actual suicides and compared them with a matched sample of notes written by members of fraternal groups, labor unions, and university classes who were asked to simulate a suicide note. Shneidman and Farberow then categorized the genuine suicide notes into three types—"logical," "psychotic," and "confused." The analysis of suicide notes thus far is inconclusive.

Shneidman (1968) proposed a revised classification with suicide as communication, revenge, fantasy crime, unconscious flight, magical revival, and rebirth. Colson (1973), using intensive testing, sophisticated statistical procedures, and a population which was strongly suicidal but not clinically referred found four clusters of suicidal intentions as due to: (1) loneliness and interpersonal loss, (2) health problems, (3) fear of failure and a dim future, and (4) manipulation of someone else and a personal fear of "going insane." While such lists could be multiplied, they make the important point of the heterogeneity of backgrounds for the act.

Suicide is not an act isolated from an individual's total environment. It can only be understood in the context of an individual's relationship with key figures in his life. Meerloo (1959) argues that suicide is always committed in relation to other people, or, as expressed in this chapter, has anticipated interpersonal consequences. Meerloo argues that every suicide is directed toward some survivor so as to elicit remorse, guilt, shock, or embarrassment. He also describes what he calls "psychic homicide," or one individual literally driving someone else to suicide. Wolfgang (1959) goes further in arguing that in a large number of instances murder actually represents an elicited form of suicide. Wolfgang analyzed the victim-offender relationship. In 558 consecutive criminal homicides recorded for five years by the Philadelphia police department, he classified 26 percent as victim-precipitated. These cases were homicides in which the victim provoked the murder, in some instances literally handing the murderer the weapons. Wolfgang points out the relationship between homicide, suicide, and social conditions. He concluded that the profile of the victim of victim-precipitated homicide indicates that he is "one who is a member of the lower socio-economic class" whose behavior is characterized by eliciting aggression from others and who finally succeeds in provoking his own murder.

Shneidman, Farberow, and Litman (1961) summarize their findings about suicide in terms of its "folklore" or "mythology," the generally held misconceptions about its nature. First it is *not* true that people who communicate suicidal intentions will not commit suicide. Evidence indicates that roughly 75 percent of individuals who had actually committed suicide had previously attempted or threatened it. This argues that people's verbal behavior should be taken more seriously than is usually done. Further, it is *not* true that suicide is a sudden behavior without any previous warning. In retrospect, it is clear that the suicidal individual had given many clues, warnings, and indications of his intentions. It is *not* true that improvement after a suicidal crisis means that the suicidal risk is over. Shneidman et al. discovered that almost half the people who were in a suicidal crisis and subsequently committed suicide did so within 90 days of having passed the emotional crisis and after they had seemed to be on the way to recovery. Suicidal individuals are not necessarily depressed, suffering from a disease, or mentally disturbed; nor is suicide a behavior that can be controlled by legal action, since to make suicide a crime may only alter the rate of suicidal attempts being reported.

Suicide Prevention

An interesting development in the field is the growth of suicide-prevention centers. The objective of these centers is to demonstrate to the individual, through direct personal contact or on an emergency telephone basis, that someone is interested in him and that there are ways of re-evaluating and altering the environment. As an expression of interest by people in other people, they are to be welcomed.

To the extent that the suicide centers offer the kind of psychological assistance which is generally in short supply, calls may be received from persons who wish to bypass long waiting lists for clinics or psychotherapy (Hitchcock and Wolford, 1970). These people often "feel they must frame their initial request in a suicidal context in order to get assistance." (Haughton, 1968, p. 1695.) In order to rationalize the need for the service and to obtain volunteers as well as clients, the focus of the center is on suicidal behavior and the emergency telephone interviews.

While it is difficult to assess the impact of the centers on the suicide rate, the number of callers is so high that (while the population may be one of grave risk) the vast majority would not have consummated the contemplated act whether they called or not. Thoughts of suicide are anything but rare among the general population. Lester and Lester (1971, p. vii) cite a survey in which 50 percent of students "at the University of Maine had considered, threatened, or actually attempted suicide." Schwab, Warheit, and Holzer (1972) using a southeastern adult population noted that 15.9 percent reported some degree of suicidal ideation. Leonard and Flinn (1972) using a younger population give a figure of 18 percent. Craig and Senter (1972) who interviewed undergraduates found that 30 percent had thought of suicide during the preceding academic year and 10 percent considered that their thoughts had been "very serious." Murray, using a questionnaire with an undergraduate population, reported that 40 percent had thought of killing themselves. While the methods of data collection, populations sampled, and criteria for serious suicidal ideation differ, the point is that thoughts of suicide are far from unusual. Because they provide an entry to treatment, they may be given a weight that they would not otherwise have had.

Wilkins (1970), in a follow-up study of 1,300 callers to a suicide-prevention clinic reports eight suicides, four equivocal deaths, and five "suicides" by alcohol. He cites other studies, especially Litman (1967), in which 6 percent had made one or more additional attempts. Wold (1970) reported research using 42 known suicides from among 26,000 people who had contacted the Los Angeles Center. How many other of these people had committed suicide is not known, but the rate is up to 14 times greater than expected by chance. Wold and Litman (1973) reinterviewed a random sample of the people who had called a suicide prevention center two years earlier and found that 9 of the 417 people were dead by reason of suicide, a rate up to 100 times greater than that of the general population. Sawyer, Sudak, and Hall (1972) report a suicide rate of 288 per 100,000 which is 25 times greater than expected and may either indicate that the population contacting the clinic is one of very high risk or one not well served by such clinics.

In a different manner, Nielsen and Videbech (1973) report that after a 20-fold increase in referrals, extensive use of home visits, and provision of psychiatric examinations with no wait, the suicide rate in the community served was .17 per 1000 where it had earlier been .14 per 1000. Weiner (1969) reported a similar result, and Lester (1971) points out that in a period surveyed, only one city in California had a significant change in suicide rate: Los Angeles with a famous suicide prevention center had experienced a significant increase in the suicide rate.

A different question has been raised by Maris (1969), who points out that the high-risk person is white, male, and old, while the most frequent client of the center he investigated was young, black, and female. A consistent result is reported by Greaves and Gent (1972) who found that only 2 of the 29 persons who committed suicide in an area served by a crisis intervention clinic had ever contacted it.

The suicide-prevention center does not reach the highest-risk population, and it may possibly shape the low-risk person towards the act. One immediate solution is to make the suicidal plea for help unnecessary as a reason for receiving service. In addition, we can only agree with Lester (1971, p. 47) when he writes, "If suicide prevention is to be more than an advertising gimmick and a fund-raising slogan, then it is essential that more evaluation of these services be attempted."

Self-mutilation

Lester (1972) makes the point that self-mutilation is not only an important topic in its own right but also may offer some light on suicide. Self-mutilation may be observed in "normal" people: we shave, pierce our ears, pull our beards, tattoo our bodies, etc. Further, some soldiers may shoot themselves to be withdrawn from duty, while other people take risks such as body-surfing or sky-diving, and still others find being scratched, bitten, or spanked to be sexually provocative. The point is that harming oneself may be difficult to separate from manipulating one's environment in order to reduce discomfort (as in malingering) or increase pleasure (as in masochism).

A second point is that successful treatment of self-mutilating, self-injurious, or life-endangering acts may, *by inference, support* (and not prove as experimentation would permit) a sociopsychological formulation of this category of behavior, including, by implication, suicide. Ross, Meichenbaum, and Humphrey (1971) ceased confronting a head-banger and further desensitized her to the content of her frightening dreams with resultant cessation of the target behavior. Myers and Deibert (1971) used food to develop a response incompatible with head-beating, and then extended the training beyond the eating situation. Similar procedures were used by Rubin et al. (1972), Walen (1972), Peine (1972), Peterson and Peterson (1968), and Tate (1972). Mishara and Kastenbaum (1973) found a decrease in self-injurious behavior by institutionalized elderly people in a token economy where life-enhancing behaviors were reinforced. Roback et al. (1972) taught a patient who mutilated herself by burning more adaptive methods of anger expression, while damaging inner-lip-biting was treated first by self-recording and then having the recording lead to a total relaxation response which had been taught by the therapist (Ernst, 1973). Matefy (1972) required a woman to not choke herself for two hours in order to earn cigarettes. Hughes and Panek (1973) used response-contingent shock for arm-slashing, as did Corte, Wolf, and Locke (1971) with four retardates emitting self-injurious behavior. Merbaum (1973) trained a mother to deliver aversive stimuli to a child whose beating of his face for the last five years had made it swollen, bruised, and grotesque. Adams, Klinge, and Keiser (1973), Martin and Treffry (1970), and Cautela and Baron (1973) present cases in which combined behavior-therapy techniques were used. Lovaas and Simmons (1969) used extinction and punishment with severely retarded and psychotic children, and, as in other work (Risley, 1968; Tate and Baroff, 1966) socially desirable behavior increased.

In summary, self-injurious behavior may be brought under control and altered by environmental manipulation. The procedures used are varied; the common thread in these studies is direct reeducation. In both theory and practice, work with self-injurious behavior may have implications for suicide: Lester and Lester (1971, p. 72) write that "good social integration is insurance against suicide," and we can only agree.

SUMMARY

In this chapter, we have dealt with behaviors which are not specifically incorporated into DSM-II but which are of interest and concern to many people and are the target of professional investigation. These behaviors include pornography and obscenity, smoking, gambling, suicide, and "existential" problems. Each of these is discussed in social, professional, and treatment context. Each of these topics touches on value decisions as to what is socially deviant behavior and the responsibility of a society to intervene in the conduct of the individual who may be harming himself. Society can intervene to prevent certain behaviors: What are the circumstances under which such intervention should be sanctioned? The prevention of suicide seems clearly desirable, but should social intervention go beyond that to other life-shortening behavior such as smoking? And if life is to be protected by societal manipulation, may there not also be intervention in the quality of life?

increasing prosocial behavior
"POSITIVE DEVIANCE"

28

In dealing with patterns of behavior, we have often illustrated that behavioral treatment meant helping the person to emit an effective reaction to a situation. We usually do not use only one particular response to a situation, such as aversive conditioning of drinking alcohol, but rather teach the person alternative behaviors incompatible with the changeworthy behavior. Merely reducing the emission of a response is only half the job, and usually is less important than fostering alternative behavior.

Another way of saying this is that our topic is changeworthy behavior and this includes increasing desirable behaviors as well as decreasing ones that are upsetting, self-defeating, or disruptive.

If this is so, what is special about this chapter? First, as in the foregoing chapter, there are areas of human activity that are not included in DSM-II. While we have made use of DSM-II as a sampling method and to prepare the student who will enter medicine, law, nursing, social work, teaching, and psychology where a knowledge of DSM-II is instrumental, we do not wish to be bound to DSM-II as an absolute standard.

Second, in a strict dictionary sense, abnormal means unusual. This is essentially the statistical definition discussed in the first chapter. The topics focused on in a survey of statistically rare but societally valued behaviors display the concerns of a society as much as do the definitions of "negative" abnormalities. Frequently the topics deal with concepts such as genius (Ashby and Walker, 1968), creativity (Jackson and Messick, 1968), or character (Rosen-han and London, 1968). But, the question for the scientist is not only identification of groups of people who manifest "positive" deviancy, but also the conditions that foster both the number and quality of such people and their behavioral accomplishments. *What* behaviors we wish to encourage is a matter of values and social policy (see Chapter 29 of this book and Krasner and Ullmann, 1973). At this point, however, we wish to discuss some behaviors that are currently valued by our society, not in terms of unusual people who are the result of genius, genetics, luck, etc., but in terms of conditions that foster such behavior.

A third reason for interest in this area is a matter of social survival. Society and the humans who comprise it, depend on both conformity and innovation. Conformity and cooperation make possible planning and acceptable responses to new individuals and situations. Early in this book we used the example of driving along highways; other drivers obey common expectations as to which side of the road they will choose. But environments change. Further, technological advances have changed human capabilities to move, communicate, store information, and control personal environments far beyond genetic or physiological limitations. Aside from cooperation and conformity, survival of nations and peoples requires a method for the introduction and adoption of innovation.

Associated with survival is the observation that external control seems to be absent in the majority of acts, increasingly so as humans become older. The concept of a person being "responsible" or having self-control may be the apparent absence of or long delay between an act and its consequence. A fourth reason for this chapter, then, is to approach topics such as moral choice, self-control, inhibition of immediate gratification, altruism, cooperation, help-giving, academic achievement, and work. In larger measure, it is a description and elaboration of some of the topics of what we frequently subsume under the label of "mature adult." But these mature acts need to be learned, and, by pointing out some research, we hope to indicate that such learning is similar to the learning of any behavior.

Rather than presuming people are "naturally" good, the question is how do they become good (whatever quality is used to define "good" operationally). We think that it is nice to make assertions about human potentialities, but it is better to be able to give some leads as to how these goals may be attained. In sum, then, this section picks up the challenge made to many learning and sociopsychological theorists to discuss areas of "higher" human activity.

Another reason for this chapter is that knowledge of conditions that foster prosocial behavior may lead to community applications that prepare individuals to be effective in acceptable ways so that disruptive, disturbing, seemingly irrational changeworthy behaviors may be reduced. This could be called primary prevention if we were to follow the community mental-health model discussed in the next chapter.

Our discussion of prosocial behavior will move us from the hospital and clinic into the school, the factory, the home, and the general social environment. It moves us from a medical, within the individual, model to an interaction with the environment. Another way of saying this is that we have been dealing with responses the individual makes to situations; we can and should also design and change the situations to which the individual reacts. Here we will focus not on conditions that are associated with for example, crime, but conditions that may counter such responses.

CHARACTERISTICS OF THE PROSOCIAL PERSON

As with the other patterns of behavior we have discussed, the first step is to delineate the behavior we wish to investigate. The following picture is one which is admittedly culture-bound; there is no concept or universal standard, such as Freud's genital personality or Fromm's productive orientation, although a number of efforts continue in this direction such as Maslow's (1954) self-actualizing person, Combs and Snygg's (1959) adequate personality, Shoben's (1957) normal personality, Maddi's (1967) ideal personality, and various efforts at specifying positive mental health and integration (Jahoda, 1958).

Rather, in this time and place, what general concepts can be used to describe mature, or prosocial people? First, the person is socially effective and gainfully employed. At some level, the person is cooperative, helpful, sharing, and even altruistic. He or she gives as well as gets.

Second, the person delays gratification and does not act on impulse, but rather seems to have a time-span oriented to a longer range. Some of such "impulse- and self-control" is a matter of foregoing pleasures to avoid unpleasant consequences—for example, giving up cigarettes and macadamia-nut ice-cream to avoid such aversive consequences as cancer and obesity. What we wrote on these topics in previous chapters is germane here and provides a background, but what we are interested in at this point is making some sacrifice or effort for some delayed payoff that may even be abstract, covert, and not readily apparent to an external observer.

We will cover various topics such as cooperation and sharing, helping and donating, and, underlying these, self-reinforcement, standard-setting, and conceptions of moral behavior.

After this survey, our next topic will be the area of increasing prosocial behavior in the extra-laboratory, general social environment. We will deal with three topics. The first, an overlap of Chapter 26, will be work on impulse control by self-instruction. The second will overlap and continue Chapter 24 on retardation and will deal with work; and the third will overlap with Chapter 23 on children and will deal with the formal educational process.

A final major topic will be a more general example of "positive" deviance of social innovation: the changing role of women.

SELF AND SELF-CONTROL

Because the consequences for prosocial behavior may be delayed, less public, and not obvious, it is inviting to invoke explanatory concepts such as "character" or "personality." The "impulsive" person responds to immediate stimuli and is not under control of long-range payoffs. Further, there is a fluctuation of behavior by the person called impulsive rather than persistence in the face of adversity. It should be noted that persistence in the face of adversity when observers do not understand the antecedent conditions or eventual benefits to the person or society may be called stubbornness or psychosis

When we talk of self-control, we talk of two concepts, self and control (see Krasner and Ullmann, 1973, particularly 303–26). There is a long history to the concept of self (Viney, 1967), dating from notions of the soul as the initiator of activity and the "real" individual as distinct from peripheral manifestations such as overt behavior. Mead (1934) indicated that self is derived from the interactions with other people: how the person is treated by others provides the information on which the individual builds his concept of who he is and what impact he has. Taylor (1962) emphasizes that consciousness itself is a function of activity, and Skinner (1953, p. 285) takes a view that self is "simply a device for representing a functionally unified system of responses." This formulation is similar to our definition of role.

"Self" does not initiate acts, but rather is part of a sequence of behaviors which may be conceived of as an information system with feedback loops. There are external stimuli, neurological events, decoding, evaluation, reaction, and feedback from both the external environment and the person's body of the behaviors emitted. The person observes his own behavior and its consequences in the same way he would any other person or model (Bem, 1967; Ullmann, 1969b).

Control refers to situations under which acts will or will not be made more rapidly more frequently, or more strongly. Many of these situational stimuli are acts by the individual himself. A person learns to label situations and to react in terms of these labels, from "that's a bargain" to "that's dangerous."

A person does not scan every item of potential information available at any moment. If you are reading this book, it is unlikely that you were attending to the pressure on your backside, the color of the walls, the noises from the street, etc. (although now that we mention it . . .). Stimuli must be organized, and the learning (both acquisition and extinction) of attention is crucial (see Chapter 18 and, in terms of resistance to temptation, Grim, Kohlberg, and White, 1968). If a person responds to stimuli that others consider irrelevant, he will be under a form of control that they consider "abnormal." If a person processes every item of information, he will seem "unfiltered," and will be so busy with previous information he will seem "abstracted and out of contact" at the time of new information. To the individual, it may seem that there is a stimulus input overload; to the observer, the person may have deficits in intellecutal functions such as memory or storage of information.

Through experience a person develops the sorts of acts and systems of consequences that represent the world he lives in and to which he adjusts. Again, some of these manipulations are overt: we set alarm clocks, save money, and buy airconditioning in the winter when there are sales so that we will not swelter in summer. At a national level, we pay taxes and vote for people who have plans for peace and prosperity. We are not passive; we actively strive to build a world of security, comfort, and friendship. The impact of the world we build ourselves—Adler's "guiding fiction" is a good term—may indeed start with our parents' labels of our acts; however, it is not a passive receipt of labels, but labels following acts—labels that are ultimately backed by reinforcing stimuli. One of the most widespread labels is that of being masculine or feminine: ". . . the division of society's members into age-sex categories is, perhaps, the feature of greatest importance for establishing the participation of the individual in the culture. In practically all societies, the great majority of activities and occupations are ascribed to the members of one or a very small number of age-sex categories and prohibited to members of others." (Linton, 1945, p. 63–64).

From an early age a person is taught what is manly and what is womanly. The training is pervasive and seems to indicate what is right, proper, natural, and even God-given. When a person or group of people acts in a manner not in accord with such specifications, they are unusual, upsetting, difficult to understand, and apt to be labeled in a negative fashion. For purposes of the present section, the point is that a person born and raised in a particular society rarely questions such expectations and that it takes noteworthy circumstances and individuals to pioneer activity not in line with them. A person, for example, is not born with a concept that engineering is masculine and she would be unfeminine or pushy to think of herself as working in that profession; similarly, only recently have the concepts nurse, secretary, social worker, librarian, grade-school teacher, or phone operator been divorced from female connotation, although originally telephone operators and office clerks were men. The men who venture into these professions share some of the problems faced by women venturing into traditionally "masculine" work.

HELPING STRANGERS

The following two articles appeared on successive days in the same newspaper and set the stage for the present topic. On Friday, April 9, 1971, the *Chicago Daily News,* on page three, carried the story that: "Thirty passengers aboard a CTA train sat—and did nothing—as a man assaulted and robbed a 12-year-old Glenview boy at knifepoint. . . . The attacker held a knife to the boy's neck, cutting him slightly, and forced him to hand over the dollar he had in his pocket. Then he forced the boy to commit a sex act. Some of the passengers looked away. Others watched—but none did anything to help the boy or said anything to the attacker to try to stop him."

In the Saturday and Sunday editions of the same newspaper (April 10 and 11, 1971), appeared an AP story: "Two men, armed only with tree limbs beat back a pack of wolves attacking a boy at the San Diego Zoo. . . . Jim W. Voorhis and William E. Graham, both visitors to the zoo, jumped into the wolves' enclosure when they heard the boy screaming for help."

In March, 1964 at least 38 neighbors in New York City watched and heard a young woman named Kitty Genovese being stabbed to death on the street. The assault lasted more than half an hour, yet not one person called the police. Explanations about apathy and moral decay were offered professionally and in the press. Kaplan (1972) discusses the lack of encouragement for helping behavior in our laws. A first principle defending nonintervention is the right to privacy or individualism. Why should some person, due to his foolhardiness, be allowed to impose on another? A second principle is a "why me?" concept and involves selecting a person to prosecute from among potential defendants and describing community standards for such selection. Where there is an answer to the question "why me?," people who have a clear, responsible relationship, such as employers, parents, or captains of sinking ships, are held liable. On the other hand, discouraging help-giving, the courts are unanimous in imposing liability where the attempt to help makes matters worse.

Bystander Effect

A number of social psychologists have pursued the activities of "bystanders." In one study (Latané and Darley, 1968), male undergraduates were filling out a questionnaire prior to an experiment. No other person, one, or two other men were present doing the same task. Smoke started to enter the room through the heating vent. When alone, 75 percent of the men reported the smoke, while in the three-person groups, only one of 24 people reported the smoke within the first four minutes before the room became noticeably unpleasant.

Possible explanations for the effect may be (1) that the presence of nonreacting others defines a situation that may be ambiguous—dangerous or not—as not dangerous; and (2) that the first person defining the situation as dangerous might be thought to be cowardly or "chicken."

A matter which is both an observation and an illustration of a major category of behavior—*neutralization* or *rationalization*—may be gleaned from the following quotation (Latané and Darley, 1970, p. 18):

Subjects who had not reported the smoke were also unsure about exactly what it was, but they uniformly said that they had rejected the idea that it was a fire. Instead, they hit upon an astonishing variety of alternative explanations, all sharing the common characteristic of interpreting the smoke as a nondangerous event. Many thought the smoke was either steam or airconditioning vapors, several thought it was smog, purposely introduced to simulate an urban environment, and two actually suggested that the smoke was a "truth gas" filtered into the room to induce them to answer the questionnaire accurately! Predictably, some decided that "it must be some sort of experiment" and stoically endured the discomfort of the room rather than overreact.

In another experiment (Latané and Rodin, 1969), the same results were obtained when the situation was hearing a bookcase fall on a female research assistant in the next room. Men who were alone were significantly more likely to intervene than men in groups. Again, the reports of nonintervleners are of particular interest for students of "abnormal" behavior. For example, some of the subjects who had not intervened said that they had acted in a manner to avoid embarrassing the woman. "The important thing to note is that non-interveners did not seem to feel that they had behaved callously or immorally." (Darley and Latané, 1970, p. 20.)

In another experiment (Darley and Latané, 1968), subjects were in a "communication" system in which they heard but did not see the other men. As such, the number of presumed others could be manipulated while face to face contact and observation of action could be held constant. When one of the people in the communication system had "a seizure," subjects who thought they were alone in the communication net with the person having the seizure reported the other person's distress (intervened) significantly more frequently and rapidly. Of particular import is that the nonintervening subjects later asked questions about the status of the person who had had the seizure and showed physical signs of upset; they were not untouched and indifferent. In fact, one might hypothesize that helping may be reinforcing because it terminates the conflict of whether to help or not.

Among relevant explanations, and hence variables to manipulate, are diffusion of responsibility, modeling from the other (nonhelping confederate) person both for the action and to define the situation, cost or effort required to intervene, and knowledge or competence to help the person in distress (Kazdin and Bryan, 1971; Clark and Word, (1974). In addition, Clark and Word (1972) raised the question of the ambiguity of the plea and found that when the plea was not ambiguous, at least one person in each of their groups helped. While this makes good sense, it does not explain the behaviors in New York with Kitty Genovese or in Chicago with the Transit Authority cited at the start of this section.

"Passers-by" Studies

The immediately preceding material dealt with studies that were accomplished with people recruited for experiments in a laboratory setting. A variant is to set up a situation outside the laboratory and use "passers-by" as subjects. The situation is contrived by the psychologist and the variables he considers important may be manipulated. For example, Darley and Latané (1970) report a study in which a person sitting isolated from others was approached by a young man on crutches who fell down in great pain. This situation was enacted first in a subway station and then at an airport; 83 percent of the people approached helped in the former and 41 percent in the latter location. Further analysis revealed that the key variable seemed to be familiarity with the situation. In both locations, those more familiar with the place were more likely to give assistance.

In another work by these authors (Darley and Latané, 1970), a confederate gave poor information to a person who had asked a question in the presence of a naïve subject. The naïve subject was more likely to correct the misinformation of the confederate if the questioner had asked the subject for information rather than if it were the confederate who had interrupted the informer and, further, if the confederate had given the information in a fashion which would not be an embarrassment to have corrected (e.g., "uptown, but I'm not sure"). Finally, if the confederate looked like a person who would take strong umbrage to being corrected, corrections were less frequent.

Bryan and Test (1967) and Macaulay (1970) used the situation of donations to a "Salvation Army" type Christmas pot at a market location. In general, modeling (seeing a person donate) increases the likelihood of the observer donating. The drift of these studies is that people tend to act in the way they think they should. That is, people are generally good observers of their environment and respond in a manner they think appropriate or called for by the cues they observe.

FURTHER CONDITIONS FOR HELPING. Piliavin, Rodin, and Piliavin (1969) staged help-needing scenes with the "victim" as drunk or ill, black or white, and with a helping or nonhelping model presented. The "ill" person was more likely to receive help than the "drunk" person; race had little effect unless the person was drunk; and group size did not lead to a diffusion of responsibility. Lerner, Solomon, and Brody (1971) also did not find a diffusion-of-responsibility effect when the task was asking directions at a bus stop.

Wispé and Freshly (1971) investigated the help given a young black or white female whose bag broke in a supermarket. Men helped more than women; while there was no race difference for men, white women helped more frequently than black women; and a significant number of people who saw nonhelping modeled helped anyway.

Gaertner (1973) and Gaertner and Bickman (1971) used a "wrong number" telephone caller, who, having made the connection ("No, it wasn't Ralph's garage"), asked for assistance. Male subjects were more helpful to females, blacks helped blacks and whites equally, and liberal attitudes were found to generalize to overt behavior, but weakly.

MANIPULATION OF THE SUBJECT PRIOR TO REQUEST FOR HELP. The effects of prior conditions on helping may be studied in a laboratory setting, as in Lerner's investigation (1970), in which, after observing a person receiving (supposed) aversive stimulation, observers overwhelmingly voted that the person be put into a known reward condition. But, both Lerner (1970) and Walster, Berscheid, and Walster (1970) note that the effects of observing a person in distress may be neutralized. If we wish to live in a world where there is justice, and we observe injustice, one outcome is to say that a victim "got what he deserved." More specifically, we can derogate the victim, deny responsibility for the situation, or minimize the victim's suffering. We can also try to restore equity by compensating the victim or by self-punishment.

A series of studies with college students in a laboratory situation in which a behavioral measure was taken indicate how a person who has transgressed or hurt another, even by accident, may be more likely to volunteer to help. Carlsmith and Gross (1969) found that one-fourth of the subjects who had delivered "buzzes" to confederates volunteered to help in a campaign to "save the Redwoods" while three-fourths of those who had delivered "shocks" complied with the request. Similarly, subjects who had "broken" machines (Wallace and Sadalla, 1966), who had deprived another of trading stamps in a game (Berscheid and Walster, 1967), or "knocked over" carefully arranged reference cards (Freedman, Wallinton, and Bless, 1967), complied significantly more frequently to requests for helping acts that would require time or effort, such as volunteering for charity or experimental work.

Carlsmith, Ellsworth, and Whiteside (1968, cited in Freedman, 1970, p. 157), told the subject that a clue planted by the experimenter had led to such a good performance on a test that the subject had ruined the experiment. At a later time, when asked to volunteer for future experiments, those who had "cheated" signed up more than those who had not. Subjects who had had an opportunity to "confess" and had done so did not comply (volunteer) more than the noncheating controls. The person may not necessarily have to be made to feel bad about himself; a warm glow of success or pleasant feeling may also increase generosity (Isen, 1970; Isen and Levin, 1972).

From the work covered so far, we may say that the person's prior experiences, his competence to deal with the situation, the situation itself in terms of who needs help, who is helping, and the cost of helping, as well as the types of appeals, avenues open, and many other variables influence the overt act of helping a person in distress or volunteering either to help with work or money. Helping activity is human activity and is dependent upon what the person brings to the situation in terms of prior experience and the nature of the immediate situation. It is not an invariant characteristic of the person, but a situation-specific act that may be manipulated.

Field Experiments: Good Citizens

How honest are people? What is the best way to approach them? Dorris (1972) approached coin dealers with a collection by a naïve seller. Under one condition, evidence was provided that the seller had been previously exploited by another dealer, while this was not true for the other half of the subjects. Within these groups half were divided into a "moral-appeal" condition in which the seller would trust the dealer even though afraid of exploitation and not seek other appraisals, and a neutral-appeal condition that did not include the worry about exploitation. The moral appeal was more effective in obtaining a high initial bid, increased eyecontact, and the dealer standing closer. Previous exploitation by another dealer led to more discussion of the coin that had been sold to a prior dealer and less devaluation of the remaining coins, but did not directly alter the price.

Schaps (1972) had a female confederate limp or not limp into a shoe store due to a broken heel; she had to buy shoes right there. Half the shoe stores were crowded, half were relatively empty. Since the person with the limp would have to buy, she was "dependent." Salesmen working on commission would require time assisting her and this would cut down their rate of pay, that is, it would "cost" them. The store being filled or not filled was thus called the "cost" condition, and limping or not limping was the "dependent" condition. The service obtained was the same for the nonlimping person whether the store had many or few customers. Compared to the service for the nonlimping customer the service for the limping woman was better when the store was relatively empty, and worse when it was relatively full. In short, helping a dependent person was influenced by the cost to the person giving the service.

Reporting shoplifters may be one aspect of becoming involved in law functions. Gelfand et al. (1973) staged shoplifts by conventionally dressed versus hippie, youth-culture attired female confederates in upper- and low-income neighborhood stores. Of the people who noticed the shoplifting, 28 percent reported it; middle-aged males and people raised in rural rather than city environments were most likely to report the shoplifting. The dress of the shoplifter made a difference in likability ratings, but not in rate of reports.

Darley and Batson (1973) studied the influences on the behavior of people finding a shabbily dressed old man slumped on the side of the road (the parable of the Good Samaritan). A person not in a hurry may stop and offer help. A person in a hurry is likely to keep going.

These studies indicate ways that aspects of good citizenship may be studied outside the institutional setting, using actions as dependent variables.

Summary

People help others. It is hard to define altruism: it involves providing something of value to another for no obvious extrinsic gain. To demand that there be no intrinsic return to the individual requires the proof of the null hypothesis, an impossibility in empirical science. Krebs (1970), Bryan and London (1970), Macaulay and Berkowitz (1970), Rosenhan (1972) Wispé (1972), and Bryan (1972) provide major sources of information on the topic. Weiss et al. (1971) used alleviation and avoidance of another person's distress as a reinforcing consequence and duplicated typical parameters of learning. That is, altruistic behavior is rewarding.

Aspects of Moral Behavior

Morality deals with "right" conduct and conformity to rules. In Chapter 10 we discussed rules and the need to learn them. In this section we will deal with the emission of an act that follows rules. There is a definite element of self-control and delay of gratification in general concepts of morality. For example, the Random House unabridged dictionary (p. 930) equates sexual virtue with chastity. Following Kanfer (1971; Kanfer and Karoly, 1972) self-regulation may be viewed as an input-output system with feedback loops involving steps of self-monitoring, self-evaluation, and self-reinforcement. The person observes the environment and his own responses, evaluates and compares them with some standard, and categorizes the consequences. People may and do introduce additional stimuli to bring their behavior under control (Stuart,

1972). Among these stimuli are external ones, such as restriction of acts to certain times, places, and interpersonal relationships (e.g., marriage), or internal ones, such as contingency contracts a person makes with himself (Watson and Tharp, 1972).

Operationally, what is observed are behaviors such as resistance to temptation, delay of gratification, and standards for reinforcing oneself.

When in common parlance we use the term "self-control" or "delay of gratification," we usually refer to a situation in which there is high-probability behavior (the pleasure of a drink or cigarette) in which the person doesn't partake. This contrast of high- and low-probability behaviors is almost opposite to the Premack principle: the person does something, at least in the immediate situation, seemingly not as reinforcing as what might have been done. The individual engages in self-evaluation of his own behavior, that is he judges how close or different his current or future performance would be to some pre-set standard. Therefore, we have to see how standards may be set or changed. And crucial to this are the behaviors the person emits to himself as audience: his contracts and his reactions to situations which in turn provide stimuli. That is, the person produces some cues himself.

The concept of a person providing himself stimuli through his responses is not a novel one to this volume. In rational-emotive therapy the person observes his own behavior, including what he says to himself, expects, or gives as reasons for the acts that he wishes to change, and analyzes, relabels, and eventually performs new operations. That is, he evaluates how well his acts, including his thoughts (statements to himself), meet standards. In assertive training, the person observes his own behavior and that of others to determine what is a legitimate act and whether his own behavior meets this standard. Frequently we restructure physiological responses. A person's own physiological response may serve as a stimulus: "This is making me up tight, so let's cut out." The person may record his own behavior, and its antecedents and consequences. Again, he evaluates his responses, those he recorded, and the very responses which comprise the recording process. He may restructure the response-stimulus of feeling anxious and look for it as something which provides him with information. (For further material on this topic see Chapters 14 and 16.)

Rules

"Moral rules form the yardstick against which we evaluate the rules of any particular activity." (Wright, 1971, p. 13.) A person must learn these rules, and this in turn means that they must be clear enough to learn; they must be feasible in terms of being carried out, and must have some consequence so that they are worth a child's learning and adults' teaching. Punishment [1] (response-contingent aversive stimuli) reduces emission of acts; favorable consequences contingent upon acts increases them. The child learns the types of act likely to lead to each and is often helped by seeing others (modeling; e.g., Bandura, in press). He is also helped by the adults' labels and explanations, and even, on occasion, such as touching stoves, by reality. He learns labels and responds to them, and strives to institute conditions that lead to favorable labels and outcomes: he will work for smiles, praise, good grades and responsibilities that lead to increased salary. The ability to predict others, take roles, and empathize are significant aspects of this process (Selman, 1971; Hogan, 1973). Much of this has been discussed in Chapter 2 and in Krasner and Ullmann (1973). The person may learn to apply the same labels that others do to him and react, at least

---

[1] See Cheyne and Walters (1969), Katz (1971), Zimmerman and Krauss (1971), and Grusec and Ezrin (1972) for some of the research in this area.

in part, as if conditions had been reinstituted: The discriminative stimulus becomes a reinforcing one worth working or paying (delay of gratification, response cost) for. This formulation is quite close to that of Staats (1970); although we emphasize the operant components. The foregoing work may be summarized by a quotation from Wright (1972, p. 42): "Having discovered the principles underlying his parents' use of praise, the child comes to praise himself in a similar way. Thus the recognition that an act is 'good' can be its own reward."

One problem in the area of moral behavior is to devise an operational definition (Pittel and Mendelsohn, 1966). With different definitions of moral behavior, we find different correlates of morality, especially as regards age, sex, IQ, desire to create a favorable impression, and culture (Johnson, Dokecki, and Mowrer, 1972).

What is considered correct moral behavior varies over time, although Gorsuch and Smith (1972) noted relative stability of college students' evaluations over 30 years, other than increased liberalism in the area of sexual expression.

Work by Piaget (1948) hypothesized stages of moral development. Kohlberg (1963) has suggested six general stages: first, fear of punishment; second, to protect a selfish need; third, being good to win approval; fourth, respect for law and order as ends in themselves; fifth, law as a method for preserving human rights; and sixth, following abstract principles. Here morality becomes an approach to problems rather than a specific set of actions, and thus it may be stylistic and cut across situations.

Some Empirical Studies

If moral behavior is a method of approach to situations, similar in development and maintenance to other operants, then it should differ when various aspects of the situation are manipulated by different experimental conditions. This is indeed the situation. Among the topics are *self-reward* (particularly varying modeling and incentives) (Bandura and Kupers, 1964; Allen and Liebert, 1969; Liebert and Ora, 1968: Kanfer and Duerfeldt, 1968; McMains and Liebert, 1968), *resistance to temptation* (Bandura and Mischel, 1965; Cheyne, Goyeche, and Walters, 1969; Mischel, Ebbesen and Zeiss, 1972; Hartig and Kanfer, 1973; Mischel, in press), and *self-instruction* (i.e. talking to oneself) (O'Leary, 1968; Meichenbaum and Goodman, 1969; Higa, 1973).

Delay of gratification or resistance to temptation usually involves a situation which, while unpleasant in itself, still concerns approach to some positive stimulus. Kanfer and Goldfoot (1966), Kanfer and Seidner (1973), and Staub, Tursky, and Schwartz (1971), illustrate self-control in the face of an unpleasant or aversive stimuli. Guilt is a frequently used concept, but, as pointed out by Johnson and Kalafat (1969), it is difficult to measure. Further, Johnson et al. (1968) found guilt not significantly related to other measures, while resistance to temptation was significantly associated with favorable adjustment. Johnson and his colleagues (1968) point out that theories of "psychopathology" show much more concern about guilt than about resistance to temptation and that a reversal might prove fruitful.

The object of these studies is that of investigating and documenting whether moral behavior can be changed at all, and, if one wishes to attempt to do so, of determining the best strategy for so doing. But above all, a person is not necessarily moral or immoral; moral behavior is, rather, human behavior; that is, it may be studied in the context of natural science.

Tracy and Cross (1973) used a session of role-playing to expose subjects to moral reasoning of a level higher than their pretest levels. At posttest, the effect was an increase in level of measured moral maturity. Keasey (1973) found that exposure to a more mature model had an immediate but not a long-term effect, and Bandura and McDonald (1963), Cowan et al. (1969), and Crowley (1968) also found that moral judgment could be changed through behavior influence procedures.

One of the most enduring lines of inquiry in psychology is whether lying and cheating (deceit) is a trait or a response to situations. In Hartshorne and May's (1928) work, children who were below average in athletics were more deceitful when athletic prowess was the issue; children from less wealthy backgrounds were less trustworthy in money matters; and children with low grades were more likely to cheat in academic situations. Johnson and Gormly (1971) found that students for whom a task was more important cheated more.

Aronson and Mettee (1968) gave false feedback to subjects about a personality test they had taken and found that more people in the induced low self-esteem condition cheated than those in the high self-esteem condition. Cheating in experiments increases when the risk of being caught decreases (Kanfer and Duerfeldt, 1968; Hill and Kochendorfer, 1969) or, when if caught, the risk of punishment is slight (Rettig and Pasamanick, 1964; Rettig and Suiha, 1966). Dienstbier and Munter (1971) gave college students two different lists of side effects for a placebo and then a vocabulary test supposedly predictive of success in college on which they had an opportunity to cheat. Of the subjects expecting arousal side effects, 49 percent cheated compared with 27 percent of the subjects expecting benign effects.

Essentially, deceit is an inconsistency between actions and standards and, especially for lying, between words and deeds. Risley and Hart (1968) and Israel and O'Leary (1973) investigated the conditions leading to congruence of words and deeds in nursery school children. In a clinical situation, Flowers (1972) successfully treated cheating by reinforcing accurate self-assessment and self-report of work on tests. In short, people can be trained to make accurate statements rather than necessarily having to be punished for lying.

To summarize our observations in this area, behavior evaluated as moral is a function of various aspects of the situation and the person's capacity to deal with those situations. Different aspects of the situations may be manipulated or the person may be trained in acts that make behavior called moral more likely.

SPECIFIC POSITIVE BEHAVIORS

Whether as amelioration or as prevention, societies need to encourage the development of prosocial behaviors. We have previously noted that helping behavior was influenced by different situational and presituational conditions. This is as true for adults as well as children (Staub, 1970, 1971a; Severy and Davis, 1971; Grusec, 1972). Recently, sharing and generosity have been investigated with modeling, role-playing, and incentives being used as behavior-influence variables (Bryan and Walbek, 1970; Elliott and Vasta, 1970; Fouts, 1972; Harris, 1970; Staub, 1971b; Presbie and Kanareff, 1970; Presbie and Coiteux, 1971).

Cooperation is akin to sharing, and a classic work is by Azrin and Lindsley (1956), in which two people were required to operate an apparatus, and each had to help the other in order to obtain a favorable outcome for themselves. Mithaug and Burgess (1968) and Hart et al. (1968) further investigated different reinforcement-contingency effects, and Altman (1971) showed that such laboratory-developed cooperative responses generalized to a free-play situation. Klotz and Shantz (1973) also obtained generalization of cooperative responses after approving instances of cooperation with emotionally disturbed boys.

Reciprocal positive social interaction is

a basis for good morale or prolonged contacts; it is a step forward from cooperation *per se*. Charlesworth and Hartup (1967) observed the reinforcing behaviors of nursery school children and found that reinforcement, as expected, led to continuation of activity. Hartup, Glazer, and Charlesworth (1967) showed that social acceptance in the nursery school was associated with the amount of positive reinforcement the child gave to others. Direct application of such results is illustrated by Simkins (1971), who investigated conditions of baseline, noncontingent points, extinction, contingent points, and social reinforcement. The target behavior was interacting with a peer, as distinct from being isolated by 9-to-12-year-old females at a school for "disturbed" children. Points given contingently, which were later discounted for items on a reinforcement menu, had a greater effect than points given noncontingently and instructions, special incentives, and social reinforcement increased the effect of contingent reinforcement. Paloutzian et al. (1971) used prompting and reinforcement to train severely retarded children to imitate novel social responses of a model in order to increase positive social interactions with peers. After training, the experimental group showed a significantly higher level of social behavior than the control group, and the gain generalized from the training situation to the ward setting. Carlin and Armstrong (1968) report experiences consistent with those of Simkins and Paloutzian et al.

In the Classroom

A major element in socialization in current American society is the school. By the time a person has graduated from high school, he has spent half his "waking" hours for two-thirds of his life in this environment. The school is a method of passing on information about how to live in the culture. Obviously, such an institution is necessary as a channel for cultural continuity.[2] To the extent that jobs have been segmented and functions specialized, the family no longer performs this task.

In the school setting, we may distinguish two broad areas. The first is stylistic—dealing with people and tasks. The second is one of content, the particular material to be learned. Both aim to prepare the individual for emission of behavior that will be of assistance in getting along with other people in the future, in earning a living, and coping with new problems. The method of teaching and the content taught supplement each other.

Failure of a school system in accomplishing its tasks places the student at great disadvantage for the remainder of his life. Skills which are necessary for a more satisfying life are not mastered and may even become so aversive to the individual that they are denigrated. Put differently, a person may fail to develop skills to the extent of being disruptive in school and unqualified for work. He may be blamed for his lack of preparation by some diagnostic label; this preserves the dignity of school officials in the face of their own incompetence. Such labels may further exclude the individual. It is hard to say whether a person has a school problem because he has a behavior problem, or he has a behavior problem because he has a problem with school. We think that the latter occurs often, quite possibly in the majority of instances. It is a waste for society as well as a serious disservice to the individual. A first question, then, is whether we can improve educational settings. (See Krasner and Krasner, 1973; and Krasner and Ullmann, 1973, Chapter 14.)

Token Economy in the Classroom

The use of a token economy in the classroom context has a number of conse-

---

[2] Even such an obvious observation, however, is is not without challenge. Illich (1970) and others argue for "deschooling" society.

quences.[3] The first is that it makes the students' responses more meaningful to themselves and to others. The consequences of such a result may be increasing use of symbolic (social) reinforcers, increasing delay between reinforcer and back-up reinforcer, increased complexity of required act prior to reinforcer, increased self-monitoring, fading of teacher, use of peer pressure, development of self-programming and self-reinforcement, and training in methods of approaching problems rather than specific solutions. Eventually, the acts learned become instrumental in obtaining further positive consequences and, it is hoped, some tasks become pleasant in themselves (e.g., reading).

Intellectual Targets

In the work just mentioned, the object was to create an interpersonal setting in which productive work would increase. In this, as in the prior and next sections, the students comprise special populations: delinquents, retardates, special-classroom or disruptive children, and minority groups called disadvantaged.

A major desirable behavioral objective for most educators is that of *reading*. If reading is subvocal speech and the person sounds out every word, his reading rate will be limited. Hardyck, Petrinovich, and Ellsworth (1966) used surface electromyograms

[3] Much of this work is stimulated by and an elaboration of the concepts of B. F. Skinner (1968) and Sidney Bijou (1965; Birnbrauer et al., 1965a, 1965b). The effects of applying token economies in the classroom have been studied with retardates (Zimmerman, Zimmerman, and Russell, 1969), disruptive behaviors (O'Leary and Becker, 1967; Sulzbacher and Houser, 1968; Quay et al., 1966), problems in reading (Winett et al., 1971), and minority and socially disadvantaged groups (Sloggett, 1971). For an overview, see O'Leary and Drabman (1971).

Major anthologies of work in educational settings have been edited by O'Leary and O'Leary (1972) and Klein, Hapkiewicz, and Roden (1973), who, among themselves, present close to an additional 100 articles.

to measure and provide feedback when there was laryngeal muscle activity. This provided rapid and long-lasting cessation of subvocalization and increased reading speed. It can be conceptualized as an application of biofeedback (see Chapter 16). Hewett, Mayhew, and Rabb (1967) and Rydberg (1971) worked with retardates, and Staats and Butterfield (1965) with culturally deprived juvenile delinquents to increase reading skills.

Akin to reading are language skills, and Odom, Liebert, and Fernandez (1969), Carroll, Rosenthal, and Brysh (1972), Sapon (1967), and Smith, Brethower, and Cabot (1969) have demonstrated the effect of direct retraining on language skills, particularly with retardates (who pose a greater challenge). Usually, tangible reinforcers, such as money or food, are more effective, particularly at the start, than social or highly symbolic rewards.

A major area of concern is that a person not passively learn, but rather be encouraged in ways of gathering information and approaching problems. A salient topic, then, is the *question-asking* behavior of children. Martin (1970) provides validation of this need. Rosenthal, Zimmerman, and their coworkers (Rosenthal, Zimmerman, and Durning, 1970; Rosenthal and Zimmerman, 1972, in press; Zimmerman and Pike, 1972) have assessed modeling and reinforcement in the question-asking behavior of young, Mexican-American school children and observed not only acquisition but also generalization of altered question-asking.

Akin to question-asking are matters of approach to problems and styles of organizing material. Here, the same direct training with special groups may be noted (Jacobson et al., 1971; Rosenthal, Alford, and Rasp, 1972; Zimmerman and Rosenthal, 1972; Rosenthal et al., 1970; Rosenthal, Feist, and Durning, 1972; Rosenthal and Kellogg, 1973; Blank and Solomon, 1968; Baird and Lee, 1969; Shure, Spivak, and Jaeger, 1971). Aside from the presumed usefulness of the techniques taught, this work has implications for the activities called thinking. It demonstrates that patterns of cognitive behavior or personal "style" may be increased. As such, it has theoretical as well as practical meaning.

How to Approach Situations

We have indicated at a general level that various conditions may increase self-imposed standards, self-reinforcement, delay of gratification, and patterns of approach to problems. A number of workers have applied these concepts and findings to work in the classroom setting (see above; e.g., O'Leary and O'Leary, 1972; and Klein, Hapkiewicz and Roden, 1973). Meichenbaum and Goodman (1971), following up their previous work (1969a, 1969b) taught "impulsive" children to talk to themselves, first openly and then covertly or silently. The remarks were of the pattern:

Okay, what is it I have to do? You want me to copy the picture with different lines. I have to go slow and be careful. Okay, draw the line down, down, good; then to the right, that's it; now down some more and to the left. Good, I'm doing fine so far. Remember go slow. Now back up again. No, I was supposed to go down. That's okay. Just erase the line carefully. . . . Good, even if I make an error I can go on slowly and carefully. Okay, I have to go down now. Finished. I did it. [Meichenbaum and Goodman, 1971, p. 117.]

In summary, the goals of the training procedure were to develop for the impulsive child a cognitive style or learning set in which the child could "size up" the demands of a task, cognitively rehearse, and then guide his performance by means of self-instructions, and when appropriate reinforce himself. [Meichenbaum and Goodman, 1971, p. 117.]

The reader may wish to note the various techniques embedded in the training; modeling by the experimenter, information, standard-setting, self-reinforcement, and self-programming to set up the task. Beyond this, the emission of responses may so slow down the person, by adding a link in the sequence of responses, that he attends to a wider range of stimuli and makes better choices. Subtasks for effectiveness in this type of program include having the person attend to the model, repeat the model's instructions to himself (through response-contingent reinforcement, if so required), and have the final product be meaningful and worthwhile. Further steps are the fading of the experimenter and the teaching of times when the new style is appropriate to other situations, that is, encouragement and training of generalization.

Stumphauzer (1970, 1972) has worked directly with delinquents and young prison inmates to increase delay of gratification. In the latter (1972) work, he used prestigious inmates as models, and in the former, a sequence of conditions of a baseline, reinforcement of delay choices, then reinforcement of immediate choices, and, finally, a second reinforcement of delay choices. The results support the work just described.

Other articles consistent with these findings are by Tyler (1967), Santogrossi et al. (1973), Giebink, Stover, and Fahl (1968), Drabman, Spitalnik, and O'Leary (1973), and Egeland (1974).

The Classroom as a Planned Environment

Efforts to increase prosocial behaviors in the classroom are influenced by behavior modification developments such as the token economy and changes in theoretical concepts about the nature and goals of the classroom (e.g., Silberman, 1970).

The classroom is being viewed increasingly as a planned environment (Krasner and Krasner, 1973). This concept involves combining of behavior change principles that we have been describing throughout with concepts derived from those approaching the classroom as a structured but open ecology (Sarason, 1971; Weber, 1971; Stephens, 1974).

As the view to the nature and goals of

classroom changes, the roles of teacher, student, parent, and teacher aide change. The teacher becomes a designer of environments; parents participate in such designs; the role of the student changes from that of a passive recipient of knowledge to that of an active influencer of his own environment (Krasner and Hutchison, 1974; Krasner et al., in press).

Work

Specific retraining for employment in the general market makes use of concepts of the token economies observed with hospitalized psychiatric patients and in the classroom. It should be explicit that most adults work in a complex token economy: they receive pay-checks or cash on a schedule that is, in the example of college professors, a fixed interval of too little, too late. Studies aimed at retraining people for work have been reported for retardates by Evans and Spradlin (1966), Schroeder (1972), and Kliebhan (1967); for long-term hospitalized psychiatric patients by Ayllon and Azrin (1968), Atthowe and Krasner (1968), and Ogburn, Fast and Tiffany (1972); for multiply handicapped (Zimmerman et al., 1969a, 1969b); a military setting (Ellsworth and Colman, 1969, 1970); and the hard-core unemployed (Sandler and Turner, 1973).

Caring for the Environment

Care for the environment is a goal that reflects concern for other people and, at times, means learning a new pattern of behavior. Geller, Farris, and Post (1973) report that use of prompting (see Chapter 4) at the grocery store increased the purchase of returnable bottles by an average of 25 percent. Burgess, Clark, and Hendee (1971), using theaters as their locales, and Clark, Burgess, and Hendee (1972), working at campgrounds, found that incentives could reduce dramatically the amount of littering. Kohlenberg and Phillips (1973) repeated this work in a public park. Wilson and Hopkins (1973) used quietly played popular music as a reinforcer contingent on a low level of noise in junior high school classrooms and demonstrated the effectiveness of this procedure in reducing "noise pollution." This type of work is only in its beginnings, but what we have learned about the arrangement of the environment, reinforcing contingencies, and generalization of alternative behavior indicates that there should be more effective techniques than general appeals and threat of fines.

Behavior Therapy Procedures as Part of Other Treatment Programs

Frequently, sound medical advice is not followed. The patient's cooperation in terms of changed behavior is needed. An example is weight reduction, discussed in Chapter 15; merely handing a person a diet is not as effective as providing training that supports the behaviors involved in changing eating habits. Kerr and Meyerson (1964), Zifferblatt (1972), and Couch and Allen (1973) survey the applications of behavior therapy techniques applied to occupational therapy and physical rehabilitation settings. Schwartz (1973) provides an example of teaching proper walking and posture, while Abramson and Wunderlich (1972) and Lattal (1969) took as their target dental hygiene. Lattal's results of making swimming contingent upon tooth brushing may be compared with more typical appeals (Evans et al., 1970). A final example in this area is the design of a machine by Azrin and Powell (1969) that made a noise when medication was to be taken. Turning off the noise delivered the pill to the person's hand and increased the extent to which the prescription was followed. The work in this area, as in the others reviewed in the immediately preceding sections, offers by example the challenge to apply behavioral concepts to promote prosocial activities.

CHANGING ROLES, CHANGING SOCIETY: WOMEN'S LIB AS CREATIVE DEVIANCE

At the start of this book, we noted that the abnormal label is used when a person does the unexpected, is difficult to understand, is upsetting, but does not necessarily break written rules (and, in fact, may, as in the case of the women's liberation movement, be insisting on consistency and equality of legal interpretation in terms of job opportunities, pay, and abortion [Cisler, 1970; Dreifus, 1970; Ellis, 1970, pp. 163–67; Kanowitz, 1969; and Schulder, 1970]). The pioneers of change often are few in numbers (i.e., statistically rare), upsetting to others, and themselves dissatisfied enough to make sacrifices for change. They meet various tests of the definition of "deviant" or "abnormal" but the impact of their difference from expectation is eventually found to be beneficial. Whether in dealing with the creation of ideas as in science, objects as in art, or life-styles as in utopias (Krasner and Ullmann, 1973) difference is an element, but not the entirety, of worthwhile change.

As indicated in Chapter 21 on sex, the majority of behavior, and even much of gender identity, is learned. As noted earlier in this chapter, every society limits activities on the basis of sex and age categories.[4] Documentation of the cumulative effect of derogation over thousands of years is beyond the scope of the present volume (Bem and Bem, 1970; Bird, 1969; Bernard, 1971; Gross, 1968; Morgan, 1970) and may be reflected in literature (Hays, 1966) as well as contemporary statistics.[5] The focus of the present material is an indication of the conditions, acts, and results (in behavioral terms, antecedents, behaviors, and consequents, that is, a functional analysis) of the positive deviance.

Micossi (1970) makes two important points. One is the frequently noted similarity of the role of women to that of other subjugated groups, such as blacks. The second point is that the problem is social and not biological. A subsidiary point is that women participate in their own abuse and one ideal of adjustment is being a happy slave. An empirical observation made by Micossi, as others (e.g., Bernard, 1971, pp. 203–4), is that women's liberation is at present preponderantly a white, educated, and middle-class phenomenon.

A first step towards conversion to women's liberation delineated by Micossi is that the woman must be aware of forms of self-expression and self-esteem that deviate from the prescribed sex role. We might note that a first step in most social movements (Blumer, 1964) is that there is discontent or recognition of a problem. Micossi relates such awareness to higher education and parents who encouraged careers and advanced schooling. Achievements different from the feminine mystique (Friedan, 1970) of homemaker and middle-class wifely role were measures of self-esteem rather than popularity and "dumb" feminity. To Micossi's analysis of this point we should add that both mid-nineteenth-century and mid-twentieth-century women's movements had as their model black liberation efforts: "The women's rights movement had its official beginning in 1848, when several hundred

---

[4] A nonacademic indication of the impact of ascribed status on individual behavior is from Mary McConnell Borah, who was quoted on her hundredth birthday: "One thing I've learned after living 100 years is that every man is different, but husbands are all alike." (*Champaign-Urbana Courier*, October 25, 1970.)

[5] Of the endless citations possible, the one we think most revealing is from the *New York Times* editorial of 1915: "The grant of suffrage to women is repugnant to instincts that strike their roots deep in the order of nature. It runs counter to human reason, it flouts the teachings of experience and the admonitions of common sense." (Cited in Komisar, 1972, p. 108.) Not only is this an illustration of sexism, it highlights a view of human nature that takes what the writer wishes to be true as true. Finally, the awful event has taken place, and the most tragic effect is that things are still so much as they were.

women and sympathetic men met at Seneca Falls in upstate New York for a convention called by two active abolitionists, Elizabeth Cady Stanton and Lucretia Mott." (Brown and Seitz, 1970, p. 15.) "Many women got their political and 'soap box' training from the antislavery movement, but ironically, the first major women's rights convention was called as a result of their exclusion from participation in antislavery societies on an equal basis with men." (Komisar, 1972, 86–87.)

A century later, "The original organizational impetus for the Women's Liberation Movement came from the shock of having . . . equality denied to them by radical men, and they have not recovered. Radical to begin with, they were further radicalized by their treatment, first in the civil rights movement and then in the student protest movement." (Bernard, 1971, 208.) Other authors (e.g., Ware, 1970, p. 16) pinpoint the time as the summer of 1967 in Chicago: "Women activists came full circle in the shock of recognizing they had been the house niggers in the New Left."

Given the availability of alternative roles, the next factor is a recognition of discrepancies between present and possible actions. This leads to a major step in social movements, that of delineating the problem—in Micossi's formulation, the development of a political problem-solving perspective. Given the background of the 1960's, models of such a perspective were readily available.

Micossi makes the point that as a further precondition to conversion to women's liberation, the people had to have a background of defiance of tradition. Encouragement of intellectual creativity in home, school, and in the civil rights movements of the sixties, provided such a background. There was also decreased support of the traditional role behavior and contact with people who supported and defined a new "appropriate" role.

An important technique in women's liberation is enhanced consciousness of the role of women. Small groups of women may share their experiences about self-centered, domineering, insensitive men, and their frustrations and anger. There is a redefinition of events so that they recognize that they are part of a pattern of male domination. An order and a rationale is given to what was previously amorphous; a rhetoric is adopted; and a new role is developed in which it is inappropriate not to feel anger.[6] The similarities of consciousness-raising sessions to forms of psychotherapy and indoctrination (cf. Frank, 1961) are striking. The effects are also strikingly similar:

Looking at herself and her past in this new way is followed by a rise in self-esteem. A woman begins to like herself more. This happens because the self-hatred that comes with failure and disappointment is hurled outward in a liberating catharsis. Society is held to blame for much of her frustration. And freed from guilt and self-doubt, converts often remark on their "new strength," an exhilarating feeling of "wholeness" or "a greater sense of myself and my potential." [Micossi p. 87.]

The language and concepts of sensitivity-encounter groups and psychoanalysis provide the model and method of expression.

The redefinition includes the evaluation of men in terms of their chauvinism, and feelings of closeness to other women (although condescension to the unliberated is also noticeable); "institutions such as the

---

[6] The fineness of the analysis is illustrated by response to etiquette or chivalry (Hole and Levine, 1971, pp. 216–18): being treated differently, as when placed on a pedestal, means denial of human (equal) status. Men opening or holding doors for women (Shenker, 1973) may be a denigrating political act: "Professor Walum complained that this stylized ritual—impregnated with sexual, patriarchal and hierarchical overtones—puts men and women in their places. The male 'communicates his independence by actively meeting the challenge of the door and overcoming it,' stereotypically displaying 'the male virtues of physical strength, mechanical ability, worldliness, self-confidence, and efficacy.'" Our earlier remarks on nonverbal behavior, especially in regards to assertion are relevant in this context.

university, government, legal system, occupational structure and the church are appraised according to their support of the traditional sex role and their manifestations of discrimination." (p. 88.) In addition to reformulating interactions from the new point of view, there are new acts: "her behavior must change to align with these new images." (p. 89.) It is in this context that there is an active display of commitment. There is a great range to such action (e.g., Hole and Levine, 1971, pp. 77–166). It may take the form of working within the system towards changing laws dealing with abortion, rape, property rights in marriage, taxation, child-care centers, or equality of employment. It may at times take the form of acts which seem tempests in teapots when waves need to be made, such as attacks on symbols involving clothing or advertising. Such acts, however, by drawing attention, are considered educational in purpose.

In addition, the new acts validate the new role in the person's own eyes. "These kinds of actions served to educate politicians as well as the general public, partly because the media are much more likely to publicize protest actions (television requires 'visual appeal') than to discuss legislative or legal demands. And they forced men and women all over the country to confront the issues and talk about them for the first time." (Komisar, 1972, p. 135.)

These acts are steps toward a new role, and such relatively small and seemingly inconsequential acts inaugurate the commitment process (Kiesler, 1971). Of greatest importance, the expected docile behaviors are replaced by active, assertive, and, at times, aggressive ones. This may be in talking up at meetings, even though the issue introduced may seem very tangential to the points being discussed.

Micossi (p. 89) says, in this context of the more extreme convert, "she feels righteously justified in abrogating responsibility for her actions." In acting in a manner contrary not only to expectations held about women but also those of civility, traditional discourse, or scientific method (Millet, 1970; Greer, 1971; Chesler, 1972), the woman becomes the object of criticism. She may consider the criticism invalid, she may shift from the argument at hand to an attack on the critic's motives or personal adequacy (a tactic not unknown to psychoanalysts), or she may simply appeal to circumstances: "They don't deny that they may be committing injustices, but these, they say, are justifiable . . . they slough off any guilt by seeing the 'injury' as justifiable when balanced against men's calculated dehumanization of all females." (Micossi, p. 89.) At this point, for example, an interviewer argues the respondents to her questionnaire into the "correct" answers; the objectivity which is presumed in scientific endeavor gives way to enlightening the subjects to the way they should feel rather than finding out what they experienced or how they actually felt. The end justifies the means, but there is shock when such methods are repudiated by the scientific community. Such rejection, however, may be taken as validation of the central formulation of a sexist society. The person begins to create a world which fits her formulation, and for some, at an extreme, she may be shaped into a position and actions that she never intended.

We have selected the women's liberation movement for our example of creative deviants, although the structure of the careers fits that for other movements and could have been applied equally well to behavior therapists (Ullmann and Sikora, 1970; Ullmann, 1972), marijuana smokers, policemen, or Blacks. The effects of the women's liberation activities are already felt in an increased range of choices, from occupation to dress, from marriage styles to ownership of one's own body and property. The opportunity to make choices between meaningful alternatives is our definition of freedom.

At an immediately applied level, sensitivity to the social pressures on women affects target behaviors in therapy, most fundamentally in terms of what is acceptable and appropriate.[7] From practically the moment of birth, the sexes are treated differently and different patterns of behavior are encouraged (see, e.g., Freeman, 1970) in terms of dress, toys, sports, school work and material in texts,[8] and types of interpersonal styles (active versus passive). Given stereotypes of mental health and stereotypes of masculinity and femininity (Broverman et al., 1970), two problems arise. The first is that being logical, competitive, direct, aggressive, independent, skilled, adventurous, and dominant are stereotypically masculine and yet frequently valued as indicating adjustive behavior. The second problem is that women clients may be considered changeworthy if they fit this pattern and do not fit a conforming, sensitive, unambitious (save for her mate's success), submissive, interested-in-personal-appearance pattern. The manifesto for the New York Radical Femininists delineates this stereotype: "The services we supply are services to the male ego. We are rewarded according to how well we perform these services. Our skill—our profession—is our ability to be feminine—that is, dainty, sweet, passive, helpless, ever-giving and sexy." (Hole and Levine, 1971, p. 441).

Horner (1969), for example, makes the point that a man who is a success in business or a profession is likely to be evaluated as happy, but a woman who has such a success is likely to be looked at with suspicion and considered unhappy and insecure. The question for a change agent such as a therapist is whether a person is acting appropriately, and there is a clear danger that a person may be labeled in terms of values or stereotypes which are not only inaccurate but actually destructive.

SUMMARY

This chapter dealt with behaviors which usually do not find their way into books on abnormal psychology. Cooperation, sharing, helping others, altruism, self-control, good citizenship, and morality were included under the general label of "positive deviance." Influences on the occurrence of such behaviors were discussed, not because we consider them to be "abnormal," but because we consider these as highly desirable behaviors which in many instances are alternatives to behaviors usually described as "deviant." The methods for developing these behaviors are the same as those used to alter any behavior. While "positive" deviance takes us into the realm of values, it is our belief that the best way to alter behavior is to provide a satisfying alternative. As we have repeatedly noted, to decrease a behavior without teaching a new one is to do but half the job, and to do that half poorly.

---

[7] One of the hardest decisions in writing the present volume was whether to use the pronoun "he" in a general sense, or to use the genderless pronoun, "they." Quite possibly incorrectly, we chose the former; we were responding to the distancing involved in referring to people who are changeworthy as "they."

[8] There is growing evidence that the textbooks used in most elementary school classrooms are likely to present the female role in a denigrating or derogatory manner (Levy and Stacey, 1973; Saairo, Tittle, and Jacklin, 1973). This early exposure may be an important element in the development of adult sex stereotypes in both males and females.

humanism, human behavior, and the concept of abnormality

29

At the start of this book we said, "First of all, this is a book about people. It is about how people get along with other people, the things they learn to do, and the concepts other people have about such adjustments." Further, we noted that, "The central idea of this book is that the behaviors traditionally called abnormal are no different, either quantitively or qualitatively, in their development and maintenance from other learned behaviors." We view the treating of another person as abnormal to be a learned behavior; and we spent considerable time describing the conditions and consequences of such activities. In particular, we noted that, historically, a change from a moralistic model to a medical one encouraged scientific endeavor and more humane treatment. We also noted, however, that the medical model, while appropriate to some problems such as paresis, did not accurately fit the observations of the behavior of the vast majority of people who have come under the changing, expanding purview of psychiatry.

An advantage of the medical orientation is that it permits intervention for the person's own good. By extension, it may legitimize intervention in situations in which someone wishes to change another's behavior which has not violated written laws. It is a short cut in an area of activity not covered by law (Shah, 1970). In addition, for the person who wishes a change in himself, the patient role is one in which he is not directly responsible. Finally, sickness, as deviation from health, carries with it an ethical justification, a setting of things to the normal, natural, and proper way they should be. The restoration of "health" is an acceptable reason for the interventions of professional mental health practitioners such as psychiatrists or clinical psychologists.

If we take away the medical model, we must replace it with some other paradigm so that we can proceed to act in the difficult situations with which we are faced. As we learn more about the influences on behavior, we are increasingly less likely to make use of the traditional concepts of abnormality. We then are faced with the problem of guidelines for dealing with people. We cannot avoid or deny the existence of ethical problems, and to do so would be the most unethical resolution of all.

In discussing a related subject—personality as a human creation (Krasner and Ullman, 1973)—we attempted to resolve the issue. Space permits us to present only some of the conclusions of our discussion. There is no way that logic or social science can provide an absolute definition of good; rather, values are chosen (rationally or capriciously) as, for example, the value of accurate observation is the foundation of science, simply because such a value makes science possible. Further, the impact of the selection of a value deserves study rather than passive acceptance. The circular nature of the situation is illustrated by the fact that the evaluation of the selection of a value (independent variable) is in terms of another value (dependent variable).

The problem yields to no easy or absolute answers. But it is a situation which is also one of responsibility: people must select and test the values on which they base their decisions and order their lives.

If we believe that a technology of behavior influence is developing, we are faced with a choice. We may stamp it out and make it a punishable offense to pursue this line of investigation. We may decide not to do anything and to leave the application of such psychological findings to whoever wishes to use them for whatever ends he desires. Or, we may try to face the hard problems of *what* procedures may be used by *whom* to attain *what* permissible ends. We may pursue this undertaking not in an attempt to discover something already given, but to help create something new. [Krasner and Ullmann, 1973, p. 502.]

Areas of Choice (Ethical Concern)

New discoveries solve some problems, but in their very nature create new ones, or, as very frequently happens with scientific endeavor, create opportunities for choice which had not previously existed. In this section we will review some topics of this nature. Aside from the material itself, we hope to introduce some of the considerations involved in ethical choices. Hard but exciting decisions are the ones in which there are two or more values or interests in potential conflict.

Genetic Engineering

We need only look at each other to note that few, if any, of us are physically identical. Some differences in physique represent major biological anomalies that are associated with decreased physical and intellectual capacity. Other genetic defects are associated with decreased life-span, and possibly with increased likelihood of psychotic depression or schizophrenic behavior. On a positive side, longevity, physical endurance, and intellectual capacity may be associated with genetic dispensation (e.g., Hirsch, 1963, 1967). With increasing knowledge, the possibility of genetic modification through DNA manipulation (Davis, 1970; Friedmann and Roblin, 1972; *Time,* April 1971, pp. 34–43) is a distinct possibility. Problems are raised by diagnostic procedures that indicate the probabilities of a child having a defective genetic endowment. The side effects and specificity of genetic engineering are not known (Fox and Littlefield, 1971), but may be overcome by advanced technology.

The problem of who is to determine what particular traits are desirable runs throughout the area of abnormal behavior. For example: should high-risk populations be forced to take tests? Should information about a person's genetic defects be given to him or to other people who might also be at risk, such as blood relatives, future spouses, or insurance companies? (Adams, 1973). Thus, the issues raised includes confidentiality within a high-risk population as well as the basis for the selection of traits to be manipulated.

Biofeedback

Biofeedback is a form of education and has as a goal an increase in awareness and self-control. A first question is whether the procedure is safe in the hands of a person not specifically trained; that is, should a person be prevented from harming himself? A second consideration is that if a person elects to undertake a course of biofeedback, either by himself or under supervised tutelage, he must do so with *informed consent*. How much should a customer know before he can be sold either the process or the equipment? If the standards of knowledge are set too high, there follows a limitation on who will obtain the benefits of the new technology. Next, the claims for both the hardware (equipment) and the procedures for using it should be honest—the seller should not make unfounded claims. But what if the developer or seller makes honest errors in his scientific evaluations? For example, there may have been a poor research design and the results reported were obtained because of a placebo effect. Is incompetence in science unethical?

The issue of consumer protection, and beyond it, of paternalism, is highlighted by biofeedback sales to the general public. Above all, under what conditions may a person alter his own physiological environment and under what conditions should he be limited by the judgments of medical and governmental policy? The issue resembles that raised by suicide and drugs such as marijuana and heroin insofar as defining the rights of people to control their own bodies.

Population Control

There are limited, nonrenewable resources that eventually limit population size. Even before this limit is reached, an increasing population may wipe out gains made by a nation in its productivity. The methods of social science and behavior influence may be used to persuade or propagandize for implementation of population-control programs. Pressures to limit population conflict with concepts of freedom, including the one of couples having the right to decide, without pressure, how many children, if any, they wish to have. At one level, the issue is similar to the problem of the battered child: At what point may a government enter into what was previously the exclusive province of the family? In population control, it is a matter of birth; with the battered child, it is a matter of discipline. At its most crucial level, the issue is one of survival of the species versus survival of a particular lifestyle (in this case a freedom of choice in an area many consider privileged) (Callahan, 1972; Ehrlich and Holdren, 1971.) At intermediary levels, methods of control and methods to influence people to adopt birth-control methods must be evaluated ethically.

Death and Life, and Style of Life

In this final section of physiologically centered ethical problems, we may note that the very definitions of death and life are open to dispute (Morrison, 1971; Kass, 1971). The matter has been highlighted by judicial decisions on abortion, and leads to a consideration of when is life present in an individual with rights to be protected.

A different question is when may (or should) activities to prolong life cease? This involves the movement towards "death with dignity." At what point is pain so great, activity so reduced, cost so high for all concerned (utilization of limited medical resources as well as impact on surviving relatives), and the outcome so clear that positive efforts to prolong life should cease? Heroic efforts to prolong life using advanced technology are a relatively recent example of scientific technology creating an ethical problem (not unlike genetic engineering). Is there an obligation to make the utmost act in all cases? The issue is not limited to the aged; a newspaper report (Snider, 1973) notes that 43 infants over a two-and-a-half-year span were deliberately allowed to die because physicians had decided that their birth deformities could not be overcome to afford "meaningful humanhood." That the parents gave consent to cessation of positive efforts (e.g., supplemental oxygen) does not alter the ethical issue: When may one person decide to stop his efforts for another person? Of even greater interest is the introduction of the concept of "meaningful humanhood," that is, quality of life rather than life itself. Does the quality of life take precedence over life, or is it an important consideration, or no consideration at all?

We are particularly impressed by Morrison's (1971) comments that make the labeling of a person as dead, and the very reification of death, quite similar to processes observed in the area of abnormality. For purposes of ethical concerns, the most controversial statement by Morrison is:

> ... the life of the dying patient becomes steadily less complicated and rich, and, as a result, less worth living or preserving. The pain and suffering involved in maintaining what is

left are inexorably mounting, while the benefits enjoyed by the patient himself, or those he can in any way confer on those around him, are just as inexorably declining. As the costs mount higher and the benefits become smaller and smaller, one may well begin to wonder what the point of it all is. [Morrison, 1971, p. 696.]

In fact, parts of the body which might be used for transplants and extend other lives may be more alive and "valuable" than the total dying corpus. However, we must remind the reader of the potential misuse of the state's right to allow the aged or deformed to die, as evidenced in totalitarian countries such as Nazi Germany.

Hardware: Information Storage and Retrieval

Electronic devices make possible the gathering of data that invades privacy. It makes possible the combination into single, easily retrieved dosiers of all of a person's records: of his hospitalizations and treatments, his family, and his monetary dealings, etc. This may prove a blessing in collecting and collating information, particularly when a patient is not capable of volunteering it. In this regard, Glueck is an outstanding contributor (Glueck and Luce, 1968; Rosenberg and Glueck, 1967; Glueck, 1967; Rosenberg, Glueck, and Bennett, 1967). Ethical concerns arise when information is retrieved from the computer which is not the appropriate concern of an investigator. What is appropriate, in turn, is itself open to dispute. For example, if a person is receiving service from two or more government agencies, at what point is coordination of the services in his interest, and at what point might such coordination decrease his benefits? And if his benefits are decreased because he has stepped outside legal or policy guidelines, should information obtained from him (and collated on the computer) be used against him?

While computers provide educational opportunities (Cooley and Glaser, 1969; Alpert and Bitzer, 1970; Hammond, 1971), as well as manipulation of data statistically, they so extend human capabilities that they introduce new ethical problems (Weizenbaum, 1972). The two noted here are invasion of privacy and data utilization without the person's consent.

The Production of Research

The unwitting but nonetheless deleterious effects of psychological testing (e.g., using tools not standardized on the population being measured; the decisions taken thereon; the effects of labeling and "tracking") and the invasion of privacy in both institutionalized testing and behavioral research led to a series of self-searching works (e.g., Willingham, 1967; Wolfensberger, 1967; Panel, 1967), and culminated in adoption of a set of ethical principles in the conduct of research with human participants (American Psychological Association, 1973a).

The key features of the ethical principles highlight areas in which there was ethical concern. A first feature is that research workers are ethically responsible in this professional activity. A second principle, perhaps the central one, is that the research worker must inform the participant of all features of the experiment that might reasonably affect the decision to participate. Further, there should be no coercion, and the person may decline to participate or terminate his involvement at any time without aversive consequences. The research worker must be honest and open with the participant and carry out all the promises he makes. The investigator must protect the participant from harm both during the research and afterwards, including the privacy of the responses he gave.

Because the research agreement may be made between people of unequal power, for example a professor and a student in his course, the research worker has the burden of being careful not to abuse his power. The guidelines alert him to seek the counsel of his colleagues for conditions of ethical risk when he deviates from the standards for purposes of the research, as the only way to carry it out. There is an acceptance of a relative cost-to-benefit, or risk-to-gain principle: Will the gain to society of the knowledge justify the discomfort, danger, or risk to the participant? In a small way this mirrors the cost to benefit involved in the matters of death broached by Morrison (above); in a larger measure, it reflects the fact that one person may know, or think he knows, better than another.

Application of Research

This entire volume deals with the use of material that is presumably scientific to understand and respond to acts by humans. It is an application of science to social behavior. Aside from the inequality of individuals in the face of institutions, there is the inequality of knowledge, that is, unequal access to scientific information. Beyond this, information may be applied in a manner that is questionable to some while correct to others.

SPECIFYING LIMITS OF BEHAVIOR: RIGHTS OF PEOPLE

Eventually, ethical concerns are matters of guiding actions in difficult situations in which alternative decisions may be made. They are attempts to provide guidelines before the fact. To say that something was correct because it came out all right is an appeal to the concept of the ends justifying the means. Guidelines are offered to provide decisions prior to such a test. In this regard, ethical strictures are very different from scientific procedures in which data are gathered to help make decisions in the face of uncertainty.

We have mentioned guidelines in terms of the conduct of research, notably obligations to human participants. Workers in the field welcome such guidelines because they are relieved, at least in some measure, from having to work through each new instance on their own. Among the groups for whom guidelines are developing are children and parents, and patients and practitioners. In these two instances, the former (children and patients) are unequal in power to the latter (parents and practitioners); in both instances, the latter are frequently presumed to know better and to have the interests of the former at heart.

Children and Parents

Childhood, as we know it today, is a relatively recent invention, spurred by child-labor laws and compulsory education. It is a period of developing maturity without legal rights. For example, a teen-ager is essentially incompetent to make contracts or sue for redress at law; similarly, a juvenile may be incarcerated for activities, such as curfew violations, that are not crimes for adults. A minor, in the majority of juvenile court situations, does not have the same legal safeguards as an adult, in terms of requirements for evidence, although this situation is changing in the face of recent court decisions.

In the school environment, personal rights may be curtailed; this may be in matters of grooming (hair length, slacks), political expression (wearing buttons or arm bands), or privacy (search of lockers for contraband). A crucial issue at the time of this writing is the privacy of a minor's consultation with a physician without parental knowledge.

Another area of concern is the nature of the material which may be included in a student's file; a student's "attitude," undefined and without documentation, may be held against him. Such material may not be seen, much less protested, although the file may travel with the student so that he is labeled and placed at a disadvantage throughout his educational experience (in much the same manner as a hospital file may follow the patient the remainder of his life).

The topic of the battered child raises a number of questions; for example, parents are expected to guide and discipline children, and not to do so may be considered neglect. At the point at which there is physical evidence such as broken bones, discipline turns to abuse. The state sets limits on parental authority and rights and enters into the relationship between parent and child in order to protect the latter. It may lead to certain parents being considered unfit or (at an extreme) justification for breaking up a family. (Billingsley and Giovannoni, 1972).

Patients and Practitioners

Aside from privacy and fair financial treatment, a major consideration in the treatment of patients who are physically ill is that the patient, or his guardian, has the right, which is also a key one in research participation, of being fully informed and offering his consent based on fair information. These considerations have been elaborated by Ackley (1971) in regard to confidentiality of psychological consultation or the use of psychological material. Practitioners usually do not have a privilege of confidentiality; they have an *obligation*. While trial evidence that is accurate may force disclosure in limited circumstances, the need for protection is basic to the therapist-client relationship and is usually respected.

The American Psychological Association has a relatively elaborate body of guidelines for professional ethics and conduct, particularly in regard to psychotherapy. Because the code (under revision at the time of this writing) was adopted in 1952, a number of recent developments, such as the community mental health centers, the encounter-sensitivity movement, the growth of behavior therapy, and the greater awareness of socioeconomic influences and of experimenter bias are not directly treated therein. The thread that runs through the American Psychological Association guidelines is that the psychologist in the practice of his profession shall not use his role in order to satisfy illegitimate goals or legitimate goals in an illegitimate fashion. There are specific guidelines for relations with clients, the public, and other professional people, and for confidentiality. The basic guideline is protecting the client's welfare and the next is a related one of honesty. This includes the therapist neither making claims for competence he does not have nor making undocumented claims for techniques.

Increasingly, courts are affirming that if a person is incarcerated for treatment, he should receive treatment and should not be institutionalized if that treatment can be obtained (e.g., drugs) while he is in the extrainstitutional community. A related issue, on which courts are currently ruling, is that a school-age child, even if handicapped by retardation or sensory losses (e.g., deafness, blindness), has a right to an education, and classes suitable for him should be provided by the community.

In terms of detail, the most complete list of rights of those treated has been developed in the area of corrections (National Council on Crime and Delinquency, 1972). Inhumane treatments, isolation procedures, grievances, visits, judicial recourse, and disciplinary procedures are outlined. Positive rights which are to be encouraged, rather than errors to be avoided, are not yet clear; but minimal protection of human rights, includes fair and decent interaction.

Encounter-Sensitivity Training

The last decade has seen the burgeoning of encounter-sensitivity practices that may include religious, entertainment, or psychotherapeutic orientations (or combinations thereof). To the extent that they claim to be working within a scientific discipline such as psychology, psychiatry, or social science, and to the extent that they promise changes in life-style or personality and the lifting of repressions, there is implicit orientation that this procedure is psychotherapy. If this is so, certain legal and ethical guidelines come into focus. State laws certify who shall offer such services to the public. The standards of professional associations governing advertising and the limits of interpersonal interactions also come to attention. For example, professionals ordinarily do not advertise for clients. Further, undocumented, testimonial, or evaluative claims are not made about one's ability, techniques or equipment in public media.

Psychotherapeutic practice usually demands screening so that the method is suited to the needs of a client. The therapist remains responsible for what occurs in the interaction and what results therefrom. As such, the encounter-sensitivity practitioners who advertise for and do not screen clients and who do not accept any responsibility for activities within or immediately after their interactions, are acting in a manner that is at variance with ethical therapeutic practice. The documented encounter-sensitivity casualties (see Chapter 12) have led one observer to remark that if encounter were a medical preparation, it would be banned as dangerous. It might also be added that given the new standards for drug effectiveness, it would probably be banned as not living up to advertised claims.

The response of the encounter-sensitivity group practitioners is many-faceted. The first is to the issue of *responsibility*. They claim that they should be no more restricted than any other public educational (books, lectures) offering. As such, they disavow clinical practice or therapeutic intent (although this is counter to what is observed during their actual practices). Their claim is that the procedure is designed to enhance normal living: to extend awareness and to improve already normal functioning. As such, it is an interaction between consenting adults and not bound by the restrictions of clinical practice. (The deviation from this stance in actual interactions, then, is a matter of dishonesty, but not one that is an ethical issue specific to encounter-sensitivity practitioners).

Further, the very philosophy on which encounter-sensitivity is based calls for the person being authentic, that is making acts on his own volition, acts which may be dangerous, and, in fact, by definition, may lead to anxiety (due to the risk of not conforming). As such, the practitioner argues that he should not be responsible, for if he is, he encourages inauthenticity.

That acts made during encounter sessions may later cause the former group member anguish or lead to acts with other people that are not likely to be in the member's best interest are countered by two arguments. The first is that such follow-ups are *dehumanizing* since they observe and quantify individual behavior as one does in physical science. The other argument offered is that the encounter leader may be concerned, but he is *not responsible* in any legal or moral fashion. While there may be lip-service to a group member being allowed to do (and be responsible for) whatever he wishes (that he can leave at any time), in practice there is strong group pressure to remain and frequently aversive interpretation by the leader (who cannot let his group disintegrate or his knowledge be challenged) of what withdrawing from a session "means."

These issues have been addressed, in developing standards for encounter-therapy usage, by the National Training Laboratory (1969), American Medical Association Council on Mental Health (1971), and the American Psychological Association (APA, 1973b, Strassburger, 1971). The guidelines deal with such topics as the qualifications of the leader, his methods of soliciting clients, selection and screening of clients as to suitability, complete freedom from coercion at every step of the way (e.g., an employer or a teacher may not make participation a requirement), and availability of consultation or follow-up by the leader or a stand-in.

Two crucial matters are informed consent and leader responsibility. These concepts have been touched on above in our discussion of research participation. Informed consent means that the person contemplating participation must be told beforehand what will occur, how he may be affected, and that every promise made will be kept. There is no informed consent without knowledge by the participant. The leader is responsible for the accuracy of that information. A second and related matter is that the group setting and exercises of increasing intimacy may lead to unusual behaviors in the context of the larger society; the leader's responsibility for such activities, as well as his participation and personal gratification therein, require an ethical stance. It has been suggested that not only should the group leader's qualifications be openly scrutinized, but also that he should be restrained by the legal standards set for professional people in the acts of their profession and by guidelines such as those of the American Psychological Association dealing with respect for societal standards.

The following excerpt from the American Psychological Association guidelines (1973) reflects the beliefs of professionals as to the kinds of responsibility involved:

. . . it is recognized that growth groups may be used for both educational and psychotherapeutic purposes. If the purpose is primarily educational, the leader assumes the usual professional and ethical obligations of an educator. If the purpose is therapeutic, the leader assumes the same professional and ethical responsibilities he or she would assume in individual or group psychotherapy, including before and after consultation with any other therapist who may be professionally involved with the participant. In both cases, the leader's own education, training, and experience would be commensurate with these responsibilities. [APA, 1973, p. 933.]

Behavior Therapy

The major ethical problem for the behavior therapist stems from the assumption of responsibility (as distinct from the encounter-sensitivity avoidance thereof). A behavior therapist, like a teacher, has goals for his student and brings to bear the most effective technology he knows in order to attain them. (Ullmann, 1973.) The behavior therapist must decide what material he will teach and how he will teach that material. This decision is affected by the age and social competence of the client, and the social concern caused by the behavior in question. For example, in Chapter 16 we noted (Lang and Melamed, 1969) the problem involved in the change of ruminative behavior in a nine-month-old child. The informed consent of a nine-month-old child is difficult to obtain and, in this case, the child's death was highly likely. It is not a question of whether one may intervene; not to intervene is a genuine decision and act in itself, as noted above in the section on life and death. At the other extreme, there are instances of intelligent adults who have fears that were learned in situations which no longer are present and which keep them from making rational choices of alternative courses of action and sources of pleasure open to them. An example would be a college student who literally gets so uptight on exams that he is in danger of flunking out of college. Here, fully informed consent is possible and, at a realistic level, is vital for the success of a behavior-therapy intervention such as systematic desensitization.

Ethical questions are far more severe when fully informed consent is not possible, such as with children, retardates, and institutionalized people labeled psychotic. One question that is raised with outpatient adults, usually in the realm of sexual activity, is whether there are any behaviors that the therapist should *not* alter, either to increase or decrease. If all behaviors are learned, and if we take the extreme biological view that if the person can do it it is (physiologically) natural (not necessarily desirable), are there any limits to our actions? Behaviorists differ among themselves on this point.

A change in an individual's behavior is likely to have an impact on the people around him. A person who learns to assert himself, that is stick up for his legitimate human rights, is acting in a manner more likely to increase the range of situations with which he can deal pleasantly and effectively. It increases his behaviors and choices. Such assertion, however, may be considered reprehensible or an indication of deterioration by those who previously exploited him (e.g., by his employer, his wife, or others whose unreasonable demands he previously satisfied). We face the problem, then, of defining reasonable demands and legitimate human rights. When possible and relevant, the significant other who will be affected becomes a partner to the intervention. In actuality, such a procedure facilitates treatment as well as solves ethical problems, and the very confrontation of values may have benefit. But when such an ideal situation is not possible, the therapist must make a decision on his own. While community standards and regard for the rights and feelings of people other than his immediate client are crucial, eventually the therapist must accept the responsibility for making the decision whether to help in a task or not. He cannot duck the decision; nor, in a rapidly changing, pluralistic society, can he find a standard that will be a guide in all situations.

If we must act, then the question is on what basis will we make decisions. By definition, when we intervene, we change behavior. We must not fall into the trap of saying that what the person is currently doing is what he "wants" to do. "Want," in this case, usually means "reinforcing." A person does what he has been taught: what he knows how to do and what has paid off. That a person has developed a particular set of responses as a result of prior experiences and current reinforcement contingencies does not mean that the learning and maintaining environments cannot and should not be changed.

The child, retardate, or institutionalized person is not an equal in the power relationship. Our goal is that he will become such: that he will select both the payoffs and the methods for gaining such, that is, that he will become the programmer and designer of his own environment. In the interim, however, who speaks for the client and what are the safeguards? Two major concepts are applicable here. The first is that the behaviorist himself is the child's or institutionalized person's advocate. Our object is that the person will be able to deal with as many situations as possible, that he will have a genuine choice based on competence. Our effort is directed towards independence and increasing life-space. Very frequently our impact is to help the teacher or ward technician to understand the specific person, to react to him as a human being, to enrich and increase positive consequences in both the long- and short-term run. We are likely to program positive consequences for behavior that moves in a prosocial direction and to ignore, whenever possible, disruptive behavior. We have previously referred to the concepts as shaping and extinction. The point here is that we increase the target person's overall favorable consequences.

A second major concept is that the person does not live in a social vacuum. While we are advocates for our clients, we are also representatives of society, both in general and in particular. Taking the latter first: a child who disrupts a schoolroom adversely affects the learning experience of his classmates, whose welfare must also be taken into account. Withdrawal of the child from the classroom, however, may start a scenario of that person being labeled as disruptive, uneducable, or the like.

If possible we will retrain the child in the target situation and not withdraw him. (Among other things, this encourages the teacher to analyze problem situations rather than resolve difficulties by stigmatizing children.) We believe that even if the schools were as inefficient as some claim, they still are major vehicles for transmitting skills such as reading, writing, and computing, which help people get and keep jobs or enter later forms of training with increasing and diverse payoffs.

Behavioral approaches, like all other forms of social-influence technology, do not specify how they are to be applied. This leads to a search for values by which to evaluate the impact of the applications. Ultimate values are not given to us; we select them and later determine the consequences of our choices. (See Krasner and Ullmann, 1973, especially Chapter 19.)

At an applied level, questions have been raised about behavioral techniques, many of which have been dealt with in the foregoing chapters. Behavioral approaches do not aim for unquestioning conformity, but rather for effective and satisfying responses to situations. As such, questioning behavior, defining problems, listing alternative courses of action, assertion, self-programming, and building complex social relations (such that what was a terminal act becomes instrumental and role-expressive) are all encouraged as integral parts of the behavioral approach. Further questions concern the use of aversive stimuli; we can only point out the conditions under which such stimuli are used (e.g., severe, critical self-injurious behavior, and with a consenting adult outpatient) and the relative specificity and gentleness of such stimuli compared with physiological treatments such as electroconvulsive therapy and lobotomy, which stem from a medical orientation. The choice frequently is between incarceration and reeducation. For both the individual and the people represented by the word "society" who underwrite programs, reeducation is preferable. This is all the more so as one becomes familiar with typical institutional practices.

Running throughout behavioral intervention techniques is a focus on behavior and the measurement of change. The focus on overt behavior rather than hypothesized internal traits, which are at best vaguely defined and minimally related to target tasks and situations (Mischel, 1968), makes for a clearer understanding among client, therapist, and social system. The specification of what behaviors will be increased or decreased makes much easier the determination of whether the change will be desirable or not; put in different terms, the therapeutic contract is much more explicit. Second, the behavioral therapist relates what will be done, when, and for what effect, *beforehand*. The effects of treatment are also much easier to assess when the targets are overt behaviors which are explicitly defined. If such definitions cannot be devised, the program is not undertaken, that is, there is no functional response class present for the observers, much less, the trainee. Finally, not only the target response classes, but behavior in general is observed and evaluated after treatment. Because of the psychoanalytic hypothesis that direct treatment (reeducation) of overt behavior should lead to symptom substitution, behaviorists have an additional spur to follow up their cases.

Another question is what steps are taken to prepare for unforeseen and unwanted effects of intervention. The follow-up material just cited is a first measure. In addition, changed behavior, and the effects on others of this change, has a feedback effect. Rather than new unwanted behavior, which might be called symptom substitution, what is much more likely is generalization of both specific positive behaviors and general approaches to other similar situations. Second, knowing that what one does has an effect on others provides what in another time might have been called insight. Changed behavior precedes changed attitudes. Such changes are not restricted to the target person alone. Teachers, parents, and institutional workers are able to see that the people with whom they deal are not hopeless and that they may become teachers rather than custodians and baby-sitters. Specificity and measurement increase the chance of public accountability. Necessary parts of the behavioral technology, they are also major steps toward ethical practice.

While the direct, educational model of behavior therapy is a step forward at an ethical as well as technical level, all ethical problems are not resolved (e.g., Wexler, 1973; Schwitzgebel, 1970). First, learning principles as generalizations are neutral as to specific application. Second, in line with making effective responses to situations, we must deal with specific times, places, and people of different age, sex, race, education, and the like. Finally, ethics are created by people; they are a form of behavior; and they should be studied in the same manner and with the same rigor as other classes of behavior.

LAW AND MEDICINE

Many of the problems previously discussed in this book converge in the question of the legal status of individuals labeled mentally ill. Different models of abnormal behavior have consequences for the rights granted to individuals called abnormal. In most instances the medical profession conceptualizes abnormal behavior as mental illness and hence a health problem. If this view is correct, then it is the physician who should be primarily, if not exclusively, responsible for decisions involving hospitalization and discharge. In contrast, if abnormal behavior is approached from a sociopsychological framework, then questions of hospitalization primarily involve legal, behavioral, and ethical issues rather than medical ones.

The medical point of view contends that procedures necessitated by the laws about commitment in many states tend to be detrimental to the patient, especially insofar as they insist upon his personal appearance in court and hence making him a public spectacle. This, it is argued, aggravates the condition and makes it less likely that the family will seek assistance early in the "illness." In contrast, people emphasizing the importance of the legal procedures argue that there is no justification for depriving an individual of his liberty without giving him an opportunity to appear in court, testify, and even cross-examine those who would argue for his confinement.

These opposing views are manifested in various state laws which emphasize either "medical certification" as the route to involuntary commitment or judicial hospitalization with a jury determining the issue. In the former procedure all that is necessary is that a number of physicians, usually two, examine the individual and find him in need of treatment. In the latter procedure it is laymen, insofar as medicine is concerned, who make the determination.

Rea (1966; also Burris, 1969), reviewing the legal rights of the mentally ill, points out that there are three issues which add to the conflict between the medical and the legal advocates. First, in most state mental hospitals the patient is likely to encounter a custodial rather than a treatment program. If an individual is involuntarily held in an institution without adequate treatment, he is actually being punished by being deprived of liberty without having committed a crime. Second, most state laws are vague as to what behaviors justify involuntary hospitalization. In Massachusetts, for example, one may be hospitalized for "social nonconformity." The danger inherent in such laws, especially as they may be applied to unpopular opinions, is obvious (Halleck, 1972; Szasz, 1971; Liefer, 1969).

As has been discussed throughout the book, psychiatric labeling is at best tenuous. Most legal statutes do nothing to foster careful definitions of problem behavior. Third, most hospital commitments are made for an indefinite length of time without provision for periodic review. There are considerable numbers of people now in psychiatric hospitals solely because there was no requirement that their case be reviewed. All three of these points emphasize the dangers inherent in a system whereby an individual is deprived of his social rights on the basis of a medical judgment of his behavior.

Once a person is hospitalized, there are consequences that literally follow him the rest of his life. Many applications for jobs and even drivers' licenses include questions about having spent time in a mental hospital. Further, it is usually almost impossible for a patient to obtain information about his legal rights, since even key administrators may be unaware of these rights, and any attempt to find out about them is frequently treated as further evidence of illness.

An example of these concepts is the following case: In 1967 the New York Court of Claims awarded $115,000 to a 57-year-old man who had been held for 33 years in state mental institutions "through a tragic error." The individual, Stephen D., was arrested in 1925 at the age of 16 for having stolen $5 worth of candy. He violated probation by not reporting to his minister and was committed to serve a ten-year sentence. Prison officials erroneously classified him as a lowgrade moron and placed him in an institution for defective delinquents. In 1936, shortly before completing his sentence, he was transferred to an institution for the criminally insane. He was kept there until his half brother obtained his release by a writ of habeas corpus in 1960. The judge summarized Stephen D.'s experiences as follows: "In a sense, society labeled him as a subhuman, placed him in a cage with genuine subhumans, drove him insane, and then used the insanity as an excuse for holding him indefinitely."

PROBLEMS OF CHANGE: PSYCHOTHERAPY

If the role of the therapist is to remove the blocks that inhibit natural growth or to restore a "normal" state of mental health, then there need be little concern about matters of value. If, on the other hand, the role of the therapist is to directly and actively change behavior (which in itself is neither normal nor abnormal) and to rearrange environmental contingencies, then what the therapist considers socially appropriate becomes crucial. This issue applies to individual psychotherapy, community mental health programs, and the development of institutional programs such as token economies.

A review of research in the field of values and psychotherapy concludes that "the therapist communicates his values to the patient, the patient responds to such communications, certain therapists are likely to be more successful with certain patients because of the interaction of therapist-patient value orientations, therapist-patient pairs with highly discrepant value systems do not usually form an effective therapeutic team, psychotherapy may at least in part consist of a didactic situation in which the patient learns and adopts the values of the therapist, the therapist as a controller of behavior is responsible for concern with the issue of values, and mental health and psychopathology are, at least in part, value problems." (Kessel and McBrearty, 1967, pp. 682–83.)

These problems have been directly raised in the therapy deduced from a behavioral model because the object of treatment is specifically educational (Kanfer, 1965a; Krasner, 1962a, 1965c, 1968b; London, 1964; Ullmann, 1969b). The therapist's personal values, however, are transmitted in indirect therapies even though such teaching may be unwanted and the use of social influence disavowed (Rosenthal, 1955; Parloff, Iflund, and Goldstein, 1960; Petoney, 1966; Holzman, 1961; Welkowitz, Cohen, and Ortmeyer, 1967).

The therapist teaches the individual to "take his place in the . . . social world." This is an explicit definition of value: normality is doing what is socially appropriate. The theoretical limitation of this definition is that normality is potentially equated with conformity. The practical limitation is that it is sometimes hard to determine a person's place in the world. A white supremacist and a black nationalist might well differ as to what the proper place of a specific person is, and the positive value of one might well be the negative value of the other. The point which cannot be escaped is that casting the therapist as a teacher raises the problem of what he shall teach. The decision of what he shall teach involves concepts of good and bad.

Are there certain areas where the therapist may *not* alter behavior? Pepinsky (1966) claims that if a therapist alters the behavior of person A for the sake of person B, he is in an ethically improper position. This is indeed what is done in much of child therapy, work with retardates, correctional procedures with criminals, and hospitalized schizophrenics. In the last two instances, the therapeutic procedures may be coercive in terms of deprived liberties. In the behavior modification literature there are reports of food deprivation of both children and adult psychotics. There are instances of the use of electric shock in a response-contingent manner with children. While it is explicitly a value judgment, it would seem strange to permit a child to do permanent damage to himself rather than use a response-contingent electric shock which imparted information definitely related to his long-term survival (Lovaas, Schaeffer, and Simmons, 1965; see Chapter 23). It is a value judgment, but it would seem strange to permit a child to lose his eyesight rather than deprive him of food for a period of time long enough to develop an effective reinforcing stimulus (Wolf, Risley, and Mees, 1965; see Chapter 23); or to permit him to starve to death rather than use an aversive stimulus (Lang and Melamud, 1969). The point, then, is that there are certain circumstances in which one person may act in the best interests of another without the latter's consistent. The question is, What are these circumstances?

It is possible to add to Pepinsky's point that whenever a change in the person receiving therapy will have an effect on another person, the therapist is on ethically difficult grounds. If a college student who is afraid of women is treated so that he becomes "normal," the therapist bears an ethical burden. Normality in the college culture has a high probability of carrying with it behavior that parents, ministers, and deans of students disavow. The therapist is faced with more than one standard of culturally acceptable behavior, and he may well aid a person to a statistical normality which is contradictory to some other standard of approved behavior.

The ethical problem may be pushed to the limit by considering the research situation. By definition, researchers exploit (make use of for some one else's advantage) people included in the control group. Placebos which are hypothesized not to benefit the subjects but which have hope-giving elements are administered as treatment; there are experimental conditions under which manifestly valuable environmental contingencies are reversed in order to demonstrate their crucial nature. These situations pose grave ethical problems. Where Schreiber (1962; see Chapter 13) used placebo therapy for the good of his patients, in research these procedures are not intended to benefit the patient, even though they may do so (Paul, 1966; see Chapter 12). The dilemma of research is that to determine whether a treatment has genuine merit, procedures must be used during data collection that are designed *not* to benefit the patient.

COMMUNITY AS "PATIENT"

The term "social psychiatry" was probably first used by Southard in 1917; he described it as a new and promising subspecialty of psychiatry analogous to social psychology (Bell and Spiegel, 1966). Under this rubric attempts have been made to bring together psychiatrists, psychologists, social workers, parole officers, anthropologists, sociologists, teachers, and all people interested in altering deviant behavior taking place within or ascribable to social settings. The failure of the development of a model other than the medical analogue and the consequent lack of a technology other than that of individual therapy are probably the reasons why social psychiatry did not have the impact its originators hoped it might have.

Closely allied to social psychiatry, community mental health refers to a philosophy, a method of prevention, and a method of treatment.

One may integrate concepts of intrapsychic, interpersonal, and social settings into a concept of Social Breakdown Syndrome (Gruenberg, Brandon, and Kasius, 1966, pp. 150–51). That is, one may posit conditions which are likely to lead to crime, divorce, hospital admission, or other indications of social breakdown and recourse to mental health professionals. Social conditions may be thought of as leading to stress, which in turn leads to psychiatric symptoms. The miasma model, advocated by Florence Nightingale as a protest against the "germ" or conventional medical theory of discrete, uniquely caused diseases, is seriously advocated by a number of community mental health workers (Bloom, 1965) because of the interdependence of difficulties and the stress on arranging nonspecific optimal conditions. The same social conditions may be thought of as environments failing to provide opportunity for reinforced behavior. In either case, *it is assumed that social action is called for to provide a minimum quality of life.*

The pattern of this life reflects the values of the dominant middle class; the obvious physical advantages of this life and its promulgation through mass media such as television and magazines have led to its widespread acceptance. Work such as that by Mercer (1965) (reviewed in Chapter 24) makes the point that the values of the core culture are not universally accepted. Of greater importance, however, is that a welfare movement having the best intentions may lead to an unthinking paternalism which does violence to the patterns of living of the very people it was designed to help (Sulzer, 1967; Leifer, 1966).

Community psychiatry involves responsibility for prevention, treatment, and rehabilitation of mental disorders in a given population. Caplan and Caplan write that the responsibility "must extend beyond the known cases of mental disorder to the unrecognized cases of current or *future* disorder in the population." (quoted in Margolis and Bonstedt, 1970; italics added.) This raises major ethical and practical issues.

Among the ethical issues Shore and Golann (1969) point out are ones of confidentiality (sharing information outside institutional channels); consultation (is the expert responsible to the organization, the person with whom he is consulting, or the person about whom he is consulting?); competence (training suitable to the tasks assumed, documentation of procedures used); and problems of being a professional or a private citizen.

McNeil, Llewellyn, and McCollough (1970) note that "It is this comprehensive approach to a total population that calls for a consideration of ethics." (p. 23.) Among the problems these authors cite are those of individual versus social needs; threats to individual freedom; priority groups leading to rejection of ones less favored by the workers (for example, difficult cases may be avoided, or cases may be selected on the basis of racial characteristics); "overthrust" and overcontrol (overthrust may lead to the application of a mental health model where it was not previously used and may result in professional intervention that is a distortion of values: "An example of overthrust can be found in the experience of antipoverty community councils in Philadelphia. Community council leaders from the ranks of the poor proved inept, and professional antipoverty workers quickly guided council action. The antipoverty staff became the controllers of the poor rather than their advisors." [p. 27.]); and the de facto generation of public policy ("There are now hopes that community mental health can find solutions to poverty, crime, unhappiness, urban living, racial division, the healthy [proper?] way to live, and even problems of government; in essence, that mental health can cover the gamut of personal and social life." [p. 28.]). Both Roman (1971) and Kellert (1971) point out the dangers of applying medical models to sociological problems, and marshall material of the type presented throughout this volume.

In practice, the goal of community mental health is to develop programs at the federal, state, and local levels to assist individuals in the betterment of their mental health. Carter (1957) summarizes this concept as follows: "A state-wide program of community mental health includes responsibilities in three broad areas of activities: (1) the promotion of mental health by assisting people in the acquisition of knowledge, attitudes, and behavior that will foster, maintain and improve their mental health; (2) the prevention of mental disorders by control of biological, interpersonal, and social factors that jeopardize mental health; and (3) the restoration to health of those persons with mental disorders by providing treatment, aftercare, and rehabilitation services." The problem of what mental health *is,* remains.

Community mental health people often talk of primary, secondary, and tertiary prevention. *Primary prevention* involves reducing the frequency of new cases by modifying environments (Caplan and Grunbaum, 1967) and interpersonal strengths to decrease the development of difficulties. Programs of training interpersonal skills, planned parenthood, community centers, etc., may all fall under this rubric. The epidemiological technique, as illustrated by Eisner's work with juvenile delinquency, (see chapter 26) may be used to isolate correlates of "mental illness." For example, being socially isolated, unmarried, old, male, ill, and religiously unobservant may be highly associated with increased risk of suicide. If we approach suicide in terms of influencing a "mental health" social variable, it could mean the use of therapeutic communities to decrease isolation. By this reasoning, one might also suggest enforced church attendance or marriage for older people. The use of mental health to justify a change on a social variable founders on the problems of (1) changing the social milieu of an entire population for a potentially smaller target population; (2) the selection of the target itself; (3) the intellectual and political legitimacy of those who do the selection; and (4) the lack of compelling evidence that "mental illness is etiologically or sequentially associated with social conditions such as poverty or racism." (Wagenfeld, 1972, p. 195.)

Secondary prevention involves early detection and rapid intervention (treatment). Case-finding is the key technique here, although it presumes the accuracy of diagnosis and the availability of effective treatment. Caplain (1964, p. 268) illustrates the enthusiasm of some: "The psychiatrist can no longer wait for patients to come to him, because he carries equal responsibilities for all those who do not come. A significant part of his job consists of finding out who the mentally disordered are and where they are located in the community."

School children may be tested so that those likely to drop out or become behavioral difficulties are spotted and their files literally "red-tagged" so that therapeutic activities may be focused. The problem of violation of privacy is raised by this procedure. The efficacy of therapy which isolates, labels, and is presumably preventive has yet to be validated. It is quite possible that many people who would not have become problems are identified, since many of these surveys find up to one-third the school population to be high-risk. For example, Cowan and Zax (1968) write: "The designation Red-Tag was used for those youngsters who, on the basis of all available evidence, had already manifested disorders ranging from moderate to severe, or *in whom such pathology seemed incipient*. In schools we have worked in thus far that figure has run about 35 to 40 percent." (p. 51; italics added.) (The reader may note the use of "incipient pathology," a concept that justifies intervention without an overt behavioral referent, which in law is called preventive detention). The special values and groups on which the tests used were standardized lead to a violation of the values of the special subgroups to which they are applied. Not only is there an implicit derogation of the cultures from which the red-tagged are likely to be selected, there is also a major disservice in widespread labeling of people prior to the availability of a validated treatment and prior to overt acts. Rather than presuming that psychological treatment is called for by special groups of people, an effort can and should be made to provide the best possible service to all people. For example, Staats (1968) has noted that classroom problems may well be due to lack of opportunity to engage in learning activities. If a classroom is dull and irrelevant, not only will the immediate effect be behavioral problems, it will in the long run lead to people who are not prepared with skills to perform tasks necessary for earning a living. Efforts such as those of Becker (1973) and Krasner and Krasner (1973) point to the body of information (see also Chapters 23 on children's behavior and 28 on positive deviations) available to help people gain mastery without either labeling them or adhering to a medical model.

Tertiary prevention occurs once a person is in the treatment system. Efforts should be made to avoid the effects of chronicity. Institutionalization in prisons or in large psychiatric hospitals may lead to the learning of patterns of behavior that are not advantageous in the larger, noninstitutional culture. Institutions may be revised in the direction of training for independent living through skill acquisition such as the token economy, or in the direction of the total institution becoming a therapy session (Jones, 1953). Jones (1968) advocates the extension of principles of multiple leadership, decision by consensus, confrontation, feedback, and a therapeutic milieu to all social organizations. Tertiary prevention may also aim at changing attitudes toward the expsychiatric patient or prisoner so that he may more readily resume his former place in society.

Community Mental Health in Action

Problems may be isolated in terms of the locus and method of delivery of services, redefinition of services, and the modification of the community as a social environment (Kahn, 1968; Fairweather et al., 1974; Zax and Specter, 1974).

There is general consensus . . . involving one issue. Traditional treatment programs for the mentally ill have been inadequate. There are a number of goals which emerge from the philosophies which are guiding change. The following might be considered representative of these:

(a) The promotion of mental health becomes the class of activities which subsumes those of treatment of mental illness.

(b) The community is the client and partner

in the promotion and maintenance of mental health.

(c) The mental health professions have a responsibility for the reduction of illness in certain high risk populations.

(d) There must be a professional responsibility for primary prevention as well as treatment and rehabilitation.

(e) Social action becomes a primary tool of intervention. [Vance, 1971, p. 389.]

Roberts (1969) says:

Specifically it [community psychiatry] means that the psychiatrist, his staff, and his agency make the treatment of mental disorder in a given, defined community their responsibility. They are responsible for prevention of new cases, diagnosis and treatment of new and old cases, and rehabilitation of old cases. . . . What lies outside the boundaries of community psychiatry is even less well defined than the outer limits of the field. Some would include all human affairs within the borders of community psychiatric practice, since all man's activities are relevant to his present and future mental health . . . Within our definition, all social, psychological, and biological activity affecting the mental health of the population is of interest to the community psychiatrist, including programs for fostering social change, resolution of social problems, political involvement, community organization planning, and clinical psychiatric practice." [pp. 5 and 7.]

There is an implied control of humans based on psychiatric objectives: "Manifestly, the proper application of public health measures implies the planning and control of human as well as inanimate factors." (Rome, 1969, p. 43.) Halleck (1969, p. 61) sees some of the ethical implications of the community-psychiatry position as outlined above when he writes:

An unexamined and unplanned growth of community psychiatry could have at least five major undesirable results:

1. Community psychiatry could require alteration of the traditional values that have served the medical profession for over two thousand years.

2. Community psychiatry could be abused in a manner that would lead to undesirable limitations of our traditional freedoms.

3. Community psychiatry could involve the physician in political decision-making that is beyond his qualifications or interests.

4. Community psychiatry could lead to an emphasis on medical administrative skills at the expense of services that physicians alone can offer.

5. Community psychiatry, in its efforts to serve all of the citizens of the community, could paradoxically encourage the perpetuation of differential treatment according to class. [Halleck, 1969, p. 61.]

The locus of activity in community psychiatry is extended from intrapsychic phenomenon to the entire range of actors and forces that impinge on the individual. We have often noted that a person is best trained as close to the locus of the required new act as possible—in the classroom, the office, or the home, rather than in interview offices. There is agreement, then, on the change of the place in which work will be done. The difference resides in the rational for acts and the procedures to be undertaken.

A community mental health center which attempts to approach its services to the community within the behavioral model has been established in Huntsville, Alabama (Turner and Goodson, 1971, 1972, 1973). This "empirically-based" comprehensive center serves a county population of close to 200,000 people. The aim of the center is to deliver services effectively to a large number of people, utilizing paraprofessionals, using natural or existing community resources to the fullest within a research orientation which emphasizes accountability to the community. The procedures involved include many of the approaches to individual problems described throughout this book; among them are the organization around learning principles of inpatient, outpatient, alcoholism and crisis services, training, research, and staff activities (Rinn,

Tapp, and Petrella, 1973; Tarver and Turner, 1974).

Conditions of Service Delivery
Crisis Intervention

Under what conditions will service be delivered? Community psychiatry has built up a theory of *crisis intervention* (Caplan, 1964; Schulberg and Sheldon, 1968). Crises may be defined as relatively abrupt, usually time-limited situations in which the person's or family's usual method of coping becomes ineffective. In many regards, there is a similarity to panic or transient situational difficulties. The crises may be environmentally produced, as in unemployment or disaster; be the result of the individual's perception of the event; or be characterized by tension, as with important but insoluble problems, or with critical role transitions such as becoming a parent, moving to a new home, or taking a new job. In short, crisis theory seems to be a new approach to stress, and does not delimit either a special set of problems or techniques for intervention.

Who delivers services in the community is a major question to many authors in this field rather than *what* is delivered. A quasi-analytic, quasi-encounter procedure in which the procedure is to have all parties "communicate" is the typical procedure. In this situation, "indigenous non-professional" members of the target community are recruited to act as "mental" healers. The alternative is found in the training of teachers, parents, spouses, and friends in behavioral procedures that start with defined targets and counting, thus making possible direct accountability. The training of the agents is crucial, for without delivery of something of worth, community efforts create the appearance (placebo) rather than the substance of service.

Delivery *to whom* raises subsidiary ethical issues in terms of case-finding. Are the indigenous nonprofessionals supposed to be paid for recruiting people who would not otherwise have come to the attention of the mental healers? If so, how is the decision to recruit clients to be made? On the basis of what behaviors?

Rapid behavior change may come through political action; various concepts of power permeate many efforts in the field. For example, Denner and Price (1973) divide their book into sections on "the politics of defining deviance," "the politics of emerging professions," and "the politics of community control and its repercussions." This hearkens back to the "radical therapists" mentioned in Chapter 12: more than adjustment to a system is the object, and rather than change by the person, the target is change of the system.

An important area is that of the culture of poverty (Schlesinger and James, 1967). Hunt (1961, 1968, 1972) as well as Hurley (1969) and Hudson (1970) correlates poverty with underdeveloped potentiality, both in terms of nutrition as well as stimulation and encouragement of experience and manipulation. Such material led to environmental enrichment efforts such as Project Head Start. Parents have the option to make use of this agency, participate in it, and provide input. How fully informed parents are in making the decision is difficult to say, because the professionals themselves are not sure of the eventual results.

This may be contrasted with a different form of political maneuver, in which the crucial matters are who selects the target, the legitimacy of the mental healer's involvement, and the appropriateness of his tactics, particularly in regard to the people whom he claims to help. A professional person may observe facts such as those outlined by Hunt, Hurley, and Hudson. He may believe that the quickest method of relief is by governmental or political intervention; he may also note that to be effective he needs the people who will benefit to present the case, and therefore he needs to "raise their political consciousness." The person may gain his entry into the situation as a mental health worker employed to provide service to a group. With no training in *what* to provide, and finding his traditional treatment techniques inadequate and his credibility reduced by lack of success, the person may then blame the system. A technique to regain the lost constituency and self-esteem is to create a *crisis:* ". . . the powerless or non-established group must (1) recognize that it is possible to change the status quo, (2) take the necessary steps to build its support, increase its membership and improve its skills, and then, (3) act or threaten to act against its opposition." (Cohen, 1973, p. 1.) The leader makes use of disruptive acts by the group in a response-contingent manner and must be able both to inaugurate disruptions and, when a point has been won, call them off. Crises are encouraged and situations that may be politically useful are magnified rather than arbitrated. "A critical area of skill for a community action group is knowing how to forecast, generate, pursue, and resolve crises in a manner that brings positive social change." (Cohen, 1973, p. 5.) Positive social change is not defined.

Therapists, unlike activists, work for change within the systems and do not subvert them (Ullmann, 1969b). On the one hand, subversion places the professional in an ethically problematic position in terms of his employers, who contracted with him to do something different. On the other hand, more crucially, it seems improper, for example, to sacrifice an entire cycle of students at a university during a crisis that makes the system become so offensive that it collapses. This is particularly so since neither the students nor parents have consented to the tactic of crisis generation. Finally, to destroy a system without clear delineation of what will take its place also seems ethically problematical. If the alternative is known and clearly specified, it may be tested and evaluated—this we would consider experimentation and change within the system. Further, it is necessary to recognize that social institutions and systems are continually changing and evolving.

A person who has been through a crisis has indeed changed in his perceptions of other members of the community, as his attitudes follow his actions. Further, the other parties will also act differently in the future. The situation is indeed different, but whether polarization or reconciliation are the ultimate results is difficult to predict.

The ethical issues concern the extent to which mental health orientation and training legitimize the tactics of a self-proclaimed activist. What may be appropriate political action may not be justifiable under the guise of professional intervention. The activist may not tell his constituents what his plan is, that is, he may not make that disclosure that is needed for informed consent. He may mislead people for what he considers their own eventual welfare and he may not pursue the activities for which he was originally employed. His means may be such that they tarnish his goals, which may be impeccable; but his actions, if they are a model, widen the chasm rather than bridge it. An ultimate goal of the professional person is to train or educate those who come into contact with him in ways of affecting their own environment so that they increase their chances for satisfying lives.

SUMMARY

Guidelines are required for who shall take responsibility for selecting goals and how shall goals be selected. We suggest a general concept of respect for people; for their aspirations, for their way of life, for their ability to understand and decide for themselves when given information that is accurate rather than manipulative.

We wish to increase the range of realistic choices available to people. Because people are interdependent, we hope to help them find ways to become more skillful in satisfying themselves without infringing on the rights and satisfactions of others. These procedures follow an educational rather than a medical model, and one need not presume that a changeworthy condition is necessarily deviant or "sick." Rather, there must be public scrutiny of both methods and goals.

A medical model may at times be used for social control and for personal benefit. What was at one point in history a humanitarian and progressive development, over time has become an unnecessary and repressive ideology. In changing the model to a sociopsychological formulation and educational intervention, we hope to continue the goals originally envisaged by innovators in the areas of behavior called abnormal such as Pinel, Charcot, and Freud, without the distortions that have been introduced over time through stretching the medical model beyond its appropriate realm.

We can neither divorce ourselves from responsibility nor pretend to superior wisdom. Advocates of newer models, even sociopsychological ones, must be continually vigilant and aware of the potential misuse and misdirection of what are initially "good" social values. The best methods of protecting the general public we can think of are strict enforcement of professional ethical standards, use of scientific method to obtain information, and open communication so that the public is genuinely informed.

references

ABEL, G. G., LEVIS, D. J., and CLANCY, J. Aversion therapy applied to taped sequences of deviant behavior in exhibitionism and other sexual deviations: a preliminary report. *Journal of behavior therapy and experimental psychiatry,* 1970, *1,* 59–66.

ABOOD, L. G. A chemical approach to the problem of mental disease. In D. D. Jackson, ed., *The etiology of schizophrenia.* New York: Basic Books, 1960, pp. 91–110.

ABRAHAM, K. Notes on the psycho-analytical investigation and treatment of manic-depressive insanity and allied conditions (1911). In K. Abraham, *Selected papers on psycho-analysis.* London: Hogarth Press, 1949.

ABRAMOWITZ, S. I., ABRAMOWITZ, C. V., JACKSON, C., and GOMES, B. The politics of clinical judgment: what nonliberal examiners infer about women who do not stifle themselves. *Journal of consulting and clinical psychology,* 1973, *41,* 385–391.

ABRAMSON, E. E., and WUNDERLICH, R. A. Dental hygiene training for retardates: an application of behavioral techniques. *Mental retardation,* 1972, *10,* 6–8.

ABROMS, G. M. Defining milieu therapy. *Archives of general psychiatry,* 1969, *21,* 553–560.

ABSE, D. W. *Hysteria and related mental disorders.* Bristol, Eng.: Wright, 1966.

ACKLEY, S. Individual rights and professional ethics. *Professional psychology,* 1972, 209–216.

ADAMS, H. E., BUTLER, J. R., and NOBLIN, C. D. Effects of psychoanalytically derived interpretations: a verbal conditioning paradigm? *Psychological reports,* 1962, *10,* 691–694.

ADAMS, H. E., NOBLIN, C. D., BUTLER, J. R., and TIMMONS, E. O. Differential effect of psychoanalytically-derived interpretations and verbal conditioning in schizophrenics. *Psychological reports,* 1962, *11,* 195–198.

ADAMS, K. M., KLINGE, V., and KEISER, T. W. The extinction of self-injurious behavior in an epileptic child. *Behaviour research and therapy,* 1973, *11,* 351–356.

ADAMS, M. Science, technology, and some dilemmas of advocacy. *Science,* 1973, *180,* 840–842.

ADAMS, M. R. Psychological differences between stutterers and nonstutterers: a review of the experimental literature. *Journal of communication disorders,* 1969, *2,* 163-170.

ADAMS, P. L., and McDONALD, N. F. Clinical cooling out of poor people. *American journal of orthopsychiatry,* 1968, *38,* 457-463.

ADERMAN, D., and BERKOWITZ, L. Observational set, empathy, and helping. *Journal of personality and social psychology,* 1970, *14,* 141-148.

ADLER, N. Kicks, drugs, and politics. *The psychoanalytic review,* 1970, *57,* 433-441.

ADLER, N., and GOLEMAN, D. Gambling and alcoholism: symptom substitution and functional equivalents. *Quarterly journal of studies on alcoholism,* 1969, *30,* 733-736.

AGNEW, J., and BANNISTER, D. Psychiatric diagnosis as a pseudo-specialist language. *British journal of medical psychology,* 1973, *46,* 69-73.

AGRAS, S., LEITENBERG, H., and BARLOW, D. H. Social reinforcement in the modification of agoraphobia. *Archives of general psychiatry,* 1968, *19,* 423–427.

AGRAS, S., LEITENBERG, H., BARLOW, D. H., and THOMSON, L. E. Instructions and reinforcement in the modification of neurotic behavior. *American journal of psychiatry,* 1969, *125,* 1435-1439.

AGRAS, S., and MARSHALL, C. The application of negative practice to spasmodic torticollis. *American journal of psychiatry,* 1965, *122,* 579-582.

AGRAS, S., SYLVESTER, D., and OLIVEAU, D. The epidemiology of common fears and phobias. *Comprehensive psychiatry,* 1969, *10,* 151-156.

AICHHORN, A. *Wayward youth.* New York: Viking Press, 1935.

AIELLO, J. R., and JONES, S. E. Field study of the proxemic behavior of young children in three subcultural groups. *Journal of personality and social psychology,* 1971, *19,* 351-356.

AIKEN, E. G., and PARKER, W. H. Conditioning and generalization of positive self-evaluations in a partially structured diagnostic interview. *Psychological reports,* 1965, *17,* 459–464.

AKERS, R. L. Socioeconomic status and delinquent behavior: a retest. *Journal of research in crime and delinquency*, 1964, *1*, 38–46.

AKISKAL, H. S., and MCKINNEY, W. T., JR. Depressive disorders: toward a unified hypothesis. *Science*, 1973, *182*, 20–30.

ALABISO, F. Inhibitory functions of attention in reducing hyperactive behavior. *American journal of mental deficiency*, 1972, *77*, 259–282.

ALBERT, S., and DABBS, J. M., JR. Physical distance and persuasion. *Journal of personality and social psychology*, 1970, *15*, 265–270.

ALEXANDER, A. B., CHAI, H., CREER, T. L., MIKLICH, D. R., RENNE, C. M., and CARDOSO, R. DE A. The elimination of chronic cough by response suppression shaping. *Journal of behavior therapy and experimental psychiatry*, 1973, *4*, 75–80.

ALEXANDER, F. The influence of pyschologic factors upon gastro-intestinal disturbances: general principles, objectives, and preliminary results. *Psychoanalytic quarterly*, 1934, *3*, 501-509.

ALEXANDER, F. *Fundamentals of psychoanalysis*. New York: Norton, 1948.

ALEXANDER, F., and FRENCH, T. M. *Psychoanalytic therapy*, New York: Ronald Press, 1946.

ALEXANDER, F., and FRENCH, T. M. *Studies in psychosomatic medicine*. New York: Ronald Press, 1948.

ALEXANDER, F., and SELESNICK, S. T. *The history of psychiatry*. New York: New American Library, 1968.

ALEXANDER, F., and STAUB, H. *The criminal, the judge, and the public: a psychological analysis* (1929). Rev. ed.: Glencoe, Ill.: Free Press, 1956.

ALFORD, G. S., BLANCHARD, E. B., and BUCKLEY, T. M. Treatment of hysterical vomiting by modification of social contingencies: a case study. *Journal of behavior therapy and experimental psychiatry*, 1972, *3*, 209–212.

ALLEN, G. J. The behavioral treatment of test anxiety: recent research and future trends. *Behavior therapy*, 1972, *3*, 253–262.

ALLEN, G. J. Treatment of test anxiety by group-administered and self-administered relaxation and study counseling. *Behavior therapy*, 1973, *4*, 349–360.

ALLEN, K. E., and HARRIS, F. R. Elimination of a child's excessive scratching by training the mother in reinforcement procedures. *Behaviour research and therapy*, 1966, *4*, 79–84.

ALLEN, G. J., CLINSKY, J. M., and VEIT, S. W. Pressures toward institutionalization within the aide culture: a behavioral-analytic case study. *Journal of community psychology*, in press.

ALLEN, K. E., HART, B. M., BUELL, J. S., HARRIS, F. R., and WOLF, M. M. Effects of social reinforcement on isolate behavior of a nursery school child. In L. P. Ullmann and L. Krasner, eds., *Case studies in behavior modification*. New York: Holt, Rinehart and Winston, 1965, pp. 307–312.

ALLEN, M. K., and LIEBERT, R. M. Children's adoption of self-reward patterns: model's prior experience and incentive for nonimitation. *Child development*, 1969, *40*, 921–926.

ALLEN, M. K., and LIEBERT, R. M. Effects of live and symbolic deviant modeling cues on adoption of a previously learned standard. *Journal of personality and social psychology*, in press.

ALLMAN, L. R., TAYLOR, H. A., and NATHAN, P. E. Group drinking during stress: effects on drinking behavior, affect, and psychopathology. *American journal of psychiatry*, 1972, *129*, 669-678.

ALLPORT, G. W. *Personality: a psychological interpretation*. New York: Holt, 1937.

ALMOND, R., KENISTON, K., and BOLTAX, S. The value system of a milieu therapy unit. *Archives of general psychiatry*, 1968, *19*, 545–561.

ALMOND, R., KENISTON, K., and BOLTAX, S. Patient value change in milieu therapy. *Archives of general psychiatry*, 1969a, *20*, 339–351.

ALMOND, R., KENISTON, K., and BOLTAX, S. Milieu therapy process. *Archives of general psychiatry*, 1969b, *21*, 431–442.

ALPERT, D., and BITZER, D. L. Advances in computer-based education. *Science*, 1970, *167*, 1582–1590.

ALTMAN, K. Effects of cooperative response acquisition on social behavior during free-play. *Journal of experimental child psychology*, 1971, *12*, 387–395.

ALTSCHULE, M. D. *Roots of modern psychiatry: essays in the history of psychiatry*. New York: Grune & Stratton, 1957.

ALVAREZ, A. *The savage god: a study of suicide*. New York: Bantam, 1973.

AMERICAN PSYCHIATRIC ASSOCIATION. *Diagnostic and statistical manual: mental disorders* (DSM–I). Washington, D.C.: American Psychiatric Association, 1952; special printing, 1965.

AMERICAN PSYCHIATRIC ASSOCIATION. *Diagnostic and stastical manual of mental disorders*. 2nd ed. (DSM–II). Washington, D.C.: American Psychiatric Association, 1968.

AMERICAN PSYCHOLOGICAL ASSOCIATION. Ethical principles on the conduct of research with human participants. Washington, D.C.: American Psychological Association, 1973a.

AMERICAN PSYCHOLOGICAL ASSOCIATION. Guidelines for psychologists conducting growth groups. *American psychologist*, 1973b, *28*, 933.

references

ANANT, S. S. A note on the treatment of alcoholics by a verbal aversion technique. *Canadian psychologist*, 1967, *8*, 19–22.

ANANT, S. S. The use of verbal aversion (negative conditioning) with an alcoholic: A case report. *Behaviour research and therapy*, 1968b, *6*, 395–396.

ANANT, S. S. Verbal aversion therapy with a promiscuous girl: a case report. *Psychological reports*, 1968a, *22*, 795–796.

ANANT, S. S. Treatment of alcoholics and drug addicts by verbal aversion techniques. *International journal of the addictions*, 1968c, *3*, 381–388.

ANDELMAN, D. A. Job survey finds aged work well. *New York times*, 22 September 1972, p. 39.

ANDRY, R. G. *Delinquency and parental pathology*. London: Methuen, 1960.

ANTHONY, E. J. The developmental precursors of adult schizophrenia. In D. Rosenthal and S. S. Kety, eds., *The transmission of schizophrenia*. New York: Pergamon Press, 1968, pp. 293–316.

ANTHONY, E. J. A clinical evaluation of children with psychotic parents. *American journal of psychiatry*, 1969, *26*, 117–184.

APPELL, M. J., and TISDALL, W. J. Factors differentiating institutionalized from noninstitutionalized referred retardates. *American journal of mental deficiency*, 1968, *37*, 424–432.

APTER, I. M. On the psychotherapy of psychogenic impotence. In R. B. Winn, ed., *Psychotherapy in the Soviet Union*. New York: Philosophical Library, 1961, pp. 89–93.

ARANN, L., and HORNER, V. M. Contingency management in an open psychiatric ward. *Journal of behavior therapy and experimental psychiatry*, 1972, *3*, 31–37.

AREHART, J. L. The search for a heroin "cure." *Science news*, 1972, *101*, 250–251.

ARIETI, S. *Interpretation of schizophrenia*. New York: Bruner, 1955.

ARIETI, S. Manic-depressive psychosis. In S. Arieti, ed., *American handbook of psychiatry*. New York: Basic Books, 1959, pp. 419–454.

ARIETI, S. New views on the psychodynamics of schizophrenia. *American journal of psychiatry*, 1967, *124*, 453–458.

ARONSON, E., and METTEE, D. R. Dishonest behavior as a function of differential levels of induced self-esteem. *Journal of personality and social psychology*, 1968, *9*, 121–127.

ARONSON, H., and OVERALL, B. Treatment expectations of patients in two social classes. *Social work*, 1966, *11*, 35–41.

ARTHUR, A. Z. Diagnostic testing and the new alternatives. *Psychological bulletin*, 1969, *72*, 183–192.

ARTHUR, R. J. *An introduction to social psychiatry*. Baltimore: Penguin, 1971.

ARTHUR, R. J., and GUNDERSON, E. K. E. Stability in psychiatric diagnoses from hospital admission to discharge. *Journal of clinical psychology*, 1966, *22*, 140–144.

ASCOUGH, J. C., and SIPPRELLE, C. N. Operant verbal conditioning of autonomic responses. *Behaviour research and therapy*, 1968, *6*, 363–370.

ASH, P. The reliability of psychiatric diagnosis. *Journal of abnormal and social psychology*, 1949, *44*, 272–276.

ASHBY, W. R., and WALKER, C. C. Genius. In P. London and D. Rosenhan, eds., *Foundations of abnormal psychology*. New York: Holt, Rinehart and Winston, 1968, pp. 201–225.

ASHEM, B., and DONNER, L. Covert sensitization with alcoholics: a controlled replication. *Behaviour research and therapy*, 1968, *6*, 7–12.

ATKINSON, R. L., and ROBINSON, N. M. Paired-associate learning by schizophrenic and normal subjects under conditions of personal and impersonal reward and punishment. *Journal of abnormal and social psychology*, 1961, *62*, 322–326.

ATTHOWE, J. M., JR., and KRASNER, L. A preliminary report on the application of contingent reinforcement procedures (token economy on a "chronic" psychiatric ward). *Journal of abnormal psychology*, 1968, *73*, 37–43.

AULD, F., JR., and MURRAY, E. J. Content-analysis studies of psychotherapy. *Psychological bulletin*, 1955, *52*, 377–395.

AUSTIN, G. M., and GRANT, F. C. Physiologic observations following total hemispherectomy in man. *Surgery*, 1955, *38*, 239–258.

AVERILL, J. R. Grief: its nature and significance. *Psychological bulletin*, 1968, *70*, 721–748.

AYLLON, T. Intensive treatment of psychotic behaviour by stimulus satiation and food reinforcement. *Behaviour research and therapy*, 1963, *1*, 53–61.

AYLLON, T., and AZRIN, N. H. The measurement and reinforcement of behavior of psychotics. *Journal of the experimental analysis of behavior*, 1965, *8*, 357–383.

AYLLON, T., and AZRIN, N. H. *The token economy: a motivational system for therapy and rehabilitation*. New York: Appleton-Century-Crofts, 1968.

AYLLON, T., and HAUGHTON, E. Control of the behavior of schizophrenic patients by food. *Journal of the experimental analysis of behavior*, 1962, *5*, 343–352.

AYLLON, T., and HAUGHTON, E. Modification of symptomatic verbal behaviour of mental patients. *Behaviour research and therapy*, 1964, *3*, 87–97.

AYLLON, T., and KELLY, K. Effects of reinforcement on standardized test performance. *Journal of applied behavior analysis*, 1972, *5*, 477–484.

AYLLON, T., and MICHAEL, J. The psychiatric nurse as a behavioral engineer. *Journal of the experimental analysis of behavior*, 1959, *2*, 323–334.

AYLLON, T., and SKUBAN, W. Accountability in psychotherapy: a test case. *Journal of behavior therapy and experimental psychiatry*, 1973, *4*, 19–30.

AYMAN, O. Personality type of patients with arteriolar essential hypertension. *American journal of medical science*, 1933, *186*, 213–223.

AZERRAD, J., and STAFFORD, R. L. Restoration of eating behavior in anorexia nervosa through operant conditioning and environmental manipulation. *Behaviour research and therapy*, 1969, *7*, 165–171.

AZRIN, N. H., BUGLE, C., and O'BRIEN, F. Behavioral engineering: two apparatuses for toilet training retarded children. *Journal of applied behavior analysis*, 1971, *4*, 249–253.

AZRIN, N. H., and FOXX, R. M. A rapid method of toilet training the institutionally retarded. *Journal of applied behavior analysis*, 1971, *4*, 89–99.

AZRIN, N. H., and HOLZ, W. C. Punishment. In W. K. Honig, ed., *Operant behavior: areas of research and application*. New York: Appleton, 1966, pp. 380–447.

AZRIN, N. H., JONES, R. J., and FLYE, B. A synchronization effect and its application to stuttering by a portable apparatus. *Journal of applied behavior analysis*, 1968, *1*, 283–296.

AZRIN, N. H., and LINDSLEY, O. R. The reinforcement of cooperation between children. *Journal of abnormal and social psychology*, 1956, *52*, 100–102.

AZRIN, N. H., and POWELL, J. Behavioral engineering: the use of response priming to improve prescribed self-medication. *Journal of applied behavior analysis*, 1969, *2*, 39–42.

BAASTRUP, P. C. The use of lithium in manic-depressive psychosis. *Comprehensive psychiatry*, 1964, *5*, 396–408.

BABIGIAN, H. M., GARDNER, E. A., MILES, H. G., and ROMANO, J. Diagnostic consistency and change in a follow-up study of 1215 patients. *American journal of psychiatry*, 1965, *121*, 895–901.

BABST, D. V., CHAMBERS, C. D., and WARNER, A. Patient characteristics associated with retention in a methadone maintenance program. *British journal of addiction*, 1971, *66*, 195–204.

BACHRACH, A. J., ed. *Experimental foundations of clinical psychology*. New York: Basic Books, 1962.

BACHRACH, A. J., ERWIN, W. J., and MOHR, J. P. The control of eating behavior in an anorexic by operant conditioning techniques. In L. P. Ullmann and L. Krasner, eds., *Case studies in behavior modification*. New York: Holt, 1965, pp. 153–163.

BACHRACH, A. J., and KAREN, R. *Chaining: complex behavior*. 16mm. film. San Diego, Calif.: Rodentia Productions, 1966.

BACK, K. W. *Beyond words: The story of sensitivity training and the encounter movement*. New York: Russell Sage, 1972.

BACON, F. *Complete essays*. New York: Pocket Books, 1963.

BAER, D. M., PETERSON, R. F., and SHERMAN, J. A. The development of imitation by reinforcing behavioral similarity to a model. *Journal of the experimental analysis of behavior*, 1967, *10*, 405–416.

BAILEY, J., and ATCHINSON, T. The treatment of compulsive handwashing using reinforcement principles. *Behavior research and therapy*, 1969, *7*, 327–329.

BAILEY, J., and MEYERSON, L. Vibration as a reinforcer with a profoundly retarded child. *Journal of applied behavior analysis*, 1967, *2*, 135–137.

BAILEY, J. S., TIMBERS, G. D., PHILLIPS, E. L., and WOLF, M. M. Modification of articulation errors of pre-delinquents by their peers. *Journal of applied behavior analysis*, 1971, *4*, 265–281.

BAILEY, J. S., WOLF, M. M., and PHILLIPS, E. L. Home-based reinforcement and the modification of pre-delinquents' classroom behavior. *Journal of applied behavior analysis*, 1970, *3*, 223–233.

BAIRD, R. R., and LEE, H. L. Modification of conceptual style preference by differential reinforcement. *Child development*, 1969, *40*, 903–910.

BAKAN, D. *Slaughter of the innocents*. San Francisco: Jossey-Bass, 1971.

BAKER, A. A., The misfit family: a psychodrama technique used in a therapeutic community. *British journal of medical psychology*, 1952, *25*, 235–243.

BAKER, B. Camp freedom: behavior modification for retarded children in a therapeutic camp setting. *American journal of orthopsychiatry*, 1973, *43*, 418–427.

BAKER, B., and WARD, M. Reinforcement therapy for behavior problems in severely retarded children. *American journal of orthopsychiatry*, 1971, *41*, 113–125.

BAKER, B. L. Symptom treatment and symptom substitution in enuresis. *Journal of abnormal psychology*, 1969, *74*, 42–49.

BAKER, B. L., COHEN, D. C., and SAUNDERS, J. T. Self-directed desensitization for acrophobia. *Behaviour research and therapy*, 1973, *11*, 79–89.

BAKER, R. The use of operant conditioning to reinstate speech in mute schizophrenics. *Behavior research and therapy*, 1971, *9*, 329–336.

BAKWIN, H. Pseudocia peditricia. *New England journal of medicine*, 1956, *232*, 691–697.

BALDWIN, V. L. Development of social skills in retardates as a function of three types of reinforcement programs. *Dissertation abstracts*, 1967, *27*, (9-A), 2865.

BALINT, M. *The doctor, his patient, and the illness.* New York: International Universities Press, 1957.

BALL, T. S. Training generalized imitation: variations on a historical theme. *American journal of mental deficiency*, 1970, *78*, 135–141.

BALLER, W. R., CHARLES, D. C., and MILLER, E. L. Mid-life attainment of the mentally retarded: a longitudinal study. *Genetic psychology monographs*, 1967, *75*, 235–329.

BALLER, W. R., and SHALOCK, H. Conditioned response treatment of enuresis. *Exceptional children*, 1956, *22*, 233–236 and 247–248.

BALSON, P. M. Encopresis: a case with symptom substitution? *Behavior therapy*, 1973, *4*, 134–136.

BANDLER, R. J., MADARAS, G. R., and BEM, D. J. Self-observation as a source of pain perception. *Journal of personality and social psychology*, 1968, *9*, 205–209.

BANDURA, A. Psychotherapy as a learning process. *Psychological bulletin*, 1961, *58*, 143–159.

BANDURA, A. Social learning through imitation. In M. R. Jones, ed., *Nebraska symposium on motivation.* Lincoln: University of Nebraska Press, 1962, pp. 211–215.

BANDURA, A. Behavior modifications through modeling procedures. In L. Krasner and L. P. Ullmann, eds., *Research in behavior modification.* New York: Holt, 1965a, pp. 310–340.

BANDURA, A. Vicarious processes: a case of no-trial learning. In L. Berkowitz, ed., *Advances in experimental social psychology* (Vol. 2). New York: Academic Press, 1965b, pp. 1–55.

BANDURA, A. *Principles of behavior modification.* New York: Holt, Rinehart and Winston, 1969.

BANDURA, A. Psychotherapy based upon modeling principles. In A. E. Bergin and S. L. Garfield, eds., *Handbook of psychotherapy and behavior change.* New York: Wiley, 1971.

BANDURA, A. Vicarious and self-reinforcement processes. In R. Glaser, ed., *The nature of reinforcement.* Columbus, Ohio: Merrill, in press.

BANDURA, A., BLANCHARD, E. B., and RITTER, B. Relative efficacy of desensitization and modeling approaches for inducing behavioral, affective, and attitudinal changes. *Journal of personality and social psychology*, 1969, *13*, 173–199.

BANDURA, A., GRUSEC, J. E., and MENLOVE, F. L. Vicarious extinction of avoidance behavior. *Journal of personality and social psychology*, 1967, *5*, 16–23.

BANDURA, A., and KUPERS, C. J. Transmission of patterns of self-reinforcement through modeling. *Journal of abnormal and social psychology*, 1964, *69*, 1–9.

BANDURA, A., and MENLOVE, F. L. Factors determining vicarious extinction of avoidance behavior through symbolic modeling. *Journal of personality and social psychology*, 1968, *8*, 99–108.

BANDURA, A., and MCDONALD, F. J. The influence of social reinforcement and the behavior of models in shaping children's moral judgments. *Journal of abnormal and social psychology*, 1963, *67*, 274–281.

BANDURA, A., and MISCHEL, W. Modification of self-imposed delay of reward through exposure to live and symbolic models. *Journal of personality and social psychology*, 1965, *2*, 698–705.

BANDURA, A., and ROSENTHAL, T. L. Vicarious classical conditioning as a function of arousal level. *Journal of personality and social psychology*, 1966, *3*, 54–62.

BANDURA, A., and WALTERS, R. H. *Adolescent aggression.* New York: Ronald, 1959.

BANGS, J. L., and FREIDINGER, A. Diagnosis and treatment of a case of hysterical aphonia in a thirteen-year-old girl. *Journal of speech and hearing disorders*, 1949, *14*, 312–317.

BAR, A. The shaping of fluency not the modification of stuttering. *Journal of communication disorders*, 1971, *4*, 1–8.

BARAHAL, H. S. 1000 prefrontal lobotomies: five-to-ten-year follow-up study. *Psychiatric quarterly*, 1958, *32*, 653–678.

BARBER, T. X. Toward a theory of pain: relief of chronic pain by prefrontal leucotomy, opiates, placebos, and hypnosis. *Psychological bulletin*, 1959, *56*, 430–460.

BARBER, T. X. Empirical evidence for a theory of hypnotic behavior: effects on suggestibility of five variables typically included in hypnotic induction procedures. *Journal of consulting psychology*, 1965a, *29*, 98–107.

BARBER, T. X. Physiological effects of "hypnotic suggestions": a critical review of recent research (1960–1964). *Psychological bulletin*, 1965b, *63*, 201–222.

BARBER, T. X. *Suggested ("hypnotic") behavior: the trance paradigm versus an alternative paradigm.* Harding, Mass.: Medfield Foundation, 1970a.

BARBER, T. X. *LSD, marijuana, yoga, and hypnosis.* Chicago: Aldine, 1970b.

BARBER, T. X., DALAL, A. S., and CALVERLEY, D. S. The subjective reports of hypnotic subjects. *American journal of clinical hypnosis*, 1968, *11*, 74–88.

BARBER, T. X., and HAHN, K. W., JR. Hypnotic induction and "relaxation." *Archives of general psychiatry*, 1963, *8*, 295–300.

BARBER, T. X., and HAHN, K. W., JR. Experimental studies in "hypnotic" behavior: physiologic and subjective effects of imagined pain. *Journal of nervous and mental disease*, 1964, *139*, 416–425.

BARDILL, D. R. Behavior contracting and group therapy with preadolescent males in a residential treatment setting. *International journal of group psychotherapy*, 1972, *22*, 333–342.

BARKER, J. C., THORPE, J. G., BLAKEMORE, C. B., LAVIN, N. I., and CONWAY, C. G. Behavior therapy in a case of transvestism, *Lancet*, 1961, *1*, 510.

BARKER, R. *Ecological psychology*. Stanford, Calif.: Stanford University Press, 1968.

BARKER, R. G., and SCHOGGEN, P. *Qualities of community life*. San Francisco, Calif.: Jossey-Bass, 1973.

BARKER, R. G., and WRIGHT, H. F. *Midwest and its children*. New York: Harper and Row, 1955.

BARLOW, D. H., and AGRAS, W. S. Fading to increase heterosexual responsiveness to homosexuals. *Journal of applied behavior analysis*, 1973, *6*, 355–366.

BARNETT, I. The successful treatment of an exhibitionist: a case report. *International journal of offender therapy and comparative criminology*, 1972, *16*, 125–129.

BARNHART, J. E. The acquisition of cue properties by social and nonsocial events. *Child development*, 1968, *39*, 1237–1245.

BARON, R. A., and LIEBERT, R. M., eds. *Human social behavior*. Homewood, Ill.: Dorsey, 1971.

BARRETT, B. H. Reduction in rate of multiple tics by free operant conditioning methods. *Journal of nervous and mental disease*, 1962, *135*, 187–195.

BARRETT, J. E., JR., KURIANSKY, J., and GURLAND, B. Community tenure following emergency discharge. *American journal of psychiatry*, 1972, *128*, 958–964.

BARRISH, H. H., SAUNDERS, M., and WOLF, M. M. Good behavior game: effects of individual contingencies for group consequences on disruptive behavior in a classroom. *Journal of applied behavior analysis*, 1969, *2*, 119–124.

BARTLETT, D., ORA, J. P., BROWN, E., and BUTLER, J. The effects of reinforcement on psychotic speech in a case of early infantile autism, age 12. *Journal of behavior therapy and experimental psychiatry*, 1971, *2*, 145–149.

BARTON, A. H., ed. *Communities in disaster: a sociological analysis of collective stress situations*. Garden City: N.Y.: Doubleday, 1969.

BARTON, E. S. Inappropriate speech in a severely retarded child: a case study in language conditioning and generalization. *Journal of applied behavior analysis*, 1970, *3*, 299–307.

BARTON, R. *Institutional neurosis*. Bristol, Eng.: Wright, 1959.

BASS, B. M. Conformity, deviation, and a general theory of interpersonal behavior. In I. A. Berg and B. M. Bass, eds., *Conformity and deviation*. New York: Harper, 1961, pp. 38–100.

BATCHELOR, I. R. C. *Henderson and Gillespie's textbook of psychiatry*. London: Oxford University Press, 1969.

BATTLE, E. S., and LACEY, B. A context for hyperactivity in children, over time. *Child development*, 1972, *43*, 757–773.

BAUM, M. Extinction of avoidance responding through response prevention (flooding). *Psychological bulletin*, 1970, *74*, 276–284.

BAUMEISTER, A. A., and FOREHAND, R. Effects of extinction of an instrumental response on stereotyped body rocking in severe retardates. *Psychological record*, 1971, *21*, 235–240.

BAUMEISTER, A. A., and WARD, L. C. III. Effects of rewards upon the reaction times of mental defectives. *American journal of mental deficiency*, 1967, *71*, 801–805.

BAYES, M. A. Behavioral cues of interpersonal warmth. *Journal of consulting and clinical psychology*, 1972, *39*, 333–339.

BAYMONT, H. Modern legal test of insanity attacked by one of its drafters. *New York times*, 30 August, 1970.

BAYNES, T. E., JR. Continuing conjectural concepts concerning civil commitment criteria. *American psychologist*, 1971, *26*, 489–495.

BAZELL, R. J. Drug abuse: methadone becomes the solution and the problem. *Science*, 1973, *179*, 772–775.

BEACH, F. It's all in your mind. *Psychology today*, 1969, *3*, 33–35 and 60.

BECK, A. T. *Depression: clinical, experimental, and theoretical aspects*. New York: Harper, 1967.

BECK, A. T., WARD, C. H., MENDELSON, M., MOCK, J. E., and ERBAUGH, J. K. Reliability of psychiatric diagnosis. 2: A study of consistency of clinical judgments and ratings. *American journal of psychiatry*, 1962, *119*, 351–357.

BECK, J. C., MACHT, L. B., LEVINSON, D. J., and STRAUSS, M. A controlled experimental study of the therapist-administrator split. *American journal of psychiatry*, 1967, *124*, 467–474.

BECKER, C. L. *Everyman his own historian*. New York: Crofts, 1935.

BECKER, H. S. *Outsiders: studies in the sociology of deviance*. New York: Free Press, 1963.

BECKER, P. W., and CESAR, J. A. Use of beer in geriatric psychiatric patient groups. *Psychological reports,* 1973, *33,* 182.

BECKER, W. C. A genetic approach to the interpretation and evaluation of the process-reactive distinction in schizophrenia. *Journal of abnormal social psychology,* 1956, *53,* 229-236.

BECKER, W. C. The process-reactive distinction: a key to the problem of schizophrenia? *Journal of nervous and mental disease,* 1959, *129,* 442-449.

BECKER, W. C. Consequences of different kinds of parental discipline. In M. L. Hoffman and L. Hoffman, eds., *Review of child development research.* Lafayette, Ind.: Society for Research in Child Development, 1964.

BECKER, W. C. Applications of behavior principles in typical classrooms. In C. E. Thoresen, ed., *Behavior modification in education.* National Society for the Study of Education, 72nd Yearbook. Chicago: University of Chicago Press, 1973, pp. 77-106.

BECKER, W. C., MADSEN, C. H., JR., ARNOLD, C. R., and THOMAS, D. R. The contingent use of teacher attention and praise in reducing classroom behavior problems. *Journal of special education,* 1967, *1,* 287-307.

BECKER, W. C., and MCFARLAND, R. L. A lobotomy prognosis scale. *Journal of consulting psychology,* 1955, *19,* 157-162.

BEDNAR, R. L., ZELHART, P. F., GREATHOUSE, L., and WEINBERG, S. Operant conditioning principles in the treatment of learning and behavior problems with delinquent boys. *Journal of counseling psychology,* 1970, *17,* 492-497.

BELKNAP, I. *Human problems of a state mental hospital.* New York: McGraw-Hill. 1956.

BELL, N. W., and SPIEGEL, J. P. Social psychiatry: vagaries of a term. *Archives of general psychiatry,* 1966, *14,* 337-345.

BEM, D. J. An experimental analysis of self-persuasion. *Journal of experimental social psychology,* 1965, *1,* 199-218.

BEM, D. J. Self-perception: the dependent variable of human performance. *Organizational behavior and human performance,* 1967, *2,* 105-121.

BEM, S. L., and BEM, D. J. Training the woman to know her place: the power of a nonconscious ideology. In D. J. Bem, *Beliefs, attitudes and human affairs.* Belmont, Calif.: Brooks/Cole, 1970.

BENDER, L. Psychopathic behavior disorders in children. In R. Lindner and R. Seliger, eds., *Handbook of correctional psychology.* New York: Philosophical Library, 1947, pp. 360-377.

BENDER, L. The life course of children with schizophrenia. *American journal of psychiatry,* 1973, *130,* 783-786.

BENEDICT, P. K., and JACKS, I. Mental illness in primitive societies. *Psychiatry,* 1954, *17,* 377-389.

BENEDICT, R. Anthropology and the abnormal. *Journal of general psychology,* 1934, *10,* 59-82.

BENSBERG, G. J., COLWELL, C. N., and CASSEL, R. H. Teaching the profoundly retarded self-help activities by shaping behavior techniques. *American journal of mental deficiency,* 1965, *69,* 674-679.

BENSON, H., SHAPIRO, D., TURSKY, B., and SCHWARTZ, G. E. Decreased systolic blood pressure through operant conditioning techniques in patients with essential hypertension. *Science,* 1971, *173,* 740-741.

BENTLER, P. M. An infant's phobia treated with reciprocal inhibition therapy. *Journal of child psychology and psychiatry,* 1962, *3,* 185-189.

BENTZ, W. K. The relationship between educational background and the referral role of ministers. *Sociology and social research,* 1967, *51,* 199-208.

BERG, I. A., and BASS, B. M., eds., *Conformity and deviation.* New York: Harper, 1961.

BERGER, S. M. Conditioning through vicarious instigation. *Psychological review,* 1962, *69,* 450-466.

BERGNER, L., and SUSSER, M. W. Low birth weight and prenatal nutrition: an interpretive review. *Pediatrics,* 1970, *46,* 946-966.

BERK, L. E. Effects of variations in the nursery school setting on environmental constraints and childrens' modes of adaption. *Child development,* 1971, *42,* 839-869.

BERKLEY, H. J. *A treatise on mental diseases.* New York: D. Appleton, 1900.

BERKOWITZ, B. P., and GRAZIANO, A. M. Training parents as behavior therapists: a review. *Behaviour research and therapy,* 1972, *10,* 297-317.

BERKOWITZ, L. The contagion of violence: an S-R mediational analysis of some effects of observed aggression. In W. J. Arnold and M. M. Page, eds., *Nebraska symposium on motivation,* 1970. Lincoln: University of Nebraska Press, 1970, pp. 95-135.

BERKOWITZ, S., SHERRY, P., and DAVIS, B. Teaching self-feeding skills to profound retardates using reinforcement and fading procedures. *Behavior therapy,* 1971, *2,* 62-67.

BERMAN, P. A., and BRADY, J. P. Miniaturized metronomes in the treatment of stuttering: a survey of clinicians' experience. *Journal of behavior therapy and experimental,* 1973, *4,* 117-119.

BERNARD, J. *Women and the public interest.* Chicago: Aldine, 1971.

BERNAL, M. E., DURYEE, J. S., PRUETT, H. L., and BURNS, B. J. Behavior modification and the brat syndrome. *Journal of consulting and clinical psychology,* 1968, *32,* 447-455.

BERNARD, J. L., and EISENMAN, R. Verbal conditioning in sociopaths with social and monetary reinforcement. *Journal of personality and social psychology,* 1967, *6,* 203–206.

BERNE, E. *Games people play.* New York: Grove, 1964.

BERNHARDT, A. J., HERSEN, M., and BARLOW, D. H. Measurement and modification of spasmodic torticollis: an experimental analysis. *Behavior therapy,* 1972, *3,* 294–297.

BERNSTEIN, B. Social class, speech systems, and psychotherapy. *British journal of sociology,* 1964, *15,* 54–64.

BERNSTEIN, D. A. Modification of smoking: an evaluative review. *Psychological bulletin,* 1969, *71,* 418–440.

BERNSTEIN, D. A. The modification of smoking behavior: a search for effective variables. *Behaviour research and therapy,* 1970a, *8,* 133–146.

BERNSTEIN, D. A. Problems in behavioral fear assessment in psychotherapy outcome research. Paper presented to Western Psychological Association, Los Angeles, 1970b.

BERNSTEIN, D. A. Behavioral fear assessment: anxiety or artifact? In H. Adams and I. P. Unikel, eds., *Issues and trends in behavior therapy.* Springfield, Ill.: Charles C Thomas, 1973.

BERNSTEIN, D. A., and BEATTY, W. E. The use of in vivo desensitization as part of a total therapeutic intervention. *Journal of behavior therapy and experimental psychiatry,* 1971, *2,* 259–265.

BERNSTEIN, D. A., and PAUL, G. Some comments on therapy analogue research with small animal phobias. *Behavior therapy and experimental psychiatry,* 1971, *2,* 225–237.

BERSCHEID, E., and WALSTER, E. When does a harmdoer compensate a victim? *Journal of personality and social psychology,* 1967, *6,* 435–441.

BEST, J. A., and STEFFY, R. A. Smoking modification procedures tailored to subject characteristics. *Behavior therapy,* 1971, *2,* 177–191.

BEVAN, J. R. Learning theory applied to the treatment of a patient with obsessional ruminations. In H. J. Eysenck, ed., *Behaviour therapy and the neuroses.* New York: Pergamon Press, 1960, pp. 165–169.

BEVAN, W. On growing old in America. *Science,* 1972, *177.*

BEWLEY, T., JAMES, I., FEVRE, C., MADDOCKS, P., and MAHON, T. Maintenance treatment of narcotic addicts (not British nor a system, but working now). *The international journal of the addictions,* 1972, *7,* 597–612.

BEXTON, W. H., HERON, W., and SCOTT, T. H. Effects of decreased variation in the sensory environment. *Canadian journal of psychology,* 1954, *8,* 70–77.

BEYME, F. Hyperesthesia of taste and touch treated by reciprocal inhibition. *Behaviour research and therapy,* 1964, *2,* 7–14.

BHATTACHARYYA, D. D. and SINGH, R. Behavior therapy of hysterical fits. *American journal of psychiatry,* 1971, *128,* 602–606.

BIANCHI, G. N. Pattern of hypochondriasis: a principal components analysis. *British journal of psychiatry,* 1973, *122,* 541–548.

BIANCO, F. J. Rapid treatment of two cases of anorexia nervosa. *Journal of behavior therapy and experimental psychiatry,* 1972, *3,* 223–224.

BICKMAN, L. Social roles and uniforms: clothes make the person. *Psychology today,* 1974, 7, 49–51.

BIDERMAN, A. D., and ZIMMER, H., eds., *The manipulation of human behavior.* New York: Wiley, 1961.

BIEBER, I., DAIN, H. J., DINCE, P. R., DRELLICH, M. G., GRAND, H. G., GRUNDLACH, R. H., KREMER, M. W., RIFKIN, A. H., WILBUR, C. B., and BIEBER, T. B. *Homosexuality: a psychoanalytical study.* New York: Basic Books, 1962.

BIEBER, T. On treating male homosexuals. *Archives of general psychiatry,* 1967, *16,* 60–63.

BIGGS, B. and SHEEHAN, J. Punishment or distraction: operant stuttering revisited. *Journal of abnormal psychology,* 1969, *74,* 256–262.

BIGLOW, G., COHEN, M. LIEBSON, I., and FAILLACE, L. A. Abstinence or moderation? choice by alcoholics. *Behavior research and therapy,* 1972, *10,* 209–214.

BIJOU, S. W. Experimental studies of child behavior, normal and deviant. In L. Krasner and L. P. Ullmann, eds., *Research in behavior modification.* New York: Holt, Rinehart and Winston, 1965, pp. 56–81.

BIJOU, S. W. A functional analysis of retarded development. In N. R. Ellis, ed., *International review of research in mental retardation* (Vol. 1). New York: Academic Press, 1966, pp. 1–19.

BIJOU, S. W. Behavior modification in the mentally retarded: application of operant conditioning principles. *Pediatric clinics of North America,* 1968, *15,* 969–987.

BIJOU, S. W. Behavior modification in teaching the retarded child. In C. E. Thoresen, ed., *Behavior modification in education.* National Society for the Study of Education, 72nd Yearbook. Chicago: University of Chicago Press, 1973, pp. 259–290.

BIJOU, S. W., AINSWORTH, M. H., and STOCKEY, M. R. The social adjustment of mentally retarded girls paroled from the Wayne County Training

School. *American journal of mental deficiency*, 1943, *47*, 422–428.

Bijou, S. W., Peterson, R. F., Harris, F. R., Allen, K. E., and Johnston, M. S. Methodology for experimental studies of young children in natural settings. *Psychological record*, 1969, *19*, 177–210.

Bijou, S. W., and Peterson, R. F. The psychological assessment of children: a functional analysis. In P. McReynolds, ed., *Advances in psychological assessment*. Vol. 2. Palo Alto, Calif.: Science and Behavior Books, 1971, 63–78.

Billingsley, A., and Giovannoni, J. M. *Children of the storm*. New York: Harcourt Brace Jovanovich, 1972.

Bird, C. (with Briller, S. W.) *Born female*. New York: Pocket Books, 1969.

Birk, L. Social reinforcement in psychotherapy. *Conditional reflex*, 1968, *3*, 116–123.

Birky, H. J., Chambliss, J. E., and Wasden, R. A comparison of residents discharged from a token economy and two traditional psychiatric programs. *Behavior therapy*, 1971, *2*, 46–51.

Birnbrauer, J. S. Preparing "uncontrollable" retarded children for group instruction. Paper read at American Educational Research Association Convention, 1967.

Birnbrauer, J. S., Bijou, S. W., Wolf, M. M., and Kidder, J. D. Programed instruction in the classroom. In L. P. Ullmann and L. Krasner, eds., *Case studies in behavior modification*. New York: Holt, Rinehart and Winston, 1965a, pp. 358–363.

Birnbrauer, J. S., Wolf, M. M., Kidder, J. D., and Tague, C. E. Classroom behavior of retarded pupils with token reinforcement. *Journal of experimental child psychology*, 1965b, *2*, 219–235.

Bittner, E. Police discretion in emergency apprehension of mentally ill persons. *Social problems*, 1967, *14*, 278–292.

Blackburn, H. L. Factors affecting turnover rates in mental hospitals. *Hospital and community psychiatry*, 1972, *23*, 268–271.

Blacker, K. H., Jones, R. T., Stone, G. C., and Pfefferbaum, D. Chronic users of LSD: the "acid-heads." *American journal of psychiatry*, 1968, *125*, 341–351.

Blacker, M., and Schacht, L. S. Activity patterns of psychiatric residents at a staff conference. *Archives of general psychiatry*, 1970, *23*, 56–60.

Blackwell, B. and Shepard, M. Prophylactic lithium: another therapeutic myth? an examination of the evidence to date. *Lancet*, 1968, *1*, 968–971.

Blake, B. G. The application of behaviour therapy to the treatment of alcoholism. *Behaviour research and therapy*, 1965, *3*, 75–85.

Blake, B. G. A follow-up of alcoholics treated by behaviour therapy. *Behaviour research and therapy*, 1967, *5*, 89–94.

Blake, P. and Moss, T. The development of socialization skills in an electively mute child. *Behaviour research and therapy*, 1967, *5*, 349–356.

Blakemore, C. B., Thorpe, J. G., Barker, J. C., Conway, C. G., and Lavin, N. I. The application of faradic aversion conditioning in a case of transvestism. *Behaviour research and therapy*, 1963a, *1*, 29–34.

Blakemore, C. B., Thorpe, J. G., Barker, J. C., Conway, C. G., and Lavin, N. I. Follow-up note to: the application of faradic aversion conditioning in a case of transvestism. *Behaviour research and therapy*, 1963b, *1*, 191.

Blank, M., and Solomon, F. A. Tutorial language program to develop abstract thinking in socially disadvantaged preschool children. *Child development*, 1968, *39*, 379–389.

Blashfield, R. An evaluation of the DMS-II classification of schizophrenia as a nomenclature. *Journal of abnormal psychology*, 1973, *82*, 382-389.

Blau, P. M. *Bureaucracy in modern society*. New York: Random House, 1956.

Blau, P. M., and Scott, W. R. *Formal organizations*. San Francisco: Chandler, 1962.

Blinder, B. J., Freeman, D. M. A., and Stunkard, A. J. Behavior therapy of anorexia nervosa: effectiveness of activity as a reinforcer of weight gain. *American journal of psychiatry*, 1970, *126*, 1093–1098.

Bliss, E. L., and Branch, C. H. H. *Anorexia nervosa*. New York: Hoeber, 1960.

Blitch, J. W., and Haynes, S. N. Multiple behavioral techniques in a case of female homosexuality. *Journal of behavior therapy and experimental psychiatry*, 1972, *3*, 319–322.

Blitz, B., Dinnerstein, A. J., and Lowenthal, M. Performance on the pain apperception test and tolerance for experimental pain: a lack of relationship. *Journal of clinical psychology*, 1968, *24*, 73.

Bloch, H. A., and Prince, M. *Social crisis and deviance*. New York: Random House, 1967.

Bloch, H. S. Army clinical psychiatry in the combat zone—1967–1968. *American journal of psychiatry*, 1969, *126*, 289–298.

Bloom, B. L. "The "medical model," miasma theory, and community mental health. *Community mental health journal*, 1965, *1*, 333–338.

Bloom, B. L., Lang, E. M., and Goldberg, H. Factors associated with accuracy of prediction of posthospitalization adjustment. *Journal of abnormal psychology*, 1970, *76*, 243–249.

BLOOM, S. W. *The doctor and his patient.* New York: Russell Sage Foundation, 1963.

BLUM, R. H., and ASSOCIATES. *Utopiates: the use and users of LSD 25.* New York: Atherton, 1964.

BLUM, R. H., and BLUM, E. M. *Alcoholism: modern psychological approaches to treatment.* San Francisco: Jossey-Bass, 1967.

BLUMBERG, S., and GILLER, D. W. Some verbal aspects of primary-process thought: a partial replication. *Journal of personality and social psychology,* 1956, *1,* 517–520.

BLUMENTHAL, S., and BERGNER, L. Suicide and newspapers: a replicated study. *American journal of psychiatry,* 1973, *130,* 468–471.

BLUMER, H. Collective behavior. In J. Gould and W. L. Kolb, eds., *Dictionary of the social sciences.* New York: Free Press, 1964, pp. 100–101.

BOARDMAN, W. K. Rusty: a brief behavior disorder. *Journal of consulting psychology,* 1962, *26,* 293–297.

BOAS, F. *Race, language, and culture.* New York: Macmillan, 1940.

BOCKOVEN, J. S. *Moral treatment in American psychiatry.* New York: Springer, 1963.

BOER, A. P., and SIPPRELLE, C. N. Induced anxiety in the treatment for LSD effects. *Psychotherapy and psychosomatics,* 1969, *17,* 108–113.

BOLEN, D. W., and BOYD, W. H. Gambling and the gambler: a review and preliminary findings. *Archives of general psychiatry,* 1968, *18,* 617–629.

BOND, I. K., and EVANS, D. R. Avoidance therapy: its use in two cases of underwear fetishism. *Canadian medical association journal,* 1967, *96,* 1160–1162.

BOND, I. K., and HUTCHINSON, H. C. Application of reciprocal inhibition therapy to exhibitionism. *Canadian medical association journal,* 1960, *83,* 23–25.

BORDIN, E. S. Inside the therapeutic hour. In E. A. Rubinstein and M. B. Parloff, eds., *Research in psychotherapy.* Washington, D.C.: American Psychological Association, 1959, pp. 235–246.

BOREN, J. J., and COLMAN, A. D. Some experiments on reinforcement principles within a psychiatric ward for delinquent soldiers. *Journal of applied behavior analysis,* 1970, *3,* 29–37.

BORKOVEC, T. D., and FOWLES, D. C. Controlled investigation of the effects of progressive and hypnotic relaxation on insomnia. *Journal of abnormal psychology,* 1973, *82,* 153–158.

BORNSTEIN, P. H., and SIPPRELLE, C. N. Group treatment of obesity by induced anxiety. *Behaviour research and therapy,* 1973, *11,* 339–341.

BOSTOW, D. E., and BAILEY, J. B. Modification of severe disruptive and aggressive behavior using brief timeout and reinforcement procedures. *Journal of applied behavior analysis,* 1969, *2,* 31–37.

BOUCHER, M. L. Effect of seating distance on interpersonal attraction in an interview situation. *Journal of consulting and clinical psychology,* 1972, *38,* 15–19.

BOUDIN, H. M. Contingency contracting as a therapeutic tool in the deceleration of amphetamine use. *Behavior therapy,* 1972, *3,* 604–608.

BOULOUGOURIS, J. C., and BASSIAKOS, L. Prolonged flooding in cases with obsessive-compulsive neurosis. *Behaviour research and therapy,* 1973, *11,* 227–231.

BOURNE, P. G. Some observations on the psychosocial phenomena seen in basic training. *Psychiatry,* 1967, *30,* 187–196.

BOURNE, P. G. *Men, stress and Vietnam.* Boston: Little, Brown, 1970.

BOWEN, M. A family concept of schizophrenia. In D. D. Jackson, ed., *The etiology of schizophrenia.* New York: Basic Books, 1960, pp. 346–372.

BOWEN, W. T., SOSKIN, R. A., and CHOTLOS, J. W. Lysergic acid diethylamide as a variable in the hospital treatment of alcoholism. *Journal of nervous and mental disease,* 1970, *150,* 111–118.

BOWLBY, J. *Maternal care and mental health.* Genva: World Health Organization, 1952.

BOWLBY, J., AINSWORTH, M., BOSTON, M., and ROSENBLUTH, D. The effects of mother-child separation, a follow-up study. *British journal of medical psychology,* 1956, *29,* 211–247.

BOWMAN, K. M., and BLAU, A. Psychotic states following head and brain injury in adults and children. In S. Brock, ed., *Injuries of the skull, brain, and spinal cord.* Baltimore: Williams & Wilkins, 1943, pp. 294–341.

BOWMAN, K. M., and ENGLE, B. Review of psychiatric progress: geriatrics. *American journal of psychiatry,* 1960, *116,* 629–630.

BOWMAN, L. *The American funeral.* Washington, D.C.: Public Affairs Press, 1959.

BOZARTH, J. D., and DALY, W. C. Three occupational groups and their perceptions of mental retardates. *Mental retardation,* 1969, *7,* 10–12.

BRAATZ, G. A. Preference in transivity as an indicator of cognitive slippage in schizophrenia. *Journal of abnormal psychology,* 1970, *75,* 1–6.

BRACELAND, F. J., ed., Special section: follow-up studies. *American journal of psychiatry,* 1966, *122,* 1088–1124.

BRACKBILL, Y. Extinction of the smiling response in infants as a function of reinforcement schedule. *Child development,* 1958, *29,* 115–124.

BRADY, J. P. Brevital-relaxation treatment of frigidity. *Behaviour research and therapy,* 1966, *4,* 71–77.

BRADY, J. P. On the use of brevital induced relaxation in the treatment of frigidity. Colloquium, State University of New York, Stony Brook, 1967.

BRADY, J. P. A behavioral approach to the treatment of stuttering. *American journal of psychiatry,* 1968, *125,* 843–848.

BRADY, J. P. Studies on the metronome effect of stuttering. *Behaviour research and therapy,* 1969, *7,* 197–204.

BRADY, J. P. Metronome-conditioning speech retraining for stuttering. *Behavior therapy,* 1971, *2,* 129–150.

BRADY, J. P., and LIND, D. L. Experimental analysis of hysterical blindness. *Archives of general psychiatry,* 1961, *4,* 331–339.

BRAGINSKY, B. M., and BRAGINSKY, D. D. Schizophrenic patients in the psychiatric interview: an experimental study of their effectiveness at manipulation. *Journal of consulting psychology,* 1967, *31,* 543–547.

BRAGINSKY, B. M., BRAGINSKY, D. D., and RING, K. *Methods of madness: the mental hospital as a last resort.* New York: Holt, Rinehart and Winston, 1969.

BRAGINSKY, B. M., GROSSE, M., and RING, K. Controlling outcomes through impression-management: an experimental study of the manipulative tactics of mental patients. *Journal of consulting psychology,* 1966, *30,* 295–300.

BRAGINSKY, D. D., and BRAGINSKY, B. M. *Hansels and Gretels: studies of children in institutions for the mentally retarded.* New York: Holt, Rinehart and Winston, 1971.

BRAGINSKY, D. D., and BRAGINSKY, B. M. The intelligent behavior of mental retardates: a study of their manipulation of intelligence test scores. *Journal of personality,* 1972, *40,* 558–563.

BRAND, D. Beyond the blues. *Wall Street Journal,* 7 April 1972, p. 1.

BRAUSCHI, J. T., and WEST, L. J. Sleep deprivation. *Journal of the American medical association,* 1959, *171,* 11–14.

BRAWLEY, E. R., HARRIS, F. R., ALLEN, K. E., FLEMING, R. S., and PETERSON, R. F. Behavior modification of an autistic child. *Behavioral science,* 1969, *14,* 87–97.

BREASTED, M. *Oh! sex education.* New York: New American Library, Signet, 1971.

BRECHER, E. M. *The sex researchers.* Boston: Little, Brown, 1969.

BRECHER, E. M. *Licit and illicit drugs.* Boston: Little, Brown, 1972.

BREUER, J., and FREUD, S. Studies on hysteria (1893–1895). In *The standard edition of the complete psychological works of Sigmund Freud* (Vol. 2). London: Hogarth Press and the Institute of Psycho-Analysis, 1962.

BRICKER, W. A. Identifying and modifying behavioral deficits. *American journal of mental deficiency,* 1970, *75,* 16–21.

BRIDGER, W. H. Contributions of conditioning principles to psychiatry. In *Pavlovian conditioning and American psychiatry* (GAP Symposium No. 9). New York: Group for the Advancement of Psychiatry, 1964, pp. 181–198.

BRIERLEY, H. The treatment of hysterical spasmodic torticollis by behaviour therapy. *Behaviour research and therapy,* 1967, *5,* 139–142.

BRIGHAM, T. A., and SHERMAN, J. A. An experimental analysis of verbal imitation in preschool children. *Journal of applied behavior analysis,* 1968, *1,* 151–158.

BRILL, N. G. Gross stress reaction. II: Traumatic war neurosis. In A. M. Freedman and H. I. Kaplan, eds., *Comprehensive textbook of psychiatry.* Baltimore: Williams & Wilkins, 1967, 1031–1035.

BROADHEAD, G. D. Socioeconomic traits in mildly retarded children of differential diagnosis. *Rehabilitation literature,* 1973, *34,* 104–107.

BROCK, T. C. On interpreting the effects of transgression upon compliance. *Psychological bulletin,* 1969, *72,* 138–145.

BRODY, J. E. Drug fails tests in schizophrenia. *New York Times,* 25 June 1966, p. 11.

BROMBERG, W. *The mind of man: a history of psychotherapy and psychoanalysis.* New York: Harper, 1959.

BROOKSHIRE, R. H. Speech pathology and the experimental analysis of behavior. *Journal of speech and hearing disorders,* 1967, *32,* 215–227.

BROOKSHIRE, R. H. Control of "involuntary" crying behavior emitted by a multiple sclerosis patient. *Journal of communication disorders,* 1970, *3,* 171–176.

BROUGHTON, R. J. Sleep disorders: disorders of arousal? *Science,* 1968, *159,* 1070–1078.

BROVERMAN, I. K., BROVERMAN, D. M., CLARKSON, F. E., ROSENKRANTZ, P. S., and VOGEL, S. R. Sex-role stereotypes and clinical judgments of mental health. *Journal of consulting and clinical psychology,* 1970, *34,* 1–7.

BROWN, C., and SEITZ, J. "You've come a long way, baby": historical perspectives. In R. Morgan, ed., *Sisterhood is powerful.* New York: Vintage, 1970, pp. 3–28.

BROWN, G. M., QUARRINGTON, B., and STANCER, H. C. A re-evaluation of glucose tolerance in schizophrenia. *Journal of psychiatric research,* 1969, *6,* 261–270.

BROWN, J. S. A comparative study of deviations from sexual mores. *American sociological review,* 1952, *17,* 138.

BROWN, P., and ELLIOT, R. Control of aggression in a nursery school class. *Journal of experimental child psychology,* 1965, *2,* 103–107.

BROWN, R. A., PACE, Z. S., and BECKER, W. C. Treatment of extreme negativism and autistic behavior in a 6-year-old boy. *Exceptional children,* 1969, *35,* 115–122.

BROWN, R. L. The effects of aversive stimulation on certain conceptual error responses of schizophrenics. *Dissertation abstracts,* 1961, *22,* 629.

BROWNFIELD, E. D., and KEEHN, J. D. Operant eyelid conditioning in trisomy-18. *Journal of abnormal psychology,* 1966, *71,* 413–415.

BROWNING, R. M. Behaviour therapy for stuttering in a schizophrenic child. *Behaviour research and therapy,* 1967, *5,* 27–35.

BROWNING, R. M. Treatment effects of a total behavior modification program with five autistic children. *Behaviour research and therapy,* 1971, *9,* 319–327.

BRUCH, H. Obesity and orality. *Contemporary psychoanalysis,* 1969, *5,* 129–144.

BRUEHL, D., and SOLAR, D. Systematic variation in the clarity of demand characteristics in an experiment employing a confederate. *Psychological reports,* 1970, *27,* 55–60.

BRUSH, A. L. Recent literature relative to psychiatric aspects of gastro-intestinal disorders. *Psychosomatic medicine,* 1939, *1,* 423-428.

BRUTTEN, E., and SHOEMAKER, D. *The modification of stuttering.* Englewood Cliffs, N.J.: Prentice-Hall, 1967.

BRYAN, J. H. Why children help: a review. In L. G. Wispe, ed., Positive forms of social behavior. *Journal of social issues,* 1972, *3,* 1–229.

BRYAN, J. H. and LONDON, P. Altruistic behavior by children. *Psychological bulletin,* 1970, *73,* 200–211.

BRYAN, J. H., and TEST, M. A. Models and helping: naturalistic studies in aiding behavior. *Journal of personality and social psychology,* 1967, *6,* 400–407.

BRYAN, J. H., and WALBEK, N. H. Preaching and practicing generosity: children's actions and reactions. *Child development,* 1970, *41,* 329–353.

BUCHER, B. D. A pocket-portable shock device with application to nailbiting. *Behaviour research and therapy,* 1968, *6,* 389–392.

BUCHER, B., and FABRICATORE, J. Use of patient-administered shock to suppress hallucinations. *Behavior therapy,* 1970, *1,* 382–385.

BUCKNER, H. The transvestic career path. *Psychiatry,* 1970, *33,* 381–389.

BUDZYNSKI, T. H., and STOYVA, J. M. An instrument for producing deep muscle relaxation by means of analog information feedback. *Journal of applied behavior analysis,* 1969, *2,* 231-237.

BUDZYNSKI, T. H., and STOYVA, J. M. Biofeedback techniques in behavior therapy. In D. Shapiro et al., eds., *Biofeedback and self-control.* Chicago: Aldine, 1972.

BUDZYNSKI, T. H., STOYVA, J. M., and ADLER, C. S. Feedback-induced muscle relaxation: application to tension headache. *Journal of behavior therapy and experimental psychiatry,* 1970, *1,* 205–211.

BUDZYNSKI, T. H., STOYVA, J. M., ADLER, C. S., and MULLANEY, D. J. EMG biofeedback and tension headache: a controlled outcome study. *Psychosomatic medicine,* 1973, *35,* 484–496.

BUEHLER, R. E., PATTERSON, G. R., and FURNISS, J. M. The reinforcement of behaviour in institutional settings. *Behaviour research and therapy,* 1966, *4,* 157–167.

BUGENTAL, J. F. T. *The search for authenticity: an existential-analytic approach to psychotherapy.* New York: Holt, Rinehart and Winston, 1966.

BURCHARD, J. D. Systematic socialization: a programmed environment for the habilitation of antisocial retardates. *Psychological record,* 1967, *17,* 461–476.

BURCHARD, J. D., and TYLER, V. The modification of delinquent behaviour through operant conditioning. *Behaviour research and therapy,* 1965, *2,* 245–250.

BURGESS, E. P. Elimination of vomiting behavior. *Behaviour research and therapy,* 1969, *7,* 173–176.

BURGESS, R. L., BURGESS, J. M., and ESVELDT, K. C. An analysis of generalized imitation. *Journal of applied behavior analysis,* 1970, *3,* 39–46.

BURGESS, R. L., CLARK, R. N., and HENDEE, J. C. An experimental analysis of antilitter procedures. *Journal of applied behavior analysis,* 1971, *4,* 71–75.

BURKE, B. D., and YATES, A. J. Stuttering: theoretical and therapeutic considerations: I. Some implications of recent research findings to the theory of stuttering. *Australian psychologist,* 1967, *2.*

BURNHAM, W. H. *The normal mind.* New York: Appleton, 1924.

BURRIS, D. S., ed. *The right to treatment.* New York: Springer, 1969.

BURROW, T. *The social basis of consciousness.* New York: Harcourt, Brace, 1927.

BURTON, R. The anatomy of melancholy (F. Dell

and P. Jordan-Smith, eds.). New York: Tudor, 1927.

Buss, A. H. *Psychopathology*. New York: Wiley, 1966.

Buss, A. H., and Daniell, E. F. Stimulus generalization and schizophrenia. *Journal of abnormal psychology*, 1967, *72*, 50–53.

Butterfield, E. C., Barnett, C. D., and Bensberg, G. J. Some objective characteristics of institutions for the mentally retarded: implications for attendant turnover rate. *American journal of mental deficiency*, 1966, *70*, 786–794.

Butterfield, E. C., and Zigler, E. Preinstitutional social deprivation and IQ changes among institutionalized retarded children. *Journal of abnormal psychology*, 1970, *75*, 83–89.

Bycel, B. Help for compulsive gamblers comes from their fellow victims. *Champaign-Urbana courier*, 16 May 1971, p. 35.

Bykov, K. M. *Cerebral cortex and internal organs*. Translated by W. A. H. Gantt. New York: Chemical Publishing Co., 1957.

Byrne, D. The relationship between humor and the expression of hostility. *Journal of abnormal and social psychology*, 1955, *53*, 84–89.

Cahoon, D. D., and Crosby, C. C. A teaching approach to chronic drug use: Sources of reinforcement. *Behavior therapy*, 1972, *3*, 64–71.

Calfee, A. J. The differential effects of verbal reinforcement on a verbal and a non-verbal task in process and reactive hospitalized neuropsychiatric patients. Unpublished doctoral dissertation, U.C.L.A., 1965.

Calhoun, J., and Koenig, K. P. Classroom modification of elective mutism. *Behavior therapy*, 1973, *4*, 700–702.

Callahan, D. Ethics and population limitation. *Science*, 1972, *175*, 487–494.

Cameron, N. A. The functional psychoses. In J. McV. Hunt, ed., *Personality and the behavior disorders* (Vol. 2). New York: Ronald Press, 1944, pp. 861–921.

Cameron, N. A. *The psychology of behavior disorders*. New York: Houghton, 1947.

Cameron, N. A. *Personality development and psychopathology: a dynamic approach*. Boston: Houghton Mifflin, 1963.

Cameron, N. A. Paranoid reactions. In A. M. Freedman and H. I. Kaplan, eds., *Comprehensive textbook of psychiatry*. Baltimore: Williams & Wilkins, 1967, pp. 665–675.

Cameron, N. A., and Magaret, A. *Behavior pathology*. New York: Houghton, 1951.

Cameron, P., and Titus, D. The happiness of retarded children. *Proceedings of the 81st annual convention of the American Psychological Association*, Montreal, Canada, 1973, *8*, 803–804.

Campbell, L. M., III. Variation of thought-stopping in a twelve-year-old boy: a case report. *Journal of behavior therapy and experimental psychiatry*, 1973, *4*, 69–70.

Campion, E., and Tucker, G. A note on twin studies, schizophrenia and neurological impairment. *Archives of general psychiatry*, 1973, *29*, 460–464.

Cancro, R., and Pruyser, P. W. A historical review of the development of the concept of schizophrenia. *Bulletin of the Menninger clinic*, 1970, *34*, 61–70.

Cannon, W. B. *Bodily changes in pain, hunger, fear, and rage*. 2nd ed. New York: Appleton, 1929.

Caplan, G. *Principles of preventive psychiatry*. New York: Basic Books, 1964.

Caplan, G., and Grunebaum, H. Perspectives on primary prevention: a review. *Archives of general psychiatry*, 1967, *17*, 331–346.

Caplan, R. B. *Psychiatry, and the community in nineteenth century America*. New York: Basic Books, 1969.

Carden, N. L., and Sehramel, D. J. Observations of conversion reactions seen in troops involved in the Vietnam conflict. *American journal of psychiatry*, 1966, *123*, 21–31.

Carey, F. Report: mental problems common in U.S. *Champaign-Urbana courier*, 24 April 1972, p. 9.

Carlin, A. S., and Armstrong, H. E. Rewarding social responsibility in disturbed children: a group play technique. *Psychotherapy: theory, research and practice*, 1968, *5*, 169–174.

Carlsmith, J. M., et al. Dissonance reduction following forced attention to the dissonance. *Proceedings of the 77th annual convention of the American Psychological Association*, 1969, *4*, 321–322.

Carlsmith, J. M., and Gross, A. E. Some effects of guilt on compliance. *Journal of personality and social psychology*, 1969, *11*, 232–239.

Carlson, C. G., Hersen, M., and Eisler, R. M. Token economy programs in the treatment of hospitalized adult psychiatric patients. *Journal of nervous and mental disease*, 1972, *155*, 192–204.

Carlson, C. S., Arnold, C. R., Becker, W. C., and Madsen, C. H. The elimination of tantrum behavior of a child in an elementary classroom. *Behaviour research and therapy*, 1968, *6*, 117–119.

Carnegie, D. *How to stop worrying and start living*. New York: Simon & Schuster, 1948.

Carnegie, D. *How to win friends and influence people*. New York: Simon & Schuster, 1936.

CARP, F. M. Senility or garden variety maladjustment? *Journal of gerontology*, 1969, *24*, 203–208.

CARR, E. H. *What is history?* New York: Random House, 1961.

CARTER, D. B., and ALLEN, D. C. Evaluation of the placebo effect in optometry. *American journal of optometry and archives of American academy of optometry*, 1973, *50*, 94–104.

CARTER, J. W., JR. The training needs of psychologists in community health programs at state and local levels. In C. R. Strother, ed., *Psychology and mental health*. Washington: American Psychological Association, 1957.

CASE, H. W. Therapeutic methods in stuttering and speech blocking. In H. J. Eysenck, ed., *Behaviour therapy and the neuroses*. New York: Pergamon Press, 1960, pp. 207–220.

CASSELL, S. Effect of brief puppet therapy upon the emotional responses of children undergoing cardiac catheterization. *Journal of consulting psychology*, 1965, *29*, 1–8.

CATTELL, R. B., and SCHEIER, I. H. *Neuroticism and anxiety*. New York: Ronald Press, 1961.

CAUTELA, J. R. Covert sensitization. *Psychological reports*, 1967, *20*, 459–468.

CAUTELA, J. R. Behavior therapy and the need for behavioral assessment. *Psychotherapy: theory, research and practice*, 1968, *5*, 175–179.

CAUTELA, J. R. A classical conditioning approach to the development and modification of behavior in the aged. *Gerontologist*, 1969, *9*, 109–113.

CAUTELA, J. R. Covert reinforcement. *Behavior therapy*, 1970a, *1*, 33–50.

CAUTELA, J. R. Covert negative reinforcement. *Journal of behavior therapy and experimental psychiatry*, 1970b, *1*, 273–278.

CAUTELA, J. R., and BARON, M. G. Multifaceted behavior therapy of self-injurious behavior. *Journal of behavior therapy and experimental psychiatry*, 1973, *4*, 125–131.

CAVAN, R. S., ed. *Readings in juvenile delinquency*. Philadelphia: Lippincott, 1964.

CAVANAUGH, D. Improvement in the performance of schizophrenics on concept formation tasks as a function of motivational change. *Journal of abnormal and social psychology*, 1958, *57*, 8–12.

CENTERWELL, S. A., and CENTERWELL, W. R. A study of children with Mongolism reared in the home compared with those reared away from home. *Journal of child psychology and psychiatry*, 1960, *1*, 23–36.

CERMAK, S. A., STEIN, F., and ABELSON, C. Hyperactive children and an activity group model. *American journal of occupational therapy*, 1973, *27*, 311–315.

CHAFETZ, M. E. Addictions. III: alcoholism. In A. M. Freedman and H. I. Kaplan, eds., *Comprehensive textbook of psychiatry*. Baltimore: Williams & Wilkins, 1967, 1011–1026.

CHAMBERS, D. A. Conditioning in psychotics. *Acta psychiatrica scandinavica*, 1965, *41*, 1–41.

CHAPEL, J. L. Treatment of a case of school phobia by reciprocal inhibition. *Canadian psychiatric association journal*, 1966, *12*, 25–28.

CHAPMAN, J. D. Frigidity: rapid treatment by reciprocal inhibition. *Journal of the American osteopathic association*, 1968, *67*, 871–878.

CHAPMAN, L. J., DAY, D., and BURSTEIN, A. The process-reactive distinction and prognosis in schizophrenia. *Journal of nervous and mental disease*, 1961, *133*, 383–391.

CHAPMAN, L. J., and CHAPMAN, J. P. The genesis of popular but erroneous psychodiagnostic observations. *Journal of abnormal psychology*, 1967, *72*, 193–204.

CHAPMAN, L. J., and CHAPMAN, J. P. Illusory correlation as an obstacle to the use of valid psychodiagnostic signs. *Journal of abnormal psychology*, 1969, *74*, 271–280.

CHAPMAN, L. J., CHAPMAN, J. P., and BRELJE, T. Influence of the experimenter on pupillary dilation to sexually provocative pictures. *Journal of abnormal psychology*, 1969, *74*, 396–400.

CHAPMAN, R. F., SMITH, J. W., and LAYTON, T. A. Elimination of cigarette smoking by punishment and self-management training. *Behaviour research and therapy*, 1971, *9*, 255–264.

CHARLES, D. C. Adult adjustment of some deficient American children–II. *American journal of mental deficiency*, 1957, *62*, 300–304.

CHARLESWORTH, R., and HARTUP, W. W. Positive social reinforcement in the nursery school peer group. *Child development*, 1967, *38*, 1017–1024.

CHASE, L. S. and SILVERMAN, S. Prognosis in schizophrenia: an analysis of prognostic criteria in 150 schizophrenics treated with metrazol or insulin. *Journal of nervous and mental disease*, 1943, *98*, 464–473.

CHASSEN, J. B. Population and sample: a major problem in psychiatric research. *American journal of orthopsychiatry*, 1970, *40*, 456–462.

CHATEL, J. C., and PEELE, R. A centennial review of neurasthenia. *American journal of psychiatry*, 1970, *126*, 1404–1411.

CHEEK, F. E., FRANKS, C. M., LAUCIUS, J., and BURTLE, W. Behavior modification training for wives of alcoholics. *Quarterly journal of studies in alcohol*, 1971, *32*, 456–461.

CHERRY, C., and SAYERS, B. Experiments upon the

total inhibition of stammering by external control, and some clinical results. *Journal of psychosomatic research,* 1956, *1,* 233–246.

CHESLER, P. *Women and madness.* New York: Avon Books, 1972.

CHEYNE, J. A., GOYECHE, J. R. M., and WALTERS, R. H. Attention, anxiety, and rules in resistance-to-deviation in children. *Journal of experimental child psychology,* 1969, *8,* 127–139.

CHEYNE, J. A., and WALTERS, R. H. Intensity of punishment, timing of punishment, and cognitive structure as determinants of response inhibition. *Journal of experimental child psychology,* 1969, *7,* 231–244.

CHIEN, C. P. Psychiatric treatment for geriatric patients: "pub" or drug? *American journal of psychiatry,* 1971, *127,* 1070–1075.

CHOUKAS, M. *Propaganda comes of age.* Washington, D.C.: Public Affairs Press, 1965.

CHRISTENSEN, D.E., and SPRAGUE, R. L. Reduction of hyperactive behavior by conditioning procedures alone and combined with methylphenidate. *Behaviour research and therapy,* 1973, *2,* 331–333.

CHURCH, R. M. The varied effects of punishment on behavior. *Psychological review,* 1963, *70,* 369–402.

CHURCHILL, D. W., and BRYSON, C. Q. Looking and approach behavior of psychotic and normal children as a function of adult attention or preoccupation. *Comprehensive psychiatry,* 1972, *13,* 171–177.

CHURCHMAN, C. W. *The systems approach.* New York: Dell, 1969.

CISLER, L. Abortion law repeal (sort of) : a warning to women. In S. Stambler, ed., *Women's liberation: blueprint for the future.* New York: Ace, 1970, pp. 72–81.

CLANCY, J., VANDERHOOF, E., and CAMPBELL, P. Evaluation of an aversive technique as a treatmnet for alcoholism: controlled trial with Succinylcholine-induced apnea. *Quarterly journal of studies on alcohol,* 1967, *28,* 476–485.

CLARIZIO, H. Stability of deviant behavior through time. *Mental hygiene,* 1968, *52,* 288–293.

CLARK, D. F. Fetishism treated by negative conditioning, *British journal of psychiatry,* 1963a, *109,* 404-407.

CLARK, D. F. The treatment of hysterical spasm and agoraphobia by behaviour therapy. *Behaviour research and therapy,* 1963b, *1,* 245–250.

CLARK, D. F. A note on avoidance conditioning techniques in sexual disorder. *Behaviour research and therapy,* 1965, *3,* 203–206.

CLARK, D. F. Behaviour therapy of Gilles de la Tourette's syndrome. *British journal of psychiatry,* 1966, *112,* 771–778.

CLARK, M., LACHOWICZ, J., and WOLF, M. M. A pilot basic education program for school dropouts incorporating a token reinforcement system. *Behaviour research and therapy,* 1968, *6,* 183–188.

CLARK, R. D., III., and WORD, L. E. Why don't bystanders help? because of ambiguity? *Journal of personality and social psychology,* 1972, *24,* 392–400.

CLARK, R. D., III., and WORD, L. E. Where is the apathetic bystander? situational characteristics of the emergency. *Journal of personality and social psychology,* 1974, *29,* 279–287.

CLARK, R. N., BURGESS, R. L., and HENDEE, J. C. The development of anti-litter behavior in a forest campground. *Journal of applied behavior analysis,* 1972, *5,* 1–5.

CLARK, W. C., and YANG, J. C. Acupunctural analgesia? evaluation by signal detection theory. *Science,* 1974, *184,* 1096–1098.

CLAUSEN, J. A., and YARROW, M. R. Paths to the mental hospital. *Journal of social issues,* 1955, *11,* 25–32.

CLECKLEY, H. *The mask of sanity.* 4th ed. St. Louis: Mosby, 1964.

CLEGHORN, R. A. Hysteria—multiple manifestations of semantic confusion. *Canadian psychiatric association journal,* 1969a, *14,* 539–551.

CLEGHORN, R. A. Hysterical personality and conversion: theoretical aspects. *Canadian psychiatric association journal,* 1969b, *14,* 553–567.

CLELAND, C. C., and PECK, R. F. Intra-institutional administrative problems: a paradigm for employee stimulation. *Mental retardation,* 1967, *5,* 2–8.

CLEMENT, P. W. Operant conditioning in group therapy with children. *Journal of school health,* 1968, *38,* 271–278.

CLEMENT, P. W. Elimination of sleepwalking in a seven-year-old boy. *Journal of consulting and clinical psychology,* 1970, *34,* 22–26.

CLEMENT, P. W., FAZZONE, R. A., and GOLDSTEIN, B. Tangible reinforcers and child group therapy. *Journal of the American academy of child psychiatry,* 1970, *9,* 409–427.

CLEMENT, P. W., and MILNE, D. C. Group play therapy and tangible reinforcers used to modify the behavior of eight-year-old boys. *Proceedings of the 75th Annual Convention of the American Psychological Association,* 1967, 241–242.

CLEMENTS, C. B., and MCKEE, J. M. Programmed instruction for institutionalized offenders: contingency management and performance contracts. *Psychological reports,* 1968, *22,* 957–964.

CLEMENT, S. Minimal brain dysfunction in children.

NINDB Monograph No. 3. PHS Bull. No. 1415. Washington, D.C.: Dept. of Health, Education and Welfare, 1966.

CLEMMER, D. *The prison community.* New York: Holt, Rinehart and Winston, 1968.

CLINARD, M. B. and QUINNEY, R. *Criminal behavior systems: a typology.* New York: Holt, Rinehart and Winston, 1967.

CLORE, G. L., and JEFFERY, K. McM. Emotional role playing, attitude change, and attraction toward a disabled person. *Journal of personality and social psychology,* 1972, *23,* 105–111.

CLOWARD, R. A. Illegitimate means, anomic, and deviant behavior. *American sociological review,* 1959, *24,* 164–176.

COAN, R. W. Personality variables associated with cigarette smoking. *Journal of personality and social psychology,* 1973, *26,* 86–104.

COBLENTZ, S. Earthquake, fire and flood (in the eyes of childhood). *Pacific spectator,* 1950, *4,* 144–152.

COE, W. C., and SARBIN, T. R. An experimental demonstration of hypnosis as role enactment. *Journal of abnormal psychology,* 1966, *71,* 400–406.

COHEN, A. K. *Deviance and control.* Englewood Cliffs, N.J.: Prentice-Hall, 1966.

COHEN, B. D. Motivation and performance in schizophrenia. *Journal of abnormal and social psychology,* 1956, *52,* 186–190.

COHEN, E. S., and KRAFT, A. C. The restorative potential of elderly long-term residents of mental hospitals. *Gerontologist,* 1968, *8,* 264–268.

COHEN, H. L., and FILIPCZAK, J. *A new learning environment.* San Francisco: Jossey-Bass, 1971.

COHEN, H. L., FILIPCZAK, J. A., BIS, J. S., and COHEN, J. E. *Contingencies applicable to special education of delinquents.* Silver Spring, Md.: Institute for Behavioral Research, 1966.

COHEN, M. LIEBSON, I., and FAILLACE, L. A. Controlled drinking by chronic alcoholics over extended periods of free access. *Psychological reports,* 1973, *32,* 1107–1110.

COHEN, M., LIEBSON, I., and FAILLACE, L. A. A technique for establishing controlled drinking in alcoholics. *Diseases of the nervous system,* 1972, *33,* 46–49.

COHEN, R. The effects of group interaction and progressive hierarchy presentation on desensitization of test anxiety. *Behaviour research and therapy,* 1969, *7,* 15–26.

COHEN, R. L., and RICHARDSON, C. H. A retrospective study of case attrition in a child clinic. *Social psychiatry,* 1970, *5,* 77–83.

COHEN, S. I., and REED, J. L. The treatment of "nervous diarrhea" and other conditioned autonomic disorders by desensitization. *British journal of psychiatry,* 1968, *114,* 1275–1280.

COLBY, K. M. Psychotherapeutic processes. In P. Farnsworth, O. McNemar, and Q. McNemar, eds., *Annual review of psychology.* Palo Alto, Calif.: Annual Reviews, 1964, pp. 347–370.

COLEMAN, J. C. *Abnormal psychology and modern life.* 3d ed. Chicago: Scott, Foresman, 1964. (With W. E. BROEN, JR.)

COLEMAN, J. C. *Abnormal psychology and modern life.* 4th ed. Glenview, Ill.: Scott, Foresman, 1972.

COLLMANN, R. D., and NEWLYN, D. Employment success of mentally dull and intellectually normal ex-pupils in England. *American journal of mental deficiency,* 1957, *61,* 484–490.

COLMAN, A. D., and BAKER, S. L., JR. Utilization of an operant conditioning model for the treatment of character and behavior disorders in a military setting. *American journal of psychiatry,* 1969, *125,* 1395–1403.

COLSON, C. E. Olfactory aversion therapy for homosexual behavior. *Journal of behavior therapy and experimental psychiatry,* 1972, *3,* 185–187.

COLSON, C. An objective-analytic approach to the classification of suicidal motivation. *Acta psychiatrica scandinavica,* 1973, *49,* 105–113.

COMBS, A. W. and SNYGG, D. *Individual behavior.* New York: Harper, 1959.

COMFORT, A. *The anxiety makers.* New York: Dell, 1969.

COMMISSION ON OBSCENITY AND PORNOGRAPHY. *The report of the commission on obscenity and pornography.* New York: Bantam, 1970.

COMMONS, M. L., PAUL, S. M., and FARGO, G. A. Developing speech in an autistic boy using operant techniques to increase his rate of vocal-verbal responding. Paper read at the Western Psychological Association Convention, 1966.

COMTOIS, D. R., and HOLLAND, H. O. Operant conditioning: one year's experience with habit training the severely and profoundly retarded. Unpublished manuscript. Mount Pleasant State Home and Training School, Michigan, 1966.

CONGDON, M. H., HAIN, J., and STEVENSON, I. A case of multiple personality illustrating the transition from role playing. *Archives of general psychiatry,* 1972, *27,* 497–504.

CONGER, J. C. The treatment of encopresis by the management of social consequences. *Behavior therapy,* 1970, *1,* 386–390.

CONGER, J. J. Reinforcement theory and the dynamics of alcoholism. *Quarterly journal of studies on alcohol,* 1956, *17,* 296–305.

CONLEY, R. W., CONWELL, M., and ARRILL, M. B. An approach to measuring the cost of mental illness. *American journal of psychiatry*, 1967, *124*, 755-762.

COOK, C., and ADAMS, H. E. Modification of verbal behaviour in speech deficient children. *Behaviour research and therapy*, 1966, *4*, 265-271.

COOKE, G., JOHNSTON, N., and POGANY, E. Factors affecting referral to determine competency to stand trial. *American journal of psychiatry*, 1973, *130*, 870-875.

COOKE, O. The court study unit: patient characteristics and differences between patients judged competent and incompetent. *Journal of clinical psychology*, 1969, *25*, 140-143.

COOLEY, W. W., and GLASER, R. The computer and individualized instruction. *Science*, 1969, *166*, 574-582.

COOPER, A. B., and EARLY, D. F. Evolution in the mental hospital: review of a hospital population. *British medical journal*, 1961, *1*, 1600-1603.

COOPER, A. J. Conditioning therapy in hysterical retention of urine. *British journal of psychiatry*, 1965, *111*, 575-577.

COOPER, E. B. Recovery from stuttering in a junior and senior high school population. *Journal of speech and hearing research*, 1972, *15*, 632-638.

COOPER, J. B. Emotion in prejudice. *Science*, 1959, *130*, 314-318.

COOPER, J. E. A study of behaviour therapy in thirty psychiatric patients. *Lancet*, 1963, *1*, 411-415.

COOPER, J. E., GELDER, M. G., and MARKS, I. M. Results of behaviour therapy in 77 psychiatric patients. *British medical journal*, 1965, *1*, 1222-1225.

COOPER, J. E., KENDELL, R. E., GURLAND, B. J., SARTORIUS, N., and FARKAS, T. Cross-national study of the mental disorders: some results of the first comparative investigation. *American journal of psychiatry*, 1969, *125*. (Supplement No. 10), 21-29.

COPPEN, A., et al. Prophylactic lithium in affective disorders. *Lancet*, 1971, *2*, 275-279.

CORTE, H. E., WOLF, M. M., and LOCKE, B. J. A comparison of procedures for eliminating self-injurious behavior of retarded adolescents. *Journal of applied behavior analysis*, 1971, *4*, 201-213.

COTLER, S. B. Sex differences and generalization of anxiety reduction with automated desensitization and minimal therapist interaction. *Behaviour research and therapy*, 1970, *8*, 273-285.

COTLER, S. B. The use of differential behavioral techniques in treating a case of compulsive gambling. *Behavior therapy*, 1971, *2*, 579-584.

COTTRELL, W. F. Death by dieselization. *American sociological review*, 1951, *16*, 358-365.

COUCH, R. H., and ALLEN, C. M. Behavior modification in rehabilitation facilities: a review. *Journal of applied rehabilitation counseling*, 1973, *4*, 88-95.

COWAN, P. A., HODDINOTT, B. A., and WRIGHT, B. A. Compliance and resistance in the conditioning of autistic children: an exploratory study. *Child development*, 1965, *36*, 913-923.

COWAN, P. A., LANGER, J., HEAVENRICH, J., and NATHANSON, M. Social learning and Piaget's cognitive theory of moral development. *Journal of personality and social psychology*, 1969, *11*, 261-274.

COWDEN, R. C., and FORD, L. I. Systematic desensitization with phobic schizophrenics. *American journal of psychiatry*, 1962, *119*, 241-245.

COWEN, E. L., and ZAX, M. Early detection and prevention of emotional disorder: conceptualizations and programming. In J. W. Carter, Jr., ed., *Research contributions from psychology to community mental health*. New York: Behavioral Publications, 1968, pp. 46-59.

CRAIG, K. D. Physiological arousal as a function of imagined, vicarious, and direct stress experiences. *Journal of abnormal psychology*, 1968, *73*, 513-520.

CRAIG, K. D., and LOWERY, H. J. Heart-rate components of conditioning vicarious autonomic responses. *Journal of personality and social psychology*, 1969, *11*, 381-387.

CRAIG, L. E., and SENTER, R. J. Student thoughts about suicide. *Psychological record*, 1972, *22*, 355-358.

CRAIGHEAD, W. E., and MERCATORIS, M. Mentally retarded residents as paraprofessionals: a review. *American journal of mental deficiency*, 1973, *78*, 339-347.

CRAIGHEAD, W. E., MERCATORIS, M., and BELLAK, B. The use of mentally retarded residents as behavioral observers. *Journal of applied behavior analysis*, in press.

CRAIGHEAD, W. E., O'LEARY, K. D., and ALLEN, J. S. Teaching and generalization of instruction-following in an "autistic" child. *Journal of behavior therapy and experimental psychiatry*, 1973, *4*, 171-176.

CRAIK, K. H. Environmental psychology. In, *New directions in psychology*, IV. New York: Holt, Rinehart and Winston, 1970, pp. 1-121.

CRANE, A. R. The development of moral values in children. *British journal of educational psychology*, 1958, *28*, 201-208.

CREER, T. L. The use of a time-out from positive reinforcement procedure with asthmatic children. *Journal of psychosomatic research*, 1970, *14*, 117-120.

CRIDER, A., SHAPIRO, D., and TURSKY, B. Reinforcement of spontaneous electrodermal activity. *Journal of comparative and physiological psychology*, 1966, *61*, 20-27.

CRONBACH, L. J. *Essentials of psychological testing.* 3rd ed. New York: Harper & Row, 1970.

CROSS, H. J. The outcome of psychotherapy: a selected analysis of research findings. *Journal of consulting psychology,* 1964, *28,* 413–417.

CROSS, K. W., HARRINGTON, J. A., and MAYER-GROSS, W. A survey of chronic patients in a mental hospital. *Journal of mental science,* 1957, *103,* 146–171.

CROWLEY, P. M. Effect of training upon objectivity of moral judgment in grade-school children. *Journal of personality and social psychology,* 1968, *8,* 228–232.

CRUICKSHANK, W. M., ed. *Psychology of exceptional children and youth.* 3rd ed. Englewood Cliffs, N.J.: Prentice-Hall, 1971.

CRUTCHFIELD, R. S. Conformity and character. *American psychologist,* 1955, *10,* 191–198.

CUBER, J. F. *Sociology.* 5th ed. New York: Appleton, 1963.

CULL, J. Conformity behavior in schizophrenics. *Journal of social psychology,* 1971, *84,* 45–49.

CUMMING, J., and CUMMING, E. Social equilibrium and social change in the large mental hospital. In M. Greenblatt, D. J. Levinson and R. H. Williams, eds., *The patient and the mental hospital.* Glencoe, Ill.: Free Press, 1957, 49–72.

CURLEE, R. F., and PERKINS, W. H. Conversational rate control therapy for stuttering. *Journal of speech and hearing disorders,* 1969, *34,* 245–250.

CURRAN, D., and PARR, D. Homosexuality: an analysis of 100 male cases seen in private practice. *British medical journal,* 1957, *1,* 797–801.

CURTIS, R. H., and PRESLY, A. S. The extinction of homosexual behaviour by covert sensitization: a case study. *Behaviour research and therapy,* 1972, *10,* 81–83.

DAIN, N. *Concepts of insanity in the United States, 1789–1865.* New Brunswick, N.J.: Rutgers University Press, 1964.

DALY, D. A., and FRICK, J. V. The effects of punishing stuttering expectations and stuttering utterances. *Behavior therapy,* 1970, *1,* 228–239.

DALY, D. D., and BARRY, M. J., JR. Musicogenic epilepsy. *Psychosomatic medicine,* 1957, *19,* 399–408.

DARLEY, J. M., and BATSON, C. D. "From Jerusalem to Jericho": a study of situational and dispositional variables in helping behavior. *Journal of personality and social psychology,* 1973, *27,* 100–108.

DARLEY, J. M., and DARLEY, S. A. *Conformity and deviation.* Morristown, N.J.: General Learning Press, 1973.

DARLEY, J. M., and LATANÉ, B. Bystander intervention in emergencies: diffusion of responsibility. *Journal of personality and social psychology,* 1968, *8,* 377–383.

DARLEY, J. M., and LATANÉ, B. Norms and normative behavior: field studies interdependence. In J. Macaulay and L. Berkowitz, eds., *Altruism and helping behavior.* New York: Academic Press, 1970, pp. 83–101.

DARNTON, R. *Mesmerism and the end of the enlightenment in France.* Cambridge, Mass.: Harvard University Press, 1968.

DARWIN, C. *The origin of species by means of natural selection* (1859). New York: Modern Library.

DAVIDSON, A. R., and STEINER, I. D. Reinforcement schedules and attributed freedom. *Journal of personality and social psychology,* 1971, *19,* 357–366.

DAVIDSON, H. A. The semantics of psychotherapy. *American journal of psychiatry,* 1958, *115,* 410–413.

DAVIDSON, J. R., and DOUGLASS, E. Nocturnal enuresis: a special approach to treatment. *British medical journal,* 1950, *1,* 1345–1347.

DAVIS, B. D. Prospects for genetic intervention in man. *Science,* 1970, *170,* 1279–1283.

DAVIS, J. M., and FARINA, A. Humor appreciation as social communication. *Journal of personality and social psychology,* 1970, *15,* 175–178.

DAVIS, K. Extreme social isolation of a child. *American journal of sociology,* 1940, *45,* 554–565.

DAVIS, N. J. Labeling theory in deviance research: a critique and reconsideration. *Sociological quarterly,* 1972, *13,* 447–474.

DAVISON, G. C. Differential relaxation and cognitive restructuring in therapy with a "paranoid schizophrenic" or "paranoid state." *Proceedings of the 74th annual convention of the American psychological association,* 1966, p. 177.

DAVISON, G. C. The elimination of a sadistic fantasy by a client-controlled conditioning technique: a case study. *Journal of abnormal psychology,* 1968a, *73,* 84–90.

DAVISON, G. C. Systematic desensitization as a counterconditioning process. *Journal of abnormal psychology,* 1968b, *73,* 91–99.

DAVISON, G. C., and KRASNER, L. *Behavior therapy with an autistic child.* 16mm. sound film. Public Health Service Audiovisual Facility, Communicable Disease Center, Atlanta, Georgia, #MIS-895, 1964.

DAVISON, G. C., and LIEBERT, R. M. *Behavior therapy for homosexuality.* Penn State: Psychological Cinema Register, 1972.

DAVISON, G. C., TSUJIMOTO, R. N., and GLAROS, A. G. Attribution and the maintenance of behavior change in falling asleep. *Journal of abnormal psychology,* 1973, *82,* 124–133.

DAVISON, G. C., and VALINS, S. Maintenance of self-attributed and drug attributed behavior change.

Journal of personality and social psychology, 1969, *11*, 25–33.

DAWS, P. P. The aetiology of mental disorder. *Bulletin of the British psychological society*, 1967, *20*, 45–47.

DAWSON, E. B., MOORE, T. D., and MCGANITY, W. J. The mathematical relationship of drinking water, lithium, and rainfall to mental hospital admissions. *Diseases of the nervous system*, 1970, *31*, 811–820.

DAYAN, M. Toilet training retarded children in a state residential institution. *Mental retardation*, 1964, *2*, 116–117.

DEKKER, E., PELSER, H. E., and GROEN, J. Conditioning as a cause of asthmatic attacks; a laboratory study. *Journal of psychosomatic research*, 1957, *2*, 97–108.

DEKKER, E., and GROEN, J. Reproducible psychogenic attacks of asthma: a laboratory study. *Journal of psychosomatic research*, 1956, *1*, 58–67.

DEL CASTILLO, J. The influence of language upon symptomatology in foreign-born patients. *American journal of psychiatry*, 1970, *127*, 242–244.

DELEON, G., and MANDELL, W. A comparison of conditioning and psychotherapy in the treatment of functional enuresis. *Journal of clinical psychology*, 1966, *22*, 326–330.

DEMENT, W. C. But I still cannot sleep at night. *The Stanford alumni almanac*, 1972, 3–6.

DEMENT, W. C. The effect of dream deprivation. *Science*, 1960, *131*, 1705–1707.

DEMENT, W. C. Experimental dream studies. In J. Masserman, ed., *Science and psychoanalysis. Vol. VII. Development and research.* New York: Grune & Stratton, 1964, 129–162.

DEMENT, W. C. An essay on dreams: the role of physiology in understanding their nature. *New directions in psychology II.* New York: Holt, Rinehart and Winston, 1965.

DEMOOR, W. Systematic desensitization versus prolonged high intensity stimulation (flooding). *Journal of behavior therapy and experimental psychiatry*, 1970, *1*, 45–52.

DEMYER, M. K., CHURCHILL, D. W., PONTIUS, W., and GILKEY, K. M. A comparison of five diagnostic systems for childhood schizophrenia and infantile autism. *Journal of autism and childhood schizophrenia*, 1971, *1*, 175–189.

DEMYER, M. K., et al. Prognosis in autism: a follow-up study. Journal of *autism and childhood schizophrenia*, 1973, *3*, 199–246.

DENGROVE, E. Behavior therapy of the sexual disorders. *Journal of sex research*, 1967, *3*, 49–61.

DENNEY, D., QUASS, R. M., RICH, D. C., and THOMPSON, J. K. Psychiatric patients on medical wards: I. Prevalence of illness and recognition of disorders by staff personnel. *Archives of general psychiatry*, 1966, *14*, 530–535.

DENNIS, W., and NAJARIAN, P. Infant development under environmental handicap. *Psychological monographs*, 1957, *71*, 7 (whole no. 436).

DENZIN, N. K., and SPITZER, S. P. Paths to the mental hospital and staff predictions of patient role behavior. *Journal of health and human behavior*, 1966, *7*, 265–271.

DEPARTMENT OF HEALTH AND SOCIAL SECURITY. *On the state of the public health.* London: Her Majesty's Stationery Office, 1971.

DEUTSCH A. *The mentally ill in America.* Garden City, N.Y.: Doubleday, 1937.

DEVRIES, A. G. Model for the prediction of suicidal behavior. *Psychological reports*, 1968, *22*, 1285–1302.

DEXTER, L. A. On the politics and sociology of stupidity in our society. In H. S. Becker, ed., *The other side.* New York: Free Press, 1964, pp. 37–49.

DIAMOND, B. L. The psychiatrist as advocate. *Journal of psychiatry and law*, 1973, *1*, 5–21.

DICAPRIO, N. S. Essentials of verbal satiation therapy: a learning-theory-based therapy. *Journal of counseling psychology*, 1970, *17*, 419–424.

DICKEN, C and FORDHAM, M. Effect of reinforcement of self-references in quasi-therapeutic interviews. *Journal of counseling psychology*, 1967, *14*, 145–152.

DIELMAN, T. E., CATTELL, R. B., and LEPPER, C. Dimensions of problem behavior in the early grades. *Journal of consulting and clinical psychology*, 1971, *37*, 243–249.

DIENSTBEIR, R. A., and MUNTER, P. O. Cheating as a function of the labeling of natural arousal. *Journal of personality and social psychology*, 1971, *17*, 208–213.

DIETZE, D. Staff and patient criteria for judgments of improvement in mental health. *Psychological reports*, 1966, *19*, 379–387.

DILLEHAY, R. C., and JERNIGAN, L. R. The biased questionnaire as an instrument of opinion change. *Journal of personality and social psychology*, 1970, *15*, 144–150.

DIMASCIO, A., BOYD, R. W., and GREENBLATT, M. Physiological correlates of tension and antagonism during psychotherapy: a study of "interpersonal physiology." *Psychosomatic medicine*, 1957, *19*, 99–104.

DINNERSTEIN, A. J., and HALM, J. Modification of placebo effects by means of drugs: effects of aspirin and placebo on self-rated moods. *Journal of abnormal psychology*, 1970, *75*, 308–314.

DINOFF, M., HORNER, R. F., KURPIEWSKI, B. S., RICK-

ARD, H. C., and TIMMONS, E. O. Conditioning verbal behavior of a psychiatric population in a group therapy-like situation. *Journal of clinical psychology,* 1960, *16,* 371–372.

DISCIPIO, W. J. Modified progressive relaxation and homosexuality. *British journal of medical psychology,* 1968, *41,* 267–272.

DISCIPIO, W. J., GLICKMAN, H., and HOLLANDER, M. A. Social learning and operant techniques with hospitalized psychotics. *Proceedings of 81st annual convention of the American Psychological Association, 1973,* pp. 453–454.

DITTES, J. E. Extinction during psychotherapy of GSR accompanying "embarrassing" statements. *Journal of abnormal and social psychology,* 1957a, *54,* 187–191.

DITTES, J. E. Galvanic skin response as a measure of patient's reaction to therapist's permissiveness. *Journal of abnormal and social psychology,* 1957b, *55,* 295–303.

DIXON, J. C. Depersonalization phenomena in a sample population of college students. *British journal of psychiatry,* 1963, *109,* 371–375.

DMITRUK, V. M., COLLINS, R. W., and CLINGER, D. L. The "Barnum effect" and acceptance of negative personal evaluation. *Journal of consulting and clinical psychology,* 1973, *41,* 192–194.

DODDS, E. R. *The Greeks and the irrational.* Berkeley: University of California Press, 1951.

DOERING, C. R., and RAYMOND, A. F. Reliability of observation in psychiatric and related characteristics. *American journal of orthopsychiatry,* 1934, *4,* 249–257.

DOHRENWEND, B. P., and DOHRENWEND, B. S. *Social status and psychological disorder: a causal inquiry.* New York: Wiley, 1969.

DOHRENWEND, B. S. Life events as stressors: a methodological inquiry. *Journal of health and social behavior,* 1973a, *14,* 167–175.

DOHRENWEND, B. S. Social status and stressful life events. *Journal of personality and social psychology,* 1973b, *28,* 225–235.

DOLAND, D. J., and ADELBERG, K. The learning of sharing behavior. *Child development,* 1967, *38,* 695–700.

DOLE, V. P. Methadone maintenance treatment for 25,000 heroin addicts. *Journal of the American medical association,* 1971, *215,* 1131–1134.

DOLE, V. P., and NYSWANDER, M. A medical treatment for diacetylmorphine (heroin) addiction—a clinical test with methadone hydro-chloride. *Journal of the American medical association,* 1965, *198,* 646–650.

DOLLAR, B. L., and SUTTON, B. Reinforcement therapy: the consequation of asocial behavior in a children's psychiatric hospital. *Revista interamericana de psicologia,* n.d., *300,* 309.

DOLLARD, J., DOOB, L. W., MILLER, N. E., MOWRER, O. H., and SEARS, R. R. *Frustration and aggression.* New Haven: Yale University Press, 1939.

DOLLARD, J., and MILLER, N. E. *Personality and psychotherapy.* New York: McGraw-Hill, 1950.

DONNER, L. Automated group desensitization—a follow-up report. *Behaviour research and therapy,* 1970, *8,* 241–247.

DORCUS, R. M., and SHAFFER, G. W. *Textbook of abnormal psychology.* 3rd ed. Baltimore: Williams & Wilkins, 1945.

DORIS, J., and FIERMAN, E. Humor and anxiety. *Journal of abnormal and social psychology,* 1955, *53,* 59–62.

DORRIS, J. W. Reactions to unconditional cooperation: a field study emphasizing variables neglected in laboratory research. *Journal of personality and social psychology,* 1972, *22,* 387–397.

DOUBROS, S. G. Behavior therapy with high level, institutionalized, retarded adolescents. *Exceptional children,* 1966, *33,* 229–233.

DOUBROS, S. G., and DANIELS, G. J. An experimental approach to the reduction of overactive behaviour. *Behaviour research and therapy,* 1966, *4,* 251–258.

DOUGLAS, V. I., and SANDERS, F. A. A pilot study of Rimland's diagnostic check list with autistic and mentally retarded children. *Journal of child psychology and psychiatry,* 1968, *9,* 105–109.

DRABMAN, R. S., SPITALNIK, R., and O'LEARY, K. D. Teaching self-control to disruptive children. *Journal of abnormal psychology,* 1973, *82,* 10–16.

DRAGUNS, J. G., LEAMAN, L., and ROSENFELD, J. M. Symptom expression in Christian and Buddist hospitalized psychiatric patients of Japanese descent in Hawaii. *Journal of social psychology,* 1971, *85,* 155–161.

DRAGUNS, J. G. and PHILLIPS, L. *Culture and psychopathology: the quest for a relationship.* Morristown, N.J.: General Learning Press, 1972.

DRAGUNS, J. G., PHILLIPS, L., BROVERMAN, I. K., CAUDILL, W., and NISHIMAE, S. Symptomatology of hospitalized psychiatric patients in Japan and in the U.S.: a study of cultural differences. *Journal of nervous and mental disease,* 1971, *152,* 3–16.

DRASH, P. Habilitation of the retarded child: a remedial program. *The journal of special education,* 1972, *6,* 149-160.

DRASH, P., and LEIBOWITZ, J. Operant conditioning of speech and language in the nonverbal retarded child. *Pediatric clinics of North America,* 1973, *20,* 233–242.

DREGER, R. M., et al. Behavioral classification project. *Journal of consulting psychology,* 1964, *28,* 1–13.

DREIBLATT, I. S., and WEATHERLEY, D. An evaluation of the efficacy of brief-contact therapy with hospitalized psychiatric patients. *Journal of consulting psychology*, 1965, *29*, 513-519.

DREIFUS, C. Women's lib hits the courts: the great abortion suit. In, S. Stambler, ed. *Women's liberation: blueprint for the future.* New York: Ace, 1970, pp. 57-72.

DREIKURS, R. Early experiments with group psychotherapy: a historical review. *American journal of psychotherapy*, 1959, *13*, 882-891.

DREIKURS, R. The Adlerian approach to therapy. In M. I. Stein, ed., *Contemporary psychotherapies*, New York: Free Press, 1961.

DRISCOLL, J. P. Transsexuals. *Trans-action*, 1971, *8*, 28-37.

DUBEY, E. Intensive treatment of the institutionalized ambulatory geriatric patient. *Geriatrics*, 1968, *23*, 170-177.

DUNBAR, F. *Emotions and bodily changes.* New York: Columbia University Press, 1954.

DUNCAN, S., JR. Some signals and rules for taking speaking turns in conversations. *Journal of personality and social psychology*, 1972, *23*, 283-292.

DUNHAM, H. W. Sociocultural studies of schizophrenia. *Archives of general psychiatry*, 1971, *24*, 206-214.

DUNHAM, H. W. Current status of ecological research in mental disorder. In A. M. Rose, ed., *Mental health and mental disorder.* New York: Norton, 1955, 168-179.

DUNHAM, H. W. Epidemiology of psychiatric disorders, as a contribution to medical ecology. *Archives of general psychiatry*, 1966, *14*, 1-19.

DUNHAM, H. W., and WEINBERG, S. K. *The culture of the state mental hospital.* Detroit: Wayne State University Press, 1960.

DUNLAP, K. A. A revision of the fundamental law of habit formation. *Science*, 1928, *67*, 360-362.

DUNLAP, K. A. Repetition in the breaking of habits. *Scientific monthly*, 1930, *30*, 66-70.

DUNLAP, K. A. *Habits: their making and unmaking.* New York: Liveright, 1932.

DUNN, L. M. Special education for the mildly retarded: is much of it justifiable? *Exceptional children*, 1968, *35*, 5-22.

D'ZURILLA, T. J. Persuasion and praise as techniques for modifying verbal behavior in a "real-life" group setting. *Journal of abnormal psychology*, 1966, *71*, 369-376.

EATON, J. W., and WEIL, R. J. *Culture and mental disorders.* Glencoe, Ill.: Free Press, 1955.

EDELMAN, R. I. Operant conditioning treatment of encopresis. *Journal of behavior therapy and experimental psychiatry*, 1971, *2*, 71-73.

EDGERTON, R. B. On the "recognition" of mental illness. In S. C. Plog and R. B. Edgerton, eds., *Changing perspectives in mental illness.* New York: Holt, Rinehart and Winston, 1969, pp. 48-72.

EDLUND, C. V. Changing classroom behavior of retarded children: using reinforcers in the home environment and parents and teachers as trainers. *Mental retardation*, 1971, *9*, 33-36.

EDLUND, C. V. The effect on the behavior of children, as reflected in the IQ scores, when reinforced after each correct response. *Journal of applied behavior analysis*, 1972, *5*, 317-319.

EDMONSON, B., LELAND, H., DEJUNG, J. E., and LEACH, E. M. Increasing social cue interpretations (visual decoding) by retarded adolescents through training. *American journal of mental deficiency*, 1967, *71*, 1017-1024.

EDWARDES, A. *The jewel in the lotus.* New York: Julian Press, 1959.

EDWARDES, A., and MASTERS, R. E. L. *The cradle of erotica.* New York: Julian Press, 1962.

EDWARDS, M., and LILLY, R. T. Operant conditioning: an application to behavioral problems in groups. *Mental retardation*, 1966, *4*, 18-20.

EDWARDS, N. B. Case conference: assertive training in a case of homosexual pedophilia. *Journal of behavior therapy and experimental psychiatry*, 1972, *3*, 55-63.

EDWARDS, R. P., ALLEY, G. R., and SNIDER, B. Academic achievement and minimal brain dysfunction in mentally retarded children. *Exceptional children*, 1971, *37*, 539-540.

EFRAN, J. S. Looking for approval: effects on visual behavior of approbation from persons differing in importance. *Journal of personality and social psychology*, 1968, *10*, 21-25.

EFRON, R. The conditioned inhibition of uncinate fits. *Brain*, 1957, *80*, 251-262.

EFRON, R. The effect of olfactory stimuli in arresting uncinate fits. *Brain*, 1956, *79*, 267-281.

EGELAND, B. Training impulsive children in the use of more efficient scanning techniques. *Child development*, 1974, *45*, 165-171.

EGOLF, D. B., SHAMES, G. H., JOHNSON, P. R., and KASPRISIN-BURRELLI, A. The use of parent-child interaction patterns in therapy for young stutterers. *Journal of speech and hearing disorders*, 1972, *37*, 222-232.

EGOLF, D. B., SHAMES, G. H., and SELTZER, H. N. The effects of time-out on the fluency of stutterers in group therapy. *Journal of communication disorders*, 1971, *4*, 111-118.

EHRENBERG, R., and GULLINGSRUD, M. J. O. Electroconvulsive therapy in elderly patients. *American journal of psychiatry*, 1955, *111*, 743-747.

EHRLICH, P. R., and HOLDREN, J. P. Impact of population growth. *Science*, 1971, *171*, 1212-1217.

EICHENWALD, H. F., and FRY, P. C. Nutrition and learning. *Science*, 1969, *163*, 644-648.

EIDUSON, B. T. Retreat from help. *American journal of orthopsychiatry*, 1968, *38*, 910-921.

EISENBERG, L. Child psychiatry: the past quarter century. *American journal of orthopsychiatry*, 1969, *39*, 389-401.

EISENDORFER, C. Experimental studies. In C. Eisendorfer and M. P. Lawton, eds., *The psychology of adult development and aging*. Washington, D.C.: American Psychological Association, 1973, 71-73.

EISENTHAL, S., FARBEROW, N. L., and SHNEIDMAN, E. S. Follow-up of neuropsychiatric patients in suicide observation status. *Public health reports*, 1966, *81*, 977-990.

EISLER, R. M., MILLER, P. M., and HERSEN, M. Components of assertive behavior. *Journal of clinical psychology*, 1973, *29*, 295-299.

EISNER, V. *The delinquency label: the epidemiology of juvenile delinquency*. New York: Random House, 1969.

EKMAN, P. Research as therapy? *Journal of nervous and mental disease*, 1961, *133*, 229-232.

EKMAN, P. Body position, facial expression and verbal behavior during interviews. *Journal of abnormal and social psychology*, 1964, *68*, 295-301.

EKMAN, P., and FRIESEN, W. V. Head and body cues in the judgment of emotions: a reformulation. *Perceptual and motor skills*, 1967, *24*, 711-724.

EKMAN, P., and FRIESEN, W. V. Constants across cultures in the face and emotion. *Journal of personality and social psychology*, 1971, *17*, 124-129.

ELDER, S. T., RUIZ, Z. R., DEABLER, H. L., and DILLENKOFFER, R. L. Instrumental conditioning of diastolic blood pressure in essential hypertensive patients. *Journal of applied behavior analysis*, 1973, *6*, 377-382.

ELKIN, T. E., HERSEN, M., EISLER, R. M., and WILLIAMS, J. G. Modification of caloric intake in anorexia nervosa: an experimental analysis. *Psychological reports*, 1973, *32*, 75-78.

ELLIOT, R., and VASTA, R. The modeling of sharing: effects associated with vicarious reinforcement, symbolization, age, and generalization. *Journal of experimental child psychology*, 1970, *10*, 8-15.

ELLIS, A. *Homosexuality: its causes and cure*. New York: Lyle Stuart, 1965.

ELLIS, A. *Reason and emotion in psychotherapy*. New York: Lyle Stuart, 1962.

ELLIS, J. *Revolt of the second sex*. New York: Lancer, 1970, pp. 141-168.

ELLIS, N. C., and SELLS, S. B. An analysis of psychiatric diagnosis in a military mental hygiene clinic. *Journal of clinical psychology*, 1964, *20*, 354-356.

ELLSWORTH, P. C., and CARLSMITH, J. M. Effects of eye contact and verbal content on affective response to a dyadic interaction. *Journal of personality and social psychology*, 1968, *10*, 15-20.

ELLSWORTH, P. C., CARLSMITH, J. M., and HENSON, A. The stare as a stimulus to flight in human subjects: a series of field experiments. *Journal of personality and social psychology*, 1972, *21*, 302-311.

ELLSWORTH, P. D., and COLMAN, A. D. The application of operant conditioning principles to work experience. *American journal of occupational therapy*, 1969, *23*, 495-501.

ELLSWORTH, P. D., and COLMAN, A. D. Reinforcement systems to support work behavior. *American journal of occupational therapy*, 1970, *24*, 1-7.

ELLSWORTH, R., ARTHUR, G., KROEKER, D., and CHILDERS, B. Psychiatric patients' behavior and adjustment as appraised in the community and hospital setting. *Proceedings, 75th annual convention of the American Psychological Association*, 1967, pp. 199-200.

ELLSWORTH, R., MARONEY, R., KLETT, W., GORDON, H., and GUNN, R. Milieu characteristics of successful psychiatric treatment programs. *American journal of orthopsychiatry*, 1971, *41*, 427-441.

EMPEY, L. T., and ERICKSON, M. L. Hidden delinquency and social status. *Social forces*, 1966, *44*, 546-554.

ENGEL, B. T. Clinical applications of operant conditioning techniques in the control of the cardiac arrhythmias. *Seminars in psychiatry*, 1973, *5*, 433-438.

ENGEL, B. T. Comment on self-control of cardiac functioning: a promise as yet unfulfilled. *Psychological bulletin*, 1974, *81*, 43-44.

ENGEL, B. T., and CHISM, R. A. Operant conditioning of heart rate speeding. *Psychophysiology*, 1967, *3*, 418-426.

ENGEL, B. T., and HANSEN, S. P. Operant conditioning of heart rate slowing. *Psychophysiology*, 1966, *3*, 176-187.

ENGELHARDT, D. M., MARGOLIS, R. A., RUDORFER, L., and PALEY, H. M. Physician bias and the double-blind. *Archives of general psychiatry*, 1969, *20*, 315-320.

ENGLE, K. B., and WILLIAMS, T. K. Effect of an ounce of vodka on alcoholics' desire for alcohol.

Quarterly journal of studies on alcohol, 1972, *33,* 1099–1105.

ENGLISH, H. B., and ENGLISH, A. C. *A comprehensive dictionary of psychological and psychoanalytical terms.* New York: McKay, 1958.

ENNIS, B. J., and FRIEDMAN, P. R., eds., *Legal rights of the mentally handicapped,* 3 vols. Washington, D. C.: Practicing Law Institute, 1973.

ENNIS, B. J., and SIEGEL, L. *The rights of mental patients.* New York: Discus/Avon, 1973.

ENRIGHT, J. B., and JAECKLE, W. R. Psychiatric symptoms and diagnosis in two subcultures. *International journal of social psychiatry,* 1963, *9,* 12–17.

EPSTEIN, L. H., and HERSEN, M. Behavioral control of hysterical gagging. *Journal of clinical psychology,* 1974, *30,* 102–104.

ERICKSON, G. D., and GUSTAFSON, G. J. Controlling auditory hallucinations. *Hospital and community psychiatry,* 1968, *19,* 327–329.

ERIKSON, K. T. Patient role and social uncertainty: a dilemma of the mentally ill. *Psychiatry,* 1957, *20,* 263–274.

ERLENMEYER-KIMLING, L. Studies on the offspring of two schizophrenic parents. In D. Rosenthal and S. S. Kety, eds., *The transmission of schizophrenia.* New York: Pergamon Press, 1968.

ERLENMEYER-KIMLING, L. Comments on past and present in genetic research on schizophrenia. *The psychiatric quarterly,* 1972, *46,* 363–370.

ERNST, F. A. Self-recording and counterconditioning of a self-mutilative compulsion. *Behavior therapy,* 1973, *4,* 144–146.

ESSEN-MÖLLER, E. Psychiatrishe untersuchungen an einer serie von Zwillingen. *Acta psychiatrica et neurologica,* 1941, suppl. 23.

ESSEN-MÖLLER, E. Individual traits and morbidity in a Swedish rural population. *Acta psychiatrica et neurologica scandinavia,* 1956, suppl. 100.

ESSER, A. H. Behavioral changes in working chronic schizophrenic patients. *Diseases of the nervous system,* 1967, *28,* 433–440.

ESTES, W. K. An experimental study of punishment. *Psychological monographs,* 1944, *57,* whole No. 263.

ESTES, W. K., and STRAUGHAN, J. H. Analysis of a verbal conditioning situation in terms of statistical learning theory. *Journal of experimental psychology,* 1954, *47,* 225–234.

ETZEL, B. C., and GEWIRTZ, J. L. Experimental modification of caretaker-maintained high-rate operant crying in a 6- and 20-week-old infant. (Infans tyrannotearus) : extinction of crying with reinforcement of eye contact and smiling. *Journal of experimental child psychology,* 1967, *5,* 303–317.

ETZIONI, A., ed., *Complex organizations.* New York: Holt, Rinehart and Winston, 1961.

ETZIONI, A. *Modern organizations.* Englewood Cliffs, N.J.: Prentice-Hall, 1964.

EVANS, D. R., and BOND, I. K. Reciprocal inhibition therapy and classical conditioning in the treatment of insomnia. *Behaviour research and therapy,* 1969, *7,* 323–325.

EVANS, F. J. The power of a sugar pill. *Psychology today,* 1974, *7,* 55–59.

EVANS, G. W., and OSWALT, G. L. Acceleration of academic progress through the manipulation of peer influence. *Behaviour research and therapy,* 1968, *6,* 189–195.

EVANS, G. W., and SPRADLIN, J. E. Incentives and instructions as controlling variables of productivity. *American journal of mental deficiency,* 1966, *71,* 129–132.

EVANS, R. I., and ROZELLE, R. M. eds., *Social psychology in life.* Boston: Allyn and Bacon, 1970.

EVANS, R. I., ROZELLE, R. M., LASATER, T. M., DEMBROWSKI, T. M., and ALLEN, B. P. Fear arousal, persuasion, and actual versus implied behavioral change: new perspective utilizing a real-life dental hygiene program. *Journal of personality and social psychology,* 1970, *16,* 220–227.

EWALT, J. R., and FARNSWORTH, D. L. *Textbook of psychiatry.* New York: McGraw-Hill, 1963.

EWALT, J. R., STRECKER, E. A., and EBAUGH, F. A. *Practical clinical psychiatry.* 8th ed. New York: McGraw-Hill, 1957.

EWING, J. A. Addictions. II: Non-narcotic addictive agents. In A. M. Freedman and H. I. Kaplan, eds., *Comprehensive textbook of psychiatry.* Baltimore: Williams & Wilkins, 1967, pp. 1003-1011.

EYSENCK, H. J. The effects of psychotherapy: an evaluation. *Journal of consulting psychology,* 1952, *16,* 319–324.

EYSENCK, H. J. *The dynamics of anxiety and hysteria.* New York: Prager, 1957.

EYSENCK, H. J. Learning theory and behaviour therapy. *Journal of mental science,* 1959, *105,* 61–75.

EYSENCK, H. J. ed., *Behaviour therapy and the neuroses.* New York: Pergamon Press, 1960.

EYSENCK, H. J. Classification and the problem of diagnosis. In H. J. Eysenck, ed., *Handbook of abnormal psychology.* New York: Basic Books, 1961a, pp. 1–31.

EYSENCK, H. J. The effects of psychotherapy. In H. J. Eysenck, ed., *Handbook of abnormal psychology.* New York: Basic Books, 1961b, pp. 697–725.

EYSENCK, H. J., and RACHMAN, S. *The causes and cures of neurosis.* San Diego, Calif.: Knapp, 1965.

FABREGA, H., JR., RUBEL, A. J., and WALLACE, C. A. Working class Mexican psychiatric out-patients: some social and cultural features. *Archives of general psychiatry,* 1967, *16,* 704–712.

FABREGA, H., JR., and WALLACE, C. A. How physicians judge symptom statements: a cross-cultural story. *Journal of nervous and mental disease,* 1968, *145,* 486–491.

FADIMAN, J., and KEWMAN, D. *Exploring madness: experience, theory, and research.* Monterey, Calif.: Brooks/Cole, 1973.

FAILLACE, L. A., VOURLEKIS, A., and SZARA, S. Hallucinogenic drugs in the treatment of alcoholism: a two-year follow-up. *Comprehensive psychiatry,* 1970, *1,* 51–56.

FAIRWEATHER, G. W., SANDERS, D. H., TORNATZKY, L. G., and HARRIS, R. N. *Creating change in mental health organizations.* Elmsford, N. Y.: Pergamon Press, 1974.

FAIRWEATHER, G. W., and SIMON, R. A further follow-up comparison of psychotherapeutic programs. *Journal of consulting psychology,* 1963, *27,* 186.

FALLIK, A., and SIGAL, M. Hysteria: the choice of symptom site. *Psychotherapy and psychosomatics,* 1971, *19,* 310–318.

FARBER, B., *Mental retardation: its social context and social consequences.* Boston: Houghton Mifflin, 1968.

FARBER, I. E., HARLOW, H. F., and WEST, L. J. Brainwashing, conditioning, and DDD (debility, dependency, and dread). *Sociometry,* 1957, *20,* 271–285.

FARINA, A. *Schizophrenia.* Morristown, N. J.: General Learning Press, 1972.

FARIS, R. E. L. Ecological factors in human behavior. In J. McV. Hunt, ed., *Personality and the behavior disorders.* Vol. 2. New York: Ronald Press, 1944, pp. 736–757.

FARIS, R. E. L., and DUNHAM, H. W. *Mental disorders in urban areas.* Chicago: University of Chicago Press, 1939.

FARLEY, J. WOODRUFF, R. A., JR., and GUZE, S. B. The prevalence of hysteria and conversion symptoms. *British journal of psychiatry,* 1968, *114,* 1121–1125.

FEINSILVER, D. B., and GUNDERSON, J. G. Psychotherapy for schizophrenics—is it indicated? A review of the relevant literature. *Schizophrenia bulletin,* 1972, *6,* 11–23.

FELDMAN, H. W. Ideological supports to becoming and remaining a heroin addict. *Journal of health and social behavior,* 1968, *9,* 131–139.

FELDMAN, M. P. Aversion therapy for sexual deviations: a critical review. *Psychological bulletin,* 1966, *65,* 65–79.

FELDMAN, M. P., and MACCULLOCH, M. J. A systematic approach to the treatment of homosexuality by conditioned aversion. Preliminary report. *American journal of psychiatry,* 1964, *121,* 167–171.

FELDMAN, M. P., and MACCULLOCH, M. J. The application of anticipatory avoidance learning to the treatment of homosexuality. I: Theory, technique and preliminary results. *Behaviour research and therapy,* 1965, *2,* 165–183.

FELDMAN, M. P., and MACCULLOCH, M. J. *Homosexual behaviour: therapy and assessment.* Oxford: Pergamon Press, 1971.

FENICHEL, O. *The psychoanalytic theory of neurosis.* New York: Norton, 1945.

FERDINAND, T. N. *Typologies of delinquency: a critical analysis.* New York: Random House, 1966.

FERGUSON, T., and KERR, A. W. After-histories of boys educated in special school for mentally-handicapped children. *Scottish medical journal,* 1958, *3,* 31–38.

FERINDEN, W., JR., and HANDEL, D. V. Elimination of soiling behavior in an elementary school child through the application of aversive techniques. *Journal of school psychology,* 1970, *8,* 267–269.

FERNALD, W. E. The imbecile with criminal instincts. *American journal of insanity,* 1908, *65,* 731–749.

FERNANDEZ, J., FISCHER, I., and RYAN, E. The token economy: a living-learning environment. *British journal of psychiatry,* 1973, *122,* 453-455.

FERSTER, C. B. Positive reinforcement and behavior deficits of autistic children. *Child development,* 1961, *32,* 437–456.

FERSTER, C. B. Classification of behavioral pathology. In L. Krasner and L. P. Ullmann, eds., *Research in behavior modification.* New York: Holt, Rinehart and Winston, 1965, 6–26.

FERSTER, C. B. A functional analysis of depression. *American psychologist,* 1973, *28,* 857–870.

FERSTER, C. B., and DEMYER, M. K. The development of performances in autistic children in an automatically controlled environment. *Journal of chronic diseases,* 1961, *13,* 312–345.

FERSTER, C. B., NURNBERGER, J., and LEVITT, E. B. The control of eating. *Journal of mathetics,* 1962, *1,* 87–109.

FERSTER, C. B., and SIMONS, J. Behavior therapy with children. *Psychological record,* 1966, *16,* 65–71.

FESTINGER, L. *A theory of cognitive dissonance.* Evanston, Ill.: Row, Peterson, 1957.

FESTINGER, L. Behavioral support for opinion change. *Public opinion quarterly,* 1964, *28,* 404–417.

FICHTLER, H., and ZIMMERMAN, R. R. Changes in reported pain from tension headaches. *Perceptual and motor skills,* 1973, *36,* 712.

FIELD, M. J. *Search for security: an ethnopsychiatric study of rural Ghana.* Evanston, Ill.: Northwestern University Press, 1960.

FIEVE, R. R. Prophylaxis of bipolar manic-depressive illness. Read before the Collegium Internationale Neuro-Psychopharmacologicum Meeting. Copenhagen, August 1972.

FINELY, W. W., BESSERMAN, R. L., BENNETT, L. P., CLAPP, R. K., and FINLEY, P. M. The effect of continuous, intermittent, and "placebo" reinforcement on the effectiveness of the conditioning treatment for enuresis nocturna. *Behavior research and therapy,* 1973, *11,* 289–297.

FINEMAN, K. R. Shaping and increasing verbalizations in an autistic child in response to visual-color simulation. *Perceptual and motor skills,* 1968a, *27,* 1071–1074.

FINEMAN, K. R. An operant conditioning program in a juvenile detention facility. *Psychological reports,* 1968b, *22,* 1119–1120.

FINEMAN, K. R., and FERJO, J. Establishing and increasing verbalizations in a deaf schizophrenic child through use of contingent visual-color reinforcement. *Perceptual and motor skills,* 1969, *29* 647–652.

FISH, B. The "one child, one drug" myth of stimulants in hyperkinesis. *Archives of general psychiatry,* 1971, *25,* 193–203.

FISH, J. M. *Placebo therapy: a practical guide to social influence in psychotherapy.* San Francisco: Jossey-Bass, 1974.

FISKE, D. W., and GOODMAN, G. The posttherapy period. *Journal of abnormal psychology,* 1965, *70,* 169–179.

FISKE, D. W., HUNT, H. F., LUBORSKY, L., ORNE, M. T., PARLOFF, M. B., and TUMA, A. H. Planning of research on effectiveness of psychotherapy. *American psychologist,* 1970, *25,* 727–737.

FITZGIBBONS, D. J., and SHEARN, C. R. Concepts of schizophrenia among mental health professionals: a factor-analytic study. *Journal of consulting and clinical psychology,* 1972, *38,* 288–295.

FIXSEN, D. L., PHILLIPS, E. L., and WOLF, M. M. Achievement place: experiments in self-government with pre-delinquents. *Journal of applied behavior analysis,* 1973, *6,* 31–47.

FLANAGAN, B., GOLDIAMOND, I., and AZRIN, N. H. Instatement of stuttering in normally fluent individuals through operant procedures. *Science,* 1959, *130,* 979–981.

FLANDERS, J. P. A review of research on imitative behavior. *Psychological bulletin,* 1968, *69,* 316–337.

FLAVELL, J. E. Reduction of stereotypes by reinforcement of toy play. *Mental retardation,* 1973, *11,* 21–23.

FLOWERS, J. V. Behavior modification of cheating in an elementary school student: a brief note. *Behavior therapy,* 1972, *3,* 311–312.

FONTANA, A. F., and COREY, M. Culture conflict in the treatment of "mental illness" and the central role of patient leader. *Journal of consulting and clinical psychology,* 1970, *34,* 244-249.

FONTANA, A. F., and GESSNER, T. Patients' goals and the manifestation of psychopathology. *Journal of consulting and clinical psychology,* 1969, *33,* 247–253.

FONTANA, A. F., GESSNER, T., and LORR, M. How sick and what treatment: patient presentation and staff judgments. *American journal of psychotherapy,* 1968, *22,* 26–34.

FONTANA, A. F., and KLEIN, E. B. Self-presentation and the schizophrenic "deficit." *Journal of consulting and clinical psychology,* 1968, *32,* 250–256.

FONTANA, A. F., KLEIN, E. B., LEWIS, E., and LEVINE, L. Presentation of self in mental illness. *Journal of consulting and clinical pyschology,* 1968, *32,* 110–119.

FONTANA, A. F., MARCUS, J. L., NOEL, B., and RAKUSIN, J. M. Prehospitalization coping styles of psychiatric patients: the goal-directedness of life events. *Journal of nervous and mental disease,* 1972, *155,* 311–321.

FONTANA, V. J. *The maltreated child: the maltreatment syndrome.* 2nd ed. Springfield, Ill.: Charles C. Thomas, 1971.

FOOKES, B. H. Some experiences in the use of aversion therapy in male homosexuality, exhibitionism, fetishism, and transvestism. *British journal of psychiatry,* 1969, *115,* 339–341.

FORD, C. S., and BEACH, F. A. *Patterns of sexual behavior,* New York: Harper, 1951.

FORD, J. D. Training parents to use behavioral procedures: a review. Unpublished manuscript, State University of New York, Stony Brook, New York, 1974.

FOREMAN, P. B. Panic theory. *Sociology and social research,* 1953, *37,* 295–304.

FORSTER, F. M. Conditional reflexes and sensory-evolved epilepsy: the nature of the therapeutic process. *Conditional reflex,* 1969, *4,* 103–114.

FORTUNE, R. F. *Sorcerers of Dobu.* New York: Dutton, 1932.

FOSBURGH, L. Has he a right to jump? *Honolulu star bulletin,* 10 October 1973, p. D-3.

FOUCAULT, M. *Madness and civilization.* New York: Mentor, 1967.

FOUTS, G. T. Charity in children: the influence of "charity" stimuli and an audience. *Journal of experimental child psychology,* 1972, *13,* 303-309.

FOUTS, R. S. Acquisition and testing of gestural signs in four young chimpanzees. *Science,* 1973, *180,* 978-980.

FOWLER, O. S., *Sexual science.* Philadelphia: National Publishing Co., 1870.

FOWLER, R. L., and KIMMEL, H. D. Operant conditioning of the GSR. *Journal of experimental psychology,* 1962, *63,* 563-567.

FOWLER, R. S., JR., CHAWLA, N. S., LEHMANN, J. F., and TINDALL, V. L. An application of behavior therapy to a program of debilitating vertigo. *Behavior therapy,* 1971, *2,* 589-591.

FOWLER, R. S., FORDYCE, W. E., and BERNI, B. Operant conditioning in chronic illness. *American journal of nursing,* 1969, *69,* 1226-1228.

FOX, M. S., and LITTLEFIELD, J. W. Reservations concerning gene therapy. *Science,* 1971, *173,* 195.

FOX, R. G. The XYY offender: a modern myth? *Journal of criminal law, criminology and police science,* 1971, *62,* 59-73.

FOXX, R. M., and AZRIN, N. H. The elimination of autistic self-stimulatory behavior by overcorrection. *Journal of applied behavior analysis,* 1973, *6,* 1-14.

FRANK, G. H. The role of the family in the development of psychopathology. *Psychological bulletin,* 1965, *64,* 191-205.

FRANK, G. H. Psychiatric diagnosis: a review of research. *Journal of genetic psychology,* 1969, *81,* 157-176.

FRANK, J. D. *Persuasion and healing.* Baltimore: Johns Hopkins Press, 1961.

FRANK, J. D. Therapeutic factors in psychotherapy. *American journal of psychotherapy,* 1971, *25,* 350-361.

FRANK, J. D. The bewildering world of psychotherapy. *Journal of social issues,* 1972, *28,* 27-43.

FRANKEL, A. S., and BARRETT, J. Variations in personal space as a function of authoritarianism, self-esteem, and racial characteristics of a stimulus situation. *Journal of consulting and clinical psychology,* 1971, *37,* 95-98.

FRANKS, C. M., ed., *Conditioning techniques in clinical practice and research.* New York: Springer, 1964.

FRANKS, C. M. Conditioning and conditioned aversion therapies in the treatment of the alcoholic. *International journal of the addictions,* 1966, *1,* 61-98.

FRANKS, C. M., and LEIGH, D. The conditioned eyeblink response in asthmatic and nonasthmatic subjects. *Journal of psychosomatic research,* 1959, *4,* 88-98.

FRANZ, S. I. *Nervous and mental reeducation.* New York: Macmillan, 1924.

FRAZIER, S. H., and CARR, A. C. Phobic reaction. In A. M. Freedman and H. I. Kaplan, eds., *Comprehensive textbook of psychiatry.* Baltimore: Williams & Wilkins, 1967, pp. 899-911.

FREDERICK, C. J. Treatment of a tic by systematic desensitization and massed response evocation. *Journal of behaviour therapy and experimental psychiatry,* 1971, *2,* 281-283.

FREEDMAN, A. M., KAPLAN, H. I., and SADOCK, B. J. *Modern synopsis of comprehensive textbook of psychiatry.* Baltimore: Williams & Wilkins, 1972.

FREEDMAN, D. X. On the use and abuse of LSD. *Archives of general psychiatry,* 1968, *18,* 330-347.

FREEDMAN, J. L. Transgression, compliance, and guilt. In J. Macaulay and L. Berkowitz, eds., *Altruism and helping behavior.* New York: Academic Press, 1970, pp. 155-161.

FREEDMAN, J. L., WALLINTON, S., and BLESS, E. Compliance without pressure: the effect of guilt. *Journal of personality and social psychology,* 1967, *7,* 117-124.

FREEDMAN, N., BLASS, T., RIFKIN, A., and QUITKIN, F. Body movements and the verbal encoding of aggressive affect. *Journal of personality and social psychology,* 1973, *26,* 72-85.

FREEDMAN, R. V., and GRAYSON, H. M. Maternal attitudes in schizophrenia. *Journal of abnormal and social psychology,* 1955, *50,* 45-52.

FREEDMAN, S. J., GRUNEBAUM, H. U., and GREENBLATT, M. Perceptual and cognitive changes in sensory deprivation. In P. Solomon et al., eds., *Sensory deprivation: a symposium held at Harvard Medical School.* Cambridge, Mass.: Harvard University Press, 1961, pp. 58-71.

FREEMAN, H. L. The tranquilizing drugs. In L. Bellak, ed., *Schizophrenia: a review of the syndrome.* New York: Logos Press, 1958, pp. 473-500.

FREEMAN, H. L., and KENDRICK, D. C. A case of cat phobia: treatment by a method derived from experimental psychology. *British medical journal,* 1960, *2,* 497-502.

FREEMAN, J. Growing up girlish. *Trans-action,* 1970, *8,* 36-43.

FREEMAN, T., CAMERON, J. L., and McGHIE, A. *Chronic schizophrenia.* New York: International Universities Press, 1958.

FREEMAN, W. Psychosurgery. In S. Arieti, ed., *American handbook of psychiatry*. Vol. II. New York: Basic Books, 1959, pp. 1521–1541.

FREEMAN, W., and WATTS, J. W. The frontal lobes and consciousness of the self. *Psychosomatic medicine*, 1941, *3*, 111–119.

FREUD, A. *The ego and mechanisms of defense*. New York: International Universities Press, 1946.

FREUD, A., and BURLINGHAM, D. *Infants without families*. New York: International Universities Press, 1944.

FREUD, S. *New introductory lectures in psychoanalysis* (1932). New York: Norton, 1933.

FREUD, S. A case of paranoia running counter to the psychoanalytical theory of the disease (1915). In *Collected papers*. Vol. 2. London: Hogarth Press, 1950, pp. 150–161.

FREUD, S. Certain neurotic mechanisms in jealousy, paranoia and homosexuality (1922). In *Collected papers*. Vol. 2. London: Hogarth Press, 1950, 232–243.

FREUD, S. Analysis of a phobia in a five-year-old boy (1909). In *Collected papers*. Vol. 3. London: Hogarth Press, 1953, pp. 149–289.

FREUD, S. Mourning and melancholia (1917). In *The standard edition of the complete psychological works of Sigmund Freud*. Vol. 14. London: Hogarth Press and the Institute of Psycho-Analysis, 1957.

FREUD, S. The intepretation of dreams (1900). In *The standard edition of the complete psychological works of Sigmund Freud*. Vols. 4 and 5. London: Hogarth Press and the Institute of Psycho-Analysis, 1962.

FREUD, S. *The question of lay analysis* (1926–1927). New York: Doubleday, 1964.

FREUND, K. Some problems on the treatment of homosexuality. In H. J. Eysenck, ed., *Behaviour therapy and the neurosis*. New York: Pergamon Press, 1960, pp. 312–326.

FRIEDAN, B. *The feminine mystique*. New York: Dell, 1970.

FRIEDMAN, A. S. Minimal effects of severe depression on cognitive functioning. *Journal of abnormal and social psychology*, 1964, *69*, 237–243.

FRIEDMAN, D. The treatment of impotence by brevital relaxation therapy. *Behaviour research and therapy*, 1968, *6*, 257–261.

FRIEDMANN, T., and ROBLIN, R. Gene therapy for human disease? *Science*, 1972, *175*, 949–955.

FROMM, E. *Escape from freedom*. New York: Rinehart, 1941.

FROMM, E. *Man for himself*. New York: Rinehart, 1947.

FRUMKIN, R. M. Occupation and major mental disorders. In A. M. Rose, ed., *Mental health and mental disorder*. New York: Norton, 1955, pp. 136–160.

FULLER, P. R. Operant conditioning of a vegetative human organism. *American journal of psychology*, 1949, *62*, 587–590.

FUNDIA, T. A., DRAGUNS, J. G., and PHILLIPS, L. Culture and psychiatric symptomatology: a comparison of Argentine and United States patients. *Social psychiatry*, 1971, *6*, 11–20.

FURST, J. B., and COOPER, A. Combined use of imaginal and interoceptive stimuli in desensitizing fear of heart attacks. *Journal of behavior therapy and experimental psychiatry*, 1970, *1*, 87–89.

GAERTNER, S. L. Helping behavior and racial discrimination among liberals and conservatives. *Journal of personality and social psychology*, 1973, *25*, 335–341.

GAERTNER, S. L., and BICKMAN, L. Effects of race on the elicitation of helping behavior: the wrong number technique. *Journal of personality and social psychology*, 1971, *20*, 218–222.

GAGNON, J. H., and SIMON, W. *The sexual scene*. Chicago: Aldine, 1970.

GAGNON, J. H., and SIMON, W. They're going to learn in the street anyway. *Psychology today*, 1969, *3*, 46–47; 71.

GAL, P. Mental disorders of advanced years. *Geriatrics*, 1959, *14*, 224–228.

GALLE, O. R., GOVE, W. R., and MCPHERSON, J. M. Population density and pathology: what are the relations for man? *Science*, 1972, *176*, 23–30.

GALLINEK, A. The nature of affective and paranoid disorders during the senium in the light of electric convulsive therapy. *Journal of nervous and mental disease*, 1948, *108*, 293–303.

GANDOLFO, R. L. Role of expectancy, amnesia, and hypnotic induction in the performance of posthypnotic behavior. *Journal of abnormal psychology*, 1971, *77*, 324–328.

GANTT, W. H. *Experimental basis for neurotic behavior*. New York: Hoeber, 1944.

GANTT, W. H. Autonomic conditioning. In J. Wolpe, A. Salter, and L. J. Reyna, eds., *The conditioning therapies*. New York: Holt, Rinehart and Winston, 1964, pp. 115–124.

GANZER, V. J., SARASON, I. G., GREEN, C. T., and RINKE, C. Effects of model's and observer's hostility on Rorschach, interview, and test performance. *Journal of projective techniques and personality assessment*, 1970, *34*, 302–315.

GARAI, J. E. Sex differences in mental health. *Genetic psychology monographs*, 1970, *81*, 123–142.

GARDNER, J. E. Behavior therapy treatment approach to a psychogenic seizure case. *Journal of consulting psychology*, 1967, *31*, 209–212.

GARDNER, J. E. A blending of behavior therapy techniques in an approach to an asthmatic child. *Psychotherapy: theory, research and practice*, 1968, *5*, 46–49.

GARDNER, R. A., and GARDNER, B. T. Teaching sign language to a chimpanzee. *Science*, 1969, *165*, 664–672.

GARDNER, W. I. *Behavior modification in mental retardation*. New York: Aldine, 1971.

GARFIELD, S. L., and BERGIN, A. E. Personal therapy, outcome and some therapist variables. *Psychotherapy*, 1971, *8*, 251–253.

GARFIELD, Z. H., DARWIN, P. L., SINGER, B. A., and McBREARTY, J. F. Effect of "in vivo" training on experimental desensitization of a phobia. *Psychological reports*, 1967, *20*, 515–519.

GARLAND, L. H. Studies on the accuracy of diagnostic procedures. *American journal of roentgenology, radium therapy, and nuclear medicine*, 1959, *82*, 25–38.

GARLINGTON, W. K., and COTLER, S. B. Systematic desensitization of test anxiety. *Behaviour research and therapy*, 1968, *6*, 247–256.

GARMEZY, N., and RODNICK, E. H. Premorbid adjustment and performance in schizophrenia; implication for interpreting heterogeneity in schizophrenia. *Journal of nervous and mental disease*, 1959, *129*, 450–465.

GARRATT, F. N., LOWE, C. R., and McKEOWN, T. Investigation of the medical and social needs of patients in mental hospitals. II. type of accommodation and staff required. *British journal of preventive and social medicine*, 1958, *12*, 23–41.

GASTAUT, H., and BROUGHTON, R. J. Conclusions concerning the mechanisms of enuresis nocturna. *Electroencephalography and clinical neurophysiology*, 1964, *16*, 626.

GAUPP, L. A., STERN, R. M., and RATLIFF, R. G. The use of aversion-relief procedures in the treatment of a case of voyeurism. *Behavior therapy*, 1971, *2*, 585–588.

GAURON, E. F., and DICKINSON, J. K. Diagnostic decision making in psychiatry. I: information usage. *Archives of general psychiatry*, 1966a, *14*, 225–232.

GAURON, E. F., and DICKINSON, J. K. Diagnostic decision making in psychiatry. II: diagnostic styles. *Archives of general psychiatry*, 1966b, *14*, 233–237.

GAURON, E. F., and DICKINSON, J. K. The influence of seeing the patient first on diagnostic decision making in psychiatry. *American journal of psychiatry*, 1969, *126*, 199–205.

GAZZANIGA, M. S. The split brain in man. *Scientific American*, 1967, *217*, 24–29.

GEBHARD, P. H., et al. *Sex offenders: an analysis of types*. New York: Harper, 1965.

GEBHARD, P. H., POMEROY, W. B., MARTIN, C. E., and CHRISTENSON, C. V. *Pregnancy, birth and abortion*. New York: Harper & Row, 1958.

GEER, J. H., and KATKIN, E. S. Treatment of insomnia using a variant of systematic desensitization: a case report. *Journal of abnormal psychology*, 1966, *71*, 161–164.

GEER, J. H., and TURTELTAUB, A. Fear reduction following observation of a model. *Journal of personality and social psychology*, 1967, *6*, 327–331.

GELDER, M. G., and MARKS, I. M. Desensitization and phobias: a cross-over study. *British journal of psychiatry*, 1968, *114*, 323–328.

GELDZAHLER, H. *American painting in the twentieth century*. New York: Metropolitan Museum of Art, 1965.

GELFAND, D. M., GELFAND, S., and DOBSON, W. R. Unprogrammed reinforcement of patients' behaviour in a mental hospital. *Behaviour research and therapy*, 1967, *5*, 201–207.

GELFAND, D. M., HARTMAN, D. P., WALDER, P., and PAGE, B. Who reports shoplifters? A field-experimental study. *Journal of personality and social psychology*, 1973, *25*, 276–288.

GELFAND, S., ULLMANN, L. P., and KRASNER, L. The placebo response: an experimental approach. *Journal of nervous and mental disease*, 1963, *136*, 379–387.

GELLER, E. S., FARRIS, J. C., and POST, D. S. Prompting a consumer behavior for pollution control. *Journal of applied behavior analysis*, 1973, *6*, 367–376.

GENTRY, W. D. *In vivo* desensitization of an obsessive cancer fear. *Journal of behavior therapy and experimental psychiatry*, 1970a, *1*, 315–318.

GENTRY, W. D. Effect of time-out from positive reinforcement on aggressive behavior in young children. *Psychological reports*, 1970b, *26*, 283–288.

GEPPERT, T. V. Management of nocturnal enuresis by conditioned response. *Journal of American Medical Association*, 1953, *152*, 381–383.

GERARD, D. L., SAENGER, G., and WILE, R. The abstinent alcoholic. *Archives of general psychiatry*, 1962, *6*, 83–95.

GERBER, I. Practitioners' perceptual consistency of mental patients' behavioral characteristics. *Journal of social psychology*, 1967, *72*, 129–134.

GERGEN, K. J. *The concept of self*. New York: Holt, Rinehart and Winston, 1971.

GERICKE, O. L. Practical use of operant conditioning

procedures in a mental hospital. *Psychiatric studies and projects,* 1965, *3,* 1–10.

GERSHAM, L. Case conference: a transvestite fantasy treated by thought-stopping, covert sensitization, and aversive shock. *Journal of behavior therapy and experimental psychiatry,* 1970, *1,* 153–161.

GIALLOMBARDO, R., ed., *Juvenile delinquency: a book of readings.* New York: Wiley, 1966.

GIBSON, H. B. Self-reported delinquency among school boys and their attitudes to the police. *British journal of social and clinical psychology,* 1967, *6,* 168–173.

GIL, D. G. *Violence against children: physical child abuse in the United States.* Cambridge, Mass.: Harvard University Press, 1970.

GILES, D. K., and WOLF, M. M. Toilet training institutionalized, severe retardates: an application of operant behavior modification techniques. *American journal of mental deficiency,* 1966, *70,* 766–780.

GILLIS, L. S., LEWIS, J. B., and SLABBERT, M. Psychiatric disorder amongst the colored people of the cape peninsula. *British journal of psychiatry,* 1968, *114,* 1575–1578.

GILLISON, T. H., and SKINNER, J. L. Treatment of nocturnal enuresis by the electric alarm. *British medical journal,* 1958, *2,* 1268–1272.

GINOTT, H. G. The private practice of child therapy. In G. D. Goldman and G. Stricker, eds., *Practical problems of a private psychotherapy practice.* Springfield, Ill.: Charles C Thomas, 1972, pp. 28–50.

GIOVANNONI, J. M., and GUREL, L. Socially disruptive behavior of ex-mental patients. *Archives of general psychiatry,* 1967, *17,* 146–153.

GIOVANNONI, J. M., and ULLMANN, L. P. Characteristics of family care homes. *International journal of social psychiatry,* 1961, *7,* 299–306.

GIOVANNONI, J. M., and ULLMANN, L. P. Conceptions of mental health held by psychiatric patients. *Journal of clinical psychology,* 1963, *19,* 398–400.

GIRARDEAU, F. L., and SPRADLIN, J. E. Token rewards on a cottage program. *Mental retardation,* 1964, *2,* 345–351.

GITTELMAN, M. Behavior rehearsal as a technique in child treatment. *Journal of child psychology and psychiatry,* 1965, *6,* 251–255.

GLASNER, S. Benign paralogical thinking. *Archives of general psychiatry,* 1966, *14,* 94–99.

GLASS, B. *Science and ethical values.* Chapel Hill: University of North Carolina Press, 1965.

GLASS, D. C., COHEN, S. and SINGER, J. E. Urban din fogs the brain. *Psychology today,* 1973, *6,* 92–99.

GLASS, L. B., and BARBER, T. X. A note on hypnotic behavior, the definition of the situation and the placebo effect. *Journal of nervous and mental disease,* 1961, *132,* 539–541.

GLASSCOTE, R. M., CUMMING, E., HAMMERSLEY, D. W., OZARIN, L. D., and SMITH, L. H. *The psychiatric emergency: a study of patterns of service.* Washington, D. C.: Joint Information Service, 1966.

GLUECK, B. C., JR. Automation and social change. *Comprehensive psychiatry,* 1967, *8,* 441–449.

GLUECK, B. C., JR., and LUCE, G. The computer as psychiatric aid and research tool. *Mental health program reports,* 1968, *2,* 353–372.

GLUECK, S. *Law and psychiatry.* Baltimore: Johns Hopkins Press, 1966.

GLUECK, S., and GLUECK, E. T. *Unraveling juvenile delinquency.* Cambridge, Mass.: Commonwealth Fund, 1950.

GLUECK, S., and GLUECK, E. T. *Family environment delinquency.* Boston: Houghton, 1962.

GOFFMAN, E. *Asylums.* Garden City, N.Y.: Doubleday Anchor, 1961.

GOLCHROS, H. I. The sexually oppressed. *Social work,* 1972, *17,* 16–23.

GOLD, S., and NEUFELD, I. L. A learning approach to the treatment of homosexuality. *Behaviour research and therapy,* 1965, *2,* 201-204.

GOLDBERG, D. P., and BLACKWELL, B. Psychiatric illness in general practice: a detailed study using a new method of case identification. *British medical journal,* 1970, *2,* 439–443.

GOLDBERG, L. R. Diagnosticians vs. diagnostic signs: the diagnosis of psychosis vs. neurosis from the MMPI. *Psychological monographs,* 1965, *79* (No. 9, whole #602).

GOLDBERG, L. R. Simple models or simple processes? Some research on clinical judgments. *American psychologist,* 1968, *23,* 483–496.

GOLDBERG, L. R. Man versus model of man: a rationale, plus some evidence, for a method of improving on clinical inferences. *Psychological bulletin,* 1970, *73,* 422–432.

GOLDEN, J., MANDEL, N., GLUECK, B. C., JR., and FEDER, Z. A summary description of fifty "normal" white males. *American journal of psychiatry,* 1962, *119,* 48–56.

GOLDFRIED, M. R., and MERBAUM, M., eds., *Behavior change through self-control.* New York: Holt, Rinehart and Winston, 1973.

GOLDHAMER, H., and MARSHALL, A. W. *Psychosis and civilization.* New York: Free Press, 1949.

GOLDIAMOND, I. Self-control procedures in personal behavior problems *Psychological reports,* 1965a, *17,* 851–868.

GOLDIAMOND, I. Stuttering and fluency as manipulatable operant response classes. In L. Krasner and L. P. Ullmann, eds., *Research in behavior modification.* New York: Holt, Rinehart and Winston, 1965b, pp. 106-156.

GOLDING, S. L., and RORER, L. G. "Illusory correlation" and the learning of clinical judgment. *Oregon research institute bulletin,* 1971, *11,* No. 10.

GOLDMAN, R. K., and MENDELSOHN, G. A. Psychotherapeutic change and social adjustment: a report of a national survey of psychotherapists. *Journal of abnormal psychology,* 1969, *74,* 164-172.

GOLDSCHMID, M. L., and DOMINO, G. Differential patient perception among various professional disciplines. *Journal of consulting psychology,* 1967, *31,* 548-550.

GOLDSTEIN, A. P. *Therapist-patient expectancies in psychotherapy.* New York: Pergamon Press, 1962.

GOLDSTEIN, A. P. *Psychotherapeutic attraction.* Elmsford, N.Y.: Pergamon Press, 1971.

GOLDSTEIN, A. P. *Structured learning therapy: toward a psychotherapy for the poor.* New York: Academic Press, 1973.

GOLDSTEIN, A. P., HELLER, K., and SECHREST, L. B. *Psychotherapy and the psychology of behavior change.* New York: Wiley, 1966.

GOLDSTEIN, A. P., MARTENS, J., HUBBEN, J., VAN BELLE, H. A., SCHAAF, W., WIERSMA, H., and GOEDHART, A. The use of modeling to increase independent behavior. *Behaviour research and therapy,* 1973, *11,* 31-42.

GOLDSTEIN, A. S. *The insanity defense.* New Haven: Yale University Press, 1967.

GOLDSTEIN, D., FINK, D., and METTEE, D. R. Cognition of arousal and actual arousal as determinants of emotion. *Journal of personality and social psychology,* 1972, *21,* 41-51.

GOLEMBIEWSKI, R. T. *Behavior and organization.* Chicago: Rand McNally, 1962.

GOLIN, M. By one's own hand. *Medicolegal digest,* September 1960, 17-22.

GOODE, E. Multiple drug use among marijuana smokers. *Social problems,* 1969, *17,* 48-64.

GOODKIN, R. A. Changes in word production, sentence production and relevance in an aphasic through verbal conditioning. *Behaviour research and therapy,* 1969a, *7,* 93-99.

GOODKIN, R. A. Procedure for training spouses to improve the functional speech of aphasic patients. Paper presented at convention of the American Psychological Association, Washington, D.C., September 1969b.

GOODLET, G. R., GOODLET, M. M., and DREGE, K. Modification of disruptive behavior of two young children and follow-up one year later. *Journal of school psychology,* 1970, *8,* 60-63.

GOODWIN, D. W., ALDERSON, P., and ROSENTHAL, R. Clinical significance of hallucinations in psychiatric disorders: a study of 116 hallucinatory patients. *Archives of general psychiatry,* 1971, *24,* 76-80.

GOORNEY, A. B. Treatment of a compulsive horse race gambler by aversion therapy. *British journal of psychiatry,* 1968, *114,* 329-333.

GORDON, J. E. MARTIN, B., and LUNDY, R. M. GSR's during repression, suppression, and verbalization in psychotherapeutic interviews. *Journal of consulting psychology,* 1959, *23,* 243-251.

GORDOVA, T. N., and KOVALEV, N. K. Unique factors in the hypnotic treatment of chronic alcoholism. In R. B. Winn, ed., *Psychotherapy in the Soviet Union,* New York: Philosophical Library, 1961, pp. 136-140.

GORHAM, D. R., GREEN, L. W., CALDWELL, L. R., and BARTLETT, E. R. Effect of operant conditioning techniques on chronic schizophrenics. *Psychological reports,* 1970, *27,* 223-234.

GORSUCH, R. L., and SMITH, R. A. Changes in college students' evaluations of moral behavior: 1969 versus 1939, 1949 and 1958. *Journal of personality and social psychology,* 1972, *24,* 381-391.

GOSLIN, D. A. Standardized ability tests and testing. *Science,* 1968, *159,* 851-855.

GOTTHEIL, E., ALTERMAN, A. I., SKOLODA, T. E., and MURPHY, B. F. Alcoholics' patterns of controlled drinking. *American journal of psychiatry,* 1973, *130,* 418-422.

GOTTMAN, J. M., and LEIBLUM, S. R. *How to do psychotherapy and how to evaluate it.* New York: Holt, Rinehart and Winston, 1974.

GOTTSCHALK, L. A., SPRINGER, K. J., and GLESER, G. C. Experiments with a method of assessing the variations in intensity of certain psychologic states occurring during the psychotherapeutic interview. In L. A. Gottschalk, ed., *Comparative psycholinguistic analysis of two psychotherapeutic interviews.* New York: International Universities Press, 1961.

GOUGH, H. G. A sociological theory of psychopathy. *American journal of sociology,* 1948, *53,* 359-366.

GRACE, W. J., and GRAHAM, D. T. Relationship of specific attitudes and emotions to certain bodily diseases. *Psychosomatic medicine,* 1952, *14,* 242-251.

GRACE, W. J., WOLF, S., and WOLFF, H. G. *The human colon.* New York: Hoeber, 1951.

GRAHAM, D. T., LUNDY, R. M., BENJAMIN, L. S., and KABLER, F. K. Some specific attitudes in initial research interviews with patients having different "psychosomatic" diseases. *Psychosomatic medicine,* 1962, *24,* 257-266.

GRAHAM, S. R. The influence of therapist character structure upon Rorschach changes in the course of psychotherapy. *American psychologist,* 1960, *15,* 415 (abstract).

GRANDA, A. M., and HAMMACK, J. T. Operant behavior during sleep. *Science,* 1961, *133,* 1485–1486.

GRANT, V. The development of a theory of heredity. *American scientist,* 1956, *44,* 158–179.

GRAUBARD, P. S. Utilizing the group in teaching disturbed delinquents to learn. *Exceptional children,* 1969, *39,* 267–272.

GRAYSON, H. M., and OLINGER, L. B. Simulation of "normalcy" by psychiatric patients on the MMPI. *Journal of consulting psychology,* 1957, *21,* 73–77.

GRAZIANO, A. M., and KEAN, J. E. Programmed relaxation and reciprocal inhibition with psychotic children. *Proceedings of the 75th convention of the American Psychological Association,* 1967, 253–254.

GREAVES, G., and GENT, L. Comparison of accomplished suicides with persons contacting a crisis intervention clinic. *Psychological reports,* 1972, *31,* 290.

GREENACRE, P. Conscience in the psychopath. *American journal of orthopsychiatry,* 1945, *15,* 495–509.

GREENBERG, R. P., GOLDSTEIN, A. P. and PERRY, M. A. The influence of referral information upon patient perception in a psychotherapy analogue. *Journal of nervous and mental disease,* 1970, *150,* 31–36.

GREENBLATT, D. J., and SHADER, R. I. Meprobamate: a study of irrational drug use. *American journal of psychiatry,* 1971, *127,* 1297–1303.

GREENE, F. M. Programmed instruction techniques for the mentally retarded. In N. R. Ellis, ed., *Internatoinal review of research in mental retardation.* Vol. 2. New York: Academic Press, 1967, pp. 209–239.

GREENE, R. J., and HOATS, D. L. Reinforcing capabilities of television distortion. *Journal of applied behavior analysis,* 1969, *2,* 139–141.

GREENE, R. J., HOATS, D. L., and HORNICK, A. J. Music distortion: a new technique for behavior modification. *Psychological record,* 1970, *20,* 107–109.

GREENE, W. A. Operant conditioning of the GSR using partial reinforcement. *Psychological reports,* 1966, *19,* 571–578.

GREENHOUSE, L. Elderly emerging as a major voting bloc. *Champaign-Urbana courier,* 25 February 1971, p. 8.

GREENSPOON, J., and GERSTEN, C. D. A new look at psychological testing: psychological testing from the standpoint of a behaviorist. *American psychologist,* 1967, *22,* 848–853.

GREER, G. *The female eunuch.* New York: McGraw-Hill, 1971.

GRICE, D. G. Patient sex differences and selection for individual psychotherapy. *Journal of nervous and mental disease,* 1969, *148,* 124–133.

GRIFFITT, W., and VEITCH, R. Hot and crowded: influences of population density and temperature on interpersonal affective behavior. *Journal of personality and social psychology,* 1971, *17,* 92–98.

GRIM, P. F., KOHLBERG, L., and WHITE, S. H. Some relationships between conscience and attentional processes. *Journal of personality and social psychology,* 1968, *8,* 239–252.

GRIMALDI, K. E., and LICHTENSTEIN, E. Hot, smoky air as an aversive stimulus in the treatment of smoking. *Behaviour research and therapy,* 1969, *7,* 275–282.

GRINKER, R. R., MILLER, J., SABSHIN, M., NUNN, R., and NUNNALLY, J. C. *The phenomena of depression.* New York: Hoeber, 1961.

GRINSPOON, L. *Marihuana reconsidered.* Cambridge, Mass.: Harvard University Press, 1971.

GRIPP, R. F., and MAGARO, P. A. A token economy program evaluation with untreated control ward comparisons. *Behaviour research and therapy,* 1971, *9,* 137–149.

GRISELL, J. L., and ROSENBAUM, G. Effects of auditory intensity on schizophrenic reaction time. *American psychologist,* 1963, *18,* 394.

GRISWOLD, R. L., PACE, N., and GRUNBAUM, B. W. Metabolic concomitants of schizophrenia. *Comprehensive psychiatry,* 1969, *10,* 1–15.

GROSS, E. Plus ça change . . . ? The sexual structure of occupations over time. *Social problems,* 1968, *16,* 198–208.

GROSS, H. S., HERBERT, M. R., KNATTERUD, G. L., and DONNER, L. The effect of race and sex on the variation of diagnosis and disposition in a psychiatric emergency room. *Journal of nervous and mental disease,* 1969, *148,* 638–642.

GROSS, M. M., ROSENBLATT, S. M., MALENOWSKI, B., BROMAN, M., and LEWIS, E. Classification of alcohol withdrawal syndromes. *Quarterly journal of studies on alcohol,* 1972, *33,* 400–407.

GROSSBERG, J. M. Behavior therapy: a review. *Psychological bulletin,* 1964, *62,* 73–88.

GROSZ, H. J., and ZIMMERMAN, J. Experimental analysis of hysterical blindness: a follow-up report and new experimental data. *Archives of general psychiatry,* 1965, *13,* 255–260.

GROSZ, H. J., and ZIMMERMAN, J. A second detailed case study of functional blindness: further demonstration of the contribution of objective psychological laboratory data. *Behavior therapy,* 1970, *1,* 115–123.

GROSZ, H. J., and GROSSMAN, K. G. The sources of observer variation and bias in clinical judgments:

I. the item of psychiatric history. *Journal of nervous and mental disease*, 1964, *138*, 105–113.

GROSZ, H. J., and GROSSMAN, K. G. Clinician's response style: a source of variation and bias in clinical judgments. *Journal of abnormal psychology*, 1968, *73*, 207–214.

GROUP FOR THE ADVANCEMENT OF PSYCHIATRY. *Psychiatrically deviated sex offenders*. Report no. 9, February 1950.

GROUP FOR THE ADVANCEMENT OF PSYCHIATRY. *Criminal responsibility and psychiatric expert testimony*. Report no. 26, May 1954.

GROUP FOR THE ADVANCEMENT OF PSYCHIATRY. *Report on homosexuality with particular emphasis on this problem in governmental agencies*. Report no. 30, December 1955.

GROUP FOR THE ADVANCEMENT OF PSYCHIATRY. *Psychopathological disorders in childhood: theoretical considerations and a proposed classification*. Report no. 62, June 1966a.

GROUP FOR THE ADVANCEMENT OF PSYCHIATRY. *Sex and the college student*. New York: Atheneum, 1966b.

GROUP FOR ADVANCEMENT OF PSYCHIATRY. *The right to abortion: a psychiatric view*. New York: Scribner, 1972.

GROVES, I. D., and CARROCCIO, D. F. A self-feeding program for the severely and profoundly retarded. *Mental retardation*, 1971, *9*, 10–12.

GRUENBERG, E. M. Foreword. In *DSM-II*. Washington, D.C.: American Psychiatric Association, 1968, pp. vii-x.

GRUENBERG, E. M., BRANDON, S., and KASIUS, R. V. Identifying cases of the social breakdown syndrome. *Millbank fund quarterly*, 1966, 44 (No. 1, part 2), 150–154.

GRUSEC, J. E. Demand characteristics of the modeling experiment: altruism as a function of age and aggression. *Journal of personality and social psychology*, 1972, *22*, 139–148.

GRUSEC, J. E., and EZRIN, S. A. Techniques of punishment and the development of self-criticism. *Child development*, 1972, *43*, 1273–1288.

GUESS, D., and RUTHERFORD, G. Experimental attempts to reduce stereotyping among blind retardates. *American journal of mental deficiency*, 1967, *71*, 984–986.

GUGGENHEIM, F. G., POLLIN, W., STABENAU, J. R., and MOSHER, L. R. Prevalence of physical illness in parents of identical twins discordant for schizophrenia. *Psychosomatic medicine*, 1969, *31*, 288–299.

GUGGENHEIM, P. *Confessions of an art addict*. New York: Macmillan, 1960.

GUNDERSON, E. K. E., ARTHUR, R. J., and RICHARDSON, J. W. Military status and mental illness. *Military medicine*, 1968, *133*, 543–549.

GUREL, L., and ULLMANN, L. P. Quantitative differences in response to TAT cards: the relationship between transcendence score and number of emotional words. *Journal of projective techniques*, 1958, *22*, 399–401.

GUREL, L. M., WILBUR, J. C., and GUREL, L. Personality correlates of adolescent clothing styles. *Journal of home economics*, 1972, *64*, 42–47.

GURLAND, B. J. A broad clinical assessment of psychopathology in the aged. In C. Eisdorfer and M. P. Lawton, eds., *The psychology of adult development and aging*. Washington, D.C.: American Psychological Association, 1973, pp. 343–377.

GUTHRIE, E. R. *The psychology of learning*. New York: Harper, 1935.

GUTHRIE, E. R. *The psychology of human conflict*. New York: Harper, 1938.

GUTHRIE, E. R. Conditioning: a theory of learning in terms of stimulus, response, and association. In *The psychology of learning* (Chapter I). National Social Studies Education, 1942, 41st yearbook (Part 2), pp. 17–60.

GUTHRIE, G. M. *Culture and mental disorder*. Reading, Mass.: Addison-Wesley, 1973.

GUTRIDE, M. E., GOLDSTEIN, A. P., and HUNTER, G. F. The use of modeling and role playing to increase social interaction among asocial psychiatric patients. *Journal of consulting and clinical psychology*, 1973, *40*, 408–415.

GUZE, S. B. The diagnosis of hysteria: what are we trying to do? *American journal of psychiatry*, 1967, 124, 491–498.

GUZE, S. B., and ROBINS, E. Suicide and primary affective disorders. *British journal of psychiatry*, 1970, *117*, 437–438.

HAAS, H., FINK, H., and HARTFELDER, G. The placebo problem. *Psychopharmacology service center bulletin*, 1963, *2*, 1–65.

HAASE, R. F., and TEPPER, D. T. Nonverbal components of empathic communication. *Journal of counseling psychology*, 1972, *19*, 417–424.

HAGEN, R. L. Group therapy versus bibliotherapy in weight reduction. *Dissertation abstracts international*, 1970, *31*, 2985–2986.

HAGGARD, H. W. *Devils, drugs, and doctors*. New York: Harper, 1929.

HAGNELL, O. Personal communication, 1964. cited in A. H. Leighton, Discussion. In A. V. S. DeReuck and R. Porter, eds., *Transcultural psychiatry*. Boston: Little, Brown, 1965, p. 83.

HALL, E. T. *The hidden dimension*. New York: Doubleday, 1966.

HALL, E. T. *The silent language.* New York: Fawcett World Library, 1969.

HALL, G. S. *Adolescence.* New York: Appleton, 1907.

HALL, R. V., and BRODEN, M. Behavior changes in brain-injured children through social reinforcement. *Journal of experimental child psychology,* 1967, *5,* 463-479.

HALLAM, R., and RACHMAN, S. Theoretical problems of aversion therapy. *Behaviour research and therapy,* 1972, *10,* 341-353.

HALLECK, S. L. Community psychiatry: some troubling questions. In L. M. Roberts, S. L. Halleck, and F. Loeb, eds., *Community psychiatry.* New York: Doubleday, 1969, pp. 58-71.

HALLECK, S. L. *The politics of therapy.* New York: Harper & Row, 1972.

HALLECK, S. L. Legal and ethical aspects of behavior control. *American journal of psychiatry,* 1974, *131,* 381-385.

HALLER, B. L. Some factors related to the adjustment of psychopaths on parole from a state hospital. *Smith college studies of social work,* 1942, *13,* 193-194.

HALLSTEN, E. A., JR. Adolescent anorexia nervosa treated by desensitization. *Behaviour research and therapy,* 1965, *3,* 87-91.

HALSAM, J. *Observations on madness and melancholy.* London, 1798.

HAMILTON, G. V. *An introduction to objective psychopathology.* St. Louis: Mosley, 1925.

HAMILTON, J., and STANDAHL, J. Suppression of stereotyped screaming behavior in a profoundly retarded institutionalized female. *Journal of experimental child psychology,* 1969, *7,* 114-121.

HAMILTON, J. W., and STEPHENS, L. Y. Reinstating speech in an emotionally disturbed, mentally retarded young woman. *Journal of speech and hearing disorders,* 1967, *32,* 383-389.

HAMILTON, J., STEPHENS, L., and ALLEN, P. Controlling aggressive and destructive behavior in severely retarded institutionalized residents. *American journal of mental deficiency,* 1967, *71,* 852-856.

HAMMER, M. Influence of small social networks as factors on mental hospital admissions. *Human organization,* 1963, *22,* 243-251.

HAMMER, M., and KAPLAN, A. M. *The practice of psychotherapy with children.* Homewood, Ill.: Dorsey Press, 1967.

HAMMER, M., SALZINGER, K., and SUTTON, S. *Psychopathology: contributions from the social, behavioral and biological science.* New York: Wiley-Interscience, 1973.

HAMMOND, A. L. Narcotic antagonists: new methods to treat heroin addiction. *Science,* 1971, *173,* 503-506.

HAMMOND, K. R. Computer graphics as an aid to learning. *Science,* 1971, *172,* 903-908.

HANEY, C. A., and MICHIELUTTE, R. Selective factors operating in the adjudication of incompetency. *Journal of health and social behavior,* 1968, *9,* 233-242.

HANSON, R. W., and ADESSO, V. J. A multiple behavioral approach to male homosexual behavior: a case study. *Journal of behavior therapy and experimental psychiatry,* 1972, *3,* 323-325.

HARE, R. D. Psychopathy, fear arousal and anticipated pain. *Psychological reports,* 1965, *16,* 499-502.

HARE, R. D. *Psychopathy: theory and research.* New York: Wiley, 1970.

HARLOW, H. The formation of learning sets. *Psychological review,* 1949, *56,* 51-65.

HARMATZ, M. G. Verbal conditioning and change on personality measures. *Journal of personality and social psychology,* 1967, *5,* 175-185.

HARMATZ, M. G. Observational study of ward staff havior. *Exceptional children,* 1973, *39,* 554-558.

HARMATZ, M. G., and LAPUC, P. Behavior modification of overeating in a psychiatric population. *Journal of consulting and clinical psychology,* 1968, *32,* 583-587.

HAROLDSON, S. K., MARTIN, R. R. and STARR, C. D. Time-out as a punishment for stuttering. *Journal of speech and hearing research,* 1968, *11,* 560-566.

HARRIS, F. R., JOHNSTON, M. K., KELLEY, C. S., and WOLF, M. M. Effects of positive social reinforcement on regressed crawling of a nursery school child. *Journal of educational psychology,* 1964, *55,* 35-41.

HARRIS, M. B. Self-directed program for weight control: a pilot study. *Journal of abnormal and social psychology,* 1969, *74,* 263-270.

HARRIS, M. B. Reciprocity and generosity: some determinants of sharing in children. *Child development,* 1970, *41,* 313-328.

HART, B. M., ALLEN, K. E., BUELL, J. S., HARRIS, F. R., and WOLF, M. M. Effects of social reinforcement on operant crying. *Journal of experimental child psychology,* 1964, *1,* 145-153.

HART, B. M., REYNOLDS, N. J., BAER, D. M., BRAWLEY, E. R., and HARRIS, F. R. Effect of contingent and non-contingent reinforcement on the cooperative play of a preschool child. *Journal of applied behavior analysis,* 1968, *1,* 73-76.

HART, B. M., and RISLEY, T. R. Establishing use of descriptive adjectives in the spontaneous speech of disadvantaged preschool children. *Journal of applied behavior analysis,* 1968, *1,* 109-120.

HART, H. L. A. *Law, liberty and morality.* New York: Vintage, 1966.

HARTIG, M., and KANFER, F. H. The role of verbal self-instructions in children's resistance to temptation. *Journal of personality and social psychology,* 1973, *25,* 259–267.

HARTLAGE, L. C. Subprofessional therapists' use of reinforcement versus traditional psychotherapeutic techniques with schizophrenics. *Journal of consulting and clinical psychology,* 1970, *34,* 181–183.

HARTOGS, R., and FANTEL, H. *Four-letter word games: the psychology of obscenity.* New York: Dell, 1968.

HARTSHORNE, H., and MAY, M. A. *Studies in deceit.* New York: Macmillan, 1928.

HARTUNG, J. R. A review of procedures to increase verbal imitation skills and functional speech in autistic children. *Journal of speech and hearing disorders,* 1970, *35,* 203–217.

HARTUP, W. W., GLAZER, J. A., and CHARLESWORTH, R. Peer reinforcement and sociometric status. *Child development,* 1967, *38,* 1017–1024.

HARWAY, N. I., DITTMANN, A. T., RAUSH, H. L., BORDIN, E. S., and RIGLER, D. The measurement of depth of interpretation. *Journal of consulting psychology,* 1955, *19,* 247–253.

HASLAM, M. H. The treatment of an obsessional patient by reciprocal inhibition. *Behaviour research and therapy,* 1965a, *2,* 213–216.

HASLAM, M. H. The treatment of psychogenic dyspareunia by reciprocal inhibition. *British journal of psychiatry,* 1965b, *111,* 272–279.

HASLETON, S. Marihuana: a brief review. *Australian and New Zealand journal of psychiatry,* 1972, *6,* 41–45.

HASTINGS, D. W. *Impotence and frigidity.* Boston: Little, Brown, 1963.

HASTINGS, D. W. Can specific training procedures overcome sexual inadequacy? In R. Brecher and E. Brecher, eds., *An analysis of human sexual response.* New York: New American Library, 1966, pp. 221–235.

HATHAWAY, S. R. The personality inventory as an aid in the diagnosis of psychopathic inferiors. *Journal of consulting psychology,* 1939, *3,* 112–117.

HAUGEN, G. B., DIXON, H. H., and DICKEL, H. A. *A therapy for anxiety tension reactions.* New York: Macmillan, 1958.

HAUGHTON, A. B. Suicide prevention programs—the current scene. *American journal of psychiatry,* 1968, *124,* 1692–1696.

HAUGHTON, E., and AYLLON, T. Production and elimination of symptomatic behavior. In L. P. Ullmann and L. Krasner, eds., *Case studies in behavior modification.* New York: Holt, Rinehart and Winson, 1965.

HAUSER, A. *The social history of art.* 4 vols. New York: Vintage, 1958.

HAUSER, A. *The philosophy of art history.* New York: World (Meridan Ed.), 1963.

HAUSERMAN, N., WALEN, S. R., and BEHLING, M. Reinforced racial integration in the first grade: a study in generalization. *Journal of applied behavior analysis,* 1973, *6,* 193–200.

HAUSERMAN, N., ZWEBACK, S., and PLOTKIN, A. Use of concrete reinforcement to facilitate verbal initiations in adolescent group therapy. *Journal of consulting and clinical psychology,* 1972, *38,* 90–96.

HAUTALUOMA, J. Syndromes, antecedents, and outcomes of psychosis: a cluster-analytic study. *Journal of consulting and clinical psychology,* 1971, *37,* 332–344.

HAWKINS, R. P., PETERSON, R. F., SCHWEID, E., and BIJOU, S. W. Behavior therapy in the home: amelioration of problem parent-child relations with the parent in a therapeutic role. *Journal of experimental child psychology,* 1966, *4,* 99–107.

HAWKS, D. V. The dimensions of drug dependence in the United Kingdom. *International journal of the addictions,* 1971, *6,* 135–160.

HAWLEY, A. H. Ecology and population. *Science,* 1973, *179,* 1196–1201.

HAYES, K. J. Genes, drives, and intellect. *Psychological reports,* 1962, *10,* 299–342.

HAYNES, S. N. Contingency management in a municipally-administered anti-abuse program for alcoholics. *Journal of behavior therapy and experimental psychiatry,* 1973, *4,* 31–32.

HAYNES, S. N., and GEDDY, P. Suppression of psychotic hallucinations through time-out. *Behavior therapy,* 1973, *4,* 123–127.

HAYS, H. R. *The dangerous sex: the myth of feminine evil.* New York: Pocket Books, 1966.

HAYS, P. *New horizons in psychiatry.* Baltimore: Penguin, 1964.

HAZELRIGG, L., ed., *Prison within society.* Garden City, N. Y.: Doubleday, 1969.

HEAP, R. F., BOBLITT, W. E., MOORE, C. H., and HORD, J. E. Behavior-milieu therapy with chronic neuropsychiatric patients. *Journal of abnormal psychology,* 1970, *76,* 349–354.

HEATH, C. W. *What people are: a study of normal young men.* Cambridge, Mass.: Harvard University Press, 1945.

HEBB, D. O. Intelligence in man after large removals of cerebral tissue: report of four left frontal lobe cases. *Journal of general psychology,* 1939, *21,* 73–87.

HEBB, D. O. Man's frontal lobes: a critical review.

Archives of neurology and psychiatry, 1945, *54,* 10–24.

HEDBERG, A. G. The treatment of chronic diarrhea by sytematic desensitization: a case report. *Journal of behavior therapy and experimental psychiatry,* 1973, *4,* 67–68.

HEINE, R. W. A comparison of patients' reports on psychotherapeutic experience with psychoanalytic, nondirective, and Adlerian therapists. *American journal of psychotherapy,* 1953, *7,* 16–23.

HEKMAT, H. Reinforcing values of interpretations and reflections in a quasi-therapeutic interview. *Journal of abnormal psychology,* 1971, *77,* 25–31.

HEKMAT, H., and LEE, Y. B. Conditioning of affective self-references as a function of semantic meaning of verbal reinforcers. *Journal of abnormal psychology,* 1970, *76,* 427–433.

HEKMAT, H., and THEISS, M. Self-actualization and modification of affective self-disclosures during a social conditioning interview. *Journal of counseling psychology,* 1971, *18,* 101–105.

HEKMAT, H., and VANIAN, D. Behavior modification through covert semantic desensitization. *Journal of consulting and clinical psychology,* 1971, *36,* 248–251.

HELLER, K. Effects of modeling procedures in helping relationships. *Journal of consulting and clinical psychology,* 1969, *33,* 522–526.

HELLER, R. F., and STRANG, H. R. Controlling bruxism through automated aversive conditioning. *Behaviour research and therapy,* 1973, *11,* 327–329.

HENDERSON, D., and BATCHELOR, I. R. C. *Henderson and Gillespie's textbook of psychiatry.* 9th ed. London: Oxford University Press, 1962.

HENDERSON, J. D., and SCOLES, P. E., JR. Conditioning techniques in a community-based operant environment for psychotic men. *Behavior therapy,* 1970, *1,* 254–251.

HENDERSON, L. J. Physician and patient as a social system. *New England journal of medicine,* 1935, *212,* 819-833.

HENDRIKSEN, S. D., and OEDING, P. Medical survey of Tristan da Cunha: results of the Norwegian scientific expedition to Tristan da Cunha 1937–1938 (No. 5). Oslo: Det Norske Videnskaps-Akademi, 1940.

HENRY, J. Space and power in a psychiatric unit. In A. F. Wessen, ed., *The psychiatric hospital as a social system.* Springfield, Ill.: Charles C Thomas, 1964, 20–34.

HERGUTH, R. J. People. *Chicago daily news,* 13 May 1969, p. 13.

HERGUTH, R. J. Herguth's people. *Chicago daily news,* 7 August 1970, p. 15.

HERRON, W. G. The process-reactive classification of schizophernia. *Psychological bulletin,* 1962, *59,* 329–343.

HERSEN, M. Treatment of a compulsive and phobic disorder through a total behavior therapy program: a case study. *Psychotherapy: theory, research and practice,* 1968, *5,* 220–225.

HERSEN, M. Nightmare behavior: a review. *Psychological bulletin,* 1972, *78,* 37–48.

HERSEN, M., EISLER, R. M., SMITH, B. S., and AGRAS, W. S. A token reinforcement ward for young psychiatric patients. *American journal of psychiatry,* 1972, *129,* 228–233.

HERSEN, M., EISLER, R. M., ALFORD, G. S., and AGRAS, W. S. Effects of token economy on neurotic depression: an experimental analysis. *Behavior therapy,* 1973, *4,* 392–397.

HERSEN, M., EISLER, R. M., MILLER, P. M., JOHNSON, M. B., and PINKSTON, S. G. Effects of practice, instructions, and modelling on components of assertive behaviour. *Behaviour research and therapy,* 1973, *11,* 443–451.

HERSEN, M., and GREAVES, S. T. Rorschach productivity as related to verbal reinforcement. *Journal of personality assessment,* 1971, *35,* 436–441.

HERSEN, M., MATHERNE, P. M., GULLICK, E. L., and HARBERT, T. L. Instructions and reinforcement in the modification of a conversion reaction. *Psychological reports,* 1972, *31,* 719–722.

HERSEN, M., MILLER, P. M., and EISLER, R. M. Interactions between alcoholics and their wives; a descriptive analysis of verbal and nonverbal behavior. *Studies of alcohol,* 1973, *34,* 516–519.

HESS, E. H., SELTZER, A. L., and SHLIEN, J. M. Pupil response of hetero- and homosexual males to pictures of men and women: a pilot study. *Journal of abnormal psychology,* 1965, *70,* 165–168.

HESTON, L. L. Psychiatric disorders in foster home reared children of schizophrenic mothers. *British journal of psychiatry,* 1966, *112,* 819–825.

HETHERINGTON, E. M., and WRAY, N. P. Aggression, need for social approval, and humor preferences. *Journal of abnormal and social psychology,* 1964, *68,* 685–689.

HEWETT, F. M. Teaching speech to an autistic child through operant conditioning. *American journal of orthopsychiatry,* 1965, *35,* 927–936.

HEWETT, F. M., MAYHEW, D., and RABB, E. An experimental reading program for neurologically impaired, mentally retarded, and severely emotionally disturbed children. *American journal of orthopsychiatry,* 1967, *37,* 35–48.

HIGA, W. R. Self-instructional versus direct training in modifying children's impulsive behavior. Unpublished doctoral dissertation, University of Hawaii, 1973.

HIGGINS, J. The concept of process-reactive schizophrenia: criteria and related research. *Journal of nervous and mental disease,* 1964, *138,* 9–25.

HIGGINS, J., and PETERSON, J. C. Concept of process-reactive schizophrenia: a critique. *Psychological bulletin,* 1966, *66,* 201–206.

HIGGINS, R. L., and MARLATT, G. A. The effects of anxiety arousal upon the consumption of alcohol by alcoholics and social drinkers. *Journal of consulting and clinical psychology,* 1973, *41.*

HILGARD, E. R. *Introduction to psychology.* 3rd ed. New York: Harcourt, 1962.

HILGARD, E. R. *Hypnotic susceptibility.* New York: Harcourt, 1965.

HILGARD, E. R. Individual differences in hypnotizability. In J. E. Gordon, ed., *Handbook of clinical and experimental hypnosis.* New York: Macmillan, 1967, 391–443.

HILGARD, E. R., and BOWER, G. H. *Theories of learning.* 3rd ed. New York: Appleton, 1966.

HILL, J. P., and KOCHENDORFER, R. A. Knowledge of peer success and risk of detection as determinants of cheating. *Developmental psychology,* 1969, *1,* 121–128.

HINDE, R. A. *Non-verbal communication.* New York: Cambridge University Press, 1972.

HINGTGEN, J. N., and COULTER, S. K. Auditory control of operant behavior in mute autistic children. *Perceptual and motor skills,* 1967, *25,* 561–565.

HINGTGEN, J. N., COULTER, S. K., and CHURCHILL, D. W. Intensive reinforcement of imitative behavior in mute autistic children. *Archives of general psychiatry,* 1967, *17,* 36–43.

HINGTGEN, J. N., SANDERS, B. J., and DEMYER, M. K. Shaping cooperative responses in early childhood schizophrenics. In L. P. Ullmann and L. Krasner, eds., *Case studies in behavior modification.* New York: Holt, Rinehart and Winston, 1965, 130–138.

HIPPLER, A. E. Fusion and frustration: dimensions in the cross-cultural ethnopsychology of suicide. *American anthropologist,* 1969, *71,* 1074–1087.

HIRSCH, J. Behavior genetics and individuality understood. *Science,* 1963, *142,* 1436–1442.

HIRSCH, J. Behavior-genetic or "experimental" analysis: the challenge of science versus the lure of technology. *American psychologist,* 1967, *22,* 118–130.

HITCHCOCK, J., and WOLFORD, J. A. Alternatives to the suicide prevention approach to mental health. *Archives of general psychiatry,* 1970, *22,* 547–549.

HNATIOW, M., and LANG, P. J. Learned stabilization of cardiac rate. *Psychophysiology,* 1965, *1,* 330–336.

HOAKEN, P. C. S. Monozygotic twins discordant for schizophrenia. *Psychiatric quarterly,* 1969, *43,* 612–621.

HOBBES, T. *Leviathan* (1651).

HOCH, P. H., and KNIGHT, R. P. *Epilepsy.* New York: Grune and Stratton, 1947.

HODGSON, R., RACHMAN, S., and MARKS, I. M. The treatment of chronic obsessive-compulsive neurosis: follow-up and further findings. *Behaviour research and therapy,* 1972, *10,* 181–189.

HOFFER, A., and POLLIN, W. Schizophrenia in the NAS-NRC panel of 15,909 veteran twin pairs. *Archives of general psychiatry,* 1970, *23,* 469–477.

HOGAN, R. Moral conduct and moral character: a psychological perspective. *Psychological bulletin,* 1973, *79,* 217–232.

HOGAN, R. A., and KIRCHNER, J. H. Preliminary report of the extinction of learned fears via short-term implosive therapy. *Journal of abnormal psychology,* 1967, *72,* 106–109.

HOKANSON, J., and BURGESS, M. Effects of physiological arousal level, frustration, and task complexity on performance. *Journal of abnormal and social psychology,* 1964, *68,* 698–702.

HOLAHAN, C. J., and SAEGERT, S. Behavioral and attitudinal effects of large-scale variation in the physical environment of psychiatric wards. *Journal of abnormal psychology,* 1973, *82,* 454–462.

HOLDEN, C. Alcoholism: on-the-job referrals mean early detection, treatment. *Science,* 1973, *179,* 363.

HOLE, J., and LEVINE, E. *Rebirth of feminism.* New York: Quadrangle, 1971.

HOLLANDER, M. A., and PLUTCHIK, R. A reinforcement program for psychiatric attendants. *Journal of behavior therapy and experimental psychiatry,* 1972, *3,* 297–300.

HOLLANDER, M., PLUTCHIK, R., and HORNER, V. Interaction of patient and attendant reinforcement programs: the "piggyback" effect. *Journal of consulting and clinical psychology,* 1973, *41,* 43–47.

HOLLINGSHEAD, A. B. and REDLICH, F. C. Social stratification and psychiatric disorders. *American sociological review,* 1953, *18,* 163–169.

HOLLINGSHEAD, A. B., and REDLICH, F. C. *Social class and mental illness.* New York: Wiley, 1958.

HOLLINGWORTH, H. L. *Abnormal psychology.* New York: Ronald Press, 1930.

HOLMES, D. J. *The adolescent in psychotherapy.* Boston: Little, Brown, 1964.

HOLMES, D. S. Differential change in affective intensity and the forgetting of unpleasant personal experiences. *Journal of personality and social psychology* 1970, *15,* 234–239.

Holmes, D. S. Repression or interference? A further investigation. *Journal of personality and social psychology*, 1972, *22*, 163–170.

Holmes, D. S., and Appelbaum, A. S. Nature of prior experimental experience as a determinant of performance in a subsequent experiment. *Journal of personality and social psychology*, 1970, *14*, 195–202.

Holmes, D. S., and Schallow, J. R. Reduced recall after ego threat: repression or response competition. *Journal of personality and social psychology*, 1969, *13*, 145–152.

Holmes, F. B. An experimental investigation of a method of overcoming children's fears. *Child development*, 1936, *7*, 6–30.

Holmes, T. H. and Rahe, R. H. The social readjustment rating scale. *Journal of psychosomatic research*, 1967, *11*, 213–218.

Holt, E. B. *The Freudian wish and its place in ethics.* New York: Henry Holt, 1915.

Holt, R. R., and Luborsky, L. *Personality patterns of psychiatrists: a study of methods of selecting psychiatrists.* New York; Basic Books, 1958.

Holz, W. C., Azrin, N. H., and Ayllon, T. Elimination of behavior of mental patients by response-produced extinction. *Journal of the experimental analysis of behavior*, 1963, *6*, 407–412.

Holzman, M. S. The significance of the value systems of patient and therapist for the outcome of psychotherapy. Unpublished doctoral dissertation, University of Washington, 1961.

Homans, G. C. *Social behavior: its elementary forms.* New York: Harcourt, 1961.

Homme, L. E. Control of coverants, the operants of the mind. *Psychological reports*, 1965, *15*, 501–511.

Homme, L. E. Coverant control therapy: a special case of contingency management. Paper read at Rocky Mountain Psychological Association Convention, 1966.

Homme, L. E., DeBaca, P. C. Devine, J. V., Steinhorst, R., and Rickert, E. J. Use of the Premack principle in controlling the behavior of nursery school children. *Journal of the experimental analysis of behavior*, 1963, *6*, 544.

Honigfeld, G. Non-specific factors in treatment. I: review of placebo reactions and placebo reactors. *Diseases of the nervous system*, 1964a, *25*, 145–156.

Honigfeld, G. Non-specific factors in treatment. II: review of social-psychological factors. *Diseases of the nervous system*, 1964b, *25*, 225–239.

Hook, E. B. Behavioral implications of the human XYY genotype. *Science*, 1973, *179*, 139–150.

Hooker, E. The adjustment of the male overt homosexual. *Journal of projective techniques*, 1957, *21*, 18–31.

Hooker, E. The homosexual community. In *Proceedings of the XIV international congress of applied psychology.* Vol. 2. Personality research. Copenhagen: Munksgaard, 1962.

Horan, J. J. and Johnson, R. G. Coverant conditioning through a self-management application of the Premack principle: its effect on weight reduction. *Journal of behavior therapy and experimental psychiatry*, 1971, *2*, 243–249.

Horner, M. A bright woman is caught in a double bind. *Psychology today*, 1969, *3*, 36–38.

Hornstein, H. A. The influence of social models on helping. In J. Macaulay and L. Berkowitz, eds., *Altruism and helping behavior.* New York: Academic Press, 1970, 29–41.

Horton, L. E. Generalization of aggressive behavior in adolescent delinquent boys. *Journal of applied behavior analysis*, 1970, *3*, 199–203.

Horton, P. C. Normality—toward a meaningful concept. *Comprehensive psychiatry*, 1971, *12*, 54–66.

Houston, B. K. Review of the evidence and qualifications regarding the effects of hallucinogenic drugs on chromosomes and embryos. *American journal of psychiatry*, 1969, *126*, 251–254.

Howard, J. *Please touch: a guided tour of the human potential movement.* New York: McGraw-Hill, 1970.

Huddle, D. D. Work performances of trainable adults as influenced by competition, cooperation, and a monetary reward. *American journal of mental deficiency*, 1967.

Hudson, L., ed., *The ecology of human intelligence.* Baltimore: Penguin, 1970.

Huessy, H. R., Marshall, C. D., and Gendron, R. A. Five hundred children followed from grade 2 through grade 5 for the prevalance of behavior disorder. *Acta paedopsychiatrica*, 1973, *39*, 301–309.

Huff, F. W. The desensitization of a homosexual. *Behaviour research and therapy*, 1970, *8*, 99–102.

Hughes, J. T., and Panek, M. Aversive conditioning of a chronic arm slasher with electric shock. *Behavior therapy*, 1973, *4*, 755.

Hull, C. L. *Principles of behavior.* New York: Appleton, 1943.

Hull, C. L. *Essentials of behavior.* New Haven: Yale University Press, 1951.

Hullen, R. P., McDonald, R., and Allsopp, M. N. Prophylactic lithium in recurrent affective disorders. *Lancet*, 1972, *1*, 1044–1046.

Humphreys, L. *Out of the closets: the sociology of homosexual liberation.* Englewood Cliffs, New Jersey: Prentice-Hall, 1970.

HUMPHREYS, L. New styles in homosexual manliness. *Trans-action,* 1971, *8,* 38–46; 64–66.

HUNDZIAK, M., MAURER, R. N., and WATSON, L. S. Operant conditioning in toilet training severely mentally retarded boys. *American journal of mental deficiency,* 1964, *70,* 120–124.

HUNT, G. M., and AZRIN, N. H. A community-reinforcement approach to alcoholism. *Behaviour research and therapy,* 1973, *11,* 91–104.

HUNT, J. McV. *Intelligence and experience.* New York: Ronald Press, 1961.

HUNT, J. McV., ed. *Human intelligence.* New Brunswick, N. J.: Transaction Books, 1972.

HUNT, J. McV., and COFER, C. N. Psychological deficit. In J. McV. Hunt, ed., *Personality and the behavior disorders.* Vol. II. New York: Ronald Press, 1944, pp. 971–1032.

HUNT, M. *Sexual behavior in the 70's.* New York: Playboy Press, 1974.

HUNT, R. G. Social class and mental illness: some implications for clinical theory and practice. *American journal of psychiatry,* 1960, *116,* 1065–1069.

HUNT, W., and MATARAZZO, J. Three years later: recent developments in the experimental modification of smoking behavior. *Journal of abnormal psychology,* 1973, *81,* 107–114.

HUNT, W. A., and WALKER, R. E. Schizophrenics' judgments of schizophrenic test responses. *Journal of clinical psychology,* 1966, *22,* 118–120.

HUNTER, R., and MACALPINE, I., eds., *Three hundred years of psychiatry, 1535–1860.* London: Oxford University Press, 1963.

HURLEY, R. *Poverty and mental retardation: a causal relationship.* New York: Random House, 1969.

HUSTED, J., WALLIN, K., and WOODEN, H. The psychological evaluation of profoundly retarded children with the use of concrete reinforcers. *Journal of psychology,* 1971, *77,* 173–179.

HUSTON, P. E., and LOCHER, L. M. Manic-depressive psychosis: course when treated and untreated with electric shock. *Archives of neurology and psychiatry,* 1948 *60,* 37–48.

HUTT, M. L., and GIBBY, R. G. *Patterns of abnormal behavior.* Boston: Allyn & Bacon, 1957.

HUXLEY, A. *The devils of Loudon.* New York: Harper, 1952.

IMPERI, L. L., KLEBER, H. D., and DAVIS, J. S. Use of hallucinogenic drugs on campus. *Journal of the American medical association,* 1968, *204,* 1021–1024.

INCE, L. P. Effects of fixed-interval reinforcement on the frequency of a verbal response class in a quasi-counseling situation. *Journal of counseling psychology,* 1968a, *15,* 140–146.

INCE, L. P. Densensitization with an aphasic patient. *Behaviour research and therapy,* 1968b, *6,* 235–237.

INGHAM, R. J., and ANDREWS, G. An analysis of a token economy in stuttering therapy. *Journal of applied behavior analysis,* 1973, *6,* 219–230.

INKELES, A., and BAUER, R. A. Keeping up with the news. In B. Berelson and M. Janowitz, eds., *Reader in public opinion and communication.* 2nd ed. New York: Free Press, 1966, 556–587.

IRONSIDE, R., and BATCHELOR, I. R. C. The ocular manifestations of hysteria in relation to flying. *British journal of ophthalmology,* 1945, *29,* 88–98.

ISAACS, W., THOMAS, J., and GOLDIAMOND, I. Application of operant conditioning to reinstate verbal behavior in psychotics. *Journal of speech and hearing disorders.* 1960, *25,* 8–12.

ISEN, A. M. Success, failure, attention and reaction to others: the warm glow of success. *Journal of personality and social psychology,* 1970, *15,* 294–301.

ISEN, A. M. and LEVIN, P. F. Effect of feeling good on helping: cookies and kindness. *Journal of personality and social psychology,* 1972, *21,* 384–388.

ISHIYAMA, T., and BROWN, A. F. Modifications in the role-image of the chronic psychotic patient as a function of social pressures. *Journal of health and human behavior,* 1966, *7,* 203–211.

ISRAEL, A. C., and O'LEARY, K. D. Developing correspondence between children's words and deeds. *Child development,* 1973, *44,* 575–581.

ITTELSON, W. H., PROSHANSKY, H. M., and RIVLIN, L. G. The environmental psychology of the psychiatric ward. In H. M. Proshansky, W. H. Ittelson, and L. G. Rivlin, eds., *Environmental psychology: man and his physical setting.* New York: Holt, Rinehart and Winston, 1970, pp. 419–438.

IVERSEN, W. *O the times! O the manners!* New York: Morrow, 1965.

JACKSON, B. The revised diagnostic and statistical manual of the American psychiatric association. *American journal of psychiatry,* 1970, *127,* 65–73.

JACKSON, B. T. A case of voyeurism treated by counterconditioning. *Behaviour research and therapy,* 1969, *7,* 133–134.

JACKSON, C. W., JR., and KELLY, E. L. Influence of suggestion and subjects' prior knowledge in research on sensory deprivation. *Science,* 1962, *135,* 211–212.

JACKSON, C. W., JR., and POLLARD, J. C. Sensory deprivation and suggestion: a theoretical approach. *Behavioral science,* 1962, *7,* 332–342.

JACKSON, D. D., ed. *The etiology of schizophrenia.* New York: Basic Books, 1960.

JACKSON, D. D., BLOCK, J., BLOCK, J., and PATTERSON,

V. Psychiatrists' conceptions of the schizophrenogenic parent. *Archives of neurology and psychiatry,* 1958, *79,* 448–459.

JACKSON, D. D., and WEAKLAND, J. Conjoint family therapy: some considerations on theory, technique and results. *Psychiatry,* 1961, *24,* 30–45.

JACKSON, J. Toward the comparative study of mental hospitals; characteristics of the treatment environment. In A. F. Wessen, ed., *The psychiatric hospital as a social system.* Springfield, Ill.: Charles C Thomas, 1964, 35–87.

JACKSON, P. W., and MESSICK, S. Creativity. In P. London and D. Rosenhan, eds., *Foundations of abnormal psychology.* New York: Holt, Rinehart and Winston, 1968, pp. 226–250.

JACKSON, R. N. Employment adjustment of educable mentally handicapped ex-pupils in Scotland. *American journal of mental deficiency,* 1968, *72,* 924–930.

JACOB, R. G., O'LEARY, K. D., and PRICE, G. H. Behavioral treatment of hyperactive children: an alternative to medication. Unpublished manuscript. State University of New York, Stony Brook, 1974.

JACOBS, N. The phantom slasher of Tapei: mass hysteria in a non-Western society. *Social problems,* 1965, *12,* 318–328.

JACOBSON, E. *Progressive relaxation.* Chicago: University of Chicago Press, 1938.

JACOBSON, L. I., BERGER, S. E., BERGMAN, R. L., MILLHAM, J., and GREESON, L. E. Effects of age, sex, systematic conceptual learning, acquisition of learning sets and programmed social interaction on the intellectual and conceptual development of preschool children from poverty backgrounds. *Child development,* 1971, *42,* 1399–1415.

JAHODA, M. *Current concepts of positive mental health.* New York: Basic Books, 1958.

JAKOBOVITS, L. A. Mediation theory and the "single-stage" S-R model: different? *Psychological review,* 1966, *73,* 376–381.

JAKOVLJEVIC, V. Transkulturno-psihijatricka proucavanja u Gvineji. *Neuropsihijatrija,* 1963, *11,* 21–38.

JAKUBASCHK, J., and WERNER, J. Reliability of psychiatric diagnoses: a preliminary inquiry. *Psychological abstracts,* 1974, *51,* 669.

JAKUBOWSKI, P. A. Expectancy and the effects of consistent and inconsistent contingent social reinforcement. Unpublished doctoral dissertation, University of Illinois 1968.

JAKUBOWSKI, S. P. Facilitating the growth of women through assertive training. *Counseling psychologist,* 1973, *4,* 23–27.

JAMES, B. Case of homosexuality treated by aversion therapy. *British medical journal,* 1962, *1,* 768–770.

JANET, P., *The mental state of hystericals.* New York: Putnam, 1901.

JANET, P. *The major symptoms of hysteria.* New York: Macmillan, 1920.

JANKOWSKI, K., GRZESIUK, L., and MARKIEWICZ, L. Psychophysiological aftereffects of prolonged stay in psychiatric hospital. Warsaw, Poland: State Sanatorium for Nervous Diseases, 1970.

JARVIK, L. F., KLODIN, V., and MABSUYAMA, S. S. Human aggression and the extra Y chromosome: fact or fantasy? *American psychologist,* 1973, *28,* 674–682.

JELLINEK, E. M. *The disease concept of alcoholism.* New Haven: Hillhouse Press, 1960.

JENKINS, R. L. Diagnoses, dynamics, and treatment in child psychiatry. In R. L. Jenkins and J. O. Cole, eds., Diagnostic classification in child psychiatry. *Psychiatric research report No. 18,* 1964, 91–120.

JERSILD, A. T., and HOLMES, F. B. Methods of overcoming children's fears. *Journal of psychology,* 1935, *1,* 75–104.

JESNESS, C. F., and DeRISI, W. J. Some variations in techniques of contingency management in a school for delinquents. In J. S. Stumphauzer, ed., *Behavior therapy with delinquents.* Springfield, Ill.: Charles C Thomas, 1973, pp. 196–235.

JOHNS, J. H., and QUAY, H. C. The effect of social reward on verbal conditioning in psychopathic and neurotic military offenders. *Journal of consulting psychology,* 1962, *26,* 217–220.

JOHNSON, C. D., and GORMLY, J. Achievement, sociability, and task importance in relation to academic cheating. *Psychological reports,* 1971, *28,* 302.

JOHNSON, D. M. The "phantom anesthetist" of Mattoon: a field study of mass hysteria. *Journal of abnormal and social psychology,* 1945, *40,* 175–186.

JOHNSON, F. G. LSD in the treatment of alcoholism. *American journal of psychiatry,* 1969, *126,* 481–487.

JOHNSON, R. C., ACKERMAN, J. M., FRANK, H., and FIONDA, A. J. Resistance to temptation, guilt following yielding, and psychopathology. *Journal of consulting and clinical psychology,* 1968, *32,* 169–175.

JOHNSON, R. C., DOKECKI, P. R., and MOWRER, O. H., eds., *Conscience, contract, and social reality: theory and research in behavioral science.* New York: Holt, Rinehart and Winston, 1972.

JOHNSON, R. C., and KALAFAT, J. D. Projective and sociometric measures of conscience development. *Child development,* 1969, *40,* 655.

JOHNSON, R. J. Operant reinforcement of an autonomic response. *Dissertation abstracts,* 1963, *24,* 1255–1256.

JOHNSON, S. M., and SECHREST, L. Comparison of

desensitization and progressive relaxation in treating test anxiety. *Journal of consulting and clinical psychology,* 1968, *32,* 280–286.

JOHNSON, W. *Stuttering in children and adults: thirty years of research at the University of Iowa.* Minneapolis: University of Minnesota Press, 1965.

JOHNSTON, M. K., KELLEY, C. S. HARRIS, F. R., and WOLF, M. M. An application of reinforcement principles to development of motor skills of a young child. *Child development,* 1966, *37,* 379–387.

JOHNSTON, N., SAVITZ, L., and WOLFGANG, M. E. *The sociology of punishment and correction.* New York: Wiley, 1962.

JONES, E. *The life and work of Sigmund Freud.* Vol. 1. New York: Basic Books, 1953.

JONES, E. *The life and work of Sigmund Freud.* Vol. 2. New York: Basic Books, 1955.

JONES, H. *Crime in a changing society.* Baltimore: Penguin, 1967.

JONES, H. G. The application of conditioning and learning techniques to the treatment of a psychiatric patient. *Journal of abnormal and social psychology,* 1956, *52,* 414–420.

JONES, H. G. Continuation of Yates' treatment of a tiqueur. In H. J. Eysenck, ed., *Behaviour therapy and the neuroses.* New York: Pergamon, 1960a, pp. 250–258.

JONES, H. G. The behavioural treatment of enuresis nocturna. In H. J. Eysenck, ed., *Behaviour therapy and the neuroses.* New York: Pergamon, 1960b, pp. 377–403.

JONES, K., and SIDEBOTHAM, R. *Mental hospitals at work.* London: Routledge & Kegan Paul, 1962.

JONES, K. L., SHAINBERG, L. W., and BYER, C. O. *Drugs and alcohol.* New York: Harper & Row, 1969.

JONES, M. *The therapeutic community.* New York: Basic Books, 1953.

JONES, M. *Beyond the therapeutic community: social learning and social psychiatry.* New Haven: Yale University Press, 1968.

JONES, M. C. A laboratory study of fear: the case of Peter. *Pediatrics seminar,* 1924a, *31,* 308–315.

JONES, M. C. The elimination of children's fears. *Journal of experimental psychology,* 1924b, *7,* 382–390.

JONES, N. F., and KAHN, M. W. Patient attitudes as related to social class and other variables concerned with hospitalization. *Journal of consulting psychology,* 1964, *28,* 403–408.

JONES, N. F., and KAHN, M. W. Dimensions and consistency of clinical judgment as related to the judges' level of training. *Journal of nervous and mental disease,* 1966, *142,* 19–24.

JONES, R. A. Volunteering to help: the effects of choice, dependence, and anticipated dependence. *Journal of personality and social psychology,* 1970, *14,* 121–129.

JONES, R. J., and AZRIN, N. H. Behavioral engineering: stuttering as a function of stimulus duration during speech synchronization. *Journal of applied behavior analysis,* 1969, *2,* 223–229.

JONES, S. E., and AIELLO, J. R. Proxemic behavior of black and white first- third- and fifth-grade children. *Journal of personality and social psychology,* 1973, *25,* 21–27.

JORDAN, B. T., and KEMPLER, B. Hysterical personality: an experimental investigation of sex-role conflict. *Journal of abnormal psychology,* 1970, *75,* 172–176.

JOURARD, S. M., and FRIEDMAN, R. Experimenter-subject "distance" and self-disclosure. *Journal of personality and social psychology,* 1970, *15,* 278–282.

JOURARD, S. M., and JOFFE, P. E. Influence of an interviewer's disclosure on the self-disclosing behavior of interviewees. *Journal of counseling psychology,* 1970, *17,* 252–257.

JUDSON, H. F. The British and heroin. *The New Yorker,* Sept. 24 and Oct. 1, 1973.

KADUSHIN, C. *Why people go to psychiatrists.* New York: Atherton, 1969.

KAHANA, B., and KAHANA, E. Changes in mental status of elderly patients in age-integrated and age-segregated hospital milieus. *Journal of abnormal psychology,* 1970, *75,* 177–181.

KAHN, E. J. Verbal conditioning of positive and negative self-reference statements under three types of experimenter intervention. *Proceedings of the 75th annual convention of the American Psychological Association,* 1967, 257–258.

KAHN, M., and BAKER, B. Desensitization with minimal therapist contact. *Journal of abnormal psychology,* 1968, *73,* 198–200.

KAHN, M., BAKER, B. L., and WEISS, J. M. Treatment of insomnia by relaxation training. *Journal of abnormal psychology,* 1968, *73,* 556–558.

KAHN, R. L. Implications of organizational research for community mental health. In J. W. Carter, Jr., ed., *Research contributions from psychology to community mental health.* New York: Behavioral publications, 1968, pp. 60–74.

KAHN, R. L., and PERLIN, S. Dwelling-unit density and use of mental health services. *Proceedings of the 75th annual convention of the American Psychological Association,* 1967, 175–176.

KALE, R. J., KAYE, J. H., WHELAN, P. A., and HOPKINS, B. L. The effects of reinforcement on the modification, maintenance and generalization of social responses of mental patients. *Journal of applied behavior analysis*, 1968, *1*, 307–314.

KALES, A., and KALES, J. Evaluation, diagnosis, and treatment of clinical conditions related to sleep. *Journal of the American medical association*, 1972, *213*, 2229–2235.

KALINOWSKY, L. B., and HOCH, P. H. *Shock treatments and other somatic procedures in psychiatry*. New York: Grune & Stratton, 1946.

KALINOWSKY, L. B., and HOCH, P. H. *Somatic treatment in psychiatry: pharmacotherapy, convulsive, insulin, surgical and other methods*. New York: Grune & Stratton, 1961.

KALISH, H. I. Behavior therapy. In B. B. Wolman, ed., *Handbook of clinical psychology*. New York: McGraw-Hill, 1965.

KALISH, R. A. Suicide: an ethnic comparison. Hawaii: *Bulletin of suicidology*, in press.

KALLMANN, F. J. The genetic theory of schizophrenia: an analysis of 691 twin index families. *American journal of psychiatry*, 1946, *103*, 309–322.

KALLMANN, F. J. *Heredity in health and mental disorder*. New York: Norton, 1953.

KAMIN, L. J. Heredity, intelligence, politics, and psychology. Unpublished manuscript, Princeton University, 1973.

KAMMAN, G. F., LUCERO, R. J., MEYER, B. T., and RECHTSCHAFFEN, A. Critical evaluation of a total push program for regressed schizophrenics in a state hospital. *Psychiatric quarterly*, 1954, *28*, 650–667.

KANFER, F. H. Issues and ethics in behavior manipulation. *Psychological reports*, 1965a, *16*, 187–196.

KANFER, F. H. Vicarious human reinforcement: a glimpse into the black box. In L. Krasner and L. P. Ullmann, eds., *Research in behavior modification*. New York: Holt, 1965b, pp. 3–40, 244–267.

KANFER, F. H. Behavior modification: an overview. In C. E. Thoresen, ed., *Behavior modification in education*. National Society for the Study of Education, 72nd Yearbook. Chicago: University of Chicago Press, 1973.

KANFER, F. H., and DUERFELDT, P. H. Comparison of self-reward and self-criticism as a function of types of prior external reinforcement. *Journal of personality and social psychology*, 1968, *8*, 261–278.

KANFER, F. H., and GOLDFOOT, D. A. Self-control and tolerance of noxious stimulation. *Psychological reports*, 1966, *18*, 79–85.

KANFER, F. H., and MARSTON, A. R. Conditioning of self-reinforcing responses: an analogue to self-confidence training. *Psychological reports*, 1963a, *13*, 63–70.

KANFER, F. H., and MARSTON, A. R. Determinants of self-reinforcement in human learning. *Journal of experimental psychology*, 1963b, *66*, 245–254.

KANFER, F. H., and NEWMAN, A. Self-attribution of false emotional feedback and observational learning, in press.

KANFER, F. H., and SASLOW, G. Behavioral analysis. *Archives of general psychiatry*, 1965, *12*, 529–539.

KANFER, F. H., and SASLOW, G. Behavioral diagnosis. In C. M. Franks, ed., *Behavior therapy: appraisal and status*. New York: McGraw-Hill, 1969, 417–444.

KANFER, F. H., and SEIDNER, M. L. Self-control: factors enhancing tolerance of noxious stimulation. *Journal of personality and social psychology*, 1973, *25*, 381–389.

KANNER, L. Autistic disturbances of affective contact. *Nervous child*, 1943, *2*, 217–250.

KANNER, L. Behavior disorders in childhood. In J. McV. Hunt, ed., *Personality and the behavior disorders*. Vol. 2. New York: Ronald Press, 1944, 761–793.

KANNER, L. *Child psychiatry*. 3rd ed. Springfield, Ill.: C. C. Thomas, 1957.

KANNER, L. Emotionally disturbed children: a historical review. *Child development*, 1962, *33*, 97–102.

KANNER, L. *A history of the care and study of the mentally retarded*. Springfield, Ill.: C. C. Thomas, 1964.

KANNER, L., RODRIGUEZ, A., and ASHENDEN, B. How far can autistic children go in matters of social adaptation? *Journal of autism and childhood schizophrenia*, 1972, *2*, 9–33.

KANOUSE, D. E. *Language, labeling, and attribution*. Morristown, N. J.: General Learning Press, 1971.

KANOWITZ, L. *Women and the law: the unfinished revolution*. Albuquerque: University of New Mexico Press, 1969.

KANT, H. S., and GOLDSTEIN, M. J. Pornography. *Psychology today*, 1970, *4*, 58–61, 76.

KANTOR, R. E., WALLNER, J. M., and WINDER, C. L. Process and reactive schizophrenia. *Journal of consulting psychology*, 1953, *17*, 157–162.

KANTOR, R. E., and WINDER, C. L. The process-reactive continuum: a theoretical proposal. *Journal of nervous and mental disease*, 1959, *129*, 429–434.

KANTOROVICH, N. An attempt at associative-reflex therapy in alcoholism. *Psychological abstracts*, 1930, *4*, 493.

KAPLAN, B., ed., *The inner world of mental illness*. New York: Harper and Row, 1964.

KAPLAN, B. J. Malnutrition and mental deficiency. *Psychological bulletin*, 1972, *78*, 321–334.

KAPLAN, H. I., and KAPLAN, H. S. Current theoretical concepts in psychomatic medicine. *American journal of psychiatry*, 1959, *115*, 1091–1096.

KAPLAN, H. I., and SADOCK, B. J. The status of the paranoid today: his diagnosis, prognosis and treatment. *Psychiatric quarterly*, 1971, *45*, 528–541.

KAPLAN, J. A legal look at pro-social behavior: what can happen for failing to help or trying to help someone. In L. G. Wispe, ed., *Positive forms of social behavior, the journal of social issues*, 1972, *28*, 219–226.

KAPP, F. T., ROSENBAUM, M., and ROMANO, J. Psychological factors in men with peptic ulcer. *American journal of psychiatry*, 1946, *103*, 700–704.

KARACKI, L., and LEVINSON, R. B. A token economy in a correctional institution for youthful offenders. *The Howard journal of penology and crime prevention*, 1970, *13*, 20–30.

KAREN, R. L., and MAXWELL, S. J. Strengthening self-help behavior in the retardate. *American journal of mental deficiency*, 1967, *71*, 546–550.

KARKALAS, Y., and HARBANS, L. A double-blind comparison with placebo. *Psychosomatics*, 1970, *11*, 107–111.

KARKALAS, Y., and LAL, H. Imiyramine pamoate in hospitalized depressives: a double-bind comparison with placebo. *Psychosomatics*, 1970, *11*, 107–111.

KARPMAN, B. On the need of separating psychopathy into two distinct clinical types: the symptomatic and the idiopathic. *Journal of criminal psychopathology*, 1941, *3*, 112–137.

KASL, S. V., and SCHLINGENSLIEPEN, W. Effects of educational discrepancy in parents on self-reported mental health of male college students. *Journal of clinical psychology*, 1970, *26*, 64–65.

KASPRISIN-BURRELLI, A., EGOLF, D. B., and SHAMES, G. H. A comparison of parental verbal behavior with stuttering and nonstuttering children. *Journal of communication disorders*, 1972, *5*, 335–346.

KASS, L. R. Death as an event: a commentary on Robert Morison. *Science*, 1971, *173*, 798–702.

KASTENBAUM, R. Wine and fellowship in aging: an exploratory action program. *Journal of human relations*, 1965, *13*, 266–277.

KATAHN, M., STRENGER, S., and CHERRY, N. Group counseling and behavior therapy with test-anxious college students. *Journal of consulting psychology*, 1966, *30*, 544–549.

KATCHADOURIAN, H. A., and LUNDE, D. T. *Fundamentals of human sexuality*. New York: Holt, Rinehart and Winston, 1972.

KATKIN, E. S. *Instrumental autonomic conditioning*. Morristown, N. J.: General Learning Press, 1971.

KATKIN, E. S., and MURRAY, E. N. Instrumental conditioning of automatically mediated behavior: theoretical and methodological issues. *Psychological Bulletin*, 1968, *70*, 52–68.

KATZ, R. Case conference: rapid development of activity in a case of chronic passivity. *Journal of behavior therapy and experimental psychiatry*, 1971, *2*, 187–193.

KATZ, R. C. Interactions between the facilitative and inhibitory effects of a punishing stimulus in the control of children's hitting behavior. *Child development*, 1971, *42*, 1433–1446.

KAUFMAN, K. F., and O'LEARY, K. D. Reward, cost, and self-evaluation procedures for disruptive adolescents in a psychiatric hospital school. *Journal of applied behavior analysis*, 1972, *5*, 293–309.

KAUFMAN, L. N. The development of a proverb scale for the measurement of thinking pathology in schizophrenia and a further investigation of the process-reactive dimension. Unpublished master's thesis. University of Illinois, 1960.

KAUFMAN, M. E. The formation of a learning set in institutional and noninstitutional children. *American journal of mental deficiency*, 1963, *67*, 601–605.

KAUFMAN, M. E. The effects of institutionalization on development of stereotyped and social behaviors in mental defectives. *American journal of mental deficiency*, 1967, *71*, 581–585.

KAZDIN, A. E. Role of instructions and reinforcement in behavior change in token reinforcement programs. *Journal of educational psychology*, 1973, *64*, 63–71.

KAZDIN, A. E. Self-monitoring and behavior change. In M. J. Mahoney and C. E. Thoresen, eds., *Self-control: power to the person*. Monterey, Calif.: Brooks/Cole, 1974, 218–246.

KAZDIN, A. E. Effects of covert modeling and model reinforcement on assertive behavior. *Journal of abnormal psychology*, in press.

KAZDIN, A. E., and BOOTZIN, R. R. The token economy: an evaluative review. *Journal of applied behavior analysis*, 1972, *5*, 343–372.

KAZDIN, A. E., and BRYAN, J. H. Competence and volunteering. *Journal of experimental social psychology*, 1971, *7*, 87–97.

KAZDIN, A. E., and POLSTER, R. Intermittent token reinforcement and response maintenance in extinction. *Behavior therapy*, 1973, *4*, 386–391.

KEANE, D. A survey of the graduates of a residential school for the retarded. *Australian journal of mental retardation*, 1972, *2*, 127–131.

KEASEY, C. B. Experimentally induced changes in moral opinions and reasoning. *Journal of personality and social psychology*, 1973, *26*, 30–38.

KEEHN, J. D. Brief case-report: reinforcement

therapy of incontinence. *Behaviour research and therapy*, 1965, *2*, 239.

KEEHN, J. D. Translating behavioral research into practical terms for alcoholism. *Canadian psychologist*, 1969, *10*, 438-446.

KEEHN, J. D. Reinforcement of alcoholism: schedule control of solitary drinking. *Quarterly journal of studies on alcohol*, 1970, *31*, 28-39.

KEEHN, J. D., KUECHLER, H. A., and WILKINSON, D. Behavior therapy in a transactional context: the case of a blind drunk. *American journal of mental deficiency*, 1973, *77*, 147-149.

KEITH-LEE, P., and SPIEGEL, D. E. The relationships between perceived hostility in cartoons and acting-out behavior among psychotic, criminal, and normal women. Paper read at Western Psychological Association Convention, 1966.

KELLAM, A. M. P. Shoplifting treated by aversion to a film. *Behaviour research and therapy*, 1969, *7*, 125-127.

KELLERT, S. R. The lost community in community psychiatry. *Psychiatry*, 1971, *34*, 168-179.

KELLEY, H. H., CONDRY, J. C., DAHLKE, A. E., and HILL, A. H. Collective behavior in a simulated panic situation. *Journal of experimental social psychology*, 1965, *1*, 20-54.

KELLEY, H. H. Attribution theory in social psychology. *Nebraska symposium on motivation*, 1967, *15*, 192-238.

KELLY, F. D. Communicational significance of therapist proxemic. *Journal of consulting and clinical psychology*, 1972, *39*, 345.

KELLY, F. S., FARINA, A., and MOSHER, D. L. Ability of schizophrenic women to create a favorable or unfavorable impression on an interviewer. *Journal of consulting and clinical psychology*, 1971, *36*, 404-409.

KELLY, G. A. *The psychology of personal constructs*. 2 vols. New York: Norton, 1955.

KEMPE, C. H., SILVERMAN, F. N., STEELE, B. F., DROEGEMUELLER, W., and SILVER, H. K. The battered child syndrome. *Journal of the American medical association*, 1962, *181*, 17-24.

KENDALL, R. E. The classification of depressive illness: the uses and limitations of multivariate analysis. *Psychiatria, neurologia, neurochiurgia*, 1969, *72*, 207-216.

KENDIG, I., and RICHMOND, W. V. *Psychological studies in dementia praecox*. Ann Arbor: Edwards, 1940.

KENDRICK, S. R., and MCCULLOUGH, J. P. Sequential phrases of covert reinforcement and covert sensitization in the treatment of homosexuality. *Journal of behavior therapy and experimental psychiatry*, 1972, *3*, 229-231.

KENNARD, E. A. Psychiatry, administrative psychiatry, administration: a study of a veterans hospital. In M. Greenblatt, D. J. Levinson, and R. H. Williams, eds., *The patient and the mental hospital*. Glencoe, Ill.: Free Press, 1957, 36-45.

KENNEDY, R. J. R. *The social adjustment of morons in a Connecticut city*. Hartford, Conn.: State Office Building, 1948.

KENNEDY, W. A. *Intelligence and economics: a confounded relationship*. Morristown, N.J.: General Learning Press, 1973.

KEPNER, E. Application of learning theory to the etiology and treatment of alcoholism. *Quarterly journal of studies on alcohol*, 1964, *25*, 279-291.

KERCHOFF, A. C., and BACK, K. W. The bug. *Psychology today*, 1969, *3*, 46-49.

KERCHOFF, A. C., BACK, K. W., and MILLER, N. Sociometric patterns in hysterical contagion. *Sociometry*, 1965, *28*, 2-15.

KERR, N., and MEYERSON, L. *Learning theory and rehabilitation*. New York: Random House, 1964.

KERR, N., MEYERSON, L., and MICHAEL, J. A. procedure for shaping vocalizations in a mute child. In L. P. Ullmann and L. Krasner, eds., *Case studies in behavior modification*. New York: Holt, 1965, pp. 366-370.

KESSEL, N., and WALTON, H. *Alcoholism*. Baltimore: Penguin, 1965.

KESSEL, P., and MCBREARTY, J. F. Values and psychotherapy: a review of the literature. *Perceptual and motor skills*, 1967, *25*, 669-690.

KESSLER, J. W. *Psychopathology of childhood*. Englewood Cliffs, N.J.: Prentice-Hall, 1966.

KETY, S. S. Recent biochemical theories of schizophrenia. In D. D. Jackson, ed., *The etiology of schizophrenia*. New York: Basic Books, 1960, pp. 120-145.

KETY, S. S., ROSENTHAL, D., WENDER, P. H., and SCHULZINGER. F. Mental illness in the biological and adoptive families of adopted schizophrenics. *American journal of psychiatry*, 1971, *128*, 302-306.

KEUP, W., SETO, T. A., and GONDA, O. Non-specificity of the "gray" spot (indole derivative) in the urine of schizophrenics. *Diseases of the nervous system*, 1970, *31*, 476-478.

KEUTZER, C. S. Behavior modification of smoking: the experimental investigation of diverse techniques. *Behaviour research and therapy*, 1968, *6*, 137-157.

KEUTZER, C. S., LICHTENSTEIN, E., and MEES, H. L. Modification of smoking behavior: a review. *Psychological bulletin*, 1968, *70*, 520-533.

KIESLER, C. A. *The psychology of commitment*. New York: Academic Press, 1971.

KIESLER, C. A., NISBETT, R. E., and ZANNA, M. P. On

inferring one's beliefs from one's behavior. *Journal of personality and social psychology*, 1969, *11*, 321–327.

KIEV, A. Transcultural psychiatry: research problems and perspectives. In S. C. Plog and R. B. Edgerton, eds., *Changing perspectives in mental illness*. New York: Holt, Rinehart and Winston, 1969, pp. 106–128.

KIEV, A. *Transcultural psychiatry*. New York: Free Press, 1972.

KIFNER, J. The drug scene: many students now regard marijuana as a part of growing up. *New York times*, 11 January 1968, p. 18.

KILOH, L. G. Depressive illness. *British medical journal*, 1968, *4*, 813–815.

KIMMEL, E., and KIMMEL, H. D. A replication of operant conditioning of the GSR. *Journal of experimental psychology*, 1963, *65*, 212–213.

KIMMEL, H. D. Instrumental conditioning of autonomically mediated behavior. *Psychological bulletin*, 1967, *67*, 337–345.

KIMMEL, H. D., and HILL, F. A. Operant conditioning of the GSR. *Psychological reports*, 1960, *7*, 555–562.

KIMMEL, H. D., and KIMMEL, E. An instrumental conditioning method for the treatment of enuresis. *Journal of behavior therapy and experimental psychiatry*, 1970, *1*, 121–123.

KIMURA, B. Vergleichende untersuchungen uber depressive erkrankungen in Japan und in Deutschland. *Fortschritte der neurologie und psychiatrie*, 1965, *33*, 202–215.

KIMURA, B. Phanomenologie des schulderlebnisses in einer vergleichenden psychiatrischen sicht. *Aktvelle fragen der psychiatrie und neurologie*, 1967, *6*, 54–65.

KING, C. W. *Social movements in the United States*. New York: Random House, 1956.

KING, G. F. Differential autonomic responsiveness in the process-reactive classification of schizophrenia. *Journal of abnormal and social psychology*, 1958, *56*, 160–164.

KING, G. F., ARMITAGE, S. G., and TILTON, J. R. A therapeutic approach to schizphrenics of extreme pathology: an operant-interpersonal method. *Journal of abnormal and social psychology*, 1960, *61*, 276–286.

KING, S. H. *Perceptions of illness and medical practice*. New York: Russell Sage Foundation, 1962.

KINKEAD, E. *In every war but one*. New York: Norton, 1959.

KINSEY, A. C., POMEROY, W. B., and MARTIN, C. E. *Sexual behavior in the human male*. Philadelphia: Saunders, 1948.

KINSEY, A. C., POMEROY, W. B., MARTIN, C. E., and GEBHARD, P. H. *Sexual behavior in the human female*. New York: Saunders, 1953.

KINTZ, B. L., DELPRATO, D. J., METTEE, D. R., PERSONS, C. E., and SCHAPPE, R. H. The experimenter effect. *Psychological bulletin*, 1965, *63*, 223–232.

KINZEL, A. F. Body-buffer zone in violent prisoners. *American journal of psychiatry*, 1970, *127*, 59–64.

KLEE, G. D. Lysergic acid diethylamide (LSD-25) and ego functions. *Archives of general psychiatry*, 1963, *8*, 461–474.

KLEIN, H. E., and TEMERLIN, M. K. On expert testimony in sanity cases. *Journal of nervous and mental disease*, 1969, *149*, 435–438.

KLEIN, R. D., HAPKIEWICZ, W. G., and RODEN, A. H., eds., *Behavior modification in educational settings*. Springfield, Ill.: Charles G. Thomas, 1973.

KLEINER, R. J., and PARKER, S. Goal-striving, social status, and mental disorder: a research review. *American sociological review*, 1963, *28*, 189–203.

KLEINER, R. J., TUCKMAN, J., and LAVELL, M. Mental disorder and status based on race. *Psychiatry*, 1960, *23*, 271–274.

KLEITMAN, N. *Sleep and wakefulness* (Rev. ed). Chicago: University of Chicago Press, 1963.

KLEMME, H. L. Heart rate response to suggestion in hypnosis. Unpublished manuscript. Topeka, Kansas: V. A. Hospital, 1963.

KLERMAN, G. L. Clinical research in depression. *Archives of general psychiatry*, 1971, *24*, 305–319.

KLERMAN, G. L., SHARAF, M. R., HOLZMAN, M., and LEVINSON, D. J. Sociopsychological characteristics of resident psychiatrists and their use of drug therapy. *American journal of psychiatry*, 1960, *117*, 111–117.

KLIEBHAN, J. M. Effects of goal-setting and modeling on job performance of retarded adolescents. *American journal of mental deficiency*, 1967, *72*, 220–226.

KLINE, N. S. Clinical experience with iproniazid (marsilid). *Journal of clinical and experimental psychopathology*, 1958, *19*, 72–79.

KLINGER, B. I. Effect of peer model responsiveness and length of induction procedure on hypnotic responsiveness. *Journal of abnormal psychology*, 1970, *75*, 15–18.

KLOTZ, J., and SHANTZ, D. W. Cooperative behavior of emotionally disturbed boys as a function of contingent application of social approval. *Journal of behavior therapy and experimental psychiatry*, 1973, *4*, 33–37.

KNIGHT, E. M. A descriptive comparison of markedly aggressive and submissive children. *Smith college studies in social work*. Vol. 4. 1933.

KNIGHT, J. A., FRIEDMAN, T. I., and SULIANTI, J.

Epidemic hysteria: a field study. *American journal of public health*, 1965, *55*, 858–865.

KNOWLES, P. L., PRUTSMAN, T. D., and RADUEGE, V. Behavior modification of simple hyperkinetic behavior and letter discrimination in a hyperactive child. *Journal of school psychology*, 1968, *6*, 157–160.

KOGAN, K. L., and WIMBERGER, H. C. Behavior transactions between disturbed children and their mothers. *Psychological reports*, 1971, *28*, 395–404.

KOHLBERG, L. The development of children's orientations toward a moral order. *Vita humana*, 1963, *6*, 11–33.

KOHLENBERG, R. J. The punishment of persistent vomiting: a case study. *Journal of applied behavior analysis*, 1970, *3*, 241–245.

KOHLENBERG, R. J. Behavioristic approach to multiple personality: a case study. *Behavior therapy*, 1973, *4*, 137–140.

KOHLENBERG, R., and PHILLIPS, T. Reinforcement and rate of litter depositing. *Journal of applied behavior analysis*, 1973, *6*, 391–396.

KOHN, M. L. Social class and schizophrenia: a critical review and a reformulation. *Schizophrenia bulletin*, 1973, *7*, 60–79.

KOKASKA, C. J. The occupational status of the educable mentally retarded: a review of follow-up studies. *Journal of special education*, 1968, *2*, 369–377.

KOLB, L. C. *Noyes' modern clinical psychiatry.* 7th ed. Philadelphia: Saunders, 1968.

KOMECHAK, M. G. Extinction of vomiting behavior in a retarded child. Duplicated material. Child Study Center, Fort Worth, Texas, 1971.

KOMISAR, L. *The new feminism.* New York: Warner, 1972.

KONDAS, O. Reduction of examination and "stage fright" by group desensitization and relaxation. *Behaviour research and therapy*, 1967, *5*, 275–281.

KONECNI, V. J. Some effects of guilt on compliance. *Journal of personality and social psychology*, 1972, *23*, 30–32.

Koos, E. L. *The health of Regionville.* New York: Columbia University Press. 1954.

KOPEL, S. A., and ARKOWITZ, H. S. Role playing as a source of self-observation and behavior change. *Journal of personality and social psychology*, 1974, *29*, 677–686.

KOTTKE, L. The aged are mobilizing here. *Chicago daily news*, 30 November 1970, p. 15.

KRAEPELIN, E. *Lectures on clinical psychiatry.* Translated, revised, and edited by Thomas Johnstone. London: Bailliere, Tindall and Cox, 1904.

KRAEPELIN, E. *Textbook of psychiatry.* 8th ed. New York: Macmillan, 1923.

KRAEPELIN, E. *One hundred years of psychiatry.* New York: Citadel Press, 1972.

KRAFT, T. A case of homosexuality treated by systematic desensitization. *American journal of psychotherapy*, 1967, *21*, 815–821.

KRAFT, T. Successful treatment of a case of chronic barbiturate addiction. *British journal of addiction*, 1969, *64*, 115–120.

KRAFT, T. Treatment of compulsive shoplifting by altering social contingencies. *Behaviour research and therapy*, 1970a, *8*, 393–394.

KRAFT, T. Treatment of drinamyl addiction. *Journal of nervous and mental disease*, 1970b, *156*, 138–144.

KRAFT, T. Social anxiety model of alcoholism. *Perceptual and motor skills*, 1971, *33*, 797–798.

KRAFT, T., and AL-ISSA, I. Alcoholism treated by desensitization: a case study. *Behaviour research and therapy*. 1967a, *5*, 69–70.

KRAFT, T., and AL-ISSA, I. Behavior therapy and the treatment of frigidity. *American journal of psychotherapy*, 1967b, *21*, 116–120.

KRAFT, T., and AL-ISSA, I. The use of methohexitone sodium in the systematic desensitization of premature ejaculation. *British journal of psychiatry*, 1968, *114*, 351–352.

KRAINES, S. H. *The therapy of the neuroses and psychoses.* Philadelphia: Lea and Febiger, 1948.

KRAMER, J. C. Introduction to the problem of heroin addiction in America. *Journal of psychodelic drugs*, 1971, *4*, 15–22.

KRAMER, J. C. Controlling narcotics in America. Part two: medicine or the law? *Drug forum*, 1972, *1*, 153–167.

KRAMER, M. Introduction: the historical background of ICD-8. In *DSM-II*. Washington, D.C.: American Psychiatric Association, 1968, pp. xi–xv.

KRAMER, T. J., and RILLING, M. Differential reinforcement of low rates: a selective critique. *Psychological bulletin*, 1970, *74*, 225–254.

KRAPFL, J. E., and NAWAS, M. M. Client-therapist relationship factor in systematic desensitization. *Journal of consulting and clinical psychology*, 1969, *33*, 435–439.

KRASNER, L. Personality differences between patients classified as psychosomatic and as non-psychosomatic. *Journal of abnormal and social psychology*, 1953, *48*, 190–198.

KRASNER, L. The use of generalized reinforcers in psychotherapy research. *Psychological reports*, 1955, *1*, 19–25.

KRASNER, L. A technique for investigating the relationship between the behavior cues of the examiner and the verbal behavior of the patient. *Journal of consulting psychology*, 1958a, *22*, 364–366.

KRASNER, L. Studies of the conditioning of verbal behavior. *Psychological bulletin*, 1958b, *55*, 148–170.

KRASNER, L. Behavior control and social responsibility. *American psychologist*, 1962a, *17*, 199–204.

KRASNER, L. The therapist as a social reinforcement machine. In H. H. Strupp and L. Luborsky, eds., *Research in psychotherapy*. Vol. 2. Washington, D.C.: American Psychological Association, 1962b.

KRASNER, L. Operant conditioning techniques with adults: from the laboratory to "real life" behavior modification. Paper read at the American Psychological Association Convention, 1965a.

KRASNER, L. Psychotherapy as a laboratory. *Psychotherapy: theory, research and practice*, 1965b, *2*, 104–107.

KRASNER, L. The behavioral scientist and social responsibility: no place to hide. *Journal of social issues*, 1965c, *21*, 9–30.

KRASNER, L. Verbal conditioning and psychotherapy. In L. Krasner and L. P. Ullmann, eds., *Research in behavior modification*. New York: Holt, 1965d, 211–228.

KRASNER, L. Behavior modification research and the role of the therapist. In L. A. Gottschalk and A. H. Auerbach, eds., *Methods of research in psychotherapy*. New York: Appleton, 1966a.

KRASNER, L. The translation of operant conditioning procedures from the experimental laboratory to the psychotherapeutic interaction. Paper read at the American Psychological Association Convention, 1966b.

KRASNER, L. Assessment of token economy programmes in psychiatric hospitals. In N. H. Miller and R. Porter, eds., *Learning theory and psychotherapy*. London: CIBA Foundation, 1968.

KRASNER, L. Behavior modification: values and training. In C. M. Franks, ed., *Assessment and status of the behavior therapies*. New York: McGraw-Hill, 1969.

KRASNER, L., FORD, J. D., HARPIN, R. E., and KRASNER, M. The human behavior lab as an environmental design procedure. In J. D. Krumboltz and C. E. Thoresen, eds., *Behavioral counseling methods*, in press.

KRASNER, L., and HUTCHISON, W. R. Helping people change by designing environments. Unpublished manuscript, 1974, State University of New York at Stony Brook, New York.

KRASNER, L., and KRASNER, M. Token economies and other planned environments. In C. E. Thoresen, ed., *Behavior modification in education*. National Society for the Study of Education, 72nd Yearbook. Chicago: University of Chicago Press, pp. 351–381, 1973.

KRASNER, L., KNOWLES, J. B., and ULLMANN, L. P. Effect of verbal conditioning of attitudes on subsequent motor performance. *Journal of personality and social psychology*, 1965, *1*, 407–412.

KRASNER, L., and ULLMANN, L. P. Variables affecting report of awareness in verbal conditioning. *Journal of psychology*, 1963, *56*, 193–202.

KRASNER, L., and ULLMANN, L. P., eds. *Research in behavior modification*. New York: Holt, Rinehart and Winston, 1965.

KRASNER, L. and ULLMANN, L. P. *Behavior influence and personality*. New York: Holt, Rinehart and Winston, 1973.

KRASNER, L., ULLMANN, L. P., and FISHER, D. Changes in performance as related to verbal conditioning of attitudes toward the examiner. *Perceptual motor skills*, 1964, *19*, 811–816.

KRASNER, L., ULLMANN, L. P. and WEISS, R. L. Studies in role perception. *Journal of general psychology*, 1964, *71*, 367–371.

KRASNER, L., ULLMANN, L. P., WEISS, R. L., and COLLINS, B. J. Responsivity to verbal conditioning as a function of three different examiners. *Journal of clinical psychology*, 1961, *17*, 411–415.

KRAUSS, H. H. Schizophrenia: a self-fulfilling, labeling process. *Psychotherapy: theory, research and practice*, 1968, *5*, 240–245.

KRAUSS, H. H. and KRAUSS, B. J. Cross-cultural study of the thwarting-disorientation theory of suicide. *Journal of abnormal psychology*, 1968, *73*. 353–357.

KRAUSS, H. H., and TESSER, A. Social contexts of suicide. *Journal of abnormal psychology*, 1971, *78*, 222–228.

KREITMAN, N. The reliability of psychiatric diagnosis. *Journal of mental science*, 1961, *107*, 876–886.

KREITMAN, N., SAINSBURY, P., MORRISSEY, J., TOWERS, J., and SCRIVENER, J. The reliability of psychiatric assessment: an analysis. *Journal of mental science*, 1961, *107*, 887–908.

KRINGLEN, E. Discordance with respect to schizophrenia in monozygotic male twins: some genetic aspects. *Journal of nervous and mental disease*, 1964, *138*, 26-31.

KRINGLEN, E. Schizophrenia in twins: an epidemiological-clinical study. *Psychiatry*, 1966, *29*, 172–184.

KROLL, J. A reappraisal of psychiatry in the middle ages. *Archives of general psychiatry*, 1973, *26*, 276–283.

KROP, H. Modification of hyperactive behavior of a brain-damaged, emotionally disturbed child. *Training school bulletin*, 1971, *68*, 49–51.

KRUMBOLTZ, J. D., and THORESEN, C. E. The effect of behavioral counseling in group and individual settings on information-seeking behavior. *Journal of counseling psychology*, 1964, *11*, 324–333.

KRUMBOLTZ, J. D., and THORESEN, C. E., eds., *Behavioral counseling.* New York: Holt, Rinehart and Winston, 1969.

KUBANY, E. S., and SLOGETT, B. B. The role of motivation in test performance and remediation. *Journal of learning disabilities,* 1971, *4,* 426–429.

KUGEL, R. B., and REQUE, D. A. A comparison of Mongoloid children. *Journal of the American medical association,* 1961, *175,* 959–961.

KUHN, T. S. *The structure of scientific revolutions.* 2nd ed. Chicago: University of Chicago Press, 1970.

KUMAR, K., and WILKINSON, J. C. Thought stopping: a useful treatment in phobias of "internal stimuli." *British journal of psychiatry,* 1971, *119,* 305–307.

KUMASAKA, Y. The lawyer's role in involuntary commitment. New York's experience. *Mental hygiene,* 1972 *56,* 21–29.

KURLAND, A. A. Maryland alcoholics: follow-up study 1. *Psychiatric research reports,* March 1968.

KUSHNER, M. Desensitization of a post-traumatic phobia. In L. P. Ullmann and L. Krasner, eds., *Case studies in behavior modification.* New York: Holt, Rinehart and Winston, 1965a, pp. 193–196.

KUSHNER, M. The reduction of a long-standing fetish by means of aversive conditioning. In L. P. Ullmann and L. Krasner, eds., *Case studies in behavior modification.* New York. Holt, Rinehart and Winston, 1965b, pp. 239–242.

KUSHNER, M., and SADLER, M. Aversion therapy and the concept of punishment. *Behaviour research and therapy,* 1966, *4,* 179–186.

KUTNER, L. The illusion of due process in commitment proceedings. *Northwestern university law review,* 1962, *57,* 383–399.

LABRECHE, G., TURNER, J., and ZABO, L. J. Social class and participation in outpatient care by schizophrenics. *Community mental health journal,* 1969, *5,* 394–402.

LACEY, J. I. The evaluation of autonomic responses: toward a general solution. *Annals of the New York Academy of Science,* 1956, *67,* 123–164.

LACEY, J. I. Psychophysiological approaches to the evaluation of psychotherapeutic process and outcome. In E. A. Rubinstein and M. B. Parloff, eds., *Research in psychotherapy.* Washington, D.C.: American Psychological Association, 1959.

LACEY, J. I., BATEMAN, D. E., and VANLEHN, R. Autonomic response specificity. *Psychosomatic medicine,* 1953, *15,* 8–21.

LADRIERE, M., and SZCZEPKOWSKI, T. R. Marijuana: its meaning to a college population. *Journal of psychology,* 1972, *8,* 173–180.

LAFAVE, H. G., STEWART, A. R., GRUNBERG, F., and MACKINNON, A. A. The Weyburn experience: reducing intake as a factor in phasing out a large mental hospital. *Comprehensive psychiatry,* 1967, *8,* 239–248.

LAHEY, B. B., MCNEES, M. P., and MCNEES, M. C. Control of an obscene "verbal tic" through time-out in an elementary classroom. *Journal of applied behavior analysis,* 1973, *6,* 101–104.

LAING, R. D. Is schizophrenia a disease? *International journal of social psychiatry,* 1964, *10,* 184–193.

LAING, R. D. *The politics of experience.* New York: Pantheon, 1967.

LAIRD, J. D. Self-attribution of emotion: the effects of expressive behavior on the quality of emotional experience. *Journal of personality and social psychology,* 1974, *29,* 475–486.

LAKE, R. Twelve steps for alcoholics. *Today's health,* November 1957, *35,* 18–19.

LAKIN, M., and LIEBERMAN, M. A. Diagnostic information and psychotherapists' conceptualization. *Journal of clinical psychology,* 1965, *21,* 385–388.

LAL, H. and LINDSLEY, O. R. Therapy of chronic constipation in a young child by rearranging social contingencies. *Behaviour research and therapy,* 1968, *6,* 484–485.

LAMBERD, W. G. The treatment of homosexuality as a monosymptomatic phobia. *American journal of psychiatry,* 1969, *126,* 512–518.

LAMBO, T. A. Schizophrenic and borderline states. In A. V. S. DeReuck and R. Porter, eds., *Transcultural psychiatry.* Boston: Little, Brown, 1965, 62–75.

LAMONTAGNE, Y., and MARKS, I. M. Psychogenic urinary retention: treatment by prolonged exposure. *Behavior therapy,* 1973, *4,* 581–585.

LAMY, R. E. Social consequences of mental illness. *Journal of consulting psychology,* 1966, *30,* 450–455.

LANDIS, C., and BOLLES, M. M. *Textbook of abnormal psychology.* New York: Macmillan, 1950.

LANG, P. J. The effect of aversive stimuli on reaction time in schizophrenia. *Journal of abnormal and social psychology,* 1959, *59,* 263–268.

LANG, P. J. Behavior therapy with a case of nervous anorexia. In L. P. Ullmann and L. Krasner, eds., *Case studies in behavior modification.* New York: Holt, Rinehart and Winston, 1965a, pp. 217–221.

LANG, P. J. Experimental studies of desensitization psychotherapy. In J. Wolpe, A. Salter, and L. J. Reyna, eds., *The conditioning therapies.* New York: Holt, Rinehart and Winston, 1965b, pp. 38–53.

LANG, P. J., and LAZOVIK, A. D. Experimental desensitization of a phobic. *Journal of abnormal and social psychology,* 1963, *66,* 519–525.

LANG, P. J., LAZOVIK, A. D., and REYNOLDS, D. J. Desensitization, suggestibility and pseudotherapy.

Journal of abnormal and social psychology, 1965, *70*, 395–402.

LANG, P. J., and MELAMED, B. G. Case report: avoidance conditioning of an infant with chronic ruminative vomiting. *Journal of abnormal psychology*, 1969, *74*, 1–8.

LANG, P. J., MELAMED, B. G., and HART, J. A psychophysiological analysis of fear modification using an automated desensitization procedure. *Journal of abnormal psychology*, 1970, *76*, 220–234.

LANG, P. J., STROUFE, L. A., and HASTINGS, J. E. Effects of feedback and instructional set on the control of cardiac-rate variability. *Journal of experimental psychology*, 1967, *75*, 425–431.

LANGSLEY, D. G., MACHOTKA, P., and FLOMENHAFT, K. Avoiding mental hospital admission: a follow-up study. *American journal of psychiatry*, 1971, *127*, 1391–1394.

LANYON, R. I. Behavior change in stuttering through systematic desensitization. *Journal of speech and hearing disorder*, 1969, *34*, 253–260.

LANYON, R. I., and GOODSTEIN, L. D. *Personality assessment.* New York: Wiley, 1971.

LANYON, R. I., MANOSEVITZ, M., and IMBER, R. R. Systematic desensitization: distribution of practice and symptom substitution. *Behaviour research and therapy*, 1968, *6*, 323–329.

LARSEN, D. E., and ABU-LABAN, B. Norm qualities and deviant drinking behavior. *Social problems*, 1968, *15*, 441–450.

LARSEN, K. S., COLEMAN, D., FORBES, J., and JOHNSON, R. Is the subject's personality or the experimental situation a better predictor of a subject's willingness to administer shock to a victim? *Journal of personality and social psychology*, 1972, *22*, 287–295.

LARSON, D. E. An adaptation of the Feldman and MacCulloch approach to treatment of homosexuality by the application of anticipatory avoidance learning. *Behaviour research and therapy*, 1970, *8*, 209–210.

LASAGNA, L., MOSTELLER, F., FELSINGER, J. M., and BEECHER, H. K. A study of the placebo response. *American journal of medicine*, 1954, *16*, 770–779.

LASHLEY, K. S. The human salivary reflex and its use in psychology. *Psychological review*, 1916, *23*, 446–464.

LASKY, D. I., and DOWLING, M. The release rates of state mental hospitals as related to maintenance costs and patient-staff ratio. *Journal of clinical psychology*, 1971, *27*, 272–277.

LASKY, J. J., HOVER, G. L., SMITH, P. A., BOSTIAN, D. W., DUFFENBACK, S. C., and NORD, C. L. Post-hospital adjustment as predicted by psychiatric patients and by their staff. *Journal of consulting psychology*, 1959, *23*, 213–218.

LATANÉ, B., and DARLEY, J. M. Group inhibition of bystander intervention. *Journal of personality and social psychology*, 1968, *10*, 215–221.

LATANÉ, B., and DARLEY, J. M. Social determinants of bystander intervention in emergencies. In J. Macauley and L. Berkowitz, eds., *Altruism and helping behavior.* New York: Academic Press, 1970, pp. 13–27.

LATANÉ, B., and RODIN, J. A lady in distress: inhibiting effects of friends and strangers on bystander intervention. *Journal of experimental social psychology*, 1969, *5*, 189–202.

LATANÉ, B., and SCHACHTER, S. Adrenalin and avoidance learning. *Journal of comparative and physiological psychology*, 1962, *55*, 369–372.

LATTAL, K. A. Contingency management of toothbrushing behavior in a summer camp for children. *Journal of applied behavior analysis*, 1969, *2*, 195–198.

LATTIMORE, R., trans. *The odes of Pindar.* Chicago: University of Chicago Press, Phoenix Books, 1947.

LAUVER, P. J., KELLEY, J. D., and FROEHLE, T. C. Client reaction time and counselor verbal behavior in an interview setting. *Journal of counseling psychology*, 1971, *18*, 26–30.

LAVIN, N. I., THORPE, J. G., BARKER, J. C., BLAKEMORE, C. B., and CONWAY, C. G. Behavior therapy in a case of tranvestism. *Journal of nervous and mental disease*, 1961, *133*, 346–353.

LAWSON, R. B., GREEN, R. T., RICHARDSON, J. S., MCCLURE, G., and PADINA, R. J. Token economy program in a maximum security correctional hospital. *Journal of nervous and mental disease*, 1971, *152*, 199–205.

LAZARUS, A. A. New methods in psychotherapy: a case study. *South African medical journal*, 1958, *32*, 660–663.

LAZARUS, A. A. The elimination of children's phobias by deconditioning. In H. J. Eysenck, ed., *Behaviour therapy and the neuroses.* New York: Pergamon Press, 1960, 114–122.

LAZARUS, A. A. Group therapy of phobic disorders by systematic desensitization. *Journal of abnormal and social psychology*, 1961, *63*, 504–510.

LAZARUS, A. A. The treatment of chronic frigidity by systematic desensitization. *Journal of nervous and mental disease*, 1963, *136*, 272–278.

LAZARUS, A. A. The treatment of a sexually inadequate man. In L. P. Ullmann and L. Krasner, eds., *Case studies in behavior modification.* New York: Holt, Rinehart and Winston, 1965a, 243–245.

LAZARUS, A. A. Towards the understanding and

effective treatment of alcoholism. *South African medical journal*, 1965b, *39*, 736–741.

LAZARUS, A. A., and ABRAMOVITZ, A. The use of "emotive imagery" in the treatment of children's phobias. *Journal of mental science*, 1962, *108*, 191–195.

LAZARUS, A. A., and RACHMAN, S. The use of systematic desensitization in psychotherapy. In H. J. Eysenck, ed., *Behaviour therapy and the neuroses*. New York: Pergamon, 1960, 181–187.

LEAF, W. B., and GAARDER, K. R. A simplified electromyograph feedback apparatus for relaxation training. *Journal of behavior therapy and experimental psychiatry*, 1971, *2*, 39–43.

LEARY, T., and GILL, M. The dimensions and a measure of the process of psychotherapy: a system for the analysis of the content of clinical evaluations and patient-therapist verbalizations. In E. A. Rubinstein and M. B. Parloff, eds., *Research in psychotherapy*. Washington, D.C.: American Psychological Association, 1959.

LEAVITT, H. J. *Managerial psychology*. Rev. ed. Chicago: University of Chicago Press, 1964.

LECKY, P. *Self-consistency*. New York: Island Press, 1945.

LEE, S. D., and TEMERLIN, M. K. Social class, diagnosis, and prognosis for psychotherapy. *Psychotherapy: theory, research, and practice*, 1970, *7*, 181–185.

LEHRMANN, N. S. Follow-up of brief and prolonged psychiatric hospitalization. *Comprehensive psychiatry*, 1961, *2*, 227–240.

LEIDERMAN, P. H., MENDELSON, J. H., WEXLER, D., and SOLOMON, P. Sensory deprivation: clinical aspects. *American medical association archives of internal medicine*, 1958, *101*, 389–396.

LEIFER, R. Community psychiatry and social power. *Social problems*, 1966, *14*, 16–22.

LEIFER, R. *In the name of mental health*. New York: Science House, 1969.

LEIGHTON, A. H. Discussion. In A. V. S. DeReuck and R. Porter, eds., *Transcultural psychiatry*. Boston: Little, Brown, 1965, 83.

LEIGHTON, A. H., LAMBO, T. A., HUGHES, C. C., LEIGHTON, D. C., MURPHY, J. M., and MACKLIN, D. B. *Psychiatric disorder among the Yoruba*. Ithaca, N.Y.: Cornell University Press, 1963a.

LEIGHTON, A. H., LAMBO, T. A., HUGHES, C. C., LEIGHTON, D. C., MURPHY, J. M., and MACKLIN, D. B. Psychiatric disorder in West Africa. *American journal of psychiatry*, 1963b, *120*, 521–527.

LEIGHTON, D. C., HARDING, J. S., MACKLIN, D. B., HUGHES, C. C., and LEIGHTON, A. H. Psychiatric findings of the Stirling County study. *American journal of psychiatry*, 1963a, *119*, 1021–1026.

LEIGHTON, D. C., HARDING, J. S. MACKLIN, D. B., MACMILLAN, A. M., and LEIGHTON, A. H. *The character of danger: Stirling County study*. Vol. 3. New York: Basic Books, 1963b.

LEITENBERG, H. Is time-out from positive reinforcement an aversive event? A review of experimental evidence. *Psychological bulletin*, 1965, *64*, 428–441.

LEITENBERG, H. The use of single case methodology in psychotherapy research. *Journal of abnormal psychology*, 1973, *82*, 87–101.

LEITENBERG, H., AGRAS, S. BUTZ, R., and WINCZE, J. Relationship between heart rate and behavioral change during the treatment of phobias. *Journal of abnormal psychology*, 1971, *78*, 59–68.

LEITENBERG, H., AGRAS, S. W., and THOMSON, L. E. A sequential analysis of the effect of selective positive reinforcement in modifying anorexia nervosa. *Behaviour research and therapy*, 1968, *6*, 111–118.

LEJEUNE, J., GAUTIER, M., and TURPIN, R. Le mongolisme, premier exemple d'aberration autosomique humaine. *Annales génétiques*, 1959, *2*, 41–59.

LEMBERGER, H. SILBERSTEIN, S. D., AXELROD, J., and KOPIN, I. J. Marihuana: studies on the disposition and metabolism of Delta-9-Tetrahydrocannabinol in man. *Science*, 1970, *170*, 1320–1322.

LEMERE, F.. VOEGTLIN, W. L., BROZ, W. R., O'HOLLAREN, P., and TUPPER, W. E. Conditioned-reflex treatment of chronic alcoholism. VII: technique. *Diseases of the nervous system*, 1942, *3*, 243–247.

LEMERT, E. M. *Social pathology*, New York: McGraw-Hill, 1951.

LEMERT, E. M. Paranoia and the dynamics of exclusion, *Sociometry*, 1962, *25*, 2–25.

LEMERT, E. M. *Human deviance, social problems, and social control*. Englewood Cliffs, N.J.: Prentice-Hall, 1967.

LEMKAU, P. V. Alcoholism, a medical and a social problem. *Maryland State medical journal*, 1952, *1*, 467–473.

LEMKAU, P. V., and CROCETTI, G. M. Epidemiology. In A. M. Freedman and H. I. Kaplan, eds., *Comprehensive textbook of psychiatry*. Baltimore: Williams & Wilkins. 1967.

LEMKE, H., and MITCHELL, R. D. Controlling the behavior of a profoundly retarded child. *American journal of occupationl therapy*, 1972, *26*, 261–264.

LENT, J. The application of operant procedures in the modification of behaviors of retarded children in a free social situation. Paper read at Symposium on research on the modification of deviant behavior in children, A.A.A.S. Meeting, Berkeley, California, 1965.

LEON, C. A., CLIMENT, C. E., ESTRADA, H., and JARAMILLO, R. Assessment instruments for studying the prevalence of mental disorder. *Social psychiatry,* 1970, *5,* 212–215.

LEONARD, C. V., and FLINN, D. E. Suicidal ideation and behavior in youthful nonpsychiatric populations. *Journal of consulting and clinical psychology,* 1972, *38,* 366–371.

LERNER, M. J. The desire for justice and reactions to victims. In J. Macaulay and L. Berkowitz, eds., *Altruism and helping behavior.* New York: Academic Press, 1970, 205–229.

LERNER, R. M., SOLOMON, H., and BRODY, S. Helping behavior at a busstop. *Psychological reports,* 1971, *28,* 200.

LESSER, E. Behaviour therapy with a narcotics user: a case report. *Behaviour research and therapy,* 1967, *5,* 251–252.

LESSE, S. Placebo reactions and spontaneous rhythms; their effects on the results of psychotherapy. *Archives of general psychiatry,* 1964, *10,* 497–505.

LESTER, D. Attempts to predict suicidal risk using psychological tests. *Psychological bulletin,* 1970a, *74,* 1–17.

LESTER, D. Social disorganization and completed suicide. *Social psychiatry,* 1970b, *5,* 175–176.

LESTER, D. Suicide and homicide: bias in the examination of the relationship between suicide and homicide rates. *Social psychiatry,* 1971a, *6,* 80–82.

LESTER, D. The evaluation of suicide prevention centers. *International behavioural scientist,* 1971b, *3,* 40–47.

LESTER, D. Self-mutilating behavior. *Psychological bulletin,* 1972, *78,* 119–128.

LESTER, G., and LESTER, D. *Suicide: the gamble with death.* Englewood Cliffs, N.J.: Prentice-Hall, 1971.

LEURET, F. *Traitement moral de la folie.* Paris: J. B. Ballière, 1840.

LEVIN, S. M., HIRSCH, I. S., SHUGAR, G., and KAPCHE, R. Treatment of homosexuality and heterosexual anxiety with avoidance conditioning and systematic desensitization: data and case report. *Psychotherapy: theory, research and practice,* 1968, *5,* 160–168.

LEVINE, D. Rorschach genetic-level and mental disorder. *Journal of projective techniques,* 1959, *23,* 436–439.

LEVINE, E. M. The twist: a symptom of identity problems as social pathology. *Israel annals of psychiatry and related disciplines,* 1966, *4,* 198–210.

LEVINSON, B. L., SHAPIRO, D., SCHWARTZ, G. E., and TURSKY, B. Smoking elimination by gradual reduction. *Behavior therapy,* 1971, *2,* 477–487.

LEVINSON, T., and SERENY, G. An experimental evaluation of "insight therapy" for the chronic alcoholic. *Canadian psychiatric association journal,* 1969, *14,* 143–146.

LEVITT, E. E. The results of psychotherapy with children: an evaluation. *Journal of consulting psychology,* 1957, *21,* 189–196.

LEVITT, E. E. Psychotherapy with children: a further evaluation. *Behaviour research and therapy,* 1963, *1,* 45–51.

LEVITZ, L. S., and ULLMANN, L. P. Manipulation of indications of disturbed thinking in normal subjects. *Journal of consulting and clinical psychology,* 1969, *33,* 633–641.

LEVY, L., and ROWITZ, L. Ecological attributes of high and low mental hospital utilization areas in Chicago. *Social psychiatry,* 1971, *6,* 20–28.

LEVY, M. R., and KAHN, M. W. Interpreter bias on the Rorschach test as function of patients' socioeconomic status. *Journal of projective techniques and personality assessment,* 1970, *14,* 106–112.

LEWIN, K. Group decision and social change. In T. M. Newcomb and E. L. Hartley, eds., *Readings in social psychology.* New York: Holt, Rinehart and Winston, 1947, 330–344.

LEWIN, K., DEMBO, T., FESTINGER, L., and SEARS, P. S. Level of aspiration. In J. McV. Hunt, ed., *Personality and the behavior disorders.* Vol. I. New York: Ronald Press, 1944, 333–378.

LEWINSOHN, P. M., and ATWOOD, G. E. Depression: a clinical-research approach. *Psychotherapy: theory, research and practice,* 1969, *6,* 166–171.

LEWINSOHN, P. M., and GRAF, M. Pleasant activities and depression. *Journal of consulting and clinical psychology,* 1973, *41,* 261–268.

LEWINSOHN, P. M., and LIBET, J. Pleasant events, activity schedules, and depressions. *Journal of abnormal psychology,* 1972, *79,* 291–295.

LEWINSOHN, P. M. LOBITZ, W. C., and WILSON, S. "Sensitivity" of depressed individuals to aversive stimuli. *Journal of abnormal psychology,* 1973, *8,* 259–263.

LEWINSOHN, P. M., and SHAFFER, M. Use of home observations as an integral part of the treatment of depression: preliminary report and case studies. *Journal of consulting and clinical psychology,* 1971, *37,* 87–94.

LEWINSOHN, P. M., WEINSTEIN, M. S., and ALPER, T. A behavioral approach to the group treatment of depressed persons: a methodological contribution. *Journal of clinical psychology,* 1970, *26,* 525–532.

LEWINSOHN, P. M., WEINSTEIN, M. S., and SHAW, D. A. Depression, a clinical–research approach. In R. D. Rubin and C. M. Franks, eds., *Advances in behavior therapy, 1968.* New York. Academic Press, 1969.

LEWIS, A. Paranoia and paranoid: a historical perspective. *Psychological medicine*, 1970, *1*, 5–12.

LEWIS, J. H., and SARBIN, T. R. Studies in pyschosomatics: the influence of hypnotic stimulation on gastric hunger contractions. *Psychosomatic medicine*, 1943, *5*, 125–131.

LEWITTES, D. J., MOSELLE, J. A., and SIMMONS, W. L. Sex role bias in clinical judgments based on Rorschach interpretations. *Proceedings of the 81st Annual Convention of the American Psychological Association*, 1973, *8*, 497–498.

LEY, P. The reliability of psychiatric diagnosis: some new thoughts. *British journal of psychiatry*, 1971, *121*, 41–43.

LIBB, J. W., HOUSE, C., and GREEN, M. Charting and contingency management procedures in a children's home. *Child care quarterly*, 1973, *2*, 113–123.

LIBERMAN, R. P. Aversive conditioning of drug addicts: a pilot study. *Behaviour research and therapy*, 1968, *6*, 229–231.

LIBERMAN, R. P. Behavioural group therapy: a controlled clinical study. *British journal of psychiatry*, 1971, *119*, 535–544.

LIBERMAN, R. P., and RASKIN, D. E. Depression: a behavioral formulation. *Research digest*, 1972, *10*, 41–43.

LIBERMAN, R. P., TEIGEN, J., PATTERSON, R., and BAKER, V. Reducing delusional speech in chronic, paranoid schizophrenics. *Journal of applied behavior analysis*, 1973, *6*, 57–64.

LIDDELL, H. S. Pavlov, the psychiatrist of the future. *Journal of Mt. Sinai Hospital*, 1936, *3*, 101–104.

LIDDELL, H. S. The influence of experimental neuroses on respiratory function. In H. A. Abramson, ed., *Somatic and psychiatric treatment of asthma*. Baltimore: Williams & Wilkins, 1951, 126–147.

LIDDELL, H. S. *Emotional hazards in animals and man*. Springfield, Ill.: C. C. Thomas, 1956.

LIEBERT, R. M., FERNANDEZ, L. E., and GILL, L. Effects of a "friendless" model on imitation and prosocial behavior. *Psychonomic science*, 1969, *16*, 81–82.

LIEBERT, R. M. and ORA, J. P., JR. Children's adoption of self-reward patterns: incentive level and method of transmission. *Child development*, 1968, *39*, 537–544.

LIEBSON, E. Conversion reaction: a learning theory approach. *Behaviour research and therapy*, 1969, *7*, 217–218.

LIEF, H. I. Anxiety reaction. In A. M. Freedman and H. I. Kaplan, eds., *Comprehensive textbook of psychiatry*. Baltimore: Williams & Wilkins, 1967, pp. 857–870.

LIFTON, R. J. Home by ship: reaction patterns of American prisoners of war repatriated from North Korea. *American journal of psychiatry*, 1954, *110*, 732–739.

LIFTON, R. J. "Thought reform" of western civilians in Chinese communist prisons. *Psychiatry*, 1956, *19*, 173–195.

LIFTON, R. J. Chinese communist thought reform. In *Group processes: transactions of the third conference*. New York: Josiah Macy, Jr., Foundation, 1957a, 219–311.

LIFTON, R. J., Thought reform of Chinese intellectuals: a psychiatric evaluation. *Journal of social issues*, 1957b, *13*, 5–20.

LIFTON, R. J. *Thought reform and the psychology of totalism: a study of "brainwashing" in China*. New York: Norton, 1961.

LILLY, J. C. Mental effects of reduction of ordinary levels of physical stimuli on intact, healthy persons. *Psychiatric research reports*, 1956, *5*, 1–9.

LIN, T. Discussion. In A. V. S. DeReuck and R. Porter, eds., *Transcultural psychiatry*. Boston: Little, Brown, 1965, 22.

LINDESMITH, A. L., and STRAUSS, A. A. *Social psychology*. New York: Dryden Press, 1949.

LINDESMITH, A. L., and STRAUSS, A. L. Critique of culture-personality writings. *American sociological review*, 1950, *15*, 587–600.

LINDNER, R. *Rebel without a cause—the hypnoanalysis of a criminal psychopath*. New York: Grune & Stratton, 1944.

LINDSLEY, O. R. Operant conditioning methods applied to research in chronic schizophrenia. *Psychiatric research reports*, 1956, *5*, 118–153.

LINDSLEY, O. R. Characteristics of the behavior of chronic psychotics as revealed by free-operant conditioning methods. *Diseases of the nervous system*, Monograph supplement, 1960, *21*, 66–78.

LINDSLEY, O. R. Direct measurement and functional definition of vocal hallucinatory symptoms. *Journal of nervous and mental disease*, 1963, *136*, 293–297.

LINN, E. L. Agents, timing, and events leading to mental hospitalization. *Human organization*, 1961, *20*, 92–98.

LINN, E. L. The community, the mental hospital, and psychotic patients' unusul behavior. *Journal of nervous and mental disease*, 1968, *145*, 492–499.

LINN, L. S. State hospital environment and rates of patient discharge. *Archives of general psychiatry*, 1970, *23*, 346–351.

LINSKY, A. S. Community structure and depressive disorders. *Social problems*, 1969, *17*, 120–131.

LINSKY, A. S. Theories of behavior and the image of the alcoholic in popular magazines, 1960–1966. *Public opinion quarterly*, 1971, *34*, 573–581.

Linton, R. *The cultural background of personality.* New York: Appleton, 1945.

Lipowski, Z. J. Psychosomatic medicine in a changing society: some current trends in theory and research. *Comprehensive psychiatry,* 1973, *14,* 203–216.

Lipscomb, W. R. Survey measurements of the prevalence of alcoholism. *Archives of general psychiatry,* 1966, *15,* 455–461.

Litman, R. Community action in the prevention of suicide. In L. Yochelson, ed., *Symposium on suicide.* George Washington University School of Medicine, 1967, pp. 142–150.

Little, L. K. Effects of the interpersonal interaction on abstract thinking performance in schizophrenics. *Journal of consulting psychology,* 1966, *30,* 158–164.

Little, S. C., and McAvoy, M. Electroencephalographic studies in alcoholism. *Quarterly journal of studies on alcohol,* 1952, *13,* 9–15.

Liversedge, L. A., and Sylvester, J. D. Conditioning techniques in the treatment of writer's cramp. In H. J. Eysenck, ed., *Behaviour therapy and the neuroses.* New York: Pergamon, 1960, 327–333.

Lloyd, K. E., and Garlington, W. K. Weekly variations in performance on a token economy psychiatric ward. *Behaviour research and therapy,* 1968, *6,* 407–410.

Lloyd, K. E., Russell, H. K., and Garmize, L. M. Operant conditioning in trisomy 18: replication and extension. *Journal of abnormal psychology,* 1970, *75,* 338–341.

Lobb, L. G., and Schaeffer, H. H. Successful treatment of anorexia nervosa through isolation. *Psychological reports,* 1971, *30,* 245–246.

Lobitz, W. C., and LoPiccolo, J. New methods in the behavioral treatment of sexual dysfunction. *Journal of behavior therapy and experimental psychiatry,* 1972, *3,* 265–271.

Loeb, M. B. Role definition in the social world of a psychiatric hospital. In M. Greenblatt, D. J. Levinson, and R. H. Williams, eds., *The patient and the mental hospital.* Glencoe, Ill.: Free Press, 1957.

Loether, H. J. *Problems of aging.* Belmont, Calif.: Dickenson, 1967.

Loew, C. A., and Silverstone, B. M. A program of intensified stimulation and response facilitation for the senile aged. *Gerontologist,* 1971, *11,* 341–347.

Logan, D. L., Kinsinger, J., Shelton, G., and Brown, J. M. The use of multiple reinforcers in a rehabilitation setting. *Mental retardation,* 1971, *9,* 3–6.

Lombroso, C. *Crime, its causes and remedies.* Translated by H. P. Horton. Boston: Little, Brown, 1911.

Lomont, J. F., Gilner, F. H., Spector, N. J., and

Skinner, K. K. Group assertion training and group insight therapies. *Psychological reports,* 1969, *25,* 463–470.

London, P. *The modes and morals of psychotherapy.* New York: Holt, Rinehart and Winston, 1964.

London, P., and Rosenhan, D., eds. *Foundations of abnormal psychology.* New York: Holt, Rinehart and Winston, 1968.

Loney, J. An MMPI measure of maladjustment in a sample of "normal" homosexual men. *Journal of clinical psychology,* 1971, *27,* 486–488.

Loney, J. Background factors, sexual experiences, and attitudes toward treatment in two "normal" homosexual samples. *Journal of consulting and clinical psychology,* 1972, *38,* 57–65.

Long, J. D., and Williams, R. L. The comparative effectiveness of group and individually contingent free time with inner-city junior high school students. *Journal of applied behavior analysis,* 1973, *6,* 465–474.

Loomis, S. D., Bohnert, P. J., and Huncke, S. Prediction of EEG abnormalities in adolescent delinquents. *Archives of general psychiatry,* 1967, *17,* 494–497.

Lorei, T. W. Staff ratings of the relative importance of the consequences of release from or retention in a psychiatric hospital. *Journal of consulting and clinical psychology.* 1970, *34,* 48–53.

Lorenz, M. Expressive behavior and language patterns. *Psychiatry,* 1955, *18,* 355–366.

Lorr, M., and Klett, C. J. Life history differentia of five acute psychotic types. In M. Roff and D. F. Kicks, eds., *Life history research in psychopathology.* Minneapolis: University of Minnesota Press, 1970.

Lorr, M., Klett, C. J., and McNair, D. M. *Syndromes of psychosis.* New York: Pergamon, 1963.

Lorr, M., Wittman, P., and Schanberger, W. An analysis of the Elgin prognostic scale. *Journal of clinical psychology,* 1951, *7,* 260–263.

Losen, S. M. The differential effects of censure on the problem-solving behavior of schizophrenics and normal subjects. *Journal of personality,* 1961, *29,* 258–272.

Loudon, J. B. Social aspects of ideas about treatment. In A. V. S. DeReuck and R. Porter, eds., *Transcultural psychiatry.* Boston: Little, Brown, 1965, 137–161.

Lovaas, O. I. Effect of exposure to symbolic aggression on aggressive behavior. *Child development,* 1961, *32,* 37–44.

Lovaas, O. I., Berberich, J. P. Perloff, B. F., and Schaeffer, B. Acquisition of imitative speech by schizophrenic children. *Science,* 1966a, *151,* 705–707.

Lovaas, O. I., Freitag, G. Gold, V. J., and Kas-

SORLA, I. C. Experimental studies in childhood schizophrenia: analysis of self-destructive behavior. *Journal of experimental child psychology*, 1965, *2*, 67–84.

LOVAAS, O. I., FREITAG, G., KINDER, M. I., RUBENSTEIN, B. D., SCHAEFFER, B., and SIMMONS, J. Q. Establishment of social reinforcers in two schizophrenic children on the basis of food. *Journal of experimental child psychology*, 1966b, *4*, 109–125.

LOVAAS, O. I., FREITAS, L., NELSON, K., and WHALEN, C. The establishment of imitation and its use for the development of complex behaviour in schizophrenic children. *Behaviour research and therapy*, 1967, *5*, 171–181.

LOVAAS, O. I., and KOEGEL, R. L. Behavior therapy with autistic children. In C. E. Thoreson, ed., *Behavior modification in education*. National Society for the Study of Education, 72nd Yearbook. Chicago: University of Chicago, 1973, pp. 230–258.

LOVAAS, O. I., KOEGEL, R., SIMMONS, J. Q., and LONG, J. S. Some generalization and follow-up measures on autistic children in behavior therapy. *Journal of applied behavior analysis*, 1973, *6*, 131–166.

LOVAAS, O. I., SCHAEFFER, B., and SIMMONS, J. Q. Building social behavior in autistic children by use of electric shock. *Journal of experimental research in personality*, 1965, *1*, 99–109.

LOVAAS, O. I., and SIMMONS, J. Q. Manipulation of self-destruction in three retarded children. *Journal of applied behavior analysis* 1969, *2*, 143–157.

LOVELL, W. S. Breath tests for determining alcohol in the blood. *Science*, 1972, *178*, 264–272.

LOVIBOND, S. H. Intermittent reinforcement in behaviour therapy. *Behaviour research and therapy*, 1963a, *1*, 127–132.

LOVIBOND, S. H. The mechanism of conditioning treatment of enuresis. *Behaviour research and therapy*, 1963b, *1*, 17–21.

LOVIBOND, S. H. Aversive control of behavior. *Behavior therapy*, 1970, *1*, 80–91.

LOVIBOND, S. H., and CADDY, G. Discriminated aversive control in the moderation of alcoholics' drinking behavior. *Behavior therapy*, 1970, *1*, 437–444.

LOWIE, R. H. *Social organization*. New York: Rinehart, 1948.

LOWINGER, P., and DOBIE, S. The attitudes of the psychiatrist about his patient. *Comprehensive psychiatry*, 1968, *9*, 627–632.

LOWREY, L. G. Delinquent and criminal personalities. In J. McV. Hunt, ed., *Personality and the behavior disorders*. Vol. 2. New York: Ronald Press, 1944.

LUBORSKY, L., CHANDLER, M., AUERBACH, A. H.,

COHEN, J., and BACHRACH, H. M. Factors influencing the outcome of psychotherapy: a review of quantitative research. *Psychological bulletin*, 1971, *75*, 145–185.

LUCE, G. G., and SEGAL, J. *Sleep*. New York: Coward-McCann, 1966.

LUCKEY, R. E., WATSON, C. M., and MUSSICK, J. K. Aversive conditioning as a means of inhibiting vomiting and rumination. *American journal of mental deficiency*, 1968, *73*, 139–142.

LUDWIG, A. M., MARK, A. J., and HILL, P. A. Chronic schizophrenics as behavioral engineers. *Journal of nervous and mental disease*, 1971, *152*, 31–44.

LUPARELLO, T., LYONS, H. A., BLEECKER, E. R., and MCFADDEN, E. R., JR. Influences of suggestion on airway reactivity in asthmatic subjects. *Psychosomatic medicine*, 1968, *30*, 819–825.

LUTKER, E. R. Treatment of migraine headache by conditioned relaxation: a case study. *Behavior therapy*, 1971, *2*, 592–593.

LUTZKER, J. R. Reinforcement control of exhibitionism in a profoundly retarded adult. *Proceedings of the 81st annual convention of the American Psychological Association*, 1973, *8*, 931–932.

LYERLY, S. B., ROSS, S., KRUGMAN, A. D., and CLYDE, D. J. Drugs and placebos: the effects of instructions upon performance and mood under amphetamine sulphate and chloral hydrate. *Journal of abnormal and social psychology*, 1964, *68*, 321–327.

LYKKEN, D. F. A study of anxiety in the sociopathic personality. *Journal of abnormal and social psychology*, 1957, *55*, 6–10.

LYLE, J. G. The effect of an institution environment upon the verbal development of imbecile children. *Journal of mental deficiency research*, 1959, *3*, 121–128.

LYLE, J. G. The effect of an institution environment upon the verbal development of imbecile children. II: speech and language. *Journal of mental deficiency research*, 1960, *4*, 1–13.

LYONS, R. D. Science's knowledge on the misuse of drugs and how they act is found to lag. *The New York times*, 9 January, 1968, p. 18.

LYNES, R. *The tastemakers*. New York: Harper, 1954.

MACANDREW, C., and EDGERTON, R. B. *Drunken comportment*. Chicago: Aldine, 1970.

MACAULAY, J. R. A shill for charity. In J. Macaulay and L. Berkowitz, eds., *Altruism and helping behavior*. New York: Academic Press, 1970, pp. 43–59.

MACAULAY, J. R. and BERKOWITZ, L., eds., *Altruism*

and helping behavior. New York: Academic Press, 1970.

MacCulloch, M. J., Birtles, C. J., and Feldman, M. P. Anticipatory avoidance learning for the treatment of homosexuality: recent developments and an automatic aversion therapy system. Behavior therapy, 1971, 2, 151–169.

MacCulloch, M. J., Williams, C., and Birtles, C. J. The successful application of aversion therapy to an adolescent exhibitionist. Journal of behavior therapy and experimental psychiatry, 1971, 2, 61–66.

MacCubrey, J. Verbal operant conditioning with young institutionalized Down's Syndrome children. American journal of mental deficiency, 1971, 75, 696–701.

MacDonald, M. L. Teaching assertion: a paradigm for therapeutic intervention. Psychotherapy: theory, research and practice, in press.

MacDonald, M. L., and Butler, A. K. Reversal of helplessness: producing walking behavior in nursing home wheelchair residents using behavior modification procedures. Journal of gerontology, 1974, 29, 97–106.

MacDonald, W. S., Gallimore, R., and MacDonald, G. Contingency counseling by school personnel: an economical model of intervention. Journal of applied behavior analysis, 1970, 3, 175–182.

MacGregor, R., Ritchie, A., Sennano, A., Schuster, F., McDanald, E., and Goolishiam, H. Multiple impact therapy with families. New York: McGraw-Hill, 1969.

MacKay, C. Extraordinary popular delusions and the madness of crowds. 841, 1852. Reprint. New York: Noonday Press, 1962.

Maddi, S. R. The existential neurosis. Journal of abnormal psychology, 1967, 72, 311–325.

Madsen, C. H., Jr. Positive reinforcement in the toilet training of a normal child: a case report. In L. P. Ullmann and L. Krasner, eds., Case studies in behavior modification. New York: Holt, Rinehart and Winston, 1965, pp. 305–307.

Madsen, C. H., Jr., and Ullmann, L. P. Innovations in the desensitization of frigidity. Behaviour research and therapy, 1967, 5, 67–68.

Magaro, P., and Staples, S. Schizophrenic patients as therapists: an expansion of the prescriptive treatment system based upon premorbid adjustment, social class and A-B status. Psychotherapy: theory, research, and practice, 1972, 9, 351–358.

Maher, B. A. Principles of psychopathology. New York: Mc-Graw-Hill, 1966.

Mahl, G. F. Chronic fear and gastric secretion of HCL in dogs. Psychosomatic medicine, 1949, 11, 30–44.

Mahl, G. F. Disturbances and silences in the patient's speech in psychotherapy. Journal of abnormal and social psychology, 1956, 53, 1–15.

Mahl, G. F. Measuring the patient's anxiety during interviews from "expressive" aspects of his speech. Transactions of New York Academy of Sciences, 1959, 21, 249–257.

Mahoney, M. J. The self-management of covert behavior: a case study. Behavior therapy, 1971, 2, 575–578.

Mahoney, M. J., Moura, N. G. M., and Wade, T. C. Relative efficacy of self-reward, self-punishment, and self-monitoring techniques for weight loss. Journal of consulting and clinical psychology, 1973 40, 404–407.

Mahoney, K., Wagenen, R. K., and Meyerson, L. Toilet training of normal and retarded children. Journal of applied behatvior analysis, 1971, 4, 173–181.

Mahrer, A. R., and Mason, D. J. Changes in number of self-reported symptoms during psychiatric hospitalization. Journal of consulting psychology, 1965, 29, 285.

Makarenko, A. S. Road to life. London: Stanley Nott, 1936.

Maletzky, B. M. "Assisted" covert sensitization: a preliminary report. Behavior therapy, 1973, 4, 117–119.

Maley, R. F., Feldman, G. L., and Ruskin, R. S. Evaluation of patient improvement in a token economy treatment program. Journal of abnormal psychology, 1973, 82, 141–144.

Maliver, B. L. The encounter game. New York: Stein and Day, 1973.

Malleson, N. Panic and phobia. A possible method of treatment. Lancet, 1959, 1, 225–227.

Malmo, R. B. Experimental studies of mental patients under stress. In M. L. Reymert, ed., Feelings and emotions. New York: McGraw-Hill, 1950, 169–180.

Malmo, R. B., Davis, J. F., and Barza, S. Total hysterical deafness: an experimental case study. Journal of personality, 1952, 21, 188–204.

Malmo, R. B., and Shagass, C. Physiologic study of symptom mechanisms in psychiatric patients under stress. Psychosomatic medicine, 1949, 11, 25–29.

Mandler, G., Preven, D. W., and Kuhlman, C. K. Effects of operant reinforcement on the GSR. Journal of the experimental analysis of behavior, 1962, 5, 317–321.

Manis, M. Houts, P. S., and Blake, J. B. Beliefs about mental illness as a function of psychiatric status and psychiatric hospitalization. Journal of abnormal and social psychology, 1963, 67, 226–233.

MANN, J. Encounter: a weekend with intimate strangers. New York: Grossman, 1970.

MANN, L., and JANIS, I. L. A follow-up study on the long-term effects of emotional role playing. *Journal of personality and social psychology*, 1968, *8*, 339–342.

MANN, R. A. The behavior therapeutic use of contingency contracting to control an adult behavior problem: weight control. *Journal of applied behavior analysis*, 1972, *5*, 99–109.

MANN, R. A., and MOSS, G. R. The therapetiuc use of a token economy to manage a young and assaultive inpatient population. *Journal of nervous and mental disease*, 1973, *157*, 1–9.

MARCH, J. G., and SIMON, H. A. *Organizations*. New York: Wiley, 1958.

MARCOS, L. R., URCUYO, L., KESSELMAN, M., and ALPERT, M. The language barrier in evaluating Spanish-American patients. *Archives of general psychiatry*, 1973, *29*, 655–659.

MARDONES, R. J. On the relationship between deficiency of B vitamins and alcohol intake in rats. *Quarterly journal of studies on alcohol*, 1951, *12*, 563–575.

MARGOLIN, S. G. Genetic and dynamic psychophysiological processes. In F. Deutsch, ed., *The psychosomatic concept in psychoanalysis*. New York: International Universities Press, 1953, pp. 3–36.

MARGOLIS, P. M., and BONSTEDT, T. What is community psychiatry? *Diseases of the nervous system*, 1970, 31, 251–258.

MARIS, R. W. The sociology of suicide prevention: policy implications of differences between suicidal patients and completed suicides. *Social problems*, 1969, *17*, 132–149.

MARK, J. C. The attitudes of the mothers of male schizophrenics toward child behavior. *Journal of abnormal and social psychology*, 1958, *48*, 185–189.

MARKS, I. M. Aversion therapy. *British journal of medical psychology*, 1968, *41*, 47–52.

MARKS, I. M., and GELDER, M. G. Transvestism and fetishism: clinical and psychological changes during faradic aversion. *British journal of psychiatry*, 1967, *113*, 711–729.

MARKS, I., GELDER, M. and BANCROFT, J. Sexual deviants two years after electric aversion. *British journal of psychiatry*, 1970, *117*, 173–185.

MARKS, I. M., RACHMAN, S., and GELDER, M. G. Methods for assessment of aversion treatment in fetishism with masochism. *Behaviour research and therapy*, 1965, *3*, 253–258.

MARKS, J., SCHALOCK, R., and SONADA, B. Reinforcement versus relationship therapy for schizophrenics. *Proceedings of the 75th annual convention of the American Psychiatric Association*, 1967, 237–238.

MARQUIS, N. Orgasmic reconditioning: changing sexual object choice through controlling masturbation fantasies. *Journal of behavior therapy and experimental psychiatry*, 1970, *1*, 263–271.

MARMOR, J. Psychoanalytic therapy as an educational process. In J. H. Masserman, ed., *Science and psychoanalysis*. Vol. 5, *Psychoanalytic education*. New York: Grune & Stratton, 1962, 286–299.

MARR, J. N., MILLER, E. R., and STRAUB, R. R. Operant conditioning of attention with a psychotic girl. *Behaviour research and therapy*, 1966, *4*, 85–87.

MARRONE, R. L., MERKSAMER, M. A., and SALZBERG, P. M. A short duration group treatment of smoking behavior by stimulus saturation. *Behaviour research and therapy*, 1970, *8*, 347–352.

MARSDEN, G. Content-analysis studies of therapeutic interviews: 1954 to 1964. *Psychological bulletin*, 1965, *63*, 298–321.

MARSELLA, A. J., KINZIE, D., and GORDON, P. Ethnic variations in depression patterns among Americans of Caucasian, Chinese, and Japanese ancestry. Unpublished manuscript, University of Hawaii, presented at Conference III on Culture and Mental Health in Asia and the Pacific, East-West Center, Honolulu, Hawaii, March, 1971.

MARSHALL, G. R. Toilet training of an autistic eight-year-old through conditioning therapy: a case report. *Behaviour research and therapy*, 1966, *4*, 242–245.

MARTIN, B., LUNDY, R. M., and LEWIN, M. H. Verbal and GSR responses in experimental interviews as a function of three degrees of "therapist" communication. *Journal of abnormal and social psychology*, 1960, *60*, 234–240.

MARTIN, F. M., BROTHERSTON, J. H. F., and CHAVE, S. P. W. Incidence of neurosis in a new housing estate. *British journal of preventive and social medicine*, 1957, *11*, 196–202.

MARTIN, G. L., ENGLAND, G., KAPROWSKY, E., and PILEK, V. Operant conditioning of kindergarten-class behavior in autistic children. *Behaviour research and therapy*, 1968, *6*, 281–294.

MARTIN, G. L., ENGLAND, G., KAPROWSKY, E., and PILEK, V. Operant conditioning in dressing behavior of severely retarded girls. *Mental retardation*, 1971, *9*, 24–31.

MARTIN, G. L., and TREFFRY, D. Treating self-destruction and developing self-care with a severely retarded girl: a case study. *Psychological aspects of disability*, 1970, *17*, 125–131.

MARTIN, J. A. The control of imitative and nonimitative behaviors in severely retarded children through "generalized instruction following." *Journal of experimental child psychology,* 1971, *11,* 390–400.

MARTIN, J. M., and FITZPATRICK, J. P. *Delinquent behavior: a redefinition of the problem.* New York: Random House, 1964.

MARTIN, R. R., and HAROLDSON, S. K. The effects of two treatment procedures. *Journal of communication disorders,* 1969, *2,* 115–125.

MARTYN, M. M., and SHEEHAN, J. Onset of stuttering and recovery. *Behaviour research and therapy,* 1968, *6,* 295–307.

MARWIT, S. J. Communication of tester bias by means of modeling. *Journal of projective techniques and personality assessment,* 1969, *33,* 345–352.

MARZAGAO, L. R. Systematic desensitization treatment of kleptomania. *Journal of behavior therapy and experimental psychiatry,* 1972, *3,* 327–328.

MASLING, J. The influence of situational and interpersonal variables in projective testing. *Psychological bulletin,* 1960, *57,* 65–85.

MASLOW, A. H. *Motivation and personality.* New York: Harper, 1954.

MASLOW, A. H. *Toward a psychology of being.* 2nd ed. Princeton, N.J.: Van Nostrand, 1968.

MASSERMAN, J. H., JACQUES, M. G., and NICHOLSON, M. R. Alcohol as a preventive of experimental neuroses. *Quarterly journal of studies on alcohol,* 1945, *6,* 281–299.

MASSERMAN, J. H., and PECHTEL, C. Neuroses in monkeys. *Annals of New York Academy of Science,* 1953, *56,* 253–265.

MASSERMAN, J. H., and YUM, K. S. An analysis of the influence of alcohol on experimental neuroses in cats. *Psychosomatic medicine,* 1946, *8,* 36–52.

MASSIE, H. N., and BEELS, C. C. The outcome of the family treatment of schizophrenia. *Schizophrenia bulletin,* 1972, *6,* 24–36.

MASTERS, J. C. Treatment of "adolescent rebellion" by the reconstruction of stimuli. *Journal of consulting and clinical psychology,* 1970, *35,* 213–216.

MASTERS, J. C., and MILLER, D. E. Early infantile autism: a methodological critique. *Journal of abnormal psychology,* 1970, *75,* 342–343.

MASTERS, J. C., and MORRIS, R. J. Effects of contingent and noncontingent reinforcement upon generalized imitation. *Child development,* 1971, *42,* 385–397.

MASTERS, W. H., and JOHNSON, V. E. *Human sexual response.* Boston: Little, Brown, 1966.

MASTERS, W. H., and JOHNSON, V. E. *Human sexual inadequacy.* Boston: Little, Brown, 1970.

MATEFY, R. E. Operant conditioning procedure to modify schizophrenic behavior: a case report. *Psychotherapy: theory, research, and practice,* 1972, *9,* 226–230.

MATHER, M. D. The treatment of an obsessive-compulsive patient by discrimination learning and reinforcement of decision-making. *Behaviour research and therapy,* 1970, *8,* 315–318.

MATSON, F. W. Humanistic theory: the third revolution in psychology. In F. W. Matson, ed., *Without/within: behaviorism and humanism.* Monterey, California: Brooks/Cole, 1973.

MAUGH, T. H. II. Narcotic antagonists: the search accelerates. *Science,* 1972, *177,* 249–250.

MAUGH, T. LSD and the drug culture: new evidence of hazard. *Research news,* 23 March 1973.

MAUSNER, B., and PIATT, E. S. *Smoking: a behavioral analysis.* Elmsford, N.Y.: Pergamon Press, 1971.

MAWDSLEY, C., and MANC, M. B. Epilepsy and television. *Lancet,* 28 January 1961, pp. 190–191.

MAX, L. W. Breaking up a homosexual fixation by the conditioned reaction technique: a case study. *Psychological bulletin,* 1935, *32,* 734 (abstract).

MAY, E. Drugs without crime: a report on the British success with heroin addiction. *Harper's magazine,* July 1971, 60–65.

MAY, R., ed. *Existential psychology.* New York: Random House, 1961.

MAYER, J. *Overweight.* Englewood Cliffs, New Jersey: Prentice-Hall, 1968.

MAYER, L. Das Verbrechen in Hypnose und seine Auflärungsmethoden. München: Lehmanns, 1937. Cited in M. T. Orne. Antisocial behavior and hypnosis: problems of control and validation in empirical studies. In G. H. Estabrooks, ed., *Hypnosis: current problems.* New York: Harper, 1962.

MAYER, M. P. *The lawyers.* New York: Harper, 1967.

MAYO, C., HAVELOCK, R. G., and SIMPSON, D. L. Attitudes toward mental illness among psychiatric patients and their wives. *Journal of clinical psychology,* 1971, *27,* 128–132.

MAZIK, K., and MACNAMARA, R. Operant conditioning at the training school. *Training school bulletin,* 1967, *63,* 153–158.

MCCARTHY, J. F. The differential effects of praise and censure upon the verbal responses of schizophrenics. *American psychologist,* 1964, *19,* 459 (abstract).

MCCLURE, R. F. Reinforcement of verbal social behavior in moderately retarded children. *Psychological reports,* 1968, *23,* 371–376.

MCCONNELL, O. L. Control of eye contact in an autistic child. Paper read at Southeastern Psychological Association, 1967.

McCord, J., and McCord, W. The effects of parental role model on criminality. *Journal of social issues*, 1958, *14*, 66–75.

McCord, W., and McCord, J. *Psychopathy and delinquency*. New York: Grune and Stratton, 1956.

McCord, W., and McCord, J. *The psychopath: an essay on the criminal mind*. Princeton, N.J.: Van Nostrand, 1964.

McCord, W., McCord, J., and Gudeman, J. *Origins of alcoholism*. Stanford, Calif.: Stanford University Press, 1960.

McCord, W., McCord, J., and Zola, I. *Origins of crime*. New York: Columbia University Press, 1959.

McCullough, T. A. H. Theories of hysteria. *Canadian psychiatric association journal*, 1969, *14*, 635–637.

McDonald, F. J. Behavior modification in teacher education, In C. E. Thoreson, ed., *Behavior modification in education*. National Society for the Study of Education, 72nd Yearbook. Chicago: University of Chicago Press, 1973.

McFall, R. M. Effects of self-monitoring on normal smoking behavior. *Journal of consulting and clinical psychology*, 1970, *35*, 135–142.

McFall, R. M., and Lillesand, D. B. Behavior rehearsal with modeling and coaching in assertion training. *Journal of abnormal psychology*, 1971, *77*, 313–323.

McFall, R. M. and Marston, A. R. An experimental investigation of behavior rehearsal in assertive training. *Journal of abnormal psychology*, 1970, *76*, 295–303.

McFall, R. M., and Twentyman, C. T. Four experiments on the relative contributions of rehearsal, modeling, and coaching to assertion training. *Journal of abnormal psychology*, 1973, *81*, 199–218.

McGarry, A. L., and Kaplan, H. A. Overview: current trends in mental health law. *American journal of psychiatry*, 1973, *130*, 621–630.

McGinn, N., Harburg, E., Julius, S., and McLeod, J. Psychological correlates of blood pressure. *Psychological bulletin*, 1964, *61*, 209–219.

McGinnies, E., and Ferster, C. B., eds. *The reinforcement of social behavior*. Boston: Houghton Mifflin, 1971.

McGoldrick, E. J., Jr. *Management of the mind*. Boston: Houghton, 1954.

McGuigan, F. J. The experimenter: a neglected stimulus object. *Psychological bulletin*, 1963, *60*, 421–428.

McGuigan, F. J. Covert oral behavior and auditory hallucinations. *Psychophysiology*, 1966, *3*, 73–80.

McGuigan, F. J. Covert oral behavior during the silent performance of language tasks. *Psychological bulletin*, 1970, *74*, 309-326.

McGuire, R. J., and Vallance, M. Aversion therapy by electric shock: a simple technique. *British medical journal*, 1964, *1*, 151–153.

McInnis, T. L., and Ullmann, L. P. Positive and negative reinforcement with short- and long-term hospitalized schizophrenics in a probability learning situation. *Journal of abnormal psychology*, 1967, *72*, 157–162.

McKenzie, B., and Day, R.H. Operant learning of visual pattern discrimination in young infants. *Journal of experimental child psychology*. 1971, *11*, 45–53.

McMains, M. J., and Liebert, R. M. Influence of discrepancies between successively modeled self-reward criteria on the adoption of a self-imposed standard. *Journal of personality and social psychology*, 1968, *8*, 166–171.

McManus, M. Group desensitization of test anxiety. *Behaviour research and therapy*, 1971, *9*, 51–56.

McNamara, J. R. The use of self-monitoring techniques to treat nailbiting. *Behaviour research and therapy*, 1972, *10*, 193–194.

McNeil, J. N., Llewellyn, C. E., and McCoullough, T. E. Community psychiatry and ethics. *American journal of orthopsychiatry*, 1970, *40*, 22–29.

McNeil, J. S., and Giffen, M. B. Military retirement: the retirement syndrome. *American journal of psychiatry*, 1967, *123*, 848–854.

McNeill, W. H. *The rise of the west*. New York: Mentor, 1965.

McReynolds, L. V. Application of timeout from positive reinforcement for increasing the efficiency of speech training. *Journal of applied behavior analysis*, 1969, *2*, 199–205.

McReynolds, P. Anxiety, perception and schizophrenia. In D. D. Jackson, ed., *The etiology of schizophrenia*. New York: Basic Books, 1960.

McReynolds, P. Relations between psychological and physiological indices of anxiety. Paper read at Midwestern Psychological Association Convention, 1967.

McReynolds, W. T. Token economy: patient and staff changes. *Behaviour, research and therapy*, 1972, *10*, 29–34.

McReynolds, W. T., and Coleman, J. Token economy: patient and staff changes. *Behaviour research and therapy*, 1972, *10*, 29–34.

McWilliams, S. A., and Tuttle, R. J. Long-term psychological effects of LSD. *Psychological bulletin*, 1973, *79*, 341–351.

Mead, G. H. *Mind, self, and society: from the stand-*

point of a social behaviorist. Chicago: University of Chicago Press, 1934.

MEAD, M. *Sex and temperament in three primitive societies.* New York: Morrow, 1935.

MEALIEA, W. L., JR., and NAWAS, M. M. The comparative effectiveness of systematic desensitization and implosive therapy in the treatment of snake phobia. *Journal of behavior therapy and experimental psychiatry,* 1971, *2,* 85–94.

MEARES, A. *A system of medical hypnosis.* Philadelphia: Saunders, 1960.

MECHANIC, D. Some factors in identifying and defining mental illness. *Mental hygiene,* 1962, *46,* 66–74.

MEDNICK, S. A. A learning theory approach to research in schizophrenia. *Psychological bulletin,* 1958, *55,* 316–327.

MEDNICK, S. A., and SCHULSINGER, F. Factors related to breakdown in children at high risk for schizophrenia. In M. Roff and D. F. Ricks, eds., *Life history research in psychopathology.* Vol. 1. Minneapolis: University of Minnesota Press, 1970, 51–93.

MEDVEDEV, Z., and MEDVEDEV, R. *A question of madness.* New York: Vintage Books, 1972.

MEEHL, P. E. *Clinical versus statistical prediction.* Minneapolis: University of Minnesota Press, 1954.

MEEHL, P. E. Psychotherapy. In C. P. Stone, ed., *Annual review of psychology.* Vol. 6. Stanford, Calif.: Annual Reviews, 1955, pp. 357–378.

MEEHL, P. E. Schizotaxia, schizotypy, schizophrenia. *American psychologist,* 1962, *17,* 827–838.

MEEKER, W. B., and BARBER, T. X. Toward an explanation of stage hypnosis. *Journal of abnormal psychology,* 1971, *77,* 61–70.

MEERLOO, J. A. M. Suicide, menticide, and psychic homicide. *American medical association archives of neurology and psychiatry,* 1959, *81,* 360–362.

MEES, H. L. Sadistic fantasies modified by aversive conditioning and substitution: a case study. *Behaviour research and therapy,* 1966, *4,* 317–320.

MEHLMAN, B. The reliability of psychiatric diagnosis. *Journal of abnormal and social psychology,* 1952, *47,* 577–578.

MEHRABIAN, A. Significance of posture and position in the communication of attitude and status relationships. *Psychological bulletin,* 1969, *71,* 359–372.

MEHRABIAN, A. *Silent messages.* Belmont, Calif.: Wadsworth, 1971.

MEHRABIAN, A., and DIAMOND, S. G. Effects of furniture arrangement, props, and personality on social interaction. *Journal of personality and social psychology,* 1971, *20,* 18–30.

MEICHENBAUM, D. H. Effects of social reinforcement on the level of abstraction in schizophrenics. *Journal of abnormal and social psychology,* 1966a, *71,* 354–362.

MEICHENBAUM, D. H. Sequential strategies in two cases of hysteria. *Behaviour research and therapy,* 1966b, *4,* 89–94.

MEICHENBAUM, D. H. The effects of instructions and reinforcement on thinking and language behaviors of schizophrenics. Unpublished doctoral dissertation, University of Illinois, 1966c.

MEICHENBAUM, D. H. The effects of instructions and reinforcement on thinking and language behavior of schizophrenics. *Behaviour research and therapy,* 1969, *7,* 101–114.

MEICHENBAUM, D. H. Cognitive modification of test anxious college students. *Journal of consulting and clinical psychology,* 1972, *39,* 370–380.

MEICHENBAUM, D. H. Cognitive factors in behavior modification: modifying what clients say to themselves. In R. D. Rubin, J. P. Brady, and J. D. Henderson, eds., *Advances in behavior therapy.* Vol. 4. New York: Academic Press, 1973, pp. 21–36.

MEICHENBAUM, D. H., BOWERS, K. S., and ROSS, R. R. A behavioral analysis of teacher expectancy effect. *Journal of personality and social psychology,* 1969, *13,* 306–316.

MEICHENBAUM, D. H., and CAMERON, R. Training schizophrenics to talk to themselves: a means of developing attentional controls. *Behavior therapy,* 1973, *4,* 515–534.

MEICHENBAUM, D. H., GILMORE, J. B., and FEDORAVICIUS, A. Group insight versus group desensitization in treating speech anxiety. *Journal of consulting and clinical psychology,* 1971, *36,* 410–421.

MEICHENBAUM, D. H., and GOODMAN, J. Reflection-impulsivity and verbal control of motor behavior. *Child development,* 1969, *40,* 785–797.

MEICHENBAUM, D. H., and GOODMAN, J. Training impulsive children to talk to themselves: a means of developing self-control. *Journal of abnormal psychology,* 1971, *77,* 115–126.

MEICHENBAUM, D. H., and SMART, I. Use of direct expectancy to modify academic performance and attitudes of college students. *Journal of counseling psychology,* 1971, *18,* 531–535.

MEISELS, M. and GUARDO, C. J. Development of personal space schemata. *Child development,* 1969, *40,* 1167–1178.

MELLO, N. K., and MENDELSON, J. H. Operator analysis of drinking patterns of chronic alcoholics. *Nature,* 1965, *206,* 43–46.

MELLO, N. K., and MENDELSON, J. H., A quantitative analysis of drinking patterns in alcoholics. *Archives of general psychiatry,* 1971, *25,* 527–539.

MELTZER, L., MORRIS, W. N., and HAYES, D. P.

Interruption outcomes and vocal amplitude: explorations in social psychophysics. *Journal of personality and social psychology*, 1971, *18*, 392–402.

MENDEL, W. M. Tranquilizer prescribing as a function of the experience and availability of the therapist. *American journal of psychiatry*, 1967, *124*, 54–60.

MENDEL, W. M., and RAPPORT, S. Determinants of the decision for psychiatric hospitalization. *Archives of general psychiatry*. 1969, *20*, 321–328.

MENDELS, J. *Concepts of depression*. New York: Wiley, 1970.

MENDELS, J., ed. *Biological psychiatry*. New York: Wiley Interscience, 1973.

MENDELSON, M., HIRSCH, S., and WEBBER, C. S. A critical examination of some recent theoretical models in psychosomatic medicine. *Psychosomatic medicine*, 1956, *18*, 363–373.

MENNINGER, K. A. Foreword. In E. S. Shneidman and N. L. Farberow, eds., *Clues to suicide*. New York: McGraw-Hill, 1957.

MENNINGER, K. The contributions of psychoanalysis to American psychiatry. In B. H. Hall, ed., *A psychiatrist's world*. New York: Viking Press, 1959.

MENNINGER, K. Psychiatrists use dangerous words. *Saturday evening post*, 25 April 1964, pp. 12–14.

MENNINGER, K., with M. MAYMAN and P. PRUYSER. *The vital balance*. New York: Viking Press. 1963.

MERBAUM, M. The modification of self-destructive behavior by a mother-therapist using aversive stimulation. *Behavior therapy*, 1973, *4*, 442–447.

MERBAUM, M., and SOUTHWELL, E. A. Conditioning of affective self-references as a function of the discriminative characteristics of experimenter intervention. *Journal of abnormal psychology*, 1965, *70*, 180–187.

MERCER, J. R. Social system perspective and clinical perspective: frames of reference for understanding career patterns of persons labelled as mentally retarded. *Social problems*, 1965, *13*, 18–34.

MERCER, J. R. IQ: the lethal label. *Psychology today*, 1972, *6*, 44.

MERRENS, M. R., and RICHARDS, W. S. Acceptance of generalized versus "bona fide" personality interpretations. *Psychological reports*, 1970, *27*, 691–694.

MERTENS, G. C., and FULLER, G. B. Conditioning of motor behavior in "regressed" psychotics. I: an objective measure of personal habit training with "regressed" psychotics. *Journal of clinical psychology*, 1963, *19*, 333–337.

MERTENS, G. C., and FULLER, G. B. *Manual for the alcoholic*. Minnesota: Wilmar State Hospital, 1964a.

MERTENS, G. C., and FULLER, G. B. *Manual for the therapist*. Minnesota: Wilmar State Hospital, 1964b.

MERTON, R. K. The self-fulfilling prophecy. *Antioch review*, 1948, *8*, 193–210.

MERTON, R. K. Bureaucratic structure and personality. In R. K. Merton, *Social theory and social structure*. rev. ed. Glencoe, Ill.: Free Press, 1957.

MESSENGER, J. C. Sex and repression in an Irish folk community. In D. S. Marshall and R. C. Suggs, eds., *Human sexual behavior*. New York: Basic Books, 1971, pp. 3–37.

METZ, J. R. Conditioning generalized imitation in autistic children. *Journal of experimental child psychology*, 1965, *2*, 389–399.

METZ, J. R. Conditioning social and intellectual skills in autistic children. In J. Fisher and R. E. Harris, eds., *Reinforcement theory in psychological treatment—a symposium. California mental health research monograph*, 1966, *8*, 40–49.

MEYER, R. G. Delay therapy: two case reports. *Behavior therapy*, 1973, *4*, 709–711.

MEYER, V. The treatment of two phobic patients on the basis of learning principles. *Journal of abnormal and social psychology*, 1957, *55*, 261–266.

MEYER, V., and MAIR, J. M. M. A new technique to control stammering: a preliminary report. *Behaviour research and therapy*, 1963, *1*, 251–254.

MEYERHOFF, H., ed. *The philosophy of history in our time*. Garden City, N.Y.: Doubleday, 1959.

MICHAEL, S. T. The family with problems, social class and the psychiatrist. *International journal of social psychiatry*, 1967, *13*, 93–100.

MICOSSI, A. L. Conversion to women's lib. *Transaction*, 1970, *8*, 89–90.

MIKLICH, D. R. Operant conditioning procedures with systematic desensitization in a hyperkinetic asthmatic boy. *Journal of behavior therapy and experimental psychiatry*, 1973, *4*, 177–182.

MIKULAS, W. L. *Behavior modification: an overview*. New York: Harper & Row, 1972.

MIKULIC, M. A. Reinforcement of independent and dependent patient behaviors by nursing personnel: an exploratory study. *Nursing research*, 1971, *20*, 162–165.

MILBY, J. B., JR. Modification of extreme social isolation by contingent social reinforcement. *Journal of applied behavior analysis*, 1970, *3*, 149–152.

MILES, C. G., CONGREVE, G. R., GIBBONS, R. J., MARSHAM, J., DEVENYI, R., and HICKS, R. C. An experimental pilot study of the effects of daily cannabis smoking on socio-economic behavior. Paper presented at the 30th International Congress on Alcoholism and Drug Dependence, Amsterdam, September 1972.

MILGRAM, S. Behavioral study of obedience. *Journal*

of abnormal and social psychology, 1963, *67,* 371–378.

MILGRAM, S. Some conditions of obedience and disobedience to authority. *Human relations,* 1965, *18,* 57–76.

MILGRAM, S. *Obedience to authority.* New York: Harper & Row, 1974.

MILLER, A. L. Treatment of a child with *Gilles de la Tourette's* syndrome using behavior modification techniques. *Journal of behavior therapy and experimental psychiatry,* 1970, *1,* 319–321.

MILLER, B. A., POKORNY, A. D., VALLES, J., and CLEVELAND, S. E. Biased sampling in alcoholism treatment research. *Quarterly journal of studies on alcohol,* 1970, *31,* 97–107.

MILLER, D., and SCHWARTZ, M. County lunacy commission hearings: some observations of commitments to a state mental hospital. *Social problems,* 1966, *14,* 26–35.

MILLER, D. R. Optimal psychological adjustment: a relativistic interpretation. *Journal of consulting and clinical psychology,* 1970, *35,* 290–295.

MILLER, E. A note on the visual performance of a subject with unilateral functional blindness. *Behaviour research and therapy,* 1968, *6,* 115–116.

MILLER, H., and TRIPODI, T. Information accrual and clinical judgment. *Social work,* 1967, *12,* 63–69.

MILLER, H. R. WISC performance under incentive conditions: case report. *Psychological reports,* 1969, *24,* 835–838.

MILLER, L. K. A note on the control of study behavior. *Journal of experimental child psychology,* 1964, *1,* 108–110.

MILLER, L. R., and MILLER, O. L. Reinforcing self-help group activities of welfare recipients. *Journal of applied behavior analysis,* 1970, *3,* 57–64.

MILLER, N. E. Liberalization of basic S-R concepts: extensions to conflict behavior, motivation and social learning. In S. Koch, ed., *Psychology: a study of a science.* Vol. 2. New York: McGraw-Hill, 1959.

MILLER, N. E. Learning of visceral and glandular responses. *Science,* 1969, *163,* 434–445.

MILLER, N. E., and DICARA, L. Instrumental learning of heart-rate changes in curarized rats: shaping and specificity to discriminative stimulus. *Journal of comparative and physiological psychology,* 1967, *63,* 12–19.

MILLER, P. M. The use of behavioral contracting in the treatment of alcoholism: a case report. *Behavior therapy,* 1972, *3,* 593–596.

MILLER, P. M. Behavioral treatment of drug addiction: a review. *The international journal of the addictions,* 1973, *8,* 511–520.

MILLER, P. M. An experimental analysis of retention control training in the treatment of nocturnal enuresis in two institutionalized adolescents. *Behavior therapy,* 1973, *4,* 288–294.

MILLER, P. M., and BARLOW, D. H. Behavioral approaches to the treatment of alcoholism. *Journal of nervous and mental disease,* 1973, *157,* 10–20.

MILLER, P. M., HERSEN, M., EISLER, R. M., EPSTEIN, L. H., and WOOTEN, L. S. Relationship of alcohol cues to the drinking behavior of alcoholics and social drinkers: an analogue study. *The psychological record,* 1974, *24,* 61–66.

MILLER, R. J., LUNDY, R. M., and GALBRAITH, G. G. Effects of hypnotically-induced hallucinations of a color filter. *Journal of abnormal psychology,* 1970, *76,* 316–319.

MILLER, W. B. The impact of a "total community" delinquency control project. *Social problems,* 1962, *10,* 168–191.

MILLER, W. R., and SELIGMAN, M. E. P. Depression and the perception of reinforcement. *Journal of abnormal psychology,* 1973, *82,* 62–73.

MILLETT, K. *Sexual politics.* Garden City, N.Y.: Doubleday, 1970.

MILLS, J., and MINTZ, P. M. Effect of unexplained arousal on affiliation. *Journal of personality and social psychology,* 1972, *24,* 11–13.

MILLS, K. C., SOBELL, M. B., and SCHAEFER, H. H. Training social drinking as an alternative to abstinence for alcoholics. *Behavior therapy,* 1971, *2,* 17–18.

MINARD, J. G., BAILEY, D. E., and WERTHEIMER, M. Measurement and conditioning of perceptual defense, response bias, and emotionally biased recognition. *Journal of personality and social psychology,* 1965, *2,* 661–668.

MINGE, M. R., and BALL, T. S. Teaching of self-help skills to profoundly retarded patients. *American journal of mental deficiency,* 1967, *71,* 864–868.

MINTZ, A. Non-adaptive group behavior. *Journal of abnormal and social psychology,* 1951, *46,* 150–159.

MISCHEL, W. *Personality and assessment.* New York: Wiley, 1968.

MISCHEL, W. Processes in delay of gratification. In L. Berkowitz, ed., *Advances in experimental social psychology.* Vol. 7. New York: Academic Press, in press.

MISCHEL, W., EBBESEN, E. B., and ZEISS, A. R. Cognitive and attentional mechanisms in delay of gratification. *Journal of personality and social psychology,* 1972, *21,* 204–218.

MISHARA, B. L., and KASTENBAUM, R. Self-injurious behavior and environmental change in the institutionalized elderly. *Aging and human development,* 1973, *4,* 133–145.

MISHLER, E. G., and SCOTCH, N. A. Sociocultural factors in the epidemiology of schizophrenia. *Psychiatry*, 1963, *26*, 315–351.

MISHLER, E. G., and WAXLER, N. E. Decision processes in psychiatric hospitalization: patients referred, accepted, and admitted to a psychiatric hospital. *American sociological review*, 1963, *28*, 576–587.

MISKIMINS, R. W., and WILSON, L. T. The revised suicide potential scale. *Journal of consulting and clinical psychology*, 1969, *33*, 258.

MITCHELL, K. R. A psychological approach to the treatment of migraine. *British journal of psychiatry*, 1971a, *119*, 533–534.

MITCHELL, K. R. A note on treatment of migraine using behavior therapy techniques. *Psychological reports*, 1971b, *28*, 171–172.

MITCHELL, W. S., and STOFFELMAYR, B. E. Application of the Premack principle to the behavioral control of extremely inactive schizophrenics. *Journal of applied behavior analysis*, 1973, *6*, 419–423.

MITFORD, J. *The American way of death*. New York: Simon and Schuster, 1963.

MITHAUG, D. E., and BURGESS, R. L. The effects of different reinforcement contingencies in the development of social cooperation. *Journal of experimental child psychology*, 1968, *6*, 402–426.

MOCKBRIDGE, N. *The scrawl of the wild: what people write on walls and why*. New York: Paperback Library, 1969.

MODELL, A. H., and POTTER, H. W. Human figure drawings of patients with essential hypertension, peptic ulcer, and bronchial asthma. *Psychosomatic medicine*, 1949, *11*, 282–292.

MODIGLIANI, A. Embarrassment, facework, and eye contact: testing a theory of embarrassment. *Journal of personality and social psychology*, 1971, *17*, 15–24.

MOGAN, J., and O'BRIEN, J. S. The counterconditioning of a vomiting habit by sips of gingerale. *Journal of behavior therapy and experimental psychiatry*, 1972, *3*, 135–137.

MOGEL, S., and SCHIFF, W. "Extinction" of a head-bumping symptom of eight years' duration in two minutes: a case report. *Behaviour research and therapy*, 1967, *5*, 131–132.

MOLONEY, J. C. *The battle for mental health*. New York: Philosophical Library, 1952.

MONEY, J. Sexual amorphism and homosexual gender identity. *Psychological bulletin*, 1970, *74*, 425–440.

MONEY, J., and ERHARDT, A. A. *Man and woman, boy and girl*. Baltimore: Johns Hopkins University Press, 1973.

MONSOUR, D. J. Management of chronic alcoholism in the Army. *Bulletin of United States Army medical department*, 1948, *8*, 882–887.

MONTAGU, A. *The anatomy of swearing*. New York: Macmillan, 1967.

MOOD, R. W., JR. Effects of foreknowledge of death in the assessment from case history material of intent to die. *Journal of consulting and clinical psychology*, 1970, *34*, 129–133.

MOORE, M. The treatment of alcoholism. *New England journal of medicine*, 1939, *221*, 489–493.

MOORE, N. Behaviour therapy in bronchial asthma: a controlled study. *Journal of psychosomatic research*, 1965, *9*, 257–276.

MOORE, R., and GOLDIAMOND, I. Errorless establishment of visual discrimination using fading procedures. *Journal of the experimental analysis of behavior*, 1964, *7*, 269–272.

MOORE, R. A., BENEDEK, E. P., and WALLACE, J. G. Social class, schizophrenia and the psychiatrist. *American journal of psychiatry*, 1963, *120*, 149–154.

MOORE, R. F., ALBERT, R. S., MANNING, M. J., and GLASSER, B. A. Explorations in alternatives to hospitalization. *American journal of psychiatry*, 1962, *119*, 560–569.

MOORE, W. H., JR., and RITTERMAN, S. I. The effects of response contingent reinforcement and response contingent punishment upon the frequency of stuttered verbal behavior. *Behavior research and therapy*, 1973, *11*, 43–48.

MORENO, J. L. *Who shall survive? A new approach to the problems of human interrelations*. Washington, D.C. Nervous and Mental Disease Publishing Co., 1934. Rev. ed., Beacon House, 1954.

MORGAN, J. J. B. *The psychology of abnormal people*. New York: Longmans, Green, 1928.

MORGAN, J. J. B., and WITMER, F. J. The treatment of enuresis by the conditioned reaction technique. *Journal of genetic psychology*, 1939, *55*, 59–65.

MORGAN, R., ed. *Sisterhood is powerful*. New York: Vintage, 1970.

MORGANSTERN, K. P. Implosive therapy and flooding procedures: a critical review. *Psychological bulletin*, 1973, *79*, 318–334.

MORGENSTERN, F., PEARCE, J., and DAVIES, B. The application of aversion therapy to tranvestism. Paper read at Reading Conference of British Psychological Society, 1963.

MORGENTHALER, F. Introduction to panel on disturbances of male and female identity as met with in psychoanalytic practice. *International journal of psychoanalysis*, 1969, *50*, 109–112.

MORISON, R. S. Death: process or event? *Science*, 1971, *173*, 694–698.

MOSHER, L. R., and GUNDERSON, J. G. Special report:

schizophrenia, 1972. *Schizophrenia bulletin*, 1973, *7*, 12–52.

Moss, F. A. Note on building likes and dislikes in children. *Journal of experimental psychology*, 1924, *7*, 475–478.

Moss, G. R., and BOREN, J. H. Depression as a model for behavioral analysis. *Comprehensive psychiatry*, 1972, *13*, 581–590.

Moss, G. R., RADA, R. T., and APPEL, J. B. Positive control as an alternative to aversion therapy. *Journal of behavior therapy and experimental psychiatry*, 1970, *1*, 291–294.

MOTTO, J. A. Newspaper influence on suicide: a controlled study. *Archives of general psychiatry*, 1970, *23*, 143–148.

MOWRER, O. H. What is normal behavior? In L. A. Pennington and I. A. Berg, eds., *An introduction to clinical psychology*. New York: Ronald Press, 1948, 17–46.

MOWRER, O. H. Changes in verbal behavior during psychotherapy. In O. H. Mowrer, ed., *Psychotherapy: theory and research*. New York: Ronald Press, 1953.

MOWRER, O. H., and LAMOREAUX, R. Avoidance conditioning and signal duration. *Psychological monographs*, 1942, *54*, 5 (whole no. 247).

MOWRER, O. H., and MOWRER, W. M. Enuresis: a method for its study and treatment. *American journal of orthopsychiatry*, 1938, *8*, 436–459.

MOWRER, O. H., and VIEK, P. An experimental analogue of fear from a sense of helplessness. *Journal of abnormal and social psychology*, 1948, *43*, 193–200.

MUELLER, L. Many don't believe man has set foot on the moon. *Champaign-Urbana courier*, 14 July 1970, p. 20.

MUENCH, G. A. A follow-up of mental defectives after eighteen years. *Journal of abnormal and social psychology*, 1944, *39*, 407–418.

MULHERN, T., and BAUMEISTER, A. A. An experimental attempt to reduce stereotypy by reinforcement procedures. *American journal of mental deficiency*, 1969, *74*, 69–74.

MULLEN, F. G., JR. The treatment of a case of dysmenorrhea by behavior therapy techniques. *Journal of nervous and mental disease*, 1968, *147*, 371–376.

MULLER, C. The overmedicated society: forces in the marketplace for medical care. *Science*, 1972, *176*, 488–492.

MURPHY, F. J., SHIRLEY, M. M., and WITMER, H. L. The incidence of hidden delinquency. *American journal of orthopsychiatry*, 1946, *16*, 686–696.

MURPHY, H. B. M., WITTOKER, E. W., and CHANCE, N. A. Crosscultural inquiry into the symptomatology of depression: a preliminary report. *International journal of psychiatry*, 1967, *3*, 6–15.

MURPHY, H. B. M., WITTOKER, E. W., FRIED, J., and ELLENBERGER, H. A crosscultural survey of schizophrenic symptomatology. *International journal of social psychiatry*, 1963, *9*, 237–249.

MURPHY, I. C. Extinction of an incapacitating fear of earthworms. *Journal of clinical psychology*, 1964, *20*, 396–398.

MURPHY, J. M. Psychotherapeutic aspects of shamanism on St. Lawrence Island, Alaska. In A. Kiev, ed., *Magic, faith and healing: studies in primitive psychiatry today*. New York: Free Press, 1964, pp. 53–83.

MURPHY, J. M., and LEIGHTON, A. H. Native conceptions of psychiatric disorder. In J. M. Murphy and A. H. Leighton, eds., *Approaches to crosscultural psychiatry*. Ithaca, N.Y.: Cornell University Press, 1965, pp. 64–107.

MURRAY, D. C. Suicidal and depressive feelings among college students. *Psychological reports*, 1973, *33*, 175–181.

MURRAY, E. J. A content-analysis method for studying psychotherapy. *Psychological monographs*, 1956, *70*, 13 (whole no. 420).

MURRAY, H. A. *Explorations in personality*. New York: Oxford University Press, 1938.

MUSTO, D. F. *The American disease*. New Haven: Yale University Press, 1973.

MUTIMER, D. D., and ROSEMIER, R. A. Behavior problems of children as viewed by teachers and the children themselves. *Journal of consulting psychology*, 1967, *31*, 583–587.

MUZEKARI, L. H., and KAMIS, E. The effects of videotape feedback and modeling on the behavior of chronic schizophrenics. *Journal of clinical psychology*, 1973, *29*, 313–315.

MYERS, J. J., JR., and DEIBERT, A. N. Reduction of self-abusive behavior in a blind child by using a feeding response. *Journal of behavior therapy and experimental psychiatry*, 1971, *2*, 141–144.

MYERS, J. K., LINDENTHAL, J. J., PEPPER, M. P., and OSTRANDER, D. R. Life events and mental status: a longitudinal study. *Journal of health and social behavior*, 1972, *13*, 398–406.

MYERS, J. K., and ROBERTS, B. H. *Family and class dynamics in mental illness*. New York: Wiley, 1959.

MYERS, J. K., and SCHAFFER, L. Social stratification and psychiatric practice: a study of an out-patient clinic. *American sociological review*, 1954, *19*, 307–310.

NACHSHON, I., DRAGUNS, J. G., BROVERMAN, I. K., and PHILLIPS, L. The reflection of acculturation in psychiatric symptomatology: a study of an Israeli child guidance clinic population. *Social psychiatry,* 1972, *7,* 109–118.

NARROL, H. G. Experimental application of reinforcement principles to the analysis and treatment of hospitalized alcoholics. *Quarterly journal of studies on alcohol,* 1967, *28,* 105–115.

NASH, M. M., and ZIMRING, F. M. Prediction of reaction to placebo. *Journal of abnormal psychology,* 1969, *74,* 568–573.

NATHAN, P. E., ANDBERG, M. M., BEHAN, P. O., and PATCH, V. D. Twenty-two observers and one patient: a study of diagnostic reliability. *Journal of clinical psychology,* 1969, *25,* 9–15.

NATHAN, P. E., MARLAND, J., and LINDSLEY, O. R. Receptive communication in psychiatric nurse supervision. *Journal of counseling psychology,* 1965, *12,* 259–267.

NATHAN, P. E., and O'BRIEN, J. S. An experimental analysis of the behavior of alcoholics and nonalcoholics during prolonged experimental drinking: a necessary precursor of behavior therapy? *Behavior therapy,* 1971, *2,* 455–476.

NATHAN, P. E., SAMARAWEERA, A., ANDBERG, M. M., and PATCH, V. D. Syndromes of psychosis and psychoneurosis. *Archives of general psychiatry,* 1968, *19,* 704–716.

NATHAN, P. E., SCHNELLER, P., and LINDSLEY, O. R. Direct measurement of communication during psychiatric admission interviews. *Behaviour research and therapy,* 1964, *2,* 49–57.

NATHAN, P. E., ZARE, N. C., FERNEAU, E. W., and LOWENSTEIN, L. M. Effects of congener differences in alcoholic beverages on the behavior of alcoholics. *Quarterly journal of studies on alcohol supplement,* 1970, *5,* 87–100.

NATIONAL TRAINING LABORATORY INSTITUTE. *Standards for the Use of Laboratory Method in NTL Institute Programs.* Washington, D.C.: NTL Institute, 1969.

NAWAS, M. M. "Existential" anxiety treated by systematic desensitization: a case study. *Journal of behavior therapy and experimental psychiatry,* 1971, *2,* 291–295.

NEALE, D. H. Behaviour therapy and encopresis in children. *Behaviour research and therapy,* 1963, *1,* 139–149.

NEALE, J. M., and LIEBERT, R. M. Reinforcement therapy using aides and patients as behavioral technicians: a case report of a mute psychotic. *Perceptual and motor skills,* 1969, *28,* 835–839.

NEISWORTH, J. T., and MOORE, F. Operant treatment of asthmatic responding with the parent as therapist. *Behavior therapy,* 1972, *3,* 95–99.

NELSON, J. D., GELFAND, D. M., and HARTMANN, D. P. Children's aggression following competition and exposure to an aggressive model. *Child development,* 1969, *40,* 1085–1097.

NELSON, R. O., and EVANS, I. M. The combination of learning principles and speech therapy techniques in the treatment of noncommunicating children. *Journal of child psychology and psychiatry,* 1968, *9,* 111–124.

NEMIAH, J. C. Anorexia nervosa: a clinical psychiatric study. *Medicine,* 1950, *29,* 225–268.

NEMIAH, J. C. *Foundations of psychopathology.* New York: Oxford University Press, 1961.

NEMIAH, J. C. Conversion reaction. In A. M. Freedman and H. I. Kaplan, eds., *Comprehensive textbook of psychiatry.* Baltimore: Williams & Wilkins, 1967a, 871–885.

NEMIAH, J. C. Obsessive-compulsive reaction. In A. M. Freedman and H. I. Kaplan, eds., *Comprehensive textbook of psychiatry.* Baltimore: Williams & Wilkins, 1967b, 912–928.

NESBITT, P. D. Smoking, physiological arousal, and emotional response. *Journal of personality and social psychology,* 1973, *25,* 137–144.

NEWMAN, R. C., II, and POLLACK, D. Proxemics in deviant adolescents. *Journal of consulting and clinical psychology,* 1973, *40,* 6–8.

NEWTON, R. D. Alcoholism as a neurotic symptom. *British journal of addiction,* 1949, *46,* 79–92.

NEY, P. Operant conditioning of schizophrenic children. *Canadian psychiatric association journal,* 1967, *12,* 9–15.

NEY, P. G., PALEVSKEY, A. E., MARKELY, J. Relative effectiveness of operant conditioning and play therapy in childhood schizophrenia. *Journal of autism and childhood schizophrenia,* 1971, *1,* 337–349.

NICASSIO, F. J., LIBERMAN, R. P., PATTERSON, R. L., RAMIREZ, E., and SANDERS, N. The treatment of tics by negative practice. *Journal of behavior therapy and experimental psychiatry,* 1972, *3,* 281–288.

NIELSEN, J., and VIDEBECH, T. Suicide frequency before and after introduction of community psychiatry in a Danish island. *British journal of psychiatry,* 1973, *123,* 35–39.

NIHIRA, K. Importance of environmental demands in the measurement of adaptive behavior. In K. E. Eyman, C. E. Meyers, and G. Tarjan, eds., *Sociobehavioral studies in mental retardation: papers in honor of Harvey F. Dingman.* University of Southern California, Los Angeles: American Association on Mental Deficiency Monographs, 1973, pp. 101–116.

NOLAN, J. D., and PENCE, C. Operant conditioning principles in the treatment of a selectively mute child. *Journal of consulting and clinical psychology,* 1970, *35,* 265–268.

NORDQUIST, V. M., and WAHLER, R. G. Naturalistic

treatment of an autistic child. *Journal of applied behavior analysis*, 1973, *6*, 79–87.

NORMAN, A., and BROMAN, H. S. Volume feedback and generalization techniques in shaping speech of an electively mute boy: a case study. *Perceptual and motor skills*, 1970, *31*, 463–470.

NOSANCHUK, T. A., and LIGHTSTONE, J. Canned laughter and public and private conformity. *Journal of personality and social psychology*, 1974, *29*, 153–157.

NOYES, A. P., and KOLB, L. C. *Modern clinical psychiatry*. 6th ed. Philadelphia: Saunders, 1963.

NUNNALLY, J. C., JR. *Popular conceptions of mental health*. New York: Holt, 1961.

NUNNALLY, J. C., DUCHNOWSKI, A. J., and PARKER, R. K. Association of neutral objects with rewards: effect on verbal evaluation, reward expectancy, and selective attention. *Journal of personality and social psychology*, 1965, *1*, 270–274.

NUNNALLY, J. C., and FAW, T. T. The acquisition of conditioned reward value in discrimination learning. *Child development*, 1968, *39*, 159–166.

NURNERGER, J. I., and ZIMMERMAN, J. Applied analysis of human behavior: an alternative to conventional motivational inferences and unconscious determination in therapeutic programming. *Behavior therapy*, 1970, *1*, 59–69.

NYDEGGER, R. V. The elimination of hallucinatory and delusional behavior by verbal conditioning and assertive training: a case study. *Journal of behavior therapy and clinical psychiatry*, 1972, *3*, 225–227.

NYE, F. I., SHORT, J. F., and OLSEN, V. J. Socioeconomic status and delinquent behavior. *American journal of sociology*, 1958, *63*, 381–389.

NYSWANDER, M. History of a nightmare. In D. Wakefield, ed., *The addict*. Greenwich, Conn.: Fawcett, 1963, pp. 20–32.

OBER, D. C. Modification of smoking behavior. *Journal of consulting and clinical psychology*, 1968, *32*, 543–549.

OBLER, M. Systematic desensitization in sexual disorders. *Journal of behavior therapy and experimental psychiatry*, 1973, *4*, 93–101.

O'BRIEN, F., AZRIN, N. H., and BUGLE, C. Training profoundly retarded children to stop crawling. *Journal of applied behavior analysis*, 1972, *5*, 131–137.

O'BRIEN, F., BUGLE, C., and AZRIN, N. H. Training and maintaining a retarded child's proper eating. *Journal of applied behavior analysis*, 1972, *5*, 67–72.

O'BRIEN, J. S., RAYNES, A. E., and PATCH, V. D. An operant reinforcement system to improve ward behavior in inpatient drug addicts. *Journal of behavior therapy and experimental psychiatry*, 1971, *2*, 239–242.

O'BRIEN, P., and AZRIN, N. H. Developing proper mealtime behaviors of the institutionalized retarded. *Journal of applied behavior analysis*, 1972, *5*, 389–399.

O'BRIEN, R., AZRIN, N. H., and HENSON, K. Increased communications of chronic mental patients by reinforcement and by response priming. *Journal of applied behavior analysis*, 1969, *2*, 23–29.

O'CONNELL, W. The adaptive functions of wit and humor. *Journal of abnormal and social psychology*, 1960, *61*, 263–270.

ODEGARD, O. Patterns of discharge and readmission in psychiatric hospitals in Norway, 1926–1955. *Mental hygiene*, 1961, *45*, 185–193.

OGBURN, K. D., FAST, D., and TIFFANY, D. The effects of reinforcing working behavior. *American journal of occupational therapy*, 1972, *26*, 32–35.

O'KELLY, L. I., and MUCKLER, F. A. *Introduction to psychopathology*. Englewood Cliffs, N.J.: Prentice-Hall, 1955.

O'LEARY, K. D. The effects of self-instruction on immoral behavior. *Journal of experimental child psychology*, 1968, *6*, 297–301.

O'LEARY, K. D., and BECKER, W. B. Behavior modification of an adjustment class: a token reinforcement program. *Exceptional children*, 1967, *33*, 637–642.

O'LEARY, K. D., and DRABMAN, R. Token reinforcement programs in the classroom: a review. *Psychological bulletin*, 1971, *5*, 379–398.

O'LEARY, K. D., and O'LEARY, S. G., eds. *Classroom management: the successful use of behavior modification*. Elmsford, N.Y.: Pergamon Press, 1972.

O'LEARY, K. D., O'LEARY, S. G., and BECKER, W. C. Modification of a deviant sibling interaction pattern in the home. *Behaviour research and therapy*, 1967, *5*, 113–120.

OLSEN, R. W. Sex differences among retarded hospital admissions: fact or artifact? *Mental retardation*, 1967, *5*, 6–9.

OLSON, K. A., and KELLEY, W. R. Reduction of compulsive masturbation by electrical-aversive conditioning to verbal cues: a case report. *Canadian psychiatric association journal*, 1969, *14*, 303–305.

OLSON, R. P., and GREENBERG, D. J. The effects of contingency-contracting and decision-making groups with chronic mental patients. *Journal of consulting and clinical psychology*, in press.

OLTMAN, J. E., McGARRY, J. J., and FRIEDMAN, S. Parental deprivation and the "broken home" in dementia praecox and other mental disorders. *American journal of psychiatry*, 1952, *108*, 685–694.

O'NEILL, M., and KEMPLER, B. Approach and avoidance responses of the hysterical personality to sexual stimuli. *Journal of abnormal psychology*, 1969, *74*, 300–305.

OPLER, M. K., and SINGER, J. L. Ethnic differences in behavior and psychopathology: Italian and Irish. *International journal of social psychiatry*, 1959, *2*, 11–23.

ORLANSKY, H. Infant care and personality. *Psychological bulletin*, 1949, *46*, 1–48.

ORNE, M. T. The nature of hypnosis: artifact and essence. *Journal of abnormal and social psychology*, 1959, *58*, 277–299.

ORNE, M. T. On the social psychology of the psychological experiment: with particular reference to demand characteristics and their implication. *American psychologist*, 1962, *17*, 776–783.

ORNE, M. T., and EVANS, F. J. Social control in the psychological experiment: antisocial behavior and hypnosis. *Journal of personality and social psychology*, 1965, *1*, 189–200.

ORNE, M. T., and SCHEIBE, K. E. The contribution of nondeprivation factors in the production of sensory deprivation effects: the psychology of the panic button. *Journal of abnormal and social psychology*, 1964, *68*, 3–12.

ORNSTEIN, R. E., ed. *The nature of human consciousness*. San Francisco: Freeman, 1973.

ORWELL, G. *1984*. New York: Harcourt, 1949.

OSBORNE, J. G. Free-time as a reinforcer in the management of classroom behavior. *Journal of applied behavior analysis*, 1969, *2*, 113–118.

OSGOOD, C. E., SUCI, G. J., and TANNENBAUM, P. H. *The measurement of meaning*. Urbana: University of Illinois Press, 1957.

OSLER, W. *The principles and practice of medicine*. New York: Appleton, 1892.

OSMUNDSEN, J. A. Drug said to aid schizophrenics. *The New York times*, 31 March 1966, p. 41.

OSTROW, M., and OSTROW, M. Bilaterally synchronous paroxysmal slow activity in the encephalograms of non-epileptics. *Journal of nervous and mental disease*, 1946, *103*, 346–358.

OSWALD, I. Induction of illusory and hallucinatory voices with consideration of behavior therapy. *Journal of mental science*, 1962, *108*, 196–212.

OTIS, R. E., MORCOMBE, J. E., and PITTMAN, W. E. Improving a Korsakoff patient's recall of information with a cigarette reward. *Newsletter for research in psychology*, 1970, *12*, 12–13.

OTTENBERG, P., STEIN, M., LEWIS, J., and HAMILTON, C. Learned asthma in the guinea pig. *Psychosomatic medicine*, 1958, *20*, 395–400.

OVESEY, L., and GAYLIN, W. Psychotherapy of male homosexuality. *American journal of psychotherapy*, 1965, *19*, 382–396.

OVID. *The art of love*. Translated by Rolfe Humphries. Bloomington: Indiana University Press (Midland) and London: Calder and Boyars, 1957.

OWEN, D. R. The 47, XYY male: a review. *Psychological bulletin*, 1972, *78*, 209–233.

PACKARD, E. P. W. *Modern persecution*. Hartford: Case, Lockwood and Brainard, 1875.

PACKARD, F. R. History of the school on Salernum. In *The school of Salernum*. English version by Sir John Harington. London: Humphrey Milford, 1922.

PAGE, J. D. *Psychopathology: the science of understanding deviance*. Chicago: Aldine-Atherton, 1971.

PALMER, J., and McGUIRE, F. L. The use of unobtrusive measures in mental health research. *Journal of consulting and clinical psychology*, 1973, *40*, 431–436.

PALMORE, G., LENNARD, H. L., and HENDIN, H. Similarities of therapist and patient verbal behavior in psychotherapy. *Sociometry*, 1959, *22*, 12–22.

PALOUTZIAN, R. F., HASAZI, J., STEIFEL, J., and EDGAR, C. L. The promotion of positive social interaction in severely retarded young children. *California mental health research digest*, 1970, *8*, 192–193.

PALOUTZIAN, R. F., HASAZI, J., STREIFEL, J., and EDGAR, C. L. Promotion of positive social interaction in severely retarded young children. *American journal of mental deficiency*, 1971, *75*, 519–524.

PANEK, D. M. Word association learning by chronic schizophrenics under conditions of reward and punishment. Paper read at Western Psychological Association convention, 1967.

PANEL ON PRIVACY AND BEHAVIORAL RESEARCH. Privacy and behavioral research. *Science*, 1967, *155*, 535–538.

PAPAGEORGIOU, M. G. Forms of psychotherapy in use in ancient Greece and among the population of modern Greece. *Psychotherapy and psychosomatics*, 1969, *17*, 114–118.

PARIS, S. G., and CAIRNS, R. B. An experimental and ethological analysis of social reinforcement with retarded children. *Child development*, 1972, *43*, 717–729.

PARLOFF, M. B., IFLUND, B., and GOLDSTEIN, N. Communications of "therapy values" between therapist and schizophrenic patients. *Journal of nervous and mental disease*, 1960, *130*, 193–199.

PARRINO, J. J. Reduction of seizures by desensitization. *Journal of behavior therapy and experimental psychiatry*, 1971, *2*, 215–218.

PARRISH, M., LUNDY, R. M., and LEIBOWITZ, H. W. Hypnotic age-regression and magnitudes of the

Ponzo and Poggendorff illusions. *Science*, 1968, *159*, 1375–1376.

PARRY-JONES, W. L., SANTER-WESTSTRATE, H. C., and CRAWLEY, R. C. Behaviour therapy in a case of hysterical blindness. *Behaviour research and therapy*, 1970, *8*, 79–85.

PARSON, B. N. Operant conditioning principles applied in the teaching of cursive writing skills. Paper read at Western Psychological Association convention, 1964.

PARSONS, T. Illness and the role of the physician: a sociological perspective. *American journal of orthopsychiatry*, 1951, *21*, 452–460.

PARTRIDGE, G. E. A study of 50 cases of psychopathic personality. *American journal of psychiatry*, 1928, *7*, 953–973.

PASAMANICK, B. A survey of mental disease in an urban population. IV: an approach to total prevalance rates. *Archives of general psychiatry*, 1961, *5*, 151–155.

PASAMANICK, B., DINITZ, S., and LEFTON, M. Psychiatric orientation and its relation to diagnosis and treatment in a mental hospital. *American journal of psychiatry*, 1959, *116*, 127–132.

PASCAL, G. R. The use of relaxation in short-term psychotherapy. *Journal of abnormal and social psychology*, 1947, *42*, 226–242.

PASCAL, G. R., and SWENSON, C. Learning in mentally ill patients under unusual motivation. *Journal of personality*, 1952, *21*, 240–249.

PASCHALIS, A. P., KIMMEL, H. D., and KIMMEL, E. Further study of diurnal instrumental conditioning in the treatment of enuresis nocturna. *Journal of behavior therapy and experimental psychiatry*, 1972, *3*, 253–256.

PATTERSON, G. R. A learning theory approach to the treatment of the school phobic child. In L. P. Ullmann and L. Krasner, eds., *Case studies in behavior modification*. New York: Holt, Rinehart and Winston, 1965a, pp. 279–285.

PATTERSON, G. R. An application of conditioning techniques to the control of a hyperactive child. In L. P. Ullmann and L. Krasner, eds., *Case studies in behavior modification*. New York: Holt, 1965b, 370–375.

PATTERSON, G. R. Multiple evaluations of a parent-training program. Paper presented at the International symposium on behavior modification. Minneapolis, October 1972.

PATTERSON, G. R., and BRODSKY, G. A behaviour modification programme for a child with multiple problem behaviours. *Journal of child psychology and psychiatry*, 1966, *7*, 277–295.

PATTERSON, G. R., COBB, J. A., and RAY, R. S. A social engineering technology for retraining the families of aggressive boys. In H. E. Adams and I. P. Unikel, eds., *Issues and trends in behavior therapy*. Springfield, Ill.: Thomas, 1973, 139–210.

PATTERSON, G. R., JONES, R., WHITTIER, J., and WRIGHT, M. A. A behaviour modification technique for the hyperactive child. *Behaviour research and therapy*, 1965, *2*, 217–226.

PATTERSON, G. R., LITTMAN, R. A., and BRICKER, W. Assertive behavior in children: a step toward a theory of aggression. *Society for research in child development monographs*, 1967, *32*, (#5, serial #113).

PATTERSON, R. L., and TEIGEN, J. R. Conditioning and post-hospital generalization of nondelusional responses in a chronic psychotic patient. *Journal of applied behavior analysis*, 1973, *6*, 65–70.

PATTISON, E. M. A critique of abstinence criteria in the treatment of alcoholism. *International journal of social psychiatry*, 1968, *14*, 268–276.

PAUL, G. L. *Insight vs. desensitization in psychotherapy*. Stanford, Calif.: Stanford University Press, 1966.

PAUL, G. L. Insight versus desensitization in psychotherapy two years after termination. *Journal of consulting psychology*, 1967a, *31*, 333–348.

PAUL, G. L. Strategy of outcome research in psychotherapy. *Journal of consulting psychology*, 1967b, *31*, 109–118.

PAUL, G. L. Outcome of systematic desensitization. I: background, procedures and uncontrolled reports of individual treatment. In C. M. Franks, ed., *Assessment and status of the behavior therapies*. New York: McGraw-Hill, 1968a, pp. 53–104

PAUL, G. L. Outcome of systematic desensitization. II: controlled investigations of individual treatment, technique variations, and current status. In C. M. Franks, ed., *Assessment and status of the behavior therapies*. New York: McGraw-Hill, 1968b, pp. 105–159.

PAUL, G. L., and BERNSTEIN, D. A. *Anxiety and clinical problems: systematic desensitization and related techniques*. New York: General Learning Press, 1972.

PAUL, G. L., and SHANNON, D. T. Treatment of anxiety through systematic desensitization in therapy groups. *Journal of abnormal psychology*, 1966, *71*, 124–135.

PAYKEL, E. S. Classification of depressed patients: a cluster analysis derived grouping. *British journal of psychiatry*, 1971, *118*, 275–288.

PAYKEL, E. S., and WEISSMAN, M. M. Social adjustment and depression. *Archives of general psychiatry*, 1973, *28*, 659–663.

PAYNE, R. W., MATTUSSEK, P., and GEORGE, E. I. An experimental study of schizophrenic thought disorder. *Journal of mental science*, 1959, *195*, 627-652.

PECHTEL, C., and MASSERMAN, J. H. Cerebral localization: not where but in whom? *American journal of psychiatry*, 1959, *116*, 51-54.

PEDERSEN, D. M., and SHEARS, L. M. A review of personal space research in the framework of general systems theory. *Psychological bulletin*, 1973, *80*, 367-388.

PEDRINI, B. C., and PEDRINI, D. T. Reinforcement procedures in the control of encopresis: a case study. *Psychological reports*, 1971, *28*, 937-938.

PEINE, H. A. The elimination of a child's self-injurious behavior at home and school. *SALT: School application of learning theory*, 1972, *4*, 36-47.

PELLEGRINI, R. J. Some effects of seating position on social perceptions. *Psychological reports*, 1971, *28*, 887-893.

PENICK, S. B., FILION, R., FOX, S., and STUNKARD, A. J. Behavior modification in the treatment of obesity. *Psychosomatic medicine*, 1971, *33*, 49-55.

PEPINSKY, H. B. Help-giving in search of a criterion. In E. Landy and A. M. Kroll, eds., *Guidance in American education*. Vol. 3. Cambridge, Mass.: Harvard University Press, 1966.

PERKINS, W. H., and CURLEE, R. F. Clinical impressions of portable masking unit effects in stuttering. *Journal of speech and hearing disorders*, 1969, *34*, 360-362.

PERLS, F., HEFFERLINE, R. F., and GOODMAN, P. *Gestalt therapy*. New York: Julian Press, 1951.

PERRY, D. G., and PERRY, L. C. Denial of suffering in the victim as a stimulus to violence in aggressive boys. *Child development*, 1974, *45*, 55-62.

PERSONS, R. W., and PERSONS, C. E. Some experimental support of psychopathic theory: a critique. *Psychological reports*, 1965, *16*, 745-749.

PERZAN, R. S., BOULANGER, F., and FISCHER, D. G. Complex factors in inhibition of defecation: review and case study. *Journal of behavior therapy and experimental psychiatry*, 1972, *3*, 129-133.

PETERSON, D. R. Behavior problems of middle childhood. *Journal of consulting psychology*, 1961, *25*, 205-209.

PETERSON, D. R., and BECKER, W. C. Family interaction and delinquency. In H. C. Quay, ed., *Juvenile delinquency: research and theory*. Princeton, N.J.: Van Nostrand, 1965, pp. 63-99.

PETERSON, D. R., and LONDON, P. A role for cognition in the behavioral treatment of a child's eliminative disturbance. In L. P. Ullmann and L. Krasner, eds., *Case studies in behavior modification*. New York: Holt, Rinehart and Winston, 1965, pp. 289-294.

PETERSON, L. W. Operant approach to observation and recording. *Nursing outlook*, 1967, *15*, 27-32.

PETERSON, R. F. Imitation: a basic behavioral mechanism. In H. N. Sloane, Jr., and B. D. MacAulay, eds., *Operant procedures in remedial speech and language training*. Boston: Houghton, 1968, 61-74.

PETERSON, R. F., MERWIN, M. R., MOYER, T. S., and WHITHURST, G. J. Generalized imitation: the effects of experimenter absence, differential reinforcement and stimulus complexity. *Journal of experimental child psychology*, 1971, *12*, 114-128.

PETERSON, R. F., and PETERSON, L. R. The use of positive reinforcement in the control of self-destructive behavior in a retarded boy. *Journal of experimental child psychology*, 1968, *6*, 351-360.

PETERSON, R. F., and WHITEHURST, G. J. A variable influencing the performance of generalized imitative behaviors. *Journal of applied behavior analysis*, 1971, *4*, 1-9.

PETONEY, P. Value changes in psychotherapy. *Human relations*, 1966, *19*, 39-45.

PETRONI, F. A. Social class, family size, and the sick role. *Journal of marriage and the family*, 1969, *31*, 728-735.

PETRONI, F. A., and GRIFFIN, C. The influence of social class and family size on adult psychiatric outpatients. *Bulletin of the Menninger clinic*, 1970, *34*, 148-160.

PFEIFFER, E., EISENSTEIN, R. B., and DOBBS, E. G. Mental competency evaluation for the federal courts: I. methods and results. *Journal of nervous and mental disease*, 1967, *144*, 320-328.

PHELAN, J. G., TANG, T., and HEKMAT, H. Some effects of various schedules of verbal reinforcement on self-reference responses. *Journal of psychology*, 1967, *67*, 17-24.

PHILLIPS, B. S. *The aging in a central Illinois community*. Urbana: University of Illinois Press, 1962.

PHILLIPS, D. L. The "true prevalence" of mental illness in a New England state. *Community mental health journal*, 1966, *2*, 35-40.

PHILLIPS, D. L., and CLANCY, K. J. Response biases in field studies of mental illness. *American sociological review*, 1970, *35*, 503-515.

PHILLIPS, E. L. *Psychotherapy: a modern theory and practice*. Englewood Cliffs, N.J.: Prentice-Hall, 1956.

PHILLIPS, E. L. Parent-child psychotherapy: a follow-up study comparing two techniques, *Journal of psychology*, 1960, *49*, 195-202.

PHILLIPS, E. L. Logical analysis of childhood behavior problems and their treatment. *Psychological reports*, 1961, *9*, 705-712.

PHILLIPS, E. L. Achievement place: token reinforcement procedures in a home-style rehabilitation setting for "pre-delinquent" boys. *Journal of applied behavior analysis,* 1968, *1,* 213–223.

PHILLIPS, E. L., PHILLIPS, E. A., FIXSEN, D. L., and WOLF, M. M. Achievement place: modification of the behaviors of pre-delinquent boys within a token economy. *Journal of applied behavior analysis,* 1971, *4,* 45–59.

PHILLIPS, E. L., and WIENER, D. N. *Short-term psychotherapy and structured behavior change.* New York: McGraw-Hill, 1966.

PHILLIPS, J. S. The relationship between two features of interview behavior comparing verbal content and verbal temporal patterns of interaction. Unpublished doctoral dissertation. Washington University, St. Louis, 1957.

PHILLIPS, L. Case history data and prognosis in schizophrenia. *Journal of nervous and mental disease,* 1953, *117,* 515–525.

PHILLIPS, R. E., JOHNSON, G. D., and GEYER, A. Self-administered systematic desensitization. *Behaviour research and therapy,* 1972, *10,* 93–96.

PIAGET, J. *The moral judgment of the child.* Glencoe, Ill.: Free Press, 1948.

PIERROL, R., and SHERMAN, G. *Barnabus, the Barnard rat: demonstration.* New York: Barnard College, 1958.

PIETSCH, D., MORROW, J. E., and SCHLESINGER, R. The effects of token reinforcers on the behavior of institutionalized female retardates. Paper read at American Psychological Association convention, 1967.

PIHL, R. O. Conditioning procedures with hyperactive children. *Neurology,* 1967, *17,* 421–423.

PILIAVIN, I. M., and BRIAR, S. Police encounters with juveniles. *American journal of sociology,* 1964, *70,* 206–214.

PILIAVIN, I. M., RODIN, J., and PILIAVIN, J. A. Good samaritanism: an underground phenomenon? *Journal of personality and social psychology,* 1969, *13,* 289–299.

PILIAVIN, I. M., and WERTHAM, C. Gang members and the police. In D. Bordua, ed., *The police.* New York: Wiley, 1967, 59–98.

PILIAVIN, J. A., and PILIAVIN, I. M. Effect of blood on reactions to a victim. *Journal of personality and social psychology,* 1972, *23,* 353–361.

PILLARD, R. C. Marihuana. *New England journal of medicine,* 1970, *283,* 294–303.

PINNEAU, S. R. A critique on the articles by Margaret Ribble. *Child development,* 1950, *21,* 203–228.

PINNEAU, S. R. The infantile disorders of hospitalism and anaclitic depression. *Psychological bulletin,* 1955, *52,* 429–452.

PINTO, R. A case of movement epilepsy with agoraphobia treated successfully by flooding. *British journal of psychiatry,* 1972, *121,* 287–288.

PIPER, T. J., and MACKINNON, R. C. Operant conditioning of a profoundly retarded individual reinforced via a stomach fistula. *American journal of mental deficiency,* 1969, *73,* 627–630.

PITTEL, S. M., and MENDELSOHN, G. A. Measurement of moral values: a review and critique. *Psychological bulletin,* 1966, *66,* 22–35.

PIVINCKI, D. and CHRISTIE, R. G. Body build characteristics in psychotics. *Comprehensive psychiatry,* 1968, *9,* 574–580.

PLATONOV, K. I. *The word as a physiological and therapeutic factor.* Moscow: Foreign Languages Publishing House, 1959.

PLATT, E. S., KRASSEN, E., and MAUSNER, B. Individual variation in behavioral change following role playing. *Psychological reports,* 1969, *24,* 155–170.

PLOG, S. C., and EDGERTON, R. B., eds., *Changing perspectives in mental illness.* New York: Holt, Rinehart and Winston, 1969.

PLUNKETT, R. J., and GORDON, J. E. *Epidemiology and mental illness.* New York: Basic Books, 1960.

POKORNY, A. D., and OVERALL, J. E. Relationships of psychopathology to age, sex, ethnicity, education, and marital status in state hospital patients. *Journal of psychiatric research,* 1970, *7,* 143–152.

POKORNY, A. D., SHEEHAN, D., and ATKINSON, J. Drinking water, lithium, and mental hospital admissions. *Diseases of the nervous system,* 1972, *33,* 649–652.

POLAK, P. Patterns of discord: goals of patients, therapists, and community members. *Archives of general psychiatry,* 1970, *23,* 277–283.

POLAK, P. R. the crisis of admission. *Social psychiatry,* 1967, *2,* 150–157.

POLANI, P. E. Abnormal sex chromosomes and mental disorder. *Nature,* 1969, *223,* 680–686.

POLIN, A. T. The effect of flooding and physical suppression as extinction techniques on an anxiety-motivated avoidance locomotor response. *Journal of psychology,* 1959, *47,* 235–245.

POLLIN, W., ALLEN, M. G., HOFFER, A., STABENAU, J. R., and HRUBEC, Z. Psychopathology in 15,909 twins: evidence for a genetic factor in the pathogensis of schizophrenia and its relative absence in psychoneurosis. *American journal of psychiatry,* 1969, *126,* 597–610.

POLLIN, W., STABENAU, J. R., MOSHER, L., and TUPIN, J. Life history differences in identical twins discordant for schizophrenia. *American journal of orthopsychiatry,* 1966, *36,* 492–509.

POMEROY, W. B. The Masters-Johnson report and

the Kinsey tradition. In R. Brecher and E. Brecher, eds., *An analysis of human sexual repsonse.* New York: Signet, 1966, 111–123.

PORTER, R. B., and MILAZZO, T. C. A comparison of mentally retarded adults who attended a special class with those who attended regular school classes. *Exceptional children,* 1958, *24,* 410–412.

PORTERFIELD, A. L. *Youth in trouble.* Fort Worth, Texas: Leo Polishman Foundation, 1946.

POSER, E. G., FENTON, G. W., and SCOTTON, L. The classical conditioning of sleep and wakefulness. *Behaviour research and therapy,* 1965, *3,* 259–264.

POTKAY, C. R. The role of personal history data in clinical judgment: a selective focus. *Journal of personality assessment,* 1973, *37,* 203–212.

POWDERMAKER, F. B., and FRANK, J. B. *Group psychotherapy: studies in methodology of research and therapy.* Cambridge, Mass.: Harvard University Press, 1953.

POWELL, B., GOODWIN, D., and BREMER, D. Drinking experience versus personality factors as predictors of tolerance for alcohol. *The British journal of psychiatry,* 1973, *122,* 415–418.

PREMACK, D. Toward empirical behavior laws. I: positive reinforcement. *Psychological review,* 1959, *66,* 219–233.

PREMACK, D. Language in chimpanzees? *Science,* 1971, *172,* 808–822.

PRESBIE, R. J. and COITEUX, P. F. Learning to be generous or stingy: imitation of sharing behavior as a function of model generosity and vicarious reinforcement. *Child development,* 1971, *42,* 1033–1038.

PRESBIE, R. J., and KANAREFF, V. T. Sharing in children as a function of the number of shares and reciprocity. *Journal of genetic psychology,* 1970, *116,* 31–44.

PRESTHUS, R. *The organizational society.* New York: Knopf, 1962.

PREU, P. W. The concept of psychopathic personality. In J. McV. Hunt, ed., *Personality and the behaviour disorders.* Vol. 2. New York: Ronald Press, 1944.

PRICE, R. H. Psychological deficit versus impression management in schizophrenic word association performance. *Journal of abnormal psychology,* 1972, *79,* 132–137.

PRICE, R. H., and DENNER, B., eds. *The making of a mental patient.* New York: Holt, Rinehart and Winston, 1973.

PRICE, W. H. Sex determination, mental subnormality, crime and delinquency in males. *Journal of mental subnormality,* 1969, *15* (June, part I).

PRIEN, R. F., CAFFEY, E. M., and KLETT, C. J. Prophylactic efficacy of lithium carbonate in manic-depressive illness. *Archives of general psychiatry,* 1973, *28,* 337–341.

PROCTOR, J. T. Hysteria in childhood. *American journal of orthopsychiatry,* 1958, *28,* 394–407.

PRONKO, N. H. *Textbook of abnormal psychology.* Baltimore: Williams & Wilkins, 1963.

PRONKO, N. H., and BOWLES, J. W., JR. *Empirical foundations of psychology.* New York: Rinehart, 1951.

PROSHANSKY, H. M., ITTELSON, W. H., and RIVLIN, L. G., eds., *Environmental psychology.* New York: Holt, Rinehart and Winston, 1970.

PSHONIK, A. T. *The cerebral cortex and the receptor functions of the organism.* Moscow: Sovetskaia nauka. 1952.

PUE, A. F., HOARE, R., and ADAMSON, J. D. The "pink spot" and schizophrenia. *Canadian psychiatric association journal,* 1969, *14,* 397–401.

PUMPIAN-MINDLIN, E. The position of psychoanalysis in relation ot the biological and social sciences. In E. Pumpian-Mindlin, ed., *Psychoanalysis as science.* Stanford, Calif.: Stanford University Press, 1952.

PUMROY, D. K., and PUMROY, S. S. Systematic observation and reinforcement technique in toilet training. *Psychological reports,* 1965, *16,* 467–471.

QUARANTELLI, E. L. The nature and conditions of panic. *American journal of sociology,* 1954, *60,* 267–275.

QUARTI, C. and RENAUD, J. A new treatment of constipation by conditioning: a preliminary report. In C. M. Franks, ed., *Conditioning techniques in clinical practice and research.* New York: Springer, 1964, 219–227.

QUAY, H. C., ed., *Research in psychopathology.* Princeton, N.J.: Van Nostrand, 1963a.

QUAY, H. C. Some basic considerations in the education of emotionally disturbed children. *Exceptional children,* 1963b, *30,* 27–31.

QUAY, H. C. Personality dimensions in delinquent males as inferred from the factor analysis of behavior ratings. *Journal of research in crime and delinquency,* 1964, *1,* 33–37.

QUAY, H. C. Psychopathic personality as pathological stimulation-seeking. *American journal of psychiatry,* 1965, *122,* 180–183.

QUAY, H. C. Dimensions of problem behavior in children and their interaction in the approaches to behavior modification. In N. C. Haring and R. J. Whelan, eds., The learning environment: relationship to behavior modification and implications for special education. *Kansas studies in education,* 1966, *16,* 6–13.

QUAY, H. C. Patterns of aggression, withdrawal and

immaturity. In H. C. Quay and J. S. Werry, eds., *Psychopathological disorders of childhood.* New York: Wiley, 1972, pp. 1-29.

QUAY, H. C., and HUNT, W. A. Psychopathy, neuroticism and verbal conditioning: a replication and extension. *Journal of consulting psychology,* 1965, *29,* 283.

QUAY, H. C., SPRAGUE, R. L., WERRY, J. S., and McQUEEN, N. M. Conditioning visual orientation of conduct problem children in the classroom. *Journal of experimental child psychology,* 1967, *5,* 512-517.

RABINER, E. L., GOMEZ, E., and GRALNICK, A. The therapeutic community as an insight catalyst: expanding the transferential field. *American journal of psychotherapy,* 1964, *18,* 244-258.

RABKIN, L. Y., ed., *Psychopathology and literature.* San Francisco: Chandler, 1966.

RABKIN, L. Y., and LYTLE, C. Further information on the ecology of service. *Journal of consulting psychology,* 1966, *30,* 146-150.

RACHMAN, S. Sexual disorders and behavior therapy. *American journal of psychiatry,* 1961, *118,* 235-240.

RACHMAN, S. Introduction to behaviour therapy. *Behaviour research and therapy,* 1963a, *1,* 3-15.

RACHMAN, S. Spontaneous remission and latent learning. *Behaviour research and therapy,* 1963b, *1,* 133-137.

RACHMAN, S. Studies in desensitization. I: the separate effects of relaxation and desensitization. *Behaviour research and therapy,* 1965, *3,* 245-251.

RACHMAN, S. Sexual fetishism: an experimental analogue. *Psychological record,* 1966a, *16,* 293-296.

RACHMAN, S. Studies in desensitization. II. flooding. *Behaviour research and therapy,* 1966b, *4,* 1-6.

RACHMAN, S. *The effects of psychotherapy.* New York: Pergamon Press, 1971a.

RACHMAN, S. Obsessional ruminations. *Behaviour research and therap,* 1971b, *9,* 229-235.

RACHMAN, S., HODGSON, R., and MARKS, I. M. The treatment of chronic obsessive-compulsive neurosis. *Behaviour research and therapy,* 1971, *9,* 237-247.

RACHMAN, S., HODGSON, R., and MARZILLIER, J. Treatment of an obsessional-compulsive disorder by modelling. *Behaviour research and therapy,* 1970, *8,* 385-392.

RACHMAN, S., and TEASDALE, J. *Aversion therapy and behavior disorders: an analysis.* Coral Gables, Fla.: University of Miami Press, 1969.

RACKENSPERGER, W., and FEINBERG, A. M. Treatment of a severe handwashing compulsion by systematic desensitization: a case report. *Journal of behavior therapy and experimental psychiatry,* 1972, 123-127.

RADICAL THERAPIST COLLECTIVE. *The radical therapist.* New York: Ballantine, 1971.

RADÓ, S. The problem of melancholia. *International journal of psychoanalysis,* 1928, *9,* 420-438.

RAFI, A. A. Learning theory and the treatment of tics. *Journal of psychosomatic research,* 1962, *6,* 71-76.

RAINES, G. N., and ROHRER, J. H. The operational matrix of psychiatric practice. I: consistency and variability in interview impressions of different psychiatrists. *American journal of psychiatry,* 1955, *111,* 721-733.

RAINEY, C. A. An obsessive-compulsive neurosis treated by flooding in vivo. *Journal of behavior therapy and experimental psychiatry,* 1972, *3,* 117-121.

RAINWATER, L. The revolt of the dirty-worker. *Trans-action,* 1967, *5,* 2.

RAINWATER, L. Marital sexuality in four "cultures of poverty." In D. S. Marshall and R. C. Suggs, eds., *Human sexual behavior.* New York: Basic Books, 1971, pp. 187-205.

RAMEY, C. T., and OURTH, L. L. Delayed reinforcement and vocalization rates of infants. *Child development,* 1971, *42,* 291-297.

RANDOLPH, T. G. The descriptive features of food addiction. Addictive eating and drinking. *Quarterly journal of studies on alcohol,* 1956, *17,* 198-224.

RASKIN, N., and EHRENBERG, R. Senescence, senility and Alzheimer's disease. *American journal of psychiatry,* 1956, *113,* 133-136.

RATLIFF, R. G., and STEIN, N. H. Treatment of neurodermatitis by behavior therapy: a case study. *Behaviour research and therapy,* 1968, *6,* 397-399.

RAUSCH, H. L., and BORDIN, E. S. Warmth in personality development and in psychotherapy. *Psychiatry,* 1957, *20,* 351-363.

RAVEN, P. H., BERLIN, B., and BREEDLOVE, D. E. The origins of taxonomy. *Science,* 1971, *174,* 1210-1213.

RAVENSBORG, M. R. An operant conditioning approach to increasing interpersonal awareness among chronic schizophrenics. *Journal of clinical psychology,* 1972, *28,* 411-413.

RAY, I. *Medical jurisprudence of insanity.* Boston: Little, Brown, 1838.

RAY, O. S. *Drugs, society, and human behavior.* St. Louis: C. V. Mosby, 1972.

RAYMOND, M. J. Case of fetishism treated by aversion therapy. *British medical journal,* 1956, *2,* 854-857.

RAYMOND, M. J. The treatment of addiction in aversion conditioning with apomorphine. *Behaviour research and therapy,* 1964, *1,* 287-291.

RAYMOND, M. J., and O'KEEFFE, K. A case of pinup fetishism treated by aversion conditioning. *British journal of psychiatry,* 1965, *111,* 579–581.

RAZANI, J. Ejaculatory incompetence treated by deconditioning anxiety. *Journal of behavior therapy and experimental psychiatry,* 1972, *3,* 65–67.

RAZRAN, G. The observable unconscious and the inferable conscious in current Soviet psychophysiology: interoceptive conditioning, semantic conditioning, and the orienting reflex. *Psychological review,* 1961, *68,* 81–147.

RAZRAN, G. Russian physiologists' psychology and American experimental psychology. *Psychological bulletin,* 1965, *63,* 42–64.

REA, R. B. The rights of the mentally ill: a proposal for procedural changes in hospital admission and discharge. *Psychiatry,* 1966, *29,* 213-226.

REDD, W. H. Attention span and generalization of task-related stimulus control effects of reinforcement contingencies. *Journal of experimental child psychology,* 1972, *13,* 527–539.

REDD, W. H., and BIRNBRAUER, J. S. Adults as discriminative stimuli for different reinforcement contingencies with retarded children. *Journal of experimental child psychology,* 1969, *7,* 440–447.

REES, L. The importance of psychological, allergic and infective factors in childhood asthma. *Journal of psychosomatic research,* 1964, *7,* 253–262.

REESE, E. P. *The analysis of human operant behavior.* Dubuque, Iowa: Wm. Brown, 1966.

REGAN, D. T., WILLIAMS, M., and SPARLING, S. Voluntary expiation of guilt: a field experiment. *Journal of personality and social psychology,* 1972, *24,* 42–45.

REHM, L. P., and MARSTON, A. R. Reduction of social anxiety through modification of self-reinforcement: an instigation therapy technique. *Journal of consulting and clinical psychology,* 1968, *32,* 565–574.

REICH, C. A. *The greening of America.* New York: Random House, 1970.

REID, J. B., HAWKINS, N., KEUTZER, C., MCNEAL, S. A., PHELPS, R. E., REID, K. M., and MEES, H. L. A marathon behavior modification of a selectively mute child. *Journal of child psychology and psychiatry,* 1967, *8,* 27–30.

REIMANIS, G., KRUGMAN, A. D., and LASKY, J. J. Compliance and noncompliance during long-term institutionalization. *Perceptual and motor skills,* 1965, *21,* 895–903.

REISINGER, J. J. The treatment of "anxiety-depression" via positive reinforcement and response cost. *Journal of applied behavior analysis,* 1972, *5,* 125–130.

REISMAN, D., GLAZER, N., and DENNY, R. *The lonely crowd.* New Haven, Conn.: Yale University Press, 1950.

REISS, A. J. The social integration of queers and peers. In H. S. Becker, ed., *The other side: perspectives on deviance.* New York: Free Press, 1964, 181–210.

REISS, A. J. The study of deviant behavior: where the action is. In M. Lefton, J. K. Skipper, Jr., and C. H. McCaghy, eds., *Approaches to deviance.* New York: Appleton-Century-Crofts, 1968, 56–66.

REISS, A. J., and RHODES, A. L. The distribution of juvenile delinquency in the social class structure. *American sociological review,* 1961, *26,* 720–732.

REISS, S., and REDD, W. H. Generalization of the control of screaming behavior in an emotionally disturbed, retarded female. *Proceedings of the 78th annual convention of the American Psychological Association,* 1970, pp. 741–742.

REITLINGER, G. *The economics of taste.* New York: Holt, Rinehart and Winston, 1961.

REITZ, W. E., and KEIL, W. E. Behavioral treatment of an exhibitionist. *Journal of behavior therapy and experimental psychiatry,* 1971, *2,* 67–69.

RENNER, J. A., and RUBIN, M. L. Engaging heroin addicts in treatment. *American journal of psychiatry,* 1973, *130,* 976–980.

RENNIE, T. Prognosis in manic-depressive psychoses. *American journal of psychiatry,* 1942, *98,* 801–814.

RENSHAW, D. C. Depression in the 1970's. *Diseases of the nervous system,* 1973, *34,* 241–245.

RESNICK, J. H. Effects of stimulus satiation on the overlearned maladaptive response of cigarette smoking. *Journal of consulting and clinical psychology,* 1968, *32,* 501–505.

RETTIG, S., AND PASAMANICK, B. Differential judgment of ethical risk by cheaters and noncheaters. *Journal of abnormal and social psychology,* 1964, *69,* 109–113.

RETTIG, S., and SUIHA, J. B. P. Bad faith and ethical risk sensitivity. *Journal of personality,* 1966, *34,* 275–286.

REYNOLDS, N. J., and RISLEY, T. R. The role of social and material reinforcers in increasing talking of a disadvantaged preschool child. *Journal of applied behavior analysis,* 1968, *1,* 253–262.

RHYNE, L. D., and ULLMANN, L. P. Graffiti: a nonreactive measure? *Psychological record,* 1972, *22,* 255–258.

RICE, D. G., ABROMS, G. M., and SAXMAN, J. H. Speech and physiological correlates of "flat" affect. *Archives of general psychiatry,* 1969, *20,* 566–572.

RICE, H. K., and MCDANIEL, M. W. Operant behavior in vegetative patients. *Psychological record,* 1966, *16,* 279–281.

RICE, H. K., MCDANIEL, M. W., STALLINGS, V. D., and GATZ, M. J. Operant behavior in vegetative patients II. *Psychological record*, 1967, *17*, 449–460.

RICHARDSON, R., KARKALAS, Y., and LAL, H. Application of operant procedures in treatment of hallucinations in chronic psychotics. In R. D. Rubin, H. Fensterheim, J. D. Henderson, and L. P. Ullmann, eds., *Advances in behavior therapy*. New York: Academic Press, 1972, pp. 147–150.

RICHARDSON, T. A. Hypnotherapy in frigidity and para-frigidity problems. *Journal of the American society of psychosomatic medicine and dentistry*, 1968, *15*, 88–96.

RICHMOND, J. B. and LUSTMAN, S. L. Autonomic function in the neonate. I: implications for psychosomatic theory. *Psychosomatic medicine*, 1955, *17*, 269–275.

RICKARD, H. C., DIGNAM, P. J., and HORNER, R. F. Verbal manipulation in a psychotherapeutic relationship. *Journal of clinical psychology*, 1960, *16*, 364–367.

RICKARD, H. C., and DINOFF, M. A follow-up note on "verbal manipulation" in a psychotherapeutic relationship. *Psychological reports*, 1962, *11*, 506.

RICKARD, H. C., and MUNDY, M. B. Direct manipulation of stuttering behavior: an experimental-clinical approach. In L. P. Ullmann and L. Krasner, eds., *Case studies in behavior modification*. New York: Holt, Rinehart and Winston, 1965, pp. 268–274.

RICKELS, K., and ANDERSON, F. L. Attrited and completed lower socioeconomic class clinic patients in psychiatric drug therapy. *Comprehensive psychiatry*, 1967, *8*, 90–99.

RIFKIN, B. G. The treatment of cardiac neurosis using systematic desensitization. *Behaviour research and therapy*, 1968, *6*, 239–241.

RIMLAND, B. *Infantile autism*. New York: Appleton, 1964.

RIMM, D. C. Thought stopping and covert assertion in the treatment of phobias. *Journal of consulting and clinical psychology*, 1973, *41*, 466–467.

RIMM, D. C., and MASTERS, J. C. *Behavior therapy: techniques and empirical findings*. New York: Academic Press, 1974.

RINN, R. C., TAPP, L., and PETRELLA, R. Behavior modification with outpatients in a community mental health center. *Journal of behavior therapy and experimental psychiatry*, 1973, *4*, 243–247.

RIOCH, M. J. ELKES, C., FLINT, A. A., UDANSKY, B. S., NEWMAN, R. G., and SILBER, E. National Institute of Mental Health pilot study in training mental health counselors. *American journal of orthopsychiatry*, 1963, *33*, 678–689.

RISLEY, T. R. The effects and side effects of punishing the autistic behaviors of a deviant child. *Journal of applied behavior analysis*, 1968, *1*, 21–34.

RISLEY, T. R., and HART, B. Developing correspondence between the non-verbal and verbal behavior of preschool children. *Journal of applied behavior analysis*, 1968, *1*, 267–281.

RISLEY, T. R., and WOLF, M. M. Establishing functional speech in echolalic children. *Behaviour research and therapy*, 1967, *5*, 73–88.

RITCHIE, G. G., JR. The use of hypnosis in a case of exhibitionism. *Psychotherapy: theory, research and practice*, 1968, *5*, 40–43.

RITSCHL, C., MONGRELLA, J., and PRESBIE, R. J. Group time-out from rock and roll music and out-of-seat behavior of handicapped children while riding a school bus. *Psychological reports*, 1972, *31*, 967–973.

RITTER, B. The use of contact desensitization, demonstration-plus-participation and demonstration-alone in the treatment of acrophobia. *Behaviour research and therapy*, 1969a, 7, 157–164.

RITTER, B. Treatment of acrophobia with contact desensitization. *Behaviour research and therapy*, 1969b, 7, 41–45.

ROBACK, H. B. Insight: a bridging of the theoretical and research literatures. *The Canadian psychologist*, 1974, *15*, 61–88.

ROBACK, H., FRAYN, D., GUNBY, L., and TUTERS, K. A multifactorial approach to the treatment and ward management of a self-mutilating patient. *Journal of behavior therapy and experimental psychiatry*, 1972, *3*, 189–193.

ROBBINS, L. *Deviant children grown up*. Baltimore: Williams & Wilkins, 1966.

ROBERTS, A. H. Self-control procedures in modification of smoking behavior: replication. *Psychological reports*, 1969, *24*, 675–676.

ROBERTS, L. M. Introduction. In L. M. Roberts, S. L. HALLECK, and M. B. LOEB, eds., *Community psychiatry*. New York: Doubleday, 1969.

ROBERTS, W. W. Normal and abnormal depersonalization. *Journal of mental science*, 1960, *106*, 478–493.

ROBINS, E. Antisocial and dyssocial personality disorders. In A. M. Freedman and H. I. Kaplan, eds., *Comprehensive textbook of psychiatry*. Baltimore: Williams & Wilkins, 1967, 951–958.

ROBINSON, H. B., and ROBINSON, N. M. *The mentally retarded child*. New York: McGraw-Hill, 1965.

ROBINSON, J. C., and LEWINSOHN, P. M. Experimental analysis of a technique based on the Premack principle changing verbal behavior of depressed individuals. *Psychological reports*, 1973, *32*, 199–210.

ROCK, R. S., JACOBSON, M. A., and JANOPAUL, R. M.

Hospitalization and discharge of the mentally ill. Chicago: University of Chicago Press, 1968.

RODIN, M. J. The informativeness of trait descriptions. *Journal of personality and social psychology,* 1972, *21,* 341–344.

RODNICK, E. H., and GARMEZY, N. An experimental approach to the study of motivation in schizophrenia. In M. R. Jones, ed., *Nebraska symposium on motivation.* Lincoln: University of Nebraska Press, 1957, pp. 109–184.

ROETHLISBERGER, F. J., and DICKSON, W. J. *Management and the worker.* Cambridge, Mass.: Harvard University Press, 1939.

ROGAWSKI, A. S., and EDMUNDSON, B. Factors affecting the outcome of psychiatric interagency referral. *American journal of psychiatry,* 1971, *127,* 925–934.

ROGERS, C. R. *Counseling and psychotherapy: newer concepts in practice.* Boston: Houghton, 1942.

ROGERS, C. R. *Client-centered therapy: its current practice, implications and theory.* Boston: Houghton, 1951.

ROGERS, C. R. A theory of therapy, personality, and interpersonal relationships, as developed in the client-centered framework. In S. Koch, ed., *Psychology: a study of a science.* Vol. II: *general systematic formulations, learnings, and special processes.* New York: McGraw-Hill, 1959.

ROGERS, C. R. *On becoming a person: a therapist's view of psychotherapy.* Boston: Houghton, 1961.

ROGERS, C. R., and DYMOND, R. F., eds., *Psychotherapy and personality change.* Chicago: University of Chicago Press, 1954.

ROGERS, C. R., and SKINNER, B. F. Some issues concerning the control of human behavior: a symposium. *Science,* 1956, *124,* 1057–1066.

ROHAN, W. P. A follow-up study of hospitalized problem drinkers. *Diseases of the nervous system,* 1970, 31, 259–267.

ROHAN, W. P., and PROVOST, R. J. Re-establishment of eating habits in a blind and brain damaged patient: a case report. *Journal of psychiatric nursing,* 1966, *4,* 458–461.

ROMAN, P. M. Labeling theory and community psychiatry. *Psychiatry,* 1971, *34,* 378–390.

ROME, H. P. Barriers to the establishment of comprehensive community mental health centers. In L. M. Roberts, S. L. Halleck, and M. B. Loeb, eds., *Community psychiatry.* New York: Doubleday, 1969, pp. 58–71.

ROME, H. P. The aging system: its historical shadows and substance. *Psychiatric annals,* 1972, *2,* 12–27.

Roos, P. Development of an intensive habit-training unit at Austin State School. *Mental retardation,* 1965, *3,* 12–15.

Roos, P. Initiating socialization programs for socially inept adolescents. *Mental retardation,* 1968, *6,* 13–17.

Roos, P., and OLIVER, M. Evaluation of operant conditioning with institutionalized retarded children. Unpublished manuscript. Austin, Tex.: Austin State School, 1965.

ROPER, G. *Madness in society.* New York: Harper & Row, 1969.

ROPER, G., RACHMAN, S., and HODGSON, R. An experiment on obsessional checking. *Behaviour research and therapy,* 1973, *11,* 271–277.

ROSE, A. M., and STUB, H. G. Summary of studies on the incidence of mental disorders. In A. M. Rose, ed., *Mental health and mental disorder.* New York: Norton, 1955, pp. 87–116.

ROSEN, B. M., BARN, A. K., and CRAMER, M. Demographic and diagnostic characteristics of psychiatric out-patient clinics in the U.S.A., 1961. *American journal of orthopsychiatry,* 1964, *34,* 455–468.

ROSEN, E., FOX, R. E., and GREGORY, I. *Abnormal psychology.* Philadelphia: W. B. Saunders Co., 1972.

ROSEN, E., and GREGORY, I. *Abnormal psychology.* Philadelphia: Saunders, 1965.

ROSEN, M., and WESNER, C. A behavioral approach to Tourette's syndrome. *Journal of consulting and clinical psychology,* 1973, *41,* 308–312.

ROSENBAUM, G. Reaction time indices of schizophrenic motivation: a cross-cultural replication. *British journal of psychiatry,* 1967, *113,* 537–541.

ROSENBAUM, G., GRISELL, J. L., and MACKAVEY, W. R. Effects of biological and social motivation on schizophrenic reaction time. *Journal of abnormal and social psychology,* 1957, *54,* 364–368.

ROSENBERG, B. G., and SUTTON-SMITH, B. *Sex and identity.* New York: Holt, Rinehart and Winston, 1972.

ROSENBERG, H. *The anxious object.* New York: New American Library, 1969.

ROSENBERG, H. *Artworks and packages.* New York: Dell, 1971.

ROSENBERG, M., and GLUECK, B. C., JR. Further developments in automation of behavioral observations on hospitalized psychiatric patients. *Comprehensive psychiatry,* 1967, *8,* 468–475.

ROSENBERG, M., GLUECK, B. C., JR., and SENNETT, W. L. Automation of behavioral observations on hospitalized psychiatric patients. *American journal of psychiatry,* 1967, *123,* 926–929.

ROSENHAN, D. L. On the social psychology of hypnosis research. In J. E. Gordon, ed., *Handbook of experimental and clinical hypnosis.* New York: Macmillan, 1967, pp. 481-510.

ROSENHAN, D. L. On being sane in insane places. *Science,* 1973, *179,* 250-258.

ROSENHAN, D. L., and LONDON, P. Character. In P. London and D. Rosenhan, eds., *Foundations of abnormal psychology.* New York: Holt, Rinehart and Winston, 1968, pp. 251-288.

ROSENTHAL, C. S. Deviation and social change in the Jewish community of a small Polish town. *American journal of sociology,* 1954, *60,* 177-181.

ROSENTHAL, D. Changes in some moral values following psychotherapy. *Journal of consulting psychology,* 1955, *19,* 431-436.

ROSENTHAL, D. Some factors associated with concordance and discordance with respect to schizophrenia in monozygotic twins. *Journal of nervous and mental disease,* 1959, *129,* 1-10.

ROSENTHAL, D. Problems of sampling and diagnosis in the major twin studies of schizophrenia. *Journal of psychiatric research,* 1962, *1,* 116-134.

ROSENTHAL, D. *Genetics of psychopathology.* New York: McGraw Hill, 1971a.

ROSENTHAL, D. A program of research on heredity in schizophrenia. *Behavioral science,* 1971b, *16,* 191-201.

ROSENTHAL, D., and FRANK, J. D. Psychotherapy and the placebo effect. *Psychological bulletin,* 1956, *53,* 294-302.

ROSENTHAL, R. On the social psychology of the psychological experiment: the experimenter's hypotheses as unintended determinants of experimental results. *American scientist,* 1963, *51,* 268-283.

ROSENTHAL, R. *Experimenter effects in behavioral research.* New York: Appleton, 1966.

ROSENTHAL, R. Covert communication in the psychological experiment. *Psychological bulletin,* 1967, *5,* 356-367.

ROSENTHAL, R., and FODE, K. L. The effect of experimenter bias on the performance of the albino rat. *Behavioral sciences,* 1963a, *8,* 183-189.

ROSENTHAL, R., and FODE, K. L. Psychology of the scientist. V: Three experiments in experimenter bias. *Psychological reports,* 1963b, *12,* 491-511.

ROSENTHAL, R., and JACOBSON, L. Teachers' expectancies: determinants of pupils' I.Q. gains. *Psychological reports,* 1966, *19,* 115-118.

ROSENTHAL, R., and JACOBSON, L. *Pygmalion in the classroom.* New York: Holt, Rinehart and Winston, 1968.

ROSENTHAL, R., and LAWSON, R. A longitudinal study of the effects of experimenter bias on the operant learning of laboratory rats. *Journal of psychiatric research,* 1964, *2,* 61-72.

ROSENTHAL, T., FEIST, J., and DURNING, K. Separate model versus experimenter as model in vicarious concept attainment. *The journal of experimental education,* 1972, *41.*

ROSENTHAL, T., and KELLOGG, J. S. Demonstration versus instructions in concept attainment by mental retardates. *Behaviour research and therapy,* 1973, *11,* 299-302.

ROSENTHAL, T. L. Response-contingent versus fixed punishment in aversion conditioning of pedophilia: a case study. *Journal of nervous and mental disease,* in press.

ROSENTHAL, T. L. Severe stuttering and maladjustment treated by desensitization and social influence. *Behaviour research and therapy,* 1968, *6,* 125-130.

ROSENTHAL, T. L., ALFORD, G. S., and RASP, L. Concept attainment, generalization, and retention through observation and verbal coding. *Journal of experimental child psychologist,* 1972, *13,* 183-194.

ROSENTHAL, T. L., COXON, M., HURT, M., JR., ZIMMERMAN, B. J., and GRUBBS, C. F. Pedagogical attitudes of conventional and specially-trained teachers. *Psychology in the schools,* 1970, *7,* 61-66.

ROSENTHAL, T. L., and HERTZ, L. Effects of minimal models on inkblot percepts. *Australian journal of psychology,* 1972, *24,* 353-361.

ROSENTHAL, T. L., and WHITE, G. M. On the importance of hair in students' clinical inferences. *Journal of clinical psychology,* 1972, *28,* 43-46.

ROSENTHAL, T. L., ZIMMERMAN, B. J., and DURNING, K. Observationally induced changes in children's interrogative classes. *Journal of personality and social psychology,* 1970, *16,* 681-688.

Ross, L., RODIN, J., and ZIMBARDO, P. G. Toward an attribution therapy: the reduction of fear through induced cognitive emotional misattribution. *Journal of personality and social psychology,* 1969, *12,* 279-288.

Ross, N. W. *Three ways of Asian wisdom.* New York: Simon & Schuster, 1966.

Ross, R. R., MEICHENBAUM, D. H., and HUMPHREY, C. Treatment of nocturnal headbanging by behavior modification techniques: a case report. *Behaviour research and therapy,* 1971, *9,* 151-154.

Ross, S. A. Effects of intentional training in social behavior on retarded children. *American journal of mental deficiency,* 1969, *73,* 912-919.

ROSZAK, T. *The making of a counter culture.* New York: Doubleday, 1969.

ROTHMAN, D. J. *The discovery of the asylum.* Boston: Little, Brown, 1971.

ROTHSCHILD, D. Senile psychoses and psychoses with cerebral arteriosclerosis. In O. J. Kaplan, ed.,

Mental disorders in later life. Stanford, Calif.: Stanford University Press, 1945, 233–279.

ROTTER, J. B. *Social learning and clinical psychology.* Englewood Cliffs, N.J.: Prentice-Hall, 1954.

ROUÉCHÉ, B. *Alcohol.* New York: Grove, 1960.

ROUTH, D. K., and KING, K. M. Social class bias in clinical judgment. *Journal of consulting and clinical psychology*, 1972, *38*, 202–207.

ROVEE, C. K., and ROVEE, D. T. Conjugate reinforcement of infant exploratory behavior. *Journal of experimental child psychology*, 1969, *8*, 33–39.

ROWDEN, D. W. MICHEL, J. B., DILLEHAY, R. C., and MARTIN, H. W. Judgments about candidates for psychotherapy: the influence of social class and insight-verbal ability. *Journal of health and social behavior*, 1970, *11*, 51–58.

ROWLAND, L. W. Will hypnotized persons try to harm themselves or others? *Journal of abnormal and social psychology*, 1939, *4*, 114–117.

RUBENSTEIN, C. The treatment of morphine addiction in tuberculosis by Pavlow's conditioning method. *American review of tuberculosis*, 1931, *24*, 682–685.

RUBIN, G., GRISWALD, K., SMITH, I., and DeLEONARDO, C. A case study in the remediation of severe self-destructive behavior in a 6-year-old mentally retarded girl. *Journal of clinical psychology*, 1972, *28*, 424–426.

RUBIN, V. Discussion. In A. V. S. DeReuck and R. Porter, eds., *Transcultural psychiatry.* Boston: Little, Brown, 1965, p. 355.

RUBOVITS, P. C., and MAEHR, M. L. Pygmalion analyzed: toward an explanation of the Rosenthal-Jacobson findings. *Journal of personality and social psychology*, 1971, *19*, 197–203.

RUDESTAM, K. E. Stockholm and Los Angeles: a cross-cultural study of the communication of suicidal intent. *Journal of consulting and clinical psychology*, 1971, *36*, 82–90.

RUDOLPH, F. *The American college and university: a history.* New York: Vintage, 1965.

RUESCH, J. *Duodenal ulcer.* Berkeley: University of California Press, 1948.

RUESCH, J., HARRIS, R. E., and BOWMAN, K. M. Pre- and post-traumatic personality in head injuries. *Research publications, association for research in nervous and mental disease*, 1945, *24*, 507–544.

RUITENBEEK, H. M. *The new group therapies.* New York: Avon, 1970.

RUITENBEEK, H. M. Introduction-Radical therapy: what is it all about? In H. M. Ruitenbeek, ed., *Going crazy: the radical therapy of R. D. Laing and others.* New York: Bantam, 1972.

RUMBAUT, R. D. The first psychiatric hospital of the western world. *American journal of psychiatry*, 1972, *128*, 1305–1309.

RUSH, B. *Medical inquiries and observations upon the diseases of the mind.* Philadelphia: Kimber & Richardson, 1812.

RUSHING, R. H. *Art as an investment.* New York: Bonanza, 1961.

RUSSELL, J. C., CLARK, A. W., and VAN SOMMERS, P. Treatment of stammering by reinforcement of fluent speech. *Behaviour research and therapy*, 1968, *6*, 447–453.

RUSSO, S. Adaptations in behavioral therapy with children. *Behaviour research and therapy*, 1964, *2*, 43–47.

RUTTER, M. Childhood schizophrenia reconsidered. *Journal of autism and childhood schizophrenia*, 1972, *2*, 315–337.

RUTNER, I. T., and BUGLE, C. An experimental procedure for the modification of psychotic behavior. *Journal of consulting and clinical psychology*, 1969, *33*, 651–653.

RYAN, W. *Blaming the victim.* New York: Vintage, 1971.

SABATASSO, A. P., and JACOBSON, L. I. Use of behavioral therapy in the reinstatement of verbal behavior in a mute psychotic with chronic brain syndrome: a case study. *Journal of abnormal psychology*, 1970, *76*, 322–324.

SACHS, L. B., BEAN, H., and MORROW, J. E. Comparison of smoking treatments. *Behavior therapy*, 1970, *1*, 465–471.

SAENGER, G. *The adjustment of severely retarded adults in the community.* Albany, N.Y.: Interdepartmental Health Resources Board, 1957.

SAENGER, G. Psychiatric patients in America and the Netherlands: a transcultural comparison. *Social psychiatry*, 1968, *1*, 149–164.

SAENGER, G. Factors in recovery of untreated psychiatric patients. *Psychiatric quarterly*, 1970, *44*, 13–25.

SAGARIN, E. *The antomy of dirty words.* New York: Stuart, 1962.

SAGARIN, E. *Odd man in. Societies of deviants in America.* Chicago: Quadrangle, 1969.

SAILOR, W., GUESS, D., RUTHERFORD, G., and BAER, D. M. Control of tantrum behavior by operant techniques during experimental verbal training. *Journal of applied behavior analysis*, 1968, *1*, 237–243.

St. Augustine: the confessions. New York: Cardinal Edition, Pocket Books, 1952.

SAJWAJ, T., LIBET, J., and AGRAS, S. Lemon juice therapy: the control of life-threatening rumination in a six-month-old infant. *Journal of applied behavior analysis*, in press.

SAJWAJ, T., TWARDOSZ, S., and BURKE, M. Side effects of extinction procedures in a remedial preschool. *Journal of applied behavior analysis*, 1972, 5, 163–175.

SALTER, A. *Conditioned reflex therapy*. New York: Farrar, Straus, 1949, and Capricorn, 1961.

SALZINGER, K. An hypothesis about schizophrenic behavior. *American journal of psychotherapy*, 1971, 25, 601–614.

SALZINGER, K., FELDMAN, R. S. COWAN, J. E., and SALZINGER, S. Operant conditioning of verbal behavior of two young speech-deficient boys. In L. Krasner and L. P. Ullmann, eds., *Research in behavior modification*. New York: Holt, Rinehart and Winston, 1965, pp. 82–105.

SALZINGER, K., FELDMAN, R. S., and PORTNOY, S. Training parents of brain-injured children in the use of operant conditioning procedures. *Behavior therapy*, 1970, 1, 4–32.

SALZINGER, K., and PISONI, S. Reinforcement of affect responses of schizophrenics during the clinical interview. *Journal of abnormal and social psychology*, 1958, 57, 84–90.

SALZINGER, K., and PISONI, S. Some parameters of the conditioning of verbal affect responses in schizophrenic subjects. *Journal of abnormal and social psychology*, 1961, 63, 511–516.

SALZINGER, K., PORTNOY, S., and FELDMAN, R. S. Experimental manipulation of continuous speech in schizophrenic patients. *Journal of abnormal and social psychology*, 1964, 68, 508–516.

SALZMAN, L. F., GOLDSTEIN, R. H., ATKINS, R., and BABIGIAN, H. Conceptual thinking in psychiatric patients. *Archives of general psychiatry*, 1966, 14, 55–59.

SAMAAN, M. The control of nocturnal enuresis by operant conditioning *Journal of behavior therapy and experimental psychiatry*, 1972, 3, 103–105.

SANDERS, J. Senior power: how the aged are getting militant. *Chicago daily news*, 30 November 1970, p. 15.

SANDIFER, M. G., HORDERN, A., and GREEN, L. M. The psychiatric interview: the impact of the first three minutes. *American journal of psychiatry*, 1970, 126, 968–973.

SANDIFER, M. G., HORDERN, A., TIMBURY, G. C., and GREEN, L. M. Psychiatric diagnosis: a comparative study in North Carolina, London, and Glasgow. *British journal of psychiatry*, 1968, 114, 1–9.

SANDIFER, M. G., JR., PETTUS, C., and QUADE, D. A study of psychiatric diagnosis. *Journal of nervous and mental disease*, 1964, 139, 350–356.

SANDLER, J., and TURNER, W. L. Vocational preparation of the hardcore unemployed: the token economy. *Rehabilitation counseling bulletin*, 1973, 79–97.

SANTOSTEFANO, S., and STAYTON, S. Training the preschool retarded child in focusing attention: a program for parents. *American journal of orthopsychiatry*, 1967, 37, 732–743.

SAPER, B. Spotlight on behavior: learning alternatives to pot, acid, speed, and scag. *The psychiatric quarterly*, 1971, 45, 610–617.

SAPON, S. M. Contingency management in the modification of verbal behavior in disadvantaged children. Paper presented at American Psychological Association convention, 1967.

SARASON, I. G. Verbal learning, modeling, and juvenile delinquency. *American psychologist*, 1968, 23, 254–266.

SARASON, I. G. *Abnormal psychology: the problem of maladaptive behavior*. New York: Appleton-Century-Crofts, 1972.

SARASON, I. G., GANZER, V. J., and SINGER, M. The effects of modeled self-disclosure on the verbal behavior of persons differing in defensiveness. *Journal of consulting and clinical psychology*, 1972, 39, 483–490.

SARASON, S. B. *The culture of the school and the problem of change*. Boston: Allyn & Bacon, 1971.

SARBIN, T. R. Contributions to role-taking theory. I: hypnotic behavior. *Psychological review*, 1950, 57, 255–270.

SARBIN, T. R. Anxiety: reification of a metaphor. *Archives of general psychiatry*, 1964a, 10, 630–638.

SARBIN, T. R. Role theoretical interpretation of psychological change. In P. Worchel and D. Byrne, eds., *Personality change*. New York: Wiley, 1964b, 176–219.

SARBIN, T. R. Hypnosis as a behavior modification technique. In L. Krasner and L. P. Ullmann, eds., *Research in behavior modification*. New York: Holt, Rinehart and Winston, 1965, pp. 343–357.

SARBIN, T. R. The historical background of the concept of hallucination. *Journal of the history of the behavioral sciences*, 1967, 3, 339–358.

SARBIN, T. R. Schizophrenia: from metaphor to myth. Unpublished manuscript, University of California at Santa Cruz, 1971.

SASLOW, G., and MATARAZZO, J. D. A technique for studying changes in interview behavior. In E. A. Rubinstein, and M. B. Parloff, eds., *Research in psychotherapy*. Washington, D.C.: American Psychological Association, 1959.

SATRAM, R., and GOLDSTEIN, M. N. Pain perception: modification of threshold of intolerance and cortical potentials by cutaneous stimulation. *Science*, 1973, 180, 1201–1202.

SATTLER, J. M. Racial "experimenter effects" in experimentation, testing, interviewing, and psychotherapy. *Psychological bulletin,* 1970, *73,* 137–160.

SAUL, L. J. Hostility in cases of essential hypertension. *Psychosomatic medicine,* 1939, *1,* 153–161.

SAUL, L. J., ROME, H., and LEUSER, E. Desensitization of combat fatigue patients. *American journal of psychiatry,* 1946, *102,* 476–478.

SAWYER, J. B., SUDAK, H. S., and HALL, S. R. A follow-up of 53 suicides known to a suicide prevention center. *Life threatening behavior,* 1972, *2,* 227–238.

SAYEGH, Y., and DENNIS, W. The effect of supplementary experience upon the behavioral development of infants in institutions. *Child development,* 1965, *36,* 81–90.

SCANDURA, J. R. Role of rules in behavior: toward an operational definition of what (rule) is learned. *Psychological review,* 1970, *77,* 516–533.

SCHAAP, C. M., and DANA, R. H. Experimental treatment of phobias by systematic desensitization. *Psychological reports,* 1968, *23,* 969–970.

SCHACHT, L. S., and BLACKER, M. Leadership effect on the staff conference process. *Archives of general psychiatry,* 1969, *20,* 358–364.

SCHACHTER, S. The interaction of cognitive and physiological determinants of emotional state. In L. Berkowitz, ed., *Advances in experimental social psychology.* Vol. 1. New York: Academic Press, 1964.

SCHACHTER, S., and SINGER, J. E. Cognitive, social and physiological determinants of emotional state. *Psychological review,* 1962, *69,* 379–399.

SCHACHTER, S., and WHEELER, L. Epinephrine, chlorpromazine, and amusement. *Journal of abnormal and social psychology,* 1962, *65,* 121–128.

SCHAEFER, H. H., and MARTIN, P. L. Behavioral therapy for "apathy" of hospitalized schizophrenics. *Psychological reports,* 1966, *19,* 1147–1158.

SCHAEFER, H. H., and MARTIN, P. L. *Behavioral therapy.* New York: McGraw-Hill, 1969.

SCHAEFER, H. H., NOBELL, M. R., and MILLS, K. C. Some sobering data on the use of self-confrontation with alcoholics. *Behavior therapy,* 1971, *2,* 28–39.

SCHAPS, E. Cost, dependency and helping. *Journal of personality and social psychology,* 1972, *21,* 74–78.

SCHEFF, T. J. *Being mentally ill.* Chicago: Aldine, 1966a.

SCHEFF, T. J. Users and non-users of a student psychiatric clinic. *Journal of health and human behavior,* 1966b, *7,* 114–121.

SCHEFF, T. J., and SUNDSTROM, E. The stability of deviant behavior over time: a reassessment. *Journal of health and social behavior,* 1970, *11,* 37–43.

SCHEIN, E. H., SCHNEIER, I., and BARKER, C. H. *Coercive persuasion.* New York: Norton, 1961.

SCHELL, R. E., STARK, J., and GIDDAN, N. J. Development of language behavior in an autistic child. *Journal of speech and hearing disorders,* 1967, *32,* 51–64.

SCHIMEL, J. L. Some practical considerations in treating male sexual inadequacy. *Medical aspects of human sexuality.* March 1971, pp. 24–31.

SCHIMEL, J. L., SALZMAN, L., CHODOFF, P., GRINKER, R. R., SR., and WILL, O. A., JR. Changing styles in psychiatric syndromes: a symposium. *American journal of psychiatry,* 1973, *130,* 146–155.

SCHLESINGER, B., and JAMES, G. M. Psychiatry and poverty: a selected review of the literature. *Canadian medical association journal,* 1969, *101,* 470–477.

SCHLOSS, G. A., SIROKA, R. W., and SIROKA, E. K. Some contemporary origins of the personal growth group. In R. W. Siroka, E. K. Siroka, and G. A. Schloss, eds., *Sensitivity training and group encounter.* New York: Grosset & Dunlap, 1971, pp. 3–10.

SCHMAUK, F. J. Punishment, arousal, and avoidance learning in sociopaths. *Journal of abnormal psychology,* 1970, *76,* 325–335.

SCHMIDT, E., CASTELL, D., and BROWN, P. A retrospective study of 42 cases of behaviour therapy. *Behaviour research and therapy,* 1965, *3,* 9–19.

SCHMIDT, H. O., and FONDA, C. P. The reliability of psychiatric diagnosis: a new look. *Journal of abnormal and social psychology,* 1956, *52,* 262–267.

SCHNURER, A. T., RUBIN, R. R., and ROY, A. Systematic desensitization of anorexia nervosa seen as a weight phobia. *Journal of behavior therapy and experimental psychiatry,* 1973, *4,* 149–153.

SCHOFIELD, W. *Psychotherapy: the purchase of friendship.* Englewood Cliffs, N.J.: Prentice-Hall, 1964.

SCHOLANDER, T. Treatment of an unusual case of compulsive behavior by aversive stimulation. *Behavior therapy,* 1972, *3,* 290–293.

SCHOOLER, C., and CAUDILL, W. Symptomatology in Japanese and American schizophrenics. *Ethnology,* 1964, *3,* 172–177.

SCHOPLER, J., and LAYTON, B. Determinants of the self-attribution of having influenced another person. *Journal of personality and social psychology,* 1972, *22,* 326–332.

SCHORER, C. E. Improvement with and without psychotherapy. *Diseases of the nervous system,* 1970, *31,* 155–160.

SCHORER, C. E., LOWINGER, P., SULLIVAN, T., and HARTLAUB, G. H. Improvement without treatment. *Diseases of the nervous system,* 1968, *29,* 100–104.

SCHREIBER, Y. L. A method of indirect suggestion as used in hysteria. In R. B. Winn, ed., *Psychotherapy in the Soviet Union*. New York: Philosophical Library, 1962, 85–86.

SCHROEDER, S. R. Parametric effects of reinforcement frequency, amount of reinforcement, and required response force on sheltered workshop behavior. *Journal of applied behavior analysis*, 1972, *5*, 431–441.

SCHULBERG, H. C., and SHELDON, A. The probability of crisis and strategies for preventive intervention. *Archives of general psychiatry*, 1968, *18*, 553–558.

SCHULDER, D. B. Women and the law. In S. Stambler, ed., *Women's liberation: blueprint for the future*. New York: Ace, 1970, pp. 85–89.

SCHULDT, W. J. Psychotherapists' approach-avoidance responses and clients' expressions of dependency. *Journal of counseling psychology*, 1966, *13*, 178–183.

SCHULER, E. A., and PARENTON, V. J. A recent epidemic of hysteria in a Louisiana high school. *Journal of social psychology*, 1963, *17*, 221–235.

SCHULTZ, D. P. *Panic behavior*. New York: Random House, 1964.

SCHUR, E. M. *Crimes without victims: deviant behavior and public policy: abortion, homosexuality, drug addiction*. Englewood Cliffs, N.J.: Prentice-Hall, 1965a.

SCHUR, E. M. Drug addiction in England and America. In D. Wakefield, ed., *The addict*. Greenwich, Conn.: Fawcett, 1965b.

SCHUR, E. M. *Labeling deviant behavior: its sociological implications*. New York: Harper & Row, 1971.

SCHWAB, J. J. Depressive illness: a sociomedical syndrome. *Psychosomatics*, 1971, *12*, 385–389.

SCHWAB, J. J., BROWN, J. M., HOLZER, C. E., and SOKOLOF, M. Current concepts of depression: the sociocultural. *International journal of social psychiatry*, 1968, *14*, 226–234.

SCHWAB, J. J., WARHEIT, G. J., and HOLZER, C. E. Suicidal ideation and behavior in a general population. *Diseases of the nervous system*, 1972, *33*, 745–748.

SCHWARTZ, A. N., and HAWKINS, H. L. Patient models and affect statements in group therapy. *Proceedings of the 75th Annual Convention of the American Psychological Association*, 1967, 265–266.

SCHWARTZ, F. Use of positive reinforcement to attain proper walking in a severely retarded child. *SALT: School application of learning theory*, 1973, *5*, 31–38.

SCHWARTZ, G. Clinical applications of biofeedback: some theoretical issues. Paper presented at the third annual Brockton symposium on behavior therapy, April 21, 1972, pp. 35–56.

SCHWARTZ, G. E. Voluntary control of human cardiovascular integration and differentiation through feedback and reward. *Science*, 1972, *175*, 90–93.

SCHWARTZ, G. E., SHAPIRO, D., and TURSKY, B. Learned control of cardiovascular integration in man through operant conditioning. *Psychosomatic medicine*, 1971, *33*, 57–62.

SCHWARTZ. S. H. Elicitation of moral obligation and self-sacrificing behavior: an experimental study of volunteering to be a bone marrow donor. *Journal of personality and social psychology*, 1970, *15*, 283–293.

SCHWARTZ, S. H., and CLAUSEN, G. T. Responsibility, norms, and helping in an emergency. *Journal of personality and social psychology*, 1970, *16*, 299–310.

SCHWITZGEBEL, R. A new approach to reducing adolescent crime. *Federal probation*, March 1960, pp. 20–24.

SCHWITZGEBEL, R. Reduction of adolescent crime by a research method. *Journal of correctional psychiatry and social therapy*, 1961, *7*, 212–215.

SCHWITZGEBEL, R. Delinquents with tape recorders. *New society*, January 1963, pp. 14–16.

SCHWITZGEBEL, R. *Street-corner research: an experimental approach to the juvenile delinquent*. Cambridge, Mass.: Harvard University Press, 1964.

SCHWITZGEBEL, R. Short-term operant conditioning of adolescent offenders on socially relevant variables. *Journal of abnormal psychology*, 1967, *72*, 134–142.

SCHWITZGEBEL, R. K. Ethical and legal aspects of behavioral instrumentation. *Behavior therapy*, 1970, *1*, 498.

SCHWITZGEBEL, R. K., and KOLB, D. A. *Changing human behavior: principles of planned intervention*. New York: McGraw-Hill, 1974.

SCHWITZGEBEL, R. L. Survey of electromechanical devices for behavior modification. *Psychological bulletin*, 1968, *70*, 444–459.

SCHWITZGEBEL, R., and KOLB, D. A. Inducing behaviour change in adolescent delinquents. *Behaviour research and therapy*, 1964, *1*, 297–304.

SCHWITZGEBEL, R., SCHWITZGEBEL, R., PAHNKE, W. N., and HURD, W. S. A program of research in behavioral electronics. *Behavioral science*, 1964, *9*, 233–238.

SCODEL, A. Passivity in a class of peptic ulcer patients. *Psychological monographs*, 1953, *10* (whole no. 360).

SCOTT, A. Growing old in America. *Honolulu star bulletin and advertiser*, 17 December 1972.

SCOTT, P. M., BURTON, R. V., and YARROW, M. R. Social reinforcement under natural conditions. *Child development*, 1967, *38*, 53–63.

SCOTT, R. A. *The making of blind men.* New York: Russell Sage, 1969.

SCOTT, R. W., PETERS, R. D., GILLESPIE, W. J., BLANCHARD, E. B., EDMUNSON, E. D., and YOUNG, L. D. The use of shaping and reinforcement in the operant acceleration and deceleration of heart rate. *Behaviour research and therapy*, 1973, *11*, 179–185.

SCOTT, W. A. Research definitions of mental health and mental illness. *Psychological bulletin*, 1958a, *55*, 29–40.

SCOTT, W. A. Social psychological correlates of mental illness and mental health. *Psychological bulletin*, 1958b, *55*, 65–87.

SCRIGNAR, C. B. Food as the reinforcer in the outpatient treatment of anorexia nervosa. *Journal of behavior therapy and experimental psychiatry*, 1971, *2*, 31–36.

SEAGER, C. P. Treatment of compulsive gamblers by electrical aversion. *British journal of psychiatry*, 1970, *117*, 545–553.

SEARS, R. R. Experimental analysis of psychoanalytic phenomena. In J. McV. Hunt, ed., *Personality and the behavior disorders.* Vol. 1. New York: Ronald Press, 1944, pp. 306–332.

SEARS, R. R. A theoretical framework for personality and social behavior. *American psychologist*, 1951, *6*, 476–483.

SEARS, R. R., and COHEN, L. H. Hysterical anaesthesia, analgesia and asterognosis. *Archives of neurology and psychiatry*, 1933, *29*, 260–271.

SEARS, R. R., MACCOBY, E. E., and LEVIN, H. *Patterns of child rearing.* Evanston, Ill.: Row, Peterson, 1957.

SEBECK, T. A. Animal communication. *Science*, 1965, *147*, 1006–1014.

SECHENOV, I. M. *Reflexes of the brain* (1863). Reprinted in *Selected Works.* Moscow: Bookmiga, 1935.

SECHREST, L. Exercise as an operant response for retarded children. *Journal of special education*, 1968, *2*, 311–317.

SECHREST, L. Philippine culture, stress, and psychopathology. In, W. Caudill and T. Lin, eds., *Mental health research in Asia and the Pacific.* Honolulu: East-West Center, 1969, pp. 306–334.

SEEMAN, W. P. Psychiatric diagnosis: an investigation of interperson-reliability after didactic instruction. *Journal of nervous and mental disease*, 1953, *118*, 541–544.

SEGAL, H. A. Initial psychiatric findings of recently repatriated prisoners of war. *American journal of psychiatry*, 1954, *111*, 358–363.

SEITZ, F. C. Five psychological measures of neurotic depression: a correlation study. *Journal of clinical psychology*, 1970, *26*, 504–505.

SEITZ, F. C. Behavior modification techniques for treating depression. *Psychotherapy: theory, research and practice*, 1971a, *8*, 181–184.

SEITZ, F. C. A behavior modification approach to depression: a case study. *Psychology*, 1971b, *8*, 58–63.

SEITZ, F. C. Behavior modification of depression. *Proceedings of the annual convention of the American Psychological Association*, 1971c, *6*, 425–426.

SELIGMAN, M. E. P. Depression and learned helplessness. In R. J. Friedman and M. M. Katz, eds., *The psychology of depression: contemporary theory and research*, 1973.

SELMAN, R. L. The relation of role taking to the development of moral judgment in children. *Child development*, 1971, *42*, 79–91.

SELYE, H. *The stress of life.* New York: McGraw-Hill, 1956.

SEMANS, J. H. Premature ejaculation. *Southern medical journal*, 1956, *49*, 353–357.

SERBER, M. Shame aversion therapy. *Journal of behavior therapy and experimental psychiatry*, 1970, *1*, 213–215.

SERBER, M. Teaching the nonverbal components of assertive training. *Journal of behavior therapy and experimental psychiatry*, 1972, *3*, 179–183.

SEVERY, L. J., and DAVIS, K. E. Helping behavior among normal and retarded children. *Child development*, 1971, *42*, 1017–1031.

SEWELL, W. H. Infant training and personality of the child. *American journal of sociology*, 1952, *58*, 150–159.

SHADER, R. I. Behavioral treatment of enuresis nocturna. *Diseases of the nervous system*, 1968, *29*, 334–335.

SHAH, S. A. Community mental health and the criminal justice system: some issues and problems. *Mental hygiene*, 1970, *54*, 1–12.

SHAKOW, D. The role of classification in the development of the science of psychopathology with particular reference to research. In (anonymous editor) *The role and methodology of classification in psychiatry and psychopathology.* Washington, D.C.: Government Printing Office, Public Health Service Publication, 1968, #1584, 116–143.

SHAMES, G. H. Dysfluency and stuttering. *Pediatric clinics of North America*, 1968, *15*, 691–704.

SHAMES, G. H., EGOLF, D. B., and RHODES, R. C. Experimental programs in stuttering therapy. *Journal of speech and hearing disorders*, 1969, *34*, 30–47.

SHAMES, G. H., and SHERRICK, C. E., JR. A discussion of nonfluency and stuttering as operant behavior.

Journal of speech and hearing disorders, 1963, 28, 3–18.

SHANNON, D. T. Clinical patterns of defense as revealed in visual recognition thresholds. Journal of abnormal and social psychology, 1962, 64, 370–377.

SHAPIRO, A. K. The placebo effect in the history of medical treatment: implications for psychiatry. American journal of psychiatry, 1959, 116, 298–304.

SHAPIRO, A. K. A contribution to a history of the placebo effect. Behavioral science, 1960, 5, 109–135.

SHAPIRO, A. K., SHAPIRO, E., WAYNE, H. L., CLARKIN, J., and BRUNN, R. D. Tourette's syndrome: summary of data on 34 patients. Psychosomatic medicine, 1973, 35, 419–435.

SHAPIRO, D., CRIDER, A., and TURSKY, B. Differentiation of an autonomic response through operant reinforcement. Psychonomic science, 1964, 1, 147–148.

SHAPIRO, D., and SCHWARTZ, G. E. Biofeedback and visceral learning: clinical applications. Seminars in psychiatry, 1972, 4, 171–184.

SHAPIRO, D., TURSKY, B., GERSHOM, E., et al. Effects of feedback and reinforcement on the control of human systolic blood pressure. Science, 1969, 163, 588–589.

SHARMA, S. L. A historical background of the development of nosology in psychiatry and psychology. American psychologist, 1970, 25, 248–253.

SHAVER, K. G. Defensive attribution: effects of severity and relevance on the responsibility assigned for an accident. Journal of personality and social psychology, 1970, 14, 101–113.

SHAW, C. R. The jack-roller. Chicago: University of Chicago Press, 1930.

SHAW, C. R., and MCKAY, H. D. Juvenile delinquency and urban areas. Chicago: University of Chicago Press, 1942.

SHAW, F. J. Some postulates concerning psychotherapy. Journal of consulting psychology, 1948, 12, 426–431.

SHAW, W. H. Treatment of a schizophrenic speech disorder by operant conditioning in play therapy. Canadian psychiatric association journal, 1969, 14, 631–634.

SHEAN, G. Perceptual conformity and responsiveness to social reinforcement in chronic schizophrenics. Journal of abnormal psychology, 1973, 82, 174–177.

SHEARN, D. Operant conditioning of heart rate. Science, 1962, 137, 530–531.

SHEEHAN, J. G. The modification of stuttering through nonreinforcement. Journal of abnormal and social psychology, 1951, 46, 51–63.

SHEEHAN, J. G. Rorschach changes during psychotherapy in relation to personality of the therapist. American psychologist, 1953, 8, 434–435 (abstract).

SHEEHAN, J. G., HADLEY, R., and GOULD, E. Impact of authority on stuttering. Journal of abnormal psychology, 1967, 72, 290–293.

SHEEHAN, J. G., and MARTYN, M. M. Stuttering and its disappearance. Journal of speech and hearing research, 1970, 13, 279–289.

SHEEHAN, P. W. Factors affecting mediation of E-bias effects in verbal conditioning. Psychological reports, 1970, 27, 647–650.

SHEEHAN, P. W., and BOWMAN, L. Peer model and experimenter expectancies about appropriate response as determinants of behavior in the hypnotic setting. Journal of abnormal psychology, 1973, 82, 112–123.

SHELLHAAS, M. D., and NIHIRA, K. Factor analysis of reasons retardates are referred to an institution. American journal of mental deficiency, 1969, 74, 171–179.

SHELLHAAS, M. D., and NIHIRA, K. Factor analytic comparisons of reasons retardates are institutionalized in two populations. American journal of mental deficiency, 1970, 74, 626–632.

SHENKER, I. Who is first through a door is no open and shut matter. New York times, 31 August 1973, p. 27.

SHEPERD, M., BROOKE, E. M., COOPER, J. E., and LIN, T. An experimental approach to psychiatric diagnosis. Acta psychiatrica Scandinavica, 1968, 44 (Supp. 201).

SHERMAN, J. A. Use of reinforcement and imitation to reinstate verbal behavior in mute psychotics. Journal of abnormal and social psychology, 1965, 70, 155–164.

SHERR, L. Sex books losing sock? Chicago daily news, 2 December 1971, p. 27.

SHERWOOD, J. J., and NATAUPSKY, M. Predicting the conclusions of Negro-white intelligence research from biographical characteristics of the investigator. Journal of personality and social psychology, 1968, 8, 53–58.

SHIBUTANI, T. Improvised news. Indianapolis: Bobbs-Merrill, 1966.

SHIELDS, J., and SLATER, E. Heredity and psychological abnormality. In H. J. Eysenck, ed., Handbook of abnormal psychology. New York: Basic Books, 1961, 298–343.

SHLIEN, J. M. An experimental investigation of time-limited client-centered therapy. University of Chicago counseling center paper, 1958, 2 (23).

SHLIEN, J. M., MOSAK, H. H., and DREIKURS, R. Effect of time limits: a comparison of client-centered and Adlerian psychotherapy. American psychologist, 1960, 15, 415 (abstract).

SHLIEN, J. M., MOSAK, H. H., and DREIKURS, R. Effect of time limits: a comparison of two psychotherapies. *Journal of counseling psychology,* 1962, *9,* 31–34.

SHNEIDMAN, E. S. Classification of suicidal phenomena. *Bulletin of suicidology,* July 1968, 1–9.

SHNEIDMAN, E. S., and FARBEROW, N. L., eds., *Clues to suicide.* New York: McGraw-Hill, 1957a.

SHNEIDMAN, E. S., and FARBEROW, N. L. Some comparisons between genuine and simulated suicide notes in terms of Mowrer's concepts of discomfort and relief. *Journal of general psychology,* 1957b, *56,* 251–256.

SHNEIDMAN, E. S., FARBEROW, N. L., and LITMAN, R. E. The suicide prevention center. In N. L. Farberow and E. S. Shneidman, eds., *The cry for help.* New York: McGraw-Hill, 1961.

SHNEIDMAN, E. S., FARBEROW, N. L., and LITMAN, R. E. *The psychology of suicide.* New York: Science House, 1970.

SHOBEN, E. J., JR. Psychotherapy as a problem in learning theory. *Psychological bulletin,* 1949, *46,* 366–392.

SHOBEN, E. J., JR. Toward a concept of the normal personality. *American psychologist,* 1957, *12,* 183–189.

SHORE, M. F., and GOLANN, S. E. Problems of ethics in community mental health: a survey of community psychologists. *Community mental health journal,* 1969, *5,* 452–460.

SHURE, M. B., SPIVAK, G., and JAEGER, M. Problem-solving thinking and adjustment among disadvantaged preschool children. *Child development,* 1971, *42,* 1791–1803.

SIDMAN, M. Normal sources of pathological behavior. *Science,* 1960, *132,* 61–68.

SIEGELMAN, M. Adjustment of homosexual and heterosexual women. *British journal of psychiatry,* 1972, *120,* 477–481.

SIEGLER, M., OSMOND, H., and NEWELL, S. Models of alcoholism. *Quarterly journal of studies on alcohol,* 1968, *29,* 571–591.

SILBERMAN, C. *Crisis in the classroom.* New York: Random House, 1970.

SILBERT, R. Psychiatric patients in the admitting emergency room. *Archives of general psychiatry,* 1964, *11,* 24–30.

SILVERMAN, I., SHULMAN, A. D., and WIESENTHAL, D. L. Effects of deceiving and debriefing psychological subjects on performance in later experiments. *Journal of personality and social psychology,* 1970, *14,* 203–212.

SILVERMAN, J. Scanning-control mechanism and "cognitive filtering" in paranoid and non-paranoid schizophrenia. *Journal of consulting psychology,* 1964, *28,* 385–393.

SILVERMAN, J., BERG, P. S. D., and KANTOR, R. Some perceptual correlates of institutionalization. *Journal of nervous and mental disease,* 1966, *141,* 651–657.

SIMKINS, L. D. Modification of duration of peer interactions in emotionally disturbed children. *Journal of social psychology,* 1971, *84,* 287–299.

SIMPSON, R. K., FITZ, E., SCOTT, B., and WALKER, L. Delirium tremens: a preventable iatrogenic phenomenon. *Journal of the American osteopathic association,* 1969, *68,* 123–130.

SIMS, G. K., and LAZARUS, A. A. The use of random auditory stimulation in the treatment of a manic-depressive patient. *Behavior therapy,* 1973, *4,* 128–133.

SINETT, E. R., STIMPERT, W. E., and STRAIGHT, E. A five-year follow-up study of psychiatric patients. *American journal of orthopsychiatry,* 1965, *35,* 573–580.

SINGER, B. D., and OSBORN, R. W. Social class and sex differences in admission patterns of the mentally retarded. *American journal of mental deficiency,* 1970, *75,* 160–162.

SINGER, E. *Key concepts in psychotherapy.* New York: Basic Books, 1970.

SINGER, J. E. Sympathetic activation, drugs, and fear. *Journal of comparative and physiological psychology,* 1963, *56,* 612–615.

SINGER, K., and WONG, M. Alcoholic psychoses and alcoholism in the Chinese: a study of 100 consecutive cases admitted to a psychiatric hospital in Hong Kong. *Quarterly journal of studies on alcohol,* 1973, *34,* 878–886.

SIPPRELLE, C. N. Induced anxiety. *Psychotherapy: theory, research and practice,* 1967, *4,* 36–40.

SIQUELAND, E. R., and DE LUCIA, C. A. Visual reinforcement of nonnutritional sucking in human infants. *Science,* 1969, *165,* 1144–1146.

SIQUELAND, E. R., and LIPSITT, L. P. Conditioned head-turning in human newborns. *Journal of experimental child psychology,* 1966, *3,* 356–376.

SKEA, S., DRAGUNS, J. G., and PHILLIPS, L. Ethnic characteristics of psychiatric symptomatology within and across regional groupings: a study of an Israeli child guidance clinic population. *Israel annals of psychiatry and related disciplines,* 1969, *7,* 31–42.

SKERLY, N. The mid-life crisis of life after 40. *Honolulu star-bulletin and advertiser,* 17 June 1973, p. D-4.

SKIBA, E. A., PETTIGREW, L. E., and ALDEN, S. E. A behavioral approach to the control of thumb-sucking in the classroom. *Journal of applied behavior analysis,* 1971, *4,* 121–125.

SKINNER, B. F. *The behavior of organisms.* New York: Appleton, 1938.

SKINNER, B. F. *Walden Two.* New York: Macmillan, 1948.

SKINNER, B. F. *Science and human behavior.* New York: Macmillan, 1953.

SKINNER, B. F. *Verbal behavior.* New York: Appleton, 1957.

SKINNER, B. F. *Cumulative record.* New York: Appleton, 1959.

SKINNER, B. F. What is the experimental analysis of behavior? *Journal of experimental analysis of behavior,* 1966, *9,* 213–218.

SKINNER, B. F. *Beyond freedom and dignity.* New York: Knopf, 1971.

SKRZYPEK, G. J. The effect of perceptual isolation and arousal on anxiety, complexity preference and novelty preference in psychopathic and neurotic delinquents. Unpublished doctoral dissertation, University of Illinois, 1967.

SLACK, C. W. Experimenter-subject psychotherapy: a new method of introducing intensive office treatment for unreachable cases. *Mental hygiene,* 1960, *44,* 238–256.

SLADE, H. C. The concept of neurasthenia. *Canadian psychiatric association journal,* 1968, *13,* 281–282.

SLADE, P. D. The effects of systematic desensitization on auditory hallucinations. *Behaviour research and therapy,* 1972, *10,* 85–91.

SLAVSON, S. R. *Analytic group psychotherapy.* New York: Columbia University Press, 1950.

SMALL, S. M. Concept of hysteria: history and reevaluation. *New York: state medical journal,* 1969, *69,* 1886–1872.

SMELSER, N. J. *Theory of collective behavior.* New York: Free Press, 1962.

SMITH, J. J. A medical approach to problem drinking, preliminary report. *Quarterly journal of studies on alcohol,* 1949, *10,* 251–257.

SMITH, K., PUMPHREY, M. W., and HALL, J. C. The "last straw": the decisive incident resulting in the request for hospitalization in 100 schizophrenic patients. *American journal of psychiatry,* 1963, *120,* 228–232.

SMITH, P. *The historian and history.* New York: Knopf, 1964.

SMITH, R. E., DIENER, E., and BEAMAN, A. L. Demand characteristics and the behavioral avoidance measure of fear in behavior therapy analogue research. *Behavior therapy,* in press.

SNIDER, A. J. Decision on alcoholism deplored by the AMA. *Chicago daily news,* 19 June 1968, p. 22.

SNIDER, A. J. Deformity or death for hopeless infants. *Honolulu star-bulletin,* 31 October 1973, p. D-8.

SNYDER, C. R., and LARSON, G. R. A further look at student acceptance of general personality interpretations. *Journal of consulting and clinical psychology,* 1972, *38,* 384–388.

SNYDER, W. U. Client-centered therapy. In L. A. Pennington and I. A. Berg, eds., *An introduction to clinical psychology.* 2nd ed. New York: Ronald Press, 1954.

SOBELL, L. C., SOBELL, M. B., and CHRISTELMAN, W. C. The myth of "one drink." *Behaviour research and therapy,* 1972, *10,* 119–123.

SOBELL, M. B., SCHAEFFER, H. H., and MILLS, K. C. Differences in baseline drinking behaviors between alcoholics and normal drinkers. *Behaviour research and therapy,* 1972, *10,* 257–268.

SOBELL, M. B., and SOBELL, L. C. Individualized behavior therapy for alcoholics: rationale, procedures, preliminary results and appendix. *California mental health research monograph,* 1972, *13,* 1–81.

SOBELL, M. B. and SOBELL, L. C. Individualized behavior therapy for alcoholics. *Behavior therapy,* 1973, *4,* 49–72.

SOCARIDES, C. W. A provisional theory of aetiology in male homosexuality. *International journal of psychoanalysis,* 1968, *49,* 27–37.

SOKOLOW, E. N. *Perception and the conditioned reflex.* New York: Pergamon, 1963.

SOLD, R. Forced retirement, a hazard to your health. *Honolulu star-bulletin,* 14 December 1972. p. E-5.

SOLOMON, P., et al., eds., *Sensory deprivation.* Cambridge, Mass.: Harvard University Press, 1961.

SOLOMON, R. L. Punishment. *American psychologist,* 1964, *19,* 239–253.

SOLOMON, R. L., KAMIN, L. J., and WYNNE, L. C. Traumatic avoidance learning: the outcomes of several extinction procedures with dogs. *Journal of abnormal and social psychology,* 1953, *48,* 291–302.

SOLOMON, R. L., and WYNNE, L. C. Traumatic avoidance learning: acquisition in normal dogs. *Psychological monographs,* 1953, *67* (4), whole No. 354.

SOLOMON, R. L., and WYNNE, L. C. Traumatic avoidance learning: the principles of anxiety conservation and partial irreversibility. *Psychological review,* 1954, *61,* 353–385.

SOLYOM, L., MCCLURE, D. J., HESELTINE, G. F. D., LEDWIDGE, B., and SOLYOM, C. Variables in the aversion relief therapy of phobics. *Behavior therapy,* 1972, *3,* 21–28.

SOLYOM, L., and MILLER, S. B. Reciprocal inhibition by aversion relief in the treatment of phobias. *Behavior research and therapy,* 1967, *5,* 313–324.

SOMMER, R. *Personal space.* Englewood Cliffs, N.J.: Prentice-Hall, 1969.

SOMMER, R. *Tight spaces: hard architecture and how to humanize it.* Englewood Cliffs, New Jersey: Prentice-Hall, 1974.

SOMMER, R., and OSMOND, H. Symptoms of institutional care. *Social problems,* 1961, *8,* 254–263.

SOMMER, R., and ROSS, H. Social interaction on a geriatrics ward. *Journal of social psychiatry,* 1958, *4,* 128–133.

SOURS, J. A. Clinical studies in anorexia nervosa syndrome. *New York state journal of medicine,* 1968, *68,* 1363–1369.

SOUTHARD, E. E. Alienists and psychiatrists. *Mental hygiene,* 1917, *1,* 567–571.

SPADONI, A. J., and SMITH, J. A. Milieu therapy in schizophrenia: a negative result. *Archives of general psychiatry,* 1969, *20,* 547–551.

SPANOS, N. P., and BARBER, T. X. "Hypnotic" experiences as inferred from subjective reports: auditory and visual hallucinations. *Journal of experimental research in personality,* 1968, *3,* 136–150.

SPANOS, N. P., MCPEAKE, J. D., and CARTER, W. Effects of pretesting on response to a visual hallucination suggestion in hynotic subjects. *Journal of personality and social psychology,* 1973, *28,* 293–297.

SPEISMAN, J. C. Depth of interpretation and verbal resistance in psychotherapy. *Journal of consulting psychology,* 1959, *23,* 93–99.

SPENCE, K. W. *Behavior theory and learning: selected papers.* Englewood Cliffs, N.J.: Prentice-Hall, 1960.

SPERRY, R. W. The great cerebral commissure. *Scientific American,* 1964, *210,* 42–52.

SPIRO, H. R. Chronic fictitious illness: Munchausen's syndrome. *Archives of general psychiatry,* 1968, *18,* 569–579.

SPITZ, R. A. Anaclitic depression. *Psychoanalytic study of the child,* 1946, *2,* 113–117.

SPITZER, R., and ENDICOTT, J. Diagno, II: Further developments in a computer program for psychiatric diagnosis. *American journal of psychiatry,* 1969, supplement, *125,* 12–20.

SPITZER, R. L., and WILSON, P. T. A guide to the American psychiatric association's new diagnostic nomenclature. *American journal of psychiatry,* 1968, *124,* 1619–1629.

SPITZER, S. P., and DENZIN, N. K., eds., *The mental patient: studies in the sociology of deviance.* New York: McGraw-Hill, 1968.

SPRADLIN, J. E., and GIRARDEAU, F. L. The behavior of moderately and severely retarded persons. In N. R. Ellis, ed., *International review of research in mental retardation.* Vol. 1. New York: Academic Press, 1966, 257–298.

SROLE, L., LANGNER, T. S., MICHAEL, S. T., OPLER, M. K., and RENNIE, T. A. C. *Mental health in the metropolis. Midtown Manhattan study.* Vol. I. New York: McGraw-Hill, 1962.

SROUFE, L. A. The diversification of minimal brain dysfunction. *Contemporary psychology,* 1972, *17,* 264–266.

STAATS, A. W. *Human learning.* New York: Holt, Rinehart and Winston, 1964.

STAATS, A. W. A case in and a strategy for the extension of learning principles to problems of human behavior. In L. Krasner and L. P. Ullmann, eds., *Research in behavior modification.* New York: Holt, Rinehart and Winston, 1965, pp. 27–55.

STAATS, A. W. *Learning, language, and cognition.* New York: Holt, Rinehart and Winston, 1968.

STAATS, A. W. Social behaviorism, human motivation, and the conditioning therapies. In B. Maher, ed., *Progress in experimental personality research.* Vol. 5. New York: Academic Press, 1970, pp. 111–168.

STAATS, A. W., and BUTTERFIELD, W. H. Treatment of nonreading in a culturally deprived juvenile delinquent: an application of reinforcement principles. *Child development,* 1965, *36,* 925–942.

STAATS, A. W., MINKE, K. A., GOODWIN, W., and LAWTON, J. Cognitive behavior modification: "Motivated learning" reading treatment with subprofessional therapy-technicians. *Behaviour research and therapy,* 1967, *5,* 283–299.

STAINBROOK, E. Psychosomatic medicine in the nineteenth century. *Psychosomatic medicine,* 1952, *14,* 211–227.

STAINBROOK, E. The community of the psychiatric patient. In S. Arieti, ed., *American handbook of psychiatry.* Vol. 1. New York: Basic Books, 1959, 150–160.

STAMPFL, T. G., and LEVIS, D. J. Essentials of implosive therapy: a learning-theory-based psychodynamic behavioral therapy. *Journal of abnormal psychology,* 1967, *72,* 496–503.

STANFORD, S. Madamhood as a vocation. In C. H. McCaghy, J. K. Skipper, Jr. and M. Lefton, eds., *In their own behalf: voices from the margin.* New York: Appleton, 1968, 204–207.

STANTON, A. H., and SCHWARTZ, M. S. *The mental hospital.* New York: Basic Books, 1954.

STAPLES, E. A., and WILENSKY, H. A controlled Rorschach investigation of hypnotic age regression. *Journal of projective techniques and personality assessment,* 1968, *32,* 246–252.

STARK, J. Language training for the autistic child using operant conditioning procedures. *Journal of communication disorders,* 1972, *5,* 183-194.

STARK, J., MEISEL, J., and WRIGHT, T. Modifying maladaptive behavior in a non-verbal child. *British journal of disorders of communication,* 1969, *4,* 38-43.

STARR, B. J., and KATKIN, E. S. The clinician as an aberrant actuary: illusory correlation and the incomplete sentences blank. *Journal of abnormal psychology,* 1969, *74,* 670-675.

STARY, O., BARANKOVA, M., and OBRDA, K. Le traitement reflexe des paralysies spasmodiques. *Annales medico-psychologiques,* 1968, *1,* 777.

STAUB, E. A child in distress: the influence of age, and number of witnesses on children's attempts to help. *Journal of personality and social psychology,* 1970, *14,* 130-140.

STAUB, E. Helping a person in distress: the influence of implict and explicit "rules" of conduct on children and adults. *Journal of personality and social psychology,* 1971a, *17,* 137-144.

STAUB, E. The use of role playing and induction, in children's learning of helping and sharing behavior. *Child development,* 1971b, *42,* 805-816.

STAUB, E., TURSKY, B., and SCHWARTZ, G. E. Self-control and predictability: their effects on reactions to aversive stimulation. *Journal of personality and social psychology,* 1971, *18,* 157-162.

STEDMAN, G. Theories of depersonalization: a reappraisal. *British journal of psychiatry,* 1970, *117,* 1-14.

STEDMAN, J. M. An extension of the Kimmel treatment method for enuresis to an adolescent: a case report. *Journal of behavior therapy and experimental psychiatry,* 1972, *3,* 307-309.

STEFFY, R. A., and BECKER, W. C. Measurement of the severity of disorder in schizophrenia by means of the Holtzman inkblot test. *Journal of consulting psychology,* 1961, *25,* 555.

STEFFY, R. A., HART, J., DRAW, M., TORNEY, D., and MARLETT, N. Operant behaviour modification techniques applied to a ward of severely regressed and aggressive patients. *Canadian psychiatric association journal,* 1969, *14,* 59-67.

STEFFY, R. A., MEICHENBAUM, D., and BEST, J. A. Aversive and cognitive factors in the modification of smoking behavior. *Behaviour research and therapy,* 1970, *8,* 115-125.

STEIN, K. B. Psychotherapy patients as research subjects: problems in cooperativeness, representativeness, and generalizability. *Journal of consulting and clinical psychology,* 1971, *37,* 99-105.

STEIN, K. B., SARBIN, T. R., and KULIK, J. A. Further validation of antisocial personality types. *Journal of consulting and clinical psychology,* 1971, *36,* 177-182.

STEINMAN, W. M. The strengthening of verbal approval in retardates by discrimination training. *Journal of experimental child psychology,* 1968, *6,* 100-112.

STEINMAN, W. M. Generalized imitation and the discrimination hypothesis. *Journal of experimental child psychology,* 1970, *10,* 79-99.

STEINMAN, W. M., and BOYCE, K. D. Generalized imitation as a function of discrimination difficulty and choice. *Journal of experimental child psychology,* 1971, *11,* 251-265.

STEKEL, W. *How to understand your dreams.* New York: Eton, 1951.

STENGEL, E. *Suicide and attempted suicide.* Baltimore: Penguin, 1964.

STEPHAN, C., STEPHANO, S., and TALKINGTON, L. Use of modeling in survival skill training with educable mentally retarded. *Training school bulletin,* 1973, *70,* 63-68.

STEPHENS, J. H., ASTRUP, C., and MANGRUM, J. C. Prognostic factors in recovered and deteriorated schizophrenics. *American journal of psychiatry,* 1966, *122,* 1116-1121.

STEPHENS, J. H., ASTRUP, C., and MANGRUM, J. C. Prognosis in schizophrenia. *Archives of general psychiatry,* 1967, *16,* 693-698.

STEPHENS, L. S. *The teacher's guide to open education.* N.Y.: Holt, Rinehart and Winston, 1974.

STERMAN, M. B., and FRIAR, L. Suppression of seizures in an epileptic following sensori-motor EEG feedback training. *Electroencephalography and clinical neurophysiology,* 1972, *33,* 89-95.

STERN, J. A., and MCDONALD, D. G. Physiological correlates of mental disease. In P. R. Farnsworth, O. McNemar, and Q. McNemar, eds., *Annual review of psychology.* Palo Alto, Calif.: Annual Reviews, 1965, pp. 225-264.

STERN, J. A., WINOKUR, G., GRAHAM, D. T., and GRAHAM, F. K. Alterations in physiological measures during experimentally induced attitudes. *Journal of psychosomatic research,* 1960, *5,* 73-82.

STERN, P. J. *The abnormal person and his world.* Princeton, N.J.: Van Nostrand, 1964.

STERN, R. Treatment of a case of obsessional neurosis using thought-stopping technique. *British journal of psychiatry,* 1970, *117,* 441-442.

STERNBACH, R. A. Psychosomatic diseases. In G. D. Shean, ed., *Studies in abnormal behavior.* Chicago: Rand McNally, 1971, pp. 136-154.

STEVENS, J. R. Endogenous conditioning to abnormal cerebral electrical transients in man. *Science,* 1962, *131,* 947-976.

STEVENSON, H. W., and FAHEL, L. S. The effect of social reinforcement on the performance of institutionalized and non-institutionalized normal and feeble-minded children. *Journal of personality*, 1961, *29*, 136–147.

STEVENSON, I. Processes of "spontaneous" recovery from the psychoneuroses. *American journal of psychiatry*, 1961, *117*, 1057–1064.

STEVENSON, I., and WOLPE, J. Recovery from sexual deviations through overcoming non-sexual neurotic responses. *American journal of psychiatry*, 1960, *116*, 737–742.

STEWART, D. J., and PATTERSON, M. L. Eliciting effects of verbal and nonverbal cues on projective test responses. *Journal of consulting and clinical psychology*, 1973, *41*, 74–77.

STEWART, J. L. Cross-cultural studies and linguistic aspects of stuttering. *Journal of the all-India institute of speech and hearing*, 1971, *2*, 1–6.

STEWART, R. A. C. Modeling in psychotherapy. *Indian journal of applied psychology*, 1969, *6*, 55–61.

STIEPER, D. R., and WIENER, D. N. The problem of interminability in outpatient psychotherapy. *Journal of consulting psychology*, 1959, *23*, 237–242.

STOECKLE, J. D., ZOLA, I. K., and DAVIDSON, G. E. The quantity and significance of psychological distress in medical patients: some preliminary observations about the decision to seek medical aid. *Journal of chronic diseases*, 1964, *17*, 959–970.

STOFFELMAYR, B. E. The treatment of a retching response to dentures by counteractive reading aloud. *Journal of behavior therapy and experimental psychiatry*, 1970, *1*, 163–164.

STOLLER, R. J. *Sex and gender*. New York: Science House, 1968.

STOLLER, R. J. Pornography and perversion. *Archives of general psychiatry*, 1970, *22*, 490–499.

STOLLER, R. J., and GEERTSMA, R. H. The consistency of psychiatrists' clinical judgments. *Journal of nervous and mental disease*, 1963, *137*, 58–66.

STOLZ, S. B., and WOLF, M. M. Visually discriminated behavior in a "blind" adolescent retardate. *Journal of applied behavior analysis*, 1969, *2*, 65–77.

STONE, A. A., and STONE, S. S., eds., *The abnormal personality through literature*. Englewood Cliffs, N.J.: Prentice-Hall, 1966.

STONE, S. Psychiatry through the ages. *Journal of abnormal and social psychology*, 1937, *32*, 131–160.

STORMS, M. D., and NISBETT, R. E. Insomnia and the attribution process. *Journal of personality and social psychology*, 1970, *16*, 319–328.

STOUFFER, G. A. W., JR. Behavior problems of children as viewed by teachers and mental hygienists. *Mental hygiene*, 1952, *36*, 271–285.

STOUFFER, G. A. W., JR. The attitudes of secondary school teachers toward certain behavior problems of children. *School review*, 1956, *64*, 358–362.

STRASSBURGER, F. Ethical guidelines for encounter groups. *American psychological association monitor*, 1971, *2*, 3 and 32.

STRASSMAN, H. D., THALER, M. B., and SCHEIN, E. H. A prisoner of war syndrome: apathy as a reaction to severe stress. *American journal of psychiatry*, 1956, *112*, 998-1003.

STRAUGHAN, J. H. Treatment with child and mother in playroom. *Behaviour research and therapy*, 1964, *2*, 37–41.

STRAUGHAN J. H., POTTER, W. K., JR., and HAMILTON, S. H., JR. The behavioral treatment of an elective mute. *Journal of child psychology and psychiatry*, 1965, *6*, 125–130.

STRECKER, E. A., and CHAMBERS, F. T., JR. *Alcohol: one man's meat*. New York: Macmillan, 1938.

STRICKLAND, C. G., and ARRELL, V. M. Employment of the mentally retarded. *Exceptional children*, 1967.

STRICKLAND, J. F. The effect of motivation arousal on humor preferences. *Journal of abnormal and social psychology*, 1959, *59*, 278–281.

STROEBEL, C. F., and GLUECK, B. C., JR. Computer derived global judgments in psychiatry. *American journal of psychiatry*, 1970, *126*, 1057–1066.

STRONG, E. K., JR., and TUCKER, A. C. The use of vocational interest scales in planning a medical career. *Psychological monographs*, 1952, *66*, 9 (whole no. 341).

STRUPP, H. H. The performance of psychiatrists and psychologists in a therapeutic interview. *Journal of clinical psychology*, 1958, *14*, 219–226.

STUART, R. B. Behavioral control of overeating. *Behaviour research and therapy*, 1967, *5*, 357–365.

STUART, R. B. Operant-interpersonal treatment for marital discord. *Journal of consulting and clinical psychology*, 1969, *33*, 675–682.

STUART, R. B. Behavioral contracting within the families of delinquents. *Journal of behavior therapy and experimental psychiatry*, 1971a, *2*, 1–11.

STUART, R. B. A three-dimensional program for the treatment of obesity. *Behaviour research and therapy*, 1971b, *9*, 177–186.

STUART, R. B. Behavioral contracting with delinquents: a cautionary note. *Journal of behavior therapy and experimental psychiatry*, 1972a, *3*, 161–169.

STUART, R. B. Situational versus self-control. In R. D. Rubin, H. Fensterheim, J. D. Henderson, and

L. P. Ullmann, eds., *Advances in behavior therapy III.* New York: Academic Press, 1972b, pp. 129–146.

STUMPHAUZER, J. S. Application of reinforcement contingencies with a 23-year-old anorexic patient. *Psychological reports,* 1969, *24,* 109–110.

STUMPHAUZER, J. S. Increased delay of gratification in young prison inmates through imitation of high-delay peer models. *Journal of personality and social psychology,* 1972, *21,* 10–17.

STUMPHAUZER, J. S., ed. *Behavior therapy with delinquents.* Springfield, Ill.: Thomas, 1973.

SUINN, R. M. The desensitization of test-anxiety by group and individual treatment. *Behaviour research and therapy,* 1968, *6,* 385–387.

SULLIVAN, H. S. *The interpersonal theory of psychiatry.* New York: Norton, 1953.

SULLIVAN, H. S. *The psychiatric interview.* New York: Norton, 1954.

SULLIVAN, H. S. *Clinical studies in psychiatry.* New York: Norton, 1956.

SULZER, E. S. Behavior modification in adult psychiatric patients. In L. P. Ullmann and L. Krasner, eds., *Case studies in behavior modification.* New York: Holt, Rinehart and Winston, 1965, pp. 196–199.

SULZER, E. S. Individual freedom, law, and social welfare. *Community mental health journal,* 1967, *3,* 49–52.

SUTCLIFFE, J. P. "Credulous" and "sceptical" views of hypnotic phenomena, a review of certain evidence and methodology. *International journal of clinical and experimental hypnosis,* 1960, *8,* 73–101.

SUTKER, P. B. Vicarious conditioning and sociopathy. *Journal of psychology,* 1970, *76,* 380–386.

SWANSON, J. C. Models of drug abuse behavior. *Drug forum,* 1972, *1,* 227–231.

SWATOS, W. H., JR. Opiate addiction in the late nineteenth century: a study of the social problem, using medical journals of the period. *International journal of the addictions,* 1972, *7,* 739–753.

SYKES, D. H., DOUGLAS, V. I., and MORGANSTERN, G. Sustained attention in hyperactive children. *Journal of child psychology and psychiatry and allied disciplines,* 1973, *14,* 213–220.

SYKES, G. M. *Crime and society.* New York: Random House, 1956.

SYKES, G. M. *The society of captives.* New York: Atheneum, 1969.

SYLVESTER, J. D., and LIVERSEDGE, L. A. Conditioning and the occupational cramps. In H. J. Eysenck, ed., *Behaviour therapy and the neuroses.* New York: Pergamon, 1960, 334–348.

SZASZ, T. S. Psychoanalysis and the autonomic nervous system. *Psychoanalytic review,* 1952, *39,* 115–151.

SZASZ, T. S. Some observations on the relationship between psychiatry and the law. *American Medical Association archives of neurology and psychiatry,* 1956, *75,* 297.

SZASZ, T. S. *Pain and pleasure: a study of bodily feelings.* New York: Basic Books, 1957.

SZASZ, T. S. *The myth of mental illness: foundations of a theory of personal conduct.* New York: Hoeber-Harper, 1961.

SZASZ, T. S. *Law, liberty, and psychiatry: an inquiry into the social uses of mental health practices.* New York: Macmillan, 1963.

SZASZ, T. S. The moral dilemma of psychiatry: autonomy or heteronomy? *American journal of psychiatry,* 1964, *121,* 521–528.

SZASZ, T. S. *Psychiatric justice.* New York: Macmillan, 1965a.

SZASZ, T. S. *The ethics of psychoanalysis: the theory and method of autonomous psychotherapy.* New York: Basic Books, 1965b.

SZASZ, T. S. Discussion of Dr. Robbins' paper. In L. D. Eron, ed., *The classification of behavior disorders.* Chicago: Aldine, 1966a, 38–41.

SZASZ, T. S. The psychiatric classification of behavior: a strategy of personal constraint. In L. D. Eron, ed., *The classification of behavior disorders.* Chicago: Aldine, 1966b, 125–170.

SZASZ, T. S. *Ideology and insanity.* Garden City, N.Y.: Doubleday, Anchor Books, 1970.

SZASZ, T. S. *The manufacture of madness.* New York: Dell, 1971.

SZUREK, S. A. Notes on the genesis of psychopathic personality. *Psychiatry,* 1942, *5,* 1–6.

TALBOT, N. Panic in school phobia. *American journal of orthopsychiatry,* 1957, *27,* 286–295.

TALKINGTON, L. W., and HALL, S. M. Use of a frustration technique to reinstate speech in nonverbal retarded. *American journal of mental deficiency,* 1968, *73,* 496–499.

TALKINGTON, L. W., HALL S., and ALTMAN, R. Use of a peer modeling procedure with severely retarded subjects on a basic communication response. *Training school bulletin,* 1973, *69,* 145–149.

TANNENBAUM, F. *Crime and the community.* Boston: Ginn, 1938.

TANNER, B. A. A case report on the use of relaxation and systematic desensitization to control multiple compulsive behaviors. *Journal of behavior therapy and experimental psychiatry,* 1971, *2,* 267–272.

TART, C. T. States of consciousness and state-specific sciences. *Science,* 1972, *176,* 1203–1210.

TARVER, J., and TURNER, A. J. Behavior modification techniques for families of patients with behavioral problems. *American journal of nursing*, 1974, *74*, 282–283.

TASTO, D. L., and HINKLE, J. E. Muscle relaxation treatment for tension headaches. *Behaviour research and therapy*, 1973, *11*, 347–349.

TATE, B. G. Case study: control of chronic self-injurious behavior by conditioning procedures. *Behavior therapy*, 1972, *3*, 72–83.

TATE, B. G., and BAROFF, G. S. Aversive control of self-injurious behaviour in a psychotic boy. *Behaviour research and therapy*, 1966, *4*, 281–287.

TAWNEY, R. H. *Religion and the rise of capitalism*. New York: Harcourt, 1926.

TAYLOR, D. W., JR. Treatment of excessive frequency of urination by desensitization. *Journal of behavior therapy and experimental psychiatry*, 1972, *3*, 311–313.

TAYLOR, G. P., and PERSONS, R. W. Behavior modification techniques in a physical medicine and rehabilitation center. *Journal of psychology*, 1970, *74*, 117–124.

TAYLOR, J. C. *The behavioral basis of perception*. New Haven, Conn.: Yale University Press, 1962.

TAYLOR, J. G. A behavioral interpretation of obsessive-compulsive neurosis. *Behaviour research and therapy*, 1963, *1*, 237–244.

TAYLOR, L. A club for parents who lose their cool. *Honolulu star-bulletin*, 7 September 1972a, p. F2.

TAYLOR, L. An introduction to Emily Post. *Honolulu star-bulletin*, 11 October 1972b, p. B–1.

TEAL, D. *The gay militants*. New York: Stein and Day, 1971.

TELFORD, C. W. and SAWREY, J. M. *The exceptional individual*. 2nd ed. Englewood Cliffs, N.J.: Prentice-Hall, 1972.

TEMERLIN, M. K. Suggestion effects in psychiatric diagnosis. *Journal of nervous and mental disease*, 1968, *147*, 349–353.

TERRACE, H. S. Discrimination learning with and without "errors." *Journal of the experimental analysis of behavior*, 1963, *6*, 1–27.

TEUBER, H. L., and POWERS, E. Evaluating therapy in a delinquency prevention program. In Association for Research in Nervous and Mental Disease, *Psychiatric treatment*. Baltimore: Williams & Wilkins, 1953, 138–147.

THALHOFER, N. N. Responsibility, reparation, and self-protection as reasons for three types of helping. *Journal of personality and social psychology*, 1971, *19*, 144–151.

THARP, R. G., and WETZEL, R. J. *Behavior modification in the natural environment*. New York: Academic Press, 1969.

THOMAS, D. Prognosis of depression with electric treatment. *British medical journal*, 1954, *2*, 950–954.

THOMAS, E. J., ed., *Behavior modification procedure: a sourcebook*. Chicago: Aldine, 1974.

THOMAS, E. J., ABRAMS, K. S., and JOHNSON, J. B. Self-monitoring and reciprocal inhibition in the modification of multiple tics of Gilles de la Tourette's syndrome. *Journal of behavior therapy and experimental psychiatry*, 1971, *2*, 159–171.

THOMPSON, D. W. *Psychology in clinical practice*. Cleveland: Howard Allen, 1965.

THOMPSON, E. E. Effectiveness of different techniques in training schizophrenic patients to give common associations. Paper read at Midwestern Psychological Association convention, 1967.

THOMPSON, N. L., JR., MCCANDLESS, B. R., and STRICKLAND, B. R. Personal adjustment of male and female homosexuals and heterosexuals. *Journal of abnormal psychology*, 1971, *78*, 237–240.

THOMPSON, T., GRABOWSKI, J., ERICKSON, E., and JOHNSON, R. Development and maintenance of a behavior modification program for institutionalized profoundly retarded adult males. *Psychological aspects of disability*, 1970, *17*, 117–124.

THOMPSON, V. A. *Modern organization*. New York: Knopf, 1963.

THORESEN, C. E., and MAHONEY, M. J. *Behavioral self-control*. New York: Holt, Rinehart and Winston, 1974.

THORNDIKE, E. L. *The psychology of learning*. New York: Teachers College, 1913.

THORNE, D. E. Is the hypnotic trance necessary for performance of hypnotic phenomena? *Journal of abnormal psychology*, 1967, *72*, 233–239.

THORPE, J. G., SCHMIDT, E., BROWN, P. T., and CASTELL, D. Aversion-relief therapy: a new method for general application. *Behaviour research and therapy*, 1964, *2*, 71–82.

THORPE, L. P., and KATZ, B. *The psychology of abnormal behavior: a dynamic approach*. New York: Ronald Press, 1948.

THRONE, J. M. The assessment of intelligence towards what end? Presented to the annual meeting of the American Academy on Mental Retardation, Washington, D.C., May 1970.

THURSTON, J. R., and MUSSEN, P. H. Infant feeding gratification and adult personality. *Journal of personality*, 1951, *19*, 449–458.

THURSTONE, L. L., and THURSTONE, T. G. *Factorial studies of intelligence*. (Psychometric monographs, No. 2.) Chicago: University of Chicago Press, 1941.

TIEBOUT, H. M. The syndrome of alcohol addiction. *Quarterly journal of the study of alcohol*, 1945, *5*, 535–546.

TIEDE, T. Brandeis prof says citizens get too old to vote. *Champaign-Urbana courier*, 3 November 1970, p. 19.

TIENARI, P. Psychiatric illnesses in identical twins. *Acta psychiatrica scandinavica*, 1963, *39* (supplementum 171).

TILKER, H. A. Socially responsible behavior as a function of observer responsibility and victim feedback. *Journal of personality and social psychology*, 1970, *14*, 95–100.

TIME.- The cell: unraveling the doble helix and the secret of life. *Time*, 19 April 1971, pp. 34–43.

TINTERA, J. W. Office rehabilitation of the alcoholic. *New York state journal of medicine*, 1956, *56*, 3896–3902.

TOCH, H. *The social psychology of social movements*. Indianapolis: Bobbs-Merrill, 1965.

TOCH, H., and SMITH, H. C., eds., *Social perception*. Princeton, N.J.: Van Nostrand, 1968.

TODD, F. J. Coverant control of self-evaluative responses in the treatment of depression: a new use for an old principle. *Behavior therapy*, 1972, *3*, 91–94.

TOEPFER, C., REUTER, J., and MAURER, C. The design and evaluation of an obedience training program for mothers of preschool children. *Journal of consulting and clinical psychology*, 1972, *39*, 194–198.

TOMKINS, S. S. Psychological model for smoking behavior. *American journal of public health*, 1966, *56*, 17–20.

TOMLINSON, J. R. The treatment of bowel retention by operant procedures: a case study. *Journal of behavior therapy and experimental psychiatry*, 1970, *1*, 83–85.

TOPHOFF, M. Massed practice, relaxation, and assertion training in the treatment of a Gilles de la Tourette's syndrome. *Journal of behavior therapy and experimental psychiatry*, 1973, *4*, 71–73.

TORREY, E. F. *The mind game: witchdoctors and psychiatrists*. New York: Bantam, 1973a.

TORREY, E. F. Is schizophrenia universal? An open question. *Schizophrenia bulletin*, 1973b, *7*, 53–59.

TOWBIN, A. P. Self-care unit: some lessons in institutional power. *Journal of consulting and clinical psychology*, 1969, *33*, 561–570.

TRACHTMAN, J. P. Socio-economic class bias in Rorschach diagnosis: contributing psychosocial attributes of the clinician. *Journal of personality assessment*, 1971, *35*, 229–240.

TRACY, J. J., and CROSS, H. J. Antecedents of shift in moral judgment. *Journal of personality and social psychology*, 1973, *26*, 238–244.

TRAMONTANA, J., and STIMBERT, V. E. Some techniques of behavior modification with an autistic child. *Psychological reports*, 1970, *27*, 498.

TREDGOLD, A. F. *Mental deficiency*. Baltimore: William Wood, 1915.

TROFER, S. A., and TART, C. T. Experimenter bias in hypnotist performance. *Science*, 1964, *145*, 1330–1331.

TROTTER, S. Biofeedback helps epileptics control seizures. *A. P. A. monitor*, 1973, *4*, 5.

TRUAX, C. B. Effective ingredients in psychotherapy: an approach to unraveling the patient-therapist interaction. *Journal of counseling psychology*, 1963, *10*, 256–263.

TRUAX, C. B. Reinforcement and nonreinforcement in Rogerian psychotherapy. *Journal of abnormal psychology*, 1966a, *71*, 1–9.

TRUAX, C. B. Therapist empathy, warmth, and genuineness and patient personality change in group pychotherapy: a comparison between interaction unit measures, time sample measures, and patient perception measures. *Journal of clinical psychology*, 1966b, *22*, 225–229.

TRUAX, C. B. Therapist interpersonal reinforcement and client self-exploration and therapeutic outcome in group pychotherapy. *Journal of counseling psychology*, 1968, *15*, 225–231.

TRUE, J. E. Learning of abstract responses by process and reactive schizophrenic patients. *Psychological reports*, 1966, *18*, 51–55.

TSENG, W. S. The development of psychiatric concepts in traditional Chinese medicine. *Archives of general psychiatry*, 1973a, *29*, 569–575.

TSENG, W. S. The concept of personality in Confucian thought. *Psychiatry*, 1973b, *36*, 191–202.

TUCKER, G., HARROW, M., and HOFFMAN, B. Perceptual experiences in schizophrenic and nonschizophrenic patients. *Archives of general psychiatry*, 1969, 20, 159–166.

TUCKMAN, J., and KLEINER, R. J. Discrepancy between aspiration and achievement as a predictor of schizophrenia. *Behavioral science*, 1962, *7*, 443–447.

TUCKMAN, J., and YOUNGMAN, W. F. Assessment of suicide risk in attempted suicides. In H. L. P. Resnik, ed., *Suicidal behaviors: diagnosis and management*. Boston: Little, Brown, 1968, pp. 190–197.

TUCKMAN, J., YOUNGMAN, W. F., and KREIZMAN, G. Multiple suicide attempts. *Community mental health journal*, 1968, *4*, 164–170.

TURNBULL, J. W. Asthma conceived as a learned

response. *Journal of psychosomatic research*, 1962, 6, 59-70.

TURNER, A. J., and GOODSON, W. H. *Programs and evaluations.* Huntsville, Ala.: Huntsville-Madison County Mental Health Center, 1971, 1972, 1973.

TURNER, R. J., RAYMOND, J., ZABO, L. J., and DIAMOND, J. Field survey methods in psychiatry: the effects of sampling strategy upon findings in research on schizophrenia. *Journal of health and social behavior*, 1969, 10, 289-297.

TURNER, R. J. and WAGENFELD, M. O. Occupational mobility and schizophrenia: an assessment of the social causation and social selection hypotheses. *American sociological review*, 1967, 32, 104-113.

TURNER, R. K., YOUNG, G. C., and RACHMAN, S. Treatment of nocturnal enuresis by conditioning techniques. *Behaviour research and therapy*, 1970, 8, 367-381.

TURNER, W. J., and MERLIS, S. Clinical correlations between electroencephalography and anti-social behavior. *Medical times*, 1962, 90, 505-511.

TWARDOSZ, S., and SAJWAJ, T. Multiple effects of a procedure to increase sitting in a hyperactive, retarded boy. *Journal of applied behavior analysis*, 1972, 5, 73-78.

TWICHELL, T. E. A behavioral syndrome. *Science*, 1971, 174, 135-136.

TYHURST, L. Displacement and migration: a study in social psychiatry. *American journal of psychiatry*, 1951, 107, 561-568.

TYLER, V. O., JR. Application of operant token reinforcement to academic performance of an institutionalized delinquent. *Psychological reports*, 1967, 21, 249-260.

TYLER, V. O., JR., and BROWN, G. D. The use of swift, brief isolation as a group control device for institutionalized delinquents. *Behaviour research and therapy*, 1967, 5, 1-9.

TYLER, V. O., JR., and BROWN, G. D. Token reinforcement of academic performance with institutionalized delinquent boys. *Journal of educational psychology*, 1968, 59, 164-168.

ULLMAN, A. D. The psychological mechanism of alcohol addiction. *Quarterly journal of studies on alcohol*, 1952, 13, 602-608.

ULLMANN, L. P. Productivity and the clinical use of TAT cards. *Journal of projective techniques*, 1957a, 21, 399-403.

ULLMANN, L. P. Selection of neuropsychiatric patients for group psychotherapy. *Journal of consulting psychology*, 1957b, 21, 277-280.

ULLMANN, L. P. Clinical correlates of facilitation and inhibition of response to emotional stimuli. *Journal of projective techniques*, 1958, 22, 341-347.

ULLMANN, L. P. On the relationship between the amount of hospitalization and self-assertion. *American psychologist*, 1958, 13, 327 (abstract).

ULLMANN, L. P. Untestability of schizophrenics upon admission to psychiatric hospitals. *Journal of clinical psychology*, 1961, 17, 199-202.

ULLMANN, L. P., An empirically derived MMPI scale which measures facilitation-inhibition of recognition of threatening stimuli. *Journal of clinical psychology*, 1962, 18, 127-132.

ULLMANN, L. P. *Institution and outcome: a comparative study of psychiatric hospitals.* New York: Pergamon, 1967a.

ULLMANN, L. P. Abnormal psychology without anxiety. Paper read at Western Psychological Association convention, 1967b.

ULLMANN, L. P. From therapy to reality. *The counseling psychologist*, 1969a, 1, 68-72.

ULLMANN, L. P. Making use of modeling in the therapeutic interview. In R. D. Rubin and C. M. Franks, eds., *Advances in behavior therapy, 1968.* New York: Academic Press, 1969b, 175-182.

ULLMANN, L. P. Behavior therapy as social movement. In C. M. Franks, ed., *Behavior therapy: appraisal and status.* New York: McGraw-Hill, 1969c, 495-523.

ULLMANN, L. P. On cognitions and behavior therapy. *Behavior therapy*, 1970, 1, 201-204.

ULLMANN, L. P. A behavioral comment on the experiential response. *Psychotherapy: theory, research and practice*, 1972a, 9, 199-203.

ULLMANN, L. P. Who are we? In R. D. Rubin, H. Fensterheim, J. D. Henderson, and L. P. Ullmann, eds., *Advances in behavior therapy.* New York: Academic Press, 1972b, 213-223.

ULLMANN, L. P. A behavioral comment on social intervention. Paper presented at conference on the ethics of social intervention. Seattle, Battelle Institute, May 1973.

ULLMANN, L. P., and BERKMAN, V. C. Types of outcome in the family care placement of mental patients. *Social work*, 1959, 4, 72-78.

ULLMANN, L. P., BOWEN, M. E., GREENBERG, D. J., MACPHERSON, E. C., MARCUM, H. B., MARX, R. O., and MAY, J. S. The effect on rapport of experimenters' approach and avoidance responses to positive and negative self-references. *Behaviour research and therapy*, 1968, 6, 355-362.

ULLMANN, L. P., and ECK, R. A. Inkblot perception and the process-reactive distinction. *Journal of clinical psychology*, 1965, 21, 311-313.

ULLMANN, L. P. FORSMAN, R. G., KENNY, J. W., MCINNIS, T. L. JR., UNIKEL, I. P., and ZEISSET, R. M. Selective reinforcement of schizophrenics' interview responses. *Behaviour research and therapy*, 1965, *2*, 205–212.

ULLMANN, L. P., and FORSYTH, R. P. Responses by normal and schizophrenic subjects under positive and negative examiner reinforcement in a probability learning situation. *American psychologist*, 1959, *14*, 407–408 (abstract).

ULLMANN, L. P., and GUREL, L. Validity of symptom rating from psychiatric records. *Archives of general psychiatry*, 1962, *7*, 130–134.

ULLMANN, L. P., and GIOVANNONI, J. M. The development of a self-report measure of the process-reactive continuum. *Journal of nervous and mental disease*, 1964, *138*, 38–42.

ULLMANN, L. P., and HUNRICHS, W. A. The role of anxiety in psychodiagnosis: replication and extension. *Journal of clinical psychology*, 1958, *14*, 276–279.

ULLMANN, L. P., and KEMP, C. H. Home intervention programs. In D. Harshbarger and R. F. Maley, eds., *Behavior analysis: an integrative approach to mental health programs*. Kalamazoo, Mich.: Behaviordelia, 1974, pp. 143–147.

ULLMANN, L. P., and KRASNER, L. Introduction: What is behavior modification? In L. P. Ullmann and L. Krasner, eds., *Case studies in behavior modification*. New York: Holt, Rinehart and Winston, 1965a, pp. 1–63.

ULLMANN, L. P., and KRASNER, L., eds., *Case studies in behavior modification*. New York: Holt, Rinehart and Winston, 1965b.

ULLMANN, L. P., and KRASNER, L. *A psychological approach to abnormal behavior*. Englewood Cliffs, N.J.: Prentice-Hall, 1969.

ULLMANN, L. P., KRASNER, L., and COLLINS, B. J. Modification of behavior through verbal conditioning: effects in group therapy. *Journal of abnormal and social psychology*, 1961, *62*, 128–132.

ULLMANN, L. P., KRASNER, L., and EDINGER, R. L. Verbal conditioning of common associations in long-term schizophrenic patients. *Behaviour research and therapy*, 1964, *2*, 15–18.

ULLMANN, L. P., KRASNER, L., and EKMAN, P. Verbal conditioning of emotional words: effects on behavior in group therapy. *Research reports*. Palo Alto, Calif.: Veterans Administration, 1961, No. 15.

ULLMANN, L. P., KRASNER, L., and GELFAND, D. M. Changed content with a reinforced, response class. *Psychological reports*, 1963, *12*, 819–829.

ULLMANN, L. P., KRASNER, L., and SHERMAN, M. MMPI items associated with pleasantness of emotional words used in thematic storytelling. *Research reports*. Palo Alto, Calif.: Veterans Administration, 1963, No. 25.

ULLMANN, L. P., and LIM, D. T. Case history material as a source of the identification of patterns of response to emotional stimuli in a study of humor. *Journal of consulting psychology*, 1962, *26*, 221–225.

ULLMANN, L. P., and MCFARLAND, R. L. Productivity as a variable in TAT protocols—a methodological study. *Journal of projective techniques*, 1957, *21*, 80–87.

ULLMANN, L. P., and SIKORA, J. P. An extension of Coleman, Katz, and Menzel's *Medical innovation* using behavior therapists. Western Psychological Association convention, Los Angeles, 1970.

ULLMANN, L. P., and STRAUGHAN, J. H. Probability learning in schizophrenic males. Paper read at Western Psychological Association convention, 1959.

ULLMANN, L. P., WEISS, R. L., and KRASNER, L. The effect of verbal conditioning of emotional words on recognition of threatening stimuli. *Journal of clinical psychology*, 1963, *19*, 182–183.

ULRICH, R., STACHNIK, T., and MABRY, J., eds. *Control of human behavior*. Glenview, Ill.: Scott-Foresman, 1966.

ULRICH, R., STACHNIK, T., and MABRY, J., eds. *Control of human behavior: from cure to prevention*. Glenview, Ill.: Scott-Foresman, 1970.

UNGER, S. N. Mescaline, LSD, psilocybin and personality change: a review. *Psychiatry*, 1963, *26*, 111–125.

UNGERLEIDER, J. T., FISHER, D. D., and FULLER, M. The dangers of LSD. *Journal of the American medical association*, 1966, *197*, 389–392.

UPI. 1 of 4 U.S. elderly live in poverty. *Chicago daily news*, 26 November 1971.

UPI. Top of list. *Honolulu star-bulletin*, 1 September 1973, p. A-3.

UPPER, D. A "ticket" system for reducing ward rules violations on a token economy program. *Journal of behavior therapy and experimental psychiatry*, 1973, *4*, 137–140.

UPPER, D., and MEREDITH, L. A stimulus control approach to the modification of smoking. *Proceedings of the 78th annual convention of the American Psychological Association*, 1970.

UPPER, D., and NEWTON, J. G. A weight-reduction program for schizophrenic patients on a token economy unit: two case studies. *Journal of behavior therapy and experimental psychiatry*, 1971, *2*, 113–115.

VAIL, D. J., LUCERO, R. J., and BOEN, J. R. The relationship between socioeconomic variables and major mental illness in the counties of a midwestern state. *Community mental health journal*, 1966, *2*, 211–212.

VALINS, S. Cognitive effects of false heart-rate feedback. *Journal of personality and social psychology,* 1966, *4,* 400–408.

VALINS, S. Emotionality and information concerning internal reactions. *Journal of personality and social psychology,* 1967, *6,* 458–463.

VALINS, S., and NISBETT, R. E. *Attribution processes in the development and treatment of emotional disorders.* Morristown, N.J.: General Learning Press, 1971.

VANCE, E. T. Community mental health—labyrinth or highroad? *Contemporary psychology,* 1971, *16,* 389.

VAN DYKE, H. B. The weapons of panacea. *Scientific monthly,* 1947, *64,* 322–326.

VAN EGEREN, L. F., FEATHER, B. W., and HEIN, P. L. Desensitization of phobias: some psychophysiological propositions. *Psychophysiology,* 1971, *8,* 213–228.

VEDDER, C. B. *Juvenile offenders.* Springfield, Ill.: C. C. Thomas, 1963.

VEITH, I. Psychiatric nosology: from Hippocrates to Kraepelin. *American journal of psychiatry,* 1957, *114,* 385–391.

VEITH, I. *Hysteria, the history of a disease.* Chicago: University of Chicago Press, 1965.

VEITH, I. Education for morality: sex education—Victorian style. *Bulletin of the Menninger clinic,* 1970, *34,* 292–303.

VENN, J. R., and SHORT, J. G. Vicarious classical conditioning of emotional responses in nursery school children. *Journal of personality and social psychology,* 1973, *28,* 249–255.

VENTURI, L. *History of art criticism.* New York: Dutton, 1964.

VERDEN, P., and SHATTERLY, D. Alcoholism research: the disease concept and normal drinking in ex-alcoholics. *Mental hygiene,* 1971, *55,* 331–356.

VERNON, J. A., McGILL, T. E., GULICK, W. L., and CANDLAND, D. K. The effect of human isolation upon some perceptual and motor skills. In P. Solomon et al., eds., *Sensory deprivation: a symposium held at Harvard medical school.* Cambridge, Mass.: Harvard University Press, 1961, 41–57.

VERNY, T. R. Analysis of attrition rates in a psychiatric out-patient clinic. *Psychiatric quarterly,* 1970, *44,* 37–48.

VINEY, L. Self: the history of a concept. *Journal of the history of behavioral science,* 1967, *5,* 349–359.

VINOKUR, A., and SELZER, M. I. Life events, stress, and mental illness. *Proceedings of the 81st annual convention of the American Psychological Association,* 1973, pp. 329–330.

VOGEL, W., KUN, K. J., and MESHORER, E. Effects of environmental enrichment and environmental deprivation on cognitive functioning in institutionalized retardates. *Journal of consulting psychology,* 1967, *31,* 570–576.

VOLKAN, V. Typical findings in pathological grief. *Psychiatric quarterly,* 1970, *44,* 231–250.

VOLKART, E. Bereavement and mental health. In A. H. Leighton, J. A. Clausen, and R. N. Wilson, eds., *Explorations in social psychiatry.* New York: Basic Books, 1957, 281–307.

VOLPE, A., and KASTENBAUM, R. Beer and TLC. *American journal of nursing,* 1967, *67,* 100–103.

VUKELICH, R., and HAKE, D. F. Reduction of dangerously aggressive behavior in a severely retarded resident through a combination of positive reinforcement procedures. *Journal of applied behavior analysis,* 1971, *4,* 215–225.

WAELDER, R. *Basic theory of psychoanalysis.* New York: International Universities Press, 1960.

WAGENEN, R. K., MEYERSON, L., KERR, N. J., and MAHONEY, K. Field trials of a new procedure for toilet training. *Journal of experimental child psychology,* 1969, *8,* 147–159.

WAGENFELD, M. O. The prevention of mental illness: a sociological perspective. *Journal of health and social behavior,* 1972, *13,* 195–203.

WAGNER, B. R. The training of attending and abstracting responses in chronic schizophrenics. *Journal of experimental research in personality,* 1968, *3,* 77–88.

WAGNER, M. K. Comparative effectiveness of behavior rehearsal and verbal reinforcement for effecting anger expressiveness. *Psychological reports,* 1968, *22,* 1079–1080.

WAGNER, M. K., and BRAGG, R. A. Comparing behavior modification approaches to habit decrement-smoking. *Journal of consulting and clinical psychology,* 1970, *34,* 258–263.

WAHLER, R. G. Behavior therapy with oppositional children: attempts to increase their parents' reinforcement value. Paper read at Southeastern Psychological Association convention, 1967.

WAHLER, R. G., and ERICKSON, M. Child behavior therapy: a community program in Appalachia. *Behaviour research and therapy,* 1969, *7,* 71–78.

WAHLER, R. G., SPERLING, M. R., THOMAS, M. R., TEETER, N. C., and LUPER, H. L. The modification of childhood stuttering: some response-response relationships. *Journal of experimental child psychology,* 1970, *9,* 411–428.

WAHLER, R. G., WINKEL, G. H., PETERSON, R. F., and MORRISON, D. C. Mothers as behaviour therapists for their own children. *Behaviour research and therapy,* 1965, *3,* 113–124.

WALDER, L. O. Teaching parents to modify the behaviors of their autistic children. Paper read at the American Psychological Association convention, 1966.

WALDER, L., COHEN, S., BREITER, D., DARTON, P., HIRSCH, I., and LIEBOWITZ, J. Teaching behavioral principles to parents of disturbed children. In A. M. Graziano, ed., *Behavior therapy with children*. Chicago: Aldine-Atherton, 1971, 382–387.

WALEN, S. R. Jactatio capitis. *Acta paedopsychiatrica*, 1972, *39*, 66–68.

WALKER, P. C., and JOHNSON, R. F. Q. The influence of presleep suggestions on dream content: evidence and methodological problems. *Psychological bulletin*, 1974, *81*, 362–370.

WALLACE, C. J., DAVIS, J. R., LIBERMAN, R. P., and BAKER, V. Modeling and staff behavior. *Journal of consulting and clinical psychology*, 1973, *41*, 422–425.

WALLACE, J., and SADALLA, E. Behavior consequences of transgression. I: the effects of social recognition. *Journal of experimental research in personality*, 1966, *1*, 187–194.

WALLERSTEIN, J. S., and WYLE, C. J. Our law-abiding law-breakers. *Probation*, 1947, *25*, 107–112.

WALLIN, J. E. W. *Minor mental maladjustments in normal people*. Durham, N.C.: Duke University Press, 1939.

WALSTER, E., BERSCHEID, E., and WALSTER, G. W. The exploited: justice or justification. In J. Macaulay and L. Berkowitz, eds., *Altruism and helping behavior*. New York: Academic Press, 1970, pp. 179–204.

WALTER, H. I., and GILMORE, S. K. Placebo versus social learning effects in parent training procedures designed to alter the behavior of aggressive boys. *Behavior therapy*, 1973, *4*, 361–377.

WALTERS, R. H., and BROWN, M. A test of the high-magnitude theory of aggression. *Journal of experimental child psychology*, 1964, *1*, 376–387.

WALTON, D. Relevance of learning theory to the treatment of an obsessive-compulsive state. In H. J. Eysenck, ed., *Behaviour therapy and the neuroses*. New York: Pergamon Press, 1960a, pp. 153–164.

WALTON, D. Strengthening of incompatible reactions and the treatment of a phobic state in a schizophrenic patient. In H. J. Eysenck, ed., *Behaviour therapy and the neuroses*. New York: Pergamon Press, 1960b. pp. 170–180.

WALTON, D. The application of learning theory to the treatment of a case of bronchial asthma. In H. J. Eysenck, ed., *Behaviour therapy and the neuroses*. New York: Pergamon, 1960c, pp. 188–189.

WALTON, D. The application of learning theory to the treatment of neuro-dermatitis. In H. J. Eysenck, ed., *Behaviour therapy and the neuroses*. New York: Pergamon Press, 1960d, pp. 272–274.

WALTON, D. Experimental psychology and the treatment of a ticquer. *Journal of child psychology and psychiatry*, 1961a, *2*, 148–155.

WALTON, D. The application of learning theory to the treatment of a case of somnambulism. *Journal of clinical psychology*, 1961b, *17*, 96–99.

WALTON, D., and BLACK, D. A. The application of learning theory to the treatment of stammering. *Journal of psychosomatic research*, 1958, *3*, 170–179.

WALTON, D., and BLACK, D. A. The application of modern learning theory to the treatment of chronic hysterical aphonia. *Journal of psychosomatic research*, 1959, *3*, 303–311.

WALTON, D., and MATHER, M. D. The application of learning principles to the treatment of obsessive-compulsive states in the acute and chronic phases of illness. *Behaviour research and therapy*, 1963, *1*, 163–174.

WANDERER, Z. W. Existential depression treated by desensitization of phobias: strategy and transcript. *Journal of behavior therapy and experimental psychiatry*, 1972, *3*, 111–116.

WARD, C. H., BECK, A. T., MENDELSON, M., MOCK, J. E., and ERBAUGH, J. K. The psychiatric nomenclature. *Archives of general psychiatry*, 1962, *7*, 198–205.

WARE, C. *Woman power: the movement for women's liberation*. New York: Tower, 1970.

WARM, J. S., KANFER, F. H., KUWADA, S., and CLARK, J. L. Motivation in vigilance: the effects of self-evaluation and experimenter controlled feedback. In press.

WARREN, S. A., and MONDY, L. W. To what behaviors do attending adults respond? *American journal of mental deficiency*, 1971, *75*, 449–455.

WASIK, B. H. The application of Premack's generalization on reinforcement to the management of classroom behavior. *Journal of experimental child psychology*, 1970, *10*, 33–43.

WASIK, B. H., SENN, K., WELCH, R. H., and COOPER, B. R. Behavior modification with culturally deprived school children: two case studies. *Journal of applied behavior analysis*, 1969, *2*, 181–194.

WATKINS, J. T. Treatment of chronic vomiting and extreme emaciation by an aversive stimulus: case study. *Psychological reports*, 1972, *31*, 803–805.

WATSON, D. L., and THARP, R. G. *Self-directed behavior: self-modification for personal adjustment*. Monterey, Calif.: Brooks/Cole, 1972.

WATSON, D. L., THARP, R. G., and KRISBERG, J. Case study in self-modification: suppression of inflammatory scratching while awake and asleep. *Journal of behavior therapy and experimental psychiatry*, 1972, *3*, 213–215.

WATSON, J. B. Psychology as a behaviorist views it. *Psychological review*, 1913, *20*, 158–177.

WATSON, J. B. *Psychology from the standpoint of a behaviorist*. Philadelphia: Lippincott, 1919.

WATSON, J. B., and RAYNOR, R. Conditioned emotional reactions. *Journal of experimental psychology*, 1920, *3*, 1–14.

WATSON, L. S., JR. Application of operant conditioning techniques to institutionalized severely and profoundly retarded children. *Mental retardation abstracts*, 1967, *4*, 1–18.

WATSON, S. G. Judgment of emotion from facial and contextual cue combinations. *Journal of personality and social psychology*, 1972, *24*, 334–342.

WAUGH, E. *The loved one*. Boston: Little, Brown, 1948.

WAXLER, C. Z., and YARROW, M. R. Factors influencing imitative learning in preschool children. *Journal of experimental child psychology*, 1970, *9*, 115–130.

WEBER, L. *The English infant school and informal education*. Englewood Cliffs, N.J.: Prentice-Hall, 1971.

WEBSTER, D. R., and AZRIN, N. H. Required relaxation: a method of inhibiting agitative-disruptive behavior of retardates. *Behaviour research and therapy*, 1973, *11*, 67–78.

WEBSTER, R. L., and LUBKER, B. B. Interrelationships among fluency producing variables in stuttered speech. *Journal of speech and hearing research*, 1968, *11*, 754–766.

WECKOWICZ, T. E., CROPLEY, A. J., and MUIR, W. An attempt to replicate the results of a factor analytic study in depressed patients. *Journal of clinical psychology*, 1971, 30–31.

WEGROCKI, H. J. A critique of cultural and statistical concepts of abnormality. *Journal of abnormal and social psychology*, 1939, *34*, 166–178.

WEIDNER, F. In vivo desensitization of a paranoid schizophrenic. *Journal of behavior therapy and experimental psychiatry*, 1970, *1*, 79–81.

WEIL, A. T., ZISBERG, N. E., and NELSEN, J. M. Clinical and psychological effects of marijuana in man. *Science*, 1968, *162*, 1234.

WEIL, G., and GOLDFRIED, M. R. Treatment of insomnia in an eleven-year-old child through self-relaxation. *Behavior therapy*, 1973, *4*, 282–294.

WEINBERG, G. *Society and the healthy homosexual*. New York: St. Martin's Press, 1972.

WEINBERG, S. K. *Society and personality disorders*. New York: Prentice-Hall, 1952.

WEINBERG, S. K. *Incest behavior*. New York: Citadel Press, 1955.

WEINER, H. Response cost and the aversive control of human operant behavior. *Journal of the experimental analysis of behavior*, 1963, *6*, 415–421.

WEINER, H., THALER, M., REISER, M. F., and MIRSKY, I. A. Etiology of duodenal ulcer. I: relation of specific psychological characteristics to rate of gastric secretion (serum pepsinogen). *Psychosomatic medicine*, 1957, *19*, 1–10.

WEINER, I. B. Behavior therapy in obsessive-compulsive neurosis: treatment of an adolescent boy. *Psychotherapy: theory, research and practice*, 1967, *4*, 27–29.

WEINER, I. W. The effectiveness of a suicide prevention program. *Mental Hygiene*, 1969, *53*, 357–363.

WEINGAERTNER, A. H. Self-administered aversive stimulation with hallucinating hospitalized schizophrenics. *Journal of consulting and clinical psychology*, 1971, *36*, 422–429.

WEINSTEIN, E. A., ECK, R. A., and LYERLY, O. G. Conversion hysteria in Appalachia. *Psychiatry*, 1969, *32*, 334–341.

WEINSTEIN, S., and TEUBER, H. L. Effects of penetrating brain injury on intelligence test scores. *Science*, 1957, *125*, 1036–1037.

WEINTRAUB, W., and ARONSON, H. The application of verbal behavior analysis to the study of psychological dense mechanisms: IV speech pattern associated with depressive behavior. *Journal of nervous and mental diseases*, 1967, *44*, 22–28.

WEISBERG, P. Student acceptance of bogus personality interpretations differing in level of social acceptability. *Psychological reports*, 1970, *27*, 743–746.

WEISBERG, P., PASSMAN, R. H., and RUSSELL, J. E. Development of verbal control over bizarre gestures of retardates through imitative and nonimitative reinforcement procedures. *Journal of applied behavior analysis*, 1973, *6*, 487–497.

WEISS, E., and ENGLISH, O. S. *Psychosomatic medicine*. Philadelphia: Saunders, 1943.

WEISS, R. F., BOYER, J. L., COLWICK, J. T. and MORAN, D. J. A delay of reinforcement gradient and correlated reinforcement in the instrumental conditioning of conversational behavior. *Journal of experimental psychology*, 1971, *90*, 33–38.

WEISS, R. F., BUCHANAN, W., ALSTATT, L., and LOMBARDO, J. P. Altruism is rewarding. *Science*, 1971, *171*, 1262–1263.

WEISS, R. L., EKMAN, P., ULLMANN, L. P., and KRASNER, L. The context of reinforcement in verbal conditioning. *Journal of clinical psychology*, 1965, *21*, 99–100.

WEISS, R. L., KRASNER, L., and ULLMANN, L. P. Responsivity to verbal conditioning as a function of emotional atmosphere and pattern of reinforcement. *Psychological reports,* 1960, *6,* 415–426.

WEISS, R. L., KRASNER, L., and ULLMANN, L. P. Responsivity of psychiatric patients to verbal conditioning: "success" and "failure" conditions and pattern of reinforced trials. *Psychological reports,* 1963, *12,* 423–426.

WEISS, T. and ENGEL, B. T. Operant conditioning of heart rate in patients with premature ventricular contractions. *Psychosomatic medicine,* 1971, *33* (4), 301–321.

WEISSMAN, H. N. The psychiatric team as a differential decision-maker with child patients. *Psychological reports,* 1969, *25,* 11–17.

WEITZ, S., ed. *Nonverbal communication.* New York: Oxford, 1974.

WEITZENHOFFER, A. M. The production of antisocial acts under hypnosis. *Journal of abnormal and social psychology,* 1949, *44,* 420–422.

WEITZENHOFFER, A. M. *Hypnotism, an objective study in suggestibility.* New York: Wiley, 1953.

WEITZENHOFFER, A. M., and HILGARD, E. R. *Stanford hypnotic susceptibility scale.* Palo Alto, Calif.: Consulting Psychologists Press, 1959.

WEIZENBAUM, J. On the impact of the computer on society. *Science,* 1972, *176,* 609–614.

WELKOWITZ, J., COHEN, J., and ORTMEYER, D. Value systems similarity: investigation of patient-therapist dyads. *Journal of consulting psychology,* 1967, *31,* 48–55.

WELLS, W. R. Experiments in the hypnotic production of crimes. *Journal of psychology,* 1941, *11,* 63–102.

WELSH, G. S., and DAHLSTROM, W. G., eds. *Basic readings on the MMPI in psychology and medicine.* Minneapolis: University of Minnesota Press, 1956.

WENDER, P. H. *Minimal brain dysfunction in children.* New York: Wiley, 1971.

WENGER, D. I., and FLETCHER, C. R. The effect of legal counsel on admissions to a state mental hospital: a confrontation of professions. *Journal of health and human behavior,* 1969, *10,* 66–72.

WERRY, J. S. The conditioning treatment of enuresis. *American journal of psychiatry,* 1966, *123,* 226–229.

WERRY, J. S., and COHRSSEN, J. Enuresis—an etiological and therapeutic study. *Journal of pediatrics,* 1965, *67,* 423–431.

WERRY, J. S. Childhood psychosis. In H. C. Quay and J. S. Werry, eds., *Psychopathological disorders of childhood.* New York: Wiley, 1972, pp. 173–233.

WERTHAM, F. Psychoauthoritarianism and the law. *University of Chicago law review,* 1955, *22,* 336.

WEST, L. J. Dissociative reaction. In A. M. Freedman and H. I. Kaplan, eds., *Comprehensive textbook of psychiatry.* Baltimore: Williams & Wilkins. 1967, 885–899.

WETZEL, R. Use of behavioral techniques in a case of compulsive stealing. *Journal of consulting psychology,* 1966, *30,* 367–374.

WETZEL, R. J., BAKER, J., RONEY, M., and MARTIN, M. Outpatient treatment of autistic behavior. *Behaviour research and therapy,* 1966, *4,* 169–177.

WEXLER, D. B. Token and taboo: behavior modification, token economies, and the law. *Behaviorism,* 1973, *1,* 1–24. (Also in *California law review,* 1973, *61,* 81–109).

WHALEN, C. K., and HENKER, B. A. Creating therapeutic pyramids using mentally retarded patients. *American journal of mental deficiency,* 1969, *74,* 331–337.

WHALEN, C. K., and HENKER, B. A. Pyramid therapy in a hospital for the retarded: methods, program evaluation and long-term effects. *American journal of mental deficiency,* 1971, *75,* 414–434.

WHITE, J. C., JR., and TAYLOR, D. J. Noxious conditioning as a treatment for rumination. *Mental retardation,* 1967, *5,* 30–33.

WHITE, J. G. The use of learning theory in the psychological treatment of children. *Journal of clinical psychology,* 1959, *15,* 227–229.

WHITE, R. W. Prediction of hypnotic susceptibility from a knowledge of subject's attitude. *Journal of psychology,* 1937, *3,* 265–277.

WHITE, R. W. A preface to the theory of hypnotism. *Journal of abnormal and social psychology,* 1941, *36,* 477–505.

WHITEHORN, J. C. Goals of psychotherapy. In E. A. Rubinstein and M. B. Parloff, eds., *Research in psychotherapy.* Washington, D.C.: American Psychological Association, 1959.

WHITING, J. W. M., and CHILD, I. L. *Child training and personality: a cross-cultural study.* New Haven, Conn.: Yale University Press, 1953.

WHITING, J. W. M., and MOWRER, O. H. Habit progression and regression—a laboratory study of some factors relevant to human socialization. *Journal of comparative psychology,* 1943, *36,* 229–253.

WHITLOCK, C. Note on reading acquisition: an extension of laboratory principles. *Journal of experimental child psychology,* 1966, *3,* 83–85.

WHITMAN, T. L. Aversive control of smoking behavior in a group context. *Behaviour research and therapy,* 1972, *10,* 97–104.

WHITMAN, T. L., CAPONIGRI, V., and MERCURIO, J. Reducing hyperactive behavior in a severely retarded child. *Mental retardation,* 1971, *9,* 17–19.

WHITMAN, T. L., ZAKARAS, M., and CHARDOS, S.

Effects of reinforcement and guidance procedures on instruction-following behavior of severely retarded children. *Journal of applied behavior analysis*, 1971, *4*, 283–290.

WHITNEY, L. R., and BARNARD, K. E. Implications of operant learning theory for nursing care of the retarded child. *Mental retardation*, 1966, *4*, 26–29.

WICKER, A. W. Attitudes versus actions: the relationship of verbal and overt behavioral responses to attitude objects. *Journal of social issues*, 1969, *25*, 41–78.

WICKES, I. G. Treatment of persistent enuresis with the electric buzzer. *Archives of disease in childhood*, 1958, *33*, 160–164.

WICKMAN, E. K. *Children's behavior and teachers' attitudes.* New York: Commonwealth Fund, 1929.

WICKRAMESKERA, I. The application of learning theory to the treatment of a case of sexual exhibitionism. *Psychotherapy: theory, research and practice*, 1968, *5*, 40–43.

WIENER, D. N. The effect of arbitrary termination on return to psychotherapy. *Journal of clinical psychology*, 1959, *15*, 335–338.

WIESEN, A. E., HARTLEY, G., RICHARDSON, C., and ROSKE, A. The retarded child as a reinforcing agent. *Journal of experimental child psychology*, 1967, *5*, 109–113.

WIESEN, A. E., and WATSON, E. Elimination of attention-seeking behavior in a retarded child. *American journal of mental deficiency*, 1967, *72*, 50–52.

WIGGINS, N., HOFFMAN, P. J., and TABER, T. Types of judges and cue utilization in judgments of intelligence. *Journal of personality and social psychology*, 1969, *12*, 52–59.

WIGGINS, S. L., and SALZBERG, H. C. Conditioning against silences and therapist-directed comments in group psychotherapy using auditory stimulation. *Psychological reports*, 1966, *18*, 591–599.

WIGNALL, C. M., and KOPPIN, I. L. Mexican-American usage of state mental hospital facilities. *Community mental health journal*, 1967, *3*, 137–148.

WIKLER, A. Some implications of conditioning theory for problems of drug abuse. *Behavioral science*, 1971, *16*, 92–97.

WILKINS, J. A follow-up study of those who called a suicide prevention center. *American journal of psychiatry*, 1970, *127*, 155–161.

WILKINS, W. Desensititization: social and cognitive factors underlying the effectiveness of Wolpe's procedure. *Psychological bulletin*, 1971, *76*, 311–317.

WILKINS, W. Expectancy of therapeutic gain: an empirical and conceptual critique. *Journal of consulting and clinical psychology*, 1973, *40*, 69–77.

WILLIAMS, C. D. The elimination of tantrum behavior by extinction procedures. *Journal of abnormal and social psychology*, 1959, *59*, 269.

WILLIAMS, W. S., and JACO, E. G. An evaluation of functional psychoses in old age. *American journal of psychiatry*, 1958, *114*, 910–916.

WILLINGHAM, W. W., ed. Invasion of privacy in research and testing. *Journal of educational measurement*, 1967, *4*, 1–31.

WILLIS, R. W., and EDWARDS, J. A. A study of the comparative effectiveness of systematic desensitization and implosive therapy. *Behaviour research and therapy*, 1969, *7*, 387–395.

WILMER, H. A. *Social psychiatry in action.* Springfield, Ill.: Thomas, 1958.

WILNER, D. M., PRICE-WALKLEY, R., PINKERTON, T. C., and TAYBACK, M. *The housing environment and family life.* Baltimore: Johns Hopkins University Press, 1962.

WILSON, C. W., and HOPKINS, B. L. The effect of contingent music on the intensity of noise in junior high home economics classes. *Journal of applied behavior analysis*, 1973, *6*, 269–275.

WILSON, D. P., KNAPP, S. C., DONDIS, E., and FEDER, Y. G. Course of mental illness in candidates for state hospitalization. *California mental health research digest*, 1964, *2*, 40–42.

WILSON, E., ed. *Sacred books of the past.* Rev. ed. New York: Wiley, 1945.

WILSON, F. S., and WALTERS, R. H. Modification of speech output of near-mute schizophrenics through social-learning procedures. *Behaviour research and therapy*, 1966, *4*, 59–67.

WILSON, M. L., and GREENE, R. L. Personality characteristics of female homosexuals. *Psychological reports*, 1971, *28*, 407–412.

WINCZE, J. P. A comparison of systematic desensitization and "vicarious extinction" in a case of frigidity. *Journal of behavior therapy and experimental psychiatry*, 1971, *2*, 285–289.

WINCZE, J. P., LEITENBERG, H., and AGRAS, W. S. The effects of token reinforcement and feedback on the delusional verbal behavior of chronic paranoid schizophrenics. *Journal of applied behavior analysis*, 1972, *5*, 247–262.

WINDER, C. L. On the personality structure of schizophrenics. *Journal of abnormal and social psychology*, 1952, *47*, 86–100.

WINDER, C. L. Psychotherapy. In P. R. Farnsworth and Q. McNemar, eds., *Annual review of psychology*. Vol. 8. Palo Alto, Calif.: Annual Reviews, 1957, pp. 309–330.

WINE, J. Test anxiety and direction of attention. *Psychological bulletin*, 1971, *76*, 92–104.

WINETT, R. A. Parameters of deposit contracts in the modification of smoking. *Psychological record*, 1973, *23*, 49–60.

WINETT, R. A., RICHARDS, C. S., KRASNER, L., and KRASNER, M. Child monitored token reading program. *Psychology in the schools*, 1971, *8*, 259–262.

WINETT, R. A., and WINKLER, R. C. Current behavior modification in the classroom: be still, be quiet, be docile. *Journal of applied behavior analysis*, 1972, *5*, 499–504.

WING, J. K. Institutionalism in mental hospitals. *British journal of social and clinical psychology*, 1962, *1*, 38–51.

WINKLER, R. C. Ward management of chronic psychiatric patients by a token reinforcement system. *Journal of applied behavior analysis*, 1970, *3*, 47–55.

WINKLER, R. C. The relevance of economic theory and technology to token reinforcement systems. *Behaviour research and therapy*, 1971, *9*, 81–88.

WINKLER, R. C. An experimental analysis of economic balance, savings and wages in a token economy. *Behavior therapy*, 1973, *4*, 22–40.

WINKLER, R. C., and KRASNER, L. The contribution of economics to token economies. Paper presented to the Eastern Psychological Association, New York, April 15, 1971.

WINOKUR, G. Genetic findings and methodological considerations in manic depressive disease. *British journal of psychiatry*, 1970, *117*, 267–274.

WINOKUR, G. Types of depressive illness. *British journal of psychiatry*, 1972, *120*, 265–266.

WINOKUR, G. Depression in the menopause. *American journal of psychiatry*, 1973, *130*, 92–93.

WINOKUR, G., CADORET, R., DORZAB, J., and BAKER, M. Depressive disease: a genetic study. *Archives of general psychiatry*, 1971, *24*, 135–144.

WIRT, R. D., and BRIGGS, P. F. The meaning of delinquency. In H. C. Quay, ed., *Juvenile delinquency*. Princeton, N.J.: Van Nostrand, 1965, pp. 1-26.

WISOCKI, P. A. Treatment of obsessive-compulsive behavior by covert sensitization and covert reinforcement: a case report. *Journal of behavior therapy and experimental psychiatry*, 1970, *3*, 233–239.

WISOCKI, P. A. The successful treatment of a heroin addict by covert conditioning techniques. *Journal of behavior therapy and experimental psychiatry*, 1973, *4*, 55–61.

WISPÉ, L. G., ed. Positive forms of social behavior. *Journal of social issues*, 1972, *3*, 1–229.

WISPÉ, L. G., and FRESHLEY, H. B. Race, sex and sympathetic helping behavior: the broken bag caper.
Journal of personality and social psychology, 1971, *17*, 59–65.

WITMER, L. Clinical psychology. *Psychological clinics*, 1907, *1*, 1–9.

WITTENBORN, J. R. Symptom patterns in a group of mental hospital patients. *Journal of consulting psychology*, 1951, *15*, 290–302.

WITTENBORN, J. R., and BAILEY, C. The symptoms of involutional psychosis. *Journal of consulting psychology*, 1952, *16*, 13–17.

WITTENBORN, J. R., HOLZBERG, J., and SIMON, B. Symptom correlates for descriptive diagnosis. *Genetic psychology monographs*, 1953, *47*, 237–301.

WITTENBORN, J. R., KIREMITCI, N., and WEBER, E. S. P. The choice of alternative antidepressants. *The journal of nervous and mental disease*, 1973, *156*, 97–108.

WITTER, C. Drugging and schooling. *Trans-action*, 1971, *8*, 31–34.

WITTKOWER, E. D. Perspectives in transcultural psychiatry. *International journal of psychiatry*, 1969, *8*, 811–824.

WITTMAN, M. P. A scale for measuring prognosis in schizophrenic patients. *Elgin papers*, 1941, *4*, 20–33.

WITZIG, J. S. The group treatment of male exhibitionists. *American journal of psychiatry*, 1968, *125*, 179–185.

WOHLWILL, J. F., and CARSON, D. H., eds., *Environment and the social sciences: perspectives and applications*. Washington, D.C.: American Psychological Association, 1972.

WOLBERG, L. R. The "spontaneous" mental cure. *Psychiatric quarterly*, 1944, *18*, 105–117.

WOLD, C. I. Demographic analysis of callers to the Los Angeles suicide prevention center. Paper read at first annual conference on suicidology, Chicago, March 1968.

WOLD, C. I. Characteristics of 26,000 suicide prevention center patients. *Bulletin of suicidology*, 1970, *6*, 24–28.

WOLD, C. I., and LITMAN, R. E. Suicide after contact with a suicide prevention center. *Archives of general psychiatry*, 1973, *28*, 735–739.

WOLF, M. M., BIRNBRAUER, J. S., WILLIAMS, T., and LAWLER, J. A note on apparent extinction of the vomiting behavior of a retarded child. In L. P. Ullmann and L. Krasner, eds., *Case studies in behavior modification*. New York: Holt, Rinehart and Winston, 1965, pp. 364–366.

WOLF, M. M., GILES, D. K., and HALL, V. R. Experiments with token reinforcement in a remedial classroom. *Behaviour research and therapy*, 1968, *6*, 51–64.

WOLF, M. M., RISLEY, T., JOHNSTON, M., HARRIS, F. R., and ALLEN, K. E. Application of operant conditioning procedures to the behaviour problems of an autistic child: a follow-up and extension. *Behaviour research and therapy*, 1967, *5*, 103–111.

WOLF, M. M., RISLEY, T., and MEES, H. L. Application of operant conditioning procedures to the behaviour problems of an autistic child. *Behaviour research and therapy*, 1964, *1*, 305–312.

WOLF, S., CARDON, P. V., SHEPARD, E. M., and WOLFF, H. G. *Life stress and essential hypertension.* Baltimore: Williams & Wilkins, 1955.

WOLF, S., and PINSKY, R. H. Effects of placebo administration and occurrence of toxic reactions. *Journal of the American medical association*, 1954, *155*, 339–341.

WOLF, S., and WOLFF, H. G. *Human gastric function.* New York: Oxford University Press, 1947.

WOLFENSBERGER, W. Ethical issues in research with human subjects. *Science*, 1967, *155*, 47–51.

WOLFF, R. The systematic application of the satiation procedure to delusional verbiage. *Psychological record*, 1971, *21*, 459–463.

WOLFF, W. T., and MERRENS, M. R. Behavioral assessment: a review of clinical methods. *Journal of personality assessment*, 1974, *38*, 3–16.

WOLFGANG, M. E. Suicide by means of victim-precipitated homicide. *Journal of clinical and experimental psychopathology and quarterly review of psychiatry and neurology*, 1959, *20*, 335–349.

WOLLERSHEIM, J. P. Effectiveness of group therapy based on learning principles in the treatment of overweight women. *Journal of abnormal psychology*, 1970, *76*, 462–474.

WOLMAN, B. B. *The unconscious mind.* Englewood Cliffs, N.J.: Prentice-Hall, 1968.

WOLPE, J. Reciprocal inhibition as the main basis of psychotherapeutic effects. *American medical association archives of neurology and psychiatry*, 1954, *72*, 205–226.

WOLPE, J. *Psychotherapy by reciprocal inhibition.* Stanford, Calif.: Stanford University Press, 1958.

WOLPE, J. The systematic desensitization treatment of neuroses. *Journal of nervous and mental disease*, 1961, *132*, 189–203.

WOLPE, J. Isolation of a conditioning procedure as the crucial psychotherapeutic factor: a case study. *Journal of nervous and mental disease*, 1962, *134*, 316–329.

WOLPE, J. Behaviour therapy in complex neurotic states. *British journal of psychiatry*, 1964, *110*, 28–34.

WOLPE, J. Transcript of initial interview in a case of depression. *Journal of behavior therapy and experimental psychiatry*, 1970, *1*, 71–78.

WOLPE, J. Dealing with resistance to thought-stopping: a transcript. *Journal of behavior therapy and experimental psychiatry*, 1971a, *2*, 121–125.

WOLPE, J. Neurotic depression: experimental analog, clinical syndrome, and treatment. *American journal of psychotherapy*, 1971b, *25*, 362–368.

WOLPE, J. Correcting misconceptions in a case of frigidity: a transcript. *Journal of behavior therapy and experimental psychiatry*, 1971c, *2*, 251–258.

WOLPE, J. *The practice of behavior therapy.* New York: Pergamon Press, 1973.

WOLPE, J., and LAZARUS, A. A. *Behavior therapy techniques: a guide to the treatment of neuroses.* New York: Pergamon Press, 1966.

WOLPE, J., and RACHMAN, S. Psychoanalytic "evidence": a critique based on Freud's case of little Hans. *Journal of nervous and mental disease*, 1960, *130*, 135–148.

WOLPE, J., and THERIAULT, N. Francois Leuret: a progenitor of behavior therapy. *Journal of behavior therapy and experimental psychiatry*, 1971, *2*, 19–21.

WOLPIN, M., and RAINES, J. Visual imagery, expected roles and extinction as possible factors in reducing fear and avoidance behaviour. *Behaviour research and therapy*, 1966, *4*, 25–37.

WOOD, K. A case of dancing mania. In B. Roueche, ed., *Curiosities of medicine.* Boston: Little, Brown, 1958, pp. 237–243.

WOODRUFF, R. A., JR. Hysteria: an evaluation of objective diagnostic criteria by the study of women with chronic medical illness. *British journal of psychiatry*, 1967, *114*, 1115–1119.

WOODRUFF, R. A., JR., CLAYTON, P. J., and GUZE, S. B. Hysteria: an evaluation of specific diagnostic criteria by the study of randomly selected psychiatric clinic patients. *British journal of psychiatry*, 1969, *115*, 1243–1248.

WOODRUFF, R. A., JR., GOODWIN, D. W., and GUZE, S. B. *Psychiatric diagnosis.* New York: Oxford University Press, 1974.

WOODWARD, J. L. Changing ideas on mental illness and its treatment. *American sociological review*, 1951, *16*, 443–454.

WOODWARD, M. The diagnosis and treatment of homosexual offenders. *British journal of delinquency*, 1958, *9*, 44–59.

WORLD HEALTH ORGANIZATION. *Alcohol and alcoholism: report of an expert committee.* Geneva: W.H.O. technical report series, 1958, No. 94.

WOY, J. R., and EFRAN, J. S. Systematic desensitization and expectancy in the treatment of speaking anxiety. *Behaviour research and therapy*, 1972, *10*, 43–49.

WRIGHT, D. Social reinforcement and maze learning in children. *Child development*, 1968, *39*, 177–183.

WRIGHT, L. Components of positive mental health. *Journal of consulting and clinical psychology*, 1971, *36*, 277–280.

WRIGHT, L. Aversive conditioning of self-induced seizures. *Behavior therapy*, 1973, *4*, 712–713.

WRIGHT, L., NUNNERY, A., EICHEL, B., and SCOTT, R. Behavioral tactics for reinstating natural breathing in infants with tracheostomy. *Pediatric research*, 1969, *3*, 275–278.

WULBERT, M., NYMAN, B. A., SNOW, D., and OWEN, Y. The efficacy of stimulus fading and contingency management on the treatment of elective mutism: a case study. *Journal of applied behavior analysis*, 1973, *6*, 435–441.

WYNNE, R. D. The influence of hospitalization on the verbal behaviour of chronic schizophrenics. *British journal of psychiatry*, 1963, *109*, 380–389.

WYRWICKA, W., STERMAN, M. B., and CLEMENTE, C. D. Conditioning of induced electroencephalographic sleep patterns in the cat. *Science*, 1962, *137*, 616–618.

YABLONSKY, L. *The tunnel back: Synanon.* New York: Macmillan, 1965.

YALOM, I. D., and LIEBERMAN, M. A. A study of encounter group casualties. *Archives of general psychiatry*, 1971, *25*, 16–30.

YAMAGAMI, T. The treatment of an obsession by thought-stopping. *Journal of behavior therapy and experimental psychiatry*, 1971, *2*, 133–135.

YAMAMOTO, J., JAMES, Q. C., BLOOMBAUM, M., and HATTEM, J. Racial factors in patient selection. *American journal of psychiatry*, 1967, *124*, 630–636.

YAMAMOTO, J., JAMES, Q. C., and PALLEY, N. Cultural problems in psychiatric therapy. *Archives of general psychiatry*, 1968, *19*, 45–49.

YAP, P. M. The culture-bound reactive syndromes. In W. Caudill and T. Lin, eds., *Mental health research in Asia and the Pacific*. Honolulu: East-West Center Press, 1969.

YARROW, L. J. Maternal deprivation: toward an empirical and conceptual re-evaluation. *Psychological bulletin*, 1961, *58*, 459–490.

YATES, A. J. Symptoms and symptom substitution. *Psychological review*, 1958a, *65*, 371–374.

YATES, A. J. The application of learning theory to the treatment of tics. *Journal of abnormal and social psychology*, 1958b, *56*, 175–182.

YATES, A. J. Psychological deficit. In P. R. Farnsworth, O. McNemar, and Q. McNemar, eds., *Annual review of psychology*. Palo Alto, Calif.: Annual Reviews, 1966, *17*, 111–144.

YEN, S. Operant therapy for excessive checking. *Canadian journal of behavioral science*, 1971, *3*, 194–197.

YOELL, W., STEWART, D., WOLPE, J., GOLDSTEIN, A., and SPEIERER, G. Marriage, morals, and therapeutic goals: a discussion. *Journal of behavior therapy and experimental psychiatry*, 1971, *2*, 127–132.

YOUNG, B. W. Self-control of smoking: a structured reduction program comparing the effects of a personal smoking pattern, self-reinforcement and continual regulation. Unpublished doctoral dissertation, University of Hawaii, 1973.

YOUNG, G. C., and MORGAN, R. T. T. Overlearning in the conditioning treatment of enuresis: a long-term follow-up study. *Behaviour research and therapy*, 1972b, *10*, 419–420.

YOUNG, I. L., and GOLDSMITH, A. O. Treatment of encopresis in a day treatment program. *Psychotherapy: theory, research and practice*, 1972, *9*, 231–235.

YOUNG, R. D., and FRYE, M. Some are laughing; some are not—why? *Psychological reports*, 1966, *18*, 747–754.

ZAIDEL, S. F., and MEHRABIAN, A. The ability to communicate and infer positive and negative attitudes facially and vocally. *Journal of experimental research in personality*, 1969, *3*, 233–241.

ZANNA, M. P., KIESLER, C. A., and PILKONIS, P. A. Positive and negative attitudinal affect established by classical conditioning. *Journal of personality and social psychology*, 1970, *14*, 321–328.

ZARLOCK, S. P. Social expectations, language, and schizophrenia. *Journal of humanistic psychology*, 1966, *6*, 68–74.

ZARLOCK, S. P. Emergence of schizophrenia from social biases of perception. *Perceptual and motor skills*, 1972, *34*, 835–846.

ZAX, M., and SPECTER, G. A. *An introduction to community psychology.* New York: Wiley, 1974.

ZEILER, M. D., and JERVEY, S. S. Development of behavior: self-feeding. *Journal of consulting and clinical psychology*, 1968, *32*, 164–168.

ZEISSET, R. M. Desensitization and relaxation in the modification of psychiatric patients' interview behavior. *Journal of abnormal psychology*, 1968, *73*, 18–24.

ZEITLYN, B. B. The therapeutic community—fact or fantasy? *British journal of psychiatry*. 1967, *113*, 1083–1086.

ZIEGLER, F. J., IMBODEN, J. B., and MEYER, E. Contemporary conversion reactions: a clinical study. *American journal of psychiatry*, 1960, *116*, 901–909.

ZIFFERBLATT, S. M. The effectiveness of modes and schedules of reinforcement on work and social behavior in occupational therapy. *Behavior therapy,* 1972, *3,* 567–578.

ZIGLER, E. Familial mental retardation: a continuing dilemma. *Science,* 1967, *155,* 292–298.

ZIGLER, E., and DELABRY, J. Concept-switching in middle-class, lower-class, and retarded children. *Journal of abnormal and social psychology,* 1962, *65,* 267–273.

ZIGLER, E., and PHILLIPS, L. Psychiatric diagnosis and symptomatology. *Journal of abnormal and social psychology,* 1961, *63,* 69–75.

ZILBOORG, G., and HENRY, G. W. *A history of medical psychology.* New York: Norton, 1941.

ZIMET, C. N., and BRACKBILL, G. A. The role of anxiety in psychodiagnosis. *Journal of clinical psychology,* 1956, *12,* 173–177.

ZIMET, C. N., and FINE, H. J. Perceptual differentiation and two dimensions of schizophrenia. *Journal of nervous and mental disease,* 1959, *129,* 435–441.

ZIMMERMAN, B. J., and ROSENTHAL, T. Concept attainment, transfer, and retention through observation and rule-provision. *Journal of experimental child psychology,* 1972, *14,* 139–150.

ZIMMERMAN, E. H., and ZIMMERMAN, J. The alteration of behavior in a special classroom situation. *Journal of the experimental analysis of behavior,* 1962, *5,* 59–60.

ZIMMERMAN, E. H., ZIMMERMAN, J., and RUSSELL, C. D. Differential effects of token reinforcement on instruction-following behavior in retarded students instructed as a group. *Journal of applied behavior analysis,* 1969, *2,* 101–112.

ZIMMERMAN, J., and GROSZ, H. J. "Visual" performance of a functionally blind person. *Behaviour research and therapy,* 1966, *4,* 119–134.

ZIMMERMAN, J., and KRAUSS, H. H. Source and magnitude of censure in predictions of unethical behavior. *Psychological reports,* 1971, *28,* 727–732.

ZIMMERMAN, J., OVERPECK, C., EISENBERG, H., and GARLICK, B. J. Operant conditioning in a sheltered workshop. *Rehabilitation literature,* 1969a, *30,* 326–334.

ZIMMERMAN, J., STUCKEY, T. E., GARLICK, B. J., and MILLER, M. Effects of token reinforcement on productivity in multiply handicapped clients in a sheltered workshop. *Rehabilitation literature,* 1969b, *30,* 34–41.

ZIV, A. Children's behavior problems as viewed by teachers, psychologists, and children. *Child development,* 1970, *41,* 871–879.

ZOLA, I. K. Culture and symptoms—an analysis of patients' presenting complaints. *American sociological review,* 1966, *31,* 615–630.

ZUBEK, J. P., ed. *Sensory deprivation.* New York: Appleton-Century-Crofts, 1969.

ZUBEK, J. P., PUSHKAR, D., SANSOM, W., and GOWING, J. Perceptual changes after prolonged sensory isolation (darkness and silence). *Canadian journal of psychology,* 1961, *15,* 83–100.

ZUBIN, J. A cross-cultural approach to psychopathology and its implications for diagnostic classification. In L. D. Eron, ed.. *The classification of behavior disorders.* Chicago: Aldine, 1966.

ZUBIN, J. Foundations of gerontology: history, training, and methodology. In C. Eisdorfer and M. P. Lawton, eds., *The psychology of adult development and aging.* Washington, D.C.: American Psychological Association, 1973, pp. 31–10.

ZUNG, W. K. A self-rating depression scale. *Archives of general psychiatry,* 1965, *12,* 63–70.

ZUSMAN, J. Some explanations of the changing appearance of psychotic patients: antecedents of the social breakdown syndrome concept. *International journal of psychiatry,* 1967a, *3,* 216–237.

ZUSMAN, J. The psychiatrist as a member of the emergency room team. *American journal of psychiatry,* 1967b, *123,* 1394–1401.

ZUSMAN, J. Sociology and mental illness: some neglected implications for treatment. In A. Kiev, ed., *Social psychiatry.* Vol. 1. New York: Science House, 1969.

ZWEIG, S. *Mental healers: Franz Anton Mesmer, Mary Baker Eddy, Sigmund Freud.* New York: Frederick Ungar, 1932.

ADDITIONAL REFERENCES

ANDERSON, K. A. The "shopping" behavior of parents of mentally retarded children. The professional person's role. *Mental retardation,* 1971, *9,* 3–5.

BLUM, A. F., and ROSENBERG, L. Some problems involved in professionalizing social interaction: the case of psychotherapeutic training. *Journal of health and social behavior,* 1968, *9,* 72–85.

BRENER, J., and KLEINMAN, R. A. Learned control of decreases in systolic blood pressure. *Nature* (London), *228,* 1063.

CARON, R. F. Visual reinforcement of headturning

in young infants. *Journal of experimental child psychology*, 1967, *5*, 489–511.

CARROLL, W. R., ROSENTHAL, T. L., and BRYSH, C. G. Social transmission of grammatical parameters. *Journal of educational psychology*, 1972, *63*, 589–596.

CLORE, G. L., and BYRNE, D. A reinforcement-affect model of attraction. In T. L. Huston, ed., *Perspective on interpersonal attraction*, New York: Academic Press, 1974.

COLSON, C. E. Effects of different explanations of disordered behavior on treatment referrals. *Journal of consulting and clinical psychology*, 1970, *34*, 432–435.

DALTON, K. Children's hospital admissions and mother's menstruation. *British medical journal*, 1970, *2*, 17–18.

DENNER, B., and PRICE, R. P., eds. *Community mental health: social action and reaction*. New York: Holt, Rinehart and Winston, 1973.

DOWD, S. A., and ABELSON, R. M. Schedule transitions in the operant conditioning of chronic schizophrenics. Unpublished manuscript. Orono, Maine: University of Maine, 1973.

FISCHER, E. H., and TURNER, J. LeB. Orientations to seeking professional help: development and research utility of an attitude scale. *Journal of consulting and clinical psychology*, 1970, *35*, 79–90.

FORBERG, F. K. *The manual of exotica sexualia*. North Hollywood, Calif.: Brandon House, 1965.

FELDSTEIN, J. H., and WITRYOL, S. L. The incentive value of uncertainty reduction for children. *Child development*, 1971, *42*, 793–804.

FREEMAN, W. *The psychiatrists*. New York: Grune & Stratton, 1968.

GANNON, L., and STERNBACH, R. A. Alpha enhancement and a treatment for pain: a case study. *Journal of behavior therapy and experimental*

GARDNER, W. I. *Behavior modification in mental retardation*. Chicago: Aldine-Atherton, 1971.

GARMEZY, N. Vulnerable adolescents: implications derived from studies of an internalizing-externalizing symptom dimension. In J. Zubin and A. M. Freedman, eds., *Psychopathology of adolescence*. New York: Grune & Stratton, 1969.

GEIS, G., ed. *White-collar criminal: the offender in business and the professions*. New York: Atherton, 1968.

GIEBINK, J. W., STOVER, D. O., and FAHL, M. A. Teaching adaptive responses to frustration to emotionally disturbed boys. *Journal of consulting and clinical psychology*, 1968, *32*, 366–368.

GROB, G. N. *Mental institutions in America: Social policy to 1875*. New York: Free Press, 1973.

HARDYCK, C. D., PETRINOVICH, L. F., and ELLSWORTH, D. W. Feedback of speech muscle activity during silent reading: rapid extinction. *Science*, 1968, *154*, 1467–1468.

HARTH, R. Attitudes and mental retardation. Review of the literature. *Training school bulletin*, 1973, 150–164.

HARTOGS, R. (with FANTEL, H.) *Four-letter games: The psychology of obscenity*. New York: Dell, 1968.

HOOD, R. W. Effects of foreknowledge of death in the assessment from case history material of intent to die. *Journal of consulting and clinical psychology*, 1970, *34*, 129–133.

HOPKINS, B. L. Effects of candy and social reinforcement, instructions, and reinforcement schedule leaning on the modification and maintenance of smiling. *Journal of applied behavior analysis*, 1968, *1*, 121–129.

HUNT, J. McV. Toward the prevention of incompetence. In J. W. Carter, Jr., ed., *Research contributions from psychology to community mental health*. New York: Behavioral Publications, 1968.

ILLICH, I. D. *Deschooling society*. New York: Harper & Row. 1970.

JACKSON, B. Treatment of depression by self-reinforcement. *Behavior therapy*, 1972, *3*, 298–307.

JOHNSON, C. A. and KATZ, R. C. Using parents as change agents for their children: a review. *Journal of child psychology and psychiatry*, 1973, *14*, 181–200.

JONES, R. J., and AZRIN, N. H. An experimental application of a social reinforcement approach to the problem of job-finding. *Journal of applied behavior analysis*, 1973, *6*, 345–353.

KAMIYA, J., DICARA, L. V., BARBER, T., MILLER, N. E., SHAPIRO, D., and STOYVA, J. *Biofeedback and self-control: an Aldine reader on the regulation of bodily processes and consciousness*. Chicago: Aldine, 1971.

KANFER, F. H., and KAROLY, P. Self-control: a behavioristic excursion into the lion's den. *Behavior therapy*, 1972, *3*, 398–416.

KAREN, A. L., and BOWER, R. C. A behavioral analysis of a social control agency: Synanon. *Journal of research in crime and delinquency*, 1968, *5*, 18–34.

KASTENBAUM, R., and DURKEE, S. Elderly people view old age. In R. Kastenbaum, ed., *New thoughts on old age*. New York: Springer, 1964.

KAZDIN, A. E. The effect of response cost in suppressing behavior in a prepsychotic retardate. *Journal of behavior therapy and experimental psychiatry,* 1971, *2,* 137-140.

KEMP, C. H. Parents as therapists. Paper presented at the annual meeting of the American Association for Mental Deficiency, Minneapolis, May 1972.

KREBS, D. L. Altruism: an examination of the concept and a review of the literature. *Psychological bulletin,* 1970, *73,* 258-302.

LAING, R. D., and ESTERSON, A. *Sanity, madness, and the family.* New York: Basic Books, 1964.

LEVY, B., STACEY, J. Sexism in the elementary school: a backward and forward look. *Phi Delta Kappan,* 1973, *55,* 105-109.

LINN, L. S. Psychopathology and experience with marijuana. *British journal of addiction,* 1971, *67,* 55-64.

MACDONALD, M. L. The forgotten Americans: a sociopsychological analysis of aging and nursing homes. *American journal of community psychology,* 1973, *1,* 272-294.

MACKEY, R. A. Personal concepts of the mentally ill among caregiving groups. *Mental hygiene,* 1969, *53,* 245-252.

MCGLOTHIN, W. H., ARNOLD, D. O., and ROWAN, P. K. Marihuana use among adults. *Psychiatry, Washington, D. C.,* 1970, *33,* 433-443.

MIRIN, S. M., et al. Casual versus heavy use of marijuana: a redefinition of the marijuana problem. *American journal of psychiatry,* 1971, *127,* 1134-1140.

NAWAS, M. M., and BRAUN, S. H. The use of operant techniques for modifying the behavior of the severely and profoundly retarded. I: Introduction and initial phase. *Mental retardation,* 1970a, *8,* 2-6.

NAWAS, M. M., and BRAUN, S. H. The use of operant techniques for modifying the behavior of the severely and profoundly retarded. II: The techniques. *Mental retardation,* 1970b, *8,* 18-24.

NAWAS, M. M., and BRAUN, S. H. An overview of behavior modification with the severely and profoundly retarded. III: Maintenance of change and epilogue. *Mental retardation,* 1970c, *8,* 4-11.

O'DELL, S. Training parents in behavior modification: a review. *Psychological bulletin,* 1974, *81,* 418-433.

ODOM, R. D., LIEBERT, R. N., and FERNANDEZ, L. E. Effects of symbolic modeling on the syntactical productions of retardates. *Psychonomic Science,* 1969, *17,* 104-105.

O'MALLEY, J. E., ANDERSON, W. H., and LAZARE, A. Failure of outpatient treatment of drug abuse. I: Heroin. *American journal of psychiatry,* 1972, *128,* 865-868.

OVESEY, L., and GAYLIN, W. Psychotherapy of male homosexuality: prognosis, selection of patients, techniques. *American journal of psychotherapy,* 1965, *19,* 382-396.

PHILLIPS, D. L. Rejection: a possible consequence of seeking help for mental disorders. *American sociological review,* 1963, *28,* 968-972.

RACHLIN, H. C., and FRANKEL, M. Choice, rate of response, and rate of gambling. *Journal of experimental psychology,* 1969, *80,* 444-449.

RAVEN, P. H., BERLIN, P., and BREEDLOVE, D. E. The origins of taxonomy. *Science,* 1971, *174,* 1210-1213.

REISINGER, J. J. The treatment of "anxiety-depression" via positive reinforcement and response cost. *Journal of applied behavior analysis,* 1972, *5,* 125-130.

RIGGS, F. W. The comparison of whole political systems. In R. T. Holt and J. E. Turner, eds. *The methodology of comparative research.* New York: Free Press, 1970.

RITVO, E. R., ORNITZ, E. M., WALLER, R. D., and HANLEY, J. Correlation of psychiatric diagnoses and EEG findings: a double blind study of 184 hospitalized children. *American journal of psychiatry,* 1970, *126,* 988-996.

ROBBINS, R. C., MERCER, J. R., and MEYERS, C. E. The school as a selecting-labeling system. *California mental health research digest,* 1967, *5,* 124-125.

ROSEN, G. *Madness in society.* New York: Harper & Row, 1969.

ROSENTHAL, T. L., and KELLOGG, J. S. Demonstration versus instructions in concept attainment by mental retardates. *Behavior research and therapy,* 1973, *11,* 299-302.

ROUTH, D. K., and ROBERTS, R. D. Minimal brain dysfunction in children: failure to find evidence for a behavioral syndrome. *Psychological reports,* 1972, *31,* 307-314.

RYDBERG, S. Beginning reading discrimination taught at IQ 35 by conditioning. *Perceptual and motor skills,* 1971, *32,* 163-166.

SAAIRO, T. N., TITTLE, C. K., and JACKLIN, C. N. Sex role sterotyping in the public schools. *Harvard educational review,* 1973, *43,* 386-416.

SAMEROFF, A., and ZAX, M. Schizotaxia revisited: model issues in the etiology of schizophrenia. *American journal of orthopsychiatry,* 1973, *43,* 744-754.

SANTOGROSSI, D. A., O'LEARY, K. D., ROMANCZYK,

R. G., and KAUFMAN, K. F. Self-evaluation by adolescents in a psychiatric hospital school token program. *Journal of applied behavior analysis*, 1973, *6*, 277–287.

SCHEFF, T. J., and SUNDSTROM, E. The stability of deviant behavior over time: a reassessment. *Journal of health and social behavior*, 1970, *11*, 37–43.

SCHULDER, D. B. Women and the law. In S. Stambler, ed., *Women's liberation: blueprint for the future*. New York: Ace, 1970.

SHAPIRO, D. et. al., eds. *Biofeedback and self-control, 1972*. Chicago: Aldine, 1973.

SHEAN, G. D., and ZEIDBERG, A. Token reinforcement therapy: a comparison of matched groups. *Journal of behavior therapy and experimental psychiatry*, 1971, *2*, 107–110.

SHEPPARD, W. C. Operant control of infant vocal and motor behavior. *Journal of experimental child psychology*, 1969, *7*, 36–51.

SILVER, L. B. A proposed view on the etiology of the neurological learning disability syndrome. *Journal of learning disabilities*, 1971, *4*, 123–133.

SIMMONS, L. Cross-cultural views of the aged. In R. Kastenbaum, ed., *New thoughts on old age*. New York: Springer, 1964, 229–236.

SINES, J. O., PAUKER, J. R., SINES, L. K., and OWEN, D. R. Identification of clinically relevant dimensions of children's behavior. *Journal of consulting and clinical psychology*, 1969, *33*, 728–734.

SMEETS, P. M. Reducing vomiting in a retardate. *American institute for mental studies*, 1970, *67*.

SMITH, D. E. P., BRETHOWER, D., and CABOT, R. Increasing task behavior in a language arts program by providing reinforcement. *Journal of experimental child psychology*, 1969, *8*, 45–62.

SNORTUM, J. R. Probability learning and gambling behavior in the psychopathic deviate. *Journal of general psychology*, 1968, *79*, 47–57.

SPEVACK, M., PIHL, R., and ROWAN, T. Behavior therapies in the treatment of drug abuse: some case studies. *The psychological record*, 1973, *23*, 179–184.

SPIEGEL, D. E., KEITH-SPIEGEL, P., and GRAYSON, H. N. Behavior of the typical mental patient as seen by eight groups of hospital personnel. *Journal of psychiatric research*, 1967, *5*, 317–325.

SPINETTA, J., and RIGLER, D. The child-abusing parent: a psychological review. *Psychological bulletin*, 1972, *77*, 296–304.

SUCHOTLIFF, L. C. Relation of formal thought disorder to the communication deficit in schizophrenics. *Journal of abnormal psychology*, 1970, *76*, 250–257.

SULZBACHER, S. I., and HOUSER, J. E. A tactic to eliminate disruptive behavior in the classroom: group contingent consequences. *American journal of mental deficiency*, 1968, *73*, 88–90.

SUTHERLAND, R. H. *White collar crime*. New York: Dryden, 1949.

THARP, R. G., WATSON, D., and KAYA, J. Self-modification of depression. *Journal of consulting and clinical psychology*, 1974, *42*, 624.

THIO, A. Class bias in the sociology of deviance. *American sociologist*, 1973, *8*, 1–12.

THOMASON, I. G., and RATHOD, N. H. Aversion therapy for heroin dependence. *Lancet*, 1968, *2*, 382–384.

TOBAN, E. Professional and nonprofessional mental health workers' mode of persuading clients to seek institutional services. *Journal of consulting and clinical psychology*, 1970, *34*, 177–180.

VISCOTT, D. S. *The making of a psychiatrist*. Greenwich, Conn.: Fawcett, 1973.

WARREN, S. A., and TURNER, D. R. Attitudes of professionals and students toward exceptional children. *Training school bulletin*, 1966, *62*, 136–144.

WEINBERG, M. S. Sexual modesty, social meanings and the nudist camp. *Social problems*, 1965, *12*, 311–318.

WILSON, E., ed. *Sacred books of the east*. Rev. ed. New York: Wiley, 1945.

WRIGHT, D. *The psychology of moral behaviour*. Baltimore: Penguin, 1972.

WYSOCKI, B. A., and WYSOCKI, A. C. Behavior symptoms as a basis for a new diagnostic classification of problem children. *Journal of clinical psychology*, 1970, *26*, 41–45.

YALOM, I. D., and LIEBERMAN, M. A. A study of encounter group casualties. *Archives of general psychiatry*, 1971, *25*, 16–30.

ZIMMERMAN, B. J., and PIKE, E. O. Effects of modeling and reinforcement on the acquisition and generalization of question-asking behavior. *Child development*, 1972, *43*, 892–907.

name index

Abel, G. G., 384, 434, 435
Abelson, C., 498
Abelson, R. M., 380
Abesso, V. J., 439
Abood, L. G., 139
Abraham, K., 390
Abramovitz, A., 485
Abramowitz, C. V., 214
Abramowitz, S. I., 214
Abrams, K. S., 294
Abramson, E. E., 597
Abroms, G. M., 266, 369
Abse, D. W., 252
Abu-Laban, B., 451
Ackley, S., 608
Adams, H. E., 241fn, 374, 525
Adams, K. M., 581
Adams, M., 604
Adams, M. R., 292
Adams, P. L., 99
Adamson, J. D., 344fn
Adelberg, K., 495fn
Adler, Alfred, 398fn
Adler, C. S., 298
Adler, N., 155, 227, 462fn, 569, 586
Agras, W. S., 235, 269, 276, 277, 294, 296, 298, 374, 438
Agnew, J., 208
Agrippa, Cornelius, 128
Aichorn, A., 554
Aiello, J. R., 90
Aiken, E. G., 241fn
Ainsworth, M.H., 516
Akers, R. L., 556
Akiskal, H. S., 397
Alabiso, F., 498
Albert, S., 90
Albertus Magnus, 55
Alden, S. E., 295
Alderson, P., 333
Alexander, F. G., 2, 18fn, 127fn, 135fn, 154, 285, 312, 315, 321, 390, 546, 547
Alford, G. S., 297, 595
Al-Issa, I., 430, 431, 456
Allen, C. M., 597
Allen, D. C., 100fn
Allen, G. J., 275, 367fn, 493
Allen, J., S., 506

Allen, K. E., 322, 480
Allen, M. K., 85fn, 592
Allen, P., 525
Alley, G. R., 496
Allman, L. R., 454
Allport, G. W., 156, 163fn, 166, 167
Altman, K., 593
Almond, R., 369
Alper, T., 399
Alpert, D., 606
Altman, R., 525
Altschule, M. D., 134fn
Alvarez, A., 577, 578
Anant, S. S., 440, 441, 455
Andelman, D. A., 537
Anderson, M. H., 467
Anderson, F. L., 99
Anderson, K. A., 520
Andrews, G., 292
Andry, R. G., 558
Anthony, E. J., 345
Aphrodite, 121
Appel, J. B., 434
Appell, M. J., 200, 520
Applebaum, A. S., 113
Appollo, 121
Apter, I. M., 430
Arann, L,. 384
Archimatheus, 103fn
Arehart, J. L., 467
Aretaeus, 389
Arieti, S., 346, 396, 397
Aristotle, 32, 36, 52, 55, 127
Arkowitz, H. S., 234
Arlidge, 136, 366
Armitage, S. G., 375
Armstrong, H. E., 594
Arnold, C. R., 494
Arnold, D. O., 465
Aronson, E., 593
Aronson, H., 99, 187fn, 266
Arrell, V. M., 516
Arrill, M. B., 5
Arthur, A. Z., 203fn
Arthur, R. J., 184, 184fn, 212
Asclepius, 121
Ascough, J. C., 317

Ash, P., 208
Ashby, W. R., 583
Ashem, B., 455
Ashenden, B., 502
Astrup, C., 340
Atkinson, R. L., 65, 341fn, 347
Atthowe, J. M., Jr., 240, 329, 382, 383, 384, 597
Atwood, G. E., 264, 266, 399
Auld, F., Jr., 227
Austin, G. M., 533
Averill, J. R., 265
Averroes, 127
Avezoar, 127
Avicenna, 127
Ayllon, T., 47, 71, 72, 72fn, 73fn, 74, 75, 76, 77, 78, 214, 240, 322, 374, 381, 382, 384, 455, 482, 506, 597
Ayman, O., 103
Azerrad, J., 296
Azrin, N. H., 240, 291, 292, 375, 381, 382, 394, 455, 457, 482, 495fn, 499, 500, 511, 524, 525, 561, 563, 593, 597

Baastrup, P. C., 399
Babigian, H. M., 208
Babst, D. V., 467
Bachrach, A. J., 80, 81, 148, 295, 297, 323
Back, K. W., 229, 253, 254
Bacon, Francis, 50
Baer, D. M., 84, 505
Bagnone, F., 107fn
Bailey, C., 394
Bailey, J., 70, 281
Bailey, J. B., 561
Bailey, J. S., 480, 561
Bailly, 108, 109
Baird, R. R., 595
Bakan, D., 483
Baker, B., 241, 525, 528
Baker, B. L., 241, 293, 499
Baker, R., 80fn, 379, 380
Baker, S. L., 560
Bakwin, H., 177
Baldwin, V. L., 527, 528
Balint, M., 363
Ball, T. S., 85, 85fn, 524
Baller, W. R., 498, 516
Balson, P. M., 500
Bancroft, J., 433
Bandler, R. J., 91fn
Bandura, A., 44, 84, 84fn, 233, 236, 242, 265, 272, 276, 487, 488, 491, 558, 559, 575, 591, 592, 593
Bangs, J. L., 258
Bannister, D., 208
Bar, A., 291
Barahal, H. S., 144
Barankova, M., 536
Barber, T. X., 110, 111, 111fn, 113, 312fn, 319, 320
Bardill, D. R., 238

Bargilai, 394fn
Barker, C. H., 307
Barker, J. C., 434
Barker, R. G., 38, 39, 118fn
Barlow, D. H., 276, 277, 294, 438, 454
Barn, A. K., 473
Barnard, K., 524
Barnett, C. D., 198
Barnett, I., 435
Barnhart, J. E., 85fn
Baroff, G. S., 481, 507, 508, 510, 581
Baron, M. G., 581
Baron, R. A., 148
Barrett, B. H., 294
Barrett, J., 90fn
Barrett, J. E., 370
Barrish, H. H., 498
Barry, M. J., 541
Bartholomaeus of Salerno, 125
Bartlett, D., 504, 505
Barton, A. H., 303
Barton, E. S., 525
Barton, R., 176
Barton, W., 329
Barza, S., 260fn
Bass, B. M., 148, 200
Bassiakos, L., 282
Batchelor, I. R. C., 23, 143, 163, 253, 331, 332, 357, 361, 413, 432, 452, 464, 470, 483, 489, 490, 532
Bateman, D. E., 314
Batson, C. D., 590
Battle, E. S., 496
Bauer, R. A., 51fn
Baum, M., 278
Baumeister, A. A., 214, 525
Bayes, M. A., 91
Bayle, A. L. J., 139, 140
Baynes, T. E., 19
Bazell, R. J., 467
Beach, F., 420, 421, 423, 426
Beaman, A. L., 113
Bean, H., 570
Beard, G. M., 286, 294
Beatty, W. E., 273
Beck, A. T., 204, 205, 206, 264, 397
Beck, J. C., 200, 395
Becker, C. L., 40
Becker, H. S., 207, 464
Becker, W. B., 85, 494, 595
Becker, W. C., 144, 339, 340, 348, 372, 395, 396, 462fn, 480, 482, 494, 495, 506, 525, 559, 618
Becker, P. W., 539
Bednar, R. L., 560
Beels, C. C., 380
Beers, C., 150, 365
Belknap, I., 364
Behling, M., 563
Bekhterev, V. M., 144

name index

Bell, N. W., 138, 616
Bellack, B., 386
Bem, D. J., 91*fn*, 242, 412, 585, 598
Bem, S. L., 598
Bemis, M., 137*fn*
Bender, L., 502, 549
Benedek, E. P., 187*fn*
Benedict, P. K., 351
Benedict, R., 116, 180, 181, 192
Bensberg, G. J., 198, 524
Benson, H., 316
Bentler, P. M., 484
Bentz, W. K., 191*fn*
Berg, I. A., 148
Berg, P. S., 367*fn*
Berger, S. M., 271
Bergin, A. E., 236
Bergner, L., 37*fn*, 578
Berk, L. E., 90
Berkley, H. J., 471, 472
Berkman, V. C., 125*fn*
Berkowitz, B. P., 480
Berkowitz, L., 168, 590
Berkowitz, S., 524
Berlin, B., 43*fn*
Berman, P. A., 292
Bernal, M. E., 493
Bernard, J. L., 550, 559, 598
Berne, E., 451
Bernhardt, A. J., 294
Bernheim, H., 132
Berni, B., 537
Bernstein, D. A., 99*fn*, 113, 113*fn*, 167, 240, 273, 570
Berscheid, E., 589
Best, J. A., 570
Bevan, J. R., 282
Bevan, W., 537
Bewley, T., 462
Bexton, W. H., 105*fn*
Beyme, F., 260*fn*
Bhattacharyya, D. D., 260*fn*
Bianchi, G. N., 285
Bianco, F. J., 296
Bickman, L., 90*fn*, 588
Biderman, A. D., 148
Bieber, T., 436*fn*, 439
Biggs, B., 292
Biglow, G., 457
Bijou, S. W., 84*fn*, 203, 203*fn*, 516, 522, 523, 525, 526, 595
Billingsley, A., 608
Binet, A., 149, 215
Bird, C., 598
Birk, L., 277
Birky, H. J., 384
Birnbrauer, J. S., 75*fn*, 525, 526, 528, 595*fn*
Birtles, C. J., 434, 438
Bittner, E., 178

Bitzer, D. L., 606
Black, D. A., 259, 292
Blackburn, H. L., 367*fn*
Blacker, K. H., 466
Blacker, M., 200
Blackwell, B., 185*fn*, 398
Blake, B. G., 455
Blake, J. B., 179, 369
Blake, P., 259*fn*
Blakemore, C. B., 434
Blanchard, E. B., 231, 236, 242, 276, 297
Blank, M., 595
Blashfield, R., 350
Blau, A., 534
Blau, P. M., 39, 39*fn*, 197
Bless, E., 589
Bleuler, E., 332, 339
Blinder, B. J., 296
Bliss, E. L., 295
Blitch, J. W., 436
Blitz, B., 111*fn*
Bloch, H. A., 50*fn*
Bloch, H. S., 304
Bloom, B. L., 616
Bloom, S. W., 364, 365
Blum, A. F., 197
Blum, R. H., 465
Blumberg, S., 359
Blumenthal, S., 578
Blumer, H., 598
Boardman, W. K., 494
Boas, F., 116*fn*
Bockoven, J. S., 135, 136, 137, 138, 150, 380
Boen, J. R., 187*fn*
Boer, A. P., 466
Bohnert, P. J., 549
Bolen, D. W., 569
Bolles, M. M., 332
Bolsi, F., 546
Boltax, S., 369
Bonaparte, Napoleon, 540
Bond, I. K., 293, 433, 435
Bonet, T., 390
Bonstedt, T., 616
Bootzin, R. R., 386
Borah, M. M., 598*fn*
Bordin, E. S., 227
Boren, J. H., 399
Boren, J. J., 560
Borge, Victor, 180
Borkovec, T. D., 293
Bornstein, P. H., 298
Bostow, D. E., 561
Boucher, M. L., 91
Boudin, H. M., 466
Boulanger, F., 500
Boulougouris, J. C., 282
Bourne, P. G., 185, 300

Bowen, W. T., 380, 453
Bowen, R. C., 467
Bowers, K. S., 113
Bowlby, J., 397, 549
Bowman, K. M., 534, 539
Bowman, L., 110, 395
Boyce, K. D., 85
Boyd, D. W., 569
Boyd, R. W., 227
Bozarth, J. D., 199fn, 520
Braatz, G. A., 332
Braceland, F. J., 245
Brackbill, G. A., 212, 402
Brackbill, Y., 46
Brady, J. P., 255, 292, 431
Bragg, R. A., 570
Braginsky, B. M., 175fn, 207, 348, 355, 516, 521, 522
Braginsky, D. D., 175fn, 207, 348, 355, 516, 521, 522
Braid, J., 132
Branch, C. H., 295
Brand, D., 263
Brandon, S., 616
Brandt, L. W., 227
Braun, S. H., 528
Brauschi, J. T., 309
Brawley, E. R., 504
Breasted, M., 422fn
Brecher, E. M., 459, 463, 467
Breedlove, D. E., 43fn
Brelje, T., 106, 169
Brener, J., 316
Brethower, D., 595
Breuer, J., 133, 152, 153
Briar, S., 555
Bricker, 203fn
Bricker, W., 491
Bridger, W. H., 368
Brierely, H., 260fn, 294
Brigham, T. A., 85
Brill, N. G., 304
Broadhead, G. D., 496
Broden, M., 537
Brodsky, G. A., 480, 494
Brody, J. E., 102
Brody, S., 588
Broen, W. E., 182
Broman, H. S., 255fn
Bromberg, W., 109fn
Bronner, A. F., 149
Brookshire, R. H., 290, 537
Broughton, R. J., 252
Broverman, D. M., 601
Broverman, I. K., 601
Brown, A. F., 355
Brown, C., 599
Brown, G. D., 560
Brown, G. M., 344fn
Brown, J. S., 436fn

Brown, M., 491, 492
Brown, P., 245, 492, 493
Brown, R. A., 506
Brown, R. L., 347
Brownfield, E. D., 524
Browning, R. M., 480, 504
Bruehl, D., 113fn
Brush, A. L., 315
Brutten, E., 292
Bryan, J. H., 397, 588, 590, 593
Brysh, C. G., 595
Bryson, C. Q., 504
Bucher, B., 295, 379
Buckley, T. M., 297
Buckner, H., 434
Buddha, 238fn
Budzynski, T., 298, 312fn, 325
Buehler, R. E., 367fn
Bugental, J. F. T., 228
Bugle, C., 379, 499, 524, 525
Burchard, J. D., 493, 503, 528, 559, 560
Burgess, E. P., 297
Burgess, J. M., 85
Burgess, M., 316
Burgess, R. L., 85, 593, 597
Burke, B. D., 290
Burke, M., 164
Burlingham, D., 549
Burnham, W. H., 145, 146, 147, 475
Burns, Robert, 333
Burris, D. S., 21fn, 613
Burrow, T., 371
Burstein, A., 340
Burton, Robert, 121, 128, 285, 394, 395, 402, 403, 472, 574
Burton, R. V., 493
Buss, A. H., 208, 315, 331, 332, 342, 346, 347, 423, 552
Butler, A. K., 540
Butler, J., 136
Butler, J. R., 241fn
Butterfield, E. C., 198, 367fn
Butterfield, W. H., 495fn, 595
Bycel, B., 569
Byer, C. O., 444fn, 445
Bykov, K. M., 323, 324
Byrne, D., 74, 168

Cabot, P., 595
Caddy, G., 456
Caelius Aurelianus, 123, 123fn
Caesar, Julius, 540
Cahoon, D. D., 466
Cairns, R. B., 523
Calfee, A. J., 353
Calhoun, J., 259fn
Callahan, D., 605
Calverley, D. S., 113

name index

Cameron, N. A., 147, 163, 265, 343, 359, 390, 404, 405, 406, 410, 413
Cameron, P. 516, 567
Cameron, R., 361, 379
Campbell, L. M., III, 282
Campbell, P., 453
Campion, E., 345
Camus, Albert, 577
Cancro, R., 339
Cannon, W. B., 316
Caplan, G., 616, 617, 620
Caplan, R. B., 57, 137*fn*, 138
Caponigri, V., 498
Carden, N. L., 253
Carey, F., 5
Carlin, A. S., 594
Carlsmith, J. M., 90*fn*, 589
Carlson, C. G., 386
Carlson, C. S., 476*fn*
Carnegie, Dale, 277, 281
Caron, R. F., 47*fn*
Carp, F. M., 538
Carr, A. C., 269, 269*fn*
Carr, E. H., 40*fn*, 116*fn*
Carroccio, D. F., 524
Carroll, W. K., 595
Carson, D. H., 38*fn*
Carter, D. B., 100*fn*
Carter, J. W., Jr., 617
Carter, W., 111*fn*
Case, H. W., 42
Cassel, R. H., 524
Cassell, S., 486
Castell, D., 245
Cattell, J. McK., 149
Cattell, R. B., 170, 474
Caudill, W., 185
Cautela, J. R., 220, 238, 455, 539, 581
Cavan, R. S., 557
Cavanaugh, D., 347
Celsus, 123
Centerwell, S. A., 367*fn*
Centerwell, W. R., 367*fn*
Cermak, S. A., 498
Cesar, J. A., 539
Chafetz, M. E., 446
Chambers, C. D., 467
Chambers, D. A., 367*fn*
Chambliss, J. E., 384
Chapman, J. D., 106, 431
Chapman, J. P., 106, 169, 219
Chapman, L. J., 106, 169, 219, 340
Chapman, R. F., 570
Charcot, Jean-Martin, 132, 153, 250, 260, 622
Chardos, S., 525
Charles, D. C., 516
Charles II (England), 103
Charlesworth, R., 594

Chase, L. S., 340
Chassan, J. B., 58*fn*
Chatel, J. C., 286-87
Cheek, F. E., 457
Cherry, C., 292
Cherry, N., 275
Chesler, P., 187, 600
Cheyne, A. A., 591*fn*, 592
Chiargui, 135*fn*
Chien, C. P., 539
Chism, R. A., 316
Chotlos, J. W., 453
Choukas, M., 238, 412, 413
Christelman, W. C., 457
Christensen, D.E., 498
Christie, R. G., 344*fn*
Church, R. M., 481
Churchill, D. W., 504, 505
Churchman, C. W., 118*fn*
Cicero, 124
Cisler, L., 598
Clancy, J., 434, 453
Clancy, K. J., 61*fn*
Clarizio, H., 208, 471
Clark, A. W., 291
Clark, D. F., 260*fn*, 294, 434
Clark, M., 562
Clark, R. D., III, 588
Clark, R. N., 597
Clark, W. C., 111*fn*
Clausen, J. A., 362*fn*
Clayton, P. J., 252*fn*
Cleckley, H., 547, 551
Cleghorn, R. A., 253, 414
Cleland, C. C., 385
Clement, P. W., 263*fn*, 486
Clemente, C. D., 318
Clements, C. B., 496, 560
Clemmer, D., 556
Clinard, M. B., 556
Clinsky, J. M., 367*fn*
Clore, G. L., 74, 234
Cloward, R. A., 188*fn*
Coan, R. W., 570
Cobb, J. A., 480, 562
Coblentz, S., 303
Coe, W. C., 110
Cofer, 348
Cohen, A. K., 196, 197, 199
Cohen, D. C., 241
Cohen, E. S., 536
Cohen, H. L., 554, 560
Cohen, J., 615
Cohen, L. H., 260*fn*
Cohen, M., 457, 621
Cohen, R., 275
Cohen, R. L., 99
Cohen, S., 38*fn*

Cohen, S. I., 325
Coiteux, P. F., 593
Colby, K. M., 245
Coleman, J. C., 5fn, 163, 182, 269, 384, 540
Collins, B. J., 374, 376
Collins, R. W., 218
Collmann, R. D., 516
Colman, A. D., 560, 597
Colson, C., 191fn, 438, 578
Columbus, C., 251fn
Colwell, C. N., 524
Combs, A. W., 584
Comfort, A., 472
Commons, M. L., 504
Comtois, D. R., 528
Confucius, 121
Congdon, M. H., 263fn
Conger, J. C., 500
Conger, J. J., 450
Conley, R. W., 5
Connolly, John, 339, 371
Conwell, M., 5
Cook, C., 525
Cooke, G., 21
Cooke, O., 21, 21fn
Cooley, W. W., 606
Cooper, A., 285
Cooper, A. B., 330
Cooper, D. G., 380
Cooper, E. B., 291
Cooper, J. B., 318
Cooper, J. E., 185, 245, 325, 434
Coppen, A., 399
Corey, M., 355
Corte, H. E., 581
Cotler, S. B., 241, 275, 569
Cottrell, W. F., 189
Coulter, S. K., 504, 505
Counch, R. H., 597
Cowan, P. A., 506, 593, 618
Cowden, R. C., 377
Craig, K. D., 318
Craig, L. E., 579
Craighead, W. E., 386, 506, 523
Craik, K. H., 38
Cramer, M., 473
Crane, A. R., 556
Crato, 285
Crawley, R. C., 260fn
Creer, T. L., 323
Crider, A., 317
Croce, Benedetto, 40fn
Crocetti, G. M., 184
Cronbach, L. J., 203fn
Cropley, A. J., 393
Crosby, C. C., 466
Cross, H. J., 99fn, 244, 330, 592
Crowley, P. M., 593

Cruickshank, W. M., 293
Crutchfield, R. S., 197
Cuber, J. F., 39fn
Cull, J., 365fn
Cumming, E., 371
Cumming, J., 371
Curlee, R. F., 292
Curran, D., 439
Curtis, R. H., 438

Dabbs, J. M., Jr., 90
Dahl, 111fn
Dain, N., 136, 137
Dalal, A. S., 113
Dalton, K., 475
Daly, D. A., 291
Daly, D. D., 541
Daly, W. C., 199fn, 520
Dameron, L. E., 504
Dana, R. H., 276
Daniell, E. F., 347
Daniels, G. J., 494, 525
Darley, J. M., 41fn, 587, 588, 590
Darley, S. A., 41fn
Darnton, R., 133fn
Darwin, Charles, 149, 152, 471
Davidson, A. R., 91
Davidson, G. E., 185fn
Davidson, H. A., 58
Davidson, J. R., 498
Davies, 394fn
Davies, B., 434
Davis, B., 524
Davis, B. D., 604
Davis, J. F., 260fn
Davis, J. M., 168
Davis, K., 549
Davis, K. E., 593
Davis, N. J., 43fn
Davison, G. C., 105fn, 234, 275, 293, 413, 435, 438, 494, 506
Daws, P. P., 118
Dawson, E. B., 65
Day, D., 340
Day, R. H., 47fn
Dayan, M., 500
Dederich, C. E., 466, 467
Deibert, A. N., 580
Dekker, E., 322
de la Tourette, Gilles, 182, 294, 295
DelCastillo, J., 208
DeLeon, G., 499
Deleuze, 133
DeLucia, C. A., 70
Dement, W. C., 168, 293
DeMoor, W., 278
DeMyer, M. K., 501, 502, 503
Dendy, T., 133

name index

Dengrove, E., 430, 434, 435
Denner, B., 176, 620
Denney, D., 185*fn*
Dennis, W., 523
Denny, R., 397
Denzin, N. K., 176, 362*fn*
DeRisi, W. J., 560
Descartes, Rene, 123
Deutsch, A., 409*fn*
Devries, A. G., 576
Dexter, L. A., 515, 516
Diamond, B. L., 231*fn*
Diamond, S. G., 90*fn*
DiCaprio, N. S., 241*fn*
DiCara, L., 316
Dickel, H. A., 235
Dicken, C., 241*fn*
Dickens, Charles, 136
Dickenson, J. K., 208, 212
Dickson, W. J., 228
Diehl, P., 103
Dielman, T. E., 474
Diener, E., 113
Dienstbeir, R. A., 593
Dietze, D., 199*fn*
Dignam, P. J., 374
Dillehay, R. C., 113*fn*
DiMascio, A., 227
Dinitz, S., 212
Dinnerstein, A. J., 105*fn*, 111*fn*
Dinoff, M., 374
Dionysus, 121
DiScipio, W. G., 376, 438
Dittes, J. E., 320
Dix, Dorothea, 129, 137, 409*fn*
Dixon, H. H., 235
Dixon, J. C., 286
Dmitruk, V. M., 218
Dobbs, E. G., 21
Dobie, S., 212
Dobson, W. R., 367*fn*
Dodds, E. R., 121*fn*
Doering, C. R., 208
Dohrenwend, B. P., 185, 300
Dohrenwend, B. S., 185, 300
Dokecki, P. R., 592
Doland, D. J., 495*fn*
Dole, V. P., 467
Dollard, J., 118, 147, 163, 170, 491
Domino, G., 199*fn*
Donner, L., 275, 455
Doreus, R. M., 261
Doris, J., 168
Dorris, J. W., 589
Doubros, S. G., 494, 525
Douglas, V. I., 498, 502
Douglass, E., 498
Dowd, S. A., 380

Dowling, M., 367*fn*
Down, 517
Drabman, R. S., 595*fn*, 596
Draguns, J. G., 185
Drash, P., 525, 526
Drege, K., 493
Dreger, R. M., 473
Dreiblatt, I. S., 367*fn*
Dreifus, C., 598
Dreikurs, R., 227, 398
Driscoll, J. P., 428
Dubey, E., 536
Duerfeldt, P. H., 592, 593
Dunbar, F., 315
Duncan, S., Jr., 91
Dunham, H. W., 185, 186, 348, 364, 366, 380, 381
Dunlap, K., 146, 237, 294
Dunn, L. M., 520
Durkee, S., 538
Durkheim, E., 576, 577
Durning, K., 595
Dymond, R. F., 244
D'Zurilla, T. J., 228

Eagleton, Thomas, 36*fn*
Early, D. F., 330
Eaton, J. W., 182, 397
Ebaugh, F. A., 143
Ebbesen, E. B., 592
Eck, R. A., 253, 340
Edelman, R. I., 500
Edgar, C. L., 85
Edgerton, R. B., 10, 451
Edinger, R. L., 83*fn*, 373
Edlund, C. V., 214, 523
Edmonson, B., 90
Edmundson, B., 199
Edwardes, A., 420, 426
Edwards, J. A., 278
Edwards, M., 525
Edwards, N. B., 440
Edwards, R. P., 496
Efran, J. S., 90*fn*, 246
Efron, R., 541
Egeland, B., 596
Egolf, D. B., 290, 291
Ehrenberg, R., 539
Ehrhardt, A. A., 423
Ehrlich, Paul, 140
Ehrlich, P. R., 605
Eichenwald, H. F., 37*fn*
Eiduson, B. T., 99
Eisdorfer, C., 535
Eisenberg, L., 472
Eisenman, R., 500
Eisenstein, R. B., 21
Eisenthal, S., 576
Eisler, R. M., 234, 386, 454, 457

Eisner, V., 555, 557, 617
Ekman, P., 90, 90fn, 198, 374, 376
Elder, S. T., 317, 325
Elkin, T. E., 297
Elliotson, J., 131
Elliott, R., 492, 493, 593
Ellis, A., 232, 234, 284, 439, 440
Ellis, J., 598
Ellis, N. C., 212
Ellsworth, D. W., 595
Ellsworth, P. C., 90, 589
Ellsworth, P. D., 597
Ellsworth, R., 362fn, 367fn
Empey, L. T., 546
Endicott, J., 185
Engel, B. T., 316, 325
Engelhardt, D. M., 56fn
Engelman, E., 168
Engle, B., 539
Engle, K. B., 451
English, A. C., 170, 482
English, H. B., 170, 482
English, O. S., 315
Ennis, B., 22, 22fn
Enright, J. B., 185
Epictetus, 238fn
Epstein, L. H., 297
Erasmus, 127
Erickson, G. D., 379
Erickson, M., 480, 562
Erickson, M. L., 546
Erikson, K. T., 196
Erlenmeyer-Kimling, L., 344, 345
Ernst, F. A., 294, 581
Eros, 121
Erwin, W. J., 295, 323
Esdaile, J., 487
Esmarch, 140
Esquirol, J. E. D., 139, 472
Essen-Möller, E., 184, 343
Esser, A. H., 375
Esterson, A., 380
Estes, W. K., 341fn, 481
Esveldt, K. C., 85
Etzel, B. C., 47fn
Etzioni, A., 39fn, 40fn, 197
Evans, D. R., 293, 433
Evans, F. J., 100, 112
Evans, G. W., 498, 525, 597
Evans, I. M., 504
Evans, R. I., 148
Ewalt, J. R., 143
Ewing, J. A., 444
Eysenck, H. J., 37, 37fn, 63fn, 117fn, 147, 172, 209, 243, 244, 271, 272, 440, 484, 499, 550, 591
Ezrin, S. A., 591fn

Fabrega, H., 185, 207

Fabricatore, J., 379
Fadiman, J., 4
Fahel, L. S., 367fn
Fahl, M. A., 596
Faillace, L. A., 453, 457
Fairweather, G. W., 245, 618
Fallik, A., 255
Falret, J. P., 390
Farber, I. E., 306, 522
Farberow, N. L., 575, 576, 578
Fargo, G. A., 504
Farina, A., 168, 344fn, 348, 355
Faris, R. E. L., 185, 186, 348
Farley, J., 252fn
Farnsworth, D. L., 143
Farris, J. C., 597
Fast, D., 597
Faulkner, William, 192
Faw, T. T., 75fn
Fazzone, R. A., 486
Feather, B. W., 274
Fechner, Gustav, 152
Fedoravicius, A., 228, 275
Feinberg, A. M., 281
Feinsilver, D. B., 380
Feist, J., 595
Feldman, G. L., 384
Feldman, H. W., 462fn
Feldman, M. P., 437, 438, 439
Feldman, R. S., 374, 537, 542
Feldstein, J. H., 70
Fenichel, O., 162, 290, 429
Fenton, G. W., 293
Ferdinand, T. N., 556
Ferguson, T., 516
Ferinden, W., 500
Ferjo, K. R., 80fn, 504
Fernald, W. E., 545
Fernandez, J., 384
Fernandez, L. E., 85fn, 595
Ferster, C. B., 148, 203fn, 264, 298, 503, 506
Festinger, L., 192, 242, 307, 482
Fichtler, H., 326
Field, M. J., 395
Fierman, E., 168
Fieve, R. R., 390, 399
Filipczak, J., 554
Fine, H. J., 340
Fineman, K. R., 80fn, 504, 560
Fink, D., 105fn
Fink, H., 103, 104
Finley, W. W., 499
Fischer, D. G., 500
Fischer, E. H., 191fn
Fischer, I., 384
Fish, J. M., 100fn, 496
Fisher, D., 110, 439
Fiske, D. W., 244, 245

name index

Fitzgibbons, D. J., 350
Fitzpatrick, J. P., 555, 556, 557
Fixsen, D. L., 561
Flanagan, B., 291
Flanders, J. P., 84*fn*
Flavell, J. E., 525
Flechsig, P., 405
Fletcher, C. R., 21
Flinn, D. E., 579
Flomenhaft, K., 356
Flowers, J. V., 593
Flye, B. A., 292
Fode, K. L., 112*fn*
Fonda, C. P., 203, 204, 206, 208, 213
Fontana, A. F., 200, 300, 348, 355, 483
Fookes, B. H., 433, 434
Forberg, F. K., 420
Ford, C. S., 420, 421, 426
Ford, J. D., 480
Ford, L. I., 377
Fordham, M., 241*fn*
Fordyce, W. E., 537
Forehand, R., 525
Foreman, P. B., 302, 303
Forster, F. M., 542
Forsyth, R. P., 341*fn*
Fortune, R. F., 181
Fosburgh, L., 578
Foucault, M., 129*fn*
Fournier, A., 140
Fouts, G. T., 593
Fouts, R. S., 90
Fowler, O. S., 422, 426
Fowler, R. L., 317
Fowler, R. S., 537, 542
Fowles, D. C., 293
Fox, M. S., 604
Fox, R. E., 15*fn*, 489, 501, 502
Fox, R. G., 548
Foxx, R. M., 500, 511
Frank, G. H., 217, 299, 346, 482, 550
Frank, J., 180
Frank, J. B., 228
Frank, J. D., 97*fn*, 104*fn*, 199, 239, 308, 363, 599
Frankel, A. S., 90
Frankel, M., 569
Franklin, Benjamin, 109
Franks, C. M., 148, 322, 455
Fray, 37*fn*
Frazier, S. H., 269, 269*fn*
Frederick, C. J., 294
Freedman, A. M., 330, 332, 513
Freedman, D. X., 466
Freedman, J. L., 589
Freedman, R. V., 346
Freedman, S. J., 105*fn*
Freeman, D.M.A., 296
Freeman, H. L., 273

Freeman, J., 601
Freeman, T., 361, 370
Freeman, W., 59, 143, 144, 534
Freidan, B., 598
Freidinger, A., 258
French, T. M., 154, 285, 312
Freshley, H. B., 588
Freud, Anna, 159
Freud, Sigmund, 43, 117, 127, 128, 131, 132, 133, 148, 149, 150, 152, 153, 154, 155, 156, 160, 162, 164, 165, 168, 169, 170, 172, 173, 197, 220, 225, 227, 228, 250, 252, 390, 404, 405, 420, 426, 460, 471, 549, 569, 576, 577, 584, 622
Freund, K., 439, 440
Friar, L., 542
Frick, J. V., 291
Friedman, A. S., 393, 394*fn*
Friedman, D., 430
Friedman, N., 90
Friedman, P. R., 22*fn*
Friedman, R., 90
Friedman, S., 483
Friedman, T., 604
Friedman, T. I., 253, 254
Friesen, W. V., 90
Froehle, T. C., 238
Fromm, E., 190, 584
Frumkin, R. M., 187
Frye, M., 169
Fuller, G. B., 375, 456
Fuller, P. R., 524
Fundia, T. A., 185
Furniss, J. M., 367*fn*
Furst, J. B., 285

Gaarder, K. R., 298
Gaertner, S. L., 588
Gagnon, J. H., 425
Gal, P., 539
Galbraith, G. G., 111*fn*
Galen, 55, 123*fn*, 124, 127, 349
Galle, O. R., 38*fn*, 187*fn*
Gallimore, R., 562
Gallinek, A., 539
Galton, Francis, 149
Gandolfo, R. L., 111
Gannon, L., 326
Gantt, W. H., 316, 322
Ganzer, V. J., 213, 241*fn*, 251*fn*
Garai, J. E., 186
Gardner, B. T., 90*fn*
Gardner, J. E., 323, 542
Gardner, R. A., 90*fn*
Gardner, W. I., 525
Garfield, John, 545
Garfield, S. L., 273
Garland, L. H., 176
Garlington, W. K., 275, 383

Garmezy, N., 340, 345, 347
Garmize, L. M., 524
Garratt, F. N., 330
Gastaut, H., 252
Gaupp, L. A., 435
Gauron, E. F., 208, 212
Gautier, M., 517
Gaylin, W., 436fn
Gazzaniga, M. S., 534
Gebhard, P. H., 425
Geddy, P., 379
Geer, J. H., 293
Geertsman, R. H., 208
Geis, G., 556
Gelder, I. M., 245, 433
Gelder, M. G., 276
Geldzahler, H., 575fn
Gelfand, D. M., 367fn, 374, 492, 590
Gelfand, S., 111fn, 367fn
Geller, E. S., 597
Gendron, R. A., 496
Genovese, Kitty, 586
Gent, L., 580
Gentry, W. D., 273, 285, 493
George, E. I., 332
Geppert, T. V., 498
Gerard, D. L., 452
Gerard, R. W., 139
Gerber, I., 197, 199fn
Gergen, K. J., 91
Gersham, L., 434
Gersten, C. D., 203fn
Gesell, A. L., 149
Gessner, T., 200, 348
Gewirtz, J. L., 47
Geyer, A., 241
Giallombardo, R., 557
Gibby, R. G., 163
Gibson, H. B., 556
Giddan, J. J., 504
Giebink, J. W., 596
Giffen, M. B., 304fn
Gil, D. G., 483
Giles, D. K., 500, 528
Gill, L., 85fn
Gill, M., 227
Giller, D. W., 359
Gillis, L. S., 184fn
Gillison, T. H., 498
Gilmore, J. B., 228, 275
Gilmore, S. K., 480
Ginott, H. G., 486fn
Giovannoni, J. M., 125fn, 179, 330, 340, 608
Girardeau, F. L., 526, 527, 528
Gittelman, M., 486
Glaros, A. G., 293
Glaser, R., 606
Glasner, S., 333
Glass, D. C., 38

Glass, L. B., 110
Glasscote, R. M., 9, 9fn, 330, 337
Glazer, J. A., 594
Glazer, N., 397
Gleser, G. C., 227
Glickman, H., 376
Glueck, B. C., Jr., 203fn, 546, 606
Glueck, E. T., 558
Glueck, S., 20, 558
Goddard, H. H., 149, 472
Goffman, E., 193, 363
Golchros, H. I., 432
Gold, S., 438
Goldberg, D. P., 185fn
Goldberg, L. R., 203fn
Goldiamond, I., 79, 81fn, 84fn, 237, 259fn, 291, 292, 298
Goldfoot, D. A., 592
Goldfried, M. R., 84fn, 238, 293
Goldhamer, H., 182
Golding, S. L., 219
Goldman, R. K., 245
Goldschmid, M. L., 199fn
Goldsmith, A. O., 500
Goldstein, A. P., 98, 136, 148, 199, 240, 376, 415
Goldstein, A. S., 22fn
Goldstein, B., 486
Goldstein, D., 105fn
Goldstein, M. J., 566
Goldstein, M. N., 111
Goldstein, N., 615
Goleman, D., 569
Golembiewski, R. T., 39fn
Golman, S. E., 616
Gomez, R., 369
Gonda, O., 344fn
Goode, E., 464
Goodkin, R. A., 537, 542
Goodlet, G. R., 493
Goodlet, M. M., 493
Goodman, G., 245
Goodman, J., 592, 596
Goodman, P., 228, 284
Goodson, 619
Goodstein, L. D., 203fn
Goodwin, D. W., 13, 13fn, 333
Goorney, A. B., 569
Gordon, J. E., 184fn, 320
Gordon, P., 390
Gordova, T. N., 455
Gorham, D. R., 384
Gormly, J., 593
Gorsuch, R. L., 592
Goslin, D. A., 218
Gottheil, E., 457
Gottman, J. M., 220
Gottschalk, L. A., 227, 230
Gough, H. G., 216, 550
Gould, E., 292

name index

Gove, W. R., 38, 187*fn*
Goyeche, J. R. M., 592
Grace, W. J., 227, 316
Graf, M., 266
Graham, D. T., 316
Graham, S. R., 231
Graham, W., 586
Gralnick, A., 369
Granda, A. M., 319
Grant, F. C., 533
Grant, V., 55
Graubard, P. S., 498
Gray, John P., 137
Grayson, H. M., 355
Grayson, H. N., 199*fn*, 346
Graziano, A. M., 480, 505
Greatraks, Valentine, 107*fn*
Greaves, G., 580
Greaves, S. T., 214
Green, L. M., 206
Green, L. N., 212
Green, M., 238
Greenacre, P., 549
Greenberg, 240
Greenberg, D. J., 384
Greenberg, R. P., 199
Greenblatt, D. J., 143
Greenblatt, M., 105*fn*, 227
Greene, F. M., 495*fn*
Greene, R. J., 70, 235
Greene, R. L., 436*fn*
Greenhouse, L., 537
Greenspoon, J., 203*fn*
Greer, G., 600
Gregory, I., 15, 314, 489, 501, 502
Griesinger, Wilhelm, 140
Griffin, C., 99*fn*
Griffit, W., 90
Grim, P. F., 585
Grimaldi, K. E., 235
Grinker, R. R., 392
Grinspoon, L., 464
Gripp, R. F., 384
Grisell, J. L., 347
Griswold, R. L., 344*fn*
Grob, G. N., 35
Groen, J., 322
Gross, A. E., 589
Gross, E., 598
Gross, M. M., 448
Grossberg, J. M., 233
Grosse, M., 355
Grossman, K. G., 212
Grosz, H. J., 212, 256*fn*
Groves, I. D., 524
Gruenberg, E. M., 616
Grunbaum, B. W., 344*fn*
Grunbaum, H., 617
Grunebaum, H. U., 105*fn*

Grusec, J. E., 487, 591*fn*, 593
Grzesiuk, L., 367*fn*
Guardo, C. J., 90
Guess, D., 525
Guggenbuhl, Johann Jacob, 141
Guggenheim, F. G., 346
Guggenheim, P., 4
Guillotin, Joseph Ignace, 109
Guiteau, C. J., 545
Gullingsrud, M. J. O., 539
Gunderson, E. K. E., 184*fn*, 212, 496
Gunderson, J. G., 345, 380
Gurel, L., 90, 208, 330, 374
Gurland, B. J., 370, 535, 536
Gustafson, G. J., 379
Guthrie, E. R., 144, 147, 240
Guthrie, G. M., 182
Gutride, M. E., 376
Guze, S. B., 13, 13*fn*, 251*fn*, 252*fn*, 576

Haas, H., 103, 103*fn*, 104
Haase, R. F., 91
Haddock, A. J., 412
Hadley, R., 292
Hagen, R. L., 298
Haggard, H. W., 103*fn*, 313
Hagnell, O., 184
Hahn, K. W., Jr., 111, 320
Hain, J., 263*fn*
Hake, D. F., 561
Halbert, Sara, 411, 412
Hall, E. T., 38, 90
Hall, G. S., 149, 426, 471
Hall, J. C., 337
Hall, R. V., 537
Hall, S., 525
Hall, S. M., 70*fn*
Hall, S. R., 580
Hall, V. R., 528
Hallam, R., 236
Halleck, S. L., 22*fn*, 231*fn*, 613, 619
Haller, B. L., 549
Hallsten, E. A., Jr., 297
Halm, J., 105*fn*
Hamilton, G. V., 146
Hamilton, J., 525
Hamilton, J. W., 525
Hamilton, S. H., Jr., 525
Hammack, J. T., 319
Hammer, M., 362*fn*, 486*fn*
Hammond, A. L., 468
Hammond, K. R., 606
Handel, D. V., 500
Haney, C. A., 178
Hansen, S. P., 316
Hanson, R. W., 439
Hapkiewicz, W. G., 495, 595*fn*, 596
Hardyck, C., 595

Hare, R. D., 548, 549, 552
Harington, Sir John, 103*fn*
Harlow, H. F., 306, 397
Harmatz, M. G., 241*fn*, 298, 385
Haroldson, S. K., 291
Harris, F. R., 322, 480, 493
Harris, M. B., 298, 593
Harris, R. E., 534
Harrow, M., 361
Hart, B. M., 493, 562, 593
Hart, H. L. A., 179, 425
Hart, J., 241
Hartage, L. C., 374, 384
Hartfelder, G., 103, 104
Harth, R., 520
Hartig, M., 592
Hartmann, D. P., 492
Hartogs, R., 568
Hartshorne, H., 593
Hartung, J. R., 505
Hartup, W. W., 594
Harvey, William, 55*fn*
Harway, N. I., 227
Hasazi, J., 85*fn*
Haslam, M. H., 139, 276*fn*, 282, 431, 433
Hasleton, S., 464
Hastings, J. E., 316
Haugen, G. B., 235
Haughton, A. B., 47, 579
Haughton, E., 74, 75, 76, 77, 374
Hauser, A., 116*fn*
Hauserman, N., 228, 563
Hautaluoma, J., 209
Havelock, R. G., 179
Hawkins, H. L., 377
Hawkins, R. P., 477, 478*fn*, 479
Hawks, D. V., 462
Hawley, A. H., 40*fn*
Hayes, D. P., 91*fn*
Hayes, K. J., 519
Hayner, 97
Haynes, S. N., 379, 436, 455
Hays, H. R., 598
Hays, P., 119*fn*
Hazelrigg, L., 556
Healey, William, 149, 471
Heap, R. F., 370, 384
Hebb, D. O., 534
Hecker, E., 339
Hedberg, A. G., 325
Hefferline, R. F., 228, 284
Hein, P. L., 274
Heine, R. W., 231
Hekmat, H., 241*fn*
Hell, Fr. Maximilian, 107
Heller, K., 148, 237
Heller, R. R., 295
Hendee, J. C., 597

Henderson, D., 23, 432, 532
Henderson, J. D., 384
Henderson, L. J., 363
Hendin, H., 231
Henker, B., 386
Henriksen, S. D., 253
Henry, G. W., 116*fn*, 121*fn*, 124*fn*, 125*fn*, 127*fn*, 128*fn*, 140
Henry, J., 197
Henson, A., 90
Henson, K., 375
Herguth, R. J., 104*fn*
Heron, W., 105*fn*
Herron, W. G., 240
Hersen, M., 214, 234, 260*fn*, 266, 282, 293, 294, 297, 386, 454, 457
Hertz, L., 213
Hess, E. H., 106
Heston, L., 344*fn*
Hetherington, e.M., 168
Hewett, F. M., 80*fn*, 495, 504, 595
Higa, W. R., 592
Higgins, J., 340
Higgins, R. L., 454
Hilgard, E. R., 110, 482
Hill, F. A., 316
Hill, J. P., 593
Hill, P. A., 385
Hinde, R. A., 90
Hingtgen, J. N., 504, 505
Hinkle, J. E., 298
Hippler, A. E., 576*fn*
Hippocrates, 122, 124, 127, 129, 389
Hirsch, J., 604
Hirsch, S., 314
Hitchcock, J., 579
Hnatiow, M., 316
Hoaken, P. C. S., 346
Hoare, R., 344*fn*
Hoats, D. L., 70*fn*, 235
Hoch, P. H., 398, 540
Hoddinott, B. A., 506
Hodgson, R., 280*fn*, 282
Hoffbauer, 134
Hoffer, A., 102*fn*, 345
Hoffman, B., 361
Hoffman, P. J., 203*fn*
Hogan, R., 591
Hogan, R. A., 277, 278
Hogarth, William, 129
Hokanson, J., 316
Holahan, C. J., 370
Holden, C., 445
Holdren, J. P., 605
Hole, J., 599*fn*, 600, 601
Holland, H. O., 528
Holland, J., 290
Hollander, M. A., 376, 385

name index

Hollingshead, A. B., 99*fn*, 186, 187
Hollingworth, H. L., 45, 147, 156, 294
Hollister, L., 143
Holmes, D. J., 483
Holmes, D. S., 113, 168*fn*
Holmes, F. B., 146, 147, 244, 475, 476, 484, 485
Holmes, T. H., 300
Holt, R. R., 196, 199
Holz, W. C., 482
Holzberg, J., 209
Holzer, C. E., 579
Holzman, M. S., 615
Homans, G. C., 118*fn*
Homburger, 472
Homme, L. E., 270, 298, 489
Honigfeld, G., 101*fn*, 103
Hood, R. W., Jr., 208*fn*
Hook, E. B., 548
Hooker, E., 436, 436*fn*
Hope, Bob, 329
Hopkins, B. L., 524, 597
Horan, J. J., 298
Hordern, A., 206, 212
Horner, M., 601
Horner, R. F., 374
Horner, V. M., 384, 385
Horney, Karen, 154
Hornick, A. J., 70*fn*
Horton, L. E., 561
Horton, P. C., 18
House, C., 238
Houser, J. E., 595*fn*
Houston, P. E., 466
Houts, P. S., 179, 369
Howard, J., 229
Howe, Samuel Gridley, 141
Hudson, L., 620
Huessey, H. R., 496
Huff, F. W., 438
Hughes, J. T., 581
Hull, Clark L., 294
Hullen, R. P., 399
Humphrey, C., 580
Humphreys, L., 435, 436*fn*
Humphries, 146*fn*
Huncke, S., 549
Hundziak, M., 500
Hunrichs, W. A., 333, 402
Hunt, G. M., 348, 457, 570
Hunt, J. McV., 519, 620
Hunt, M., 421, 422
Hunt, R. G., 99*fn*
Hunt, W. A., 550
Hunter, G. F., 376
Hurd, W. S., 561
Hurley, R., 620
Husted, J., 524

Huston, P. E., 398
Hutchison, H. C., 435
Hutchison, W. R., 597
Hutt, M. L., 163
Huzley, A., 149, 253

Iflund, B., 615
Illich, I., 594*fn*
Imber, R. R., 165
Imboden, J. B., 255
Impier, L. L., 466
Ince, L. P., 241*fn*, 542
Ingham, R. J., 292
Inkeles, A., 51*fn*
Innocent VIII, 126
Ireland, W. W., 142
Ironside, R., 253
Isaacs, W., 79, 237, 259*fn*
Isen, A. M., 589
Ishiyama, T., 355
Israel, A. C., 593
Itard, Jacques, 85, 141
Ittelson, W. H., 38, 370
Iversen, W., 568

Jacklin, C. N., 601*fn*
Jacks, I., 351
Jackson, B., 27, 265
Jackson, C. W., Jr., 106*fn*
Jackson, D. D., 343, 346, 380
Jackson, J., 10
Jackson, P. W., 583
Jackson, R. N., 516
Jaco, E. G., 539
Jacob, R. G., 498
Jacobs, N., 253
Jacobson, E., 235, 595
Jacobson, L., 112
Jacobson, L. I., 80*fn*
Jacobson, M. A., 10, 10*fn*, 18*fn*, 19, 19*fn*
Jaeckle, W. R., 185
Jaeger, M., 487, 595
Jahoda, M., 14, 17, 584
Jakovljevic, V., 185
Jakubaschk, J., 208
Jakubowski-Spector, P., 434*fn*
James I, (England), 313
James, B., 439
James, G. M., 620
James, William, 150
Janet, Pierre, 133, 133*fn*, 250, 260, 262
Janis, L., 570
Jankowski, K., 367*fn*
Janopaul, R. M., 10, 10*fn*, 18*fn*, 19, 19*fn*
Jarvik, L. F., 548
Jeffrey, K. McM., 234
Jellinek, E. M., 447, 450

Jernigan, L. R., 113fn
Jersild, A. T., 146, 147, 244, 475, 476, 484, 485
Jervey, S. S., 524
Jesness, C. F., 560
Joffee, P. E., 241fn
Jofre, Fr. Juan Gilabert, 129
Johns, J. H., 550
Johnson, C. A., 480
Johnson, C. D., 593
Johnson, D. M., 253
Johnson, G. D., 241
Johnson, J. B., 294
Johnson, R. C., 466, 592
Johnson, R. F. Q., 293
Johnson, R. G., 298
Johnson, R. J., 317
Johnson, S. M., 275
Johnson, V. E., 38, 234, 420, 421, 422, 425, 427, 429, 430, 431, 438
Johnson, W., 291
Johnston, Cecil, 412
Johnston, M. K., 493
Johnston, N., 21, 556
Jones, E., 168, 369, 460, 618
Jones, H., 555, 556
Jones, H. G., 163, 294, 324
Jones, K., 362fn
Jones, K. L., 444fn, 445
Jones, M., 228, 554, 618
Jones, M. C., 145, 146, 147, 236, 276, 475
Jones, N. F., 99fn, 212
Jones, R. J., 292, 563
Jones, S. E., 90fn
Jordan, B. T., 415
Jourard, S. M., 90fn, 241fn
Judson, H. F., 462
Jung, Carl G., 154, 155, 214, 228, 426

Kadushin, C., 98, 98fn, 99, 206
Kahana, B., 538
Kahana, E., 538
Kahlbaum, 339
Kahn, E. J., 241fn
Kahn, M., 241, 293
Kahn, M. W., 99fn, 212, 213
Kahn, R. L., 187fn, 618
Kalafat, J. D., 592
Kale, R. J., 375
Kales, A., 293
Kales, J., 293
Kalinwosky, L. B., 398
Kalish, H. I., 233
Kallmann, F. J., 343
Kamin, L. J., 36fn
Kamis, E., 380
Kamiya, J., 312fn, 316
Kamman, G. F., 370
Kanareff, V. T., 593

Kanfer, F. H., 44fn, 91fn, 203fn, 233, 272, 590, 592, 593, 614
Kanner, L., 141, 472, 473, 501, 502
Kanouse, D. E., 43fn
Kanowitz, L., 598
Kant, E., 123
Kant, H. S., 566
Kant, Immanuel, 133
Kantor, R., 367fn
Kantor, R. E., 340
Kantorovich, N., 146
Kaplan, A. M., 486fn
Kaplan, B., 4fn
Kaplan, B. J., 37fn
Kaplan, H. A., 22fn
Kaplan, H. I., 314, 330, 332, 413, 513
Kaplan, H. S., 314
Kaplan, J. A., 587
Kapp, F. T., 315
Karacki, L., 560
Karen, R., 80, 81
Karen, R. L., 467, 524
Karkalas, Y., 104, 379
Karoly, P., 590
Karpman, B., 547
Kasprisin-Burelli, A., 291
Kasius, R. V., 616
Kasl, S. V., 191fn
Kass, L. R., 605
Kassorla, I., 377
Kastenbaum, R., 538, 539, 540, 580
Katahn, M., 275
Katchadourian, H. A., 427
Katkin, E. S., 219, 293, 312fn, 316
Katz, R. C., 415, 492, 480, 591fn
Kaufman, K. F., 561
Kaufman, L. N., 372
Kaufman, M. E., 367fn
Kazdin, A. E., 79fn, 234, 238, 386, 525
Kazdin, A. L., 588
Kaya, J., 266
Kean, J. E., 505
Keane, D., 516
Keasey, C. B., 592
Keehn, J. D., 260fn, 450, 500, 524
Keil, W. E., 438
Keiser, T. W., 581
Keith-Lee, P., 168
Kellam, A. M. P., 281
Kellert, S. R., 617
Kelley, H. H., 91, 302, 412
Kelley, J. D., 238
Kelley, W. R., 441
Kellogg, J. S., 595
Kelly, E. L., 106fn
Kelly, F.D., 91
Kelly, F. S., 348, 355
Kelly, G. A., 234, 284

name index

Kelly, K., 214
Kemp, C. H., 480
Kempe, C. H., 483
Kempler, B., 415
Kendall, R. E., 393
Kendig, I., 333
Kendrick, D. C., 273, 438
Keniston, K., 369
Kennard, E. A., 370
Kennedy, R. J. R., 516
Kennedy, W. A., 40
Kent-Rosanoff, 384
Kepner, E., 450
Kerchoff, A. C., 253, 254
Kerr, N., 504, 525, 597
Kessel, N., 446, 447, 448, 451
Kessel, P., 614
Kessler, J. W., 486*fn*
Kety, S. S., 101*fn*, 344*fn*
Keup, W., 344*fn*
Keutzer, C. S., 570
Kewman, D., 4*fn*
Kiesler, C. A., 74, 91*fn*, 113*fn*, 412, 600
Kieth-Spiegel, T., 199*fn*
Kiev, A., 175*fn*, 182
Kiloh, L. G., 263, 264
Kimmel, E., 316, 317, 499
Kimmel, H. D., 316, 317, 499
Kimura, B., 185
King, C. W., 190
King, G. F., 340, 375, 376
King, K. M., 212
King, S. H., 347
Kinkead, E., 306
Kinsey, A. C., 189, 211, 405, 420, 421, 423, 424, 435, 436, 437, 438, 567
Kintz B. L., 213
Kinzel, A. F., 90
Kinzie, D., 390
Kirchner, J. H., 277, 278
Kleibhan, J. M., 525, 597
Klein, E. B., 348
Klein, H. E., 213
Klein, R. D., 495, 595*fn*, 596
Kleiner, R. J., 186, 187
Kleinman, R. A., 316
Kleitman, N., 168
Klemme, H. L., 319
Klerman, G. L., 198, 390
Klett, C. J., 209, 338
Kline, N. S., 102*fn*
Klinge, V., 581
Klinger, B., 110
Klodin, V., 548
Klotz, J., 593
Knight, E. M., 549
Knight, J. A., 253, 254
Knight, R. P., 540

Knowles, J. B., 110*fn*
Knowles, P. L., 498
Knox, S., 9
Koch, S., 152, 545
Kochendorfer, R. A., 593
Koegel, R., 502
Koenig, K. P., 259*fn*
Kogan, K. L., 482
Kohlberg, L., 585, 592
Kohlenberg, R., 597
Kohlenberg, R. J., 252*fn*, 297
Kohn, M. L., 362
Kokaska, C. J., 516
Kolb, D. A., 233, 561
Kolb, L. C., 143, 159, 163, 215, 257-58, 262, 283, 331, 357, 373, 413, 471
Komechak, M. G., 297
Komisar, L., 598*fn*, 599, 600
Kondas, O., 246, 292
Koos, E. L., 98, 182
Kopel, S. A., 234
Koppin, I. L., 187*fn*
Kottke, L., 537
Kovalev, N. K., 455
Kraemer, 126
Kraepelin, E., 96, 97, 97*fn*, 134, 139, 209, 339, 390, 390*fn*, 404
Kraines, S. H., 429
Kraft, A. C., 536
Kraft, T., 282, 430, 431, 438, 456, 466
Kramer, J. C., 460, 461
Kramer, T. J., 79*fn*
Krapfl, J. E., 241
Krasner, L., 17*fn*, 36*fn*, 44*fn*, 75, 83*fn*, 110*fn*, 111*fn*, 112*fn*, 118*fn*, 147, 148, 167, 200, 224, 228, 240, 241, 250, 298, 315, 329, 373, 374, 376, 381, 382, 383, 384, 431, 495, 506, 548, 550, 583, 585, 591, 594, 596, 597, 598, 603, 604, 612, 614, 618
Krasner, M., 594, 596
Krassen, E., 570
Kraus, 525
Krauss, B. J., 576*fn*
Krauss, H. H., 348, 576*fn*, 591*fn*
Krebs, D. L., 590
Kreitman, N., 208
Kreizman, G., 576
Kringlen, E., 343
Krisberg, J., 322
Krisppy, R. L., 427
Kroll, J., 126*fn*
Krop, H., 498
Krugman, A. D., 365*fn*
Krumboltz, J. D., 237, 572
Kubany, E. S., 214
Kuechler, H. A., 260*fn*
Kugel, R. B., 367*fn*
Kuhlman, C. K., 316
Kuhn, T. S., 35

Kulik, J. A., 557
Kumar, K., 238
Kumasaka, Y., 21
Kun, K. J., 367fn
Kupers, C. J., 592
Kuriansky, J., 370
Kurland, A. A., 453
Kushner, M., 164, 321, 430, 433, 435
Kutner, L., 177

Labreche, G., 99fn
Lacey, B., 496
Lacey, J. I., 227, 314, 316
Lachowicz, J., 562
LaDriere, M., 464
Lafave, H. G., 356
Lafayette, Marquis de, 109
Lahey, B. B., 294
Laing, R. D., 350fn, 380
Laird, J. D., 169
Lakin, M., 212
Lal, H., 104, 379, 500
Lamberd, W. G., 438
Lambo, T. A., 183
Lamontagne, Y., 325
Lamy, R. E., 176
Landis, C., 332
Lang, P. J., 241, 297, 316, 317, 323, 347, 542, 610, 615
Langsley, D. G., 356
Lanyon, R. I., 165, 203fn, 292
Lapuc, P., 298
Larsen, D. E., 451
Larsen, K. S., 167
Larson, D. E., 438
Larson, G. R., 218
Lasagna, L., 102, 103
Lasky, J. J., 365fn, 367fn
Latané, B., 319, 587, 588
Lattal, K. A., 597
Lattimore, R., 575
Lauver, P. J., 238
Lavell, M., 187
Lavin, N. I., 434
Lavoisier, Antoine, 109
Lawson, R., 112fn
Lawson, R. B., 560
Layton, B., 91fn
Layton, T. A., 570
Lazare, A., 467
Lazarus, A. A., 234, 274, 275, 282, 284, 393, 429, 430, 431, 485, 490
Leaf, W. B., 298
Leaman, L., 185
Leary, T., 191, 227
Leavitt, H. J., 39fn
Lecky, P., 192
Lee, H. L., 595
Lee, S. D., 213

Lee, Y. B., 241fn
Lefton, M., 212
Lehrmann, N. S., 97fn, 363
Leiblumb, S. R., 220
Leibowitz, H. W., 111fn
Leibowitz, J., 525
Leiderman, P. H., 105fn
Leifer, R., 22fn, 97fn, 616
Leigh, D., 322
Leighton, A. H., 183, 184, 189
Leighton, D. C., 184
Leitenberg, H., 67fn, 240, 276, 277, 296, 374, 481
Lejeune, J., 517
Lemberger, H., 465
Lemere, F., 455
Lemert, E. M., 189, 190, 193, 194, 207, 404, 406, 407, 409, 410
Lemkau, P. V., 184
Lemke, H., 524
Lennard, H. L., 231, 467
Lent, J., 528
Leon, C. A., 61fn
Leonard, C. V., 579
Lepper, C., 474
Lerner, R. M., 588, 589
Leser, E., 466
Lesse, S., 440
Lester, D., 576, 576fn, 579, 580, 581
Lester, G., 576, 579, 581
Leuret, Francis, 134
Leuser, E., 305
Levin, P. F., 589
Levin, S. M., 438
Levine, D., 340
Levine, E., 599fn, 600, 601
Levinson, B. L., 570
Levinson, R. B., 560
Levinson, T., 453
Levis, D. J., 277, 434
Levitt, E. B., 298
Levitt, E. E., 244
Levitz, L. S., 361, 569
Levy, B., 601fn
Levy, L., 186
Levy, M. R., 213
Lewin, K., 95fn, 228
Lewinsohn, P. M., 264, 265, 266, 397, 399
Lewis, A., 402, 404
Lewis, J. B., 184fn
Lewis, J. H., 111
Lewittes, D. J., 214
Ley, P., 208
Libb, J. W., 238
Liberman, R. P., 228, 265, 374, 386, 466
Libet, J., 235, 265, 266, 298
Lichtenstein, E., 235, 570
Liddell, H. S., 316, 322
Liebault, Ambroise-Auguste, 132

name index

Lieberman, M. A., 212, 230, 231
Liebert, R. M., 80fn, 85fn, 148, 234, 259fn, 592, 595
Liebson, I., 260fn, 455, 457
Lief, H. I., 285
Liefer, 613
Lifton, R. J., 306, 307
Lightstone, J., 169
Lillesand, D. B., 234, 380
Lilly, J. C., 105fn, 306
Lilly, R. T., 525
Lim, D. T., 168
Lima, 143
Lin, T., 183
Lind, D. L., 255
Lindesmith, A. L., 302
Lindner, R., 549
Lindsley, O. R., 357, 361, 495fn, 500, 593
Linebarger, 412, 413
Linn, E. L., 182, 362fn
Linn, L. S., 367fn, 464
Linsky, A. S., 397, 449
Linton, R., 116fn, 175fn, 586
Lipowski, Z. J., 311
Lippmann, W., 412
Lipsitt, L. P., 47fn
Litman, R., 575, 578, 579, 580
Little, L. K., 372
Littlefield, J. W., 604
Littmen, R. A., 491
Liversedge, L. A., 287, 288
Llewellyn, C. E., 616
Llewellyn, K., 188fn
Lloyd, K. E., 383, 384, 524
Lobb, L. G., 292
Lobitz, W. C., 399, 430, 431
Locher, L. M., 398
Locke, B. J., 581
Locke, John, 144
Loeb, M. B., 363
Loether, H. J., 536
Loew, C. A., 539, 540
Logan, D. L., 525
Lombroso, C., 546
Lomont, J. F., 234
London, P., 500, 583, 590, 614
Loney, J., 436fn
Long, J. D., 562
Loomis, S. D., 549
LoPiccolo, J., 430, 431
Lorei, T. W., 199fn
Lorenz, M., 414
Lorr, M., 200, 209, 338, 339, 340
Losen, S. M., 347
Loudon, J. B., 183
Louis XVI, 109
Lovaas, O. I., 480, 481, 502, 504, 505, 507, 508, 510, 581, 615

Lovell, W. S., 453fn
Lovibond, S. H., 236, 456, 498, 499
Lowe, C. R., 101fn
Lower, H. J., 318
Lowie, R. H., 39fn, 116fn
Lowinger, P., 212
Lowrey, L. G., 545
Lubker, B. B., 292
Luborsky, L., 196, 199, 244, 245
Luce, G. G., 252, 309, 606
Lucero, R. J., 187fn
Luckey, R. E., 297
Ludwig, A. M., 385
Lunde, D. T., 427
Lundy, R. M., 111fn, 320
Luparello, T., 322
Luther, Martin, 141
Lutker, E. R., 542
Lutzker, J. R., 435
Lyerly, O. G., 105fn, 253
Lykken, D. F., 547, 548
Lyle, J. G., 367fn
Lynes, R., 116fn
Lyons, R. D., 464, 465
Lysenko, T. D., 411
Lytie, C., 191fn

Mabry, J., 148
MacAndrew, C., 451
Macaulay, J. R., 588, 590
MacCubrey, J., 525
MacCulloch, M. J., 434, 437, 438, 439
MacDonald, M. L., 233, 434fn, 538, 540
MacDonald, W. S., 562
MacGregor, R., 380
Machotka, P., 356
MacKavey, W. R., 347
MacKay, C., 107fn, 108fn, 133fn, 501, 526
Mackey, R. A., 199fn
Mackinnon, R. C., 524
Madaras, G. R., 91fn
Maddi, S. R., 571, 584
Madsen, C. H., Jr., 431, 435, 494, 500
Maehr, M. L., 113
Magaret, A., 147, 265, 342
Magaro, P., 380, 384
Maher, B. A., 49, 170, 171, 299, 346, 357, 450, 552
Mahl, G. F., 227, 316
Mahoney, K. 500
Mahoney, M. J., 84fn, 281, 298
Maimonides, 127
Mair, J. M. M., 292
Maisel, R., 177
Makarenko, A. S., 554
Maletzky, B. M., 438
Maley, R. F., 384
Malinowski, B. K., 116fn
Maliver, B. L., 230, 231, 232fn

Malleson, N., 146, 277
Malmo, R. B., 260fn, 314, 316
Manc, M. B., 541
Mandell, W., 499
Mandler, G., 316
Mangrum, J. C., 340
Manis, M., 179, 369
Mann, J., 229
Mann, L., 570
Mann, R. A., 298, 560
Manosevitz, M., 165
March, J. G., 39fn
Marcos, L. R., 208
Margolis, P. M., 616
Marie Antoinette, 109
Maris, R. W., 580
Mark, J. C., 346
Markely, J., 510
Markiewicz, L., 367fn
Marks, I. M., 236, 245, 276, 282, 325, 433
Marks, J., 384
Marlatt, G. A., 454
Marmor, J., 241
Marquis, J. N., 234, 438
Marr, J. N., 504
Marrone, R. L., 570
Marsden, G., 227
Marsella, A. J., 390
Marshall, A., 182
Marshall, C., 294
Marshall, C. D., 496
Marshall, G. R., 500
Marston, A. R., 44fn, 234, 284
Martin, B., 320
Martin, C. E., 211, 421
Martin, G. L., 494, 524, 581, 595
Martin, J. A., 85
Martin, J. M., 555, 556, 557
Martin, P. L., 75fn, 374, 375, 377
Martin, R. R., 291
Martyn, M. M., 291
Marwit, S. J., 213
Marx, A. J., 385
Marzagão, L. R., 282
Marzillier, J., 282
Masling, J., 213
Maslow, A. H., 228, 584
Masserman, J. H., 322
Massie, H. N., 380
Masters, J. C., 85, 233, 238, 502
Masters, R. E. L., 426
Masters, W. H., 38, 234, 420, 421, 422, 425, 427, 429, 430, 431, 438
Matarazzo, J. D., 227, 570
Matefy, R. E., 380, 581
Mather, M. D., 276fn, 280fn, 292
Matson, F. W., 232fn
Matsuyama, S. S., 548

Mattussek, P., 332
Maugh, T., 468
Maurer, R. N., 500
Mausner, B., 570
Mawdsley, C., 541
Max, L. W., 146, 439
Maxwell, Clark, 152
Maxwell, S. J., 524
May, M. A., 593
May, R., 228, 230, 396
Mayer, J., 298
Mayer, M. P., 188fn
Mayhew, D., 495fn, 595
Mayo, C., 179
Mazik, K., 525
McBrearty, J. F., 614
McCandless, B. R., 436fn
McCarthy, J. F., 341fn
McClure, R. F., 525
McConnell, O. L., 505
McCord, J., 545, 548, 549, 551fn, 558, 559
McCord, W., 545, 548, 549, 551fn, 558, 559
McCullough, J. P., 438
McCullough, T. A. H., 253
McCullough, T. E., 616
McDaniel, M. W., 524
McDonald, F. J., 495, 593
McDonald, N. F., 99
McFall, R. M., 234, 284, 380, 570
McFarland, R. L., 144, 374, 407, 408
McGanity, W. J., 65
McGarry, A. L., 22fn
McGarry, J. J., 483
McGinnies, E., 148
McGlothlin, W. H., 465
McGuigan, F. J., 213, 241fn, 360
McGuire, F. L., 367fn
McGuire, R. J., 433
McInnis, T. L., 341
McKay, H. D., 558
McKee, J. M., 560
McKenzie, B., 47fn
McKinney, W. T., Jr., 397
McMains, M. J., 592
McManus, M., 275
McNair, D. M., 209, 338
McNamara, J. R., 295
McNamara, R., 525
McNees, M. P., 294
McNeil, J. N., 285
McNeil, J. S., 304fn
McNeill, W. H., 39
McPeake, J. D., 111fn
McPherson, J. M., 38fn, 187fn
McQueen, N. M., 494
McReynolds, P., 192, 342, 360, 542
McReynolds, W. T., 384, 397
McWilliams, S. A., 466

name index

Mead, G. H., 585
Mead, M., 12, 116*fn*, 181
Mealiea, W. L., Jr., 278
Mechanic, D., 177
Mednick, S. A., 345, 347
Medvedev, R., 410, 416
Medvedev, Z., 34, 410, 416
Meehl, P. E., 147, 332, 343, 346
Meeker, W. B., 111*fn*
Meerbaum, 480
Meerloo, J. A. M., 578
Mees, H. L., 237, 435, 503, 570, 615
Mehlman, B., 208
Mehrabian, A., 90*fn*
Meichenbaum, D. H., 113, 228, 238, 260, 275, 340, 361, 373, 377, 379, 486, 570, 580, 592, 596
Meisel, J., 504
Meisels, M., 90*fn*
Melamed, B. G., 241, 297, 323, 542, 610, 615
Mello, N. K., 454
Meltzer, L., 91*fn*
Mendel, W. M., 152, 198, 199
Mendels, J., 263, 264, 392
Mendelsohn, G. A., 245, 592
Mendelsohn, J. H., 454
Mendelson, M., 314
Menlove, F. L., 276, 487
Merbaum, M., 84*fn*, 238, 241*fn*, 581
Mercatoris, M., 386, 523
Mercer, J. R., 191*fn*, 515, 519, 520, 616
Mercurio, J., 498
Meredith, L., 571
Merksamer, M. A., 570
Merlis, S., 541
Merrens, M. R., 203*fn*, 218
Merrill, 215, 472
Mertens, G. C., 375, 456
Merton, R. K., 40*fn*, 95
Meshorer, E., 367*fn*
Mesmer, Frank Anton, 107, 109, 110, 122, 131
Messenger, J. C., 427
Messick, S., 583
Mettee, D. R., 105*fn*, 593
Metz, J. R., 505
Meyer, Adolf, 138, 149, 150, 339, 342, 429, 472
Meyer, E., 255
Meyer, R. G., 282
Meyer, V., 273, 292
Meyerhoff, H., 116*fn*
Meyers, C. E., 191*fn*
Meyerson, L., 70, 500, 525, 597
Michielutte, R., 178
Michael, J., 71, 72, 78
Michael, J. A., 504, 525
Michael, S. T., 182, 187*fn*
Micossi, A. L., 598, 599, 600
Miklich, D. R., 323
Mikulas, W. L., 233

Mikulic, M. A., 375
Milby, J. B., Jr., 375
Miles, G. G., 231, 466
Milgram, S., 112
Miller, B. A., 454
Miller, D., 177
Miller, D. E., 502
Miller, D. R., 18, 294
Miller, E. A., 256*fn*
Miller, E. L., 516
Miller, E. R., 504
Miller, H., 203*fn*, 474
Miller, L. K., 495*fn*
Miller, L. R., 563
Miller, N., 253
Miller, N. E., 87*fn*, 118, 147, 163, 170, 214, 312, 316, 450, 474
Miller, O. L., 563
Miller, P. M., 234, 453, 454, 457, 499
Miller, R. J., 61, 62*fn*, 111*fn*
Miller, S. B., 274
Miller, W. B., 556
Millet, K. 600
Mills, J., 105*fn*
Mills, K. C., 445, 456
Milne, D. C., 486
Minge, M. R., 524
Mintz, A., 302
Mintz, P. M., 105*fn*
Mirin, S. M., 465
Mischel, W., 167, 592, 612
Mishara, B. L., 580
Mishler, E. G., 185*fn*, 362
Miskiminis, R. W., 576
Mitchell, K. R., 542
Mitchell, R. D., 524
Mitchell, S. W., 287
Mitchell, W. S., 375
Mitford, J., 395
Mithang, D. E., 593
M'Naghten, Daniel, 20
Mockbridge, N., 568
Modell, A. H., 315
Modigliani, A., 90*fn*
Mogan, J., 297
Mogel, S., 507*fn*
Mohammed, 540
Mohr, J. P., 295, 323
Mondy, L. W., 367*fn*
Money, J., 423
Mongrella, J., 70
Moniz, 143
Montagu, A., 567
Montessori, M., 472
Moore, 140
Moore, F., 323
Moore, N., 323
Moore, R., 81*fn*

Moore, R. A., 187fn
Moore, R. F., 362
Moore, T. D., 65
Moore, W. H., Jr., 291
Morcombe, J. E., 536
More, Sir Thomas, 127
Morel, B. A., 339
Moreno, J. L., 227, 228
Morgan, J. J. B., 112fn, 498
Morgan, R., 598
Morgan, R. T. T., 498
Morganstern, K. P., 278
Morganthaler, F., 436fn
Morgenstern, F., 434
Morgenstern, G., 498
Morris, R. J., 85
Morris, W. N., 91fn
Morrison, R. S., 605, 606, 607
Morrow J., E., 528, 570
Moselle, J. A., 214
Mosher, D. L., 348, 355
Mosher, L. R., 345
Moss, F. A., 475
Moss, G. R., 399, 434, 560
Moss, T., 259fn
Mott, Lucretia, 599
Motto, J. A., 578
Mowrer, O. H., 146, 227, 235, 498, 592
Mowrer, W. M., 146, 498
Muckler, F. A., 328
Mueller, L., 411
Muench, G. A., 516
Muir, W., 393
Mulhern, T., 525
Muller, C., 462fn
Munchaussen, 257fn
Mundy, M. B., 479
Munter, P. O., 593
Murphy, F. J., 556
Murphy, H. B., 273, 350, 351
Murphy, H. B. M., 185
Murphy, J. M., 120fn, 183
Murray, E. J., 227
Murray, E. N., 312fn, 316, 579
Murray, George, 518
Murray, H. A., 149
Mussick, J. K., 297
Musto, D. F., 460, 461
Mutimer, D. D., 199fn
Muzekari, L. H., 380
Myers, J. J., Jr., 580
Myers, J. K., 99fn, 187fn, 300
Myerson, L., 504

Nachshon, I., 185
Najarian, P., 523
Narrol, H. G., 455
Nash, M. M., 538

Nataupsky, M., 114
Nathan, P. E., 208, 212, 213, 357, 454
Nawas, M. M., 241, 278, 528, 573
Neale, J. M., 80fn, 259fn, 500
Needelman, 504
Neisworth, J. T., 323
Nelson, J. D., 492
Nelson, J. M., 465
Nelson, R. O., 504
Nemiah, J. C., 16, 252fn, 254, 256, 269, 279, 279fn, 297
Nesbitt, P. D., 570
Nessen, 140
Neufeld, I. L., 438
Neumann, 134
Newell, S., 450fn
Newlyn, D., 516
Newman, A., 91
Newman, R. C., II, 90
Newton, J. G., 298
Ney, P., 510
Nicassio, F. J., 294
Nicol, 501
Nielsen, J., 580
Nightingale, Florence, 137, 616
Nihira, K., 200, 523
Nisbitt, R. E., 43fn, 91fn, 293
Noanchuck, T. A., 169
Noblin, C. D., 241fn
Noguchi, H., 140
Nolan, J. D., 80fn, 571
Nordquist, V. M., 480, 504
Norman, A., 259fn
Noyes, A. P., 143, 215, 253, 257, 258, 262, 283, 331, 357, 358, 373, 413, 471
Nunnally, J. C., 75fn, 179, 203fn
Nurnberger, J., 298
Nurnberger, J. I., 203fn
Nydegger, R. V., 378
Nye, F. I., 556
Nyswander, M., 460, 461, 467

Ober, D. C., 228, 570
Obler, M., 431
Obrda, K., 536
O'Brien, F., 375, 499, 524, 525
O'Brien, J. S., 297, 466
O'Brien, P., 524
O'Connell, W., 168
Odegard, O., 362fn
O'Dell, S., 480
Odom, R. D., 595
Oeding, P., 253
Ogburn, K. D., 597
O'Keefe, K., 433
O'Kelly, L. I., 328
O'Leary, K. D., 85, 480, 494, 495, 498, 506, 525, 561, 592, 593, 595fn, 596

name index

O'Leary S. G., 480, 495, 595fn, 596
Oliveau, D., 269
Oliver, M., 528
Olsen, R. W., 200
Olsen, V. J., 556
Olson, K. A., 441
Olson, R. P., 384
Oltman, J. E., 483
O'Malley, J. E., 467
O'Neill, M., 415
Opler, M. K., 185
Ora, J. P., Jr., 592
Orne, M. T., 105, 105fn, 106, 110; 111, 112, 254, 358
Ornitz, E. M., 501
Ornstein, R. E., 574fn
Ortmeyer, D., 615
Orwell, George, 306
Osborn, R. W., 200
Osborne, J. G., 70
Osler, W., 102
Osmond, H., 176, 450fn
Osmundsen, J. A., 102fn
Ostrow, M., 549
Oswald I, 441
Oswalt, G. L., 498
Otis, R. E., 536
Ottenberg, P., 322
Ourth, L. L., 47fn
Overall, B., 99fn, 187fn
Overall, J. E., 186
Ovesey, L., 436
Ovid, 146fn
Owen, D. R., 548

Pace, N., 344fn
Pace, Z. S., 506
Packard, E. P. W., 408, 409, 409fn, 410
Packard, F. R., 103fn
Page, J. D., 315
Pahnke, W. N., 561
Palevsky, A. E., 510
Palmer, J., 367fn
Palmore, G., 231
Paloutzian, R. F., 85fn, 523, 594
Panek, D. M., 373, 384
Panek, M., 581
Panel, 606
Papageorgiou, M. G., 119fn
Paracelsus, 107fn, 128, 129
Parenton, V. J., 253
Paris, S. G., 523
Parker, S., 186, 187
Parker, W. H., 241fn
Parloff, M., 232fn
Parloff, M. B., 615
Parr, D., 439
Parrino, J. J., 542
Parrish, M., 111fn

Parry-Jones, W. L., 260fn
Parson, B. N., 96, 495fn
Partridge, G. E., 549
Pasamanick, B., 184fn, 212, 593
Pascal, G. R., 305, 347
Paschalis, A. P., 499
Passman, R. H., 525
Pasteur, Louis, 152
Patch, V. D., 466
Patterson, G. R., 367fn, 480, 485, 486, 491, 494, 497, 498, 525, 562
Patterson, R. L., 374, 480
Pattison, E. M., 457
Paul, G., 113fn, 240
Paul, G. L., 228, 235, 245, 246, 259fn, 274, 275, 504, 615
Pavlov, I. P., 144, 316, 318
Paykel, E. S., 264, 390, 393
Payne, R. W., 332
Pearce, J., 434
Pechtel, C., 322
Peck, R. F., 385
Pedersen, D. M., 90fn
Pedrini, B. C., 500
Pedrini, D. T., 500
Peel, Robert, 20
Peele, R., 286, 287
Peine, H. A., 580
Pellegrini, R. J., 90fn
Pence, C., 80fn
Penick, S. B., 298
Pepinsky, H. B., 615
Pereire, 141
Pergy, M. A., 199
Perkins, W. H., 292
Perlin, S., 187fn
Perls, F., 228, 284
Perry, D. G., 491
Perry, L. C., 491
Persons, C. E., 550
Persons, R. W., 537, 550
Perzan, R. S., 500
Pestalozzi, 472
Peterson, D. R., 500, 551, 559
Peterson, G. J., 85
Peterson, J. C., 340
Peterson, L. R., 580
Peterson, L. W., 524
Peterson, R. F., 84, 84fn, 85fn, 203fn, 505, 580
Petoney, P., 615
Petrella, R., 619, 620
Petrinovich, L. F., 595
Petroni, F. A., 41fn, 99fn
Pettigrew, L. E., 295
Pettus, C., 205
Pfeiffer, E., 21
Phelan, J. G., 241fn
Phillips, B. S., 538

Phillips, D. L., 61fn
Phillips, E. L., 184fn, 227, 480, 484, 561
Phillips, L., 185, 209, 210, 211, 340
Phillips, R. E., 241
Phillips, T., 597
Piaget, J., 592
Pick, Arnold, 532
Pierrol, R., 80
Pietsch, D., 528
Pihl, R. O., 466, 494
Pike, E. O., 595
Piliavin, I. M., 90fn, 555, 588
Piliavin, J. A., 90fn, 588
Pilkonis, P. A., 74
Pillard, R. C., 465
Pindar, 575
Pinel, Phillipe, 122, 127, 129, 133, 134, 135, 150, 339, 545, 622
Pinsky, R. H., 104
Pinto, R., 542
Piper, T. J., 524
Pisoni, S., 374
Pittel, S. M., 592
Pittman, W. E., 536
Pivnicki, D., 344fn
Plato, 19, 122
Platonov, K. I., 316, 318
Platt, E. S., 570
Plog, S. C., 10fn
Plotkin, A., 228
Plunkett, R. J., 184fn
Plutarch, 124, 391, 577
Plutchik, R., 385
Pogany, E., 21
Pokorny, A. D., 65, 186
Polak, P. R., 200, 361
Polani, P. E., 548fn
Pollack, D., 90
Pollard, J. C., 106fn
Pollin, W., 343, 345, 346
Polster, R., 79fn
Pomeroy, W. B., 211, 421
Porter, R. B., 516
Porterfield, A. L., 556
Portnoy, S., 374, 537, 542
Poser, E. G., 293
Post, D. S., 597
Poteete, J. A., 566
Potkay, C. R., 217
Potter, W. K., Jr., 525
Powdermaker, F. B., 228
Powell, B., 454
Powell, J., 597
Pratt, J. H., 227
Premack, D., 90fn, 381, 489
Presbie, R. J., 70fn, 593
Presly, A. S., 438
Presthus, R., 39fn

Preven, D. W., 316
Price, G. H., 498
Price, R. H., 176, 348, 620
Price, W. H., 548fn
Prien, R. F., 398
Prince, M., 50fn
Pritchard, 545
Proctor, J. T., 253, 256
Pronko, N. H., 175, 534, 541
Proshansky, H. H., 38, 370
Protopopov, V., 318
Provost, R. J., 536
Prutsman, T. D., 498
Pruyser, P., 339
Pue, A. F., 344fn
Pumphrey, M. W., 337
Pumroy, D. K., 500
Pumroy, S. S., 500
Puysegur, Marquis de, 131, 250, 260
Pythagoras, 122, 124fn

Quade, D., 205
Quarantelli, E. L., 303
Quarrington, B., 344fn
Quarti, C., 325
Quay, H. C., 208, 474, 494, 525, 550, 551, 553, 554, 595fn
Quinney, R., 556

Rabb, E., 495fn, 595
Rabelais, Francois, 128
Rabiner, E. L., 369
Rabkin, L. Y., 4fn, 191fn
Rachlin, H. C., 569
Rachmann, S., 37fn, 117fn, 147, 163, 172, 225, 235, 236, 244, 271, 272, 278, 280fn, 282, 430, 432, 433, 440, 471fn, 484, 499
Rackensperger W., 281
Rada, R. T., 434
Radó, S., 390
Raduege, V., 498
Rafi, A. A., 294
Rahe, R. H., 300
Raines, G. N., 208, 278
Rainey, C. A., 282
Rainwater, L., 364fn, 427
Ramey, C. T., 47fn
Ramsey, Arthur Michael, 53fn
Rank, Otto, 155
Rapport, S., 199
Raskin, D. E., 265
Raskin, N., 539
Rasp, L., 595
Rathod, N. H., 466
Ratliff, R. G., 322, 435
Raush, H. L., 227
Raven, P. H., 43fn

name index

Ravensborg, M. R., 376
Ray, I., 545
Ray, O. S., 449fn, 460, 461
Ray, R. S., 480, 562
Raymond, A. F., 208
Raymond, M. J., 432, 433, 466
Raynes, A. E., 466
Raynor, R., 69, 144, 270, 475, 475fn
Razani, J., 429
Razran, G., 144, 316, 318
Rea, R. B., 613
Redd, W. H., 74, 75fn, 525
Redlich, F. C., 99fn, 186, 187
Reed, J. L., 325
Rees, L., 314
Reese, E. P., 69
Rehm, L. P., 234, 284
Reich, C. A., 133fn, 229, 230
Reid, J. B., 259fn
Reil, Johann Christian, 133
Reimanis, G., 365fn
Reisinger, J. J., 266, 399, 480
Reisman, D., 397
Reiss, A. J., 51, 436, 556
Reiss, S., 525
Reitlinger, G., 116fn
Reitz, W. E., 438
Renner, J. A., 467
Reque, D. A., 367fn
Resnick, J. H., 570
Retting, S., 593
Reynolds, N. J., 562, 563
Rhazes, 127
Rhodes, A. L., 556
Rhodes, R. C., 290
Rhyne, L. D., 568
Rice, D. G., 266
Rice, H. K., 524
Richards, W. S., 218
Richardson, C. H., 99fn
Richardson, J. W., 184fn
Richardson, R., 379
Richmond, W. V., 333
Rickard, H. C., 374, 479
Rickels, K., 99fn
Rifkin, B. G., 285
Riggs, F. W., 370
Rigler, D., 483
Rilling, M., 79fn
Rimland, B., 502
Rimm, D. C., 233, 238
Ring, K., 175fn, 355
Rinn, R. C., 619, 620
Risley, T. R., 237, 503, 505, 507, 562, 563, 581, 593, 615
Ritchie, G. G., Jr., 435
Ritschl, C., 70fn
Ritter, B., 236, 242, 276

Ritterman, S. I., 291
Ritvo, E. R., 501
Rivlin, L. G., 38
Roback, H. B., 241, 580
Robbins, L., 208
Robbins, R. C., 191fn
Roberts, A. H., 571, 619
Roberts, B. H., 187fn
Roberts, R. D., 497
Roberts, W. W., 286
Robins, E., 549, 576
Robinson, H. B., 517, 542
Robinson, J. C., 266
Robinson, N. M., 341fn, 347, 517, 542
Roblin, R., 604
Rock, R. S., 10, 10fn, 18fn, 19, 19fn
Roden, A. H., 495, 595fn, 596
Rodin, J., 43fn, 587, 588
Rodin, M. J., 167
Rodnick, E. H., 340, 347
Rodriguez, A., 502
Roethlisberger, F. J., 228
Rogawski, A. S., 199
Rogers, C., 226, 227, 228, 231, 232, 244, 245, 247
Rohan, W. P., 453, 536
Roman, P. M., 43fn, 617
Romano, J., 315
Rome, H., 305
Rome, H. P., 538, 619
Roos, P., 524, 528, 562
Roper, G., 179, 280fn
Rorer, L. G., 219
Rosario, Victor, 411, 412
Rose, A. M., 186
Rosen, B. M., 473
Rosen, E., 15fn, 314, 489, 501, 502
Rosen, G., 19fn, 149, 471
Rosen, M., 295
Rosenbaum, 143, 498
Rosenbaum, G., 347, 357
Rosenbaum, M., 315
Rosenberg, B. G., 423
Rosenberg, H., 116fn
Rosenberg, L., 197
Rosenberg, M., 606
Rosenfeld, J. M., 185
Rosenhan, D. L., 29, 30, 110, 110fn, 320, 583, 590
Rosenthal, C. S., 189
Rosenthal, D., 104fn, 117fn, 231, 343, 345, 615
Rosenthal, R., 112, 112fn, 213, 225, 333
Rosenthal, T. L., 90fn, 199fn, 213, 272, 292, 434, 595
Ross, H., 370
Ross, L., 42, 43fn
Ross, N. W., 238fn
Ross, R. R., 113, 580
Ross, S. A., 523
Roszak, T., 229

Rothman, D. J., 35fn, 136
Rothschild, D., 539
Rouéché, B., 449
Routh, D. K., 212, 497
Rovee, C. K., 47fn
Rovee, D. T., 47fn
Rowan, P. K., 465
Rowan, T., 466
Rowden, D. W., 99fn
Rowitz, L., 186
Roy, A., 297
Rozelle, R. M., 148
Rubin, G., 580
Rubin, M. L., 467
Rubin, R. R., 297
Rubin, V., 183
Rubovits, P. C., 113
Rudestam, K. E., 575-76
Rudolph, F., 188
Ruesch, J., 315, 534
Ruitenbeck, H. M., 227, 231fn
Rumbaut, R. D., 129fn
Rush, Benjamin, 116fn, 135, 140, 545
Ruskin, R. S., 384
Russell, C. D., 525, 595fn
Russell, H. K., 524
Russell, J. C., 291
Russell, J. E., 525
Russell-Jenkins, 384
Russo, S., 479
Rutherford, G., 525
Rutner, I. T., 379
Rutter, M., 502
Ryan, E., 384
Ryan, W., 350
Rydberg, S., 595

Saairo, T. N., 601fn
Sach, L. B., 570
Sadalla, E., 589
Sadler, M., 435
Sadock, B. J., 330, 332, 413, 513
Saegert, S., 370
Saenger, G., 185, 244, 452, 516
Sagarin, E., 436fn, 567
Sailor, W., 476fn
St. Augustine, 81
Sajwaj, T., 164, 235, 298
Salter, A., 284, 440
Salzberg, H. C., 228
Salzberg, P. M., 570
Salzinger, K., 343, 368, 374, 504, 537, 542
Salzman, L. F., 333
Samaan, M., 499
Sameroff, A., 345
Sanders, F. A., 502
Sanders, J., 537
Sandifer, M. G., 205, 206, 208, 212

Sandler, J., 597
Santer-Westrate, H. C., 260fn
Santogrossi, D. A., 596
Santostefano, S., 525
Saper, B., 466
Sapon, S. M., 495fn, 595
Sarason, I. G., 241fn, 562, 596
Sarbin, T. R., 110, 111, 170, 349, 360, 521, 557
Saslow, G., 203fn, 227
Satran, R., 111
Sattler, J. M., 213
Saul, L. J., 305
Saunders, J. T., 241
Saunders, M., 498
Savitz, L., 556
Sawrey, J. M., 293
Sawyer, J. B., 580
Saxman, J. H., 266
Sayegh, Y., 523
Sayers, B., 292
Scandura, J. R., 188fn
Schaap, C. M., 276
Schacht, L. S., 200
Schacter, S., 104, 170, 191, 240, 255, 319
Schaefer, H. H., 75fn, 374, 375, 377
Schaeffer, H. H., 297, 445, 456, 507, 508, 510, 615
Schaffer, L., 99fn
Schallow, J. R., 168fn
Schalock, R., 384, 498
Schanberger, W., 339, 340
Schaps, E., 590
Schaudinn, F., 140
Scheff, T. J., 12, 176, 177, 191fn, 192, 207, 208, 209, 330, 348, 362, 471
Scheibe K. E., 105, 106, 254
Scheier, I. H., 170
Schein, E. H., 306, 307, 366
Schell, R. E., 504
Schiff, W., 507fn
Schimel, J. L., 207, 427
Schlesinger, B., 620
Schlesinger, R., 528
Schlingensliepen, W., 191fn
Schloss, G. A., 227
Schmauk, F. J., 548
Schmidt, E., 245, 438
Schmidt, H. O., 203, 204, 206, 208, 213
Schneider, I., 307, 332
Schnurer, A. T., 297
Schofield, W., 97, 97fn, 225
Schoggen, P., 39fn
Scholander, T., 542
Scholes, P. E., Jr., 384
Schooler, C., 185
Schopler, J., 91fn
Schorer, C. E., 244, 244fn
Schreber, Daniel Paul, 405
Schreiber, Y. L., 258, 615

name index

Schroeder, S. R., 597
Schulberg, H. C., 620
Schulder, D. B., 598
Schuldt, W. J., 241fn
Schuler, E. A., 253
Schultz, D. P., 302
Schulzinger, F., 345
Schur, E. M., 207, 425, 462
Schutz, W., 229
Schwab, J. J., 390, 579
Schwann, T., 140
Schwartz, A. N., 377
Schwartz, F., 597
Schwartz, G. E., 316, 317, 318, 321, 592
Schwartz, M., 177
Schwartz, M. S., 198
Schwitzgebel, R., 561, 562, 613
Schwitzgebel, R. K., 233, 561
Schwitzgebel, R. L., 426
Scotch, N. A., 185fn
Scott, Charles, 568
Scott, P. M., 493
Scott, R. A., 92, 93fn, 94fn, 95fn
Scott, R. W., 317
Scott, Reginald, 128, 129
Scott, T. H., 105fn
Scott, W. A., 11, 187fn
Scott, Sir Walter, 280
Scott, W. R., 39fn
Scotton, L., 293
Scrignar, C. B., 296
Seager, C. P., 569
Sears, R. R., 91, 260fn
Seashore, C., 229
Sebatasso, A. P., 80
Sebeck, T. A., 90
Sechenov, I. M., 144
Sechrest, L. B., 148, 185, 275, 525
Seeman, W. P., 208
Segal, H. A., 306
Segal, J., 252, 309
Seguin, E., 85, 141
Sehramel, D. J., 253
Seidner, M. L., 592
Seitz, F. C., 266, 393, 399
Seitz, J., 599
Selesnick, S. T., 2, 18, 127fn, 135fn
Seligman, M. E. P., 264, 397, 574
Sells, S. B., 212
Selman, R. L., 591
Seltzer, A. L., 106
Seltzer, H. N., 291
Selye, H., 117, 314
Selzer, M. I., 300
Semans, J. H., 430
Sennett, W. L., 606
Senter, R. J., 579
Serber, M., 234, 438

Sereny, G., 453
Seto, T. A., 344fn
Severy, L. J., 593
Sewell, W. H., 483
Shader, R. I., 143, 499
Shaffer, G. W., 261, 266
Shagass, C., 314
Shah, S. A., 603
Shainberg, L. W., 444fn, 445
Shakespeare, William, 214
Shakow, D., 396
Shames, G. H., 290, 291
Shannon, D. T., 228, 274, 275, 374, 410
Shantz, D. W., 593
Shapiro, A. K., 100, 101, 295, 312fn
Shapiro D., 312, 316, 317, 318, 321, 325
Sharma, S. L., 35
Shatterly, D., 457
Shaw, C. R., 195, 558
Shaw, D. A., 179, 266
Shaw, F. J., 147
Shaw, W. H., 504
Shean, G. D., 380, 384
Shearn, C. R., 350
Shearn, D., 317
Shears, L. M., 90
Sheehan, J. G., 113, 231, 291, 292
Sheehan, P. W., 65, 110
Sheldon, A., 620
Shellhaas, M. D., 200
Shenker, I., 599fn
Shepard, M., 398
Sheperd, M., 205
Sheppard, W. C., 47fn
Sherman, G., 80
Sherman, J. A., 84, 85, 236, 377, 505
Sherman, M., 374
Sherr, L., 567
Sherrick, C. E., 290
Sherry, P., 524
Sherwood, J. J., 114
Shibutani, T., 413
Shields, J., 343
Shirley, M. M., 556
Shlien, J. M., 106
Shneidman, E. S., 575, 576, 578, 579
Shoben, E. J., Jr., 14, 15, 17, 147, 584
Shoemaker, D., 292
Shore, M. F., 616
Short, J. F., 556
Short, J. G., 87
Shulman, A. D., 113
Shure, M. B., 487, 595
Sidebotham, R., 362fn
Sidman, M., 70, 526
Siegel, L., 22
Siegelman, M., 436fn
Siegler, M., 450fn

Sigal, M., 255
Sikora, J. P., 600
Silberman, C., 596
Silbert, R., 185fn
Silver, L. B., 496
Silverman, I., 113, 263
Silverman, J., 341, 357, 367fn
Silverman, S., 340
Silverstone, B. M., 539, 540
Simkins, L. D., 594
Simmons, J. Q., 507, 508, 510, 581, 615
Simmons, L., 538
Simmons, W. L., 214
Simon, B., 209
Simon, H. A., 39
Simon, R., 245
Simon, Théodore, 149
Simon, W., 215, 425
Simons, J., 506
Simpson, D. L., 179
Simpson, R. K., 448
Sims, G. K., 399
Sines, J. O., 474
Sinett, E. R., 245
Singer, B. D., 200
Singer, E., 59, 163
Singer, J. E., 38, 104, 170, 191, 240, 255, 319
Singer, J. L., 185
Singer, K., 448
Singer, M., 241fn
Singh, R., 260fn
Sipprelle, C. N., 298, 317
Siqueland, R. E., 47, 70
Siroka, E. K., 227
Siroka, R. W., 227
Skea, S., 185
Skerly, N., 537
Skiba, E. A., 295
Skinner, B. F., 69, 75fn, 84, 118fn, 144, 147, 203fn, 226, 231, 232, 481, 585, 595fn
Skinner, J. L., 498
Skrzypek, G. J., 551
Skuban, W., 506
Slabbert, M., 184fn
Slack, C. W., 561
Slade, H. C., 286
Slade, P. D., 377
Slater, E., 343
Slavson, S. R., 228
Sloggett, B. B., 214, 595fn
Small, S. M., 253
Smart, I., 113, 466
Smeets, P. M., 297
Smelser, N. J., 51
Smith, D. E. P., 595
Smith, H. C., 148
Smith, J. A., 369, 377
Smith, J. W., 570

Smith, K., 337
Smith, P., 40, 116
Smith, R. A., 592
Smith, R. E., 113
Snider, A. J., 22, 605
Snider, B., 496
Snortum, J. R., 569
Snyder, C. R., 218, 464
Snyder, W. U., 226
Snygg, D., 584
Sobell, L. C., 453, 456, 457
Sobell, M. B., 445, 453, 456, 457
Socarides, C. W., 436fn
Socrates, 121
Sokolow, E. N., 317
Solar, D., 113
Solomon, F. A., 595
Solomon, H., 588
Solomon, P., 105
Solomon, R. L., 270, 481
Solyom, L., 274
Sommer, R., 38, 39, 90, 176, 370
Sonada, B., 384
Sonnenstein, 134
Soranus, 123
Soskin, R. A., 453
Sours, J. A., 295
Southard, E. E., 616
Southwell, E. A., 241fn
Spadoni, A. J., 369, 377
Spanos, N. P., 111
Specter, G. A., 618
Speisman, J. C., 227
Sperry, R. W., 534
Spevack, M., 466
Spiegel, D. E., 168, 199fn
Spiegel, J. P., 616
Spinetta, J., 483
Spinoza, Baruch, 133
Spiro, H. R., 257fn
Spitalnik, R., 596
Spitz, R. A., 46, 397
Spitzer, R., 185
Spitzer, R. L., 27
Spitzer, S. P., 176, 362fn
Spivak, G., 487, 595
Spradlin, J. E., 525, 526, 527, 597
Sprague, R. L., 494, 498
Sprenger, J., 126
Springer, K. J., 227
Srole, L., 184, 186
Staats, A. W., 74, 144, 148, 318, 412, 495fn, 562, 592, 595, 618
Stacey, J., 601fn
Stachnik, T., 148
Stafford, R. L., 296
Stainbrook, E., 96, 97fn, 311

name index

Stampfl, T. G., 277
Stancer, H. C., 344*fn*
Standahl, J., 525
Stanton, A. H., 198
Stanton, Elizabeth Cady, 599
Staples, E. A., 111*fn*
Staples, S., 380
Stark, J., 504
Starr, B. J., 219
Starr, C. D., 291
Stary, O., 536
Staub, E., 592, 593
Staub, H., 546, 547
Stayton, S., 525
Stedman, G., 286
Stedman, J. M., 499
Steffy, R. A., 340, 384, 570
Stein, N. H., 322
Stein, F., 498
Stein, K. B., 61, 557
Steiner, I. D., 91
Steinhardt, W. B., 281
Steinman, W. M., 85, 523
Stekel, W., 231
Stengel, E., 575, 577
Stephan, C., 525
Stephano, S., 525
Stephens, J. H., 340
Stephens, L. Y., 525
Stephens, L. S., 596
Sterman, M. B., 318, 542
Stern, P. J., 163
Stern, R., 238
Stern, R. M., 435
Stern, W., 215
Sternbach, R. A., 314, 326
Stevens, J. R., 319
Stevenson, H. W., 367*fn*
Stevenson, I., 244, 263*fn*, 439, 440
Stewart, D. J., 214, 496
Stewart, J. L., 291
Stewart, R. A., 237
Stimbert, V. E., 504
Stimpert, W. E., 245
Stockey, M. R., 516
Stoddard, 526
Stoebel, 203*fn*
Stoeckle, J. D., 185*fn*
Stoffelmayr, B. E., 297, 375
Stoller, R. J., 208, 428, 567
Stolz, S. B., 256*fn*
Stone, A. A., 4
Stone, S. S., 4
Storms, M. D., 293
Stouffer, G. A. W., Jr., 199*fn*
Stover, D. O., 596
Stoyva, J. M., 298, 312*fn*, 325
Straight, E., 245

Strang, H. R., 295
Strassburger, F., 609
Strassman, H. D., 306, 366
Straub, R. R., 504
Straughan, J. H., 341*fn*, 479, 525
Strauss, A. A., 302
Strecker, E. A., 143
Streifel, J., 85
Strenger, S., 275
Strickland, B. R., 436*fn*
Strickland, C. G., 516
Strickland, J. F., 168
Strong, E. K., Jr., 196
Stroufe, L. A., 316, 496
Strupp, H. H., 227
Stuart, R. B., 238, 298, 428, 562, 590
Stub, H. G., 186
Stumphauzer, J. S., 296, 562, 596
Stunkard, A. J., 296
Suchotliff, L. C., 384
Sudak, H. S., 580
Suiha, J. B. P., 593
Suinn, R. M., 165
Sulianti, J., 253, 254
Sullivan, H. S., 154, 155, 225, 227, 247, 404
Sulzbacher, S. I., 504, 595*fn*
Sulzer, E. S., 457, 616
Sundstrom, E., 208, 471
Susser, M. W., 37
Sutcliffe, J. P., 109
Sutherland, E. H., 556
Sutker, P. B., 548
Sutton-Smith, B., 423
Swanson, J. C., 460
Swatos, W. H., Jr., 460
Swensen, C., 347
Sydenham, 254
Sykes, D. H., 498
Sykes, G. M., 555
Sylvester, D., 269
Sylvester, J. D., 287, 288
Szara, S., 453
Szasz, T. S., 22, 97, 116, 132, 170, 177, 212, 356, 409*fn*, 411, 412, 462*fn*, 613
Szczepkowski, T. R., 464
Szurek, S. A., 549

Taber, T., 203*fn*
Talkington, L. W., 70, 525
Tang, T., 241*fn*
Tannenbaum, F., 196
Tanner, B. A., 282
Tapp, L., 619, 620
Tart, C. T., 113*fn*, 574*fn*
Tarver, J., 620
Tasto, D. L., 298
Tate, B. G., 481, 507, 508, 510, 580, 581
Tawney, R. H., 190

Taylor, D. J., 297, 321
Taylor, G. P., 537
Taylor, H. A., 454
Taylor, J. C., 585
Taylor, J. G. A., 282
Taylor, L., 91, 324, 483
Teadale, J., 236
Teal, D., 436fn
Teigen, J. R., 374
Telford, C. W., 293
Temerlin, M. K., 28, 29, 203fn, 213
Tepper, D. T., 91
Terman, L., 149, 215, 472
Terrace, H. S., 81
Tesser, A., 576fn
Test, M. A., 588
Thaler, M. B., 306, 366
Tharp, R. G., 84, 238, 266, 322, 562, 591
Theiss, M., 241fn
Theriant, N., 134fn
Thio, A., 182
Thomas, D., 398
Thomas, D. R., 494
Thomas, E. J., 233, 294
Thomas, J., 79, 237, 259fn
Thomason, I. G., 466
Thompson, D. W., 433
Thompson, E. E., 373
Thompson, N. L., Jr., 436fn
Thompson, T., 524
Thompson, V. A., 39
Thomson, L. E., 276, 296
Thoreson, C. E., 84, 237, 572
Thorndike, E. L., 144
Thorne, D. E., 110, 514
Thorpe, J. G., 274, 433, 434, 437
Thorpe, L. J., 162
Tiede, T., 538
Tienari, P., 343
Tiger, Joseph, 412
Tilton, J. R., 375
Timbury, G. C., 206
Tisdall, W. J., 200, 520
Tissot, 426
Tittle, C. K., 601fn
Titus, D., 516
Toban, E., 191fn
Toch, H., 148, 191, 192
Todd, Eli, 450
Todd, F. J., 265, 399
Toepfer, C., 480
Tomkins, S. S., 570
Tomlinson, J. R., 500
Tophoff, M., 294
Torrey, E. F., 119fn, 239, 351, 356
Towbin, A. P., 355
Trachtman, J. P., 214
Tracy, J. J., 592

Tramontana, J., 504
Tredgold, A. F., 545
Treffert, 501
Treffry, D., 581
Tripodi, T., 203fn
Trofer, S. A., 113fn
Trotter, S., 542
Truax, C. B., 227
True, J. E., 373
Tseng, W. S., 121fn
Tsujimoto, R. N., 293
Tucker, A. C., 196
Tucker, G., 345, 361
Tuckman, J., 187, 576
Tuke, W. H., 129, 135
Turnbull, J. W., 322
Turner, A. J., 619, 620
Turner, D. R., 520
Turner, J., 99
Turner, J. LeB., 191fn
Turner, R. J., 61, 187
Turner, R. K., 499
Turner, W. J., 541
Turner, W. L., 597
Turpin, R., 517
Tursky, B., 316, 317, 592
Tuttle, R. J., 466
Twardosz, S., 164, 498
Twentyman, C. T., 284
Twitchell, T. E., 496
Tyler, V. O., Jr., 493, 495fn, 503, 560, 596

Ullman, A. D., 448
Ullmann, L. P., 17, 24, 36, 36fn, 40, 44, 63, 83, 91, 95, 97fn, 110fn, 111 fn, 112, 118, 125, 138, 147, 148, 167, 168, 179, 188, 199, 200, 207, 208, 212, 220, 224, 228, 237, 238, 250, 281, 298, 333, 340, 341, 341fn, 361, 365fn, 366, 367fn, 373, 374, 376, 377, 378, 402, 410, 431, 480, 548, 550, 568, 571, 573, 575, 583, 585, 591, 594, 598, 600, 603, 604, 610, 612, 614, 621
Ullmann, M., 422fn
Ulrich, R., 148
Unger, S. N., 465
Upper, D., 298, 384, 571

Vail, D. J., 187fn
Valins, S., 43, 105, 319
Vallance, M., 433
Vance, E. T., 619
Vanderhoof, E., 453
Van Deusen, 286
Van Dyke, H. B., 103
Van Egeren, L. F., 274
Van Gogh, Vincent, 541
Vanian, D., 241fn
VanLehn, R., 314
Van Sommers, P., 291
Vasta, R., 593

name index

Vedder, C. B., 558
Veit, S. W., 367fn
Veitch, R., 90
Veith, I., 122, 123, 422fn, 253
Venn, J. R., 87
Venturi, L., 116
Veray, T. R., 99fn
Verden, P., 457
Vernon, J. A., 105fn
Videbech, T., 580
Viek, P., 235
Viney, L., 585
Vinokur, A., 300
Viscott, D. S., 197, 199
Vives, Juan Luis, 127, 127fn, 128
Voegtlin, W. L., 455
Vogel, W., 367fn
Volkan, V., 265
Volkart, E., 396
Volpe, A., 539
Von Feuchtersleben, Ernst, 134
Von Helmholtz, H. L. F., 152
Von Krafft-Ebing, Richard, 140
Vonnegut, Kurt, 566
Voorhis, J., 586
Vourlekis, A., 453
Vukelich, R., 561

Waelder, R., 155
Wagenen, R. K., 500
Wagenfeld, M. O., 187, 617
Wagner, B. R., 361
Wagner, M. K., 234, 570
Wagner-jauregg, Julius, 141
Wahler, R. G., 292, 478, 480, 494, 504, 562
Walbek, N. H., 593
Walder, L. O., 480
Walen, S. R., 563, 580
Walker, C. C., 583
Walker, P. C., 293
Wallace, C. A., 207
Wallace, C. J., 237, 385
Wallace, J., 589
Wallace, J. G., 187fn
Wallerstein, J. S., 189, 546
Wallin, J. E. W., 475fn
Wallin, K., 524
Wallington, S., 589
Wallner, J. M., 340
Walster, E., 589
Walter, H. L., 480
Walters, R. H., 377, 491, 492, 558, 559, 591fn, 592
Walton, D., 259, 262, 276fn, 282, 292, 294, 321, 323
Walton, H., 446, 447, 448, 451
Walum, 599fn
Wanderer, Z. W., 573
Ward, C. H., 205
Ward, D. R., 131

Ward, L. C., III, 214
Ward, M., 525
Ware, C., 599
Warheit, G. J., 579
Warm, J. S., 91
Warner, A., 467
Warren, S. A., 367fn, 520
Wasden, R., 384
Washington, George, 568
Wasik, B. H., 490, 562
Wassermann, A., 140
Watkins, J. T., 298
Watson, C. M., 297
Watson, D., 266
Watson, D. L., 84, 238, 322, 591
Watson, E., 79
Watson, J. B., 69, 144, 270, 475, 475fn
Watson, L. S., Jr., 500, 525
Watson, S. G., 90
Watts, J. W., 143, 144
Waugh, E., 395
Waxler, C. Z., 85
Waxler, N. E., 362
Weatherly, D., 367fn
Webber, C. S., 314
Weber, M., 596
Webster, D. R., 561
Webster, R. L., 292
Weckowicz, T. E., 393
Wegrocki, H. J., 16, 17, 17fn
Weil, A. T., 465
Weil, G., 293
Weil, R. J., 182, 397
Weinberg, G., 432
Weinberg, M. S., 46
Weinberg, S. K., 364, 366, 380, 381
Weiner, I. B., 282
Weiner, I. W., 79fn, 580
Weingaertner, A. H., 379
Weinstein, E. A., 253
Weinstein, M. S., 399
Weintraub, W., 266
Weisberg, W. P., 218, 525
Weiss, E., 315
Weiss, J. M., 293
Weiss, R. F., 91, 590
Weiss, R. L., 374, 550
Weiss, T., 325
Weissman, H. N., 200
Weissman, M. M., 390
Weitz, S., 90
Weitzenhoffer, A. M., 261
Weizenbaum, J., 606
Welkowitz, J., 615
Wender, P. H., 496
Wenger, D. I., 21
Werner, J., 208

name index

Werry, J. S., 494, 499, 501
Wertham, F., 555
Wesner, C., 295
West, L. J., 250, 252, 306, 309
Wetzel, R. J., 480, 494, 562
Wexberg, L. E., 450
Wexler, D. B., 613
Weyer, Johann, 128
Whalen, R. J., 386
Wheatland, J., 380
Wheeler, L., 319
White, G. M., 90
White, J. C., Jr., 297, 321
White, J. G., 494
White, S. H., 585
Whitehorn, J. C., 231
Whitehurst, G. J., 85
Whiteside, 589
Whitlock, C., 495fn
Whitman, T. L., 498, 525, 570
Whitney, L. R., 524
Wicker, A. W., 242
Wickes, I. G., 498
Wickman, E. K., 199fn
Wickrameskera, I., 435
Wiesen, A. E., 79, 495fn
Wiesenthal, D. L., 113
Wiggins, N., 203fn
Wiggins, S. L., 228
Wignall, C. M., 187fn
Wikler, A., 460
Wilbur, J. C., 90
Wile, R., 451
Wilensky, H., 111
Wilkins, J., 579
Wilkins, W., 239, 274
Wilkinson, D., 260fn
Wilkinson, J. C., 238
Williams, C., 434
Williams, C. D., 47, 48, 237, 484
Williams, D. P., 362
Williams, R. L., 562
Williams, T. K., 451
Williams, W. S., 539
Willingham, W. W., 606
Willis, R. W., 278
Wills, Thomas, 139
Wilmer, H. A., 369
Wilson, C. W., 597
Wilson, E., 44
Wilson, F. S., 377
Wilson, L. T., 576
Wilson, M. L., 436fn
Wilson, P. T., 27
Wilson, S., 399
Wimberger, H. C., 482
Wincze, J. P., 374, 431
Winder, C. L., 340, 341

Wine, J., 240
Winett, R. A., 570, 595fn
Wing, J. K., 176
Winkler, R. C., 383
Winokur, G., 390, 394fn
Wisocki, P. A., 282, 466
Wispé, L. G., 588, 590
Witmer, F. J., 498
Witmer, H. L., 556
Witmer, L., 148, 149, 471
Witryol, S. L., 70
Wittenborn, J. R., 209, 394
Witter, C., 496
Wittkower, E. D., 182
Wittman, M. P., 339
Wittman, P., 339, 340
Witzig, J. S., 435
Wohlwill, J. F., 38
Wolberg, L. R., 440
Wold, C. I., 579
Wolf, M. M., 237, 256, 297, 480, 498, 500, 503, 504, 505, 528, 561, 562, 581, 615
Wolf, S., 104, 227, 315, 321
Wolfensberger, W., 606
Wolff, H. G., 104, 227, 315
Wolff, R., 374, 474
Wolff, W. T., 203fn
Wolfgang, M. E., 556, 578
Wolford, J. A., 579
Wollersheim, J. P., 228, 298
Wolman, B. B., 155, 163
Wolpe, J. 134, 146, 147, 164, 225, 234, 235, 238, 264, 274, 281, 283, 284, 323, 324, 399, 429, 430, 431, 435, 439, 440, 471fn
Wolpin, M., 278
Wong, M., 448
Wooden, H., 524
Woodruff, R. A., Jr., 13, 13fn, 251fn, 252fn
Woodward, J. L., 179
Woodward, M., 439
Woodward, Samuel, 450
Woodworth, R., 216
Word, L. E., 588
Woy, J. R., 246
Wray, N. P., 168
Wright, B. A., 506
Wright, D., 214, 592
Wright, H. F., 39
Wright, L., 18, 323, 542, 591
Wright, T., 504
Wulbert, M., 259fn
Wunderlich, R. A., 597
Wundt, Wilhelm, 152
Wyle, C. J., 189, 546
Wynne, L. C., 270
Wynne, R. D., 267fn
Wyrwicka, W., 318

name index

Wysocki, A. C., 474
Wysocki, B. A., 474

Yablonsky, L., 467
Yalom, I. D., 228, 230, 231
Yamagami, T., 282
Yamamoto, J., 99
Yang, J. C., 111
Yap, P. M., 182
Yarrow, L. J., 366
Yarrow, M. R., 85, 362fn, 493
Yates, A. J., 146, 163, 237, 290, 294, 535
Yen, S., 281
Yoell, W., 432
Young, B. W., 571
Young, G. C., 498, 499
Young, I. L., 500
Young, R. D., 169
Youngman, W. F., 576

Zabo, L. J., 99
Zaidel, S. F., 90
Zakaras, M., 525
Zanna, M. P., 74, 91
Zarlock, S. P., 354, 355, 371
Zax, M., 345, 618

Zeidberg, A., 384
Zeiler, M. D., 524
Zeiss, A. R., 592
Zeisset, R. M., 377
Zeitlyn, B. B., 369
Ziegler, F. J., 255
Zifferblatt, S. M., 597
Zigler, E., 209, 210, 211, 367fn, 519
Zilboorg, G., 116fn, 121fn, 124, 125, 127 128, 140
Zimbardo, P. G., 43
Zimet, C. N., 212, 340, 402
Zimmer, H., 148
Zimmerman, B. J., 595, 597
Zimmerman, E. H., 237, 490, 525, 595fn
Zimmerman, J., 203fn, 237, 256fn, 490, 525, 591fn, 595fn
Zimmerman, R. R., 326
Zimring, F. M., 538
Zisberg, N. E., 465
Ziv, A., 199fn
Zola, I. K., 182, 185fn, 549, 559
Zubek, J. P., 105fn, 106
Zubin, J., 180, 208, 537
Zung, W. K., 390
Zusman, J., 118, 185fn, 371
Zweback, S., 228

subject index

Abnormal behavior:
  clergy treatment of, 125, 126
  definitions, 2, 3
    legal, 18-22
    medical, 18
    operational, 11-15
    separate behavior, 15-16
    statistical, 17-18
    unitary behavior, 15-16
  early formulations and treatment, 116-29
  learning to be normally abnormal, 187-96
  likely conditions of, 33-34
Abnormal psychology:
  as convenient term, 5
  definitions, 15-17
  historical introduction to, 116-29
    China, 121
    development of asylums, 129
    the dissenters, 127-29
    Greco-Roman period, 123-24
    the Greeks, 121-23
    India, 120-21
    Middle Ages, 124-27
    models, 116-19
    Near East, 127
    primitive man, 119-20
  importance of, 3
  misinformation about, 4-5
  modern approaches to, 131-50
    behavioral, 144-48
    forerunners of psychotherapy, 131-34
    moral treatment, rise and decline, 135-39
    organic point of view, 139-44
    the professions, 148-50
  percent of population involved, 4
  purposes of studying, 4-5
  questions touched on, 6
  traditional, 3
Abnormality, 2, 175
  psychiatric emergency, definition, 9-11
  social events leading to label, 180-87
Abortion, 605
Abstinence syndrome, 444
Abstraction formation, 84-85
Abstract reasoning, emphasis on, 515
Abuse, as social evaluation, 445
Accurate empathy, 236

Achievement Place, 560-61
Acquired reinforcers, 74, 75
Acting-out, as variable, 474
Acute alcohol intoxication, 446
Acute brain disorders, 531
Acute depression, 391
Acute mania, 390, 391
Acute schizophrenic episode, 336
Addiction, 402
  definition, 444-45
Addictive behavior, 444-68
  alcoholism, 444-58
  drug addiction, 458-68
Adequate working performance, 375
Adjustment reaction of childhood, 473
Adoption studies, and schizophrenia, 344-45
Affect, 359
  in schizophrenia, 331
Affective behavior:
  depression, 397-99
  sociopsychological formulation, 394-97
Aggression/hostility in children, 491-95
Aggressive rule breaking, and children, 208
Aging process:
  as chronic brain syndrome, 537-40
  related to brain damage, 535-36
Aide culture, 380-81
Alabama Federal District Court, 21
Alchemy, 125
Alcohol paranoid state, 446
Alcoholic, definitions, 446
Alcoholic deterioration, 446
Alcoholic hallucinosis, 446
Alcoholics Anonymous, 452, 453, 458
Alcoholism, 146, 447
  alpha, 447
  beta, 447
  chronic, 447
  delta, 447
  drinking patterns, 447
  effects of, 447-49
  gamma, 447
  history of, 449-50
  learning theory formulations, 450
  as pharmacological addiction, 447
  sampling problems, 61-62
  sociopsychological formulation of, 451-52

757

Alcoholism *(cont.)*
  statistics (U.S.), 446
  theories of, 450
  treatment, 452-58
    aversion procedures, 455-56
    behavioral approach, 453-54
    desensitization, 456
    operant and controlled approaches, 456-57
    social-group approaches, 457-58
    social learning procedures, 454
Algonquin Indians, 181
Alpha alcoholism, 447
Alpha Scale for literate English-speaking recruits, 149
Alpha training, 326
Altruistic suicide, 577
Alzheimer's disease, 532
Ambivalence, in schizophrenia, 331
American Indians, rules among, 190
American Journal of Insanity, The, 137
American Law Institute, 20
American Medical Association:
  Council on Mental Health, 609
  formulation of retardation, 522, 523
American Psychiatric Association, 3, 13, 18, 22, 23, 30, 249, 336, 418
American Psychological Association, 606, 608, 609, 610
Amnesia, in fugue, 252
Amok (homicidal rampage), 181
Amphetamines, 432
  effects of, 464
Amurakh mania, 181
Anaclitic depression, 46
Anal character, 157-58
Analog information biofeedback, 325-26
Anal stage, 156
Anatomy of Melancholy (Burton), 121, 128, 285, 394*fn*, 402
Anglo-Saxon legal system, 555
Anomic suicide, 577
Anomie theory, in diagnosis, 348
Anorexia nervosa, 290, 295-98
Antabuse, 143
  therapy, 455
Anthropologie (Kant), 133
Antisocial behavior, 544-54 *(See also* Psychopathy)
Antisocial disorders, 25-26
Antisocial labeling, 544
Antisocial reaction, 402
Antisocial tendencies, as variable, 474
Anxiety, 158, 162
  alternative to concept, 171
  and antisocial personality, 547-48
  as chief characteristic of neuroses, 249-50
  concepts of, 170-71
  and symptom, 165-66
Anxiety dimension, in schizophrenia, 341-42

Anxiety neurosis, 25, 268
  definition, 282
Anxiety-relief responses, 235
  in children, 490
  technique, 273-74
Anxious intropunitiveness, as symptom, 338
Apathy, experiments in, 373-75
Aphasic speech, 537
Aphonia, 259-60
Apologizing behavior, 49
Apomorphine, 432, 434, 455
Apoplexy, ancient view of, 123
Appalachia, 253
Aqua vitae, 449
As I Lay Dying (Faulkner), 192
Ashanti, 395
Assertion of the predicate, 368
Assertion-structured therapy, 484
Assertive responses, training of, 233-34, 283-84
Association, in schizophrenia, 331
Asthenic personality, 415
Asthma *(See* Bronchial asthma)
Astrology, 125
Asylums, development of, 129
Ataractic drugs, 142-43
Attention, 84-85
  approaches to, 357-58
  extinction of, 367-68
  as generalized reinforcer, 75-79
  as operaant response to stimulus, 45-46
  in schizophrenia, 332, 333
  training of, 85-86
Attention-placebo group, 245, 246
Attitude change, and behavior change, 242-43
Attitudes, effect on psychosomatic symptoms, 316
Attitudinal patterns, of alcohol consumption, 451-52
Attribution theory, 43*fn*, 412
Aura, 540
Autism, 322
  behavioral approaches to, 503-11
  in children, 501-11
Automatic negativism, 359
Automatic obedience, 359
Autonomic functioning, and conditioning procedures, 317-18
Autonomic patterns, inherited, 314-15
Average, as designation of central tendency, 62
Aversive procedures:
  for alcoholism, 455-56
  and children, 490-91
  drug addiction, 466
Aversive stimuli:
  behavior terminating, 71-72
  in child training, 481-82
  as treatment, 281
  of homosexual behavior, 437-39
Aversive verbalization, 377-78
Avoidance, 70

subject index

Avoidance learning, and psychopaths, 547-48
Ayur-Veda, 121
Ayurvedic treatment, 356

Back-up reinforcing stimulus, 74
Baquet, 108
Barbiturates, 459
  effects of, 463-64
Barnum effect, 218
Base rates, 63, 218
Battered child syndrome, 483
Bed-wetting (*See* Enuresis)
Behavior influence:
  definition, 224
  technology of, 604
Behavior labeling, consequences of, 35-36
Behavior modification, 224-47
  and attitude change, 242-43
  concepts of behavioral change, 224-25
  definition, 224
  and delinquency, 562-63
  diagnostic questions, 220-21
  evocative therapy:
    as behavioral technique, 226-27, 236
    dissatisfaction with, 227-32
    from Freud to Rogers, 225-27
    group therapy, 227-31
  implicit demand characteristics, 239-43
  method of change, 233-39
  psychotherapy:
    evaluations of effectiveness, 243-46
    as process of control, 231-32
Behaviour Research and Therapy, 147
Behavior reversal, 486-87
Behavior scales:
  concomitant, 375
  idiosyncratic, 375
  mutually exclusive, 375
Behavior study, schizophrenic patients, 354-55
Behavior therapy, 15
  assessment procedures, 232
  and changeworthy behavior, 597
  compared to seduction, 278
  definition, 224
  ethical problems, 610-13
  fearful behavior, children, 484-87
  increased use of, 147-48
  method of change, 233-39
  responses:
    cognitions, 238
    development of relaxation, 235
    extinction, 237
    negative practice, 237
    other techniques, 239
    positive reinforcement, 237
    satiation, 237
    self-modification, 237-38
    stimulus deprivation 237

Behavior therapy (*cont.*)
  responses (*cont.*)
    training of assertive, 233-34
    use of conditioned avoidance, 235-36
    use of sexual, 234
  shaping, 258-59
Behaviors:
  addictive, 444-68
  of alcoholics, 445-47
  aversive to others; learning of, 48-50
  changing or altering, 51-52
  children's, 470-511
  concept of, 69
  demographic evaluative characteristics, 50-51
  in depression, 394-97
  depressive, 391-93
  development and maintenance of pro-social, 36-38
  evaluation of as changeworthy, 42-50
  fearful, in children, 475-89
  labeling, 175-80
  manic, 390-91
  no criteria for involutional melancholia, 394
  overdetermined, 157
  paranoid, 402-13
  physical approaches to change, 142-44
  professional labeling, 35
  psychopathic, 544-54
  sexual, 418-42
  shaping of, 79-81
  specifying limits of, 607-13
    behavior therapy, 610-13
    children and parents, 607-608
    encounter sensitivity training, 608-10
    patients and practitioners, 608
  terms used for, 4
Behavioral approaches:
  autism, 503-11
  to alcoholism, 453-54
  development of, 144-48
  retardation, 522-24
Behavioral decisions, data for, 219-21
Behavioral setting:
  concept of, 39
  physical and social, 38-40
  social organizations, 39-40
Behaviorist, as advocate, 611
Behavioristic theory, of schizophrenia, 342-43
Belle indifference, 251, 256
Bellevue Hospital, 411
Bernheim-Charcot controversy, 132-33
Beta alcoholism, 447
Beta Scale of illiterates, 149
Bicêtre Hospital (Paris), 135
Binet intelligence scales, 215
Biochemical theories, of schizophrenia, 346
Biofeedback technique, 312, 604-605
Biography of Freud (Jones), 168
Biosocial theory, of schizophrenia, 342

Bizarre verbalization (*See* Aversive verbalization)
Bleuler's four A's, 332
Blindness:
    hysterical, 255-56
    as learned social role, 92-95
Blocked striving, influence of, 167-68
Bodily function, as factor in behavior, 37-38
Boston Psychopathic Hospital, 396
Boston State Hospital, 396
Bourneville's disease, 517
Braginskys' paradigm, 521-22
Brain function, and sociopathy, 549
Brain syndromes, 531-42
    aging process, 537-40
    assessment of damage, 535-36
    classification, 531-32
    effects of brain tissue removal, 533-34
    epilepsy, 540-42
    organic diseases, 532-33
    senile dementia, 539-40
    treatment, 536-37
Brainwashing, 306-308
British Mental Deficiencies Act (1913), 545
Bronchial asthma, 322-23
Bruxism, 295
Bughouser, learning to be, 196-200
Bureaucracy, possible effects on behavior, 39-40
Bystander effect, 587-88

Cambridge-Somerville study of delinquency, 558
Cameron's formulation of paranoia, 405-406
Camp Butner, N.C. Intensive Training Program, 559-60
Cannabis sativa, 459
Capture-recapture method, 459
Carbon dioxide therapy, 283
Cardiac arrhythmias, 325
Cardiac neurosis, 285
Career, definition, 192
Castration anxiety, 156
Catatonic behavior, situational nature of, 363-64
Catharsis, 153, 155
Censor, in dreams, 158
Cephalagia (headache), 298
Cerebral angiomatosis, 517
Cerebral traumas, and retardation, 513
Chaining (*See* Response chaining)
Champaign-Urbana Courier, 309, 598*fn*
Changeworthy behavior, 583-601
    children, 470-71
    ethical considerations, 440-41
Character, linked to gratification, 157
Chastity belt, male, 426
Chauvinism, 599
Cheating, 593
Chicago Daily News, 2, 117, 567, 586
Child, problem of defining term, 473, 473*fn*
Child labor laws, 471

Child psychiatry, history and development, 471-72
Child Psychiatry, 472
Childhood and adolescence, behavior disorders of, 26
Children's behavior, 470-511
    ability to overcome problems, 470-71
    autism, 501-11
    battered child syndrome, 483
    in classroom, 495
    conduct problems, 489-95
    desensitization practices, 484-85
    fearful behavior, 475-89
    historical development, 471-72
    hyperactivity, 495-98
    parental attitudes, 482-83
    problems of description, 472-75
    punishment, 481-82
    rights of, 607-608
    schizophrenic, 501-10
    toilet training, 498-501
    training parents, 477-81
China, behavioral beliefs, 121
Chlorpromázine, 143
Chorea lasciva, 128
Chronic alcoholism, 447
Chronic brain disorders, 531
Chronological age (C.A.), 215
City Directory, New Haven, 186
Civilian disaster, 303-304
Classical conditioning, 233
Classroom behavior, 495, 594-95, 596-97
    and retardates, 525-26
Clinical psychologist, definition, 148
Clinical psychology, definition, 148-49
Clonic stage, of epileptic seizure, 540
Closed system, 269
Cocaine, 459, 460
    effects of, 464
Cognitions, 238
Cognitive slippage, 332, 343, 368
Cognitive theory, of schizophrenia, 342
Coma, 540
Commission on Obscenity and Pornography, 567
Commitment, 18
    procedures for, 19-20
Commonwealth Fund, 472
Communist brainwashing techniques, 307-308
Community psychiatry, 616-21
    in action, 618-20
    crisis intervention, 620-21
    primary prevention, 617
    secondary prevention, 617-18
    tertiary prevention, 618
Compensation, 160
Competency, 18-19
Compulsive personality, 402
Compulsory education, effect on children, 471
Conceptual disorganization, as symptom, 338-39
Conditionability, and sociopath, 550

subject index

Conditioned avoidance responses, 235-36
Conditioned response, 69
Conditioned stimulus, 69
Conditioning, as origin of psychophysiological disorders, 316-19
Conditioning, concept of, 46
Conduct problems, in children, 489-95
Confessions (St. Augustine), 81
Conflict, as concept, 82
Conforming, as trainee behavior, 197-200
Consciousness-raising, 599-600
Consciousness III, 133, 230
Conscious-unconscious, concept integral to personality, 168
Consistency, 66
    internal, 66
Constipation, 325
Consumer protection and biofeedback, 605
Contact desensitization, 276
Contingent negative reinforcement, 373
Contingent positive reinforcement, 373
Contingent tokens, as behavioral control, 383
Control, as concept, 585-86
Control groups, 5, 6, 56
Controlled drinking approach to alcoholism, 456-57
Conversion type, hysterical neurosis, 251
Cooperative retreats, for treatment of retardates, 522
Coprophilia, 435
Coral Gables VA Hospital, 321
Core culture, and behavior models, 519-20
Cost, of human activity, 70
Counter-culture, 195, 229
Court of King's Bench, 179
Covert conditioning, in drug addiction, 466
Covert sensitization, 427
Craft palsies, 268
Creative deviance, 598-601
Cretinism, 518-19
Crime, types, 556-57
Criminal behavior, changing legal definition, 555
Criminal responsibility, 18, 20-22
Crisis intervention, 620-21
    clinic, 580
Cues, identification of, 90
Cultural-familial retardation, 519-22
Cultural patterns, effect on behavior, 39
Culture-boundedness, 14
Culture shock, 303
Curability of Insanity (Butler), 136
Cursing, 567-68
Customary law, 555
Cyclothymic personality, 25, 401, 414

Dancing manias, 126
Dangerous Drug Act (Great Britain, 1920), 462
Data, for behavioral decisions, 219-21
Data collection, 219
Death, ethical questions, 605-606

Debility-Dependency-Dread (DDD), 306
Deceit, 593
Decency-indeceny, as variable, 421
Decision-making, 55-57
Defense mechanisms, 159-60
Delay therapy, 282
Delinquency (*See* Juvenile Delinquency)
Delirious mania, 390, 391
Delirium tremens (DT's), 446, 448
Delphic oracle, 121
Delta alcoholism, 447
Delusions, 338, 359, 403
    of reference, 403, 405-406
    in schizophrenia, 333
Demand characteristics, of experimental situation, 105-106
Dementia praecox, first coined, 339
Demographic characteristics as evaluation of behavior, 50-51
Demonology, 128-29
Department of Health and Social Security, 462
Dependent variable, 57
Depersonalization, 268, 359
    behavior, 285-86
    in schizophrenia, 333
Depression:
    definition, 389
    factor analysis, 392-93
    sociopsychological formulation, 394-97
    treatment of, 397-99
    types, 391-93
Depressive neurosis, 25, 263-66
Depressive stupor, 391
Descriptive statistics, 64
Desensitization, 282
    and alcoholism, 456
    cat phobia, 273
    in practice, 484-85
De subventione pauperium (Vives), 127-28
Deviance, 175
    definition, 2
    primary, 193
    secondary, 193
    social roles and, 89-114
        enactments, 89-95
        expectancy, 95-96
        experimenter bias, 112-14
        hypnosis, 107-12
        out-patient psychotherapy, 97-100
        performance, 95-96
        placebo responses, 100-107
        role-taking, 90-92
        sick role, 96-97
    Women's Lib as creative, 598-601
Dhammapada, or Path of Virtue, 44*fn*
Diagnostic categories, reasons for use of, 3
Diagnostic criteria:
    determination of, 203-205

Diagnostic criteria *(cont.)*
  sub-types, 203-204
Diagnostic practices, 176-77
Diagnostic and Statistical Manual, Mental Disorders
    (DSM-I), 22, 23, 26, 27, 165, 166, 170, 203, 205,
    249, 285, 286, 496, 571
  addiction, 444
  anorexia nervosa, 295*fn*
  definitions of neurosis, 249-50
  mental deficiency, 513
  obsessive-compulsive behavior, 278-79
  paranoia, 403, 404
  passive-aggressive personality, 415
  personality disorders, definitions, 401, 402
  psychophysiological disorders, 311
  sexual deviation, 418
  sociopathic personality disturbance, 544
  sociopathic reactions, 547
Diagnostic and Statistical Manual, Mental Disorders
    (DSM-II), 23, 24, 25, 26, 27, 28, 165, 203*fn*,
    249, 350, 475, 565, 571, 583
  affective disorders, 389
  alcoholism, 444, 445
  antisocial personality, 544
  anxiety neurosis, 282
  asthenic personality, 415
  brain syndromes, 531
  categories, 24-27
  children's disorders, 473
  compared to DSM-I, 27
  cyclothymic personality, 414
  delirium tremens, 448
  depersonalization neurosis, 285-86
  depressive neurosis, 263
  drug dependence, 444, 459
  explosive personality, 415
  genito-urinary reactions, 324
  hyperkinetic reaction, 496
  hypochondriacal behavior, 285
  hysterical neurosis, 251
  hysterical personality, 414
  inadequate personality, 414
  involutional melancholia, 393
  mental illness and health, 28
  mental retardation, 513, 514
  neurasthenia, 286
  neuroses, 249-50
  obsessive-compulsive neurosis, 278-79
  obsessive-compulsive personality, 414
  other neuroses, 287-88
  paranoia, 403-404
  passive-aggressive personality, 415
  personality disorders, 401, 402
  phobic neurosis, 268, 269
  psychophysiological disorders, 311
  psychosis, 328
  schizoid personality, 414

Diagnostic and Statistical Manual, Mental Disorders
    (DSM-II) *(cont.)*
  schizophrenia, 331
    childhood type, 501
    types, 334, 335, 336, 337
  sexual deviation, 418, 419
  special symptoms, 290
  transient situational disturbance, 299-301
Diffuse anxious behavior, 282-85
  definitions, 282-83
  treatment techniques, 283-85
Direct retraining, as treatment, 272
Direct training, in delinquency, 562
Disciplinary problems, as variable, 474
Discovery of Witchcraft, The (Scott), 128
Discrimination, 70
  stimuli, 73-74
    function of, 73-75
Disease, definition, 13
Disorientation, symptoms of, 339
Displacement, 159
  as definition of phobia, 269
Dissenters, psychological thought of, 127-29
Dissociation, 159-60
Dissociative behavior, reformulation of, 260-61
Dissociative reaction, definition, 166
Dissociative type, hysterical neurosis, 251-52
District of Columbia Circuit Court of Appeals, 21
Dizygotic twins, and schizophrenia, 343, 345
DNA manipulation, 604
Dollard-Miller-Hullian drive model, 450
Double approach-avoidance situation, 83
Double-blind experiment, 56
Double conditioning treatment paradigm, 385-86
Down's syndrome (Mongolism), 517
Draw-a-person test, 219
Dreaming, 122, 158-59
  latent content, 158
  manifest content, 158
Drinking, patterns of, 447
Drive theory, 163
Drug addiction, 194, 458-68
  amphetamines, 464
  barbiturates, 463-64
  cocaine, 464
  hallucinogenic, 465-66
  heroin, 463
  historical background, 459-62
  marijuana, 464-65
  morphine, 463
  treatment, 466-68
    in Great Britain, 462
  usage, 459
Drugs *(See also* Names of drugs)
  effects of addicting, 463-66
  energizers, 142-43
  tranquilizers, 142-43
  in treating depression, 398-99

subject index

Drugs *(cont.)*
  usage of addictive, 459
  used for children, 485
Dyssocial behavior, 27, 402, 554-63
  sociopsychological formulation of, 555-56

Earthquakes, as shock stimuli, 303
Echolalia, 333, 506
Echopraxia, 333
Ecological considerations as factors in behavior, 38
Ecological studies of mental disorders, 185-86
Economic context, effect on behavior, 40-41
Effort, in schizophrenia, 333
Ego, development of, 156
Ego decompensation, 158
Ego and Mechanisms of Defense, The (Freud), 159
Egoistic suicide, 577
Egyptians, 252
Ejaculatio praecox, 428, 430
Ejaculatory incompetence, 431
Electroconvulsive therapy (ECT), 143
Electrodermal activity, operant reinforcement of, 317
Electroencephalogram (EEG), 541, 550
  as diagnostic tool, 549
  sleep patterns, 319
Electromyogram (EMG), use of, 325
Electronic data storage, ethical concerns, 606
Electroshock therapy (EST)
  for depression, 398
  first use of, 59-60
Emergency:
  psychiatric, 9-10
  social, 10-11
Emetine hydrochloride, use of, 455
Emotional re-education, 154, 155
Emotional stimuli, labeling of, 319
Emotionally unstable personality, 402
Emotions, effect on body function, 315-16
Emotive imagery technique, 485
Empirical approaches to diagnosis, 209-12
Enacted law, 555
Encephalitis, 519
  epidemic, 533
Encopresis, 500
Encounter grouping, 228-31
Encounter-sensitivity training, 608-10
Encyclopedia Britannica, 128
Energizers, 142-43
  and treatment of mania, 398
Enuresis, 42, 146, 498-500
Environment, care for, 597
Epidemics of hysterical behavior, 253-54
Epidemiology, 183-85
Epilepsy:
  ancient view of, 121, 125
  grand mal, 540
  Jacksonian seizure, 541

Epilepsy *(cont.)*
  musicogenic, 541
  petit mal, 540-41
  psychomotor, 541
  treatment procedures, 541-42
Epileptoid personality disorder, 415
Episodic excessive drinking, 445
Equanil, 444
Esalen, 229
Eskimos, 181
  belief about disease, 120
Espanto, 182
Ether, 259
Ethical problems, 603-22
Ethics (Aristotle), 32
Ethnic psychoses, 181-82
Evocative therapy, 224-25, 226-27
  as behavioral technique, 236
  dissatisfaction with, 227-32
Exceptional children, 520
Excessive drinking, as behavior, 447
Excitement, as symptom, 338
Exhibitionism, 435
Existential movement, 228
Existential problems, 565
  behavioral approach to, 571-75
Existential verbalizations, 573
Expectancy, 95-96
  definition, 95
  self-fulfilling prophecy, 95-96
Expectation, 574-75
Experience-producing drives, 519
Experimental group, 56
Experimenter bias, 112-14
Experiments, general considerations, 378
Explosive personality, 415
Exposure-positive condition, 487
Expression, behavior surrounding, 264
Extinction, 164
  children, 484
  and classroom behavior, 490
  of a response, 237
Extinction, concept of, 46
Eysenck's theory, 550

Factor analysis:
  children's behavior, 473-74
  of depressive behavior, 392-93
  uselessness for involutional melancholia, 394
Fading of behavior, 81
Failure, as factor in depression, 395
Family (*See also* Parents)
  possible role in schizophrenia, 346-47
  and sociopathy, 549-50
  treatment of schizophrenia, 380
Father rejection, as pattern in delinquency, 558
Fearful behavior:
  battered child syndrome, 483

Fearful behavior (cont.)
  behavioral techniques, 484-87
  modeling, 487-88
  overcoming, 475-76
  parental attitudes, 482-83
  punishment, 481-82
  training parents, 477-81
Federal Bureau of Narcotics and Dangerous Drugs, 459
Feeding problems, 295-98
Feral children, 549
Fetishism, 271, 424
Fevers, induced, 141
Fires, as shock stimuli, 303
First signal system activity, 368
Fixation, 157
Fixed interval schedule, 79
Fixed ratio of reinforcement, 79
Flagellants, 126
Fleeing behavior, 302
Flooding, 278, 282
Floods, as shock stimuli, 303
Folkways, 555
Follow through, 470
Forgetting, as anxiety release, 158
Four humors, the, 122
Free association, as major technique, 153
Free-floating anxiety, 158
Freud's formulation of paranoia, 404-405
"Friends and Supporters of Psychotherapy," 98
Frigidity, 418 (See also Orgasmic dysfunction)
Fugue, 252
  illustrative cases, 261-63
Functional psychosis, definition, 328
Furor, Ciceronian category, 124

Galactosemia, 518
Galvanic skin response (GSR), 170, 318, 320
  conditioning, with psychopaths, 547-48
Gamblers Anonymous, 569
Gambling, 565
  theories and approaches, 569-70
Gamma alcoholism, 447
Gang, and delinquent behavior, 558
Ganser syndrome, 251fn, 257fn, 299
Gastro-intestinal reactions, 323-24
Generalization:
  concept of, 69-70
  in first signal system activity, 368
  justification of, 57, 58-59
Generalized reinforcers, 75-81
Genetic endowment, as factor in behavior, 36-37
Genetic engineering, 604
Genetic theories, of schizophrenia, 343-46
Genital sexuality, 420
Genital stage, 156
Genito-urinary reactions, 324-25
Georgehospital, 129

George Washington University, 446
Georgia Supreme Court, 567
German measles, 518
Gestalt Psychology (Perls, Hefferline, and Goodman), 228
Ghana, 395
Gheel colony, 125
Ghetto riots, 190
Gilles de la Tourette syndrome, 182, 294-95
Glamors, 129
Golden Gate Bridge, 578
Good citizens field experiments, 589-90
Goose flesh, 313
Grand mal epilepsy, 540
Grandiose expansiveness, as symptom, 339
Grandiosity, delusion of, 403
Gray Panthers, 537
Greco-Roman period, psychological thought in, 123-24
Greeks:
  hysteria among, 252, 257
  psychological thought in, 121-23
  use of alcohol, 449
Griggs vs. Duke Power Company, 217
Group delinquent reaction, 473
Group for the Advancement of Psychiatry, 20, 21
Group reward program, for hyperactive child, 498
Group therapy, 227-31
  by desensitization, 274-76
Guiding fiction, 586
Guria, 181

Habitual excessive drinking, 445-46
Habituation, definition, 444
Hallucinations, 359-60
  in schizophrenia, 333
  self-shock procedures, 379
  sleep deprivation, 309
  verbal conditioning, 378-79
Hallucinogens, 459
  effects of, 465-66
Hand-washing, 281
Hara-kiri, 577
Harrison Narcotics Act (1914), 461
Harvard University, 188
Hashish, 459
Headaches, 325-26
Head Start, 470, 620
Healthy talk, 377
Hebephrenia, 339
Hebephrenic type of schizophrenia, 334-35
Hellenic period, 123-24
Helping, conditions for, 588-89
Hepatitis, 463
Heredity:
  and psychophysiological disorders, 314
  and the sociopath, 548
Heretics, 126

subject index

Heroin, 460, 461
  effects, 463
  treatment, 466-67
Heterosexual coitus, as standard, 419
Hollywood, 329
Homosexuality, 13, 271, 405, 418, 419, 435-40
  definition, 435
  female, 436
  treatment, 436-40
  type of activity, 436
Honolulu Star Bulletin, 19, 427
Hospital Général (Paris), 129*fn*
Hospitalization, conditions affecting, 199-200
Hospitalization dimension, in schizophrenia, 341
Hospitals:
  behavior beyond, 371-72
  effects of practices, 369-71
  impact of administrative changes, 356
  learned patient behaviors, 364, 365, 366
  moral treatment, 366
  patient conformity roles, 363-64
  and schizophrenia, 361-66, 366-69
  ward environment, 365
Hostile belligerence, as symptom, 338
House of Lords, 179
Huckleberry Finn (Twain), 448
Humanism, 603-22
Humor:
  aggressive, 168-69
  as partial anxiety release, 158-59
  role-expressive behavior, 169
Huntington's chorea, 531-32
Hutterites, 182
Hydrocephaly, 519
Hyperactivity, 495-98
  treatment, 497-98
  as variable, 474
Hyperkinetic reaction, 473
Hypertension, 325
Hypnosis, 107-112
  definition (Braid), 132
  and dissociative behavior, 260-61
  Mesmer and, 107-109
  nature of, opposing views, 109-110
  and physiological change, 319-21
  role enactments, 110-11
  and temple healing, 122
Hypnotic trance, 107
Hypochondriasis, 268
Hypochondriacal neurosis, 25, 285
Hypodermic needle, invention of, 460
Hypomania, 390-91
Hysteria:
  clinical observations, 257-63
  definitions:
    behavioral reformulation, 253-54
    conversion, 251
    dissociative, 251-52

Hysteria *(cont.)*
  definitions *(cont.)*
    sociopsychological formulation, 254-57
  derivation of word, 253
  early definition, 125
  epidemic, 253-54
  Freud's early theory, 153, 252*fn*
  Janet's treatment, 133
  placebo effects and, 254-55
  as sexual disease, 131
  treatment:
    behavioral, 258-66
    earliest recorded, 257-58
    placebo use, 258
Hysterical blindness, 255-56
Hysterical personality, 414-15

Iatrogenic deviations, 361
Iatrogenic effects, 36
Id impulses, 156
Identification mechanism, 159
Ideological theory of schizophrenia, 348
Idiocy, nineteenth century views on, 141-42
Illusory correlation, 219
Imitation, 84-85 (See also Modeling)
Implosion, 277-78
Impotence, 418, 428-31
  ejaculatio praecox, 428
  treatment, 430-31
Impression management, 207
  theory of schizophrenia, 347-48
Inadequate personality, 401, 414
  definition, 25
Incest, 440
Incompetency, 18-19
Inconsistency, 66
Incubi, 128
Independent variable, 57
India, behavioral beliefs in, 120-21
Inference, as procedure, 63
Inferential statistics, 64
Influence of the Planets on the Human Body by Means of a Magnetic Fluid, The, (Mesmer), 107
Informal expectations, 189
  as discriminative stimuli, 190
Informed consent, 604, 610
Inherited autonomic patterns theory, 314-15
Inhibition of inhibitions approach, 145-46
Innate characteristics, linked to psychopathy, 545-46
Inorun syndrome, 183
Insania, Ciceronian category, 124
Insight, 153, 155, 240-41
Insight-oriented psychotherapy, 245, 246
Insomnia, 293
Institutionalization:
  adverse effects with, 367
  with retardates, 367*fn*

Insulin, 259
Intelligence quotient, (IQ), 495, 496
  as diagnostic tool in retardation, 514-16
  testing children, 472
Intelligent behavior, search for definition of, 522-23
Interference, 332
  theory of schizophrenia, 342
International Classification of Disease (ICD), 23, 24, 27
International Journal of Group Psychotherapy, 232*fn*
Interoceptive conditioning, 318
Interpretation, 153
Interval, of reinforcement, 79
Intoxication, definition, 445
Intrapsychic activity, 163
Introduction to Objective Psychopathology, An (Hamilton), 146
Introverts, 271
Involutional melancholia, 393-94
Irrelevant reactions, 271
Irritability, concept of, 311

Jackroller, The (Shaw), 195, 555
Jackrolling, 195
Jacksonian epileptic seizure, 541
Jaundice, 313
Jealousy, 405
Johns Hopkins University, 471
Judge Baker Foundation, 149
Juramentado, 182
Juvenile delinquency, 555
  approaches, 556-63
  prevention, 562-63
  treatment, 559-62

Kaufman proverbs, 372-73
Kere (anxiety reaction), 181
Kinsey report, 189
Kleptomania, 281-82
Klinefelter's syndrome, 548*fn*
Koran, 141
Korean War, 304
  hysterical behavior in, 253
Korsakov's psychosis, 446, 448-49, 537
Ku Klux Klan, 556
Kwakiutl, 181

Labels, as behavioral influence, 3
Labeling:
  antisocial, 544
  as behavior, 175-80
    diagnostic practices, 176-77
    public information and, 179-80
    as social act, 175
    social function, 177-79
  dyssocial, 555-56

Labeling *(cont.)*
  general considerations, 33-34
  impact of, 45
  irrational and inaccurate, 284-85
  and language, 83-84
  learning how and when to label, 43-44
  problems of, in personality disorders, 415-16
  of psychotics, 329-30
  self-labeling, 44-45
  as step in being normally abnormal, 192-96
Ladies Directory (Shaw), 179
Langdon-Down disease, 514
Language:
  conditions for understanding, 81-82
  labeling and, 83-84
  and sex, 425
  skills as desirable behavior, 595
  verbalization as stimulus, 83
Laros, 19
Latah, 182
Latency period, 156
Laws:
  as discriminative stimuli, 189, 190
  and medical practices, 613-14
Lay analysts, 149
Lead poisoning, 518
Leader responsibility, 609, 610
Learned helplessness, 264
Learning:
  to be a bughouser, 196-200
  to be normally abnormal, 187-96
    labeling, 192-96
    rule learning and following, 191-92
    rules, 188-91
  definition, 69
  principles of, 69-87
    abstraction formation, 84-85
    behavior terminating an aversive stimulus, 71-72
    discriminative stimuli, 73-75
    fading, 81
    generalized reinforcers, 75-81
    imitation, 84-85
    interrelation of operant and respondent behavior, 86-87
    language, 81-84
    modeling, 84-85
    prompting, 81
    reinforcement schedules, 79
    satiation effects, 72-73
    shaping of behavior, 79-81
    training of attention, 85-86
  role of, 41-42
  tension-reducing theory of, 225-26
Learning approaches, and abnormality, 118
Learning disturbance, 293
Learning models, types of, 233
Learning theory, in diagnosis, 348

subject index

Legal definitions:
  abnormality, 18
  sexual normality, 421
Lemert's formulation of paranoia, 406-10
Les Invalides Hospital (Paris), 577
Lethargy, ancient view of, 123
Libido, 156, 157
  in mania, 390
Life, 427
Linguistic analysis, as approach to schizophrenia, 349-50
Lithium carbonate, as treatment for depression, 398
Lobotomy, 143-44
LSD, 459, 548, 574
  compared to functional psychoses, 466
  effects of, 465-66
Lying, 593

McGill University, 105
Magnetic therapy (Mesmer), 107-109, 131
Making of Blind Men (Scott), 92
Maladaptive behaviors, 16
  sequence of, 164-65
Maladjustment, definition, 12
Malingering, 196, 257, 257*fn*
Malleus malleficarum (Sprenger and Kraemer), 126, 127, 128, 129
Malnutrition, and alcoholism, 447-48
Manhattan State Hospital, 57
Mania:
  amurakh, 181
  ancient view of, 123-24
  dancing, 126
  menerik, 181
Manic behavior, 390-91
Manic-depressive illness:
  circular type, 389
  definition, 389
  depressed type, 389
  history, 389-90
  manic type, 389
  sociopsychological formulation, 394-97
Manie sans délire, 545
Marijuana, 459, 461
  effects of, 464-65
  radioactive tracers and, 465
  social environment and, 191-92
Marital maladjustment, 27
Masochism, 49, 433, 435
Masturbation, 426-27
  as a cause of paresis, 140
  in children, 471
Matteawan State Hospital for the Criminal Insane, 411
Mature adult, as label, 584
Meaningful humanhood, 605
Medical analogue theories, of abnormality, 117-18
Medical certification, 613

Medical definition of normality, 18
Meditation, 326
Melancholia, 389-90
  involutional, 393-94
Memoirs of My Nervous Illness (Schreber), 405
Menerik mania, 181
Meningitis, 519
Menopause, and melancholia, 394, 394*fn*
Mental age (M.A.), 215
Mental disorders:
  cross-cultural incidence of, 182-83
  ecological studies, 185-86
  epidemiological studies, 183-85
  social class studies, 186-87
Mental health:
  community, 616-21
  as positive striving, 14-15
Mental health workers:
  conditions affecting responses, 198-99
  conditions leading to careers, 196
  shaping of, 196-200
  training situations, 197-98
  turnover rate, 198
Mental hospitals:
  admissions criteria, 200
  growth of, 135-36
Mental illness:
  acute, 16
  annual cost of, 5
  changing public reaction toward, 179-80
  chronic, 16
  definitions of, 11-13
    objective psychological tests, 14
    subjective psychological reports, 13-14
    in terms of social conformity, 16-17
  legal responsibility of questioned by Cicero, 124
  maladaptive social behavior and, 16
  question of hospital admission, 361-62
  separate behavior, 15-16
  unitary behavior, 15-16
"Mental Illness in Primitive Societies," 351
"Mental illness test," 355
Mental retardation, 513-28
  behavioral treatment, 524-26
  behavioral view, 522-24
  Braginskys' paradigm, 521-22
  as category, 24
  clinical subcategories, 513-19
  cultural-familial, 519-22
  diagnosis of, 514-16
  and organic viewpoint, 141-42
  physiological defects, 517-19
  token-economy work, 526-28
Meprobamate, 444
Mescaline, 465
Mesmerism, 131-32
Methadone hydrochloride, 143
  in drug addiction, 467-68

Methedrine, 259
Metropolitan Museum of Art, 575fn
Miasma model, 616
Microcephaly, 519
Micro-economy, drug addiction, 466
Middle Ages, psychological thought in, 124-27
Midtown Study, 207
Migraine headache, 326, 542
Milieu control, 306-307
Miltown, 444
Minimal brain dysfunction, 496-97
Mind that Found Itself, A (Beers), 365
Minnesota Multiphasic Personality Inventory Test (MMPI), 216, 217
M'Naghten Rule, 20
Modeling, 84-85, 276, 282
  autism, 505
  children's behavior, 487-88
  neutral context, 487
  positive context, 487
Modern Persecution (Packard), 407
Mongolism (Down's syndrome), 117, 514, 517
Monozygotic twins, and schizophrenia, 343, 345
Montreal Children's Hospital, 501
Moral anxiety, 158
Moral behavior:
  aspects of, 590-91
  empirical studies, 592-93
  rules, 591-92
Moral derangement, 545
Moral imbeciles, 26
  definition, 545
Moral insanity, 545
Moral treatment, 135-36, 356, 407, 408
  decline of, 137-39
  in hospitals, 366
Morality-immorality, as variable, 421
Morbidity, 22, 23
Mores, 555
Morphine, 444, 460
  effects of, 463
Motivational theory, of schizophrenia, 347
Motor disturbances, 338
Mourning, and depression, 392, 395-96
Multiple personality, 252
Multiple sclerosis, 531, 537
Munchausen's syndrome, 257fn
Mundugumor, 12, 181
Musicogenic epilepsy, 541
Muteness, 338
Mutilation, sexual, 418

Nail-biting, 295
Nancy School, The, 132
Narcoanalysis, 259
National Commission on Marijuana and Drug Abuse, 462

National Committee for Mental Hygiene (1909), 150, 472
National Council on Crime and Delinquency, 608
National Institute of Mental Health, 398, 459
National Institutes of Health Public Mental Hospital Report, 206
National Training Laboratory (NTL), 228, 609
National Training School for Boys, 560
Natural causes, Hippocrates' interest in, 122
Natural selection, 41
Nazi Germany, 606
Near East, psychological thought in, 127
Negative practice, 237
Negative transference, 154
Nembutal, 463
Neologism, 338
  in schizophrenia, 333
Neoplasms, and retardation, 514
Neural integrative defect, 343
Neurasthenia, 268
Neurasthenic behavior, 286-87
Neurasthenic neurosis, 25
Neurocirculatory asthenia, 286
Neurodermatitis, 321-22
Neurofibromatoses, 517
Neuropathologists, in nineteenth century, 138-39
Neuroses, 249-66
  as category, 25
  depressive, 263-66
    definition, 263
    treatment, 265-66
  existential, 571
  hysterical, 250-63
    clinical observations and treatment, 257-63
    definitions, 250-57
  other, 287-88
  subcategories, DSM-II, 250
  war, 304-305
  writers' cramp, 287-88
Neurotic anxiety, 158
Neurotic delinquent, 554
Neutral condition experiment, 169
Neutralization behavior, 587
New Hampshire Rule, 20
New Haven study, 186-87
New South Wales, 383
New York Court of Claims, 614
New York Radical Feminists, 601
New York State Mental Hygiene Law, 21
New York Times, The, 101, 411, 598fn
Nicotinamide adenine dinucleotide (NAD), 346
Niemann-Pick's disease, 514
1984 (Orwell), 306
Nocturnal emission, ancient view of, 123
Noncontingent positive reinforcement, 373
Nonpsychotic mental disorders, as category, 25
Nonspecific psychiatric conditions, as category, 26-27
Nonverbal behaviors, 234

subject index

Normal Mind, The (Burnham), 145
Normality:
  concept of, 181
  learning to be abnormal, 187-96
    labeling, 192-96
    rule learning and following, 191-92
    rules, 188-91
  medical definition of, 18
  psychoanalytic definition of, 18
  and role-playing, 261
  sexual, definitions, 419-23
    biological, 420
    legal, 421
    religious, 421
    statistical, 421
No-treatment control group, 245, 246
Null hypothesis, use in experiments, 63

Obedience, testing of, 112
Objective anxiety, 158
Obscenity, 565
  cursing, 567-68
  wall-writing, 568-69
Observational learning, 233
Observations on Madness and Melancholy (Haslam), 139
Obsessive-compulsive behaviors, 268, 278-82
  definitions, 278-79
  reformulation, 279-80
  treatment of, 280-82
Obsessive-compulsive neurosis, 25
Obsessive-compulsive personality, 414
Occupational maladjustment, 27
Oedipus complex, 156, 429
Offensiveness, definition, 566
On Acute and Chronic Disease (Caelius), 123
Operant behavior, interrelation to respondent behavior, 86-87
Operant concepts:
  approach to alcoholism, 456-57
  and depressive behavior, 265
Operant conditioning, 69, 70, 233, 276-77
  sexual behavior, 424
Operant-interpersonal group, 376
Operant period, 46
Operant stimulus generalization, 73-74
Opiates, effects of, 463
Opium, 459
  historical background, 460, 461
Oral character, 157
Oral stage, 156
Organic basis for illnesses, 139-44
  mental retardation and, 141-42
  physical approaches to behavioral change, 142-44
Organic brain syndromes, 328
  classification of, 24-25
Organic disorders, reliability of psychiatric diagnosis, 203-12

Organizing material, as desirable skill, 595-96
Orgasmic dysfunction, 418, 431
Oriental superstitions, 120-21
Origin of the Species, The (Darwin), 152
Overanxious reaction, 473
Overdetermined behavior, 157
Overeating, 295, 298
Overinclusion (fantasy), 342
Overt behavior, 46-48
Overwhelming situation, concept of, 299-301

Pain thresholds, change in under hypnosis, 111
Panic, and transient situational disturbance, 302-303
Panic anxiety, 158
Paranoia:
  behavior, 402-403
  Cameron's formulation, 405-406
  definitions of states, 403-404
  Freud's formulation, 404-405
  Lemert's formulation, 406-10
  sociopsychological formulation, 410-13
  treatment, 413
Paranoiac tendencies, 474
Paranoid ideation, 309
Paranoid-nonparanoid dimension, of schizophrenia, 341
Paranoid personality, 25, 401, 402-13
Paranoid projection, as symptom, 338
Parental attitudes, definition and research on, 482-83
Parents, as behavior therapists, 476, 477-81
Parents Anonymous, 483
Parent-training programs, 477-81
Paresis:
  discovery of cause and cure, 139-41
  as medical model, 117
Parkinson's disease, 532-33
Parsons State Hospital and Training Center, 526
Passers-by Studies, 588-89
Passive-aggressive personality, 402, 415
Passive demonstration, in autism, 505
Paternalism, and biofeedback, 605
Pathological intoxication, 446
Patients, rights of, 608
Pavlovian conditioning, 69
Pedophilia, 433, 440
Pennsylvania Hospital, 135
Peptic ulcer, 323-24
Perceptual distortion, as symptom, 338
Performance, as concept, 95-96
Performance anxiety, 259*fn*
Persecution, as delusion, 403
Personal behavior, placing limits on, 565-81
Personal hygiene, as behavior area, 375
Personality, 162
  concepts of, 166-70
    as mediating variable, 167
    as set of responses, 167
    as stimulus, 166-67

Personality (cont.)
  conscious-unconscious, 168
  definition, 166
Personality disorders:
  as category, 25
  cyclothymic personality, 414
  paranoid personality, 401-16
    formulations, 404-10
    sociopsychological formulation, 410-12
    states, 403-404
    treatment, 413
Personality inventories, 216-17
Personality pattern disturbance types, 401
Personality trait disturbance types, 401-402
Petit mal seizure, 540-41
Phaedrus (Plato), 121
Phallic stage, 156
Phenylketonuria (PKU), 514, 518
Philosophy, approaches to psychotherapy, 133-34
Phobias:
  definition, 268-69
  instigation and termination of, with children, 475-76
Phobic anxiety, 158
Phobic behaviors, 268-88
  treatment procedures, 272-78
Phobic neurosis, 25
  definition, 282
Physical approaches, to behavior change, 142-44
Physiological addiction, criteria, 444
Piblokto, 181
Pick's disease, 532
Placebo effects, 56, 56fn
Placebo object, 56fn
Placebo responses, 100-107
Placebos:
  administrator characteristics, 102-103
  definitions, 56, 100-101
  effectiveness, 103-104
  partial list, 103
  reaction and role enactment, 104-105
  reactors, 103
  as treatment for hysteria, 258
Playboy, 319, 435
Pleasure principle, 156
Political context, effect on behavior, 40-41
Population control, 605
Population density, effect on behavior, 38-39
Pornography, 565-67
  arousal responses, 567
  definition, 565
  users, 566-67
Positive reinforcement, of selected responses, 237
Positive transference, 154
Postnatal injury, 519
Postural changes, in schizophrenia, 333
Poverty culture, 620

Power of the Mind, Through Simple Determination, to Become Master over Morbid Ideas, The (Kant), 133
Prefrontal lobotomy, 143-44
Premack principle, 238, 281, 381
  statement of, 489
  use in treatment of neurosis, 265
Prematurity, and retardation, 514
Prenatal injury, 519
President's Panel on Mental Retardation, 521
Primary deviation, 193
Primary gain, 251fn
Primary impotence, 430
Primary reinforcer, food as, 72
Primary reinforcing stimuli, 70
Primitive man, 119-20
Prisoners of war, 305-308
Prisonization, 556
Privacy, invasion of, 606
Process-reactive dimension, in schizophrenia, 339-40
Project CASE, 560
Projection, as defense mechanism, 404
Projection mechanism, 159
Projective tests, 214-15
Prompting, 81
Propaganda, as area of social psychology, 412
Propaganda Analysis Bulletin, 412
Prosocial behaviors:
  characteristics, 584-85
  development and maintenance of, 36-38
  helping strangers, 586-93
  physiological bases of, 36-38
  positive deviance, 583-601
  self and self-control, 585-86
  specific positive behaviors:
    approaching situations, 596
    behavior therapy process, 597
    care for environment, 597
    in classroom, 594-95, 596-97
    intellectual skills, 595-96
    work, 597
  Women's Lib as creative deviance, 598-601
Prosocial person, characteristics of, 584-85
Protest behavior, 47
Proverbs, abstract interpretation of, 373
Prurient interest, definition, 566
Pseudopatients experiment, 29-30
Psilocybin, 465
Psychiatric diagnosis:
  as criterion for mental illness, 12
  empirical approaches to, 209-12
  psychological tests, 213-17
  reliability of, 203-209
    evaluation, 208-209
    consistency over time and place, 207-208
  suggestion effects in, 28-29
Psychiatric disorders, and retardation, 514
Psychiatric emergency, 9-11

subject index

Psychiatric treatment, time limit problem, 22
Psychiatrists, definition, 148
Psychoanalysis:
    Freud and, 152-60
    as intellectual system, 172
    relation between theory and treatment procedure, 155
    as theory, 155-60
    as treatment, 153-55
Psychoanalyst, definition, 148
Psychoanalytic definition of normality, 18
Psychoanalytic theory, in diagnosis, 348
Psychobiology, 139
Psychodiagnostics, 147
Psychological dependency, definition, 444-45
Psychological tests, 213-17
    advantages, 13-14, 213-14
    considerations, 217-19
        baserates, 218
        data collection, 219
        illusory correlation, 219
    to define mental illness, 14
    personality inventories, 216-17
    projective, 214-15
    standardized, 215-16
Psychological theories, of origin of psychophysiological disorders, 315-16
Psychologist, definition, 148
Psychomotor epilepsy, 541
Psychomotor retardation, as system, 338
Psychopathic inferiority, 545
Psychopathology of Everyday Life (Freud), 168
Psychopathy:
    brain function and, 459
    characteristics of behavior, 546-48
    conditionability, 550
    development of behavior, 552-53
    family relations, 549-50
    hereditary factors, 548
    history of label, 545-46
    professional concept, 545-46
    role-taking, 550
    sociopsychological formulation, 551-54
    stimulation-seeking, 550-51
Psychophysiological disorders, 311-26
    behavioral environment, 313-14
    as category, 26
    clinical applications, 321-26
    hypnosis and physiological change, 319-21
    internal physical environment, 313-14
    theories of origin, 314-19
Psychoses:
    affective disorders, 389-400
    alcoholic, 446
    definition, 24
    general discussion, 328-30
    labeling and mis-labeling patients, 329-30
    not attributed to physical conditions, 25

Pychoses *(cont.)*
    psychotic depressive reaction, 389
Psycho-social deprivation, and retardation, 514
Psychosomatic disorders (*See also* Psychophysiological disorders)
    caution in use of concept, 312-13
    definitions, 311
    history of concept, 311-12
Psychosurgery, 143
    prefrontal lobotomy, 143-44
Psychotherapy:
    as behavioral control process, 231-32
    evaluations of effectiveness, 243-46
    features, 239
    forerunners of, 131-34
        Bernheim-Charcot controversy, 132-33
        philosophy, 133-34
    outpatient, 97-100
    problems of change, 614-16
Psychotherapy by Reciprocal Inhibition (Wolpe), 147
Psychotherapy sessions, first recording of, 226-27
Psychotic depressive reaction, 389
Puberty, 156
Public information, and labeling, 179-80
Punishment:
    aspect of labeling, 193-94
    children, 481-82
Pygmalion effect, 113, 207

Question of Lay Analysis, The (Freud), 152

Race, as social variable, 186, 187
Radical therapy, 231*fn*
Ramayana, 120
Random sampling, 60
Rape, 424-25, 440
Rapport, use as treatment, 273
Rater reliability, of psychiatric diagnosis, 203
Ratio of reinforcement, 79
Rational-Emotive Therapy (RT), 232
Rationalized behavior, 587
Rationalization mechanism, 159
Reaction formation, 158, 159, 160
Reactive depression, clinical contexts, 264-65
Reactive inhibition, 277
Reading, as desirable behavior, 595
Reality principle, 156
Reciprocal inhibition, 146
Recreation therapy, 375-76
Redintegration, 45
Red-tape method, 281
Reference, delusions of, 403, 405-406
Regression, 157
Regressive theories of schizophrenia, 342, 346
Reinforcement, 69-71
    and aversive behaviors, 48-50
    as concept, 46-48
    schedules, 79

Reinforcement *(cont.)*
  stimuli, 70
    in hospital situation, 364-65
Relaxation responses, 235
Reliability, 65-66
  rater, 65
  test-retest, 66
Religion and Psychiatry Institute, 99fn
Religious definitions, sexual normality, 421
Repetition compulsion, 160
Reporting (Ross), 42
Repression, 160, 168
Reproduction, and sexual normality, 420
Research, ethical considerations, 606-607
Resensitization, 164
Reserpine, 142
Residual type schizophrenic reaction, 337
Resistance, 153-54
Respiratory functions, treatment procedures, 322-23
Respondent behavior, interpretation to operant behavior, 86-87
Respondent concepts, and depressive behavior, 265
Respondent conditioning, 69
  sexual behavior, 424
Response chaining, 80-81
Response reinforcement model, and alcoholism, 450
Responsibility, of insane individual, 22
Rest cure, 287
Retardation (*See* Mental retardation)
Right behavior, as label, 33
Riots, ghetto, 190
Robinson v. California, 463
Role:
  concept of, 89
  definition of concept, 99-100
  as term, 175fn
Role expressive acts, sexual, 425-26
Roles:
  behavior associated with, 195-96
  social expectations and responses, 177-79
Role-taking, 90-92
  and sociopathy, 550
Romans, aversion procedure for alcohol, 455
Roper survey, 179
Rorschach Test, 44, 149, 214, 215
Rouse v. Cameron, 21
Rubella, and retardation, 518
Rules:
  characteristics and problems of, 188-91
  learning and following, 191-92
Rumor, as area of social psychology, 413
Rumpelstiltskin principle, 239
Runaway reaction, 473

Sadism, 433, 435
St. Basil of Caesarea (hospital), 129
St. Elizabeth's Hospital, 287
St. Mary of Bethlehem (hospital), 129

Salpêtrière Hospital (Paris), 132
Salvarsan, 140
Sampling, 60-62
San Hipolito (hospital), 129
Satiation, 237, 574, 574fn
  effects of, 72-73
Savings behavior, 383
Scattering, in schizophrenia, 333
Schizoid personality, 25, 401, 414
Schizophrenia, 25
  anxiety dimension, 341-42
  catatonic type, 335-36
    agitated, 336
    stuporus, 335-36
  in childhood, 337, 501-11
  chronic undifferentiated type, 336-37
  descriptions of, 330-34
  effect of drugs on, 370-71
  effects of hospital practices, 369-71
  experiments in sociopsychological model, 372-78
  factor analysis of symptomatic behavior, 338-39
  family treatment, 380
  hebephrenic type, 334-35
  the hospital and, 362-69
  latent type, 337-38
  length of residence in hospital, 341
  linguistic analysis as approach to, 349-50
  paranoid-nonparanoid dimension, 341
  paranoid type, 335
  predisposition to, 345-46
  process-reactive dimension, 339-40
  question of hospital admission, 361-62
  residual type, 337
  responsiveness to social circumstances, 355
  schizo-affective type, 337
  simple type, 334
  situational nature of catatonic behavior, 353-54
  sociopsychological formulation, 353-61
  task manipulation treatment, 379-80
  theories:
    biochemical, 346
    biosocial, 342
    cognitive, 342
    disorganization and defective role-taking, 342-43
    genetic, 343-46
    ideological-sociological, 348-49
    impression management, 347-48
    interference, 342
    motivational, 347
    regressive, 346
    sociopsychological, 353-78
  types, 334-38
  viability of concept, 350-51
Schizophrenia Bulletin, 371, 372
Schizotaxia, 343
Schizotypic personality organization, 343
Science and Human Behavior (Skinner), 147
Scientific method, 55-67

subject index

Scientific method *(cont.)*
   decision making, 55-57
   operational definitions, 57-60
   reliability, 65-66
   sampling, 60-62
   single case use, 66-67
   statistical analysis, 62-65
   validity, 66
Secondary deviance, 193
Secondary gain, 251*fn*
Secondary impotence, 430
Secondary reinforcers, 74, 75
Self, 585-86
Self-attribution, 169
Self-control, 585-86
Self-fulfilling prophecy, as situation definition, 95-96
Self-help behavior, for retarded, 524-25
Self-injurious response behavior (SIR), 507-508
Self-instruction, 592
Self-labeling, 44-45
Self-modification, 237-38
   as treatment for depression neurosis, 266
Self-multilation, 580-81
Self-references, conditioning effect, 374
Self-regulation, 233
Self-relaxation instructions, as therapy, 293
Self-reward, 592
Semantic conditioning, 318
Semantic dementia, 551
Senile dementia, 539-40
Senility, problems of definition, 538
Sensate focus, 427
Sensitivity training, 228
Sensory deprivation phenomena, 360
Separate behavior, 15-16
Sex, as social variable, 186-87
Sexual behavior, 418-42
   definitions of normality, 419-23
   deviational, 26, 402, 432-40
      exhibitionism, 435
      fetishism, 432-33
      homosexuality, 435-40
      masochism, 433, 435
      sadism, 433, 435
      transvestism, 434
      voyeurism, 435
   ejaculatory incompetence, 431
   ethical considerations, 440-41
   impotence, 428-31
   orgasmic dysfunction, 431
   sociopsychological approach, 423-40
Sexual responses, use of, 234
Shamans, 119-20
Shaping:
   of behavior, 79-81
   as behavior therapy, 258-59
   in children, 485-86
Shock reaction, 303

Shock therapy (*See* Electroconvulsive therapy)
Sick role, 96-97, 175*fn*
   false enactment of, 196
Sick talk, 377-78
Similarities Test, 373
Simple depression, 391
Sing Sing prison, 546
Situations:
   avoidance of punishing, 270, 271, 272
   fear of, 270-71, 272
   misidentification of, 270
Skills, possession of in order to perform correctly, 42-43
Skinnerian conditioning, 69
Slaughterhouse Five (Vonnegut), 566
Sleep deprivation, 309
Sleep problems, 293
Slips of the tongue, as anxiety release, 158
Sluggishness, as variable, 474
Smiling response, influences on, 46-47
Smith College, 149
Smoking, 295, 565
   theories and treatments, 570-71
Social Breakdown Syndrome, 616
Social class, and mental disorders, 186-87
Social conformity, as questionable basis for mental illness, 16-17
Social context, as variable affecting task performance, 358
Social emergency, 9-10
Social events, cross-cultural considerations, 180-83
Social group approach, to alcoholism, 457-58
Social interactions, as behavior area, 375
Social location, effect on behavior, 39
Social maladjustment, 27
Social merit, definition, 566
Social organization, effects on behavior, 39-40
Social psychiatry, as term, 616
Social reform, effects on children, 471
Social Research Group, 446
Social roles, 89-114
   enactments, 89-95
   expectancy, 95-96
   experimenter bias, 112-14
   hypnosis, 107-12
   outpatient psychotherapy, 97-100
   performance, 95-96
   placebo responses, 100-107
   relationship to physiological concomitants, 313-14
   role-taking, **90-92**
   sick, 96-97
Social security, 537
Social stimuli, sequence of correct response to, 42-43
Social theories, about abnormality, 118
Social variables, 186-87
Social withdrawal, 474
   experiments in, 375-76
Socialization, 195

Socialization theory, in diagnosis, 348
Societies of Harmony, 133
Socioeconomic status, and mental disorders, 186-87
Sociological theory, of schizophrenia, 348-49
Sociopathic personality disturbance, 401
　types, 402
Sociopathy (See Psychopathy)
Sociopsychological formulations:
　alcoholism, 451-52
　depression, 394-97
　dyssocial behavior, 555-56
　existential problems, 572-75
　paranoia, 410-13
　to phobic behaviors, 269-72
　psychopathic behaviors, 551-54
　schizophrenia:
　　applying concepts: treatment, 378-80
　　background, 353-56
　　formulation, 356-61
　　token economies, 380-87
　to sexual behavior, 423-40
Sociopsychological model, experiments in, 372-78
Somatic verbalization, 77
Somatic weakness, as cause of disorder, 314
Somnambulism, 252
　illustrative cases, 262-63
South Wales, work in, 183
Spasmodic paralysis, 536
Spasmodic torticollis, 294
Special symptom behaviors, 290-99
　as category, 26
Speech problems, 290-93
　as variable, 474
Speech therapy, 525
Spiritus vitae, 128
Split brain operations, 534
Standard deviation, 64
Standardized tests, 215-16
Stanford-Binet Intelligence Test, 36, 149, 214, 477
Statistical analysis, 62-65
Statistical definition of abnormality, 17-18
Status, definition, 175fn
Statutory rape, 424
Stimulation-seeking theory, of psychopathy, 550-51
Stimuli, attention and orientation to, 45-46
Stimulus deprivation, 237
Street corner research, 561
Stress, and behavioral difficulties, 300-301
Stress theory, of psychophysiological disorders, 314
Structured learning therapy, 376
Students for a Democratic Society, 556
Sturge-Weber-Dimitri's disease, 517
Stuttering, 290-92
Sublimation, 157, 160
Subtypes, of labels, 203-204
Succubi, 128
Suggestion, 132

Suicide, 565
　categories, 576
　prevention, 579-80
　research problems, 576
　self-mutilation, 580-81
　theories, 576-79
Superego, 156
Superintendent-physicians, in early mental hospitals, 137-38
Supernatural theories, about abnormality, 116-17
Superstitious behavior, 47
Suppression, 160
Susruta, 121
Susto, 182
Suttee, 577
Symptom:
　anxiety and, 165-66
　concept and theories, 162-65
　substitution, 163-65
Symptomatic behavior, factor analysis, 338-39
Synanon, 466-67
Synesthesia, 465
Syphilis:
　related to paresis, 140-41
　and retardation, 518
Systematic desensitization, 235, 274, 281, 485
　experimental evidence of effectiveness, 245-46
　by machine, 241
　package of procedures, 240

Table Talk (Luther), 141
Talmud, 141
Tangential speech, 338
Tantrum behavior, 503-504
Target behavior, 77, 221 ,
Tasks, in token economies, 384
Taxonomy, definition, 43fn
Tay-Sach's disease, 514
Temptation, resistance to, 592
Tension headache, 326
Tepoztlan, 427
Test anxiety, 274-75
Texas State Mental Hospitals, 65
Textbook of Psychiatry (Kraepelin), 139, 390fn
Thalidomide, 518
Thematic Apperception Test (TAT), 149, 214
Therapeutic community, notions of, 369
Thinking, disorganization of, 372-73
Thinking disorder, probable increase under hospitalization, 368
Thinning, of reinforcement schedule, 79
Thought control, 306
Thought reform, 306
Thumb-sucking, 295
Tic, 293-94
Time, 34, 188, 194, 298, 321, 427, 567, 604
Time-out-from reinforcement, 70
Tofranil, use in depression, 398

subject index

Toilet training, 156, 498-501
Token-earning behavior, 383
Token economies, 329, 380-87
   categories, 384
   comparison study, 384
   composition of, 381
   and delinquency, 560-61
   evaluations, 386
   reinforcement procedures, 382
   and staff training, 384-86
   as treatment for retardates, 526-28
Tonic stage, of epileptic seizure, 540
Trance, attempted definition, 107
Tranquilizers, 142-43
   and mania, 398
   as treatment, 283
Transference, 154
   interpretation, 154-55
Transference cures, 163
Transient situational disturbances, 299-303
   as category, 26
   general discussion, 301-302
   panic as paradigm of, 302-303
Transvestism, 271, 433-35
Travels in America (Dickens), 136
Treatment:
   aggression/hostility, 491-95
   alcoholism, 452-58
   aphonia, 258-59
   behavioral, for retarded, 524-26
   bronchial asthma, 322-23
   delinquency, 559-62
   depersonalization behavior, 286
   of depression, 397-99
   depressive neurosis, 265-66
   diffuse anxious behavior, 283-85
   drug addiction, 466-68
   gastro-intestinal reactions, 323-24
   genito-urinary reactions, 324-25
   headaches, 325-26
   homosexual behavior, 436-40
   hyperactivity, 497-98
   hypertension, 325
   hypochondriacal behavior, 285
   hysteria, 252, 254-55, 257-58
   hysterical blindness, 256
   obsessive-compulsive behavior, 280-82
   organic brain disorders, 536-37
   paranoia, 413
   skin problems, 321-22
   stuttering, 291-93
Treatment procedures:
   anxiety-relief responses, 273-74
   contact desensitization, 276
   direct retraining, 272
   desensitization in practice, 273
   group therapy by desensitization, 274-76
   implosion, 277-78

Treatment procedures *(cont.)*
   modeling, 276
   operant conditioning, 276-77
   reactive inhibition, 277
   self-modification procedures, 266
   systematic desensitization, 274
   token-economy work with retardates, 526-28
   use of rapport, 273
   verbal conditioning, 378-79
Trichotillomania, 280
Trisomy-21 anomaly (Mongolism), 517
True psychopath, description of, 553-54
Tuberous sclerosis, 517

Ufufunyane, 181
Ulcers, 315
   peptic, 323-24
Unconditional positive regard, 227
Unconditioned stimulus, 69
Unconscious, concept of, 159
Underactivity, as behavior pattern, 264
Unitary behavior, 15-16
U.S. Congress, 460, 461
U.S. Supreme Court, 461, 565
University of Maine, 579
University of North Carolina Medical School Psychiatric Unit, 253
University of Pennsylvania, 148, 471
Unsocialized aggressive reaction, 473
Urban renewal, 303-304
Urination, frequency reduction, 324
Utica State Hospital, 137

Validity, 66
Value, therapists' definition of, 615-16
Variable interval schedules, 79
Variable ratio, of reinforcement, 79
Variables:
   dependent, 57
   independent, 57
Verbal behavior, of schizophrenics, 374
Verbal conditioning:
   and control of heart rate, 317
   summary, 378
Verbal operant conditioning, 75-79, 241*fn*
Verbal therapy, 375-76
Verbalization:
   aversive, 377-78
   effects of as stimulus, 83
Vertigo, 542
Veterans Administration, 63, 398
Vicarious reinforcement (*See* Modeling)
Videotape feedback, used as therapy, 380
Viet Nam, hysterical behavior in, 253
Vocational selection problems, 572
Vomiting, 297-98, 321
von Recklinghausen's disease (neurofibromatosis), 517

Voodoo, 183
Voyeurism, 435
Walden Two (Skinner), 481
Wall-writing, 568-69
War neurosis, 304-305
Waxy flexibility, in schizophrenia, 333
Weak-will theories, about abnormality, 117
Wechsler-Bellevue Intelligence Tests, 66, 214, 333
Wechsler Scales of Intelligence, 373
Weight-Watchers, Inc., 194
Wernicke's syndrome, 448, 449
White House Conference on the Care of Dependent Children, 150
White House Special Action Office for Drug Abuse, 459
Why People Go to Psychiatrists (Kadushin), 98
Windigo psychosis, 181
Witchcraft, detection and treatment, 126-27
Witch's Hammer, The (See Malleus malleficarum)
Withdrawing reaction, 473
Women's Liberation, 598-601
  conscious-raising, 599-600
  history, 598-99
Worcester State Hospital, 137*fn*, 396, 397
Word associations, 373
  test, 154, 214-155
Words, as stimuli, 318

Work:
  retraining for, 597
  as therapy, 525
Work of the Digestive Glands (Pavlov), 316
World Health Organization, 446, 464
  International Classification of Diseases, 23
World War I, 304, 472, 533
  hysterical behavior in, 253
  personality inventory use, 216
  screening procedures, 149
World War II, 238, 304, 402
  and group treatment, 227-28
  hysterical behavior in, 253
  screening procedures, 149
Writers' cramp, 287-88
Wyatt v. Stickney, 21

XYY effect, 548

Yale Cross-Cultural Index, 420
Yoga, 326
York Retreat (England), 135
Yoruba, 183

Zen Buddhism, 188
Zhosa, 181
Zulus, 181